Register Now for (to Your E

MW00785307

Your print purchase of *Psychosocial Aspects of Disability, Second Edition,* **includes online access to the contents of your book**—increasing accessibility, portability, and searchability!

Access today at:

http://connect.springerpub.com/content/book/978-0-8261-8063-6 or scan the QR code at the right with your smartphone and enter the access code below.

DUDKTHD6

EYCBa2121

Scan here for quick access.

LS

SPRINGER / PUBLISHING COMPANY

View all our products at springerpub.com

The Psychological and Social Impact of Illness and Disability

Irmo Marini, PhD, DSc, CRC, CLCP, is professor in the School of Rehabilitation at the University of Texas—Rio Grande Valley in Edinburg, Texas. He obtained his PhD in rehabilitation from Auburn University and a master's degree in clinical psychology from Lakehead University in Thunder Bay, Ontario, Canada. He is a 2009 recipient of the National Council on Rehabilitation Education's Distinguished Career Award in rehabilitation education, and 2010 recipient of the American Rehabilitation Counseling Association's James F. Garrett Distinguished Career Award in rehabilitation research. In 2012, Dr. Marini was bestowed an honorary doctorate of science (honoris causa) from his alma mater Lakehead University, and was the recipient of the 2013 National Council on Rehabilitation Education's Educator of the Year award. In 2015, he was the recipient of the Patricia McCollom Distinguished Career Award in life care planning research. He is the coauthor and coeditor of seven books, more than 40 book chapters, and more than 80 refereed journal publications. He is the former chair of the Commission on Rehabilitation Counselor Certification, and former president of the American Rehabilitation Counseling Association.

Mark A. Stebnicki, PhD, LPC, DCMHS, CRC, CCM, CCMC, is a professor and coordinator of the Military and Trauma Counseling Certificate Program, which he developed in the Department of Addictions and Rehabilitation Services at East Carolina University. He holds a doctoral and a master's degree in rehabilitation counseling. Dr. Stebnicki is a licensed professional counselor in North Carolina and holds four national certifications: diplomate in clinical mental health specialist in trauma counseling through the American Mental Health Counselors Association (AMHCA), certified rehabilitation counselor, certified case manager, and certified clinical military counselor. In 2016, Dr. Stebnicki developed a military counseling training program for the state of North Carolina. The CCMC credential indicates professional counselors are trained to work with the medical, psychosocial, vocational, and mental health needs of active-duty personnel, veterans, and their family members.

Dr. Stebnicki is also certified by the Washington, DC-based crisis response team, National Organization for Victim Assistance (NOVA), and North Carolina's American Red Cross Disaster Mental Health crisis team. Dr. Stebnicki is an active teacher, researcher, and practitioner with more than 30 years' experience working with the mental health and psychosocial rehabilitation needs of persons who have traumatic stress, chronic illnesses, and disabilities.

Dr. Stebnicki has written eight books, most recent is *Disaster Mental Health Counseling: Responding to Trauma in a Multicultural Context* (2017, Springer Publishing). He has more than 28 articles in peer-reviewed journals, and has presented at more than 100 regional, state, and national conferences, seminars, and workshops, on such topics as youth violence, traumatic stress, empathy fatigue, and the psychosocial aspects of adults with chronic illnesses and disabilities.

Dr. Stebnicki has served on multiple professional counseling and accreditation boards. He served on the crisis response team for the Westside Middle School shootings in Jonesboro, Arkansas (March 24, 1998), and has done many stress debriefings with private companies, schools, and government employees after incidents of workplace violence, hurricanes, tornadoes, and floods. His youth violence program, the Identification, Early Intervention, Prevention, and Preparation (IEPP) Program, was awarded national recognition by the American Counseling Association (ACA) Foundation for its vision and excellence in the area of youth violence prevention. Other accolades include consulting with former President Bill Clinton's staff on addressing the students of Columbine High School after their critical incident (April 20, 1999).

The Psychological and Social Impact of Illness and Disability

Seventh Edition

IRMO MARINI, PhD, DSc, CRC, CLCP

MARK A. STEBNICKI, PhD, LPC, DCMHS, CRC, CCM, CCMC

Editors

SPRINGER PUBLISHING COMPANY

Springer Publishing Company, LLC
11 West 42nd Street
New York, NY 10036
www.springerpub.com

Acquisitions Editor: Sheri W. Sussman
Compositor: Newgen KnowledgeWorks

ISBN: 978-0-8261-6161-1
e-book ISBN: 978-0-8261-6162-8

Instructor's Materials: Qualified instructors may request supplements by emailing textbook@springerpub.com:
Instructor's Manual: 978-0-8261-6163-5
Instructor's PowerPoints: 978-0-8261-6164-2
17 18 19 20 21/ 5 4 3 2 1

The author and the publisher of this Work have made every effort to use sources believed to be reliable to provide information that is accurate and compatible with the standards generally accepted at the time of publication. The author and publisher shall not be liable for any special, consequential, or exemplary damages resulting, in whole or in part, from the readers' use of, or reliance on, the information contained in this book. The publisher has no responsibility for the persistence or accuracy of URLs for external or third-party Internet websites referred to in this publication and does not guarantee that any content on such websites is, or will remain, accurate or appropriate.

Library of Congress Cataloging-in-Publication Data
Names: Marini, Irmo, editor. | Stebnicki, Mark A., editor.
Title: The psychological and social impact of illness and disability /
  [edited by] Irmo Marini, PhD, DSc, CRC, CLCP and Mark A. Stebnicki, PhD,
  LPC, DCMHS, CRC, CCM, CCMC.
Description: Seventh edition. | New York, NY : Springer Publishing Company, [2018]
Identifiers: LCCN 2017024596 | ISBN 9780826161611 (paper back)
Subjects: LCSH: People with disabilities—United States—Psychology. | People with
  disabilities—Rehabilitation—United States. | People with disabilities—Family relationships—
  United States. | People with disabilities—Sexual behavior—United States. | People with
  disabilities—United States—Public opinion. | Public opinion—United States.
Classification: LCC HV1553 .P75 2018 | DDC 305.9/080973—dc23
LC record available at https://lccn.loc.gov/2017024596

Contact us to receive discount rates on bulk purchases.
We can also customize our books to meet your needs.
For more information please contact: sales@springerpub.com

Printed in the United States of America by McNaughton & Gunn.

How fortunate I have been all my life to be loved by two families unconditionally. How lucky to have an abundance of great friends, the privilege to try to inspire and be inspired by thousands of students, and to have close friends and colleagues, such as Mark and Bonnie Stebnicki, on this journey. And how lucky to have my wife and life partner, Darlene, who stubbornly never gave up on me and inspired me to live life large and find my flow.

—Irmo

To my family, who has been with me from the beginning of my career; my wife, Bonnie; daughter, Sarah; and son, Mark; and to a deep friendship with my closest friend and colleague, Irmo, and his wife, Darlene, I owe much gratitude.

—Mark

Contents

Contributors

Richard F. Antonak, PhD
Vice Provost for Research
Department of Counseling and School
    Psychology
University of Massachusetts
Boston, Massachusetts

Tosca Appel, MS
Newton, Massachusetts

Michael R. Benz, PhD
Center on Disability and Development
Department of Educational Psychology
Texas A&M University
College Station, Texas

Martin G. Brodwin, PhD, CRC
California State University
Los Angeles, California

Susanne M. Bruyère, PhD, CRC
Director, Yang-Tan Institute on Employment
    and Disability
ILR School
Cornell University
Ithaca, New York

Elizabeth Cardoso, PhD, CRC
Hunter College
New York, New York

Lindsey N. Cooper, PsyD
Staff Psychologist
Veterans Affairs North Texas Health
    Care System
Dallas, Texas

Sarah Cooper, PhD
Clinical Psychology Post Doctoral Fellow
PSIMED Corrections, Inc.
Nova Southeastern University
Fort Lauderdale, Florida

Sergio Cuevas, PhD
PhD Candidate
School of Rehabilitation
University of Texas—Rio Grande Valley
Edinburg, Texas

Alfred H. DeGraf, EdD
Fort Collins, Colorado

Paul Egan, MS
Dracut, Massachusetts

Danielle D. Fox, PhD
PhD Candidate
School of Rehabilitation
University of Texas—Rio Grande Valley
Edinburg, Texas

Bret A. Glass, PhD
Department of Educational, School, and
    Counseling Psychology
University of Missouri—Columbia
Columbia, Missouri

**Lloyd R. Goodwin, Jr., PhD, LCAS,
CRC, MAC, CCS, ACS**
Professor
Department of Addictions and Rehabilitation
    Studies
East Carolina University
Greenville, North Carolina

Noreen M. Graf, RhD, CRC
School of Rehabilitation
University of Texas—Rio Grande Valley
Edinburg, Texas

Cheryl Grenwelge, PhD
Center on Disability and Development
Department of Educational Psychology
Texas A&M University
College Station, Texas

Debra A. Harley, PhD, CRC
Department of Special Education and
    Rehabilitation Counseling
University of Kentucky
Lexington, Kentucky

Nicholas D. Holder, BS
Doctoral Candidate in Clinical Psychology
Veterans Affairs North Texas Health
    Care System
University of Texas Southwestern
    Medical Center
Dallas, Texas

Ryan P. Holliday, MA
Doctoral Candidate in Clinical Psychology
Veterans Affairs North Texas Health
    Care System
University of Texas Southwestern
    Medical Center
Dallas, Texas

Alexia Holovatyk, BS
Center for Psychological Studies
Nova Southeastern University
Fort Lauderdale, Florida

Jamylah Jackson, PhD, ABPP
Director of Psychology Training and Associate
    Professor of Psychiatry
Veterans Affairs North Texas Health
    Care System
University of Texas Southwestern
    Medical Center
Dallas, Texas

Brick Johnstone, PhD
Department of Health Psychology
University of Missouri—Columbia
Columbia, Missouri

Charlene M. Kampfe, PhD
Professor Emeritus
University of Arizona
Tucson, Arizona

Hanoch Livneh, PhD, CRC
Professor Emeritus
Portland State University
Portland, Oregon

Rosamond H. Madden, MSc, AM
Senior Research Fellow
Centre for Disability Research and Policy
University of Sydney
Sydney, New South Wales, Australia

**Irmo Marini, PhD, DSc,
CRC, CLCP**
Professor
School of Rehabilitation
University of Texas—Rio Grande Valley
Edinburgh, Texas

Gillian Mayersohn, PhD
Center for Psychological Studies
Nova Southeastern University
Fort Lauderdale, Florida

Michael J. Millington, PhD, CRC
Senior Lecturer
Rehabilitation Counselling
University of Sydney
Sydney, Australia

Gerardo Mireles, PhD
Center on Disability and Development
Department of Educational Psychology
Texas A&M University
College Station, Texas

Chris Moy, MS
Scranton, Pennsylvania

Robert J. Neumann
Chicago, Illinois

Kim Nguyen-Finn, PhD, LPC-S
PhD Candidate
School of Rehabilitation
University of Texas—Rio Grande Valley
Edinburg, Texas

Barry Nierenberg, PhD, ABPP
Center for Psychological Studies
Nova Southeastern University
Fort Lauderdale, Florida

Carol S. North, MD, MPE
Medical Director, The Altschuler Center for
Education & Research
Metrocare Services
The Nancy and Ray L. Hunt Chair in Crisis
Psychiatry and Professor of Psychiatry
Director, Division of Trauma & Disaster
University of Texas Southwestern Medical
Center
Dallas, Texas

Margaret A. Nosek, PhD
Center for Research on Women With
Disabilities
Department of Physical Medicine and
Rehabilitation
Baylor College of Medicine
Houston, Texas

Richard E. Oliver, PhD, FASAHP
Dean Emeritus
School of Health Professions
University of Missouri—Columbia
Columbia, Missouri

David B. Peterson, PhD, CRC, NCC
Licensed Clinical Psychologist and
Professor
California State University
Los Angeles, California

Rick Peterson, PhD
Center on Disability and Development
Department of Educational Psychology
Texas A&M University
College Station, Texas

Michael A. Rembis, PhD
Director of the Center for Disability
Studies
University of Buffalo (SUNY)
Buffalo, New York

J. Aaron Resch, PhD
Center on Disability and Development
Department of Educational Psychology
Texas A&M University
College Station, Texas

David S. Riggs, PhD
Department of Medical and Clinical
Psychology
University Services University of the Health
Sciences
Bethesda, Maryland

Shelley A. Riggs, PhD
Department of Psychological Science
University of North Texas
Denton, Texas

Maria G. Romero, PhD, CRC
Department of Psychology
University of Texas—Rio Grande Valley
Edinburg, Texas

Breeze Rueda, PhD, LPC
PhD Candidate
School of Rehabilitation
University of Texas—Rio
Grande Valley
Edinburg, Texas

Sophia Serpa, MS
Center for Psychological Studies
Nova Southeastern University
Fort Lauderdale, Florida

Manisha Sharma, PhD
PhD Candidate
School of Rehabilitation
University of Texas—Rio
Grande Valley
Edinburg, Texas

Frances W. Siu, PhD, CRC
California State University
Los Angeles, California

David W. Smart, PhD
Professor Emeritus
Counseling and Psychological Services Center
Brigham Young University
Provo, Utah

Julie F. Smart, PhD, CRC
Professor Emeritus
Department of Special Education and
Rehabilitation
Utah State University
Logan, Utah

Evan Smith, MS
Center for Psychological Studies
Nova Southeastern University
Fort Lauderdale, Florida

Linda Stacey
Framingham, Massachusetts

**Mark A. Stebnicki, PhD, LPC,
DCMHS, CRC, CCM, CCMC**
Professor and Coordinator, Military
    and Trauma Counseling Certificate
    Program
Department of Addictions and
    Rehabilitation
East Carolina University
Greenville, North Carolina

Alina M. Surís, PhD, ABPP
Senior Clinical Psychologist Researcher
    and Professor of Psychiatry
Veterans Affairs North Texas Health Care
    System
University of Texas Southwestern
    Medical Center
Dallas, Texas

Judy Teplow, MSW
Canton, Massachusetts

Chia Vang
PhD Candidate
School of Rehabilitation
University of Texas—Rio Grande Valley
Edinburg, Texas

Sara VanLooy, BA
Research Assistant
Yang-Tan Institute on Employment and
    Disability
ILR School
Cornell University
Ithaca, New York

John S. Wadsworth, PhD, CRC
College of Education
The University of Iowa
Iowa City, Iowa

Robert P. Winske, MS
Boston, Massachusetts

Beatrice A. Wright, PhD
University of Kansas
Lawrence, Kansas

Dalun Zhang, PhD
Center on Disability and Development
Department of Educational Psychology
Texas A&M University
College Station, Texas

Foreword

*I*n reviewing the seventh edition of *The Psychological and Social Aspects of Illness and Disability* I have come to believe that the publication of this updated edition could not come to the field of rehabilitation counseling at a more important time. This book provides a much-needed comprehensive discussion and analysis regarding the importance of the interaction between the psychological and social aspects that impact individuals and their rehabilitation outcomes. One might say that as this book is in its seventh edition, this type of discussion has already occurred. That is true, but the timing of the release of this updated version is important because the text indirectly provides a conceptual framework to guide rehabilitation counseling practitioners and students in developing an understanding of how psychological and social factors interact to impact individuals and their rehabilitation outcomes. In reviewing this seventh edition, several things stood out that make the book important, timely, and a significant contribution to the literature on rehabilitation counseling.

The first thing I did as I examined the text, was to look back at the previous editions and their forewords, several written by Professor Art Del Orto, who was one of the original editors of this book. In Professor Del Orto's initial edition and subsequent forewords, he provided a very rich review of the emergence of the research related to psychological and social aspects of disability, the key figures in this research, and how this research and those important figures impacted him as a scholar. By reexamining this informative history, one gains an understanding of how this important area of study emerged and has contributed to rehabilitation counseling research and practice. Understanding history is important because it grounds us and helps us appreciate our roots and our identity as a profession. Addressing how psychological and social factors interact with one's level of functioning to impact societal participation is one of the key pillars that distinguishes rehabilitation counseling from other helping professions. However, one thing that struck me as I was reviewing the seventh edition was how this current text informs the future by providing direction to rehabilitation counseling students, practitioners, and researchers. This text provides new and emerging information regarding how personal and environmental factors interact across the spectrum to impact individuals and outcomes. This text brings to life the *International Classification of Functioning, Disability, and Health* (ICF; World Health Organization, 2001) for rehabilitation counselors and provides contemporary information that can be used to educate, guide practice, and provide the foundation for emerging research related to the psychosocial aspects of disability and chronic disease. Emerging areas, such as working with veterans, refugees, and the aging workforce, along with many others, are covered and provide important information for rehabilitation counselors to use to address the emerging psychosocial issues and needs of the individuals they serve.

Building on my initial reaction, my second thought, maybe even more relevant, was that by indirectly grounding this text in the *ICF* framework, this book directly minimizes the medical model that unfortunately still guides rehabilitation counseling today. This text highlights the importance of psychological and social factors in human behavior, while eliminating the need to focus on identifying the appropriate and highly valued diagnosis to explain behavior and guide treatment. This text provides rehabilitation counselors with the necessary knowledge needed to conceptualize how personal, environmental, and functioning impact behavior and encourage rehabilitation counselors to develop and implement interventions that leverage resources, empower individuals, and ameliorate environmental barriers. This is in stark contrast to the medical model, which places a premium on establishing the correct diagnosis, using the derived diagnosis as the foundation of treatment, and focusing interventions exclusively on the individual. This difference is important and timely as students, practitioners, and scholars are continually having to deal with mixed messages from professional organizations and accreditation and licensure bodies that may cloak themselves in the guise of rehabilitation values while truly espousing the fundamental tenets of the medical model. This text provides a powerful and informative resource for students, practitioners, and scholars in developing and reinforcing rehabilitation counseling principles that guide rehabilitation counseling education, practice, and research.

Finally, a major strength of this book is its focus on new directions that will impact the provision of rehabilitation counseling education, practice, and research. Providing scholarly discussions of emerging issues, such as empathy resilience, and emerging populations, such as refuges and those who are obese, provides rehabilitation counselors at all levels with important information that will guide future education, practice, and research. In addition, the rich discussion of areas of grief, sexuality, family, culture, social justice, parenting, trauma, veterans, and religion allows students to be grounded in both theoretical and practical issues that impact overall psychosocial functioning. Finally, providing the historical context of how people with disabilities have been treated and the impact of individual and societal attitudes are critical so that emerging trends can be fully appreciated and all levels of rehabilitation professionals have a comprehensive foundation for understanding the psychosocial aspects of disability and the impact that rehabilitation counseling, when guided by conceptually sound principles, can have on maximizing societal participation of those with chronic health conditions and disabilities.

Overall, I would like to offer my sincere appreciation for the editorial work of Irmo Marini and Mark Stebnicki, as they have done a masterful job in collecting a group of chapters that provide contemporary, cutting-edge information regarding psychological and social aspects of chronic health and disability in a historically and theoretically relevant context. This book will become the formative text that guides the education of a new generation of rehabilitation counselors while informing current rehabilitation counseling practice and research. It is important to note that this book provides all levels of rehabilitation counselors with the much-needed resources necessary to begin to fulfill an *ICF*-based approach to chronic health and disability while minimizing a diagnostically based conceptualization that unfortunately still permeates much of today's education, research, and practice.

David R. Strauser, PhD
Department of Kinesiology and Community Health
College of Applied Health Sciences
University of Illinois at Urbana–Champaign
Champaign, Illinois

REFERENCE

World Health Organization. (2001). *International classification of functioning, disability and health: ICF*. Geneva, Switzerland: Author.

Preface

*I*t was the fall of 2010 when we first received a call from Art Dell Orto, the original coeditor of the first five editions of *The Psychological and Social Impact of Illness and Disability* (1977, 1984, 1991, 1999, and 2007), who asked us to carry on this work. Art indicated that he was not only retiring after an outstanding career at Boston University, but also retiring from many of his professional projects as well. The original edition of this work began with Art Dell Orto, professor, Boston University, and Bob Marinelli, professor, West Virginia University, who edited the first four editions, then Paul Power, professor emeritus, University of Maryland, worked on the fifth edition. Irmo and I have been friends with Art and many of his colleagues over our careers and were flattered, grateful, and honored to be asked to continue editing this exceptional work. When the book first appeared in 1977, few books existed on the topic of psychosocial aspects of chronic illness and disability. Irmo and I had written several chapters in the previous editions of this work based on our research and practice within this speciality area. However, to be asked to edit and bequeathed this work is much like Captain Kirk of the Starship *Enterprise* asking Lt. Commander and First Science Officer Mr. Spock to take over the helm. Indeed, this body of work had to continue through the constellation of books on rehabilitation, counseling, and psychology with full thrusters and warp-drive full on.

Irmo hired and mentored me in my first job as an assistant professor in the Department of Psychology and Counseling at Arkansas State University. I was fortunate to be hired directly out of my doctoral program at the Rehabilitation Institute, Southern Illinois University, Carbondale, back in 1995. As any doctoral candidate can attest, it is critical to have good mentors to guide you through the process of teaching, research, and service, and to prepare you for a publish-or-perish job at a teaching institution. It is equally important that one's first experience in academia also have good mentors to guide one through the real-world experiences of teaching, research, and service.

At my first job in academia, after 11 years of working in rehabilitation, counseling, and behavioral health, I met Irmo, an outstanding mentor; our personalities meshed into one unified brain, we thought, felt, and behaved in the same way on virtually every topic. We never perceived our time together at Arkansas State or currently as simply being "working colleagues"; our friendship runs deep and there are no real boundaries between work and play. It is a culture that few are fortunate to experience, where metaphorically work-is-play and play-is-work. Within a culture like this, the end product usually results in the second edition of a book being better than the first, and the seventh edition being better than the sixth.

This brings us forward to the seventh edition, in which we developed materials based on the talents of many authors and communicated this in a readable and usable manner. Approximately two thirds of the chapters are new and/or updated. In keeping with the formula from previous editions, we have maintained the foundation of seminal works of early authors; many present-day authors have leaned on these works for theoretical constructs, models, and practice with the intention of working with persons with chronic illnesses and disabilities. Other sections of *The Psychological and Social Impact of Illness and Disability* feature emerging populations, for whom services are required to support the mental, physical, and spiritual well-being of the individuals and groups who are aged, disabled, or have acquired disabilities because of extraordinarily stressful and traumatic events such as combator, natural disasters, and critical incidents such as terrorism. It also addresses the negative impact of societal inequities, oppression, poverty, and disability on those most in need. Overall, this text addresses the medical, physical, psychosocial, and vocational aspects of a rather unique culture of individuals. Living with chronic illnesses and disabilities is a daily challenge, but one that many meet with resilience and perseverance. It is anticipated that this nexus of material enrich the knowledge, awareness, and skills of both students and instructors in the fields of rehabilitation, counseling, psychology, and the allied health sciences.

Finally, a psychosocial text concerning illness and disability would not be complete without the stories and perspectives of resilient persons with disabilities who have lived the experience. Irmo and I have retained the majority of these poignant personal accounts written by persons with disabilities and/or their loved ones who care for them. Based on these revealing personal accounts and experiences of disability, each section of the book contains keystone and foundational material that has good intentions for learning and professional practice. The Appendices contain exercises to enhance learning. The insights shared in the seventh edition continue to give students and practitioners a different perspective of life with a chronic illness and disability in the United States.

Supplemental materials in the form of an Instructor's manual and PowerPoint presentations are available for qualified instructors and can be requested by emailing: textbook@springerpub.com

---

Acknowledgments

We would like to most humbly thank several key people who made this book possible. Editorial Director of Behavioral Sciences extraordinaire, Sheri W. Sussman, who has guided and supported us through several Springer Publishing books, made this experience as stress-free as possible with her sarcastic humor and tremendous wisdom. We would like to also thank Assistant Editor Mindy Chen for diligently keeping us organized, updated, and on time. Accolades as well go to Joanne Jay, VP of Production, and her production team for the nuts-and-bolts support, all in all making yet another Springer product a flawless work of knowledge. A special thank you to a most respected colleague, Arthur Dell Orto, who, after 35 years entrusted us to carry on with his, Bob Marinelli, and Paul Power's best-selling textbook. Dr. Dell Orto's numerous book contributions to the field span his career and have elevated thousands of educators and counselors alike in various disciplines. This seventh edition maintains at least a third of these scholars' previous ideas from earlier editions. We also would like to acknowledge Darlene Marini, who once again took on the tedious task of inputting the reference lists for certain chapters. In addition, Irmo is also appreciative of his two research assistants—doctoral student Breeze Rueda and graduate student Rigel Pinon—their assistance in scouring the literature for the most up-to-date, relevant publications for his chapters. Finally and most important, we acknowledge the select group of authors who have contributed to this seventh edition. Their expertise and field research elevates the social consciousness on disability studies. Similarly, we would like to thank the authors for their personal stories regarding the lived experience of having a disability or sharing a life with someone who is disabled. The seventh edition of this textbook would not have been as successful without these personal perspectives.

Irmo Marini
Mark A. Stebnicki

I

Historical Perspectives on Illness and Disability

*T*he first part of this book addresses disability from a sociological or social psychological perspective, focusing on exploring disability from the outside looking inward. A major premise for contemporary scholars in the field has been to examine the impact of the environment on the individual with a disability and his or her family. Somatopsychology and ecological and minority models of disability emphasize the positive and all-too-often negative psychosocial implications that societal attitudes, physical barriers, and social inequities can have on persons with disabilities. For this reason, we first explore past treatment of persons with disabilities before proceeding to discuss why and how those with disabilities and their families respond, react, adjust, or adapt to their situations. The empirical literature over the past 35 years has documented a fairly consistent set of conclusions on this matter. Perceived negative societal attitudes and physical barriers in many, but not all, cases have a negative impact on the self-concept and mental health of persons with disabilities. Conversely, positive societal attitudes and minimal barriers in many, but not all, cases lead to better adaptation for such persons.

MAJOR HIGHLIGHTS IN PART I

- As detailed in Chapter 1, the historical record includes many instances in which U.S. immigration and disability laws excluded, detained, or even sterilized persons deemed unfit to become Americans. Medical developments and political ideology help guide medical and mental health care policies that reflect disability rights. The debate surrounding issues, such as selective genetics and assisted suicide, suggests newer health care policies are on the horizon. Given the current political landscape, however, there are some signs of reverting back to the days of the precivil and disability rights movements. In this climate, understanding our past can assist us in constructing a positive future that is fair and just for persons with illnesses and disabilities.
- Negative societal attitudes toward persons with disabilities are evident and have been reflected in disability policy and legislation. Chapter 2 discusses why society as a whole is anxious, reluctant, resistant, and in some cases afraid of people with disabilities and those who are different. Understanding the misperceptions that surround people with disabilities and how these attitudes originated is critical to understanding how we can move forward. The authors of this chapter explore aspects of the conscious and subconscious human psyche at the root of societal perceptions of disability.

- The historical treatment of persons with psychiatric disabilities in the United States is particularly noteworthy, given the harsh treatment, discrimination, and institutional repression that have ensued. Psychiatric disability or mental illness has arguably been perceived and treated more harshly than any other diagnosed disability. Chapter 3 describes early beliefs of psychological illness as demonic possession, the involuntary confinement of the mentally ill in subhuman "institutions," use of prefrontal lobotomies, and debate about the legal definition of *torture*. In the United States today, persons with a history of mental illness are often homeless or incarcerated. Indeed, psychiatric disability is a category unto itself. In this chapter, the author chronicles the often brutal and inhumane history of treatment toward those with psychiatric disabilities and what happens to individuals when they are perceived as less than human.

- Chapter 4 explores the four primary models of disability: biomedical, functional, environmental, and sociopolitical. Depending on one's frame of reference regarding disability, each model presents a philosophical and treatment approach to working with persons with disabilities that not only impacts rehabilitation professionals' attitudes but also their emphasis on how they go about counseling and/or treating their patients/clients. This framework often lays the foundation for how persons with disabilities interrelate with professionals as well.

- Chapter 5 discusses guidelines for rehabilitation professionals that include treating others with dignity and respect, advocacy for the removal of environmental barriers, fundamental civil rights for all persons, and the importance of self-help organizations. The longevity and foundational roots of research in this area attest to the leadership in the field regarding psychosocial aspects of disability. The material assembled here, as a whole, provides tangible evidence for assisting persons with disabilities in rehabilitation practice.

1

History of Treatment Toward Persons With Disabilities in America

Danielle D. Fox and Irmo Marini

*D*espite the common ideal that the United States is a land of opportunity, the early history of America was not necessarily a welcoming one for everyone. The fear of diluting American bloodlines with potential hereditary diseases or illnesses had a huge impact on public and governmental beliefs and attitudes. This fear, combined with the eugenics movement of the early 19th century, led American lawmakers to pass laws that specifically restricted certain people or groups from entering the United States and, within some city ordinances, even kept them out of public view. Early American lawmakers believed that by doing this, they were protecting the welfare of the country and Americans as a whole. The purpose of this chapter is to review the history of treatment toward people with disabilities (PWDs) in the United States.

> Give me your tired, your poor, your huddled masses yearning to breathe free, the wretched refuse of your teeming shore. Send these, the homeless, tempest-tosst to me. (Lazarus, 1883)

This is a section of the 14-line sonnet that is engraved on the Statue of Liberty in New York City. The statue was completed in 1886 and the verse was actually inscribed on her in 1945. These words symbolized an American ideal against oppression to all immigrants who entered the United States during the early 20th century. In reality, however, American immigration legislation and practice during that time was in direct opposition to the intended message engraved on the Statue of Liberty.

EARLY IMMIGRATION LEGISLATION

"It is often said, and with truth, that each of the different alien peoples coming to America has something to contribute to American civilization. But what America needs is desirable additions to, and not inferior substitutions for, what it already possesses" (Ward, 1924, p. 103). Early immigration literature and the apparent attitudes and treatment toward PWDs, as well as certain other immigrant populations, were blatantly prejudiced and discriminatory. Antidisability sentiment became more evident with immigration restriction, which began as early as the development of the first North

American settlements. It was after 1838, when a large influx of immigrants came to the United States, that the issue of disability became more pressing to the early American settlers (Treadway, 1925).

Antidisability legislation began in 1882 and continued through 1924, with some of the original laws in effect until the 1980s. The concept behind early immigration legislation was to prevent the immigration of people who were considered undesirable. Early Americans believed that preventing people considered undesirable from entering the United States was a means of protecting not only the people but also the welfare of the country as a whole (Ward, 1907). Baynton (2005) states, "disability was a crucial factor in deciding whether or not an immigrant would be allowed to enter the United States" (p. 34). The term *"undesirable "*was used to describe people from any race, ethnicity, or religion, and/or with a disability, who were believed to be more likely to pass on less-than-desirable traits to their offspring. The purpose of early immigration legislation was to protect the American bloodlines, and, according to early lawmakers, this meant excluding people based on any trait that could be considered as undesirable. Baynton (2005) states,

> One of the driving forces behind early federal immigration law, beginning with the first major Immigration Act in 1882, was the exclusion of people with mental and physical defects (as well as those considered criminal or immoral, problems seen at the time as closely related to mental defect). (p. 32)

This marked the beginning of the exclusion of PWDs in America.

In the years following 1882, early American lawmakers became more and more concerned about the bloodlines of immigrants seeking entrance into the United States and their possible effect on the bloodlines that were already present. With the 1891 revised Immigration Act, a key wording change made restrictions even more discretionary regarding excluding PWDs. Baynton (2005, p. 33) notes that the original 1882 law wording was "any lunatic, idiot, or any person *unable* to take care of himself or herself without becoming a public charge"; the phrase changed in the 1891 law from *unable* to *"likely* to become a public charge." In 1894, the Immigration Restriction League (IRL) was established in Boston. The primary focus of the IRL was to "carry on a general educational campaign for more effective restriction and selection" (Ward, 1924, p. 102). According to Ward, the league's fears were that the United States was becoming an "asylum for the poor and the oppressed of every land" (p. 100). Ward went on to explain:

> Americans began to realize that the ideal of furnishing an asylum for all the world's oppressed was coming into conflict with changed economic and social conditions. The cold facts were that the supply of public land was practically exhausted; that acute labor problems, aggravated by the influx of ignorant and unskilled aliens, had arisen; that the large cities were becoming congested with foreigners; that large numbers of mentally and physically unfit, and of the economically undesirable, had come to the United States. (p. 102)

As such, by 1896, literacy requirements were imposed on all immigrants entering the United States, and then from 1903 through 1907, immigration laws were broadened and became more restrictive in scope. However, it was only after the 1917 revisions to the 1907 Immigration Act had occurred that more specific and harsher discriminatory language appeared in legislation. Before this, in 1903, persons with epilepsy were added to the list, as well as individuals who met the 1903 wording: "persons who have been insane within 5 years previous [or] who have had two or more attacks of insanity at any time previously" (Baynton, 2005, p. 33). Treadway (1925) cites the exclusionary language of the law in the 1907 Act:

> The insane; idiots; imbeciles; feebleminded; chronic alcoholics; constitutional psychopathic inferiors; the mentally defective whose defect would modify their ability to earn a living; those with loathsome or dangerous contagious diseases, and those over sixteen years of age who were without a reading knowledge of some language. (p. 351)

The 1907 Act was also the first in which the law required a medical certificate for persons judged to be "mentally or physically defective, such mental or physical defect being of a nature which *may affect* the ability of such alien to earn a living" (Baynton, 2005, p. 33).

The subsequent years saw increasing restrictions, including financial penalties on transport companies and ship captains for the transportation of immigrants considered "unfit" for entry into the United States (Barkan, 1991; Baynton, 2005; Treadway, 1925). In an attempt to gain better control of the immigration situation, ship captains at ports of entry were to examine prospective immigrants for "defects." Although they were neither physicians nor did they have any medical experience, the purpose of their inspections was to medically examine the immigrants. If a disability, either mental or physical, was observed or perceived, the ship captain at transit or the inspector at entry ports was authorized to either deny departure from the immigrant's country of origin or deny entry into the United States. If an immigrant was granted departure from his or her country of origin and, on arrival, entry into the United States was denied, the immigrant was to be deported back to his or her country of origin at the expense of the transport company that brought the individual (Baynton, 2005). For this reason, many ship captains in all likelihood denied numerous individuals for various vague reasons in order to not be fined or potentially lose their jobs. Baynton notes:

> Inspectors prided themselves on their ability to make a "snapshot diagnosis" as immigrants streamed past them single file. For most immigrants, a normal appearance usually meant an uneventful passage through the immigration station. An abnormal appearance, however, meant a chalked letter on the back. Once chalked, a closer inspection was required—L for lameness, K for suspected hernia, G for goiter, X for suspected mental illness, and so on. (p. 37)

This process allowed for the discrimination and/or refusal of immigrants based on suspected impairments whether or not any impairment was present. The commissioner general of immigration in his 1907 report regarding the governing immigration laws essentially laid out that the primary reason for the laws was to exclude anyone with a disability or anyone perceived as having a disability. The commissioner wrote, "The exclusion from this country of the morally, mentally, and physically deficient is the principal object to be accomplished by the immigration laws" (Baynton, p. 34). In order to exclude those with physical disabilities, the regulations stated that inspectors were to observe individuals at rest and then in motion to detect any irregularities or abnormalities in gait. Again, the wording for excluding individuals was vague and granted the inspectors full discretion in excluding anyone they wished. Baynton wrote about an Ellis Island medical inspector whose job was to "detect poorly built, defective or broken down human beings" (p. 34). A few examples of the physical impairments listed included spinal curvature, varicose veins, poor eyesight, hernia, flat feet, bunions, deafness, arthritis, hysteria, and, simply, poor physical development. Once again, as with all age-old debates on eugenics, ethnocentricity, and exactly who was considered the weaker species, there was no consistent consensus.

During this period, individuals were often excluded based on size or physical stature, or lack thereof, and abnormal sexual development. In addition, the commissioner and IRL, among others, were concerned about the public charge or becoming an economic drain because of perceived discrimination from employers in hiring. The surgeon general in a letter to the commissioner noted that such persons were:

> A bad economic risk ... known to their associates who make them the butt of coarse jokes to their own despair, and to the impairment of the work in hand. Among employers, it is difficult for these unfortunates to get or retain jobs, their facial and bodily appearance at least in adult life, furnishing a patent advertisement of their condition. (Baynton, 2005, p. 38)

In all, it is difficult to determine exactly how many immigrants were excluded either before or on entering the United States. Baynton (2005) cites statistics that increased over the years and notes that the actual numbers were likely much higher. The number of individuals excluded because they were likely to become a public charge or were mentally or physically defective in 1895 was 1,720; in 1905 the number was greater than 8,000, and by 1910 it rose to more than 16,000. Individuals from certain countries in particular were denied more often than the others. Individuals from Slovakia were viewed as slow witted, Jews were seen as having poor physique and being neurotic, and those of Portuguese, Greek, or Syrian ethnicity were described as undersized (Baynton, 2005).

For those individuals who were somehow allowed entry to the United States, or were born in the United States with any type of perceived or real impairment, life was not generally favorable regarding societal attitudes. Specifically, Longmore and Goldberger (2000) noted court rulings in which railroads and public transit systems were essentially granted permission to deny access to transportation for these impaired people. School laws were upheld segregating PWDs by not alllowing them to attend school or requiring that they be taught in a segregated room. Employers were also permitted to discriminate in hiring those with disabilities, and all public venues such as restaurants, theaters, and so on, could deny access and frequently did so. For all intents and purposes, many of those with disabilities during the early 20th century were relegated to being shut-ins in their own homes, and when venturing out were subject to ridicule and indignant comments.

Many PWDs were outraged by these political and societal attitudes and the blatant efforts to prejudice and discriminate against them. For many, it was not only the negative attitudes of being devalued and dehumanized, but also the discrimination of being excluded from the workforce. Longmore and Goldberger (2000) cite the historic accounts during the spring of 1935 after 5 years of the Great Depression, in which a number of persons with physical and other disabilities demanded their voices be heard and protested against New York City's Emergency Relief Bureau demanding jobs. Forming the League of the Physically Handicapped (LPH), this group focused on discrimination issues as opposed to their medical impairments. Media coverage back then was also largely discriminatory and prejudiced. Longmore and Goldberger cite how media and popular culture portrayals during the 1920s and 1930s perceived PWDs as villains, victims, sinners, charity cases, unsightly objects, dangerous denizens of society, and unworthy citizens (p. 896).

Franklin D. Roosevelt was a member of the LPH, and although he largely hid his own paralysis from polio at age 39 years, he strived for the rehabilitation of those with disabilities. He epitomized what persons with a disability "can" do and is arguably one of America's greatest presidents, having presided for 12 years over troubling times, including the Great

Depression, the signing of the 1935 Social Security Act, and World War II (Gallagher, 1994). In his book, *FDR's Splendid Deception,* Gallagher cites how Roosevelt was intuitively aware of the negative societal attitudes toward disability and aware that if the public knew of both the extent of his disability and chronic pain, he would be perceived as a weak, ineffective leader. As such, Roosevelt had agreements with the media not to photograph or film him in his wheelchair or while ambulating with his leg braces. Ironically, he did not really have a disability agenda and in fact tried to reduce vocational rehabilitation funding by 25%, which was ultimately not supported by Congress (Gallagher, 1994).

THE EUGENICS MOVEMENT IN AMERICA

Driving the ideology of the early immigration Acts was Charles Darwin's highly influential 1859 book, *On the Origin of Species by Means of Natural Selection, or the Preservation of Favored Races in the Struggle of Life*, which initially set out to explain the concept of heredity in plants and animals. Darwin refrained from applying his beliefs to humans out of fear of the reaction from the ruling religions. Sir Francis Galton, a cousin of Darwin's, whose own studies primarily focused on mathematics and meteorology, was inspired by Darwin's work and the implications of it. Galton applied mathematics to the study of heredity as a whole, and through this application he established not only some of the techniques of modern statistics but also the basis for what he later called *eugenics* (Pearson, 1995). Galton, who coined the term *eugenics* in 1883, believed that natural selection could rid mankind of problems such as disease, criminality, alcoholism, and poverty (Farrell, 1979). Farrell states that when Galton introduced the word *eugenics* in 1883 he did so with the following explanation:

> We greatly want a brief word to express the science of improving stock, which is by no means confined to questions of judicious mating, but which, especially in the case of man, takes cognizance of all influences that tend in however remote a degree to give to the more suitable races or strains of blood a better chance of prevailing speedily over the less suitable than they otherwise would have had. The word eugenics sufficiently expresses the idea; it is at least a neater word and a more generalized one than viriculture which I once ventured to use. (p. 112)

The concept of eugenics reached America around 1900, and many prominent politicians, physicians, and academics agreed with Galton's premise of essentially restricting the promulgation of those considered the weaker species. The notion of protecting and preserving healthy American bloodlines for the betterment of future generations was idealistic in theory and would later prove extremely difficult to implement. The central question contemplated for these powerful and predominantly Caucasian White males was to decide who exactly was the weaker species, and how exactly could these undesirables be restricted from bearing children (Marini, 2011a). President Theodore Roosevelt also embraced eugenics in the United States along with other highly influential people such as Alexander Graham Bell, John Harvey Kellogg, and J. C. Penney, to name a few (Pearson, 1995).

STERILIZATION IN THE UNITED STATES

Evidence of eugenic ideals became more obvious with the passage of sterilization laws in the early 20th century, the primary goal of which was to "improve the quality of the nation's citizenry by reducing the birth rate of individuals they considered to be "fee-bleminded" (Largent, 2002, p. 190). The term *feebleminded* was used at this time to describe anyone with any type of observed or perceived mental or physical disability. Eugenics continued to gain strength and support through the first quarter of the 20th century with 27 of the 48 states adopting sterilization laws (Farrell, 1979). The state of Indiana was at the forefront of the sterilization movement, being the first to implement eugenic sterilization laws in 1907.

Although the first sterilization law was passed in 1907, Osgood (2001) noted that unauthorized sterilization of the so-called defectives had already occurred in institutions in several states as early as the 1890s (p. 257). In 1909, the state of Oregon also implemented eugenic sterilization laws, 5 years after Dr. Bethenia Owens-Adair had proposed sterilization in Oregon as a means of dealing with persons considered to be criminals and/or insane (Largent, 2002). Noll (2005) reports that the use of intelligence testing in the 1920s allowed medical and mental health doctors to more accurately identify "feeblemindedness." As the years progressed, more states adopted eugenic sterilization laws, and, as the United States entered World War II, the nation's state mental health and prison authorities reported more than 38,000 sterilizations (Largent, 2002, p. 192). In the 1920s, the most notable Supreme Court sterilization case was *Buck v. Bell*. In 1927, Carrie Buck, a 17-year-old Virginia girl, became pregnant and was institutionalized by her foster parents in the Virginia State Colony for Epileptics and Feeble-Minded. Carrie's mother had already been committed and was deemed feebleminded and subsequently sterilized. Because Carrie's mother was deemed feebleminded, Carrie was also deemed feebleminded and was sterilized as well. Carrie had a younger sister who, under the pretense that she was undergoing an appendectomy, was also sterilized as a result of her mother's perceived mental capacity. Although there was no evidence to the accusations that Carrie Buck was promiscuous, the case went to the U.S. Supreme Court where Judge Oliver Wendell Holmes, Jr., reported in an 8 to 1 decision that the state of Virginia was supported by its sterilization law and further stated, "three generations of imbeciles are enough" (Carlson, 2009, p. 178). The case of Carrie Buck was not an isolated incident at the time, and although other cases similar in nature were found in other states to be unconstitutional, *Buck v. Bell* was never overturned. Despite the injustice associated with forced sterilization of people considered to be developmentally disabled, mentally ill, or simply criminals, sterilization laws lasted well into the 1980s in some states (Largent, 2002). Although there was a focus on eugenic sterilization laws, other laws that specifically targeted persons with mental and physical disabilities were being passed.

THE UGLY LAWS

> Any person who is diseased, maimed, mutilated or in any way deformed so as to be an unsightly or disgusting object, or an improper person to be allowed in or on the streets, highways, thoroughfares or public places in this city shall not therein or thereon expose himself or herself to public view under penalty of one dollar for each offense. On the conviction of any person for a violation of this section, if it shall seem proper and just, the fine provided for may be suspended, and such person detained at the police station, where he shall be well cared for, until he can be committed to the county poor house. (Coco, 2010, p. 23)

This was a City of Chicago ordinance, originally passed in 1881. Unsightly beggar ordinances passed between the years 1867 and 1913 were otherwise known as *Ugly Laws*.

The first unsightly beggar ordinance was passed in San Francisco in 1867. Although these ordinances had been in place for 14 years before the passage of the Chicago ordinance, it is the most well known and considered "the most egregious example of discrimination against people with physical disabilities in the United States" (Coco, 2010, p. 23). The passing of these ordinances and laws allowed some insight into how disability was perceived. PWDs were generally thought of as a burden to society as they lacked the ability to care for themselves or contribute in any way to society. This perception, however, was largely contingent on one's social standing and social contribution (Schweik, 2009, as cited in Coco, 2010). Although unsightly beggar ordinances were commonplace in cities throughout the country, Chicago's unsightly beggar ordinance remained on the law books until 1973 (Coco, 2010).

However, the soldiers returning from World War II with various disabilities provide a good example of how some PWDs were perceived. For example, soldiers were often viewed with sympathy but were nevertheless respected because of their contribution, whereas a civilian born with a disability would often not be perceived in the same way. The Industrial Revolution in the United States further increased the number of Americans with disabilities, as factory workers began to sustain injuries leading to chronic conditions. Without effective workers compensation laws early on, injured workers had to sue their employers, with the vast majority often losing their suits for contributory negligence and for knowingly accepting the hazards of the job, otherwise known as "assumption of risk" (Marini, 2011b).

For some PWDs with facial or physical deformities, performing in circus freak shows became the only employment they could obtain. These PWDs appeared to be more highly regarded and were often considered to be prominent citizens despite the fact that in certain parts of the country, where Ugly Laws were adopted, they were unable to show themselves in public.

MOVEMENT TOWARD EQUALITY

As disability discrimination and sterilization laws were being passed concerning PWDs, helpful legislation was also being passed. The 1920s brought about the Smith–Fees Act (P.L. 66–236), allowing services to PWDs such as vocational guidance, occupational adjustment, and placement services. In 1935 the Social Security Act (P.L. 74–271) was passed and the State-Federal Vocational Rehabilitation Program was established as a permanent program (Parker, Szymanski, & Patterson, 2005). Despite this early legislation and numerous additional laws over time designed to protect and employ PWDs in the workforce, the unemployment rate for PWDs has been dismally held at around 70%. Yelin (1991) noted that the lowest unemployment rate for PWDs was actually during World War II because many able-bodied Americans were involved in the war and manufacturing jobs for the war effort increased dramatically. Once the war was over, however, tens of thousands of able-bodied men and women in the armed services returned home looking for work, and thousands of workers with disabilities were subsequently replaced and suddenly unemployed. There was a shift in who was entering the workforce in the United States (Longmore & Goldberger, 2000).

The year 1943 marked the passage of landmark legislation with the Vocational Rehabilitation Act Amendments (P.L. 113), essentially increasing the amount of state vocational services available to PWDs (Parker et al., 2005). The Vocational Rehabilitation Act Amendments also broadened the definition of disability, allowing persons with mental illness or psychiatric disabilities to be eligible for services. Disability rights continued to make progress for the next 30 years without much fanfare, but unemployment rates remained relatively the same as they are today.

The 1973 Rehabilitation Act was also considered to be landmark legislation for PWDs, especially since President Nixon was considering abolishing the state/federal Vocational Rehabilitation program altogether. After much debate and considerable outcry from disability groups, President Nixon signed into law what is believed to be the first civil rights laws for PWDs, from which the 1990 Americans with Disabilities Act (ADA) was designed. Again, there was increased funding for public vocational rehabilitation programs and affirmative action in the hiring of federal employees (Parker et al., 2005). Although this landmark employment legislation was unprecedented, it was extremely difficult for employees to sue and win their claims against discriminatory employers. Colker (1999) noted that 94% of all court trials were decided in the employer's favor. The statistic remains high even today, as much of the burden of proof lies with the suing employee. Separately, sections 501 to 504 of the Act also addressed access to transportation, removal of architectural barriers, and physical access to all newly constructed federal buildings. Perhaps one of the most criticized aspects of the 1973 Act was the fact that there was no enforcement entity designed to check whether policies were being followed or implemented.

In 1975, the Rehabilitation Act was combined with the Education for All Handicapped Children Act (P.L. 94–142), now known as the Individuals with Disabilities Education Act (IDEA). IDEA allowed for opportunities such as equal access to public education for all children with disabilities in the least restrictive environment. IDEA also allowed for children with disabilities to be tested through multiple means, such as being tested in their native language. The law also gave parents the right to view their children's school records (Olkin, 1999). The 1986 revision of IDEA extended services to provide early intervention for children from birth to preschool, help with equipment purchases, and provide legal assistance to families with children with disabilities (Olkin, 1999).

Perhaps the single most important legislation to date concerning the civil rights of PWDs was the 1990 passage of the Americans with Disabilities Act (ADA) by President George H. W. Bush. The Act contains five titles: employment, extended access to state and federal government services including public or paratransit transportation access, public accommodations for physical access to all public venues (e.g., restaurants, theaters, sporting events), access to telecommunications (e.g., closed captioning, theater audio loops), and a miscellaneous title. The ADA has arguably been deemed a success as far as making communities more accessible; however, there continues to be complaints and lawsuits filed daily owing to employers and businesses that continue to knowingly or unknowingly discriminate (Blackwell, Marini, & Chacon, 2001). Some PWDs continue to see the glass as half empty regarding physical access and societal attitudes; others see it as half full (Marini, 2001). The United States Equal Employment Opportunity Commission's charge statistics website (n.d.) indicates that since 2009, there have been over 20,000 to 25,000 filed disability employment discrimination claims annually.

CURRENT PULSE ON AMERICA REGARDING DISABILITY

Attitudes, physical access, and the laws regarding PWDs have unquestionably improved in the last century. The eugenics movement essentially died down after World War II, primarily because of Social Darwinism and the Nazi extermination of an estimated 250,000

German citizens and war veterans with disabilities (Marini, 2011a). In America, many eugenicists realized that this extremist version was essentially a slippery slope and that continued forced sterilization, as well as forbidding those with epilepsy, mental illness, or mental retardation from marrying, could potentially lead them down a similar path.

Current attitudes of Americans without disabilities toward those with disabilities suggest contradictory sentiments of both admiration and pity (Harris, 1991). Most likely influenced by media portrayals, the sentiment of admiration can be easily explained when we watch a documentary on FDR, Wilma Rudolph, Christopher Reeve, or Stephen Hawking. Conversely, the pity sentiment occurs when one watches any televised charitable event, particularly *Jerry's Kids Muscular Dystrophy* Labor Day telethon. Although Americans generally believe that it is right to hire a qualified individual with a disability, many nondisabled persons still believe that PWDs are fundamentally "different" from those without disabilities (Harris, 1991).

As previously noted, how much better conditions and attitudes toward those with disabilities have become is still open to debate. Although many outside observers anecdotally argue that PWDs get free benefits and health care without making a contribution to society, others are quick to point out a different reality. Specifically, with an approximate 65% unemployment rate and two thirds of those with disabilities indicating they would work if they could, this population has one of the highest poverty rates in America (Rubin & Roessler, 2008). Single minority females with children having a disability have the highest rate of poverty, along with single minority female parents with a disability (Brault, 2012). More than 25% of African Americans and Hispanics live under the federal poverty rate, and approximately 30% of caregivers who have a child with a disability live in poverty as well (Annual Disability Statistics Compendium, 2014; United States Department of Health and Human Services, 2014). This is compared to approximately 13% of those Caucasian families without a disabled loved one.

Although physical barriers and community access have improved exponentially since the 1990 ADA, several studies of persons with physical disabilities suggest that the United States still has a long way to go to become barrier free. Specifically, two recent studies have found that even 22 years after the ADA was signed into law, persons with physical disabilities still cite physical access barriers as the number one frustration (Graf, Marini, & Blankenship, 2009; Marini, Bhakta, & Graf, 2009). Negative and ambivalent societal attitudes were not far behind in the rankings as perceived by those with disabilities. Although many outsiders or those without disabilities and no experience with disability view the proverbial glass as half-full, many persons with disabilities (insiders who live the experience) continue to see the glass as half empty (Marini, 2011a). Many experience daily frustrations with health care, education, public accommodations, transportation, and employment. These are among the ongoing daily hassles many Americans with disabilities face (O'Day & Goldstein, 2005).

Eugenics has taken a different form in the 21st century. Today, scientists are improving medical technology to remove the so-called defective genes responsible for various neuromuscular diseases while an unborn fetus is still in the embryo stage (Marini, 2011a). Likewise, parents are now able to abort a fetus that may result in a child having a developmental disability and essentially start over. Roberts, Stough, and Parrish (2002) found that when referred by their physician for genetic testing in relation to potential fetus birth defects, 65% of mothers elected to abort such a child. However, when mothers were provided with information and educational counseling about the disease or disability, many changed their minds. The authors found little effort to educate and counsel expectant mothers takes place in genetic testing clinics. Designer babies are also medically possible now, meaning parents can select gender, eye, and hair color.

In one extreme example of the quest for the perfect human, a *Playboy* photographer auctioned off a supermodel's egg and 5 million people visited the website in one morning, offering $42,000 for the egg (Smart, 2009). For those who can afford to pay for a designer baby, the option has arrived.

The survival-of-the-fittest concept and natural selection in the 21st century appear to have morphed into a survival of the financially fittest ideology. The ramifications of the 2008 Great Recession, continual middle-class decline into poverty, and historical government actions to cut social programs like Social Security, Medicare, and Medicaid ultimately leave those who need the most assistance to fend for themselves (Huffington, 2010; Reich, 2010). Today the have-nots are no longer sterilized or exterminated, but live on the fringe of society with poor living conditions, poor health care access and treatment, unemployment or underemployment, and food insufficiency. Indeed, the most disenfranchised of us, largely including those minorities with disabilities, may see their life expectancy shortened by 20+ years depending on one's ZIP Code (Bloch et al., 2017). With the aging of America and millions of baby boomers moving into their golden years, the financial portfolios of these individuals dictate what the quality of their lives will be, like at no time before in American history. Although Americans are living longer and healthier lives, those with disabilities and little income may face even greater precarious times ahead.

REFERENCES

Annual Disability Statistics Compendium. (2014). Poverty in the US. Retrieved from http://disability compendium.org/statistics/poverty

Barkan, E. (1991). Reevaluating progressive eugenics: Herbert Spencer Jennings and the 1924 immigration legislation. *Journal of the History of Biology, 24*(1), 91–112.

Baynton, D. (2005). Defectives in the land: Disability and American immigration policy, 1882–1924. *Journal of American Ethnic History, 24*(30), 31–44.

Blackwell, T. M., Marini, I., & Chacon, M. (2001). The impact of the Americans with Disabilities Act on independent living. *Rehabilitation Education, 15*(4), 395–408.

Bloch, J., Holzmann, C., Koczan, D., Helmke, B. M., & Bullerdiek, J. (2017). Factors affecting the loss of MED12-mutated leiomyoma cells during in vitro growth. *Oncotarget, 8*(21), 34762–34772.

Brault, M. W. (2012). Americans with disabilities: 2010. In *Current population reports* (Report No. P70-131). Washington, DC: U.S. Census Bureau.

Carlson, E. (2009). Three generations, no imbeciles: Eugenics, the Supreme Court, and *Buck v. Bell*. *Quarterly Review of Biology, 84*(2), 178–180.

Coco, A. P. (2010). Diseased, maimed, mutilated: Categorizations of disability and an ugly law in late nineteenth-century Chicago. *Journal of Social History, 44*(1), 23–37.

Colker, R. (1999). The Americans with Disabilities Act: A windfall for defendants, *Harvard Civil Rights–Civil Liberties Law Review,* 34, 99.

Darwin, C. (1859). *On the origin of species by means of natural selection, or the preservation of favoured races in the struggle for life* (American ed.). New York, NY: D. Appleton & Co.

Farrell, L. A. (1979). The history of eugenics: A bibliographical review. *Annals of Science, 36*(2), 111–123.

Gallagher, H. G. (1994). *FDR's splendid deception*. Arlington, TX: Vandamere.

Graf, N. M., Marini, I., & Blankenship, C. (2009). 100 words about disability. *Journal of Rehabilitation, 75*(2), 25–34.

Harris, L. (1991). *Public attitudes toward persons with disabilities*. New York, NY: Lou Harris and Associates.

Huffington, A. (2010). *Third World America: How our politicians are abandoning the middle class and betraying the American dream*. New York, NY: Crown Publishers.

Largent, M. (2002). The greatest curse of the race: Eugenic sterilization in Oregon 1909–1983. *Oregon Historical Quarterly, 103*(2), 188–209.

Lazarus, E. (1883). The new colossus. Retrieved from http://xroads.virginia.edu/~CAP/LIBERTY/lazarus.html

Longmore, P. K., & Goldberger, D. (2000). The League of the Physically Handicapped and the Great Depression: A case study in the new disability history. *Journal of American History, 87*(3), 888–921.

Marini, I. (2001). ADA continues to be tested and tweaked. *SCI Psychosocial Process, 13*(2), 69–70.

Marini, I. (2011a). The history of treatment towards persons with disabilities. In I. Marini, N. M. Glover-Graf, & M. J. Millington (Eds.), *Psychosocial aspects of disability: Insider perspectives and counseling strategies* (pp. 3–32). New York, NY: Springer Publishing.

Marini, I. (2011b). The psychosocial world of the injured worker. In I. Marini, N. M. Glover-Graf, & M. J. Millington (Eds.), *Psychosocial aspects of disability: Insider perspectives and counseling strategies* (pp. 235–255). New York, NY: Springer Publishing.

Marini, I., Bhakta, M. V., & Graf, N. (2009). A content analysis of common concerns of persons with physical disabilities. *Journal of Applied Rehabilitation Counseling, 40*(1), 44–49.

Noll, S. (2005). The public face of Southern institutions for the "feeble-minded." *Public Historian, 27*(2), 25–41.

O'Day, B., & Goldstein, M. (2005). Advocacy issues and strategies for the 21st century. *Journal of Disability Policy Studies, 15*(4), 240–250.

Olkin, R. (1999). *What psychotherapists should know about disability*. New York, NY: Guilford Press.

Osgood, R. (2001). The menace of the feebleminded: George Bliss, Amos Butler, and the Indiana Committee on mental defectives. *Indiana Magazine of History, 97*(4), 253–277.

Parker, R., Szymanski, E., & Patterson, B. (2005). *Rehabilitation counseling: Basics and beyond* (4th ed.). Austin, TX: PRO-ED.

Pearson, W. R. (1995). Comparison of methods for searching protein sequence databases. *Protein Science, 4*, 1145–1160.

Reich, R. B. (2010). *Aftershock: The next economy and America's future*. New York, NY: Alfred A. Knopf.

Roberts, C. D., Stough, L. M., & Parrish, L. H. (2002). The role of genetic counseling in the elective termination of pregnancies involving fetuses with disabilities. *Journal of Health Psychology, 7*, 183–193.

Rubin, S. E., & Roessler, R. T. (2008). Philosophical and economic considerations in regard to disability rights and support for rehabilitation programs. In S. E. Rubin & R. T. Roessler (Eds.), *Foundations of the vocational rehabilitation process* (pp. 143–165). Austin, TX: PRO-ED.

Smart, J. (2009). *Disability, society, and the individual*. Austin, TX: PRO-ED.

Treadway, W. (1925). Our immigration policy and the nation's mental health. *The Scientific Monthly, 21*(4), 347–354.

U.S. Department of Health and Human Services. (2014). 2014 poverty guidelines. Retrieved from http:// aspe.hhs.gov/poverty/14poverty.cfm

The U.S. Equal Employment Opportunity Commission. (n.d.). Charge statistics. Retrieved from https:// www .eeoc.gov/eeoc/statistics/enforcement/charges.cfm

Ward, R. (1907). The new immigration act. *North American Review, 185*(619), 587–593.

Ward, R. (1924). Our new immigration policy. *Foreign Affairs, 3*(1), 99–111.

Yelin, E. H. (1991). The recent history and immediate future of employment among persons with disabilities. In J. West (Ed.), *The Americans with Disabilities Act: From policy to practice* (pp. 129–149). New York, NY: Milbank Memorial Fund.

2

On the Origins of Negative Attitudes Toward People With Disabilities*

HANOCH LIVNEH

*I*n the past quarter of a century, several attempts have been made to categorize the different sources of negative attitudes toward individuals with disabling conditions. Among these attempts, the works of Gellman (1959); Raskin (1956); Siller, Chipman, Ferguson, and Vann (1967); and Wright (1960) are often singled out. In addition, a plethora of theoretical and empirical work has been directed toward the narrower goal of advancing and supporting a specific cause (often referred to as *root* or *base*) for negative attitudes toward disability (see Goffman, 1963; Meng, 1938; Parsons, 1951; Schilder, 1935).

The main objective of this chapter is twofold: to integrate the major approaches in the domain of attitudinal sources toward people with disabilities and to offer a new classification system by which these attitudes can be better conceptualized and understood.

Of the four main classifications, earlier attempts by Raskin (1956) and Gellman (1959) were more narrowly conceived. Both offered a fourfold classification system for the roots of prejudicial attitudes toward those who are blind (Raskin) and those who are disabled in general (Gellman). Raskin perceived these attitudes to be determined by psychodynamic, situational, sociocultural, and historical factors. Gellman, on the other hand, viewed the prejudicial roots as stemming from social customs and norms, child-rearing practices, recrudescence of neurotic childhood fears in frustrating and anxiety-provoking situations, and discrimination-provoking behavior by persons with disabilities.

Wright (1960), in a comprehensive literature review, discussed attitudes toward atypical physique according to the following categories: general requiredness of cause–effect relations (i.e., phenomenal causality between certain "sinful behaviors" and disability as an "unavoidable punishment"), negative reaction to the different and strange, childhood experiences, and prevailing socioeconomic factors. Siller and colleagues (1967), based on their extensive attitudinal study, reported the existence of 13 aversive content categories toward those with disabilities, using both empirical and clinical

*From *Rehabilitation Literature,43*(11–12) (1982), 338–347. Reprinted with permission. Published by the National Easter Seal Society, Chicago, IL, currently Easterseals/easterseals.com.

findings. Their discussion, however, often confuses components of attitudinal correlates (such as functional limitations or attribution of negative qualities) with attitudinal sources (e.g., aesthetic–sexual aversion, fear it could happen to self).

This chapter attempts to deal exclusively with attitudinal sources. In other words, only approaches—both theoretical and empirical—that can be perceived in terms of cause (attitudinal source or root) and effect (negative or aversive reaction or attitude) relationships will be dealt with. Also, the classification system of the different attitudinal sources combines both process- (psychodynamic mechanisms) and content- (sociocultural factors) related formulations. It was felt that any attempt to separate the two would be rather arbitrary.

SOCIOCULTURAL CONDITIONING

Pervasive social and cultural norms, standards, and expectations often lead to the creation of negative attitudes toward the disabled population. Among the frequently mentioned contributing factors are:

1. **Emphasis on concepts such as "body beautiful," "body whole," youth, health, athletic prowess, personal appearance, and wholeness:** These highly stressed societal standards are often institutionalized into cultural customs, which are to be conformed to by members of society (Gellman, 1959; Roessler & Bolton, 1978; Wright, 1960).

2. **Emphasis on personal productivity and achievement:** Individuals in most Western countries are judged on the basis of their ability to be socially and economically competitive (Hanks & Hanks, 1948; Safilios-Rothschild, 1968).

3. **Prevailing socioeconomic level:** The importance of socioeconomic factors in creating an atmosphere within which attitudes toward individuals with disabilities are often nourished was emphasized by Safilios-Rothschild (1968). The level of societal development (Jordan & Friesen, 1968), the rate of unemployment, beliefs concerning the origins of poverty, and the importance attached to the nation's welfare economy and security are all contributing factors affecting attitudes toward people with disabilities.

4. **Society's delineation of the "sick role" phenomenon:** Whereas the occupant of the "sick role" is exempt from normal societal obligations and responsibilities, the length of time a disabled person remains in this role is associated with negative attitudes (Parsons, 1951, 1958; Thoreson & Kerr, 1978).

5. **The status degradation attached to disability:** The social deviance and inferred stigma of having a physical disability bear heavily on society's attitudes toward those affected (see Davis, 1961; Freidson, 1965; Goffman, 1963; Safilios-Rothschild, 1970; Wolfensberger, 1972, 1976; Worthington, 1974; Yamamato, 1971). The cultural values held by members of society are often based on the perception of any form of "imputed deviancy," including disability, as a sign of marginal status. The person with a disability is, therefore, viewed as an "outsider," an "offender," or as "different" (Barker, 1948; Gove, 1976; Kutner, 1971). Wolfensberger (1972, 1976) regards the devalued or deviant status as a negative role imposed on the stigmatized person and views the sources of this deviancy as stemming from physical, behavioral, and attribution-based characteristics. Yamamato (1971) goes as far as to suggest that society needs the deviants as a symbol of evil and intangible dangers.

CHILDHOOD INFLUENCES

The importance of infancy and early childhood experiences, in terms of both child-rearing practices and early parental influences (verbal and behavioral), is often stressed (Gellman, 1959; Wright, 1960). The impact of early experiences and their related emotions and cognitions play a major role in influencing the growing child's belief and value system. Parental and significant others' actions, words, tone of voice, gestures, and so forth, are transmitted, directly or indirectly, to the child and tend to have a crucial impact on the formation of attitudes toward disability.

Rearing practices, which emphasize the importance of health and normalcy, and which threaten any infringement of health rules with sickness, illness, and long-term disability, result in aversion toward individuals who are affected (Gellman, 1959; Wright, 1960). Childhood stages of development (oral, anal, phallic, and genital) are wrought with anxiety-laden premises regarding the etiology of certain illnesses; therefore, the association with ongoing disabilities and disabled persons, as past transgressors, is readily made.

PSYCHODYNAMIC MECHANISMS

Several mainly unconscious psychological processes have been advanced in the literature as explanatory mechanisms for the attitudes manifested by the "nondisabled" toward the "disabled." Although most of these mechanisms are apparently shown during early childhood (Gellman, 1959; Siller et al., 1967; Yamamato, 1971) and may, therefore, be regarded as related to childhood experiences, it was felt that because of their significance in creating and maintaining these attitudes such a separation is warranted.

1. **Requirement of mourning:** The person with a disability is expected to grieve the loss of a body part or function. He or she "ought" to suffer and slowly adjust to such a misfortune (Dembo, Leviton, & Wright, 1956, 1975; Kutner, 1971; Sussman, 1969; Thoreson & Kerr, 1978; Wright, 1960). The nondisabled individual has a need to safeguard his or her values, by wanting the disabled individual to suffer, and show the appropriate grieving, so as to protect one's own values of the importance of a functioning body (Dembo et al., 1956, 1975). Any attempt on the disabled person's part to deny or reject the "suffering role" is met with negative attitudes. The mechanism of rationalization is clearly operative in this case.

2. **Unresolved conflict over scopophilia and exhibitionism:** Psychoanalytic thought stresses the importance of vision in early psychosexual and ego development (Blank, 1957). The significance of sight, both in terms of pleasure of looking at and being looked upon in the pregenital stages, is stressed in the psychoanalytic literature. Any resolved conflicts related to these developmental stages may be triggered as a consequence of the approach/fascination–avoidance/repulsion conflict often associated with the sight of a disabled person.

3. **Negative attributes resulting from the "spread phenomenon":** Attributing certain negative characteristics to those with disabilities frequently results when the mechanism of the "halo effect" or "spread phenomenon" is in operation (Wright, 1960). The generalization from one perceived characteristic (e.g., physical disability) to other, unrelated characteristics (e.g., emotional or mental maladjustment) is referred to as "spread" and explains the too-often-pervasive negative correlates of a pure physical deviance (Kutner, 1971; Thoreson & Kerr, 1978).

4. **Associating responsibility with etiology:** The attribution of personal–moral accountability to the cause of a disabling condition results in negative attitudes. If an individual can be held responsible for an imputed deviance, certain social management approaches are then suggested (punishment, control, "rehabilitation," correction, etc.), which are frequently embedded with negative connotations (Freidson, 1965; Safilios-Rothschild, 1970; Yamamato, 1971). Again, the operation of a rationalization mechanism is evident here.

5. **Fear of social ostracism:** Siller and colleagues (1967) suggest this category as an extension of the "guilty by association" phenomenon. The nondisabled person fears that an association with disabled persons may be interpreted by others as implying some psychological maladjustment on his or her own part. The internalization of others' values and beliefs, which tends to weaken one's ego boundaries, coupled with projection onto others of unwanted personal attributes is the main operating mechanism.

6. **Guilt of being "able-bodied":** Guilt of "enjoying" one's body intactness in addition to possible injustices directed toward persons with disabilities (e.g., the belief in the disabled person's responsibility for the condition, lack of involvement in charitable activities) may result in attempts at atonement or further dissociation from the presence of disabled individuals (Siller et al., 1967; Wright, 1960).

DISABILITY AS A PUNISHMENT FOR SIN

The triad of sin, punishment, and disability can be conceived as a component of the earlier discussion of psychodynamic mechanisms operating in the creation of aversive reactions toward disability. Because of their importance in elucidating the roots of negative attitudes toward people with disabling conditions and the various versions of their interrelatedness, which are advanced in the literature, it seems justifiable to treat these concepts under a separate heading.

1. **Disability as a punishment for sin:** Alexander's (1938) concept of "emotional syllogism," when applied here (Siller et al., 1967; Wright, 1960), stresses the consequential appropriateness between physical deformity and a sinful person. The source of the disabled person's suffering is attributed to either a personally committed evil act or to an ancestral wrongdoing (Sigerist, 1945).

2. **The individual with a disability as a dangerous person:** Meng (reported in Barker, Wright, Meyerson, & Gonick, 1953) attributed fear and avoidance of those who are physically disabled to three unconscious mechanisms: (a) the belief that a disability is a punishment for a transgression and, therefore, that the disabled person is evil and dangerous; (b) the belief that a disability is an unjust punishment and that, therefore, the person is motivated to commit an evil act to balance the injustice; and (c) the projection of one's unacceptable impulses on the disabled person, which results in perceiving the latter as evil and dangerous (see also Siller et al., 1967; Thoreson & Kerr, 1978). Thus, although in the previous section suffering was perceived as being a punishment for an evil deed, in the present section physical deviance is viewed as the cause, the consequence of which is felt to be a sinful and evil act ("a twisted mind in a twisted body").

3. **The nondisabled person fearing imminent punishment:** If the notion of disability as a punishment is warranted, then the nondisabled person who anticipates, often realistically, retribution for past personal misdeeds avoids the person with disabilities because of guilt of not being punished or the fear of imminent punishment by association (Gellman, 1959).

4. Vicarious self-punishment offered by the punished disabled person: An extension of the aforementioned formula was offered by Thurer (1980). The sinning disabled person, in fiction or reality, is perceived to be an easy target for one's own projections. Because the disabled individual was punished for the sin committed and because the nondisabled person unconsciously identifies with the sin, he or she is also punished, albeit vicariously, and the felt guilt is, therefore, lessened. The externalization of one's inner conflicts on a punished target assists in controlling them. The result is, therefore, the repelling–gratifying conflict of feelings that ensues as a result of seeing, hearing, or reading about a disabled individual.

ANXIETY-PROVOKING UNSTRUCTURED SITUATIONS

The role of unfamiliar situations in creating anxiety and confusion was stressed by Hebb (1946) and Heider (1944). Similarly, on initial interaction with a disabled person, the nondisabled person is often faced with an unstructured situation in which most socially accepted rules and regulations for proper interaction are not well defined. These ambiguous situations tend to disrupt both cognitive–intellectual processes as well as the more fundamental perceptual–affective mechanisms.

1. **Cognitively unstructured situations:** The nondisabled person interacting with a disabled individual faces uncertain social outcomes engendered by the new and, therefore, cognitively vague situation (Heider, 1958). The unfamiliarity presents an incongruent cognitive gestalt, which disrupts the established basic rules of social interaction and may cause withdrawal from such a situation (Yamamato, 1971) or create strain in this interaction (Siller et al., 1967). The often reported findings in the literature—that the lack of factual knowledge and information about disabling conditions tends to lead to negative attitudes (Anthony, 1972; English, 1971a, 1971b; English & Oberle, 1971)—also support this contention.
2. **Lack of affective preparedness:** There is an apparent fearful and negative reaction, on a visceral level, to the different and strange (Hebb, 1946; Heider, 1958; Siller et al., 1967). Strange and mutilated bodies trigger a conflict in the observer because of incompatible perceptions (Hebb, 1946). People tend to resist the strange because it does not fit into the structure of an expected life space (Heider, 1958) and because of a lack of affective readiness (Worthington, 1974; Yamamato, 1971). Siller et al. (1967) perceived it to exemplify their negative atypicality category, which creates in the observer a feeling of distress. Lack of experiential contact and exposure to persons with disabilities is a contributing factor to the origination of such an attitude (Anthony, 1972; English, 1971a, 1971b).

AESTHETIC AVERSION

The impact of a purely aesthetic–sexual aversion, triggered by the sight of a visibly disabled person, has been stressed by several authors (Heider, 1958; Siller & Chipman, 1964a; Siller et al., 1967). These feelings of repulsion and discomfort are felt when nondisabled persons come in contact with certain disabilities (such as amputations, body deformities, cerebral palsy, or skin disorders [Richardson, Hastorf, Goodman, & Dornbusch, 1961; Safilios-Rothschild, 1970; Siller, 1963]). The importance of aesthetic–sexual aversion as a basis for negative attitudinal formation was also reported in Siller and colleagues' (1967) study, in which the felt aversion referred to the direct and conscious reactions experienced on sensory and visceral levels. The role played by aesthetic attractiveness was also demonstrated by Napoleon, Chassin, and Young (1980) as a predisposing factor in judging a person's degree of mental illness.

THREATS TO BODY IMAGE INTEGRITY

The concept of body image as the mental representation of one's own body was originally coined by Schilder (1935). Several related formulations were proposed regarding the importance of the body image concept (i.e., self-image, body cathexis, and body satisfaction) as an explanatory vehicle in understanding attitudes toward people with disabilities.

1. **Threat to the body image:** Schilder (1935) argued that, via the mechanism of identification, seeing a person with a physical disability creates a feeling of discomfort because of the incongruence between an expected "normal" body and the actual perceived reality. The viewer's own unconscious and somatic body image may, therefore, be threatened because of the presence of the disabled individual (Menninger, 1949).
2. **Reawakening of castration anxiety:** The psychoanalytic concept of castration anxiety, as applied to explaining the formation of negative attitudes toward persons with disabilities, stresses the stirring up of archaic castration fears in the presence of analogous situations (such as direct loss of a leg or an eye or an indirect loss of a certain body function [Chevigny & Braverman, 1950; Fine, 1978; Maisel, 1953; Siller et al., 1967; Wright, 1960]).
3. **Fear of losing one's physical integrity:** Profound anxiety about becoming disabled plays a crucial part in forming prejudicial attitudes toward those who are. When faced with a disabled person, the nondisabled individual becomes highly anxious because the original fear of potential bodily harm is rekindled (Safilios-Rothschild, 1968, 1970). Roessler and Bolton (1978), capitalizing on Gellman's (1959) original discussion, believe that nondisabled persons, being fearful of disablement and loss of self-control, feel intense discomfort that arouses additional anxiety when in contact with a visibly disabled person. The result is avoidance of disabled persons and attempts at segregating and isolating them. Similar ideas were advanced by Siller et al. (1967), who viewed the fear that the disability could happen to oneself as a basis for an aversive attitude toward people who are disabled.
4. **Separation anxiety:** Although somewhat related to castration anxiety and fear of losing physical integrity, separation anxiety, in the sense of object loss, is another unconscious source leading to negative attitudes toward disability (Siller et al., 1967). The loss of a body part or function may trigger, in the viewer, narcissistic concerns and unresolved infantile anxieties, which often evolve around possible separation from parental figures (Siller, 1964b).
5. **Fear of contamination or inheritance:** The fear that social interaction with disabled people may lead to contamination provokes aversive attitudes (Siller et al., 1967). This refers to avoiding those with disabilities on both superficial interactive levels (social intercourse) and more in-depth relationships (marriage, having children, etc.).

MINORITY GROUP COMPARABILITY

The view that attitudes toward the disabled population parallel those manifested toward minority groups, in general, was advocated by Barker and colleagues (1953) and further elaborated on by Wright (1960). This view holds that disabled people, as a marginal group (Barker, 1948; Sussman, 1969), trigger negative reactions in the nondisabled majority. Being perceived as marginal, or as a member of a minority group, carries with it the same stereotypic reactions of occupying a devalued and inferior status shared by ethnic, racial, and religious groups (Chesler, 1965; Cowen, Bobrove, Rockway, & Stevenson, 1967; Cowen, Underberg, & Verrillo, 1958; Yuker, 1965). The resulting attitude can, therefore, be categorized as being discriminatory and prejudiced in nature, and as advocating isolation and segregation of disabled persons from the remaining population (Safilios-Rothschild, 1970; Wright, 1960).

DISABILITY AS A REMINDER OF DEATH

The parallelism between reactions toward those who are disabled and feelings associated with dying (anxiety, fear, and dread) was suggested by several authors (Endres, 1979; Leviton, 1972; Livneh, 1980; Parkes, 1975; Siller, 1976). The contention is that the loss of a body part or a physical function constitutes the death of a part, which in the past was integrally associated with one's ego (Bakan, 1968). The anxiety associated with death is, therefore, rekindled at the sight of a disabled person. The disabled groups, both literally and symbolically, serve as a denial of our primitive, infantile omnipotence (Ferenczi, 1956) and as a reminder of our mortality.

PREJUDICE-INVITING BEHAVIORS

Gellman (1959) and Wright (1960) discussed the effect of certain provoking behaviors, by persons with disabilities, on discriminatory practices toward them. These provoking behaviors may be categorized into two general classes:

1. **Prejudice by invitation (Roessler & Bolton, 1978):** Specific behaviors by disabled individuals (being dependent; seeking secondary gains; acting fearful, insecure, or inferior) create and strengthen certain prejudicial beliefs in the observer. Wright (1960) similarly traced these behaviors to the physically disabled person's expectations of being treated in depreciating ways, and as a result set the person up in situations in which he or she will be devalued.
2. **Prejudice by silence:** Lack of interest on the disabled person's part or lack of effective public relations campaigns or self-help groups representing the interests and concerns of specific disability groups to combat the public's ignorance is a way of fostering stereotypic and negative attitudes on the latter's part.

THE INFLUENCE OF DISABILITY-RELATED FACTORS

Several disability-connected variables were reported in the literature as affecting attitudes toward disabled persons. The association of these variables with certain negative perceptions was both empirically studied (Barker, 1964; Siller, 1963) and theoretically discussed (Freidson, 1965; Safilios-Rothschild, 1970).

The major reported variables include:

1. **Functionality versus organicity of disability:** Barker (1964) found that a dichotomy exists between the public's perceptions regarding certain personality traits attached to functional (alcoholism) or organic (blindness, cancer) disabilities. Siller (1963)

concluded that those disabilities having the least functional implications were also those reacted to least negatively. Similar conclusions were reached in the context of occupational settings in which employers preferred physically disabled individuals (e.g., those with paraplegia) to the more functionally impaired persons (such as those who were mentally retarded or emotionally disabled [Barker, 1964; Rickard, Triandis, & Patterson, 1963; Safilios-Rothschild, 1970]).

2. **Level of severity:** Usually the more severe a disability is, the more negatively it is perceived (Safilios-Rothschild, 1970; Shontz, 1964; Siller, 1963). Severity is, of course, related to the level of functional limitation involved.

3. **Degree of visibility:** Generally, the more visible a disability is, the more negative an attitude it tends to trigger (Safilios-Rothschild, 1970; Shontz, 1964; Siller, 1963).

4. **Degree of cosmetic involvement:** Generally, the more the cosmetic implication inherent in the disability, in terms of aesthetic characteristics (see also "Aesthetic Aversion"), the less favorably it is reacted to (Siller, 1963).

5. **Contagiousness versus noncontagiousness of disability:** Safilios-Rothschild (1970) discussed the influence of contagious disabilities on the degree of prejudice directed toward them. The more contagious a disability is, the more fear of personal contraction is aroused and the more negative, therefore, is the ensuing reaction.

6. **Body part affected:** The importance of the body part affected by the disability, in terms of both personal and social implications, was suggested by Safilios-Rothschild (1970) and Weinstein, Vetter, and Sersen (1964).

7. **Degree of predictability:** The factor of imputed prognosis or probability of curability was studied and discussed by Freidson (1965), Safilios-Rothschild (1970), and Yamamato (1971). On the whole, the more curable and therefore predictable the disability is, the less negatively it is perceived.

The final category to be briefly discussed includes the association of certain demographic and personality variables of the nondisabled population with negative attitudes toward disabled persons. Because this category has been the target of extensive empirical research in past years and because most of these studies are correlational rather than causal in nature, discussion will only revolve around their main findings. It should be noted that although the conclusions drawn by the studies of the authors are only suggestive and cannot be generalized beyond their participating populations, most authors regarded the respondents' personal variables under study as determinants of attitudes toward disability due to their enduring and deeply ingrained qualities (such as sex, intelligence, self-concept, and anxiety level).

DEMOGRAPHIC VARIABLES ASSOCIATED WITH ATTITUDES

Several major reviews of studies investigating demographic correlates of negative attitudes toward people with disabilities (English, 1971b; McDaniel, 1969; Ryan, 1981) have reached these conclusions concerning the following variables:

1. **Gender:** Females display more favorable attitudes toward individuals who are physically disabled than males (Chesler, 1965; Freed, 1964; Siller, 1963, 1964a; Yuker, Block, & Younng, 1966).

2. **Age:** There appear to be two inverted U-shaped distributions when age-related differences toward persons with disabilities are measured (Ryan, 1981). Attitudes are, generally, more positive at late childhood and adulthood, and less favorable attitudes

are recorded at early childhood, adolescence, and old age (Ryan, 1981; Siller, 1963; Siller & Chipman, 1964b; Siller et al., 1967).

3. **Socioeconomic status:** Higher income groups manifest more favorable attitudes toward the emotionally and mentally disabled than lower income groups (English, 1971b; Jabin, 1966); however, no differences were found regarding physical disabilities (Dow, 1965; English, 1971b; Lukoff & Whiteman, 1964; Whiteman & Lukoff, 1965).

4. **Educational level:** In spite of age-confounding research difficulties, most studies concluded that educational level is positively correlated with more favorable attitudes toward persons with disabling conditions (Horowitz, Rees, & Horowitz, 1965; Jabin, 1966; Siller, 1964a; Tunick, Bowen, & Gillings, 1979).

PERSONALITY VARIABLES ASSOCIATED WITH ATTITUDES

Research on the association of several personality traits and characteristics in the non-disabled population with respect to negative attitudes toward disabled people was summarized and reported by several authors (e.g., English, 1971b; Kutner, 1971; McDaniel, 1969; Pederson & Carlson, 1981; Safilios-Rothschild, 1970). Major findings include the following:

1. **Ethnocentrism:** Chesler (1965), Cowen, Brobrove, et al. (1967), Cowen, Underberg, et al. (1958), Lukoff and Whiteman (1964), Noonan (1967), Whiteman and Lukoff (1965), and Yuker (1965), following Wright's (1960) formulation of the comparability between attitudes toward persons with disabilities and attitudes toward ethnic and religious minorities, in general, found that high ethnocentrism was related to the lack of acceptance of the disabled population.

2. **Authoritarianism:** Jabin (1966), Lukoff and Whiteman (1964), Noonan, Barry, and Davis (1970), Tunick et al. (1979), and Whiteman and Lukoff (1965) reported a positive correlation between accepting attitudes toward disabled persons and low authoritarianism (see also Dembo et al.'s [1956] theoretical discussion).

3. **Aggression:** Meng's (1938) original hypothesis suggested that the projection of one's aggressive and hostile desires on those with disabilities will lead to the belief that disabled persons are dangerous and, as a result, to prejudicial attitudes toward them. Jabin (1966), Siller (1964b), and Siller et al. (1967) confirmed this hypothesis in independent studies, concluding that less-aggressive individuals express more positive attitudes toward this group.

4. **Self-insight:** Siller (1964a) and Yuker (1962) reported findings that suggested a moderate relationship between the need for introspection, as a measure of insightfulness, and empathetic understanding of people who are disabled.

5. **Anxiety:** The degree of manifest anxiety was found to be associated with attitudes toward disabled persons. Jabin (1966), Kaiser and Moosbruker (1960), Marinelli and Kelz (1973), Siller (1964a), Siller et al. (1967), and Yuker, Block, and Campbell (1960) demonstrated that a high level of manifest anxiety is positively correlated with rejection of disabled individuals.

6. **Self-concept:** Several studies (e.g., Epstein & Shontz, 1962; Jabin, 1966; Siller, 1964a; Yuker, 1962; Yuker et al., 1966) reported a relationship between positive self-concept and a more accepting attitude toward disability. It seems that persons who are more secure and confident in their own selves also tend to feel more positive and accepting of disabled persons.

7. **Ego strength:** Similar to self-concept, ego strength was found to be related to attitudes toward people with disabilities. Siller (1963, 1964b) and Siller et al. (1967) reported on the relationship between ego weakness and rejection of the disabled, while Noonan et al. (1970) found a trend in this direction, albeit not statistically significant.

8. **Body and self-satisfaction:** Several studies (Cormack, 1967; Epstein & Shontz, 1962; Fisher & Cleveland, 1968; Leclair & Rockwell, 1980; Siller, 1964b) concluded that lack of satisfaction with one's own body (low "body-cathexis" score) is related, and probably a contributing factor, to the development of negative attitudes toward physically disabled persons. Siller (1964b), Siller et al. (1967), and Yuker et al. (1966) expanded the body-cathexis concept to successfully argue that a positive perception of one's self is related to the acceptance of disabled individuals. People with positive and secure self-concepts tend to show more positive and accepting attitudes toward those with disabilities, while people with low self-concepts often reject them (see also section on "Threats to Body Image Integrity" in this chapter).

9. **Ambiguity tolerance:** The ability of nondisabled persons to better tolerate ambiguity was found to be positively correlated with acceptance of physically disabled persons (Feinberg, 1971).

10. **Social desirability:** The need for social approval and acceptance by others was positively associated with acceptance of people having disabilities (Doob & Ecker, 1970; Feinberg, 1967; Jabin, 1966; Siller et al., 1967).

11. **Alienation:** Alienated individuals tend to be more hostile toward, and rejecting of, disabled persons (Jabin, 1966).

12. **Intelligence level:** English (1971b) tentatively concluded, from his review of related studies, that there may be a relationship between the nondisabled intellectual capacity and acceptance of disability.

SUMMARY AND CONCLUSIONS

The present chapter has attempted to outline a classification system according to which a number of sources or negative attitudes toward people with disabilities was categorized and discussed.

The major categories included (a) conditioning by sociocultural norms that emphasize certain qualities not met by the disabled population; (b) childhood influences in which early life experiences foster the formation of stereotypic adult beliefs and values; (c) psychodynamic mechanisms that may play a role in creating unrealistic expectations and unresolved conflicts when interacting with disabled persons; (d) perception of disability as a punishment for a committed sin or as a justification for committing a future evil act, which triggers unconscious fears in the nondisabled person; (e) the inherent capacity of unstructured social, emotional, and intellectual situations to provoke confusion and anxiety; (f) the impact of a basic aesthetic–sexual aversion, created by the sight of the visibly disfigured, on the development of negative attitudes; (g) the threat to the conscious body and unconscious body image triggered by the mere presence of physically disabled individuals; (h) the devaluative and stereotypical reactions fostered by the marginality associated with being a member of a minority group; (i) the unconscious and symbolic parallelism between disability and death as a reminder of man's transient existence; (j) prejudice-provoking behaviors by persons with disabilities that result in discriminatory practices toward them; (k) disability-related factors (e.g., levels of functionality, visibility, and severity) that may contribute to specific negative attitudes; and (l) observer-related factors, both demographic (sex, age) and personality-connected (ethnocentrism, authoritarianism), which may foster the development of negative attitudes.

The classification system suggested suffers one major drawback. There is a certain degree of overlap among several of the categories (e.g., castration anxiety, viewed here as a threat to body image, may well be conceived as belonging to the childhood influences category; or anxiety provoked by unstructured situations may be regarded as just another psychologically operated mechanism if viewed phenomenologically rather than environmentally based). It should be noted, however, that because of the often highly abstract and conjectural nature of several of these categories, at present there is no escape from resorting to a certain level of arbitrariness when attempting to adopt such a classification model.

No attempt was made in the present discussion to suggest the matching of certain attitude-changing techniques (informative, experiential, and persuasive) with the categories discussed. Several excellent articles have been written on strategies to combat negative attitudes toward people with disabilities and toward minority groups in general (see Allport, 1954; Anthony, 1972; Clore & Jeffery, 1972; English, 1971a; Evans, 1976; Finkelstein, 1980; Hafer & Narcus, 1979; Kutner, 1971; Safilios-Rothschild, 1968; Wright, 1960, 1980).

It seems to this author that because of the complexity of the interacting factors that contribute to the creation of negative attitudes toward this group, any attempt at change, in order to be successful, must first be cognizant of the fact that because attitudes are learned and conditioned over many years, any experimental study of short duration, hoping to change attitudes, is futile at best. Attempts to modify the prevailing negative attitudes have been generally unsuccessful (Roessler & Bolton, 1978). They will probably continue to follow such an inevitable course as long as researchers and clinicians look for quick and easy results and solutions.

REFERENCES

Alexander, F. G. (1938). Remarks about the relation of inferiority feelings to guilt feelings. *International Journal of Psychoanalysis, 19*, 41–49.

Allport, G. W. (1954). *The nature of prejudice.* New York, NY: Addison-Wesley.

Anthony, W. A. (1972). Societal rehabilitation: Changing society's attitudes toward the physically and mentally disabled. *Rehabilitation Psychology, 19*, 117–126.

Bakan, D. (1968). *Disease, pain and sacrifice: Toward a psychology of suffering.* Chicago, IL: University of Chicago Press.

Barker, R. G. (1948). The social psychology of physical disability. *Journal of Social Issues, 4*, 28–38.

Barker, R. G. (1964). Concepts of disabilities. *Personnel & Guidance Journal, 43*, 371–374.

Barker, R. G., Wright, B. A., Meyerson, L., & Gonick, M. R. (1953). *Adjustment to physical handicap and illness: A survey of the social psychology of physique and disability (rev. ed.).* New York, NY: Social Science Research Council.

Blank, H. R. (1957). Psychoanalysis and blindness. *The Psychoanalytic Quarterly, 26*(1), 1–24.

Chesler, M. A. (1965). Ethnocentrism and attitudes toward the physically disabled. *Journal of Personality and Social Psychology, 2*(6), 877–882.

Chevigny, H., & Braverman, S. (1950). *The adjustment of the blind.* New York, NY: Yale University Press.

Clore, G. L., & Jeffery, K. M. (1972). Emotional role playing, attitude change, and attraction toward a disabled person. *Journal of Personality and Social Psychology, 23*(1), 105–111.

Cormack, P. A. (1967). The relationship between body cognition and attitudes expressed toward the visibly disabled. *Rehabilitation Counseling Bulletin, 11*(2), 106–109.

Cowen, E. L., Bobrove, P. H., Rockway, A. M., & Stevenson, J. (1967). Development and evaluation of an attitude to deafness scale. *Journal of Personality and Social Psychology, 6*(2), 183–191.

Cowen, E. L., Underberg, R. P., & Verrillo, R. T. (1958). The development and testing of an attitude to blindness scale. *Journal of Personality and Social Psychology, 48*, 297–304.

Davis, F. (1961). Deviance disavowal: The management of strained interaction by the visibly handicapped. *Social Problems, 9*(2), 121–132.

Dembo, T., Leviton, G. L., & Wright, B. A. (1956). Adjustment to misfortune; a problem of social-psychological rehabilitation. *Artificial Limbs, 3*(2), 4–62.

Dembo, T., Leviton, G. L., & Wright, B. A. (1975). Adjustment to misfortune—A problem of social psychological rehabilitation. *Rehabilitation Psychology, 22*, 1–100.

Doob, A. N., & Ecker, B. P. (1970). Stigma and compliance. *Journal of Personality and Social Psychology, 14*(4), 302–304.

Dow, T. E. (1965). Social class and reaction to physical disability. *Psychological Reports, 17*(1), 39–62.

Endres, J. E. (1979). Fear of death and attitudinal dispositions toward physical disability. *Dissertation Abstracts International, 39*, 7161A. (University Microfilm No. 79–11, 825)

English, R. W. (1971a). Combating stigma toward physically disabled persons. *Rehabilitation, Research & Practice Review, 2*, 19–27.

English, R. W. (1971b). Correlates of stigma toward physically disabled persons. *Rehabilitation, Research & Practice Review, 2*, 1–17.

English, R. W., & Oberle, J. B. (1971). Toward the development of new methodology for examining attitudes toward disabled persons. *Rehabilitation Counseling Bulletin, 15*(2), 88–96.

Epstein, S. J., & Shontz, F. C. (1962). Attitudes toward persons with physical disabilities as a function of attitudes towards one's own body. *Rehabilitation Counseling Bulletin, 5*(4), 196–201.

Evans, J. H. (1976). Changing attitudes toward disabled persons: An experimental study. *Rehabilitation Counseling Bulletin, 19*(4), 572–579.

Feinberg, L. B. (1967). Social desirability and attitudes toward the disabled. *Personnel & Guidance Journal, 46*(4), 375–381.

Feinberg, L. B. (1971). *Social desirability and attitudes toward the disabled.* Unpublished manuscript, Syracuse University, Syracuse, New York.

Ferenczi, S. (1956). Stages in the development of the sense of reality. In S. Ferenczi (Ed.), *Contributions to psychoanalysis* (rev. ed.). New York, NY: Dover.

Fine, J. A. (1978). *Castration anxiety and self concept of physically normal children as related to perceptual awareness of attitudes toward physical deviance.* Unpublished doctoral dissertation, New York University, New York.

Finkelstein, V. (1980). *Attitudes and disabled people: Issues for discussion. International exchange of information in rehabilitation* (Monograph No. 5). New York, NY: World Rehabilitation Fund.

Fisher, S., & Cleveland, S. E. (1968). *Body image and personality* (2nd rev. ed.). New York, NY: Dover.

Freed, E. X. (1964). Opinions of psychiatric hospital personnel and college students toward alcoholism, mental illness, and physical disability: An exploratory study. *Psychological Reports, 15*(2), 615–618.

Freidson, E. (1965). Disability as social deviance. In M. B. Sussman (Ed.), *Sociology and rehabilitation* (pp. 71–99). Washington, DC: American Sociological Association.

Gellman, W. (1959). Roots of prejudice against the handicapped. *Journal of Rehabilitation, 40*(1), 4–6, 25.

Goffman, E. (1963). *Stigma: Notes on management of spoiled identity.* Englewood Cliffs, NJ: Prentice Hall.

Gove, W. R. (1976). Societal reaction theory and disability. In G. L. Albrecht (Ed.), *The sociology of physical disability and rehabilitation* (pp. 57–91). Pittsburgh, PA: University of Pittsburgh Press.

Hafer, M., & Narcus, M. (1979). Information and attitude toward disability. *Rehabilitation Counseling Bulletin, 23*(2), 95–102.

Hanks, J. R., & Hanks, L. M. (1948). The physically handicapped in certain non-occidental societies. *Journal of Social Issues, 4*, 11–20.

Hebb, D. O. (1946). On the nature of fear. *Psychological Review, 53*(5), 259–276.

Heider, F. (1944). Social perception and phenomenal causality. *Psychological Review, 51*, 358–374.

Heider, F. (1958). *The psychology of interpersonal relations.* New York, NY: John Wiley.

Horowitz, L. S., Rees, N. S., & Horowitz, M. W. (1965). Attitudes toward deafness as a function of increasing maturity. *The Journal of Social Psychology, 66*, 331–336.

Jabin, N. (1966). Attitudes towards the physically disabled as related to selected personality variables. *Dissertation Abstracts, 27*(2-B), 599.

Jordan, J. E., & Friesen, E. W. (1968). Attitudes of rehabilitation personnel toward physically disabled persons in Colombia, Peru, and the United States. *Journal of Social Psychology, 74*(2), 151–161.

Kaiser, P., & Moosbruker, J. (1960). *The relationship between attitudes toward disabled persons and GSR.* Unpublished manuscript, Human Resources Center, Albertson, NY.

Kutner, B. (1971). The social psychology of disability. In W. S. Neff (Ed.), *Rehabilitation psychology* (pp. 143–167). Washington, DC: American Psychological Association.

Leclair, S. W., & Rockwell, L. K. (1980). Counselor trainee body satisfaction and attitudes toward counseling the physically disabled. *Rehabilitation Counseling Bulletin, 23*(4), 258–265.

Leviton, D. (1972). *Education for death or death becomes less a stranger.* Paper presented at the American Psychological Association convention, Honolulu, HI.

Livneh, H. (1980). Disability and monstrosity: Further comments. *Rehabilitation Literature, 41*(11–12), 280–283.

Lukoff, I. F., & Whiteman, M. (1964). *Attitudes toward blindness.* Paper presented at the American Federation of Catholic Workers for the Blind meeting, New York, NY.

Maisel, E. (1953). *Meet a body.* Unpublished manuscript, Institute for the Crippled and Disabled, New York, NY.

Marinelli, R. P., & Kelz, J. W. (1973). Anxiety and attitudes toward visibly disabled persons. *Rehabilitation Counseling Bulletin, 16*(4), 198–205.

McDaniel, J. W. (1969). *Physical disability and human behavior.* New York, NY: Pergamon Press.

Meng, H. (1938). Zur sozialpsychologie der Krperbeschädigten: Ein beitrag zum problem der praktischen psychohygiene. *Schweizer Archives fr Neurologie und Psychiatrie, 40*, 328–344.

Menninger, W. C. (1949). Emotional adjustments for the handicapped. *Crippled Children, 27*, 27.

Napoleon, T., Chassin, L., & Young, R. D. (1980). A replication and extension of "physical attractiveness and mental illness." *Journal of Abnormal Psychology, 89*(2), 250–253.

Noonan, J. R. (1967). *Personality determinants in attitudes toward disability.* Unpublished doctoral dissertation, University of Florida, Gainesville, FL.

Noonan, J. R., Barry, J. R., & Davis, H. C. (1970). Personality determinants in attitudes toward visible disability. *Journal of Personality, 38*(1), 1–15.

Parkes, C. M. (1975). Psycho-social transitions: Comparison between reactions to loss of a limb and loss of a spouse. *British Journal of Psychiatry: The Journal of Mental Science, 127*, 204–210.

Parsons, T. (1951). *The social system.* Glencoe, IL: Free Press.

Parsons, T. (1958). Definitions of health and illness in the light of American values and social structure. In E. G. Jaco (Ed.), *Patients, physicians, and illness* (pp. 165–187). Glencoe, IL: Free Press.

Pederson, L. L., & Carlson, P. M. (1981). Rehabilitation service providers: Their attitudes towards people with physical disabilities, and their attitudes towards each other. *Rehabilitation Counseling Bulletin, 24*(4), 275–282.

Raskin, N. J. (1956). *The attitude of sighted people toward blindness.* Paper presented at the National Research Council on Blindness.

Richardson, S. A., Hastorf, A. H., Goodman, N., & Dornbusch, S. M. (1961). Cultural uniformity in reaction to physical disabilities. *American Sociological Review, 26*(2), 241–247.

Rickard, T. E., Triandis, H. C., & Patterson, C. H. (1963). Indices of employer prejudice toward disabled applicants. *Journal of Applied Psychology, 47*(1), 52–55.

Roessler, R., & Bolton, B. (1978). *Psychosocial adjustment to disability.* Baltimore, MD: University Park Press.

Ryan, K. M. (1981). Developmental differences in reactions to the physically disabled. *Human Development, 24*(4), 240–256.

Safilios-Rothschild, C. (1968). Prejudice against the disabled and some means to combat it. *International Rehabilitation Review, 4*, 8–10, 15.

Safilios-Rothschild, C. (1970). *The sociology and social psychology of disability and rehabilitation.* New York, NY: Random House.

Schilder, P. (1935). *The image and appearance of the human body.* London, England: Kegan Paul, Trench, Trubner.

Shontz, F. C. (1964). Body-part size judgement. *VRA Project No. 814, Final Report.* Lawrence: University of Kansas.

Sigerist, H. E. (1945). *Civilization and disease.* Ithaca, NY: Cornell University Press.

Siller, J. (1963). Reactions to physical disability. *Rehabilitation Counseling Bulletin, 7*(1), 12–16.

Siller, J. (1964a). Personality determinants of reaction to the physically disabled. *American Foundation for the Blind Research Bulletin, 7*, 37–52.

Siller, J. (1964b). Reactions to physical disability by the disabled and the non-disabled. *American Psychologist, Research Bulletin, 7*, 27–36 (American Foundation for the Blind).

Siller, J. (1976). Attitudes toward disability. In H. Rusalem & D. Maliken (Eds.), *Contemporary vocational rehabilitation* (pp. 67–79). New York, NY: New York University Press.

Siller, J., & Chipman, A. (1964a). Factorial structure and correlates of the attitude towards disabled persons scale. *Educational and Psychological Measurement, 24*(4), 831–840.

Siller, J., & Chipman, A. (1964b). *Perceptions of physical disability by the non-disabled.* Paper presented at the American Psychological Association Meeting, Los Angeles, CA. (Reported in Safilios-Rothschild, C., 1970.)

Siller, J., Chipman, A., Ferguson, L. T., & Vann, D. H. (1967). *Studies in reaction to disability: XI. Attitudes of the non-disabled toward the physically disabled.* New York: New York University, School of Education.

Sussman, M. B. (1969). Dependent disabled and dependent poor: Similarity of conceptual issues and research needs. *Social Service Review, 43*(4), 383–395.

Thoreson, R. W., & Kerr, B. A. (1978). The stigmatizing aspects of severe disability: Strategies for change. *Journal of Applied Rehabilitation Counseling, 9*(2), 21–25.

Thurer, S. (1980). Disability and monstrosity: A look at literary distortions of handicapping conditions. *Rehabilitation Literature, 41*(1–2), 12–15.

Tunick, R. H., Bowen, J., & Gillings, J. L. (1979). Religiosity and authoritarianism as predictors of attitude toward the disabled: A regression analysis. *Rehabilitation Counseling Bulletin, 22*(5), 408–418.

Weinstein, S., Vetter, R., & Sersen, E. (1964). *Physiological and experiential concomitants of the phantom.* VRA Project No. 427, Final Report. New York, NY: Albert Einstein College of Medicine.

Whiteman, M., & Lukoff, I. F. (1965). Attitudes toward blindness and other physical handicaps. *Journal of Social Psychology, 66,* 135–145.

Wolfensberger, W. (1972). *The principle of normalization in human services.* Toronto, ON, Canada: National Institute on Mental Retardation.

Wolfensberger, W. (1976). The normalization principle. In S. A. Grand (Ed.), *Severe disability and rehabilitation counseling training.* Washington, DC: National Council on Rehabilitation Education.

Worthington, M. E. (1974). Personal space as a function of the stigma effect. *Environment and Behavior, 6*(3), 289–294.

Wright, B. A. (1960). *Physical disability: A psychological approach.* New York, NY: Harper & Row.

Wright, B. A. (1980). Developing constructive views of life with a disability. *Rehabilitation Literature, 41*(11–12), 274–279.

Yamamato, K. (1971). To be different. *Rehabilitation Counseling Bulletin, 14*(3), 180–189.

Yuker, H. E. (1962). *Yearly psycho-social research summary.* Albertson, NY: Human Resources Center.

Yuker, H. E. (1965). Attitudes as determinants of behavior. *Journal of Rehabilitation, 31*(6), 15–16.

Yuker, H. E., Block, J. R., & Campbell, W. J. (1960). *A scale to measure attitudes toward disabled persons: Human resources study no. 5.* Albertson, NY: Human Resources Center.

Yuker, H. E., Block, J. R., & Young, J. H. (1966). *The measurement of attitudes toward disabled persons.* Albertson, NY: Human Resources Center.

3

History of Treatment Toward Persons With Psychiatric Disabilities

KIM NGUYEN-FINN

*P*erhaps the most stigmatized and misunderstood group of people with disabilities are those who live with a psychiatric or mental illness. People with psychiatric disabilities warrant their own historical account which differs from Fox and Marini's history in Chapter 1, primarily because throughout history those with mental illness have at times been demonized, misunderstood as witches, put in prisons, and often subjected to inhumane treatment. The purpose of this chapter is to explore this history from the Middle Ages to the present day, noting the trials and tribulations of a population that continues to remain poorly understood and misperceived by the general public.

MENTAL ILLNESS TREATMENT SINCE THE MIDDLE AGES

The premodern era and early modern period, specifically from the Middle Ages to the 1800s, saw much cruel and inhumane treatment toward people with mental illness and mental retardation. Those who were viewed as mentally ill were often labeled as witches and burned at the stake (Dix, 1904; Gilman, 1988; Rosen, 1968; Shorter, 1997). Many were accused of demonic possession and subjected to exorcism, beaten, flogged, ridiculed, chained, or otherwise treated with fear and derision (Dix, 1904; Gilman, 1988; Rosen, 1968; Shorter, 1997). However, to view the treatment of those with mental illness during the Middle Ages solely through the modern lens would be unduly harsh. One must be mindful of the historical and cultural context of the general population and their knowledge, or lack thereof, of mental illness. People during the Middle Ages knew little in terms of the causes and treatment of diseases and even less so about mental illness. Physicians of this time period viewed disease and disability as often being caused by an imbalance of humors in the body, a belief inherited from the ancient Greeks. The theory was that the body is composed of four humors—blood, phlegm, yellow bile, and black bile. For instance, "madness" and "melancholy" were often viewed as caused by an excess of black bile (Gilman, 1988; Rosen, 1968). One possible treatment for imbalanced humor was bloodletting (Rosen,

1968)—a process of drawing blood from a patient to balance the humors and restore health. That which could not be explained by an imbalance of humors was believed to be an evil brought forth by sin committed by the sufferer, demons, or Satan or a spell cast by a witch and thus requiring to be cured by the Church or with magical herbs and incantations (Obermann, 1965).

The *Canon Episcopi,* a document that received a great deal of attention in the early medieval period, asserted that a belief in witches and sorcery, especially the idea that women rode on animals in the night, was a satanic delusion (Hansen, as cited in Rosen, 1968). A later document of the Middle Ages, the *Malleus Maleficarum (Hammer of Witches)*, revised the notion that a belief in witchcraft was brought about by Satan to assert that witches indeed carried out Satan's orders and espoused procedures for identifying, putting to trial, and forcing confessions out of witches (Rosen, 1968). These two documents show a shift in societal beliefs about mental illness. The *Canon Episcopi* asserted that those who believed in witchcraft had a mental illness; later, the *Malleus Maleficarum* stated that the accused likely were the ones with mental illness. In reality, accusations of witchcraft were often the result of petty jealousy, social or familial conflicts, spurned sexual advances, suggestion, delusions, and mental illness. Indeed, some accused witches seem to be described in accounts during the period of the Inquisition as elderly women afflicted with dementia. In cases of demonic possession, one may find symptoms of the accused that are consistent with dysthymia, paranoia, mania, compulsive disorders, epilepsy, schizophrenia, and senile dementia (Rosen, 1968).

Care for the mentally ill was essentially the responsibility of relatives so long as the individuals did not cause a disturbance or were deemed too dangerous to be cared for at home (Rosen, 1968; Shorter, 1997). If they could not be cared for, authorities would confine the person viewed as insane to an asylum, a hospital, a prison, or a workhouse (Rosen, 1968; Shorter, 1997). Cases have been noted of accused witches being recognized as actually mentally ill and transferred to hospitals (Lea, as cited in Rosen, 1968). One of the oldest hospitals to treat people with psychiatric disabilities was the Priory of Saint Mary of Bethlehem, or Bethlem, which was founded in the 13th century in Europe. As centuries passed, the institution began to focus almost entirely on those with mental illness, and its name gradually morphed from Bethlem to "Bedlam"; the hospital remained in use as an asylum until 1948 (Shorter, 1997). Institutions of this time often did little more than warehouse people with psychiatric disabilities to keep them away from the public.

Much of the treatment for this population during the Middle Ages was often moral or religious in nature and sometimes included fasting, prayer, and pilgrimages to shrines; for the latter, financial assistance was often provided by religious groups (Rosen, 1968). Two stained-glass windows from this time period found in the Canterbury Cathedral illustrate a man suffering from mental illness and depict prayer as a treatment; one window caption states, "Mad he comes," whereas the other reads, "He prays. Sane he goes away" (Torrey & Miller, 2001). Ibn Sīnā, or Avicenna, as he was known in the Western world, was a Persian physician who lived in the late first century or early second century and promoted treatments for ailments such as melancholia and "lovesickness." These included moisturizing the body, assisting with good sleep hygiene, promoting good nutrition, giving laxatives to reduce the toxins accumulated in the colon (which was believed to drive a person to madness; Shorter, 1997), and assisting in focusing on other matters and activities as a healthy distraction (Ibn Sīnā, 12th century/2010). Some of these treatments are like those espoused by mental health professionals of today.

COLONIAL AMERICA

Conditions for people with psychiatric disabilities did not fare much better in the American colonies. Similar to the circumstances during the Middle Ages, care for this population was the family's responsibility if they had a family to care for them (Torrey & Miller, 2001). Those less fortunate who were held in institutions were often subjected to extremely unhygienic conditions, flogged, jeered at, confined to workhouses, and manacled and chained to walls or floors. In extreme cases, people with psychiatric disabilities were shackled for years until they lost use of their limbs and gradually died for lack of food (Shorter, 1997). Occasionally, if a family could not adequately care for or control what they deemed a "distracted person," a colonial town would construct a small house (generally approximately 5' × 7') to confine the individual (Shorter, 1997). Eventually, asylums began to be built in the United States to house those with psychiatric disabilities. In 1729, the Boston Almshouse became the first institution in America to separate those with mental illness in a ward dedicated to psychiatric patients (Shorter, 1997). The first psychiatric hospital was opened in 1773 in Williamsburg, Virginia, with 30 beds (Shorter, 1997; Torrey & Miller, 2001), partly modeled after Bethlem in England (Scull, 1981).

By contrast, although not a belief shared by all American Indian tribes, some looked on those with possible mental illness with high regard, believing them to possess "special gifts," especially those with psychoses (Grandbois, 2005; Obermann, 1965; Thompson, Walker, & Silk-Walker, 1993). Other tribes viewed mental illness similarly to European Americans as resulting from supernatural possession, soul loss (the loss of part of the soul or life force due to trauma or substance abuse), or internal or external imbalance (Grandbois, 2005; Thompson et al., 1993). In other tribes, those who displayed behavior outside of their cultural norm because of a mental or physical disability were treated as if they had misbehaved and were punished accordingly (Thompson et al., 1993). Yellow Bird (2001) asserts that Indian nations do not generally have a word for *mentally ill*; what is translated as *crazy* means a humorous person or someone too angry to think clearly. With the expansion of the territory of the "White man," Western views and standards of practice in addressing mental illness also spread. The first asylum for a specific ethnic group was established in 1899 for the Northern Plains tribes, the Hiawatha Asylum for Insane Indians in Canton, South Dakota (Yellow Bird, 2001).

MENTAL ILLNESS IN 19TH-CENTURY AMERICA

In the 1800s, there was a huge rise in the number of those confined to asylums. The number of beds in each of the institutions increased to the low hundreds (Shorter, 1997). Braslow (1997) states that as more asylums were being built, still more were needed. Physicians of this time had scant training in diagnosing and treating mental illness (Caplan, 1969), but believed that they would be able to cure 80% of all such cases (Yanni, 2003). Indeed, they were so confident in their work that in 1853, psychiatrists who formed the American Organization of Asylum Physicians refused any association with the American Medical Association as they held other physicians in lower regard (Shorter, 1997).

The asylums of the early 19th century were largely therapeutic institutions providing moral treatment (Yanni, 2003). This treatment modality emphasized a positive change in environment (including staying within the asylum), an avoidance of immoral behavior and temptations, living a healthy lifestyle through exercise and proper nutrition, and abiding by a consistent daily schedule. Attendants were also instructed to show respect to patients, refrain from chaining them, and encourage supervised vocational and leisure activities (Yanni, 2003). Proponents of moral treatment also founded the *American Journal of Insanity,* a publication that aimed to educate citizens about mental illness and disability, as well as combat stigma and the abuses of those with a psychiatric disability (Caplan, 1969). However, in reality, moral therapy in its truest form was practiced in only a few institutions.

Patients of this time period were still being treated with physical therapies, including those designed to balance the humors. Records show that even up to the 1830s blistering, by which a patient's skin was burned with caustic substances to extract poisonous humors, was still being performed (Shorter, 1997). Treatment also used laxatives, bleeding, opiates, and hydrotherapy, or therapeutic baths, which came into vogue during this period (Shorter, 1997; Yanni, 2003).

Physicians tried to link disorders with treatments, but were limited in their scope of understanding. Phrenology became a popular diagnostic and predictive tool and was developed through the belief that a direct relationship existed between the shape and size of the skull and mental illness and disability (Gilman, 1988). Categorizing mental illness as chronic or curable was of paramount importance as it enabled physicians to focus only on the few patients they believed could be successfully treated (Caplan, 1969). During this period, diagnosing illness could also be viewed as a way of identifying and compartmentalizing people who appeared different from the rest of society. Common diagnoses included melancholia, mania, idiocy, and paresis (a condition with symptoms of dementia, seizures, and muscle impairment resulting from syphilis; Braslow, 1997). Shorter (1997) writes of one doctor from Albany, New York, who described what he termed "insane ear" or bloodied blisters within the ear to be a symptom of mental illness. In reality, the blisters were the result of asylum workers clubbing patients' heads (Shorter, 1997).

MENTAL ILLNESS AND TREATMENT AT THE TURN OF THE CENTURY

Moral treatments began to decline in the second half of the 19th century in favor of somatic therapies and behavioral control techniques (Braslow, 1997). Behavior that was deemed loud, offensive, or otherwise obnoxious by hospital staff was frequently managed by restraint, punishment, or sedative. Patients were physically restrained through the use of straightjackets, strapped to their beds—sometimes for years—confined in cells, and wrapped tightly in wet sheets (Braslow, 1997; Dix, 1904; Shorter, 1997). Criticized as another form of restraint, medications were administered to sedate patients and control symptoms of mental illness (Braslow, 1997; Shorter, 1997). Drugs in use during the 19th century included narcotics and the sedatives bromide, chloral hydrate, and hyoscine (Ackerknecht, as cited by Braslow, 1997). The most popular drug in use in the majority of asylums at this time was chloral hydrate (Caplan, 1969). Chloral hydrate, an addictive sedative related to chloroform, was especially popular among women, whose families were too embarrassed to commit them to an asylum, as a home remedy for psychosis, anxiety, and sleeping difficulties (Shorter, 1997). Physicians and psychiatrists often diagnosed females with hysteria.

Forced sterilization to control reproduction began to be employed and continued through the 1940s (Braslow, 1997). The eugenics movement has been likened to Nazi Germany's efforts to control the quality of future generations and involved the mass sterilization of those deemed to have a mental illness or hereditary-linked disability (Braslow, 1997). Patients were often considered incurable and their offspring were at risk of inheriting the disease (Braslow, 1997). Originally, however, laws allowing for forced sterilization made no mention of offspring. For example, the original 1909 California law known as the "Asexualization Act" stated that patients could be involuntarily sterilized if it benefited the physical, mental, or moral condition of any inmate (Braslow, 1997). Nearly 10 years later, an amendment was introduced that stated involuntary sterilization may be performed on persons confined to an asylum if they had a disorder or disability that might be inherited and could be transmitted to descendents. This law broadened physicians' ability to decide about patients' reproductive capabilities (Braslow, 1997). Many viewed forced sterilization as an economic issue. One such individual, Horatio M. Pollock, a statistician for the New York State Hospital Commission, wrote in 1921 that the United States loses over $200 million each year as a result of mental illness and less than a quarter of those afflicted are curable. Pollock (1921) further states that mental illness heredity is an accepted fact and thus the limitation of reproduction by "defective stock" should be employed to reduce the burden on taxpayers.

Sterilization was not only used to control the population of those with a psychiatric illness, but some physicians believed it to be therapeutic. In the case of men, physicians asserted that by severing the vas deferens, the testicles compensated by increasing the production of a hormone that was thought to make the patient feel physically and mentally invigorated (Money, 1983). For women, sterilization was often an ill-guided, but more socially acceptable, attempt at reducing the psychological strain of having more pregnancies than desired (Braslow, 1997). Research at this time also posits that genital abnormalities were seen as common among those with mental illness or disability—a way of nature ensuring that these individuals did not reproduce—while physicians believed that vasectomies could provide a cure (Gibbs, 1923).

Hydrotherapy, based on the idea that water had healing properties, became a widely used mode of treatment that remained in use until 1940 (Braslow, 1997). Hydrotherapeutic techniques were modeled after hot or cold mineral spring spas, long used as a curative, and consisted mainly of wet-sheet packs and hours of hot continuous baths (Braslow, 1997; Shorter, 1997). Patients who underwent wet-sheet packs were tightly wrapped in either cold or hot water-drenched sheets in which they had to remain until the treatment administration was deemed completed (Braslow, 1997). Continuous bath treatments required patients to remain in a bathtub with limbs bound until they appeared to be more tranquil (Winslow, as cited in Braslow, 1997).

THE SHIFTING PUBLIC VIEW OF PSYCHIATRY

Although treatments were changing through the end of the 19th century, so was the public's perception of psychiatry. By the 1900s as therapy and treatment reverted back to confinement, physicians who were specialized in mental illness were deemed in poor light (Shorter, 1997). The profession was considered to be dangerous, and quality entrants into the field were scarce (Caplan, 1969). There was a huge increase in the number of patients in mental hospitals in the United States (150,000 in 1904, or 2 for every 1,000 in the population; U.S. Bureau of the Census, 1975, as cited in Shorter, 1997). Psychiatrists in the United States lacked the education to address the mental health needs of their patients as less than 10% of psychiatrists graduated from a respected medical school and 20% had never attended a medical school lecture (Stevens, as cited in Shorter, 1997). Mental hospitals also struggled to hire attendants and other staff who were even minimally qualified (Caplan, 1969). Further, the negative perceptions of those with mental illness persisted. The "us versus them" attitude against those perceived to have a psychiatric illness increased with the rise in the number of immigrants in America and its asylums, particularly against Irish immigrants, whom psychiatrists claimed were prone to mental illness because of their irascibility and excessive indulgence in alcohol (Torrey & Miller, 2001).

Not surprising, the quality of mental health care in the United States had reached a new low during this time. Physicians who did not know how to treat mental illnesses and disabilities resorted to simply warehousing patients; reformers and former patients began to speak publicly about the treatment of those in mental institutions, which they viewed as little more than prisons. One early mental health reformer, Dorothea Dix, traveled throughout New England in the early 1840s investigating the treatment of the "insane poor" and prisoners (Shorter, 1997). Dix was spurred to activism in 1841 after teaching a class of female prisoners at a jail near Boston, Massachusetts, and was exposed to the unheated and squalid conditions in which the women presumed to be insane were confined (Torrey & Miller, 2001). Dix spoke in 1843 to the Massachusetts legislature and described how the "insane poor" were kept naked, chained, beaten with rods and whipped, and appeared filthy and disheveled. Dix (1904) also reported about those confined to cages, cellars, stalls or pens in stables, and closets. In her speech to the legislature, she related how she visited an almshouse and met a woman who was kept for years in a cellar and had wasted down to bone. Dix was told the woman had to be kept there because of violent tendencies. Dix's impassioned descriptions of the suffering of prisoners and those with mental illness helped raise the public's awareness of the needs of the "insane poor" and convinced states' legislatures across the country to increase funding for mental health needs (Torrey & Miller, 2001; Yanni, 2003).

Others spoke of their personal experiences in the nation's mental institutions. Packard (1868) wrote "The Prisoners' Hidden Life, or Insane Asylums Unveiled" in 1868 after being freed from an asylum following being involuntarily committed by her husband after a disagreement with him about religious beliefs (Eghigian, 2010). Lawsuits were being successfully brought forward against asylums for false imprisonment (Caplan, 1969). A few newspapers had reporters committed in mental institutions so that they could investigate patients' treatment firsthand and report on it (Caplan, 1969). In 1889, the *Chicago Times* sent a reporter into Jefferson Asylum in Cook County. The newspaper reported abuses ranging from verbal abuse to assault to murder, which spurred public outrage and an investigation by authorities (Caplan, 1969).

Another former patient, Clifford Beers, who wrote *A Mind That Found Itself* in 1907 (Beers, as cited in Clifford W. Beers Guidance Clinic, Inc., 2009), spent 798 days in confinement after a failed suicide attempt. Rosen (1968) argues that Beers's work played a tremendous part, if not the most important part, in the development of the modern mental health movement. Recounting his nearly 3-year confinement in a state mental institution, Beers describes witnessing beatings, days spent in cold cells wearing only underwear, and being restrained so tightly that his hands went numb. The story of how a Yale-educated man could be degraded with shockingly brutal treatment resonated with the public. Beers founded the National Committee for Mental Hygiene in 1909 to improve the care of patients in mental institutions, promote research, and disseminate information on the prevention and treatment of mental illnesses (Caplan, 1969; Rosen, 1968).

The work of Beers and other reformers helped make substantive changes in the field of mental health. For example, *asylum* would no longer be used to refer to mental hospitals, a sign of the change in focus from confinement to treatment (Caplan, 1969). In addition, patients were afforded the opportunity to appeal the decision to commit them, and institutions were directed to keep up with the latest knowledge through the purchase of updated medical books and subscriptions to scientific medical journals (Caplan, 1969).

Initially, however, psychiatrists responded to critics indignantly and with charges of ignorance and hypocrisy. They accused reformers of unjustly frightening the public away from receiving care and tarnishing psychiatrists' reputations (Caplan, 1969). Reformers were dismissed as ill-educated concerning proper behavioral management techniques and treatment modalities for mental disorders, and accused of hypocritically refusing to care for those with mental illness or disability themselves (Caplan, 1969). Other physicians, including neurologists, were cast as jealous individuals who lacked the qualifications to work in a mental hospital (Caplan, 1969).

DEVELOPMENT OF TREATMENTS IN THE 20TH CENTURY

Although psychiatrists initially scoffed at the notion that the quality of the care they provided in mental hospitals was subpar, research was conducted in the treatment of mental illness that brought about improvements. Physicians continued to develop and work toward improvement of somatic treatments for psychiatric disabilities in the early part of the 20th century. Physicians of this time period largely believed that fevers could treat a wide range of psychiatric illnesses (Braslow, 1997). Fevers were also believed by many physicians to kill the bacteria that causes syphilis, and fever therapy for paresis was in use until the early 1960s (Braslow, 1997). Interestingly, Wagner-Jauregg (1927), a winner of the Nobel Prize for physiology and medicine for his work in the development of this treatment, states that fever alone does not destroy the spirochaetes in that, sometimes, it will return once the fever has passed.

Other treatments included shock therapies. In the 1930s, some physicians used insulin to induce hypoglycemic coma in patients as a treatment for mental illness after noticing that patients who were difficult to manage became sedate and more cooperative with insulin (Braslow, 1997; Shorter, 1997). Insulin had previously been used to relieve depression and stimulate the appetite, as well as relieve diabetic symptoms (Shorter, 1997). Researchers could not agree why producing physiological shock through the use of insulin seemed to produce a positive effect (Braslow, 1997), but its use gradually rose in popularity. More than 100 mental hospitals in the United States housed insulin units by the 1960s (Shorter, 1997).

Metrazol injections, which produced seizures or convulsions, began to be administered (Braslow, 1997). Thus began the start of convulsive therapies. Physician–researchers have been unable to definitively state why convulsive therapies work, but continue to use the procedure in specific cases. Some theorize that fear of the treatment itself induced improvement (Braslow, 1997). Shorter (1997) reports that physician–researchers of the 1920s noted that when patients who had epilepsy developed schizophrenia, they experienced fewer epileptic seizures. They posited that there must be a correlation; thus, by inducing epileptic-like seizures, symptoms of schizophrenia might be reduced (Shorter, 1997). Initially, camphor, a naturally produced chemical that was sometimes used to treat psychosis in the 18th century, was used to shock the body to convulse (Shorter, 1997). The drug metrazol was developed and used in place of camphor (Shorter, 1997). The use of metrazol was fraught with problems, however, because physicians could not predict the onset or the intensity of the convulsions, which were reported to be agonizingly painful for the patients who experienced them and the hospital staff who witnessed them (Braslow, 1997; Shorter, 1997).

Later, seizures were induced in patients by passing electrical currents through electrodes on each of the temples and deemed to be safe (Braslow, 1997; Shorter, 1997). The use of electroshock therapy or electroconvulsive therapy (ECT) soon expanded from treating symptoms of schizophrenia to treating a wide array of mental illnesses such as depression, senile psychosis, melancholia, and alcohol abuse (Braslow, 1997). Although ECT remains in use today as an acceptable psychiatric intervention for mental illness, it is not without critics (Braslow, 1997). A large portion of the criticism lies in the fact that more women than men (50%–75%) are administered ECT. Another criticism is that ECT alters the physician–patient relationship to one of control and discipline (Braslow, 1997).

Psychosurgery, based on the viewpoint that the cause of mental illness or disease originated in the frontal lobe, began to gain ground in the 1930s (Braslow, 1997). Prefrontal lobotomy or leucotomy entails cutting the white matter in the frontal lobes of the brain, thought to be associated with insight, and severing its connection with the thalamus, thought to control emotion, and thereby reducing mental pain (Freeman & Watts, 1947). Surgery initially involved pouring alcohol onto the white matter of the frontal lobe through two holes that were drilled into the skull (Braslow, 1997). The neurologist Egas Moniz developed the prefrontal leucotomy based on observations of wartime head injuries, autopsies, and animal experiments and for which he later received the Nobel Prize (Eghigian, 2010). Moniz's procedure utilized an instrument called a *leukotome*, which is a rod affixed with a steel loop at one end that was inserted into the skull through holes drilled to cut the brain's white matter (Braslow, 1997). Freeman and Watts, two American physician–researchers, developed the transorbital lobotomy in which an ice pick is inserted into the eye socket of the patient and then the brain tissue is destroyed by tapping the ice pick with a hammer (Eghigian, 2010; Shorter, 1997). Freeman and Watts (1947) assert that prefrontal lobotomy is most successful with those patients whose mental illness may be anxiety disorder, depression, or excitability with schizophrenia, but is not successful for those with substance-use disorders, epilepsy, organic brain disease, and criminality. They also relayed doubts about the benefits of lobotomy with severe schizophrenia (Grob, 1991a). Moniz also questioned the effectiveness of leucotomy on schizophrenia, believing the surgery to be most successful on those with affective disorders (Grob, 1991a). Mahli and Bartlett (as cited in Juckel, Uhl, Padberg, Brüne, & Winter, 2009) reported that of those with certain psychiatric disabilities who underwent prefrontal leucotomy or lobotomy, approximately 67% had schizophrenia and 20% had an affective disorder. Shorter (1997) notes that lobotomies did indeed tend to calm patients with management problems. Psychosurgery, however, is also not without its hazards. It is not only dangerous to perform this surgery, but side effects of this treatment include a decline in social skills and judgment, loss of mental capacity, avolition or apathy, and a change in personality, such as loss of interest in previously enjoyed activities and changes in temperament (Juckel et al., 2009).

With the advent of talk therapy, psychological practice began its shift from being solely hospital based and became office based (Shorter, 1997). Outpatient psychiatric clinics were started in the 1920s, and by 1934 the practice of group psychotherapy began to be conducted (Shorter, 1997). Psychotherapy became the preferred treatment for middle and upper socioeconomic class individuals who were relatively high functioning, while somatic therapies tended to be used more often on those of the lower classes (Grob, 1991a).

The early 20th century witnessed the development of psychoanalysis, or the "talking cure." Sigmund Freud, a Viennese psychiatrist, developed an insight-oriented method of therapy (Shorter, 1997). According to Freud, neuroses are caused by repressed childhood memories, especially those of a sexual nature, as well as subconscious conflicts (Shorter, 1997). The goal of psychoanalysis is to bring the subconscious to consciousness and have the patient address the psychic conflict in a safe environment (Freud, 1910). Freud's theory of psychoanalysis conflicted with his contemporaries' views. Freud's focus on the individual, unconscious thoughts and urges, and childhood sexual development was in direct contradiction and thus ripe for criticism (Oberndorf, 1953). Despite its criticisms and limitations, Freud's work continues to have a major influence on contemporary therapeutic theories and practices (Corey, 1996). A significant assertion of psychotherapeutic theories is that the decision to undergo treatment rests with the patient.

Psychotherapy has also continued to evolve. Carl Rogers's client-centered therapy represented a fundamental shift in working with patients from Freudian and Jungian psychoanalysis. Rogers asserted that it is the client who has the ability and insight to know his or her problems, and how to put forth the issues, thus making the client the expert. The psychotherapist is simply there to be a sounding board and reassure the client's progress (Rogers, 1961). Psychotherapy also does not discount the benefits of somatic treatments, but it affirms a combination with appropriate drug therapy as the most effective treatment modality for mental illness today (Shorter, 1997).

Gains in understanding brain chemistry and more effective psychotropic medication for the treatment of mental illness were being made as well. The first neurotransmitter was isolated in the early 1920s, and soon thereafter the chemical acetylcholine was found to have an effect on nerve impulse transmissions between neurons (Shorter, 1997). Chlorpromazine, an antihistamine that would have a major impact on psychiatry, was developed in 1951 and initially was used as a sedative for psychiatric patients, but was found to also reduce psychosis. Today, chlorpromazine is more commonly known as an antipsychotic medication under the brand name Thorazine. Soon, other antipsychotic medications along with antidepressants and mood stabilizers were being developed and marketed. The success of psychotropic medications in reducing once debilitating symptoms of mental illness has allowed more and more individuals to lead productive lives outside institutions (Shorter, 1997).

THE SECOND WORLD WAR AND ITS INFLUENCE ON MENTAL HEALTH

Psychiatrists' wartime experiences expanded knowledge about mental health and the importance of the environment in both disorder development and treatment (Grob, 1991b); they applied what they learned during World War II (WWII) to their rehabilitation and therapeutic efforts (Grinker & Spiegel, as cited in Grob, 1991b). The war necessitated that those unfit for military service for physical and mental reasons be screened out, and those serving and who required rehabilitation as psychological casualties needed treatment (Grob, 1991a). The screening out of recruits aroused controversy and was not wholly successful. Approximately 1.75 million potential recruits were rejected by the Selective Service (Grob, 1991a) and an additional 500,000 were discharged for mental reasons (Pickren, 2005). These high numbers raised questions about prevalence of mental illness, the screening criteria's validity, and personal privacy (Grob, 1991a). The problems with screenings, however, did successfully highlight the need for additional research in the field and the importance of prevention of mental health problems (Grob, 1991a). The U.S. government began to assist the funding of psychological research on a large scale, which further shaped public perception of mental illness and treatment (Pickren, 2005). Psychiatrists serving during the war successfully utilized a more holistic approach to treatment, providing supportive counseling in conjunction with prescribing adequate sleep, good nutrition, and rest close to the patient's unit and support system (Grob, 1991b).

The successful treatment of psychiatric issues for returning veterans helped elevate the profession, and, in 1944, psychiatry was designated as a medical specialty within the Office of the Surgeon General (Grob, 1991b). Additional physicians were recruited into its ranks—at the outbreak of WWII, there were 35 psychiatrists serving in the military; the number swelled to 2,400 by 1945 (Grob, 1991b). Psychiatrists who were transitioning to civilian life at the end of the war began to enter academia, government, private practice, and public service, and carried with them their unique knowledge and approaches (Grob, 1991a). Indeed, the end of WWII brought with it a renewed sense of hope within the mental health field and the intellectual and institutional means to effect substantive changes. It also produced fresh challenges that needed to be addressed. One year after the end of hostilities, 60% of the Veterans Affairs (VA) hospital patients were WWII veterans presenting with mental disorders (Brand, 1965). The rising number of those in need of quality mental health services spurred the VA, along with the American Psychological Association (APA) and several universities, to work together to develop a doctoral clinical psychology program (Miller, 1946). Of significance, the National Mental Health Act was passed in the same year, which assisted states in the implementation of services for the diagnosis, prevention, and treatment of mental illnesses, as well as provided for research, training, and the formation of the National Institute of Mental Health (NIMH; Grob, 1991a; Pickren, 2005).

CLASSIFICATION OF MENTAL ILLNESS

The APA started to devise a standard nosology for mental disorders in 1948 (Shorter, 1997), but the first standardized nosology for mental illness, *The Statistical Manual for the Use of Institutions for the Insane,* was developed in 1918 by the American Medico-Psychological Association in collaboration with the National Committee for Mental Hygiene at the request of the U.S. Bureau of the Census (Grob, 1991b). Categorizing mental illnesses was found useful in that the public health statistical data regarding disorders could be collected and used in public policy development to uncover future trends and to show recidivism and recovery rates with different treatments or hospitals. The use of diagnoses in the development of treatment plans was not as important at this time (Grob, 1991b). Over time, the inadequacy of the earlier classification systems was made increasingly apparent. In 1952, the American Psychiatric Association (APA) published the *Diagnostic and Statistical Manual of Mental Disorders,* this volume is now referred to as the *DSM-I* (APA, 1952), which, like previous classification systems, reflected the intellectual, cultural, and political viewpoints on mental illness of its day (Grob, 1991b). Since its initial publication, there have been several revisions and the *DSM* continues to be used as the standard diagnostic tool by a wide array of mental health researchers and clinicians in a variety of settings (*DSM-5;* APA, 2013). Critics of the *DSM,* however, have cited that the resource fails to fully capture a holistic picture of an individual's circumstances. As such, in coordination with the WHO, the APA has endorsed a more holistic resource that can be cross-referenced with almost any disability and that takes into account an individual's external environment and medical and psychological problems (Peterson, 2010). Specifically, the International Classification of Functioning represents the most contemporary source available to mental health professionals in holistically assessing an individual's situation (Peterson, 2010).

DEINSTITUTIONALIZATION

There were 131 state-funded mental hospitals at the turn of the 20th century to house 126,137 patients; by 1941, there were 419,374 patients, but the number of hospitals had increased by only 181 (Braslow, 1997). With the overcrowding of mental hospitals, the need for an alternative to institutions became apparent. The increase in the use of drug therapies gave rise to the notion that individuals with mental illness could integrate back into the community if their symptoms were managed (Shorter, 1997). In addition, WWII evidenced how successful treatments outside of institutions were, and psychiatrists who served worked to incorporate mental health care into community treatment and prevention efforts of mental illnesses (Grob, 1991a; Kelly, 2005). The antipsychiatry movement further drove the shift to deinstitutionalization. The movement in large part comprised mental health professionals themselves who were critical about overuse of psychotropic medications, the viewpoint that behaviors simply outside of the norm implied mental disorders, and what they considered inferior institutional practices (Eghigian, 2010; Grob & Goldman, 2006). Deinstitutionalization also appeared to be strongly influenced by financial reasons as Medicaid payments gave states impetus to move patients to nursing homes (Mechanic & Rochefort, 1990).

Programs and centers with a community health focus began to rise. The Menninger Clinic in Topeka, Kansas, was started by William and Karl Menninger, brothers who served as psychiatrists in WWII; their model became a respected form of mental health care (Kelly, 2005). In 1955, Public Law 84–182 established the Mental Health Study Act, which examined mental health care in the United States (Kelly, 2005). The final report contributed to the development of the Community Mental Health Centers Act of 1963 (Stockdill, 2005). This Act required community mental health centers to provide inpatient and outpatient services, partial hospitalizations, emergency services, training and education, and consultation services (Mechanic & Rochefort, 1990; Stockdill, 2005). Thousands of institutionalized patients were placed with their families for care at home; however, the difficulty of patient monitoring and the lack of case management and coordination of care plagued the community mental health clinics (Grob & Goldman, 2006). New York recognized that patients needed a transition period between hospitalization and reintegration into the family and community and developed aftercare clinics in 1954 (Carmichael, as cited in Grob & Goldman, 2006). Halfway houses, which were either linked to hospitals or founded by mental health professionals or laypeople, were created to also help patients' transition back into the community (Grob & Goldman, 2006). Underfunding and what many perceived as disinterest by professionals for the rehabilitation and support of the reintegration into the community of those with severe mental illness posed major problems for halfway houses (Grob & Goldman, 2006). As an alternative, independent living communities for those with mental illnesses called "Fairweather Community Lodge Programs" were developed in California in the 1960s (Kelly, 2005). George Fairweather created his lodges believing that those with severe psychiatric illnesses can remain deinstitutionalized if they live and work together collaboratively (Kelly, 2005). Other treatment facilities started and still in use today are supervised apartments, board and care facilities, and group homes (Mechanic & Rochefort, 1990). Outpatient programs such as Assertive Community Treatment (ACT) have also come into use to serve the needs of those with severe and persistent mental illness living in the community (National Alliance on Mental Illness [NAMI], 2006). ACT programs provide highly intensive, multifaceted care available 24 hours/7 days per week with a low service provider to consumer ratio and have been shown to reduce the number of hospitalizations (NAMI, 2006). Between 1965 and 1975, the number of patients in state mental hospitals decreased an average of 8.6% per year (Mechanic & Rochefort, 1990). As the population in state mental hospitals reduced, general hospitals experienced a dramatic rise in the registration of patients with mental illness, necessitating the development of specialized psychiatric units as these hospitals were forced to house patients in surgical or emergency wards (Mechanic & Rochefort, 1990).

Reintegration into the community occurred on a large scale during the late 1960s; most of those released had been admitted to the hospitals in later life or had a lengthy confinement (Grob & Goldman, 2006). Disability and health insurance provided financial assistance and mental health benefits for individuals so that they may remain with their families (Mechanic & Rochefort, 1990). Moreover, the introduction of Medicaid and Medicare in 1966 gave states the incentive to transition patients from hospitals to nursing homes as these social programs provided for the care of elderly patients with mental illness or dementia in nursing homes (Mechanic & Rochefort, 1990). In addition, Medicaid often provided funds for short-term inpatient care in general hospitals (Mechanic & Rochefort, 1990).

DISILLUSIONMENT WITH THE PROMISES OF DEINSTITUTIONALIZATION

In time, deinstitutionalization produced less-than-positive results. The concepts of using the least restrictive method of care and that those with severe and persistent mental disorders would be treated in the community rather than the psychiatric institution meant that an increasing number of individuals would receive inadequate care as the community clinics were not poised to address their needs (Grob & Goldman, 2006; Mechanic & Rochefort, 1990). Many of those who would have been institutionalized in the past were forced to function independently in the community, and these individuals were frequently cited as being noncompliant with treatment, denying their mental illnesses, taking their medications irregularly, being aggressive, self-medicating with alcohol or drugs, and lacking social skills (Grob & Goldman, 2006).

The massive slash of funding for welfare programs in the 1980s further hindered mental health care efforts and precipitated a rise in the number of those with mental illness among the homeless and prison population (Mechanic & Rochefort, 1990). Although a direct correlation with the cuts to social programs is difficult to make, roughly one third of the nation's homeless population and 14% of county inmates in the 1980s were documented to have a psychiatric diagnosis (Torrey, as cited in Shorter, 1997). These figures contrast radically with the prevalence of severe mental illness in the general population at that time, which was about 2.8% (National Advisory Mental Health Council, 1993). According to the U.S. Department of Justice (DOJ), more than half of all inmates in 2005 had either a diagnosis of a mental disorder or met the criteria for one based on symptoms; these included psychotic disorders, major depressive disorders, and symptoms of mania (James & Glaze, 2006). In contrast, about 11% of adults in the general population now meet the criteria for a mental disorder according to the National Epidemiologic Survey on Alcohol and Related Conditions, 2001 to 2002 (James & Glaze, 2006).

MENTAL ILLNESS AND THE CRIMINAL JUSTICE SYSTEM

According to the U.S. DOJ, inmates with mental health problems are more likely to have violent records and are generally given longer sentences (James & Glaze, 2006). Although those with severe and persistent mental illness may and do commit criminal acts, many encounter law enforcement during mental crises or because they are exhibiting bizarre and/or disturbing behaviors in public (Lamberti & Weisman, 2004). Definite gains have been made in raising awareness of the unique needs of those with mental illness among law enforcement professionals. The Crisis Intervention Team (CIT) of the Memphis, Tennessee, Police Department is a model jail diversion program used in other communities as well. CIT officers volunteer to be educated about signs and symptoms of mental disorders and are trained in de-escalation techniques, community mental health and social service resources, and empathy of those with mental illness (Slate & Johnson, 2008). CIT programs have resulted in fewer arrests of those with severe mental illness, as well as fewer officer and detainee injuries (Lamberti & Weisman, 2004). Other police departments have experimented with using mental health professionals or social workers in crisis response (Lamberti & Weisman, 2004). The Law Enforcement and Mental Health Project Act of 2000 authorized funding for the development of "mental health courts" as an alternative for those with severe mental illness and to promote treatment and supervision for the accused (Lamberti & Weisman, 2004). They were also designed to curb reoffending among those with severe mental illness and divert them into community-based treatment (Redlich, Steadman, Monahan, Robbins, & Petrila, 2006).

Despite these improvements, the treatment of those with mental illness within the criminal justice system remains a concern. Suicide is the leading cause of death among inmates in jails and the third leading cause in prisons (Lamberti & Weisman, 2004). Some studies on inmates document that more than half of those who died by suicide had a history of mental illness (Lamberti & Weisman, 2004). These inmates with mental illness are also more likely to have disciplinary problems and be involved in altercations with other inmates while incarcerated (Hayes, 1995). As many view prisons and jails as a source of punishment rather than treatment, psychotherapy and medication management are lacking for many inmates. Depending on the facility type (local jail, state or federal prison), only 17% to 35% of inmates with mental disorders are provided mental health services (James & Glaze, 2006). To prevent recidivism, prisons and jails face the challenging task of coordinating with community mental health and social services on release of inmates with mental illness for employment, housing, and mental health assistance (Lamberti & Weisman, 2004).

ABUSE OF PERSONS WITH MENTAL ILLNESS

Not only do a high number of prisoners have a psychiatric disability, but those with mental illness also appear to be more vulnerable to sexual and physical abuse. Those incarcerated in prisons or jails were two to three times more likely to have been sexually or physically abused than other inmates (James & Glaze, 2006). Although causality cannot be stated, O'Hare, Shen, and Sherrer (2010) found that of those they interviewed with severe mental illness, 51.8% reported physical abuse, 41.7% reported sexual abuse, and a greater number of women than men reported they were abused. Those with severe mental illness also may engage in high-risk behaviors such as running away and substance abuse, which puts them at greater risk for repeated abuse (O'Hare et al., 2010). In addition, people with severe mental illness are more likely to live in high-crime areas that can further expose them to risk of decompensation (Schwartz, Bradley, Sexton, Sherry, & Ressler, 2005). Those with severe mental illness are particularly vulnerable to revictimization from the judicial system, given the difficulty in prosecuting based on a witness statement from someone with delusions, a history of engaging in multiple episodes of unprotected sex while having a manic episode, or having been severely impaired as a result of self-medication with drugs or alcohol (O'Hare et al., 2010). This also illustrates the negative public perceptions those with mental illness continue to face.

SOCIAL SECURITY BENEFICIARIES

The number of persons diagnosed with a psychiatric disability continues to grow rapidly, and psychiatric disability is the number one disability on Social Security benefit rolls (Marini, Feist, & Miller, 2004). Psychiatric disability continues to be the disability with the fastest growing percentage of beneficiaries, currently estimated to be approximately 28% of disabled workers and 41% of those on Supplemental Security Disability Income plus those on Social Security Income (Vercillo, 2011). Of more than 75% of beneficiaries with this diagnosis, half are younger than 30 years and the other half are aged between 30 and 39, thus representing the youngest population among beneficiaries (Marini et al., 2004). This is an alarming increase considering more than 50 million individuals are on the Social Security benefit rolls, and less than 1% of them ever return to gainful employment.

CONTINUED STIGMA AGAINST PEOPLE WITH MENTAL ILLNESS

Link, Phelan, Bresnahan, Stueve, and Pescosolido (1999) studied people's perceptions of mental illness and their thoughts on causes of mental disorders, dangerousness of those with mental illness, and preferred social distance. Link et al. (1999) found that Americans continue to perceive individuals with mental illness to be dangerous and desire minimal contact with them. In terms of causality of mental illness, more people today share the views of mental health professionals that disorders are caused by a variety of complex factors, including environment, biology, and social experiences (Link et al., 1999). A study by Corrigan and colleagues (2000) found that among their participants, physical illness such as cancer was viewed benignly and depression was the only mental illness seen as nonthreatening and more acceptable. Those with cocaine addiction, psychotic disorders, and mental retardation were perceived negatively and were discriminated against in the study (Corrigan et al., 2000).

One classic study focused on the stigmatizing attitudes against people with mental illness among mental health professionals. Rosenhan (1973) studied normal and abnormal behaviors, noting that differences existed among cultures. From this, he wondered whether the symptomatic criteria for diagnoses are met solely because they are exhibited by the individual or based on the environment or context (Rosenhan, 1973). Eight healthy individuals were admitted to 12 different mental hospitals across the United States as pseudopatients. Each pseudopatient falsely reported only his or her name, employment, and psychosocial history, and proffered fake symptoms of hearing voices such as a "thud" sound (Rosenhan, 1973). Further, while in the wards, the pseudopatients behaved as they normally do, were compliant, and reported to the hospital staff that they no longer experienced symptoms when asked (Rosenhan, 1973). Although the individuals were very high functioning in their daily lives, and the group included a graduate student in psychology, a psychiatrist, three psychologists, a pediatrician, a housewife, a painter, and Rosenhan himself, each was discharged with a diagnosis of schizophrenia in remission, implying that all members of the group were perceived as having schizophrenia throughout their hospitalization. In addition, the pseudopatients were treated dismissively by hospital staff; their questions were ignored completely and, in one instance, a nurse adjusted her bra in front of male patients as if they were not present. At other times, they were verbally and physically abused. It is interesting to note that it was other patients who detected the pseudopatients as being sane (Rosenhan, 1973). The Rosenhan study demonstrated that behaviors of the pseudopatients were judged in the context of the diagnostic label they were given and the hospital setting they were confined to (Hock, 2005).

CURRENT ISSUES REGARDING MENTAL ILLNESS AND ITS TREATMENT

Efforts are being made through public policy, advocacy organizations, and private individuals to raise awareness of mental illness, reduce its stigma, and combat discrimination against those with the disability. For example, more Americans are seeking treatment for mental health and emotional issues; 13.4% of adults in 2008 received inpatient, outpatient, or prescription medication treatment, a steady increase from previous years (NIMH, 2011). However, the costs for mental health care have also been increasing. Between 1996 and 2006, the total expenditure for mental health care in the United States rose from $35.2 to $57.5 billion (NIMH, 2011). As a comparison, the cost of care for those with cancer was also $57.5 billion in 2006 (NIMH, 2011). The WHO estimates that in 2004, the burden of disability (the number of years lost due to the disability and measured in disability-adjusted life years) for neuropsychiatric disorders in the United States and Canada together accounted for the greatest number (49%), followed by cardiovascular diseases, the second leading contributor (NIMH, 2011; WHO, 2011).

In their effort to raise awareness and encourage help-seeking behaviors, NIMH organized the, now annual, National Depression Screening Day in 1991 (NIMH, 2011; Shorter, 1997). Each year since its inception, approximately half a million individuals are screened annually (Screening for Mental Health, Inc., 2011). The U.S. surgeon general released a landmark publication, *Mental Health—A Report of the Surgeon General,* in 1999 (cited in Grob & Goldman, 2006), emphasizing that mental illnesses are valid conditions and treatments have been shown to be effective (Grob & Goldman, 2006). In addition, the report included the importance of reducing stigma and attitudinal barriers to help-seeking behaviors, tailoring intervention to the individual's cultural background, and the need for more clinicians to be trained in research-based treatments such as cognitive behavioral therapy (Office of the Surgeon General, 2011).

Another government agency, the Department of Veterans Affairs, is making promising efforts on treatment and preventative measures for mental illness. The global war on terrorism (GWT) and its fronts in Afghanistan and Iraq have highlighted the need for improved mental health services as an increasing number of psychiatric casualties are returning to civilian life. For example, the VA disseminates to health care providers and mental health clinicians evidence-based clinical practice guidelines for mental and physical health issues (U.S. Department of Veterans Affairs, 2011). Furthermore, taking into account the stigma against disclosing emotional concerns among service members and their resulting hesitancy to go to a mental health center, the VA expanded its primary care services to be better equipped to address veterans' clinical mental health needs (Committee on Veterans Affairs, 2007). According to the U.S. Department of Defense (DOD), as of July 2011, there were close to 45,000 servicemen wounded in action in the GWT, many of whom were diagnosed with a mental disability such as posttraumatic stress disorder (DOD, 2011). As veterans are returning to civilian life with service-related emotional disabilities, greater protections have been placed to help ensure they are provided equal treatment and opportunities.

In 1990, the Americans with Disabilities Act (ADA) was passed by Congress to provide equal opportunity and protection against discrimination on the basis of physical and mental disabilities (DOJ, 1990). For veterans and other individuals diagnosed with a mental illness, the ADA means that they have a right to reasonable accommodations, such as having a service dog trained to ease heightened anxiety and for the dog to be allowed to accompany them, flexible work schedules that enable them to attend counseling sessions, to have instructions provided in writing, to have tasks broken down to more manageable increments, extended deadlines, and additional breaks for those with memory impairments or difficulty focusing (DOJ, 2010).

Chamberlin (1993) noted that the ADA's inclusion of mental disabilities aroused controversy at the time and exposed some prejudices. Some of those who debated the bill questioned whether individuals with mental illnesses are reliable employees, or whether they are dangerous, unstable, undependable, and lazy. Despite the controversy, the ADA was passed into law and individuals with mental disabilities were afforded the same protections as those with physical disabilities. Since its inception, the ADA has undergone several revisions to strengthen its language and enforceability (DOJ, 2009).

Although those with mental illness still face multiple challenges, such as discrimination, stigma, lack of access to treatment, and disability (Mechanic & Rochefort, 1990), barriers are being reduced and treatments are being improved. Individuals and organizations, both public and private, continue to strive to raise public awareness and lobby for the needs of those with mental illness. A growing number of treatment options are available, including psychiatric hospitals (long- or short-term inpatient), emergency services (short-term acute care), private practice psychotherapists and psychiatrists, community mental health centers (comprehensive and state funded), community support services (halfway houses, quarter-way houses, day treatment centers), medication management, and self-help. Holistic treatment approaches are also being used as a way of improving the quality of mental health care, combining skills training, a social support system, environmental and behavioral modification, vocational assistance, and medication. With the variety of options available, more Americans are receiving mental health treatment than ever before (Shorter, 1997). Although gaps remain, the definite gains in efforts to prevent and effectively treat mental illness through the years are worthy to note.

REFERENCES

American Psychiatric Association. (1952). *The diagnostic and statistical manual of mental disorders.* Washington, DC: Author.

American Psychiatric Association. (2013). *Diagnostic and statistical manual of mental disorders* (5th ed.). Arlington, VA: American Psychiatric Press.

Brand, J. L. (1965). The National Mental Health Act of 1946: A retrospective. *Bulletin of the History of Medicine, 39,* 231–245.

Braslow, J. (1997). *Mental ills and bodily cures: Psychiatric treatment in the first half of the twentieth century.* Berkley: University of California Press.

Caplan, R. B. (1969). *Psychiatry and the community in nineteenth-century America: The recurring concern with the environment in the prevention and treatment of mental illness.* New York, NY: Basic Books.

Chamberlin, J. (1993). Psychiatric disabilities and the ADA: An advocate's perspective. In L. O. Gostin & H. A. Beyer (Eds.), *Implementing the Americans with Disabilities Act: Rights and responsibilities of all Americans* (pp. 223–227). Baltimore, MD: Paul H. Brookes Publishing.

Clifford W. Beers Guidance Clinic, Inc. (2009). *Clifford Beers—His legacy.* Retrieved from http://www .cliffordbeers.org/wp-content/uploads/2013/03/CBC-Timeline-Landscape-03-06-2013-Revision.pdf

Committee on Veterans Affairs. (2007). *DoD/VA collaboration and cooperation to meet the needs of returning service members: Hearing before the Committee on Veterans Affairs, United States Senate, One Hundred Tenth Congress, first session,* January 23, 2007. Washington, DC: U.S.

Government Printing Office. Retrieved from https://books.google.com/books?id=6nFKzHCodmw C&pg=PR1&lpg=PR1&dq=Committee+on+Veterans+Affairs.+(2007).+DoD/+VA+collaboration+and +cooperation+to+meet+the+needs+of+returning+service+members:+Hearing+before+the+Commit tee+on+Veterans+Affairs,+United+States+Senate,+One+Hundred+Tenth+Congress,+first+session,+ January+23,+2007.+Washington,+DC:+U.S.+Government+Printing+Office&source=bl&ots=eppr-W -umG&sig=87mbR-ErVIxYHzszH1LyIlC_1tc&hl=en&sa=X&ved=0ahUKEwiu2vzv65_WAhWB5yYK HeEzCr4Q6AEILTAB#v=onepage&q&f=false

Corey, G. (1996). *Theory and practice of counseling and psychotherapy* (5th ed.). Pacific Grove, CA: Brooks/Cole Publishing.

Corrigan, P. W., River, L. P., Lundin, R. K., Wasowski, K. U., Campion, J., Mathisen, J., . . . Kubiak, M. A. (2000). Stigmatizing attributions about mental illness [Electronic version]. *Journal of Community Psychology, 28*(1), 91–102. doi:10.1002/(SICI)1520-6629(200001)28:1<91::AID-JCOP9>3.0.CO;2-M

Dix, D. (1904). Memorial to the legislature of Massachusetts. Retrieved from https://archive.org/details/ memorialtolegisl00dixd

Eghigian, G. (2010). *From madness to mental health: Psychiatric disorder and its treatment in Western civilization.* New Brunswick, NJ: Rutgers University Press.

Freeman, W., & Watts, J. W. (1947). Psychosurgery during 1936–1946. *Archives of Neurology & Psychiatry, 58*(4), 417–425. doi:10.1001/archneurpsyc.1947.02300330029002

Freud, S. (1910). The origin and development of psychoanalysis. *American Journal of Psychology, 21*(2), 181–218. doi: 10.2307/1413001

Gibbs, C. E. (1923). Sex development and behavior in male patients with dementia praecox [Electronic version]. *Archives of Neurology & Psychiatry, 9*, 73–87.

Gilman, S. L. (1988). *Disease and representation: Images of illness from madness to AIDS.* Ithaca, NY: Cornell University Press.

Grandbois, D. (2005). Stigma of mental illness among American Indian and Alaska Native Nations: Historical and contemporary perspectives [Electronic version]. *Issues in Mental Health Nursing, 26*, 1001–1024. doi:10.1080/01612840500280661

Grob, G. N. (1991a). *From asylum to community: Mental health policy in modern America.* Princeton, NJ: Princeton University Press.

Grob, G. N. (1991b). Origins of *DSM-I*: A study in appearance and reality [Electronic version]. *American Journal of Psychiatry, 148*(4), 421–431. doi:10.1176/ajp.148.4.421

Grob, G. N., & Goldman, H. H. (2006). *The dilemma of federal mental-health policy: Radical reform or incremental change?* New Brunswick, NJ: Rutgers University Press.

Hayes, L. M. (1995). *Prison suicide: An overview and guide to prevention.* Washington, DC: National Center on Institutions and Alternatives, U.S. Department of Justice.

Hock, R. R. (2005). *Forty studies that changed psychology: Explorations into the history of psychological research* (5th ed.). Upper Saddle River, NJ: Pearson/Prentice Hall.

Ibn Sīnā. (2010). Lovesickness. In G. Eghigian (Ed.), *From madness to mental health: Psychiatric disor- der and its treatment in Western civilization* (pp. 50–52). New Brunswick, NJ: Rutgers University Press. (Original work published 12th c.)

James, D. J., & Glaze, L. E. (2006). *Mental health problems of prison and jail inmates* [Electronic ver- sion]. Bureau of Justice Statistics Special Report. Retrieved from https://www.bjs.gov/content/pub/ pdf/mhppji.pdf

Juckel, G., Uhl, I., Padberg, F., Brüne, M., & Winter, C. (2009). Psychosurgery and deep brain stimula- tion as *ultima ratio* treatment for refractory depression [Electronic version]. *European Archives of Psychiatry and Clinical Neuroscience, 259*, 1–7. doi:10.1007/s00406-008-0826-7

Kelly, J. G. (2005). The National Institute of Mental Health and the founding of the field of community psychology. In W. E. Pickren & S. F. Schneider (Eds.), *Psychology and the National Institute of Mental Health: A historical analysis of science, practice, and policy* (pp. 223–260). Washington, DC: American Psychological Association.

Lamberti, J. S., & Weisman, R. L. (2004). Persons with severe mental disorders in the criminal justice system: Challenges and opportunities [Electronic version]. *Psychiatric Quarterly, 75*(2), 151–164. doi:10.1023/B:PSAQ.0000019756.34713.c3

Link, B. G., Phelan, J. C., Bresnahan, M., Stueve, A., & Pescosolido, B. A. (1999). Public conceptions of mental illness: Labels, causes, dangerousness, and social distance [Electronic version]. *American Journal of Public Health, 89*, 1328–1333. doi: 10.2105/AJPH.89.9.1328

Marini, I., Feist, A., & Miller, E. (2004). Vocational expert testimony for the Social Security Administration: Observations from the field. *Journal of Forensic Vocational Analysts, 7*(1), 25–34.

Mechanic, D., & Rochefort, D. A. (1990). Deinstitutionalization: An appraisal of reform [Electronic ver- sion]. *Annual Review of Sociology, 16*, 301–327. doi:10.1146/annurev.so.16.080190.001505

Miller, J. G. (1946). Clinical psychology in the Veterans Administration [Electronic version]. *American Psychologist, 1*, 181–189. doi: http://dx.doi.org/10.1037/h0055143

Money, J. (1983). The genealogical descent of sexual psychoneuroendocrinology from sex and health theory: The eighteenth to the twentieth centuries [Electronic version]. *Psychoneuroendocrinology, 8*, 391–400. doi:10.1016/0306-4530(83)90018-5

National Advisory Mental Health Council. (1993). Health care reform for Americans with severe mental illness: Report of the National Advisory Mental Health Council. *American Journal of Psychiatry, 150*(10), 1447–1465.

National Alliance on Mental Illness. (2006). *Grading the states: A report on America's health care system for serious mental illness.* Retrieved from https://www.nami.org/grades

Obermann, C. E. (1965). *A history of vocational rehabilitation in America* (2nd ed.) [Electronic version]. Minneapolis, MN: T.S. Denison & Company. Retrieved from https://www.bjs.gov/content/pub/pdf/mhppji.pdf.

Oberndorf, C. P. (1953). *A history of psychoanalysis in America.* New York, NY: Harper & Row.

Office of the Surgeon General. (2011). *Mental health: A report of the surgeon general.* Retrieved from http://www.surgeongeneral.gov/library/mentalhealth/home.html

O'Hare, T., Shen, C., & Sherrer, M. (2010). High-risk behaviors and drinking-to-cope as mediators of lifetime abuse and PTSD symptoms in clients with severe mental illness [Electronic version]. *Journal of Traumatic Stress, 23*, 255–263. doi:10.1002/jts.20515

Packard, E. P. W. (1868). The prisoners' hidden life, or insane asylums unveiled. Retrieved from http://hdl.handle.net/10111/UIUCOCA:prisonershidden00pack

Peterson, D. B. (2010). *Psychological aspects of functioning, disability, and health.* New York, NY: Springer Publishing.

Pickren, W. E. (2005). Science, practice, and policy: An introduction to the history of psychology and the National Institute of Mental Health. In W. E. Pickren & S. F. Schneider (Eds.), *Psychology and the National Institute of Mental Health: A historical analysis of science, practice, and policy.* (pp. 3–16). Washington, DC: American Psychological Association.

Pollock, H. M. (1921). Eugenics as a factor in the prevention of mental disease. *State Hospital Quarterly, 7*, 13–19.

Redlich, A. D., Steadman, H. J., Monahan, J., Robbins, P. C., & Petrila, J., (2006). Patterns of practice in mental health courts: A national survey [Electronic version]. *Law and Human Behavior, 30*, 347–362. doi:10.1007/s10979-006-9036-x

Rogers, C. (1961). *On becoming a person.* Boston, MA: Houghton Mifflin.

Rosen, G. (1968). *Madness in society: Chapters in the historical sociology of mental illness.* Chicago, IL: The University of Chicago Press.

Rosenhan, D. L. (1973). On being sane in insane places [Electronic version]. *Science, 179*, 250–258. Retrieved from http://www.jstor.org/stable/1735662

Schwartz, A., Bradley, R., Sexton, M., Sherry, A., & Ressler, K. (2005). Posttraumatic stress disorder among African Americans in an inner city mental health clinic [Electronic version]. *Psychiatric Services, 56*, 212–215. doi:10.1176/appi.ps.56.2.212

Screening for Mental Health, Inc. (2011). *National Depression Screening Day (NDSD).* Retrieved from http://www.mentalhealthscreening.org/events/national-depression-screening-day.aspx

Scull, A. (1981). The discovery of the asylum revisited: Lunacy reform in the new American republic. In A. Skull (Ed.), *Madhouses, mad-doctors, and madmen: The social history of psychiatry in the Victorian Era* (pp. 144–165). Philadelphia: University of Pennsylvania Press.

Shorter, E. (1997). *A history of psychiatry: From the era of the asylum to the age of prozac.* New York, NY: John Wiley.

Slate, R. N., & Johnson, W. W. (2008). *The criminalization of mental illness: Crisis & opportunity for the justice system.* Durham, NC: Carolina Academic Press.

Stockdill, J. W. (2005). National mental health policy and the community mental health centers, 1963–1981. In W. E. Pickren & S. F. Schneider (Eds.), *Psychology and the National Institute of Mental Health: A historical analysis of science, practice, and policy* (pp. 261–294). Washington, DC: American Psychological Association.

Thompson, J. W., Walker, R. D., & Silk-Walker, P. (1993). Psychiatric care of American Indians and Alaska Natives. In A. C. Gaw (Ed.), *Culture, ethnicity and mental illness* (pp. 189–243). Washington, DC: American Psychiatric Press.

Torrey, E. F., & Miller, J. (2001). *The invisible plague: The rise of mental illness from 1750 to present.* New Brunswick, NJ: Rutgers University Press.

U.S. Bureau of the Census. (1975). *Historical statistics of the United States, Colonial times to 1970, Bicentennial Edition, Part 2.* Washington, DC: Author, 1, 84, tab. B-427.

U.S. Department of Defense. (2011). *U.S. casualty status.* Retrieved from http://www.defense.gov/news/casualty.pdf

U.S. Department of Justice. (1990). *Americans with Disabilities Act.* Retrieved from http://www.ada.gov/archive/adastat91.htm

U.S. Department of Justice. (2009). *Americans with Disabilities Act of 1990, as amended.* Retrieved from http://www.ada.gov/pubs/adastatute08mark.htm

U.S. Department of Justice. (2010). *ADA: Know your rights: Returning service members with disabilities.* Retrieved from http://www.ada.gov/servicemembers_adainfo.html

U.S. Department of Veterans Affairs. (2011). *VA/DoD Clinical practice guidelines.* Retrieved from https://www.healthquality.va.gov

Vercillo, A. (2011). *Social Security vocational expert testimony and psychiatric impairments.* Presentation August 3, International Association of Rehabilitation Professionals webinar.

Wagner-Jauregg, J. (1927). The treatment of dementia paralytica by malaria inoculation. Retrieved from https://www.nobelprize.org/nobel_prizes/medicine/laureates/1927/wagner-jauregg-lecture.html

World Health Organization. (2011). *Global burden of disease (GBD).* Retrieved from http://www.who.int/healthinfo/global_burden_disease/en

Yanni, C. (2003). The linear plan for insane asylums in the United States before 1866. *Journal of the Society of Architectural Historians, 62*(1), 24–49.

Yellow Bird, P. (2001). Wild Indians: Native perspective on the Hiawatha Asylum for Insane Indians. Retrieved from https://www.power2u.org/downloads/NativePerspectivesPeminaYellowBird.pdf

4

Models of Disability: Implications for the Counseling Profession*

JULIE F. SMART AND DAVID W. SMART

*D*isability is a natural part of human existence and is growing more common as a larger proportion of the U.S. population experiences some type of disability (Americans with Disabilities Act [ADA], 1990; Bowe, 1980; Employment and Disability Institute, 1996; Pope & Tarlov, 1991; Trieschmann, 1987; U.S. Department of Education, Office of Special Education and Rehabilitation Services, National Institute on Disability and Rehabilitation Research, 2000). Owing to medical advances and technology, wider availability of health insurance, and a generally higher standard of living that provides more services and support, people who would have died in the past now survive with a disability. In the same way that the viewpoints, experiences, and history of various ethnic/linguistic/cultural groups have been incorporated into the broader American culture, people with disabilities wish to have their social context and experiences become a valued and acknowledged part of American life. These contributions will strengthen and enrich the lives of those who do not experience disability (Akabas, 2000). In the past, clients with disabilities were served primarily by rehabilitation counselors, probably because of the misconception that the client's disability was the sole or, at minimum, the most important concern. However, because disability is both a common and a natural fact of life and because all individuals, including people with disabilities, have multiple identities, roles, functions, and environments, clients with disabilities require the services of counselors in all specialty areas: aging and adult development; gay, lesbian, bisexual, and transsexual issues; multicultural concerns; community mental health; school counseling; group counseling; marriage and family counseling; career counseling; and spiritual, ethical, and religious values.

To meet minimum standards of practice, therefore, counselors will be required to become proficient in the disability issues (Hayes, 2001; Hulnick & Hulnick, 1989). Indeed, Humes, Szymanski, and Hohenshil (1989) suggested that counselors have not facilitated the personal growth and development of their clients with disabilities: "The

---

*From "Models of disability: Implications for the counseling profession," by J. F. Smart and D. W. Smart, 2006, *Journal of Counseling & Development, 84,* 29–40. ACA. Reprinted with permission.

literature includes many testimonies of persons with disabilities … who have achieved successful careers despite roadblocks they perceived to have been imposed by counselors" (p. 145). However, in spite of this need, which continues to grow, very few university counseling programs provide adequate training about disability issues (Kemp & Mallinckrodt, 1996; Olkin, 1999; Pledger, 2003).

This lack of training and the resulting failure to provide services may be due to the powerful influence of models of disability, because these models determine in which academic disciplines the experience of disability is studied and taught. Thomas (2004) made the point that only rehabilitation counselors are trained in disability issues. A growing interest in models of disability has emerged in recent years, led by a variety of counseling practitioners, educators, and policy makers (Bickenbach, Chatterji, Badley, & Üstün, 1999; Humes et al., 1989; Melia, Pledger, & Wilson, 2003; Olkin & Pledger, 2003; J. F. Smart, 2004, 2016; Tate & Pledger, 2003). Examining these changing models can assist the counseling profession, and individual practitioners, to reorient service provision. Counselor educators and counseling practitioners, regardless of specialty, theoretical orientation, or professional setting, should recognize that disability is never entirely a personal, subjective, and idiosyncratic experience, nor is disability a completely objective, standardized, and universal experience.

The conceptualization of disability as an attribute located solely within an individual is changing to a paradigm in which disability is thought to be an interaction among the individual, the disability, and the environment (both social and physical; Dembo, 1982; Higgins, 1992). Typically, the disability is not the single defining characteristic of the individual; rather, the disability is one of several important parts of the individual's self-identity. When counselors dismiss or ignore the disability, a critical part of the client's self-identity must remain unexplored. On the other hand, counselors may tend to overemphasize the salience of the disability and automatically assume that the disability is the "presenting problem" or the cause and source of all the client's concerns. Indeed, the "roadblocks" referred to by Humes et al. (1989) may be caused by a lack of understanding, training, and experience with disability issues. Many individuals with disabilities view their disability as a valued part of their self-identity, see positive aspects in the disability, and would choose not to eliminate the disability if they had this option. In contrast, few counselors conceptualize the client's disability as a source of self-actualization.

In this chapter, we draw both theoretical and practice implications, which may assist practitioners and educators in gaining a clearer understanding of counseling clients who have disabilities, from four broad models of disability. Intended as a broad overview of the major models and an introductory discussion of ways in which these models can affect the profession of counseling, we present several different ways of conceptualizing the experience of disability. The four broad models discussed here are (a) the Biomedical Model, (b) the Functional Model, (c) the Environmental Model, and (d) the Sociopolitical Model. In this chapter, the Functional Model and the Environmental Model are presented together because both are interactive models; stated differently, these two models define disability as an interaction between the individual and his or her environment and functions. Furthermore, it is these two models, the Functional and Environmental, that are most closely related to the practice of counseling. The Sociopolitical Model is considered separately because it is the newest of the models; more important, this model conceptualizes people with disabilities as belonging to a minority group of individuals who have not yet received their full civil rights.

THE BIOMEDICAL MODEL

The Biomedical Model of disability has a long history, is the most well known to the general public, and carries with it the power and prestige of the well-established medical profession. This model, rooted in the scientific method and the benefactor of a long tradition, has had dominance in shaping the understanding of disability. The strength of the Biomedical Model lies in its strong explanatory power, which far exceeds the explanatory power of other models. Moreover, this model defines disability in the language of medicine, lending scientific credibility to the idea that disabilities are wholly an individual experience. Because of this "individualization," "privatization," and "medicalization" of disability, the Biomedical Model has encouraged investigators to remain silent on issues of social justice. Indeed, this model is not considered to be an interactional model because the definition, the "problem," and the treatment of the disability are all considered to lie within the individual with the disability. In addition, interprofessional collaboration is rarely implemented when the disability is medicalized.

Underlying the Biomedical Model is the assumption that pathology is present, and, in addition, disabilities are objective conditions that exist in and of themselves. This "objectification" process opens the door to the possibility of dehumanizing the person because attention is focused on the supposed pathology (Albrecht, 1992; Longmore, 1995). Bickenbach (1993) described this definition of disability as deviance:

> The most commonly held belief about [this model of] disablement is that it involves a defect, deficiency, dysfunction, abnormality, failing, or medical "problem" that is located in an individual. We think it is so obvious as to be beyond serious dispute that disablement is a characteristic of a defective person, someone who is functionally limited or anatomically abnormal, diseased, or pathoanatomical, someone who is neither whole nor healthy, fit nor flourishing, someone who is biologically inferior or subnormal. The essence of disablement, in this view, is that there are things wrong with people with disabilities. (p. 61)

It is interesting that Bickenbach considered the Biomedical Model to have roots in the religious model of disability, in which biological wholeness was viewed as virtue and righteousness. The combination of religion and science in the Biomedical Model has had a formidable influence.

Furthermore, there is a clear-cut normative aspect to the Biomedical Model in that the disability is considered to be a biological inferiority, malfunction, pathology, and deviance when compared with (or normed on) individuals without disabilities (McCarthy, 1993). Thus, the individual with a disability, regardless of personal qualities and assets, understands that he or she belongs to a devalued group. Frequently when clients with an identified disability seek professional services, such as counseling, they understand that, in the view of others, a life with a disability is worth less investment (McCarthy, 2003). Joanne Wilson, the commissioner for the Rehabilitation Services Administration from 2002 to 2005, is blind. She summarized the devaluation and the normative aspect of having a disability when she stated, "It's not quite respectable to have a disability" (Joanne Wilson, personal communication October 15, 2003). Furthermore, many individuals with disabilities may see no value in trying to integrate into a society that automatically discounts and pathologizes them. Taken to its extreme, the normative aspect of this model views a perfect world as a world without disabilities, and the possibility exists of providing the medical profession the mandate with which to eliminate disabilities and the people who experience them (Singer, 2000).

The Biomedical Model places people with disabilities in stigmatizing categories, therefore allowing the "general public" to view them as their category—"the blind," "quads" (individuals with quadriplegia), or "the mentally ill" (Nagi, 1969). Regardless of the category, categorized people are viewed as their category and not as individuals. Schur (1971) described the effects of categorization:

> Others respond to devalued persons in terms of their membership in the stigma-laden category. Individual qualities and actions become secondary.... Individuals of devalued categories are treated as being ... substitutable for each other.... Stigmatized persons, then, are little valued as persons. Classificatory status tends to displace alternative criteria of personal worth.... Others may claim license—implicitly, if not explicitly—to treat stigmatized individuals in exploitative and degrading ways. (pp. 30–31)

This categorization according to disability type has had many pervasive, institutional, and systematic consequences, some of which have resulted in inferior services or a lack of services from the counseling professions. In addition, this categorization has fragmented people with disabilities from their own community and robbed them of a collective history (Hahn, 1985, 1988, 1993). Categorization has also successfully taught society to focus on the disability category rather than the universal problems and challenges faced by people with all types of disabilities. Because of the strength and prestige of the Biomedical Model, both the general public and individuals with disabilities have come to see people with disabilities as categories.

In the Biomedical Model, the disability exists totally within the individual, and, accordingly, the individual responsible for the "problem" should also be totally responsible for the solution (Kiesler, 1999). This view, therefore, has the authority to relieve society of any responsibility to accord civil rights to individuals with disabilities. After all, the disability is the individual's flaw and tragedy. A disability is thought to be bad luck, but it is the individual's bad luck. Society often communicates to people with disabilities: "This is how the world is. Take it or leave it." Not only does the Biomedical Model legitimize prejudice and discrimination, but to the general public, its treatment of people with disabilities often does not appear to be prejudicial and stigmatizing. For example, when individuals with disabilities are not integrated into the workplace, schools, and other social institutions, their absence is usually not noticed. After all, according to this attribution theory, individuals with disabilities are thought to be responsible for their stigmatization. Clinicians have attempted to include environmental issues in their classification/diagnostic systems; however, the degree of prejudice and discrimination experienced or the lack of accommodations is typically not considered when medical professionals determine the level of severity of the disability or render a percentage of impairment.

In the traditional view of the Biomedical Model, both the cause of the disability and the solution and treatment rest with the individual. Liachowitz (1988) described an additional responsibility placed on individuals with disabilities: "Recent medical textbooks go further and construe disability as a variable dependent upon characteristics of motivation and adaptability as well as the limiting residue of disease and injury" (p. 12). Individuals concerned with the rights of people with disabilities derisively refer to this as the "Try Harder" syndrome. One hundred years ago, people with disabilities were often given moral and religious education in an attempt to "rehabilitate" them (Byrom, 2004).

These aspects of the Biomedical Model—the pathologizing, the objectification, the categorization, and the individualization of a disability—are dependent on the diagnosis and classification systems used by the medical professions. Certainly, the diagnostic systems of the medical professions are the most objective, standardized, reliable, and morally neutral assessments compared with those of the other models (American Psychiatric Association, 2013; Peterson, 2002; World Health Organization, 1980, 2001). Medical diagnoses are, however, only as valid as the classification systems used, and further, medical diagnoses can be subjective, impressionistic, value-laden judgments of individuals (Clendinen & Nagourney, 1999; Kirk & Kutchins, 1992; D. W. Smart & J. F. Smart, 1997a). L. Eisenberg (1996) stated, "Diagnostic categories and classification schemes are acts of the imagination rather than real things in the world. ... We must not mistake this for reality itself" (p. xv), whereas Stone (1984), in a chapter titled "Disability as a Clinical Concept," referred to these systems as "false precision" and stated that medical diagnoses are not the product of "a scientific procedure of unquestionable validity, free from error" (p. 111). Stone concluded by pronouncing the determination of a diagnosis as "an unattainable quest for neutrality" (p. 111). Disability scholars (Albrecht, 1992; Reno, Mashaw, & Gradison, 1997) have posited that all diagnoses are based on the dual concepts of clinical neutrality and clear-cut measures of "normality" and that neither complete clinical neutrality nor absolutely clear-cut measures exist.

The Biomedical Model of disability does not provide a strong basis for the treatment and policy considerations of chronic conditions, which include most disabilities (J. F. Smart, 2005a, 2005b). Because of the long history of the two-outcome paradigm of medicine—total cure or the death of the individual—medical professionals work best with acute injuries rather than chronic, long-term disabilities. Vestiges of this two-outcome paradigm remain in insurance payment policies, which dictate that payments for services—such as counseling—are withdrawn once medical stabilization has been achieved and progress toward a full recovery has terminated. This has a kind of reasonableness, because the business of medical insurance was originally based on the Biomedical Model, with physicians acting as gatekeepers and policy makers.

Furthermore, because of the Biomedical Model's lack of attention to the individual's environment and its focus on the individual, this model is less useful for mental and psychiatric disabilities, which are episodic and very responsive to context and environment (Stefan, 2001). In short, the Biomedical Model is much stronger, in both diagnosis and treatment, when dealing with physical disabilities. This narrow emphasis presents difficulties because the definition of disability is enlarging and evolving beyond that of only physical disabilities to include such impairments as learning disabilities, mental illness, and other disorders.

The Biomedical Model is often conceived to be a model of experts in control (J. F. Smart, 2016), therefore reducing individuals with disabilities to the role of passive and compliant patients. Because most individuals with disabilities do not possess the expertise, knowledge, education, and experience of physicians, they may not be accorded respect as decision makers. For example, many individuals with disabilities have consistently reported that "doctors always underestimate the quality of my life." Thus, the subordinate, dependent, and inferior status of people with disabilities is reinforced by the power differential inherent in the Biomedical Model. Conrad (2004) described another result of the use of medical experts:

> Because of the way the medical profession is organized and the mandate it receives from society, decisions related to medical diagnoses and treatment are virtually controlled by the medical professions.... By defining a problem as medical, it is removed from the public realm where there can be discussion by ordinary people and put on a plane where only medical people can discuss it. (p. 22)

As would be expected, much of the current conceptualization of disability is a reaction against the Biomedical Model (Brant & Pope, 1997; Gill, Kewman, & Brannon, 2003; Pope & Tarlov, 1991; Scotch, 1988). In spite of its shortcomings, no one, including proponents of the other models, suggests totally abandoning the Biomedical Model, nor is any intentional harm on the part of the medical profession implied. Indeed, the medical profession itself is moving away from many of the assumptions of this model. Furthermore, in the final analysis, it is the broader society that has endowed the medical professions and the Biomedical Model of disability with the appearance of reality, science, and objectivity.

FUNCTIONAL AND ENVIRONMENTAL MODELS

The Functional and Environmental models are considered together in this chapter because both are interactional models. In these two models, it makes no sense to discuss the definition of disability, or the ways in which to intervene, without first considering the functions of both the individual and the individual's environment. Therefore, biology becomes less important. Disability is defined in relation to the skills, abilities, and achievements of the individual in addition to biological/organic factors. Thus, these models do recognize the biological factors of a disability. Disadvantages or limitations such as poverty or a lack of education, although social ills, are not considered to be disabilities. Also, although everyone is required to successfully negotiate difficult environments, to undertake demanding functions, and to experience disadvantages, not everyone has a disability.

These two models are considered to be interactive models because the disability (of the individual) interacts with functions and environment (Dembo, 1982; Tanenbaum, 1986; Thomason, Burton, & Hyatt, 1998). Therefore, the definition of *disability*, the causal attribution, and the solution attribution are not found wholly within the individual (or his or her disability). Instead, adherents of these models of disability recognize the importance of biology, but also posit that the environment can cause, contribute to, and exaggerate disability. Furthermore, these models do not view the "problem" of disability as located totally within the individual, suggesting that many of the difficulties of disability are also located outside the individual, specifically within the environment and its functional requirements (Wolfensberger, 1972). If the location of the problem shifts, the onus for the solution of the problem also shifts. By viewing the definition, the cause, and the difficulties of disability as interactional, helping professionals can aim interventions at adapting the environmental and functional demands to the needs of the individual with a disability in addition to "rehabilitating" the individual.

Causal attribution differs also, but it is safe to state that for most individuals the Biomedical Model's conception of causation is much easier to understand. As we have pointed out, in the Biomedical Model, the causes and solutions to the disability are found in the individual, and generally the social solution and the built environment are ignored. In contrast, the Environmental and Functional models of disability posit that society can cause disabilities, exaggerate disabilities, and, in the words of some disability scholars, "make disabilities" (Higgins, 1992). Two examples illustrate these models. Itzhak Perlman, the world-famous violinist and a survivor of polio, stated that people with disabilities experience two problems: (a) the physical inaccessibility of the environment and (b) the attitudes of the people without disabilities toward disability and people with disabilities (J. F. Smart, 2004). As difficult as these problems are, it can be seen that neither problem concerns the disability itself (or the individual with the disability). Indeed, one of the results of the ADA has been the increased public awareness that many of the problems and obstacles experienced by people with disabilities are caused by their environments. Also, it can be seen that for Perlman's major professional function, playing the violin, his difficulty in walking is not a functional disability. The definition of disability varies with the roles expected of the individual. In addition, it can be seen that both of Perlman's difficulties can be ameliorated.

World War II and the resulting demands for a large number of military personnel changed both the functional and environmental definitions of disability. During World War I and World War II, many men who had been residents of institutions for the long-term care of individuals with mental retardation entered the U.S. military and fought in the wars' battles. Sobsey (1994) told of 13 men from such an institution in Connecticut who, in spite of being labeled as having mental retardation, enlisted to fight in World War II. Four of these men were promoted to higher ranks, and seven were wounded in action. In spite of their war records, most of these men returned to the institution after the war. Sobsey concluded, "wars and labor shortages have repeatedly redefined who has mental retardation" (p. 132). It can be seen that nothing in the disability or the individual changed, but rather changes in the environment occurred.

These two examples also illustrate the disabling effects of prejudice and discrimination, and therefore in both the Environmental and Functional models, the potential exists for incorporating some degree of societal prejudice and discrimination when attempting to render a rating of the severity of a disability. For example, a young African American man with schizophrenia would probably experience more prejudice and discrimination than a European American man who is blind. Medical ratings of the level of severity of these two disabilities might be relatively equal, but the difficulties experienced are probably much greater for the man with schizophrenia, mostly because of societal attitudes. Schizophrenia is a disability that is considered highly stigmatizing, and blindness is not. Furthermore, other perceived characteristics of the individual who "carries" the disability label (such as racial/cultural/ethnic identification, gender, sexual orientation, or age) intersect with the public perception of the disability.

There is a tendency to think that each individual's environment and functions are exclusively unique to that individual. However, broad, general changes in both environment and function can affect the daily life of an individual with a disability. For example, in a society based on physical labor such as farming or mining, a physical disability presents more difficulties than a cognitive disability, but in a service-, information-, and technology-based economy, a physical disability does not cause as many difficulties as does a cognitive disability. Liachowitz (1988) in her book, *Disability as a Social Construct: Legislative Roots,* made a compelling argument that literally overnight the federal government has the capability to define disability and, therefore, to determine who has a disability. Nazi Germany is an extreme but clear-cut illustration of the Environmental Model and its power to shape the response to disability. Because of the political–social environment (Nazism), "Aryan" Germans with disabilities were systematically mass murdered by their government (Friedlander, 1995; Gallagher, 1990).

The causal attributions of these two models are not as sharply defined and as easily understandable as those of the Biomedical Model; certainly, one of the strengths of the Biomedical Model is its strong explanatory power. Nonetheless, both the Functional Model and the Environmental Model possess strengths that the Biomedical Model does not. In addition, the bases of the Functional and Environmental models are more closely related to the theoretical assumption and practice orientations of most counselors.

Viewing the client as a complete person with skills, abilities, and demands and conceptualizing the client within a context allow the counselor to see the client as more than a disability. If the disability is not the only factor in the equation of disability, then the diagnoses and labels attached to the individual will not acquire as much power to define the individual to himself or herself and to others. It will be more difficult to dehumanize people with disabilities and to think of the person with a disability as "not one of us." Labels and diagnoses, and the professionals who render them, will not be as powerful as they once were.

In contrast to the Biomedical Model, the Environmental and Functional models deal more flexibly with psychiatric disabilities that are episodic, highly responsive to context and environment, and exist along a spectrum, which theoretically could be the cause for hope—people with mental disabilities are frequently strong, talented, competent, and capable, and their environments can be structured in a way to support and increase their strengths, talents, competence, and capabilities (Stefan, 2001, p. 10).

Because an individual's cultural identification defines his or her functions, roles, and environment to a great extent, the Functional and Environmental models provide a better basis from which to understand and respond to the disabilities experienced by individuals who are not White, middle-class, heterosexual, male, or European American (D. W. Smart & J. F. Smart, 1997b; J. F. Smart & D. W. Smart, 1997). The Functional and Environmental models are also more appropriate for chronic conditions, which most disabilities are. With chronic conditions, after medical stabilization, the treatment focus is on maintaining the highest quality of life, avoiding secondary disabilities and complications, supporting independence, acquiring the appropriate assistive technology, and assisting the individual in negotiating developmental tasks. It can be seen that most of these interventions require functional and environmental adaptations—rather than focusing solely on "rehabilitating" the individual.

In the Functional and Environmental models, it is more difficult to dehumanize individuals with disabilities because of the following factors: (a) categorization by disability type is less likely; (b) the power differential is reduced when the individual is viewed as a total person and not as a stigmatized, medicalized category; and (c) partial responsibility for the response to the disability devolves on "society" to provide a physically accessible and nonprejudiced environment.

Perhaps most important, the discomfort, anxiety, defensiveness, and existential angst experienced because of the fear of acquiring a disability are decreased when individuals without disabilities take the opportunity to associate with friends, colleagues, and clients with disabilities. Thus, by viewing the individual as more than the disability and conceptualizing the environment and the functional requirements as major determinants of the difficulties experienced by people with disabilities, the fear of acquiring a disability will be greatly reduced.

THE SOCIOPOLITICAL MODEL

The Sociopolitical Model, also referred to as the *Minority Model of Disability* (Hahn, 1985, 1988, 1991, 1996, 1997; Kleinfield, 1979), is the most recently developed model and, more important, is a fundamental and radical change from the previous models. The Sociopolitical Model (in contrast to the Biomedical Model and the Environmental and Functional models) has the capability to explain and describe more of the day-to-day life of people with disabilities. Certainly, for most people with disabilities, the prejudice and discrimination found in the broader society are more of an obstacle than are medical impairments or functional limitations.

Madeline Will (cited in Weisgerber, 1991), former assistant secretary for education and head of the Office of Special Education and Rehabilitation Services, underscored this:

> Most disabled people [*sic*] ... will tell you that despite what everyone thinks, the disability itself is not what makes everything different. What causes the difficulties are the attitudes society has about being disabled, attitudes that make a disabled person embarrassed, insecure, uncomfortable, dependent. Of course, disabled people [*sic*] rarely talk about the quality of life. But it has precious little to do with deformity and a great deal to do with society's own defects. (p. 6)

In this model, people with disabilities view themselves as members of a U.S. minority group. Indeed, some disability rights advocates have described Americans with disabilities as "foreigners in their own country" (Higgins, 1992). The hallmarks of this model include self-definition, self-determination, the elimination (or reduction) of the prejudice and discrimination (sometimes referred to as "handicapism"), rejection of medical diagnoses and categories, and the drive to achieve full equality and civil rights under U.S. law.

The Sociopolitical Model refuses to accept the inferior, dependent, and stigmatizing definition of disability; furthermore, in this model, disability is defined as a social construction in that the limitations and disadvantages experienced by people with disabilities have nothing to do with the disability, but are only social constructions and therefore unwarranted. If society constructs disability, society can also deconstruct disability. Stigmatization, prejudice, discrimination, inferiority, and handicapism are not inevitable, natural, or unavoidable consequences of disabilities. Inherent in this definition of disability are three aspects: (a) people with disabilities must define disability; (b) people with disabilities must refuse to allow "experts" or "professionals" to define the disability, determine the outcomes of their lives, or judge the quality of their lives; and (c) people with disabilities refuse the "disabled role" of deviance and pathology. Although in the past, professionals defined disabilities and the experiences available to individuals with disabilities, disability rights advocates assert their rights to self-definition and self-determination. It can be seen that much of the Sociopolitical Model seeks to displace the "expert in control" basis of the Biomedical Model.

In the past, the disabled role was determined by people who did not have disabilities and therefore had no experience in managing a disability on a day-to-day basis. Individuals with disabilities were expected to learn the rules of this role; to live the rules; and, most important, to believe in the rules. The rules and expectations of this role, although unwritten, were strongly enforced, and individuals who did not comply with these expectations often experienced severe consequences, including the lack of services and social isolation. These rules included the following: always be cheerful; face the disability with courage, optimism, and motivations; manage the disability as well as possible (in the view of others); adhere to medical and rehabilitation regimens; request only those accommodations and assistance that others feel are necessary; make others comfortable with the disability; and keep all aspirations at a reasonable level, or stated differently, do not ask for much. Often, a person with a disability who is perceived to have adopted the disabled role is considered to be a "Tiny Tim" by disability rights advocates.

Adherents of the Sociopolitical Model resist medical categorization by diagnosis and, indeed, view this categorization to be a source of prejudice and discrimination (although they acknowledge that prejudice and discrimination were not the intention of the medical profession). According to the Sociopolitical Model, categorization has resulted in (a) teaching individuals who bear the diagnoses to accept the meanings of these labels as their self-identity, (b) allowing the general public to avoid focusing on the universal problems of people with all types of disabilities, (c) fragmenting the disability community so that it cannot form broad coalitions with which to effect sociopolitical changes, and (d) leading "society" to believe that disability is inferiority and that, therefore, the prejudice and discrimination toward people with disabilities are inevitable consequences of the inferiority.

Thus, the Sociopolitical Model minimizes dependence on an academic discipline or professional area of expertise, and it does not consider causal attribution to be a relevant concern. This model is considered to be an interactional model. Disability, in this model, is not viewed as a personal tragedy, but as a public concern.

Many scholars and researchers state that the prejudice and discrimination directed toward people with disabilities have been more pervasive than the prejudice and discrimination directed toward any other group of people, and, further, much of this has been due to the Biomedical Model. In their book, Fleischer and Zames (as cited in McCarthy, 2003) pointed out the tendency to overlook prejudice against persons with disabilities:

> In *The Anatomy of Prejudices* (1996), Elisabeth Young-Bruehl analyzes what she believes to be "the four prejudices that have dominated American life and reflection in the past half-century—anti-Semitism, racism, sexism, and homophobia." No reference is made to disability discrimination. Misrepresented as a health, economic, technical, or safety issue rather than discrimination, prejudice based on disability frequently remains unrecognized. (p. 210)

Albrecht (1992) summarized,

> More *recent* studies suggest that prejudice against impaired persons is more intense than that against other minorities. Bowe (1980) concludes that employer attitudes toward impaired workers are "less favorable than those toward elderly individuals, minority group members, ex-convicts, and student radicals," and Hahn (1988) finds that handicapped persons are victims of greater animosity and rejection than many other groups in society. (p. 245)

Proponents of the Sociopolitical Model assert that this prejudice and discrimination against individuals with disabilities is long-standing, systematic, and institutionalized in American life. The ADA (1990) states,

> Individuals with disabilities are a discrete and insular minority who have been faced with restrictions and limitations, subjected to a history of purposeful unequal treatment, and relegated to a position of political powerlessness in our society, based on characteristics that are beyond the control of such individuals and resulting from stereotypical assumptions not truly indicative of the individual ability of such individuals to participate in and contribute to society. (Seventh Finding)

The ADA (1990) further asserts, "Unlike individuals who have experienced discrimination on the basis of race, color, sex, national origin, religion, or age, individuals who have experienced discrimination on the basis of disability have often had no legal recourse to redress such discrimination" (Fourth Finding). Moreover, it is the prejudices, stereotypes, and stigma, and not the disability itself, that are the true handicap and obstacle.

Much like other civil rights movements in the United States and, indeed, building on the history and the methods of the successes of African Americans and the women's movement, the disability rights advocates view the only commonality among people with disabilities as being the prejudice and discrimination they experience. If the occurrence of the disability appears to be unfair and unpredictable, then society's response to disability can nevertheless be equitable, moral, and predictable. A perfect world is not a world without disabilities, but a world in which accommodations and services are provided to people with disabilities, and, more important, disability is not viewed as inferiority.

THE POWER OF MODELS

Lack of Interagency Collaboration

All four broad models answer the question, "What is a disability?" (Berkowitz, 1987). Because each model provides a different answer to this question, the needs of the individual with a disability are also determined differently in each of the models (Bickenbach, 1993). All four models contain a definition of disability that reduces it to a single dimension, thus ignoring and excluding other important aspects. Therefore, all of these models are considered to be reductionistic, unidimensional, and somewhat time bound and culture bound. As a result, these incomplete definitions of disability may impede the type of interagency collaboration that has the potential to provide a range of services to individuals with disabilities. In addition, funding policies (which pay for services) are often based on these unidimensional definitions. Occasionally, the meanings ascribed to the disability experience by professional service providers and funding agencies may remain invisible simply because these meanings are not questioned or challenged.

Despite these basic differences, three of the models of disability lump individuals into categories such as "the blind," "the mentally ill," or "quads" (M. G. Eisenberg, Griggins, & Duval, 1982; Wright, 1991). Furthermore, the simple act of "placing" or "assigning" people to categories robs them of their individuality; to counteract this, counselors can assist clients with disabilities in dealing with the effects of automatic categorization.

These definitions of disability vary with the purposes, values, and needs of the definers. Zola's (1993) chapter, "Disability Statistics, What We Count and What It Tells Us," provides an excellent introduction to the varying definitions of disability. Zola's title clearly communicates that definitions (and statistics) of disability are a reflection of the values and needs of the defining group, and because of this, none of the models can be entirely value free or morally neutral.

Blaming the Victim

Models ask the questions, "Who is responsible for the disability" and "Who is responsible for the solution?" (Berkowitz & Hill, 1986; Yelin, 1992). Again, each model answers these questions differently. Determining the onset or acquisition of the disability attempts to understand *how* the disability occurred, or, more precisely stated, the etiology of the disability. Often, the search for the etiology or cause of the disability becomes distorted, resulting in implicit or explicit blame, fault, and moral accountability placed on the individual or his or her parents. Nonetheless, for purposes of calculating financial benefits and allocation of services, many disability programs require a clear-cut causal attribution. It is true that regardless of etiology or causal attribution, the treatment of a particular type and severity of disability is almost identical. However, the response of the general population, and hence the personal experience of the person with the disability, is a result of the public's assumptions of causal attribution. For example, an individual who is born with spina bifida is often considered a victim, whereas a person who acquires a spinal cord injury in combat is thought to be a hero, and a person who acquires a spinal cord injury while intoxicated and speeding on a motorcycle, without a helmet, is viewed as a culprit. The attribution of responsibility also determines which professions serve people with disabilities (Albrecht, 1981; Davis, 1997; Reno et al., 1997).

The history of these models can be easily traced simply by looking at the attributions of cause and responsibility in each model and the resulting formulation and implementation of policies and services. Furthermore, these attributions have had a profound effect on the lack of counseling services provided to people with disabilities, simply because the Biomedical Model of disability has dominated. Most important, attribution theory (Heider, 1958) has the power to individualize and privatize the experience of disability by looking for (and seemingly finding) both the cause and the solution for the disability wholly within the individual rather than within the social system. Attribution theories that privatize disability (rather than viewing disability as a public concern) often view the individual as a "patient," a "victim," or both.

The models described in this chapter place varying emphasis on the medical, functional, environmental, and sociopolitical needs and rights of the person with a disability. Three of the models emphasize definitions of disability rather than determining ways in which to intervene. In order for needs to be met, they must be clearly defined (Zola, 1989). For example, in the Biomedical Model, needs are considered to be solely medical; in the Environmental and Functional models, the needs are thought to be those of adapting the environment and functional requirements to fit the requirements of the individual with the disability; and in the Sociopolitical Model, the needs are considered to be full social integration and civil rights. The counseling interventions that flow from each model dictate different responses from the counselor. In order to be even minimally effective, counselors should understand the implications of each model for their manner of practice.

Shaping Self-Identities and Daily Lives

One model, the Biomedical Model, provides labels, diagnoses, categories, and theories of causation and responsibility that are derived from seemingly authoritative and prestigious sources. Diagnostic categories, however, can often be distorted to become stereotypes and uninformed assumptions (Clendinen & Nagourney, 1999). Moreover, these stereotypes are continually socially reinforced in the media and in the educational system, eventually becoming an accepted part of the social environment and, consequently, often remain unidentified and unquestioned (Stone, 1984). The individual with a disability may come to accept these diagnoses, and occasionally the stereotypes, as self-identifiers (Goffman, 1963). Often the individual with a disability is required to label himself or herself with a negative diagnosis or other label to be declared eligible for services and benefits. If disability is thought to be an unbearable personal tragedy, the individual (with a disability) is often effectively taught to be both inferior and dependent.

Despite the fact that these models are only representations of reality, and not reality itself, the assumptions, definitions, and history of each model are so persuasive and long-standing that they are often mistaken for fact (Hannah & Midlarsky, 1987). In addition, the personal daily functioning of the individual with a disability is determined, in large part, by assumptions derived from these models. Where the individual lives, how (and if) the individual is educated, the type and quality of professional services offered, and the degree of social integration afforded the individual are all influenced by the model of disability that is implemented.

Determining Which Academic Disciplines Teach About the Disability Experience

The disability experience, despite the large number of individuals with disabilities, remains invisible in most university curricula (Bauman & Drake, 1997; Hogben & Waterman, 1997). Students in counseling training programs, with the exception of rehabilitation counseling (Thomas, 2004), are typically not required to learn about people with disabilities. Simply because disability has been considered solely a biological and medical concern, only medical schools and the allied health professions have offered course work in disability issues. The "medicalization" of the disability experience has effectively kept the history and viewpoints of people with disabilities outside the realm of counseling education and professional training. Models of disability have provided the explanatory rationale for academic disciplines and therefore most graduates of counseling programs do not possess competencies to provide services to clients with disabilities. Olkin and Pledger (2003) reported that students are trained *not* to notice the absence of disability issues. In their view, the lack of disability information "in curricula, and among peers and professors—is a powerful statement about the marginalization of people with disabilities" (p. 297). Furthermore, research on disability and people with disabilities, including rigorously designed and executed studies, is often of questionable value because of negative and biased assumptions toward disability. Certainly, any disability-related research study is only as valid as the model of disability on which it is based. Myerson (1988) provided the following summary:

> The number of investigations that are flawed from inception by prejudicial commonsense assumptions, by theoretical bias, or by methodological error remains high. ... These errors are functions, in great part, not of [the researchers'] incompetence in the mechanics of research, but of asking the wrong questions, of incorrect notions of the meaning of disability to those who live with it, and of lack of understanding.... A particular source of error is the narrowly trained clinician who believes that clinical criteria are appropriate measures of problems that arise from systematic social injustice. (pp. 182–183)

Myerson concluded that "like others, to the extent that their thinking incorporates cultural myths, [researchers] become prisoners of plausible but erroneous hypotheses" (p. 183).

IMPLICATIONS FOR THE COUNSELING PROFESSION

Biology is still a factor in the equation of disability; however, biology does not matter as much as has been previously thought (J. F. Smart, 2005c). For counselors, this assumption has important implications because for the client with a disability, self-identity and the conceptualization of his or her life situation are derived from these basic concepts. In contrast, many professionals may, consciously or unconsciously, ascribe more importance to the biological and physical aspects of the disability than the client does. The individual with a disability certainly does not conceive of his or her life in these four neatly (and artificially) explained models. However, counselors can, albeit unintentionally, reinforce the status quo by unquestioningly accepting the assumptions, including expectations for the client's self-actualization, of these models and their labels and diagnoses. Clients with disabilities, on the other hand, may enter the counseling relationship with the expectation of receiving inaccurate (and often negative) diagnoses and inadequate services, often provided in offices that are inaccessible. Nevertheless, counselors are in a unique position to recognize the interplay of personal characteristics and environmental factors in a developmental context. Furthermore, counselors have long recognized the value of empowerment for all clients. The following is a listing of some implications for the counseling profession.

1. Counselors should engage in an ongoing examination of clients' feelings about the experience of disability and the resulting interaction of the counselor's own identity with that of the client. Taken to the extreme, the counselor may focus more on himself or herself if the disability of the client arouses feelings of existential angst, anxiety, and defensiveness, much of which is a result of the widely held view of the Biomedical Model of disability. If the counselor views disability as a tragic inferiority, then he or she will more likely experience a negative, emotional response to the client with a disability. Countertransference, and other emotional reactions to the disability of the client, may prevent the counselor from fully understanding the client and therefore negatively affect the counseling relationship.

2. Counselors should recognize that most individuals with disabilities do not accept the basic tenets of the Biomedical Model of disability. Rather, they may view the disability as a valued part of their identity, see positive aspects in having the disability, do not view the disability as tragic or limiting or being an inferiority, and would not choose to eliminate the disability if they could. At times, it may be necessary to ask the client about his or her identity as a person with a disability. Counselors must recognize that clients with disabilities want respect and not sympathy (Harris, 1992). Indeed, sympathy and lowered expectations may be considered to be stigmatizing and prejudicial; sympathy and lowered expectations toward people with disabilities often result in withholding helpful and honest feedback, reduce the range of opportunities open to the individual, foster dependence, and subtly communicate the message to clients with a disability that standards will be lowered for them because they are not perceived (by the counselor) to be capable.

3. Counselors should recognize that the disability is simply one part of the individual's identity. As does everyone, the client with a disability has multiple identities and multiple roles. Disability is not the "master status." Furthermore, a deeper and more complete understanding of the client's varied identities, functions, and environments will facilitate the implementation of the Environmental and Functional models of disability in the counseling process. Disability identity also constantly shifts and develops, as do all identities.

4. Counselors know that empowerment refers to the processes and outcomes relating to issues of control, critical awareness, and participation (Perkins & Zimmerman, 1995). For clients with disabilities, empowerment values provide a belief system that governs how our clients and we as professionals can work together. Based on this paradigm shift, there are substantial changes to be made to our practice. ... Empowerment values include attention toward health, adaptation, and competence, and the enabling environment. As professionals, our goal is to promote our clients' full participation and integration into their communities. The collaboration ... is itself an empowering process (Tate, 2001, p. 133).

5. As with any other client, the counselor may occasionally need to guard against imposing his or her values on the client with a disability (Norcross, 2002). Clients with disabilities have, at times, interpreted their counselors' guidance as a type of the "Try Harder Syndrome," or some individuals with disabilities have felt themselves to have been given the negative label by counselors of denying their disability. Often, clients with disabilities are not denying the presence, implications, or permanence of the disability, but rather they are denying the "disabled role" of pathology, inferiority, and deviance. Therefore, these clients may terminate counseling prematurely because they have felt misjudged.

6. The power differential between counselor and client with a disability should be addressed. Often, the power differential is increased when the client has a disability and the counselor does not. If the counselor subscribes to the Biomedical Model, with its strong normative emphasis, this increased power differential may impede the establishment of rapport and trust. Furthermore, this power imbalance in the therapeutic setting may simply reflect the broader world in which the client functions.

7. Counselors should listen to their clients and be willing to hear about experiences of prejudice and discrimination experienced by their clients with disabilities. Learning the basic tenets of the Sociopolitical Model of disability will provide counselors with some introductory understanding of this stigmatization and discrimination, and, accordingly, counselors will be able to set aside some of their preconceived notions concerning the experiences of their clients with disabilities. Counselors should recognize that many clients with disabilities may not seek services at counseling agencies because they understand that often the counselors at these agencies may reinforce the prejudice and discrimination of the broader culture. On the other hand, counselors need to avoid attributing all the client's issues and problems to prejudice and discrimination. Nonetheless, for most people with disabilities, self-identification as a person with a disability does not automatically translate into group consciousness or political action (Scotch, 1988).

8. Counselors should recognize that, for many of them, their professional training may be inadequate to prepare them with the skills and competencies to work with clients with disabilities. Also, some theoretical approaches and counseling practices have their basis in the Biomedical Model and therefore simply "adapting" these approaches and orientations for clients with disabilities may be at best ineffective and at worst harmful. Stated differently, the little professional training counselors have received may be faulty and ill conceived. Counselors who do not have adequate training must seek opportunities for additional education.

9. Counselors should examine their willingness to broaden their vision about the experience of disability. On one hand, counselors may have strong needs to be knowledgeable, skilled, and helpful, but on the other hand, counselors may view disability as ambiguous and inferior. Students in counseling programs should seek out course work (such as is available in rehabilitation counseling programs) and other workshops that focus on disability issues. Certainly, information about a client's identity and feelings about his or her disability must come from that individual, but obtaining a broad knowledge of the topic of disability is imperative. It is not ethical or appropriate to expect clients with disabilities to teach counselors about the world of disability.

10. Both outreach efforts and collaborative learning among counseling professions can be achieved by learning which agencies people with disabilities typically go to for assistance (such as state vocational rehabilitation offices) and then establishing professional relationships with these agencies.

11. Professionals, in all aspects of counseling, should intervene at institutional and political levels when appropriate and possible. Although individual counseling and support for clients with disabilities can make a contribution to the larger society, advocating for changes in systems and policies, alerting the public to manifestations of prejudice and discrimination in the media, and advocating for environmental accessibility can also be valuable contributions. Counselors, both as individuals and as part of statewide, regional, or national professional organizations, can create change.

12. Counselors should recognize that it is necessary to clearly articulate the assumptions about models of disability that underlie research studies. Research can be more sharply focused if the basic assumptions and values about people with disabilities are made clear. Articulating these values as they relate to one or more of the four models of disability would help both researchers and consumers of research evaluate the research findings.

In order to provide ethical and effective services to clients with disabilities, counseling professionals in all aspects of the field will be required to examine the ways in which they conceptualize the experience of disability. For some counseling professionals, many of these ideas, derived from the models of disability, may be new and different ways of responding to people with disabilities. For others, these ideas will provide a useful adjunct to the counseling services or the counseling training and education they provide.

REFERENCES

Akabas, S. H. (2000). Practice in the world of work. In P. Allen-Meares & C. Garvin (Eds.), *The handbook of social work: Direct practice* (pp. 449–517). Thousand Oaks, CA: Sage.

Albrecht, G. L. (Ed.). (1981). *Cross national rehabilitation policies: A sociological perspective.* Beverly Hills, CA: Sage.

Albrecht, G. L. (1992). *The disability business: Rehabilitation in America.* Newbury Park, CA: Sage.

American Psychiatric Association. (2013). *Diagnostic and statistical manual of mental disorders* (5th ed.). Arlington, VA: American Psychiatric Press.

Americans with Disabilities Act of 1990, 42 U.S.C.A. § 12101.

Bauman, H. D. L., & Drake, J. (1997). Silence is not without voice: Including deaf culture within the multicultural curricula. In L. J. Davis (Ed.), *Disability studies reader* (pp. 307–314). New York, NY: Routledge.

Berkowitz, M. (1987). *Disabled policy: America's programs for the handicapped.* London, England: Cambridge University Press.

Berkowitz, M., & Hill, M. A. (Eds.). (1986). *Disability and the labor market: Economic problems, policies, and programs.* Ithaca, NY: Cornell University Press.

Bickenbach, J. E. (1993). *Physical disability and social policy.* Toronto, ON, Canada: University of Toronto.

Bickenbach, J. E., Chatterji, S., Badley, E. M., & Ustün, T. B. (1999). Models of disablement, universalism and the International Classification of Impairments, Disabilities and Handicaps. *Social Science & Medicine, 48*(9), 1173–1187.

Bowe, F. (1980). *Rehabilitation America: Toward independence for disabled and elderly people.* New York, NY: Harper & Row.

Brant, E. N., & Pope, A. M. (Eds.). (1997). *Enabling America: Assessing the role of rehabilitation science and engineering.* Washington, DC: National Academies Press.

Byrom, B. (2004). A pupil and a patient: Hospital schools in progressive America. In S. Danforth & S. D. Taff (Eds.), *Crucial readings in special education* (pp. 25–37). Upper Saddle River, NJ: Pearson/Merrill, Prentice Hall.

Clendinen, D., & Nagourney, A. (1999). *Out for good: The struggle to build a gay rights movement in America.* New York, NY: Simon & Schuster.

Conrad, P. (2004). The discovery of hyperkinesis: Notes on the medicalization of deviant behavior. In S. Danforth & S. D. Taff (Eds.), *Crucial readings in special education* (pp. 18–24). Upper Saddle River, NJ: Pearson/Merrill, Prentice Hall.

Davis, L. J. (1997). Constructing normalcy: The bell curve, the novel, and the invention of the disabled body in the nineteenth century. In L. J. Davis (Ed.), *Disability studies reader* (pp. 307–314). New York, NY: Routledge.

Dembo, T. (1982). Some problems in rehabilitation as seen by a Lewinian. *Journal of Social Issues, 38,* 131–139.

Eisenberg, L. (1996). Foreword. In J. E. Mezzich, A. Kleinman, H. Fabrega Jr., & D. L. Parron (Eds.), *Culture and psychiatric diagnosis: ADSM-IV perspective* (pp. xiii–xv). Washington, DC: American Psychiatric Association.

Eisenberg, M. G., Griggins, C., & Duval, R. J. (Eds.). (1982). *Disabled people as second-class citizens.* New York, NY: Springer Publishing.

Employment and Disability Institute. (1996). National health interview survey. Retrieved from http://www.disabilitystatistics.org

Friedlander, H. (1995). *The origins of Nazi genocide: From euthanasia to the final solution.* Chapel Hill: University of North Carolina Press.

Gallagher, H. G. (1990). *By trust betrayed: Patients, physicians, and the license to kill in the Third Reich.* New York, NY: Holt.

Gill, C. J., Kewman, D. G., & Brannon, R. W. (2003). Transforming psychological practice and society. Policies that reflect the new paradigm. *American Psychologist, 58*(4), 305–312.

Goffman, E. (1963). *Stigma: Notes on the management of spoiled identity.* Englewood Cliffs, NJ: Prentice Hall.

Hahn, H. (1985). Toward a politics of disability: Definitions, disciplines, and policies. *Social Science Journal, 22*, 87–105.

Hahn, H. (1988). The politics of physical differences: Disability and discrimination. *Journal of Social Issues, 44*, 39–47.

Hahn, H. (1991). Alternative views of empowerment: Social services and civil rights. *Journal of Rehabilitation, 57*, 17–19.

Hahn, H. (1993). The political implications of disability definitions and data. *Journal of Disability Policy Studies, 4*, 41–52.

Hahn, H. (1996). Antidiscrimination laws and social research on disability: The minority group perspectives. *Behavioral Sciences and the Law, 14*, 41–59.

Hahn, H. (1997). Advertising the acceptable employment image: Disability and capitalism. In L. J. Davis (Ed.), *The disability studies reader* (pp. 172–186). New York, NY: Routledge.

Hannah, M. E., & Midlarsky, E. (1987). Differential impact of labels and behavioral descriptions on attitudes toward people with disabilities. *Rehabilitation Psychology, 32*, 227–238.

Harris, R. (1992). Musing from 20 years of hard earned experience. *Rehabilitation Education, 6*, 207–212.

Hayes, P. A. (2001). *Addressing cultural complexities in practice: A framework for clinicians and counselors.* Washington, DC: American Psychological Association.

Heider, F. (1958). *The psychology of interpersonal relations.* New York, NY: John Wiley.

Higgins, P. C. (1992). *Making disability: Exploring the social transformation of human variation.* Springfield, IL: Charles C Thomas.

Hogben, M., & Waterman, C. K. (1997). Are all of your students represented in their textbooks? A content analysis of coverage of diversity issues in introductory psychology textbooks. *Teaching of Psychology, 24*, 95–100.

Hulnick, M. R., & Hulnick, H. R. (1989). Life's challenges: Curse or opportunity? Counseling families of persons with disabilities. *Journal of Counseling & Development, 68*, 166–170.

Humes, C. W., Szymanski, E. M., & Hohenshil, T. H. (1989). Roles of counseling in enabling persons with disabilities. *Journal of Counseling & Development, 68*, 145–150.

Kemp, N. T., & Mallinckrodt, B. (1996). Impact of professional training on case conceptualization of clients with a disability. *Professional Psychology: Research and Practice, 27*, 378–385.

Kiesler, D. J. (1999). *Beyond the disease model of mental disorders.* Westport, CT: Praeger.

Kirk, S. A., & Kutchins, H. (1992). *The selling of the DSM: The rhetoric of science in psychiatry.* New York, NY: Aldine Degruyter.

Kleinfield, S. (1979). *The hidden minority: A profile of handicapped Americans.* Boston, MA: Atlantic Monthly Press.

Liachowitz, C. H. (1988). *Disability as a social construct: Legislative roots.* Philadelphia: University of Pennsylvania Press.

Longmore, P. K. (1995). Medical decision making and people with disabilities: A clash of cultures. *Journal of Law, Medicine & Ethics, 23*(1), 82–87.

McCarthy, H. (1993). Learning with Beatrice A. Wright: A breath of fresh air that uncovers the unique virtues and human flaws in us all. *Rehabilitation Education, 10*, 149–166.

McCarthy, H. (2003). The disability rights movement: Experiences and perspectives of selected leaders in the disability community. *Rehabilitation Counseling Bulletin, 46*, 209–223.

Melia, R. P., Pledger, C., & Wilson, R. (2003). Disability and rehabilitation research. Opportunities for participation, collaboration, and extramural funding for psychologists. *American Psychologist, 58*(4), 285–288.

Myerson, L. (1988). The social psychology of physical disability. *Journal of Social Issues, 44*, 173–188.

Nagi, S. Z. (1969). *Disability and rehabilitation: Legal, clinical, and self-concepts and measurements.* Columbus: Ohio State University Press.

Norcross, J. C. (Ed.). (2002). *Psychotherapy relationships that work: Therapist contributions and responsiveness to patient needs.* New York, NY: Oxford University Press.

Olkin, R. (1999). *What psychotherapists should know about disability.* New York, NY: Guilford Press.

Olkin, R., & Pledger, C. (2003). Can disability studies and psychology join hands? *American Psychologist, 58*(4), 296–304.

Perkins, D. D., & Zimmerman, M. A. (1995). Empowerment theory, research, and application. *American Journal of Community Psychology, 23*(5), 569–579.

Peterson, D. B. (2002). *International Classification of Functioning, Disability and Health (ICF): A primer for rehabilitation psychologists.* Unpublished manuscript, New York University.

Pledger, C. (2003). Discourse on disability and rehabilitation issues. Opportunities for psychology. *American Psychology, 58*(4), 279–284.

Pope, A. M., & Tarlov, A. R. (1991). *Disability in America: Toward a national agenda for prevention.* Washington, DC: National Academies Press.

Reno, V. P., Mashaw, J. L., & Gradison, B. (Eds.). (1997). *Disability: Challenges for social insurance, health care financing, and labor market policy.* Washington, DC: National Academy of Social Insurance.

Schur, E. M. (1971). *Labeling deviant behavior: Its sociological implications.* New York, NY: Harper & Row.

Scotch, R. K. (1988). Disability as a basis for a social movement: Advocacy and the politics of definition. *Journal of Social Issues, 44,* 159–172.

Singer, P. (2000). *Writings on an ethical life.* New York, NY: Ecco.

Smart, D. W., & Smart, J. F. (1997a). *DSM-IV* and culturally sensitive diagnosis: Some observations for counselors. *Journal of Counseling & Development, 75,* 392–398.

Smart, D. W., & Smart, J. F. (1997b). The racial/ethnic demography of disability. *Journal of Rehabilitation, 63,* 9–15.

Smart, J. F. (2004). Models of disability: The juxtaposition of biology and social construction. In T. F. Riggar & D. R. Maki (Eds.), *Handbook of rehabilitation counseling* (pp. 25–49). New York, NY: Springer Publishing.

Smart, J. F. (2005a). Challenges to the biomedical model of disability: Changes to the practice of rehabilitation counseling. *Directions in Rehabilitation Counseling, 16,* 33–43.

Smart, J. F. (2005b). The promise of the International Classification of Functioning, Disability, and Health (ICF). *Rehabilitation Education, 19,* 191–199.

Smart, J. F. (2005c). *Tracing the ascendant trajectory of models of disability: Confounding competition or a cross-model approach?* Unpublished manuscript, Utah State University, Logan.

Smart, J. F. (2016). *Disability, society and the individual* (3rd ed.). Austin, TX: PRO-ED.

Smart, J. F., & Smart, D. W. (1997). Culturally sensitive informed choice in rehabilitation counseling. *Journal of Applied Rehabilitation Counseling, 28,* 32–37.

Sobsey, D. (1994). *Violence and abuse in the lives of people with disabilities: The end of silent acceptance.* Baltimore, MD: Brookes.

Stefan, S. (2001). *Unequal rights: Discrimination against people with mental disabilities and the Americans with Disabilities Act.* Washington, DC: American Psychiatric Association.

Stone, D. A. (1984). *The disabled state.* Philadelphia, PA: Temple University Press.

Tanenbaum, S. J. (1986). *Engineering disability: Public policy and compensatory technology.* Philadelphia, PA: Temple University Press.

Tate, D. G. (2001). Hospital to community: Changes in practice and outcomes. *Rehabilitation Psychology, 46,* 125–138.

Tate, D. G., & Pledger, C. (2003). An integrative conceptual framework of disability. New directions for research. *American Psychology, 58*(4), 289–295.

Thomas, K. R. (2004). Old wine in a slightly cracked new bottle. *American Psychology, 59*(4), 274–275; author reply 275.

Thomason, T., Burton, J. F., Jr., & Hyatt, D. R. (Eds.). (1998). *New approaches to disability in the workplace.* Madison: University of Wisconsin Press.

Trieschmann, R. (1987). *Aging with a disability.* New York, NY: Demos Medical Publishing.

U.S. Department of Education, Office of Special Education and Rehabilitation Services, National Institute on Disability and Rehabilitation Research. (2000). *Long-range plan 1999–2003.* Washington, DC: Author.

Weisgerber, R. S. (1991). *Quality of life for persons with disabilities.* Gaithersburg, MD: Aspen.

Wilson, J. (2003, October). *Johnny Lingo: Helping clients to fulfill their potential.* Speech given at the national training conference of the National Council on Rehabilitation Education/Rehabilitation Services Administration/Council of State Administrators of Vocational Rehabilitation, Arlington, VA.

Wolfensberger, W. (1972). *The principle of normalization in human services.* Toronto, ON, Canada: National Institute on Mental Retardation.

World Health Organization. (1980). *International Classification of Impairments, Disabilities, and Handicaps: A manual of classification relating to the consequences of disease.* Geneva, Switzerland: Author.

World Health Organization. (2001). *International Classification of Impairments, Disabilities, and Handicaps: A manual of classification relating to the consequences of disease.* Geneva, Switzerland: Author.

Wright, B. A. (1991). Labeling: The need for greater person-environment individuation. In C. R. Snyder & D. R. Forsythe (Eds.), *Handbook of social and clinical psychology* (pp. 469–487). Elmsford, NY: Pergamon.

Yelin, E. H. (1992). *Disability and the displaced worker.* New Brunswick, NJ: Rutgers University Press.

Young-Bruehl, E. (1996). *The anatomy of prejudices.* Cambridge, MA: Harvard University Press.

Zola, I. K. (1989). Toward the necessary universalizing of a disability policy. *Milbank Q, 67*(Suppl. 2 Pt 2), 401–428.

Zola, I. K. (1993). Disability statistics, what we count and what it tells us. *Journal of Disability Policy Studies, 4,* 9–39.

5

*Changes in Attitudes Toward People With Handicaps**

BEATRICE A. WRIGHT

AFFIRMATION OF HUMAN RIGHTS

A most important document appeared in 1948 when the General Assembly of the United Nations adopted the Universal declaration of Human Rights. That declaration not only affirmed that it is possible for all of humanity to agree in general on what is important to every human being but, more than that, it also forthrightly stated that "every individual and every organ of society" has a responsibility to promote the matters contained in the Declaration.

Since then, in fact, different persons and organs of society have formulated principles to serve as guidelines for action to ensure the fuller realization of human dignity. In 1973, the American Hospital Association published a "Patient's Bill of Rights" consisting of 12 points. These rights are considered to be so fundamental that every patient in a hospital setting is to be informed of them. The rights include such items as the right of the patient to respectful care and to consideration of privacy, the right to receive information necessary to give informed consent to any procedure or treatment, and the right to be advised if the hospital proposes to engage in human experimentation affecting his or her care. The document concludes with this significant emphasis. "No catalog of rights can guarantee for the patient the kind of treatment he has a right to expect .... [For such treatment] must be conducted with an overriding concern for the patient, and, above all, the recognition of his dignity as a human being" (American Hospital Association, 1973, p. 41).

In addition to the rights of patients in general, a formulation of the basic rights of the mentally ill and the mentally retarded was published in 1973 (Mental Health Law

---

*From "Changes in attitudes toward people with handicaps," by B. A. Wright, 1973, *Rehabilitation Literature, 34*, 354–368. Copyright ©1973 by the National Easter Seal Society for Crippled Children and Adults. Reprinted by permission of the Editor. Also published in *The Psychological and Social Impact of Illness and Disability*, 1st Edition, 1977.

Project, 1973). These rights are articulated in three broad categories, namely, the right to treatment, the right to compensation for institution-maintaining labor, and the right to education. Prototype court cases are presented to show that litigation can be a valuable tool and catalyst in protecting the rights of the mentally handicapped.

A set of 18 value-laden beliefs and principles published in 1972 provides guidelines for rehabilitation of people with disabilities (Wright, 1972). The general tenor of these principles may be conveyed by citing a few of them:

1. Every individual needs respect and encouragement; the presence of a handicap, no matter how severe, does not alter these fundamental rights.
2. The assets of the person must receive considerable attention in the rehabilitation effort.
3. The active participation of the client in the planning and execution of his or her rehabilitation program is to be sought as fully as possible.
4. The severity of a handicap can be increased or diminished by environmental conditions.
5. Involvement of the client with the general life of the community is a fundamental principle guiding decisions concerning living arrangements and the use of resources.
6. All phases of rehabilitation have psychological aspects.
7. Self-help organizations are important allies in the rehabilitation effort.

For each of these principles, implications for action are elaborated. For example, principle 1 further asserts that "A person is entitled to the enrichment of his life and the development of his abilities whether these be great or small and whether he has a long or short time to live" (Wright, 1972, p. xi). "A Bill of Rights for the Disabled" (Abramson & Kutner, 1972), published in 1972, highlights 16 rights that apply to such areas as health, education, employment, housing, transportation, and civil rights. To take transportation as an example, it is resolved that programs and standards be established for the "modification of existing mass transportation systems and the development of new specially designed demand-schedule transportation facilities" (Abramson & Kutner, 1972, p. 99).

"A Bill of Rights for the Handicapped" was recently adopted by the United Cerebral Palsy Association (UCPA, 1973). Among the 10 rights listed are the right to health and educational services, the right to work, the right to barrier-free public facilities, and the right to petition social institutions and the courts to gain such opportunities as may be enjoyed by others but denied the handicapped because of oversight, public apathy, or discrimination.

Also in accord with the stress on civil rights is the recent declaration of intent by the Canadian Rehabilitation Council for the Disabled, which delineates 14 areas to which these rights pertain. These areas include treatment, education, recreation, transportation, housing, spiritual development, legal rights, and economic security.

Accepting the handicapped person as a full human being means accepting him or her as having the full range of human needs, including those involving the sexual areas of life. The past few years have witnessed a much greater awareness of the importance of this matter. A brief summary of specialized studies and conferences in a number of countries was presented at the Twelfth World Congress of Rehabilitation International in 1972 (Chigier, 1972). In this enlightening presentation, Chigier listed six rights with regard to sexual behavior of individuals in general and then traced the extent to which persons with disabilities are assisted or prevented from achieving these rights. Among the rights examined were the right to be informed about sexual matters, the right to sexual expression, the right to marry, and the right to become parents. Although recognizing certain problems that come with greater freedom in these areas, the thrust of the analysis is directed toward constructive solutions that will enable severely disabled and mentally retarded persons to realize these rights more fully. Also in 1972, a beautiful article appeared on management of psychosexual readjustment in the spinal cord-injured male (Hohmann, 1972). It deals specifically with the kinds of sexual activities open to the cord-injured person and how the possibilities for sexual fulfillment can be enhanced between two people who care for each other.

Legislation helps to give reality to principles of human rights by making provision for the financing and administration of relevant services. The First International Conference on Legislation Concerning the Disabled was held in 1971. The principles guiding the recommendations reflect changing attitudes toward people with handicaps. For example, it is pointed out that "the ultimate objective of all legislation for the disabled is complete integration of the disabled in the community and to enable the disabled person to lead as normal a life as possible regardless of productive capacity" (First International Conference on Legislation Concerning the Disabled, 1972, p. 19). The conference further emphasized that real progress can be achieved only when legislation is designed to foster "respect for the personality and human rights of the individual" (First International Conference on Legislation Concerning the Disabled, 1972, p. 19).

MANIFESTATIONS IN PRACTICE

Fortunately, the explicit expression of principles and ideals set forth in the aforementioned documents is increasingly becoming manifest in practice. Let us consider, as an example, the concept of integration, which has been regarded as a principle that can more fully ensure the realization of human rights for most people. What is necessary to appreciate is that, once integration becomes a guiding principle, certain matters are not at issue until they quickly assume vital importance. The location of institutions and the houses in which handicapped people can live becomes important because their location within communities enables participation of the handicapped in community offerings. Architectural barriers become an issue because their elimination enables people with a wide range of physical abilities to have access to events within buildings at large. The organization of services becomes a challenge because integration rather than segregation is fostered when special needs can be met within general community facilities, such as hospitals, comprehensive rehabilitation centers, schools, recreation areas, churches, and community centers. Transportation assumes special significance because integration requires that the person have a way to get to the integrated facilities that exist. And, when these issues receive sufficient attention, ways to improve the situation become apparent.

A case in point is the increasing accommodation of handicapped children within regular schools (Telford & Sawrey, 1972). Helping to make such integration a reality are special classes, resource teachers, and teacher aides. The following conclusion, based on a review of children with hearing impairments, is also applicable to children with other handicapping conditions: Lest there be a too-ready overgeneralization, however, I hasten to add that this conclusion does not obviate the need for special groupings of children in particular instances and for special purposes.

Integration is not an answer for all circumstances. It will ill serve handicapped children unless their special needs are met through necessary accommodations within the community setting that nurtures a climate of full respect for the dignity of each individual. Nor must integration imply that, where handicapped people are integrated within general community settings, there is no need for handicapped people to get together. Sharing and solving mutual problems, participating in specially designed activities together, and finding needed companionship are some of the rewards that can be provided by self-help, recreation, and other groups. This does not mean that people should be forced to join such groups, that the groups are appropriate for all people with handicaps, or that these groups should preempt association with people who are not handicapped. But it does mean that such groups should not be discredited as fostering segregation, as limiting adaptation to a nonhandicapped world, or as implying overconcern with personal problems. It does mean that groups like these should be valued for providing the opportunity for people to meet together, have fun together, and to affirm and assert themselves together.

A second example of change in practice is the greater involvement of people with handicaps in leadership positions in agencies working on their behalf. Agencies are increasingly recognizing that handicapped people themselves have special contributions to make in the development of services directed toward meeting the needs and enriching the lives of clients. The UCPA, for example, has enumerated the kinds of roles that adults with cerebral palsy are especially equipped to fill by virtue of their special vantage point (United Cerebral Palsy Associations, 1971). It is explicitly pointed out that adults with cerebral palsy should serve on boards of directors and on *all* committees, that they can help with educating parents, that they can provide constructive role models and share personal experiences with young cerebral palsied children and teenagers, and that in-service training programs for such leadership roles are important just as are other in-service training efforts. A recent survey conducted by the UCPA of New York on "The Status of the Cerebral Palsied Adult as a Board, Committee, or Staff Member in UCPA Affiliates" revealed that one or more cerebral palsied adults were on the board of directors in 24% of the 227 local agencies who replied and served as staff members in 16% (United Cerebral Palsy Associations, 1971). It was urged that these percentages be increased.

A third reflection in practice of the affirmation of human dignity is the enormously significant effort on the part of people with handicaps to speak out and act on their own behalf, an effort that so clearly parallels the efforts of other minority groups. Sometimes the effort has taken the form of individual action, as in the case of a blind woman who, in 1964, filed a complaint in criminal court against being refused restaurant service because she was accompanied by her seeing-eye dog. Sometimes the protest involved civil disobedience, as in 1967 when a group of seven persons were refused restaurant service because four of them were blind and had guide dogs. They refused to leave the premises; after the owner contacted the Health Department, they were allowed to remain. Sometimes the effort involved street demonstrations, as in 1970 when a group of university paraplegic students undertook a 100-mile wheelchair trek to promote employment of the handicapped.

Sometimes the effort was extended beyond a single issue to include wide-ranging problems of concern to large numbers of people with handicaps. Thus, in 1970, after winning the case of a young woman confined to a wheelchair who had been refused a teaching license, the law institute that was involved extended its services to all cases of infringement of civil rights of the handicapped. Among these new cases were a bedridden man who was refused an absentee ballot in a federal election and a blind man who was denied a teacher's license. Recently, a National Center for Law and the Handicapped was established. Sometimes the effort on the part of the handicapped solicited the support of an entire community, as in the case of the Committee for the Architecturally Handicapped, organized by two University of Kansas students. Curb cuts in town and on campus, the remodeling of buildings, the revamping of architectural plans for new construction, and the appearance of the international symbol of access attest to the success of this effort.

Parent groups have had a long and impressive history of involvement on behalf of children with disabilities; currently, people with handicaps themselves are gaining the sense of strength and accomplishment that comes from actively participating in advancing their own cause. The number of self-help and mutual-aid groups keeps growing. There are publications by people with handicaps for people with handicaps, such as *Accent on Living, Rehabilitation Gazette* (formerly *Toomey j Gazette*), *Paraplegia News,* and *The Braille Technical Press. Stuttering,* published for specialists in the field of speech pathology, primarily consists of papers presented at an annual conference by speech pathologists who stutter. All of these efforts reflect a greater readiness on the part of people with handicaps to acknowledge their own handicaps and to become actively involved with improving their circumstances and increasing understanding of their problems.

PROSPECTS

Attitudes toward the handicapped have seen such marked change since World War II that I believe the reader will be able to guess whether the article from which the following is quoted was published before 1950 or after. It deals with the birth of a child with Down syndrome (Mongolian mental retardation):

> The problems presented by the arrival into a family of one of these accidents of development are many.... Because the mongolian is so incompetent in the ordinary technics of living, his mother soon becomes a complete slave to his dependency. As a result, she devotes all of her time to his necessary care, neglecting her other household duties, her other children ... , and inevitably, her husband. The effect of all this is that all other satisfying areas of living are blotted out.... With the passing years, ... [the mongol's] brothers and sisters refuse to bring other children into the house, ... and are obsessed with a feeling of family shame no matter how unjustifiable it may be.... There is only one adequate way to lessen all this grief, fortunately a measure which most experienced physicians will agree to, and that is immediate commitment to an institution at the time of diagnosis.... When the diagnosis has been made in a newborn the mother is told that the baby is not strong enough to be brought to her at present.... Next, the father is asked to meet the physician immediately, bringing with him any close relatives ... the nature of the problem is explained, ... emphasizing its seriousness ... and that immediate placement outside the family provides the only hope of preventing a long series of family difficulties.... [The mother] is asked, not to make the decision, but to accept the one which has already been made by the close relatives.... It means that the physician must take the lead in precipitating an immediate crisis in order to prevent much more serious difficulties later on. This is preventive medicine. (Aldrich, 1947)

The cues that one had in guessing correctly? There were many. In this article, the emphasis was on institutionalizing the child rather than on seeking ways to make it feasible for him to remain with his family, at least during his early years; the main responsibility for deciding the issue rested with the physician rather than with those directly concerned, that is, the family; gross devaluating generalizations were made concerning the devastating effects of having such a child; no consideration was given for the capacity of families, with the help of community resources, to be able to accept and adapt to new circumstances. It is not likely that the article in question could be published in a responsible professional journal today, an indication of how attitudes have changed in the past quarter of a century, even though, to be sure, there continue to be frequent breeches of the new directions in actual life settings.

We have seen how the ideals of human dignity and basic civil rights are being reflected in what is being said and done regarding people with handicaps. But how much can we count on continued progress? Not very much, I would argue. To assert otherwise would be to invite apathy. There is no guarantee that the right of each individual to respect and encouragement in the enrichment of his or her life will increasingly be honored, or that people with handicaps will increasingly have an important voice in influencing conditions that affect their lives. Although we can affirm that the changing attitudes described previously are durable insofar as they are regarded as expressions of basic human rights, we must also recognize that they are fragile insofar as they are subject to the vicissitudes of broad-sweeping social and political circumstances. The lives of handicapped people are inextricably a part of a much wider socioeconomic political and ethical society affecting the lives of all people. It is therefore essential for all of us to remain vigilant to protect and extend the hard-won gains of recent decades and to be ready to counter undermining forces. Vigilance requires thoughtful action guided by continuing reevaluation of the effectiveness of present efforts and alertness to needs of changing conditions.

REFERENCES

Abramson, A. S., & Kutner, B. (1972). A bill of rights for the disabled. *Archives of Physical Medicine and Rehabilitation, 53*(3), 99–100.

Aldrich, C. A. (1947). The pediatrician looks at personality. *American Journal of Orthopsychiatry, 17*, 571–574. doi:10.1111/j.1939-0025.1947.tb05036.x

American Hospital Association. (1973). *A patient's bill of rights.* Retrieved from http://www.injured worker.org/Library/Patient_Bill_of_Rights.htm

Canadian Council for Rehabilitation of the Disabled. (1973). A declaration of intent. *Rehabilitation Digest, 4*(4), 4–5.

Chigier, E. (1972). *Sexual adjustment of the handicapped.* In Proceedings preview: Twelfth World Congress of Rehabilitation International (Vol. 1, pp. 224–227), Sydney, Australia.

First International Conference on Legislation Concerning the Disabled. (1972). *International Rehabilitation Review, Second Quarter, 23*(2), 18–19.

Hohmann, G. W. (1972). Considerations in management of psychosexual readjustment in the cord injured male. *Rehabilitation Psychology, 19*, 250–258.

Mental Health Law Project. (1973). *Basic rights of the mentally handicapped.* Washington, DC: Author.

Telford, C. W., & Sawrey, J. M. (1972). *The exceptional individual* (2nd ed.). Englewood Cliffs, NJ: Prentice Hall.

United Cerebral Palsy Associations. (1971). Survey shows few CP adults involved in UCP decision making. *Crusader, 6*, 2.

United Cerebral Palsy Associations. (1973). A bill of rights for the handicapped. *Crusader, 3*, 1–6.

Wright, B. A. (1972). Value-laden beliefs and principles for rehabilitation psychology. *Rehabilitation Psychology, 19*(1), 38–45.

Wright, B. A. (1973). Changes in attitudes toward people with handicaps. *Rehabilitation Literature, 34*, 354–368.

II

The Personal Impact of Disability

*P*art II offers insights into the personal impact of illness and disability on individuals by looking closely at several unique psychosocial life experiences. This section blends a focus on the issues with theory and practice for rehabilitation professionals. Building on themes introduced in the previous editions of this book, contributors in this section explore disability from a sociological and cultural perspective. It is difficult to approach the topic of psychosocial rehabilitation without looking inward at the potential implications and interrelationships between the individual and his or her environment when living with a disability. Thus, the current authors discuss various theories of adaptation to disability, the unique experiences faced by women with disabilities, gender differences regarding sexuality, multicultural and family perspectives of disability, and quality of life (QOL) issues for those with disabilities.

MAJOR HIGHLIGHTS IN PART II

- Chapter 6 provides rehabilitation professionals with a primer on the psychosocial adaptation to chronic illness and disability (CID). The authors discuss some of the major reactions to congenital and adventitious disabilities, including stress and threats to body image, grieving the loss, stages of adjustment, various coping mechanisms of adapting to disability, and intervention strategies. Common psychometric measures are described that assist readers in assessing an individual's adaptation to CID.
- Chapter 7 explores the differences in psychosocial adjustment between persons with a congenital disability and those who sustain an adventitious disability later in life. It summarizes seven major theories of psychosocial adaptation to disability—the stage model, chaos theory, ecological model, disability centrality model, somatopsychological model, recurrent or integrated model, and transactional model—that offer different but ultimately overlapping explanations. This comparative view is a highlight of the book, synthesizing the author's previous writings on this topic.
- The author of Chapter 8 discusses the unique challenges faced by women with disabilities and the social inequities they continue to experience in 21st-century America. This population often receives poor or inadequate health care, is frequently viewed as being helpless, and experiences isolation, lack of social connectedness, abuse, and stress. For some women, the psychosocial impact of disability leads to poor self-esteem or self-worth, depression, and anxiety. The author offers

recommendations that counselors can use to help minimize or eradicate some of these societal inequities and barriers for women.

- Chapter 9 deals with sensitive issues relating to sexuality and disability. It explores the definition of sexuality as well as common myths and misconceptions regarding the impact of disability on a person's sexuality. The author examines sexuality from a social model perspective, noting that traditional ideas of what constitutes sexuality have been replaced by a new "normal," representing a broader spectrum of preferences and displays of sexuality.

- Chapter 10 presents current research on cross-cultural counseling issues, focusing on the need for professional counselors to be understanding, tolerant, and aware of race, ethnicity, worldview, and spirituality, as well as cultural perceptions of disability, when working with clients and theirfamilies. The authors explore gender differences as well as implications for counselors in working with the major cultural groups in the United States.

- Chapter 11 explores the theoretical and contextual definition of QOL in relation to the temporal context of community living and personal experiences. The impact of positive coping on adaptation to disability is discussed in relation to QOL and managing life stresses during three relevant periods. Future-oriented, positively valenced, and postdisability coping skills and the salutary impact on QOL are also discussed.

6

Psychological Adaptation to Chronic Illness and Disability: A Primer for Counselors*

Hanoch Livneh and Richard F. Antonak

*C*hronic illnesses and disabling conditions are common occurrences in the lives of many individuals. It has been estimated that approximately 54 million Americans (about one in five) have physical, sensory, psychiatric, or cognitive disabilities that interfere with their daily living (Bowe, 2000). Furthermore, (a) more than 9 million Americans with disabilities are unable to work or attend school; (b) costs of annual income support (e.g., Supplemental Security Income and Social Security disability insurance) and medical care provided by the U.S. government to assist people with disabilities are about $60 billion; (c) disabilities are higher among older people, minorities, and lower socioeconomic groups; and (d) eight of the 10 most common causes of death in the United States are associated with chronic illness (Eisenberg, Glueckauf, & Zaretsky, 1999; Stachnik, Stoffelmayr, & Hoppe, 1983).

Many disability- and nondisability-related factors interact to create a profound effect on the lives of individuals with chronic illness and disabilities (CID). Among these, the most commonly recognized factors include the degree of functional limitations, interference with the ability to perform daily activities and life roles, uncertain prognosis, the prolonged course of medical treatment and rehabilitation interventions, the psychosocial stress associated with the incurred trauma or disease process itself, the impact on family and friends, and the sustained financial losses (e.g., reduced income and increased medical bills).

The intent of this article is to provide the reader with an overview of (a) the dynamics (i.e., process) of psychosocial adaptation to CID, (b) methods commonly used to assess psychosocial adaptation to CID, and (c) intervention strategies applied to people with CID.

THE DYNAMICS OF PSYCHOSOCIAL ADAPTATION TO CID

The onset of CID is typically associated with a disease process (e.g., multiple sclerosis [MS] and cancer) or a traumatic injury (spinal cord injury and traumatic brain

*H. Livneh and R. Antonak, Psychological adaptation to chronic illness and disability: A primer for counselors, 2005, *Journal of Counseling & Development*, 83, 12–20. ACA. Reprinted with permission.

injury). CID is also dichotomized into congenital, or evident at birth (e.g., spina bifida and cerebral palsy), and adventitious, or acquired later in life (Parkinson's disease and amputation). In this chapter, we focus on psychosocial adaptation to acquired disabling conditions.

This overview of the literature on psychosocial adaptation to CID is grouped under three headings: basic concepts, CID-triggered reactions, and CID-related coping strategies.

BASIC CONCEPTS

The concepts of stress, crisis, loss and grief, body image, self-concept, stigma, uncertainty and unpredictability, and quality of life (QOL) are included here.

Stress

Individuals with CID normally face an increase in both the frequency and severity of stressful situations (Falvo, 1999; Horowitz, 1986). Increased stress is experienced because of the need to cope with daily threats that include, among others, threats to (a) one's life and well-being; (b) body integrity; (c) independence and autonomy; (d) fulfillment of familial, social, and vocational roles; (e) future goals and plans; and (f) economic stability (Falvo, 1999).

Crisis

The sudden onset of many medical impairments and disabilities (e.g., myocardial infarction, spinal cord injury, traumatic brain injury, and amputation) and that of life-threatening diagnoses or loss of valued functions (e.g., cancer and vision impairment) is highly traumatic. As such, these conditions constitute a psychosocial crisis in the life of the affected person (Livneh & Antonak, 1997; Moos & Schaefer, 1984). Although crisis, by definition, is time limited (e.g., Janosik, 1984), during its presence, life is affected by disturbed psychological, behavioral, and social equilibrium. The psychological consequences of crisis are, in contrast, long lasting and may even evolve into pathological conditions such as posttraumatic stress disorder (PTSD).

Loss and Grief

The crisis experienced following the onset of a traumatic or progressive CID triggers a mourning process for the lost body part or function. In a manner parallel to that evidenced following the loss of a loved one, the individual exhibits feelings of grief, bereavement, and despair (Parkes, 1975; B. A. Wright, 1983). The term *chronic sorrow* has often been used to depict the grief experienced by persons with CID (Burke, Hainsworth, Eakes, & Lindgren, 1992; Davis, 1987). Unlike grief associated with non-bodily losses, CID serves as a constant reminder of the permanency of the condition. Furthermore, daily triggering events act to remind the affected person of the permanent disparity between past and present or future situations (Teel, 1991).

Body Image

Body image has parsimoniously been defined as the unconscious mental representation or schema of one's own body (Schilder, 1950). It evolves gradually and reflects interactive forces exerted by sensory (e.g., visual, auditory, and kinesthetic), interpersonal (e.g., attitudinal), environmental (e.g., physical conditions), and temporal factors. CID, with its impact on physical appearance, functional capabilities, experience of pain, and social roles, is believed to alter, even distort, one's body image and self-concept (Bramble & Cukr, 1998; Falvo, 1999). Successful psychosocial adaptation to CID is said to reflect the integration of physical and sensory changes into a transformed body image and self-perception. Unsuccessful adaptation, in contrast, is evidenced by experiences of physical and psychiatric symptoms such as unmitigated feelings of anxiety and depression, psychogenic pain, chronic fatigue, social withdrawal, and cognitive distortions (Livneh & Antonak, 1997).

Self-Concept

One's self-concept and self-identity are linked to body image and are often seen as conscious, social derivatives of it (Bramble & Cukr, 1998; McDaniel, 1976). However, self-concept and self-identity may be discordant for many individuals with visible disabilities. The sense of self (i.e., self-identity), which is privately owned and outwardly presented, may be denied in social interactions with others who respond to the person as "disabled" first (i.e., focusing on appearance rather than identity), thereby losing sense of the person's real self (Kelly, 2001). The person's self-esteem, representing the evaluative component of the self-concept, gradually shows signs of erosion and negative self-perceptions following such encounters.

Stigma

The impact of stereotypes and prejudice acts to increase stigma toward people with CID (Corrigan, 2000; Falvo, 1999). Restrictions imposed by CID lead to deviations from several societal norms and expectations (e.g., utilization of health care services and occupational stability). They are, therefore, viewed negatively by society and result in stigmatizing perceptions and discriminatory practices. Moreover, when internalized by people with CID, these stigmatizing encounters with others result in increased life stress, reduced self-esteem, and withdrawal from social encounters, including treatment and rehabilitation environments (Falvo, 1999; B. A. Wright, 1983).

Uncertainty and Unpredictability

Although the course of some CIDs is rather stable or predictable (e.g., amputation and cerebral palsy), most conditions may be regarded as neither stable nor predictable (e.g., epilepsy, cancer, diabetes mellitus, and MS). Put differently, the insidious and variable course of these conditions is fraught with intermittent periods of exacerbation and remissions, unpredictable complications, experiences of pain and loss of consciousness, and alternating pace of gradual deterioration. Indeed, the concept of "perceived uncertainty in illness" was coined by Mishel (1981, p. 258) to depict how uncertainty, or the inability to structure personal meaning, results if the individual is unable to form a cognitive schema of illness-associated events. Medical conditions, such as cancer and MS, which are marked by heightened levels of perceived uncertainty regarding disease symptoms, diagnosis, treatment, prognosis, and relationships with family members, were found to be associated with decreased psychosocial adaptation (Mishel, 1981; Wineman, 1990).

Quality of Life

The ultimate psychosocial outcome in rehabilitation practice is believed to be that of post-CID QOL (Crewe, 1980; Roessler, 1990). As a global and multifaceted construct, QOL includes the following functional domains (Flanagan, 1982; Frisch, 1999): (a) intrapersonal (e.g., health, perceptions of life satisfaction, and feelings of well-being), (b) interpersonal (e.g., family life and social activities), and (c) extrapersonal (e.g., work activities and housing). In the context of adaptation to CID, for QOL, there are typically assumptions in two primary domains: successful restructuring of previously disrupted psychosocial homeostasis and attainment of an adaptive person–environment (reality) congruence. Furthermore, QOL is considered to be linked to a more positive self-concept and body image, as well as to an increased sense of control over CID, and QOL is negatively associated with perceived stress and feelings of loss and grief (Dijkers, 1997; Falvo, 1999).

CID-TRIGGERED RESPONSES

Clinical observations and empirical research on the psychosocial process of adaptation to CID have been marred by conflicting findings and heated debate. In this section, we focus on the most frequently experienced psychosocial reactions to CID as cited in the rehabilitation research and disability studies literature.

Shock

This short-lived reaction marks the initial experience following the onset of a traumatic and sudden injury or the diagnosis of a life-threatening or chronic and debilitating disease. The reaction is characterized by psychic numbness, cognitive disorganization, and dramatically decreased or disrupted mobility and speech.

Anxiety

This reaction is characterized by a panic-like feature on initial sensing of the nature and magnitude of the traumatic event. Reflecting a state-like (i.e., situationally determined) response, it is accompanied by confused thinking, cognitive flooding, and a multitude of physiological symptoms, including rapid heart rate, hyperventilation, excess perspiration, and irritable stomach.

Denial

This reaction, also regarded as a defense mechanism mobilized to ward off anxiety and other threatening emotions, involves the minimization and even complete negation of the chronicity, extent, and future implications associated with the condition. Denial involves selective attention to one's physical and psychological environments. It includes wishful thinking, unrealistic expectations of (full or immediate) recovery, and, at times, blatant neglect of medical advice and therapeutic or rehabilitation recommendations. Although denial may successfully mitigate anxiety and depression when used selectively and during the initial phases of adaptation, its long-term impact is often considered maladaptive and life threatening (Krantz & Deckel, 1983; Meyerowitz, 1983).

Depression

This reaction, commonly observed among people with CID, is considered to reflect the realization of the permanency, magnitude, and future implications associated with the loss of body integrity, chronicity of condition, or impending death. Feelings of despair, helplessness, hopelessness, isolation, and distress are frequently reported during this time. Although depression has been found to be a widespread reaction among persons with CID (e.g., Rodin, Craven, & Littlefield, 1991; Turner & Noh, 1988), it is still unclear if it is (as some theoreticians and clinicians argue) a prerequisite to ultimate acceptance of the condition or attaining successful psychosocial adaptation (Wortman & Silver, 1989).

Anger/Hostility

The action of anger/hostility is frequently divided into internalized danger (i.e., self-directed feelings and behaviors of resentment, bitterness, guilt, and self-blame) and externalized hostility (i.e., other- or environment-directed retaliatory feelings and behaviors; Livneh & Antonak, 1997). When internally directed, self-attributions of responsibility for the condition's onset or failure to achieve successful outcomes are evident. In contrast, externally oriented attributions of responsibility tend to place blame for the CID onset or unsuccessful treatment efforts on other people (e.g., medical staff and family members) or aspects of the external environment (e.g., inaccessible facilities and attitudinal barriers). The behaviors commonly observed during this time include aggressive acts, abusive accusations, antagonism, and passive-aggressive modes of obstructing treatment.

Adjustment

This reaction, also referred to in the literature as reorganization, reintegration, or reorientation, is composed of several components: (a) an earlier cognitive reconciliation of the condition, its impact, and its chronic or permanent nature; (b) an affective acceptance, or internalization, of oneself as a person with CID, including a new or restored sense of self-concept, renewed life values, and a continued search for new meanings; and (c) an active (i.e., behavioral) pursuit of personal, social, and/or vocational goals, including successful negotiation of obstacles encountered during the pursuit of these goals.

CID-ASSOCIATED COPING STRATEGIES

The literature on CID-related coping strategies is vast (Moos, 1984; Zeidner & Endler, 1996). In this section, only a cursory overview of the most commonly reported strategies, directly related to coping with CID, is undertaken. First, however, the concept of coping is briefly discussed and its relevance to CID is illustrated.

Coping has been viewed as a psychological strategy mobilized to decrease, modify, or diffuse the impact of stress-generating life events (Billings & Moos, 1981; Lazarus & Folkman, 1984). Foremost, among the defining characteristics of coping are those of (a) including both stable (i.e., trait-like) and situationally determined (i.e., state-like) elements; (b) accessibility to conscious manipulation and control; (c) hierarchical organization that spans the range from macroanalytic, global styles of coping (e.g., locus of control and optimism), to microanalytic, specific behavioral acts; and (d) being structurally multifaceted, including affective, cognitive, and behavioral aspects (Krohne, 1993; Zeidner & Endler, 1996). In addition, clinical and empirical studies of coping emphasize its (a) amenability to assessment by psychometric measures (there are currently more than 20 psychological measures that purport to assess from two to almost 30 coping styles and strategies) and (b) divergent theoretical underpinnings (the nature of coping has been viewed differently by clinicians from various theoretical persuasions, including psychodynamic, interpersonal, and cognitive behavioral).

Research on coping with CID has spanned a wide range of conditions such as cancer, heart disease, spinal cord injury, epilepsy, MS, amputation, rheumatoid arthritis, and diabetes, as well as the experience of pain. It is commonly assumed in these research endeavors the existence of two broad categories of coping strategies, namely, disengagement and engagement coping strategies.

Disengagement Coping Strategies

These strategies refer to coping efforts that seek to deal with stressful events through passive, indirect, even avoidance-oriented activities such as denial, wish-fulfilling fantasy, self- and other-blame, and resorting to substance abuse (Tobin, Holroyd, Reynolds,

& Wigal, 1989). This group of coping strategies is often associated with higher levels of psychological distress (i.e., increased negative affectivity), difficulties in accepting one's condition, and generally poor adaptation to CID.

Engagement Coping Strategies

These strategies refer to coping efforts that defuse stressful situations through active, direct, and goal-oriented activities such as information seeking, problem solving, planning, and seeking social support (Tobin et al., 1989). This group of coping strategies is commonly linked to higher levels of well-being, acceptance of condition, and successful adaptation to CID.

During the chronic, but often remitting and exacerbating, course of medical conditions and physical disabilities, coping strategies are differentially adopted to meet the fluctuating demands necessitated by the changing physical, psychosocial, spiritual, economic, and environmental needs of the person. The rehabilitation and disability studies literature suggests that coping strategies could occupy several roles in their relationship to psychosocial adaptation to CID. These include (a) direct or causal, such that their use might differentially determine or influence psychosocial adaptation; (b) indirect or mediating, such that their use acts to mediate between certain demographic (e.g., age), disability-related (e.g., severity or duration of condition), or personality (e.g., level of perceived uncertainty) variables, and outcomes of adaptation to CID; and (c) outcome variables, such that the type and valence of coping strategies are an indicator of how successful psychosocial adaptation is.

ASSESSMENT OF PSYCHOSOCIAL ADAPTATION TO CID

Over the past half century, a large number of measures of psychosocial adaptation to and coping with CID have been reported in the literature. In this section, only those psychometrically sound measures most frequently reported in the literature are reviewed. Readers may refer to the study by Livneh and Antonak (1997) for a comprehensive discussion of these and other measures.

GENERAL MEASURES OF ADAPTATION TO CID

Millon Behavioral Health Inventory

The Millon Behavioral Health Inventory (MBHI; Millon, Green, & Meagher, 1979) is a 150-item self-report questionnaire, organized into 20 clinical scales. The scales are classified into four domains: (a) coping styles, (b) psychogenic attitudes, (c) psychosomatic complaints, and (d) a prognostic index. The MBHI seeks to (a) describe the psychological styles of medical service recipients, (b) examine the impact of emotional and motivational needs and coping strategies on disease course, and (c) suggest a comprehensive treatment plan to decrease the impact of deleterious psychological reactions. The strengths of the MBHI include its sound psychometric (i.e., reliability and validity) properties, clinical usefulness, and applicability to a wide range of medical and rehabilitation settings. Weaknesses include empirically unconfirmed domain structure and potential reactivity influences and response bias.

Psychosocial Adjustment to Illness Scale

The Psychosocial Adjustment to Illness Scale (PAIS; Derogatis, 1977; Derogatis & Lopez, 1983) is a 46-item instrument designed to measure psychosocial adaptation to medical illnesses and chronic diseases. The scale can be administered both as a semistructured psychiatric interview by a trained clinician and as a self-report measure (PAIS-SR). In addition to an overall adjustment score, seven subscales are provided: health care orientation, vocational environment, domestic environment, sexual relationships, extended family relationships, social environment, and psychological distress (i.e., indicating reactions of anxiety, depression, guilt, and hostility, as well as levels of self-esteem and body image). The strengths of the PAIS include the psychometric robustness of its scales, having both self-report and clinician interview forms, and the availability of norm scores for several medical conditions (e.g., cancer, MS, and renal failure). Weaknesses include lack of data on possible response bias influences.

Acceptance of Disability Scale

The Acceptance of Disability (AD; Linkowski, 1971) scale is a 50-item, 6-point, summated rating scale developed to measure the degree of AD as theorized by Dembo, Leviton, and Wright (1956). Items are summed to yield a single score representing changes in one's value system following the onset of physical disability.

Major strengths inherent in the AD scale include its theory-driven rationale, reliability, and use in a large number of English-speaking and non–English-speaking countries. Weaknesses are suggested by the lack of investigation of its factorial structure, its unidimensional approach to a complex construct, and lack of data on response bias influences.

Sickness Impact Profile

The Sickness Impact Profile (SIP; Bergner et al., 1976; Gilson et al., 1975) comprises 136 items that yield, in addition to scores on 12 subscales, a global scale score; three scales can be combined to create a physical dimension score (i.e., ambulation, mobility, and body care and movement), four scales can be combined and yield a psychosocial dimension score (i.e., social interaction, alertness behavior, emotional behavior, and communication), and the five remaining scales are viewed as independent categories and are typically scored separately (i.e., sleep and rest, eating, work, home management, and recreation and pastimes). Respondent-perceived impact of sickness is measured by directing the respondent to choose descriptors of currently experienced, sickness-related behavioral dysfunction.

The strengths of the SIP include its comprehensive and rigorous psychometric development and properties, extensive use with patients diagnosed with a variety of physical and health conditions, and the availability of a Spanish-language version. Weaknesses may be related to its yet-to-be tested factorial structure and susceptibility to defensiveness and response set.

Reactions to Impairment and Disability Inventory

The Reactions to Impairment and Disability Inventory (RIDI; Livneh & Antonak, 1990) is a 60-item, multidimensional, self-report summated rating scale. Its intended use is to investigate eight clinically reported classes of psychosocial reactions to the onset of CID. The eight psychosocial reaction scales are shock, anxiety, denial, depression, internalized anger, externalized hostility, acknowledgment, and adjustment. The strengths of the RIDI include its comprehensive psychometric development, scale reliability, and multidimensional perspective on adaptation to CID. Weaknesses are suggested by scant concurrent validity data, lack of normative data across disabling conditions, and potential confounding effects of response bias influences.

Handicap Problems Inventory

The Handicap Problems Inventory (HPI; G. N. Wright & Remmers, 1960) is a 280-item checklist of problems believed to be attributed to the presence of physical disability. Respondents are asked to mark those problems that are caused or exacerbated by the existence of the condition. Items on the inventory are grouped into four life domains: personal, family, social, and vocational subscales. The strengths of the HPI include domain comprehensiveness, its documented internal reliability estimates, and available normative data. Weaknesses include lack of supportive data on its validity, possible response bias, and its inordinate length.

SPECIFIC MEASURES OF ADAPTATION TO CID

A sizeable number of measures related to psychosocial adaptation to specific CIDs have been reported in the rehabilitation and disability studies literature. As a result of space constraints, these measures are not reviewed here. Interested readers may refer to the study by Livneh and Antonak (1997) for a comprehensive review of these scales. Readers may also wish to directly consult the following:

1. Measures of adaptation to cancer that include the Mental Adjustment to Cancer Scale (Watson et al., 1988).
2. Measures of adaptation to diabetes that include the Diabetic Adjustment Scale (Sullivan, 1979).
3. Measures on adaptation to epilepsy and seizure disorders that include the Washington Psychosocial Seizure Inventory (Dodrill, Batzel, Queisser, & Temkin, 1980).
4. Measures of adaptation to traumatic brain injury that include the Portland Adaptability Inventory (Lezak, 1987).
5. Measures of adaptation to rheumatoid arthritis that include the Arthritis Impact Measurement Scale (Meenan, 1982, 1986).
6. Measures of adaptation to spinal cord injuries that include the psychosocial questionnaire for spinal cord injured persons (Bodenhamer, Achterberg-Lawlis, Kevorkian, Belanus, & Cofer, 1983).
7. Measures of adaptation to visual impairments that include the Nottingham Adjustment Scale (Dodds, Bailey, Pearson, & Yates, 1991).
8. Measures of adaptation to hearing impairments that include the social-emotional assessment inventory for deaf and hearing-impaired students (Meadow, Karchmer, Peterson, & Rudner, 1980).

Counselors and clinicians who consider adopting traditional psychological measures (e.g., the Minnesota Multiphasic Personality Inventory, Beck Depression Inventory, and Spielberger's State-Trait Anxiety Inventory) to address psychosocial adaptation to CID must be cognizant of the following two issues:

1. Physical and physiological symptoms (e.g., fatigue, weakness, and sleep problems) directly associated with a number of CIDs (e.g., spinal cord injury, MS, and Parkinson's disease) often mimic indicators of depression and anxiety among members of these populations. Counselors who work with people with CID should therefore (a) pay careful attention and differentiate, whenever possible, the more authentic indicators of depression and anxiety (typically cognitive and affective correlates) from those associated with the condition's physiological concomitants and (b) gain understanding of the literature that has examined the confounding effects of CID-triggered physiological

symptoms on the scoring and interpretation of traditional psychological measures (e.g., Morrison, 1997; Pollak, Levy, & Breitholtz, 1999; Skuster, Digre, & Corbett, 1992).

2. Most traditional psychological and psychiatric measures lack scoring norms based on responses from populations of people with CID. This lack of normative data for people with CID renders these measures suspicious, even misleading, when their findings are interpreted indiscriminately. Counselors who adopt, or contemplate modifying, psychological tests for use with people with CID should carefully review the *Standards for Educational and Psychological Testing* (American Psychological Association, 1999) and Bolton (2001) for specific suggestions on this matter.

INTERVENTION STRATEGIES FOR PEOPLE WITH CID

Numerous theory-driven, reaction-specific, and clinically documented intervention strategies to assist people with CID successfully adapt to their conditions have been reported in the literature. In the following section, we review the major approaches to psychosocial interventions applied to people with CID.

Theory-Driven Interventions

These interventions focus on the clinical applications of widely recognized personality theories and therapeutic models to persons with CID and the perceived merits of their use with this population. Among the more commonly applied theories are psychoanalytic, individual (Adlerian), Gestalt (Perls), rational-emotive-behavioral (Ellis), cognitive (Beck), and behaviorist (Riggar, Maki, & Wolf, 1986; Thomas, Butler, & Parker, 1987).

When adopting theory-driven interventions, clinicians typically follow a three-step sequence. First, core concepts from a particular theory (e.g., defense mechanisms, feelings of inferiority, unfinished life situations, and irrational beliefs) are identified and examined. Second, the usefulness of these concepts, within the context of psychosocial adaptation to CID (e.g., understanding the process of grieving for loss of body parts or functions), is scrutinized. Third, the benefits derived from these concepts, for practical counseling interventions, for people with CID are assessed and, if deemed appropriate, are applied to their life situations. Readers may wish to refer to the study by Chan, Thomas, and Berven (2002); English (1971); Livneh and Antonak (1997); Livneh and Sherwood (1991); and Shontz (1978) for detailed reviews of these interventions.

Psychosocial Reaction-Specific Interventions

These eclectic interventions aim at offering a logical match between specific psychotherapeutic strategies and those reactions (or experiences) evoked during the process of adaptation to CID (e.g., anxiety, depression, denial, and anger). Worded differently, the counselor seeks to link specific counseling strategies with clinically observed, or client-reported, psychosocial reactions (Dunn, 1975; Livneh & Antonak, 1997; Livneh & Sherwood, 1991). It is generally argued that strategies regarded as supportive, affective-insightful, or psychodynamic in nature (e.g., person-centered therapy, Gestalt therapy, and Jungian therapy) may be more useful during earlier phases of the adaptation process. In contrast, strategies viewed as more active-directive, goal-oriented, or cognitive behavioral in nature (e.g., cognitive therapy, behavioral therapy, and coping skills training) may be more beneficial during the later stages (Dunn, 1975; Livneh & Antonak, 1997; Marshak & Seligman, 1993). To illustrate this rationale, two examples are provided. First, disability or loss-triggered depression can be approached by encouraging the client to vent feelings associated with grief, isolation, guilt, shame, and mourning for the lost function (e.g., mobility, vision, and health). Protracted depression can be further managed by reinforcing social contacts and activities and by practicing self-assertiveness, self-determination, and independent living skills. Second, reactions (feelings and behaviors) of self-directed or other-directed anger may be dealt with by teaching and practicing anger expression in socially sanctioned forms, such as the pursuit of artistic endeavors and, if feasible, sports-related activities. Other strategies could include practicing behavior modification techniques to reduce physically and verbally aggressive acts.

Global Clinical Interventions

These comprehensive clinical interventions are geared toward assisting people with specific CIDs (e.g., cancer, heart disease, and spinal cord injury) in successfully adapting to their condition and its impact on their lives. More specifically, these interventions provide the client and his or her family and significant others with emotional, cognitive, and behavioral support. In addition, these interventions equip the client with adaptive coping skills that could be successfully adopted when facing stressful life events and crisis situations. Among the most commonly encountered global clinical interventions are the following:

1. **Assisting clients to explore the personal meaning of the CID:** These strategies rest heavily on psychodynamic principles and focus on issues of loss, grief, mourning, and suffering. Emphasis is also placed on encouraging clients to vent feelings leading to acceptance of condition permanency, altered body image, and realization of decreased functional capacity. A three-phase approach by Rodin et al. (1991) to treating depression in medically impaired individuals best illustrates this strategy (i.e., assisting clients in expressing grief and mourning, providing clients with opportunities to seek personal meaning of their CID, and training clients to attain a sense of mastery over their emotional experiences).

2. **Providing clients with relevant medical information:** These strategies emphasize imparting accurate information to clients on their medical condition, including its present status, prognosis, anticipated future functional limitations, and, when applicable, vocational implications. These approaches are best suited for decreasing the initial levels of heightened anxiety and depression, as well as the potentially damaging effects of unremitting denial (Ganz, 1988; Razin, 1982).

3. **Providing clients with supportive family and group experiences:** These strategies permit clients (usually with similar disabilities or common life experiences) and, if applicable, their family members or significant others to share common fears, concerns, needs, and wishes. These experiences also allow clients to acquire greater insight and to gain social support and approval from other group participants, family members, and professional helpers. Common group modalities include educational groups, psychotherapeutic groups, coping-skills training groups, and social support groups (Roback, 1984; Seligman, 1982; Telch & Telch, 1985). A group model by Subramanian and Ell (1989) for heart patients best exemplifies this approach because it incorporates (a) information on heart conditions and disability management, (b) coping-skills training to manage stressful life situations, and (c) cognitive skills teaching to manage maladaptive emotions.

4. **Teaching clients adaptive coping skills for successful community functioning:** These strategies, in a similar vein to those of group-based coping-skills training, focus on instilling in clients coping skills that allow them to face a wide range of stressful conditions typically encountered by people with CID in physical, social, educational, and vocational settings. These skills include assertiveness, interpersonal relations, decision making, problem solving, stigma management, and time management skills. Craig and coauthors (Craig, Hancock, Chang, & Dickson, 1998; Craig,

Hancock, Dickson, & Chang, 1997) have used a cognitive behavioral therapy coping program to train clients who have sustained a spinal cord injury. The authors' multifaceted approach uses relaxation techniques, visualization techniques, cognitive restructuring, and social and self-assertiveness skills training to help participants cope with psychosocial difficulties encountered on release into the community.

SUMMARY

Approximately one in every five Americans is currently diagnosed with CID. People with CID often encounter physical, psychological, social, educational, financial, and vocational barriers that greatly interfere with their QOL. In this chapter, we have attempted to provide counselors with the most useful and pragmatic concepts, processes, assessment tools, and intervention strategies related to psychosocial adaptation to CID.

When working with individuals who have sustained CID, counselors are commonly called to draw on their expertise in the areas of (a) stress, crisis, and coping with loss and grief; (b) the impact of traumatic events on self-concept, body image, and QOL; and (c) the effects of disability-linked factors (e.g., uncertainty and unpredictability) and societal reactions (e.g., stigma and prejudice) on psychosocial adaptation to CID.

Counselors must also be cognizant of, and demonstrate clinical acumen when observing, clients' psychosocial reactions to their conditions and the external environment. Several CID-triggered responses (at times described as phases) have been discussed. These include (a) reactions of shorter duration that are more commonly experienced earlier in the adaptation process (e.g., shock and anxiety); (b) reactions of longer duration that normally suggest distressed and unsuccessful coping efforts (e.g., depression and anger); and (c) reactions that signal successful adaptation to the condition and renewed life homeostasis (adjustment).

Of the many measures available for assessing psychosocial adaptation to CID, six have been reviewed in this chapter. They were selected because of their (a) applicability to a wide range of CIDs, (b) sound psychometric development and structure, (c) frequent citations in the rehabilitation and disability studies literature, and (d) clinical and research potential.

Assessment of clients' levels of psychosocial adaptation to their condition should pave the way to appropriate selection of intervention strategies. To this end, the chapter concludes with an overview of four psychosocial strategies most commonly applied to counseling people with CID. Interventions based on innovative applications of traditional personality and psychotherapeutic interventions were reviewed. Subsequently, interventions that seek to address reactions linked to the onset of CID (e.g., anxiety, depression, and anger) were highlighted. Finally, global, eclectic, clinical approaches that were typically developed for specific disabilities (e.g., cancer, heart conditions, and spinal cord injury) were illustrated. The last group of interventions offers the counselor fertile ground for applying comprehensive, multifaceted approaches geared to meet the wide range of psychological, social, and vocational needs of clients with CID.

REFERENCES

American Psychological Association. (1999). *Standards for educational and psychological testing* (4th ed.). Washington, DC: Author.
Bergner, M., Bobbitt, R. A., Kressel, S., Pollard, W. E., Gilson, B. S., & Morris, J. R. (1976). The sickness impact profile: Conceptual formulation and methodology for the development of a health status measure. *International Journal of Health Services, 6*(3), 393–415.

Billings, A. G., & Moos, R. H. (1981). The role of coping responses and social resources in attenuating the stress of life events. *Journal of Behavioral Medicine, 4*(2), 139–157.

Bodenhamer, E., Achterberg-Lawlis, J., Kevorkian, G., Belanus, A., & Cofer, J. (1983). Staff and patient perceptions of the psychosocial concerns of spinal cord injured persons. *American Journal of Physical Medicine, 62*(4), 182–193.

Bolton, B. (Ed.). (2001). *Handbook of measurement and evaluation in rehabilitation* (3rd ed.). Gaithersburg, MD: Aspen.

Bowe, F. (2000). *Physical, sensory, and health disabilities: An introduction.* Upper Saddle River, NJ: Merrill.

Bramble, K., & Cukr, P. (1998). Body image. In I. M. Lubkin (Ed.), *Chronic illness: Impact and interventions* (4th ed., pp. 283–298). Boston, MA: Jones & Bartlett.

Burke, M. L., Hainsworth, M. A., Eakes, G. G., & Lindgren, C. L. (1992). Current knowledge and research on chronic sorrow: A foundation for inquiry. *Death Studies, 16*, 231–245.

Chan, F., Berven, N. L., & Thomas, K. R. (Eds.). (2002). *Counseling theories and techniques for rehabilitation health professionals.* New York, NY: Springer Publishing.

Corrigan, P. W. (2000). Mental health stigma as social attribution: Implications for research methods and attitude change. *Clinical Psychology: Science and Practice, 7*, 48–67.

Craig, A. R., Hancock, K., Chang, E., & Dickson, H. (1998). The effectiveness of group psychological intervention in enhancing perceptions of control following spinal cord injury. *The Australian and New Zealand Journal of Psychiatry, 32*(1), 112–118.

Craig, A. R., Hancock, K., Dickson, H., & Chang, E. (1997). Long-term psychological outcomes in spinal cord injured persons: Results of a controlled trial using cognitive behavior therapy. *Archives of Physical Medicine and Rehabilitation, 78*(1), 33–38.

Crewe, N. M. (1980). Quality of life–the ultimate goal in rehabilitation. *Minnesota Medicine, 63*(8), 586–589.

Davis, B. H. (1987). Disability and grief. *Social Casework, 68*, 352–357.

Dembo, T., Leviton, G. L., & Wright, B. A. (1956). Adjustment to misfortune; a problem of social-psychological rehabilitation. *Artificial Limbs, 3*(2), 4–62.

Derogatis, L. R. (1977). *Psychological adjustment to illness scale.* Baltimore, MD: Clinical Psychometric Research.

Derogatis, L. R., & Lopez, M. (1983). *Psychosocial adjustment to illness scale (PAIS & PAIS-SR): Scoring, procedures and administration manual.* Baltimore, MD: Clinical Psychometric Research.

Dijkers, M. (1997). Quality of life after spinal cord injury: A meta analysis of the effects of disablement components. *Spinal Cord, 35*(12), 829–840.

Dodds, A. G., Bailey, P., Pearson, A., & Yates, L. (1991). Psychological factors in acquired visual impairment: The development of a scale of adjustment. *Journal of Visual Impairment and Blindness, 85*, 306–310.

Dodrill, C. B., Batzel, L. W., Queisser, H. R., & Temkin, N. R. (1980). An objective method for the assessment of psychological and social problems among epileptics. *Epilepsia, 21*(2), 123–135.

Dunn, M. E. (1975). Psychological intervention in a spinal cord injury center: An introduction. *Rehabilitation Psychology, 22*, 165–178.

Eisenberg, M. G., Glueckauf, R. L., & Zaretsky, H. H. (Eds.). (1999). *Medical aspects of disability: A handbook for the rehabilitation professional.* New York, NY: Springer Publishing.

English, R. W. (1971). The application of personality theory to explain psychological reactions to physical disability. *Rehabilitation Research and Practice Review, 3*, 35–47.

Falvo, D. (1999). *Medical and psychosocial aspects of chronic illness and disability* (2nd ed.). Gaithersburg, MD: Aspen.

Flanagan, J. C. (1982). Measurement of quality of life: Current state of the art. *Archives of Physical Medicine and Rehabilitation, 63*(2), 56–59.

Frisch, M. B. (1999). Quality of life assessment/intervention and the quality of life inventory. In M. E. Maruish (Ed.), *The use of psychological testing for treatment planning and outcome assessment* (pp. 1277–1331). Mahwah, NJ: Erlbaum.

Ganz, P. A. (1988). Patient education as a moderator of psychological distress. *Journal of Psychosocial Oncology, 6*, 181–197.

Gilson, B. S., Gilson, J. S., Bergner, M., Bobbitt, R. A., Kressel, S., Pollard, W. E., & Vesselago M. (1975). The sickness impact profile: Development of an outcome measure of health care. *American Journal of Public Health, 65*, 1304–1310.

Horowitz, M. J. (1986). *Stress response syndromes* (2nd ed.). Northvale, NJ: Aronson.

Janosik, E. H. (1984). *Crisis counseling: A contemporary approach.* Belmont, CA: Wadsworth.

Kelly, M. P. (2001). Disability and community: A sociological approach. In G. L. Albrecht, K. D. Seelman, & M. Bury (Eds.), *Handbook of disability studies* (pp. 396–411). Thousand Oaks, CA: Sage.

Krantz, D. S., & Deckel, A. W. (1983). Coping with coronary heart disease and stroke. In T. G. Burish & L. A. Bradley (Eds.), *Coping with chronic disease: Research and applications* (pp. 85–112). New York, NY: Academic Press.

Krohne, H. W. (Ed.). (1993). *Attention and avoidance.* Seattle, WA: Hugrefe & Huber.

Lazarus, R. S., & Folkman, S. (1984). *Stress, appraisal, and coping.* New York, NY: Springer Publishing.

Lezak, M. D. (1987). Relationship between personality disorders, social disturbance, and physical disability following traumatic brain injury. *Journal of Head Trauma and Rehabilitation, 2*(1), 57–59.

Linkowski, D. C. (1971). A scale to measure acceptance of disability. *Rehabilitation Counseling Bulletin, 14,* 236–244.

Livneh, H., & Antonak, R. F. (1990). Reactions to disability: An empirical investigation of their nature and structure. *Journal of Applied Rehabilitation Counseling, 21*(4), 13–21.

Livneh, H., & Antonak, R. F. (1997). *Psychosocial adaptation to chronic illness and disability.* Gaithersburg, MD: Aspen.

Livneh, H., & Antonak, R. (2005). Psychological adaptation to chronic illness and disability: A primer for counselors. *Journal of Counseling & Development, 83,* 12–20.

Livneh, H., & Sherwood, A. (1991). Application of personality theories and counseling strategies to clients with physical disabilities. *Journal of Counseling & Development, 69,* 525–538.

Marshak, L. E., & Seligman, M. (1993). *Counseling persons with physical disabilities: Theoretical and clinical perspectives.* Austin, TX: PRO-ED.

McDaniel, J. W. (1976). *Physical disability and human behavior* (2nd ed.). New York, NY: Pergamon Press.

Meadow, K. P., Karchmer, M. A., Peterson, L. M., & Rudner, L. (1980). *Meadows/Kendall social-emotive assessment inventory for deaf students: Manual.* Washington, DC: Gallaudet College, Pre-College Programs.

Meenan, R. F. (1982). The AIMS approach to health status measurement: Conceptual background and measurement properties. *Journal of Rheumatology, 9*(5), 785–788.

Meenan, R. F. (1986). New approaches to outcome assessment: The AIMS questionnaire for arthritis. *Advances in Internal Medicine, 31,* 167–185.

Meyerowitz, B. E. (1983). Postmastectomy coping strategies and quality of life. *Health Psychology, 2,* 117–132.

Millon, T., Green, C. J., & Meagher, R. B. (1979). The MBHI: A new inventory for the psycho-diagnostician in medical settings. *Professional Psychology, 10,* 529–539.

Mishel, M. H. (1981). The measurement of uncertainty in illness. *Nursing Research, 30*(5), 258–263.

Moos, R. H. (Ed.). (1984). *Coping with physical illness: New perspectives* (Vol. 2). New York, NY: Plenum.

Moos, R. H., & Schaefer, J. A. (1984). The crisis of physical illness. In R. H. Moos (Ed.), *Coping with physical illness: New perspectives* (Vol. 2, pp. 3–31). New York, NY: Plenum.

Morrison, J. (1997). *When psychological problems mask medical disorders: A guide for psychotherapists.* New York, NY: Guilford Press.

Parkes, C. M. (1975). Psychosocial transitions: Comparison between reactions to loss of a limb and loss of a spouse. *British Journal of Psychiatry, 127,* 204–210.

Pollak, J., Levy, S., & Breitholtz, T. (1999). Screening for medical and neuro developmental disorders for the professional counselor. *Journal of Counseling & Development, 77,* 350–358.

Razin, A. M. (1982). Psychosocial intervention in coronary artery disease: A review. *Psychosomatic Medicine, 44*(4), 363–387.

Riggar, T. F., Maki, D. R., & Wolf, A. W. (Eds.). (1986). *Applied rehabilitation counseling.* New York, NY: Springer Publishing.

Roback, H. B. (Ed.). (1984). *Helping patients and their families cope with medical problems.* San Francisco, CA: Jossey-Bass.

Rodin, G., Craven, J., & Littlefield, C. (1991). *Depression in the medically ill: An integrated approach.* New York, NY: Brunner/Mazel.

Roessler, R. T. (1990). A quality of life perspective on rehabilitation counseling. *Rehabilitation Counseling Bulletin, 34,* 82–91.

Schilder, P. (1950). *The image and appearance of the human body.* New York, NY: Wiley.

Seligman, M. (1982). Introduction. In M. Seligman (Ed.), *Group psychotherapy and counseling with special populations* (pp. 1–26). Baltimore, MD: University Park Press.

Shontz, F. C. (1978). Psychological adjustment to physical disability: Trends in theories. *Archives of Physical Medicine and Rehabilitation, 59*(6), 251–254.

Skuster, D. Z., Digre, K. B., & Corbett, J. J. (1992). Neurologic conditions presenting as psychiatric disorders. *The Psychiatric Clinics of North America, 15*(2), 311–333.

Stachnik, T., Stoffelmayr, B., & Hoppe, R. B. (1983). Prevention, behavior change, and chronic disease. In T. G. Burish & L. A. Bradley (Eds.), *Coping with chronic disease: Research and applications* (pp. 447–473). New York, NY: Academic Press.

Subramanian, K., & Ell, K. O. (1989). Coping with a first heart attack: A group treatment model for low-income Anglo, Black, and Hispanic patients. *Social Work in Groups, 11,* 99–117.

Sullivan, B. J. (1979). Adjustment in diabetic adolescent girls: I. Development of the Diabetic Adjustment Scale. *Psychosomatic Medicine, 41*(2), 119–126.

Teel, C. S. (1991). Chronic sorrow: Analysis of the concept. *Journal of Advanced Nursing, 16*(11), 1311–1319.

Telch, C. S., & Telch, M. J. (1985). Psychological approaches for enhancing coping among cancer patients: A review. *Clinical Psychology Review, 5,* 325–344.

Thomas, K., Butler, A., & Parker, R. M. (1987). Psychosocial counseling. In R. M. Parker (Ed.), *Rehabilitation counseling: Basics and beyond* (pp. 65–95). Austin, TX: PRO-ED.

Tobin, D. L., Holroyd, K. A., Reynolds, R. V., & Wigal, J. K. (1989). The hierarchical factor structure of the coping strategies inventory. *Cognitive Therapy and Research, 13,* 343–361.

Turner, R. J., & Noh, S. (1988). Physical disability and depression: A longitudinal analysis. *Journal of Health and Social Behavior, 29*(1), 23–37.

Watson, M., Greer, S., Young, J., Inayat, Q., Burgess, C., & Robertson, B. (1988). Development of a questionnaire measure of adjustment to cancer: The MAC scale. *Psychological Medicine, 18*(1), 203–209.

Wineman, N. M. (1990). Adaptation to multiple sclerosis: The role of social support, functional disability, and perceived uncertainty. *Nursing Research, 39*(5), 294–299.

Wortman, C. B., & Silver, R. C. (1989). The myths of coping with loss. *Journal of Consulting and Clinical Psychology, 57*(3), 349–357.

Wright, B. A. (1983). *Physical disability—A psychosocial approach.* New York, NY: Harper & Row.

Wright, G. N., & Remmers, H. H. (1960). *Manual for the handicap problems inventory.* Lafayette, IN: Purdue Research Foundation.

Zeidner, M., & Endler, N. S. (Eds.). (1996). *Handbook of coping: Theory, research, applications.* New York, NY: Wiley.

7

Theories of Adjustment and Adaptation to Disability

Irmo Marini

*T*his chapter explores one of the most profound and important empirical questions that researchers have regarding the psychological and sociological impact of disability: How do persons with disabilities react to their situation, and why do some actually excel, whereas others become indefinitely incapacitated both mentally and physically? To begin with, there is some debate regarding appropriate terminology. Some experts, such as Olkin (1999), do not agree with the term *adjustment* to disability. Olkin argues that the concept of *adjusting* is a pathological term presuming something is wrong and implies persons with disabilities must successfully negotiate or transition through a series of stages to finally accept their situation. He is not a proponent of the stage model of disability, but rather believes that individuals "respond" to their disability throughout their lives, and that final adjustment or acceptance does not exist. Other experts, such as Livneh (1991), do support a stage-like model and believe that persons with later onset or adventitious disabilities often do transition through stages and reach a level of final adjustment or acceptance; however, they may experience setbacks. Still other experts, such as Vash and Crewe (2003), describe how some persons with disabilities may actually "transcend" beyond their disability once they acknowledge or come to terms with their situation, accept the implications, and embrace the experience.

In this chapter, the terms *adjustment, adaptation, reaction*, and *response* are used interchangeably; despite the fact that they may be different concepts, they have overlapping definitions. When used, they essentially refer to individuals with disabilities in their attempts to come to terms with their disability. Certain terms like *adjustment* and *adaptation* also have a temporal or time component to them (Livneh & Antonak, 1997). In other words, one would typically need to be adapting before he or she can reach final adjustment. Livneh and Antonak describe psychosocial adaptation as:

> An evolving, dynamic, general process through which the individual gradually
> approaches an optimal state of person-environment congruence manifested
> by (1) active participation in social, vocational, and avocational pursuits;
> (2) successful negotiation of the physical environment; and (3) awareness of
> remaining strengths and assets as well as existing functional limitations. (p. 8)

The concept of *adjustment*, as however, is defined as:

a particular phase (e.g., set of experiences and reactions) of the psychosocial adaptation process. As such, adjustment is the clinically and phenomenologically hypothesized final phase—elusive as it may be—of the unfolding process of adaptation to crisis situations including the onset of chronic illness and disability. It is alternatively expressed by terms such as (1) reaching and maintaining psychosocial equilibrium; (2) achieving a state of reintegration; (3) positively striving to reach life goals; (4) demonstrating positive self-esteem, self-concept, self regard, and the like; and, (5) experiencing positive attitudes toward one's self, others, and the disability. (p. 8)

Also, as discussed in Chapter 2, each and every day we experience thoughts, emotions, and behaviors that may or may not be in congruence with each other (e.g., we can be emotionally upset about something, but behaviorally smile and pretend nothing is wrong). Each of the aforementioned concepts involves an emotional, cognitive, and behavioral response. When Olkin (1999) states that individuals respond to their disability, it means that they actually feel and think something while they are responding. Likewise, when individuals accept their circumstances, this again involves certain cognitions, behaviors, and emotions that accompany successful adaptation. Therefore, persons who are believed to have genuinely adapted to their disabilities should otherwise experience congruent feelings of contentment, thoughts of self-confidence with their disability identity, and some type of overt accompanying measurable behaviors such as socializing more, developing assertiveness, being employed, volunteering or attending school, and having the desire and confidence to date, if relevant.

Overall, seven common theories of adaptation to a traumatic physical disability are explored in this section. Some proposed theories have stronger evidence-based empirical support, whereas others rely on more qualitative and case study accounts, as well as clinical observation. This chapter first explores persons born with a congenital disability, and questions whether such individuals actually experience any type of adjustment process since they have no preinjury, nondisabled experience with which to compare their situation. Olkin (1999) shares her life experience as an individual born with polio, and prefers to describe her experience as "in response" to life circumstances she interfaces with in her external environment. Yet, others born with a disability report different developmental experiences. As this phenomenon of adaptation to a congenital disability is less understood or written about in the literature, we lead off with this investigation. The remainder of the chapter explores the following seven theories of adjustment: stage models (Livneh, 1991), somatopsychology (Lewin, 1935; Trieschmann, 1988; Wright, 1983), the disability centrality model (DCM; Bishop, 2005), ecological models (Livneh & Antonak, 1997; Trieschmann, 1988; Vash & Crewe, 2004), recurrent or integrated model (Kendall & Buys, 1998), transactional model of coping (Lazarus & Folkman, 1984b), and chaos theory (Parker, Schaller, & Hansmann, 2003).

RESPONSE TO DISABILITY FOR PERSONS WITH CONGENITAL DISABILITIES

Although there is a plethora of conceptual and empirical literature regarding the adjustment or adaptation to an acquired disability, far less attention has been directed toward the psychosocial impact of a congenital disability, or those disabilities people have at birth (Varni, Rubenfeld, Talbot, & Setoguchi, 1989). Some researchers anecdotally believe that as individuals born with a disability have no predisability background to compare with or a loss of function to grieve, they generally do not have any apparent difficulties adjusting (Olkin, 1999). In actuality, the available literature is inconsistent in these findings (Cadman, Boyle, Szatmari, & Offord, 1987; Olkin, 1999; Trask et al., 2003; Varni et al., 1989; Wallander, Varni, Babani, Banis, & Wilcox, 1989; Witt, Riley, & Coiro, 2003).

From a psychosocial development standpoint, theoretically, we all generally pass through a number of critical life cycle stages of development (Erikson, Erikson, & Kivnick, 1986). Erikson et al. unfortunately did not take into account when a disability occurs; however, as he was a former student of psychodynamics, he would likely view the individual as experiencing some pathology at various stages. Statistically, data from the 1994 to 1995 National Health Interview Surveys, Disability Supplement population study (Witt et al., 2003), indicates that psychological maladjustment was 10% to 15% higher among children with chronic illness and disability (CID) as opposed to otherwise healthy children in the early 1970s (Pless, Roghmann, & Haggerty, 1972). As previously indicated, however, the level of severity of the disability has little impact on response (Wallander & Varni, 1998). In the 1994 to 1995 national health survey of biological mothers, the psychosocial statuses of 3,362 disabled and nondisabled children and adolescents aged 6 to 17 years were assessed. Children with psychiatric disabilities were excluded. Poor maternal health or mental health, child-perceived family burden (scored by answering yes to one or more of three questions asking whether family disruptions in work status, sleep patterns, or financial problems occurred), and living in poverty were all positively associated with reported maladjustment of the children. Mothers of children with disabilities were more likely to be divorced, separated, or never married, as well as in poorer health and depressed, as opposed to mothers with a nondisabled child. In addition, children with communication or learning limitations also were positively associated with poor adjustment. Conversely, Varni and colleagues (1989) found that family cohesion, organization, and moral–religious emphasis were all predictors of positive psychological and social adaptation in 42 children with congenital or acquired limb disabilities. Researchers also found that increased parental distress, such as wishful thinking and self-blame, were associated with an increased distress among children and adolescents with cancer. It appears that environmental or external influences such as emotionally stable family support and cohesion are key factors that predict child adaptation.

Olkin (1999) notes that even among well-meaning or well-intended parents, children with disabilities can still run into adjustment problems. Specifically, Olkin discusses the "conspiracy of silence," where well-meaning parents intentionally withhold information or ignore discussing important topics with their child regarding his or her prognosis, sexuality, and so forth, because the parents perceive that it upsets their child. Similarly, some parents overprotect them by not allowing opportunities for their child to compete or attempt new experiences for fear of him or her failing. This undermines the child's ability to handle stress and be exposed to new experiences, ultimately hurting the child as he or she becomes an adult (Hogansen, Powers, Geenen, Gil-Kashiwabara, & Powers, 2008). By being sheltered, some children with disabilities are often less physically independent, having had everything done for them; as a result, they may experience low self-esteem and greater social anxiety and immaturity (Holmbeck et al., 2002; Levy, 1966; Thomasgard, 1998). Seligman (1975) uses the concept of "learned helplessness" to describe instances where individuals repeatedly have things done for them over time, essentially learning to be helpless and unable to perform tasks or activities they could otherwise be capable of performing had they been taught or empowered to learn.

In reverting back to the Erikson and colleagues (1986) theory of psychosocial development, some children with congenital disabilities might otherwise experience psychosocial difficulties with shame or self-doubt (Erikson's *autonomy versus shame*) at an early age as a result of not being allowed, or physically able, to explore their environment (Kivnick, 1991). This can carry over during school-age years (Erikson's *industry versus inferiority* stage) where children with severe disabilities are unable to master their environment, and at times come under ridicule from fellow students (Connors & Stalker, 2007; Kivnick, 1991). Adolescents with disabilities can experience a particularly awkward and difficult time (Erikson's *identity versus identity confusion*). Generally believed to be a time when they develop a sense of identity, Kivnick (1991) notes how adolescents' general acceptance of their disability and mastery over their environment dictates the strength of their identity. If adolescents have been unable to master and/or explore their environment, they may theoretically succumb to societal expectations about disability. Other potentially problematic areas during teenage years include body changes like puberty and body image, peer relations, sexuality, and rejection (S. E. Davis, Anderson, Linkowski, Berger, & Feinstein, 1991; Gordon, Tschopp, & Feldman, 2004; Hofman, 1975; Rousso, 1996). Livneh and Antonak (2007) cite the importance of body image on one's self-esteem, and note how persons with disabilities may be particularly vulnerable to poor body image perceptions. Not being viewed as "different" becomes critically important to the psychosocial well-being of adolescents; as the alternative, rejection and ridicule can be devastating to their self-esteem (Bramble, 1995; Connors & Stalker, 2007; S. E. Davis et al., 1991; Gordon et al., 2004; Howland & Rintala, 2001; Rousso, 1996).

Despite what appears to be a number of societal attitude barriers for persons growing up with an acquired or congenital disability, overall reports of happiness, contentment, and life satisfaction are mixed, but generally positive (Albrecht & Devlieger, 1999; Allman, 1990; C. B. Cohen & Napolitano, 2007; Connors & Stalker, 2007; Freedman, 1978; Lucas, 2007; Marinic & Brkljacic, 2008). Connors and Stalker (2007), for example, in interviewing 26 children aged 7 to 15 years found that despite the children citing public reactions of sometimes being stared at, condescended to, harassed, and being pitied, they otherwise reported seeing themselves in a positive way and basically as similar to nondisabled children. However, as Thomasgard (1998) and others have found, parental perceptions and projections of their child's psychosocial well-being is frequently viewed much more negatively than the child views his or her own circumstances (Holmbeck et al., 2002; Trask et al., 2003), sometimes leading to parental guilt.

Marinic and Brkljacic (2008) surveyed 397 persons with varying types of disabilities compared to 913 nondisabled Croatians regarding levels of happiness and well-being. Of the group with disabilities, approximately 22% were either born with their disability or acquired it before the age of 7 years. The authors correlated happiness among both groups with life satisfaction by measuring happiness with the Fordyce scale (1988) and subjective well-being (SWB) using the Personal Wellbeing Index (Cummins, 2006), which measures satisfaction with life domains. The results indicated that both groups showed positive happiness and satisfaction with the majority of life domains; however, happiness levels of persons with disabilities were lower than the control group in several areas. Less than 15% of persons with disabilities rated themselves as "extremely happy" compared to 40% of the nondisabled control group. Overall happiness score means on a 10-point scale, with 10 being extremely happy, showed the disability group ($M = 6.14$) scored slightly lower compared to the control group ($M = 7.8$). In contrast, Myers and Diener (1996) conducted a meta-analysis of 916 research projects from 45 countries with over one million participants, finding that people on average are moderately happy and score a mean of 6.75/10 on the same scale. Participants in the Marinic and Brkljacic (2008) study also scored moderately satisfied regardless of the disability. The disabled group, however, scored significantly different in the areas of happiness and physical safety and community acceptance. The authors opine that safety of the physical environment and positive or negative societal attitudes had an impact on their happiness, whereas this generally is not a consideration for persons without disabilities.

Overall, persons born with a disability are statistically at a greater risk of substance abuse problems, twice as likely to drop out of school, and more likely to be living in poverty than children without disabilities (Helwig & Holicky, 1994; Olkin, 1999). Research indicates that family and community support are critical in the positive psychosocial development of children and adolescents. When family cohesion, stability, and nurturing are dysfunctional, the likelihood increases for children to grow up with greater levels of adjustment problems. In addition, the person–environment interaction has time and again in numerous studies proved to be critical regarding individual self-concept and adaptation to disability. There is, however, what Freedman (1978) describes as the "disability paradox," whereby persons with disabilities who otherwise perceive themselves as having successfully coped with environmental and societal barriers, and believe that they have emerged even stronger than others, generally report a very high quality of life (QOL) and level of happiness (Weinberg, 1988).

THEORIES OF ADJUSTMENT AND ADAPTATION TO ACQUIRED DISABILITIES

A Brief History of Adjustment Theories

This section addresses seven various models of adjustment, adaptation, or reaction to an acquired disability some time later in life. Again, some models have stronger evidence-based empirical support, while others are supported by clinical observation or qualitative self-report methods. As this line of academic study has evolved, some of the earliest theories on adjustment to disability were postulated by Dembo, Leviton, and Wright (1956), and later expanded upon by Wright (1960, 1983). Successful versus unsuccessful adjustment was initially conceptualized within a "coping" versus "succumbing" framework. Essentially, Dembo and colleagues (1956) theorized that successful coping involved assisting clients to recognize what they functionally could do as opposed to dwelling on what they no longer could do, emphasizing personal accomplishments, taking direct control of one's life, successfully negotiating physical and social access barriers, enjoying and expanding on social activities that one enjoys, and appropriately dealing with negative life experiences. Conversely, poor adjustment was described as succumbing to one's disability by dwelling on the past, focusing on one's limitations rather than assets, and passively accepting the disabled role as defined by society (e.g., helpless, pitied, incapable).

Wright (1983) refined her earlier theory by equating adjustment or acceptance to disability by emphasizing the values and beliefs individuals ascribe to their condition. Wright distinguished between successfully reevaluating one's disabling circumstances as opposed to devaluing or denigrating oneself with the onset of a physical disability. She proposed four reevaluation changes that must occur for successful adaptation. Specifically, (a) subordination of physique or placing less self-worth emphasis on one's physical appearance, (b) containing or minimizing the "spread" effect of the disability to other unaffected functions and activities, (c) enlarging one's scope of values and interests consistent with our abilities, and (d) transforming from comparative to asset values. In other words, instead of comparing oneself to those without disabilities, it is better to focus more on the remaining abilities and qualities one can engage in rather than the functions one can no longer engage in. Wright's thinking on adjustment to disability went through a transformation as well. In her 1983 classic, *Physical Disability: A Psychosocial Approach*, Wright affirms the significance of the social environment and interpersonal relationships on adjustment, whereas in her 1960 book titled *Physical Disability: A Psychological Approach*, she focused mostly on the psychodynamics of adjustment and the individual. Although psychologists have been criticized for ignoring the impact of environmental barriers and negative societal attitudes on an individual's adjustment, Wright began to acknowledge this relationship early on.

Stage Models

Livneh (1986, 1991) provides a succinct summary and synthesis of more than 40 explicit and implicit stage models of adjustment, described as a reaction to a sudden and unexpected permanent physically disabling condition. The variations of this model range in theory from three to 10 stages, but most commonly four to six stages. Livneh cites several authors regarding a number of shared assumptions or rules of thumb applicable to these models. Several of the more pertinent assumptions are: (a) adjustment is not a static, but rather a dynamic ongoing process, despite the concept that adaptation is considered to be the final outcome (Kahana, Fairchild, & Kahana, 1982); (b) the initial insult causes a psychological disequilibrium that typically restabilizes over time; (c) most individuals sequentially transition through time-limited stages by coming to terms psychologically with whatever trauma has occurred to them; (d) although most individuals experience most stages, others may not; (e) not everyone transitions through all stages sequentially; some individuals skip stages, some regress backwards to a previous stage, some can become stuck in a stage for long periods, while others may never reach the final adjustment stage (Gunther, 1969, 1971); (f) experiencing different stages separately and sequentially does not always occur, as some individuals may be observed to be in overlapping stages (Dunn, 1975) without any particular timeline, and often fluctuate based on individual circumstances and coping mechanisms; (g) observations at each stage can be correlated with certain cognitions, emotions, and behaviors; and (h) although stages are self-triggered, appropriate behavioral, psychosocial, and environmental interventions (counseling) can positively affect coping strategies to successfully transition toward adaptation (Livneh, 1991, pp. 113–114).

The five stages of adjustment to a sudden onset physical disability postulated by Livneh (1991) are formulated as follows.

Initial Impact

This first stage generally involves individual and often family reaction during the initial hours and days following a sudden and severe bodily trauma such as a spinal cord injury, limb amputation, heart attack, or sudden onset of a life-threatening disease. Two substages are commonly identified: *shock* and *anxiety*. *Shock* is described as a surreal experience in which thought process are disorganized, disoriented, and confused, as many individuals in shock have difficulty concentrating and are unable to make simple decisions (Gunther, 1971; Livneh & Antonak, 1997; Shands, 1955). Thought processes are disorganized, disoriented, and confused, and many individuals have difficulty concentrating and are unable to make simple decisions (Livneh & Antonak, 1997; Shands, 1955). *Anxiety* is described as overwhelming and can trigger a panic attack or hysteria-like behavior in extreme reaction cases. Some empirical support for these two reactions exists in the cross-sectional study by Livneh and Antonak (1991) with 214 rehabilitation facility inpatient and outpatient participants with various conditions including spinal cord injury, cerebrovascular accidents, and multiple sclerosis. Participants distinguished between past and present reactions to their disability, indicating earlier adaptation phases were reported significantly more frequently in the past than present, including shock, anxiety, depression, internalized anger, and externalized hostility.

Defense Mobilization

This stage is characterized by two substages as well: *bargaining* and *denial.* Bargaining is described as a religious or spiritual attempt to negotiate with God or a higher power to be cured with the expectation of full recovery. In essence, the individual (and often the family) pray for survival and/or recovery with a promise to pay penance for any past wrongdoing (Livneh, 1991). In addition, in return for a cure or recovery, individuals may promise to donate to the church, do charitable work, and so forth. Livneh describes bargaining as being short term in nature, whereas denial is seen as lasting longer. Although bargaining and denial are seen as overlapping, denial is viewed as a more "extensive level of suppression or negation of the disability and its ramifications in order to maintain self integrity" (p. 119). Related to this is the extensively studied and debated coping dimensions of problem- versus emotion-focused coping (Carver, Scheier, & Weintraub, 1989; Folkman & Moskowitz, 2004).

Problem-focused coping is described as a more task-oriented, constructive, and positive way of dealing with stressful events whereby an individual recognizes the problem, thinks of strategies to solve it, weighs the pros and cons of the decision, decides, and implements the chosen strategy (Cheng, Kuan, Li, & Ken, 2010; Endler & Parker, 1990). *Emotion-focused coping* is described as a coping strategy to minimize or reduce the negative emotions associated with the stressor by denying, avoiding, or engaging in distracting activities (Folkman & Lazarus, 1980, 1985). The debate has centered around which coping strategy is more appropriate for alleviating an individual's distress. Typically, problem-focused coping has received greater support; however, emotion-focused coping appears best in instances where an individual experiences some emotionally overwhelming and extreme trauma for which he or she has little control over, and the problem cannot be solved. More recently, researchers suggested that both coping domains cannot be clearly distinguished from one another, and may overlap and represent variations of one another (Endler & Parker, 1990; Folkman & Moskowitz, 2004). Cheng and colleagues (2010) in their study of 180 undergraduate students regarding problem- and emotion-focused coping strategies defined *certainty emotions* (such as anger, disgust, happiness, and contentment) as eliciting problem-focused coping because they perceived being in control of the situation. "Uncertainty emotions" (hope, surprise, worry, fear, and sadness) most often that elicited emotion-focused coping when the event was perceived as uncontrollable. These findings were originally supported by Folkman and Lazarus (1980) and have since been affirmed by Nabi (2003) and C. A. Smith and Ellsworth (1985).

Denial is the other major substage cited during this period (Livneh, 1991; Livneh & Antonak, 1997). Denial is a defense mechanism to protect the self from overwhelming fear and sadness by optimistically hoping things will get better and temporarily escaping the immense emotional sadness and fear of the unknown. Smart (2009) notes that denial can take three forms: denying the presence of the disability, denying the implications of the disability, or denying the permanency of the disability (p. 393). Livneh (1991) cites additional cognitions, behaviors, and emotions during this stage including distorting facts and selective attention to good news, repressing unacceptable realities, constantly seeking information, setting unrealistic goals, having unrealistic expectations, refusing to modify the home or talk to persons with similar disabilities, and evading future planning with the belief that it will not be necessary (Dunn, 1975; Falek & Britton, 1974; Gunther, 1971; Naugle, 1991). Ironically, persons in denial have been observed with a range of emotions including cheerfulness and happiness at one end as they unrealistically hope for recovery (Parker, 1979), to despair and anger during moments of realizing the permanency of their disability (Weller & Miller, 1977). Meyerowitz (1980), however, noted that denial can be adaptive as well, protecting the individual from overwhelming life-altering news. As Livneh and Antonak (1997) cite, denial continues to be debated by researchers regarding its relative value or hindrance in adjusting to a disability. Specifically, Livneh and Antonak (1997) cite denial in the literature as either a stage or phase of adaptation in dealing with traumatic loss, or a defense mechanism that protects our ego to minimize or escape overwhelming anxiety. In this latter instance, denial is part of an emotion-focused response, which has arguably been viewed as temporarily helpful soon after injury, especially where the circumstances cannot be controlled (Meyerowitz, 1980). Theoretically, and for practical application purposes, should counselors confront patients and their family regarding the seriousness and/or grim permanency of the disability; or, should these individuals be allowed to "hope?" This is debatable. The practical application may indeed be to assist individuals by never taking their hope away, but to encourage them to continue with their rehabilitation program, therapy program, and so forth, in the event that the disability may be with them for a while. This tangible compromise could then be viewed as "healthy denial," where the individual and his or her family continue to move forward, while not being denied their hope that a miracle or medical advances may exist in the near or distant future (I. Marini, personal communication, September 14, 2009).

Initial Realization

The third stage is again also characterized by two major substages: *mourning and depression*, and *internalized anger*. Mourning or grief is typically of shorter duration where the individual grieves the loss of body function and past way of life. Depression is generally longer and future oriented, where cognitions involve fear of an often uncertain and perceived grim future. Suicidal ideation is sometimes present during this stage, as well as asking "Why me?" of God or a higher power (Kübler-Ross, 1981). The theory of mourning and depression has encountered some debate among researchers as to whether all individuals actually go through a diagnosable clinical depression, and whether going through a depression is mandatory to move on to acceptance (Trieschmann, 1988). Wortman and Silver (1989) reviewed the existing empirical evidence regarding bereavement following a physical disability, and found that not all individuals report experiencing a depression. Recently, Maciejewski, Zhang, Block, and Prigerson's (2007) grief study with 233 individuals who had suffered the death of a loved one from natural causes found participants mouned the loss of a loved one more so than they reported becoming depressed. The temporal sequence reported by grieving loved ones included disbelief that peaked at 1 month, yearning at 4 months, anger at 5 months, and a depression plateau at about 6 months post-loss. Acceptance of the loss was observed to gradually occur as time went on over a 24-month observation period. Livneh (1991) and Livneh and Antonak (1997) cite common reactive depression observations during this stage as including feelings of hopelessness, despair, anxiety, intense sadness, withdrawal, and despondency as well.

Alternatively, Worden's (2009) task of mourning concept identifies four tasks that mourners can actively work through to adapt to their loss. The first task involves accepting the reality that the loved one has died and will not return. Some mourners see their loved one in a crowd, deny he or she is dead, keep the person's possessions ready for him or her to return, and so on. The second task Worden identifies is the process of experiencing the emotional and behavioral pain. Some mourners repress painful emotions and do not allow themselves to feel the pain. Burying or avoiding such emotions can eventually lead to clinical depression. The third task involves adjusting to a world without the loved one. External adjustments include taking on the activites (e.g., paying bills, shopping, house chores) the loved one performed, while internal adjustments involve being an independent person from your loved one, concerning self-esteem, self-identity, and the like. Spiritual adjustments during this task involve making sense of the world and testing one's faith and beliefs as to why this happened. The final task is that of maintaining an enduring, healthy connection with the deceased loved one while moving on with a new life. Worden indicates that these tasks are not fixed stages, and can be experienced and worked on simultaneously because grieving is a fluid and not a static process.

Smart (2009) differentiated between how the individual mourns and/or possibly becomes depressed following a disabling injury, and the societal expectation "requirement to mourn" as hypothesized by Wright (1983). It is expected that persons with a disability should feel bad and constantly grieve their loss indefinitely because it is the presumed normal response to one's misfortune. This societal belief that an individual must mourn and continually grieve his or her loss is a common misconception, but a projected value judgment by others nonetheless regarding how they think they would feel if they became disabled. Despite studies showing that most persons with a traumatic onset disability gradually adjust to their situation over time, the societal requirement to mourn continues to be perpetuated (Livneh & Antonak, 1991; Marini, Rogers, Slate, & Vines, 1995; Silver, 1982; Wright, 1983).

Internalized anger essentially involves self-blame, guilt, and shame. The individual blames himself or herself and often views the disability as a punishment from God for some alleged wrongdoing (Hohmann, 1975; Marini & Graf, 2011). This self-blame can be amplified if the individual was indeed the cause of his or her injuries (e.g., drunk driving), which can make adjustment much more difficult (Livneh & Antonak, 1997). Suicidal ideation, risk-taking, and self-injurious behavior can occur at this stage as well. Janoff-Bulman (1979) differentiated between behavioral and characterological self-blame attributions and their perceived impact on adjustment. Behavioral self-blame refers to individuals who believe their behavior caused their injury; in such cases, individuals can adjust more readily knowing that they were, and are, in control of events. Conversely, characterological self-blame refers to individuals who attribute blame to a flaw in their character or personality, and hence believe their fate was unavoidable and deserving. Overall, research is mixed regarding self-blame attributions of disability, with some finding a positive relationship between coping and self-blame attributions (Janoff-Bulman, 1979) and others a negative relationship where individuals with a spinal cord injury were perceived as coping less well (L. Bordieri, Comninel, & Drehmer, 1989; Westbrook & Nordholm, 1986). J. E. Bordieri and Kilbury (1991) surveyed 84 rehabilitation counseling graduates using observer simulation regarding self-blame attributions. They found that characterological self-blamers were rated as coping less well, being more depressed, and having perceived less control of future life events than individuals who attributed blame to behavior.

Retaliation

In Livneh's (1991) conceptualization of the five-stage model of adjustment, retaliation is the fourth stand-alone stage with no substages. In their 1997 description of this concept, Livneh and Antonak refer to retaliation as externalized hostility. This stage essentially involves "rebelling against a perceived dependency fate . . . anger is now projected onto the external world in the form of hostility toward other people, objects, or environmental conditions" (Livneh, 1991, p. 124). During this stage, individuals may blame and lash out at perceived incompetent medical professionals for not doing enough, and/or significant others for no apparent reason because of frustration and anger. Behaviorally, individuals may become noncompliant with hospital rules, use profanity, make accusations, attempt to manipulate hospital staff and significant others, or physically strike others (Livneh & Antonak, 1997). Smart (2009) notes how some individuals may initially be angry with God about being unfairly punished. Marini and Graf (2011) surveyed 157 persons with spinal cord injury regarding their spiritual or religious beliefs and practices, and found that whereas some respondents were initially angry with God postinjury, this tended to subside over time in the majority of, but not all, cases.

Final Adjustment or Reintegration

This final stage delineates a cognitive, affective, and behavioral component. Livneh and Antonak (1997) note how acknowledgment is a cognitive reconciliation or acceptance of the disability and its permanency. A new disability self-concept is formed, and individuals seek to master their environment by problem solving. Persons who reach this stage are able to "accept him or herself as a person with a disability gain a new sense of self-concept, reappraise life values, and seek new meanings and goals" (p. 22). Emotionally, individuals are "okay" with their disability, and can talk about it without becoming upset. Behaviorally, persons in this stage begin to actively pursue social, academic, and/or vocational goals, and learn to successfully navigate physical and social environmental barriers. Livneh and Antonak (1991) found correlational support for acceptance among 214 rehabilitation patients during the temporal later phase of disability onset. Similarly, Marini et al. (1995) surveyed 63 persons with spinal cord injury during their first, second, or fifth year postinjury, finding that self-esteem increased over time as respondents became more comfortable and confident with their disability status.

Despite all the caveats to the stage model of adjustment, a number of criticisms have been cited (Kendall & Buys, 1998; Olkin, 1999; Parker et al., 2003). Some concerns relate to the dangers of counselors expecting and anticipating persons with a sudden onset of physical disabilities to go through specific stages (Kendall & Buys, 1998). Others cite the complexity of human behavior and the attempt to fit everyone through these stages when there are so many complex individual differences regarding people's coping mechanisms, environmental factors, and extenuating circumstances (Parker et al., 2003). Relatedly, some researchers argue that there exists little empirical support for the stage model of adjustment (Chan, Da Silva Cardoso, & Chronister, 2009; Olkin, 1999).

Although many injured persons have been found to progress from initially experiencing higher to lower levels of distress over time, others do not show any signs of intense distress, and some remain in a heightened level of distress for longer periods (Wortman & Silver, 1989). As discussed later with the recurrent model, some researchers argue that persons with physical disabilities do grieve the loss of bodily function and preinjury lifestyle, and that the permanency of the loss leads to recurrent and unpredictable periods of chronic sorrow (Burke, Hainsworth, Eakes, & Lindgren, 1992; B. H. Davis, 1987; Kendall & Buys, 1998; Teel, 1991).

Somatopsychology

As briefly introduced in Chapter 4, field theory postulated by Kurt Lewin (1935, 1936) centers around the belief that our self-concept or self-worth can, and is, affected by the feedback we perceive from interacting with others in our environment, referred to as our "life space." Although Lewin's original theory did not include the impact a disability has on this reciprocal interaction, researchers since then have refined the hypothesis to include the impact of disability (Barker, Wright, Meyerson, & Gonick, 1953; Dembo et al., 1956; Trieschmann, 1988; Wright, 1960, 1983). The revised theory has been encompassed as follows: *Behavior* (B) is a function (*f*) of *Psychosocial* variables such as self-esteem and coping skills (P), *Organic* factors related to the disability such as paralysis or blindness (O), and *Environmental* or physical access and attitudinal factors (E), comprising the formula $B = f(P \times O \times E)$ summarized by Trieschmann (1988). Lewin's somatopsychology theory was the first to take a more social psychological view of human behavior as opposed to focusing exclusively on individual behavior in isolation.

Specific to this theory, then, arises the central question: "How do persons with disabilities perceive themselves in Western society's mirror?" A synopsis of historical attitudes in general would suggest many persons with disabilities have been stigmatized, discriminated against, persecuted, devalued, dehumanized, and essentially treated as minorities (Chubon, 1994; Mackelprang & Salsgiver, 2009; Olkin, 1999; Smart, 2009). Arguably, for individuals who possess a more *internal locus of control*, many of these negative experiences would potentially not have as demoralizing an emotional effect as for persons who have a more *external locus of control* (Elfstrom & Kreuter, 2006; Frank & Elliott, 1989). Past research indicates that the link between locus of control and emotional well-being is mediated by coping strategies (Elfstrom & Kreuter, 2006; Frank & Elliott, 1989). These authors found that persons with spinal cord injuries who perceived that they were more in control of their life circumstances (internal locus) possessed greater levels of acceptance and emotional well-being than the group who believed their destiny was not in their hands (external locus). As Maltby, Day, and Macaskill (2007) note regarding clinical depression and various illnesses and disabilities, persons who are internally located tend to attribute their self-worth to their own efforts and internal evaluation, whereas persons who are externally located are more likely to evaluate their self-worth based on how others respond to them and believe their circumstances are controlled more by environmental influences and not themselves. Wright (1983) would otherwise view those externally located individuals who regularly experience discriminating and demoralizing attitudes of others as more susceptible to "succumbing" to the societal limitations imposed by society, thereby adjusting less well.

Some of the empirical support for this theory centers around assessing the attitudes of persons with disabilities in relation to their lived experience in the community. Li and Moore (1998) surveyed 1,266 adults with disabilities in relation to their experiences in the community. Aside from emotional support from friends and family playing a significant role in adjustment, perceived societal discrimination had a negative impact on accepting one's disability. DiTomasso and Spinner (1997) additionally found their respondents with disabilities reported greater levels of loneliness when confronted by the negative attitudes of others. Similarly, Hopps et al.'s (2001) sample of 39 adults with physical disabilities showed a high correlation between feelings of loneliness, social anxiety, and poorer social skills that they attributed to poor physical access in their community. Finally, in the qualitative survey by Graf, Marini, and Blankenship (2009) of 78 persons with spinal cord dysfunction who were asked to compose in 100 words or less what experience(s) best exemplified their living with a disability, most frequently reported anger and frustration from encountering physical access barriers in the community. Clearly, repeated negative experiences with others in society can, over time, impact how well someone adjusts to his or her disability.

Disability Centrality Model

The most recent adaptation model to CID has shown to have great promise theoretically, empirically, and with tangible clinical implications (Bishop, 2005). Drawing upon Devins's illness intrusiveness approach (Devins et al., 1983; Devins, 1994), Livneh's (2001) conceptual framework, and the value change concepts of Dembo et al. (1956) and Wright (1960, 1983), Bishop proposes the DCM. He (2005) describes six tenets as the theoretical underpinnings for DCM that factor in subjective and objective QOL satisfaction and control over one's medical and environmental circumstances. These are summarized as follows: (a) The impact of a CID can be measured by a multidimensional subjective QOL measure; (b) QOL is an individual's overall perceived subjective satisfaction of life domains that are disproportional because of individual differences regarding which domains are more important (central) to us; (c) the onset of a CID results in an initial reduction in overall QOL and centrally important satisfying activities, as well as feelings of personal control; (d) the degree of QOL reduced is dependent on how many central domains are affected; (e) individuals seek to maintain and maximize overall QOL by minimizing gaps (distress) caused by the CID; and (f) people strive to close these gaps by either changing their values and interests commensurate with their disabled abilities, employ strategies to increase perceived control over their health and environment, or alternatively do nothing to improve control or change their values (p. 223; Bishop & Feist-Price, 2002; Devins et al., 1983).

Bishop (2005) incorporates the concept of domain satisfaction and importance described by Devins and colleagues (1983) and others (Frisch, 1999; Pavot & Diener, 1993) regarding the relative significance various QOL domains may have for each individual. For example, a construction worker with a grade 9 education who sustains a tetraplegia and has derived great satisfaction from work and playing sports preinjury likely experiences a poorer adjustment if he or she can no longer engage in either domain. In contrast, a professor with the same injury is likely able to retain employment and try to compensate (develop new interests) for being unable to play sports. In both instances, the former individual would likely experience a greater reduction in satisfaction and perceived control than the professor, and hence a greater reduction in overall QOL (Frisch, 1999). Although Bishop (2005) concedes there is never a universal agreement on what all the QOL life domains should include, there has been an increased agreement over the years on certain domains, including physical and mental health, social support, employment, or a satisfying or avocational activity and economic or material well-being (Bishop & Allen, 2003; Jalowiec, 1990). Cummins (2002) differentiated between objective and subjective QOL domains. Objective indicators include more tangible domains such as employment, wage earnings, marital status, and so forth, whereas a more subjective assessment of one's QOL includes what Roessler (1990) describes as an individual's private assessment or feeling about his or her life situation. As Cummins (2005) has noted, however, there is a weak relationship between objective and subjective measures of QOL. In other words, people can have what others may think is a great job, income, marriage, and so forth, and yet those that seem to have it all score poorly on life satisfaction, subjective well-being and happiness (Dijkers, 1997; Myers & Diener, 1995).

In addition, incorporating Devins's illness intrusiveness model (Devins et al., 1983; Devins & Shnek, 2000) proposes that when individuals sustain a CID, the impact compromises psychological well-being by temporarily or permanently reducing positive or meaningful activities, as well as reducing real or perceived control to regain the positive activities or outcomes and avoid negative ones. The central question then becomes whether individuals can compensate for lost interests that once brought them enjoyment, but they can no longer engage in? With Bishop's DCM, the counselor must be able to assess what the "central" or most important life satisfaction domains are for clients, and how these can be compensated for or replaced (Groot & Van Den Brink, 2000; Misajon, 2002). This concept is similar to Wright's (1960, 1983) "value change" theory, whereby individuals who perceive a loss in one area of their lives attempt to develop new interests within their capabilities (i.e., transitioning from enjoying jogging to reading for persons with a mobility impairment). This has also been termed as "preference drift" (Groot & Van Den Brink, 2000) and "response shift" by Schwartz and Sprangers (2000).

Empirical support for DCM is building. Bishop (2005) assessed 72 college students with disabilities using the *Delighted–Terrible Scale* (Andrews & Withey, 1976), the *Ladder of Adjustment* scale (Crewe & Krause, 1990), and what Bishop (2005) describes as the *Domain Scale*, which assessed 10 domains like the QOL. Overall, the results indicated a positive correlation between QOL and psychosocial adaptation to CID. A second correlation was found between satisfaction and perceived control in relation to the impact of CID and QOL. Bishop describes counseling interventions that empower clients to assert more control over their circumstances, developing new interests or response shift, and working through the loss of satisfying activities no longer accessible.

Bishop, Shepard, and Stenhoff (2007) conducted a follow-up DCM study with 98 persons with multiple sclerosis. In this study, Bishop et al. (2007) discuss subjective quality of life (SQOL) or subjective well-being relating to the previously described QOL domains (Johnson, Amtmann, Yorkston, Klasner, & Kuehn, 2004) and psychosocial adaptation. The assessments used were the *Delighted–Terrible Scale, Ladder of Adjustment,* and the *Disability Centrality Scale* (DCS; Bishop & Allen, 2003), the latter of which measures 10 life domains, including physical health, mental health (emotional well-being, happiness, enjoyment), work/studies, leisure activities, financial situation, relationship with significant other, family relations, other social relations, autonomy/independence, and religious or spiritual expression (p. 7). Results indicated a positive correlation between scores on the self-management scale and both perceived control and QOL. The second positive correlation was found between scores on the Ladder of Adjustment scale and overall QOL satisfaction across domains. Bishop et al. (2007) again cite similar tangible counselor intervention strategies that involve assisting clients in developing new interests and asserting more control over their situation. Livneh and Antonak (1997) view the DCM as an ecological model; however, it is treated separately here because of its emphasis on perceived control and satisfaction of life domains.

Ecological Models

Chan et al. (2009) make the observation that even within the ecological models of adjustment to disability, there is overlap representing the stage or phase theory of adjustment including early reactions of shock, anxiety, and denial; intermediate reactions of depression, internalized anger, and externalized anger; and later reactions involving acknowledgment, acceptance, and adjustment (p. 58). As we conclude later, all of these proposed theories have overlapping and similar concepts.

Two theorists who summarize the complexity of ecological models best are arguably Trieschmann (1988) and Vash and Crewe (2004). These models involve a foundation of three major determining factors that consider: (a) nature of the disability, (b) characteristics of the person, and (c) environmental influences. Within each of these determining factors are subsets that require exploration by the counselor to assess what, if any, bearing each of these factors have on psychosocial adjustment. It is important to note that none of these factors may negatively influence poor adjustment; conversely, any one of these factors, in and of themselves, if deemed important by the individual, may delay or prolong adjustment. A brief summary of each is provided.

Nature of the Disability

This factor explores aspects of the disability itself and the implications of each. The first subfactor considers the *time of onset* regarding whether an individual was born with a disability or acquires it sometime later in life. Vash and Crewe (2004) discuss some potential implications for someone who is born with a disability, including being treated as an infinite child, isolated and overprotected, unable to engage in many childhood activities, and as (Olkin, 1999) describes, sometimes subjected to a "conspiracy of silence" where parents do not discuss their child's prognosis or treatment with him or her at the risk of upsetting their child. Conversely, as we explore in detail regarding the psychosocial aspects of an acquired disability, one can succumb to a whole host of other adjustment issues (Kendall & Buys, 1998; Livneh, 1991). The next subfactor, *type of onset,* concerns whether or not the disability had a sudden impact (spinal cord injury from a car accident) versus a prolonged onset (more gradual such as multiple sclerosis), and the implications of each. In the case of a sudden onset, perceived attribution of blame becomes a factor that influences adjustment. Specifically, research is mixed regarding the implications of self-induced versus other-induced attribution of blame on adjustment. Although findings indicate those who accept the responsibility of their injury may possess a more internal locus of control and therefore may adjust better, they may also be more self-critical and angry at the fact that they could have possibly prevented their accident (Athelstan & Crewe, 1979; Bulman & Wortman, 1977; Reidy & Caplan, 1994). *Functions impaired* address the relative importance each of us place on our functional abilities. For example, some individuals are most terrified to lose their sight, while others fear becoming paralyzed or losing their hearing the most. Related to this factor is the significance these abilities play in our lives. An academic whose livelihood and intrinsic interests revolve around reading may be devastated by vision loss. Wright (1983), however, reminds us of the "insider" perspective, whereby those persons who have lived and adapted to their disability emphatically disagree that it is the worst thing (bodily function) they could lose. Unfortunately, many lay public mostly perceive any disability as a tragedy, and one that they are not certain they could live with (Olkin, 1999). *Severity of the disability* essentially considers how severe the disability is, with the once assumed belief that those with more severe disabilities were likely more maladjusted (Livneh & Antonak, 1991). Although some literature finds that this may indeed be the case, it is more commonly believed now that the severity of a disability has little or no impact on how someone adjusts (Livneh & Antonak, 1997; Wallander & Varni, 1998). *Visibility of the disability* considers the reactions individuals with visible disabilities sometimes experience (wheelchair users) such as discrimination, devaluation, and being ignored (Graf et al., 2009; Marini, Bhakta, & Graf, 2009). Conversely, consider the plight of those with invisible disabilities unknown to the public (low back injuries) who may be thought of as lazy or unmotivated if unable to participate in certain activities, such as not wanting to find a job owing to ongoing chronic pain. *Stability of the disability* addresses whether the disability is stable and generally will not become worse (spinal cord injury) versus those that have an uncertain prognosis, but become progressively worse over time (Parkinson's disease; Cheng et al., 2010; Elfstrom & Kreuter, 2006; Folkman & Lazarus, 1980; Frank & Elliott, 1989). The uncertainty of waking up each morning not knowing whether one is still able to walk or see not only leaves an individual with no control over his or her situation, but also compromises making any future plans. Finally, the concept of *pain* deserves a category unto itself in addressing psychosocial adjustment. As Vash and Crewe (2004) emphasized, unlike many of the other disabilities, chronic pain is a primary or secondary debilitating condition that can have a significant negative impact on an individual's thoughts, emotions, and behaviors. Cognitively, individuals can exhibit poor concentration and attention, suicidal ideation, and reduced problem-solving abilities. Emotions often include depression, feelings of hopelessness and helplessness, and despair (Banks & Kerns, 1996; Fishbain, Cutler, Rosomoff, & Rosomoff, 1997). Behaviors have been defined as social isolation, withdrawal from activities, and, in worst case scenarios, addicted to pain prescription medications, substances, and drug abuse (Lewinsohn, Clarke, & Hops, 1990; Waters, Campbell, Keefe, & Carson, 2004).

Personal Characteristics

These determining factors involve individualized traits or characteristics. *Gender* largely considers gender differences in coping with disability, as well as societal expectations of males and females (Hwang, 1997; Livneh, 1991; Marini, 2007; Tepper, 1997). There are mixed findings regarding which gender adjusts to a disability better; however, Western societal expectations of each gender are quite clear (Charmaz, 1995; Hwang, 1997). Males are supposed to be rugged, independent, breadwinners, stoic, athletic, dominant, and tough (Charmaz, 1995; Marini, 2007; Zilbergeld, 1992), whereas women are expected to be beautiful in physical appearance, passive, homemakers, and good nurturers (Hwang, 1997). Males and females with severe disabilities may not be able to live up to some or any of these expectations, and may have difficulty adjusting if they rely on external cues (societal expectations) for affirmation of their self-concept/self-esteem (Charmez, 1995; Marini, 2007; Nosek & Hughes, 2007). *Activities affected* relates to the significance individuals place on their activities. A hockey player who becomes paralyzed and is no longer able to play sports may experience greater difficulty adjusting than a professor who has the same injury, but can still perform academic activities. Similarly, *interests/ values/goals* pertain to the differing passions people have in their lives. Those who proverbially "put all their eggs in one basket" or have few if any interests and lose the ability to engage in them likely find adjustment more stressful than those persons who have multiple interests and are still able to return to some of them (Massimini & Delle Fave, 2000; Schafer, 1996). Lewinsohn et al. (1990) indicates that when people experience a loss and withdraw from engaging in what were once pleasurable activities, there is a greater likelihood of lengthening or exacerbating a reactive depression. *Remaining resources* are described by Vash and Crewe (2004) as the abilities and traits an individual retains regardless of his or her disability. These include intelligence, motivation, sense of humor, extroversion, social poise, resilience, emotional stability, and coping strategies, all of which have been implicated in positive adjustment (see Livneh, 1991). Finally, *spiritual and philosophical base* refer to one's spiritual or religious beliefs, particularly as to whether some people believe their disability is a punishment from God or higher power, with the assumption that those who believe they are being punished have a more difficult time adjusting (Byrd, 1990; Gallagher, 1995; Graf, Marini, Baker, & Buck, 2007). Conversely, individuals who believe their disability to be a divine intervention or calling for them to serve a higher purpose for God experience lesser adjustment difficulties (Eareckson, 2001, Graf et al., 2007).

Environmental Influences

As extensively detailed earlier, environmental influences may have a significant impact on adaptation to disability (DiTomasso & Spinner, 1997; Graf et al., 2009; Hopps, Pepin, Arseneau, Frechette, & Begin, 2001; Lewin, 1936; Li & Moore, 1998; Wright, 1983). In this determining factor, Vash and Crewe (2004) as well as Trieschmann (1988) describe several contributing factors. *Family acceptance and support* becomes significant in that if a disabled loved one is viewed as a contributing family member and not devalued, this generally correlates with a more positive adjustment to the disability (Li & Moore, 1998). In addition, those families that have been shown to possess positive coping strategies and support one another typically adapt well to the disability (Trask et al., 2003). *Income* plays an important role not so much as in overall happiness, but rather in overall QOL (Diener & Seligman, 2004; Inglehart, 1990; Lykken, 1999). Once people have their basic needs met, there is relatively little difference in happiness ratings between those who are extremely wealthy and those of more modest means (Diener & Seligman, 2004); however, a higher income and adequate health care positively impact one's ability to remain healthy, as well as purchase necessary accommodations and equipment/devices (modified van, accessible home) for a better QOL. *Available community resources* refers to support from local agencies, which could include Centers for Independent Living (CILs), Veterans Affairs services, Client Assistance Programs (CAPs), access to modernized hospitals, and so forth. Individuals with severe disabilities who live in rural settings with no resources may not only have to travel long distances for appointments, but also be required to be away from home and family at times if having to remain in the city for several days (A. J. Smith, Thorngren, & Christopher, 2009). *Social support* is also critical for positive adjustment and fostering self-esteem in most, but not all, instances (Buunk & Verhoeven, 1991; Li & Moore, 1998). Schwarzer and Leppin (1992) define functional support by differentiating between instrumental support (offering financial aid), informational support (giving information and advice), and emotional support (caring, empathy, and reassurance). Functional support is further delineated by individuals' perceptions of the support they received (retrospective evaluation) and the perception of available support if needed (anticipation of getting the support) (Lakey & Cassady, 1990; Symister & Friend, 2003). Much like Yuker's (1988) extensive review of the impact of contact regarding positive and negative attitudes toward disability, empirical findings are somewhat mixed regarding the benefits of social support (Barrera, 1981; S. Cohen, 2004; Heller & Rook, 2001; Hupcey, 1998; Lazarus & Folkman, 1984a; Li & Moore, 1998). On the positive side, social support is believed to be a buffer against stress, an appropriate coping strategy, and regulates negative emotions (S. Cohen, Gottlieb, & Underwood, 2000). For example, persons who sustain a severe disability may have friends who give or loan them money, help them in finding community resources, and provide emotional support by empathizing and genuinely listening to their concerns. Conversely, having a social support system made up of people who are themselves dysfunctional, have promised to help but always have excuses, or in the worst case scenario take advantage of the person with the disability by neglecting, abusing, or stealing from him or her are all clear examples of a potentially poorer adjustment process for the disabled individual. Finally, *institutionalization* becomes a concern for those persons with severe disabilities who are unable to physically take care of themselves, do not have the funding to hire an attendant, or have no family or friends who can perform a caregiving function. In such cases, individuals are faced with temporarily or permanently having to reside in a nursing home. Aside from most Americans not wanting to live in a nursing home, the U.S. General Accounting Office (2002) published a study indicating an approximate 25% abuse rate, which either resulted in death or serious injury of nursing home residents nationwide. The forms of abuse include neglect, physical abuse, sexual abuse, and malnourishment. Clearly, individuals who have no choice but to live in a nursing home may, in the worst-case scenario, be subjected to such abuse, or minimally deprived of the freedom to control their environment and thus experience a resulting reduction in QOL (Bishop, 2005). In a best case scenario of well-run nursing homes, persons with severe disabilities may be medically well cared for as well as having a resident support network that residents would not otherwise have living alone.

Recurrent or Integrated Model of Adjustment

The recurrent or integrated model of adjustment following an acquired disability was essentially hypothesized owing to perceived shortcomings of the stage or linear model of disability (B. H. Davis, 1987; Wikler, Wasow, & Hatfield, 1981; Wortman & Silver, 1989). One of the several criticisms of the stage model was its theoretical emphasis likening the stages of grief over a deceased loved one (Kübler-Ross, 1981) to that of acquiring a disability. The main argument is that persons with acquired disabilities continue to live with their disability everyday; therefore, although the emotional upheaval subsides over time, those with acquired disabilities continue to periodically experience chronic sorrow throughout their lives. In this sense, there is never a final adjustment or adaptation stage where the disability no longer affects the individual (B. H. Davis, 1987; Kendall & Buys, 1998; Wortman & Silver, 1989).

Pertinent to this model are several key concepts. Beck's (1967) cognitive theory defines *cognitive schema* as our ingrained beliefs and assumptions regarding ourselves, others, and how the environment works (Beck & Weishaar, 1989). When a sudden and traumatic disability occurs, many individuals attempt to cling on to the comfortable, old schemas because of an overwhelming anxiety and uncertainty that the disability brings. Wright (1983) refers to this as "as if" behavior, whereby individuals attempt to minimize anxiety by denying or distorting reality and pretending as if nothing (the disability) has happened. As the old schema no longer adequately works and the individual begins to realize the implications of the disability, depression may set in (Kendall & Buys, 1998). Yoshida (1993) uses the analogy of a wildly swinging pendulum to describe the initial injury phase of anxiety, fear, and grief. Over time, however, the pendulum gradually slows to a middle set point where individuals either develop a new positive or negative schema of life with a disability (Yoshida, 1993). Positive new schema are formed when individuals with traumatic disabilities can (a) search and find meaning in the disability and in post-disability life; (b) learn to master or control their environment, the disability, and their future; and (c) protect and enhance the self by incorporating the new disability identity (Barnard, 1990; Kendall & Buys, 1998, p. 17). Conversely, negative schema can also be formed about the disability, allowing stereotypical societal expectations about disability (helpless, incapable) to influence one's self-worth (Charmaz, 1983; Stewart, 1996). Wright (1983) would describe those who develop negative schema as otherwise having succumbed to their disability.

Undoubtedly, individuals with acquired disabilities who develop a more negative schema postinjury, in all likelihood, are more susceptible to self-pity, low self-esteem, and likely more frequent episodes of chronic sorrow. Regardless, according to the theory of recurrent periods of sadness, even individuals who have developed positive schema and have otherwise been successful in their lives still experience sorrow or sadness from time to time (Kendall & Buys, 1998). As some research has shown, it is quite likely that these periods of sorrow may be facilitated from environmental influences such as a relationship rejection, job rejection, or discrimination perceived by the individual because of his or her disability (Graf et al., 2009; Li & Moore, 1998; Marini et al., 2009). Overall, response to the disability varies for everyone depending on one's coping mechanisms (Lazarus, 1993; Lazarus & Folkman, 1984b).

Transactional Model of Coping

The most frequently cited and empirically supported theory of coping with stressful events is that of Lazarus and Folkman's transactional theory (1984a, 1984b). The authors define coping as "constantly changing cognitive and behavioral alternatives to manage specific external and/or internal demands that are appraised as taxing or exceeding the resources of the person" (1984a, p. 141). These appraisal efforts are constantly changing as the individual interacts with his or her environment back and forth like watching a tennis match. Central to transactional theory are two major components of a sequential appraisal process salient to when people encounter a stress-inducing event. The first component, referred to as *primary appraisal,* is an individual's assessment as to whether a situation is stressful or not. Key to this appraisal is the motivational strength attributed to various personal goals (goal relevance) the stressor may pose, otherwise called goal congruence or incongruence. Individuals assess whether the stressful event is deemed beneficial or harmful/threatening to the goal, specifically in the case of disability. Will the goal of maintaining optimal health be compromised by the stressful event? If not, no coping mechanisms are required and the individual returns to a state of emotional equilibrium. If, however, the situation is deemed as harmful or threatening, the individual moves into the *secondary appraisal* component. At this level, individuals assess their options for coping and expectations about what will happen (Lazarus, 1993). The three subcomponents involved are (a) blame or who the event is attributable to; (b) coping potential as to whether the individual has any control to change the circumstances of the event and whether he or she can influence the person–environment relationship; and (c) future expectations regarding perceptions as to how the situation plays out. At both levels of appraisal, Lazarus and Folkman (1984a) discuss problem- versus emotion-focused coping strategies defined earlier. The authors suggest that emotion focused coping is more likely when individuals perceive they have no control over the situation, and that the stressful event (e.g., disability) is indeed harmful or threatening to achieving or blocking one's goals. Positive-focused coping has previously been shown to be more effective in the long run as far as adaptive coping strategies, particularly in situations where individuals can insert some control over their situation to minimize or eliminate the stressor (Carver et al., 1989; Cheng et al., 2010; Folkman & Lazarus, 1991; Folkman & Moskowitz, 2004; Groomes & Leahy, 2002; Nilsson, 2002; Provencher, 2007).

Overall, the transactional model of coping has excellent application in understanding how persons with CID react and cope with a catastrophic injury resulting in significant functional loss and reduction in critical QOL domains (Bishop, 2005). In many such injuries, most individuals indeed do not have control over the situation, have initially little or no control over their health status, and, in the case of permanently disabling injuries such as a spinal cord injury or traumatic brain injury, are unable to perceive a positive future. Similarly, in cases where parents learn that their child is born with cerebral palsy, muscular dystrophy, or some other disabling condition, they too are likely to experience very similar emotions, cognitions, and behaviors as those with the disability (e.g., shock, anxiety, denial, anger, acceptance) (Livneh & Antonak, 2005).

Chaos Theory of Adjustment

Chaos and complexity theory (CCT) of adjustment is essentially the human application response of a phenomenon originally hypothesized from the disciplines of mathematics, meteorology, engineering, physics, biology, geography, astronomy, and chemistry (Livneh & Parker, 2005, p. 19). Its origination appears to lie with mathematician and meteorologist Edward Lorenz back in the 1960s, when he famously coined the term *butterfly effect*, essentially explaining how a butterfly flapping its wings in Brazil could ultimately end up causing a tornado in Texas a month later (Gleick, 1987). This theory, in addition to Rene Thom's (1975) multidimensional and nonlinear catastrophe theory, forms the basis for its eventual application to human behavior.

An intriguing major concept about CCT is that, despite its complexity and initial perceptions of random, unorganized sets of behavior, there is indeed an ordered and deterministic set of rules (Chamberlain, 1998). Several concepts must first be understood and are briefly defined here. *Nonlinearity* is often referred to as "sensitive dependence on initial conditions" (Butz, 1997). Nonlinear behavior is described as a nonrepetitive, unpredictable, aperiodic, and unstable phase that experiences critical junctions of instability called *bifurcation points* (Capra, 1996). These bifurcation points might otherwise be analogous to watching ice crack on a lake. Specifically, there is no order to when the ice will cease in one direction and fork off to another. Bifurcation of behavior after an acute injury is representative of the anxiety, fear and shock, and individual experiences during crisis, but with each critical bifurcation point (fork), it allows for growth, stability, and new behavior to result (Chamberlain, 1998). *Fixed-point attractors* are stable and predictable set points that Livneh and Parker (2005, p. 20) describe as synonymous with watching water approaching a drain. *Limited cycle or periodic attractors* are predictable open and closed loops, with donut-shaped trajectories where the system approaches two separate points periodically but is unable to escape the cycle (p. 20). *Strange attractors* are indicative of the unpredictable and unstable chaotic trajectories that demonstrate the sensitive dependence on initial conditions and bifurcates over time (Capra, 1996). The fixed point attractors, limited cycle attractors, and strange attractors all constitute the first, second, and third order changes, respectively.

Dynamic systems are neither random nor determined systems interconnected with one another that depend on the system itself (the individual), the environment, and the interaction between the two (similar to somatopsychology). Complex systems are open systems in that they exchange and lose energy, information, and material through interacting with their environment (Cambel, 1993). In order to survive, the system must reduce internal disorder or entropy (decay), while drawing energy from the environment. The level of entropy (minimal versus extreme) represents the degree of chaos occurring within the system or individual in human application. There are, however, closed systems where the entropy cannot be dissipated and new energy cannot enter from the environment. In closed systems that are isolated from renewable environmental energy, maximum entropy continues (Kossmann & Bullrich, 1997). This may otherwise be a representation of what Livneh (1991) describes as "getting stuck" in a certain stage of psychosocial adjustment. *Self-organization* is defined by Livneh and Parker (2005) as open systems with nonlinear trajectories that experience dramatic changes following a stressor (injury), spontaneously develop new structures and behaviors (schema), and experience internal feedback loops that ultimately self-organize, stabilize, and develop new ways of adaptation (p. 21; Capra, 1996). *Self-similarity* involves similar patterns within chaotic systems such as the fact that no two snowflakes are alike; however, they all have six sides. Self-similar patterns are called "fractals," which are determined patterns essentially fixed inside of the chaos (Mandelbrot, 1977).

In aligning the hard science of chaos theory with human behavior, Livneh and Parker (2005) indicate that under everyday conditions, most persons without disabilities essentially function under a state of cognitive and behavioral equilibrium. When a crisis occurs, however, we generally react in a more complex and unpredictable manner. Chaos is described as an indication of this overwhelming anxiety, capable of facilitating emotions such as depression and anger (Butz, 1997). As a result of these distressing emotions, adaptation involves a series of bifurcation points that is unpredictable and may be observed with varying degrees of maladjustment in different people (Francis, 1995). There are, however, some "self-similar" observations (e.g., shock, anxiety, denial, anger) that can be observed in most individuals. As time goes on, the individual generally reorganizes his or her cognitions, emotions, and behaviors to restore preinjury equilibrium. Interactions with the environment (others) can have a positive or negative effect on the individual's adjustment that may either slow, stall, or facilitate adaptation. Livneh and Parker (2005) suggest that counselors can assist persons with acquired CID to shift their focus and energy from past and present thinking to the future, with goal-directed and community-oriented participation. Clients can be encouraged to look past their health and survival mentality, and begin thinking about social, vocational, and environmental mastery activities. Finally, knowing that many individuals instinctively retrench (withdraw, succumb) following a traumatic injury, counselors can encourage clients to recognize their spontaneity and creativeness, and begin taking risks again (p. 24).

Additional Adjustment Concepts

Value Change System

Although indirectly addressed previously, there are several additional concepts and/or theories regarding acceptance of loss and disability worthy of noting. The first stems from Dembo et al. (1956) and later Wright's (1960) theory of value system changes that are necessary regarding acceptance of loss. In her later conceptualization, Wright (1983) cites four value changes that may or may not occur in any particular order for the individual. The first is *enlargement of the scope of values*. This pertains to individuals needing to refocus or let go of preinjury activities or values they are no longer able to perform, and instead expanding activities and interests to match their new abilities (e.g., an athlete who enjoyed playing sports becomes paralyzed and expands his or her values consistent with the limitations from the disability to enjoy reading). The second value change is *subordination of physique*, essentially cognitively reframing the significance of what is beautiful about oneself. Persons who place great importance on their physical appearance and ability must be able to redefine remaining attributes (e.g., intelligence, personality) as becoming most important. The third value change, *containment of disability effects,* pertains to persons with disabilities not allowing the disability to "spread" to other parts of their being, and assertively correcting those without disabilities who assume this to be so. For example, someone with a physical disability may be presumed as also being mentally retarded. Numerous personal reports exist regarding a waitress asking a nondisabled companion what his or her wheelchair-using partner would like to eat, based on the assumption that the individual is incapable of ordering for himself or herself. The fourth value change needing to occur for successful adjustment is *transformation from comparative to asset values*, involving cognitive reframing as well. Asset values are more intrinsic and personal regarding what the individual finds to be valuable and needs to change in his or her life to sustain asset values. Comparative values, however, are evaluations we make on comparing what we have with what is supposedly normal and in relation to what others have. Therefore, refocusing on one's own assets without comparing to what other nondisabled persons perceive as normal or standard needs to occur. Dembo et al. (1956) hypothesized in their coping with disability framework that, in order for persons with disabilities to successfully adapt and not ultimately succumb to the disability, they must be able to focus on the things they can do, take control of shaping their life, recognize personal accomplishments, manage negative life experiences, minimize physical and social barriers, and participate in activities that are pleasurable.

Good-Fortune Comparison

This concept refers to some sense of relief persons with CID experience when they meet and/or perceive other persons with severe disabilities are much worse off than they. This is referred to as the "downward comparison," whereby one's perceived good fortune is from the belief that he or she could have sustained a more severe disability (Shotton, Simpson, & Smith, 2007). In a Shotton et al. (2007) study of psychosocial adjustment, appraisal, and coping strategies of nine persons with traumatic brain injuries (TBI), one of the significant findings was the comfort participants expressed in knowing their injuries could have been much worse. Psychologically, this realization assisted these individuals to enjoy what abilities they had remaining as opposed to what they had lost.

Conceptualized Synthesis of the Seven Theories of Adjustment to an Acquired Disability

Having explored both the old and contemporary theories and concepts of psychosocial adjustment (adaptation, response, or reaction) to disability, what then are the major overlapping areas that appear to be consistently supported empirically? In other words, what cognitions, behaviors, and emotions do most persons who acquire a CID go through immediately following, then long after sustaining, a disability? We attempt to synthesize the areas of agreement various authors have conceptualized in essentially explaining the same process. The references for these conclusions are found within this chapter and therefore not all are repeated here.

First, following a traumatic, acquired injury with permanent long-term functional implications, all humans experience some type of reaction. They may or may not experience Livneh's (1991) five stages of adjustment in the exact sequential order initially proposed; however, the caveats Livneh noted with the stage theory make these cognitions, behaviors, and emotions more probable since he indicated some people skip stages, regress back to a previous stage, overlap stages, and can become stuck in a stage. In analyzing this initial time period following injury, most people are overwhelmed with shock and anxiety, synonymous with Parker et al.'s (2003) chaos theory in describing bifurcation points. This also overlaps with Yoshida's (1993) analogy of a wildly swinging pendulum initially following a trauma to explain the response to overwhelming anxiety and shock as part of the recurrent model (Kendall & Buys, 1998). This type of response lasts differing lengths of time for different people, based on personality traits and strengths of coping strategies, family stability and support, and type of interactions with the environment or community.

Second, as Lazarus and Folkman (1984a) have hypothesized, in appraising whether a severe injury is considered to be harmful or a threat to the individual's well-being, unquestionably it is harmful and does threaten the individual's well-being. The disabling injury is largely not under an individual's direct control, and, as Cheng et al. (2010) found, we tend to levitate toward using emotion-focused coping because this is a situation we are unable to problem solve our way out of by self-repairing our bodily injuries. We therefore must rely on our physicians, and sometimes pray or bargain with God in the meantime, for a full recovery with or without medical intervention. Interestingly, Levin's (2001) analysis of more than 200 epidemiological studies regarding religion/spirituality and its impact on mental and physical health found positive relationships between religious participation and beliefs in relation to dealing with CID more positively.

Third, some or most individuals experience a clinical reactive depression of a mild, moderate, or severe nature from the loss of perceived and/or real preinjury functioning and QOL. Unquestionably, the majority of people grieve the loss of bodily function and previous way of life; however, whether these same people fall under the clinical diagnosis for depression varies from person to person. Again, synonymous with Parker et al.'s (2003) bifurcation points (Which way do the cracks in the ice go?), it depends on the personality traits and strengths in coping, family stability and support, and types of interactions with the environment regarding how one adjusts. The person–environment interaction is essentially the theoretical framework for somatopsychology as well as the "dynamic systems" concept of Parker and colleagues' explanation of chaos theory. The ecological model is a more complex model, but essentially is similar to somatopsychology, noting the interplay between aspects of the disability involving the person, personal characteristics and resources to cope, and the interplay with environmental forces (Trieschmann, 1988; Vash & Crewe, 2004). Basically, then, whatever occurs after what is considered a normal grief response (generally 3 to 6 months) may be classified as noteworthy to address in counseling (Livneh & Antonak, 1991; Silver, 1982). Suicidal ideation and suicide completion are statistically higher for persons with disabilities, so although not everyone becomes depressed, some disability groups are more likely to think about suicide as an option compared to the general public (e.g., spinal cord injury vs. deafness).

Fourth, the occurrence of anger, be it internal or external, is a factor. Do most people with an acquired disability at some point after their injury become angry? Olkin (1999) discusses the contradictory societal perception of persons with disabilities as expected to be happy and grateful for the charitable crumbs thrown their way; however, conversely, they are also required to indefinitely mourn their loss as well. She further asserts that society does not tolerate, accept, or understand anger from people with disabilities, but that whatever negative emotion is displayed, it is somehow always thought to be related or salient to the disability. Clinical observation and empirical studies suggest anger is a response, whether a short-term transitional occurrence or long-term periodic state (Graf et al., 2009; Livneh & Antonak, 1991; Marini et al., 2009). Livneh (1991) initially described self-blame and anger at God or a higher entity for causing the injury or not being able to prevent it. When the higher entity or medical profession is unable to cure impairments from the disability, the anger is redirected outwardly toward medical staff, family, and God or the higher power (Graf et al., 2007; Graf & Marini, 2011). What few researchers have addressed, however, is not so much anger, but the combination of sheer boredom and frustration persons with acquired disabilities feel during their first weeks and months of recovery, and later when they encounter environmental barriers and negative societal attitudes (Graf et al., 2009; Marini et al., 2009). Initially, the boredom and frustration persons with an acute injury experience waiting for the few minutes every day to see the doctor can be aggravating for many. Once out in the community, people with disabilities periodically become angry and frustrated in their interactions with others in the community regarding wheelchair parking violators, inaccessible washrooms, rude or condescending medical staff, long waiting times to see a doctor, and so forth (Graf et al., 2009; Marini et al., 2009).

Fifth, and perhaps the most controversial, is whether persons with acquired or congenital disability eventually experience some type of final adjustment, adaptation, or transcendence to their disability (Livneh, 1991; Vash & Crewe, 2004). In defense of stage theory, Livneh (1991) noted the caveat that some individuals can regress back to an earlier stage. This is otherwise understood to mean that periodic setbacks can occur. Indeed, this is essentially very similar to the concept of periodic "chronic sorrow" that Kendall and Buys (1998) maintain in the recurrent model of adjustment. It is also synonymous with Parker et al.'s (2003) chaos theory concept of "self-organization," where individuals encounter a bad event and adapt or change what is necessary and within their control to adjust to the situation. The larger question becomes, what causes these periodic instances of chronic sorrow? Only two answers are plausible: (a) The individual experiences additional or recurrent health problems (e.g., loss of sight with diabetes, severe pressure sore requiring surgery for spinal cord injury); or (b) someone or something in the person's "life space" interacting with the environment upsets the individual. In the first instance, this potential health setback and subsequent sadness is an otherwise normal reaction. If these setbacks do not occur, it has already been demonstrated in various empirical studies that persons with disabilities revert to preinjury levels of emotions after roughly 2 months (Brickman & Campbell, 1971; Silver, 1982). The second instance concerns a negative experience with others or from encountering an environmental barrier; these causes are both socially constructed. A prejudicial or discriminatory attitude reminds the person with a disability that he or she not only has a disability, but that he or she is even devalued by some people because of it (Li & Moore, 1998). Such interactions may well hurt the individual and can cause temporary sadness and/or anger as well. Similarly, when individuals with disabilities encounter an inaccessible restaurant or public place, it reminds them of their disability and the environmental barriers imposed on them that deny their civil rights (Graf et al., 2009; Marini et al.,

2009). Regardless, many persons without disabilities in society automatically assume that when someone with a disability appears upset, it is somehow salient to the disability, and this may indirectly be so (e.g., requirement of mourning; Wright, 1983).

Finally, how do persons with disabilities reach any type of successful adjustment, adaptation, response, or reaction to their disability? For stage theory proponents, it is by successfully transitioning through the various stages over time and coming to terms with the disability. As with the grieving process, time heals. For somatopsychology proponents, it is that critical person–environment interaction where the individual possesses the personal characteristics and coping skills to succeed, and learns to control and master his or her environment. Disability centrality proponents also postulate mastering one's environment and substituting new and interesting activities that are central for sustaining satisfaction and QOL in place of those pleasurable activities no longer accessible because of the limitations imposed by the disability. Ecological models are more complex, but again similar to somatopsychology in that psychosocial adjustment depends on the interplay of an individual's personal characteristics and coping abilities, aspects of the disability itself, and environmental influences including family and community support.

Overall, all models arguably converge into one at some point, or certainly overlap enough to provide counselors with some good insights as to what persons with disabilities may experience. For those with congenital disabilities, there does not appear to be a transitional stage of adjustment. It is more likely that this population experiences periodic sorrow if they allow themselves to sometimes wish that they could do all the activities someone without a disability supposedly can do. Such cognitions, however, from the literature appear to be rare (Connors & Stalker, 2007). In addition, it appears that emotional upsets may otherwise have an external cause such as being ridiculed or reminded of one's minority status. Again, this would hopefully be a rare occurrence, and the literature suggests that persons with congenital disabilities are otherwise generally happy and satisfied with their QOL. For those with acquired disabilities, there is for a time an emotional instability in grieving the loss of bodily function and preinjury lifestyle. This does appear to stabilize in most cases over time, and it does so when individuals can cognitively reframe (adapt new cognitive schema) about their situation and what is important in life. This is accomplished by letting go of, and not dwelling on, what one used to be able to do, but instead focusing on new interests, values, and goals commensurate with remaining disability assets. The perception of being in control and mastering one's environment is central to reestablishing self-esteem. And, as discussed in the "disability paradox" theory (Freedman, 1978) and later in this text on positive psychology, persons who have not only survived their disability but become very successful in spite of it otherwise perceive themselves as stronger than most nondisabled persons. It therefore seems appropriate to end this chapter with Nietzsche's (1889) classic quote, "what does not kill me, makes me stronger," otherwise experienced as posttraumatic growth.

REFERENCES

Albrecht, G. L., & Devlieger, P. J. (1999). The disability paradox: High quality of life against all odds. *Social Science & Medicine, 48,* 977–988.

Allman, A. (1990). *Subjective well-being of people with disabilities: Measurement issues.* (Unpublished master's thesis), University of Illinois.

Andrews, F., & Withey, S. (1976). Developing measures of perceived life quality: Results from several national surveys. *Social Indicators Research, 1,* 1–26.

Athelstan, G. T., & Crewe, N. M. (1979). Psychological adjustment to spinal cord injury as related to manner of onset of disability. *Rehabilitation Counseling Bulletin, 22,* 311–319.

Banks, S. M., & Kerns, R. D. (1996). Explaining high rates of depression in chronic pain: A diathesis-stress framework. *Psychological Bulletin, 119,* 95–110.

Barker, R. G., Wright, B. A., Meyerson, L., & Gonick, M. R. (1953). *Adjustment to physical handicap: A survey of the social psychology of physique and disability* (2nd ed.). New York, NY: Social Science Research Council.

Barnard, D. (1990). Healing the damaged self: Identity, intimacy, and meaning in the lives of the chronically ill. *Perspectives in Biology and Medicine, 33,* 535–546.

Barrera, M. (1981). Social support in adjustment of pregnant adolescents: Assessment issues. In B. H. Gottlieb (Ed.), *Social networks and social support* (pp. 69–96). Beverly Hills, CA: Sage.

Beck, A. T. (1967). *Depression: Causes and treatment.* Philadelphia: University of Pennsylvania Press.

Beck, A. T., & Weishaar, M. (1989). Cognitive therapy. In A. Freeman, K. M. Simon, L.E. Beutler, & H. Arkowitz (Eds.), *Comprehensive handbook of cognitive therapy* (pp. 21–36). New York, NY: Plenum.

Bishop, M. (2005). Quality of life and psychosocial adaptation to chronic illness and acquired disability: A conceptual and theoretical synthesis. *Journal of Rehabilitation, 71*(2), 5–13.

Bishop, M., & Allen, C. A. (2003). Epilepsy's impact on quality of life: A qualitative analysis. *Epilepsy & Behavior, 4*(3), 226–233.

Bishop, M., & Feist-Price, S. (2002). Quality of life assessment in the rehabilitation counseling relationship: Strategies and measures. *Journal of Applied Rehabilitation Counseling, 33*(1), 35–41.

Bishop, M., Shepard, L., & Stenhoff, D. M. (2007). Psychosocial adaptation and quality of life in multiple sclerosis: Assessment of the disability centrality model. *Journal of Rehabilitation, 73*(1), 3–12.

Bordieri, L., Comninel, M., & Drehmer, D. (1989). Client attributions for disability: Perceived adjustment, coping and accuracy. *Rehabilitation Psychology, 34,* 271–278.

Bordieri, J. E., & Kilbury, R. (1991). Self-blame attributions for disability and perceived rehabilitation outcomes. *Rehabilitation Bulletin, 34*(4), 1–12.

Bramble, K. (1995). Body image. In I. M. Lubkin (Ed.), *Chronic illness: Impact and interventions* (pp. 285–299). Boston, MA: Jones & Bartlett.

Brickman, P., & Campbell, D. T. (1971). Hedonic relativism and planning the good society. In M. H. Appley (Ed.), *Adaptation-level theory* (pp. 287–305). New York, NY: Academic Press.

Bulman, R., & Wortman, C. B. (1977). Attributions of blame and coping in the "real world": Severe accident victims respond to their lot. *Journal of Personality and Social Psychology, 35,* 351–363.

Burke, M. L., Hainsworth, M. A., Eakes, G. G., & Lindgren, C. L. (1992). Current knowledge and research on chronic sorrow: A foundation for injury. *Death Studies, 16,* 231–245.

Butz, M. (1997). *Chaos and complexity: Implications for psychological theory and practice.* Washington, DC: Taylor & Francis.

Buunk, B. P., & Verhoeven, K. (1991). Companionship and support at work: A microanalysis of the stress-reducing features of social interaction. *Basic and Applied Social Psychology, 12,* 243–258.

Byrd, E. K. (1990). A study of biblical depiction of disability. *Journal of Applied Rehabilitation Counseling, 21*(4), 52–53.

Cadman, D., Boyle, M., Szatmari, P., & Offord, D. R. (1987). Chronic illness, disability, and mental health and social well-being: Findings of the Ontario child health study. *Pediatrics, 79,* 805–813.

Cambel, A. B. (1993). *Applied chaos theory.* New York, NY: Academic Press.

Capra, F. (1996). *The web of life.* New York, NY: Anchor Books.

Carver, C. S., Scheier, M. F., & Weintraub, J. K. (1989). Assessing coping strategies: A theoretically based approach. *Journal of Personality and Social Psychology, 56,* 267–283.

Chamberlain, L. (1998). An introduction to nonlinear dynamics. In L. Chamberlain & M. Butz (Eds.), *Clinical chaos: A therapist's guide to nonlinear dynamics and therapeutic change* (pp. 3–14). Philadelphia, PA: Brunner/Mazel.

Chan, F., Da Silva Cardoso, E., & Chronister, J. A. (2009). *Understanding psychosocial adjustment to chronic illness and disability.* New York, NY: Springer Publishing.

Charmaz, K. (1983). Loss of self: A fundamental form of suffering in the chronically ill. *Sociology of Health and Illness, 5,* 168–195.

Charmaz, K. (1995). Identity dilemmas of chronically ill men. In D. Sabo & D. Gordon (Eds.), *Men's health and illness: Gender, power, and the body* (pp. 266–291). Thousand Oaks, CA: Sage.

Cheng, Y., Kuan, F., Li, C., & Ken, Y. (2010). A comparison between the effect of emotional certainty and uncertainty on coping strategies. *Social Behavior and Personality, 38*(1), 53–60.

Chubon, R. A. (1994). *Social and psychological foundations of rehabilitation.* Springfield, IL: Charles C Thomas.

Cohen, C. B., & Napolitano, D. (2007). Adjustment to disability. *Disability and Social Work Education: Practice and Policy Issues, 6*(1/2), 135–155.

Cohen, S. (2004). Social relationships and health. *American Psychologist, 59,* 676–684.

Cohen, S., Gottlieb, B. H., & Underwood, L. G. (2000). In S. Cohen, L. Underwood, & B. H. Gottlieb (Eds.), *Social support measurement and intervention* (pp. 3–25). New York, NY: Oxford University Press.

Connors, C., & Stalker, K. (2007). Children's experiences of disability: Pointers to a model of childhood disability. *Disability & Society, 22*(1), 19–33.

Crewe, N. M., & Krause, J. S. (1990). An eleven-year follow-up of adjustment to spinal cord injury. *Rehabilitation Psychology, 35*(4), 205–210.

Cummins, R. A. (2002). *Caveats on the comprehensive quality of life scale (and a suggested alternative).* Melbourne, Australia: Deakin University School of Psychology.

Cummins, R. A. (2005). Moving from the quality of life concept to a theory. *Journal of Intellectual Disability Research, 49,* 699–706.

Cummins, R. A. (2006). *Personal Well-being Index* (4th ed.). Melbourne, Australia: Deakin University.

Davis, B. H. (1987). Disability and grief. *Social Casework, 68,* 352–357.

Davis, S. E., Anderson, C., Linkowski, D. C., Berger, K., & Feinstein, C. F. (1991). In R. P. Marinelli & A. E. Dell Orto (Eds.), *The psychological & social impact of disability* (pp. 70–80). New York, NY: Springer Publishing.

Dembo, T., Leviton, G., & Wright, B. A. (1956). Adjustment to misfortune: A problem in social psychological rehabilitation. *Artificial Limbs, 3,* 4–62.

Devins, G. M. (1994). Illness intrusiveness and the psychosocial impact of lifestyle disruptions in chronic life-threatening disease. *Advances in Renal Replacement Therapy, 1,* 251–263.

Devins, G. M., Blinik, Y. M., Hutchinson, T. A., Hollomby, D. J., Barre, P. E., & Guttmann, R. D. (1983). The emotional impact of end-stage renal disease: Importance of patients' perceptions of intrusiveness and control. *International Journal of Psychiatry in Medicine, 13,* 327–343.

Devins, G. M., & Shnek, Z. M. (2000). Multiple sclerosis. In R. G. Frank & T. R. Elliott (Eds.), *Handbook of rehabilitation psychology* (pp. 163–184). Washington, DC: American Psychological Association.

Diener, E., & Seligman, M. E. (2004). Beyond money: Toward an economy of well-being. *Psychological Science in the Public Interest, 5,* 1–31.

Dijkers, M. (1997). Measuring quality of life. In M. J. Fuhrer (Ed.), *Assessing medical rehabilitation practices: The promise of outcome research* (pp. 153–180). Baltimore, MD: Paul H. Brooks.

DiTomasso, E., & Spinner, B. (1997). Social and emotional loneliness: A re-examination of Weiss' typology of loneliness. *Personality and Individual Differences, 22,* 417–427.

Dunn, M. E. (1975). Psychological intervention in a spinal cord injury center: An introduction. *Rehabilitation Psychology, 22*(4), 165–178.

Eareckson, J. (2001). *An unforgettable story.* Grand Rapids, MI: Zondervan.

Elfstrom, M. L., & Kreuter, M. (2006). Relationships between locus of control, coping strategies and emotional well-being in persons with spinal cord lesion. *Journal of Clinical Psychology in Medical Settings, 13*(1), 93–104.

Endler, N. S., & Parker, J. D. A. (1990). Multidimensional assessment of coping: A critical evaluation. *Journal of Personality and Social Psychology, 58,* 844–854.

Erikson, E. H., Erikson, J. M., & Kivnick, H. Q. (1986). *Vital involvement in old age.* New York, NY: W. W. Norton.

Falek, A., & Britton, S. (1974). Phases in coping: The hypothesis and its implications. *Social Biology, 21*(1), 1–7.

Fishbain, D. D., Cutler, R. B., Rosomoff, H. L., & Rosomoff, R. S. (1997). Chronic pain associated depression: Antecedent or consequences of chronic pain? A review. *Clinical Journal of Pain, 13,* 116–137.

Folkman, S., & Lazarus, R. S. (1980). An analysis of coping in a middle-aged community sample. *Journal of Health and Social Behavior, 21,* 219–239.

Folkman, S., & Lazarus, R. S. (1985). If it changes it must be a process: Study of emotion and coping during three stages of a college examination. *Journal of Personality and Social Psychology, 48,* 150–170.

Folkman, S., & Lazarus, R. S. (1991). Coping and emotions. In A. Monet & R. S. Lazarus. (Eds.), *Stress and coping* (pp. 207–227), New York, NY: Columbia University Press.

Folkman, S., & Moskowitz, J. T. (2004). Coping: Pitfalls and promise. *Annual Review of Psychology, 55,* 745–774.

Fordyce, M. (1988). A review of results on the happiness measures: A 60-second index of happiness and mental health. *Social Indicators Research, 20,* 355–381.

Francis, S. E. (1995). Chaotic phenomena in psychophysiological self-regulation. In R. Robertson & A. Combs (Eds.), *Chaos theory in psychology and the life sciences* (pp. 253–265). Mahwah, NJ: Erlbaum.

Frank, R. G., & Elliott, T. R. (1989). Spinal cord injury and health locus of control beliefs. *Paraplegia, 27,* 250–256.

Freedman, J. (1978). *Happy people.* New York, NY: Harcourt Brace Jovanovich.

Frisch, M. B. (1999). Quality of life assessment/intervention and the quality of life inventory (QOLI). In M. R. Maruish (Ed.), *The use of psychological testing for treatment planning and outcome assessment* (2nd ed., pp. 1227–1331). Hillsdale, NJ: Erlbaum.

Gallagher, H. G. (1995). *By trust betrayed: Patients, physicians, and the license to kill in the Third Reich* (Rev. ed.). Arlington, TX: Vandamere.

Gleick, J. (1987). *Chaos: Making a new science.* New York, NY: Viking.

Gordon, P. A., Tschopp, M. K., & Feldman, D. (2004). Addressing issues of sexuality with adolescents with disabilities. *Child and Adolescent Social Work Journal, 21*(5), 513–527.

Graf, N. M., Marini, I., Baker, J., & Buck, T. (2007). The perceived impact of religious and spiritual beliefs for persons with chronic pain. *Rehabilitation Counseling Bulletin, 51,* 21–33.

Graf, N. M., Marini, I., & Blankenship, C. J. (2009). 100 words about disability. *Journal of Rehabilitation, 75*(2), 25–34.

Groomes, D. A. G., & Leahy, M. J. (2002). The relationships among the stress appraisal process, coping disposition and level of acceptance of disability. *Rehabilitation Counseling Bulletin, 46,* 14–23.

Groot, W., & Van Den Brink, H. M. (2000). Life satisfaction and preference drift. *Social Indicators Research, 50,* 315–328.

Gunther, M. S. (1969). Emotional aspects. In D. Ruge (Ed.), *Spinal cord injuries* (pp. 93–108). Springfield, IL: Charles C Thomas.

Gunther, M. S. (1971). Psychiatric consultation in a rehabilitation hospital: A regression hypothesis. *Comprehensive Psychiatry, 12*(6), 572–585.

Heller, K., & Rook, K. S. (2001). Distinguishing the theoretical functional of social ties: Implications for support interventions. In B. R. Sarason & S. Duck (Eds.), *Personal relationships: Implications for clinical and community psychology* (pp. 119–139). New York, NY: Wiley.

Helwig, A. A., & Holicky, R. (1994). Substance abuse in persons with disabilities: Treatment considerations. *Journal of Counseling and Development, 72,* 227–233.

Hofman, A. D. (1975). The impact of illness in adolescence and coping behavior. *Acta Paediatrica Scandinavica, 256* (Suppl.), 29–33.

Hogansen, J., Geenen, S., Powers, L. E., & Gil-Kashiwabara, E. (2008). Gender matters in transition to adulthood: A survey study of adolescents with disabilities and their families. *Psychology in the Schools, 45*(4), 1–17.

Hohmann, G. W. (1975). Psychological aspects of treatment and rehabilitation of the spinal cord injured person. *Clinical Orthopedics, 112,* 81–88.

Holmbeck, G. N., Johnson, S. Z., Wills, K. E., McKernon, W., Rose, B., Erklin, S., & Kemper, T. (2002). *Journal of Consulting & Clinical Psychology, 70*(1), 96–111.

Hopps, S., Pepin, M., Arseneau, I., Frechette, M., & Begin, G. (2001). Disability related variables associated with loneliness among people with disabilities. *Journal of Rehabilitation, 67*(3), 42–48.

Howland, C. A., & Rintala, D. H. (2001). Dating behaviors of women with physical disabilities. *Sexuality and Disability, 19,* 41–70.

Hupcey, J. E. (1998). Clarifying the social support theory-research linkage. *Journal of Advanced Nursing, 27,* 1231–1241.

Hwang, K. (1997). Living with a disability: A woman's perspective. In M. L. Sipski & C. J. Alexander (Eds.), *Sexual function in people with disability and chronic illness* (pp. 119–130), Gaithersburg, MD: Aspen.

Inglehart, R. (1990). *Modernization and postmodernization: Cultural, economic, and political change in societies.* Princeton, NJ: Princeton University Press.

Jalowiec, A. (1990). Issues in using multiple measures of quality of life. *Seminars in Onocology Nursing, 6,* 271–277.

Janoff-Bulman, R. (1979). Characterological versus behavioral self-blame: Injuries into depression and rape. *Journal of Personality and Social Psychology, 37,* 1798–1809.

Johnson, K. L., Amtmann, D., Yorkston, K., Klasner, E. R., & Kuehn, C. M. (2004). Medical, psychological, social, and programmatic barriers to employment for people with multiple sclerosis. *Journal of Rehabilitation, 70,* 38–49.

Kahana, E., Fairchild, T., & Kahana, B. (1982). Adaptation. In D. J. Mangen & W. A. Peterson (Eds.), *Research instruments in clinical gerontology: Vol 1. Clinical and social psychology.* (pp. 145–193). Minneapolis: University of Minnesota Press.

Kendall, E., & Buys, N. (1998). An integrated model of psychosocial adjustment following acquired disability. *Journal of Rehabilitation, 64,* 16–20.

Kivnick, H. Q. (1991). Disability and psychosocial development in old age. In R. P. Marinelli & A. E. Dell Orto (Eds.), *The psychological & social impact of disability* (pp. 92–102). New York, NY: Springer Publishing.

Kossmann, M. R., & Bullrich, S. (1997). Systematic chaos: Self-organizing systems and the process of change. In F. Masterpasqua & P. A. Pena (Eds.), *The psychological meaning of chaos: Translating theory into practice* (pp. 199–224). Washington, DC: American Psychological Association.

Kübler-Ross, E. (1981). *Living with death and dying.* New York, NY: Macmillian.

Lakey, B., & Cassady, P. B. (1990). Cognitive processes in perceived social support. *Journal of Personality and Social Psychology, 59,* 337–343.

Lazarus, R. S. (1993). Coping theory and research: Past, present, and future. *Psychosomatic Medicine, 55,* 234–247.

Lazarus, R. S., & Folkman, S. (1984a). *Stress, appraisal, and coping.* New York, NY: Springer Publishing.

Lazarus, R. S., & Folkman, S. (1984b). Coping and adaptation. In W. D. Gentry (Ed.), *Handbook of behavioral medicine* (pp. 282–325). New York, NY: Guilford Press.

Levin, J. (2001). *God, faith, and health: Exploring the spirituality healing connection.* Hoboken, NJ: Wiley.

Levy, D. (1966). *Maternal overprotection.* New York, NY: W. W. Norton.

Lewin, K. (1935). *A dynamic theory of personality.* New York, NY: McGraw-Hill.

Lewin, K. (1936). *Principles of topological psychology.* New York, NY: McGraw-Hill.

Lewinsohn, P. M., Clarke, G. N., & Hops, H. (1990). Cognitive-behavioral treatment for depressed adolescents. *Behavior Therapy, 21,* 385–401.

Li, L., & Moore, D. (1998). Acceptance of disability and its correlates. *Journal of Social Psychology, 138*(1), 13–25.

Livneh, H. (1986). A unified approach to existing models of adaptation to disability: Part I-A model adaptation. *Journal of Applied Rehabilitation Counseling, 17,* 5–16.

Livneh, H. (1991). On the origins of negative attitudes toward people with disabilities. In R. P. Marinelli & A. E. Dell Orto (Eds.), *The psychological & social impact of disability.* New York, NY: Springer Publishing.

Livneh, H. (2001). Psychosocial adaptation to chronic illness and disability: A conceptual framework. *Rehabilitation Counseling Bulletin, 44*(3), 151–160.

Livneh, H., & Antonak, R. F. (1991). Temporal structure of adaptation to disability. *Rehabilitation Counseling Bulletin, 34*(4), 298–320.

Livneh, H., & Antonak, R. F. (1997). *Psychosocial adaptation to chronic illness and disability.* Gaithersburg, MD: Aspen.

Livneh, H., & Antonak, R. F. (2005). Psychosocial adaptation to chronic illness and disability: A primer for counselors. *Journal of Counseling & Development, 83,* 12–20.

Livneh, H., & Antonak, R. F. (2007). Psychological adaptation to chronic illness and disability: A primer for counselors. In A. E. Dell Orto & P. W. Power (Eds.), *The psychological and social impact of illness and disability* (5th ed., pp. 125–144). New York, NY: Springer Publishing.

Livneh, H., & Parker, R. M. (2005). Psychological adaptation to disability: Perspectives from chaos and complexity theory. *Rehabilitation Counseling Bulletin, 49*(1), 17–28.

Lucas, R. E. (2007). Adaptation and the set-point model of subjective well-being: Does happiness change after major life events? *Current Directions in Psychological Science, 16,* 75–79.

Lykken, D. (1999). *Happiness.* New York, NY: Golden Books.

Maciejewski, P. K., Zhang, B., Block, S., & Prigerson, H. G. (2007). An empirical examination of the stage theory of grief. *Journal of the American Medical Association, 297,* 716–723.

Mackelprang, R., & Salsgiver, R. (2009). *Disability: A diversity model approach in human service practice.* Pacific Grove, CA: Brooks/Cole.

Maltby, J., Day, L., & Macaskill, A. (2007). *Personality individual differences and intelligence.* Harlow, UK: Pearson/Prentice Hall.

Mandelbrot, B. (1977). *The fractal geometry of nature.* New York, NY: W. H. Freeman.

Marini, I. (2007). Cross-cultural counseling issues of males who sustain a disability. In A. E. Dell Orto & P. W. Power (Eds.), *The psychological and social impact of illness and disability* (5th ed., pp. 194–213). New York, NY: Springer Publishing.

Marini, I., Bhakta, M. V., & Graf, N. (2009). A content analysis of common concerns of persons with physical disabilities. *Journal of Applied Rehabilitation Counseling, 40*(1), 44–49.

Marini, I., & Graf, N. M. (2011). Spirituality and SCI: Attitudes, beliefs, and practices. *Rehabilitation Counseling Bulletin, 54*(2), 89–92.

Marini, I., Rogers, L., Slate, J. R., & Vines, C. (1995). Self-esteem differences among persons with spinal cord injury. *Rehabilitation Counseling Bulletin, 38*(3), 198–205.

Marinic, M., & Brkljacic, T. (2008). Love over gold—the correlation of happiness level with some life satisfaction factors between persons with and without physical disability. *Journal of Developmental Physical Disability, 20,* 527–540.

Massimini, F., & Delle Fave, A. (2000). Individual development in a bio-cultural perspective. *American Psychologist, 55,* 24–33.

Meyerowitz, B. E. (1980). Psychosocial correlates of breast cancer and its treatments. *Psychological Bulletin, 87,* 108–131.

Misajon, R. A. (2002). *The homeostatic mechanism: Subjective quality of life and chronic pain.* Unpublished doctoral dissertation, Deakin University, Victoria, Australia.

Myers, D. G., & Diener, E. (1995). Who is happy? *Psychological Science, 6,* 10–19.

Myers, D. G., & Diener, E. (1996). The pursuit of happiness: New research uncovers some anti-intuitive insights into how many people are happy—And why. *Scientific American, 27*(4), 70–72.

Nabi, R. L. (2003). Exploring the framing effects of emotion. *Communication Research, 30,* 224–247.

Naugle, R. I. (1991). Denial in rehabilitation: Its genesis, consequences, and clinical management. In R. P. Marinelli & A. E. Dell Otto (Eds.), *The psychological and social impact of disability.* (pp. 139–151). New York, NY: Springer Publishing.

Nietzsche, F. (1889). *Twilight of the idols.*(R. J. Hollingdale, trans.). Leipzig, Germany: C. G. Nesmeer.

Nilsson, D. H. (2002). "What's the problem?": A conceptual and empirical exploration adjustment to health condition and adjustment to hospitalization as indicators for intervention for social workers in health-care settings (Unpublished DSW thesis), La Trobe University, Melbourne, Australia.

Nosek, M. A., & Hughes, R. B. (2007). Psychosocial issues of women with physical disabilities. In A.E. Dell Orto & P. W. Power, *The psychological and social impact of illness and disability* (5th ed., pp. 156–175). New York, NY: Springer Publishing.

Olkin, R. (1999). *What psychotherapists should know about disability.* New York, NY: Guilford Press.

Parker, R. M. (1979). *Assessing adjustment to disability through determining predominant feeling states.* Paper presented at the American Rehabilitation Counseling Association Meeting, Las Vegas, NV.

Parker, R. M., Schaller, J., & Hansmann, S. (2003). Castastrophe, chaos, and complexity models and psychosocial adjustment to disability. *Rehabilitation Counseling Bulletin, 46*(4), 234–241.

Pavot, W., & Diener, E. (1993). Review of the satisfaction with life scale. *Psychological Assessment, 5,* 164–172.

Pless, I. B., Roghmann, K., & Haggerty, R. J. (1972). Chronic illness, family functioning, and psychological adjustment: A model for the allocation of preventive mental health services. *International Journal of Epidemiology. 1,* 271–277.

Provencher, H. L. (2007). Role of psychological factors in studying recovery from a transactional stress-coping approach: Implications for mental health nursing practices. *International Journal of Mental Health Nursing, 16,* 188–197.

Reidy, K., & Caplan, B. (1994). Causal factors in spinal cord injury: Patients' evolving perceptions and associations with depression. *Archives of Physical Medicine & Rehabilitation, 75*(8), 837–842.

Roessler, R. T. (1990). A quality of life perspective on rehabilitation counseling. *Rehabilitation Counseling Bulletin, 34,* 82–90.

Rousso, H. (1996). Sexuality and positive sense of self. In D. M. Krotoski, M. A. Nosek, & M. A. Turk (Eds.), *Women with physical disabilities: Achieving and maintaining health and well-being* (pp. 109–116). Baltimore, MD: Paul H. Brookes.

Schafer, W. (1996). *Stress management for wellness.* Orlando, FL: Harcourt Brace.

Schwartz, C. E., & Sprangers, M. A. (2000). *Adaptation to changing health: Response shift in quality of life research.* Washington, DC: American Psychological Association.

Schwarzer, R., & Leppin, A. (1992). Social supports and mental health: A conceptual and empirical overview. In L. Montada, S. Filipp, & M. J. Lerner (Eds.), *Life crises and experiences of loss in adulthood* (pp. 435–458). Hillsdale, NJ: Eribaum.

Seligman, M. E. P. (1975). *Helplessness.* San Francisco, CA: W. H. Freeman.

Shands, H. C. (1955). An outline of the process of recovery from severe trauma. *Archives of Neurology and Psychiatry, 73,* 403–409.

Shotton, L., Simpson, J., & Smith, M. (2007). The experience of appraisal, coping and adaptive psychosocial adjustment following traumatic brain injury: A qualitative investigation. *Brain Injury, 21*(8), 857–869.

Silver, R. L. (1982). *Coping with an undesirable life event: A study of early reactions to physical disability* (Unpublished doctoral dissertation), Northwestern University, Evanston, IL.

Smart, J. (2009). *Disability, society, and the individual.* Austin, TX: PRO-ED.

Smith, A. J., Thorngren, J., & Christopher, J. C. (2009). Rural mental health counseling. In I. Marini, & M. Stebnicki (Eds.), *The professional counselor's desk reference* (pp. 263–273). New York, NY: Springer Publishing.

Smith, C. A., & Ellsworth, P. C. (1985). Patterns of cognitive appraisal in emotions. *Journal of Personality and Social Psychology, 48,* 813–838.

Stewart, J. R. (1996). Applying Beck's cognitive therapy to Livneh's model of adaptation to disability. *Journal of Applied Rehabilitation Counseling, 27,* 40–45.

Symister, P., & Friend, R. (2003). The influence of social support and problematic support on optimism and depression in chronic illness: A prospective study evaluating self-esteem as a mediator. *Health Psychology, 22,* 123–129.

Teel, C. S. (1991). Chronic sorrow: Analysis of the concept. *Journal of Advanced Nursing, 16,* 1311–1319.

Tepper, M. S. (1997). Living with a disability: A man's perspective. In M. L. Sipski & C. J. Alexander (Eds.), *Sexual function in people with disability and chronic illness* (pp. 119–130), Gaithersburg, MD: Aspen.

Thom, R. (1975). *Structural stability and morphogenesis: An outline of a general theory of model* (H. Fowler, Trans.). Reading, PA: Benjamin.

Thomasgard, M. (1998). Parental perceptions of child vulnerability, overprotection, and parental psychological characteristics. *Child Psychiatry & Human Development, 28*(4), 223–240.

Trask, P. C., Paterson, A. G., Trask, C. L., Bares, C. B., Birt, J., & Maan, C. (2003). Parent and adolescent adjustment to pediatric cancer: Associations with coping, social support, and family function. *Journal of Pediatric Oncology Nursing, 20*(1), 36–47.

Trieschmann, R. (1988). *Spinal cord injuries: Psychological, social, and vocational rehabilitation* (2nd ed.). New York, NY: Demos Medical Publishing.

U.S. General Accounting Office. (2002). *Nursing homes: More can be done to protect residents from abuse* (GAO/HEHS02-312). Washington, DC U.S. Government Printing Office.

Varni, J. W., Rubenfeld, L. A., Talbot, D., & Setoguchi, Y. (1989). Family functioning, temperament, and psychologic adaptation in children with congenital or acquired limb deficiencies. *Pediatrics, 84*(2), 323–330.

Vash, C. L. (1981). *The psychology of disability.* New York, NY: Springer Publishing.

Vash, C. L., & Crewe, N. M. (2003). *Psychology of disability* (2nd ed., pp. 288–299). New York, NY: Springer Publishing.

Wallander, J. L., & Varni, J. W. (1998). Effects of pediatric chronic physical disorders on child and family adjustment. *Journal of Child Psychology and Psychiatry, 39,* 29–46.

Wallander, J. L., Varni, J. W., Babani, L., Banis, H. T., & Wilcox, K. T. (1989). Family resources as resistance factors for psychological maladjustment in chronically ill and handicapped children. *Journal of Pediatric Psychology, 14,* 157–173.

Waters, S. J., Campbell, L. C., Keefe, F. J., & Carson, J. W. (2004). The essence of cognitive-behavioral pain management. In R. H. Dworkin & W. S. Breitbart (Eds.), *Psychosocial aspects of pain: A handbook for health care providers* (pp. 261–283). Seattle, WA: IASP Press.

Weinberg, N. (1988). Another perspective: Attitudes of people with disabilities. In H. E. Yuker (Ed.), *Attitudes toward persons with disabilities* (pp. 141–153). New York, NY: Springer Publishing.

Weller, D. J., & Miller, P. M. (1977). Emotional reactions of patient, family, and staff in acute-care period of spinal cord injury: Part 1. *Social Work in Health Care, 24*(4), 369–377.

Westbrook, M., & Nordholm, L. (1986). Reactions to patient's self or chance-blaming attributions for illnesses having life-style involvement. *Journal of Applied Social Psychology, 16,* 428–446.

Wikler, L., Wasow, M., & Hatfield, E. (1981). Chronic sorrow revisited: Parent versus professional depiction of the adjustment of mentally retarded children. *American Journal of Orthopsychiatry, 51,* 63–70.

Witt, W. P., Riley, A. W., & Coiro, M. J. (2003). Childhood functional status, family stressors, and psychosocial adjustment among school-aged children with disabilities in the United States. *Archives of Pediatrics and Adolescent Medicine, 157*(7), 687–695.

Worden, J. W. (2009). *Grief counseling and grief therapy: A handbook for the mental health practitioner* (4th ed.). New York, NY: Springer Publishing.

Wortman, C. B., & Silver, R. C. (1989). The myths of coping with loss. *Journal of Consulting and Clinical Psychology, 57*(3), 349–357.

Wright, B. A. (1960). *Physical disability: A psychological approach.* New York, NY: Harper & Row.

Wright, B. A. (1983). *Physical disability: A psychosocial approach* (2nd ed.). New York, NY: Harper & Row.

Yoshida, K. K. (1993). Reshaping of self: A pendular reconstruction of self identity among adults with traumatic spinal cord injury. *Sociology of Health and Illness, 15,* 217–245.

Yuker, H. E. (1988). *Attitudes toward persons with disabilities.* New York, NY: Springer Publishing.

Zilbergeld, B. (1992). *The new male sexuality.* New York, NY: Bantam Books.

8

Psychosocial Disparities Faced by Women With Physical Disabilities*

MARGARET A. NOSEK

Women with disabilities constitute one of the largest and most disadvantaged populations in the United States. Despite the magnitude of the psychological, social, physical, and environmental challenges they face across the life span and the disproportional share of health care costs they incur, only a small fraction of research on disability topics is dedicated to their concerns. Women like me, who live with disabilities, are nevertheless in every corner of the country, at every socioeconomic level, part of every minority, in every type of relationship, and in every vocation, living as successfully as they can. A careful look places these women in one category or another, but most do not even identify as having a disability. It did not take me very long to realize I had a disability, but it took decades before I understood what it meant to be a woman.

The major driving force in my career has been my desire to make that journey toward successful living a little easier for my sisters in disability. As the founder and executive director of the Center for Research on Women with Disabilities, I have had a hand in dozens of research projects over the past 20 years, substantiating our many disadvantages with population-based statistics, survey data, and interviews with hundreds of women with various types of disability. I have networked with and studied the research of others, looking for theories and connections that might help us understand why we face such enormous socioeconomic and health disparities. It is not enough to say it is because of our disability! If that were so, why then are some women with relatively minor disabling conditions totally devastated by them in every aspect of their lives, yet other women with very severe limitations are able to achieve their vocational and family goals and manifest fulfillment? Across almost all of our studies, disability type, age at onset, and severity of limitations have consistently failed to explain the difference in outcome variables. All that we have learned points to one undeniable truth— disability is a complex phenomenon, but psychological and social factors make all the difference in the outcomes.

The purpose of this chapter is to help rehabilitation counselors understand the myriad factors that affect the psychological and social health of women with disabilities.

*M. A. Nosek and R. B. Hughes, Psychosocial issues of women with physical disabilities: The continuing gender debate, 2003, *Rehabilitation Counseling Bulletin, 46*, 224–233. Reprinted by permission of SAGE Publications, Inc.

After giving some background on the historical roots of the rehabilitation response to women and a description of the demographic and health characteristics of this population, I present a heuristic, holistic model for understanding the reality of our lives and strategies for helping us achieve optimal health. The pivotal construct of self-esteem is discussed first, followed by social connectedness, its polar opposite—abuse—and the consequences of disparities—stress and depression. The chapter ends with recommendations on strategies that the rehabilitation researchers and practitioners can use to include gender in their examination of individual and program outcomes, and thereby advance the field.

HISTORY OF RESEARCH ON WOMEN WITH DISABILITIES

The study of disability and rehabilitation has made its most significant advances during and after periods of war, and therefore has been primarily concerned with the health and vocational problems of men. Guidelines for clinical treatment and interventions for reintegration into society have been developed for the most part based on the needs of men with spinal cord injury, amputation, and other adventitious musculoskeletal problems. Any services rendered to women used male norms and approached the needs of women according to traditional social roles. In case of issues related to congenital disabling conditions, such as cerebral palsy, spina bifida, or neuromuscular disorders, and adult-onset chronic disabling conditions, such as joint and connective tissue disorders (arthritis, lupus) or multiple sclerosis, gender has rarely been considered important in research or intervention development.

Interest in examining the needs of women with disabilities took an early focus on sexuality in response to the overwhelming preponderance of literature on the fertility and erectile dysfunction of spinal cord injured men (Charlifue, Gerhart, Menter, Whiteneck, & Manley, 1992; Griffith & Trieschmann, 1975). When the sexuality of women with disabilities was studied, it was often narrowly defined as fertility, pregnancy, labor, and delivery as demonstrated by the number of studies on menstruation, fertility, pregnancy, and childbirth (Axel, 1982; Carty & Conine, 1988; Comarr, 1976; Jackson & Varner, 1989; Jackson & Wadley, 1999; Leavesley & Porter, 1982; Verduyn, 1986). Women's self-reports indicate that if their fertility was not compromised, they were made to feel as if no other aspects of sexuality should matter (Cole, 1975). In one of the few early studies dealing specifically with sexual issues of women with spinal cord injuries, Charlifue and colleagues (1992) discovered that 69% of 231 women surveyed were satisfied with their postinjury sexual experiences but were not content with the sexual information provided during rehabilitation, feeling a need for more literature, counseling, and peer support. In another early study of gynecologic health care of women with disabilities, 91% had received breast and pelvic examinations and Papanicolaou smears, but only 19% had received counseling about sexuality; women with paralysis, impaired motor function, or obvious physical deformity were rarely offered contraceptive information or methods (Beckmann et al., 1989). Only one third believed that their health care provider knew enough about their disability to provide adequate sexual information.

The study of health and wellness in the context of disability for women is a relatively new avenue of investigation, opened only after challenges to entrenched stereotypes that disability is the opposite of health and that gender is far less important than the characteristics of the disability itself. Interest in research on women with disabilities followed a decade after the rise of interest in women's health and wellness, and the prevention of secondary conditions in people with disabilities after the deficit in the literature was noted by several researchers and feminist disability rights activists (Altman, 1985; Barnartt, 1982; Deegan & Brooks, 1985; Fine & Asch, 1985). According to Altman (1996), before 1990, there was only one publication on the demographics about women with disabilities using national population-based data and a few on access to benefits by women with disabilities. Although some information about women with disabilities could be found in publications about people with disabilities in general (LaPlante, 1991; McNeil, 1997), Altman (1996) was the first to examine statistical information about risks, causes, and consequences of disability among women at the national level. Aside from one very useful compilation of data from multiple national statistical data sources and individual research studies on the demographics, education, employment, and health status of girls and women with disabilities (Jans & Stoddard, 1999), there have been very few efforts to examine population-based data sets for statistics related to women with disabilities. Notable advances have been made in refining the wording of disability definitions in national surveys, and many analyses have been conducted to reveal the changing demographics of the disabled population (Brault, 2008; Waldrop & Stern, 2003), yet no detailed information has been published about gender differences in these statistics.

DEMOGRAPHIC AND HEALTH STATISTICS

There is a distinct lack of consistency in the few studies that have examined national data sets to describe the population of women with disabilities. Data from the 1994–1995 Survey of Income and Program Participation (Jans & Stoddard, 1999; McNeil, 1997) use a functional- and employment-based definition of disability and show that women with disabilities comprise 21% of the population of women in the United States, outnumbering men with disabilities (28.6 million vs. 25.3 million). Using the new set of definitions (hearing, visual, cognitive, ambulatory, self-care, and independent living disability), data from the 2008 American community survey show somewhat lower statistics, with 12.4% of all women in the United States (nearly 19 million) and 11.7% of all men (17.1 million) having some type of disability (Erickson, Lee, & von Schrader, 2009). Quite a different disability rate surfaces when the definition of physical functioning (in terms of nine daily activities) in the National Health Interview Survey data set is used: 17% of women (19.9 million) in 2006 had at least one physical difficulty compared with 12% of men (12.3 million), and more women than men had difficulty performing each of the nine physical activities. When results are considered by single race, sex, and ethnicity, non-Hispanic Black women were more likely to find at least one of the nine physical activities very difficult or impossible to do compared with the other single race-sex or single race-ethnicity groupings (Pleis & Lethbridge-Cejku, 2006, p. 9). People who have difficulty in physical function comprise only one subset of the disabled population; therefore, the actual number of women with any kind of disability-related limitation may be much greater than reported earlier.

According to the 1994 and 1995 National Health Interview Survey (Chevarley, Thierry, Gill, Ryerson, & Nosek, 2006), women with three or more functional limitations, compared to women in general, were less likely to be married (40% vs. 63%); more likely to be living alone (35% vs. 13%); more likely to have only a high school education or less (78% vs. 54%); less likely to be employed (14% vs. 63%); more likely to be living in households below the poverty level (23% vs. 10%), particularly in the 18 to 44 years age group; and less likely to have private health insurance (55% vs. 74%). Other studies (Jans & Stoddard, 1999; McNeil, 1997) have shown that men earn substantially higher monthly incomes than women whether or not they have a disability ($2,190 vs. $1,470 for men vs. women without disabilities; $1,262 vs. $1,000 for men vs. women with severe disabilities). Men with work disabilities are more likely to receive benefits from Social Security (30.6% vs. 25.6%), but women with work disabilities are more likely to receive food stamps, Medicaid, and housing assistance.

In terms of health care needs, women with functional limitations, especially younger women, are more likely to see a specialist, delay getting care because of cost, and are unable to get care for general medical conditions or surgery, mental health needs, dental needs, prescription medicine, or eyeglasses. Although hypertension, depression, stress, smoking, and being overweight are concerns for women in general, these problems are significantly greater among women with functional limitations (Chevarley et al., 2006). Nearly a third of women with three or more functional limitations rate their overall health as poor compared to less than 1% of women with no limitations.

The prevalence of disability is highly correlated with age, with 40% of women 65 years and older having at least one functional limitation. The most prevalent disabling condition in women is back disorder (15.3%), followed by arthritis (13.3%), cardiovascular disease (9.7%), asthma (5.3%), orthopedic impairment of lower extremity (4.2%), mental disorders (3.3%), diabetes (3.3%), and learning disability and mental retardation (2.5%). Men are also most often disabled by back disorders (15.9%), but the list varies from there, with cardiovascular disease (11.4%), followed by orthopedic impairment of lower extremity (6.1%), arthritis (5.8%), asthma (5.4%), learning disability and mental retardation (5.0%), mental disorders (4.6%), and diabetes (2.9%) (LaPlante & Carlson, 1996). In case of disabilities resulting from trauma, such as spinal cord injury (DeVivo & Chen, 2011) and brain injury (TBI National Data and Statistics Center, 2010), men outnumber women, 4 to 1. Women, however, have a greater prevalence of many physically disabling health conditions compared to men, such as joint and connective tissue disorders (rheumatoid arthritis, fibromyalgia) (Lawrence et al., 2008), systemic lupus erythematosus (Bernatsky et al., 2009), osteoporosis (Johnell & Kanis, 2006), and multiple sclerosis (Noonan et al., 2010).

The most limiting characteristic shared by a high percentage of women with physical disabilities is that of low economic status. For women with disabilities aged 16 to 64 years, nearly two and a half times as many live in poverty as do their counterparts with no disability (28.1% vs. 11.9%) (U.S. Census Bureau, 2006). Women with disabilities share the economic-related problems of women in general, including low wages and occupational segregation (Schaller & DeLaGarza, 1995). They may, however, also experience restricted career opportunities associated with the nature of their disabilities, gender plus disability socialization experiences, and a lack of role models or mentors (Patterson, DeLaGarza, & Schaller, 1998). Women with gradual-onset disabilities, such as arthritis, fibromyalgia, lupus, multiple sclerosis, and neuromuscular disorders, may live on the edge of poverty because they are unable to maintain their level of employment as symptoms increase. Reducing their hours or changing jobs usually means lower pay and no health insurance. Earning even a minimal salary makes them ineligible for government-funded health care (Medicaid, Medicare). Women with early-onset disabilities or traumatic injuries, who have no other means of support from spouse or family, often cannot afford to work. They must maintain a state of poverty in order to qualify for the government-funded medical, personal assistance, food, and housing benefits they need to survive. The health care that is available to them through Medicaid is the lowest tier in the dysfunctional health care system of this country (Nosek, 2010b). Those who have disabilities that are severe enough to make working unfeasible qualify for Social Security and Medicare and fair far better.

Despite an increasing number of publications purporting to characterize the population of people with disabilities, consistent and detailed reports of findings about the number of women with disabilities living in the United States and their specific demographic and health characteristics are not available. Despite a substantial amount of federal funding allocated to identifying and removing health disparities and developing health promotion interventions, women with disabilities have not garnered a position on the priority list. Indeed, they are not even considered a health disparities population (Nosek & Simmons, 2007).

The demographic characteristics of the population of women with disabilities will change substantially in the coming years because of the improved survival rate of low birth-weight newborns, resulting in higher rates of children with activity limitation and permanent disability (National Center for Health Statistics, 2006), as well as the aging and functional decline of baby boomers. The combination of longer life expectancy and increased disability rates is expected to more than triple the number of persons aged 65 years and older with severe or moderate disabilities in the coming 50 years (Siegel, 1996). Our society does not seem prepared for the rapidly expanding population of women with disabilities across the life span who may face serious and worsening social disadvantages (Nosek, 2006).

To illustrate more specifically the need to examine the disability-related needs of women, we now present evidence from the literature and our own studies about five major psychosocial problems that are disproportionately severe for women with disabilities compared to men with disabilities and women in general. The topics to be discussed are depression, stress, self-esteem, social connectedness, and abuse.

A MODEL FOR UNDERSTANDING HEALTH IN THE CONTEXT OF DISABILITY FOR WOMEN

There has been considerable discussion of the disability relevance of health and wellness models that include biological, psychological, social, and spiritual elements (Myers & Sweeney, 2004; Nosek, 2005; Roberts & Stuifbergen, 1998). After putting these together with what I have learned from many years of living and studying independent living (Nosek & Fuhrer, 1992) and feminism (Nosek, 2010a), I am convinced that there has not been enough attention placed on context, particularly for women. Context is not only the environment but the entirety of a woman's past experience and current living situation in our patriarchal society. As a longtime student of Eastern philosophy and religion, I have come to understand that spirituality is not just one part of the analytic model; it is the whole thing (Nosek, 1995; Nosek & Hughes, 2001; Nosek et al., 2004). I have now begun to teach this model by using a tetrahedron, a three-sided pyramid, as a visual aid. The visible faces represent in equal measure the biological, psychological, and social elements of being. Without any one of them, the integrity of the structure cannot be maintained. The part that is not visible is the base of the tetrahedron, which represents context. Without considering that element, it is impossible to understand why women with disabilities experience such extreme health disparities. The entire structure, including the base and all that surrounds it, is a manifestation of spirituality or, as some would prefer to phrase it, the feeling of essence or connection with a higher power (Figure 8.1).

This heuristic allows for a holistic approach to health promotion. I describe the construct of context as including factors that are either internal to the individual or external in the environment and tend not to be easily changed, but some of them can be modified through management strategies (Nosek, 2005). These include health history, disability characteristics, demographics, relationships, values and beliefs, life experiences, and environmental resources. The category of environmental resources encompasses many aspects of the micro-, meso-, exo-, and macrosystems in which people with disabilities live, including access to financial resources, education level, the built and natural environment, technology, information from the print and broadcast media and the Internet, instrumental social support and services, and access to health care services. At the Center for Research on Women with Disabilities, we postulate that psychological factors, such as self-esteem and self-efficacy, together with social connectedness can mediate the effect of context on health behaviors and health outcomes (Figure 8.2). By creating and testing health promotion interventions that offer information, goal setting and action planning, and opportunities for women with disabilities to connect with one another, women can be empowered to improve their health behaviors and health outcomes. To date, we have had success in using this approach to address general health promotion, aging and health promotion, self-esteem enhancement, stress reduction, and self-management of depression for women with physical disabilities. Attending face-to-face workshops, however, is difficult for some women who deal with significant mobility impairments, transportation and environmental barriers, lack of personal assistance, and interference in their daily lives from pain and fatigue. To circumvent these participation barriers, we have begun testing the effectiveness of offering our

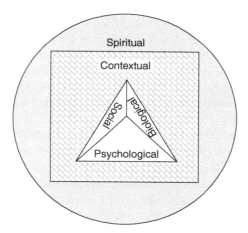

FIGURE 8.1 A contextual model of health.

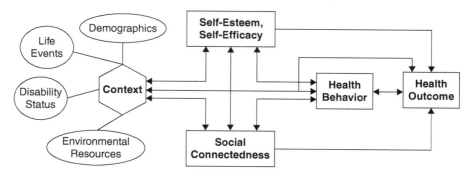

FIGURE 8.2 A health-promotion model for women with physical disabilities.

intervention programs using the Internet, both via interactive websites and 3D immersive virtual environments, such as Second Life.

SELF-ESTEEM

Self-esteem and its related constructs appear to play a central role in the psychological well-being of persons with functional limitations (O'Leary, Shoor, Lorig, & Holman, 1988), including women with physical disabilities (Abraido-Lanza, Guier, & Colon, 1998). It can be threatened at times of declining health and increased functional limitation associated with the development of secondary health conditions such as pain, fatigue, and other new symptoms (Burckhardt, 1985; Mahat, 1997; Schlesinger, 1996; Taal, Rasker, & Wiegman, 1997). In the context of disability, self-worth may be compromised by internalizing the devaluation that society tends to assign physical impairment (Wright, 1960).

The literature offers convincing evidence that positive self-esteem is fundamental to psychological and social well-being. It has been defined as a comparison of accomplishment to hopes, and a personal awareness and recognition of all of one's being (James, 1890; May, 1953). The effect of interpersonal feedback and the environment is a link to a sense of belongingness, societal contribution, and gaining approval from significant others (Adler, Ansbacher, & Ansbacher, 1979). Our research suggests that this is particularly true for women with disabilities (Nosek, 1996; Nosek, Hughes, Swedlund, Taylor, & Swank, 2003).

Feminist theory posits that for women "the primary experience of self is relational, that is, the self is organized and developed in the context of important relationships" (Surrey, 1991, p. 51). As a result of this relational context of sense of self, a woman's perception about how others view her disability may become internalized and incorporated into her definitions and evaluation of self, resulting in low self-esteem.

Disability is a stigmatizing phenomenon as shown by the lower levels of self-esteem observed among individuals with disabilities compared to those without disabilities (Craig, Hancock, & Chang, 1994; Felton, Revenson, & Hinrichsen, 1984; Magill-Evans & Restall, 1991; Walsh & Walsh, 1989). When combined with women's social devaluation, its effects on the sense of self can be profound. The relevant literature portrays a woman who is challenged to accommodate increased needs for personal assistance; to grieve multiple losses, increased vulnerabilities, and externally imposed invisibility; to maintain self-efficacy for inclusion; to test self-evaluation as opposed to societal devaluation equating functional abilities with personal value; and to deal with environmental factors such as barriers to employment and health care, interpersonal violence, and inaccessibility. Yet, clinical experience suggests many women who acquire disability at birth or later develop and maintain positive self-worth. The literature on self-esteem in the context of disability fails to explain these differences and the connections between self-esteem and health outcomes, particularly as related to gender. Our national study of women with physical disabilities revealed that this population experiences low self-esteem and the problems associated with it, such as depression, unemployment, social isolation, limited opportunities to establish satisfying relationships, and emotional, physical, and sexual abuse (Nosek, Howland, Rintala, Young, & Chanpong, 2001).

People with disabilities must continually cope with assaults to their self-esteem by negative societal attitudes, which would have us believe that individuals with disabilities are "ill, pitiful, asexual, and incapable of employment" (Perduta-Fulginiti, 1996, p. 298). Finally, the literature validates our clinical picture of women who—like those in our face-to-face group intervention studies—must mobilize fierce, personal efficacy for coping with, and connecting to, the contextual experience of disability. The link of self-esteem with health status is evidenced by decreased self-esteem related to symptom exacerbation, increased functional limitation, and/or the emergence of secondary health conditions (Gatten, Brookings, & Bolton, 1993; Maynard & Roller, 1991; Schlesinger, 1996).

Self-esteem in adulthood has been linked to childhood experiences. We explored relations among a set of precursor variables (age, education, severity of disability, and childhood experiences, including overprotection, familial affection, and school environment) and a set of adult outcome variables (intimacy, employment, and health maintenance behavior) (Nosek et al., 2003). We hypothesized that variables related to one's sense of self (self-cognition, social isolation, and self-esteem) would mediate the effects of the precursor variables on adult outcomes. The sample included 881 women—475 with physical disabilities and 406 without disabilities, aged 18 to 65 years who were Caucasian (82%), African American (9%), or other ethnic minority women (9%). Our findings indicated that the women with disabilities had significantly less education, were more overprotected during childhood, and had lower rates of salaried employment than the women without disabilities. Additionally, women with disabilities had significantly lower self-esteem and self-cognition and greater social isolation. The self variables did prove to mediate the effect of the precursors on the outcomes in a number of ways. Self-esteem, for example, mediated the impact of family affection and school environment on intimacy and mediated the impact of some of the precursor variables on employment and health maintenance.

Self-esteem appears to be a malleable factor in women with disabilities. We developed a psychoeducational, peer-led, self-esteem enhancement program for women with disabilities (Hughes, Taylor, Robinson-Whelen, Swedlund, & Nosek, 2004). In collaboration with five centers for independent living (CIL), we recruited 102 participants and randomly assigned them to either CIL services alone or CIL services plus the program on self-esteem. The results indicated that participants in the intervention showed significantly greater improvement on two measures of self-esteem: self-efficacy and depression. The two groups did not differ significantly on social connectedness. We concluded that women with physical disabilities can benefit from peer-led self-esteem enhancement interventions and that such interventions should be incorporated into CIL services.

SOCIAL CONNECTEDNESS

Intimate relationships and other sources of connectedness and support may offer people with disabilities an important validation of self-worth (Crisp, 1996); however, social isolation has been strongly associated with health problems and mortality (Berkman & Syme, 1979). Relationships often provide positive social support that serves important functions for the well-being of people with physical disabilities (Patrick, Morgan, & Charlton, 1986). Social isolation is regarded by some as a very common secondary condition associated with any primary disability (Coyle, Santiago, Shank, Ma, & Boyd, 2000; Ravesloot, Seekins, & Walsh, 1997). Physical restrictions, such as fatigue and pain, may discourage people from making contact and connecting with others. Common knowledge and clinical experience suggest that the combination of multiple environmental barriers, negative societal messages, and diminished social opportunities may lead women with disabilities to become disconnected and isolated from sources of support and intimacy, employment opportunities, and health-promoting opportunities.

Part of the theoretical foundation for our intervention research is the importance of social connectedness and self-efficacy in relation to self-esteem and other outcomes. First, social connectedness serves as a foundation for self-esteem in women (Jordan, Kaplan, Miller, Stiver, & Surrey, 1991). Feminist theory postulates that women's groups may reduce social isolation by offering participants an opportunity to share common life experiences and connect more effectively with one another (Burden & Gottlieb, 1987; Jordan et al., 1991; McManus, Redford, & Hughes, 1997; Walker, Sechrist, & Pender, 1987) and address topics difficult to discuss in mixed-gender groups (Enns, 1992). In the context of disability, greater self-esteem has been associated with better integration in social networks (Crisp, 1996). Women with physically disabling and chronic health conditions appear to benefit from the presence of mutually supportive relationships with one another (Crigger, 1996; Fine & Asch, 1988; Hughes, Nosek, Howland, Groff, & Mullen, 2003; Hughes et al., 2004; Hughes, Robinson-Whelen, Taylor, & Hall, 2006; Reid-Cunningham, Snyder-Grant, Stein, Tyson, & Halen, 1999). In our group intervention studies, we have drawn successfully on the use of peer leaders, a practice grounded in the independent living movement with its emphasis on role modeling, consumer participation, and empowerment (Nosek & Fuhrer, 1992).

In our group intervention studies, women shared how they yearn for and benefit from opportunities to develop caring relationships with one another, to heal their shared multiple losses, and to strive for optimal wellness. Women with physically disabling conditions may clearly benefit from the resources of supportive relationships (Hughes, Swedlund, Petersen, & Nosek, 2001).

ABUSE

It took a long time for abuse against women with disabilities to surface in the research literature. For most of history, it was an accepted practice and sometimes even encouraged; women with disabilities were safe targets because they were less able to fight back and less likely to be believed (Pelletier, 1989). Canadians were the first to take a serious look at the issue. Disabled Women's Network Canada/Réseau d'action des femmes handicapées du Canada (DAWN-RAFH) conducted a survey of the needs and concerns of women with disabilities in 1989 and analyzed responses from 245 women (Pelletier, 1989). They found that 40% had been raped, abused, or assaulted and 64% had been verbally abused; girls with disabilities had a less than equal chance of escaping violence; women with disabilities had little access to services for victims of violence; and women with multiple disabilities reported being multiply abused. They also asked about perpetrators, reporting of violence, and response to violence, as well as passing an organizational action agenda related to these findings. Sadly, abuse of women with disabilities is a little different in the United States 20 years later, but at least we can describe it more accurately.

Although early research focused primarily on physical, sexual, and emotional violence against women with disabilities, additional forms of disability-specific violence have now been documented (Nosek, Foley, Hughes, & Howland, 2001; Powers, Hughes, & Lund, 2009). Examples include destruction of medical equipment and communication devices, withholding, stealing or overdosing of medications, physical neglect, and financial abuse (Curry, Powers, Oschwald, & Saxton, 2004; Gilson, DePoy, & Cramer, 2001; McFarlane et al., 2001; Saxton et al., 2001). Rates of abuse vary considerably across studies depending on the definitions used and the types of disabilities represented in the sample. A comparison of the abuse experienced by a large sample of women with disabilities with their nondisabled women friends found comparable rates of abuse (Young, Nosek, Howland, Chanpong, & Rintala, 1997). Most studies, however, show significantly higher rates of violence among women with disabilities (Powers et al., 2009) and that they are more likely to experience physical and sexual violence (Brownridge, 2006; Martin et al., 2006; Powers et al., 2002; Smith, 2008), increased severity of violence (Brownridge, 2006; Nannini, 2006; Nosek, Howland, & Hughes, 2001), multiple forms of violence (Curry et al., 2004; Martin et al., 2006; Nosek, Foley, et al., 2001), and longer duration of violence (Nosek, Howland, & Hughes, 2001). A consistent theme across the research is the complex intersections of disabled women's experience of impairment, poverty, isolation, reliance on others for support, discrimination, and other factors that may restrict women's violence awareness, safety-promoting behavior, and access to resources (Copel, 2006; Hassouneh-Phillips, McNeff, Powers, & Curry, 2005; Nosek, Hughes, Taylor, & Taylor, 2006).

Contrary to what some may believe, disability does not serve as a protective factor against abuse for women (Nosek, Howland, & Hughes, 2001). We strongly recommend that counselors use a very simple screening tool that we developed, the Abuse Assessment Screen—Disability (McFarlane et al., 2001), which includes four items assessing physical, sexual, and disability-related abuse in the past year. We found that women who were positive for abuse tended to be younger, had more education, had greater mobility impairments, were more socially isolated, and reported more symptoms of depression (Nosek et al., 2006). This important topic is discussed in greater detail in Chapter 23.

STRESS

Women in the general population have reported higher levels of perceived stress than their male counterparts (Cohen & Williamson, 1988). We also know that having a physical disability constitutes a chronic life strain (Turner & Wood, 1985). Thus, women with physical disabilities are at increased risk for experiencing stress and its negative health consequences as a result of being both female and having a disability (Coyle et al., 2000; Hughes, Taylor, Robinson-Whelen, & Nosek, 2005; Rintala, Hart, & Fuhrer, 1996). Hughes, Taylor, and colleagues (2005), who observed elevated levels of perceived stress in a sample of 415 women with physical disabilities, reported that greater perceived stress was linked with lower levels of social support, greater pain limitations, and recent experience with abuse. According to an analysis of data from the National Health Interview Survey, 1992 and 1994, women with disabilities (three or more functional limitations) are 10 times more likely to report having difficulty with day-to-day stress than women with no limitations (21% vs. 2%) when age was adjusted (Chevarley et al., 2005).

Stress reflects the extent to which individuals perceive their lives to be unpredictable, uncontrollable, and overloading (Cohen & Williamson, 1988). Although everyone lives with some degree of stress, its impact on people with disabilities may be more severe because of the fact that they often have a more vulnerable physical and psychological health status (Turner & Noh, 1988), and fewer resources to buffer the effects of stress. Social support, which has been well studied as a stress buffer (Cohen & Wills, 1985), is often lacking or inadequate among women with disabilities (Crewe & Clarke, 1996; Rintala et al., 1996). Hughes and colleagues found that, after controlling for demographics and disability characteristics, perceived stress is greater for women with physical disabilities who have less social support, greater pain, and an experience with abuse in the past year (Hughes, Robinson-Whelen, Taylor, Petersen, & Nosek, 2005).

Elevated blood pressure, chronic pain, and irritable bowel syndrome are generally acknowledged as being associated with high levels of stress, but less known is its effect on worsening disability symptoms. Stress has been associated with greater disability among those with arthritis (Weinberger, Tierney, Booher, & Hiner, 1990), elevated depressive symptomatology in spinal cord injury (Hughes et al., 2001; Rintala et al., 1996), greater symptom severity in systemic lupus erythematosus (Adams, Dammers, Saia, Brantley, & Gaydos, 1994), increased disease progression in multiple sclerosis (Schwartz et al., 1999), and exacerbations of disease activity in rheumatoid arthritis (Zautra et al., 1998).

A task force of the American Psychological Association (APA) asserted that women are likely to experience stress related to social isolation, poverty, violence, and other forms of victimization and chronic health problems (McGrath, Keita, Strickland, & Russo, 1990). Women with disabilities are often faced with the uncertainty of health problems; lack of physical fitness related to mobility limitations, pain, and illness; inadequate nutrition; abuse and violence; environmental barriers in health care settings and the workplace; and unemployment, lower wages, and poverty (Crewe & Clarke, 1996; Nosek, 2000). Other stressors related to a woman's disability include the need for personal assistance, changes in appearance, interruption of daily activities, and increased planning, time, and effort for activities of daily living (Crewe & Clarke, 1996).

Only one effort to date has been made to develop an intervention that helps women with disabilities manage stress. Hughes and colleagues together with women with disabilities modified the standard approach to stress management to include elements of feminist theory and peer role modeling from the independent living movement. This intervention offers information, opportunities to practice coping and management skills, goal setting, and action planning to increase self-efficacy, social connectedness, and peer support. When the intervention was tested in a randomized clinical trial, the intervention group showed greater improvement on measures of stress, pain, and role limitations owing to physical health compared to the wait-listed control group. Perceived stress was supported as a mediator of the effect of the intervention on mental health. There was also support for social connectedness and self-efficacy as mediators of the relation between the intervention and perceived stress (Hughes et al., 2006).

DEPRESSION

Depression is a complex phenomenon among women who live with the culturally devalued status of being female and having a disability (Fine & Asch, 1988; Gill, 1996; Nosek, Hughes, & Robinson-Whelen, 2008). As women, they are twice as likely to experience depression as men (Coyle & Roberge, 1992; Rintala et al., 1996; U.S. Department of Health and Human Services, 1999) primarily because of women's experience of being female in our culture (McGrath et al., 1990), including gender-based roles and socialization experiences (Fedele, 1994; Jordan et al., 1991; Miller, 1976). As women living with disabilities, they may experience disproportionately high rates of depressive symptomatology compared to other women, with estimates ranging from 30% to 59% (Chevarley et al., 2006; Ferguson & Cotton, 1996; Hughes et al., 2001; U.S. Department of Health and Human Services, 2000; Ward et al., 1999). Younger women with three or more functional limitations are more frequently depressed (30%) than women without disabilities (4%) and are eight times more likely to report having experienced major depression in the past year (Chevarley et al., 2006).

Some of the somatic criteria for depression (e.g., fatigue, sleep disturbance) are also common disability-related symptoms that may lead to overestimating depression (Aikens et al., 1999). On the other hand, those same symptoms can mask psychological distress (Franklin, 2000) and leave depression in women with disabilities under-detected and undertreated. Depression has been associated with conditions that often accompany disability, such as cerebral involvement or medications for the underlying disease (Cameron, 1987), pain (Kraaimaat, Van Dam-Baggen, & Bijlsma, 1995; Tate, Forchheimer, Kirsch, Maynard, & Roller, 1993), and environmental factors (Turner & Noh, 1988), such as social isolation (Murphy, Dickens, Creed, & Bernstein, 1999).

Hughes and colleagues examined depression in a sample of 443 women with physical disabilities living in the community, the majority of whom had minority backgrounds and low income (Hughes, Robinson, et al., 2005). Using the self-report Beck Depression Inventory II (BDI-II; Beck, Steer, & Brown, 1996) cutoff for significant depressive symptomatology (greater than 17), 51% of the respondents scored in the mildly depressed range or higher and 31% scored in the moderately or severely depressed range. Women classified as depressed compared to nondepressed women were significantly younger and had shorter duration of disability. Only 44% of the women classified as depressed on the BDI-II had received recent treatment for depression, and those identified as Hispanic were the least likely to have received treatment.

Rural women with physical disabilities may face even greater barriers to mental health than their urban counterparts because of greater social and geographical isolation, lack of access to health-related resources, transportation problems, and communication barriers (Levine, Lishner, Richardson, & Porter, 2001; Mulder et al., 2000). A study of 135 rural women with physical disabilities who exceeded the cutoff for depression on the BDI-II indicated that most of the women reported moderate to severe depression, and nearly one out of five reported thoughts of suicide (Hughes, Nosek, & Robinson-Whelen, 2007).

CONCLUSIONS

The life situation of women with disabilities is complex and permeated with attitudinal, social, and economic obstacles to psychosocial well-being. The evidence is irrefutable that women with disabilities are a substantial segment of the population and face more serious disadvantages than men with disabilities or women in general in achieving their life goals. Population-based research has documented very high rates of mental and physical health problems among women with disabilities, yet attention to these problems in the clinical research literature is minimal and far out of proportion to their magnitude.

The field of rehabilitation counseling has been slow to rouse regarding the importance of recognizing gender differences in the experience of disability and developing approaches that have proven to be effective in counseling women. The way of women is holistic with a very strong emphasis on mutual benefit and social connectedness. As rehabilitation counseling as a profession has its roots in the wars of the 20th century, it is understandable that it grew out of a masculine, competitive base. To maintain its relevance for a future that is witnessing the rising status of women, rehabilitation research and counseling must develop and test new approaches that incorporate balance of biological, psychological, social, contextual, and spiritual elements.

We believe that rehabilitation researchers and practitioners are ready to take action to address the needs of women. We recommend that researchers

1. Remove unnecessary enrollment criteria that would exclude or tend to exclude women with disabling conditions, such as
   a. Limiting age to less than 65 years, unless a working-age sample is essential to the design
   b. Conducting surveys or exams in inaccessible facilities
   c. Requiring telephonic response to questions
   d. Requiring attendance at a clinic or an event.
2. Eliminate procedures that require manual dexterity or mobility when these are not essential for the phenomenon under investigation (e.g., minimum competency screens, intelligence tests).
3. During recruitment, take special measures to ensure that announcements reach minority, low-income, low-education, and sensory-impaired women.
4. Set the parameters for your study carefully and state exclusion criteria in all publications of findings.
5. Always include gender as an independent variable in all data analyses. Do not simply control for gender because that, in effect, pretends that a woman is a man.
6. Advance the careers of students who are women with disabilities by offering scholarships, giving opportunities to make presentations to academic audiences, and introducing them to leaders in their field.

We recommend that rehabilitation counselors and administrators

1. Be aware of gender bias when developing rehabilitation plans for women consumers
2. Use only those assessment instruments and tools that have been validated for both genders
3. Consider, as appropriate, the woman's life situation; if abuse is suspected, refer her to community resources for battered women
4. Be vigilant for signs of stress and depression and, as appropriate, refer for psychological counseling
5. Encourage all consumers to become involved in the independent living movement or other peer support groups
6. Include gender as a variable in analyzing consumer and program outcomes
7. Ensure that advisory boards for rehabilitation services have equal representation of women and men with disabilities

It is not difficult to see that some of these recommendations cannot be implemented until more research has been conducted. When assessment techniques that are common in rehabilitation settings have been proven valid for women, when counselors have information and training about how disability can affect women differently than men, when success is defined by the same standards for both women and men, and when as many women as men have reached the highest levels of rehabilitation research, education, administration, and practice, then we will begin to see progress toward a truly inclusive society.

REFERENCES

Abraido-Lanza, A. F., Guier, C., & Colon, R. M. (1998). Psychological thriving among Latinas with chronic illness. *Journal of Social Issues, 54,* 405–424.

Adams, S. G., Dammers, P. M., Saia, T. L., Brantley, P. J., & Gaydos, G. R. (1994). Stress, depression, and anxiety predict average symptom severity and daily symptom fluctuation in systemic lupus erythematosus. *Journal of Behavioral Medicine, 17,* 459–477.

Adler, A., Ansbacher, H. L., & Ansbacher, R. R. (Eds.). (1979). *Superiority and social interest*. New York, NY: W. W. Norton.

Aikens, J. E., Reinecke, M. A., Pliskin, N. H., Fischer, J. S., Wiebe, J. S., McCracken, L. M., & Taylor, J. L. (1999). Assessing depressive symptoms in multiple sclerosis: Is it necessary to omit items from the original Beck Depression Inventory? *Journal of Behavioral Medicine, 22*(2), 127–142.

Altman, B. M. (1985). Disabled women in the social structure. In S. E. Browne, D. Conners, & N. Stern (Eds.), *With the power of each breath* (pp. 69–76). Pittsburgh, PA: Cleis Press.

Altman, B. M. (1996). Causes, risks, and consequences of disability among women. In D. M. Krotoski, M. A. Nosek, & M. A. Turk (Eds.), *Women with physical disabilities: Achieving and maintaining health and well-being* (Vol. 35–55). Baltimore, MD: Paul H. Brookes.

Axel, S. (1982). Spinal cord injured women's concerns: Menstruation and pregnancy. *Rehabilitation Nursing, 10,* 10–15.

Barnartt, S. N. (1982). The socio-economic status of deaf women: Are they doubly disadvantaged? In J. Christiansen & K. Egelston-Dodd (Eds.), *Socioeconomic status of the deaf population* (pp. 1–31). Washington, DC: Gallaudet College.

Beck, A. T., Steer, R. A., & Brown, G. K. (1996). *Manual for Beck Depression Inventory-II*. San Antonio, TX: Psychological Corporation.

Beckmann, C. R. B., Gittler, M., Barzansky, B. M., & Beckmann, C. A. (1989). Gynecologic health care of women with disabilities. *Obstetrics and Gynecology, 74,* 75–79.

Berkman, L. F., & Syme, S. L. (1979). Social networks, host resistance, and mortality: A nine-year follow-up study of Alameda County residents. *American Journal of Epidemiology, 109,* 186–204.

Bernatsky, S., Joseph, L., Pineau, C. A., Belisle, P., Lix, L., Banerjee, D., & Clarke, A. E. (2009). Polymyalgia rheumatica prevalence in a population-based sample. *Arthritis and Rheumatism, 61*(9), 1264–1267.

Brault, M. W. (2008). *Americans with disabilities: 2005*. Washington, DC: U.S. Census Bureau.

Brownridge, D. A. (2006). Partner violence against women with disabilities: Prevalence, risk, and explanations. *Violence Against Women, 12,* 805–822.

Burckhardt, C. S. (1985). The impact of arthritis on quality of life. *Nursing Research, 34,* 11–16.

Burden, D. S., & Gottlieb, N. (1987). Women's socialization and feminist groups. In C. M. Brody (Ed.), *Women's therapy groups: Paradigms of feminist treatment* (pp. 24–39). New York, NY: Springer Publishing.

Cameron, O. G. (1987). Some guidelines for a pragmatic approach to the patient with secondary depression. In O. G. Cameron (Ed.), *Presentations of depression: Depressive symptoms in medical and other psychiatric disorders* (pp. 417–423). New York, NY: John Wiley.

Carty, E. A., & Conine, T. A. (1988). Disability and pregnancy: A double dose of disequilibrium. *Rehabilitation Nursing, 13,* 85–92.

Charlifue, S. W., Gerhart, K. A., Menter, R. R., Whiteneck, G. G., & Manley, M. S. (1992). Sexual issues of women with spinal cord injuries. *Paraplegia, 30,* 192–199.

Chevarley, F., Thierry, J. M., Gill, C. J., Ryerson, A. B., & Nosek, M. A. (2006). Health, preventive health care, and health care access among women with disabilities in the 1994–1995 National Health Interview Survey. *Women's Health Issues, 16*(6), 297–312.

Cohen, S., & Williamson, G. M. (1988). Perceived stress in a probability sample of the United States. In S.Spacapan & S. Oskamp (Eds.), *The social psychology of health: Claremont symposium on applied social psychology* (pp. 31–67). Newbury Park, CA: Sage.

Cohen, S., & Wills, T. A. (1985). Stress, social support, and the buffering hypothesis. *Psychological Bulletin, 98,* 310–357.

Cole, T. M. (1975). Spinal cord injured patients and sexual dysfunction. *Archives of Physical Medicine and Rehabilitation, 56,* 11–12.

Comarr, A. E. (1976). Sexual response of paraplegic women. *Medical Aspects of Human Sexuality, 10,* 124–128.

Copel, L. C. (2006). Partner abuse in physically disabled women: A proposed model for understanding intimate partner violence. *Perspectives in Psychiatric Care, 42*(2), 114–129.

Coyle, C. P., & Roberge, J. J. (1992). The psychometric properties of the Center for Epidemiological Studies-Depression Scale (CES-D) when used with adults with physical disabilities. *Psychology & Health, 7,* 69–81.

Coyle, C. P., Santiago, M. C., Shank, J. W., Ma, G. X., & Boyd, R. (2000). Secondary conditions and women with physical disabilities: A descriptive study. *Archives of Physical Medicine and Rehabilitation, 81*(10), 1380–1387.

Craig, A. R., Hancock, K., & Chang, E. (1994). The influence of spinal cord injury on coping styles and self-perceptions two years after the injury. *Australian and New Zealand Journal of Psychiatry, 28,* 307–312.

Crewe, N. M., & Clarke, N. (1996). Stress and women with disabilities. In D. Krotoski, M. A. Nosek, & M. A. Turk (Eds.), *Women with physical disabilities: Achieving and maintaining health and well-being* (pp. 193–202). Baltimore, MD: Paul H. Brookes.

Crigger, N. J. (1996). Testing an uncertainty model for women with multiple sclerosis. *Advances in Nursing Science, 18,* 37–47.

Crisp, R. (1996). Community integration, self-esteem, and vocational identity among persons with disabilities. *Australian Psychologist, 31,* 133–137.

Curry, M. A., Powers, L. E., Oschwald, M., & Saxton, M. (2004). Development and testing of an abuse screening tool for women with disabilities. *Journal of Aggression, Maltreatment and Trauma, 8*(4), 123–141.

Deegan, M. J., & Brooks, N. A. (Eds.). (1985). *Women and disability: The double handicap.* New Brunswick, NJ: Transaction Books, Rutgers University.

DeVivo, M. J., & Chen, Y. (2011). Trends in new injuries, prevalent cases, and aging with spinal cord injury. *Archives of Physical Medicine and Rehabilitation, 92,* 332–338.

Enns, C. Z. (1992). Self-esteem groups: A synthesis of conscious-raising and assertiveness training. *Journal of Counseling and Development, 71,* 7–13.

Erickson, W., Lee, C., & von Schrader, S. (2009). *2008 Disability Status Report: The United States.* Ithaca, NY: Cornell University Rehabilitation Research and Training Center on Disability Demographics and Statistics.

Fedele, N. (1994). *Relationships in groups: Connection, resonance, and paradox: Work in progress, No. 69.* Wellesley, MA: Stone Center Working Papers Series.

Felton, B. J., Revenson, T. A., & Hinrichsen, G. A. (1984). Stress and coping in the explanation of psychological adjustment among chronically ill adults. *Social Science and Medicine, 18*(10), 889–898.

Ferguson, S. J., & Cotton, S. (1996). Broken sleep, pain, disability, social activity, and depressive symptoms in rheumatoid arthritis. *Australian Journal of Psychology, 48*(1), 9–14.

Fine, M., & Asch, A. (1985). Disabled women: Sexism without the pedestal. In M. J. Deegan & N. A. Brooks (Eds.), *Women and disability: The double handicap* (pp. 6–22). New Brunswick, NJ: Transaction Books.

Fine, M., & Asch, A. (Eds.). (1988). *Women with disabilities: Essays in psychology, culture, and politics.* Philadelphia, PA: Temple University Press.

Franklin, D. J. (2000). Depression: Information and treatment [Electronic version]. *Psychology Information Online.*

Gatten, C. W., Brookings, J. B., & Bolton, B. (1993). Mood fluctuations in female multiple sclerosis patients. *Social Behavior and Personality, 21,* 103–106.

Gill, C. (1996). Becoming visible: Personal health experiences of women with disabilities. In D. M. Krotoski, M. A. Nosek, & M. A. Turk (Eds.), *Women with physical disabilities: Achieving and maintaining health and well-being* (pp. 5–15). Baltimore, MD: Paul H. Brookes.

Gilson, S. F., DePoy, E., & Cramer, E. P. (2001). Linking the assessment of self-reported functional capacity with abuse experiences of women with disabilities. *Violence Against Women, 7*(4), 418–431.

Griffith, E. R., & Trieschmann, R. B. (1975). Sexual functioning in women with spinal cord injury. *Archives of Physical Medicine and Rehabilitation, 56,* 18–21.

Hassouneh-Phillips, D., McNeff, E., Powers, L. E., & Curry, M. (2005). Invalidation: A central process underlying maltreatment of women with disabilities. *Women and Health, 41*(1), 33–50.

Hughes, R. B., Nosek, M. A., Howland, C. A., Groff, J., & Mullen, P. D. (2003). Health promotion workshop for women with physical disabilities: A pilot study. *Rehabilitation Psychology, 48,* 182–188.

Hughes, R. B., Nosek, M. A., & Robinson-Whelen, S. (2007). Correlates of depression in rural women with physical disabilities. *Journal of Obstetric, Gynecologic, and Neonatal Nursing, 36*(1), 105–114.

Hughes, R. B., Robinson-Whelen, S., Taylor, H. B., & Hall, J. W. (2006). Stress self-management: An intervention for women with physical disabilities. *Women's Health Issues, 16*(6), 389–399.

Hughes, R. B., Robinson-Whelen, S., Taylor, H. B., Petersen, N., & Nosek, M. A. (2005). Characteristics of depressed and non-depressed women with physical disabilities. *Archives of Physical Medicine & Rehabilitation, 86*(3), 473–479.

Hughes, R. B., Swedlund, N., Petersen, N., & Nosek, M. A. (2001). Depression and women with spinal cord injury. *Topics in Spinal Cord Injury Rehabilitation, 7*(1), 16–24.

Hughes, R. B., Taylor, H. B., Robinson-Whelen, S., & Nosek, M. A. (2005). Perceived stress in women with physical disabilities: Identifying psychosocial correlates. *Womens Health Issues, 15,* 14–20.

Hughes, R. B., Taylor, H. B., Robinson-Whelen, S., Swedlund, N., & Nosek, M. A. (2004). Enhancing self-esteem in women with physical disabilities. *Rehabilitation Psychology, 19*(4), 295–302.

Jackson, A. B., & Varner, R. E. (1989). Gynecological problems encountered in women with acute and chronic spinal cord disabilities [Abstract]. *Abstracts Digest,* 111–112.

Jackson, A. B., & Wadley, V. (1999). A multicenter study of women's self-reported reproductive health after spinal cord injury. *Archives of Physical Medicine and Rehabilitation, 80*(11), 1420–1428.

James, W. (1890). *Principles of psychology.* New York, NY: Dover.

Jans, L., & Stoddard, S. (1999). *Chartbook on women and disability in the United States: An InfoUse report.* Washington, DC: U.S. Department of Education, National Institute on Disability and Rehabilitation Research.

Johnell, O., & Kanis, J. A. (2006). An estimate of the worldwide prevalence and disability associated with osteoporotic fractures. *Osteoporosis International, 17,* 1726.

Jordan, J. V., Kaplan, A. G., Miller, J. B., Stiver, I. P., & Surrey, J. L. (1991). *Women's growth in connection.* New York, NY: Guilford Press.

Kraaimaat, F. W., Van Dam-Baggen, C. M., & Bijlsma, J. W. (1995). Depression, anxiety and social support in rheumatoid arthritic women without and with a spouse. *Psychology and Health, 10,* 387–396.

LaPlante, M. P. (1991). *Disability risks of chronic illnesses and impairments.* Washington, DC: National Institute on Disability and Rehabilitation Research, U.S. Department of Education.

LaPlante, M. P., & Carlson, D. (1996). *Disability in the United States: Prevalence and causes, 1992: Disability Statistics Report: Report 7.* Washington, DC: National Institute on Disability and Rehabilitation Research, U.S. Department of Education.

Lawrence, R. C., Felson, D. T., Helmick, C. G., Arnold, L. M., Choi, H., Deyo, R. A.,... Stone, J. H.; National Arthritis Data Workgroup. (2008). Estimates of the prevalence of arthritis and other rheumatic conditions in the United States: Part II. *Arthritis & Rheumatism, 58*(1), 26–35.

Leavesley, G., & Porter, J. (1982). Sexuality, fertility and contraception in disability. *Contraception, 26,* 417–441.

Levine, P., Lishner, D., Richardson, M., & Porter, A. (2001). Face on the data: Access to health care for people with disabilities living in rural communities. In R. M. Moore III (Ed.), *The hidden America: Social problems in rural America for the twenty-first century* (pp. 179–196). Cranbury, NJ: Associated University Press.

Magill-Evans, J. E., & Restall, G. (1991). Self-esteem of persons with cerebral palsy: From adolescence to adulthood. *American Journal of Occupational Therapy, 45,* 819–825.

Mahat, G. (1997). Perceived stressors and coping strategies among individuals with rheumatoid arthritis. *Journal of Advanced Nursing, 25,* 1144–1150.

Martin, S. L., Ray, N., Sotres-Alvarez, D., Kupper, L. L., Moracco, K. E., Dickens, P. A.,...Gizlice, Z. (2006). Physical and sexual assault of women with disabilities. *Violence Against Women, 12,* 823–837.

May, R. (1953). *Man's search for himself.* New York, NY: New American Library.

Maynard, F. M., & Roller, S. (1991). Recognizing typical coping styles of polio survivors can improve rehabilitation. *American Journal of Physical Medicine and Rehabilitation, 70,* 70–2.

McFarlane, J., Hughes, R. B., Nosek, M. A., Groff, J. Y., Swedlund, N., & Mullen, P. D. (2001). Abuse assessment screen-disability (AAS-D): Measuring frequency, type, and perpetrator of abuse towards women with physical disabilities. *Journal of Women's Health and Gender-Based Medicine, 10*(9), 861–866.

McGrath, E., Keita, G. P., Strickland, B. R., & Russo, N. F. (1990). *Women and depression: Risk factors and treatment issues: Final report.* Washington, DC: American Psychological Association's National Task Force on Women and Depression.

McManus, P. W., Redford, J. L., & Hughes, R. B. (1997). Connecting to self and others: A structured group for women. *The Journal for Specialists in Group Work, 22,* 22–30.

McNeil, J. M. (1997). *Americans with disabilities 1994–1995.* Washington, DC: U.S. Census Bureau.

Miller, J. B. (1976). *Toward a new psychology of women.* Boston, MA: Beacon Press.

Mulder, P. L., Shellenberger, S., Streigel, R., Jumper-Thurman, P., Danda, C. E., Kenkel, M. B., ... Hager, A. (2000). *The behavioral health care needs of rural women: An APA Report to Congress.* Washington, DC: American Psychological Association.

Murphy, H., Dickens, C., Creed, F., & Bernstein, R. (1999). Depression, illness perception and coping in rheumatoid arthritis. *Journal of Psychosomatic Research, 46,* 155–164.

Myers, J. E., & Sweeney, T. J. (2004). The indivisible self: An evidence-based model of wellness. *Journal of Individual Psychology, 60*(3), 234–245.

Nannini, A. (2006). Sexual assault patterns among women with and without disabilities seeking survivor services. *Women's Health Issues, 16*(6), 372–379.

National Center for Health Statistics. (2006). *Health, United States, 2006, with chartbook on trends in the health of Americans.* Hyattsville, MD: National Center for Health Statistics.

Noonan, C. W., Williamson, D. M., Henry, J. P., Indian, R., Lynch, S. G., Neuberger, J. S.,... Marrie, R. A. (2010). The prevalence of multiple sclerosis in 3 US communities. *Preventing Chronic Disease, 7*(1), A12.

Nosek, M. A. (1995). The defining light of Vedanta: Personal reflections on spirituality and disability. *Rehabilitation Education, 9*(2–3), 171–182.

Nosek, M. A. (1996). Wellness among women with physical disabilities. *Sexuality and Disability, 14*(3), 165–182.

Nosek, M. A. (2000). The John Stanley Coulter lecture. Overcoming the odds: The health of women with physical disabilities in the United States. *Archives of Physical Medicine and Rehabilitation, 81,* 135–138.

Nosek, M. A. (2005). Wellness in the context of disability. In J. Myers & T. Sweeney (Eds.), *Wellness in counseling: Theory, research, and practice*. Alexandria, VA: American Counseling Association.

Nosek, M. A. (2006). The changing face of women with disabilities: Are we ready? *Journal of Women's Health and Gender-Based Medicine, 15*(9), 996–999.

Nosek, M. A. (2010a). Feminism and disability: Synchronous agendas in conflict. In H. Landrine & N. Russo (Eds.), *Handbook of diversity in feminist psychology* (pp. 501–533). New York, NY: Springer Publishing.

Nosek, M. A. (2010b). Healthcare apartheid and quality of life for people with disabilities. *Quality of Life Research, 19*(4), 609–610

Nosek, M. A., Foley, C. C., Hughes, R. B., & Howland, C. A. (2001). Vulnerabilities for abuse among women with disabilities. *Sexuality and Disability, 19*(3), 177–190.

Nosek, M. A., & Fuhrer, M. J. (1992). Independence among people with disabilities: I. A heuristic model. *Rehabilitation Counseling Bulletin, 36*(1), 6–20.

Nosek, M. A., Howland, C., & Hughes, R. B. (2001). The investigation of abuse and women with disabilities: Going beyond assumptions. *Violence Against Women, 7*(4), 477–499.

Nosek, M. A., Howland, C. A., Rintala, D. H., Young, M. E., & Chanpong, G. F. (2001). National study of women with physical disabilities: Final report. *Sexuality and Disability, 19*(1), 5–39.

Nosek, M. A., & Hughes, R. B. (2001). Psychospiritual aspects of sense of self in women with physical disabilities. *Journal of Rehabilitation, 67*(1), 20–25.

Nosek, M. A., Hughes, R. B., Howland, C. A., Young, M. E., Mullen, P. D., & Shelton, M. (2004). The meaning of health for women with physical disabilities: A qualitative study. *Family & Community Health, 27*(1), 6–21.

Nosek, M. A., Hughes, R. B., & Robinson-Whelen, S. (2008). The complex array of antecedents of depression in women with physical disabilities: Implications for clinicians. *Disability and Rehabilitation, 30*(3), 174–183.

Nosek, M. A., Hughes, R. B., Swedlund, N., Taylor, H. B., & Swank, P. (2003). Self-esteem and women with disabilities. *Social Science and Medicine, 56*(8), 1737–1747.

Nosek, M. A., Hughes, R. B., Taylor, H. B., & Taylor, P. (2006). Disability, psychosocial, and demographic characteristics of abused women with physical disabilities. *Violence Against Women, 12*(9), 1–13.

Nosek, M. A., & Simmons, D. K. (2007). People with disabilities as a health disparities population: The case of sexual and reproductive health disparities. *California Journal of Health Promotion 5, Special Issue (Health Disparities & Social Justice),* 68–81.

O'Leary, A., Shoor, S., Lorig, K., & Holman, H. R. (1988). A cognitive behavioral treatment for rheumatoid arthritis. *Health Psychology, 7,* 527–544.

Patrick, D. L., Morgan, M., & Charlton, R. H. (1986). Psychosocial support and change in the health status of physically disabled people. *Social Science and Medicine, 22,* 1347–1354.

Patterson, J. B., DeLaGarza, D., & Schaller, J. (1998). Rehabilitation counseling practice: Considerations and interventions. In R. M. Parker & E. M. Szymanski (Ed.), *Rehabilitation counseling: Basics and beyond* (3rd ed., pp. 269–302). Austin, TX: PRO-ED.

Pelletier, J. (1989). Beating the odds: Violence and women with disabilities. Retrieved from http://www.dawncanada.net/ENG/Engodds.pdf

Perduta-Fulginiti, P. S. (1996). Impact of bladder and bowel dysfunction on sexuality and self-esteem. In D. M. Krotoski, M. A. Nosek, & M. A. Turk (Eds.), *Women with physical disabilities: Achieving and maintaining health and well-being* (pp. 287–298). Baltimore, MD: Paul H. Brookes.

Pleis, J. R., & Lethbridge-Cejku, M. (2006). Summary health statistics for U.S. adults: National Health Interview Survey, 2005. National Center for Health Statistics. *Vital Health Statistics, 10*(232).

Powers, L. E., Curry, M. A., Oschwald, M., Maley, S., Eckels, K., & Saxton, M. (2002). Barriers and strategies in addressing abuse within personal assistance relationships: A survey of disabled women's experiences. *Journal of Rehabilitation, 68*(1), 4–13.

Powers, L. E., Hughes, R. B., & Lund, E. M. (2009). Interpersonal violence and women with disabilities: A research update. *Applied Research Forum, National Online Resource Center on Violence Against Women* Retrieved from http://vawnet.org/sites/default/files/materials/files/2016-09/AR_WomenWithDisabilities.pdf

Ravesloot, C., Seekins, T., & Walsh, J. (1997). A structural analysis of secondary conditions experienced by people with physical disabilities. *Rehabilitation Psychology, 42*(1), 3–16.

Reid-Cunningham, M., Snyder-Grant, D., Stein, K., Tyson, E., & Halen, B. (1999). *Work in progress: Women with chronic illness: Overcoming disconnection.* Wellesley, MA: The Stone Center.

Rintala, D. H., Hart, K. A., & Fuhrer, M. J. (1996). Perceived stress in individuals with spinal cord injury. In D. Krotoski, M. A. Nosek, & M. A. Turk (Eds.), *Women with physical disabilities: Achieving and maintaining health and well-being* (pp. 223–242). Baltimore, MD: Paul H. Brookes.

Roberts, G., & Stuifbergen, A. K. (1998). Health appraisal models in multiple sclerosis. *Social Science & Medicine, 47,* 243–253.

Saxton, M., Curry, M. A., Powers, L. E., Maley, S., Eckels, K., & Gross, J. (2001). "Bring my scooter so I can leave you": A study of disabled women handling abuse by personal assistance providers. *Violence Against Women, 7*(4), 393–417.

Schaller, J., & DeLaGarza, D. (1995). Issues of gender in vocational testing and counseling. *Journal of Job Placement, 11,* 6–14.

Schlesinger, L. (1996). Chronic pain, intimacy, and sexuality: A qualitative study of women who live with pain. *Journal of Sex Research, 33,* 249–256.

Schwartz, C. E., Foley, F. W., Rao, S. M., Bernardin, L. J., Lee, H., & Genderson, M. W. (1999). Stress and course of disease in multiple sclerosis. *Behavioral Medicine, 25,* 110–116.

Siegel, J. (1996). Aging into the 21st century. Retrieved from http://purl.access.gpo.gov/GPO/LPS137

Smith, D. L. (2008). Disability, gender and intimate partner violence: Relationships from the behavioral risk factor surveillance system. *Sexuality and Disability 26*(1), 15–28.

Surrey, J. (1991). The self in relation: A theory of women's development. In J. V. Jordan, A. G. Kaplan, J. B. Miller, I. P. Stiver, & J. L. Surrey (Eds.), *Women's growth in connection: Writings from the stone center* (pp. 51–66). New York, NY: Guilford Press.

Taal, E., Rasker, J. J., & Wiegman, O. (1997). Group education for rheumatoid arthritis patients. *Seminars in Arthritis and Rheumatism, 26*(6), 805–816.

Tate, D. G., Forchheimer, M., Kirsch, N., Maynard, F., & Roller, A. (1993). Prevalence and associated features of depression and psychological distress in polio survivors. *Archives of Physical Medicine and Rehabilitation, 74,* 1056–1060.

TBI National Data and Statistics Center. (2010). *The traumatic brain injury model systems of care.* Englewood, CO: TBI National Data and Statistics Center.

Turner, R. J., & Noh, S. (1988). Physical disability and depression: A longitudinal analysis. *Journal of Health and Social Behavior, 29,* 23–37.

Turner, R. J., & Wood, D. W. (1985). Depression and disability: The stress process in a chronically strained population. *Research in Community and Mental Health, 5,* 77–109.

U.S. Census Bureau. (2006). B18030. Disability status by sex by age by poverty status for the civilian non-institutionalized population 5 years and over—universe: Civilian noninstitutionalized population 5 years and over for whom poverty status is determined. Retrieved from http://factfinder.census.gov/servlet/DTTable?_bm=y&-state=dt&-ds_name=ACS_2006_EST_G00_&-mt_name=ACS_2006_EST_G2000_B18030&-redoLog=true&_caller=geoselect&-geo_id=01000US&-geo_id=NBSP&-format=&-_lang=en

U.S. Department of Health and Human Services. (1999). Executive summary mental health: Culture, race, and ethnicity, a supplement to mental health: A report of the surgeon general. Retrieved from http://www.surgeongeneral.gov/library/mentalhealth/cre/execsummary-1.html

U.S. Department of Health and Human Services. (2000). *Healthy People 2010*: Understanding and improving health and objectives for improving health. http://www.healthequityks.org/download/Hllthy_People_2010_Improving_Health.pdf

Verduyn, W. H. (1986). Spinal cord injured women, pregnancy and delivery. *Paraplegia, 24,* 231–240.

Waldrop, J., & Stern, S. M. (2003). Disability status: 2000. *Census 2000 Brief.* Retrieved from http://www.census.gov/prod/2003pubs/c2kbr-17.pdf

Walker, S. N., Sechrist, K. R., & Pender, N. J. (1987). The health-promoting lifestyle profile: Development and psychometric characteristics. *Nursing Research, 36*(2), 76–81.

Walsh, A., & Walsh, P. A. (1989). Love, self-esteem, and multiple sclerosis. *Social Science & Medicine, 29,* 793.

Ward, M. M., Lotstein, D. S., Bush, T. M., Lambert, R. E., van Vollenhoven, R., & Neuwelt, C. M. (1999). Psychosocial correlates of morbidity in women with systemic lupus erythematosus. *Journal of Rheumatology, 26*(10), 2153–2158.

Weinberger, M., Tierney, W. M., Booher, P., & Hiner, S. L. (1990). Social support, stress, and functional status in patients with osteoarthritis. *Social Science and Medicine, 30,* 503–508.

Wright, B. A. (1960). *Physical disability: A psychological approach*. New York, NY: Harper & Row.

Young, M. E., Nosek, M. A., Howland, C. A., Chanpong, G., & Rintala, D. H. (1997). Prevalence of abuse of women with physical disabilities. *Archives of Physical Medicine and Rehabilitation, 78*(12, Suppl. 5), S34–S38.

Zautra, A. J., Hoffman, J. M., Matt, K. S., Yocum, D., Potter, P. T., Castro, W. L., & Roth, S. (1998). An examination of individual differences in the relationship between interpersonal stress and disease activity among women with rheumatoid arthritis. *Arthritis Care and Research, 11*(4), 271–279.

9

Beyond the Binary: Rethinking the Social Model of Disabled Sexuality*

MICHAEL A. REMBIS

Binary oppositions between straight and gay, disabled and non-disabled are inaccurate and oppressive ideologies, which obscure the continuities of disability and sexuality.

—Tom Shakespeare

I think that disability is a breed on its own, neither masculine or feminine.

—Jazz

Sex and disability, disability and sex; the two words may seem incompatible. Practitioners, caregivers, family, friends, society—rooted in what Butler (1999) has called the heterosexual matrix and what disability rights activists and scholars have called the medical model of disability—consider disabled people to be not only broken or damaged, but also incompetent, impotent, undesirable, or asexual. Their inability to perform gender and sexuality in a way that meets dominant societal expectations is seen as an intrinsic limitation, an "unfortunate" but unavoidable consequence of inhabiting a disabled body. Many disabled people who have internalized dominant, ableist, heteronormative notions of strength, beauty, sex, and sexuality continue to experience psychological insecurity and distress when confronted with their own sexuality. They may even recount feelings of anger and self-loathing when they ponder the frustration, humiliation, and hostility they face (Taleporos & McCabe, 2001). Yet there are many disabled people who consider themselves sexy and fully capable of a rich sex life, and many disabled people are in relationships that they find rewarding (Taleporos & McCabe, 2001). The complexity of disabled peoples' lives, however, remains largely unexplored and unintelligible to the nondisabled masses.

Excavating this seemingly perilous yet richly fertile terrain reveals a standpoint that has the potential to alter the future landscape of human sexualities. It is not possible to

*Beyond the binary: Rethinking the social model of disabled sexuality, *Sexuality and Disability,* 2010, *28*, 51–60. © Springer Science+Business Media, LLC. With permission of Springer.

contemplate the positionality of disabled people without thinking about gender and sexuality and we cannot theorize about gender and sexuality without considering disability, or its conceptual opposite, "ability" (McRuer, 2006). The three identities are intimately bound up with one another, inextricably interwoven and embedded in systems of compulsory, yet unattainable, "heterosexuality" and "able-bodiedness." Ultimately what becomes disabling for most people is a failure to perform gender and sexuality in a way that approximates what Butler (1999) calls the "phantasmatic idealization" of heterosexuality.

In reflecting on the complexities of (dis/abled) sexualities, a series of questions posed by Butler in the anniversary edition of *Gender Trouble* become equally relevant to disability scholars:

> What will and will not constitute an intelligible life, and how do presumptions about normative gender and sexuality determine in advance what will qualify as the "human" and the "livable"? In other words, how do normative gender presumptions work to delimit the very field of description that we have for the human? What is the means by which we come to see this delimiting power, and what are the means by which we transform it? (Butler, 1999, p. xxii)

In the end, the means through which we "see" the delimiting power of normative gender presumptions are deeply rooted in dominant notions of "ability" (or a lack thereof); transforming the "human" and the "livable" therefore requires us to move beyond the simple notions of "disabled" and "nondisabled." We must move toward a standpoint that Davis has called "dismodernism" (Davis, 2006). We must move beyond tolerance, beyond inclusion, beyond the acknowledgement of nonnormative sex and sexuality, eroticism and desire—in short, beyond the binary. The future landscape of the "human" and the "livable" must be informed by a new discourse that resurfaces the intellectual field on which gender, sexuality, and disability become politicized, materialized, and knowable.

Transforming the "human" and the "livable" depends on nothing less than a reconceptualization and rearticulation of "sex" itself. Sex as a physical, spiritual, and emotional act; sex as a signifier of bodies; and sex as the "requisite antecedent" (Tremain, 2000) of the performance of gender must be refashioned in the popular mind. Disability, it seems, offers a perfect entry point into this discussion. In many ways, disability confounds the heterosexual matrix. As Jazz, a Jordanian woman, said in Shakespeare, Gillespie-Sells, and Davies' (1996) *The Sexual Politics of Disability,* disability is neither masculine nor feminine. As such, it demands a new discourse of gender and human sexualities.

Although the social model of disabled sexuality offers a fundamental and vitally important critique of ableist assumptions concerning disabled people's sexuality, it remains limited. Following a brief history and critical overview of the most recent scholarship emerging out of the social model of disabled sexuality, the argument is made that this new scholarship, which is meant largely to challenge dominant ableist assumptions concerning disabled people's sexuality, actually serves to reinforce the heterosexual matrix. In the final section, both theoretical and practical means of moving beyond the binary and transforming the future landscape of (dis/abled) human sexualities are discussed.

THE SOCIAL MODEL OF DISABLED SEXUALITY

The (not unchallenged) institutionalization of disability studies and the proliferation of a vibrant and dynamic disability culture, both of which have their roots in disabled activism and the social model of disability (Shakespeare, 2006), have given rise to a whole new subfield, disability sexuality studies (Shakespeare, 2000). Beginning in the 1980s, feminist disability scholars and those researchers and activists committed to a social model of disability began to deconstruct dominant assumptions concerning disabled sexuality (Fine & Asch, 1981, 1988; Finger, 1992; Garland-Thomson, 1997; Hahn, 1981; Hahn, 1988a, 1988b). Although still acknowledging the embodiment of disability, they began to highlight and analyze the social, cultural, ideological, and environmental barriers to disabled people's expression of their sexuality. A decade later, a significant body of scholarship had emerged, epitomized by Shakespeare and colleagues' (1996) foundational *The Sexual Politics of Disability: Untold Desires.*

Unlike previous research, which was conducted in a clinical setting by "rehabilitation" specialists, medical professionals, and psychologists, the new disability and sexuality scholarship draws on the everyday lives of disabled people to, as Ora Prilleltensky argues, "defy stereotypes" and "name their oppression" (Prilleltensky, 2004). Rather than focus on the perceived "trauma" caused by individual "dysfunction" or an "inability to perform," the new research explores disabled peoples' sexual lives in their own words and on their own terms.

Although there is mounting evidence that shows that many people with disabilities lead positive and fulfilled sexual lives, theirs is a sexual history characterized largely by oppression and discrimination (Shakespeare et al., 1996). As Fiduccia (2000) argues, sexuality and disability research has, for years, interrogated the high rates of divorce, neglect and sterilization, the lack of privacy, sexual knowledge and access to reproductive health services, and the low rates of marriage and domestic partnering experienced by most disabled people. Stories of abuse and rape, especially among institutionalized women and men, are quite common. Ubiquitous in the literature is also evidence that the larger nondisabled population perceives disabled people as either child-like, asexual and in need of "protection," or hypersexualized and in need of control (Milligan & Neufeldt, 2001).

Disabled people themselves have recounted numerous tales of exclusion and oppression (Howland & Rintala, 2001; Karellou, 2003; Kef & Bos, 2006; O'Toole, 2000; Prilleltensky, 2003; Richards, Tepper, Whipple, & Komisaruk, 1997; Rintala et al., 1997; Whitney, 2006). A lack of access to public transport, inadequate economic resources, physical inaccessibility, and, perhaps most important, attitudinal barriers, especially among family, friends, caregivers and health care providers, colleagues, close acquaintances, and prospective mates, have kept many disabled people from experiencing and expressing their own sexuality. As Shakespeare et al. (1996) have commented, "For most disabled people, it's not how to do it which causes the main problems, it's finding someone to do it with."

Despite a long history of exclusion and oppression, emerging evidence has shown that an increasing number of disabled people are leading satisfying sex lives. It seems that after a period of adjustment, or "coming out" (Shakespeare et al., 1996), in which one embraces his or her own embodiment and forges a disability identity, many disabled people come to see themselves as sexual beings (Guldin, 2000; Potgeiter & Khan, 2005). Although their relationship with their own body and with lovers and partners may be fraught, many disabled people, as Guldin has found, note other qualities, both physical and nonphysical, that "negate, displace, or supersede" qualities seen as undesirable or lacking (Guldin, 2000). In the end, Guldin contends, "What is constructed—if not a sexy body—is nonetheless a sexy being" (Guldin, 2000). Some disabled people claim that disability has made them a *better* lover or partner (Karlen, 2002). As sexual pleasure seems to be associated with psychosocial rather than strictly physical factors (Sakellariou, 2006), some disabled people see disability as a vehicle for learning about and exploring their own sexuality, as well as that of their lover or partner, which they claim makes them a more sensitive and responsive, or in some cases creative and courageous, lover. As

Guldin found, some disabled men assert that the disability has in a way been beneficial because they are no longer the "stereotypical guy:" They claim to be better, more willing lovers, and indicate that they derive more pleasure from oral sex and "going slow," as well as other forms of eroticism and sexuality (Guldin, 2000). Richards et al. (1997) found that after a period of adjustment, disabled women also developed a positive sense of self, and they and their partners became more creative sexually, working with the disability. As one disabled woman informed Shakespeare and colleagues (1996, p. 60):

> I see my limitations as parameters; my normality, my sexuality, to be pushed right to the edge. If you are a sexually active disabled person, and comfortable with the sexual side of your life, it is remarkable how dull and unimaginative non-disabled people's sex lives can appear.

In what one researcher referred to as a "wonderful celebration of her sexual life," a female wheelchair user in a Gay Pride parade in Boston in the mid-1990s carried a sign that read, "Trached dykes eat pussy all night without coming up for air" (O'Toole, 2000).

Most disabled respondents root their willingness (some might say eagerness) to express and even celebrate their own sexuality in an increasingly visible disability culture and the burgeoning disability rights or "disability pride" movements, which they argue are changing the way some individuals view disability. Although much work remains to be done, it seems some headway is being made, albeit rather unequally. Despite changing views, some sexualities remain marginalized, both in the research literature and in life. Both straight women and lesbians, especially those with congenital—as opposed to acquired—disabilities, gay men, bisexuals, and racial/ethnic minorities continue to experience the most hostility and/or neglect (Howland & Rintala, 2001; Karellou, 2003; Kef & Bos, 2006; O'Toole, 2000; Prilleltensky, 2003; Richards, Tepper, Whipple, & Komisaruk, 1997; Rintala et al., 1997; Whitney, 2006). This is because most disability research remains wedded to dominant heteronormative and ableist notions of gender and sexuality. Ironically, much of the social research on disabled sexuality and many of the pronouncements of disabled subjects, both of which have been concerned with "defying sex/gender stereotypes" and challenging powerful cultural myths concerning disabled people, have served to reinforce, rather than challenge, the heterosexual matrix.

THE HETEROSEXUAL MATRIX AND THE LIMITS OF THE SOCIAL MODEL OF DISABLED SEXUALITY

In their effort to empower themselves and their disabled subjects, most disability activists and scholars fall short of challenging what Butler in her work on gender and sexuality has referred to as "the naturalized knowledge" that "operates as a preemptive and violent circumscription of reality" (Butler, 1999). As other scholars have noted, the social model of disability, which emerged out of a highly politicized, male dominated, activist culture assumed a White, male, heterosexual norm that mirrored larger social norms (Shakespeare, 2006). As a result, much of the disability sexuality research has also assumed gender normative heterosexuality. This can be seen most readily in the research on disabled women, which tends to focus almost exclusively on "dating," marriage, reproduction, and parenting (Barron, 1997; Buzzanell, 2003; Prilleltensky, 2004). Although critically important, this research leaves unexplored the notion that these may not be desirable life choices for many women, nor does it examine the complex responses of disabled subjects that both reinforce and challenge normative sexual constructions. Guldin observes, for example, that although disabled men may take on a "more feminine model of sexuality," they continue to root their sexuality in their ability to please women, ultimately reinforcing their identity as a heterosexual "masculine man" (Guldin, 2000). Women, too, engage in seemingly contradictory behaviors. One of Guldin's participants made a point of stating that, for a period of time, she had been a "slut" (Guldin, 2000). Although this confession challenges dominant views of disabled asexuality and undesirability, it simultaneously reinforces dominant assumptions about women's "proper" roles, and sexual propriety more generally.

Although studies are scant, work in the intersection of lesbian and queer sexualities and disability are increasingly identifying the compulsory heterosexuality that dominates both disability research and the lives of most disabled people. Whitney (2006), for example, argues that although significant progress has been made toward the recognition of disabled sexuality, most of the studies remain limited. Most folks, Whitney contends, "often assume heterosexuality" (Whitney, 2006). O'Toole is less optimistic, noting that disabled women are not just assumed to be heterosexual, but also, and perhaps more problematically, asexual (O'Toole, 2000). O'Toole also highlights the dearth of literature on the intersection of various identities, writing that:

> In general, issues for lesbians, issues for women, issues for disabled people and issues for women of color are acknowledged in the domains of gender, sexuality, disability, and race. Almost never is there discussion of how these differing issues impact a woman who has membership in multiple communities. (O'Toole, 2000, p. 208)

Disability researchers and the larger society must adopt a broader view of human sexualities, one that more accurately reflects the lived experiences of most people, if we are going to move beyond the binaries that dominate many of our lives.

Although few in number, lesbian feminists and queer theorists have offered some of the most compelling challenges to gender normativity and compulsory heterosexuality. Lesbian communities are admittedly far from utopian and egalitarian. Disabled lesbians have reported feeling isolated and discriminated against within their own communities. Yet some lesbian writers proclaim that they are the "premier role models" for the "classic" sex advice to disabled people (O'Toole, 2000). As one respondent has asserted, "Hell, lesbians should be teaching all those sex classes [for disabled people]" (O'Toole, 2000). O'Toole argues that lesbians experience a tremendous sense of sexual freedom and that lesbian sex fosters communication and experimentation, all of which are critical to disabled sex. She writes that with lesbian sex, there is "little or no pressure" to have sex at the same time, and that lesbians are not as preoccupied with sexual positions as their heterosexual counterparts. There is no equivalent of the missionary position in lesbian sex. Moreover, there is no requirement that both partners have simultaneous orgasms during lesbian sex. As one respondent replied, "In fact, there is no requirement that both partners climax [at all]. One of the freedoms with lesbian sex is the removal of a huge "duty to come" (O'Toole, 2000). O'Toole has recognized and deconstructed the violent and constraining power of the heterosexual matrix and has offered a practical way of subverting it—teaching disabled people how to have a full (some might say "lesbian") sex life. Although extremely important and valuable, the emancipatory rhetoric of lesbian feminists such as O'Toole runs the risk of replacing one set of social hierarchies with another.

In searching for alternatives to heteronormativity, one must be careful not to idealize lesbian relationships; lesbians certainly do not have a monopoly on communication; and they, like any other social group, create their own hierarchies. Yet the larger point implicit in O'Toole's work is a compelling one. Current disability sexuality researchers and activists define sexuality very narrowly, and in most cases concern themselves almost exclusively with the physical capacity of disabled people and their inability to perform gender and sexuality in a way that approximates dominant conceptions of normative heterosexuality. Whether this is seen as a "challenge" to dominant social norms or simply as an individual "failure" to meet those norms, it ultimately serves to reinforce the heterosexual matrix. The future of (dis/abled) sexualities does not depend on disabled men's ability and willingness to "challenge" dominant assumptions by admitting that they are more "feminine" in their lovemaking and that this can actually be "positive," nor does it necessarily depend on disabled women who "defy" stereotypes by marrying and bearing (or adopting) and raising children. Disability and gender and sexuality scholars, and society generally, must move beyond the binary, beyond male/female, masculine/feminine, adult/child-like, independent/dependent, nondisabled/disabled, sexual/asexual, straight/gay toward a revisioning of gender, sexuality, and disability that addresses the ways in which the maintenance of these categories works to delimit, as Butler (1999) puts it, "the very field of description that we have for the human." It is imperative that we reshape culture in a way that enables us all.

Transforming culture is certainly a long and difficult process. We can begin (and I think we have already begun) by viewing human sexualities from what Richards and colleagues (1997, p. 272) call "a holistic perspective." For them, sexuality "encompasses biological, psychological, emotional, social, cultural, and spiritual qualities, and individuals can express their sexuality in any and all of these areas." Thinking more broadly about sexuality is no doubt beneficial, but we must also work to reshape the very notion of gender, sex, sexuality, eroticism, desire, and disability, and to subvert the power relations and class structures that undergird the maintenance of these ideological constructions. Fundamentally altering the way we see the world ultimately is much more difficult than simply being more "inclusive." In the last section, a means of transforming the future landscape of (dis/abled) sexualities is offered.

DIS/ABILITY AND THE FUTURE OF SEX

I envision a future in which there are no "dis/abled sexualities," only human sexualities; a world in which difference is what we have in common; a world where limitation, interdependence, and reliance on technology are the norm; where technology is not separate from, but rather part of the body; where both the body and identity are not fixed but malleable (Davis, 2006). Davis (2006) calls this *dismodernism*. Put simply, it is a world in which we move beyond the rigid humanistic ideals of enlightenment and the equally constraining identity politics of the postmodern era. Like Davis (2006), I seek to usher in a new era and a new ethics of the body that begins with disability rather than ends with it. The goal is not the erasure of dis/abled bodies and sexualities, nor is it the incorporation of the disabled other into a humanistic ideal of the separate and independent yet equal self. We need a sweeping reclamation of dis/abled bodies that enable us to reconfigure the human and the livable in a way that makes limitation and what Davis (2006) calls "cosmopolitanism" the rule.

Transforming the future of (dis/abled) sexualities hinges on the notion that sex and disability—in all of their various materializations—are malleable, pliable, and quite often multifarious. They are not fixed or rigid, and they are not rooted in our biology. The work of Tremain (2000, 2006) is useful in this regard. Drawing primarily on Foucault and Butler, she argues, in different settings, that sex and disability (or more accurately impairment) are socially constructed; neither of them are prediscursive, natural, or transhistorical. The body, moreover, is not "sexed" or "disabled" in any significant way before its signification as such within a discourse on sexuality or impairment. The materiality or embodiment of "sex" or "disability" is thereby marked or formed by discursive practices, which, if we agree with McRuer (2006), ultimately have their roots in competing notions of gender, sexuality, and compulsory able-bodiedness. "Sex" and "disability" become politicized, naturalized, and knowable through the performance of gender and sexuality. Coming to terms with the idea that sex, gender, sexuality, and disability are discrete yet interrelated socially constructed identities embedded within larger ableist systems of knowledge and power help us move beyond the binary and challenge the ways in which the "human" and the "livable" are conceived, expressed, and constrained in modern societies.

To affect change, (dis/abled) sexualities must become intelligible through a "dismodernist" discourse that emerges organically from the "bottom up." By incorporating the voices and actions of social actors, who historically have been silenced, we can move beyond what might be considered a strictly Foucauldian formation of the "human" and the "livable." As scholars writing in other contexts have shown, Foucault's work can be helpful in elucidating the complex relationship between knowledge and power and the historically situated sets of practices that restrict the actions of humans generally and of disabled people in particular (Hughes, 2005; Tremain, 2000, 2006). Recent feminist and disability studies scholars have, however, raised considerable and important criticisms concerning the extent to which Foucault recognized and appreciated what social philosopher Hughes (2005) refers to as, "the ways in which practical sensuous activities constitute social life" (as cited in Rembis, 2010, p. 57). Hughes argues that Foucault's notion of the body as a docile locus of power underestimates the subject's role as an agent of self- and social transformation. For Foucault, the body is a medium on which history is written; it is monitored into existence; it is molded by "a great many distinct regimes" (Hughes, 2005). The body is "a product of the play of power; … power reaches into the very grain of individuals, touches their bodies and inserts itself into their actions and attitudes, their discourses, learning processes and everyday lives" (Hughes, 2005, cited in Rembis, 2010, p. 57). Hughes (2005) contends that the "active or creative subject is invisible" in Foucault's work. "The subject," for Foucault, "is a product of expert classification and regulatory techniques" (Rembis, 2010, p. 57). Hughes (2005, cited in Rembis, 2010, p. 57) argues that unlike Foucault, who makes only a "post hoc case for agency," and even then considers it "a discursive product of new reflexive technologies of power," disability scholars—and I would add scholars of gender and sexuality—must recognize that "various forms of embodied praxis" have allowed disabled people to claim the "status of subjects with agency." The new "dismodernist" discourse would recognize that agency would enable (dis/abled) people to deploy that power in transforming human sexualities.

If disabled people are going to have power, they must have access in its very broadest sense: physical and social access, access to their own bodies, and access into the consciousness of those individuals currently considered "nondisabled." The "dismodernist" revolution is largely a cultural and ideological endeavor. As Davis (2006) argues, it uses culture and symbolic production to create an ethic of liberation. Consciousness raising, tolerance, and inclusion must be rearticulated as consciousness altering, empowerment, and equity. Transforming minds, and ultimately the future landscape of (dis/abled) sexualities, can only be accomplished through research, scholarship, education, and a judicious use of media that engages in both a thick description of disabled peoples' rich, rewarding, and quite diverse lives, histories, and cultures, and a social critique that originates with disabled people themselves. The "counter-narrative" must become the dominant narrative.

Although they have made tremendous gains in all areas of access, disabled people still haunt the margins of the popular imagination. If all humans are going to occupy a "dismodern" world equally, people with a broad range of cognitive, emotional, physical, and sensory disabilities must be able to live freely. They must have full access to employment, education, transportation, entertainment, valuable resources, and perhaps most importantly to their own bodies and experiences. In many ways, disabled peoples' bodies are not their own, their very existence is at best constrained by "well-meaning" but often misguided family, friends, caregivers, colleagues, health care professionals, and politicians, and at worst directly violated by those who have power over them. Disabled bodies must cease being the objects of abuse and neglect, or of pity, sorrow, and charity, so that they might become the objects of desire and eroticism. In a "dismodern" world we all have the freedom and the power to be sexy—or not.

In a "dismodern" world, celibacy and intimate (but "platonic") friendships or partnerships will be equally "legitimate" and "acceptable" life choices. Any astute observer quickly recognizes that our modern culture is saturated with sex; it is omnipresent. In our modern lives, bodily maintenance and bodily pleasures are central to our socialization into an image conscious, youth obsessed capitalist consumer culture. Most of us demand the right to be sexual. As Shakespeare (2000) has noted, we vigorously defend "our right to choose whatever form of sexual expression or fulfillment we can find. We live in the "market of free emotions." Potential sexuality is everywhere. But do we really want more sex? Popular media would make it seem as though we do. Shakespeare has referred to this as the "Cosmo conspiracy" (Shakespeare, 2000). The reality is that most people are not having that much sex, let alone "great" sex. Australian women in relationships are having sex one to three times per week, with the majority of women having it closer to once a week. Sex is an even less frequent occurrence for women who are not in relationships (Allen, 2008). American men age 30 to 44 years reported in a 2002 national survey that they had had an average (median) of six to eight female sexual partners during their lifetime. For women, the number of male sexual partners was only about four (Mosher, Chandra, & Jones, 2005). Some surveys in Britain have found that more women preferred gardening to sex (Shakespeare, 2000). "Sex" as it is currently conceived by most people is not as important as our modern culture would have us believe and it is not critical to happiness. Most people, as Shakespeare has mentioned, "are not looking for sex itself, they are searching out intimacy, warmth, validation, connection" (Shakespeare, 2000). In a "dismodern" world free of compulsory able-bodiedness and heterosexuality such relationships are a valued part of the "human" and the "livable."

Disabled people cannot, and must not, create a "dismodern" world on their own. They must continue to build coalitions, coalitions across disability, across various sexual and racial/ethnic minorities, and with their (often) privileged "nondisabled" allies. Like Butler, I "hope for a coalition of sexual minorities that will transcend the simple categories of identity, that will refuse the erasure of bisexuality, that will counter and dissipate the violence imposed by restrictive bodily norms" (McRuer, 2006). A multiplicity of voices are needed to rearticulate and reconceptualize (dis/abled) human sexualities.

Researchers, activists, and artists need to work together to dispel powerful myths about the dominant arenas in which sexuality is performed, most notably interpersonal relationships. In a "dismodern" world, relationships that do not "conform" will be the norm. There are roughly eight million families in the United States with children younger than 18 years where one or both parents are disabled. Yet there is little research on these families and a general lack of acknowledgement of these families from the larger society (Prilleltensky, 2003). This is a direct violence committed on these families, on all disabled people. It is critical that we learn more about these families, but I would like to go one step further and ask why disabled individuals—or anyone for that matter—would want to "marry" at all (in the strict legal sense). What compels people to marry? What stakes do the interested parties, the state, and society have in legalized marriage and what one scholar has called "compulsory monogamy" (Emens, 2004)? Why are issues such as gay marriage and polygamy or polyamory so controversial? Despite the tenacious grip with which many folks cling to idyllic notions of monogamy and family, households may well be more diverse now than at any point in the past—in the Western world, at least. Gay male and lesbian couples are increasingly asserting their right to marry and have children. The number of children raised in single-parent households continues to rise. Household diversity continues to increase as reproductive technologies that enable women to have babies on their own or with a same-sex partner, and at an older age, continue to become more available and reliable. In 1995, 30% of births in the United States were to unmarried women (Coontz, 2000). Despite the myth of self-reliance that continues to dominate much of Western discourse, all parents are increasingly relying on a broad range of supports to raise their children. In 1996, more than half (54.3%) of mothers returned to work before their child's first birthday (Coontz, 2000). Whether we like to admit it or not, most people—disabled and "nondisabled"— are dependent, and most people simply fail at performing the "phantasmatic idealization" of not only heterosexuality, but also marriage and monogamy. As legal scholar Elizabeth Emens points out, "many people practice alternatives to lifelong monogamy either secretly (adultery) or serially (divorce and remarriage)" (Emens, 2004). According to research, 40% of marriages end in divorce and 50% of Americans between the ages of 16 years and 45 years admit to having been sexually unfaithful. Yet 70% of those individuals who divorce remarry, only to "fail" again (in most cases; Emens, 2004). In a "dismodern" world, we no longer see these seemingly disparate sexualities, partnerships, marriages, and family forms as "deviant." They are equally valued parts of a broad social and cultural mosaic. *They* define the "human" and the "livable."

By loosening the conceptual ties that bind our perception of "normal" relationships, we in turn open up new ways of thinking about sex and beauty. "Dismodernism" has the potential to transform a society where people are expected to live a life free of pain and discomfort; a society where strict social norms concerning beauty and physical fitness compel people to alter their bodies in drastic, often violent ways, through surgery, dieting, exercise, and other "cosmetic" procedures; a society where youth, physical prowess, and a very narrow idealization of heteronormative sexual allure are highly valued; and sexual performance is wedded to one's physicality. Sex, eroticism, and desire look very different in a "dismodern" world where "cosmopolitanism," interdependence, and a reliance on technology are the "norm." In a "dismodern" world, dis/abled bodies become "sexy" bodies.

REFERENCES

Allen, J. S. (2008). Unpublished paper presented at the International Congress on Women's Mental Health in Melbourne, 20 March 2008.

Barron, K. (1997). The bumpy road to womanhood. *Disability & Society, 12*(2), 223–240.

Butler, J. (1999). *Gender trouble: Feminism and the subversion of identity.* New York, NY: Routledge.

Buzzanell, P. M. (2003). A feminist standpoint analysis of maternity and maternity leave for women with disabilities. *Women and Language, 26*(2), 53–65.

Coontz, S. (2000). *The way we never were: American families and the nostalgia trap.* New York, NY: Basic Books.

Davis, L. J. (2006). The end of identity politics and the beginning of dismodernism. In L. J. Davis (Ed.), *The disability studies reader* (2nd ed., pp. 231–242). New York, NY: Routledge.

Emens, E. F. (2004). Monogamy's law: Compulsory monogamy and polyamorous existence. *N.Y.U. Review of Law & Social Change, 29,* 277–376.

Fiduccia, B. W. (2000). Current issues in sexuality and the disability movement. *Sexuality and Disability, 18*(3), 167–174.

Fine, M., & Asch, A. (1981). Disabled women: Sexism without the pedestal. *Journal of Sociology & Social Welfare, 6,* 233–248.

Fine, M., & Asch, A. (1988). Disability beyond stigma: Social interaction, discrimination and activism. *Journal of Social Issues, 44*(1), 3–22.

Finger, A. (1992). Forbidden fruit. *International Journal of New Technology and Research, 233*, 8–10.

Garland-Thomson, R. (1997). *Extraordinary bodies*. New York, NY: Columbia University Press.

Guldin, A. (2000). Self-claiming sexuality: Mobility impaired people and American culture. *Sexuality and Disability, 18*(4), 233–238.

Hahn, H. (1981). The social component of sexuality, disability: Some problems and proposals. *Sexuality and Disability, 4*(4), 220–233.

Hahn, H. (1988a). Can disability be beautiful? *Social Policy, 18*, 26–32.

Hahn, H. (1988b). The politics of physical differences: Disability and discrimination. *Journal of Social Issues, 44*, 39–47.

Howland, C. A., & Rintala, D. H. (2001). Dating behaviors of women with physical disabilities. *Sexuality and Disability, 19*(1), 41–70.

Hughes, B. (2005). What can a foucauldian analysis contribute to disability theory? In S. Tremain (Ed.), *Foucault and the government of disability* (pp. 78–92). Ann Arbor: University of Michigan Press.

Karellou, J. (2003). Laypeople's attitudes towards the sexuality of people with learning disabilities in Greece. *Sexuality and Disability, 21*, 64–84.

Karlen, A. (2002). Positive sexual effects of chronic illness: Case studies of women with lupus (SLE). *Sexuality and Disability, 20*(3), 191–208.

Kef, S., & Bos, H. (2006). Is love blind? Sexual behavior and psychological adjustment of adolescents with blindness. *Sexuality and Disability, 24*, 89–100.

McRuer, R. (2006). We were never identified: Feminism, queer theory, and a disabled world. *Radical History Review, 94*, 148–154.

Milligan, M. S., & Neufeldt, A. H. (2001). The myth of asexuality: A survey of social and empirical evidence. *Sexuality and Disability, 19*(2), 91–109.

Mosher, W., Chandra, A., & Jones, J. (2005). Sexual behavior and selected health measures: Men and women 15–44 years of age, United States, 2002 (Advance data from *Vital and Health Statistics*, no. 362). Hyattsville, MD: National Center for Health Statistics.

O'Toole, C. J. (2000). The view from below: Developing a knowledge base about an unknown population. *Sexuality and Disability, 18*(3), 207–224.

Potgeiter, C.-A., & Khan, G. (2005). Sexual self-esteem and body image of South African spinal cord injured adolescents. *Sexuality and Disability, 23*(1), 1–20. doi: 10.1007/s11195-004-2076-6

Prilleltensky, O. (2003). A ramp to motherhood: The experiences of mothers with physical disabilities. *Sexuality and Disability, 21*(1), 21–47.

Prilleltensky, O. (2004). *Motherhood and disability: Children and choices* (p. 45). New York, NY: Palgrave Macmillan.

Rembis, M. (2010). Beyond the binary: Rethinking the social model of disabled sexuality. *Sexuality and Disability, 28*(1), 51–60.

Richards, E., Tepper, M., Whipple, B., & Komisaruk, B. R. (1997). Women with complete spinal cord injury: A phenomenological study of sexuality and relationship experiences. *Sexuality and Disability, 15*(4), 271–283.

Rintala, D. H., Howland, C. A., Nosek, M. A., Bennett, J. L., Young, M. E., Foley, C. C., … Chanpong, G. (1997) Dating issues for women with physical disabilities. *Sexuality and Disability, 15*(4), 219–242.

Sakellariou, D. (2006). If not the disability, then what? Barriers to reclaiming sexuality following spinal cord injury. *Sexuality and Disability, 24*, 101–111.

Shakespeare, T. (1999). The sexual of disabled masculinity. *Sexuality and Disability, 17*(1), 53–64.

Shakespeare, T. (2000). Disabled sexuality: Toward rights and recognition. *Sexuality and Disability, 18*(3), 159–166.

Shakespeare, T. (2006). The social model of disability. In L. J. Davis (Ed.), *The disability studies reader* (2nd ed., pp. 197–204). New York, NY: Routledge.

Shakespeare, T., Gillespie-Sells, K., & Davies, D. (1996). *The sexual politics of disability: Untold desires* (p. 60). New York, NY: Cassell.

Taleporos, G., & McCabe, M. P. (2001). Physical disability and sexual esteem. *Sexuality and Disability, 19*(2), 131–148.

Tremain, S. (2000). Queering disabled sexuality studies. *Sexuality and Disability, 18*(4), 291–299.

Tremain, S. (2006). On the government of disability: Foucault, power, and the subject of impairment. In L. J. Davis (Ed.), *The disability studies reader* (2nd ed., pp. 185–196). London, England: Routledge.

Whitney, C. (2006). Intersections in identity—Identity development among queer women with disabilities. *Sexuality and Disability, 24*, 39–52.

10

Culture, Family, and Attitudes Toward Disability

CHIA VANG, SERGIO CUEVAS,
MANISHA SHARMA, AND BREEZE RUEDA

*T*he United States continues to grow in population, particularly among persons of minority. The U.S. Census Bureau (2010) projects America's changing demographics as well as an increase in the elderly population through 2060 at current trends. Specifically, non-Hispanic Whites are expected to experience a slower growth period by just more than 20 million people between 2024 and 2060 projections. Hispanics during this same period are expected to double to more than 128 million, representing one in three Americans by 2060. African Americans are expected to reach 60 million and see a slight increase over this time, and Asian Americans are also expected to double by 2060 to more than 34 million by that time. Non-Hispanic Whites as a group are expected to become a minority compared to all other groups combined by 2060 as well.

With these statistics in mind, it becomes all the more relevant for counselors to be knowledgeable and prepared to work with these growing populations in relation to their values, culture, family dynamics, and ultimately how they view and treat their disabled members. This chapter represents a synopsis of six different groups; Hispanic or Latino Americans, African Americans, Asian Americans, Middle Eastern Americans, European Americans, and Native Americans. Finally, it should be noted that although opinions in this chapter may suggest an entire culture believes or behaves in certain ways, please note that we are speaking in generalities and not defining exclusive group traits, noting that individual differences and opposing beliefs exist in unknown numbers. What follows in each section is a synopsis of each specific group's culture, cultural and family perspectives on disability, socioeconomic factors, and religion. Counseling implications are addressed.

LATINO AMERICANS

In 2015, there were 56.6 million Latino Americans, making them the largest ethnic or racial minority in the United States. Latino Americans may be referred to as Hispanics or Mexican Americans. Latino American origins include 63.4% Mexican, 9.5% Puerto Rican, 3.8% Salvadoran, 3.7% Cuban, 3.3% Dominican, and 2.4% Guatemalan (U.S. Census

Bureau, 2016). The rapid increase of Latino Americans is transforming the landscape of American culture (Ai, Aisenberg, Weiss, & Salazar, 2014).

Culture

Latino American culture values such beliefs as *familismo*, fatalism, collectivism, *machismo*, and *marianismo* (Ojeda & Piña-Watson, 2013). *Familismo* focuses on the attachment, respect, cooperation, and loyalty among close family members as well as extended family members (Ojeda & Piña-Watson, 2013). Fatalism is a connection to spirituality viewed as a higher power having control over individuals and their circumstances; thus, for many who sustain a disability, they may perceive this is God's way and do little to improve their circumstances (Bermúdez, Kirkpatrick, Hecker, & Torres-Robles, 2010). Collectivism includes attitudes, beliefs, and behaviors that reflect support for the family, community, and the collective unit (Booker, Gallaher, Unger, Ritt-Olson, & Johnson, 2004). Latino American families may uphold values in which the male is seen to be the head of the household and will embody hypermasculine traits that embrace traditional *machismo* (Sarmiento & Cardemil, 2009), whereas women will embody *marianismo*, which refers to the woman's responsibility to protect, nurture, dedicate, sacrifice, and sometimes even suffer for her family (Garcia-Preto, 2005). Latino American parents have expectations from their children to behave properly and be respectful to adults (Arcia, Reyes-Blanes, & Vazquez-Montilla, 2000).

Cultural Perspectives of Disability

Disability in the Latino American culture is seen as the result of a woman or a family member being cursed by an enemy or someone giving them the "evil eye" (Groce & Zola, 1993; Rogers-Adkinson, Ochoa, & Delgado, 2003). Latino Americans believe that the causes for illness are both biological and spiritual (Gurung, 2006). Latino Americans in general have much higher rates of diabetes mellitus, obesity, disability, and sedentary lifestyle compared to other groups, yet they are also one of the hardest working classes, often taking hazardous and physically demanding jobs that other Americans would not do (Haan et al., 2003). Latino American children are more frequently identified as speech–language impaired and learning disabled than European American children (Valdez, 2003). The Latino American population underutilizes community services (e.g., mental health services) more than any other group in the United States (López, Barrio, Kopelowicz, & Vega, 2012) other than perhaps Asian Americans; consequently, it is vital to consider, understand, and address their cultural values and beliefs to have a better understanding about how cultural factors play regarding disability issues. Individuals who hold the value of fatalism may believe that they do not have control over their illness or impairment and may not seek assistance, thereby hindering an individual's ability to seek treatment (Bermúdez et al., 2010).

Family Perspectives of Disability

Some Latino American families will often hide a family member with a disability and may not ask for help, which may be a matter of pride or a matter of shame, or *verguenza*, that the disability exists (World Institute on Disability, 2006). Latino American males are generally devastated on sustaining a catastrophic disability to the extent that, for many, the disability is viewed as a punishment from God (Marini, 2012). Males may face conflicts when dealing with a disability as feelings of isolation and depression may result due to perceiving they cannot express their worries or anxieties with others for fear of being viewed as weak (Marini, 2012). Latino American women with disabilities report greater levels of disablement, which may contribute to higher levels of perceived functional limitations, unemployment, and difficulties with performing daily living activities (Harrison, 2009). For many with physical disabilities and few resources to travel throughout the community, isolation from engaging in social activities is common (Divin, Volker, & Harrison, 2013). Latino American families believe that loved ones with a disability may improve faster and better under the care of family members as opposed to medical providers because they know their loved one better than anyone else (Edgerton & Karno, 1971; Guarnaccia, Martinez, & Acosta, 2005). Family is the essential primary support for Latino Americans, who may be concerned about disclosing their struggles due to perceptions of others who believe the family has sinned in some way (P. Taylor, Lopez, Martínez, & Velasco, 2012). Latino American families may adhere to child-rearing beliefs regarding disability based on cultural beliefs and customs (Cohen, 2013). Latino American children with disabilities are expected to be well behaved, clean, and respectful. Many Latino American parents nevertheless hold the belief that they must protect their child and prevent any type of illness or distress. This sometimes leads to behaviors such as allowing the child to use diapers or drink out of a baby bottle long after there is a need to do so. While accepting these behaviors, parents may disenfranchise their child with a disability, thus fostering learned helplessness and inhibiting the child from mastering self-independence and self-caring skills (Cohen, 2013).

Socioeconomic Status Effects on Disability

The growth of Latino Americans in the United States has increased the possibility of concentrated poverty and inequality (e.g., the rise in majority–minority places), rural low-income residences, and boomtowns (Burton, Garrett-Peters, & Eason, 2011; Lichter, Parisi, & Taquino, 2012; Lichter, Sanders, & Johnson, 2015). In 2015, the median income of Latino American households was $45,150, the poverty rate was 21%, and 66% of those 25 or older had at least a high school education (U.S. Census Bureau, 2016). In the United States, demographic factors such as poverty, limited access to health care, language barriers, and immigrant status contribute to underdiagnoses and poor-quality treatment of Latino American families and their children with intellectual disabilities, ultimately limiting their access to effective community and family supports (Cohen, 2013). Latino American children are among the poorest, least educated, and most disadvantaged in the nation, specifically those who are non-English speakers and noncitizens (Lichter, Johnson, Turner, & Churilla, 2012; Lichter et al., 2015).

Latino Americans with disabilities also experience unemployment at a higher rate than the White population (U.S. Bureau of Labor Statistics, 2016). Low levels of formal education among Latino Americans can increase the likelihood of being employed in jobs that are physically demanding and dangerous, which in turn can increase the likelihood of acquiring a work-related disability (Smart & Smart, 1994). About half of Latino American workers are employed in just four industries—construction; eating, drinking and lodging services; wholesale and retail trade; and professional and other business services (Kochhar, 2014). There is also a large majority who work in factories, such as meat production slaughterhouses and agriculture, which are typically extremely arduous jobs.

The Impact of Religion on Disability

Guarnaccia and colleagues (2005) found that Latino Americans rely on the church for family support. Catholicism has remained the most common religious denomination for Latino Americans (Steigenga & Cleary, 2007). Families often opt to seek help from religious services and priests, which they find to be not only more trustworthy but less stigmatizing or judgmental than are medical professionals and others (P. Taylor et al., 2012). Although many believe that a medical doctor can cure their medical conditions, only *curanderos* or healers can be trusted to cure spiritual problems (Trotter & Chavira, 1997). These latter sentiments are generally not held by the younger population of Hispanics, who have higher levels of education.

AFRICAN AMERICAN CULTURE

In 2015, the U.S. population totaled nearly 45 million African Americans (U.S. Census Bureau, 2015c). By 2060, the African American population is expected to increase to 42% with similar increases among other minorities (Colby & Ortman, 2015). African American origins exist in any of the Black racial groups in Africa such as Kenya, Nigeria, or Haiti (U.S. Census Bureau, 2011). African American relationships and families are shaped by their experiences in the United States and African cultural patterns (Dixon, 2007).

Culture

African American culture may originate from their African heritage as well as from their experience with discrimination, forced migration, and enslavement. These experiences and patterns contribute to their core cultural values, as does their strong faith (Nobles, 1980). African American culture holds cohesiveness, cooperation, community, respect for elders, and harmony with nature as meaningful values. As a cultural group, African Americans value interdependence and cooperation (D. W. Sue & Sue, 2013; White & Parham, 1990) and have a strong sense of collectivism that extends beyond family to community members (Collins, 1990; Nobles, 1980). In many African American families, parental roles are shared between parents, aunts, uncles, grandparents, ex-spouses and partners, neighbors, community members, and even older children (Hines & Boyd-Franklin, 1996). Gender roles can vary, such that the male may be the primary economic provider and the female the homemaker, or vice versa, and they may both share household and childcare responsibilities (Dixon, 2007). African American children may sometimes be expected to assist with parental responsibilities such as becoming the main source of guidance, control, and decision making (Hines & Boyd-Franklin, 2005).

Cultural Perspectives of Disability

In the African American culture, embarrassment and shame are associated with disability, and African Americans who hold negative attitudes about individuals with disabilities such as mental illness are fearful of labels and stigmas (Atkinson, 2004; Nickerson, Helms, & Terrell, 1994). Some African Americans believe that illness is the result of punishment for sin, while many others do not (Holt, Clark, & Roth, 2014). The onset of disability may obstruct or hinder the psychological and social development of an ethnic identity, which assists individuals with the acquisition of internal and external resources including resilience, self-concept perceptions, and ability to network with others (Caldwell, Kohn-Wood, Schmeelk-Cone, Chavous, & Zimmerman, 2004). Some African Americans may regard chronic illness in terms of nerves, stress, and depression (Fukukawa et al., 2004), thus referring to having a disability as difficulties in life rather than an illness that needs to be treated (Lincoln, Chatters, & Taylor, 2005). The rate of disability for African Americans is approximately 13% (National Committee to Preserve Social Security & Medicare, 2016). African Americans may have experiences with stress, depression, and discrimination from perceptions of being oppressed and discriminated against (Richter, Wilcox, Greaney, Henderson, & Ainsworth, 2002). Other common conditions experienced by African Americans and Latinos include cardiovascular disease, hypertension, diabetes, and cancer (Holt et al., 2014). Due to lack of health care and perceptions of oppression, some African Americans may seek outpatient treatment or complete treatment at lower rates (Snowden, 2001; S. Sue, Zane, & Young, 1994).

Family Perspectives of Disability

When seeking treatment for disability, Boyd-Franklin (2003) reveals African American families may become suspicious or distrustful of professionals lacking understanding of historical or here-and-now experiences with oppression (Aymer, 2013). African American men may not seek treatment because of the negative perception that seeking treatment is a sign of weakness (Thompson Sanders, Bazile, & Akbar, 2004). Similarly, African American women with a disability may experience an array of barriers, including racism and sexism, which may hinder their adjustment and treatment of the disability (Barer & Johnson, 2003; Cavenaugh, Gisen, & Steinman, 2006; King & Ferguson, 1996). Many African American women believe that issues within the family should remain within the family and not be discussed with anyone outside their household. Like many Latinos, African American women may first seek assistance from their church pastor or minister (Alvidrez, 1999; Neighbors, Musick, & Williams, 1998). African American children with disabilities may face poor self-esteem, hypochondria, depression, or embarrassment over having a disability (Wright & Phillips, 1988), have problems with identity formation (S. A. Morgan & Jackson, 1986), and have issues with realizing the limitations imposed by the disease. Children with disabilities adjust better when high achievement, such as honoring commitment, is supported by the family (Hurtig, Koepke, & Park, 1989).

Socioeconomic Status Effects on Disability

Lack of access, poor nutrition, and low health care quality experienced by many African Americans contribute to levels of poverty and influence the risk of disability (Newacheck, Stein, Bauman, & Hung, 2003). Initial efforts of African American parents to help their children with learning disabilities in their education can lead to frustration, disillusionment, and skepticism of special education, accommodations, and the educational system in general by the time these students reach high school (Harry, Allen, & McLaughlin, 1995). The Bureau of Labor Statistics (2016) shows that African American youth with disabilities, aged 16 years and older, made up 21.6% of the unemployed population in the United States. Because African American males with learning disabilities may not have access to competitive employment or educational requirements, they are limited to opportunities within educational spaces and the workforce (Booth, Butler, Richardson, Washington, & Henfield, 2016). African Americans can often be found working in areas such as education, health care, social assistance, retail trade, arts, entertainment, recreation, and food service (U.S. Census Bureau, 2015c).

The Impact of Religion on Disability

During the slavery period in the United States and elsewhere, spirituality enabled African Americans to connect with others (Jones, 1993; White, 1984). Church was a location where slaves could express themselves freely through congregation, testifying, preaching, and prayer (Holland, 2014). African Americans share many common but diverse faiths including Baptist, Catholic, Protestant, Lutheran, Seventh Day Adventist, Muslim, and others (Holland, 2014). Today, spirituality continues to resonate and be practiced in every aspect of African Americans' lives. Hence, the church is an essential element of African American spirituality, creating a profound connection among God, individuals, family, and the community (Barrett, 1974). Religion helps enhance the financial, emotional, social, and spiritual well-being of African Americans (Billingsley, 1992; Chaney, 2008a, 2008b; R. J. Taylor, Chatters, & Levin, 2004). For many African Americans, prayer, meditation, and religious reading among other behaviors and religious traditions have been associated with mental and physical health improvement as well as improvement of coping skills (Chatters, Taylor, Jackson, & Lincoln, 2008; Curtis-Boles & Jenkins-Monroe, 2000; Shorter-Gooden, 2004). A majority of African Americans view persons with disabilities as one of all God's children as opposed to being cursed.

ASIAN AMERICAN CULTURE

The Asian population in 2015 was estimated at approximately 19.4 million persons in the United States (U.S. Census Bureau, 2015b). Asian Americans are one of the fastest growing minority populations. Chinese, Filipinos, Indians, Vietnamese, and Koreans are among the largest ethnic groups that represent subgroups of Asian Americans (Tsai, Ying, & Lee, 2000). Asian Americans include groups differing in language, culture, and religious affiliations, making them a heterogeneous population much like many other minority groups (Chang, 2003).

Culture

The most common cultural value among all Asian Americans is collectivism, which means there is an interdependence of family members as a group where the needs of the family outweigh the needs of individual members (Chao, Crockett, & Russell, 2010). Asian American culture is patriarchal with the father being the head of the household and followed by the mother. Asian Americans generally follow Confucian principles that emphasize responsibility, leadership, and patriarchy (Berg & Jaya, 1993; Chang, 2003; Hamilton, 1996; U. Kim & Chun, 1994; D. Sue, 1998). Women adhere to a passive, subservient role, while children learn at an early age to respect authority and value harmonious interpersonal relationships (Chang, 2003; Chang & Myers, 1997). Asian American children are more likely to adopt American values such as independence and autonomy than do their parents (Chang, 2003).

Cultural Perspectives of Disability

Asian American perceptions toward disability may be driven based on religious beliefs from Asia including disability viewed as a punishment, curse, or sin (Chiang & Hadadian, 2010; Girimaji & Kommu, 2016). Some Asian American parents may attribute the cause of a child's disability to supernatural influences or sins committed by the child's parents or ancestors (Chan, 1998). Asian American adolescents have higher elevated levels of social anxiety compared to other ethnic groups (Brice et al., 2015). Mental health problems (e.g., depression and anxiety) are growing among Asian Americans as a result of negative attitudes held against their culture and high stress due to pressures to excel academically and in their career (J.-H. Kim & Park, 2015; Kung, 2004). As a result, Asian Americans are reluctant to seek mental health services or terminate early from the counseling compared to European Americans due to feelings of shame and embarrassment (J.-H. Kim & Park, 2015; Shea & Yeh, 2008). Researchers have reported that several factors impact counseling-seeking behavior among Asian Americans, including language barriers, communication style, family values, culture, financial resources, lack of knowledge, and access to mental health services (Kung, 2004; Yeung & Kung, 2004). Both U.S. born and foreign-born Asian Americans tend to underutilize mental health services because of the use of alternative services such as a religious or spiritual advisor, a healer, a doctor of Oriental medicine or acupuncturist, a chiropractor, or a spiritualist. This, in combination with being perceived as weak willed and the stigma of such for a mental illness, is another barrier to seeking traditional American mental health services (Le Meyer, Zane, Cho, & Takeuchi, 2009).

Family Perspectives of Disability

Asian American families may deal with disability by delaying professional help and instead turn to self-control and solving one's own problems (Boey, 1999; Congress & Kung, 2013; Loo, Tong, & True, 1989; Zhang, Snowden, & Sue, 1998). Some Asian Americans are more likely to turn to family members, friends, or church groups instead of seeking help from mental health professionals (Chang, 2003; Chin, 1998; Shin, Berkson, & Crittenden, 2000; Yeh & Wang, 2000). Women with disabilities of any minority often face a type of double discrimination due to their gender and disability (Deegan, 1981; Hanna & Rogovsky, 1991). For Asian American families with children with disabilities, shame is not present once they have positive attitudes, being well-informed of the legal protections provided through educational and community resources in the United States (Parette, Chuang, & Huer, 2004). Nevertheless, feelings of shame and embarrassment among family members and the disabled loved one are often present. When raising a child with a disability, Asian American mothers stay home and take care of their child while the father provides financially (Wang & West, 2016). Asian American children with disabilities learn familial and educational values and do not want to disappoint their parents (Ambert, 2001). Children with visible disabilities are encouraged to be the best, although competing may be a struggle and some children may be sheltered and over-protected by their parents (Yan, Accordino, Boutin, & Wilson, 2014).

Socioeconomic Status Effects on Disability

Asian Americans tend to be satisfied with their lives as they place high value on marriage, parenthood, hard work, and career success compared to other races and ethnic groups in the United States (Pew Research Center, 2013). The poverty rate is only 9% among Asian Americans, and their educational attainment is high with 30% holding at least a bachelor's degree (U.S. Census Bureau, 2015b). Asian Americans as a racial group have the highest income and are the best educated in the United States (Pew Research Center, 2013). Asian American parents invest heavily in their children's education and consider a quality education as a high priority (Saw, Berenbaum, & Okazaki, 2013; S. Sue & Okazaki, 2009). According to the U.S. Census Bureau in 2014, Asian households had the highest median income of $74,297 (DeNavas-Walt & Proctor, 2015). Types of jobs Asian Americans participate in include positions in the medical field, government, business, education, and popular culture (Coontz, Parson, & Raley, 2008).

The Impact of Religion on Disability

Religion and spirituality are diverse among Asian Americans; therefore, finding commonality can be difficult (Marini, Glover-Graf, & Millington, 2012; Millington, 2012). Confucianism, Daoism, and Hinduism are influential among East- and Southeast-Asian and Asian–Indian Americans, and many Asian Americans who report non-Christian faith practice Asian-born faiths (Ai, Huang, Bjorck, & Appel, 2013). Just as there is diversity in religion for Asian Americans, there is also a diversity in the impact of religion on disability. Similar to those who hold other strong religious faiths, Asian Americans report lower rates of depression, risky behavior, suicide, and substance abuse than those who do not practice a faith (Ai et al., 2013).

MIDDLE EASTERN AMERICANS

In the United States, it is estimated that nearly 3.5 million Americans trace their roots to an Arab country (Arab American Institute, 2010). The five primary groups of Middle Eastern Americans are Lebanese, Arab/Arabic, Egyptian, Syrian, and Iranian (Ameredia, 2006). Middle Eastern American populations are found significantly in California, New York, Florida, Washington DC, and Virginia (Ameredia, 2006). Middle Eastern Americans attempt to preserve their culture and pass it on from generation to generation, but for many recent Middle Eastern Americans, it can become difficult adapting to a new culture while retaining their traditional cultural traditions (Arab American National Museum, 2017).

Culture

Arab American families have very close relationships and maintain contact with their extended family (Arab American National Museum, 2017). Many view family as the center of all loyalty, obligation, and status of its members, where family relationships are the ultimate standard to which the individual seeks social approval and the loyalty and duty to his or her family are greater than any other social obligation (Hammad, Kysia, Rabah, Hassoun, & Connelly, 1999). Shame and honor are viewed as important for Middle Eastern Americans where individual shameful behaviors can bring dishonor to the individual and also the entire family unit. Middle Eastern American families are primarily patriarchal, in which the father makes all major family decisions (Goforth, 2011). As such, the father generally provides for food, clothing, and shelter for his wife and children (Hammad et al., 1999), and elders tend to dominate and be held in high esteem (Al Khateeb, Al Hadidi, & Al Khatib, 2014). The different roles of men, women, boys, and girls in a Middle Eastern American family may mean dressing modestly, having little socializing with children of the opposite sex, not dating, and showing respect for elders (Arab American National Museum, 2017). Arab American women roles are linked to shame and honor with their reputations; sexual behavior, asking for a divorce, challenging men's authority, or criticizing one's husband can be seen as shaming the family (Abu-Ras, 2013; Glazer & Abu-Ras, 1994). In regard to children's roles, girls predominantly follow traditional female roles and boys at the age of 5 are expected to become increasingly involved in learning aspects of the Arab American men's world (Crabtree, Husain, & Spalek, 2008).

Cultural Perspectives of Disability

Many in Arab society hold negative attitudes toward people with disabilities as a result of the lack of values and morals inherent in the society before Islam came to the Arabian Peninsula, as disabled people were neglected, considered worthless, and faced minimal interaction because of the fear of contagion (Almusa & Ferrell, 2004). Today, some Middle Eastern Americans view disability or illness as a way of God punishing them, and a disability may be construed as the family having earned the wrath of Divine Will, which might affect the social standing and marriage ability of all associated family members (Hammad et al., 1999). Also, mental illness is highly shunned and stigmatized, and while kindness and care are given to those with a mental illness under Islamic norms, mental illness is approached with fear and social avoidance under Arab social norms. Chronic disease and mental illness are considered shameful and blameworthy for the individual and for his or her family. Because of this reason, disabilities are generally not disclosed for fear that people will view the disability as a sign of a hereditary defect (Hammad et al., 1999). Significant mental health complaints and service utilization within the Arab American population have increased as they face acculturative stressors such as immigration stressors, war trauma, political exile, economic instability, communication barriers, and loss of extended family support (Amer, 2005). More recent, after 9/11 to the present under the current Republican president, some Middle Easterners face discrimination and prejudice and have incurred violence and intimidation.

Family Perspectives of Disability

Some Middle Eastern Americans may have left their countries of origin, which could lead them to a high risk of posttraumatic stress disorder (PTSD). The negative effects of PTSD on the family may include shame, fear, paranoia, and broken family ties (Kira, 1999; Nassar-McMillan, 2003). Middle Eastern men with disabilities may be assisted with education and employment, whereas girls and women are often subjected to being abused physically and sexually (Crabtree, 2006; Crabtree et al., 2008). Some Middle Eastern families feel shame giving birth to a child with a disability (Bywaters, Ali, Fazil, Wallace, & Singh, 2003). Mothers are stuck burdened with the majority of care for children with disabilities. In some cases, women with children with disabilities may be rejected or displaced (Crabtree, 2007; Crabtree et al., 2008). Families have lower expectations from children with disabilities in regard to their future (Bywaters et al., 2003).

Socioeconomic Status Effects on Disability

In general, Middle Eastern Americans have a strong commitment to family, economic, and educational achievement (Ameredia, 2006). Middle Eastern Americans, on average, are better educated, more prosperous, and more politically active than the average American in the 21st century (Minority Rights Group International, 2017). A Middle Eastern American's economic and social status is highly connected with the family's status (Goforth, 2011). Approximately 17% of Arab Americans lived in poverty in 1999 and Iraqi children statistically are more likely to be poor compared to Lebanese children (Minority Rights Group International, 2017). It is estimated that about 336,600 Arab Americans of all ages have a disability (Al Khateeb et al., 2014), and an estimated 23,400 of Arab American school-age children have a disability. In terms of education, 85% of Middle Eastern Americans have a high school diploma or higher and 4 of 10 Middle Eastern Americans have a bachelor's degree or higher (Ameredia, 2006). In 1999, the overall median earnings for Arab American men working year round and full time were $41,700, and for women it was $31,800 (Minority Rights Group International, 2017). Middle Eastern Americans work in all occupations, and are more likely to be self-employed, entrepreneurs, or to work in sales. Approximately 60% are executives, hold professional jobs, and are employed as office and sales staff (Ameredia, 2006).

The Impact of Religion on Disability

Christian Arab Americans can be influenced by Islam and non-Western ideals, and may find easier acceptance into the mainstream United States (Nassar-McMillan, 2003). In Arab American ethnic and cultural identities, religion is often infused, especially for Muslim Arab Americans (Goforth, 2011). For both Christian and Muslim Arab Americans, religion may serve as a source of prevention and coping, and Arab Americans who are affiliated with the Islamic religion might be expected not to adopt American cultural identity, may encounter greater acculturative stress, and feel greater psychological distress (Amer, 2005). It is possible that religious coping for Middle Eastern Americans has an indirect effect on anxiety and depression.

NATIVE AMERICANS

There are an estimated 5.4 million Native Americans, who comprise 1% of the population of the United States (U.S. Census Bureau, 2015a). Native Americans are the most diverse minority group with more than 500 tribes extant (Bryan, 2014). In 2000, the largest Native American tribes were Cherokee and Navajo with 730,000 and 298,000 individuals reporting affiliation, respectively (DeVoe & Darling-Churchill, 2008). Native Americans have different tribal groups with different traditions, customs, and beliefs (Vacc, DeVaney, & Brendel, 2003). Native Americans live in a variety of settings, including rural, urban, and on reservations (Vacc et al., 2003).

Culture

Although tribal groups may have some nuanced cultural differences, they also share native traditional core values that include the importance of community contribution, acceptance, sharing, cooperation, harmony and balance, attention to nature, immediacy of time, awareness of the relationship, and a deep respect for elders (Vacc et al., 2003). Native American customs typically focus on balance and harmony as essential components of wellness, and individuals who seek healing must fulfill community and family roles (Kelsey, 2013). In mainstream American society, worth and status for Native Americans are based on one's place of origin (Garrett et al., 2014). Native American families may participate in many activities of daily living in mixed-gender pairs or groups, but if a Native American family goes on a hunting or fishing trip, they do so together (Burger, Gochfeld, Jeitner, & Pittfield, 2012). The role of mothers in Native American culture is to nurture the young; however, over the past several years, the role has begun to shift to share coresponsibility with the father. Approximately the same number of men are employed as women; thus, the idea of males as the primary provider is no longer true, often because of difficulties men have in securing gainful employment (Bryan, 2014). Care for children is valued for Native Americans through constructive family adjustment; children are supported, nourished, and nurtured, thus ensuring the continuity of cultural ways. Caring for all children in the community ensures the preservation of tribal beliefs and traditions (Nichols & Keltner, 2005).

Cultural Perspectives of Disability

Disability in the indigenous Native American culture is not frowned on or stigmatized negatively, and everyone is viewed as able bodied and able to contribute to the community. The community assists people with differences in any way they may need and offers assistance necessary to enable them to participate in the community (Lovern, 2014). Native Americans identify individuals with a physical or mental difference as having a difference in functioning but not different per se, and their disability does not define who they are. Colonialization had a powerful impact on Native American lives and their ways of thinking about disability; however, having a negative attitude toward disability overall is incongruent with their traditions (Lovern, 2008). Overall, Native Americans are grounded in their traditions in the need to maintain or regain a balance in their lives and their community (Lovern, 2014).

On average, Native American women have more nonfatal chronic conditions, such as physical disabilities, depression, and anxiety disorders (Bird & Rieker, 2008; Rohlfsen, 2008; Yang & Lee, 2009), whereas men have higher odds of problems with drinking, substance abuse (Bird & Rieker, 2008; Rohlfsen, 2008), and life-threatening chronic diseases (Bird & Rieker, 2008). Among Native American children, the leading causes of disabilities are accidents, infections, and congenital abnormalities (Joe, 1997). For Native Americans with disabilities who live in rural or on a reserve setting, medical resources are usually scarce, often leaving them to drive long distances for treatment. Some Native Americans continue to use traditional and informal supports, while some utilize professional support when available (Begay, Roberts, Weisner, & Matheson, 1999). Many programs on a local or tribal level have been developed to provide appropriate cultural services to Native Americans with disabilities; however, these are often scarce (Weaver, 2015).

Family Perspectives of Disability

Native American families view people with physical or intellectual challenges as being able to afford more freedom in their behavior as they realize that a disability is beyond their control (Leung, 2003; Pengra & Godfrey, 2001). Other families often assist people with disabilities as a family's normal routine is caregiving of all community members (Leung, 2003; Pengra & Godfrey, 2001). Because of this level of community caring, Native Americans with disabilities feel loved as fully functioning members of the family and their community (Pengra & Godfrey, 2001).

Effects on Disability of Socioeconomic Status

Some socioeconomic issues of concern are poverty, high dropout rates, unemployment, poor physical health, substance use and abuse, depression, poor emotional well-being, and drastic transformations of cultural values of Native Americans (Bichsel & Mallinckrodt, 2001). A higher percentage of American Indian individuals and families live in poverty compared to White individuals and families, and the American Indian poverty rate is larger among families on reservations than among American Indian families in other areas (DeVoe & Darling-Churchill, 2008). Native Americans have the highest disability rate of any ethnic group (Ma, Coyle, Wares, & Cornell, 1999). In 2008, 12.4% of females and 11.7% of Native American males reported having a disability (Erickson, Lee, & Von Schrader, 2009). Native Americans who are part of reservation-based populations face challenges accessing social and health services, as most reservations are rural (Weaver, 2015). The single most significant health problem among Native Americans is alcohol abuse (Bryan, 2014; Carpenter, Lyons, & Miller, 1985). Living in poverty with poor nutrition, health, housing, and transportation leads to chronic stress, which causes some Native Americans to turn to alcohol and other substances (Beauvais & LaBoueff, 1985; Bryan, 2014).

Native Americans account for less than 1% of those with undergraduate and graduate degrees in the United States (Aguirre Jr. & Turner, 2001). In 2014, the median income for American Indians was $37,227 (U.S. Census Bureau, 2015a). Native American incomes are among the lowest of any cultural group in America, and they are underrepresented in white-collar jobs and found primarily in service occupations (Aguirre Jr. & Turner, 2001). A primary reason for the high unemployment rates is the lack of job opportunities on reservations; because the vast majority of reservations are in remote areas, traveling to a job site outside of the reservation boundaries becomes challenging, especially if one has limited transportation options (Bryan, 2014). Due to poverty levels and scarcity of job opportunities on reservations, many Native Americans maintain employment in the farming, forestry, fishing, and mechanical repair industries (Ambert, 2001; Schaefer, 1998).

The Impact of Religion on Disability

Native Americans view spirit as the life force; therefore, spiritual health is linked to physical health (Johnston, 2006). Spirituality and the use of a healer play a crucial role as there is an interaction and a connection at some level between Mother Earth/nature, Father Sky, and all of life through the creator (Johnston, 2006). Illness and disability are viewed as a disruption in the balance among individual beings of the universe. In terms of treatment, correcting the imbalances through traditional healers helps to restore or maintain health (Johnston, 2006). Depending on the tribe, members may respond differently to illness, disease, and disability by utilizing religious activities, medicine men, and church elders (Bryan, 2014).

EUROPEAN AMERICANS

European Americans (White) are the largest ethnic group in North America, estimating the population to be 77% (U.S. Census Bureau, 2015d). There are many diverse European American groups such as German, Irish, French, Italian, Greek, and Russian, among others (Alessandria, 2002). The European American culture currently has the most power to create, maintain, and to influence the economic, political, and institutional structures in America (Smith, 2012).

Culture

European Americans' cultural values include the importance of work, individuality, family, expression/suppression of feelings, and prescribed roles as a mode of coping with internal conflict (W. M. Lee, 1999). They are among the most individualistic people in the world (Hitchcock, 2002). Individualism reflects self-reliance and independence as highly valued principles striving for success and achievement (Katz, 1999; McGoldrick, Giordano, & Garcia-Preto, 2005). European American traditional values include family-centered views; the family is important for identity, loyalties, and social organization. Fathers have traditionally been the head of the household; however, this has changed over the last several decades. The household care of home and family has typically been centered around the mother; however, more recently with women in the workforce, fathers have begun to contribute in roles previously assigned to women (Henderson & Bryan, 2011). European American couples with special needs share responsibility for household matters such as childcare, cleaning, meal provision, and outdoor landscaping. In many cases today, however, mothers may carry more economic power than their male companions (Daniel, 2003). Children's social class reflects that of their parents, and their lives are more organized and institutionalized, but less spontaneous, free ranging, and adult-interactive than those of past generations (Adler & Adler, 1998; Ambert, 2001).

Cultural Perspectives of Disability

European American paradigms define disabled bodies as "deviant" or biological "freakery" (Thomson, 1997), which reinforces negative connotations such as inferiority, helplessness, and weakness (Lovern, 2008). Weakness is influenced in certain cases by the belief that some disabilities are self-inflicted (e.g., substance abuse, injuries sustained from drunk driving), which may be associated with the moral judgment of deserving the disability punishment (Lovern, 2008). People with disabilities of all groups in general face discrimination, and have a collective history of devaluation, marginalization, and exclusion experiences in Western society (Marini, 2012). European Americans face common conditions such as heart disease, back problems, arthritis, diabetes, and orthopedic impairments of the upper or lower extremities (Olkin, 1999). In particular, White American children are more likely to be identified as having emotional or behavioral disorders and are more likely to be receiving special education services for emotional or behavioral disorders (P. Morgan & Farkas, 2016). Mandell and Novak (2005) note that European American parents are more likely to notice general developmental delays or regression of language before social issues when a family member has autism. This could relate to the fact that language is emphasized in the Anglo culture more than social skills (Pitten, 2008).

Family Perspectives of Disability

European American families value all members of the family becoming involved in caring for a person with a disability by first handling their own negative feelings of shame, anger, self-pity, hurt, and frustration when they are present (Henderson & Bryan, 2011). European American families do what they believe is best to help and advocate for services for a disabled child in order for him or her to attain the highest level of functioning and quality of life (Ravindran & Myers, 2012). Supportive European American families are essential to help family members with adjustment and to cope with their disability and nurture self-esteem (Carr, Linehan, O'Reilly, Walsh, & McEvoy, 2016). Like other groups, Western values of male masculinity, independence, and strength are diametrically different to sustaining a disability where one might be perceived as helpless and dependent (Shuttleworth, Wedgwood, & Wilson, 2012). European American women with disabilities may face discrimination and can be viewed as weaker and more fragile than women without disabilities and incapable of caring for their children (Henderson & Bryan, 2011). European American children with disabilities face societal expectations and norms to learn sex-appropriate behavior and become socially responsible; however, a severe disability such as cerebral palsy or muscular dystrophy may inhibit social development (Henderson & Bryan, 2011).

Socioeconomic Status Effects on Disability

European Americans place high value on economic, social, political, and spiritual practices (Ravindran & Myers, 2012). Married European American couples have lower poverty rates than those who are elderly and living alone; however, rates of poverty are lowest for the 65- to 74-year age group at approximately 5% (Taeuber, 2002). The U.S. Census Bureau (2000) estimates approximately 15 million European American families reported having a member with a disability, and one million families reported raising a child with a disability. Among European Americans in 2015, 47% had at least a 2-year college degree (Kolodner, 2016). The U.S. Census Bureau (2011) cites the median family income of single European American men is more than three fifths of the median married-family income; for single European American women, it is more than two fifths. Men can be found in professional, technical, or managerial occupations, and women are more likely to be highly educated and hold professional and managerial jobs (Jacobs & Gerson, 2008).

Impact of Religion on Disability

According to the Pew Research Center (2014), 81% of the European American population identify themselves as Christians. Over half of Christian European Americans identify as Protestant and about a quarter identify as Catholic (Lugo et al., 2008; Suarez & Lewis, 2013). European Americans value religious practices as a way to cope, attempt to solve problems, and seek assistance (Lago, 2006). Adults with disabilities and parents see church as an important social institution that facilitates a personal relationship with their God (Treloar, 2002). Spiritual beliefs stabilize strength for people with disabilities and their families by finding meaning in living with a disability (Treloar, 2002). European Americans who describe themselves as religious and spiritual report fewer mental health and stress-related problems (Corrigan, McCorkle, Schell, & Kidder, 2003). Many European Americans use religion to deal with disability as it may influence ways of coping with adversity, the experience of suffering, and the meaning of symptoms (Walsh, 2009).

An increasing body of knowledge supports the benefits of religious practice on physical and mental health outcomes (Koenig et al., 2001).

Counseling Implications Regarding Cultural Differences

Although the rehabilitation counselors are all well trained on generalized counseling skills, it is imperative for counselors to have a firm understanding of the racial and ethnic differences of other populations. D. W. Sue and Sue (2013), for example, noted that when European American counselors were counseling minorities, approximately half of these initial clients never returned for a second appointment. This either assumes that the client's psychosocial difficulties were resolved, or that there was a disconnect at some level between the counselor and client. Multicultural competencies and ongoing training has been occurring now for at least 20 years.

Overall, as described in this chapter, each group has nuanced values, beliefs, cultural history that may carry with it trust issues of certain groups, and family dynamics. In the United States, European Americans have enjoyed the benefits of the majority group for more than two centuries that brings privilege to many, as well as less stigmatization, poverty, and oppression (David, 2014). The majority identify as Christians, and they primarily adhere to individualism and a strong work ethic where hard work pays off with career success (Alessandria, 2002; Boston et al., 2015; Lago, 2006).

African American history in the United States has been marred by slavery, oppression, poverty, stigmatization, and incarceration (Smiley & West, 2012). More recent, national news has placed a spotlight on alleged police violence, unjustified force, and death of African Americans for traffic stops. Overall mistrust against European Americans has heightened; this led to the creation of the Black Lives Matter movement and an overall belief in inequality of this population. Counselors need to acknowledge these conditions for many African Americans and advocate with them where necessary and within one's employment policies where blatant social inequities exist, blocking them from essential services/rights. African Americans for the most part have a strong sense of faith, which strengthens their ability to cope with stress (Nobles, 1980).

One of the several obstacles to providing effective and appropriate helping services for Native Americans is the lack of understanding of within-group differences (Good & Good, 1986). Some ways to develop help for Native Americans are to deal with personal, social, and environmental difficulties resulting from its diminishing culture and difficulties with acculturation, particularly for those who moved to urban centers (Garrett, 1999). Another obstacle is the fact that many Native Americans live in rural areas often not easily found with few if any medical and counseling facilities. Some Native Americans succumb to alcohol and other substances, with higher than average rates of unemployment, low education, and chronic illness.

There is also a need for culturally competent counseling services for Asian Americans (J.-H. Kim & Park, 2015; Kung, 2004; S. M. Lee, 1998; Leong et al., 2006; Li & Kim, 2004). Shea and Yeh (2008) have listed several stressors found in Asian American youth—intergenerational conflict, adjusting cultural identities, career development, racism, and immigration status. Therefore, the counseling services need to assist the youth population toward better adjustment both in the family and society as older generation sacred values and practices clash with new generation American cultural values (Shea & Yeh, 2008).

Multicultural counseling competence when working with Middle Eastern Americans includes being empathetic (Soheilian & Inman, 2015), counselors overcoming their own prejudices, misconceptions, and gaps in knowledge about Arab Americans, acknowledging negative societal attitudes and prejudice are heightened since 9/11 (Al Khateeb et al., 2014) and assessment of a client's acculturation status (Amer, 2005). When initially working with culturally isolated Muslim clients, counselors can help identify aspects of American culture that are consistent with their faith and support the client in establishing proactive relationships with mainstream activities and persons with similar interests (Amer, 2005). Involving the entire family and not just the client can assist counselors to establish a relationship of trust that can be meaningful for the counselor–client relationship (Hammad et al., 1999). Cultural competence has been known to be an important component in receiving school psychological services for Arab American youth and their families (Goforth, 2011).

REFERENCES

Abu-Ras, W. (2013). Working with Arab Americans. In E. P. Congress & M. J. Gonzalez (Eds.), *Multicultural perspectives in social work practice with families* (pp. 185–204). New York, NY: Springer Publishing.

Adler, P. A., & Adler, P. (1998). *Peer power: Preadolescent culture and identity*. New Brunswick, NJ: Rutgers University Press.

Aguirre Jr., A., & Turner, J. (2001). *American ethnicity: The dynamics and consequences of discrimination* (3rd ed.). New York, NY: McGraw-Hill.

Ai, A. L., Aisenberg, E., Weiss, S. I., & Salazar, D. (2014). Racial/ethnic identity and subjective physical and mental health of Latino Americans: An asset within? *American Journal of Community Psychology, 53*(1–2), 173–184.

Ai, A. L., Huang, B., Bjorck, J. P., & Appel, H. B. (2013). Religious attendance and major depression among Asian Americans from a national database: The mediation of social support. *Psychology of Religion and Spirituality, 5*(2), 78–89.

Alessandria, K. P. (2002). Acknowledging White ethnic groups in multicultural counseling. *Family Journal, 10*(1), 57–60.

Al Khateeb, J. M., Al Hadidi, M. S., & Al Khatib, A. J. (2014). Arab Americans with disabilities and their families: A culturally appropriate approach for counselors. *Journal of Multicultural Counseling & Development, 42*(4), 232–247.

Almusa, A., & Ferrell, K. (2004, April). *Blindness in Islam*. Paper presented at the Council for Exceptional Children Conference, New Orleans, LA. Retrieved from http://faculty.ksu.edu.sa/10607/DocLib5/Blindness%20in%20Islam.doc

Alvidrez, J. (1999). Ethnic variations in mental health attitudes and service use among low-income African American, Latina, and European American young women. *Community Mental Research, 19*, 535–551.

Ambert, A. (2001). *Families in the new millenium*. Needham Heights, MA: Allyn & Bacon.

Amer, M. (2005). Arab American mental health in the post September 11 era: Acculturation, stress, and coping. *Dissertation Abstracts International: Section B. Sciences and Engineering, 66*(4), 1974.

Ameredia. (2006). Middle Eastern Americans. Retrieved from http://www.ameredia.com/resources/demographics/middle_eastern.html

Arab American Institute. (2010). Demographics. Retrieved from http://www.aaiusa.org/demographics-old

Arab American National Museum. (2017). Arab American culture. Retrieved from http://www.arabamericanmuseum.org/Arab+American+Culture.id.168.htm

Arcia, E., Reyes-Blanes, M. E., & Vazquez-Montilla, E. (2000). Constructions and reconstructions: Latino parents' values for children. *Journal of Child and Family Studies, 9*(3), 333–350.

Atkinson, D. R. (2004). *Counseling American minorities* (6th ed.). New York, NY: McGraw-Hill.

Aymer, S. R. (2013). An Afrocentric approach to working with African American families. In E. P. Congress & M. J. Gonzalez (Eds.), *Multicultural perspectives in social work practice with families* (pp. 129–139). New York, NY: Springer Publishing.

Barer, B. M., & Johnson, C. (2003). Problems and problem solving among White and Black Americans. *Journal of Aging Studies, 17*(3), 323–340.

Barrett, L. E. (1974). *Soul-force: African heritage in Afro-American religion*. Garden City, NY. Anchor.

Beauvais, F., & LaBoueff, S. (1985). Drug and alcohol abuse intervention in American Indian communities. *The International Journal of the Addictions, 20*(1), 139–171.

Begay, R. C., Roberts, R. N., Weisner, T. S., & Matheson, C. (1999). Indigenous and informal systems of support: Navajo families who have children with disabilities. *Bilingual Review, 24*(1–2), 79–94.

Berg, I. K., & Jaya, A. (1993). Different and same: Family therapy with Asian-American families. *Journal of Marital and Family Therapy, 19*, 31–38.

Bermúdez, J. M., Kirkpatrick, D., Hecker, L., & Torres-Robles, C. (2010). Describing Latinos families and their help-seeking attitudes: Challenging the family therapy literature. *Contemporary Family Therapy: An International Journal, 32*(2), 155–172.

Bichsel, R. J., & Mallinckrodt, B. (2001). Cultural commitment and the counseling preferences and counselor perceptions of Native American women. *The Counseling Psychologist, 29*(6), 858–881.

Billingsley, A. (1992). *Climbing Jacob's ladder: The enduring legacies of African American families.* New York, NY: Touchstone.

Bird, C., & Rieker, P. (2008). *Gender and health: The effects of constrained choices and social policies.* New York, NY: Cambridge University Press.

Boey, K. W. (1999). Help-seeking preference of college students in urban China after the implementation of the "open-door" policy. *International Journal of Social Psychiatry, 45*(2), 104–116.

Booker, C. L., Gallaher, P., Unger, J. B., Ritt-Olson, A., & Johnson, A. (2004). Stressful life events, smoking behavior, and intentions to smoke among a multiethnic sample of sixth graders. *Ethnicity & Health, 9*(4), 369–397.

Booth, J. J., Butler, M. J., Richardson, T. V., Washington, A. R., & Henfield, M. S. (2016). School-family-community collaboration for African American males with disabilities. *Journal of African American Males in Education, 7*(1), 87–97.

Boston, Q., Dunlap, P. N., Ethridge, G., Barnes, E., Dowden, A. R., & Euring, M. J. (2015). Cultural beliefs and disability: Implications for rehabilitation counsellors. *International Journal for the Advancement of Counselling, 37*(4), 367–374.

Boyd-Franklin, N. (2003). *Black families in therapy: Understanding the African American experience.* New York, NY: Guilford Press.

Brice, C., Masia Warner, C., Okazaki, S., Ma, P. W., Sanchez, A., Esseling, P., & Lynch, C. (2015). Social anxiety and mental health service use among Asian American high school students. *Child Psychiatry and Human Development, 46*(5), 693–701.

Bryan, W. V. (2014). *Multicultural aspects of human behavior: A guide to understanding human cultural development.* Springfield, IL: Charles C Thomas.

Burger, J., Gochfeld, M., Jeitner, C., & Pittfield, T. (2012). Activity patterns and perceptions of goods, services, and eco-cultural attributes by ethnicity and gender for Native Americans and Caucasians. *International Journal of Sport Management, Recreation & Tourism, 9c*, 934–951.

Burton, L. M., Garrett-Peters, R., & Eason, J. M. (2011). Morality, identity, and mental health in rural ghettos. In L. M. Burton, S. P. Kemp, M. Leung, S. A. Matthews, & D. T. Takeuchi (Eds.), *Communities, neighborhoods, and health* (pp. 91–110). New York, NY: Springer.

Bywaters, P., Ali, Z., Fazil, Q., Wallace, L. M., & Singh, G. (2003). Attitudes towards disability amongst Pakistani and Bangladeshi parents of disabled children in the UK: Considerations for service providers and the disability movement. *Health & Social Care in the Community, 11*(6), 502–509.

Caldwell, C. H., Kohn-Wood, L. P., Schmeelk-Cone, K. H., Chavous, T. M., & Zimmerman, M. A. (2004). Racial discrimination and racial identity as risk or protective factors for violent behaviors in African American young adults. *American Journal of Community Psychology, 33*(1–2), 91–105.

Carpenter, R. A., Lyons, C. A., & Miller, W. R. (1985). Peer-managed self-control program for prevention of alcohol abuse in American Indian high school students: A pilot evaluation study. *International Journal of the Addictions, 20*(2), 299–310.

Carr, A., Linehan, C., O'Reilly, G., Walsh, P. N., & McEvoy, J. (Eds.). (2016). *The handbook of intellectual disability and clinical psychology practice.* New York, NY: Routledge.

Cavenaugh, B., Giesen, M., & Steinman, B. (2006). Contextual effects of race or ethnicity on acceptance for vocational rehabilitation of consumers who are legally blind. *Journal of Visual Impairment & Blindness, 100*(11), 132–149.

Chan, S. (1998). Families with Asian roots. In E. W. Lynch & M. J. Hanson (Eds.), *Developing cross-cultural competence: A guide for working with children and their families* (2nd ed., pp. 181–257). Baltimore, MD: Paul H. Brookes.

Chaney, C. (2008a). Religiosity and spirituality among members of an African-American church community: A qualitative analysis. *Journal of Religion and Spirituality in Social Work: Social Thought, 27*, 201–234.

Chaney, C. (2008b). The benefits of church involvement for African Americans—The perspectives of congregants, church staff and the church pastor. *Religion and Society, 10*, 1–23.

Chang, C. Y. (2003). Counseling Asian Americans. In N. A. Vacc, S. B. DeVaney, & J. M. Brendel (Eds.), *Counseling multicultural and diverse populations: Strategies for practitioners* (pp. 73–92). New York, NY: Taylor & Francis Books.

Chang, C. Y., & Myers, J. E. (1997). Understanding and counseling Korean Americans: Implications for training. *Counselor Education & Supervision, 37*(1), 35–49.

Chao, R. K., Crockett, L. J., & Russell, S. T. (2010). *Asian American parenting and parent-adolescent relationships.* New York, NY: Springer Publishing.

Chatters, L. M., Taylor, R. J., Jackson, J. S., & Lincoln, K. D. (2008). Religious coping among African Americans, Caribbean Blacks and Non-Hispanic Whites. *Journal of Community Psychology, 36*(3), 371–386.

Chiang, L. H., & Hadadian, A. (2010). Raising children with disabilities in China: The need for early interventions. *International Journal of Special Education, 25*(2), 113–118.

Chin, J. L. (1998). Mental health services and treatment. In L. C. Lee & N. W. S. Zane (Eds.), *Handbook of Asian American psychology* (pp. 485–504). Thousand Oaks, CA: Sage.

Cohen, S. R. (2013). Advocacy for the "abandonados": Harnessing cultural beliefs for Latino families and their children with intellectual disabilities. *Journal of Policy & Practice in Intellectual Disabilities, 10*(1), 71–78.

Colby, S. L., & Ortman, J. M. (2015). *Projections of the size and composition of the U.S. population: 2014 to 2060, current population reports* (P25-1143). Washington, DC: U.S. Census Bureau, 2014.

Collins, P. H. (1990). *Black feminist thought: Knowledge, consciousness, and the politics empowerment.* New York, NY: Routledge.

Congress, E. P., & Kung, W. W. (2013). Using the cultgram to assess and empower culturally diverse families. In E. P. Congress & M. J. Gonzalez (Eds.), *Multicultural perspectives in social work practice with families* (pp. 1–20). New York, NY: Springer Publishing.

Coontz, S., Parson, M., & Raley, G. (2008). *American families: A multicultural reader.* New York, NY: Routledge.

Corrigan, P., McCorkle, B., Schell, B., & Kidder, K. (2003). Religion and spirituality in the lives of people with serious mental illness. *Community Mental Health Journal, 39*(6), 487–499.

Crabtree, S. A. (2006). A comparative analysis of social work responses to child abuse in the United Arab Emirates. *International Journal of Child and Family Welfare, 9*(4), 228–237.

Crabtree, S. A. (2007). Family responses to the social inclusion of children with developmental disabilities in the United Arab Emirates. *Disability & Society, 22*(1), 49–62.

Crabtree, S. A., Husain, F., & Spalek, B. (2008). *Islam and social work: Debating values, transforming practice.* Chicago, IL: The Policy Press.

Curtis-Boles, H., & Jenkins-Monroe, V. (2000). Substance abuse in African American women. *Journal of Black Psychology, 26*(4), 450.

Daniel, R. L. (2003). Counseling men. In N. A. Vacc, S. B. DeVaney, & J. M. Brendel (Eds.), *Counseling multicultural and diverse populations: Strategies for practitioners* (pp. 189–207). New York, NY: Taylor & Francis Books.

David, E. J. R. (2014). *Internalized oppression: The psychology of marginalized groups.* New York, NY: Springer Publishing.

Deegan, M. J. (1981). Multiple minority groups: A case study of physically disabled women. *Journal of Sociology & Social Welfare, 8*(2), 274.

DeNavas-Walt, C., & Proctor, B. D. (2015). *Income and poverty in the United States: 2014. Current population report* (P60-252). Washington, DC: U.S. Census Bureau. Retrieved from https://www.census.gov/content/dam/Census/library/publications/2015/demo/p60-252.pdf

DeVoe, J. F., & Darling-Churchill, K. E. (2008). *Status and trends in the education of American Indians and Alaska Natives: 2008* (NCES 2008–084). Washington, DC: National Center for Education Statistics.

Divin, C., Volker, D. L., & Harrison, T. (2013). Intimate partner violence in Mexican-American women with disabilities: A secondary data analysis of cross-language research. *Advances in Nursing Science, 36*(3), 243–257.

Dixon, P. (2007). *African American relationships, marriages, and families: An introduction.* New York, NY: Routledge.

Edgerton, R. B., & Karno, M. (1971). Mexican-American bilingualism and the perception of mental illness. *Archives of General Psychiatry, 24*(3), 286–290.

Erickson, W., Lee, C., & Von Schrader, S. (2009). *2008 Disability status report: The United States.* Ithaca, NY: Cornell University Rehabilitation Research and Training Center on Disability Demographics and Statistics.

Fukukawa, Y., Nakashima, C., Tsuboi, S., Niino, N., Ando, F., Kosugi, S., & Shimokata, H. (2004). The impact of health problems on depression and activities in middle-aged and older adults: Age and social interactions as moderators. *Journals of Gerontology. Series B, Psychological Sciences and Social Sciences, 59*(1), P19–P26.

Garcia-Preto, N. (2005). Latino families: An overview. In M. McGoldrick, J. Giordano, & N. Garcia-Preto (Eds.), *Ethnicity and family therapy* (pp. 143–152). New York, NY: Guilford Press.

Garrett, M. T. (1999). Understanding the "medicine" of Native American traditional values: An integrative review. *Counseling and Values, 43*(2), 84–98.

Garrett, M. T., Parrish, M., Williams, C., Grayshield, L., Portman, T. A., Rivera, E. T., & Maynard, E. (2014). Invited commentary: Fostering resilience among Native American youth through therapeutic intervention. *Journal of Youth and Adolescence, 43*(3), 470–490.

Girimaji, S. C., & Kommu, J. V. S. (2016). Intellectual disability in India: Recent trends in care and services. In I. L. Rubin, J. Merrick, D. E. Graydanus, & D. R. Patel (Eds.), *Health care for people with intellectual and developmental disabilities across the lifespan* (pp. 461–470). Cham, Switzerland: Springer International Publishing.

Glazer, I. M., & Abu Ras, W. (1994). On aggression, human rights and hegemonic discourse: The case of a murder for family honor in Israel. *Sex Roles, 30*(3–4), 269–289.

Goforth, A. N. (2011). Considerations for school psychologists working with Arab American children and families. *Communique, 39*(6), 28–30.

Good, B. J., & Good, M. D. (1986). The cultural context of diagnosis and therapy: A view from medical anthropology. In M. R. Miranda & H. L. Kitano (Eds.), *Mental health research & practice in minority communities* (pp. 1–27). Washington, DC: U.S. Department of Health and Human Services.

Groce, N. E., & Zola, I. K. (1993). Multiculturalism, chronic illness, and disability. *Pediatrics, 91*(5 Pt 2), 1048–1055.

Guarnaccia, P. J., Martinez, I., & Acosta, H. (2005). Mental health in the Hispanic immigrant community: An overview. In M. J. Gonzalez & G. Gonzalez-Ramos (Eds), *Mental health care for new Hispanic immigrants: Innovative approaches in contemporary clinical practice* (pp. 21–46). Binghamton, NY: The Haworth Social Work Practice Press.

Gurung, R. (2006). *Health psychology: A cultural approach.* Belmont, CA: Wadsworth Publishing.

Haan, M. N., Mungas, D. M., Gonzalez, H. M., Ortiz, T. A., Acharya, A., & Jagust, W. J. (2003). Prevalence of dementia in older Latinos: The influence of type 2 diabetes mellitus, stroke and genetic factors. *Journal of the American Geriatrics Society, 51*(2), 169–177.

Hamilton, B. (1996). Ethnicity and the family life cycle: The Chinese-American family. *Family Therapy, 23*(3), 199–212.

Hammad, A., Kysia, R., Rabah, R., Hassoun, R., & Connelly, M. (1999). *ACCESS guide to Arab culture: Health care delivery to the Arab American community.* Dearborn, MI: ACCESS Community Health Center. Retrieved from http://www.naama.com/pdf/arab-american-culture-health-care.pdf

Hanna, W. J., & Rogovsky, B. (1991). Women with disabilities: Two handicaps plus. *Disability, Handicap & Society, 6*(1), 49–63.

Harrison, T. (2009). Health disparities among Latinas aging with disabilities. *Family & Community Health, 32*(1 Suppl.), S36–S45.

Harry, B., Allen, N., & McLaughlin, M. (1995). Communication versus compliance: African-American parents' involvement in special education. *Exceptional Children, 61*, 364–377.

Henderson, G. H., & Bryan, W. V. (2011). *Psychosocial aspects of disability.* Springfield, IL: Charles C Thomas.

Hines, P. M., & Boyd-Franklin, N. (1996). African American families. In M. McGoldrick, J. Giordano, & J. K. Pearce (Eds.), *Ethnicity and family therapy* (2nd ed., pp. 66–84). New York, NY: Guilford Press.

Hines, P. M., & Boyd-Franklin, N. (2005). African American families. In M. McGoldrick, J. Giordano, & N. Garcia-Preto (Eds.), *Ethnicity and family therapy* (pp. 87–100). New York, NY: Guilford Press.

Hitchcock, J. (2002). *Lifting the white veil: An exploration of White American culture in a multiracial context.* Roselle, NJ: Crandall, Dostie & Douglass Books.

Holland, A. W. (2014). *Cultural competence in recreation therapy: Working with African-Americans, Chinese Americans, Japanese Americans, Hmong Americans, Mexican Americans, and Puerto Rican Americans.* Enumclaw, WA: Idyll Arbo.

Holt, C. L., Clark, E. M., & Roth, D. L. (2014). Positive and negative religious beliefs explaining the religion–health connection among African Americans. *International Journal for the Psychology of Religion, 24*(4), 311–331.

Hurtig, A. L., Koepke, D., & Park, K. B. (1989). Relation between severity of chronic illness and adjustment in children and adolescents with sickle cell disease. *Journal of Pediatric Psychology, 14*(1), 117–132.

Jacobs, J. A., & Gerson, K. (2008). Work and American families. In S. Coontz, M. Parson, & G. Raley, *American families: A multicultural reader* (pp. 454–466). New York, NY: Routledge.

Joe, J. R. (1997). American Indian children with disabilities: The impact of culture on health and education services. *Families, Systems, & Health, 15*(3), 251.

Johnston, L. (2006). Native-American medicine. Retrieved from http://www.healingtherapies.info/Native-American%20Medicine.htm

Jones, A. C. (1993). *Wade in the water: The wisdom of the spirituals.* Maryknoll, NY: Orbis.

Katz, J. H. (1999). *White culture and racism: Working for organizational change in the United States. The Whiteness Papers* (3). Roselle, NJ: Center for the Study of White American Culture.

Kelsey, P. (2013). Disability and Native North American boarding school narratives: Madonna swan and Sioux sanitorium. *Journal of Literary & Cultural Disability Studies, 7*(2), 195–212.

Kim, J.-H., & Park, E.-C. (2015). Impact of socioeconomic status and subjective social class on overall and health-related quality of life. *BMC Public Health, 15,* 783.

Kim, U., & Chun, M. B. J. (1994). Educational "success" of Asian Americans: An indigenous perspective. *Journal of Applied Developmental Psychology, 15,* 329–343.

King, T., & Ferguson, S. (1996). "I am because we are": Clinical interpretations of communal experience among African American women. *Women & Therapy, 18,* 33–45.

Kira, I. A. (1999, July). *Value processing and mental health.* Paper presented at the Sixth European Congress of Psychology, Rome, Italy.

Kochhar, R. (2014). *Latino jobs growth driven by U.S. born.* Pew Research Center Hispanic Trends. Retrieved from http://www.pewhispanic.org/2014/06/19/latino-jobs-growth-driven-by-u-s-born/#

Koenig, H. G., McCullough, M. E., & Larson, D. B. (2001). *Handbook of religion and health.* New York, NY: Oxford University Press.

Kolodner, M. (2016). College degree gap grows wider between Whites, Blacks and Latinos: State funding is down and tuition is up since the recession. Retrieved from http://hechingerreport.org/25368-2

Kung, W. W. (2004). Cultural and practical barriers to seeking mental health treatment for Chinese Americans. *Journal of Community Psychology, 32*(1), 27–43.

Lago, C. (2006). *Race, culture and counseling: The ongoing challenge.* New York, NY: McGraw-Hill.

Lee, S. M. (1998). Asian Americans: Diverse and growing. *Population Bulletin, 53*(2), 1–40.

Lee, W. M. (1999). *An introduction to multicultural counseling.* Ann Arbor, MI: Taylor & Francis.

Le Meyer, O., Zane, N., Cho, Y. I., & Takeuchi, D. T. (2009). Use of specialty mental health services by Asian Americans with psychiatric disorders. *Journal of Consulting and Clinical Psychology, 77*(5), 1000–1005.

Leong, F. T. L., Inman, A. G., Ebreo, A., Yang, L. H., Kinoshita, L., & Fu, M. (Eds.). (2006). *Handbook of Asian American psychology* (2nd ed.). Thousand Oaks, CA: Sage.

Leung, P. (2003). Culture, disability, and caregiving for people with traumatic brain injury. In H. Muenchberger, E. Kendall, & J. Wright (Eds.), *Health and healing after traumatic brain injury: Understanding the power of family, friends, community, and other support systems* (pp. 215–226). Santa Barbara, CA: Praeger.

Li, L. C., & Kim, B. S. (2004). Effects of counseling style and client adherence to Asian cultural values on counseling process with Asian American college students. *Journal of Counseling Psychology, 51*(2), 158. doi:10.1037/0022-0167.51.2.158

Lichter, D. T., Johnson, K. M., Turner, R. N., & Churilla, A. (2012). Hispanic assimilation and fertility in new destinations. *The International Migration Review, 46*(4), 767–791.

Lichter, D. T., Parisi, D., & Taquino, M. C. (2012). The geography of exclusion: Race, segregation, and concentrated poverty. *Social Problems, 59,* 364–388.

Lichter, D. T., Sanders, S. R., & Johnson, K. M. (2015). Hispanics at the starting line: Poverty among newborn infants in established gateways and new destinations. *Social Forces, 94*(1), 209–235.

Lincoln, K. D., Chatters, L. M., & Taylor, R. J. (2005). Social support, traumatic events, and depressive symptoms among African Americans. *Journal of Marriage and the Family, 67*(3), 754–766.

Loo, C., Tong, B., & True, R. (1989). A bitter bean: Mental health status and attitudes in Chinatown. *Journal of Community Psychology, 17,* 283–296.

López, S. R., Barrio, C., Kopelowicz, A., & Vega, W. A. (2012). From documenting to eliminating disparities in mental health care for Latinos. *American Psychologist, 67*(7), 511–523.

Lovern, L. (2008). Native American worldview and the discourse on disability. *Essays in Philosophy, 9*(1), 14.

Lovern, L. (2014). Embracing difference: Native American approaches to disability. *Tikkun, 29,* 37–38B.

Lugo, L., Stencel, S., Green, J., Smith, G., Cox, D., & Pond, A. (2008). U.S. religious landscape survey: Religious beliefs and practices: Diverse and politically relevant. Retrieved from http://www.pewforum.org/files/2008/06/report2-religious-landscape-study-full.pdf

Ma, G. X., Coyle, C. P., Wares, D., & Cornell, D. (1999). Assessment of services to American Indians with disabilities. *Journal of Rehabilitation, 65*(3), 11.

Mandell, D. S., & Novak, M. (2005). The role of culture in families' treatment decisions for children with autism spectrum disorders. *Mental Retardation and Developmental Disabilities Research Reviews, 11*(2), 110–115.

Marini, I. (2012). Cross-cultural counseling issues of males who sustain a disability. In I. Marini & M. Stebnicki (Eds.), *The psychological and social impact of illness and disability* (pp. 151–164). New York, NY: Springer Publishing.

Marini, I., Glover-Graf, N. M., & Millington, M. J. (2012). *Psychosocial aspects of disability: Insider perspectives and strategies for counselors.* New York, NY: Springer Publishing.

McGoldrick, M., Giordano, J., & Garcia-Preto, N. (Eds.). (2005). *Ethnicity and family therapy*. New York, NY: Guilford Press.

Millington, M. J. (2012). Culturally different issues and attitudes toward disability. In I. Marini, N. M. Glover-Graf, & M. J. Millington (Eds.), *Psychosocial aspects of disability: Insider perspectives and strategies for counselors* (pp. 61–95). New York, NY: Springer Publishing.

Minority Rights Group International. (2017). Arab and other Middle Eastern Americans. Retrieved from http://minorityrights.org/minorities/arab-and-other-middle-eastern-americans

Morgan, P., & Farkas, G. (2016). Evidence and implications of racial and ethnic disparities in emotional and behavioral disorders: Identification and treatment. *Behavioral Disorders, 41*(2), 122–131.

Morgan, S. A., & Jackson, J. (1986). Psychological and social concomitants of sickle cell anemia in adolescents. *Journal of Pediatric Psychology, 11*(3), 429–440.

Nassar-McMillan, S. C. (2003). Counseling Asian Americans. In N. A. Vacc, S. B. DeVaney, & J. M. Brendel (Eds.), *Counseling multicultural and diverse populations: Strategies for practitioners* (pp. 117–139). New York, NY: Taylor & Francis.

National Committee to Preserve Social Security & Medicare. (2016). Social Security is important to African Americans. Retrieved from http://www.ncpssm.org/SocialSecurity/AfricanAmericansandSS

Neighbors, H. W., Musick, M. A., & Williams, D. R. (1998). The African American minister: Bridge or barrier to mental health care. *Health Education and Behavior, 25*, 759–777.

Newacheck, P. W., Stein, R. E., Bauman, L., & Hung, Y. Y.; Research Consortium on Children With Chronic Conditions. (2003). Disparities in the prevalence of disability between Black and White children. *Archives of Pediatrics & Adolescent Medicine, 157*(3), 244–248.

Nichols, L. A., & Keltner, B. (2005). Indian family adjustment to children with disabilities. *American Indian and Alaska Native Mental Health Research, 12*(1), 22–48.

Nickerson, K. J., Helms, J. E., & Terrell, F. (1994). Cultural mistrust, opinions about mental illness and Black students' attitude toward seeking psychological help from White counselors. *Journal of Counseling Psychology, 41*, 378–385.

Nobles, W. W. (1980). African philosophy: Foundations for Black psychology. In R. L. Jones (Ed.) *I, Black psychology* (pp. 23–36). New York, NY: Harper & Row.

Ojeda, L., & Piña-Watson, B. (2013). Day laborers' life satisfaction: The role of familismo, spirituality, work, health, and discrimination. *Cultural Diversity & Ethnic Minority Psychology, 19*(3), 270–278.

Olkin, R. (1999). *What psychotherapists should know about disability*. New York, NY: Guilford Press.

Parette, P., Chuang, S. L., & Huer, M. B. (2004). First-generation Chinese American families' attitudes regarding disabilities and educational interventions. *Focus on Autism and Other Developmental Disabilities, 97*, 114–123.

Pengra, L., & Godfrey, J. (2001). Different boundaries, different barriers: Disability studies and Lakota culture. *Disability Studies Quarterly, 21*(3), 36–53.

Pew Research Center. (2013). *The rise of Asian Americans*. Retrieved from http://www.pewsocialtrends.org/2012/06/19/the-rise-of-asian-americans

Pew Research Center Religion & Public Life. (2014). Religions: Explore religious groups in the U.S. by tradition, family and denomination. Retrieved from http://www.pewforum.org/religious-landscape-study

Pitten, K. (2008). How cultural values influence diagnosis, treatment and the welfare of families with an autistic child. *InSight: Rivier Academic Journal, 4*(1), 1–5.

Ravindran, N., & Myers, B. (2012). Cultural influences on perceptions of health, illness, and disability: A review and focus on autism. *Journal of Child & Family Studies, 21*(2), 311–319.

Richter, D. L., Wilcox, S., Greaney, M. L., Henderson, K. A., & Ainsworth, B. E. (2002). Environmental, policy, and cultural factors related to physical activity in African American women. *Women & Health, 36*(2), 91–109.

Rogers-Adkinson, D., Ochoa, T., & Delgado, B. (2003). Developing cross-cultural competence: Serving families of children with significant developmental needs. *Focus on Autism and Other Developmental Disabilities, 18*(1), 4–8.

Rohlfsen, L. S. (2008). Gender disparities in trajectories of functional, mental, and self-rated health: An analysis of older adults (Order No. 3319078). Available from ProQuest Dissertations & Theses Global (304686555). Retrieved from http://ezhost.utrgv.edu:2048/login?url=http://search.proquest.com/docview/304686555?accountid=7119

Sarmiento, I. A., & Cardemil, E. V. (2009). Family functioning and depression in low-income Latino couples. *Journal of Marital and Family Therapy, 35*(4), 432–445.

Saw, A., Berenbaum, H., & Okazaki, S. (2013). Influences of personal standards and perceived parental expectations on worry for Asian American and White American college students. *Anxiety, Stress & Coping, 26*(2), 187–202.

Schaefer, R. T. (1998). *Racial and ethnic groups* (7th ed.). New York, NY: Addison-Wesley Longman.

Shea, M., & Yeh, C. J. (2008). Asian American students' cultural values, stigma, and relational self-construal: Correlates of attitudes toward professional help seeking. *Journal of Mental Health Counseling, 30*(2), 157.

Shin, J. Y., Berkson, G., & Crittenden, K. (2000). Informal and professional support for solving psychological problems among Korean-American immigrants. *Journal of Multicultural Counseling and Development, 28*, 144–159.

Shorter-Gooden, K. (2004). Multiple resistance strategies: How African American women cope with racism and sexism. *Journal of Black Psychology, 30*(3), 406–425.

Shuttleworth, R., Wedgwood, N., & Wilson, N. J. (2012). The dilemma of disabled masculinity. *Men and Masculinities, 15*(2), 174–194.

Smart, J. F., & Smart, D. W. (1994). The rehabilitation of Hispanics experiencing acculturative stress: Implications for practice. *Journal of Rehabilitation, 60*(4), 8–12.

Smiley, T., & West, C. (2012). *The rich and the rest of us: A poverty manifesto*. New York, NY: Hay House.

Smith, C. (2012). The ethnicity of White Americans: Hidden or all-pervading? Retrieved from https://the societypages.org/sociologylens/2012/10/16/the-ethnicity-of-white-americans-hidden-or -all-pervading

Snowden, L. R. (2001). Barriers to effective mental health services for African Americans. *Mental Health Services Research, 3*(4), 181–187.

Soheilian, S. S., & Inman, A. G. (2015). Competent counseling for Middle Eastern American clients: Implications for trainees. *Journal of Multicultural Counseling & Development, 43*(3), 173–190.

Steigenga, T. J., & Cleary, E. L. (2007). *Conversion of a continent: Contemporary religious change in Latin America*. Piscataway, NJ: Rutgers University Press.

Suarez, Z. E., & Lewis, E. A. (2013). Spirituality and culturally diverse families: The intersection of culture, religion, and spirituality. In E. P. Congress & M. J. Gonzalez (Eds.), *Multicultural perspectives in social work practice with families* (3rd ed., pp. 231–244). New York, NY: Springer Publishing.

Sue, D. (1998). The interplay of sociocultural factors on the psychological development of Asians in America. In D. R. Atkinson, G. Morten, & D. W. Sue (Eds.), *Counseling American minorities* (5th ed., pp. 205–213). Boston, MA: McGraw-Hill.

Sue, D. W., & Sue, D. (2013). *Counseling the culturally diverse: Theory and practice*. Hoboken, NJ: John Wiley.

Sue, S., & Okazaki, S. (2009). Asian American journal of psychology: Asian-American educational achievements: A phenomenon in search of an explanation. *American Psychological Association, 45*(1), 45–55.

Sue, S., Zane, N., & Young, K. (1994). Research on psychotherapy with culturally diverse populations. In A. E. Bergin & S. L. Garfield (Eds.), *Handbook of psychotherapy and behavior change* (4th ed., pp. 783–820). New York, NY: John Wiley.

Taeuber, C. M. (2002). Sixty-five plus in the U.S.A. In N. A. Denton & S. E. Tolnay (Eds.), *American diversity: A demographic challenge for the twenty-first century* (p. 245). Albany: State University of New York Press.

Taylor, P., Lopez, M., Martínez, J., & Velasco, G. (2012). *When labels don't fit: Hispanics and their views of identity*. Washington, DC: Pew Hispanic Center.

Taylor, R. J., Chatters, L. M., & Levin, J. S. (2004). *Religion in the lives of African Americans*. Thousand Oaks, CA: Sage.

Thompson Sanders, V. L., Bazile, A., & Akbar, M. (2004). African Americans' perceptions of psychotherapy and psychotherapists. *Professional Psychology: Research and Practice, 35*, 19–26.

Thomson, R. G. (1997). *Exceptional bodies: Figuring physical disability*. Birmingham, England: Open University Press.

Treloar, L. L. (2002). Disability, spiritual beliefs and the church: The experiences of adults with disabilities and family members. *Journal of Advanced Nursing, 40*(5), 594–603.

Trotter, R. T., & Chavira, J. A. (1997). *Curanderismo: Mexican-American folk healing*. Athens: University of Georgia Press.

Tsai, J. L., Ying, Y. W., & Lee, P. A. (2000). The meaning of "being Chinese" and "being American" variation among Chinese American young adults. *Journal of Cross-Cultural Psychology, 31*(3), 302–332.

U.S. Bureau of Labor Statistics. (2016). Persons with a disability: Labor force characteristics—2015. Retrieved from https://www.bls.gov/news.release/pdf/disabl.pdf

U.S. Census Bureau. (2000). Disability and American Families: 2000. Retrieved from http://www .census.gov/prod/2005pubs/censr-23.pdf

U.S. Census Bureau. (2010). 2010 census shows Asians are fastest-growing race group. Retrieved from https://www.census.gov/newsroom/releases/archives/2010_census/cb12-cn22.html

U.S. Census Bureau. (2011). The White population: 2010 census briefs. Retrieved from http://www .census.gov/prod/cen2010/briefs/c2010br-05.pdf

U.S. Census Bureau. (2015a). FFF: American Indian and Alaska Native heritage month: November 2015. Retrieved from http://www.census.gov/newsroom/facts-for-features/2015/cb15-ff22.html

U.S. Census Bureau. (2015b). FFF: Asian/Pacific American heritage month: May 2015. Retrieved from http://www.census.gov/newsroom/facts-for-features/2015/cb15-ff07.html

U.S. Census Bureau. (2015c). Facts for features: Black (African-American) history month: February 2015. Retrieved from http://www.census.gov/newsroom/facts-for-features/2015/cb15-ff01.html

U.S. Census Bureau. (2015d). Quickfacts. Retrieved from https://www.census.gov/quickfacts/table/PST045216/00

U.S. Census Bureau. (2015e). 2015 American community survey 1-year estimates. Retrieved from https://factfinder.census.gov/faces/tableservices/jsf/pages/productview.xhtml?src=bkmk

U.S. Census Bureau. (2016). FFF: Hispanic heritage month 2016. Retrieved from http://www.census.gov/newsroom/facts-for-features/2016/cb16-ff16.html

Vacc, N. A., DeVaney, S. B., & Brendel, J. M. (Eds.). (2003). *Counseling multicultural and diverse populations: Strategies for practitioners*. New York, NY: Routledge.

Valdez, C. M. (2003). Placement of ethnic minority students in special education: A study of over and underrepresentation issues. *ProQuest Dissertations and Theses, 66569* (UMI No.9315947).

Walsh, F. (2009). *Spiritual resources in family therapy*. New York, NY: Guilford Press.

Wang, H., & West, E. A. (2016). Asian American immigrant parents supporting children with autism: Perceptions of fathers and mothers. *International Journal of Whole Schooling, 12*(1), 1–21.

Weaver, H. N. (2015). Disability through a Native American lens: Examining influences of culture and colonization. *Journal of Social Work in Disability & Rehabilitation, 14*(3–4), 148–162.

White, J. L. (1984). *The psychology of Blacks*. Englewood Cliffs, NJ: Prentice Hall.

White, J. L., & Parham, T. A. (1990). *The psychology of Blacks: An African American perspective*. Englewood Cliffs, NJ: Prentice Hall.

World Institute on Disability. (2006). *Latinos with disabilities in the United States*. Retrieved from http://citeseerx.ist.psu.edu/viewdoc/download;jsessionid=38308EEF709AFB8559A61D1B41A9454F?doi=10.1.1.172.1813&rep=rep1&type=pdf

Wright, D. A., & Phillips, D. J. (1988). Chesapeake and San Francisco bays: A study in contrasts and parallels. *Marine Pollution Bulletin, 19*(9), 405–413.

Yan, K. K., Accordino, M. P., Boutin, D. L., & Wilson, K. B. (2014). Disability and the Asian culture. *Journal of Applied Rehabilitation Counseling, 45*(2), 4–8. Retrieved from http://ezhost.utrgv.edu:2048/login?url=http://search.proquest.com/docview/1544866983?accountid=7119

Yang, Y., & Lee, L. C. (2009). Sex and race disparities in health: Cohort variations in life course patterns. *Social Forces, 87*(4), 2093–2124.

Yeh, C., & Wang, Y. W. (2000). Asian American coping attitudes, sources, and practices: Implications for indigenous counseling strategies. *Journal of College Student Development, 41*(1), 94–103.

Yeung, A., & Kung, W. (2004). How culture impacts on the treatment of mental illnesses among Asian Americans. *Psychiatric News, 21*(1), 34–36.

Zhang, A. Y., Snowden, L. R., & Sue, S. (1998). Differences between Asian and White Americans help seeking and utilization patterns in the Los Angeles area. *Journal of Community Psychology, 26*(4), 317–326.

11

Quality of Life and Coping With Chronic Illness and Disability: A Temporal Perspective*

Hanoch Livneh

The concept of quality of life (QOL), as a psychosocial construct, process, measure, goal, and outcome, has gained much popularity in the rehabilitation literature during the past 35 years (Bishop, 2005; Crewe, 1980; Fabian, 1991; Hershenson, 1990; Livneh, 2001; Roessler, 1990). As both a goal (i.e., assisting clients with chronic illnesses and disabilities [CIDs] to attain a better QOL) and a process–outcome indicator (i.e., assessing both subjective and objective levels of QOL during and following rehabilitation interventions), QOL has become one of the most prominent and central concepts in the field of rehabilitation (Bishop, 2005; Bishop, Smedema, & Lee, 2009; Crewe, 1980; Renwick, Brown, & Nagler, 1996). Despite the numerous theoretical, clinical, and empirical perspectives from which it has been approached, the understanding of QOL has seldom been addressed by using the dynamic, time-dependent, process-like perspective of its clinical underpinnings. The link between QOL, as a rehabilitation goal and outcome, and its unfolding temporal link to the domains of (a) community-level clinical interventions (i.e., public health, mental health, crisis intervention, and rehabilitation services) and (b) personal-level coping strategies (i.e., psychosocial adaptation and, more specifically, coping with life stresses and disability-induced functional limitations) has only scarcely been explored by rehabilitation researchers and practitioners.

More specific, within the context of improving and maintaining QOL, community-level interventions have sought to address the occurrence among the public of physical limitations (e.g., functional restrictions), psychological limitations (e.g., stressful life events), and social limitations (e.g., restricted social activities) through the establishment of a comprehensive network of interventions that are geared toward (a) prevention (future oriented; reducing the risk variables that may affect the lives of community members), (b) early intervention (present oriented, or crisis intervention; directed at people who actively experience a crisis by seeking to restore equilibrium and reduce distress), and (c) postvention (past oriented; directed at people long after the onset of stressful or crisis situation, by seeking to minimize residual impairments and limitations following resolution of crisis; Caplan, 1964; Janosik, 1984; Livneh, 1995; Slaikeu, 1990). In a similar

---

*Quality of life and coping with chronic illness and disability: A temporal perspective, *Rehabilitation Counseling Bulletin*, 2016, 59(2), 67–83. Reprinted by permission of SAGE Publications, Inc.

vein, person-level (psychosocial) interventions, mostly internally driven, but, at times, also externally initiated, include the acquisition of individualized coping skills to combat the deleterious impact of disability-imposed functional limitations and associated stressful life events: (a) before crisis onset (i.e., preventive, proactive, and anticipatory coping; or future-oriented coping), (b) during or through currently experienced crisis situations (i.e., crisis intervention, or present-oriented coping), and (c) pursuant to the resolution of crisis (i.e., reactive and residual coping, or past-oriented coping; Aspinwall, 2005; Auerbach, 1992; Folkman & Moskowitz, 2004; Schwarzer & Knoll, 2003).

In line with these notions of community-level and personal-level strategies, the aims of this chapter are to (a) familiarize the reader with the conceptual and temporal parallelism underlying the domains of community interventions and personal coping, of which rehabilitation services are an essential component, as part of their joint goal to improve QOL; and (b) provide examples from the field of psychosocial rehabilitation, and more specific coping with CID, that address the temporal nature of QOL-improving coping strategies.

COMMUNITY AND PERSONAL-LEVEL INTERVENTIONS: MANAGING STRESSFUL EVENTS AND COPING WITH CID

As suggested earlier, an often observed parallelism exists between the temporal under-gird of community-level human service interventions and personal-level coping efforts and strategies. The so-called tripartite model of therapeutic modalities, which was first conceived by Caplan (1964) to combat health impairments as well as psychopathologies, was developed to depict preventions and interventions (the two terms are often inexplicably used interchangeably; Auerbach, 1992; Janosik, 1984; Slaikeu, 1990) in the fields of public health, mental health, social services, medicine, nursing, physical therapy (PT), occupational therapy (OT), and rehabilitation (psychology and counseling). The model contains, both structurally and temporally, three distinct content domains as well as time frames. These three intervention domains, as mentioned earlier, are time dependent and customarily include preventive (i.e., primary prevention [PP] or crisis prevention), interventive (i.e., secondary prevention [SP] or crisis intervention), and postventive (i.e., tertiary prevention [TP] or rehabilitation) services. The three domains are also noted by their differential therapeutic goals, indicators, targeted service providers, and intervention strategies (for detailed treatment of various aspects of the tripartite model, the reader may also wish to consult Auerbach, 1992; Goodyear, 1976; Janosik, 1984; and Slaikeu, 1990, and more specifically the rehabilitation field; Hershenson, 1990; Hershenson et al., 1981; Livneh, 1995).

In contrast to the community-based, large-scale, broad-angle view on human health, functioning, and behavior, undertaken by fields such as community health, occupational health, medicine, and nursing, the concept of coping has traditionally been associated more specifically with individual-level processes, originated in the field of psychology and its derivatives (e.g., health psychology, medical psychology, and rehabilitation psychology and counseling). Furthermore, coping models seek to directly address the sources of life stresses by considering their "temporal ordering." They aim to explore the effectiveness of various coping strategies in minimizing physiological stress, emotional distress, cognitive distortions, and behavioral and psychological dysfunction, as they are anchored in a differentiated temporal fabric (Auerbach, 1992; Schwarzer & Knoll, 2003).

The concept of coping has been explored and described in numerous ways and has been studied in a wide range of contexts (Endler & Parker, 1990; Haan, 1977; Lazarus,

1966; Lazarus & Folkman, 1984; Martz & Livneh, 2007; Moos, 1986; Zeidner & Endler, 1996). It is essential in the understanding of coping to regard it as a dynamic and sequential process in which the various coping modalities operate, intersect, and aggregate their unique properties (Krohne, 1996; Lazarus & Folkman, 1984; Skinner, Edge, Altman, & Sherwood, 2003). Regardless of its definitional nuances, a common theme that has been overtly or covertly implied by these definitions is that coping efforts undertake different patterns and guises commensurate with the temporal orientation of the encountered stressful situation. Indeed, Auerbach (1992) argued more than two decades ago that time and temporality are intrinsic to the understanding of stress and coping. More specific, he maintained that the two (temporality and coping) are intimately linked because (a) exposure to stressful life events varies in its duration, and as a result, coping outcomes vary as well; (b) stressful life events confront individuals at different developmental life stages, and, consequently, the nature, interpretation, and modes of coping with these events vary along the life cycle (see also McGrath & Beehr, 1990); and (c) life events that occur "off-time" (unexpectedly) typically result in higher levels of stress and less effective coping, as compared with those that occur "on-time" (age-associated) or at a "bad time" concurrent with other life events and stressors (see also Schlossberg, 1981). To this list, one could also add the following: (a) coping (and its success) with stressful life events often hinges on the degree of predictability, certainty, and controllability of the encountered event, and these events differ as to their temporal properties (e.g., unlike a stressful event that has already been experienced, those anticipated are less predictable or controllable; Folkman & Moskowitz, 2004; McGrath & Beehr, 1990; Schwarzer & Knoll, 2003).

The role of temporality in the context of coping with stressful situations was first suggested by Lazarus and colleagues (Lazarus, 1966, 1991; Lazarus & Folkman, 1984; Lazarus & Launier, 1978). In their model of coping with stressful life events, they viewed coping as consisting of a range of psychological and behavioral efforts, undertaken to manage, minimize, overcome, or defuse stressful events. The deployment of coping efforts follows the individual's appraisal of the situation, which determines whether the potential threat is viewed as stressful, irrelevant, or even possibly beneficial for future well-being. These appraisals are further classified as (a) loss and harm (implying events that occurred in the past), (b) crises and ongoing stresses (indicating events of the present), and (c) challenges and threats (implying anticipated or future events). These time-associated stressful experiences further suggest that the temporal location of the stressful event may be associated with certain emotional manifestations such that, for example, appraisals of loss or harm (past orientation) may trigger feelings of depression (and possibly anger), those of threat (future orientation) may be more directly associated with apprehension and anxiety, whereas appraisals of challenge (also future orientation) may be linked to feelings of hope and benefit finding.

In the context of life following the onset of CID, coping efforts, at first glance, seem to suggest that, because CID has already occurred (i.e., the event leading to loss, damage, or injury is anchored in the past), these efforts to mitigate the event's impact should be directed toward the aftermath of the CID. Coping efforts should target overcoming the experience of lost bodily parts, functions, abilities, and so on. In reality, however, this is a rather myopic, misleading perspective because people who have sustained CID, by necessity, must deal with continuous, presently experienced crises and realizations, as well as coping with future consequences and vicissitudes of their physical and psychological conditions. Furthermore, the linear, universal, and objective passage of time in which future events gradually and uniformly mold into the present and then proceed to become part of the past (i.e., Newtonian time) is not reflective of human subjective passage of time (i.e., private or "felt" time) in which time is often experienced through cyclical, pendular, episodic, or epochal perception of events, including stressful events, crisis situations, or traumatic onset of CID (McGrath & Beehr, 1990; McGrath & Tschan, 2004; Slife, 1993). For example, a person who sustained a spinal cord injury (SCI), in addition to having to cope with losses (e.g., mobility) and imposed life changes (e.g., use of transportation) and psychological stresses necessitated by the onset of the injury (i.e., the past), in reality must cope with present, continuous stressful situations (e.g., neurological pain, respiratory difficulties, spasticity, urinary complications, inaccessible settings, architectural barriers), as well as anticipated future events (e.g., further medical complications, decreased employment opportunities, increased insurance premiums, and other financial hardships). In a somewhat similar vein, the diagnosis of life-threatening and chronic medical conditions (lung cancer, congestive heart disease) could, likewise, trigger a set of temporally influenced coping efforts, commensurate with the nature, severity, stability, and functionality of the experienced symptoms. For instance, present coping efforts may focus more squarely on mitigating the debilitating effect of anxiety, the impact on other family members, the changes required in daily activities, and the time and energy constraints imposed by the treatment regimen. In contrast, future coping efforts may be differentially applied and focus on long-term implications of the condition, its prognosis, level of (un)certainty and (un)controllability, as well as issues revolving around the anticipated long-term functional abilities and restrictions, financial burden, employability considerations, and future level of QOL. Finally, individuals with early life-induced disabling conditions (e.g., type 1 diabetes mellitus, cerebral palsy, epilepsy) may be altogether more likely to apply a different set of coping efforts, typically termed *proactive coping*. Individuals with diabetes must regularly proactively cope with such issues as continuous dietary restrictions, worries about future physical complications, fear of diabetic coma and insulin shock, and the anxiety associated with a hidden disability, unpredictable symptoms, and uncertain future. Those with cerebral palsy must also cope, proactively, with such areas as progressively worsening mobility and speech deficits, involuntary muscle spasms (e.g., contractures), feelings of shame and embarrassment, and negative public attitudes triggering social rejection. Finally, people with epilepsy find it necessary to proactively cope with concerns emanating from anxiety linked to the unpredictability and often uncontrollability of seizures, the wide range of side effects associated with many antiepileptic medications, social restrictions (on alcohol consumption and driving), and the shame and embarrassment triggered by the seizure itself and the associated public stigma. The use of coping modalities to manage these issues is marked by an early acquisition and organization of those personal and environmental resources needed to facilitate successful coping with the imminent challenges of life with CID and its anticipated, yet often unpredictable, consequences (Aspinwall, 2005; Schwarzer & Knoll, 2003).

In light of the previously noted considerations, the following sections seek to provide the reader with a more thorough review of (a) the role of temporality within community-anchored strategies to combat both physical pathologies and psychopathologies, (b) the role of temporality in coping with life stresses, and (c) selected examples from the CID literature on how temporality has been conceived in assessing coping with, and adaptation to, CID-induced life stresses (Table 11.1).

THE TEMPORAL ASPECTS OF COMMUNITY-BASED STRESS AND CRISIS

Although Caplan's (1964) original tripartite model of community-based medical and psychiatric pathology prevention was conceived half a century ago, applications of its

TABLE 11.1 CID-ORIENTED COMMUNITY INTERVENTIONS AND COPING STRATEGIES AS VIEWED FROM A TEMPORAL PERSPECTIVE

Comparative Components	Primary Prevention (Prevention)	Secondary Prevention (Intervention)	Tertiary Prevention (Postvention)	Preimpact/Proactive, Preventive Coping	Dynamic/Ongoing Coping	Postimpact/Residual Coping
Time orientation	Future; precrisis	Present; crisis is being experienced	Past; crisis occurred in recent or remote past	Future; precrisis; coping efforts in a planning stage	Present; crisis is being experienced; coping efforts are mobilized and operational	Past; crisis occurred in recent or remote past; coping efforts directed at event aftermath
Primary goals	Preventing or reducing risk of occurrence of physical and psychiatric impairments	Reducing experienced stressful events and crises, and facilitating psychological growth	Minimizing residual limitations and sustained damage, and restoring adaptive functioning	Preventing or reducing likelihood of occurrence or impact of stress or crisis on one's life	Mitigating psychological toll of currently experienced stress, crisis, injury, or health-impacting diagnosis	Reducing impact of previously sustained life crises and functional limitations, and restoring psychological equilibrium and QOL
Mechanisms/intervention strategies (examples)	Public awareness and education; health-enhancing environmental modifications	Crisis intervention; psychiatric first aid	Rehabilitation; disability minimization; skill acquisition; environmental manipulation; long-term psychotherapy	Problem-focused coping to prevent or minimize likelihood of crisis; action-oriented coping to avoid exposure to aversive events	Emotion-focused coping to defuse or minimize psychological impact; cognitive-focused coping to contain mental disorganization	Problem-focused coping to manage consequences of crisis; social-emotional coping to defuse affective distress
Intended/targeted sector	Public; focus on high-risk and more vulnerable groups	Public; family members; affected person	Affected person	Affected person	Affected person	Affected person
Practicing professions	Educators/teachers, public and occupational health providers, preventive medicine practitioners	Physicians, nurses, psychotherapists/mental health counselors, police officers	Rehab. psychologists and counselors, PTs, OTs, rehab.engineers	NA; crisis survivor and family	NA; crisis survivor and family (possibly psychotherapists and clinical rehab. and mental health professionals)	NA; crisis survivor and family (possibly mental health and rehab. professionals)

(continued)

TABLE 11.1 CID-ORIENTED COMMUNITY INTERVENTIONS AND COPING STRATEGIES AS VIEWED FROM A TEMPORAL PERSPECTIVE *(continued)*

Comparative Components	Primary Prevention (Prevention)	Secondary Prevention (Intervention)	Tertiary Prevention (Postvention)	Preimpact/Proactive, Preventive Coping	Dynamic/Ongoing Coping	Postimpact/Residual Coping
Stressful life events and crises (examples)	Genetic susceptibility; environmental pollutants and carcinogens	Injuries, accidents, natural disasters	Long-term/chronic CID, residual functional limitations and deteriorating health conditions	Age-related diseases and functional losses, retirement, upcoming medical treatment/surgery	Physical injuries, vehicular accidents, life-threatening diagnoses or illnesses, Victimization events	Aftermath of CID, aftermath of personal losses, long-term impact of bodily injuries or psychological traumas
Locus of intervention-initiating agent	External (environment; other people)	External and internal (person)	External and internal (person)	Internal (person)	Internal (person) and possibly external (other people)	Internal (person) and possibly external (other people)
Rehabilitation-related applications	Promoting physical and mental health; expanding and strengthening social networks; ensuring occupational safety practices; bolstering QOL among people with CID	Providing crisis-oriented, psychiatric first aid type services to reduce distress; gradually restoring cognitive and emotional functioning	Minimizing CID impact through use of assistive technologies; teaching and practicing life skills necessary to overcome CID impact, modifying and restructuring physical and social environments	Practicing coping (and building coping resources) to thwart or minimize likelihood of future disease/CID occurrence and exposure to aversive events and CID impact; striving to maintain accustomed levels of QOL	Applying available coping strategies to mitigate psychological/emotional impact of ongoing crises, such as injuries, accidents, painful sensations, and life-threatening diagnoses; gradually restoring previous levels of QOL	Applying available coping strategies to defuse and manage long-term consequences of CID, including chronic functional limitations, impaired vocational abilities, and long-lasting emotional distress; bolstering positive-oriented coping to regain pre-CID QOL

CID, chronic illness and disability; OTs, occupational therapists; PTs, physical therapists; QOL, quality of life; rehab., rehabilitation.

clinical acumen and practical versatility have been surprisingly lacking in the fields of rehabilitation psychology and counseling. In this section, we provide an overview of the model's three-pronged temporal nature (i.e., PPs, SPs, and TPs/interventions) and essential features.

PP

PP encompasses those strategies that seek to reduce, harness, and, if possible, prevent the occurrence of physical disabilities, chronic illnesses, and psychiatric disorders among members of the public, with particular emphasis on those who represent high-risk groups, thus ensuring a sustained positive QOL. They are, therefore, applied before the event occurrence. When viewed from a different angle, as espoused by the prevailing positive psychology framework, these interventions may also be said to represent attempts at promoting physical and psychological health, as well as positive QOL (e.g., subjective well-being, life satisfaction). The professions that best represent the type of interventions within the PP domain include, among others, public/community health, public education, occupational health, public safety, and preventive medicine. Specific intervention strategies most commonly used by proponents of PP, therefore, include public education and political campaigns to inform the public of health threats and hazards; environmental modifications to ensure the reduction, control, or elimination of detrimental environmental stimuli and stressors; and the teaching and promotion of behaviors that are known to be successfully linked to warding off future stressful situations and physical impairments and diseases. On a more constricted scale, PP strategies focus on teaching problem-solving and decision-making skills and the fostering of personal strengths, resources, and coping modalities that serve to immunize people to stress and minimize the future risk of physical and psychiatric conditions (Caplan, 1964; Hershenson, 1990; Livneh, 1995; Slaikeu, 1990).

SP

SP, or *crisis intervention* (also referred to as direct or real-time intervention), refers to those interventions that attempt to directly, immediately, and intensely reduce the effects of an ongoing life (non-chronic) crisis, and, concomitantly, promote personal resilience and growth through the crisis experience itself. Through these early intervention efforts, SP aims at restoring life equilibrium and reducing the severity and frequency of debilitating affective, cognitive, and behavioral distress experienced by community members. Crisis intervention, therefore, is equated with those efforts more traditionally referred to as short-term (crisis) therapy, intensive psychotherapy, and psychiatric first aid (Auerbach, 1992; Caplan, 1964), which aim to restore previously experienced QOL. The professional schools that most clearly represent SP interventions are medicine and nursing (i.e., urgent care), and psychiatry and psychotherapy, all seeking to reverse or curtail physical pathology (medicine and nursing) and psychiatric symptomatology (psychiatry and psychotherapy). Unlike PP, where the focus is on the community at large, SP targets selected individuals directly (i.e., those affected by the crisis experience), as well as their immediate environments (Hershenson, 1990; Livneh, 1995).

TP

TP, also known as *postvention* or *rehabilitation*, is the third and final domain (as well as therapeutic phase) of community-based intervention. It encompasses those interventions that are geared toward minimizing and, if possible reversing, the residual impact on people (typically patients or ex-patients) of long-standing and severe physical and psychiatric CIDs, whose onset has been associated with an earlier experience of crisis and its aftermath. TP is implemented long after crisis resolution (although it may be initiated relatively early following successful attainment of physical and/or psychosocial equilibrium), and its overarching goal is the restoration of pre-CID QOL. When put differently, TP focuses on the provision of supportive and ameliorative services to individuals with CID and the promotion of a better QOL (Bishop, 2005; Hershenson et al., 1981; Janosik, 1984; Livneh, 1995; Slaikeu, 1990; Wright, 1980). Among the professions that are associated with TP, the most prominent ones are medicine (for chronic conditions, physiatry, cardiology, neurosurgery, oncology, pain medicine), long-term psychotherapy, PT, OT, speech and hearing therapy (S&HT), rehabilitation engineering, and (psychosocial, vocational) rehabilitation psychology and counseling (Hershenson, 1990; Livneh, 1995).

Further analysis of the goals of TP, as mostly espoused by the fields of rehabilitation psychology and counseling, indicates that they could be further categorized into the following three domains.

CID Minimization

This goal is best reflected in those efforts that seek to minimize the CID impact on the individual by reversing the course of the CID and restoring functional capacity, including affected life skills. Typical interventions include the use of assistive technologies to improve sensory functioning, surgical procedures to correct neuromuscular and orthopedic impairments, the use of orthotic and prosthetic devices to improve mobility and manipulative functioning, and a host of CID-specific PT, OT, and S&HT procedures (Hershenson, 1990; Livneh, 1995).

Skill Acquisition

This goal is normally associated with rehabilitation efforts to compensate for the functional limitations imposed by CID through the enhancement of other, not directly implicated abilities and skills, thus often necessitating modification and reformulation of earlier life goals. More specifically, the goal is to teach and practice specific coping skills and a broad range of life skills through the adoption of psychosocial and vocational rehabilitation (VR)-based strategies that include educational, career, vocational (job-specific), and personal adjustment skills. Among the wide spectrum of coping skills training modules available, the following appear to be the most widely used: managing anxiety, depression, frustration, and anger; self-assertiveness; stigma reduction; self-concept/efficacy improvement; job searching, interviewing, and performance; time management; decision making; problem solving; money management; and medical/symptom management. Rehabilitation (postvention) services are commonly provided by rehabilitation counselors and psychologists, special educators, social workers, and recreational therapists (Hershenson, 1990; Livneh, 1995).

Environmental Manipulation

This goal is normally implemented through efforts directed at modifying and restructuring the environment to minimize the impact of CID-imposed functional restrictions. These efforts are aimed at both the physical environment (i.e., restructuring features of one's home, work, and leisure activity environments and eliminating community-based architectural barriers) and the social/attitudinal environment (i.e., combating and eliminating the stigma, prejudice, and discrimination stemming from the existence of CID). The target groups include family members, employers, and members of the public whose negative attitudes often foster additional barriers to positive QOL maintenance (Hershenson, 1990; Livneh, 1995).

In sum, the community-based primary, secondary, and tertiary interventions are mostly externally driven strategies (i.e., applied by trained professionals) geared toward preventing or minimizing the likelihood of occurrence, or reducing the impact of certain medical and psychiatric conditions before, during, or following their onset. In addition, although a logical temporal sequencing is often assumed for strategy applications (i.e., prevention → intervention → postvention), strategies normally applied later on in this model are not necessarily bound by these clinical features. People who sustained CID (by definition, function in a postvention or rehabilitation stage) are not excluded from using, and are just as likely to benefit from, preventive and interventive services for QOL enhancement that may stem from anticipated future medical complications and encountered crisis situations that may still be experienced by the person with CID.

THE TEMPORAL ASPECTS OF COPING WITH STRESS AND CID

Only scarce literature is presently available on the temporal aspects of coping efforts. Nevertheless, this body of literature suggests that these efforts to improve QOL following stressful situations (e.g., onset of CID) could be conveniently organized into three broad categories: (a) preemptive, or preimpact, coping efforts that are directed at potential future stressful live events (threats, challenges) that range from those whose occurrence spans from unlikely but possible to likely or probable; (b) crisis-experienced coping efforts directed at presently experienced, or ongoing (dynamic), stressful events and crises (including various physical injuries, bodily insults, and psychiatric crises); and (c) postimpact or postevent coping efforts directed at stressful life events (losses, harms) of the past whose impact still plays a significant role in influencing present physical, psychological, and social activities (Aspinwall, 2005; Auerbach, 1992; Livneh & Martz, 2007; McGrath & Beehr, 1990; Schwarzer & Knoll, 2003).

Preemptive or Preimpact Coping

Preemptive coping can be viewed as the person-level analogue of community-anchored PP, which, as outlined earlier, aims to reduce the likelihood of *future* occurrence of both physical and psychiatric CIDs. Preimpact coping strategies have been classified into the following: (a) preventive coping, regarded as the most temporally distal from future event occurrence; (b) proactive coping; and (c) anticipatory coping (most proximal to future event occurrence). Put differently, the extended preimpact period can be, somewhat arbitrarily, subdivided into distal anticipatory (preventive), mid-range anticipatory (proactive), and proximal anticipatory (or just anticipatory) "time zones" (Auerbach, 1992; McGrath & Beehr, 1990; Schwarzer & Knoll, 2003). As a group, all preemptive coping efforts present a rather elusive and uncertain picture because the impact or stressful experience has not yet occurred and is, therefore, not directly familiar to the person. These efforts, then, may be conceived as attempts to cognitively scan possible future scenarios and the scope of their potential impact and implications, and gradually build up (psychologically and behaviorally) those necessary resources to combat stressful life events.

Preventive Coping

Preventive coping, as its name suggests, focuses on those long-term, distant future-anchored, yet broadly anticipated events well before these events are to be encountered (e.g., retirement, age-related illnesses, expected functional losses, long-term medical insurance). These efforts, therefore, reflect coping strategies that seek to address uncertain and mostly unpredictable threats located within a distant future. The function of preventive coping, according to Auerbach (1992), is to ideally delay or, when feasible, prevent the likelihood of (a) the event occurring, (b) the impact of the event on the individual, and (c) the potential damage that the impact of such an event may impose on the individual. In the context of the health domain, Auerbach further argues that activities undertaken by the individual during preventive coping typically include (a) prevention of the occurrence of these potentially stressful or damaging events (e.g., the use of problem-focused coping); (b) prevention of exposure to those potentially aversive events, such as the use of problem-focused and action-oriented coping to avoid such exposure (e.g., carcinogenic agents, pulmonary pollutants, hearing loss-inducing environments); and (c) prevention or, at the very least, significant minimization of the detrimental consequences of such potentially damaging and stressful events, again, through the employment of mostly problem-focused efforts that seek to eliminate or reduce anticipated harmful conditions, various life losses, functional limitations, and experienced pain.

In a similar vein, Schwarzer and colleagues (Aspinwall, 2005; Schwarzer, 2000; Schwarzer & Knoll, 2003) have maintained that preventive coping is noted for its efforts to prepare the individual for adverse or stressful events through the gradual building and use of generalized resources (e.g., development of psychological strengths, accumulation of wealth, attainment of social resources and skills). These future-oriented efforts are directed at nullifying (or, at times, mostly minimizing) the severity of the potential impact and maximizing the probability of successful stress-reducing strategies.

Proactive Coping

Whereas preventive coping, ideally, seeks to *avoid* or *neutralize* the occurrence of potentially threatening stressful life events, proactive coping efforts focus more on minimizing or reducing the impact of such future-anchored events (i.e., events that are likely to occur). The available literature, however, is not always clear about such a distinction and presents a rather overlapping view of the two coping modalities. For example, Aspinwall and colleagues (Aspinwall, 2005; Aspinwall & Taylor, 1997) offer only marginal distinction between proactive and preventive coping efforts and regard both as active behavioral efforts to *prevent, eliminate, reduce,* or *modify* impending stressful events. The latter encompass events such as threatening environmental situations or taxing psychological demands, which are likely to culminate in harm, loss, or damage.

As compared with anticipatory coping (discussed in the next section), proactive coping can be best described as (a) temporally removed from the threatening event (i.e., they are used earlier in the chain of coping efforts); (b) invoking aggregation of personal and environmental resources, including the mastery of skills needed to confront threatening events; and (c) necessitating a different set of coping skills. Although proactive coping is normally better served through the use of more active coping modes, such as planning, information gathering, skill development, and goal management, anticipatory coping may, quite often, be better served through the use of more affective and social coping modes, such as emotional regulation, emotional support, and positive reappraisal to manage the upcoming stressful event (Aspinwall, 2005; Aspinwall & Taylor, 1997).

A somewhat diverging perspective was advanced by Schwarzer and Knoll (2003; Folkman & Moskowitz, 2004). These authors view proactive coping as coping efforts that involve future challenges that are "potentially self-promoting" (Folkman & Moskowitz, 2004, p. 757; Schwarzer & Knoll, 2003). In contrast, they regard preventive coping as coping efforts that portend "an uncertain threat potential in the distant future" (p. 757). Proactive coping, therefore, serves as the prototype of positive coping efforts, in which the individual builds up resources that facilitate promotion of challenging future goals and personal growth, as well as goal management and the attainment of meaningful life pursuits (Schwarzer & Knoll, 2003). These efforts, then, serve a different purpose than the one promoted by preventive coping, the latter seeking to avoid or largely minimize potential negative occurrences, such as damage to one's physique or psyche.

Anticipatory Coping

As its name implies, anticipatory coping refers to those coping efforts that are triggered by environmental and physical (e.g., bodily) cues that indicate that the individual is on a course of confronting, in the near future, an aversive life event (e.g., anxiety-provoking doctor appointment, forthcoming diagnostic test or surgery, job interview, important exam, upcoming retirement) with a high degree of certainty (Auerbach, 1992; Folkman & Moskowitz, 2004; Schwarzer & Knoll, 2003). Here, too, the individual may be more likely to use problem-focused coping to avoid such an encounter or, if this is impossible, to minimize the risk or damage (including level of stress) that such an encounter may produce (Auerbach, 1992; Janis, 1958).

Anticipatory coping is further subdivided into those efforts that confront avoidable and unavoidable life stressors (Auerbach, 1992). A somewhat similar subclassification may also be useful here, in which future life stressors are grouped into controllable and uncontrollable, changeable and non-changeable, certain and uncertain events (Krohne, 1993; Maes, Leventhal, & de Ridder, 1996; McGrath & Beehr, 1990; Mishel, 1988; Perrez & Reicherts, 1992). Avoidable (or potentially controllable) stressors according to Auerbach and others (e.g., Aspinwall & Taylor, 1997; Schwarzer & Knoll, 2003) are those stressors whose potential harm can be modified, minimized, or postponed. This can be accomplished through vigilant attention, preparation for the stressful event's eventual occurrence, acquisition of necessary information, assessment of useful alternatives, and selection of an appropriate course of action to confront those upcoming stressors. Unavoidable, or uncontrollable, stressors, however, such as eventual retirement, physical deterioration, death of spouse or oneself, and even the risk of invasive medical and surgical procedures, are those stressors that most, if not all, individuals ultimately face. According to Auerbach (1992), successful coping efforts with these imminent stressors include both cognitive-behavioral-focused modalities (e.g., information use, planning, behavior modeling) and emotional-focused modalities (e.g., seeking social support, venting emotions in a supportive environment) used to reduce apprehension, anxiety, and further stress.

Dynamic or Impact-Experienced Coping

Coping with ongoing crises may be considered the individual-level analogue of community-aimed SP, the latter seeking to mitigate the psychic toll mounted by a presently experienced crisis situation (e.g., injury, life-threatening diagnosis). Dynamic coping, or coping with presently experienced stressors or crises, includes those coping efforts where the individual is said to actively manage the stressful event. They are also described as coping efforts undertaken *during* (at the present, or at real time) directly experienced, or ongoing, stressful events, often also termed *crisis* or crisis situation. Ironically, crisis is often viewed as that period where coping, including problem-solving ability, has broken down, and, therefore, normal coping and cognitive processes are no longer capable of achieving the goal of returning the individual to a state of psychological equilibrium (Roberts, 2000; Slaikeu, 1990). The redeployment of organized and balanced coping efforts is not an instantaneous and automatic occurrence and may, therefore, require additional time to successfully detect, interpret, process, and eventually recover from the crisis experience (McGrath & Beehr, 1990). Notwithstanding this theoretical contradiction, one of the primary aims of coping efforts that ostensibly still serves the individual in crisis is to defuse or minimize the felt (emotional) impact (Hodgkinson & Stewart, 1991; James & Gilliland, 2001).

Historically, the field of coping with crisis situations has its roots in the seminal bodies of work of Eric Lindemann (1944) and Gerald Caplan (1961, 1964). Lindemann studied reactions of acute grief and bereavement among both nonpsychiatric and psychiatric patients, describing them as reflecting wave-like processes of panic and anxiety reactions that alternate with those of denial and avoidance. In his Crisis Prevention/ Intervention model, Caplan extended this body of work by developing a crisis-oriented brief psychotherapy to help individuals who experience a crisis to better confront and defuse their stress reactions during this time-limited period.

It is beyond the scope of this chapter to address the plethora of contributions made by crisis (and crisis intervention) clinicians and researchers. Briefly, however, it could be argued that to better understand crisis-experienced coping, one needs to (a) provide a broad description (rather than the formal, yet linguistically rigid, use of a succinct definition) of the term *crisis* that includes its main components and clinical features, (b) understand the initial and extended reactions to crisis, and (c) describe the primary types of crisis. These are summarized in the following paragraphs for the benefit of readers who are not well-acquainted with the literature on crisis intervention.

The Experience of Crisis

There have been many, and often inconsistent, definitions of the term *crisis*. It may, therefore, be beneficial to provide first a more general description of the term. Briefly, then, crisis can be described as a subjective reaction to an acute and intense variant of a stressful or hazardous life event or experience. By its very nature, it has an identifiable beginning (a precipitating event, or an adverse stimulus or catalyst) and is a time-limited (i.e., temporary) state[1]; a state most commonly associated with cognitive and emotional disorganization, psychological disequilibrium, extreme vulnerability, reduced functional capacity, and ultimately a *failure to cope* with the stressful situation using previously familiar and successful strategies. Crisis, then, reflects the experience of a highly stressful situation or event that creates an obstacle to the attainment of meaningful life goals, and whose resolution exceeds the individual's presently available resources and coping (i.e., problem-solving) strategies (Collins & Collins, 2005; James & Gilliland, 2001; Janosik, 1984; Roberts, 2000; Slaikeu, 1990). Other models of crisis can be found in Selye's (1976) general adaptation syndrome (alarm, resistance, and exhaustion) and Horowitz's (1986) stages of normal response (outcry, denial, intrusion, working through, and completion) versus pathological response (overwhelmed, panic, exhaustion, avoidance, flooded psyche, and psychosomatic response) to crisis situations.

Reactions to Crisis

The clinical literature has generated an exhaustive list of chaotic psychosocial reactions that are associated with the onset of crisis. Among the most frequently discussed are those that indicate cognitive and emotional distortions and behavioral malfunctioning. More specifically, the literature strongly indicates that acute reactions to crisis situations strongly parallel those observed among individuals who sustained a sudden and severe onset of CID, and that have traditionally been referred to as shock, alarm, and anxiety "phases" (alternatively referred to as reactions or responses; Hodgkinson & Stewart, 1991; Horowitz, 1986; Livneh & Antonak, 1997; Shontz, 1975). These include reactions such as disbelief, numbness, confusion, disorientation, incoherency, feeling overwhelmed, disorganized thinking and speech (all regarded as indicators of a shock response), intense fear, panic, tension, distress, subjective discomfort, and dread (all viewed as indicators of an anxiety response; Caplan, 1964; Cavaiola & Colford, 2006; Collins & Collins, 2005; James & Gilliland, 2001; Janosik, 1984; Roberts, 2000; Slaikeu, 1990). These reactions are perceived among "crisis theory" proponents as further clinical proof that during the immediate aftermath of a crisis experience, the person is temporarily unable to cope. This eventuality is believed to follow the breakdown of the network of previously used coping strategies that are now incapable of thwarting off crisis-triggered cognitive and affective disorganization.

Types of Crisis

Crisis situations are commonly subdivided into the following types.

Developmental crises. These are crises that are associated with those life stages or phases (the life cycle; for example, Erikson's psychosocial stages of development) that the individual undergoes, rather predictably, during the normal course of his or her growth and maturation. They reflect changes perceived in the individual's inner sense of self as he or she transitions through these life milestones (James & Gilliland, 2001; Janosik, 1984; Slaikeu, 1990). Examples include high school or college graduation, marriage, career change, "midlife crisis," and retirement.

Situational crises. These are crises that are directly linked to sudden onset, random, unexpected, unpredictable, uncommon, and environmentally triggered episodes, where the individual faces external events that may alter his or her life considerably and even permanently (James & Gilliland, 2001; Janosik, 1984; Slaikeu, 1990). Examples include (a) health-related crises, such as loss of body part or function, major surgery, physical injury, automobile accident, and life-threatening illness (or its diagnosis); (b) death-related crises, such as the death (by natural causes or fatal accidents), homicide, or suicide of a spouse or a loved one; (c) crime-related crises, such as physical or sexual assault, domestic violence, and any other form of victimization; (d) financial crises, such as job loss, bankruptcy, and loss of one's home; and (e) crises associated with natural or man-made disasters, such as earthquakes, floods, hurricanes, fires, and wars (James & Gilliland, 2001; Janosik, 1984; Slaikeu, 1990).

Existential crises. These crises are the result of personal anxieties and inner conflicts that are associated with significant and unresolved human issues and uncertainties. These experienced crises typically reflect subjective concerns that include, among others, the purpose and meaning (or alternatively, futility) of one's life and existence, personal responsibility, issues of dependency versus independency, freedom and freedom of choice, alienation, commitment (to others or an important cause), and connectedness to others (Cavaiola & Colford, 2006; James & Gilliland, 2001).

Postimpact Coping

Postimpact coping can best be seen as the person-level analogue of community-based TP, which embodies rehabilitation philosophy and processes and focuses on reducing and altering functional limitations acquired in the most recent as well as remote past; therefore, their resolution culminates in enhanced QOL. Postimpact, or postcrisis, coping has been traditionally viewed as including two temporally variant coping efforts. These are (a) proximal or reactive coping efforts (where the impact of harm, damage, loss, or onset of CID has been sustained within recent time), and (b) distal or residual coping efforts (where these events occurred more remotely in time; Auerbach, 1992; Folkman & Moskowitz, 2004; Livneh & Martz, 2007; Schwarzer & Knoll, 2003). No clear demarcating boundary between what is regarded as "recent" or "short-termed" and what is referred to as "remote" or "long-termed" has ever been proposed in the literature. Despite the fact that reactive coping is directed toward experiences of the immediate (short-term) past, and residual coping toward experiences long after the stressful event has occurred, in both cases primary coping strategies often include (a) problem-focused coping to manage the consequences of the event (e.g., task-oriented), (b) cognitive-focused coping to rationally assess and prioritize available alternatives (e.g., cognitive reappraisal, belief-control, meaning finding, and benefit finding), (c) social-emotional coping to defuse or moderate emotional distress and heightened anxiety (e.g., seeking social support, expressing emotions constructively), and (d) avoidance coping to divert or remove oneself from a stressful situation (e.g., social avoidance, denial, emotional venting; Amirkhan, 1990; Endler & Parker, 1994; Martz & Livneh, 2007; Moos & Holahan, 2003; Pearlin & Schooler, 1978).

Traditionally, therefore, postimpact coping can be viewed as coping efforts directed at stressful events whose aftermath resulted from physical harm or bodily injury, personal loss (e.g., marital breakup, job loss, loss of home), and, in general, chronic illnesses or disabling conditions that were experienced in the immediate or remote past and that, consequently, served to mitigate against negative affect and restore functioning and pre-impact QOL (Bishop, 2005; Kennedy, Lude, Elfström, & Smithson, 2012; Livneh, 2001; Moos & Holahan, 2007; Smedema, Catalano, & Ebener, 2010). The goal of postimpact coping efforts is, accordingly, to compensate for those sustained losses and injuries and gradually restore psychological equilibrium, leading to an improved QOL (Bishop, 2005; Bishop et al., 2009; Schwarzer & Knoll, 2003). Postimpact coping efforts could, therefore, be regarded as more realistic and tangible in nature, as compared with preimpact efforts, because the impact has already been experienced, perceived, and cognitively and emotionally processed. In the context of life following the onset of CID, these efforts could also, at first glance, be viewed as dealing with shattered plans and hopes, and essentially with the discrepancy created between "having had" (the past) and "no longer having" (present and presumably future).

In sum, then, the person-based preemptive, dynamic, and postimpact coping efforts are mostly internally derived strategies (i.e., applied by the individual himself or herself) geared toward preventing or minimizing anticipated future stressful events, confronting ongoing crisis situations, and managing the aftermath of past stressful occurrences and related CID-triggered losses. In addition, although a logical temporal sequencing is often assumed for the application of these coping modalities (i.e., preemptive → crisis-experienced → postimpact), strategies normally applied later on in this model are not necessarily restricted to this order. People who sustained personal losses, including CID (by definition, engage in postimpact coping), are not excluded from using, and are just as likely to benefit from, preemptive and crisis-experienced coping strategies that may stem from anticipated future stressful events and ongoing crisis situations that may still confront the person with CID. Indeed, research findings have shown that past-oriented coping efforts (or "getting stuck" in the past, focusing on the negative content of the past) and foreshortened future time coping (failure to project into the future) are often associated with negatively valenced coping and increased levels of psychological distress (e.g., Buckelew, Baumstark, Frank, & Hewett, 1990; Holman & Silver, 1998; Livneh & Martz, 2007; Malcarne, Compas, Epping-Jordan, & Howell, 1995; Martz, 2004). Similar findings were obtained from the literature on the relationships between negative past-oriented appraisals and psychosocial outcomes following the onset of CID. For example, appraisals of loss, including overwhelming disbelief of SCI occurrence and related negative perceptions of its impact on one's life, have been associated with higher levels of depression and anxiety, poorer social integration, and lower QOL perceptions (Dean & Kennedy, 2009; Kennedy et al., 2012; Kennedy et al., 2010). Other indicators of negative and past-oriented appraisals, including feelings of helplessness (lack of control over the future) and self-blame (focusing on self in the past), have also been found to be correlated with perceived lower QOL and life satisfaction, and even self-reported poorer mental health (Schulz & Decker, 1985; van Leeuwen et al., 2012). In a similar vein, a bourgeoning body of literature has now been amassed to document the beneficial consequences, including the salutary influences on various QOL indicators, of future- and positive-oriented coping on the lives of people with CID. These are reviewed subsequently.

Coping: Gaining From Adversity

As was argued earlier, the more traditional view of coping fails to fully recognize two important issues. First, postimpact coping is not necessarily bound by a past-oriented psychological framework, and second, it does not indubitably originate from a "loss and grief" mentality. To wit, postimpact coping efforts are not necessarily constricted in their focus to negative perceptions, cognitions, and feelings that are tied to lost past abilities and unfulfilled dreams. Indeed, adopting a *future-oriented,* positively valenced coping framework, rather than a *past-oriented,* negatively valenced approach to coping, negates focusing not only on the immutable past and therefore losses incurred, but also, and most importantly, on the future and its many opportunities for personal growth and improvement in one's QOL. A growing body of literature has now conclusively documented that the onset of CID often gives rise to positive perceptions and beliefs that, alternatively, are linked to new hopes, aspirations, and challenges. These latter positive appraisals and adaptive coping modalities have been shown to be associated with such psychosocial outcomes as psychological and social QOL, life satisfaction, and perceived well-being, and negatively linked to depression and anxiety. They have been studied and observed under terms such as *maintaining hope* (Elliott, Witty, Herrick, & Hoffman, 1991; Kennedy, Evans, & Sandhu, 2009; Kortte, Stevenson, Hosey, Castillo, & Wegener, 2012; Snyder, Lehman, Kluck, & Monsson, 2006); *benefit finding* (from adversity in general and CID, more specifically; Helgeson, Reynolds, & Tomich, 2006; Kortte, Gilbert, Gorman, & Wegener, 2010; Pakenham, 2005; Tennen & Affleck, 2002; van Leeuwen et al., 2012); *meaning searching, making, restoring,* or *finding* (Davis & Morgan, 2008; Davis, Nolen-Hoeksema, & Larson, 1998; deRoon-Cassini, de St Aubin, Valvano, Hastings, & Horn, 2009; Janoff-Bulman & Yopyk, 2004; Pakenham, 2007; Park, Edmondson, Fenster, & Blank, 2008; Park & Folkman, 1997); *purpose or meaning in life* (deRoon-Cassini et al., 2009; Reker, 1977; Thompson, Coker, Krause, & Henry, 2003); *posttraumatic growth* (or growth and resilience through adversity; Joseph & Linley, 2006; Kennedy et al., 2010; Pollard & Kennedy, 2007; Tedeschi & Calhoun, 2004; Tedeschi, Park, & Calhoun, 1998); and *challenge* (used as a generic term for Lazarus-derived, future-oriented, primary appraisal concept; Kennedy et al., 2009; Kennedy et al., 2012).

These coping efforts demonstrate that postimpact coping, despite its origination from a stressful and loss-associated past event, nevertheless is not bound by past orientation and, frequently, spans the entire range of the human temporal experience. When put differently, the post-CID experience often necessitates the engagement of both proactive (e.g., anticipating future barriers, transcending life constraints) and presently active (e.g., confronting ongoing stresses and restrictions, defusing negative affective states) sets of coping efforts to restore perceived pre-CID QOL, or any QOL level commensurate with one's present abilities, skills, plans, and hopes. Indeed, research focusing on future-oriented, positive postimpact coping, as manifested by the engagement of the earlier mentioned coping strategies of (a) sustaining hope, (b) finding benefits in the experience of CID, (c) searching and making meaning and purpose in one's life following the onset of CID, (d) sustaining self-efficacy beliefs, and, in general (e) experiencing post-CID growth has documented that positively valenced postimpact coping is uniquely meritorious in overcoming past losses and seeking to achieve a positive and satisfying level of future QOL (e.g., Carver et al., 1994; deRoon-Cassini et al., 2009; Dunn, 1996; Kortte et al., 2010; Schou, Ekeberg, Sandvik, Hjermstad, & Ruland, 2005; Smedema et al., 2010). For example, postimpact, future-oriented, positive coping modalities, such as those outlined earlier, have demonstrated their positive influence on improved QOL in a wide range of CIDs including, but not limited to, SCI (Pollard & Kennedy, 2007), traumatic brain injury (Moore, Stambrook, & Gill, 1994), multiple sclerosis (Pakenham, 2005), epilepsy (Amir, Roziner, Knoll, & Neufeld, 1999), heart disease (Garnefski, Kraaij, Schroevers, & Somsen, 2008), cancer (Manne et al., 2004), limb amputation (Oaksford, Frude, & Cuddihy, 2005), and general rehabilitation populations (Kortte et al., 2012). The recognition that positive and future-oriented coping efforts exert a powerful influence on the QOL of people with CID ushers several important implications to the field of rehabilitation. Several of these are addressed in the following paragraphs.

Implications to Rehabilitation Theory

The distinction between a past-oriented, negatively valenced and present- and/or future-oriented, positively valenced approach to postimpact (e.g., CID) coping is also implicitly, even if not always explicitly, portrayed in several of the leading models of psychosocial adaptation to CID. For example, two of the leading models of psychosocial adaptation to CID are those of Devins (Illness Intrusiveness model; Devins, Bezjak, Mah, Loblaw, & Gotowiec, 2006; Devins et al., 1993) and Bishop (Disability Centrality model; Bishop, 2005; Bishop, Stenhoff, & Shepard, 2007). Although both models share a common core of concepts and mechanisms (Bishop, by his own admission, even argues that his model is an extension of Devins's model), and one would be hard-pressed to identify any glaring discrepancies between the two, they nevertheless intimate two distinct philosophical underpinnings that are rooted in discrepant views of human nature and time perspectives. Devins's model is spawned by a traditional medical model that suggests the supremacy of concepts such as psychopathological processes, sickness, passivity, and functional deficits. These notions are clearly evidenced in the use of terms such as *intrusiveness of disease, disruption of global lifestyle, burden of illness,* and *diminished participation in valued life functions.* This philosophical framework is also anchored in the model's overarching mostly, but not inclusively, unidimensional outcome measure of adaptation to postimpact CID, that of emotional distress–emotional well-being, as reflected in indicators of QOL such as mood disturbance, depressive symptoms, pessimism, and global psychopathological symptoms (Devins et al., 1993). The Illness Intrusiveness model, therefore, focuses mostly on the impact of past losses on present functioning and the "negative" aspects of the human CID experience, including lack of personal control over positive outcomes (which indicates truncated future possibilities) and perceptions of decreased capacity to influence such life outcomes (again suggesting that future options are limited). In contrast, Bishop's model, despite recognizing some of these aspects, including the initial decrease in perceived personal control and the role played by negative emotions, nevertheless incorporates a more positive, present- and future-oriented, and holistic rehabilitation philosophy. In this model, greater emphasis is placed on the person with CID's ability to maintain satisfaction in, and positive control over, central life domains and reprioritize domain centrality to close existing gaps between present levels of experienced QOL and desired or expected (i.e., future-oriented) QOL (Bishop, 2005). Bishop's positive, future-oriented notions are clearly evidenced by his emphasis on the use of processes that increase perceived control and rearrange domain importance, such as self-management, environmental accommodations, and rehabilitation interventions, all indicating a dynamic approach to changes in centrally important domains. Furthermore, Bishop's model adopts a broader and more inclusive view of the QOL concept, as exemplified in its multidimensional view on various life domains (e.g., physical health, mental health, work, leisure activities, social relationships, spirituality) and their role in psychosocial adaptation to CID.

Implications to Rehabilitation Practice

Unlike their disengagement, mostly past-oriented postimpact coping modalities (e.g., avoidance, escape, denial, wish fulfillment, self- or other-blame), postimpact engagement coping (e.g., problem focusing, planning, positive reframing, active acceptance, seeking social support) and coping resources (e.g., hope, optimism, benefit finding, meaning making) are mostly future-oriented. Disengagement coping efforts are, in general, oriented toward past events. For example, blaming self or others for CID onset focuses on irrevocable past losses and the reasons for their occurrence. Wish fulfillment can be equated with attempts to negate or nullify the reality of CID and avoiding confrontation with a realistic CID-experienced future. In contrast, engagement coping and the use of positive coping resources are, in general, squarely anchored in present experiences and, likewise, view the future more favorably and as realistically changeable (e.g., hope, optimism, planning, seeking social support). Furthermore, whereas the former modalities largely dwell on the sustained losses and functional deficits (e.g., CID) or seek to negate their reality by adopting subterfuge mechanisms, the latter modalities focus on efforts that seek to build on remaining functions and available skills and resources.

Adoption of future-oriented postimpact engagement coping strategies and tapping into available positive coping resources have been, indeed, repeatedly documented to promote higher levels of perceived QOL among a wide range of people with CID (Elfström & Kreuter, 2006; Livneh & Wilson, 2003; McMillen & Cook, 2003; Pakenham, 2006; Sears, Stanton, & Danoff-Burg, 2003). In contrast, when postimpact coping has been limited to past-oriented (or, separately, future-truncated) disengagement coping strategies, the literature has conclusively shown decreased reports of QOL by people with CID, as indicated by higher levels of post-CID depression and anxiety and lower levels of perceived well-being and life satisfaction (e.g., Kemp & Krause, 1999; McCabe, Stokes, & McDonald, 2009; M. K. Wagner, Armstrong, & Laughlin, 1995). Rehabilitation practitioners, therefore, would benefit from promoting client awareness of their available coping resources and use of future-oriented, engagement coping strategies. In addition, discouraging client use of past-oriented, disengagement, loss-dominated coping strategies should be identified and discouraged. Postimpact, future-oriented coping intervention modules that address CID-related psychosocial adaptation have been developed and successfully implemented by Radnitz (2000), Kennedy and colleagues (Kennedy, 2008; Kennedy, Duff, Evans, & Beedie, 2003), and Sharoff (2004). These coping interventions rely, largely, on the use of cognitive restructuring and reframing skills, problem-solving skills, planning for future eventualities, and related cognitive-behavioral interventions, all seeking to bolster engagement coping skills.

Another temporally based clinical intervention that provides fruitful implications to serving individuals who sustained CID can be found in the work of Zimbardo and colleagues (Sword, Sword, Brunskill, & Zimbardo, 2014; Zimbardo & Boyd, 2008). Derived from Zimbardo's temporal theory (Zimbardo & Boyd, 2008), the authors developed an intervention modality known as *time perspective therapy (TPT)*. In this theoretical and clinical approach, time is perceived as psychological time, that is, a subjective, flexible, and dynamic concept, rather than an objective, rigid, scientifically measured duration of time. In this approach, the rehabilitation professional is concerned with the *perception* of experienced past and present events (including CID-triggering situations and currently held beliefs and perceptions), and their impact on future goals and plans, rather than with their actual temporal unfolding.

Among TPT's essential operating principles are the following: (a) Human time experience or perception can best be compartmentalized into six (originally five) time zones: past positive (focusing on "good experiences"), past negative (focusing on failures and losses), present hedonistic (focusing on pleasurable experiences), present fatalistic (focusing on inability to control life situations), future (focusing on goals and objectives), and (more recently) future transcendental (for a detailed discussion of each zone the reader is referred to Zimbardo & Boyd, 2008); (b) TP is a learned human experience and latently influences most cognitions, decisions, and behaviors; (c) humans develop time zone biases, such that they tend to over- or under-employ certain time zones when they engage in action-based judgments and decisions; (d) overuse of any time zone(s), especially past negative ("getting stuck in the past"), could have dire consequences to one's psychological well-being; and (e) individuals function best when they develop and implement a balanced and flexible TP, adapted to their current, dynamic, and continuously unfolding life situations (Sword et al., 2014; Zimbardo & Boyd, 2008). The clinical thrust of TPT, therefore, rests on the premise that past-oriented people make decisions and act according to both negative and positive (even if no longer appropriate) memories of similarly encountered situations. Future-oriented individuals, in contrast, reach their decisions and initiate behaviors based on rational assessment of anticipated consequences and probability of success.

In the context of adaptation to CID, TPT can be best implemented through both making the negative past (onset of CID, the functional losses incurred, and the experienced psychological impact) more manageable and extending the perceived timeline further into the future, a zone where the pursuit of positive goals, the use of coping resources such as hope and optimism, and the employment of future-oriented engagement coping skills all serve to balance out the time zone bias of the negative past. To keep this balance intact, the rehabilitation professional seeks to continuously juggle efforts to minimize reliance on the past negative zone (e.g., the use of past-oriented, disengagement-like coping strategies and negative thoughts), leveraging the present (mostly hedonistic) zone to initiate new and realistic life goals and plans, as well as bolstering self-confidence/efficacy, and ultimately ensuring that the positively valenced future time zone gains supremacy in the client's life (Sword et al., 2014; Zimbardo & Boyd, 2008). Although TPT is a relatively nascent therapeutic intervention, and requires additional supportive documentation of its merits, preliminary documentation of the association between time perception and psychosocial adaptation to CID (i.e., cardiac disease, diabetes) has been reported in the literature (e.g., Hamilton, Kives, Micevski, & Grace, 2003; Livneh & Martz, 2007).

Implications to VR

The field of VR has traditionally focused on helping people with CID seek and secure employment commensurate with their functional level, skills, and abilities. Two pivotal concepts that have undergirded much of the success incurred by VR are those of strengthening client (functional) life skills and motivation level. As viewed from a post-impact, future-oriented, positively valenced coping perspective, both concepts acquire additional meaning that can serve to further elucidate their importance and usefulness. Life skills have been operationalized as skills that include self-direction and determination skills, self-care skills, employment skills, work tolerance skills, and communication skills (Chan, Rubin, Lee, & Pruitt, 2003; da Silva Cardoso, Blalock, Allen, Chan, & Rubin, 2004). These skills, when acquired postimpact, exemplify future-oriented, engagement-like coping modalities, and have been shown to be positively associated with subjective well-being. Furthermore, VR services geared toward improving these life skills were also found to improve reported QOL (da Silva Cardoso et al., 2004). These findings, demonstrating the benefits accrued by the use of future-oriented vocationally adaptive skills and life-functioning skills within the world of work and their impact on clients' QOL, have prompted rehabilitation researchers (Rubin, Chan, Bishop, & Miller, 2003; Rubin, Chan, & Thomas, 2003) to maintain that QOL may be a better predictor of *long-term* rehabilitation success, because life-functioning skills, in general, and employ-ability skills, more specifically, require extended time to be fully internalized and successfully processed. It can, therefore, be argued that when applied to VR services, the careful implementation of programs that focus on future-oriented (both proximal and distal), adaptive life coping skills that seek to comprehensively instill physical (i.e., self-care), psychological (i.e., self-direction and determination), social (i.e., communication), and vocational (i.e., work tolerance, performance of specific job activities) skills is likely to promote higher perceived QOL and, relatedly, long-term vocational success. This assumed link of postimpact engagement coping strategies → functional life skills→ improved QOL → successful vocational outcomes certainly merits further exploration and verification.

The importance of the second concept, that of client motivation level, has been well recognized by practitioners in the field of VR for more than half a century, but has experienced a renewed clinical and empirical interest with the advent of the therapeutic approach known as *motivational interviewing* (MI; Miller & Rollnick, 2002; C. C. Wagner & McMahon, 2004). It is beyond the scope of this chapter to faithfully address the many features and innovations of the MI approach to VR, but its shared elements with postimpact, future-oriented coping skills must be recognized. MI can be best understood as a goal- (i.e., future-) oriented, self-determination- (i.e., adaptive coping-) enhancing, and change-of-life seeking approach to promote client motivation, explore and resolve ambivalence, and ultimately change maladaptive cognitions and behaviors and replace them with adaptive ones (Chou, Ditchman, Pruett, Chan, & Hunter, 2009; Miller & Rollnick, 2002). The MI approach emphasises on empathic listening; seeking, planning, and implementing specific goals (e.g., health-related, vocational); and committing oneself to needed changes is akin to that undertaken by rehabilitation professionals who seek to train their clients in the use of engagement-type, adaptive coping skills that focus on the judicial and proficient use of such coping strategies as using emotional and instrumental support, cognitive reframing, and active planning to enhance successful psychosocial adaptation to CID. Both approaches share a common, overarching mission that focuses on (a) promoting autonomy and responsibility in implementing changes and adaptation to life both pre-CID (e.g., health maintenance, disease prevention; see earlier discussion on PP, and preimpact and preventive coping) or following CID onset (e.g., substance abuse, SCI, cardiovascular disease); (b) relying on decision-making and problem-solving skills to chart one's therapeutic course while implementing life (e.g., health-oriented, psychosocial, vocational) changes; (c) boosting self-efficacy/confidence during the process of adaptation to CID, including the acquisition of job skills and increasing employment opportunities; and (d) encouraging hope and optimism, both perceived as future-oriented motivational tools and coping resources, when seeking behavioral changes, psychosocial adaptation, and successful employment (Chou et al., 2009; C. C. Wagner & McMahon, 2004). Bolstering client motivation and enhancing future-oriented life changes, as envisioned by proponents of the MI approach, are highly commensurate with the future-oriented, engagement coping–type therapeutic framework advocated by psychosocial rehabilitation professionals.

Both approaches have amassed an impressive body of clinical and empirical literature to support their usefulness, although they have followed separate professional routes. It is hoped that by recognizing both approaches' underlying theoretical and clinical commonalities, rehabilitation professionals from both camps seek to cross-fertilize the bodies of knowledge and strengths inherent in both approaches, thus benefitting the rehabilitation field as a whole.

Implications to Rehabilitation Research

As was observed earlier in this chapter, although postimpact coping strategies emanate from past traumatic events (e.g., injuries, life-threatening diagnoses), they are by no means exclusively past-oriented and, in fact, often focus on presently encountered obstacles and barriers, as well as anticipated future issues. Indeed, it is the latter coping orientation that has been often associated with successful psychosocial adaptation, better QOL, and positive rehabilitation outcomes. One area that the rehabilitation researchers may wish to address, and further clarify, is the nature of the relationships between these coping strategies and psychosocial adaptation. For example, do these strategies directly influence perceived QOL (e.g., life satisfaction, well-being) and other, more objective indicators of QOL (e.g., community integration, occupational success) among people with CID, or are these relationships further mediated or moderated by (a) specific psychological mechanisms such as cognitive processes, appraisal, (control) belief system, motivational level, flexibility, and range of coping modes; (b) various situational determinants; and (c) degree, duration, or severity of the stress itself (Folkman & Lazarus, 1988; Folkman & Moskowitz, 2004; Mattlin, Wethington, & Kessler, 1990; Moos & Holahan, 2003; Terry, 1994). Furthermore, it would be of interest to learn what mechanisms and post-CID experiences may exist that differentiate between these successful future-oriented coping strategies and those that are past-oriented and typically associated with poorer adaptation.

Another fruitful area for research efforts includes the study of how the use, nature, and dynamics of these post-CID future-oriented (e.g., proactive, anticipatory) coping strategies differ from future-oriented coping in the *absence* of CID, that is, coping strategies that are not triggered by traumatic onset but rather by mere anticipation and wish to prevent future events (the more traditional future-oriented coping). Researchers may also wish to consider another potential venue that focuses on investigating whether the scope, frequency, and clinical efficacy of post-CID coping strategies differ according to such CID-related characteristics as nature of onset (e.g., gradual, sudden), time of onset, duration of condition, severity of the CID, its course (e.g., stable vs. variable; predictable vs. unpredictable), and so on.

Finally, in certain situations, it is expected that both preemptive (e.g., anticipatory) and post-CID coping occur. These situations involve medical procedures such as planned surgery (e.g., limb amputation, mastectomy, open heart surgery) and side effects of administered medication (e.g., chemotherapy, radiation therapy) among others. Research could shed light on such intriguing questions as what transitions in coping strategies, from preevent to postevent, predict better psychosocial adaptation and reported QOL. When put differently, is there an "ideal" or beneficial coping transition (e.g., a particular pattern of preevent to postevent set of coping strategies) that can predict better psychosocial adaptation, as indicated by such outcome measures as assessed QOL, perceived well-being and life satisfaction, level of depression and anxiety, and even nonpsychological outcomes such as level of experienced pain, degree of functional abilities, extent of social pursuits, and community integration.

Note

1. Most crisis researchers and clinicians maintain that the typical duration of crisis ranges from 4 to 8 weeks (e.g., Janosik, 1984; Roberts, 2000; Slaikeu, 1990), but also differentiate between equilibrium restoration that is time-limited and crisis resolution that is of longer duration and necessitates the development and implementation of new and adaptive coping strategies.

REFERENCES

Amir, M., Roziner, I., Knoll, A., & Neufeld, M. Y. (1999). Self-efficacy and social support as mediators in the relation between disease severity and quality of life in patients with epilepsy. *Epilepsia, 40*(2), 216–224.

Amirkhan, J. H. (1990). A factor analytically derived measure of coping: The coping strategy indicator. *Journal of Personality and Social Psychology, 59,* 1066–1074.

Aspinwall, L. G. (2005). The psychology of future-oriented thinking: From achievement to proactive coping, adaptation, and aging. *Motivation and Emotion, 29,* 203–235.

Aspinwall, L. G., & Taylor, S. E. (1997). A stitch in time: Self-regulation and proactive coping. *Psychological Bulletin, 121*(3), 417–436.

Auerbach, S. M. (1992). Temporal factors in stress and coping: Intervention implications. In B. N. Carpenter (Ed.), *Personal coping: Theory, research, and application* (pp. 133–147). Westport, CT: Praeger.

Bishop, M. (2005). Quality of life and psychosocial adaptation to chronic illness and acquired disability: A conceptual and theoretical synthesis. *Journal of Rehabilitation, 71*(2), 5–13.

Bishop, M., Smedema, S. M., & Lee, E. J. (2009). Quality of life and psychosocial adaptation to chronic illness and disability. In F. Chan, E. Cardoso, & J. A. Chronister (Eds.), *Understanding psychosocial adjustment to chronic illness and disability: A handbook for evidence-based practitioners in rehabilitation* (pp. 521–558). New York, NY: Springer Publishing.

Bishop, M., Stenhoff, D., & Shepard, L. (2007). Psychosocial adaptation and quality of life in multiple sclerosis: Assessment of the disability centrality model. *Journal of Rehabilitation, 73*(1), 3–12.

Buckelew, S., Baumstark, K., Frank, R., & Hewett, J. (1990). Adjustment following spinal cord injury. *Rehabilitation Psychology, 35,* 101–109.

Caplan, G. (1961). *An approach to community mental health.* New York, NY: Grune & Stratton.

Caplan, G. (1964). *Principles of preventive psychiatry.* New York, NY: Basic Books.

Carver, C. S., Pozo-Kaderman, C., Harris, S. D., Noriega, V., Scheier, M. F., Robinson, D. S., ... Clark, K. C. (1994). Optimism versus pessimism predicts the quality of women's adjustment to early stage breast cancer. *Cancer, 73*(4), 1213–1220.

Cavaiola, A. A., & Colford, J. E. (2006). *A practical guide to crisis intervention.* Boston, MA: Lahaska Press.

Chan, F., Rubin, S. E., Lee, G., & Pruitt, S. (2003). Empirically derived life skill factors for program evaluation in rehabilitation. *Journal of Applied Rehabilitation Counseling, 34*(4), 15–22.

Chou, C. C., Ditchman, N., Pruett, S. R., Chan, F., & Hunter, C. (2009). Application of self-efficacy related theories in psychosocial interventions. In F. Chan, E. Cardoso, & J. A. Chronister (Eds.), *Understanding psychosocial adjustment to chronic illness and disability: A handbook for evidence-based practitioners in rehabilitation* (pp. 243–276). New York, NY: Springer Publishing.

Collins, B. G., & Collins, T. M. (2005). *Crisis and trauma: Developmental–ecological intervention.* Boston, MA: Lahaska Press.

Crewe, N. M. (1980). Quality of life—The ultimate goal in rehabilitation. *Minnesota Medicine, 63*(8), 586–589.

da Silva Cardoso, E., Blalock, K., Allen, C. A., Chan, F., & Rubin, S. E. (2004). Life skills and subjective well-being of people with disabilities: A canonical correlation analysis. *International Journal of Rehabilitation Research, 27*(4), 331–334.

Davis, C. G., & Morgan, M. S. (2008). Finding meaning, perceiving growth, and acceptance of tinnitus. *Rehabilitation Psychology, 53,* 128–138.

Davis, C. G., Nolen-Hoeksema, S., & Larson, J. (1998). Making sense of loss and benefiting from the experience: Two construals of meaning. *Journal of Personality and Social Psychology, 75*(2), 561–574.

Dean, R. E., & Kennedy, P. (2009). Measuring appraisals following acquired spinal cord injury: A preliminary psychometric analysis of the appraisals of disability. *Rehabilitation Psychology, 54*(2), 222–231.

deRoon-Cassini, T. A., de St Aubin, E., Valvano, A., Hastings, J., & Horn, P. (2009). Psychological well-being after spinal cord injury: Perception of loss and meaning making. *Rehabilitation Psychology, 54*(3), 306–314.

Devins, G. M., Bezjak, A., Mah, K., Loblaw, D. A., & Gotowiec, A. P. (2006). Context moderates illness-induced lifestyle disruptions across life domains: A test of the illness intrusiveness theoretical framework in six common cancers. *Psycho-oncology, 15*(3), 221–233.

Devins, G. M., Edworthy, S. M., Seland, T. P., Klein, G. M., Paul, L. C., & Mandin, H. (1993). Differences in illness intrusiveness across rheumatoid arthritis, end-stage renal disease, and multiple sclerosis. *The Journal of Nervous and Mental Disease, 181*(6), 377–381.

Dunn, D. S. (1996). Well-being following amputation: Salutary effects of positive meaning, optimism, and control. *Rehabilitation Psychology, 41,* 285–302.

Elfström, M., & Kreuter, M. (2006). Relationships between locus of control, coping strategies, and emotional well-being in persons with spinal cord lesion. *Journal of Clinical Psychology in Medical Settings, 13,* 89–100.

Elliott, T. R., Witty, T. E., Herrick, S., & Hoffman, J. T. (1991). Negotiating reality after physical loss: Hope, depression, and disability. *Journal of Personality and Social Psychology, 61*(4), 608–613.

Endler, N. S., & Parker, J. D. (1990). Multidimensional assessment of coping: A critical evaluation. *Journal of Personality and Social Psychology, 58*(5), 844–854.

Endler, N. S., & Parker, J. D. (1994). Assessment of multidimensional coping: Task, emotion, and avoidance strategies. *Psychological Assessment, 6,* 50–60.

Fabian, E. S. (1991). Using quality of life indicators in rehabilitation program evaluation. *Rehabilitation Counseling Bulletin, 34,* 344–346.

Folkman, S., & Lazarus, R. S. (1988). Coping as a mediator of emotion. *Journal of Personality and Social Psychology, 54*(3), 466–475.

Folkman, S., & Moskowitz, J. T. (2004). Coping: Pitfalls and promise. *Annual Review of Psychology, 55,* 745–774.

Garnefski, N., Kraaij, V., Schroevers, M. J., & Somsen, G. A. (2008). Post-traumatic growth after a myocardial infarction: A matter of personality, psychological health, or cognitive coping? *Journal of Clinical Psychology in Medical Settings, 15*(4), 270–277.

Goodyear, R. L. (1976). Counselors as community psychologists. *Personnel and Guidance Journal, 54,* 512–516.

Haan, N. (1977). *Coping and defending: Processes of self-environment organization.* New York, NY: Academic Press.

Hamilton, J. M., Kives, K. D., Micevski, V., & Grace, S. L. (2003). Time perspective and health-promoting behavior in a cardiac rehabilitation population. *Behavioral Medicine, 28*(4), 132–139.

Helgeson, V. S., Reynolds, K. A., & Tomich, P. L. (2006). A meta-analytic review of benefit finding and growth. *Journal of Consulting and Clinical Psychology, 74*(5), 797–816.

Hershenson, D. B. (1990). A theoretical model for rehabilitation counseling. *Rehabilitation Counseling Bulletin, 33,* 268–278.

Hershenson, D. B., Crater, L. A., Enoch, B. D., Gaskell, A. W., Huston, W. J., Jr., Kuljian, I. M., ... Tabb, B. (1981). Toward a theory of rehabilitation counseling. *Journal of Applied Rehabilitation Counseling, 12*(1), 23–26.

Hodgkinson, P. E., & Stewart, M. (1991). *Coping with catastrophe: A handbook of disaster management.* New York, NY: Routledge.

Holman, E. A., & Silver, R. C. (1998). Getting "stuck" in the past: Temporal orientation and coping with trauma. *Journal of Personality and Social Psychology, 74*(5), 1146–1163.

Horowitz, M. J. (1986). *Stress response syndromes* (2nd ed.). Northvale, NJ: Jason Aronson.

James, R. K., & Gilliland, B. E. (2001). *Crisis intervention strategies* (4th ed.). Belmont, CA: Brooks/Cole.

Janis, I. L. (1958). *Psychological stress.* New York, NY: John Wiley.

Janoff-Bulman, R., & Yopyk, D. J. (2004). Random outcomes and valued commitments: Existential dilemmas and the paradox of meaning. In J. Greenberg, S. L. Koole, & T. Psyzczynski (Eds.), *Handbook of experimental existential psychology* (pp. 122–138). New York, NY: Guilford Press.

Janosik, E. H. (1984). *Crisis counseling: A contemporary approach.* Monterey, CA: Wadsworth.

Joseph, S., & Linley, P. A. (2006). Growth following adversity: Theoretical perspectives and implications for clinical practice. *Clinical Psychology Review, 26*(8), 1041–1053.

Kemp, B. J., & Krause, J. S. (1999). Depression and life satisfaction among people ageing with post-polio and spinal cord injury. *Disability and Rehabilitation, 21*(5-6), 241–249.

Kennedy, P. (2008). *Coping effectively with spinal cord injury: Therapist guide.* New York, NY: Oxford University Press.

Kennedy, P., Duff, J., Evans, M., & Beedie, A. (2003). Coping effectiveness training reduces depression and anxiety following traumatic spinal cord injuries. *The British Journal of Clinical Psychology, 42*(Pt 1), 41–52.

Kennedy, P., Evans, M., & Sandhu, N. (2009). Psychological adjustment to spinal cord injury: The contribution of coping, hope and cognitive appraisals. *Psychology, Health & Medicine, 14*(1), 17–33.

Kennedy, P., Lude, P., Elfström, M. L., & Smithson, E. (2012). Appraisals, coping and adjustment pre and post SCI rehabilitation: A 2-year follow-up study. *Spinal Cord, 50*(2), 112–118.

Kennedy, P., Smithson, E., McClelland, M., Short, D., Royle, J., & Wilson, C. (2010). Life satisfaction, appraisals and functional outcomes in spinal cord-injured people living in the community. *Spinal Cord, 48*(2), 144–148.

Kortte, K. B., Gilbert, M., Gorman, P., & Wegener, S. T. (2010). Positive psychological variables in the prediction of life satisfaction after spinal cord injury. *Rehabilitation Psychology, 55*(1), 40–47.

Kortte, K. B., Stevenson, J. E., Hosey, M. M., Castillo, R., & Wegener, S. T. (2012). Hope predicts positive functional role outcomes in acute rehabilitation populations. *Rehabilitation Psychology, 57*(3), 248–255.

Krohne, H. W. (1993). *Attention and avoidance.* Seattle, WA: Hogrefe & Huber.

Krohne, H. W. (1996). Individual differences in coping. In M. Zeidner & N. S. Endler (Eds.), *Handbook of coping: Theory, research, applications* (pp. 381–409). New York, NY: John Wiley.

Lazarus, R. S. (1966). *Psychological stress and the coping process.* New York, NY: McGraw-Hill.

Lazarus, R. S. (1991). *Emotion and adaptation.* New York, NY: Oxford University Press.

Lazarus, R. S., & Folkman, S. (1984). *Stress, appraisal, and coping.* New York, NY: Springer Publishing.

Lazarus, R. S., & Launier, R. (1978). Stress-related transactions between person and environment. In L. A. Pervin & M. Lewis (Eds.), *Perspectives in interactional psychology* (pp. 287–327). New York, NY: Plenum Press.

Lindemann, E. (1944). Symptomatology and management of acute grief. *American Journal of Psychiatry, 101,* 141–148.

Livneh, H. (1995). The tripartite model of rehabilitation intervention: Basics, goals, and rehabilitation strategies. *Journal of Applied Rehabilitation Counseling, 26*(1), 25–29.

Livneh, H. (2001). Psychosocial adaptation to chronic illness and disability: A conceptual framework. *Rehabilitation Counseling Bulletin, 44,* 151–160.

Livneh, H., & Antonak, R. F. (1997). *Psychosocial adaptation to chronic illness and disability.* Gaithersburg, MD: Aspen.

Livneh, H., & Martz, E. (2007). Reactions to diabetes and their relationship to time orientation. *International Journal of Rehabilitation Research, 30*(2), 127–136.

Livneh, H., & Wilson, L. M. (2003). Coping strategies as predictors and mediators of disability-related variables and psychosocial adaptation: An exploratory investigation. *Rehabilitation Counseling Bulletin, 46,* 194–208.

Maes, S., Leventhal, H., & de Ridder, D. T. (1996). Coping with chronic diseases. In M. Zeidner & N. S. Endler (Eds.), *Handbook of coping: Theory, research, applications* (pp. 221–251). New York, NY: John Wiley.

Malcarne, V. L., Compas, B. E., Epping-Jordan, J. E., & Howell, D. C. (1995). Cognitive factors in adjustment to cancer: Attributions of self-blame and perceptions of control. *Journal of Behavioral Medicine, 18*(5), 401–417.

Manne, S., Ostroff, J., Winkel, G., Goldstein, L., Fox, K., & Grana, G. (2004). Posttraumatic growth after breast cancer: Patient, partner, and couple perspectives. *Psychosomatic Medicine, 66*(3), 442–454.

Martz, E. (2004). Do reactions of adaptation to disability influence the fluctuation of future time orientation among individuals with spinal cord injuries? *Rehabilitation Counseling Bulletin, 47,* 86–95.

Martz, E., & Livneh, H. (Eds.). (2007). *Coping with chronic illness and disability: Theoretical, empirical and clinical aspects.* New York, NY: Springer.

Mattlin, J. A., Wethington, E., & Kessler, R. C. (1990). Situational determinants of coping and coping effectiveness. *Journal of Health and Social Behavior, 31*(1), 103–122.

McCabe, M. P., Stokes, M., & McDonald, E. (2009). Changes in quality of life and coping among people with multiple sclerosis over a 2 year period. *Psychology, Health & Medicine, 14*(1), 86–96.

McGrath, J. E., & Beehr, T. A. (1990). Time and the stress process: Some temporal issues in the conceptualization and measurement of stress. *Stress Medicine, 6,* 93–104.

McGrath, J. E., & Tschan, F. (2004). *Temporal matters in social psychology: Examining the role of time in the lives of groups and individuals.* Washington, DC: American Psychological Association.

McMillen, J., & Cook, C. (2003). The positive by-products of spinal cord injury and their correlates. *Rehabilitation Psychology, 48,* 77–85.

Miller, W. R., & Rollnick, S. (2002). *Motivational interviewing: Preparing people for change* (2nd ed.). New York, NY: Guilford Press.

Mishel, M. H. (1988). Uncertainty in illness. *Image—The Journal of Nursing Scholarship, 20*(4), 225–232.

Moore, A. D., Stambrook, M., & Gill, D. G. (1994). Coping patterns associated with long-term outcome from traumatic brain injury among female survivors. *NeuroRehabilitation, 4*(2), 122–129.

Moos, R. H. (Ed.). (1986). *Coping with life crises: An integrated approach.* New York, NY: Plenum Press.

Moos, R. H., & Holahan, C. J. (2003). Dispositional and contextual perspectives on coping: Toward an integrative framework. *Journal of Clinical Psychology, 59*(12), 1387–1403.

Moos, R. H., & Holahan, C. J. (2007). Adaptive tasks and methods of coping with chronic illness and disability. In E. Martz & H. Livneh (Eds.), *Coping with chronic illness and disability: Theoretical, empirical, and clinical aspects* (pp. 107–126). New York, NY: Springer.

Oaksford, K., Frude, N., & Cuddihy, R. (2005). Positive coping and stress-related psychological growth following lower limb amputation. *Rehabilitation Psychology, 50,* 266–277.

Pakenham, K. I. (2005). Benefit finding in multiple sclerosis and associations with positive and negative outcomes. *Health Psychology, 24*(2), 123–132.

Pakenham, K. I. (2006). Investigation of the coping antecedents to positive outcomes and distress in multiple sclerosis. *Psychology & Health, 21,* 633–649.

Pakenham, K. I. (2007). Making sense of multiple sclerosis. *Rehabilitation Psychology, 52,* 380–389.

Park, C. L., Edmondson, D., Fenster, J. R., & Blank, T. O. (2008). Meaning making and psychological adjustment following cancer: The mediating roles of growth, life meaning, and restored just-world beliefs. *Journal of Consulting and Clinical Psychology, 76*(5), 863–875.

Park, C. L., & Folkman, S. (1997). Meaning in the context of stress and coping. *Review of General Psychology, 1,* 115–144.

Pearlin, L. I., & Schooler, C. (1978). The structure of coping. *Journal of Health and Social Behavior, 19*(1), 2–21.

Perez, M., & Reicherts, M. (1992). *Stress, coping and health: A situation-behavior approach, theory, methods, applications.* Seattle, WA: Hogrefe & Huber.

Pollard, C., & Kennedy, P. (2007). A longitudinal analysis of emotional impact, coping strategies and post-traumatic psychological growth following spinal cord injury: A 10-year review. *British Journal of Health Psychology, 12*(Pt 3), 347–362.

Radnitz, C. (2000). *Cognitive-behavioral therapy for persons with disabilities.* Lanham, MD: Jason Aronson.

Reker, G. T. (1977). The Purpose-in-Life test in an inmate population: An empirical investigation. *Journal of Clinical Psychology, 33*(3), 688–693.

Renwick, R., Brown, I., & Nagler, M. (Eds.). (1996). *Quality of life in health promotion and rehabilitation.* Thousand Oaks, CA: Sage.

Roberts, A. R. (2000). *Crisis intervention handbook: Assessment, treatment, and research* (2nd ed.). New York, NY: Oxford University Press.

Roessler, R. T. (1990). A quality of life perspective on rehabilitation counseling. *Rehabilitation Counseling Bulletin, 34,* 82–91.

Rubin, S. E., Chan, F., Bishop, M., & Miller, S. M. (2003). Psychometric validation of the Sense of Well-Being Inventory for program evaluation in rehabilitation. *Professional Rehabilitation, 11*(2), 54–59.

Rubin, S. E., Chan, F., & Thomas, D. L. (2003). Assessing changes in life skills and quality of life resulting from rehabilitation services. *Journal of Rehabilitation, 69*(3), 4–9.

Schlossberg, N. K. (1981). A model for analyzing human adaptation to transition. *Counseling Psychologist, 9*(2), 2–18.

Schou, I., Ekeberg, Ø., Sandvik, L., Hjermstad, M. J., & Ruland, C. M. (2005). Multiple predictors of health-related quality of life in early stage breast cancer. Data from a year follow-up study compared with the general population. *Quality of Life Research, 14*(8), 1813–1823.

Schulz, R., & Decker, S. (1985). Long-term adjustment to physical disability: The role of social support, perceived control, and self-blame. *Journal of Personality and Social Psychology, 48*(5), 1162–1172.

Schwarzer, R. (2000). Manage stress at work through preventive and proactive coping. In A. E. Locke (Ed.), *The Blackwell handbook of principles of organizational behavior* (pp. 342–355). Oxford, England: Blackwell.

Schwarzer, R., & Knoll, N. (2003). Positive coping: Mastering demands and searching for meaning. In S. J. Lopez & C. R. Snyder (Eds.), *Positive psychological assessment: A handbook of models and measures* (pp. 393–409). Washington, DC: American Psychological Association.

Sears, S. R., Stanton, A. L., & Danoff-Burg, S. (2003). The yellow brick road and the emerald city: Benefit finding, positive reappraisal coping and posttraumatic growth in women with early-stage breast cancer. *Health Psychology, 22*(5), 487–497.

Selye, H. (1976). *Stress in health and disease.* Boston, MA: Butterworths.

Sharoff, K. (2004). *Coping skills therapy for managing chronic and terminal illness.* New York, NY: Springer Publishing.

Shontz, F. C. (1975). *The psychological aspects of physical illness and disability.* New York, NY: Macmillan.

Skinner, E. A., Edge, K., Altman, J., & Sherwood, H. (2003). Searching for the structure of coping: A review and critique of category systems for classifying ways of coping. *Psychological Bulletin, 129*(2), 216–269.

Slaikeu, K. A. (1990). *Crisis intervention: A handbook for practice and research* (2nd ed.). Boston, MA: Allyn & Bacon.

Slife, B. D. (1993). *Time and psychological explanation.* New York: State University of New York Press.

Smedema, S. M., Catalano, D., & Ebener, D. J. (2010). The relationship of coping, self-worth, and subjective well-being: A structural equation model. *Rehabilitation Counseling Bulletin, 53,* 131–142.

Snyder, C. R., Lehman, K. A., Kluck, B., & Monsson, Y. (2006). Hope for rehabilitation and vice versa. *Rehabilitation Psychology, 51,* 89–112.

Sword, R. M., Sword, R. K. M., Brunskill, S. R., & Zimbardo, P. G. (2014). Time perspective therapy: A new-time based metaphor therapy for PTSD. *Journal of Loss and Trauma: International Perspectives on Stress & Coping, 19,* 197–201.

Tedeschi, R. G., & Calhoun, L. G. (2004). Posttraumatic growth: Conceptual foundations and empirical evidence. *Psychological Inquiry, 15,* 1–18.

Tedeschi, R. G., Cann, A., Taku, K., Senol-Durak, E., & Calhoun, L. G. (2017). The Posttraumatic Growth Inventory: A revision integrating existential and spiritual change. *Journal of Traumatic Stress, 30*(1), 11–18.

Tedeschi, R. G., Park, C. L., & Calhoun, L. G. (1998). *Posttraumatic growth: Positive transformations in the aftermath of crisis.* Mahwah, NJ: Lawrence Erlbaum Associates.

Tennen, H., & Affleck, G. (2002). Benefit-finding and benefit-reminding. In C. R. Snyder & S. J. Lopez (Eds.), *Handbook of positive psychology* (pp. 584–597). London, England: Oxford University Press.

Terry, D. J. (1994). Determinants of coping: The role of stable and situational factors. *Journal of Personality and Social Psychology, 66*(5), 895–910.

Thompson, N. J., Coker, J., Krause, J. S., & Henry, E. (2003). Purpose in life as a mediator of adjustment after spinal cord injury. *Rehabilitation Psychology, 48,* 100–108.

van Leeuwen, C. M., Post, M. W., Westers, P., van der Woude, L. H., de Groot, S., Sluis, T., … Lindeman, E. (2012). Relationships between activities, participation, personal factors, mental health, and life satisfaction in persons with spinal cord injury. *Archives of Physical Medicine and Rehabilitation, 93*(1), 82–89.

Wagner, C. C., & McMahon, B. T. (2004). Motivational interviewing and rehabilitation counseling practice. *Rehabilitation Counseling Bulletin, 47,* 152–161.

Wagner, M. K., Armstrong, D., & Laughlin, J. E. (1995). Cognitive determinants of quality of life after onset of cancer. *Psychological Reports, 77*(1), 147–154.

Wright, G. N. (1980). *Total rehabilitation.* Boston, MA: Little, Brown.

Zeidner, M., & Endler, N. S. (Eds.). (1996). *Handbook of coping: Theory, research, applications.* New York, NY: John Wiley.

Zimbardo, P. G., & Boyd, J. N. (2008). *The time paradox: The new psychology of time that will change your life.* New York, NY: Free Press.

III

Family Issues in Illness and Disability

*I*n this section, author draw on the most current research related to people with disabilities and their families. Issues, such as involvement, support, and coping of family members (parents, children, spouses, and partners), must be addressed to promote optimal medical, physical, mental, emotional, and psychological functioning of the person with a disability. Coping, resiliency, and psychosocial adjustment draw from the individual's support system. Hence, the attributes of family members cannot be separated from those of the individual. Indeed, as families heal, so do their loved ones with disabilites. The authors in this section look deep into relationships within the family, such as the attachment of children and adolescents with disabilities and their parents. The literature examining relationships between parents with disabilities and their children, including those of adult age, is sparse, and cultural differences are seldom discussed. To date, most of what has been explored in the literature focuses on the relationship between parents with a disability and the psychosocial needs of their children's well-being. Among the strengths of this section are chapters discussing the unique aspects and personal experiences of parenting children with disabilities, being an adult caregiver for a partner or child with a specific disability, and the related adjustment, stresses, and rewards of caregiving. The authors give voice to parents who describe their experiences caring for a loved one with a disability and coping in a family system thrown into crisis mode by the introduction of disability—an event that may threaten family members' health if not dealt with appropriately. This section also explores grief, death, and dying of terminal or elderly family members with a disability. Several authors explore risk factors within family systems, such as poverty, single parenting, deficits in family and extended family support systems, health insurance, and society's attitudinal barriers that hinder optimal psychosocial adjustment and well-being.

MAJOR HIGHLIGHTS IN PART III

- Chapter 12 offers qualitative research that demonstrates unique cultural differences, demands, and responsibilities of families parenting children with disabilities. There is no doubt that parenting with a disability or being a parent of a child with a disability can be stressful. It is interesting to note that many authors view the overall impact as not necessarily negative. Using a family systems model, readers can examine ethnographic data, caregiving roles, social occupations, and self-identities of families whose members have chronic medical and physical conditions. In-depth qualitative analysis of these families offers guidelines for rehabilitation practitioners seeking to cultivate coping and resiliency strategies among families facing such challenges. Cultural differences are also explored.

- The authors of Chapter 13 discuss the importance of parental access to information and resources about their loved one's condition and available services, as well as issues relating to community inclusion, financial barriers associated with insurance struggles and lack of government funding, and the importance of family support. This chapter is a powerful testament to the struggles families face not because of the burden of caregiving, but rather because of the need to fight against the system for support and resources—a fight that can cause frustration and stress for parents and the family unit.

- Chapter 14 delineates concepts, models, and practical applications for counselors dealing with issues of grief, loss, death, and dying. This section provides empirical support for addressing issues early on in various stages of grief. The new *Diagnostic and Statistical Manual of Mental Disorders* (*DSM-5;* American Psychiatric Association, 2013) category of Persistent Complex Bereavement Disorder is discussed, laying the foundation for clinical interviews, standardized assessments, and treatment strategies for families dealing with this form of complicated and complex grief. In addition, the author discusses the range of mental, emotional, and physical exhaustion experienced by some caregivers. Newer research is offered suggesting that the caregiver role can be quite satisfying despite the sometimes devastating effects on family members. The reader is directed to studies that have advanced the understanding of families in relation to grief, death, and dying. This newer research highlights elements of the caregiving role that can increase spiritual growth, meaning, and purpose, which ultimately assists in the grieving process.

- Approximately 85% of all caregiving in the United States is provided by unpaid family members and friends. The authors of Chapter 15 explore the pros and cons of caregiving, noting the mental and physical stress associated with having few resources or perceiving that one is alone, and conversely the rewards of having a purpose, doing something meaningful, and providing unconditional love through caring. The authors also address caregiver abuse, differences in agency care versus family care, family role changes, and the difficult decision of having to place a loved one in a nursing home.

- The authors of Chapter 16 consider family identity in relation to disability and interaction with the community. They discuss personal identity versus family identity and social identity within a social movement. The McMaster model of family functioning and the three dominant tasks of family are explored as are the *International Classification of Functioning, Disability and Health* (*ICF;* World Health Organization, 2001) domains of health conditions, activities and participation, and functions affected. Finally, methods of family coping (both negative and positive strategies), family resiliency, and strategies that counselors can use to effectively assist families are presented.

REFERENCES

American Psychiatric Association. (2013). *Diagnostic and statistical manual of mental disorders* (5th ed.). Arlington, VA: American Psychiatric Publishing.

World Health Organization. (2001). *International classification of functioning, disability and health: ICF.* Geneva, Switzerland: Author.

12

Family Adaptation Across Cultures Toward a Loved One Who Is Disabled

NOREEN M. GRAF

*T*he first experiences of supportive and social units come, most often, from the family; a unit of persons united through blood, adoption, or marriage (U.S. Census Bureau, 2000). Here, parents are obligated to provide adequate basic care for their children by supplying food, shelter, medical care, and schooling. The onset of disability in the family creates challenges for them, sometimes even to basic care obligations, depending on the resources available to, and the unique characteristics of, the members. Today, more than 65 million Americans care for a family member with a disability or illness; two thirds of them are women (American Psychological Association, 2017). This chapter discusses the impact of disability on family by examining the reactions of family members to disability, factors that influence adjustment to disability in the family, adjustment models, parenting reaction perspectives, effective family coping, the impact of disability based on the family role of the person with a disability, and cultural influence on family adaptation to disability.

DEFINING *FAMILY*

Much of the literature related to families and disability is written from the framework of the traditional family model, married parents living with children. But in fact only about 25% of American households are made up of a married man and woman and their children, and another 25% are persons living alone, many of them elderly and young unmarried persons. The remaining households are single-parent households, mixed families, same-sex parent households, extended family households, cohabiting unmarried partners, and numerous other combinations of persons living together. In the United States, an average of 2.6 persons live in a household; the average income for the household is about $52,000. The percentage of persons below the poverty level is 14.3%. Compared with families without members with disabilities, families with members with disabilities are more likely to live in poverty and have a lower median income (U.S. Census Bureau, 2010). They are also more likely to have increased medical and childcare expenses, further taxing the financial resources of these families.

Because families are the primary support systems of persons with disabilities, it is important to understand the characteristics of healthy and well-functioning units. A healthy family depends less on the structure of the family and more on particular characteristics of its members. With this in mind, families of any makeup—traditional, single-parent, extended family households, or otherwise—can be healthy families; however, a lack of financial, social, and personal resources will certainly make it more difficult to remain so. Lin (1994) described six characteristics of healthy families dealing with a disability among its members:

1. Commitment that involves the prioritization of family over self, coordination of family roles and responsibilities, working together toward mutual goals, and supporting one another
2. Togetherness, which refers to the family making arrangements for family time as in eating, playing, and celebrating together; it is less important what activities are shared as long as they are performed together
3. Appreciation and admiration of an individual's strengths, talents, and interests as well as encouragement of individual pursuits
4. Good communication that establishes a sense of belonging, diminishes frustrations, and improves marital relations; this involves listening and conflict resolution rather than avoidance of a problem situation
5. Spiritual well-being that involves the family sharing a common faith or spiritual belief that increases family cohesion
6. Coping with crisis and stress that involves the family's willingness to face the reality of difficult situations and cope effectively, systematically, and rationally.

REACTIONS OF FAMILY TO DISABILITY

Emotional Reactions

In 1962, Olshansky described *chronic sorrow* as the regret and sorrow experienced by parents at the birth of a child with a disability caused by the loss of the expected child. It was seen as an understandable sorrow that could last indefinitely as parents would reexperience sorrow at each of their child's developmental milestones. Twenty years later, Wolfensberger (1983) alternatively described *novelty shock crisis*, a state of confusion resulting from lack of information and societal reaction. This term illustrated the shift in thinking from disability as the problem in the family, to understanding that a lack of social supports was also a hindrance to caregivers. Today, the term *caregiver burden* is frequently used to assist in the understanding of the amount of responsibility placed on caregivers that can result in extraordinary stress (Zarit, Reever, & Bach-Peterson, 1980). Caregivers may need to provide assistance with daily activities even to the extent that they feel they are missing out on life that can lead to feelings of anger, resentment, and depression. They may become emotionally drained and physically exhausted due to increased financial responsibilities and may need to take over all or part of the disabled member's family responsibilities while maintaining their own.

Stress Reactions

Stress occurs when any demand placed on an individual or system exceeds the coping capacity. Initially, stress is inevitable at the onset of significant changes of any type. The stress created by disability in the family can cause it to collapse and struggle, or it may lead the family to become stronger, closer, and a better functioning system. Stress is more evident in families with disability than those without it (Hodapp & Krasner, 1995; Taanila, Syrjala, Kokkonen, & Järvelin, 2002; Wallander & Noojin, 1995) and comes from a number of difficult family challenges, including repeated medical and emotional crises, financial hardships, difficult schedules, modification of activities and goals, societal isolation, difficulty in educational placements, and marital discord (Lavin, 2001; H. I. McCubbin & Patterson, 1983). Other factors that increase stress for parents include having a greater number of children and having difficulty accessing reliable childcare (Warfield, 2005). In a study to look at the everyday lives of families with children who have chronic illnesses, families reported daily stresses as including chronic preoccupation with making health decisions, restricted social lives, and overall low vitality (Martin, Brady, & Kotarba, 1992).

As a result of the medical costs of chronic illness and disability, and the need for caretaking that can cause one family member to decrease or give up work, there can be considerable stress caused by the financial impact of disability to families. Park et al. (2003) determined that among children with disabilities who are 3 to 21 years old, 28% are living below poverty level, affecting their health, living environment, family interactions, productivity, and their emotional well-being. In addition, mothers of children with disabilities tend to have lower incomes and work fewer hours than mothers of children without disabilities (Neely-Barnes & Dia, 2008). Higher family income has been found to allow for increases in parents' coping options and adaptability, and ability to spend time supporting and nurturing their children (Mcleod & Shanahan, 1996; Yau & LiTsang, 1999).

Although stress has been noted as high in families, there is generally a decline in stress over time as the family adapts to their circumstances. In a longitudinal study that examined stress among parents of children with intellectual disabilities over a 7-year period, stress declined significantly over time in the areas of worry about speech deficits, intelligence deficits, behavior at home, behavior in public, and obtaining help. Parents in this study also had additional children without disabilities and rated the amount of stress due to the child with a disability as twice that of the amount of stress caused by a child in the home without a disability (Baxter, Cummins, & Yiolitis, 2000).

Marital Discord

Marital difficulties are frequently discussed in the literature as problematic when families experience disability. Taanila, Kokkonen, and Järvelin (1996) investigated the long-term effects of chronic illness, severe intellectual impairment, and physical disability on parents' marital relationships and found that 25% of the parents reported that their child's disability was a contributing factor to their marital impairment. Specifically, the intense demands of daily caretaking, unequal division of daily task labor, and insufficient available time for leisure activities were identified as contributing to marital discord.

Although preexisting marital discord can serve to increase family stress, severe childhood disability may also contribute to the onset of marital difficulties and be responsible for the higher rates of divorce among couples. Divorce is more likely to occur in families where one of the parents acquires a disability or a child is born with or acquires a disability. In families with children with developmental disorders, this increase is generally small, with only a 5.35% greater chance of divorce (Hodapp & Krasner, 1995). In a study of children with a chronic illness and variety of disabilities, the percentage of increase in divorce was even lower at 2.9% (Witt, Riley, & Coiro, 2003). Contrarily, Singer and Farkas (1989) found that families with infants with disabilities reported greater closeness.

FACTORS THAT INFLUENCE ADJUSTMENT TO DISABILITY IN THE FAMILY

Families have a great impact on the recovery/adjustment, well-being, and success of an individual with a disability (Degeneffe & Lynch, 2006; Kosciulek, 1994), and family competence is considered by many to be a key factor in adjustment to disability (Alston & McCowan, 1995). Power and Dell Orto (2004) noted seven family characteristics that will influence how a family reacts to disability:

1. *Risk factors* will contribute to poor functioning in a family; these include a lack of support systems, family compositions that may add to stress such as single-parent households, stressed families, or families in conflict.
2. *Protective factors*, identified as strong family connections, effective communication, and problem solving, will increase the likelihood that families will successfully adapt.
3. *Belief systems* that are moderated by religious and cultural values impact how the family manages the demands of disability, makes sense of the disability, and communicates with health professionals.
4. *Access to coping resources* includes personality strengths, previous life experiences, positive attitudes, values and religious beliefs, extended family support, and community and financial resources.
5. *Family history* involves the previous experiences in dealing with illness and disability and managing losses.
6. *Family relationships and communication styles* involve the members' ability to be open and honest with one another, to nurture each other, and to function in a well-structured manner versus members acting in isolation.
7. *Who in the family is disabled* plays a role in that dreams and expectations are affected differently based on if the member is a caretaker or dependent. Caretaker impairment will have a more detrimental impact on the family.

ADJUSTMENT MODELS

A number of models have been used to describe the process of family adaptation to disability. The Family Stress Theory was propounded by Reuben Hill in 1949 after his work with families of soldiers. His ABCX model explained how a stressor event, the family's perception of that event, and the available resources interacted to avoid or create a crisis reaction. H. I. McCubbin and Patterson (1983) expanded this model in the Double ABCX model by incorporating the use of family coping mechanisms to deal with a crisis event, recognizing an accumulation of stress on families over time, and a need to use existing and new resources and coping skills to reach positive adaptation termed *bonadaptation*.

The Family Resilience Model has also been utilized to examine family adjustment. *Resiliency* is the ability to adapt, adjust, and thrive in difficult times. In rehabilitation, resiliency refers to the ability to adapt and adjust to disability and then to achieve a successful outcome (Kosciulek, 1994; Lustig, 1997). Family resiliency refers to the family's ability to make successful adaptations. The Resiliency Model of Family Stress, Adjustment, and Adaptation (M. A. McCubbin & McCubbin, 1993; H. I. McCubbin, Thompson, & McCubbin, 1996) focuses on how families can positively adjust and cope to maintain their quality of life. The model places emphasis on the functional capacity and strengths of the family rather than on deficits. It builds on the positive assets of the family, specifically what the family is good at and then works toward increasing problem solving, coping, and adjustment. Thus, instead of assessing only the deficits and needs of the family, the counselor would assess family strengths in terms of existing resources to deal with family crisis, views, and attitudes toward the crisis, and the family's coping and problem-solving skills.

Following this assessment, the counselor assists the family in building and utilizing resources and prepares the family to the extent possible for what to expect from the rehabilitation process and assists in developing realistic expectations for recovery. Counselors will also make efforts to help the family review and reframe the occurrence of disability in the family. Families are assisted in coming to understand that their reactions to disability and feelings of stress, being overwhelmed, or angry are all normal reactions to a crisis. By reframing the event as an opportunity to work as a family to overcome obstacles, the family can become stronger, more efficient, and closer. Finally, counselors build on existing coping skills, including communication skills and work history, moving toward open family communication so that fears, misconceptions, and apprehensions about family roles can be resolved and long-term goals can be established. With open communication, family members can make decisions about who will be a caretaker and what role changes will occur. If these issues are not dealt with openly, anger and resentment may result (Frain et al., 2007).

Stage models have been used to describe the adjustment of persons to disability (Livneh & Antonak, 1990) over time. Blacher (1984) described three stages of adjustment of parents: First, an initial emotional crisis in which parents experience feelings of denial and shock; a second stage of fluctuating emotions that include anger, depression, guilt, shame, rejection of the child, and overprotection of the child; and a final stage of acceptance. A revision of this model by Anderegg, Vergason, and Smith (1992) that emphasizes the grieving process consists of three stages: confronting, adjusting, and adapting.

More recent, a number of researchers have moved beyond the notion of adjustment and adaptation phases as being the final stages or end goal and have come to incorporate an additional growth phase, recognizing that families may grow closer as a unit due to the challenges and rewards brought on by disability (Bradley, Knoll, & Agosta, 1993; Naseef, 2001). Although stage theories have the benefit of attempting to explain how people proceed toward adjustment, they have been criticized for insufficient attention to the unpredictable or recurrent and complex aspects of adjustment to disability (Kendall & Buys, 1998). Likewise, Snow (2001) and Esdaile (2009) found that mothers of children with disabilities find these theories condescending and meaningless because they do not take into account the variety of positive experiences, insights, and understandings gained from caring for a child with a disability.

PARENTING REACTION PERSPECTIVES

In reviewing the literature related to reactions of parents of children with disabilities, Ferguson (2002) described five approaches to conceptualizing parental reactions; *psychodynamic, functionalist, psychosocial, interactionist,* or *adaptational*. For a number of decades, a *psychodynamic approach* was the only lens used to describe parental reactions to disability. This led to viewing parental reactions from a pathological standpoint, viewed as either apathetic or involved and either angry or accepting. From this standpoint, parents' reactions were framed as unhealthy and neurotic. Even involvement with the child could be interpreted as resulting from underlying guilt. Justifiable anger at a lack of appropriate care could be seen as displaced anger and a lack of adjustment.

With a shift to behavioral treatment approaches in the 1960s, a *functionalist* approach frequently labeled parents' reactions as dysfunctional and children's parents were often seen as additionally disabling to the child. With the advent of the 1970s, the *psychosocial* approach to viewing disability focused on the interplay of the environment and the emotions of the parents. The emotions of shock, loneliness, stress, and grief became the focus. The work of Olshansky (1962) in the area of chronic sorrow, and Wolfensberger (1983) in the area of shock and grief are examples of using the psychosocial approach to conceptualize parental reactions. From this standpoint, parents are viewed as suffering from loss. The *interactionist* standpoint, which is an infrequent approach, views parental reactions as a function of societal stigma, fatigue, disempowerment, and poverty leading parents to feel powerless. Finally, a recent approach to viewing parental reaction is the *adaptational* approach that emphasizes supportive social policy and cultural values as essential components of parental reaction to disability. It emphasizes the adaptability and resiliency of families and recognizes coping skills and positive aspects of raising a child with a disability, including the potential of marital and spiritual growth and family harmony. From this standpoint, families can be viewed as empowered, cohesive, and adapted.

EFFECTIVE FAMILY COPING WITH DISABILITY

The emotional, financial, and social impact of disability on the family will be determined largely by how the family responds to crisis and how effectively the members manage and resolve conflict, make decisions, and meet role expectations. Families that avoid or seek to escape dealing with disability will likely experience greater disorganization and stress, whereas families that demonstrate competence in reorganizing and actively addressing issues by changing their behaviors and attitudes to meet new demands will likely have greater positive adjustment (Alston & McCowan, 1995).

In order to determine what family qualities are most helpful toward the effective adjustment of disability, H. I. McCubbin and McCubbin (1988) identified three family types: balanced, midrange, and extreme. The balanced family possesses two characteristics that render it most resilient and functional: rhythm and regenerativity. Rhythm in a family refers to established rituals, rules, and routines that allow children to have a clear understanding of what is expected of them and allows for increased closeness and bonding among family members. These families also report greater flexibility and satisfaction. Regenerativity in families refers to family coherence and hardiness. Coherence involves the emphasis placed on caring for one another, respect, loyalty, trust, pride, and common values. Hardiness involves internal control of events, activity involvement, and willingness to explore and challenge themselves (H. I. McCubbin & McCubbin, 1988). Similarly, Walsh (2003) reflected this description of resilient families, listing three factors that assist them to succeed. First, families need to be able to make sense and meaning of the difficulties they face. Second, they need to affirm their strength and maintain a positive perspective. Finally, they need a shared spiritual belief system. In addition to these characteristics, families must also be flexible, connected, and resourceful to persevere.

In a recent study, Knestrict and Kuchey (2009) investigated resiliency among families who had children with severe disabilities and found a strong connection between socioeconomic status (SES) and family resiliency. Of the families they determined to be resilient, all were in the upper family income categories. Likewise, the lowest functioning families were in the low-income category. The effect of higher SES was that families were more likely to have health insurance benefits, additional income provided for a better level of care, and the ability to access information and services. They found that more money was available to provide for respite care, home remodeling, and additional activities, such as aquatic and equine therapy, and more leisure time. The authors acknowledge the potential for state and federal programs to equalize disability services across SES levels, but point to continued funding cutbacks that limit available services.

Families have expressed a number of other needs that, if provided, could assist in family functioning, including family and social support, medical information, financial information and assistance, help explaining the disability to others, childcare, and professional support and services (Sloper & Turner, 1992; Walker, Epstein, Taylor, Crocker, & Tuttle, 1989). In a study of needs for families with a child with cerebral palsy (CP), parents desired information on services, help planning for the future, help finding community activities, and more respite time. Parents whose children used wheeled mobility expressed needing help paying for home equipment and home modifications, and finding childcare workers, respite care providers, and community recreational activities (Palisano et al., 2010).

DISABILITY IMPACT AND THE FAMILY MEMBER WITH A DISABILITY

When a Child Has a Disability

The extent of the physical impairment, the predictability of the course of the illness, and whether or not it is life threatening affect the reactions of families and children to disability. The more severe and difficult the management of the disability is, the greater the family's susceptibility to stress reactions, frustration, and feelings of being overwhelmed (Lyons, Leon, Roecker Phelps, & Dunleavy, 2010). In examining the influence of predictability of symptoms in young children with chronic illnesses on parents' stress levels, Dogson et al. (2000) found that childhood illness with unpredictable symptoms caused significantly higher levels of distress.

In addition to the disability's severity and predictability, the child's age will have an impact on emotional adjustment. Children who are very dependent on their parents, who do not have an opportunity to socialize with friends, or who are frequently absent from school due to medical conditions may be delayed in emotional and social development. If children are less socially mature, or if they have experienced rejection from peers, they may have difficulty making friends, feel rejected, and become isolated. Adolescents who are unable to achieve sufficient independence or explore friendships and intimate relationships, or whose body image is negative, may become frustrated and depressed (Falvo, 2005).

Other emotions that children and adolescents with disabilities may have are fear, grief, anger, and denial. Anger can be experienced as loud outbursts as well as moodiness, pouting, and silence. Grief may be experienced as sadness but can also be masked behind hostility and resentment toward others. Uncertainty related to medical procedures or returning to school or other social environments may trigger lingering fear and apprehension. Denial and unreasonable expectations may initially serve to protect the child from emotionally dealing with difficulties related to the disability, but they can also serve to keep the child from making efforts to adjust to the condition (Power & Dell Orto, 2004).

As with other crises, parents' initial reactions to disability onset may present as shock and denial, a time of numbness, and disbelief. These reactions are productive in that they provide psychological protection until the family members work up to psychological coping, but may also interfere with rational decision making if the parents refuse to accept the diagnosis or the permanency of a condition. Parents may then experience a number of emotions as a result of having a child with a disability, including being overwhelmed, confused, and profoundly sad (Power & Dell Orto, 2004). They may experience guilt, believing that something they did or failed to do may have caused the disability or may become depressed (Norton & Drew, 1994). Parental depression and feelings of helplessness and stress may then contribute to additional restrictions or limitations in the child with a disability (Tomasello, Manning, & Dulmus, 2010).

A number of studies have compared the impact of a birth of a child with a disability to a death in terms of adjustment because families have been noted to progress through the grief stages of shock, realization, defensive retreat, and acknowledgment (Norton & Drew, 1994; Wolfensberger, 1983). These studies suggest that parents grieve the death of the child that they anticipated and they grieve the loss of dreams they had for their child. Depending on the disability, parents may need to alter their physical, emotional, or cognitive expectations of their child. For example, for children with significant mobility impairments, parents who wished to play sports with their children may initially grieve that perception of a future loss. In addition, parents may experience anger or look to place blame on hereditary causes in themselves or their partners. If poor nutrition, drug use, or other controllable factors are suspected to have contributed to the child's disability, such as in fetal alcohol syndrome, intense guilt and societal scorn may also result (Vash & Crewe, 2004).

In a study of parents of children with intellectual disabilities, Gallagher, Phillips, Oliver, and Carroll (2008) found parents to have high levels of anxiety and depression that were most influenced by the amount of caregiver burden and their feelings of guilt. Another study by Norton and Drew (1994) identified the family hardships associated with raising a child with autism as difficulty with communication and bonding, sleep disruption, behavior problems, a need for consistent routine, respite care and problems, and future financial planning needs. The inability to effectively communicate and the child's rejection of physical contact and a seemingly noncaring attitude toward the family create difficulty in parental bonding. The child's behavior and need for consistency make traveling outside the home difficult. Children may sleep for only a few hours at night, causing sleep deprivation for parents. In addition, any disruption in routine may lead to screaming outbursts and prolonged crying. Because of the constant caregiving demands, respite is important, particularly for the primary caregiver, and siblings may be called on to provide care that can either be seen as positive role modeling or, if used to excess, may have a negative impact.

In examining caregiving burdens of families with a member with intellectual and behavioral/psychiatric problems, Maes, Broekman, Dosen, and Nauts (2003) concluded:

> Psychiatric and behavioral problems are often incomprehensible and unpredictable, which causes the parents to feel dissatisfied, inadequate to cope, insecure and reticent to act. But feelings and motivations of parents on the other hand may also have profound effects on the behavioral difficulties of their child. Parents consider the psychiatric or behavioral problems of their child to be an extra burden and feel it more difficult to raise and manage such a child in the family situation. This forces them to change the situation and to call on the help of external services. (Maes et al., 2003, p. 454)

These authors conclude that families need more resources for respite, extended social support groups for emotional support specialized training, and recognition of negative feelings.

Not all parents react in the same way to having a child with a disability; whereas some report continued discomfort with their child, others find the child has strengthened their marriage and family life (Scorgie & Sobsey, 2000). In comparing differences in the mother's and father's reactions to a child with a disability, some studies have found that mothers react with greater depression, express greater caregiver burden, and feel higher levels of stress than fathers do. They spend more hours caring for the child with a disability than fathers do. However, Hastings (2003) found that stress and depression levels were similar in mothers and fathers of children with autism, but mothers exhibited higher levels of anxiety. In an additional study, Hastings and colleagues (2005) reported that despite race or ethnicity, mothers report experiencing both greater depression and greater positive effects from parenting a child with a disability than fathers do.

In addition to parents, grandparents are increasingly being called on to care for their grandchildren with disabilities. This is especially true for African American and Latino families. Grandparents may have unique problems associated with caregiving because, unless they are the legal guardians, they have more difficulty accessing services and information (such as medical and school records) necessary for caretaking. In addition, they may have financial concerns, they may have difficulties due to aging and a need for respite, they may have problems associated with the child's parents, particularly if they have exited their child's life due to addictions or legal problems, and, they may have problems navigating social service, judicial, and educational systems (McCallion, Janicki, Grant-Griffin, & Kolomer, 2000). It is not surprising that grandparents have also been found to be susceptible to depression in some studies, but results vary and this remains unclear. What may be the most important to determining the amount of stress and caregiver burden experienced by grandparents may be strongly impacted by their beliefs and attitudes related to disability (Neely-Barnes & Dia, 2008). Positive effects of caretaking a grandchild with a disability have been noted as creating better relationships and a greater sense of connectedness, meaning, and personal growth (Gardner, Scherman, Efthimiadis, & Shultz, 2004).

The Decision to Place a Child Outside of the Home

The decision to place a child with a disability outside of the home is difficult for many parents. Several studies have demonstrated that increased stress is related to the extent of behavior problems (Maes et al., 2003) that may in turn affect the family's decision to place the child in residential care. This decision generally occurs at birth and in the transition out of high school. In a study to examine outside placement decisions of parents of young adults with severe intellectual disability, McIntyre, Blacher, and Baker (2002) found that outside home placement could be predicted by the extent of behavior problems and mental health problems of the young adult.

When a Partner Has a Disability

Because most of the caregiving falls on the spouse, the impact of disability can be overwhelming for couples. Researchers have found that among couples in which one of the partners had a spinal cord injury (SCI), the caregiving partner had equal or higher levels of stress, fatigue, resentment, and anger when compared with the partner with the disability (Chan, Lee, & Lieh-Mak, 2000; Weitzenkamp, Gerhart, Charlifue, Whiteneck, & Savic, 1997). Parker (1989) reviewed the impact of disability on the partner's caregiver and concluded that they have higher levels of stress than any other caregiver due to the psychological and social effects of caring for their partner.

When a partner acquires a cognitive disability, such as traumatic brain injury (TBI), stroke, or Parkinson's, the caregiver loses the equitable relationship and assumes a parenting role for their spouse, and they often feel as if they have gained a child and lost a spouse. The spouse caregiver must take on many of the duties of the afflicted spouse and may need to assume all of the financial burden as well and is frequently forced to make difficult financial cuts that may involve liquidating assets. In order to provide sufficient care, the caregiver may need to reduce social time with friends and family, creating social isolation. Even if the caregiver finds time to socialize, socializing may be difficult because he or she will not fit well into either the couple's socializing world or the single world. Ultimately, the strain of caretaking, financial struggles, and social isolation may lead to a marital relationship that is void of sexual relations. For some, this overwhelming change in living conditions and relations leads to separation or divorce (Parker, 1989).

Multiple sclerosis (MS) is a progressive disorder that will involve increasing reliance on others for activities of daily living and social interactions. Hakim et al. (2000) identified a number of issues related to living with MS that could affect partner relationships, including the reduction of social interactions and a shrinking number of friends, particularly as the disease progresses. In addition, the partner with MS frequently retired early and many partners believed that their own careers were inhibited due to the spouse's illness. Partners also experienced higher levels of anxiety and depression associated with greater severity of MS. Even so, the authors did not find a greater incidence of divorce among couples with MS when compared with the general population.

For persons with SCI, the divorce rates are higher than the general population whether they marry before or after they are injured and the likelihood of marriage after injury is decreased (Brain and Spinal Cord.Org, 2010). Aside from the individual's adjustment to physical changes and pain, those in partner relationships will encounter a number of lifestyle changes that affect their relationships, such as changes to sexual intimacy, independence, raising children, job security, financial security, and recreational activity involvement. The emotional responses to these changes will also affect the relationship and may include depression and anxiety, suicide ideation (an initial suicide rate of four to five times that of the general population), and alcohol and drug abuse (Craig & Hancock, 1998). In a review of the literature on partner relationships and SCI, Kreuter (2000) found that divorce rates from 8% to 48% have been reported in the literature, depending on the time since injury for participants. In general, it appears that divorce rates are higher in the first 3 years and then decline to a normal rate. DeVivo and Richards (1992) noted a number of factors that put persons with SCI at greater risk for divorce, including being nonambulatory, being female, not having any children, being young, having a previous divorce, and having an injury less than 3 years old. In a study that interviewed 55 couples with preinjury or postinjury marriages, Crewe, Athelstan, and Krumberger (1979) and DeVivo, Hawkins, Richards, and Go (1995) found more stability and life satisfaction in postinjury marriages. Kreuter, Sullivan, and Siösteen (1994) studied marriage stability following SCI and found differences based on the age of the couple; older couples had greater emotional attachment or relationship satisfaction than younger couples.

Despite the negative public perception that persons who date people with disabilities are deviant or desperate (Olkin, 1999), in a qualitative study to examine females who were dating men with SCI, Milligan and Neufeldt (1998) found that maladaptive motivations were not present. They identified a number of factors related to the disability that influenced the development of the relationships. Nondisabled participants described their partners as well adjusted to their SCI and exhibiting autonomous attitudes. These elements in combination with individual personality traits were described as important features of their attraction. Attributes of the nondisabled female partners included open-mindedness about a relationship with a person with SCI, previous experiences with disability, role flexibility, acceptance of the partner's need for assistance, commitment to foster independence, and resiliency against social disapproval.

In relation to cognitive and mental health disabilities, studies have also shown high rates of divorce. Lefley (1989) identified problem behaviors in families of persons with severe mental illness, including persons with disabilities' abuse of family members, conflicts with neighbors, noncompliance with medications and other interventions, unpredictable reactions, and mood swings. Butterworth and Rodgers (2008) reported that a number of studies have demonstrated that divorce frequently follows the acquisition of mental illness in couples where one partner has a mental illness. Causes of marital termination have been attributed to relationship dissatisfaction, marital conflict, and social causes. In couples where both partners have a mental illness, divorce rates have been shown to be eight times that of the general population.

Studies related to couples in which one partner acquires a TBI have reported varying rates of divorce ranging from 15% to 54% and dependent on factors such as the length of the relationship preinjury and how much time has elapsed since the injury. In a study that examined 120 persons with TBI, people who were more likely to stay married had been in longer-term preinjury marital relationships, were older, had less severe TBI, and their injuries were not due to violent crimes (Kreutzer, Marwitz, Hsu, Williams, & Riddick, 2007).

When a Parent Has a Disability

Early speculation related to children being raised by persons with disabilities suggested that children were in danger of negative emotions and behaviors, such as anxiety and depression, and developmental issues, such as dependency, helplessness, overcompliance, social alienation, and isolation. However, empirical literature presents no definitive evidence of these negative parenting effects. Buck and Hohmann (1983) reported that children raised by a father with SCI showed no difference from other children in terms of physical health measures, personality disturbance, body image or sexual orientation, or in interpersonal relationships. The differences noted in male children were that they were more conventional, practical, and tough-minded, but less secure than other males. Female children were found to be more self-assured, imaginative, and unconventional, but were less tough-minded and realistic than other females. Coles, Pakenham, and Leech (2007) studied children of parents with MS and noted that often these children assume caregiving roles by cleaning, cooking, shopping, budgeting, and giving emotional support. Children with a parent who has MS have also been shown to have higher levels of anxiety dysphoria, somatization, interpersonal difficulties, and hostility and less satisfaction with life (Pakenham & Bursnall, 2006). The fact that positive and negative effects are present is to be expected because children who have parents with disabilities have different growing-up experiences and challenges. However, negative differences may be directly related to a lack of financial and social supports to alleviate overburdening children.

Parents with mental retardation (MR) face problems such as poverty, lack of parenting models, isolation from families, lack of public resources, and limited experiences. For these parents, providing adequate parenting depends on long-term support (Whitman & Accardo, 1993). Incidences of neglect and abuse are due to a lack of support and resources more than cognitive deficit (Tymchuk & Andron, 1990). In a study of children whose parent(s) had MR, two thirds were diagnosed with MR or developmental delays. Most of the delays were corrected with intervention, pointing to the need for additional resources and supports. In addition, a number of studies have demonstrated the need for and efficacy of parenting skills training for parents with MR (Feldman et al., 1992; Whitman & Accardo, 1993).

Parents with sensory impairments reported difficulty in assisting children with school work and a need to rely on children as interpreters (Strom, Daniels, & Jones, 1988), and hearing children of deaf adults (CODA) often grow up in the deaf culture, learning sign language and acting as interpreters for parents. These children grow up with distinct advantages, but can also feel caught between two worlds; they sometimes describe being raised as a deaf child (Malik & Jabeen, 2016).

When a Sibling Has a Disability

Depending on the age of the child, siblings may have a number of reactions to a sister or brother with a disability. Young children may experience some fear that they may catch the disability, or they may believe they are responsible in some way for the disability due to wishful or magical thinking (Batshaw, 1991), or they may feel jealous or embarrassed of their sibling, causing abusive behaviors (Havens, 2005; Pearson & Sternberg, 1986). Poor adjustment of siblings has been attributed to high levels of family conflict, poor parent functioning, low family adaptability and cohesion, and deficit problem-solving skills and communication.

In a study of 49 siblings, Giallo and Gavidia-Payne (2006) found that they had significantly higher overall adjustment difficulties, more emotional and peer problems, and lower levels of socialization compared with the normative sample. In order to investigate how family characteristics, family routines, and problem solving influence sibling adjustment, these authors determined that (a) sibling adjustment to disability was not significantly impacted by sibling level of daily stress and coping skills, (b) level of parent stress was a predictor of sibling adjustment, (c) siblings in households with regular and consistent family routines exhibited fewer adjustment problems, and (d) siblings had better adjustment in households that demonstrated great problem-solving strategies and more effective communication.

Research involving siblings has also described some positive benefits (Hannah & Midlarsky, 1985), but siblings are often expected to assume additional responsibilities, such as providing for the inclusion, socialization, and physical care of their sibling with a disability (Skrtic, Summers, Brotherson, & Turnbull, 1984; Swenson-Pierce, Kohl, & Egel, 1987). Parents of nondisabled siblings who can provide care and socialization may benefit from the additional assistance, but some studies have determined that nondisabled siblings may be given too much responsibility for their maturity level. Charles, Stainton, and Marshall (2009) discussed the negative impact for young caregivers as including the loss of their childhood and increased stress. However, siblings report both positive and negative effects related to caregiving. In a study of school-aged siblings' stressors, siblings identified being the most stressed when they felt embarrassed in the presence of their friends, they felt the happiest when they played with their sibling, and they felt the most uplifted when their sibling expressed affection through hugs and kisses (Orfus & Howe, 2008).

Most of the literature related to siblings of persons with disabilities focuses on the childhood relationships between the disabled and nondisabled siblings. However, as the person with a disability ages and parents become too old to care for their children, the sibling may be called on to provide extensive care. Although some persons with disabilities may move into group homes, the demand for residential care far exceeds availability and waiting lists for group homes may be prohibitively long.

CULTURAL IMPACT ON FAMILY ADAPTATION

For the purposes of this section, I briefly address culture in relation to family dynamics and responses. Although it is difficult to imagine how odd U.S. culture might seem to others, examination of documents intended to explain our culture to migrating persons highlights cultural differences in family behavior and practices.

- Americans will invite strangers (people they have never met) into their homes.
- Visitors to an American home might be allowed or even encouraged to see any room of the house. It is not unusual for people who visit a home in the winter to use the bed in the master bedroom as a place to deposit their coats.
- Some entertaining might take place in the kitchen. The kitchen is not the exclusive territory of the female of the house. Men might be seen helping in the kitchen, cooking and/or cleaning up. Men might even be seen wearing aprons.
- Children may get more attention than they would in some other countries. The children might be included in a social activity, particularly if the activity entails dinner. Children may take a fairly active role in the conversation, and may even get more attention than some of the adults.
- The host might have pets, usually dogs or cats, who live in the house along with the human inhabitants, and who may be permitted to enter any part of the house and use any item of furniture as a resting place.
- The social interaction might entail much mixing of the sexes. Although it sometimes happens that women will form their own conversation groups and men theirs, there is no rigid sexual segregation at American social gatherings.
- Although they will make certain accommodations for guests, particularly for guests at a formal gathering, Americans do not have the idea that their normal lives should be entirely devoted to guests during the time the guests are visiting them. Thus, if they have other obligations that conflict with hosting, they may turn their attentions to other commitments, such as providing transportation for young children who have obligations or answering a telephone call and engaging in an extended conversation (University of Missouri–St. Louis, 2013).

Disability is defined differently across cultures in terms of the meaning of experience, family values, and interaction with social systems. Understanding cultural differences in family function is essential to understanding the adjustment process as well as understanding the strengths of family systems. Living as a minority family in the United States differs from living in the majority culture in a number of ways identified by Sue and Sue (1999). Families must frequently deal with racism and there is a greater likelihood of living in poverty. Family values, although not in conflict with the majority values, place greater emphasis on family and less emphasis on the individual. Values and dreams related to wealth, occupation, and status may differ in their meaning to minorities. They are also likely to be transitioning into assimilation and juggling two cultures. They may have come from histories that include slavery, immigration, and refugee status, and may have been forced from their countries or made difficult decisions to leave. They may also be in the process of learning or using English, which may not be a good substitute for expression.

African Americans

The African American family differs in that it uses extended family members as primary caretakers, has great flexibility in family roles, is intensely religious, and has developed coping skills to stressors brought on by racism, poverty, and unemployment (Hines & Boyd-Franklin, 1982). In addition, African American families may face health care provider diagnostic bias in terms of delayed diagnoses and experience substantial differences in health care sought and received (Burkett, Morris, Manning-Courtney, Anthony, & Shambley-Ebron, 2015). In a study of disparities among AA and Caucasian children with autism spectrum disorder, Mandell, Ittenbach, Levy, and Pinto-Martin (2007) found AA children were more likely to be misdiagnosed than Caucasian children. They were five times more likely to be improperly diagnosed with adjustment disorder and two and a half times more likely to be misdiagnosed with conduct disorder. This suggests health care providers may have race-based preconceived notions when approaching assessment, which may result in critical delays of child development and treatment.

Alston and Turner (1994) examined African American family strengths, noting strong kinship bonds that include immediate, extended, and even fictive kin. They suggest that one reason African American families do not access rehabilitation services may be that they have the capacity to support a family member with a disability through the process of adjustment to the disability. Greater role flexibility is present in African American families for a number of reasons, including the fact that Black women frequently are in a head-of-household position by choice or because a disproportionate number of men in the Black community are incarcerated, unemployed, or living out of the home. When the mother is employed, extended family members or older children are enlisted to provide for childcare and household duties. Unlike families that adhere to rigid roles, the African American family has adapted to avoid overload through role flexibility. In the case of disability in the family, members may be accustomed to assuming a variety of family roles and duties.

In addition to role flexibility, studies have found that African American family caregivers find greater satisfaction and feel less anxious and less burdened than Caucasian caregivers. In a qualitative study of 22 Black family caregivers who were caring for relatives with dementia, Lindauer, Harvath, Berry, and Wros (2016) identified the two themes of *Hanging On* and *Changed but Still Here*. These themes illustrated the high value of caring for the family member as long as possible. One participant stated, "Way back when . . . even in the struggles, and slavery, all we had is each other. So that's why we hang on to each other" (p. 5). In the second theme, participants focused on what remained of their loved one's personality as opposed to dementia-related losses. Ancestral values were seen to influence the belief that no matter how changed a person, what remained was worthy of both compassion and respect.

Religious orientation has also been noted as a strength for African Americans because it offers spiritual inspiration, social support, and an opportunity for ventilation of distress and other emotions. The church is viewed as a further extension of the family that emphasized positive outlook and increased self-esteem. It also assists in providing for basic needs, such as shelter, food, clothing, childcare, and assistance in locating work (Alston & Turner, 1994). In a recent study, Chatters, Taylor, Woodward, and Nicklett (2015) examined the influence of attendance at religious services on depression and stress among Black participants. They found social support offered through church networks acted as a protective factor against psychological distress and depressive symptoms. Thus, religion appears to serve as both emotionally and physically assistive and as a protection against psychological impairment.

Other family strengths noted by Alston and Turner (1994) are education and work ethics. African Americans value education and encourage children to succeed academically because this is considered as one of the pathways to social and economic upward mobility. Unfortunately, this is all too often an uphill battle. In their examination of special education placement in elementary and middle schools, Morgan and colleagues (2015) found:

> Minority children were consistently less likely than otherwise similar White, English-speaking children to be identified as disabled and so to receive special

education services. From kindergarten entry to the end of middle school, racial- and ethnic-minority children were less likely to be identified as having (a) learning disabilities, (b) speech or language impairments, (c) intellectual disabilities, (d) health impairments, or (e) emotional disturbances. (p. 278)

Thus, similar to the health care system, disparities are evident early-on in educational institutions, which result in a lack of appropriate educational accommodation. If behavioral disturbances are misdiagnosed, focus may be misdirected to behavioral modification and discipline.

Alston and McCowan (1995) determined that African Americans who adjust well to disability have families that are close and supportive, have strong emotional support, and have members willing to assist with activities of daily living (ADL). These authors suggested that Black families are not easily disrupted by disability and can accommodate disability while maintaining stability, humor, and generosity. They also suggest that African American families benefit from a lack of traditionally defined roles and are able to redefine and reassign family roles as needed to meet the needs of the family. Interestingly, perhaps one of the obvious cultural differences is that conflict was not predictive of poor adjustment. Black families did not view the expression of family conflict as an obstacle to adjustment. Rather, the expression of disagreement and emotions was seen as natural and acceptable.

Asian Americans

Asian Americans are a homogeneous population whose relatives have descended from a number of geographic locations, including Cambodia, China, India, Japan, Korea, Malaysia, Pakistan, the Philippine Islands, Thailand, Vietnam, and the Asian/Pacific Islander population. The core values of Asian families are family, duty to family, family welfare, family reputation, harmony, education, wisdom, knowledge, humility, work, and self-sacrifice (Lynch & Hanson, 2004). The Chinese are highly interdependent and very willing to sacrifice for family members. They seek assistance within the family context first and find seeking government assistance is intimidating as it is frequently difficult to find translators when needed or desired (Liu, 2001).

Canfei is the traditional Chinese word for disability. Its interpretation is handicap and useless. Another common word used is *Canji*, which translates to handicap and illness (Liu, 2001). Significant differences exist in the Asian American outlook related to disability. Depending on the level of acculturation, Asian parents may view children with disabilities as shameful or humiliating and may believe that they are to blame for the disability.

In a study of Chinese families in New York, Ryan and Smith (1989) determined that language barriers caused almost half the parents not to understand their child's diagnosis. Parents were also inclined to view disability as a temporary condition and many exhibited reactions of denial, guilt, and only partial acceptance. Parents attributed disability to either natural, supernatural, or metaphysical causes. Supernatural causes resulted from a belief there had been a religious or ethical violation that caused a deity to become angry. One third of the parents surveyed believed in a metaphysical cause for their child's disability and attributed disability to a lack of balance between the Yin and Yang, considered essential for health. Imbalances were felt to produce fever and chills in children, which were seen as having the potential to lead to disability. These parents used alternative medicine that included incense to remove evil spirits, acupuncture, and wearing silver bracelets.

As the family becomes more acculturated, negative attitudes are replaced with attitudes of hope and acceptance (Cho, Singer, & Brenner, 2003). In a study of first-generation Chinese families with a child with a disability, Parette, Chuang, and Huer

(2004) noted that parents were involved, valued education, were concerned about social stigma, and did not express shame about their child's disability.

Latino Families

The Latino population of the United States has increased by 50% since 1990. Because of poor health care, exposure to violence, and work in settings that expose them to greater physical risks, disability is prevalent in Latino communities (World Institute on Disability, 2004). Although every culture and every family is different, and they come to the United States from a number of Central American and South American countries, some common themes are present in Latino families, including religion, family, and gender roles. Religion is important to community and family life and most Latinos practice Catholicism, but many also have additional beliefs that are related to their countries of origin. Many Latinos believe that things that happen in their lives are beyond their control and are meant to be; they also may engage in magical thinking and have a strong belief in miracles and the power of prayer. They may believe in positive or negative spirits that can cause difficulties or bad luck in their families and marriages (de Rios, 2001; Falicov, 1998).

For Latinos, the purpose of marriage is to have children and there is little separation between the two. Family is frequently the top priority and couples tend to include children in nearly all activities and outings. Extensive interaction with large and extended families is common, and extended family is frequently relied on for social, emotional, and financial support. Perhaps due to the high value placed on family interaction, Skinner, Bailey, Correa, and Rodriguez (1999) found that many of the 150 Latina mothers in their study believed that having a child with disabilities made them better mothers. Latino families with disabilities have long been credited with viewing disability as a punishment from God (Falicov, 1998; Vega, 1990), but in a study of Mexican and Mexican American beliefs about God in relation to disability, Graf and Blankenship (2007) found that only a small minority of Mexicans and Mexican Americans believed disability to be a punishment from God. This study, and others, point to the importance of reexamining cultural values over time.

In a recent study of Latino elders, Ruiz and Ransford (2012) cautioned that there has been a decline in the ability of Hispanic families to measure up to the traditional obligations, known as familismo. Hispanic families have previously relied on large extended family networks to dutifully provide care for their own. Ruiz and Ransford's study revealed family self-reliance "may no longer be attainable" (p. 56). Elders in this study reported infrequent family contact and experiencing hardships that went unnoticed by younger family members. It is essential that health professionals examine family circumstances without making cultural assumptions. "By perpetuating an over-romanticized notion [of familismo], communities may inadvertently be contributing to a shortage of formal support services for older Latinos" (p. 56; Carrillo, Trevino, Betancourt, & Coustasse, 2001).

Disability that affects gender roles may be particularly difficult for Latinos because gender roles tend to be traditional, with the male expected to be the financial provider, to be physically and emotionally strong, and to be a protective authority figure. Women are expected to provide for the children and elderly family members and to be self-sacrificing; they are in charge of the home and children, but are expected to defer to their husbands. Although these traditional roles have begun to change for many Latinos, these traditional beliefs and roles are the foundation for current practices and beliefs (Vega, 1990). In a recent study to examine the influence of gender on Spanish family caregiving, Casado-Mejía and Ruiz-Arias (2016) noted that males became caregivers if there was not an available female to meet this role. Women caregivers experienced greater strain than males, especially if they tried to maintain employment. Women were also less likely to receive outside help than males who became caregivers.

SUMMARY

Understanding the role of the family and how it functions to enhance or to detract from the lives of people with disability is imperative because this basic social unit can provide a lifetime of love, support, encouragement, and care. It is important to assess family needs and support services so that the family does not become overwhelmed or feel isolated in their endeavors to assist their loved one and to integrate into the larger community. This involves understanding numerous differences in family reactions and functioning based on the resilience of the family, who in the family has the disability, the extent of the disability, the resources available, and cultural beliefs and practices.

REFERENCES

Alston, R. J., & McCowan, C. J. (1995). Perception of family competence and adaptation to illness among African Americans with disabilities. *Journal of Rehabilitation, 67*(1), 27–32.

Alston, R. J., & Turner, W. L. (1994). A family strengths model of adjustment to disability for African American clients. *Journal of Counseling and Development, 72,* 378–383.

American Psychological Association. (2017). Who are family caregivers? Retrieved from http://www.apa.org/pi/about/publications/caregivers/faq/statistics.aspx

Anderegg, M. L., Vergason, G. A., & Smith, M. C. (1992). A visual representation of the grief cycle for use by teachers with families of children with disabilities. *Remedial and Special Education, 13,* 17–23.

Batshaw, M. L. (1991). *Your child has a disability: A complete sourcebook of daily and medical care.* Boston, MA: Little, Brown.

Baxter, C., Cummins, R. A., & Yiolitis, L. (2000). Parental stress attributed to family members with and without disability: A longitudinal study. *Journal of Intellectual & Developmental Disability, 25,* 105–118.

Blacher, J. (1984). Sequential stages of parental adjustment to the birth of a child with handicaps: Fact or artifact? *Mental Retardation, 22*(2), 55–68.

Bradley, V., Knoll, J., & Agosta, J. (1993). *Emerging issues in family support* (Monograph No. 18). Washington, DC: American Association on Mental Retardation.

Brain and Spinal Cord.Org. (2010). Spinal cord injury statistics. Retrieved from http://www.brainandspinalcord.org/spinal-cord-injury/statistics.htm

Buck, F., & Hohmann, G. (1983). Parental disability and children's adjustment. In E. Pan, T. Backer, & C. Vash (Eds.), *Annual review of rehabilitation* (pp. 203–241). New York, NY: Springer Publishing.

Burkett, K., Morris, E., Manning-Courtney, P., Anthony, J., & Shambley-Ebron, D. (2015). African American families on autism diagnosis and treatment: The influence of culture. *Journal of Autism and Developmental Disorders, 45*(10), 3244–3254.

Butterworth, P., & Rodgers, B. (2008). Mental health problems and marital disruption: Is it the combination of husbands and wives' mental health problems that predicts later divorce? *Social Psychiatry and Psychiatric Epidemiology, 43*(9), 758–763.

Carrillo, E., Trevino, F., Betancourt, J., & Coustasse, A. (2001). Latino access to health care: The role of insurance, managed care, and institutional barriers. In M. Aguirre-Molina, C. W. Molina, & R. E. Zambrana (Eds.), *Health issues in the Latino community* (pp. 55–74). San Francisco, CA: Jossey-Bass.

Casado-Mejía, R., & Ruiz-Arias, E. (2016). Influence of gender and care strategy in family caregivers' strain: A cross-sectional study. *Journal of Nursing Scholarship, 48*(6), 587–597.

Chan, R. C., Lee, P. W., & Lieh-Mak, F. (2000). Coping with spinal cord injury: Personal and marital adjustment in the Hong Kong Chinese setting. *Spinal Cord, 38*(11), 687–696.

Charles, G., Stainton, T., & Marshall, S. (2009). Young careers: Mature before their time. *Reclaiming Children & Youth, 18,* 38–41.

Chatters, L. M., Taylor, R. J., Woodward, A. T., & Nicklett, E. J. (2015). Social support from church and family members and depressive symptoms among older African Americans. *The American Journal of Geriatric Psychiatry, 23*(6), 559–567.

Cho, S.-J., Singer, G. H. S., & Brenner, B. M. (2003). A comparison of adaptation to childhood disability in Korean immigrant and Korean mothers. *Focus on Autism and Other Developmental Disabilities, 18*(1), 9–19.

Coles, A. R., Pakenham, K. I., & Leech, C. (2007). Evaluation of an intensive psychosocial intervention for children of parents with multiple sclerosis. *Rehabilitation Psychology, 52*, 133–142.

Craig, A., & Hancock, K. (1998). Living with spinal cord injury: Longitudinal factors, interventions and outcomes. *Clinical Psychology and Psychotherapy, 5*, 102–108.

Crewe, N. M., Athelstan, G. T., & Krumberger, J. (1979). Spinal cord injury: A comparison of preinjury and postinjury marriages. *Archives of Physical Medicine and Rehabilitation, 60*(6), 252–256.

Degeneffe, C. E., & Lynch, R. T. (2006). Correlates of depression in adult siblings of persons with traumatic brain injury. *Rehabilitation Counseling Bulletin, 49*, 130–142.

de Rios, M. D. (2001). *Brief psychotherapy with the Latino immigrant client*. New York, NY: Haworth Press.

DeVivo, M. J., Hawkins, L. N., Richards, J. S., & Go, B. K. (1995). Outcomes of post-spinal cord injury marriages. *Archives of Physical Medicine and Rehabilitation, 76*(2), 130–138.

DeVivo, M. J., & Richards, J. S. (1992). Community reintegration and quality of life following spinal cord injury. *Paraplegia, 30*(2), 108–112.

Dogson, J. E., Garwick, A., Blozis, S. A., Patterson, J. M., Bennett, F. C., & Blum, R. W. (2000). Uncertainty in childhood chronic conditions and family distress in families of young children. *Journal of Family Nursing, 6*, 252–266.

Esdaile, S. A. (2009). Valuing difference: Caregiving by mothers of children with disabilities. *Occupational Therapy International, 16*(2), 122–133.

Falicov, C. J. (1998). *Latino families in therapy*. New York, NY: Guilford Press.

Falvo, D. (2005). *Medical and psychosocial aspects of chronic illness and disability*. Sudbury, MA: Jones & Barlett.

Feldman, M. A., Case, L., Garrick, M., MacIntyre-Grande, W., Carnwell, J., & Sparks, B. (1992). Teaching child-care skills to mothers with developmental disabilities. *Journal of Applied Behavior Analysis, 25*(1), 205–215.

Ferguson, P. M. (2002). A place in the family: An historical interpretation of research on parental reactions to having a child with a disability. *Journal of Special Education, 36*, 124–130.

Frain, M. P., Lee, G. K., Berven, N. L., Tansey, T., Tschopp, M., & Chronister, J. (2007). Effective use of the resiliency model of family adjustment for rehabilitation counselors. *Journal of Rehabilitation, 73*(3), 18–25.

Gallagher, S., Phillips, A. C., Oliver, C., & Carroll, D. (2008). Predictors of psychological morbidity in parents of children with intellectual disabilities. *Journal of Pediatric Psychology, 33*(10), 1129–1136.

Gardner, J. E., Scherman, A., Efthimiadis, M. S., & Shultz, S. K. (2004). Panamanian grandmothers' family relationships and adjustment to having a grandchild with a disability. *International Journal of Aging & Human Development, 59*(4), 305–320.

Giallo, R., & Gavidia-Payne, S. (2006). Child, parent and family factors as predictors of adjustment for siblings of children with a disability. *Journal of Intellectual Disability Research, 50*(Pt 12), 937–948.

Graf, N. M., & Blankenship, C. B. (2007). Mexican and Mexican Americans' beliefs about God in relation to disability. *Journal of Rehabilitation, 73*(4), 41–50.

Hakim, E. A., Bakheit, A. M., Bryant, T. N., Roberts, M. W., McIntosh-Michaelis, S. A., Spackman, A. J., … McLellan, D. L. (2000). The social impact of multiple sclerosis—A study of 305 patients and their relatives. *Disability and Rehabilitation, 22*(6), 288–293.

Hannah, M. E., & Midlarsky, E. (1985). Siblings of the handicapped: A literature review for school psychologists. *School Psychology Review, 14*, 510–520.

Hastings, R. P. (2003). Child behaviour problems and partner mental health as correlates of stress in mothers and fathers of children with autism. *Journal of Intellectual Disability Research, 47*(Pt 4–5), 231–237.

Hastings, R. P., Kovshoff, H., Ward, N. J., degli Espinosa, F., Brown, T., & Remington, B. (2005). Systems analysis of stress and positive perceptions in mothers and fathers of pre-school children with autism. *Journal of Autism and Developmental Disorders, 35*(5), 635–644.

Havens, C. A. (2005). Becoming a resilient family: Child disability and the family system. *Access Today, 17*(5).

Hines, P. M., & Boyd-Franklin, N. (1982). Black families. In M. McGoldrick, J. Pearce, & J. Giordano (Eds.), *Ethnicity and family therapy* (pp. 84–107). New York, NY: Guilford Press.

Hodapp, R. M., & Krasner, D. V. (1995). Families of children with disabilities: Findings from a national sample of eighth-grade students. *Exceptionality, 5*, 71–81.

Kendall, E., & Buys, N. (1998). An integrated model of psychosocial adjustment following acquired disability. *Journal of Rehabilitation, 64*, 16–20.

Knestrict, T., & Kuchey, D. (2009). Welcome to Holland: Characteristics of resilient families raising children with severe disabilities. *Journal of Family Studies, 15,* 227–244.

Kosciulek, J. (1994). Dimensions of family coping with head injury. *Rehabilitation Counseling Bulletin, 37,* 244–257.

Kreuter, M. (2000). Spinal cord injury and partner relationships. *Spinal Cord, 38*(1), 2–6.

Kreuter, M., Sullivan, M., & Siösteen, A. (1994). Sexual adjustment after spinal cord injury—comparison of partner experiences in pre- and postinjury relationships. *Paraplegia, 32*(11), 759–770.

Kreutzer, J. S., Marwitz, J. H., Hsu, N., Williams, K., & Riddick, A. (2007). Marital stability after brain injury: An investigation and analysis. *NeuroRehabilitation, 22*(1), 53–59.

Lavin, J. L. (2001). *Special kids need special parents: A resource for parents of children with special needs.* New York, NY: Berkley Publishing.

Lefley, H. P. (1989). Family burden and family stigma in major mental illness. *American Psychologist, 44*(3), 556–560.

Lin, P. L. (1994). *Characteristics of a healthy family.* United States Department of Education. Retrieved from http://www.eric.ed.gov/PDFS/ED377097.pdf

Lindauer, A., Harvath, T. A., Berry, P. H., & Wros, P. (2016). The meanings African American caregivers ascribe to dementia-related changes: The paradox of hanging on to loss. *The Gerontologist, 56*(4), 733–742.

Liu, G. Z. (2001). Chinese culture and disability: Information for U.S. service providers. Retrieved from http://cirrie.buffalo.edu/culture/monographs/china.php

Livneh, H., & Antonak, R. F. (1990). Reactions to disability: An empirical investigation of their nature and structure. *Journal of Applied Rehabilitation Counseling, 21,* 13–21.

Lustig, D. (1997). Families with an adult with mental retardation: Empirical family typologies. *Rehabilitation Counseling Bulletin, 41,* 138–156.

Lynch, E. W., & Hanson, M. J. (2004). *Developing cross cultural competence.* Baltimore, MD: Paul H. Brookes.

Lyons, A., Leon, S., Roecker Phelps, C., & Dunleavy, A. (2010). The impact of child symptom severity on stress among parents of children with ASD: The moderating role of coping styles. *Journal of Child & Family Studies, 10,* 516–524.

Maes, B., Broekman, T. G., Dosen, A., & Nauts, J. (2003). Caregiving burden of families looking after persons with intellectual disability and behavioural or psychiatric problems. *Journal of Intellectual Disability Research, 47*(Pt 6), 447–455.

Malik, S., & Jabeen, T. (2016). Role playing and extraversion in hearing children of deaf parents. *Science International, 28*(3), 2915–2919.

Mandell, D. S., Ittenbach, R. F., Levy, S. E., & Pinto-Martin, J. A. (2007). Disparities in diagnoses received prior to a diagnosis of autism spectrum disorder. *Journal of Autism and Developmental Disorders, 37*(9), 1795–1802.

Martin, S. S., Brady, M. P., & Kotarba, J. A. (1992). Families with chronically ill young children: The unsinkable family. *Remedial and Special Education, 13,* 6–15.

McCallion, P., Janicki, M. P., Grant-Griffin, L., & Kolomer, S. (2000). Grandparent careers II: Service needs and service provision issues. *Journal of Gerontological Social Work, 33,* 57–84.

McCubbin, H. I., & McCubbin, M. A. (1988). Typologies of resilient families: Emerging roles of social class and ethnicity. *Family Relations, 37,* 247–254.

McCubbin, H. I., & Patterson, J. M. (1983). Family transitions: Adaptation to stress. In H. I. McCubbin & C. R. Figley (Eds.), *Stress and the family: Coping with normative transitions* (Vol. 2, pp. 5–25). New York, NY: Brunner/Mazel.

McCubbin, H. I., Thompson, A. I., & McCubbin, M. (1996). *Family assessment: Resiliency, coping, and adaptation.* Madison: University of Wisconsin System.

McCubbin, M. A., & McCubbin, H. I. (1993). Family coping with health crises: The resiliency model of family stress, adjustment and adaptation. In C. Danielson, B. Hamel-Bissell, & P. Winstead-Fry (Eds.), *Families; health, and illness* (pp. 21–64). New York, NY: Mosby.

McIntyre, L. L., Blacher, J., & Baker, B. L. (2002). Behaviour/mental health problems in young adults with intellectual disability: The impact on families. *Journal of Intellectual Disability Research, 46*(Pt 3), 239–249.

Mcleod, J. D., & Shanahan, M. J. (1996). Trajectories of poverty and children's mental health. *Journal of Health and Social Behavior, 37*(3), 207–220.

Milligan, M. S., & Neufeldt, A. H. (1998). Postinjury marriage to men with spinal cord injury: Women's perspectives on making a commitment. *Sexuality & Disability, 16,* 117–132.

Morgan, P. L., Farkas, G., Hillemeier, M. M., Mattison, R., Maczugla, S., Lil, H., & Cook, M. (2015). Minorities are disproportionately underrepresented in special education: Longitudinal evidence across five disability conditions. *Educational Researcher, 44,* 278–292.

220 *The Psychological and Social Impact of Illness and Disability*

Naseef, R. A. (2001). *Special children, challenged parents: The struggles and rewards of raising a child with a disability (Revised Edition).* Baltimore, MD: Paul H. Brooks.

Neely-Barnes, S. L., & Dia, D. A. (2008). Families of children with disabilities: A review of literature and recommendations for interventions. *Journal of Early and Intensive Behavior Intervention, 5*(3), 93–107.

Norton, P., & Drew, C. (1994). Autism and potential family stressors. *American Journal of Family Therapy, 22,* 67–76.

Olkin, R. (1999). *What psychotherapists should know about disability.* New York, NY: Guilford Press.

Olshansky, S. (1962). Chronic sorrow: A response to having a mentally defective child. *Social Casework, 43,* 190–193.

Orfus, M., & Howe, N. (2008). Stress appraisal and coping in siblings of children with special needs. *Exceptionality Education International, 18,* 166–181.

Pakenham, K. I., & Bursnall, S. (2006). Relations between social support, appraisal and coping and both positive and negative outcomes for children of a parent with multiple sclerosis and comparisons with children of healthy parents. *Clinical Rehabilitation, 20*(8), 709–723.

Palisano, R. J., Almarsi, N., Chiarello, L. A., Orlin, M. N., Bagley, A., & Maggs, J. (2010). Family needs of parents of children and youth with cerebral palsy. *Child: Care, Health and Development, 36*(1), 85–92.

Parette, P., Chuang, S. L., & Huer, M. B. (2004). First-generation Chinese American families' attitudes regarding disabilities and educational interventions. *Focus on Autism and Other Developmental Disabilities, 19,* 114–123.

Park, J., Hoffman, L., Marquis, J., Turnbull, A. P., Poston, D., Mannan, H., ... Nelson, L. L. (2003). Toward assessing family outcomes of service delivery: Validation of a family quality of life survey. *Journal of Intellectual Disability Research, 47*(Pt 4–5), 367–384.

Parker, G. (1989). Spouse carers—Whose quality of life? In S. M. Baldwin, C. Godfrey, & C. Propper (Eds.), *Quality of life: Perspectives and policies* (pp. 120–130). London, UK: Routledge and Kegan Paul.

Pearson, J. E., & Sternberg, A. (1986). A mutual-help project for families of handicapped children. *Journal of Counseling and Development, 65,* 213–215.

Power, P. W., & Dell Orto, A. E. (2004). *Families living with chronic illness and disability.* New York, NY: Springer Publishing.

Ruiz, M. E., & Ransford, H. E. (2012). Latino elders reframing familismo: Implications for health and caregiving support. *Journal of Cultural Diversity, 19*(2), 50–57.

Ryan, A. S., & Smith, M. J. (1989). Parental reactions to developmental disabilities in Chinese American families. *Child and Adolescent Social Work, 6,* 283–299.

Scorgie, K., & Sobsey, D. (2000). Transformational outcomes associated with parenting children who have disabilities. *Mental Retardation, 38*(3), 195–206.

Singer, L., & Farkas, K. J. (1989). The impact of infant disability on maternal perception of stress. *Family Relations, 38,* 444–449.

Skinner, D., Bailey, D. B., Correa, V., & Rodriguez, P. (1999). Narrating self and disability: Latino mothers' construction of identities vis-a-vis their child with special needs. *Exceptional Children, 65,* 481–495.

Skrtic, T. M., Summers, J. A., Brotherson, M. J., & Turnbull, A. P. (1984). Severely handicapped children and their brothers and sisters. In J. Blancher (Ed.), *Severely handicapped young children and their families: Research in review* (pp. 215–246). New York, NY: Academic Press.

Sloper, P., & Turner, S. (1992). Service needs of families of children with severe physical disability. *Child: Care, Health and Development, 18*(5), 259–282.

Snow, K. (2001). *Disability is natural.* Woodland Park, CO: Brave Heart Press.

Strom, R., Daniels, S., & Jones, E. (1988). Parent education for deaf families. *Educational and Psychological Research, 8*(2), 117–128.

Sue, D. W., & Sue, D. (1999). *Counseling the culturally different: Theory and practice.* New York, NY: John Wiley.

Swenson-Pierce, A., Kohl, F. L., & Egel, A. L. (1987). Siblings as home trainers: A strategy for teaching domestic skills to children. *Journal of the Association for Persons With Severe Handicaps, 12,* 53–60.

Taanila, A., Kokkonen, J., & Järvelin, M. R. (1996). The long-term effects of children's early-onset disability on marital relationships. *Developmental Medicine and Child Neurology, 38*(7), 567–577.

Taanila, A., Syrjälä, L., Kokkonen, J., & Järvelin, M. R. (2002). Coping of parents with physically and/or intellectually disabled children. *Child: Care, Health and Development, 28*(1), 73–86.

Tomasello, N. M., Manning, A. R., & Dulmus, C. N. (2010). Family-centered early intervention for infants and toddlers with disabilities. *Journal of Family Social Work, 13,* 163–172.

Tymchuk, A. J., & Andron, L. (1990). Mothers with mental retardation who do or do not abuse or neglect their children. *Child Abuse & Neglect, 14*(3), 313–323.

University of Missouri–St. Louis. (2013). Key American values. Retrieved from http://www.umsl.edu/~intelstu/Admitted%20Students/Visitor%20Handbook/keyvalues.html

U.S. Census Bureau. (2000). *Census 2000 profiles of general demographic characteristics, United States.* Retrieved from http://www.census.gov/prod/cen2000/doc/ProfilesTD.pdf

U.S. Census Bureau. (2010). Americans with disabilities: 2010. Retrieved from https://www.census.gov/people/disability/publications/sipp2010.html

Vash, C. L., & Crewe, N. M. (2004). *Psychology of disability.* New York, NY: Springer Publishing.

Vega, W. A. (1990). Hispanic families in the 1980s: A decade of research. *Journal of Marriage and the Family, 52*, 1015–1024.

Walker, D. K., Epstein, S. G., Taylor, A. B., Crocker, A. C., & Tuttle, G. A. (1989). Perceived needs of families with children who have chronic health conditions. *Children's Health Care, 18*(4), 196–201.

Wallander, J. L., & Noojin, A. B. (1995). Mothers' report of stressful experiences related to having a child with a physical disability. *Children's Health Care, 24*, 245–256.

Walsh, F. (2003). Family resilience: A framework for clinical practice. *Family Process, 42*(1), 1–18.

Warfield, M. E. (2005). Family and work predictors of parenting role stress among two-earner families of children with disabilities. *Infant & Child Development, 14*, 155–176.

Weitzenkamp, D. A., Gerhart, K. A., Charlifue, S. W., Whiteneck, G. G., & Savic, G. (1997). Spouses of spinal cord injury survivors: The added impact of caregiving. *Archives of Physical Medicine and Rehabilitation, 78*(8), 822–827.

Whitman, Y. B., & Accardo, J. P. (1993). The parent with mental retardation: Rights, responsibilities and issues. *Journal of Social Work and Human Sexuality, 8*, 123–136.

Witt, W. P., Riley, A. W., & Coiro, M. J. (2003). Childhood functional status, family stressors, and psychosocial adjustment among school-aged children with disabilities in the United States. *Archives of Pediatrics & Adolescent Medicine, 157*(7), 687–695.

Wolfensberger, W. (1983). *Normalization based guidance, education and supports for families of handicapped people.* Downsview, Canada: National Institute on Mental Retardation.

World Institute on Disability. (2004). Reaching the Latino disability community. Retrieved from http://www.wid.org/programs/access-to-assets/equity/equity-e-newsletter-june-2004/reaching-the-latino-disability-community

Yau, M. K., & LiTsang, C. W. (1999). Adjustment and adaptation in parents of children with developmental disability in two parent families: A review of the characteristics and attributes. *British Journal of Developmental Disability, 45*(1), 38–51.

Zarit, S. H., Reever, K. E., & Bach-Peterson, J. (1980). Relatives of the impaired elderly: Correlates of feelings of burden. *The Gerontologist, 20*(6), 649–655.

13

Giving Parents a Voice: A Qualitative Study of the Challenges Experienced by Parents of Children With Disabilities*

J. Aaron Resch, Gerardo Mireles, Michael R. Benz, Cheryl Grenwelge, Rick Peterson, and Dalun Zhang

*N*o other single individual or health care provider has more influence on the personal health and wellness of a child with a disability than the parent (Elliott & Mullins, 2004). Parents, however, can face significant challenges because of their parenting responsibilities and the difficulties they encounter when interacting with an often unreceptive environment. Consequently, parents can be at increased risk for excessive levels of personal distress, which in turn can adversely affect the well-being of the child and the entire family unit (Plant & Sanders, 2007). This is disconcerting because the informal family caregiver provides an invaluable and irreplaceable service to society. For example, it has been estimated that the cost savings to the health care system from the informal caregiver's economic contribution amount to $196 billion annually (based on the value of the caregiver's services as of 1997; Arno, Levine, & Memmott, 1999); this figure easily exceeds the annual national spending on home health care and nursing home care (Navaie-Waliser et al., 2002).

The health and well-being of informal caregivers, such as parents, raising a child with a disability, has become a public health priority (Talley & Crews, 2007) and, given the goals of policy initiatives such as *Healthy People 2010* (U.S. Department of Health and Human Services, 2000), providing support for families has become increasingly important. Consequently, understanding the experience of parents, including what factors influence their well-being, is essential for the development of meaningful and effective interventions, services, and supports, and this is an area of inquiry that merits further investigation (Raina et al., 2005). Legislation initiatives, such as The Family Caregiver Support Act of 2001, not only encourage expanded services and assistance for

*Giving parents a voice: A qualitative study of the challenges experienced by parents of children with disabilities, *Rehabilitation Psychology*, 2010, 55(2), 139–150. © 2010 American Psychological Association. Reproduced with permission. This material was based on the work supported by a grant from the Administration on Developmental Disabilities, U.S. Department of Health and Human Services. The authors would like to give a special thanks to Mary Jane Williams, Laura Buckner, and Jill Dietrich at Family to Family in Houston, Texas, for their assistance with this study.

informal caregivers, but they also provide grants for research initiatives that specifically address caregiver well-being (Donelan et al., 2002). Psychologists, in particular, possess unique expertise that can positively contribute to the investigations and interventions into caregiver well-being, and the American Psychological Association President Carol D. Goodheart has made caregiver issues one of her top priorities (Chamberlin, 2009). Clearly, this is a topic that is beginning to receive more attention, and the extant literature suggests the issues related to caregiver well-being are receiving more scrutiny.

PARENTAL WELL-BEING

For virtually all parents, caring for a child is an experience full of triumphs and joy, as well as challenges and stress. The experiences of parents of children with disabilities are likely similar in many ways to the experiences of parents of children without disabilities, but there are some important distinctions that can cause parents of children with disabilities to be at increased risk for psychosocial distress (Parish, Rose, Grinstein-Weiss, Richman, & Andrews, 2008; Plant & Sanders, 2007). The parenting responsibilities for parents of children with disabilities often require a significant amount of time to complete, can be physically demanding, can disrupt family and social relationships, and can adversely affect caregiver employment (Brannan & Heflinger, 2006; Seltzer & Heller, 1997). Perhaps as a consequence of these additional impacts, family caregivers of children with disabilities can be at increased risk to experience depression, physical health problems, and decreased quality of life (Feldman et al., 2007; Ones, Yilmaz, Cetinkaya, & Caglar, 2005). The added challenges of caring for a child with a disability may lead to more stress and greater physical and emotional health risks for parents and their families (e.g., increased conflict with spouse; Murphy, Christian, Caplin, & Young, 2007) compared to families without a child with a disability (Feldman et al., 2007). Exacerbating all of these problems is the fact that parents of children with disabilities are less likely than other parents to practice preventive health behaviors (Navaie-Waliser et al., 2002).

Much of the previous research in the area of parent caregiver well-being has focused on challenges caused by specific caregiving tasks, the child's behavior, and the severity of the child's disability (e.g., Brannan & Heflinger, 2006; Plant & Sanders, 2007). Although these variables are important, the assumption that parent distress is primarily a result of these factors likely fails to capture the entire parent perspective. Indeed, the construct of caregiver burden ("the perception that the caregiving situation exceeds the caregiver's resources"; Chwalisz, 1992, p. 189) may more accurately capture the experiences of parents. Hence, greater attention should be given to limitations caused by environmental restrictions (Lollar, 2008). To this end, researchers (e.g., Beckman, 2002; Worcester, Nesman, Raffaele Mendez, & Keller, 2008) have suggested Bronfenbrenner's (1986) ecological framework model as an effective way to conceptualize the factors that can influence parental well-being. This model is particularly helpful in illustrating that parental well-being is influenced by myriad systemic factors. Thus, a parent's well-being is affected not only by the specific parenting tasks or child behaviors, but also by the person–environment interaction. Similar to Bronfenbrenner's model, the stress process model has been suggested as a way to further understand these complex interactions (Gaugler, Kane, & Langlois, 2000). According to this model, the parent's appraisal of a stressor as a problem combined with a lack of resources to effectively deal with the stressor will lead to maladaptive outcomes. These theories suggest that the challenges parents face are often associated with a lack of environmental receptivity. Consequently, this lack of match between parent needs and environmental support may lead to the perception among parents that their situation has exceeded their personal resources, which in turn could lead to a feeling of being burdened and overwhelmed.

Extant literature has identified areas in which there may be a mismatch between parent needs and environmental supports. One area of potential mismatch is access to accurate and helpful information, resources, and services for parent caregivers and their families. The information and resources parents need to access can be related to the needs of their child with a disability (e.g., medical care or daily living supports) or to the needs of themselves and their families (e.g., respite care or support for siblings; Chan & Sigafoos, 2001; Donelan et al., 2002; Fisman, Wolf, Ellison, & Freeman, 2000). Studies have found that obtaining accurate and useful information is a major problem encountered by parents of children with disabilities (Freedman & Boyer, 2000; Worcester et al., 2008) and their quality of life is "highly dependent on the acquisition and maintenance of necessary support services" (McCarthy & Stough, 1999, p. 485). Financial hardships may be another important factor that influences parental well-being. In general, families with children with disabilities experience much higher expenditures than other families. Newacheck and Kim (2005) found that, on average, the total annual health care expenditures for children with disabilities were more than three times as much compared to children without disabilities. Further exacerbating these monetary challenges is the finding that children with disabilities are significantly more likely to live in families considered to be poor (Parish et al., 2008). The financial strain incurred by families of children with disabilities is likely due to increased expenses related to the child's needs as well as loss of employment or inability to work because of parenting responsibilities (Murphy et al., 2007; Parish et al., 2008; Worcester et al., 2008). Inability to engage in employment can also lead to feelings of isolation, a lack of fulfillment, and low self-esteem (Shearn & Todd, 2000). Families of children with disabilities often report feeling isolated from the community (Freedman & Boyer, 2000; Worcester et al., 2008).

PURPOSE OF THE STUDY

Because parents provide such an important service to their families and to society it is vital that their experience is fully understood. To date, however, much research concerned with the well-being of parents of children with disabilities has not captured their experiences from the perspective of the parents themselves (Shewchuk & Elliott, 2000). A somewhat underused method of obtaining a rich understanding of parents' experiences is through qualitative methodology. Qualitative methods permit researchers to study selected issues in depth, and they produce a wealth of detailed information that increases understanding of the cases and situations studied (Patton, 1990). However, qualitative data-collection techniques are seldom used to investigate areas related to the well-being of parents of children with disabilities. For example, in a review of rehabilitation literature, Chwalisz, Shah, and Hand (2008) found that only 4% of qualitative studies investigated issues related to caregivers, such as parents of children with disabilities, and nearly all of those were published in international journals.

The purpose of this study was to identify specific sources of challenges related to raising a child with a disability as expressed by parents themselves. Specifically, we investigated the following research questions: (a) What are the principal stressors and challenges for parents of children with disabilities? and (b) What supports and services do parents identify as being needed to deal with the stress and challenges of their responsibilities?

METHODS

Data were collected from parents of children with disabilities using focus groups. Focus groups draw on three fundamental strengths of qualitative methods: (a) exploration and discovery, (b) context and depth, and (c) interpretation (Morgan, 1998). Focus groups were particularly useful for this study because they created "concentrated conversations that might never occur in the real world" and allowed us to obtain rich information about the parents' experiences (Morgan, 1998, p. 31).

Participants

Seven communities across a southwestern state in the United States were chosen as sites for focus group meetings. We used purposive sampling procedures (Patton, 1990) with the intention of creating a geographically (across the state), economically, racially, and culturally diverse sample. The locations for the focus groups were in both urban and rural areas. A statewide nonprofit parent organization was consulted to identify possible participants at each location. The parent organization was created by parents to offer information and resources, mentoring, and support to families of children with all types of physical and developmental disabilities. Potential participants were then contacted and were asked to participate in the study. This collaboration with the parent organization was particularly ideal for this study as it was created by parents for families of children with disabilities, chronic illness, and other special needs throughout the state. Additionally, the parent organization leaders took part in the study by cofacilitating each focus group discussion.

The focus group participants represented a variety of ethnic and cultural groups. Parents in the focus groups were primary care providers to children with various types of disabilities, but primarily children with physical, developmental, or intellectual disabilities. A total of 40 parents participated in the study. Table 13.1 provides a summary of the demographic characteristics of the sample.

Procedures

Each focus group lasted approximately 2 hours and was held between 9:00 a.m. and 2:30 p.m. Mileage reimbursement and a $100 stipend was provided to each participant. Six of the focus groups were conducted in English, and one was conducted in Spanish. At each focus group, interpretation of the focus group discussion was provided to participants that did not speak English. The focus group facilitators ensured that all individuals had an adequate opportunity to participate and respond to questions.

At each focus group all participants were asked the same questions that were derived from a written interview guide, but the moderator was allowed flexibility in responding to any concerns and asking follow-up questions and prompts. Questions were constructed by the authors following a review of the literature and they were finalized based on input from representatives of the state parent organization that collaborated with the study. Protocol questions were created to elicit (a) participants' perceptions of the biggest stressors and challenges for parents of children with disabilities and (b) the supports and services identified by parents as being needed to deal with perceived stress and challenges.

Each focus group was conducted by three project staff, with each team member serving as a cofacilitator or note taker. The first two authors were present at each focus group to ensure consistency of data collection procedures. Ethical guidelines regarding human subject research were adhered to, and this project was reviewed and approved by the institutional review board at the authors' university.

TABLE 13.1 DEMOGRAPHIC CHARACTERISTICS OF PARTICIPANTS

Demographic Characteristics	*n* (40)	Percentage
Gender		
Male	4	10.0
Female	36	90.0
Ethnicity		
Anglo	22	55.0
Hispanic	11	27.5
African American	4	10.0
Native American	2	5.0
Other	1	2.5
Education level of participant		
College graduate	18	45.0
Some college	16	40.0
High school	3	7.5
Less than high school	3	7.5
Income level of family		
< $25,000	10	25.0
$25,001–$50,000	9	22.5
$50,001–$80,000	11	27.5
$80,001–$150,000	10	25.0
Size of participant community		
Urban	15	37.5
Rural	13	32.5
Suburban	11	27.5
Unknown	1	2.5
Student's primary disability		
Autism	8	20.0
Mental disability	6	15.0
Physical impairment	5	12.5
Down syndrome	4	10.0
Communication disability	2	5.0
Muscular dystrophy	2	5.0
Pervasive developmental disorder	2	5.0
Other	11[a]	27.5
Student's primary classroom setting		
Regular classroom	17	42.5
Self-contained classroom	18	45.0
School for special needs students	1	2.5
Home school	1	2.5
NA (child no longer in school)	3	7.5

Note: Identification of a student's primary disability was provided by the parental participant.

[a] The other category includes various disabilities with only one response.

Data Analysis

Each focus group was audio recorded for later transcription. Transcripts were then entered into QSR NVivo 7 (Richards & Richards, 2006), a qualitative coding software program, to facilitate data analysis. Data were analyzed using an iterative content analysis process of data reduction, data display, and conclusion drawing/verification recommended by Miles and Huberman (1994). The data from each focus group were coded by a team of three coders. To ensure credibility and reliability, a check-coding procedure (Miles & Huberman, 1994) was used whereby each transcript was coded by a primary and secondary coder. When a consensus on how to code a particular response could not be reached by the first two coders, a third coder was used to help reach a decision.

A multilayered coding process for analyzing the data was implemented wherein the researchers developed an initial list of codes (primary codes) that were structured by the interview guide as well as relevant literature. The initial codes were subsequently categorized into superordinate (or second level) codes through an intentional process of data reduction (Miles & Huberman, 1994). The second-level codes allowed for the examination of broad thematic constructs of interest that emerged through the coding process. A theme is commonly defined as a "statement of meaning that runs through all or most of the pertinent data" (Ely, 1991, p. 150).

Validation of Results

Using QSR NVivo 7 (Richards & Richards, 2006) a series of reports were produced from the first- and second-level codes in order to (a) identify themes within focus groups and (b) compare themes across groups. The veracity of the themes was then measured through a cross-site validation process where each superordinate theme was verified across each focus group (Miles & Huberman, 1994). This process allowed us to assess the strength of each identified theme.

A member-check technique is often used when examining qualitative data to achieve credible results (Yanow & Schwartz-Shea, 2006). To examine the validity of the study's findings, a preliminary copy of this manuscript was sent to the three parent representatives of the statewide nonprofit parent organization that participated in conducting the focus groups. These three parent representatives participated in a semi-structured interview through a phone conference with members of the research team. During the member-checking process, the participants were asked whether (a) the results, interpretations, and conclusions in this manuscript accurately represented the experiences shared by the focus group participants; (b) the identified themes were representative of the challenges and experiences of the larger population of parents of children with disabilities in the state with whom they work; (c) the study appropriately portrayed the positive experiences involved when raising a child with a disability; and (d) the concept of person–environment match (i.e., degree of match between parent needs and the resources and supports in the community to meet those needs) was an appropriate explanation for the relationship between the study's key themes and varying levels of parent distress or well-being as expressed by the participants in the study.

The three parent representatives confirmed that the themes accurately captured the experiences of the focus group participants and were illustrative of the challenges experienced by other parent caregivers with whom they work. They affirmed that the degree of match between the needs of parents and the resources and support in the community to meet those needs is related to distress and well-being of parents. The three parent representatives had two other reactions to the draft manuscript that are worth noting. First, they noted that although the majority of experiences shared by participants (and quoted in the manuscript) were about families with younger children with disabilities (e.g., obtaining services from schools, working to include their children in local sports teams), the themes were equally relevant for families of young adults with disabilities; only the experiences and examples would change (e.g., obtaining services from local adult service providers, seeking inclusive employment and independent living). Second, they noted that they, and the majority of parents with whom they work, primarily think of themselves as parents and not as caregivers. Although they acknowledged and understood the use of the term *caregiver* by legislation, policy, and many professionals in the health services field, they wanted it noted that the term *caregiver* is not used by parents to self-describe their roles and responsibilities as parents. We have attempted to honor their perspective here by not using the term *caregiver* when talking exclusively about parents of children with disabilities.

RESULTS

Four major themes influencing parental well-being emerged from the data: (a) obtaining access to information and services, (b) financial barriers to obtaining services, (c) school and community inclusion, and (d) family support.

Theme One: Access to Information and Services

Access, or more pointedly lack of access, to important information and needed services was the most salient and overarching area of concern for the participants in our study. Parents indicated that they often encountered many challenges related to access. As one parent noted: "I mean it's been a fight for anything, it's unbelievable." Another parent shared the sense of rejection she often felt as she attempted to obtain services: "You have to understand where we are coming from first. We get so many no, no, no, no, no." Fighting for access and the experience of being rejected appeared to be an ever-present part of life that many parents were experiencing.

> For the past 2 and a half years we've just been fighting with the school district. We haven't made any progress, I mean we have been referred to like [participant mentions some agencies they have been referred to] and they have been able to give some help, but we are not where we need to be and I don't know how to get there ... so I feel very trapped.

During one focus group as the participants were mentioning how and where they access information, one of the parents briefly excused herself from the focus group to take a call and when she returned she reported that:

> My husband was just calling me to let us know that we lost our due process hearing. ... Our due process in trying to get services for our son.

Efforts to gain access to information and services were an aspect of the parenting role that was present immediately upon learning their child had a disability. The following comments reveal the urgency participants felt about accessing services and information as soon as possible upon learning of their child's disability.

> There's a lot of pressure when you first find out, I don't know about you all, if you felt it. ... you have to get help while they are young.
>
> You start at the overwhelmed stage. I have absolutely no idea where to begin. I can't even believe this.

This initial attempt to obtain information about their child's disability is a time-consuming and difficult process. One mother said:

> So yeah, you start to hopefully, you just start talking and then somebody else is, "oh yeah, I know somebody" ... but it's slow, it's painful.

Success in obtaining needed information and resources brought considerable relief to parents, as expressed by the following participant:

> I mean, I was like "information!" I couldn't get enough … just anything, everything. … You find something, your first help … whatever it was that [makes you go] "oh thank God, somebody can talk to me."

As previously noted, however, the parents expressed that learning where to search for information and services and then being able to access them was a process full of challenges and roadblocks. One participant summarized this when, referring to her effort to access supports and services and the subsequent challenges she encountered, she stated: "that's when it gets difficult as a parent." The difficulties associated with the process of acquiring information and services seemed to be a product of having to navigate complex human service organizations. One mother shared her experience:

> I'm sure it's the same thing when you're dealing with the [local service organization], you all go through the same thing trying to get parents to sign their children up. [You] fill out an application over here, then they go over to [different local service organization] and fill out applications over there, then [you] go to [different local service organization] … by the time you are finished you've gone at least two weeks and you are waiting for either a letter of denial or acceptance, and it's crazy.

A lack of communication and coordination among various agencies further complicates the search for information and resources, as noted by another mother when she stated:

> I mean, if you call someone and say "this is my problem, this is what I need" … they'll send you to somebody else and before you know it, you are on the phone for two hours, probably not even getting to the person you need to talk to [and then you are told], "call this number, call this number, call this number." So it would be nice to have one central place that you could go.

In addition to being complex and disorganized, parents in our study reported that the entire process of accessing services can be a demeaning experience. This was due in part to the disrespectful treatment the parents often perceived. The following comments are illustrative:

> Anytime you come upon a program you have to meet with all these people and, you know, you feel like you're … being interrogated. … You [have to] meet with all these people and you don't know what any of [them do], they don't explain their position very well. Everything sounds like it is coming from a politician somewhere and … you don't really understand it.
>
> So you're feeling like a total idiot because they're using all these big words and, you know, you're sitting there [thinking] "what are they saying?" So [the parents] get intimidated and they don't want the program … they're, you know, feeling bombarded.
>
> You feel like you are being talked down to or belittled. [Parents are] overwhelmed … you sign up for one particular program and you have to have 10 people come to your house and then [again] every six months.

Theme Two: Financial Barriers to Obtaining Services

Parents across the study reported financial barriers to obtaining needed services for their children with disabilities. Financial stressors generally concerned two types of issues: (a) direct financial strain placed upon the family's finances due to acquiring services for their child with a disability (these services were generally related to health care) and (b) inability to access needed services due to the family's financial status. Acquiring needed services for their children with disabilities was a source of strain for parents in our focus groups. For example, one participant explained that her family paid $50 per visit for therapy three times a week. She went on to state:

> If you have someone that has medical needs ... it's the cost, regardless of the deductible, you're still paying a ton of money.

Acknowledging the same source of strain, another parent in a different focus group noted that every time she took her son to seek treatment at a children's hospital in a different city, she spent over $1,000 in travel plus all the medical expenses.

Focus group participants reported that the cost of the services themselves could impede access to services and resources. One participant reported:

> parents with children with disabilities are hit with a lot of costs, and every time you go "that looks good"—money!—"that looks good"—more money! ... you know we tapped out our insurance on physical therapy.

Some participants reported that the inability to pay for services would result in their child being placed on a waiting list for those services.

The lack of being able to overcome financial barriers may lead to family stress in families who have a child with a disability. One parent related her experience with this issue. She noted:

> A lot of time people that are having financial hardships kind of shut down and really don't want to get involved in the programs, because first fear of the cost and then fear oh they're going to look down on us because they are financially hard.

Financial barriers not only serve as a strain for families, but they also may preclude access to quality services. Parents indicated that their financial status often prevented them from obtaining services for their child with a disability. When the moderator asked a group of parents if their needs were being met, several parents mentioned that this depended on their financial status. Several participants reported that they did not qualify for many services because their financial status was not in the poverty range. The following comments are illustrative of these concerns:

> You can't get anything if you're ... I mean we are working paycheck to paycheck and we don't qualify for anything, but then we can't get anything because we can't pay for it ... if you are at the poverty level, you might get some kind of help, but if you're not, you can't get any assistance if you can't afford to pay for it.
>
> The lower income bracket they are, I guess more apt to get the care that they need, but if you're in the like middle income it's more difficult to because you have to qualify.
>
> Not being able to obtain services because you are not in the lower poverty bracket. You make too much money.

Theme Three: School and Community Inclusion

The continual struggle to ensure their children with disabilities were included in their schools and communities was a strong theme among the parents in our study. The fundamental importance of inclusion was aptly noted by one mother who pointed out that as parents of children with disabilities they were *"fighting the human rights fight"* on behalf of their children. This human rights issue was fundamentally about ensuring their children were part of the community.

> [I want] everyone to see [that] my child is a person within the community. She's a person within her community that has Down Syndrome, you know, and she can still participate in some form or fashion.

In the earlier section on accessing services, we described parents' reports of their efforts to obtain the school services needed by their children. Students with disabilities have been increasingly included in mainstream school settings over the past three decades. For the parents in our study, the struggle for school inclusion was about more than being physically present and academically included. It was about having their children included in the social aspects of school, as noted by the following illustrative comment:

> Unfortunately, the school is not supporting anything. The reason I found out was because my daughter happens to attend the same school [my child with a disability attends], she'll go by and see what's going on and she said "you know [child's name] looks sad and he's sitting in there and I don't see him at lunch" … it's like they're not including him.

The sometimes successful, sometimes unsuccessful efforts to advocate for inclusion were acknowledged by many parents. After sharing an experience about her struggle to involve her child in a community program that was available to the general public, one parent commented:

> We try to make them part of the community and [sometimes we can and sometimes we cannot] that's the hardest point I think … but I was like "wow" this wasn't what I expected.

Equally frustrating to many parents were the adverse reactions of some in the community to having their children included in community activities. One father, referring to the struggle to have his son with autism included in city league baseball, shared:

> You do have some people that have strong opinions like, "they're not supposed to be here, they're not supposed to be included with us as a group."

The participants in our study also shared several stories about adverse reactions from the community that were both barriers to successful inclusion and important reasons for continuing to advocate for inclusion. The following comments illustrate the community reactions reported by participants.

> People act like they are going to catch the disability, you know they do, I mean people act like … I can't get too close because I'm going to catch it, you know, and that's hard … it's hard.
>
>   There's a lot of fear and there's fear everywhere. The other people [are] afraid of our kids … there's fear and I think a lot of the fear comes from the lack of education.

For the parents in our study, efforts to achieve community inclusion were often impeded by what the parents perceived as low expectations, as illustrated by the following comment:

> Many times, as parents, we'll go to an agency and the social worker sees the disability and she automatically labels our children. For them your child is not going to accomplish anything in life. Some people think that way and parents are confronted with those people. Unfortunately, it happens a lot of times.

In contrast to the perceived low expectations of others, the parents in our study had high expectations and positive hopes and dreams for their children's futures.

> I have an eight year old that has Down Syndrome and now I am thinking college, you know … that's my issue now, because people say, "well kids that have special needs [are] not going to go to college," [but] they are [like everyone else] … they're not just on the other side and we try to make them part of the community.

However, for some parents the high expectations, hopes, and dreams they held for a positive future for their child also included an element of fear about whether their sons/daughters would be able to be part of the community once they were no longer around. The following comments are illustrative of these concerns.

> But there's also independence. … You try to raise your child to be independent … no matter what level disability your child is, you're trying to raise them to be independent versus mommy's going to do everything … because they need to learn to be independent because mommies aren't always going to be able to take care of them.
>
> I was always like, "what is this kid going to do? I don't want her in a state school when I die." … I'm teaching her how to take care of this, because I don't know when I'm going to die, and I don't want her going to the state school. So once I die she'll be able to hire her own people and take care of herself.

The continual battle for meaningful inclusion can have consequences for parents. Several parents shared that they were personally labeled for their efforts to advocate for inclusion on behalf of their children. Referring to the consequences of her struggle to gain inclusion in a program for her son, one mother commented: "That's when I got the reputation of being a 'trouble' parent." Another participant in our study summarized her view of these consequences and how they can prevent other parents from being advocates:

> I've watched parents who I think would like to see the same kind of outcomes that our children are having as a result of what I believe are inclusive education experiences, but are not willing to put themselves in the political spot that they saw us get in. [They're] very fearful of the community backlash and so they don't.

Within this context, it is worth noting that many parents reported that they themselves often felt isolated from their respective communities. Isolation appeared to encompass a broad meaning for parents, but generally indicated that parents felt separated and disconnected from their surrounding communities and social groups, as indicated by the following comment:

> I mean, we are like friends now or mostly [friends with] parents who have other kids with disabilities and … we kind of have our own community and we share amongst [ourselves] … you become like your own little community, which you don't want to, but you kind of have to.

Theme Four: Family Support

Under most circumstances, being a parent comes with many challenges. As noted by the parents in our study, accessing information and services to meet the needs of children with disabilities, financial barriers to obtaining needed services, and ongoing efforts to ensure meaningful inclusion in schools and communities are additional challenges associated with parenting children with disabilities. These challenges can place families under stress.

The participants in our study also noted the additional stressors that parents and families may experience associated with having a family member with a disability, and with the lack of support for families as they attempt to cope with these stressors. Two family support issues emerged during data analysis: during the early stages when parents are first coping with the diagnosis of a disability, and over time as families cope with the time and unpredictability associated with the disability.

Several parents reported that they felt *"overwhelmed," "stressed,"* or *"depressed"* when they first learned about their child's diagnosis. When asked what she did after learning about her child's disability, one mother reported that she *"cried."* Another parent described the process she went through when she found out her child was diagnosed with autism. She noted:

> We find out slowly and so there's this whole, you know, denial, uh, loss of a dream kind of thing, depression, you go through a whole list of things because it's kind of a slow loss and so then you start doing your research and finding out, trying to find out things.

After the initial distress experienced by parents of children with disabilities, they have to mobilize to seek services for their child. One parent commented that she was *"paralyzed with the challenge"* of seeking services for her child. For many families, however, these initial experiences can lead to growth, action, and advocacy. Several participants in our study reported that it was this initial emotional distress that led to a change in their lives in order to obtain services for their child.

Parents noted that the extra time and occasional unpredictability of raising a child with a disability can affect the entire family, including parents, siblings, and extended family members. For example, one mother reported that she often has difficulty balancing and organizing her needs and the needs of the entire family due to the unpredictable nature of her child's disability. She commented:

> I've not led a very organized life, especially after I had [child's name] because it depends on how he's doing. … I really appreciate people who appreciate my time, because it's limited. It's not about me, I'm a mom now, and [child's name] needs come first.

Similarly, another mother explained how the unpredictability of her son's medical needs affected her and her family, even when arrangements were made in advance to participate in social activities: "If he's sick, it does not matter if I made plans a year ago … they're off."

The participants in our study also reported on the marital strain that sometimes can be experienced by parents of children with disabilities. A parent commented on her experiences:

> The divorce rate is extremely high in families with children with special needs and there are specific reasons for that. Having a child with autism when he goes off the deep end, it's a hard night, it's a very hard night and it becomes complicated with both parents, it's almost easier with just one parent.

Notably, although some participants mentioned a high divorce rate due to difficulties associated with having a child with a disability, this claim is not clearly supported by the literature. Previous research has confirmed, however, that, compared to other parents, parents of children with disabilities are more likely to experience increased marital discord (Tew, Payne, & Laurence, 1974).

Extended family can sometimes provide an important source of support for families as noted by a mother in our study who spoke about visits to grandparents by her children during the summer:

> I know in our situation we rely on my mom who lives 2 hours away, in the summertime she takes our kids one on one … we are relying on this distant grandmother to just spoil these kids rotten and give us a break. And we don't have a real severe situation in the home, we, you know, it's not intense. But, it's a wonderful break just to get to be individual with this other kid.

For many of the parents in our study, however, extended family members were not available to provide support to their families. In these circumstances, parents reported their frustration with the lack of services and supports for families with children with disabilities. In particular, services such as respite care and counseling were mentioned as being difficult to access or simply unavailable. The following comments from participants reflect how the entire family unit can be affected by the lack of support and services:

> I feel so bad for my two other children, because they understand what is wrong with him, but there's, it's, you cannot stop the meltdown sometimes and so what's not being met is an outlet for siblings … these children are living with a child with a disability and it affects them. What's not being met is support for families so that these marriages will stay together.
>
> I think counseling is a must for families, and then you have to have reliable people to watch that particular child with a disability. … Respite, a lot of times is what families need, you know … parents don't get to spend any time together and when you're dealing with situations like at our house where it is chaos at times, and not because he is a bad child, not because we are bad parents, you know, it has to do with his disability and this is sometimes what occurs, what happens, but it makes it hard.

Post Hoc Analysis: Positive Experiences

Being the parent of a child with a disability is not a devastating experience as many might assume (Ambert, 1992). On the contrary, raising a child with a disability can be as fulfilling as raising a child without a disability (King, Scollon, Ramsey, & Williams, 2000; Wilgosh, Nota, Scorgie, & Salvatore, 2004). Although much of the previous research related to parental well-being has focused on the barriers and challenges parents encounter and the potentially negative consequences of these challenges (Donelan et al., 2002), recent research has also demonstrated evidence of posttraumatic growth (Konrad, 2006), resilience (Bayat, 2007), and other benefits and rewards (Donelan et al., 2002; Green, 2007; Murphy et al., 2007) obtained through raising a child with a disability. Specifically, these studies have shown that parents often gain a greater appreciation for life, increased spirituality, increased compassion and tolerance for individual and group differences, a more united family, and a general feeling of increased mental and emotional strength.

The questions asked of participants in our study were intentionally designed to elicit information about the needs and challenges parents of children with disabilities experience. Along with this information, however, the parents in our study also shared some of their positive experiences. We would be remiss in not sharing a few of these experiences for they illustrate one of the many reasons why parents of children with disabilities fight so vigorously for information, inclusion, services, and supports: because their family and their child with a disability deserve the same opportunities as other families and children, and achieving these successes is worth the considerable effort. One father, commenting on his battle to have his son with autism included in city league baseball, shared:

> It took 3 years; he's been a clutch hitter because he is so focused. It might be different for a lot of kids to hit the ball, but to him it's no big deal. … They couldn't take from him the desire to want to play on the field and [his desire to bat]. And when he came to bat he never missed and never got nervous because of his disability. … Now, for the very first time, he has been selected to the all-star[s].

Describing how he accomplished this inclusive experience despite the initial resistance, he stated:

> It's just in educating, it's inclusion. … Once you win them [parents of children without disabilities] over, and a lot of them have common sense and they have a good heart and they don't say anything. … We are in our fourth year of him playing baseball. … It took the other kids that have been playing with him for three years to tell the coach [and] to tell their parents that they want him on their team.

Another mother shared her story about attempting to have her son involved in swimming lessons and overcoming the initial rejection:

> I was like "this isn't fair, this isn't fair, he has just as much right to take swimming lessons here for a nominal fee … but he couldn't be in a class with everybody … there's only one teacher and 6 kids … so I worked with his occupational therapist and said this is a really big concern and she got us connected with a lady in the school district and he's done it two years now and he learned how to swim last summer because she was willing to provide the one on one that he needed. . . ."

Parents often commented on the difficulties they faced in terms of their child being accepted by others at school or in the community. One mother, however, shared this experience about how her other children helped to educate their peers about their brother with a disability.

> It's been such an amazing thing to see how [my other] kids defend and stand-up and try to educate their peers, their friends about him, about the disability and what he can and can't do and don't try to make [him] special, try to make [him] like you and me.

Similarly, one participant shared a story about her child's peers making an effort to include her son in an activity:

> He was playing soccer and he never could get the ball because he was always too slow. … They were in a competition game and his team stopped the game so [he] would have a chance to kick the ball. … They were not told by anybody to do that, they had no instructions from anybody, they decided [he] needs to kick the ball at least once in the game.

Limitations

Several limitations should be noted when interpreting the findings of this study. First, it is important to note that this study was limited to parents from a single state. Although participants were selected purposefully to reflect the geographic, economic, and racial diversity of the state, only 40 total caregivers participated. Unfortunately, ethnic minorities such as Asian Americans and Native Americans were not included in the sample since they make up a small percentage of the population in the respective state. As such, these findings should be interpreted beyond these parameters with caution. Additionally, approximately two or three participants invited to attend each focus group did not show up. We did not collect data on the invited participants who declined to attend. Consequently, it is unclear how the no-shows affect the purposeful sampling. Another possible limitation is that nearly all participants (90%) were women. However, this should not significantly limit the results of this study as mothers are typically the primary care providers for children with disabilities. Nevertheless, although they are predominantly female, caregivers are not a homogeneous group. Their experiences are influenced by differences on many distinct variables such as disability type, disability severity, age of child, race, and community setting (e.g., rural vs. urban; Darling & Gallagher, 2004). An additional limitation of studies such as this is the overreliance on accessible and/or elite informants, and making inferences based on only a limited number of concrete and vivid examples (Miles & Huberman, 1994). It is possible that individuals who volunteered for this study are fundamentally different (e.g., parents who are possibly more active and involved in support groups, advocacy initiatives, etc.) than other parents. Thus, although these focus groups resulted in hundreds of pages of narrative data, caution should be taken when attempting to make inferential or conclusive statements. Another important consideration is that the parents in this study were parents of children with many different types of disabilities, indicating that there are differences in their experiences. Notably, however, the themes identified in this study were expressed by nearly all parents at each focus group regardless of the type of disability their child had. Finally, for this study we used a single method (focus groups) for collecting data. Using a single method or measure to gather data could mean that only part of the actual parent experience is being captured.

DISCUSSION

Despite these limitations, this study has several important implications for policy makers, providers, and researchers. Parents caring for a child with a disability make an invaluable contribution to their families and to society. Unfortunately, however, parents can face significant challenges that can lead to personal distress, which, in turn, can adversely affect the well-being of the child and the entire family unit. Recent federal legislation and policy are placing greater emphasis on designing and providing services and supports for parents of children with disabilities in order to enhance their well-being. To fully understand and adequately address the factors related to parental well-being, however, researchers must first capture their perspective. Particular attention should be given to the parent's perceptions of their needs, the needs of their families, and the services, supports, and barriers they identify as related to meeting those needs. In this regard, parental distress is viewed as resulting from situations in which the parenting situation exceeds the parent's resources. Conversely, well-being is enhanced by a match between parent needs and resources to meet those needs. Such an approach may have the benefit of designing policies and services that are family centered (a concept we expand in the text that follows).

The participants in our study identified four areas in which they perceive a gap between their needs, the needs of their families, and the services and supports available to address those needs: (a) obtaining access to information and resources, (b) financial barriers to obtaining services, (c) school and community inclusion, and (d) family support. The need for accurate, timely information and resources begins immediately upon learning their child has a disability. According to the parents in our study, finding information and resources to meet their family's needs is an ongoing process that is complicated by a service system that is complex and uncoordinated, and that is perceived too often as unhelpful. In addition, participants expressed that they often faced financial barriers to accessing services due to high "out-of-pocket" costs of medical and support services and because they often did not qualify for financial relief. Another challenge participants in this study shared is their fight to create inclusive school and community experiences for their children with disabilities. The resistance to meaningful inclusion that families can encounter is both a potential source of stress and a reason for continuing to challenge the status quo. For some parents in our study, school and community inclusion is a fight for basic human rights (Olkin, 1997) that has consequences not only for the present but also for the future when their children are adults. Parents, however, also expressed that efforts to create inclusive opportunities can have consequences for them in terms of being perceived as a "trouble parent" and in terms of being disconnected from the larger community beyond other families with children with disabilities. Finally, the participants in this study articulated that their well-being is intricately tied to the well-being of the entire family unit and the needs of spouses and other children in the family. Some parents in our study were able to call upon extended family to assist with the additional time demands and unpredictability of parenting a child with disabilities, and to allow parents to spend important time with other children and with one another. In the absence of extended family, the lack of respite care and other supports (e.g., counseling, support for siblings, child care) can be an additional source of stress as parents seek to balance the needs of the entire family.

To a certain extent, this study confirms the findings of recent studies that show parents of children with disabilities often feel a fundamental lack of support necessary to perform optimally as a parent (e.g., Fox, Vaughn, Wyatte, & Dunlap, 2002; Green, 2007; McCarthy & Stough, 1999; Murphy et al., 2007; Worcester et al., 2008). In contrast to other studies, however, these findings do not emphasize the role of child behavior, disability severity, or parenting tasks as the primary determinant of parental well-being. Rather, these results indicate that parent stress and well-being is also associated with a lack of match between their needs and the information, resources, and supports to respond effectively to those needs. This suggests that raising a child with a disability is not merely a personal problem. Unfortunately, disability is socially defined (Meyerson, 1948) and society has often defined disability as a personal problem. These results counter this view and instead suggest that creating favorable social and environmental situations for parents and their families is essential for positive adjustment, and initiatives that encourage family-centered support and that lead to positive outcomes are crucial in this effort (Wilgosh et al., 2004).

Family-centered care has specific characteristics for each type of professional involved in the development and delivery of services for families raising children with disabilities (i.e., researchers, policy makers, educators, and providers). The following paragraphs describe some of these characteristics, but first we wish to note what we believe to be the principal characteristic of family-centered service: collaboration between professionals and families with the explicit purpose of addressing the needs of the child while simultaneously considering the needs of the entire family (Shelton & Stepanek, 1994). Since "the family is the constant in the child's life and expert in knowing the needs of the child" (Beckman, 2002, p. 683), we assert that this collaborative approach represents the best foundation for research, policy, and intervention. Thus, the unique perspectives of parents and families raising a child with a disability should be actively solicited. Unfortunately, a "top-down" approach is often taken when theorizing and making assumptions about families raising a child with a disability (Shewchuk & Elliott, 2000), and this method prevents true collaboration, frustrating efforts to help the family and, in turn, the child with the disability. To avoid this pitfall, we suggest that researchers, service providers, and policy makers respect the singular perspective of parents by allowing them to be the experts on the "realities of their daily lives" (Mechanic, 1998, p. 284). How this is done by each professional may differ, however, and we offer the following suggestions.

The existence of services is dependent upon policies and legislation that stipulate the provision of funding and resources for families raising a child with a disability. Agosta and Melda (1995) stated that family-focused services means ". . . providing families with whatever it takes for families of people with disabilities to live as much like other families as possible" (p. 271). Central to this recommendation is that supports are made available to all family members and not just the individual with the disability. Mounting evidence points to the wisdom of providing supports for the entire family. For example, Fisman et al. (2000) discovered that siblings of children with disability are more likely to experience adjustment problems when compared to their peers and this, in turn, increases parent distress. Family support proponents are faced with three key issues related to the creation of family-focused policies: (a) the need to ensure continued involvement of families, (b) the need for increased interagency collaboration, and (c) the need to acquire a sufficient funding base (Agosta & Melda, 1995). Continued family involvement means that policy makers increase the decision-making authority of families. This does not necessarily mean that parents become the policy makers, but, rather, parents remain intimately involved in the decisions about the substance of needed services. Increased interagency collaboration signifies that service agencies improve collaboration in order to help families more efficiently navigate the service delivery systems they depend upon. Acquiring a sufficient funding base is largely self-explanatory: insufficient funds equal insufficient services, but a lack of funding is particularly problematic for the area of family support (Agosta & Melda, 1995). Braddock, Hemp, Bachleder, and Fujiuria (1995) found that, although states spent nearly $300 million on family support in 1992, this represented less than 2% of the overall funding used for people with developmental disabilities in the community service industry.

Family-centered care is also vital for the delivery of services and the implementation of interventions. Beckman (2002) posited five key principles in the provision of family-centered services: (a) empowerment, (b) providing social supports, (c) building relationships as the basis for intervention, (d) building communication, and (e) maintaining communication. Empowering families means that service providers build upon their existing strengths, help develop new strengths, and leave the decision-making ability with the family. Empowerment encourages self-determination, independence, and the ability of the family to feel like they have a measure of control as they address the challenges related to raising a child with a disability. Social support has been shown to work as a mediator between stressful life experiences and family adjustment and health (Beckman, 2002). Therefore, service providers should help and encourage families to build upon these already existing networks whenever possible. In addition, a provider who is available and compassionate can serve as an important social support for the family, and building strong relationships with families should be considered a form of intervention (Beckman, 2002). Strong relationships take time and are built on trust. Building trust is accomplished by following through on commitments, being nonjudgmental, providing complete information, maintaining confidences, and being respectful (Beckman, 2002). Building a strong line of communication is vital to family-centered care. Service providers are experts in certain areas vital to families raising a child with a disability. Similarly, only the families can provide the information about the needs of their child and family (Beckman, 2002). Each party needs information from the other to accomplish their goals and, since these relationships are often ongoing, maintaining effective communication is essential.

The decisions made by policy makers and service providers are often informed by the results of scientific research. Consequently, researchers must ensure that their conclusions are truly representative of the phenomena they are studying. In terms of research related to family-centered care, this is an area where much improvement is needed. We have three suggestions to improve future research in this area.

First, as previously mentioned, much of the research about parents raising a child with a disability has focused on child-specific factors. Although many of these studies have yielded fruit and have value, the fact remains that the child and family exist in a social/environmental context that has been largely neglected in research. The failure to address this person–environment match issue has likely been one factor that has contributed to the tendency to describe the experience of parents raising children with disabilities as one of burden and pathology. This one-sided view has several pitfalls including child blaming, further stigmatization of disability, and failure to understand a more comprehensive parent perspective.

Second, personal characteristics of the individuals and families should continue to be considered. Often research in this area focuses on important factors such as child disability severity, family socioeconomic status, parent age, and parent education level. We also suggest, however, that other individual differences (i.e., race, ethnicity, culture, and urban versus rural settings) be more closely examined in order to uncover the unique effects these differences may have on parental well-being. Moreover, the relationship between these individual differences and the environmental/social support needs identified by parents should be examined.

Third, the positive growth parents experience should not be dismissed as simply coping strategies, but rather ways in which parents grow through their unique experiences (Scorgie & Sobsey, 2000). Positive growth is often studied in research about people adjusting to disability, but has typically been neglected in research about people who provide care for individuals with disabilities. We assert that this is a mistake as emerging evidence suggests positive growth has an important role in the well-being of parents raising a child with a disability (e.g., parent's appraisal of positive growth is predictive of parental well-being outcomes; Kronenberger & Thompson, 1992; Plant & Sanders, 2007).

As a useful way to conceptualize the investigation of these three factors simultaneously, we suggest the use of a modified version of the dynamic process model recommended by Elliott and Warren (2007; Figure 13.1). This model has traditionally been used in research about individuals with disabilities adjusting to disability, but we assert that this model is also appropriate for research involving individuals caring for persons with disabilities. Of particular value is this model's simultaneous emphasis on individual characteristics as well as social/environmental characteristics. In addition, this model appropriately attends to the importance of the appraisal process when adjusting to challenging situations. Thus, the appraisal of positive growth can be considered a mediating factor in the path to parental well-being. The strength of this model is its view that adjustment to the challenges of raising a child with a disability is a dynamic process influenced by many different variables. Also, using a model such as this to conceptualize

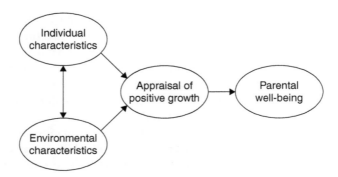

FIGURE 13.1 Modified version of the dynamic process model.

outcomes is beneficial in research because it not only describes aspects of certain processes, but it also has the potential to be prescriptive in that it can inform policy and intervention (Dunn & Elliott, 2008).

A final recommendation we offer for future research about the experiences of parents raising children with disabilities is the use of mixed methods investigative approaches. Mixed methods research has the advantage of combining both quantitative and qualitative approaches and different types of data collection techniques and can potentially provide a more effective way to capture the actual experiences of parents and their perceptions of those experiences (readers are referred to Green, 2003, 2007 for examples of using mixed methods to study the experiences of parents raising children with disabilities).

Parents experience many challenges unique to raising a child with a disability. These challenges are often the result of a mismatch between the parent's needs and the available resources. This mismatch will begin to be addressed most effectively when policy makers, researchers, and service providers collaborate with parents and families to identify a more balanced view of the needs of parents and families from their perspectives and to establish family-centered policies and services to address those needs.

REFERENCES

Agosta, J., & Melda, K. (1995). Supporting families who provide care at home for children with disabilities. *Exceptional Children, 62*, 271–282.

Ambert, A. (1992). *The effects of children on parents.* New York, NY: Haworth Press.

Arno, P. S., Levine, C., & Memmott, M. M. (1999). The economic value of informal caregiving. *Health Affairs (Project Hope), 18*(2), 182–188.

Bayat, M. (2007). Evidence of resilience in families of children with autism. *Journal of Intellectual Disability Research: JIDR, 51*(Pt 9), 702–714.

Beckman, P. J. (2002). Providing family-centered services. In M. Batshaw (Ed.), *A medical primer* (pp. 683–691). Baltimore, MD: Paul H. Brookes.

Braddock, D., Hemp, G., Bachleder, L., & Fujiuria, G. (1995). *The state of the states in developmental disabilities.* Washington, DC: American Association on Mental Retardation.

Brannan, A. M., & Heflinger, C. A. (2006). Caregiver, child, family, and service system contributors to caregiver strain in two child mental health service systems. *Journal of Behavioral Health Services & Research, 33*(4), 408–422.

Bronfenbrenner, U. (1986). Ecology of the family as a context for human development: Research perspectives. *Developmental Psychology, 22*, 723–742.

Chamberlin, J. (2009). Goodheart is APA's next president. *Monitor on Psychology, 40*, 68–69.

Chan, J. B., & Sigafoos, J. (2001). Does respite care reduce parental stress in families with developmentally disabled children? *Child and Youth Care Forum, 30*, 253–263.

Chwalisz, K. (1992). Perceived stress and caregiver burden after brain injury: A theoretical integration. *Rehabilitation Psychology, 37*, 189–203.

Chwalisz, K., Shah, R. S., & Hand, K. H. (2008). Facilitating rigorous qualitative research in rehabilitation psychology. *Rehabilitation Psychology, 53*, 387–399.

Darling, S. M., & Gallagher, P. A. (2004). Needs of and supports for African American and European American caregivers of young children with special needs in urban and rural settings. *Topics in Early Childhood Special Education, 24*, 98–109.

Donelan, K., Hill, C. A., Hoffman, C., Scoles, K., Feldman, P. H., Levine, C., & Gould, D. (2002). Challenged to care: Informal caregivers in a changing health system. *Health Affairs (Project Hope), 21*(4), 222–231.

Dunn, D. S., & Elliott, T. R. (2008). The place and promise of theory in rehabilitation psychology. *Rehabilitation Psychology, 53*(3), 254–267.

Elliot, T. R., & Mullins, L. L. (2004). Counseling families and children with disabilities. In D. Atkinson & G. Hackett (Eds.), *Counseling diverse populations* (3rd ed., pp. 151–170). New York, NY: McGraw-Hill.

Elliott, T. R., & Warren, A. M. (2007). Why psychology is important in rehabilitation. In P. Kennedy (Ed.), *Psychological management of physical disabilities* (pp. 16–39). New York, NY: Routledge.

Ely, M. (1991). *Doing qualitative research: Circles within circles*. New York, NY: Palmer Press.

Feldman, M., McDonald, L., Serbin, L., Stack, D., Secco, M. L., & Yu, C. T. (2007). Predictors of depressive symptoms in primary caregivers of young children with or at risk for developmental delay. *Journal of Intellectual Disability Research, 51*(Pt 8), 606–619.

Fisman, S., Wolf, L., Ellison, D., & Freeman, T. (2000). A longitudinal study of siblings of children with chronic disabilities. *Canadian Journal of Psychiatry. Revue Canadienne De Psychiatrie, 45*(4), 369–375.

Fox, L., Vaughn, B. J., Wyatte, M. L., & Dunlap, G. (2002). "We can't expect other people to understand": Family perspectives on problem behavior. *Exceptional Children, 68*, 437–450.

Freedman, R. I., & Boyer, N. C. (2000). The power to choose: Supports for families caring for individuals with developmental disabilities. *Health & Social Work, 25*(1), 59–68.

Gaugler, J., Kane, R., & Langlois, J. (2000). Assessment of family caregivers of older adults. In R. Kane & R. Kane (Eds.), *Assessing older persons: Measures, meaning, and practical applications* (pp. 320–359). New York, NY: Oxford University Press.

Green, S. E. (2003). "What do you mean 'what's wrong with her?'": Stigma and the lives of families of children with disabilities. *Social Science & Medicine (1982), 57*(8), 1361–1374.

Green, S. E. (2007). "We're tired, not sad": Benefits and burdens of mothering a child with a disability. *Social Science and Medicine, 64*, 150–163.

King, L. A., Scollon, C. K., Ramsey, C., & Williams, T. (2000). Stories of life transition: Subjective well-being and ego development in parents of children with Down syndrome. *Journal of Research in Personality, 34*, 509–536.

Konrad, S. C. (2006). Posttraumatic growth in mothers of children with acquired disabilities. *Journal of Loss & Trauma, 11*, 101–113.

Kronenberger, W. G., & Thompson, R. J. (1992). Psychological adaptation of mothers of children with spina bifida: Association with dimensions of social relationships. *Journal of Pediatric Psychology, 17*(1), 1–14.

Lollar, D. (2008). Rehabilitation and public health: Commonalities, barriers, and bridges. *Rehabilitation Psychology, 53*, 122–127.

McCarthy, M. G., & Stough, L. M. (1999). The qualifying game: A search for services by individuals with disabilities. *Education and Training in Mental Retardation and Developmental Disabilities, 34*, 485–498.

Mechanic, D. (1998). Public trust and initiatives for new health care partnerships. *Milbank Quarterly, 76*(2), 281–302.

Meyerson, L. (1948). Physical disability as a social psychological problem. *Journal of Social Issues, 4*, 2–10.

Miles, M. B., & Huberman, A. M. (1994). *Qualitative data analysis: An expanded sourcebook* (2nd ed.). Thousand Oaks, CA: Sage.

Morgan, D. L. (1998). *The focus group guidebook*. Thousand Oaks, CA: Sage.

Murphy, N. A., Christian, B., Caplin, D. A., & Young, P. C. (2007). The health of caregivers for children with disabilities: Caregiver perspectives. *Child: Care, Health and Development, 33*(2), 180–187.

Navaie-Waliser, M., Feldman, P. H., Gould, D. A., Levine, C., Kuerbis, A. N., & Donelan, K. (2002). When the caregiver needs care: The plight of vulnerable caregivers. *American Journal of Public Health, 92*(3), 409–413.

Newacheck, P. W., & Kim, S. E. (2005). A national profile of health care utilization and expenditures for children with special health care needs. *Archives of Pediatrics & Adolescent Medicine, 159*(1), 10–17.

Olkin, R. (1997). Human rights of children with disabilities. *Women & Therapy, 20*, 29–42.

Ones, K., Yilmaz, E., Cetinkaya, B., & Caglar, N. (2005). Assessment of the quality of life of mothers of children with cerebral palsy (primary caregivers). *Neurorehabilitation and Neural Repair, 19*(3), 232–237.

Parish, S. L., Rose, R. A., Grinstein-Weiss, M., Richman, E. L., & Andrews, M. E. (2008). Material hardship among U.S. families raising children with disabilities. *Exceptional Children, 75*, 72–91.

Patton, M. Q. (1990). *Qualitative evaluation and research methods* (2nd ed.). Newbury Park, CA: Sage.

Plant, K. M., & Sanders, M. R. (2007). Predictors of care-giver stress in families of preschool-aged children with developmental disabilities. *Journal of Intellectual Disability Research, 51*(Pt 2), 109–124.

Raina, P., O'Donnell, M., Rosenbaum, P., Brehaut, J., Walter, S. D., Russell, D., ... Wood, E. (2005). The health and well-being of caregivers of children with cerebral palsy. *Pediatrics, 115*(6), e626–e636.

Richards, T., & Richards, L. (2006). *QSR NVIVO 7* [Computer software]. Melbourne, Australia: QSR International.

Scorgie, K., & Sobsey, D. (2000). Transformational outcomes associated with parenting children who have disabilities. *Mental Retardation, 38*(3), 195–206.

Seltzer, M. M., & Heller, T. (1997). Families and caregiving across the life course: Research advances on the influence of context. *Family Relations, 46*, 395–405.

Shearn, J., & Todd, S. (2000). Maternal employment and family responsibilities: The perspectives of mothers of children with intellectual disabilities. *Journal of Applied Research in Intellectual Disabilities, 13*, 109–131.

Shelton, T. L., & Stepanek, J. S. (1994). Family-centered care for children needing specialized health and development services. *Journal of Special Education, 27*, 82–106.

Shewchuk, R., & Elliott, T. (2000). Family caregiving in chronic disease and disability: Implications for rehabilitation psychology. In R. G. Frank & T. Elliott (Eds.), *Handbook of rehabilitation psychology* (pp. 553–563). Washington, DC: American Psychological Association Press.

Talley, R. C., & Crews, J. E. (2007). Framing the public health of caregiving. *American Journal of Public Health, 97*(2), 224–228.

Tew, B. J., Payne, H., & Laurence, K. M. (1974). Must a family with a handicapped child be a handicapped family? *Developmental Medicine and Child Neurology, 16*(6 Suppl. 32), 95–98.

U.S. Department of Health and Human Services. (2000). *Healthy People 2010: Understanding and improving health* (2nd ed.). Washington, DC: U.S. Government Printing Office.

Wilgosh, L., Nota, L., Scorgie, K., & Salvatore, S. (2004). Effective life management in parents of children with disabilities: A cross-national extension. *International Journal for the Advancement of Counselling, 26*, 301–312.

Worcester, J. A., Nesman, T. M., Raffaele Mendez, L. M., & Keller, H. R. (2008). Giving voice to parents of young children with challenging behavior. *Exceptional Children, 74*, 509–525.

Yanow, D., & Schwartz-Shea, P. (2006). *Interpretation and method: Empirical research methods and the interpretive turn.* Armonk, NY: ME Sharpe.

14

Psychosocial Counseling Aspects of Grief, Death, and Dying

Mark A. Stebnicki

George Engel's (1961) classic work on grief has challenged researchers and practitioners alike in the medical and psychological community with the perplexing question of "Is grief a disease?" The idea that grief should even be considered within the classification of a medical condition helped launch the foundational work in the fields of psychosomatic medicine and the development of biopsychosocial models of significance by Engel and others that followed this research agenda (Stroebe, 2015).

Despite newer models of grief and the associated symptomatology as described by the diagnosis of Persistent Complex Bereavement Disorder in the *Diagnostic and Statistical Manual of Mental Disorders* (5th ed.; *DSM-5*; American Psychiatric Association, 2013), the nature, experience, and expression of grief may not be expressed and experienced universally. Indeed, there is a cultural significance by which grief is both experienced and expressed. Accordingly, the cultural expression of grief itself complicates the psychosocial assessment, mental health diagnosis, and treatment interventions of grief. Thus, there are many challenges for counselors as they attempt to understand the meaning of their clients' multiple losses amid the constructs, definitions, and theories that surround psychosocial adjustment to the nature of grief.

Worden (2009) reminds grief counselors that grief itself is a multidimensional or a multidetermined phenomenon. Some grievers express very little emotion after critical events of death, dying, or loss while others are overwhelmed to the point of total mental and physical incapacity. Grief is basically what the person says it is, how the person describes it, expresses it (verbally and nonverbally), and experiences it. As many seasoned grief counselors might share, establishing a person-centered and culturally sensitive rapport is essential in developing an optimal working alliance with a diverse range of individuals and groups. First and foremost, the psychosocial aspects of grief counseling require a high level of compassion and empathy by the professional counselor. The therapeutic approaches facilitated by professionals must extend beyond treating the purported mental and physical health effects that accompany grief by looking at the underlying complex factors.

Overall, the skills of working with the psychosocial aspects of grief, death, dying, and loss are essential, particularly in working with persons who have acquired chronic illness and disability. It is beyond the scope of this chapter to provide a comprehensive discussion of grief theories, models, and interventions. However, this chapter helps elucidate important psychosocial issues in death and dying as it relates to how individuals experience and express grief within the context of the person's physical, psychological, cognitive, emotional, social, cultural, and spiritual well-being.

Grief can be defined most parsimoniously as the emotional response to loss (Stroebe, Hansson, Schut, & Stroebe, 2008). However, many languages have no word for the term and constructs related to grief (Klass, 2014). The word *grief* is from the Anglo-French *gref,* which is derived from the Latin word *gravis,* which means heavy, painful, important, and the carrying of burdens. Overall, the definition itself appears to be grounded in cultural meaning (Rosenblatt, 2012).

The idea that grief should be considered within the context of a specific mental health condition has spurred debate among the disciplines of medicine, psychology, mental health, and thanatology over the last 20 years. Grief may occur in non–death-related events that involve extraordinarily stressful and traumatic events, which typically include multiples losses. Critical incidents, such as person-made (e.g., terrorism, school shootings) and natural disasters (e.g., hurricanes, floods, earthquakes) all have an accumulation of losses and should be considered within the grieving process. The psychological, emotional, physical, and spiritual cost to such critical incidents complicate the healing process but also help clarify the definition of grief (Stebnicki, 2017). Cultural and spiritual sensitivity are also critical aspects in understanding how grief is defined, expressed, and experienced during therapeutic relationships with persons grieving (Klass, 2014; Rando et al., 2012).

In search for a definition of *grief,* it may be helpful to understand how grief is measured. To assist in the constructs of measuring grief, Prigerson, Maciejewski, Reynolds, Bierhals, Newsom, Fasiczka, et al. (1995) developed a comprehensive research questionnaire, the Inventory of Complicated Grief (ICG), that measures the individual's experience of persistent grief that goes beyond the normal healing period of time. The ICG and its accompanying research may assist counselors in understanding the characteristics and symptomatology of *complicated grief.* Subsequent revisions of the ICG include the ICG-R (Prigerson & Jacobs, 2001) and the current PG-13 (Prigerson et al., 2009), which is now commonly used to measure complicated grief.

Indeed, grief and loss are mutually shared across all cultures and experienced by nearly all individuals over one's lifetime (Stebnicki, 2016c). Despite the healing aspects of grief, it is of paramount importance to note that prolonged pathological grief can become dysfunctional in one's life (Craig, 2010; Rando et al., 2012; Stroebe, 2015). The early work related to grief, death, and dying by Kübler-Ross (1975) appeared to lay some of the critical underpinnings that gave legitimacy to the experience of grieving. Kübler-Ross defined the experience of grief in terms of a model of linear progression that occurred in five stages: denial, anger, bargaining, depression, and acceptance. The underlying assumption is that grieving is a natural event and as one progresses through this process it should result in personal and psychological growth, as well as emotional healing. Although there may be shortcomings with stage models because they represent an artificial linear progression of the grieving and mourning process, the benefits of early work in this area prepared the groundwork for the modern hospice movement (Balk, 2014).

Bereaved individuals going through the grieving process, whether through a stage model or not, have many serious questions that confront them physically, emotionally, psychologically, and spiritually. Questions, such as "What will my life look like now?" "What did the deceased's life mean to me?" "How can I possibly feel safe and secure in a world such as this?" "Who am I now that this death has occurred?" and "Why do bad things happen to good people?" (Kushner, 1980; Neimeyer, Prigerson, & Davies, 2002; Worden, 2009), suggest such existential and spiritual questions challenge the personal meaning in death and dying in fundamental ways.

PERSISTENT COMPLEX BEREAVEMENT DISORDER: CRITERIA IN THE *DSM-5*

Historically, the American Psychiatric Association's (APA) *Diagnostic and Statistical Manual of Mental Disorders* (*DSM*) has not cited grief as a specific psychiatric disorder. Rather, grief has been clinically defined as a condition that can be triggered by loss and bereavement, which primarily manifests as major depressive disorder or adjustment disorder, which does not adequately cover the psychological condition itself (Murray Parkes, 2005). Recently, with the inclusion of Persistent Complex Bereavement Disorder in the new *DSM-5,* complicated grief and its co-occurring syndromes related to grief have helped lay the foundation for structured interviews, standardized assessments, and a path for the diagnosis and treatment of grief.

For many years, there has been a call for a diagnostic category in the *DSM* that reflects the symptomatology related to the grieving process (Rando et al., 2012). Accordingly, there have been systematic attempts in the research to identify, delineate, and assess grief and its co-occurring mental health conditions. Generally, the literature commonly describes other grief syndromes using the terms *absent, abnormal, compli-cated, distorted, morbid, maladaptive, atypical, intensified and prolonged, unresolved, neurotic, dysfunctional, chronic, delayed,* and *inhibited grief.* It is beyond the scope and intention of this chapter to comprehensively discuss each of the syndromes' clinical features. However, there appears to be an emphasis for the counseling profession to understand that syndromes related to *complicated grief* cannot be confined to one syndrome or disorder but rather includes multiple phenomenon for consideration when measuring ones' experience and expression of grief.

The work of Prigerson, Vanderwerker, and Maciejewski (2008; as cited by Rando et al., 2012) provides some of the foundational work underlying the category in the new *DSM-5*-termed *Persistent Complex Bereavement Disorder* (APA, 2013). The current *DSM-5* has five criteria that consider the individual's reactive distress associated with the loss and grief in close relationships. The abbreviated criterion are (a) the individual's experience of the death; (b) the clinically significant symptoms that persist for at least 12 months after the death of an adult and 6 months for children in which there is persistent yearning, sorrow, emotional pain, and preoccupation with the deceased; (c) the presentation of at least six clinically distressing symptoms on more days than not; (d) the bereaved individual's clinically significant distress is exhibited by disturbance in social, occupational, or other important psychosocial areas; and (e) the bereaved individual's reaction is out of proportion to or inconsistent with the cultural, religious, or age-appropriate norms.

In addition to criterion a–e, the *DSM-5* measures the significance of symptoms as they relate to disruption in one's social and interpersonal life. There is also the inclusion of one specifier, *traumatic bereavement,* and four differential diagnoses (i.e., normal grief, depressive disorders, posttraumatic stress disorder, and separation anxiety disorder), that assist professional counselors in comprehensively identifying the underlying cause or etiology of the *persistent and complex bereavement* such as bereavement because of homicide, suicide, degree of suffering, mutilation, injury, and the overall nature of the death as experienced by the bereaved. Given the seriousness of these clinically significant symptoms, as well as the high risk for suicide ideation, attempts, and completions, it is understandable that more therapeutic attention is required than dealing with the primary emotion of grief itself.

PSYCHOSOCIAL COUNSELING ASPECTS OF COMPLEX GRIEF

The literature related to grief, death, and dying is clear that most forms of grief syndromes are complex in nature (Murray Parkes, 2005; Prigerson et al., 2008; Rando et al., 2012; Stroebe, 2015). Counselors must reach beyond the person's primary emotion of grief in therapy to achieve optimal psychosocial therapeutic benefits with their clients. Indeed, complicated grief itself can be debilitating because complex co-occurring clinical conditions tend to develop as the result of death and loss (Prigerson & Jacobs, 2001). In fact, the *DSM-5* (APA, 2013) delineates how the functional psychological consequence of complex grief presents with co-occurring conditions such as major depressive disorder, posttraumatic stress disorder, substance use disorders, and separation anxiety disorders. The complexity of the grieving and mourning process itself lies in many other factors such as one's past experience of grieving, culturally specific issues related to the expression of grief, pre- and co-occurring mental health conditions related to the grief scenario or critical incident, and other clinical symptoms that present during therapeutic interactions (e.g., suicide ideation, persistent thoughts and preoccupation with the deceased, excessive use of substances, feelings of hopelessness, detachment, and social isolation). Accordingly, many authors recognize the complex variation within the mourning and grieving process in therapy.

Worden (2009) suggests that the goal of grief therapy is to resolve conflicts of separation to the deceased, and for the therapist to assist the bereaved in adjusting and adapting to life without their loved one. Developing a therapeutic relationship with the bereaved is the key to achieving a strong working alliance. Skilled and competent counselors understand that acknowledging the person's loss, normalizing the experience of loss and grief, dealing with other issues of complex grief at the appropriate time, and approaching clients with a compassionate and empathetic energy assist in gaining optimal therapeutic and trusting relationships.

In cases of chronic and persistent grief reactions, counselors want to identify risk factors that are related to their client's (a) medical/physical functioning (e.g., life-threatening illness, newly acquired catastrophic disability), (b) psychiatric/mental health functioning (e.g., presence of depression, anxiety, substance use, or other co-occurring conditions), and (c) level of psychosocial adjustment, support, and resources. Symptoms of clinical significance include flashbacks of the death experience; emotional and social detachment; isolation; avoidance of intrusive thoughts related to the death experience; cognitive and emotional feelings of numbness, detachment, and confusion; intense levels of bitterness, anger, and hostility; and feelings related to severe hopelessness, helplessness, and suicidal ideation.

In many models of grief and bereavement therapy there is a growing acceptance that attachment, remembering, and continuing bonds with the deceased are both natural and healthy (Koblenz, 2016; Worden, 2009). The manner in which "continuing bonds" therapy is facilitated varies. However, many proponents suggest it is important to have clients (a) connect with the deceased by making efforts to locate the deceased (e.g., heaven), (b) experiencing the deceased in dreams, (c) communicating with the deceased (e.g., speaking with them in silence, visiting the cemetery), (d) remembering the deceased often (thinking about them), and (e) attaching through a variety of objects (e.g., clothing, jewelry, home videos; Normand, Silverman, & Nickman, 1996; Rando, 1984; Worden, 2009). The absence of such approaches can lead to a lack of information about the deceased, unresolved feelings, frustration, and chronic and persistent feelings of sadness. Overall, continuing this bond with the deceased is instrumental in the mourning process and helps in assisting with increased coping and resiliency after the loss (Neimeyer, 2001).

TRAUMA AND GRIEF

The horrific terrorist attacks of September 11, 2001, and the devastation of Hurricane Katrina, which took place on August 29, 2005, are examples of extraordinarily stressful and traumatic events that left emotional, physical, spiritual, and environmental scars on the minds, bodies, and spirits of many in the United States. The desolation left in the aftermath of these and other critical events have created a type of historical trauma among Westerners that has prompted a consciousness shift within the counseling profession (Stebnicki, 2016a). It is of particular interest how we can apply models of loss, grief, death, and dying to inimitable cultural events that occur on large-scale disasters such as forest fires, catastrophic floods, school shootings, earthquakes, and other critical incidents that spark the primary emotion of loss and grief (Stebnicki, 2017).

There are multiple opportunities for professional counselors to prepare for, plan, and intervene in a variety of critical incidents that result in catastrophic loss of life. It is beyond the scope of this chapter to compare and contrast theories, models, and interventions in grief counseling, critical incident stress debriefing, or disaster mental health response. This would certainly be a fruitful area for researchers to explore in a meta-analysis as well as other research designs. The results, discussion, and conclusion of such purported studies on catastrophic loss of life in which common factors relate to symptomatology, clinical features, methods of evaluation, and interventions to facilitate with individuals' grieving multiple losses. Presently, the literature appears to mix concepts, theories, and interventions as it relates to grief counseling and trauma response.

The new *DSM-5* may be a bridge for practitioners and researchers alike dealing with issues of grief, loss, death, and dying, given the new diagnostic category of *Persistent Complex Bereavement Disorder*. Given that trauma creates a chronic, persistent, and sometimes delayed grief reaction, the diagnostic and associated clinical features may help support a diagnosis of such a mental health condition. Indeed, there are various definitions and models of disaster mental health response out of which some appear the same, similar, and different from models of grief counseling and interventions. However, competent and ethical counselors are aware of the appropriate application for diagnosing, triaging, and intervening across different settings, cultures, and types of traumatic experiences. In other words, competent mental health professionals understand the cultural and clinical differences between intervening in a rural Arkansas tornado, a California or Canadian wild fire, or a Chicago neighborhood exploding in gun violence. Likewise, the seasoned grief counselor knows how to facilitate grief therapy with children, adolescents, and adults across a variety of losses that spark persistent and complex feelings of bereavement (e.g., sudden death of a child, dying of AIDS, or death by suicide).

CHRONIC ILLNESS AND DISABILITY: A COMPLEX GRIEF RESPONSE

One particular area that has been studied a great deal is the grief and loss reaction associated with chronic illnesses and disabilities (CID). Persons with CID are served at a much greater frequency than ever before. This is primarily because of the medical advances extending life expectancy, increase in the "Baby Boomer" generation, increase in person-made (e.g., terrorism, physical assaults) and natural disasters (e.g., hurricanes, floods, earthquakes), and the ensuing wars in Iraq, Afghanistan, and multiple other geographic locations outside the United States (Stebnicki, 2017). Overall, persons with physical, cognitive, emotional, and psychiatric disabilities seek counseling services in much greater numbers than previously reported (Smart, 2016).

The U.S. Census Bureau in 2010 estimated that there are more than 56.7 million Americans with acquired CID (U.S. Census Bureau, 2010). The World Health Organization (WHO; 2016) reports about one billion persons worldwide live with a disability. Many disabilities are caused by motor vehicle accidents; falls causing catastrophic injury; acts of physical, sexual, and intimate partner violence; and war. The medical/physical injuries acquired are of a very serious nature. They typically include physical injuries such as traumatic brain injury, traumatic amputation, spinal cord injury, musculoskeletal injuries, and chronic pain conditions. Counselors could benefit greatly from having the awareness, knowledge, and skills in working with the unique psychosocial aspects of loss, mourning, and grief as they relate to persons with CID.

Many individuals who experience permanent medical–physical disabilities experience a complex level of psychosocial adjustment because of the loss of their residual functional capacity. In essence, there is a grieving and mourning process that individuals and family members go through as individuals with CID progress through the physical rehabilitation process (Marini, 2016; Smart, 2016; Stebnicki, 2017). Skilled and competent counselors understand that persons with CID experience losses in many different ways such as:

- Loss over the control of one's life and overall independence
- Loss in a sense of fairness and justice
- Loss of emotional and mental security
- Loss of mental capacity to make decisions independently
- Loss of physical capacity, body image, and ability for sexual or intimate relationships
- Loss of career identity, vocational opportunities, or ability to progress academically

Processing the multiple losses with clients can bring meaning and purpose to clients living with CID. Individuals can be empowered by understanding that they are people first and that their *dis*-ability does not define the boundaries of their mental and physical capacities and who they are as people.

The literature related to how persons with CID cope with loss is quite immense. Coping has been viewed as a psychological strategy to decrease, modify, or diffuse the impact of stress-related life events (Livneh & Antonak, 2012). The defining characteristics of coping with a CID include how the person: (a) exhibits and experiences coping as a state or trait; (b) controls or manipulates his or her coping strategies; (c) organizes his or her coping style on a range of internal–external characteristics; and (d) responds from an affective, cognitive, and/or behavioral style of coping. Falvo (2014) describes *coping strategies* in relation to CID as a subconscious mechanism to deal and cope with stress. The intent is for the person to reduce his or her level of stress and anxiety. Coping styles (e.g., denial, compensation, rationalization) are particularly relevant for persons coping with CIDs. This is because in psychosocial adjustment to disability there is a strong need for the person to bring balance, normalcy, productivity, and a certain quality of life back to optimal functioning.

From a counseling perspective, it is important to choose goals with clients and family members that relate to the person's: (a) stability, (b) progressive nature, (c) episodic nature, (d) degenerative nature, and (e) periods of exacerbation and remission of the individual's CID. Counselors who bring meaning to the loss of mental and physical capacity have opportunities to gain therapeutic leverage with their clients. Cultivating coping and resiliency skills while allowing the person to grieve and mourn the loss of his or her medical/physical and mental health can assist in empowering persons with CIDs for optimal wellness across multiple life areas.

OLDER ADULTS AND GRIEF

As Bruyere, Harley, Kampfe, and Wadsworth (2017) point out through multiple government sources, baby boomers are coming of age and are clearly in a unique developmental life space (see National Center for Health Statistics, 2012; U.S. Bureau of Labor Statistics, 2015). Currently, one in every five American workers is more than 65 years old. By 2024, persons aged 55 years and older will comprise approximately 20% of the workforce. Thus, as the number of individuals survive into older adulthood, the number of mental and physical disabilities and life stressors related to diminishing functional capacity also increases (Falvo, 2014).

As a natural part of the aging process, older individuals experience multiple losses because of mood dysregulation, cognitive decline, loss of sensory capabilities, medical and physical conditions, and loss of independence (Eisenberg, Glueckauf, & Zaretsky, 1999; Falvo, 2014; Garfield, 1979). As a result of the aging process, acquired chronic illness and disability, stress and trauma, and overall decline in mental and physical health, grief itself becomes a complicated process and is difficult to define, unlike a diagnosable condition (Parks, 2007; Prigerson, Vanderwerker, & Maciejewski, 2008; Rando et al., 2012). Consequently, grief is complicated when older individuals experience the full range of medical, physical, psychological, cognitive, social, and emotional health issues, which places older persons at-risk for any number of losses in daily functioning and independence.

Indeed, preexisting mental and physical health conditions before CID contribute much to one's wellness and resiliency (Shannonhouse, Myers, & Sweeney, 2016), especially in the case of older individuals. It may become an asset or protective factor in dealing with issues of loss and grief during older adulthood. Persons who age successfully have a better acceptance of past losses, griefs, conflicts, and a good mastery of some level of independence and control over their environment (Falvo, 2014; Kampfe, 2015). Counselors that have had training related to negative stereotypes about persons with disabilities, aging (ageism), prejudice, and attitudinal barriers against older persons (gerontophobia) can reduce the stigma, misconceptions, and fear of addressing psychosocial issues with older persons and issues related to the aging process. Thus, infusion of content related to counseling older persons within the counselor education curriculum can increase the knowledge, awareness, and skills of professional counselors to build rapport and facilitate an optimal therapeutic relationship with older individuals (Bruyere et al., 2017; Kampfe, Wadsworth, Smith, & Harley, 2005).

CAREGIVER STRESS IN THE GRIEVING PROCESS

Based on the record numbers of aging baby boomers, one of the fastest growing occupations in the United States is that of home health care aide. Family members are oftentimes caregivers for persons with CID; despite that, nearly 70% of all Americans are transferred to and die in an institution such as a hospital or a nursing home (Centers for Disease Control and Prevention [CDC], 2005). Institutions are designed to meet the acute primary medical needs of persons with CID. Most cannot offer what a concerned family member can in terms of emotional and psychosocial support. Too often, family members are viewed as a nuisance, getting in the way, rather than allies in caring for the patient (Jones, 1979). In addition, some institutional environments restrict visitation by children or the patient's friends and extended family. This can add to a source of family and caregiver stress because of the inability to provide essential emotional and psychosocial support.

The average caregiver in the United States is 63 years old and is typically caring for a spouse or family member who is aged more than 65 years (Lee & Carr, 2011). The intense person-centered nature of caregiving itself creates an emotional, physical, and spiritual exhaustion that can result in empathy fatigue (Stebnicki, 2008, 2016b). The research under certain circumstances supports the notion that family caregivers can endure a significant amount of stress (Marini, 2016). In Marini's (2012) meta-analysis of research related to caregiver stress, he found a significant number of studies that report poor health and psychosomatic conditions associated with being a caregiver. The primary factors linked to caregiver stress occur when: (a) there is little or no respite or backup assistance to perform the essential tasks and functions in the caregiver role, (b) persons with CID are verbally or physically abusive toward the caregiver, and (c) a greater number of hands-on direct care hours are spent caring for the disabled loved one. These factor increase the risk for poor health among caregivers themselves.

In Marini's (2016) review of the literature on the psychosocial impact of caregiving on caregivers, he notes the significant number of empirical and anecdotal studies in which the act of caregiving can provide meaning and purpose in one's life. Despite the impact of this demanding work, lengthy hours, and the stress associated with caregiving, it has been reported by some to be rewarding. In other words, there appears to be a life-lesson learnt in the mental-emotional process of both family and professional caregiving. There are positive experiences of caregivers, particularly when the loved one with a disability reciprocates in appreciation and gratitude. This appears to minimize the caregiver stress and burden.

When the stress of caregiving itself becomes mentally, physically, and emotionally exhausting, some caregivers may require the support of a professional counselor. Counselors working with caregiver stress can assist by offering services that are focused on (a) respite care services, (b) processing caregiver emotions that are associated with negative feelings toward their loved one, and (c) advocacy related to fragmented medical and mental health services, support groups, financial support, and managing end-of-life services and resources (Lee & Carr, 2011; Marini, 2016; Worden, 2009). Overall, minimal attention has been given to sources of caregiver stress in terms of the caregiver's reaction and experience of this highly stressful job that many times cannot be fulfilled by any other person or institution. The lack of resources for emotional, physical, and financial respite provides multiple opportunities for counselors who work with issues of death and dying to integrate family members as a natural part of psychosocial counseling.

END-OF-LIFE DECISIONS

Perhaps one of the most overlooked areas in the grief, death, and dying literature is bereavement and anticipatory grief as it relates to assisted suicide and end-of-life decisions that challenge family members. Researchers have demonstrated the significant clinical features (e.g., clinical depression, panic and anxiety, financial stress) of family members struggling with their loved ones suffering mentally, physically, and spiritually as a result of a life-threatening disability and/or anticipated death (Kevorkian, 2016; Koblenz, 2016; Lee & Carr, 2011; Michler Detmer & Lamberti, 1991; Valentine, Bauld, & Walter, 2016; Werth, 2002). Chronic and persistent mental health conditions that continue without psychosocial support and treatment place the dying individual at risk for suicide attempts or completion. Thus, these psychosocial issues should be of paramount concern for counseling professionals. Some research supports the notion that counseling clients in decisions of assisted suicide may actually lead to positive outcomes for the survivor (Worden, 2009). If the person's family is not involved in issues of assisted death, then they may have grief reactions more similar to a family survivor of someone who died alone by self-inflicted suicide (Werth, 1999).

Several issues deserve attention before counselors move forward with discussing end-of-life decisions with clients. This is because (a) oftentimes, issues related to suicide ideation and assisted suicide arise naturally within a therapeutic context; (b) counselors may have strongly held religious/spiritual beliefs and values related to end-of-life decision-making issues that may manifest as countertransference, which ultimately may harm the therapeutic relationship; and (c) there are well-defined state laws, counseling ethics, and health care policies that dictate and guide one's decision making to discontinue life or prolong treatment decisions, which can become overwhelming for clients, counselors, and family members (Kevorkian, 2016; Lee & Carr, 2011; Werth, 2002).

Counselors who provide services to the terminally ill have an ethical obligation to understand the applicable laws and health care policies that govern the termination of treatment and end-of-life decisions. First and foremost, the American Counseling Association's (ACA) *2014 Code of Ethics*, Section B.2.b.-Confidentiality of End-of-Life Decisions, states that counselors must maintain client confidentiality of any discussion related to termination of treatment, physician-assisted suicide, and issues related to end-of-life care (ACA, 2016). The 2014 ACA *Code of Ethics* indicate that, depending on the circumstance, counselors must consult with supervisors, colleagues, and/or others regarding the client's disclosure of end-of-life decisions and termination of medical treatment issues. Additional ethical considerations apply to end-of-life decisions and discontinuation of medical treatment because these issues do not constitute a direct threat or act of suicide. Rather, "physician-assisted suicide" is recognized by law in five states (Oregon, Washington, California, Montana, Vermont) and Washington, DC, thus involving the medical community.

Counselors can be of value to clients and family members when discussing issues related to end-of-life decision making. They can assist clients in exploring the risks and benefits of medical treatments, make future plans regarding their family's emotional and financial well-being, and assist clients in getting emotional and psychological closure to other critical end-of-life decisions (Corey, Schneider Corey, Corey, & Callanan, 2015). Foundational counseling skills, such as the facilitation of compassion, empathy, and family support, honor the person's decision to discontinue medical treatment or prolong life. Indeed, clients with life-threatening disabilities experience a roller coaster of emotions in dealing with the multiple losses associated with the debilitating conditions of chronic and persistent medical, physical, emotional, and spiritual pain. Some of the anticipated emotions that clients may experience related to end-of-life decisions are guilt, anger, confusion, anxiety, fear, panic, isolation, detachment, and the search for meaning (Kevorkian, 2016; Rando, 1984; Worden, 2009). Resources that are commonly used in end-stage diseases and terminal illness include, but are not limited to, caregiver support, palliative care and hospice services, mindfulness meditation, financial counseling, one-on-one religious/spiritual services, as well as many types of complementary and alternative therapies (Lee & Carr, 2011).

CONCLUSIONS

The psychosocial aspects of grief, death, and dying are overlooked in the fields of counseling and psychology. These issues are multidimensional by nature and require therapeutic attention so that the process of grieving and dying can be humanizing for the client and his or her family members. More recently, it has been recognized that the grief and loss experienced by extraordinarily stressful and traumatic non-death events such as person-made and natural disasters have similar clinical characteristics and patterns of mourning losses. Recognition in the new *DSM-5* of the Persistent Complex Bereavement Disorder diagnostic category provides legitimacy for the individual's sense of loss and mourning based on multiple events related to death and dying. It is essential that counselors address such psychosocial concerns with clients because of the added therapeutic value and ethical obligation to guide the individual and his or her family in important decisions regarding death and dying.

REFERENCES

American Counseling Association. (2016). 2014 ACA code of ethics. Retrieved from https://www.counseling.org/resources/aca-code-of-ethics.pdf

American Psychiatric Association. (2013). *Diagnostic and statistical manual of mental disorders* (5th ed.). Arlington, VA: American Psychiatric Publishing.

Balk, D. E. (2014). Taking stock: Past contributions and current thinking on death, dying, and grief. *Death Studies, 38*, 349–352.

Bruyere, S. M., Harley, D. A., Kampfe, C. M., & Wadsworth, J. S. (2017). Key concepts and techniques for an aging workforce. In I. Marini & M. A. Stebnicki (Eds.), *The psychological and social impact of illness and disability* (7th ed.). New York, NY: Springer Publishing.

Centers for Disease Control and Prevention. (2005). Work Table 309: Deaths by place of death, age, race, and sex. Retrieved from http://www.cdc.gov/nchs/data/dvs/Mortfinal2005_worktable_309.pdf

Corey, G., Schneider Corey, M., Corey, C., & Callanan, P. (2015). *Issues and ethics in the helping profession* (9th ed.). Stamford, CT: Cengage.

Craig, L. (2010). Prolonged grief disorder. *Oncology Nursing Forum, 37*(4), 401–406.

Eisenberg, M. G., Glueckauf, R. L., & Zaretsky, H. H. (1999). *Medical aspects of disability: A handbook for the rehabilitation professionals.* New York, NY: Springer Publishing.

Engel, G. L. (1961). Is grief a disease? A challenge for medical research. *Psychosomatic Medicine, 23*, 18–22.

Falvo, D. R. (2014). *Medical and psychosocial aspects of chronic illness and disability* (5th ed.). Burlington, MA: Jones & Bartlett.

Garfield, C. A. (1979). *Stress and survival: The emotional realities of life-threatening illness.* St. Louis, MO: C. V. Mosby.

Jones, R. B. (1979). Life-threatening illness in families. In C.A. Garfield (Ed.), *Stress and survival: The emotional realities of life-threatening illness.* St. Louis, MO: Mosby.

Kampfe, C. M. (2015). *Counseling older people: Opportunities and challenges.* Alexandria, VA: American Counseling Association.

Kampfe, C. M., Wadsworth, J. S., Smith, S. M., & Harley, D. A. (2005). The infusion of aging issues in the rehabilitation curriculum: A review of the literature. *Rehabilitation Education, 19*, 225–233.

Kevorkian, K. A. (2016). Counseling the terminally ill and their families. In I. Marini & M. A. Stebnicki (Eds.), *The professional counselor's desk reference* (2nd ed., pp. 469–473). New York, NY: Springer Publishing.

Klass, D. (2014). Grief, consolation, and religions: A conceptual framework. *OMEGA, 69*(1), 1–18.

Koblenz, J. (2016). Growing from grief: Qualitative experiences of parental loss. *OMEGA, 73*(3), 203–230.

Kübler-Ross, E. (1975). On death and dying. *Bulletin of the American College of Surgeons, 60*(6), 12, 15–12, 17.

Kushner, H. S. (1980). *Why do bad things happen to good people.* New York, NY: Avon Books.

Lee, C. J., & Carr, G. F. (2011). *Stepping up: A companion guide for family caregivers.* Southport, NC: Phronesis Press.

Livneh, H., & Antonak, R. F. (2012). Psychological adaptation to chronic illness and disability: A primer for counselors. In I. Marini & M. A. Stebnicki (Eds.), *The psychological and social impact of illness and disability* (6th ed.) (pp. 95–107). New York, NY: Springer Publishing.

Marini, I. (2012). Implications of social support and caregiver for loved ones with the disability. In I. Marini, N. M. Glover-Graf, & M. J. Millington (Eds.), *Psychosocial aspects of disability: Insider perspectives and strategies for counselors* (pp. 287–310). New York, NY: Springer Publishing.

Marini, I. (2016). Counseling caregivers. In I. Marini & M. A. Stebnicki (Eds.), *The professional counselor's desk reference* (2nd ed., pp. 513–517). New York, NY: Springer Publishing.

Michler Detmer, C., & Lamberti, J. W. (1991). Family grief. *Death Studies, 15*, 363–374.

Murray Parkes, C. (2005). Part I introduction to a symposium: Symposium on complicated grief. *OMEGA, 52*(1), 1–7.

National Center for Health Statistics. (2012). Healthy People 2010 final review. Retrieved from: https://books.google.com/books?hl=en&lr=&id=r8rXoEExkK8C&oi=fnd&pg=PA3&dq=U.S.+Department+of+Health+and+Human+Services,+2013&ots=xBUdakpIDZ&sig=JqNCJoT9MbbMmvMd5FAOpma bCg4#v=onepage&q=U.S.%20Department%20of%20Health%20and%20Human%20Services%2C%20 2013&f=false

Neimeyer, R. (2001). *Meaning reconstruction & the experience of loss.* Washington, DC: American Psychological Association.

Neimeyer, R., Prigerson, H. G., & Davies, B. (2002). Mourning and meaning. *American Behavioral Scientist, 46*, 235–251.

Normand, C. L., Silverman, P. R., & Nickman, S. L. (1996). Bereaved children's changing relationships with the deceased. In P. R. Silverman & S. L. Nickman (Eds.), *Continuing bonds: New understandings of grief* (pp. 87–111). Philadelphia, PA: Taylor & Francis.

Parks, C. M. (2007). Complicated grief: The debate over a new *DSM-V* category. In L. Doka (Ed.), *Living well with grief: Before and after the death* (pp. 139–152). Washington, DC: Hospice Foundation of American.

Prigerson, H. G., Horowitz, M. J., Jacobs, S. C., Parkes, C. M., Aslan, M., Goodkin, K., ... Maciejewski, P. K. (2009). Prolonged grief disorder: Psychometric validation of criteria proposed for *DSM-V* and *ICD-11*. *PLOS Medicine, 6*(8), e1000121.

Prigerson, H. G., & Jacobs, S. C. (2001). Perspectives on care at the close of life. Caring for bereaved patients: "all the doctors just suddenly go." *Journal of the American Medical Association, 286*(11), 1369–1376.

Prigerson, H. G., Maciejewski, P. K., Reynolds, C. F. III, Bierhals, A. J., Newsom, J. T., Fasiczka, A., ... Miller, M. (1995). The inventory of complicated grief: A scale to measure maladaptive symptoms of loss. *Psychiatry Research, 59*(1–2), 65–79.

Prigerson, H. G., Vanderwerker, L. C., & Maciejewski, P. K. (2008). A case for inclusion of Prolonged Grief Disorder in *DSM-V*. In M. Stroebe, R. Hanson, H. Schut, & W. Stroebe (Eds.), *Handbook of bereavement research and practice: Advances in theory and intervention* (pp. 165–186). Washington, DC: American Psychological Association.

Rando, T. A. (1984). *Grief, death, and dying: Clinical interventions for caregivers.* Champaign, IL: Research Press.

Rando, T. A., Doka, K. J., Fleming, S., Franco, M. H., Lobb, E. A., Parkes, C. M., & Steele, R. (2012). A call to the field: Complicated grief in the *DSM-5*. *Omega, 65*(4), 251–255.

Rosenblatt, P. (2012). The concept of complicated grief: Two lessons from other cultures. In M. Stroebe, H. Schut, & J. van den Bout (Eds.), *Complicated grief: Scientific foundations for health care professionals.* New York, NY: Routledge.

Shannonhouse, L. R., Myers, J. E., & Sweeney, T. J. (2016). Counseling for wellness. In I. Marini & M. A. Stebnicki (Eds.), *The professional counselor's desk reference* (2nd ed., pp. 617–623). New York, NY: Springer Publishing.

Smart, J. (2016). Counseling individuals with disabilities. In I. Marini & M. A. Stebnicki (Eds.), *The professional counselor's desk reference* (2nd ed., pp. 417–421). New York, NY: Springer Publishing.

Stebnicki, M. A. (2008). *Empathy fatigue: Healing the mind, body, and spirit of professional counselors.* New York, NY: Springer Publishing.

Stebnicki, M. A. (2016a). Disaster mental health response and stress debriefing. In I. Marini & M. A. Stebnicki (Eds.), *The professional counselor's desk reference* (2nd ed., pp. 439–447). New York, NY: Springer Publishing.

Stebnicki, M. A. (2016b). From empathy fatigue to empathy resiliency. In I. Marini & M. A. Stebnicki (Eds.), *The professional counselor's desk reference* (2nd ed., pp. 533–545). New York, NY: Springer Publishing.

Stebnicki, M. A. (2016c). Integrative approaches in counseling and psychotherapy: Foundations of mind, body, and spirit. In I. Marini & M. A. Stebnicki (Eds.), *The professional counselor's desk reference* (2nd ed., pp. 593–604). New York, NY: Springer Publishing.

Stebnicki, M. A. (2017). *Disaster mental health counseling: Responding to trauma in a multicultural context*. New York, NY: Springer Publishing.

Stroebe, M. (2015). "Is grief a disease?": Why Engel posed the question. *OMEGA-Journal of Death and Dying, 71*(3), 272–279.

Stroebe, M., Hansson, R., Schut, H., & Stroebe, W. (2008). *Handbook of bereavement research and practice: Advances in theory and intervention*. Washington, DC: American Psychological Association.

U.S. Bureau of Labor Statistics. (2015). Career outlook: Projections of the Labor Force, 2014–2024. Retrieved from http://www.bls.gov/careeroutlook/2015/article/projections-laborforce.htm

U.S. Census Bureau. (2010). Americans with disabilities report. Retrieved from https://www.census.gov/newsroom/releases/archives/miscellaneous/cb12-134.html

Valentine, C., Bauld, L., & Walter, T. (2016). Bereavement following substance misuse: A disenfranchised grief. *OMEGA, 72*(4), 283–301.

Werth, J. L. (1999). The role of the mental health professional in helping significant others of persons who are assisted in death. *Death Studies, 23*(3), 239–255.

Werth, J. L. (2002). Incorporating end-of-life issues into psychology courses. *Teaching of Psychology, 29*(2), 106–111.

Worden, J. W. (2009). *Grief counseling and grief therapy: A handbook for the mental health practitioner* (4th ed.). New York, NY: Springer Publishing.

World Health Organization. (2016). Injury-related disability and rehabilitation. Retrieved from http://www.who.int/violence_injury_prevention/disability/en

15

Family Caregiving

IRMO MARINI AND MICHAEL J. MILLINGTON

Caregiving in America is perhaps one of the most misperceived, underappreciated, sometimes stressful, and otherwise rewarding acts of unconditional love. Yet, depending on which study or author one is reading, *caregiving* is often described at one of the two contradictory ends of the spectrum; "a curse or opportunity" (Hulnick & Hulnick, 1981). Olkin (1999) and Wright (1988) are critical of some researchers' bias in presuming certain research conclusions before conducting a study, or alternatively, twisting the findings toward their bias. Olkin in particular outlines a number of research studies where the title is formulated before conducting the study, where researchers use all too common identifiers, such as "burden, caregiver burnout, and caregiver stress," regarding caring for a family member (pp. 47–48). She cites numerous studies on the concept of burden and negative implications of caring for a disabled family member as a foregone conclusion. In addition, Yuker (1994) attempted to declare a moratorium on research focusing on the horrific negative effect of caring for a child with a disability.

Wright (1988) discusses the insider versus outsider perspective. When speaking to family members of a loved one with a disability (insider perspective) versus someone who has never experienced the situation (outsider perspective), generally two different perceptions of what it must be like (outsider) versus what it is actually like (insider) to care for a loved one with a disability emerge. Overall, these studies point to insider perspectives that often translate into the benefits and rewards of caregiving, whereas many outsider perspectives continue to hold the belief that caregiving drains the emotional, physical, and financial reserves from the caregiver(s) (Argyle, 2001; Bogdan & Taylor, 1989; Heller & Factor, 1993). Although more recent national studies generally refute many of the negative aspects of caregiving (National Alliance for Caregiving and AARP [NAC/AARP], 2015), this ultimately depends on the caregiving dynamic and the situational circumstances discussed in detail later.

In this chapter, we first explore the prevalence of caregiving in America, including demographic information about who the typical caregiver is and what the situational circumstances are for these individuals. This is followed by providing a definition of the types of caregiving support generally provided by loved ones, as well as the nuanced differences between unpaid family care versus paid formal care. This segues into a brief exploration into the significant family role caregiving entails and its impact on each member. These differences lead us into exploring the negative and positive aspects of caregiving. In addition, caregiver abuse as well as the often painful decision to place a loved one in a long-term care facility are discussed. Finally, we explore strategies for counselors to be able to support family caregivers in caring for their loved one while maintaining their own mental and physical health needs.

PREVALENCE AND DEMOGRAPHICS OF CAREGIVING IN AMERICA

The 2015 Caregiving in the U.S. survey report of 1,248 caregivers cites an estimated 43.5 million unpaid adult caregivers in America; in 78% of these instances the caregivers are taking care of an adult aged 50 years or older (NAC/AARP, 2015). Sixty percent of the caregivers are women, and 82% are caring for one individual who is either a parent or a parent-in-law. The average caregiver is a 49-year-old female caring for a 69-year-old female relative with a long-term physical condition requiring some form of physical assistance. She spends an average of 24.4 hours per week providing direct care such as help bathing, dressing, running errands, and managing finances. This caregiver also provides medical assistance in terms of medication administration, wound care, or even giving injections. She is married or in a relationship, works full time, has some college education but no degree, and reports a household income of more than $54,000 per year. Regarding her own health, the average caregiver reports little or no physical or financial strain, but does report moderate levels of emotional stress (NAC/AARP, 2015).

The caregivers who indicate a greater number of caregiving hours report spending approximately 62.2 hours per week providing the same type of care described earlier (e.g., bathing, running errands). This average caregiver is female, almost 52 years old, and takes care of a 68-year-old female parent or spouse with a long-term physical condition in most cases. Approximately 50% of these caregivers are employed, have the same education as the average caregiver, are married or cohabitating, and have a household income of $45,700. The average caregiver describes her own health by noting moderate physical strain, moderate to high emotional stress, but little to no financial strain. She also reports moderate to high difficulty in performing activities of daily living (ADL), as well as experiencing some difficulty finding affordable services. As these type of caregivers themselves age (75+ years), they most often become the sole caregiver of a spouse with Alzheimer's and have to regularly communicate with the medical professionals (NAC/AARP, 2015).

At first glance, unpaid family caregivers are primarily women caring for a loved one, often with little or no assistance; this increases with age. The younger caregiver appears to be able to balance employment with part-time caregiving. In the Caregiving in the U.S. study (NAC/AARP, 2015), caregivers reported the loved one they were caring for either had a physical condition (59%), or memory problems (26%), or an emotional or mental illness (21%). The older caregiver was typically providing 44 hours or more per week of direct care or supervision, and reported higher levels of emotional and financial stress, as well as his or her own perceived poor physical health. These caregivers most often tended to be the sole provider and reported having little if any social support.

TYPES OF CAREGIVING AND SUPPORT

There is a plethora of literature regarding social support and disability, and its significance is critical to the well-being of loved ones who need assistance. Numerous theories and construct definitions exist. Cohen and Wills (1985) differentiate between structural and functional components of social support. *Structural* support is defined as the quantity and frequency of persons in the network, noting the type (partner, spouse, coworkers) and frequency in engaging with one's social network and social activities. *Functional* support is broken down into instrumental, informational, and emotional support (Chak, 1996; Cohen, 1988). Instrumental support refers to providing personal assistance with ADL, finances, and other tangible types of assistance. Informational support refers to providing information and education to assist individuals through difficult times, while emotional support pertains to listening, being empathetic, and offering counsel to individuals experiencing difficulties (Cohen, 2004).

In further defining ADL and instrumental activities of daily living (IADL), ADL include providing assistance with personal hygiene and grooming, dressing and undressing, feeding, transferring (in/out of bed, car), assistance with toileting, and ambulation. Assistance with IADL includes providing assistance with housekeeping, paying bills, managing money, meal preparation, shopping, and medications. In many instances, caregiving may also include caring for a pet or a patient's child, transportation to and from appointments, health maintenance, and being a companion. The Caregiving in the U.S. report (NAC/AARP, 2015) indicates that caregivers spent 59% of their time assisting with ADL, the most difficult of which were dealing with incontinence, assisting to/from the toilet, and bathing assistance.

Interpersonal Dynamics of Care

Millington and Marini (2016) further describe the nuanced psychological differences between unpaid proximal family care and formal distal care, or paid assistance provided by home health care agencies. Family care has a shared history, level of intimacy, emotional bond, and reciprocity. The relationships are built and trusted in most instances, and family care carries with it a sense of comfort and familiarity, as well as unconditional love (Bainbridge, Cregan, & Kulik, 2006; Bauman et al., 2006). Family caregivers generally have a more vested interest in their loved one's comfort, optimal health, and well-being. Conversely, in dysfunctional or abusive family relationships, the caregiver may be verbally or physically abusive by withholding care or medical treatment, and threaten the well-being of the family member needing assistance (Nadien, 1996).

Home care agency providers may, over time, establish a close bond with their patient and family if there is long-term consistency of care provided by that individual. However, more often than not such assistance is generally provided by rotating different providers who assist with ADL. They are paid to perform certain tasks, and not to develop a friendship, an emotional bond, or services outside of their scope of practice (e.g., caring for the patient's child). Millington and Marini (2016) note that although family and agency caregivers both perform the identical tasks of bathing, dressing, meal preparation, and so forth, the family caregiver does so out of unconditional love with the ultimate goal of comforting his or her loved one.

Regardless, be it the family or a paid agency providing the care, generally the caregiver's attitudes, beliefs, and values impact how that care is provided (Marini, 2012). Caregivers who are empathetic, value helping others, and obtain a sense of meaning doing so generally have the patient's overall health and well-being in mind. Conversely, those who see caregiving as a job, obligation, or something forced on them may directly or indirectly harm the well-being of the individual being cared for (Nosek, Foley, Hughes, & Howland, 2001; Sakakibara, Kabayama, & Ito, 2015; Washington, 2009).

Social Support

Chronister, Chou, Frain, and Cardoso (2008) conducted a meta-analysis regarding perceived social support for various rehabilitation populations. They found small effect sizes related to perceived support and physical health; medium effect sizes for psychological health, quality of life, and employment; and large effect sizes for adjustment to disability. This latter finding is supported by other studies as well, noting specifically that with strong family support, family members with disabilities generally adapt to their disability more successfully (Li & Moore, 1998; Varni, Rubenfeld, Talbot, & Setoguchi, 1989).

Lack of social support can lead to isolation. Increasing care demands can monopolize the carer's time and energy. The carer role within the family can displace other important family roles. High demand for care of one child can diminish time spent with other children, one's spouse, friends, and time spent alone with one's personal pursuits. Lack of time to participate in personal interests shrinks social environments beyond the carer role (Quittner, Glueckauf, & Jackson, 1990). Social networks providing support can erode as the situation becomes chronic. Even the spiritual network is at risk when leaders and lay members do not recognize the spiritual life of the person with a disability and worse, validate some form of social shaming. Rejection by one's religious community can create a crisis of faith and alienation in the family (Speraw, 2006).

FAMILY ROLE CHANGES

Caring responsibilities are built into existing family roles. However, disability requires a strategic renegotiation of caring roles to be effective. When it is not well considered, disability-related care tends to be disproportionately ascribed along gendered lines. Mothers are traditionally ensconced in nurturing familial roles and selfless dedication to child care. They are often primarily responsible for all facets of child development in health, education, and moral upbringing regardless of the demands on them, adequacy of resources, or their power to implement (Malacrida, 2009). In instances where there is an absent or almost absent spouse or partner, the mother role demands come increasingly at the expense of self-care and personal well-being.

Mothers with disabilities find additional struggles defending themselves in a formal care system that is predisposed to see them as unfit for parenting (Prilleltensky, 2004). Help for mothers with developmental disabilities often comes with state supervision, an assumption of incompetence, and service that usurps rather than supports the mothering role (McKeever, Angus, Lee-Miller, & Reid, 2003). Fear of the state's judgment and sanctions, including the very real threat of enforced foster care (McConnell & Llewellyn, 2002), coerces mothers into diminished and dependent roles.

Children are often active participants in care, capable of contributing to family well-being. The type and amount of care provided by children appears linked to family income (Becker, 2007), in that more is required in homes with fewer economic resources. To a point, the child's helping role can be an extension of accepted and traditional duties. As care demands increase, childhood roles undergo actual structural changes (Warren, 2007). In the extreme, the "parentification" (Stein, Reidel, & Rotheram-Borus, 1999) of the child role, especially where children are caring for parents with disabilities, can disrupt the development of traditional identities (O'Dell, Crafter, de Abreu, & Cline, 2010). A childhood spent providing personal care, performing household tasks and childcare, and acquiring supplemental family income with paid work can disrupt the customary developmental path of childhood (Earley, Cushway, & Cassidy, 2007) and challenge the development of coping skills (Pakenham, Bursnall, Chiu, Cannon, & Okochi, 2006).

Siblings find their relationships with a brother or sister with a disability redefined in childhood (Rawson, 2009). Maintaining and expanding care responsibilities throughout the life span is common (Heller & Kramer, 2009) and can compete with personal development. Sibling care is often a social negotiation. In general, siblings rise to the occasion and benefit from the relationship (Heller & Arnold, 2010). When care transitions from parent to siblings, one sibling is usually designated for the primary caring role, whereas other siblings provide indirect support, such as financial and other planning consultations (Heller & Arnold, 2010). Lone siblings are often dually encumbered as they inherit responsibilities for sibling care and simultaneously entertain approaching care issues for aging parents (Burke, Taylor, Urbano, & Hodapp, 2012).

Aging and Evolution

Transitions create challenges anew. Parental care for an adult child with a disability changes as the family moves from home care to independent living (Lindsay, 2008). In later life the aging of the parental carer becomes an issue as both mother and father face diminishing physical capacity to perform caring roles. Care becomes an issue of continuity into adulthood as parents look beyond their tenure as aging carers for a family member with developmental disabilities (Minnes, Woodford, & Passey, 2007). Sometimes grandparents reassume parental roles in child care (Pit-ten Cate, Hastings, Johnson, & Titus, 2007). This can be a beneficial role support within a network of care, but a concern when aging grandparents replace rather than support the parent in the long term. Many of the challenges facing spousal caregivers arise out of the growing psychological conflict between the desire to sustain deeply engrained roles and the reality of a relationship increasingly dominated by one-sided care, loss of function, and diminished social activity (Ducharme, Levesque, Ethier, & Lachance, 2007).

NEGATIVE IMPLICATIONS OF CAREGIVING ON CAREGIVER HEALTH

There are numerous studies examining the physical and psychological health implications of perceived caregiving stress and burden (Berglund, Lytsy, & Westerling, 2015; Brehaut et al., 2009; Roth, Perkins, Wadley, Temple, & Haley, 2009; Werner & Shulman, 2015). Although Olkin (1999) objects to some researchers' stereotypical assumptions regarding caregiver stress, many studies nevertheless report the negative health implications for caregivers who perceive themselves to be in high strain roles, particularly those caregivers who clock more hours per day with a more severely disabled loved one (Byrne, Hurley, Daly, & Cunningham, 2010; NAC/AARP, 2015; Roth et al., 2009). Byrne et al. (2010) found female caregivers of children with cerebral palsy reported poorer physical and mental health than non-caregivers, particularly those mothers who spent more time caregiving.

Brehaut and colleagues (2009) analyzed population-based data regarding caregiver health of 3,633 healthy children versus 2,485 children with health problems in Canada. Caregivers of the children with health problems reported more chronic health conditions, activity limitations, poorer health, and higher depressive symptoms. Approximately 65% of respondents had a postsecondary education with an income of $49,000 annually, and Canada has universal health care. This atypical finding differed from other studies that have shown lower income and education to be contributing factors to poorer physical and/or mental health of caregivers (Imran et al., 2010; Manuel, 2001). In further exploring physical health problems only, studies supporting specific physical health problems are generally vague other than low back pain and headaches

(Brehaut et al., 2009; Grosse, Flores, Ouyang, Robbins, & Tilford, 2009). Low back pain is often because of having to physically lift or transfer a loved one repeatedly, whereas headaches are related to worry about a variety of caregiving related matters.

Studies regarding the psychological impact of caregiving are much more common, and delineate more specifically the type of problems caregivers report, most commonly depression and anxiety (Berglund et al., 2015; Grosse et al., 2009; Imran et al., 2010; Mulvihill et al. 2005; NAC/AARP, 2015; Roth et al., 2009). Imran and associates (2010) for example, examined anxiety, depression, and family burden of 100 Pakistani primary caregivers caring for a family member with a psychiatric illness. The results indicated a high rate of depression and anxiety among male and female caregivers (86% and 85%, respectively) who expressed concerns regarding the future, fear of being alone and having the sole responsibility for the family member, coping with family member behavioral problems, social isolation, and the stigma associated with mental illness.

Sakakibara and colleagues (2015) interviewed 23 primary Japanese caregivers and found phases of acceptance of the caregiver role. In instances where caregiving was perceived as finite or short term, caregivers adapted better to the role and viewed it as their obligation. Although the sentiment was also shared with those who perceived no end to caregiving, this latter group expressed disappointment, helplessness, impatience, and having no choice but to continue providing the care indefinitely. The authors note the societal expectation in Japan that the adult children care for their aging parents, and many expect and feel an obligation to do so when the time comes, regardless of the lifestyle changes they have to make to do so.

ABUSE BY CAREGIVERS

One of the consequences of caregiver stress is that some caregivers strike back at the individual they are caring for physically or verbally (Fulmer, 1990). Payne (2005) estimates prevalence rates between 500,000 to two million cases of elder abuse or neglect annually, not including child abuse. One theory as to why abuse occurs follows the psychiatric model, which indicates the abuse is a result of some flawed characteristic of the caregiving abuser such as abusing substances or having a psychiatric illness (Miller, 1959). Coyne, Reichman, and Berbig (1993) surveyed 342 caregivers of cognitively impaired adults and found those caregivers who were more likely to abuse typically worked longer hours, had been the caregiver for many years, worked with persons requiring a higher level of care, and were more likely to be depressed. In addition, caregiver abusers reported being more likely to have been physically assaulted by their care recipients.

Nadien (1996) describes various types of abuse including physical, psychological, and material. *Physical abuse* involves "physical assault, sexual abuse, slapping, grabbing, pushing, or restraining... physical neglect pertaining to denial of food, medicine, shelter and physical assistance" (p. 159). *Psychological abuse* involves coercion, ridicule, verbal aggression, confinement, abandonment, and threats of aggression including sexual or nonsexual. *Material abuse* generally involves legal or financial abuse such as theft, exploitation, or other personal property matters; material neglect is defined as withholding legal help and information (Johnson, 1991; Nadien, 1996, 2006). Caregiver abuse may be inferred from many signs, including fractures, sprains, bruises, cigarette burns, abrasions, and overmedication. Other forms may include eating disturbances, sleeping disorders, untreated pressure sores, malnutrition or dehydration, lack of clean clothes, and denial of hearing aids, visual aids, or ambulation devices (Nadien, 2006).

Some of the general characteristics of persons with disabilities who are statistically more vulnerable to various forms of abuse include those who are more dependent for ADL, have fewer support resources, and have less power. Older women are abused more than men. In one study of caregiver abuse regarding younger persons with developmental disabilities, it appears those with more mild, moderate, or severe mental retardation who can interact have a higher frequency of abuse than those with profound mental retardation. Specifically, those individuals who interact but whose interactions involved maladaptive behavior (e.g., rebellious, hyperactive, violent or disruptive) are more frequently abused (Martin, 1982; Zirpoli, Snell, & Loyd, 2001). Nadien (2006) notes that caregivers who find the role fulfilling are less likely to abuse than caregivers who are resentful or poorly paid to do the job.

Gainey and Payne (2006) studied the role of caregiver burden in 751 suspected elder abuse cases of persons with Alzheimer's disease and compared this with other non-Alzheimer's type disabilities. They found that the impact of burden and abuse was no different between Alzheimer's and other types of disabilities, calling into question the stress or burden causation theory as to why caregivers abuse their recipients. O'Brien (1994) and others (Korbin, Anetzberger, & Eckert, 1990) have indicated that perhaps the overstressed explanation is oversimplified, noting that only some caregivers abuse, whereas most do not under similar circumstances. The authors suggest that interventions should focus not only on the caregiver in better dealing with his or her anger/frustration, but also interventions for care recipients in minimizing conflicts with the caregiver.

Finally, although strong social support is generally found to have a positive influence on recipients with disabilities, there are studies that indicate there can indeed be negative consequences with dysfunctional social supports (Abbey, Abramis, & Caplan, 1985). Persons with substance abuse problems returning to an environment where friends and family also abuse substances is an example of this occurrence. Related instances where people with disabilities are in an abusive relationship and unable to defend themselves also become more vulnerable psychologically and physically (Nosek et al., 2001). In such dysfunctional or abusive relationships, this distress can lead to depression, increased negative affect, social withdrawal, stigma, and deleterious physical well-being of the patient (Evans, Palsane, Lepore, & Martin, 1989; Nosek et al., 2001; Werner & Shulman, 2015).

THE DECISION TO MOVE A LOVED ONE INTO A NURSING HOME

What may be one of the most difficult and psychologically painful tasks for any family member to decide is having to make the decision to place a loved one into a long-term care facility (Reuss, Dupuis, & Whitfield, 2005). Numerous studies cite the psychological and financial stresses caregivers report regarding the toll of caring for a loved one at home (Grosse et al., 2009; Stevens & Thorud, 2015). The perceived stress of the caregiver, perceived and actual support or lack of it, financial constraints, severity of care of the disabled loved one (e.g., ventilator and/or feeding tube), and age of the caregiver are all significant factors in making such a decision (Fisher & Lieberman, 1999; Wackerbarth, 1999). It is not uncommon for caregivers to experience simultaneous feelings of loneliness, guilt, resentment, sense of failure, sadness, anger, loss of control, rushed decision making, and peace of mind with the process (Dellasega & Nolan, 1997; Nolan & Dellasega, 2000).

Gräsel (2002) studied caregiver physical and mental health after having placed a loved one in a long-term care facility. He interviewed 720 German primary caregivers of a loved one with dementia and followed up with 681 caregivers 1 year later after the loved one was in long-term care. Two groups were distinguished: active caregivers still caring for their loved one at home after 12 months, and caregivers who were at least 6 months past placing their loved 1 in long-term care. The active caregiving group showed no major health changes after one year, but the frequency of illnesses was up moderately with a mild increase of medication. They also did not report any increase in somatic complaints or physician visits.

For the group who was no longer providing care, their average physician visits almost doubled. Gräsel attributed this occurrence to the caregivers now having time to visit their physician. And despite their dramatic increase in physician visits, these former caregivers subjectively perceived themselves to be feeling much better and their medications had not increased. Contrary to the sense of feeling better with the perceived burden or stress of caregiving ending in Gräsel's study, other studies suggest caregivers become worse health-wise. It is not uncommon for female caregivers in particular to become lonely, guilty, depressed, and potentially physically ill (Collins, Stommel, Wang, & Given, 1994; Gaugler, Leitsch, Zarit, & Pearlin, 2000).

Reuss and colleagues (2005) surveyed family members in southern Ontario, Canada, regarding what factors were most influential in facilitating a positive transition for their loved one into a long-term care institution. Results indicated several key factors, including the experience during the waiting process, preparation for the move, ease of the actual move, control over decisions, communication throughout the process, support from others, and family and resident perceptions and attitudes toward the move. Nolan and colleagues (1996) specified that (a) when significant family members and the care recipient are able to plan and rationally prepare for the move; (b) are equal participants in actually choosing a setting; (c) have time to express reactions and sentiments about the choices; and (d) are provided information to make informed decisions about the alternatives, then final decisions and a positive transition are more likely.

POSITIVE ASPECTS OF CAREGIVING

There are far fewer studies addressing the positive aspects of caregiving for loved ones with a disability than negative ones, yet the results are meaningful and indicative of the insider perspective described by Wright (1988). A number of studies indicate that those who perform caregiving view it as an act of unconditional love that provides meaning to their lives as they sustain the comfort, safety, and quality of life for their loved one (Bogdan & Taylor, 1989; Buchanan, Radin, Chakravorty, & Tyry, 2009; Krause, Coker, Charlifue, & Whiteneck, 1999; Matheis, Tulsky, & Matheis, 2006; Sakakibara, Kabayama, & Ito, 2015). Buchanan and colleagues (2009), for example, surveyed 530 caregivers (78% were spouses, 54% male) of a loved one with multiple sclerosis. Almost half provided 20 hours or more of caregiving per week. Approximately 25% of the caregivers reported that they could benefit from counseling; over half indicated that caregiving was demanding, time-consuming, or a challenge, yet 90% reported being happy that they could help. In addition, approximately 65% indicated that caregiving was rewarding, and more than 80% expressed that they were proud of the care they provided to their loved one.

In studies related to social exchange reciprocity (Call, Finch, Huck, & Kane, 1999; Dwyer & Miller, 1990), in instances where a loved one with a disability is perceived as being able to reciprocate love, communicate, and provide companionship, caregivers generally report mutual benefits, reciprocity, and reduced perceived burden. Reid, Moss, and Hyman (2005) assessed 56 caregivers with a burden inventory, self-esteem inventory, and caregiver reciprocity scale. Results indicated that increased reciprocity such as warmth and balance was inversely related to physical, social, emotional, and developmental burden experienced by the caregivers. In addition, intrinsic motivation to provide care was more highly related when reciprocal love was perceived. Bogdan and Taylor (1989), however, described a "sociology of acceptance" of perceived reciprocation, even with caregivers whose child was profoundly developmentally disabled and unable to verbally communicate.

Lindblad, Holritz-Rasmussen, and Sandman (2007) reported similar findings in a group of 13 parents caring for a child with a disability in Sweden. In-depth narrative interviews were conducted, resulting in three overlapping themes: (a) being gratified by experiences of the child as having a natural place in relation with others, (b) being provided a room for sorrow and joy, and (c) being enabled to live an eased and spontaneous life. As with Bogdan and Taylor (1989), parents had a defined social place for their child in the family. The child was equally valued and appreciated. Parents also acknowledged the family openness and support to discuss their sadness and worries, and conversely to experience joyous occasions intermixed. Finally, the ability to live an eased and spontaneous life was described as the family social support network of grandparents and friends who would spontaneously assist with the family needs. This interdependency was appreciated and "life enriching" for all caregivers concerned (p. 244).

COUNSELOR STRATEGIES AND SUPPORTING FAMILY CAREGIVERS

The recovery movement that gave voice to the family in rehabilitation counseling extends its influence into practice through the systems of care philosophy (SOC; Cook & Kilmer, 2012). SOC was a response to family mistreatment in the fragmented panoply of services systems required in the care of children with mental health issues. Initially, SOC sought to insert community psychology practice by creating change in community entities designed to provide family support. The practices that developed within the SOC were shaped by community principles that also guided rehabilitation counseling in an emerging family practice that was (a) client-centered, (b) family-driven, (c) community based, and (d) culturally competent. Community-based rehabilitation counseling is expressed in a strengths-based case management model that focuses on the acquisition and strategic utilization of resources in accomplishing vocational and related goals (Selander & Marnetoft, 2005). Family care is the point of entry into this system for the rehabilitation counselor. Facilitating successful long-term client goals depends on a synergistic relationship with family care.

Counseling

Framed in case management, rehabilitation counseling is any service that directly or indirectly facilitates client outcomes. The family goal is to facilitate family resilience. At the client's behest, family features in two intertwined service concerns: (a) the primary participation goal of rehabilitation counseling service (e.g., supported employment) and (b) the family care system that supports the person before, during, and after the primary goal is achieved. In both service concerns, the family is engaged as a full and valued partner.

Communication and Partnership

Establishing a working alliance with the family requires clear and open communication; a safe space for self-expression; and a shared belief that everyone is heard, understood, valued, and influential. Sharing personal experiences about disability reveals care issues (Fisher, 2006), provides an opportunity to deepen trust through disclosure (Goldsmith, 2009), and creates a space for each person to find a voice. By encouraging family members to share their thoughts, emotions, and caring activities, the rehabilitation counselor develops a more holistic family profile that facilitates counselor empathy and understanding. Whether and how the family talks about its disability experience provides insight into the values and beliefs of the group and the specific perspectives of each member (Checton, Greene, Magsamen-Conrad, & Venetis, 2012).

Focus on Strengths

Motivation to act turns on the potential that exists within each person, the power of the collective, and the great untapped resources that are available in the larger community. Counseling nurtures self-efficacy and confidence through positive reframing of experience, a climate of optimism, and an accumulating history of planful successes. Helping family members reframe their stories becomes especially important in resisting disempowering social attitudes and stigma. Family members are encouraged to identify and discuss individual and collective strengths that they have otherwise taken for granted in caring for their loved one. Counselors emphasize concepts such as resilience, perseverance, altruism, meaningfulness, and faith/spirituality when appropriate.

Coping

The family's repertoire of problem solving (Nezu, Palmatier, & Nezu, 2004) and other coping skills is their bulwark against distress (Elliott, Shewchuk, & Richards, 2001). Both care and employment outcomes are pursued via a continuous process of strategic evaluation, planning, implementing, monitoring, and adapting group effort in care. Social problem solving is the preferred cognitive-behavioral coping strategy. Where plans do not come to fruition or crisis derails progress, other coping strategies are practiced to ameliorate stress and make new and constructive meaning out of otherwise untenable circumstances (Kenny & McGilloway, 2007). Failure is reframed as a learning opportunity and a step toward eventual success.

Rehabilitation counselors should engage family in contingency planning for high probability complications to the core plan. Contingency planning coordinates roles and processes in the event of a crisis, thus inoculating the family against the chaos and uncertainty. Plans may include having the emergency phone lists and trees posted, alternate "Plan B's" for predictable disruptions to daily life, and a support network of extended family and friends at the ready. As much as possible, the family strives to maintain its natural routine and rhythm with community support.

Empowerment

The fair distribution of social power is central to any social justice endeavor. Carers and care recipients alike should be intimately aware of the obligations, expectations, and authorities of their role. Their respective roles should reflect a fair distribution of obligation and authority across family members. The person should be capable of enforcing their authority and fulfilling their obligations, and reasonably satisfied with the arrangement. Within the family, empowerment comes from inclusive discussion and consensus on task delegation.

Care often takes place in a vulnerable space for the recipient. The carer has a stake in the caring task and must move with some level of autonomy. The proper balance of power is constantly being negotiated between "caring for" and "caring about." Maximizing care recipient control over the caring process is important. Where choice and self-direction are possible, they should be supported. Minimizing time spent in the care recipient role is desirable, to a point. Diversifying roles for the family member with a disability to include his or her fair share of caregiving obligations helps to balance the care load and reaffirm the interdependent nature of family life. Rehabilitation counselors encourage client independence as a family value. Learning to master one's environment is critical to one's self-esteem and prospects beyond the home.

Power is also negotiated in the family's transactions in formal care systems (Swain & Walker, 2003). Families confront byzantine health care systems as advocates for their loved ones. System empowerment can take place at a personal level in negotiations with the service providers in strategic planning, accessing service, monitoring and evaluation; or in family input into networking other forms of care across care systems (e.g., education, residential, employment, transportation). The principled push in a strengths-based model is to have families lead and control the care that enters their lives, standing as equals in the dialog with formal care professionals (Caldwell & Heller, 2007; Dempsey & Dunst, 2004).

The perceived and actual amount of power that the families can reasonably assert with health care and related community providers are dependent on several factors; some controllable, some not (Marini, 2012). Families become more empowered when they are educationally prepared and can articulate (assertively when necessary) their loved one's needs. Rehabilitation counselors can assist family members in developing appropriate medical and related service inquiries, thereby establishing a partnership of equals that affords the family the time and respect necessary to become fully informed (Yuker, 1988). Families that are more directly engaged in formal care decisions are less likely to passively defer to authority. Families may struggle with professionals who exert an authoritative medical model approach to care (whether it is appropriate or not). In such instances, rehabilitation counselors may choose to advocate on behalf of the family/client, equip the family with strategies to self-advocate for their rights, refer clients to client assistance programs (CAPs), or seek out alternative providers if necessary.

Peer Support and Advocacy

Peer support is a resource based on the resilient properties of social identity that initially emerged from the mental health recovery movement (Nelson et al., 2007). It is an empowerment model designed by people with disabilities who live engaged and inclusive lives in the presence of symptoms. They seek support and strength from each other (rather than experts) and express their well-being in coping, planning, and advancing in employment, advocacy, education, community life, and health care alternatives. Care among peers is mutual. In this model, responsibility is retained in the individual, and thus they must work for themselves and define their own goals.

Referral to a Center for Independent Living (CIL) or other peer-support groups who have persevered with similar disabilities are empowering and supportive for a newly adapting family who may otherwise feel isolated by their circumstances. The universality of experience assures families that their experience is normative and their response is common. Strength in numbers that peers represent opens the doors to untapped resources and possibilities for new solutions. Self-advocacy has a ready-made booster group that knows ways around system barriers, strategies for applying collective pressure on unresponsive services, and a louder voice for social justice change. Although the rehabilitation counseling literature rarely addresses the importance of peer support referrals, their significance cannot be overstated in assisting individuals and families to adapt in many areas of their lives (Marini, Bhakta, & Graf, 2009).

CONCLUSIONS

Family caregiving and support are perhaps the most essential elements in their disabled loved ones' adjustment for response to disability (Li & Moore, 1998). When chronic illness or disability strikes a family member, families are left to either regroup and thrive, or recoil and succumb to the negative implications of their collective misfortune. Resilient families are those who communicate and support one another, delegate caregiving responsibilities equally, maintain family routines and rituals, and advocate as needed with community resource networks. Conversely, families that become dysfunctional are those that do not communicate or support one another or deal appropriately with stress (e.g., substance abuse), as well as those whose members may verbally and/or physically abuse their disabled loved one out of resentment or frustration. Effective counseling and support strategies include focusing on family strengths, empowerment, advocacy and peer support, and instilling a strength-based approach that fosters family resilience and perseverance.

REFERENCES

Abbey, A., Abramis, D. J., & Caplan, R. D. (1985). Effects of different sources of social support and social conflict on emotional well-being. *Basic and Applied Psychology, 6*, 111–129.

Argyle, E. (2001). Poverty, disability and the role of older carers. *Disability & Society, 16*(4), 585–595.

Bainbridge, H. T., Cregan, C., & Kulik, C. T. (2006). The effect of multiple roles on caregiver stress outcomes. *Journal of Applied Psychology, 91*(2), 490–497.

Bauman, L. J., Foster, G., Silver, E. J., Berman, R., Gamble, I., & Muchaneta, L. (2006). Children caring for their ill parents with HIV/AIDS. *Vulnerable Children and Youth Studies, 1*, 56–70. doi:10.1080/17450120600659077

Becker, S. (2007). Global perspectives on children's unpaid caregiving in the family: Research and policy on "young carers" in the UK, Australia, the USA and Sub-Saharan Africa. *Global Social Policy, 7*(1), 23–50.

Berglund, E., Lytsy, P., & Westerling, R. (2015). Health and wellbeing in informal caregivers and non-caregivers: A comparative cross-sectional study of the Swedish general population. *Health and Quality of Life Outcomes, 13*, 109.

Bogdan, R., & Taylor, S. (1989). Relationships with severely disabled people: The social construction of humanness. *Social Problems, 36*, 135–148.

Brehaut, J. C., Kohen, D. E., Garner, R. E., Miller, A. R., Lach, L. M., Klassen, A. F., & Rosenbaum, P. L. (2009). Health among caregivers of children with health problems: Findings from a Canadian population-based study. *American Journal of Public Health, 99*(7), 1254–1262.

Buchanan, R. J., Radin, D., Chakravorty, B. J., & Tyry, T. (2009). Informal care giving to more disabled people with multiple sclerosis. *Disability and Rehabilitation, 31*(15), 1244–1256.

Burke, M. M., Taylor, J. L., Urbano, R., & Hodapp, R. (2012). Predictors of future caregiving by adult siblings of individuals with intellectual and developmental disabilities. *American Journal of Intellectual and Developmental Disabilities, 117*, 33–47.

Byrne, M. B., Hurley, D. A., Daly, L., & Cunningham, C. G. (2010). Health status of caregivers of children with cerebral palsy. *Child: Care, Health and Development, 36*(5), 696–702.

Caldwell, J., & Heller, T. (2007). Longitudinal outcomes of a consumer-directed program supporting adults with developmental disabilities and their families. *Intellectual and Developmental Disabilities, 45*(3), 161–173.

Call, K. T., Finch, M. A., Huck, S. M., & Kane, R. A. (1999). Care-givers burden from a social exchange perspective: Caring for older people after hospital discharge. *Journal of Marriage and the Family, 61*, 688–699.

Chak, A. (1996). Conceptualizing social support: A micro or macro perspective? *Psychologia, 39*, 74–83.

Checton, M. G., Greene, K., Magsamen-Conrad, K., & Venetis, M. K. (2012). Patients' and partners' perspectives of chronic illness and its management. *Families, Systems & Health, 30*(2), 114–129.

Chronister, J., Chou, C. C., Frain, M., & Cardoso, E. (2008). The relationship between social support and rehabilitation related outcomes: A meta-analysis. *Journal of Rehabilitation, 74*, 16–32.

Cohen, S. (1988). Psychosocial models of the role of social support in the etiology of physical disease. *Health Psychology, 7*(3), 269–297.

Cohen, S. (2004). Social relationships and health. *American Psychologist, 59*(8), 676–684.

Cohen, S., & Wills, T. A. (1985). Stress, social support, and the buffering hypothesis. *Psychological Bulletin, 98*(2), 310–357.

Collins, C., Stommel, M., Wang, S., & Given, C. W. (1994). Caregiving transitions: Changes in depression among family caregivers of relatives with dementia. *Nursing Research, 43*(4), 220–225.

Cook, J. R., & Kilmer, R. P. (2012). Systems of care: New partnerships for community psychology. *American Journal of Community Psychology, 49*(3–4), 393–403.

Coyne, A. C., Reichman, W. E., & Berbig, L. J. (1993). The relationship between dementia and elder abuse. *American Journal of Psychiatry, 150*(4), 643–646.

Dellasega, C., & Nolan, M. (1997). Admission to care: Facilitating role transition amongst family carers. *Journal of Clinical Nursing, 6*(6), 443–451.

Dempsey, I., & Dunst, C. J. (2004). Help-giving styles and parent empowerment in families with a young child with a disability. *Journal of Intellectual & Developmental Disability, 29*(1), 40–51. doi:10.1080/13668250410001662874

Ducharme, F., Levesque, L., Ethier, S., & Lachance, L. (2007). "Masculine" care: Caregiver experiences and perceptions of services helping elderly couples. *Canadian Journal of Community Mental Health, 9*, 143–159.

Dwyer, F. W., & Miller, M. K. (1990). Differences in care-giving network by area of residence: Implications for primary care-giver stress and burden. *Family Relations, 39*, 27–37.

Earley, L., Cushway, D., & Cassidy, T. (2007). Children's perceptions and experiences of care giving: A focus group study. *Counselling Psychology Quarterly, 20*, 69–80.

Elliott, T. R., Shewchuk, R. M., & Richards, J. S. (2001). Family caregiver social problem-solving abilities and adjustment during the initial year of the caregiving role. *Journal of Counseling Psychology, 48*(2), 223–232.

Evans, G. W., Palsane, M. N., Lepore, S. J., & Martin, J. (1989). Residential density and psychological health: The mediating effects of social support. *Journal of Personality and Social Psychology, 57*(6), 994–999.

Fisher, L. (2006). Research on the family and chronic disease among adults: Major trends and directions. *Families, Systems, & Health, 24*, 273–380.

Fisher, L., & Lieberman, M. A. (1999). A longitudinal study of predictors of nursing home placement for patients with dementia: The contribution of family characteristics. *The Gerontologist, 39*(6), 677–686.

Fulmer, T. (1990). The debate over dependency as a relevant predisposing factor in elder abuse and neglect. *Journal of Elder Abuse & Neglect, 2*(1/2), 51–57.

Gainey, R., & Payne, B. K. (2006). Care-giver burden, elder abuse and Alzheimer's disease: Testing the relationship. *Journal of the Health and Human Services Administration, 29*(2), 245–259.

Gaugler, J. E., Leitsch, S. A., Zarit, S. H., & Pearlin, L. I. (2000). Care-giver involvement following institutionalization: Effects of pre-placement stress. *Research on Aging, 22*, 337–359.

Goldsmith, D. J. (2009). Uncertainty and communication in couples coping with serious illness. In T. D. Afifi & W. A. Afifi (Eds.), *Uncertainty and information regulation in interpersonal contexts: Theories and applications* (pp. 204–225). New York, NY: Routledge.

Gräsel, E. (2002). When home care ends–changes in the physical health of informal caregivers caring for dementia patients: A longitudinal study. *Journal of the American Geriatrics Society, 50*(5), 843–849.

Grosse, S. D., Flores, A. L., Ouyang, L., Robbins, J. M., & Tilford, J. M. (2009). Impact of spina bifida on parental care-givers: Findings from a survey of Arkansas families. *Journal of Child Family Studies, 18*, 574–581.

Heller, T., & Arnold, C. K. (2010). Siblings of adults with developmental disabilities: Psychosocial outcomes, relationships, and future planning. *Journal of Policy and Practice in Intellectual Disabilities, 7*, 16–25.

Heller, T., & Factor, A. (1993). Aging family caregivers: Support resources and changes in burden and placement desire. *American Journal of Mental Retardation, 98*(3), 417–426.

Heller, T., & Kramer, J. (2009). Involvement of adult siblings of persons with developmental disabilities in future planning. *Intellectual and Developmental Disabilities, 47*(3), 208–219.

Hulnick, M. R., & Hulnick, H. R. (1981). Life's challenges: Curse or opportunity? In A. E. Orto, *The psychological & social impact of disability* (3rd ed., pp. 258–268). New York, NY: Springer Publishing.

Imran, N., Bhatti, R., Haider, I. I., Azhar, L., Omar, A., & Sattar, A. (2010). Caring for the care-givers: Mental health, family burden and quality of life of care-givers of patients with mental illness. *Journal of Pharmacy and Pharmaceutical Sciences, 7*(1), 23–28.

Johnson, T. F. (1991). *Elder mistreatment:Deciding who is at risk.* Westport, CT: Greenwood Press.

Kenny, K., & McGilloway, S. (2007). Caring for children with learning disabilities: An exploratory study of parental strain and coping. *British Journal of Learning Disabilities, 35*(4), 221–228.

Korbin, J. E., Anetzberger, G, J., & Eckert, J. K. (1990). Elder abuse and child abuse: A consideration of similarities and differences in intergenerational family violence. *Journal of Elder Abuse & Neglect, 1*(4), 1–14.

Krause, J. S., Coker, J., Charlifue, S., & Whiteneck, G. G. (1999). Depression and subjective well-being among 97 American Indians with spinal cord injury: A descriptive study. *Rehabilitation Psychology, 44*, 354–372.

Li, L., & Moore, D. (1998). Acceptance of disability and its correlates. *Journal of Social Psychology, 138*(1), 13–25.

Lindblad, B. M., Holritz-Rasmussen, B., & Sandman, P. O. (2007). A life enriching togetherness–meanings of informal support when being a parent of a child with disability. *Scandinavian Journal of Caring Sciences, 21*(2), 238–246.

Lindsay, P. (2008). "Sunrise, sunset"—The transition faced by the parents of adults with learning disabilities. *Advances in Mental Health and Intellectual Disabilities, 2*(3), 13–17.

Malacrida, C. (2009). Performing motherhood in a disablist world: Dilemmas of motherhood, femininity and disability. *International Journal of Qualitative Studies in Education, 22*(1), 99–117. doi:10.1080/09518390802581927

Manuel, J. C. (2001). Risk and resistance factors in the adaptation in mothers of children with juvenile rheumatoid arthritis. *Journal of Pediatric Psychology, 26*(4), 237–246.

Marini, I. (2012). Implications of social support and caregiving for loved ones with a disability. In I. Marini, N. M. Glover-Graf, & M. J. Millington (Eds.), *Psychosocial aspects of disability: Insider perspectives and counseling strategies* (pp. 287–314). New York: Springer Publishing.

Marini, I., Bhakta, M. V., & Graf, N. (2009). A content analysis of common concerns of persons with physical disabilities. *Journal of Applied Rehabilitation Counseling, 40*(1), 44–49.

Martin, H. (1982). The clinical relevance of prediction and prevention. In H. R. H. Starr, Jr. (Ed.), *Child abuse prediction: Policy implications* (pp. 175–190). Cambridge, MA: Ballinger.

Matheis, E. N., Tulsky, D. S., & Matheis, R. J. (2006). The relation between spirituality and quality of life among individuals with spinal cord injury. *Rehabilitation Psychology, 51*, 265–271.

McConnell, D., & Llewellyn, G. (2002). Stereotypes, parents with intellectual disability and child protection. *Journal of Social Welfare and Family Law, 24*(3), 297–317.

McKeever, P., Angus, J., Lee-Miller, K., & Reid, D. (2003). It's more of a production: Accomplishing mothering using a mobility device. *Disability & Society, 18*, 179–197.

Miller, D. S. (1959). [Fractures among children. I. Parental assault as causative agent]. *Minnesota Medicine, 42*, 1209–1213.

Millington, M. J., & Marini, I. (2016). Family care and support. In M. Millington & I. Marini (Eds.), *Family in rehabilitation counseling: A community-based rehabilitation approach* (pp. 87–107). New York, NY: Springer Publishing.

Minnes, P., Woodford, L., & Passey, J. (2007). Mediators of well-being in aging family carers of adults with intellectual disabilities. *Journal of Applied Research in Intellectual Disabilities, 20*(6), 539–552.

Mulvihill, B. A., Wingate, M. S., Altarac, M., Mulvihill, F. X., Redden, D. T., Telfair, J., ... Ellis, D. E. (2005). The association of child condition severity with family functioning and relationship with health care providers among children and youth with special health care needs in Alabama. *Maternal and Child Health Journal, 9*(2 Suppl.), S87–S97.

Nadien, M. B. (1996). Aging women: Issues of mental health and maltreatment. *Annals of the New York Academy of Sciences, 3*, 129–145.

Nadien, M. B. (2006). Factors that influence abusive interactions between aging women and their caregivers. *Annals of the New York Academy of Sciences, 1087*, 158–169.

National Alliance for Caregiving and American Association of Retired Persons Public Policy Institute. (2015). *Caregiving in the U.S., 2015*. Bethesda, MD: Author.

Nelson, G., Ochocka, J., Janzen, R., Trainor, J., Goering, P., & Lomorey, J. (2007). A longitudinal study of mental health consumer/survivor initiatives: Part V—Outcomes at 3 year follow-up. *Journal of Community Psychology, 35*, 655–665.

Nezu, C. M., Palmatier, A., & Nezu, A. M. (2004). Social problem-solving training for caregivers. In E. C. Chang, T. J. D'Zurilla, & L. J., Sanna (Eds.), *Social problem solving: Theory research, and training* (pp. 223–238). Washington, DC: American Psychological Association.

Nolan, M., & Dellasega, C. (2000). 'I really feel I've let him down': Supporting family carers during long-term care placement for elders. *Journal of Advanced Nursing, 31*(4), 759–767.

Nolan, M., Walker, G., Nolan, J., Williams, S., Poland, F., Curran, M., & Kent, B. C. (1996). Entry to care: Positive choice or fait accompli? Developing a more proactive nursing response to the needs of older people and their carers. *Journal of Advanced Nursing, 24*(2), 265–274.

Nosek, M. A., Foley, C. C., Hughes, R. B., & Howland, C. A. (2001). Vulnerabilities for abuse among women with disabilities. *Sexuality and Disability, 19*, 177–189.

O'Brien, M. E. (1994). Elder abuse. How to spot it–how to help. *North Carolina Medical Journal, 55*(9), 409–411.

O'Dell, L., Crafter, S., de Abreu, G., & Cline, T. (2010). Constructing 'normal childhoods': Young people talk about young carers. *Disability & Society, 25*(6), 643–655.

Olkin, R. (1999). *What psychotherapists should know about disability.* New York, NY: Guilford Press.

Pakenham, K. I., Bursnall, S., Chiu, J., Cannon, T., & Okochi, M. (2006). The psychosocial impact of caregiving on young people who have a parent with an illness or disability: Comparisons between young caregivers and non-caregivers. *Rehabilitation Psychology, 51*(2), 113–126. doi: http://dx.doi.org/10.1037/0090-5550.51.2.113

Payne, B. K. (2005). *Crime and elder abuse: An integrated perspective.* Springfield, IL: Charles C Thomas.

Pit-ten Cate, J. M., Hastings, R. P., Johnson, H., & Titus, S. (2007). Grandparent support for mothers of children with and without physical disabilities. *Families in Society, 88*(1), 141–146.

Prilleltensky, O. (2004). My child is not my carer: Mothers with physical disabilities and the wellbeing of children. *Disability & Society, 19,* 209–223.

Quittner, A. L., Glueckauf, R. L., & Jackson, D. N. (1990). Chronic parenting stress: Moderating versus mediating effects of social support. *Journal of Personality and Social Psychology, 59*(6), 1266–1278.

Rawson, H. (2009). 'I'm going to be here long after you've gone'—Sibling perspectives of the future. *British Journal of Learning Disabilities, 38,* 225–231.

Reid, C. E., Moss, S., & Hyman, G. (2005). Care-givers reciprocity: The effect of reciprocity, carer self-esteem and motivation on the experience of care-giver burden. *Australian Journal of Psychology, 57*(3), 186–196.

Reuss, G. F., Dupuis, S. L., & Whitfield, K. (2005). Understanding the experience of moving a loved one to a long-term care facility: Family members' perspectives. *Journal of Gerontological Social Work, 46*(1), 17–46.

Roth, D. L., Perkins, M., Wadley, V. G., Temple, E. M., & Haley, W. E. (2009). Family caregiving and emotional strain: Associations with quality of life in a large national sample of middle-aged and older adults. *Quality of Life Research, 18*(6), 679–688.

Sakakibara, K., Kabayama, M., & Ito, M. (2015). Experiences of "endless" caregiving of impaired elderly at home by family caregivers: A qualitative study. *BMC Research Notes, 8,* 827.

Selander, J., & Marnetoft, S. U. (2005). Case management in vocational rehabilitation: A case study with promising results. *Work (Reading, Mass.), 24*(3), 297–304.

Speraw, S. (2006). Spiritual experiences of parents and caregivers who have children with disabilities or special needs. *Issues in Mental Health Nursing, 27*(2), 213–230.

Stein, J. A., Riedel, M., & Rotheram-Borus, M. J. (1999). Parentification and its impact on adolescent children of parents with AIDS. *Family Process, 38*(2), 193–208.

Stevens, A., & Thorud, J. (2015). The symbiosis of population health and family caregiving drives effective programs that support patients and families. *Journal of the American Society on Aging, 39*(4), 34–38.

Swain, J., & Walker, C. (2003). Parent-professional power relations: Parent and professional perspectives. *Disability & Society, 18*(5), 547–560.

Varni, J. W., Rubenfeld, L. A., Talbot, D., & Setoguchi, Y. (1989). Family functioning, temperament, and psychologic adaptation in children with congenital or acquired limb deficiencies. *Pediatrics, 84*(2), 323–330.

Wackerbarth, S. (1999). What decisions are made by family care-givers? *American Journal of Alzheimer's Disease, 14*(2), 111–119.

Warren, J. (2007). Young carers: Conventional or exaggerated levels of involvement in domestic and caring tasks. *Children & Society, 21,* 136–146.

Washington, L. (2009). A contextual analysis of caregivers of children with disabilities. *Journal of Human Behavior in the Social Environment, 19*(5), 554–571.

Werner, S., & Shulman, C. (2015). Does type of disability make a difference in affiliate stigma among family caregivers of individuals with autism, intellectual disability or physical disability? *Journal of Intellectual Disability Research, 59*(3), 272–283.

Wright, B. A. (1988). Attitudes and the fundamental negative bias: Conditions and corrections. In H. E. Yuker (Ed.), *Attitudes toward persons with disabilities* (pp. 3–21). New York, NY: Springer Publishing.

Yuker, H. E. (1994). Variables that influence attitudes toward persons with disabilities: Conclusion from that data. *Psychosocial Perspectives on Disability, A Special Issue of the Journal of Social Behavior and Personality, 9,* 3–22.

Yuker, H. E. (Ed.). (1988). *Attitudes towards persons with disabilities.* New York, NY: Springer Publishing.

Zirpoli, T. J., Snell, M. E., & Loyd, B. H. (2001). Characteristics of persons with mental retardation who have been abused by care-givers. *Journal of Special Education, 21*(2), 37–40.

16

Counseling in the Context of Family Identity

MICHAEL J. MILLINGTON AND ROSAMOND H. MADDEN

Who am I (who are we) in the face of change?

*I*dentity arises out of the sum of our experiences. It gives us a sense of constancy and centeredness across the sometimes turbulent change that comes with living. This is our sense of self. It is tied closely to our sense of community. In this chapter, we trace the developmental concept of identity through its manifestations at different levels of community, revealing a complex and systemic context for rehabilitation counseling. Each level of identity (personal, social, and collective) denotes a potential point of counseling exchange with the family.

To properly frame what these counseling exchanges with the family might entail, we describe how the experience of disability challenges the family system and how that experience is inculcated at each level of identity for each participating member. The family field on which all rehabilitation counseling acts becomes more than a backdrop for client service at this point. Family context, relations, and transactions create meaning in the shared disability experience. Family changes in response to the experience and becomes an agent of change in its own right as it moves in the collective on behalf of the person with a disability. Rehabilitation counseling becomes a party to this meaning making and a partner in family efforts to redefine themselves in its wake. It is important for a family-inclusive profession to contemplate the meaning of rehabilitation counseling in the context of family identity. Counseling beyond the individual is a novel frame for rehabilitation. The essential presence of the family requires a reconsideration of the applied psychological counseling constructs that undergird current practice.

Families in rehabilitation counseling are peers and partners in a person-centered initiative to advance full community inclusion for their loved one. They enter into the relationship voluntarily and at the request of the client. They are the foremost experts in the lived experience of caring for the client, and are strategically situated to facilitate or sabotage any plan devised. They are the first community that includes the client and advocates on his or her behalf. Rehabilitation counseling in this context is a social strategy. The working alliance between the counselor and the family eschews the clinical for an intentional community of purpose that emerges from a joint-common cause: full community inclusion for the person with a disability, and support for the participating family. We join the family in a shared space of community and counsel in the context of identity because we need to know, and become part of, the network that surrounds and supports the client.

FINDING IDENTITY IN THE FAMILY

> Within the flickering inconsequential acts of separate selves dwells a sense of the whole which claims and dignifies them. In its presence we put off mortality and live in the universal. The life of the community in which we live and have our being is the fit symbol of this relationship. The acts in which we express our perception of the ties which bind us to others are its only rites and ceremonies. (Dewey, 1922, pp. 331–332)

The "rites and ceremonies" of our social relationships are the conduit through which we discover and create our world. It is the field of Lewin's (1936) life space, where our sense of self is given form in the interaction between the person and his or her unique construction of a subjective world. Translating Lewin's formula to its identity equivalent, we are a function of the environment we create ($P = f[B,E]$).

Meaning and Identity

To understand identity, we must first understand meaning and how it is made. Meaning is value given form in the objects and events of lived experience (Pearlin, 1991). We make meaning with every intentional act. We orient our lives to the act of making meaning and then impose our meanings on all phenomena we encounter. In making meaning, we conceptualize our world, our identities, and ultimately our sense of self.

Meaning is predicated on core beliefs and value-laden goals (Park & Folkman, 1997). Beliefs are an encyclopedic and personal epistemology that informs the individual's worldview and frames behavior. Personal beliefs in regard to locus of control, self-worth, and optimism are important prerequisites for initiating and sustaining action. Beliefs function at the collective level to direct group action. Families that engage in collective problem solving do so with a collective belief in an orderly and responsive universe. Conversely, families that see themselves as a cohesive group are more likely to collaborate in problem solving than one that espouses a strong belief in rugged individualism (Oliveri & Reiss, 1982). Beliefs about the social environment are part of group and individual identity, played out in the problem-solving tasks of life (Oliveri & Reiss, 1981). We act and react according to our individual and shared beliefs, whether or not they are an accurate reflection of reality.

Goals turn meaning into intent. They provide the impetus and direction of our participation. There is a goal behind every intentional act and so they are as numerous as our beliefs. They differ widely in importance, commitment, and centrality to our lives. They are hierarchical and complex in their interactions. We take on proximal goals to serve more distal ones. We invest time and energy into goals in proportion to our motivation to achieve them. Beliefs and goals provide the character of our community participation and together they make meaning in our lives.

Our self-concept is the global meaning we derive from putting these beliefs and goals to work (Schwartz, 2001). Self-concept grows and changes with experience, but comes with a bias toward stability. A stable self-concept is a secure one and we jealously guard it. Presented with a challenge to our self-concept, we are more likely to change the interpretation of the data behind the challenge than our comfortable worldview. We seek out environments that reinforce our standing beliefs. We see ourselves in a more optimistic and complimentary light than facts would support. We value concrete personal relevance over abstract ideals. We have an investment in our present identity. Actual change, even positive change, comes at a cost, that is, stress (Park & Folkman, 1997). This rather ambivalent relationship to change is what Lewin called, *quasi-stationary equilibrium* (Burnes, 2004, p. 981); the status quo tends to be well secured by environmental conditions and a kind of social inertia. Meaning crystalizes through our habits and rituals (see Costa, 2013) into a perceived (if sometimes illusory) stable and unified identity.

Personal Identity

Personal identity develops with one's cognitive abilities (Erikson, 1968) and evolves through community participation. As we grow into and out of developmental roles, our beliefs are challenged and our goals change in normative and expected ways. We experiment with identity alternatives across domains (e.g., occupation, politics; Schwartz, 2001), evaluate their fit in our lives, and make an eventual commitment to an identity, its values, and its worldview. The process of identification moves along axes of exploration and commitment (Marcia, 1966). A person's first contact with a role is usually characterized as one of diffusion. He or she has neither explored nor committed to this identity in any meaningful way, and so has no deep investment in it. Having explored the role, one may reserve commitment (moratorium) until meaning is internalized (achievement). Others may take on new roles in a leap of faith and commit without exploring (foreclosure). Their challenge comes when the role does not live up to faith-based expectations.

It follows that a personal history of evolving identities leads to the present concept of self. It is a path of challenge and self-discovery. Our motivations along the way are not always conscious (Schwartz, 2001). The forces influencing our decisions are not always clear. The impact of intense experience is not easily interpretable in the traumatic moment (Pals, 2006) or its immediate aftermath. This is why telling the creation story of our identities is a powerful act of meaning-making (King & Hicks, 2006) advanced in the narrative approach to identity development (McLean & Pasupathi, 2012).

In the theory of narrative identity, individuals construct a personal mythology out of their life experiences. They repurpose memories, interpret current events through the new narrative, and project their future in its image. Story construction gives one a sense of meaning in the present and reinforces the sense of continuity in the unfolding saga over time (McAdams, 2001). More than personal reflection, the narrative story is a social process that appreciates an audience (Weeks & Pasupathi, 2010). Identity as developmental path and socially constructed history is realized on the community stage, where opportunities for roles are found and one's stories will be heard.

Community creates the opportunity to develop personal identity through the role experiences it offers the individual. In the first community, each family role is differentiated by its function in the group and its relationship to other family roles (Deaux, 2001). The mother role, for instance, implies a specialized relationship with a child with attendant tasks and routines; suggests a series of defining relationships with other proximal roles (i.e., father, grandmother, grandfather); and may be locally defined by connections with a number of distal roles in the community (e.g., social worker, teacher). In this way, family roles are networked and interdependent.

Personal identity is drawn from a multitude of roles. Mothers are also sisters, aunts, and grandmothers within the family. Beyond the family they are workers, students, and activists. Each role comes with a different set of meanings and connections (Tajfel & Turner, 1979). Each role lays claim to its own facet of one's personal story. Some roles are more salient than others. All are in flux, multifaceted, and developmental (Cox & Lyddon, 1997). Personal identity is defined by *all* of the roles one plays in community. "Who I am" is a living history of the roles that the individual has explored and inhabited in the past, in the present, and intends to pursue in a goal-directed future. The concordance of personal meaning that the individual constructs out of the totality of role experiences is his or her unique answer to the question of identity (Skaff & Pearlin, 1992). We are the stories we tell ourselves.

Social Identity

As personal identity reflects meaning associated with individuation (*who I am*), social identity reflects meaning associated with affiliation (*who we are*). Social identity trades in a social field (Reicher, Spears, & Haslam, 2010) of the collective's values, norms, and worldview. Herein, the individual shapes, and is shaped by, a shared identity. Social identity is not secondary to personal identity or dependent on it. Social identity springs from a primal drive to belong to a social order that has its own values and meanings.

Social identity is comparative in nature. The in-group differentiates itself by its comparison to an out-group. The family is defined as much by what it stands for as what it stands against. The distinction between in-group membership and out-group status is one of boundaries. Boundaries are the social skin of identity and value keeps it in place. Membership must be seen as added value to attract and keep members in. Values must also be in place to justify keeping others out. Outsiders must be different in some meaningful way, and in this difference they must be unworthy of membership. It is human nature to discriminate along lines of affiliation. Research has shown that random assignment to groups based on arbitrary categorization is enough to induce discrimination against out-group members (Tajfel & Turner, 1986). As the salience of categorization increases, so does one's commitment to the social identity. Strong boundaries make strong identities and acts of both inclusion and exclusion are at work in group dynamics.

The psychological attraction of community inclusion is very strong. Inclusion requires members to see the world through a collective lens (J. C. Turner, 1982). In this social communion, individuals draw on the self-efficacy of the group (Bandura, 1998) and on its resources (Iyer, Jetten, Tsivrikos, Postmes, & Haslam, 2011). A group characterized by strong social identification is more cohesive, more effective in collaborative effort (Reicher & Haslam, 2009), and less prone to internal conflict (Putnam, 2000). Individual members of such a group respond to stress and threats with more resolve (Haslam & Reicher, 2006), feel more empowered in their action (Camp, Finlay, & Lyons, 2002), and sustain mental health through trauma and crises better when social identity brings meaning to suffering (Kallezi, Reicher, & Cassidy, 2009). Social identity is an essential component of self-concept (Hogg & Abrams, 1988). It is fortified by the confidence that comes from external validation and support (Stets & Burke, 2000).

Community exclusion, as social identity theory suggests, is an active force that also motivates membership and assimilation into a shared social identity. McMillan and Chavis (1986) identified "freedom from shame" as part of the socializing process and added value of established membership. In it, the candidate engages in a sharing of personal and sensitive information, or otherwise opens himself or herself to the potential for rejection by the group. It is the group prerogative at that point to share secrets, or turn its collective back. Becoming vulnerable is the risk taken and the cost of membership. The psychological value of membership is tied to the depth of the potential for shame. Shame pushes people out, but it does so with the consent of the individual. Shame is to be found wanting in some aspect of social identity and for the shamed person to accept this shortcoming as a legitimate claim. For the candidate, it is an agreed on and deserved end to community. Humiliation, on the more sinister hand, does not require cooperation from the stigmatized individual (Klein, 1991). It is the forced and public rejection of the person regardless of his or her claims to membership. If shame is the death of community, humiliation is its murder. The fear of shame and humiliation are powerful tools for maintaining social boundaries and group prejudices.

Where one's social identity is strong and commitment is high, loss of membership is catastrophic. Insiders, threatened with expulsion, will commit heinous acts against their better nature to retain their in-group status. Humiliation is ubiquitous in group dynamics, subtly applied, and implied. Demotion is nearly as good as expulsion. Any loss of resource, position, power, or face is a tool that political animals in any group will use to better their own position at the expense of others. One tool of control is to assign labels to people you wish to diminish and thus force them into spoiled identities (Goffman, 1963) that mark them permanently as outsiders.

Klein (1991) wrote of the humiliation dynamic, its powerful influence, and the psychosocial damage left in its wake. It is familiar ground for rehabilitation counselors dealing with the stigma of disability experienced by individuals. But the traditional models of personal counseling have mostly dealt with the person's individual efforts at coping with the "disabled" role to which he or she has been relegated. Social identity theory was created to address community exclusion with a community response.

Social Identity and the Social Movement

Social identity theory (Tajfel & Turner, 1979) sought to understand the psychosocial dynamics and strategies of low-status groups in dealing with stigmatized, devalued, or otherwise marginalized identities imposed by high-status groups. Theorists wanted to know how disenfranchised individuals might effectively self-advocate by participating in the collective. They identified three sociostructural characteristics that influence how minority groups respond: permeability, stability, and legitimacy. Permeability is the ability of group members to join or leave the group freely, that is, social mobility. Stability is the degree to which group status is subject to change. Legitimacy is the perception that people have concerning whether or not the group's diminished status is a valid appraisal of their character or worth. The interplay of these three characteristics defines the strategies available to group members attempting to escape stigmatization (Verkuyten & Reijerse, 2008).

Denying one's membership in a stigmatized group is a potential strategy, especially when high stability and legitimacy limit other options. People with invisible disabilities could choose to "pass." This option is codified in the Americans with Disabilities Act (ADA) after a fashion, and is commonly taught as a strategy in job seeking; that is, employers cannot ask about irrelevant characteristics in the selection process, and job seekers are conversely advised not to offer information about irrelevant physical or psychological impairments. As convenient as this strategy might be for persons not strongly committed to a disability identity, it does nothing to address the injustice that makes it necessary. In fact, "passing" supports the legitimacy of oppression and reinforces the notion of permanence by the lack of community response.

Where boundaries are impermeable and status is immoveable, options for change are limited to perspective. The stigmatized group can redefine themselves in contrast to an even more stigmatized group by accentuating what positive dimensions the dominant group might deign of value, or by redefining the meaning of membership completely. These responses are passive, but at least they maintain group cohesion.

Self-Categorization Theory and Community Building

Where group identity is salient and commitment is high, the group can organize to challenge their status under the gaze of others (Deyhle, 2009) through reinforcing, intensifying, and redefining their own social identity in terms of resistance (Latrofa, Vaes, Cadinu, & Carnaghi, 2010), actively rejecting and challenging the status quo, and advocating a new relationship in collective action (Schmitt & Branscombe, 2002). Social identity creates the possibility for a discourse with power (Clare, Rowlands, & Quin, 2008).

This advocacy-oriented approach to social identity was promulgated by self-categorization theory (J. C. Turner, Hogg, Oakes, Reicher, & Wetherell, 1987). It extends social identity theory into activism based on three insights:

- Social identity is an adaptive process that sublimates differences within a group, accentuates differences between groups, produces collective behavior, and makes cooperation and influence between members possible.
- Self-categorization is a reflection of the groups a person sees himself or herself aligned with and alienated from (us vs. them); salience of a particular category depends on its fit with personal values, meanings, and utility (J. C. Turner, 1999).
- The stronger the sense of social identity, the more likely the individual is to acquiesce to group decisions, seek comity with members, give of himself or herself, and work cooperatively toward shared goals (J. C. Turner, 1991).

Self-categorization is an active process that is reinforced through community action. From the collective perspective, stronger bonds between members generate greater emotional, physical, and social resources available to the individual. The processes that create social identity and self-categorization (e.g., sharing and cooperation) are the same means by which social capital is accumulated (Haslam, O'Brien, Jetten, Vormedal, & Penna, 2005), community is built, and social change is pursued.

Finding Family Identity in Family Systems

Family as first community provides for the origins of identity at the personal, social, and collective levels. We find the family identity in the collective, beyond individuation and affiliation of the individual. Family is a corporate identity, if boundaries hold, that acts on group needs in a social field populated with other social entities (Lewin, 1936). The plans of the collective concentrate influence and orchestrate resources in ways that support each individual and advance group meanings and goals in the marketplace. Family identity arises from these social exchanges, paralleling the processes previously described.

Family Function: McMaster Model

The McMaster model looks at family function in three family task domains (Epstein, Ryan, Bishop, Miller, & Keitner, 2003): basic, developmental, and hazardous. Basic tasks sustain the day-to-day family operations (e.g., procuring and managing food, shelter, money, transportation). Developmental tasks facilitate growth and transitions (graduation, marriage, procreation, death). Hazardous tasks respond to crisis and the unexpected (disability, job loss, bankruptcy, divorce, death). Task performance involves effective (a) problem solving, (b) communication, (c) role function, (d) affective responsiveness and involvement, and (e) behavior control.

Problem-Solving Effectiveness

The family engages in a problem-solving process to address instrumental (getting things done) and affective (feelings surrounding family function) issues that become an impediment to family function. Effective and logical steps to solution include some variant of (a) problem identification, (b) communication of problem among appropriate stakeholders, (c) generating alternative action plans, (d) specific plan identification, (e) plan implementation, (f) monitoring implementation, and (g) evaluating outcomes. The everyday problems of family are many and most are resolved without consciously moving through the steps. But the greater the novelty and risk associated with the problem, the more important a strategic approach to problem solving becomes. Systemically complex life problems do not, by definition, have simple answers. Layers of problems beneath surface symptoms require a steadfast application of problem-solving skills and the ability to learn from failure and improve on partial success. Resilient families are not differentiated by the number of problems they have, but by their commitment to the problem-solving process (Epstein et al., 2003). Problems arise with the lack of skill.

Communication

There are many channels of communication in a social system and all must be recognized for their contribution to group cohesion. Theory has focused overwhelmingly on verbal communication as the primary medium of information exchange between participants. Verbal communication of instrumental and affective content can be characterized in terms of its (a) clarity of message and (b) directness to the intended recipient. Clarity is a straightforward standard of good communication. There are no conditions in which garbling the message is a positive aspect of communication, unless confusion is the intended message. Directness is more of a style issue. In some cultures (and situationally within any culture), directness is valued under some circumstances and is considered abrupt, rude, or disrespectful in others. Within the family, there is much more to communication than meets the ear. A raised eyebrow, a handshake between cousins, even the silence that passes between any family dyad can speak volumes. Problems arise when communication is absent, garbled, mismatched as to style, or the content is toxic to the relationship in any medium of exchange.

Role Function

Family roles have specialized functions and relationships that provide structure and circulate resources into and through the family system. Some of the more important functions include (a) acquiring/generating resources, (b) nurturance and support, (c) sex and intimacy, (d) personal development and advancement (e.g., career support), and (e) family management. Family management includes decision making, boundary maintenance, distribution of resources, caregiving, role allocation (how tasks are meted out), and role accountability (responsibility to the family and the authority within the family). Role functions are negotiated for balance within the family. Problems arise when that balance is missing.

Affective Responsiveness and Affective Involvement

Responsiveness is the ability to react with appropriate emotionality to family cues. Involvement is the degree to which individuals engage emotionally, intellectually, and physically with other members. Engagement runs a continuum from complete isolation, to symbiotic loss of identity, with healthy balance usually (but not always) found in more moderate positions. The range in both depth of responsiveness and the means by which it is communicated varies widely across cultures. In the family, emotional responsiveness may vary within specific relationships; for example, compare the strength and character of the socio-emotional bonds between spouses, siblings, and along gender lines. Being role dependent, the nature of these family bonds change as roles mature and when challenged by events. Crises can bring us together or drive us apart. Problems arise at the extremes when relationships are unresponsive to the need for change.

Behavior Control

Family roles are circumscribed by hierarchy, rules, and sanctions. Well-established family structure removes uncertainty about one's place in the order of things, the consequences of one's actions, and expectations for the future. Families range from autocracy to anarchy in the expression of behavioral control, with culturally mediated democratic approaches in the productive middle (Epstein et al., 2003). Entering into this compact of roles, one trades autonomy for security. The rewards are a comforting sense of predictability and constancy, and a clearly defined social identity. Problems arise when behavior control acts against the best interests of the individual.

Family Life Cycle

Family systems are constantly evolving through time (McGoldrick & Carter, 2003), cycling through developmental transitions and shifting in composition in response to external pressures and internal forces. Local expectations vary by culture and shift on socioeconomic tides, but there are some rather consistent, almost universal themes in the arc of family life (Steinglass, Bennett, Wolin, & Reiss, 1987). Childbirth brings family members together to provide support. There is an expansion of social circles through childhood and a distancing in adolescence. Rituals mark the generational transitions from youth to adulthood, from debutante to spouse to parent, to elder, and passing on—ad infinitum. In this way, family identity is always becoming, changing in culturally patterned ways that provide a sense of constancy over time.

FINDING REHABILITATION COUNSELING IN THE FAMILY IDENTITY

Disability manifests in the family system (McKellin, 1995) through the same social exchanges that create personal, social, and collective identity. Roles change in response to disability (Yeates, Henwood, Gracey, & Evans, 2007). External relationships end (Feigin, 1994) and new relationships are formed. Crises come and go; life stabilizes around a new system; and along the way disability becomes part of the family identity (McKellin, 1995) at every level.

Experience of Disability

Disability is a complex phenomenon fundamentally captured in the interaction between health conditions (i.e., disorders or disease) and the contextual factors that embed the person in his or her environment.

Figure 16.1 represents the experience of disability from the first-person perspective. The diagram is adapted from the model espoused in the *International Classification of Functioning, Disability and Health* (*ICF*: World Health Organization [WHO], 2001, 2013). It has been inverted here to emphasize the psychosocial point of view and adapted to show the connection with the family. The family appears as a category within the individual's environment. The exchange between the person and the family is represented by the reciprocating arrow that joins them. This exchange is similarly connected to the bodily structures and functions, the activities, and ultimately the participation of the individual in the community. To demonstrate that the experience of disability in a family system does not stop at the boundary of the individual, a second *ICF* diagram has been embedded in the environmental domain, representing the experience of each family member. Disability enters the experience of each family member as a feature of his or her environment and through the social identity he or she shares with the family member with a disability. The individual experiences of disability channeled through

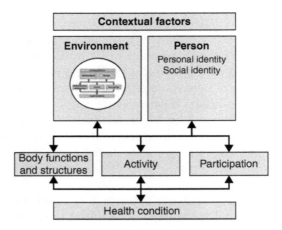

FIGURE 16.1 First-person experience of disability.

supporting family members are as systemically integrated into the *ICF* system as the direct personal experience of the client. All biopsychosocial aspects of family function are influenced by proximity to and interaction with disability. As family changes the disability experience, the experience changes the family.

Health Conditions

The instrumental characteristics of the health conditions that mediate the experience for families include onset, course, outcome expectations, and predictability (Rolland, 2012). Acute onset is most often a traumatic family event, creating a distinct moment in time that demarcates identity, before and after. Disability may be introduced at birth or later in life as a disease, complication, or traumatic injury. Gradual onset provides a gray time of transition. The course of the illness dictates the tasks of adjustment. Progressive illness dictates a constant adjustment to increasing limitations; the faster the progression, the more destabilizing the effect. In extreme circumstances, the family is in a state of continual reorganization. Where progress is intermittent, the family may develop different contingency plans for relapse and remission. Where illness prompts contemplation of death or profound loss, anticipatory grief creates avoidance behaviors that may serve to protect one from the intensity of experience, but at the cost of emotional separation and social isolation. Predictability (Rolland, 2012) is a meta-characteristic affecting all of the other attributes. Unpredictable disease creates a level of ambiguity that makes planning difficult.

Functions and Structures

Changes to body functions and structures may occur, related to one or more health conditions an individual may experience. Although these changes are sometimes a component of health outcomes, the relationship is not necessarily simple or linear. In the *ICF*, problems with body function and structure are called impairments and may relate to effects such as problems with muscle or joint functions, mental functions, loss of limbs, spinal injury, or skin damage. These are aspects of physiology and anatomy and are often seen as the domain of medical and other health professionals in treatment and rehabilitation. Although very much of the body, impairments also relate to a person's environment. The healing of muscle functions may be slow if the physical home environment is difficult to navigate, or if family support of a sometimes demanding exercise regime does not reinforce the efforts a person may need to make.

Decreasing impairment may be an end in itself. A person may consider a reduction in pain levels or a reduction in scarring and a related improvement in mental functions such as confidence as worthwhile goals. A professional may concentrate on achieving the increase in joint movement he or she considers is possible, based on his or her knowledge and experience, and consider this a worthwhile goal, assuming but not investigating possible flow-on benefits.

Impairments do not necessarily have a direct causal relationship with a person's activities or participation. For example, loss of limb may not restrict mobility with the right equipment and in the right environment. Conversely, lack of mobility may relate to a range of impairments (e.g., muscle, mental, or perceptual functions). The degree of importance a person attaches to impairments of body function and structure may relate directly to the importance he or she attaches to the range of activities that require these functions. This relationship, or perceived relationship, may thereby affect motivation in rehabilitation.

Activities and Participation

The *ICF* distinguishes between activity (the execution of a task or act) and participation (involvement in life situations). Both take place in any lifespace, from learning, to mobility, to interpersonal relationships. The model thus recognizes that a person may be undertaking activities but may never feel involved. The person may lack choice, control, or a sense of inclusion; he or she may wash dishes, but not be truly involved in discussions of the menu. The disability experience is ultimately defined in its impact on participation as the essence of community inclusion. Participation in the domains of work, education, and independent living has been the context most familiar to rehabilitation counselors to date. But if community inclusion is indeed the fundamental mission, wherever participation is diminished or denied is a domain of interest.

Stress and Disability

The reason rehabilitation counseling in is engaged is not the presence of health issues, structural or functional impairment of bodily systems, or alternatively problems in environmental or personal contextual factors. We engage because participation is not served, and so we look to the family system for ways to facilitate. We are engaging change processes. We engage the reactive change that disability has wrought on the family, and the proactive change that is the family response to disability in its midst. In both cases, the system is challenged and stress is the result. Stress can motivate, but with sufficient intensity or duration, it also creates systemic physical, psychological, and social challenges to rehabilitation and threats to personal and familial well-being. There are two models of stress that provide useful perspectives on the dynamics of disability in the family. Although both are psychosocial in application, they start from psychological and social roots, respectively.

The Transactional Model of Stress

The transactional model of stress posits that stress is not an objective feature of the person or the environment, but a subjective emotional response to the interaction between the two (Lazarus & Folkman, 1984). The process begins with an objective event. Perhaps the mother has an accident at work, or a child is born with a congenital disability. A personal appraisal of the event follows. The mother contemplates all of the consequences of lost income, the risks, and the hardships that await her rehabilitation and return to work. The parents of the child deal with the initial shock of an unexpected diagnosis and grapple with understanding present needs, while only vaguely grasping the enormity of change coming in the ensuing years. The primary appraisal addresses the question: "Is this situation a threat?" Perhaps in these cases, yes, there is a threat. The first appraisal establishes the motivational relevance of the event (Lazarus, 1993).

Risks that rise to the level of personal threat are met with an emotionally charged response (Perrewé & Zellars, 1999) and a second appraisal. Can I resolve this threat? Can I cope? The individual contemplates the meaning of the experience, the resources at his or her disposal, and the potential for response. Perhaps the worker sees a way through the experience. Rehabilitation will be a challenge, but the job is secure; the family is supportive; and the impairment can be accommodated. The woman is secure enough in her self-concept that any residual loss can be managed. Perhaps the infant's parents do not have such a positive appraisal. Specialized services and medical care are nonexistent in their rural community. The community is burdened with poverty and alcoholism has become a generational problem. The parents are estranged and underemployed. They fear that having a child with a disability will bring shame on their families. They do not have the resources, skills, or confidence to mount a response. In the absence of response, the threat and the stress remain. To the degree that stress is only partially resolved, stressors become strains (Pearlin, 1983).

The event precipitating stress can be sudden and traumatic like a heart attack, or the iconic last straw of a cumulative chronic strain (Pearlin, Lieberman, Menaghan, & Mullan, 1981). In either case, the deepest threat is existential. To discover that one is not in control, not powerful, and not respected is a direct assault to self-beliefs: self-efficacy, self-esteem, and self-worth (Aneshensel, Pearlin, & Schuler, 1993). Faced with a situation that challenges one's global beliefs and negates one's cherished goals (Park & Folkman, 1997), a person is compelled to defend his or her self-concept, create new meaning that transcends the challenge, or succumb to a spoiled identity (Wright, 1983).

The stress model that explains individual struggle is adaptable to the family system (Kelly & Steed, 2004). Caregiving demands can become primary stressors (Pearlin, Aneshensel, & LeBlanc, 1997) on the family system. The resultant strain can in turn exacerbate a litany of secondary psychosocial stressors that challenge the family identity and the roles within it (Aneshensel et al., 1993). The incremental change in spousal relationships in the context of progressive illness is a direct affront to role identity. For the individual with Alzheimer's, stress comes from feelings of loss of control and loss of meaning in the relationship. Stress for the caregiver comes from ever-increasing demands, the loss of identity in the relationship, and role engulfment (Skaff & Pearlin, 1992) with its consequent loss of social connections outside of the carer role (Aneshensel et al., 1993).

The public face of the family is also challenged. Family participation in new circles of formal care must be incorporated into present beliefs and goals. Attitudes and expectations about disability within the family's existing social network set up the potential for conflict. The micro-oppressions of a stigmatizing society are a chronic stressor on the family's emerging disability identity as well as the social identity of the person identified with the disability community (Nario-Redmond, 2010).

The transactional stress model was a major shift in psychology away from a psychomedical bias of state and trait diagnostics (Pearlin, 1983) and clinical behaviorism in favor of a psychosocial perspective of mental health that integrated cognition, affect, and social relationships (Lazarus, 1993). In defining psychological stress processes in Lewin's person X environment field, it captured the essence of identity. As Lazarus said, "Indeed, the differences between physiological and psychological stress are profound and center on an issue that psychologists have long had great difficulty dealing with, namely, *personal meaning*" (1993, p. 4, italics added). The transactional stress model has provided a solid foundation for theoretical development and practical interpretation in individual, family, and community applications (H. A. Turner & Schieman, 2008).

Conservation of Resources Model

Hobfoll offers a community variation on the psychosocial appraisal of stress (1989, 2001) that recognizes both the family and the "tribe" beyond the family as concentric frames required to capture the whole of the social experience of stress. The conservation of resource (COR) theory posits that stress "appraisals are embedded in the social context in which individuals find themselves, and that the idiographic aspects of appraisal are secondary to biological and overlearned automatic processes, on one hand, and socio-cultural processes, on the other hand" (2001, p. 341). Hobfoll does not discount the mind in the interpretation of stress. He emphasizes the importance of more fundamental aspects of the person × environment transaction.

The central tenet of COR theory is that the basic drive of people is to acquire, preserve, protect, and cultivate resources. Families are living systems constantly consuming and pursuing resources that sustain a dynamic equilibrium. This is the drive that creates the need for community because it provides the most efficient and effective structure for satisfying the many and varied needs the family has. Resources are anything of value from food and clothing, to barter and money, to space and time, to ideas and personality characteristics. Acquiring resources is crucial to recover from harm, overcome threat, and advance in the face of challenge (Lazarus, 1993). COR theory provides an economic perspective on stress that is aligned with social identity (Hobfoll, 2001) and meaning-making in the marketplace. This complements rather than contradicts the stress transaction theory and expands the construct of stress with two principles (Hobfull, 1998).

COR Principle 1: Primacy of Resource Loss

Life is lived in trade; success depends on profitable ventures. Stress occurs when resources are lost, threatened, or diminished in inefficient trade or investment. Thus, there is a negativity bias attached to loss. The perception of loss is more powerful than the perception of gain. Gains become more important in the context of previous loss, that is, there is more emotional energy invested in recouping something of value that was lost than the energy invested in its acquisition. Resource loss is more stressful than low resources; that is, there is less perceived stress in dealing with low resources if you have never experienced high resources. Positive life events are not stressful if they are equated with gain. They are only stressful inasmuch as they include loss in subevents. For example, a promotion is not stressful for the gain in prestige or cash, but in the loss of the social network of equals incurred in leaving previous employment.

COR Principle 2: The Necessity of Resource Investment

The community is a dynamic and fluid marketplace of resources and life in the community requires strategic investment. Resources must be invested to protect against future loss, recoup actual loss, and hopefully to amass resources as a form of well-being. In this psycho-socio-economic model, people who have limited resources consequently have little capacity to increase their "wealth" and suffer proportionally more from loss. Access to resources is positively correlated with capacity to orchestrate resource gain, and negatively correlated with vulnerability for loss of resources.

Those who are vulnerable to loss are vulnerable to "loss spirals," as current loss begets future loss (Hobfull, 1998, 2001). Cascading loss associated with at-risk populations exponentially exacerbates stress as vulnerable persons transact in increasingly frustrating systems with fewer and fewer resources. Families that lack a reservoir of resources tend to take a defensive approach to conservation rather than an investing approach that would have a better probability to ameliorate the loss and create gains. They do not see a way to risk-manage what they have, as they are not in a position to gamble. Consequently, they hang on without leverage and eventually lose again. There is a difference between learned helplessness and a defensive resource conservation strategy. Learned helplessness is succumbing; it is giving up. In a defensive posture, austerity is used as a coping strategy. But they eventually end up in the same place as loss spirals down and efficacy erodes. This describes the dynamics of Wright's (1983) concept of succumbing. Succumbing is a stress response of last resort, the last choice at the end of the spiral. In this way, poverty creates poverty and stress spreads from the economic to the social and psychological.

Coping, Disability, and Identity

Coping is a normal function of everyday life. Coping with disability does not engender new coping strategies, although it often requires an enhanced portfolio of options. The appraisal of harm, threat, or challenge associated with disability is multifaceted and requires a concerted coping response that varies in its orchestration across individuals, within groups, and over time. The vast potential for variance and its idiosyncratic application makes coping a personal art navigating many possible outcomes (Haslam et al., 2005). Capacity for coping depends on both access to resources and skills to mobilize them.

Social Supports

We start with social support because any internalized skill that might be brought to bear first requires an environment that is conducive to implementation. Social support provides the conduit to resources and the relationships required to solve problems and achieve goals. Social support comes from being embedded in a social network that is responsive to one's needs. This implies a deeper set of relationships and stronger socioemotional bonds than casual or formal professional connections allow (Pearlin et al., 1981, p. 340). Social support comes from one's family and friends because it is based on sustainable interdependence.

Instrumental (Problem Solving)

Problem solving is the most straightforward approach to dealing with stress, wherein one strives to resolve the problem directly. Most strategies are variations on a strategic, highly cognitive approach (Isaksen & Treffinger, 2004) that moves stepwise from problem identification, to solution finding, to plan development, to implementation, to evaluation of outcomes. Problem solving is most useful when it cycles through repeatedly as an organizational learning process. Problem solving may not be directly effective when you are not in control of the source of the problem or there is no solution to be found (Newth & Delongis, 2004).

Problem Solving With Resources

Solving problems defined within a transactional model involves resolving issues surrounding events and thus tend to be reactive. Problems and solutions in the COR theory are defined in terms of resources and more easily take on a proactive approach to problem solving. Strategic planning revolves around efforts to build reservoirs of resources and orchestrate them to best advantage in recouping loss, take preemptive action to prevent future loss and loss spirals, and encourage synergistic gain spirals that fortify a healthy social position. Immediate strategies include (a) resource replacement (get back what you lost), (b) resource substitution (lose peace at home, increase investment in work), (c) optimize what you already have, and (d) compensate for lack of fit with support (e.g., adaptive technology; social support). Emphasis on optimizing environmental resources facilitates the development of underlying personal characteristics such as self-efficacy (Freedy & Hobfoll, 1994), optimism, self-esteem, sense of coherence, learned resourcefulness, social support, and personal hardiness (Hobfoll, 2001).

Affective Coping

Alternatively, emotional response to stress can be changed. Reappraisal initiates all emotional coping. Acceptance of the situation is a positive reframing. Self-blame is a negative reframing (Gross & John, 2003). Emotional distance, avoidance, and suppression attempt to negate appraisal completely. There is a general consensus to view positive framing as superior and the others as potentially dysfunctional coping. In practice, there are times when emotional distance, avoidance, and suppression are the more healthy coping alternatives.

Meaning-Making as Coping

Rogers (1951) opined that healthy adjustment comes from being able to incorporate all of your experiences into a relationship with your self-concept. Any experience that one does not integrate becomes a threat or stress. As a major theme in this chapter, meaning-making has emerged as the loom on which we weave our identities. It follows that stressful challenges to identity send us back to the loom, and there we find a particularly potent exercise in the family processes.

Family Narrative (Stories and Myths)

Families create shared meaning in the stories they tell of themselves and of each other. There is the everyday story, like the news, that explains what we did and why. It reifies the routines of our lives, "The children were gathering eggs on Saturday morning..." puts the story in a role, at a time, in a place, for a purpose that is known in a special way to the family. The most powerful stories become family mythologies that carry deeper meaning. The communion of storytelling creates a sense of coherence among family members. It normalizes the stress-filled event and reassures the teller's place in the family by the tacit approval of the attentive audience (Pasupathi & Hoyt, 2009). The family participates in the meaning-making of the story with their asides and commentary. Shared values are accentuated. Out-group villains are vilified. Reasons for optimism are found and value is mined in lessons learned (Saltzman et al., 2011). The story of the individual becomes the story of the group, thereby reaffirming solidarity in social identity (McLean & Pasupathi, 2012) in times of adversity.

Meaning-Making in Action: Routines and Rituals

Meaning-making also takes place in cooperative action. Family life gets its sense of stability from the habits of individuals and the routines of the group (Fiese, 2006). These are the basic proximal processes (Bronfenbrenner, 1977) that construct personal and social identity. There is comfort in the pattern of routine, and a sense of competence comes from mastering it (Fiese et al., 2002). Caring for a loved one is a potent path for meaning-making. The meaning of a caring act deepens and intensifies with repetition. Loving care captured in routine creates a moment in time when the array of other demands are put into perspective. It becomes an applied and practiced acceptance of the present, and a renewal of the value of this particular relationship (Larson, 2010). The act being charged with symbolic meaning becomes more than routine; it becomes a ritual (Fiese et al., 2002).

Rituals exist for daily activities (e.g., pledge of allegiance), scheduled events (e.g., weddings), and in response to the unforeseen, providing structure to life. They are celebrations, traditions, or patterned family interactions (Costa, 2013) that communicate meaning through the generations and most importantly reify membership and create a role for everyone. Rituals around family care routines of loved ones have been shown to improve cohesion and compliance with treatment regimens (Santos, Crespo, Silva, & Canavarro, 2012). Disability is incorporated into family stories and myths, and routines and rituals through traditional family channels (Fiese et al., 2002) and thus becomes an integral feature of evolving family life (Larson, 2010).

Relational Coping

Relational coping arises out of dyads and is used to strengthen the individuals and preserve the relationship (Marin, Holtzman, DeLongis, & Robinson, 2007). Parental dyads often engage in mutual emotional support and collaborative problem solving (Donato, Iafrate, Bradbury, & Scabini, 2012) to deal with larger issues of family stress (DeLongis & Holtzman, 2005) and the logistics of disability/care within the family (Kramer, 1993). The salience of group membership acts as a buffer against stressors that attack the family (Haslam & Reicher, 2006). Relational coping is most obvious in moments of trauma, when families come together to comfort each other and to make meaning out of chaos and tragedy (Marin et al., 2007).

Manifestations of Coping: Family Resilience

Unabated stress and strain have negative biological, psychological (Haslam, 2004), and social consequences (Saltzman et al., 2011). Ineffective coping strategies only slow the rate of decline. The experience of disability often poses such risks to families. Even under the best of circumstances, it is doubtful that their first attempts at coping with the complexities of care are particularly efficacious. But they learn. Coping is social learning (Layne, Warren, Watson, & Shalev, 2007) with family at the core in both character and process (Werner & Smith, 2001). Disability is experienced as the history of a shared adaptation to adversity (Luthar, 2006). Experience begets wisdom, a portfolio of coping strategies, and a worldview infused in the social identity that bespeaks emotional lessons learned.

This positive manifestation of stress and coping is called family resilience. Walsh (2006) saw family resilience as the capacity to withstand crises, endure hardships, and grow through adversity as a functional unit. She saw this capacity coming out of family strengths tested against challenge. Family resilience, Walsh states, "involves many interactive processes over time—from a family's approach to a threatening situation, through its ability to manage disruptive transitions, to varied strategies for coping with emerging challenges in the immediate and long-term aftermath" (p. 23). Walsh (2006) found the families shared beliefs, norms, and rituals at the balanced center of family resilience. Identity is the foundation on which resilience grows.

Meaning-Making in Family Resilience

Patterson (1995) observed that the meaning-making processes were the social learning engine that turned coping experience into integrated resilience. Meaning-making builds resilience through its capacity to (a) redefine threat and challenge in the appraisal process; (b) reconstitute a coherent family identity capable of developing new coping strategies; and (c) reimagine family relationships with other groups and social systems (Patterson, 2002).

Relational Aspect of Family Resilience

The strength of family resilience is the synergistic effect of individual resilience in the collective. The individual is fortified by the confidence that comes from family membership and is thus motivated to advocate on its behalf. Responding to challenge in the collective, no one individual need master all aspects of coping, nor be particularly resilient 100% of the time (Patterson, 2002). Shared problems and orchestrated response allow that individuals can contribute according to their strengths and seek support according to their needs.

Social Support of Family Resilience

Resilience is learned, but it is not entirely a personal or group attribute. Just as individual resilience depends on family support, family resilience depends on the social support of the community (Corrigan & Phelan, 2004). The character of the family's social network determines the kind, amount, quality, and timing of informal support and care resources available. The constellation, structures, and processes of community services similarly determine the societal contribution to the raw material of family resilience (Farrell, Bowen, & Swick, 2014). Rehabilitation counseling stands among these formal resources offerings. Its value in building resilience, as with all social support, depends largely on the fit between service and need and the family's ability to turn potential into plan and practice.

Implications for Rehabilitation Counseling

Client-centered rehabilitation counseling maintains the individual with a disability at its core. All counseling activity must be maximally under client control and evaluated based on its contribution to the full community inclusion of the individual. The family is recognized as the first community, a social extension of the client that experiences threats to its collective inclusion in the community and thus has a legitimate and direct relationship with rehabilitation counseling. Family is recognized as an essential component of efficient and effective service in the present and sustaining inclusion into the future. It is the prerogative of the client to define what the family is in the collective sense, who its constituents are, and the role family members will play in the development, execution, and evaluation of rehabilitation counseling plans and services. To serve the family and the fundamental mission, rehabilitation counseling is transacted in the community with two instrumental expressions: (a) to facilitate client inclusion within the family and (b) to facilitate family inclusion in the rehabilitation process.

Working Alliance

Rehabilitation counselors approach the family as an outsider, a stranger, and worse—a stranger with an agenda. At the door, the family knows nothing of rehabilitation counseling but the stereotype and their previous experience with health care, insurance, and/or governmental systems. Imagine the family connotations of "I'm from the government and I'm here to help," or "I represent your employer and I'm here to get you back to work." The rehabilitation counselor is an outsider at entry and potentially a threat to a family in need. The counselor must often act on whatever motivation and goodwill accompanies him or her to the initial contact and begin negotiating a better relationship immediately. The counselor must form a bond of trust and communication that starts with the client (Strauser Lustig, & Donnell, 2004) and will grow into a working alliance with the family (Thompson, Bender, Lantry, & Flynn, 2007).

Preconditions for a Working Alliance

A working alliance in a group setting might as well be called community development. The rehabilitation counselor seeks a place in the family's social constellation. The rehabilitation counselor's position should be peripheral and deferent to the family dynamic, close, and trusted enough to participate in the family business of caring for the client, and emic enough as scientist–practitioners to accurately and empathetically document the family's lived experience of disability. The counselor strikes this balance not to join the family, but to become a bona fide part of the family's community.

Finding that balance under current vocational rehabilitation service structures may make this level of family communion problematic, but nevertheless, it is what is likely to be effective when the family's engaged cooperation is desired. A social model worldview is required to make this work, and it begins by embracing more egalitarian relationships and eschewing the power of the expert role. The proper relationship is a partnership of equals, with each partner to be respected and valued in his or her contribution.

The second requirement is to reject pathology. The family in community-based rehabilitation counseling is assumed to be healthy, normal, and performing to the best of their abilities. The problem that precipitated the partnership is defined as a temporary gap between where the family is and where the family wishes to be. The solution is in closing the gap, not fixing the person. The rehabilitation counselor must be slow to label behavior as maladaptive or pathological. When pathology cannot be denied and exists as a threat to self, other, or progress, it is time for a referral. The rehabilitation counselor cannot fill a dual role as family therapist and expect to succeed in either.

The third requirement is to embrace a positive, community-based psychology (see Lopez & Snyder, 2009). Rehabilitation counseling with families focuses on strengths, opportunities, and solutions. It communicates a realistic sense of optimism and models the sense of individual flexibility, group efficacy, and mutual esteem that undergirds effective collaboration. It transpires in the space where the family lives: at the kitchen table, in the workplace, at the community center. It remains consistently focused on client-controlled processes and outcomes, but everyone has a voice to be heard and a role to play.

Strategic Collaboration

Given this proactive and resilient worldview, rehabilitation counseling builds community with the family within a very focused set of shared values, meanings, beliefs, goals, and actions. The medium through which this exchange happens is instrumental problem solving. It is a normal family process and the most productive of coping strategies. The problem-solving process also mirrors brief and solution-focused counseling as well as models of the learning organization and continuous improvement logic models in quality assurance. In the identification of problems and goals, the family shares meaning. In the generation of solutions, the family explores resources. In the development of the plan, the family clarifies roles and relationships. In the implementation of the plan, the family masters the process and themselves, growing in resilience through every failure and success. In time, this effort becomes identity and part of the stories they tell about community.

REFERENCES

Aneshensel, C. S., Pearlin, L. I., & Schuler, R. H. (1993). Stress, role captivity, and the cessation of caregiving. *Journal of Health and Social Behavior, 34*(1), 54–70.

Bandura, A. (1998). Personal and collective efficacy in human adaptation and change. In J. G. Adair, D. Belanger, & K. L. Dion (Eds.), *Advances in psychological science: Vol 1. Personal, social and cultural aspects* (pp. 51–71). Hove, England: Psychology Press.

Bronfenbrenner, U. (1977). Lewinian space and ecological substance. *Journal of Social Issues, 33*, 199–212.

Burnes, B. (2004). Kurt Lewin and the planned approach to change: A re-appraisal. *Journal of Management Studies, 41*, 977–1002.

Camp, D. L., Finlay, W. M., & Lyons, E. (2002). Is low self-esteem an inevitable consequence of stigma? An example from women with chronic mental health problems. *Social Science & Medicine, 55*(5), 823–834.

Clare, L., Rowlands, J., & Quin, R. (2008). Collective strength: The impact of developing a shared social identity in early-stage dementia. *Dementia: The International Journal of Social Research and Practice, 7*, 9–30.

Corrigan, P. W., & Phelan, S. M. (2004). Social support and recovery in people with serious mental illnesses. *Community Mental Health Journal, 40*(6), 513–523.

Costa, R. P. (2013). Family rituals: Mapping the postmodern family through time, space and emotion. *Journal of Comparative Family Studies, 44*(3), 269–289.

Cox, L. M., & Lyddon, W. J. (1997). Constructivist conceptions of self: A discussion of emerging identity constructs. *Journal of Constructivist Psychology, 10*, 201–219.

Deaux, K. (2001). Social identity. In J. Worrell (Ed.), *Encylopedia of women and gender* (Vol. 2, pp. 1059–1067). New York, NY: Academic Press.

DeLongis, A., & Holtzman, S. (2005). Coping in context: The role of stress, social support, and personality in coping. *Journal of Personality, 73*(6), 1633–1656.

Dewey, J. (1922). *Human nature and conduct: An introduction to Social Psychology*. New York, NY: Holt, Rinehart and Winston. Retrieved from http://www.archive.org/details/humannaturecondu00deweiala

Deyhle, D. (2009). *Reflections in place*. Tucson: University of Arizona Press.

Donato, S., Iafrate, R., Bradbury, T. N., & Scabini, E. (2012). Acquiring dyadic coping: Parents and partners as models. *Personal Relationships, 19*, 386–400.

Epstein, N. B., Ryan, C. E., Bishop, D. S., Miller, I. W., & Keitner, G. I. (2003). The McMaster model: A view of healthy family functioning. In F. Walsh (Ed.), *Normal family processes* (3rd ed., pp. 581–607). New York, NY: Guilford Press.

Erikson, E. (1968). *Identity: Youth and crisis*. New York, NY: W. W. Norton.

Farrell, A. F., Bowen, G. L., & Swick, D. C. (2014). Network supports and resiliency among U.S. military spouses with children with special health care needs. *Family Relations, 63*(1), 55–70.

Feigin, R. (1994). Spousal adjustment to a postmarital disability in one partner. *Family Systems Medicine, 12*, 235–247.

Fiese, B. H. (2006). *Family routines and rituals*. London, England: Yale University Press.

Fiese, B. H., Tomcho, T. J., Douglas, M., Josephs, K., Poltrock, S., & Baker, T. (2002). A review of 50 years of research on naturally occurring family routines and rituals: Cause for celebration? *Journal of Family Psychology, 16*(4), 381–390.

Freedy, J. R., & Hobfoll, S. E. (1994). Stress inoculation for reduction of burnout: A conservation of resources approach. *Anxiety, Stress, and Coping, 6*, 311–325.

Goffman, E. (1963). *Stigma: Notes on the management of spoiled identity*. New York, NY: Simon & Schuster.

Gross, J. J., & John, O. P. (2003). Individual differences in two emotion regulation processes: Implications for affect, relationships, and well-being. *Journal of Personality and Social Psychology, 85*(2), 348–362.

Haslam, S. A. (2004). *Psychology in organizations: The social identity approach* (2nd ed.). London, England: Sage.

Haslam, S. A., O'Brien, A., Jetten, J., Vormedal, K., & Penna, S. (2005). Taking the strain: Social identity, social support, and the experience of stress. *British Journal of Social Psychology, 44*(Pt 3), 355–370.

Haslam, S. A., & Reicher, S. (2006). Stressing the group: Social identity and the unfolding dynamics of responses to stress. *Journal of Applied Psychology, 91*(5), 1037–1052.

Hobfoll, S. E. (1989). Conservation of resources. A new attempt at conceptualizing stress. *American Psychologist, 44*(3), 513–524.

Hobfoll, S. E. (1998). *Stress, culture, and community: The psychology and philosophy of stress*. New York, NY: Plenum.

Hobfoll, S. E. (2001). The influence of culture, community, and the nested-self in the stress process: Advancing conservation of resources theory. *Applied Psychology: An International Review, 50*(3), 337–421.

Hogg, M. A., & Abrams, D. (1988). *Social identifications: A social psychology of intergroup relations and group processes*. London, England: Routledge.

Isaksen, S. G., & Treffinger, D. J. (2004). Celebrating 50 years of reflective practice: Versions of creative problem solving, *Journal of Creative Behavior, 38*(2), 65–92.

Iyer, A., Jetten, J., Tsivrikos, D., Postmes, T., & Haslam, S. A. (2009). The more (and the more compatible) the merrier: Multiple group memberships and identity compatibility as predictors of adjustment after life transitions. *British Journal of Social Psychology, 48*(Pt 4), 707–733.

Kallezi, B., Reicher, S., & Cassidy, C. (2009). Surviving the Kosovo conflict: A study of social identity, appraisal of extreme events, and mental well-being. *Applied Psychology, 58*(1), 59–83.

Kelly, G. J., & Steed, L. G. (2004). Communities coping with change: A conceptual model. *Journal of Community Psychology, 32*(2), 201–216. doi:10.1002/jcop.10090

King, L. A., & Hicks, J. A. (2006). Narrating the self in the past and the future: Implications for maturity. *Research in Human Development, 3*, 121–138.

Klein, D. C. (1991). The humiliation dynamic: An overview. *Journal of Primary Prevention, 12*(2), 93–121.

Kramer, B. J. (1993). Expanding the conceptualization of caregiving coping: The importance of relationship-focused coping strategies. *Family Relations: Interdisciplinary Journal of Applied Family Studies, 42*, 383–391.

Larson, E. (2010). Psychological well-being and meaning-making when caregiving for children with disabilities: Growth through difficult times or sinking inward. *Open Journal of Therapy and Rehabilitation, 30*(2), 78–86.

Latrofa, M., Vaes, J., Cadinu, M., & Carnaghi, A. (2010). The cognitive representation of self-stereotyping. *Personality and Social Psychology Bulletin, 36*, 911–922.

Layne, C. M., Warren, J., Watson, P., & Shalev, A. (2007). Risk, vulnerability, resistance, and resilience: Towards an integrative conceptualization of posttraumatic adaptation. In M. M. Friedman, T. M. Keane, & P. A. Resick (Eds.), *Handbook of PTSD: Science and practice* (pp. 497–520). New York, NY: Guilford Press.

Lazarus, R. S. (1993). From psychological stress to the emotions: A history of changing outlooks. *Annual Review of Psychology, 44*, 1–21.

Lazarus, R. S., & Folkman, S. (1984). *Stress, appraisal, and coping.* New York, NY: Springer Publishing.

Lewin, K. (1936). *Principles of topological psychology.* New York, NY: McGraw-Hill.

Lopez, S. J., & Snyder, C. R. (Eds.). (2009). *Oxford handbook of positive psychology* (2nd ed.). New York, NY: Oxford University Press.

Luthar, S. S. (2006). Resilience in development: A synthesis of research across five decades. In D. Cicchetti & D. J. Cohen (Eds.), *Developmental psychopathology: Risk, disorder, and adaptation* (pp. 740–795). New York, NY: John Wiley.

Marcia, J. E. (1966). Development and validation of ego-identity status. *Journal of Personality and Social Psychology, 3*(5), 551–558.

Marin, T., Holtzman, S., DeLongis, A., & Robinson, L. (2007). Coping and the response of others. *Journal of Social and Personal Relationships, 24*, 951–969.

McAdams, D. P. (2001). The psychology of life stories. *Review of General Psychology, 5*, 100–122. doi:10.1037/1089-2680.5.2100

McGoldrick, M., & Carter, B. (2003). The family life cycle. In F. Walsh (Ed.), *Normal family processes* (3rd ed., pp. 375–398). New York, NY: Guilford Press.

McKellin, W. H. (1995). Hearing impaired families: The social ecology of hearing loss. *Social Science & Medicine, 40*(11), 1469–1480.

McLean, K. C., & Pasupathi, M. (2012). Processes of identity development: Where I am and how I got there. *Identity: An International Journal of Theory and Research, 12*(1), 8–28.

McMillan, D. W., & Chavis, D. M. (1986). Sense of community: A definition and theory. *Journal of Community Psychology, 14*(1), 6–23.

Nario-Redmond, M. R. (2010). Cultural stereotypes of disabled and non-disabled men and women: Consensus for global category representations and diagnostic domains. *British Journal of Social Psychology, 49*(Pt 3), 471–488.

Newth, S., & DeLongis, A. (2004). Individual differences, mood, and coping with chronic pain in rheumatoid arthritis: A daily process analysis. *Psychology & Health, 19*, 283–305.

Oliveri, M. E., & Reiss, D. (1981). A theory-based empirical classification of family problem-solving behavior. *Family Process, 20*(4), 409–418.

Oliveri, M. E., & Reiss, D. (1982). Families' schemata of social relationships. *Family Process, 21*(3), 295–311.

Pals, J. L. (2006). Narrative identity processing of difficult life experiences: Pathways of personality development and positive self-transformation in adulthood. *Journal of Personality, 74*(4), 1079–1109.

Park, C. L., & Folkman, S. (1997). Meaning in the context of stress and coping. *Review of General Psychology, 1*, 115–144.

Pasupathi, M., & Hoyt, T. (2009). The development of narrative identity in late adolescence and emergent adulthood: The continued importance of listeners. *Developmental Psychology, 45*(2), 558–574.

Patterson, J. M. (1995). The role of family meanings in adaptation to chronic illness and disability. In A. P. Turnbull, J. M. Patterson, S. K. Behr, D. L. Murphy, J. G. Marquis, & M. J. Blue-Banning (Eds.), *Cognitive coping, families, and disabilities* (pp. 221–238). Baltimore, MD: Brookes.

Patterson, J. M. (2002). Integrating family resilience and family stress theory. *Journal of Marriage and Family, 64*(2), 349–360.

Pearlin, L. I. (1983). Role strains and personal stress. In H. B. Kaplan (Ed.), *Psychosocial stress: Trends in theory and research* (pp. 3–32). New York, NY: Academic Press.

Pearlin, L. I. (1991). The study of coping: An overview of problems and directions. In J. Eckenrode (Ed.), *The social context of coping* (pp. 261–276). New York, NY: Plenum.

Pearlin, L. I., Aneshensel, C. S., & LeBlanc, A. J. (1997). The forms and mechanisms of stress proliferation: The case of AIDS caregivers. *Journal of Health and Social Behavior, 38*(3), 223–236.

Pearlin, L. I., Lieberman, M. A., Menaghan, E. G., & Mullan, J. T. (1981). The stress process. *Journal of Health and Social Behavior, 22*(4), 337–356.

Perrewé, P. L., & Zellars, K. L. (1999). An examination of attributions and emotions in the transactional approach to the organizational stress process. *Journal of Organizational Behavior, 20*, 739–752.

Putnam, R. D. (2000). *Bowling alone: The collapse and revival of American community*. New York, NY: Simon & Schuster.

Reicher, S., & Haslam, S. A. (2011). After shock? Towards a social identity explanation of the Milgram obedience studies. *British Journal of Social Psychology, 50*, 163–169.

Reicher, S. D., Spears, R., & Haslam, S. A. (2010). The social identity approach in social psychology. In M. S. Wetherell & C. T. Mohanty (Eds.), *Sage identities handbook* (pp. 45–62). London, England: Sage.

Rogers, C. (1951). *Client-centered therapy: Its current practice, implications and theory*. London, England: Constable.

Rolland, J. S. (2012). Mastering family challenges in serious illness and disability. In F. Walsh (Ed.), *Normal family processes* (4th ed., pp. 452–482). New York, NY: Guilford Press.

Saltzman, W. R., Lester, P., Beardslee, W. R., Layne, C. M., Woodward, K., & Nash, W. P. (2011). Mechanisms of risk and resilience in military families: Theoretical and empirical basis of a family-focused resilience enhancement program. *Clinical Child and Family Psychology Review, 14*(3), 213–230.

Schmitt, M. T., & Branscombe, N. R. (2002). The meaning and consequences of perceived discrimination in disadvantaged and privileged social groups. *European Review of Social Psychology, 12*, 167–199.

Schwartz, S. J. (2001). The evolution of Eriksonian and New-Eriksonian identity theory and research: A review and integration. *Identity, 1*(1), 7–58.

Skaff, M. M., & Pearlin, L. I. (1992). Caregiving: Role engulfment and the loss of self. *The Gerontologist, 32*(5), 656–664.

Steinglass, P., Bennett, L., Wolin, S., & Reiss, D. (1987). *The alcoholic family*. New York, NY: Basic Books.

Stets, J. E., & Burke, P. J. (2000). Identity theory and social identity theory. *Social Psychology Quarterly, 63*, 224–237.

Strauser, D. R., Lustig, D. C., & Donnell, C. (2004). The relationship between working alliance and therapeutic outcomes for individuals with mild mental retardation. *Rehabilitation Counseling Bulletin, 47*(4), 215–223.

Tajfel, H., & Turner, J. (1979). An integrative theory of intergroup conflict. In W. G. Austin & S. Worchel (Eds.), *The social psychology of intergroup relations* (pp. 33–47). Monterey, CA: Brooks/Cole.

Tajfel, H., & Turner, J. C. (1986). The social identity theory of intergroup behaviour. In S. Worchel & W. G. Austin (Eds.), *Psychology of intergroup relations* (2nd ed., pp. 7–24). Chicago, IL: Nelson-Hall.

Thompson, S. J., Bender, K., Lantry, J., & Flynn, P. M. (2007). Treatment engagement: Building therapeutic alliance in home-based treatment with adolescents and their families. *Contemporary Family Therapy, 29*(1–2), 39–55.

Turner, H. A., & Schieman, S. (Eds.). (2008). *Stress across the life course. Advances in life course research*. New York, NY: Elsevier.

Turner, J. C. (1982). Towards a cognitive redefinition of the social group. In H. Tajfel (Ed.), *Social identity and intergroup relations* (pp. 15–40). Cambridge, England: Cambridge University Press.

Turner, J. C. (1991). *Social influence*. Milton Keynes, England: Open University Press.

Turner, J. C. (1999). Some current issues in research on social identity and self categorization theories. In N. Ellemers, R. Spears, & B. Doosje (Eds.), *Social identity: Context, commitment, content* (pp. 6–34). Oxford, England: Blackwell.

Turner, J. C., Hogg, M. A., Oakes, P. J., Reicher, S. D., & Wetherell, M. S. (1987). *Rediscovering the social group: A self-categorization theory*. Oxford, England: Blackwell.

Verkuyten, M., & Reijerse, A. (2008). Intergroup structure and identity management among ethnic minority and majority groups: The interactive effects of perceived stability, legitimacy, and permeability. *European Journal of Social Psychology, 38*, 106–127.

Walsh, F. (2006). *Strengthening family resilience* (2nd ed.). New York, NY: Guilford Press.

Weeks, T. L., & Pasupathi, M. (2010). Autonomy, identity, and narrative construction with parents and friends. In K. C. McLean & M. Pasupathi (Eds.), *Narrative development in adolescence: Creating the storied self* (pp. 65–92). New York, NY: Springer Publishing.

Werner, E., & Smith, R. (2001). *Journeys from childhood to midlife: Risk, resilience, and recovery*. Ithaca, NY: Cornell University Press.

World Health Organization. (2001). *International classification of functioning, disability and health: ICF*. Geneva, Switzerland: Author.

World Health Organization. (2013). *How to use the ICF: A practical manual for using the International Classification of Functioning*. Geneva, Switzerland: Author.

Wright, B. A. (1983). *Physical disability: A psychosocial approach*. New York, NY: Harper & Row.

Yeates, G., Henwood, K., Gracey, F., & Evans, J. (2007). Awareness of disability after acquired brain injury and the family context. *Neuropsychological Rehabilitation, 17*(2), 151–173.

IV

Interventions and Resources

Since the first edition of this book was published in 1977, the literature related to topics in this section has grown significantly. Chapters included for this edition reflect the growing need in counseling, psychology, rehabilitation, and other social sciences to prepare professionals for diagnostic, treatment, and preventive interventions, and the coordination of important resources to help persons with chronic illnesses and disabilities achieve optimal levels of independent functioning.

Authors in Part IV reflect on the all-important topic of substance use disorders, for which treatment has continued to evolve since the implementation of the *Diagnostic and Statistical Manual of Mental Disorders* (*DSM-5*; American Psychiatric Association, 2013). An ongoing contemporary counseling need relates to the returning veterans from Afghanistan and Iraq; specifically, the many issues faced by them and their families in attempting to integrate back into society. Their mental and physical health issues continue to go unmet and counselors need to be uniquely knowledgeable of veteran concerns. We also continue to see advances in assistive technology (AT), which ultimately can enhance the lives and independence of those with disabilities. In order for this to happen, however, individuals must be part of the process and matched with the appropriate technology. Religion and spirituality has always played a significant role in the lives of Americans and those globally. As spirituality has traditionally been one of those neglected taboo topics for counselors to broach in session, adequate training on this topic is discussed.

MAJOR HIGHLIGHTS IN PART IV

- Chapter 17 offers current information on the treatment of substance use disorders from a biopsychosocial perspective. The author provides the most up-to-date research on principles, goals, and strategies of effective treatment; matching clients to treatment modalities; substance abuse counseling guidelines and strategies; counselor factors influencing treatment outcomes; pathways to recovery; the chronic nature of moderate to severe substance use disorders; and the influence of substance use disorders on the family.
- The impact of extraordinarily stressful and traumatic events on active-duty service members, veterans, and their family members is a critically relevant topic when providing services to those who have a combination of mental and physical

disabilities. Recent conflicts in Iraq, Afghanistan, and other countries in the Middle East have spurred the expansion of programs and services for veterans, including those with disabilities. The authors of Chapter 18 educate readers on key differences when providing services in community versus military mental health settings for this emerging population. In addition, the cultural differences among army, navy, marine, air force, coast guard, and reservist service members are included, too. Issues related to the deployment cycle are explored, along with career transition from active duty to civilian life and other critical areas with implications for treatment.

- Chaper 19 focuses on the important topic of assistive technology (AT). The expansion of AT has had a profound impact on quality of life in all areas, including, but not limited to, education, careers, employment settings, independent living, transportation, and recreational and social activities in the community. Indeed, AT has provided greater independence for persons with disabilities, as it has enabled them to perform activities not possible in the past. Overall, AT helps increase individuals' self-worth and sense of belonging and has "leveled the playing field" between people with and without disabilities.

- The authors of Chapter 20 discuss the significance of spirituality and religious support for persons with disability. Spirituality, particularly for persons with chornic illness and disability (CID), provides an increased sense of meaning and purpose, and is an important therapeutic tool for developing increased opportunites for coping and resiliency. The authors provide a comprehensive approach to integrating spirituality within the context of psychosocial-focused counseling sessions. Counseling professionals benefit from the in-depth exploration of this topic, including definitions, constructs, assessment tools, belief systems, and therapeutic advantages of integrating spiritual practices in sessions for persons with CID.

- Women with disabilities comprise a unique cultural group. Counseling professionals need awareness and knowledge of their special needs to work at optimal levels of therapeutic engagement with this particular cultural group. Chapter 21, which concludes Part IV, presents research on various topics relevant to women with disabilities that assist practitioners in developing a stronger working alliance. The authors explore women's issues, including abuse and violence against women, intimate partner violence (IPV), strategies for violence prevention, and strategies and resources that can be used to advocate within the healing process.

REFERENCE

American Psychiatric Association. (2013). *Diagnostic and statistical manual of mental disorders* (5th ed.). Arlington, VA: American Psychiatric Publishing.

17

Treatment for Substance Use Disorders

Lloyd R. Goodwin, Jr.

In 2012, 4.0 million persons aged 12 or older (1.5 percent of the population) received treatment for a problem related to the use of alcohol or illicit drugs. Of these, 1.2 million received treatment for the use of both alcohol and illicit drugs, 1.0 million received treatment for the use of illicit drugs but not alcohol, and 1.4 million received treatment for the use of alcohol but not illicit drugs.

—Substance Abuse and Mental Health Services Administration

Substance abuse treatment programs and clinical counseling approaches are designed to treat a variety of substance use disorders (SUDs). Treatment approaches may include a combination of medical (e.g., pharmacotherapy) and psychosocial approaches. Therapeutic programs for individuals with SUDs include hospital-based inpatient programs and mutual help groups (e.g., Alcoholics Anonymous and Narcotics Anonymous); detoxification programs; partial hospitalization; intensive outpatient programs; therapeutic communities; halfway houses; pharmacotherapy-based interventions such as methadone programs for opioid addicts, naltrexone for alcoholics, and nicotine-replacement therapies for tobacco addicts; employee assistance programs; prison-based programs and community-based criminal justice programs such as drug courts; boot camps; school-based programs; and specialty programs for particular populations such as adolescents, women (e.g., perinatal programs for pregnant addicts and halfway houses that accommodate children of single parents), and culturally diverse groups such as African Americans, Hispanic Americans, Asian Americans, and Native American Indians.

CLIENT–TREATMENT MATCHING

Following a comprehensive substance abuse assessment, the substance abuse counselor determines the type of substance abuse treatment program that best meets the individual's clinical needs. In many communities, the type of treatment modality that individuals are referred to may be determined more by the availability of treatment resources and the financial status of individuals, instead of ideal client–treatment matching criteria.

The American Society of Addiction Medicine's (ASAM) five levels of care. The patient placement criteria developed by the ASAM (1996) are widely used in substance abuse treatment programs. The ASAM criteria have five levels of care: Level 0.5—early intervention; Level I—outpatient services; Level II—intensive outpatient/partial hospitalization services; Level III—residential inpatient services; and Level IV—medically managed intensive inpatient services.

ASAM criteria for determining levels of care. The ASAM uses criteria along six different dimensions to determine the most appropriate level of care. These dimensions are (a) acute intoxication, (b) withdrawal potential, (c) biomedical conditions and complications, (d) emotional or behavioral conditions and complications, (e) treatment acceptance or resistance and relapse potential, and (f) recovery environment. After conducting a substance abuse assessment, a substance abuse counselor matches the client to the appropriate level of care and type of treatment. "In general, the least restrictive environment for treatment should be used unless the severity of the substance use disorder and related medical, psychiatric, and social problems is such that structured or medically monitored treatment is needed" (Daley & Marlatt, 2006, p. 39).

PRINCIPLES OF EFFECTIVE TREATMENT

Thirteen principles of effective treatment for SUDs have been described by a panel of substance abuse experts (National Institute on Drug Abuse [NIDA], 1999): (a) No single treatment is appropriate for all individuals, hence treatment settings, interventions, and services should be matched to each individual's needs and problems; (b) treatment needs to be readily available; (c) effective treatment attends to multiple needs of the individual, not just his or her drug use; (d) an individual's treatment and services plan must be assessed continually and modified as necessary to ensure that the plan meets the person's changing needs; (e) remaining in treatment for an adequate period of time is critical for treatment effectiveness; (f) counseling (individual, group, and/or family) and other behavioral therapies are critical components of effective treatment for addiction; (g) medications are an important element of treatment for many patients, especially when combined with counseling and other behavioral therapies; (h) addicted or drug-abusing individuals with coexisting mental disorders should have both disorders treated in an integrated way; (i) detoxification is only the first stage of addiction treatment and by itself does little to change long-term drug use; (j) treatment does not need to be voluntary to be effective; (k) possible drug use during treatment must be monitored continuously; (l) treatment programs should provide assessment for HIV/AIDS, hepatitis B and C, tuberculosis, and other infectious diseases as well as counseling to help patients modify or change behaviors that place themselves or others at risk; and (m) recovery from drug addiction can be a long-term process and frequently requires multiple episodes of treatment.

GOALS OF EFFECTIVE TREATMENT

Treatment goals for individuals with SUDs include motivation toward abstinence, moderation of use, or drug substitution (e.g., methadone for heroin). Supporting goals include (a) creating a healthy lifestyle that includes drugless alternatives to satisfy the same motivations to use psychoactive substances; (b) developing support systems that may include a mutual-help group such as Alcoholics Anonymous; (c) enhancing social skills, including assertion and refusal skills; (d) practicing stress management and relaxation techniques; (e) attaining stable and supportive family relationships; (f) enhancing vocational and educational functioning and career goals; (g) attaining a stable housing arrangement and financial security; (h) enhancing physical health status; (i) improving mental health status by better managing psychological and emotional issues such as shame, guilt, depression, and anxiety; (j) learning how to recognize and express feelings and increase self-esteem, self-efficacy, and more effective problem-solving and decision-making skills; (k) developing healthy leisure, recreational, and social activities; (l) resolving or avoiding legal problems; and (m) addressing relevant spiritual issues and practicing centering and transcendental practices such as meditation or prayer.

SUBSTANCE ABUSE COUNSELING

Counselors apply a variety of evidence-based treatments, counseling theories, and approaches to substance abuse problems. Some general guidelines for substance abuse counseling include the following: (a) use a respectful and positive approach with all clients; (b) view substance abuse problems on a continuum from nonproblematic to problematic use rather than as an either/or situation; (c) provide treatment that is individualized, both in goals and in methods; (d) provide multidimensional treatment that focuses on the social and environmental aspects of long-term recovery; (e) use a multicultural perspective to meet the needs of diverse client populations; (f) perform collaborative treatment planning; (g) focus on empowerment, social justice, and advocacy; (h) use ethical practice; and (i) remain open to new methods and goals as research findings become available (Lewis, Dana, & Blevins, 2015).

Stages of Change

Prochaska, Norcross, and DiClemente (1994) have described six stages of change that people go through in changing harmful behaviors, including SUDs. These stages are (a) the *precontemplation stage*, when individuals do not recognize that a problem exists; (b) the *contemplation stage*, when individuals believe that a problem might exist and give some consideration to the possibility of changing their behaviors though they are not quite ready and are ambivalent about changing; (c) the *preparation stage*, when individuals decide to change and make plans to do so; they know change is best, but they are not sure how to begin; (d) the *action stage*, when individuals take active steps toward change, such as entering treatment; (e) the *maintenance stage*, which involves activities to maintain the change such as implementing a relapse prevention plan; and (f) the *relapse stage*, when individuals return to abuse of substances. The relapse is dedramatized and the focus becomes learning from the experience and returning to an earlier stage of change and their recovery goals.

Motivational Interviewing and Motivational Enhancement Therapy

These therapies, motivational interviewing (MI; Miller & Rollnick, 1991, 2002) and motivational enhancement therapy (MET; Miller, Zweben, DiClemente, & Rychtarik, 1995), are often used by substance abuse professionals in conjunction with the stages of change model described by Prochaska et al. (1994). Both MI and MET are nonauthoritative approaches to help people free up their own motivations and resources. These approaches shift the focus away from denial and toward increasing motivation to change. Both MI and MET help counselors identify the individuals' stage of change, resolve ambivalence about change, strengthen commitment for change, and increase motivation to move through the stages of change toward successful recovery and rehabilitation.

Other Substance Abuse Counseling Strategies

Many of the individual, group, and family counseling theories and techniques used to treat other mental health problems are also used to treat individuals with SUDs. Group work, including group therapy, theme groups, and psychoeducational groups, is the counseling modality most often used in substance abuse treatment programs. Commonly used counseling strategies include stress management and relaxation skill training; skill training in areas such as assertiveness, refusal, problem solving, decision making, social and behavioral self-control, and drugless alternatives; relapse prevention planning, including identification of substance use cues and triggers such as certain people, places, and emotional states, and a plan for action when the desire to use psychoactive substances occurs; behavioral counseling, including contingency contracting and management and cue extinction procedures; and cognitive behavioral strategies that teach individuals how their thoughts (e.g., "stinking thinking"), beliefs, and injunctions may hinder their recovery. Use of a global psychological self-help method such as the six-step button therapy method (Goodwin, 1981, 2002) for identifying and removing potentially self-defeating cognitions and coping with stressors (i.e., "button-pushers") is especially helpful when individuals become emotionally distressed. It is also useful to help individuals select appropriate support networks that may include mutual-help groups such as Alcoholics Anonymous (McCrady, Horvath, & Delaney, 2003; Sias & Goodwin, 2007).

SUBSTANCE ABUSE COUNSELOR INFLUENCE ON TREATMENT OUTCOME

Although the review by Miller, Wilbourne, and Hettema (2003) focused on substance abuse treatment methods, there were also some interesting findings on substance abuse counselor variables. Counselors' rates of successful treatment outcome varied from 25% to 100%, and counselor empathy was found to be a key factor in successful treatment.

Counselor Empathy

Several studies found that the more empathy expressed by the counselor during treatment, the less likely his or her clients were to drink following treatment (Miller & Baca, 1983; Miller, Benefield, & Tonigan, 1993; Valle, 1981). In one study, counselor empathy accounted for two thirds of the variance in client outcomes at 6 months, one half at 12 months, and one quarter at 24 months. By far, the strongest predictor of clients' treatment outcomes was the counselor to whom they were assigned, even though all counselors were using the same treatment method (Miller & Baca, 1983, cited in Miller et al., 2003).

As Miller et al. (2003) point out, "It is clear that client outcomes are influenced not only by what we do in treatment but also by how we do it.... Therapist empathy is one of the better-specified determinants of effective treatment" (p. 39). Accurate empathy involves the ability to actively listen and reflect an accurate understanding of the client's experience. Miller et al. (2003) further suggest that, "[therapist empathy] has little or nothing to do with identification, with having had a similar experience oneself. Rather, empathy is skillful active listening. Its opposite, perhaps, is a 'listen-to-me' authoritarian approach" (p. 39).

Confrontation

The use of confrontation is often associated with substance abuse counseling. In one study (Miller et al., 1993) cited by Miller and colleagues (2003), the researchers "were able to predict half of the variance in clients' drinking outcomes at 12-month follow-up from one therapist behavior during treatment: The more the therapist confronted, the more the client drank" (p. 39). In the Miller et al. (1993) study,

> Therapist "confronting" responses consisted of challenging, disagreeing, head-on disputes, incredulity, emphasizing negative client characteristics, and sarcasm. ... In general, client resistance behaviors were strongly correlated with therapist confrontational responses. Positive, self-motivational client responses, on the other hand, were related to therapist listening and restructuring. (p. 458)

As Miller and colleagues (1993) pointed out, "In every study in which therapist characteristics have been systematically evaluated and effects were found, more favorable outcomes have been associated with a therapeutic style approximating what Rogers termed *accurate empathy*" (p. 455).

Shaming and Punishing

Miller and Carroll (2006) indicate that, "No scientific evidence supports belittling, shaming, and castigating addicted people; taking away their children and social benefits; and incarcerating them for extended periods" (p. 263). These strategies will often have a paradoxical effect and drive the person to increased substance abuse.

Counselor Tone of Voice

Another therapist variable affecting treatment retention and outcome is the tone of voice. One study found that the more anger in the counselor's tone of voice, the less likely clients were to stay in treatment or to change their drinking (Milmoe, Rosenthal, Blane, Chafetz, & Wolf, 1967).

Hope and Faith

Hope and faith appear to influence treatment outcomes as well. A counselor's expectation that a client will change or not can be a powerful self-fulfilling prophecy (Leake & King, 1977). Similarly, the client's own level of hope or optimism about change (i.e., self-efficacy), as well as the counselor's belief in the efficacy of the treatment, can enhance outcomes (Miller et al., 2003).

EVIDENCE-BASED TREATMENTS

The substantial research on treatment approaches for alcohol use disorders has been summarized by Miller et al. (2003). Their review of 381 controlled trials of 99 different treatment modalities, involving 75,000 clients, concluded that, "First, there is clearly reason for optimism in the treatment of alcohol use disorders. This review reveals 18 treatment methods with a positive balance of evidence" (p. 40). However, in a narrative review of the treatment outcome research, the authors noted that:

> [A]lthough the scientific literature points to a list of treatment approaches with reasonable evidence of positive benefit, this list overlaps little with those components often employed in U.S. alcoholism treatment programs. ... The negative correlation between scientific evidence and treatment-as-usual remains striking, and could hardly be larger if one intentionally constructed treatment programs from those approaches with the least evidence of efficacy. (p. 41)

Thus, most of the currently available evidence-based treatment approaches with demonstrated efficacy are infrequently used in substance abuse treatment programs. SAMHSA maintains a list of evidence-based treatments.

Cost-Effectiveness of Substance Abuse Treatment

Substance abuse treatment more than pays for itself in terms of costs to society. The California Drug and Alcohol Treatment Assessment (CALDATA) study of treatment outcomes over a 3- to 5-year period following treatment, conducted by the State of California and duplicated by several other states, found that there was continual abstinence in approximately 50% of individuals treated, crime was abated in 74% of those treated, and the state enjoyed savings of $7 to $39 for every $1 spent on treatment (Ettner et al., 2005; Inaba & Cohen, 2014; Robert Wood Johnson Foundation, 2006a). Economic studies across settings, populations, methods, and time periods have consistently found positive net economic benefits of substance abuse treatment. The primary economic benefits come from reduced crime, including incarceration and victimization costs, and posttreatment reduction in health care costs (Belenko, Patapis, & French, 2005; Robert Wood Johnson Foundation, 2006b). In addition, the most effective treatment models are not necessarily the costliest ones. One earlier study found that a more expensive treatment was not likely to produce more effective results (Holder, Longabaugh, Miller, & Rubonis, 1991). More than three-quarters of the people accessing addiction treatment receive some kind of public assistance (SAMHSA, 2013).

Treatment Outcomes

According to Dr. Alan I. Leshner, former director of the NIDA (cited in Inaba & Cohen, 2014):

> Treatment is effective. Scientifically based drug addiction treatments typically reduce drug abuse by 40% to 60%. These rates are not ideal, of course, but they are comparable to compliance rates seen with treatment for other chronic diseases, such as asthma, hypertension, and diabetes. Moreover, treatment markedly reduces undesirable consequences of drug abuse and addiction, such as unemployment, criminal activity, and HIV/AIDS or other infectious diseases, whether or not patients achieve complete abstinence. (p. 379)

Benefits to society include social, financial, and quality-of-life gains, including reductions in criminal activity, health care expenditures, dependence on public assistance, and increases in employment earnings (Carr et al., 2008).

Remission rates vary widely and are markedly different for legal and illegal substances and for different racial and ethnic groups. The proportion of dependent users in remission for at least a year increases as the time since the onset of dependence increases. The rates of remission of the various substances differ. The likelihood of quitting cocaine and marijuana is much higher than the likelihood of quitting the two legal drugs, alcohol and nicotine. For example, studies indicate that with the onset of dependence as the start date, half of those ever addicted to cocaine had quit using this substance at clinically significant levels by year 4, and the half-life for marijuana dependence was 6 years. In contrast, for alcohol, the 50% remission mark was not reached until year 16, and for cigarettes, it took on average 30 years for dependent smokers to quit. The remission rate also varied as a function of racial and ethnic group. For example, after year 3, about 50% of Whites had remitted their cocaine dependence, whereas the 50% criterion was not met until year 8 by African Americans (Heyman, 2013).

PATHWAYS OF RECOVERY

The path of many individuals with SUDs is marked by cycles of recovery, relapse, and repeated treatments, often spanning many years before ending in stable recovery, other disabilities, or death (Anglin, Hser, & Grella, 1997; Hser, Anglin, Grella, Longshore, & Prendergast, 1997; Scott, Foss, & Dennis, 2005; Simpson, Joe, & Broome, 2002; White, 1996). Between 57% and 60% of people who meet the criteria for an SUD at some time in their lives eventually achieve sustained recovery, with females quitting substances at higher rates than males (Dawson, 1996; Dennis & Scott, 2007; Heyman, 2013; Kessler, 1994; Robins & Regier, 1991). Those who abused alcohol were less likely to stop drinking than were those who were dependent on alcohol (Vaillant, 2003). Assuming the onset of illicit substance dependence at about 20 years of age, the typical person quits using substances at clinically significant levels after about 6 to 8 years from the onset of dependence and before he or she is 30 years old. However, a significant minority of individuals with illicit substance dependence continue for much longer periods of time (Heyman, 2013).

Natural Recovery

Many, if not most, individuals with substance abuse problems manage to recover on their own without the assistance of professional treatment or mutual-help groups (Burman, 1997; Humphreys, Moos, & Finney, 1995; Sobell, Ellingstad, & Sobell, 2000; Toneatto, Sobell, Sobell, & Rubel, 1999; Watson & Sher, 1998). In one review of the literature, "Estimates of the prevalence of nontreatment recoveries ranged from 87.5% to 53.7% depending on the definition of prior alcohol problems employed" (Cunningham, 1999a, p. 463). Between 80% and 90% of individuals quit smoking tobacco, one of the most addictive substances, on their own without treatment (Fiore et al., 1990; Orleans et al., 1991).

Professional Substance Abuse Treatment

The majority of all prior substance abusers have never come in contact with any drug treatment services (Cunningham, 1999a, 1999b; National Center on Addiction and Substance Abuse at Columbia University, 2012). Estimates of the ratio of untreated to treated individuals with alcohol problems in the general population range from 3:1 to 13:1 (Roizen, 1977). Only 10.8% of people with SUDs who needed treatment received treatment at a specialty facility (SAMHSA, 2013). Of those who entered a substance abuse treatment program, less than half (42.1%) completed their treatment (National Center on Addiction and Substance Abuse, 2012). Although a significant proportion of individuals recover from alcohol problems without treatment, such recoveries appear less common among individuals with more severe SUDs, particularly when addiction is accompanied by mental disorders (Cunningham, 1999a; Scott et al., 2005). A subset of individuals with SUDs suffer from a more chronic version whereby they cycle through periods of relapse, treatment reentry, recovery, and incarceration, often lasting several years (Anglin et al., 1997; Goodwin & Sias, 2014; Scott et al., 2005). Compared with individuals with alcohol-related problems who do not obtain timely help, those who enter either Alcoholics Anonymous or other treatment relatively soon after initiating help improve more quickly and achieve higher long-term remission rates (Moos & Moos, 2005; Timko, Moos, Finney, & Lesar, 2000).

Substance Abuse Counseling Interventions

In addition to mutual-help groups such as Alcoholics Anonymous and Narcotics Anonymous (Gossop, Stewart, & Marsden, 2008; Scott et al., 2005; Sias & Goodwin, 2007), several counseling approaches have shown promise in reducing SUDs, including group therapy, marital and family therapy, cognitive behavior therapy, MI and enhancement therapy, brief interventions, social skills training, relaxation training, systematic desensitization, problem solving, relapse prevention, and integrative models (French et al., 2008; Miller et al., 2003; Winters, Stinchfield, Latimer, & Lee, 2007). In one study (French et al., 2008), skill-focused psychoeducational group therapy was the least expensive and most cost-effective intervention when compared to functional family therapy, individual cognitive behavior therapy, and integrative treatment combining joint individual and family therapy for adolescents with an SUD. Substance abuse services and treatment outcomes are affected by factors in the external political and economic environment of a facility, by internal program-level variables, and by client characteristics (Ghose, 2008).

Medication-Assisted Substance Abuse Treatment

The use of medications for treating physiological and psychological symptoms related to substance withdrawal and relapse can be beneficial additions to psychosocial treatments. In recent years, a driving force for integrating pharmacotherapeutic agents into treatment for substance dependence has been the increased understanding of the effects of psychoactive substances on the brain and body. This knowledge has formed the foundation upon which researchers have developed medications designed to counteract or lessen physiological effects (Graves & Goodwin, 2008). Pharmacotherapy for SUDs is an evidence-based practice utilized primarily for individuals dependent on opioids, alcohol, and nicotine. Thomas and colleagues (2013) note that medications approved by the U.S. Food and Drug Administration (FDA) for treatment of opioid and alcohol dependency outside of a licensed methadone treatment program include short-acting and extended-release naltrexone, disulfiram, and acamprosate for alcohol dependence; and buprenorphine and short-acting and extended-release naltrexone for opioid dependence. There is a lack of consensus as to the appropriate duration of pharmacotherapy treatment.

Chronic Nature of SUDs

In a review of the substance abuse treatment outcome literature, Heyman (2013) concludes that most addicts relapse, which is to say that treatment interrupts but does not end addiction. Sixty-two percent of individuals in publicly funded substance abuse treatment in 2002 met the diagnostic criteria for dependence, 16% met the criteria for abuse, and 22% met the criteria for other substance-related problems such as acute intoxication and mental health problems aggravated by substance use. Sixty-four percent were reentering treatment: 23% for the second time, 22% for the third or fourth time, and 19% for the fifth or more time (Office of Applied Studies, 2005). Approximately half of the clients entering public or private substance abuse treatment are doing so for the first time. Clients entering substance abuse treatment for the first time tend to be younger, more educated, more steadily employed, and have less serious drug use and criminal involvement, as well as fewer family and mental health problems than clients with a prior treatment history (Anglin et al., 1997; Cacciola, Dugosh, Foltz, Leahy, & Stevens, 2005). On average, people reach sustained recovery only after three to four episodes of different kinds of treatments over a number of years (Anglin et al., 1997; Dennis, Scott, Funk, & Foss, 2005; Grella & Joshi, 1999; Hser et al., 1997; Hser, Grella, Chou, & Anglin, 1998; Scott et al., 2005). The estimated median time from first use to at least one drug-free year was 27 years, and the median time from first treatment episode to last use was 9 years in one study (Dennis et al., 2005). In sum, most individuals with SUDs require multiple treatment episodes over several years to reach stable recovery (Dennis & Scott, 2007). Psychoactive SUDs, especially those with severe SUDs, need to be viewed like other chronic relapsing disorders such as arthritis, asthma, cystic fibrosis, diabetes, heart disease, hypertension, and obesity in that they typically require long-term versus acute treatment (Goodwin & Sias, 2014). Dennis and Scott (2003) developed a Recovery

Management Checkup model to provide ongoing monitoring for relapse and reducing the time from relapse to treatment reentry. SUDs are typically chronic disorders where multiple substance use, comorbid mental disorders, and multiple treatment admissions over many years are the norm (Dennis et al., 2005).

TREATMENT DEMAND

In 2012, 23.1 million (8.9%) persons aged 12 years or older needed treatment for an illicit drug or alcohol use problem. Of these, only 10.8% received treatment at a specialty facility. There are many reasons why individuals with SUDs do not enter treatment. The primary reason for not receiving treatment among this group of persons was a lack of insurance coverage and inability to pay the cost (38.2%; SAMHSA, 2013). Other barriers to substance abuse treatment include a lack of resources to accommodate the need, lack of treatment referrals from the health care system, a misunderstanding of SUDs, negative public attitudes and behavior toward those with an SUD, privacy concerns, lack of information on how to get help, insufficient social support, conflicting time commitments, negative perceptions of the treatment process, legal barriers (National Center on Addiction and Substance Abuse at Columbia University, 2012), and the placement of treatment-seeking individuals on a waiting list.

> Substance users who wait for treatment services are less likely to enter treatment and often continue to use drugs, placing them at heightened risk for health complications such as overdose and exposure to infectious diseases such as hepatitis and HIV .... The likelihood of treatment-seeking substance abusers actually entering treatment after assessment is often less than 50%. ... In part, this is related to substance abusers' limited tolerance for treatment wait time, with longer waits associated with higher rates of pretreatment attrition ... longer wait time for an assessment is influenced by being court referred, less belief in having a substance abuse problem, and less desire for change. A shorter wait to actually enter treatment is predicted by having a case manager, being more ready for treatment, and having less severe employment and alcohol problems. (Carr et al., 2008, p. 193)

FAMILY ISSUES

Substance abuse can be viewed as a family illness. Nearly one third (32%) of respondents in one study reported past substance abuse in their immediate family. And of those households with an immediate family member who had an addiction problem, nearly half (44%) reported more than one family member with a drug problem (Hazelden Foundation, 2008). Hook (2008) estimated that substance abuse affects approximately 45% to 68% of the U.S. population. It is estimated that, in the United States, 25% of children younger than 18 years are living with a parent in need of treatment of an SUD (Kinney, 2003). Psychoactive substance use also affects future generations through women taking substances during pregnancy, the genetic transmission by substance-abusing parents, and family psychosocial effects, including modeling of parental and sibling substance abuse.

Psychoactive Substances and Pregnancy

Approximately 5.5% of U.S. women giving birth used illicit drugs and 18.8% drank alcohol sometime during their pregnancy (NIDA, 1994). Most psychoactive substances can have a deleterious effect on the developing fetus. Probably the best-known harmful effect of psychoactive substances on the developing fetus is that of *fetal alcohol syndrome* (FAS) and the less severe *fetal alcohol effects*. According to Kinney (2003), FAS is the most preventable cause of mental retardation and developmental disabilities in the United States.

Genetic Predisposition

There is an increased incidence of substance abuse in children of substance abusers versus children of non–substance-abusing parents. Heredity can influence SUDs, behavioral addictions, and some mental disorders. Studies of twins along with other human and animal studies estimate the influence of genetics on substance abuse to be between 40% and 60% (Bierut et al., 1998; Blum, Cull, Braverman, & Comings, 1996; Eisen et al., 1998; Kendler, Aggen, Tambs, & Reichborn-Kjennerud, 2006; Lynskey et al., 2006; Schuckit, 1986, 2000).

Family System, Homeostasis, and Coping Styles

Viewing the family as a system is a common perspective in mental health disciplines. Central to the family systems theory is the belief that changes in any part (i.e., any family member) of the system affect all of the others. The other family members, in response, make changes to maintain the balance within the family system. Substance abuse by a family member affects the homeostatic balance of the entire family system. Families tend to strive for homeostatic balance when confronted with the disrupting stressor of a substance-abusing family member. Families utilize numerous coping strategies to adapt to the stress within a family system. Wegscheider (1981), a student of Virginia Satir, gave titles of the *family hero, scapegoat, lost child*, and *mascot* to family roles played by children in the alcoholic family. Black (1981), another early pioneer in the promotion of treatment for children of alcoholics, defined their role behavior in two categories: (a) the misbehaving and obviously troubled children and (b) the mature, stable, overachieving, behaving children. She termed the roles of young children of alcoholics as the *responsible ones, adjusters*, and *placaters*. These roles identified by Wegscheider and Black were adaptations of the family dysfunctional communication patterns identified earlier by Satir (Bandler, Grender, & Satir, 1976; Satir, 1988) of *placater, blamer, computer (super reasonable)*, and *distracter*. Children often blame themselves for the pain in the family and try to fix it by rigidly playing out their role in the system, often at the expense of their own mental health. In times of stress, these roles tend to become rigid in an attempt to cope and survive. These childhood coping styles can last into adulthood, affect relationships, and work in both negative and positive ways, depending on how these patterns are channeled.

Three basic approaches family members adopt in living with an alcoholic are (a) keeping out of the way of the drinker and managing one's own life; (b) caregiving, counseling, and controlling; and (c) resigning and maintaining a façade. The approach most commonly chosen differs by gender and between spouse and children. The spouse is often involved in caregiving, counseling, and controlling. Children are more likely to keep out of the way of the drinker and manage their own lives. Women, more than men, are more likely to selectively keep out of the drinker's way while also engaged in caregiving, whereas men are more likely to adopt resignation. The husband is more likely to leave an alcoholic wife than vice versa, and the female alcohol-dependent member is much more likely to be divorced than is her male counterpart (Kinney, 2003).

Although substance abuse can be viewed as a symptom of a dysfunctional family system, it is difficult to determine if the substance abuse caused the family system dysfunction or is the result of a dysfunctional family system (Lawson & Lawson, 1983).

Enabling

For a variety of reasons, family members may unwittingly adopt certain behaviors that allow the substance abuse to continue. Enabling occurs whenever the actions of family members, or others, protect the substance-abusing family member from the consequences of substance abuse. While trying to cope with the embarrassment, shame, and financial consequences of living with a substance-abusing family member, family members may make excuses and cover up the consequences of substance abuse. As Kinney (2003) points out, "Ironically, while sparing the alcohol-dependent person from experiencing the consequences and thus the associated pain, the family members absorb the pain themselves" (p. 203).

Codependency

Family and friends of individuals caught up in substance abuse are usually affected to some degree. It is difficult to watch a loved one travel down a self-destructive path. Codependency refers to the phenomenon of being affected by the person with an SUD to the point that one becomes hopeful and happy when the person with the SUD takes a break from his or her substance abuse and responsibly performs his or her life functions, and becomes discouraged and distressed when the substance abuse behavior returns. In codependency, happiness or distress is dependent on the status of the person with the SUD at any given time. In its more extreme form, the codependent may attempt to meet the person with the SUD's needs to the exclusion of his or her own needs. The codependent individual may become hypervigilant and live in a chronically distressed state waiting for the person with the SUD to fall off the wagon or to receive a call from the police station asking to be bailed out. It is no wonder that many family members and friends eventually cut loose the person with an SUD from their lives for their own welfare and survival.

Boundaries and Family Rules

Families with a substance-abusing member often have many boundary issues and family rules. As Lawson and Lawson (1983) point out:

> Disengaged or rigid boundaries are frequently seen in alcoholic families with the result of isolation of family members from each other and isolation of the family from the community. The disengagement of family members is perpetuated by family rules such as: it is not safe to comment on alcoholism or drug addiction, it is not wise to confront the alcoholic or addict, and it is essential to the survival of the family to protect the alcoholic or addict so things don't get worse .... Researchers have reported that young adults and adolescents with drug problems often describe their families as chaotic and disengaged. (p. 182)

Family Therapy

Studies indicate that including the spouse or other family members in substance abuse treatment improves treatment outcomes. Family therapy appears to be effective, and in some cases better than individual therapy (Friedman, Tomko,& Utada, 1991; Joanning, Quinn, Thomas, & Mullen, 1992; Liddle et al., 2001; Liddle & Diamond, 1991; O'Farrell & Fals-Stewart, 2003; O'Farrell, Murphy, Alter, & Fals-Stewart, 2008; Piercy & Frankel, 1989; Quinn, Kuehl, Thomas, & Joanning, 1988; Rowe & Liddle, 2003; Stanton & Shadish, 1997; Szapocznik, Kurtines, Foote, Perez-Vidal, & Hervis, 1986).

SUBSTANCE ABUSE COUNSELING SPECIALISTS

Many mental health disciplines, including counseling, psychology, and psychiatry, have developed a specialty area of practice in substance abuse counseling along with specialty certifications. Furthermore, substance abuse counseling is evolving as a separate profession with its own unique body of knowledge, specialized preparation needs and competencies, certifications, licensure, and accreditation standards. The substance abuse field is at a crossroads with two evolving trends that attract substance abuse professionals. One trend is the development of substance abuse counseling as a separate profession with its own independent accreditation and licensure mechanisms. The other trend is the development of substance abuse counseling as a specialization, including specialty certification, within other, more established mental health professions (Goodwin, 2006).

The substance abuse field has an extensive body of knowledge as well as specialty assessment, counseling, and treatment strategies. Mental health professionals are advised to attain specialty preservice or continuing education preparation in order to work effectively with individuals with SUDs and their families. There are many institutions of higher education that offer substance abuse courses, including online distance education courses that are available to practitioners in the field. In addition, there are many continuing education workshops in the substance abuse area (Goodwin, 2006). Individuals with SUDs have unique issues and problems that are often life changing and sometimes life threatening and deserve qualified mental health professionals knowledgeable in the substance abuse field to serve them. Because substance use and abuse are found in every mental health, school, and health care setting, all professional counselors should attain enough education to recognize the signs and symptoms of SUDs, provide substance abuse screenings, and know when to refer to more qualified substance abuse professionals for more comprehensive assessment and treatment.

In summary, some SUDs, especially those concerning individuals with severe SUDs, are best viewed as chronic, relapsing biopsychosocial-spiritual disorders that are treatable with successful outcomes. SUDs are analogous to other chronic relapsing disorders such as asthma, hypertension, and diabetes in that recurrence of symptoms, also known as slips and relapses, often occur following acute treatments. Healing or management of the illness often requires continued monitoring and successive acute care treatments when the illness flares up. With continued care, successive treatments, and continual monitoring, individuals with SUDs can increase the interval between abusive episodes until the individual achieves either full abstinence or more responsible substance use, as well as a more stable life-fulfilling recovery (Goodwin & Sias, 2014). Successful long-term recovery requires the adoption of a healthy lifestyle and continued mindfulness that SUDs can rear their ugly heads if one becomes distressed or negligent in maintaining life-enhancing attitudes, beliefs, and behaviors. Eventually, the majority of individuals can be expected to recover from SUDs with abstinence or reductions in substance use, along with improved health and social, vocational, and spiritual functioning. With patience, persistence, tolerance, empathy, and compassion, counselors can help individuals and their families successfully recover from this devastating and potentially life-threatening disorder.

RESOURCES

Addiction Technology Transfer Centers: www.nattc.org
Center for Substance Abuse Prevention: www.samhsa.gov/about-us/who-we-are/offices-centers/csap
Center on Alcoholism, Substance Abuse, and Addictions (associated with the University of New Mexico): http://casaa.unm.edu/inst.html

Join Together (associated with Boston University; provides an online screening tool for alcohol use disorders [AUDs]): www.alcoholscreening.org/Home.aspx

National Institute on Alcoholism and Alcohol Abuse: www.niaaa.nih.gov

National Institute on Drug Abuse: www.nida.nih.gov

PROJECT CORK (associated with Dartmouth Medical School): www.projectcork.org/clinical_tools/index.html

Substance Abuse and Mental Health Services Administration: www.samhsa.gov

Treatment Research Institute (TRI): www.tresearch.org; TRI was founded by A. Thomas McLellan, PhD, one of the developers of the Addiction Severity Index; Jack Durell, MD; and a small team of colleagues from the University of Pennsylvania.

REFERENCES

American Society of Addiction Medicine. (1996). *Patient placement criteria for the treatment of substance-related disorders* (2nd ed.). Chevy Chase, MD: Author.

Anglin, M. D., Hser, Y. I., & Grella, C. E. (1997). Drug addiction and treatment careers among clients in the Drug Abuse Treatment Outcome Study (DATOS). *Psychology of Addiction Behaviors, 11*(4), 308–323.

Bandler, R., Grender, J., & Satir, V. (1976). *Changing with families*. Palo Alto, CA: Science and Behavior Books.

Belenko, S., Patapis, N., & French, M. T. (2005). *Economic benefits of drug treatment: A critical review of the evidence for policy makers*. Treatment Research Institute at the University of Pennsylvania. Retrieved from http://www.fccmh.org/resources/docs/EconomicBenefits_of_Drug_Trx_02.05_.pdf

Bierut, L. J., Dinwiddie, S. H., Begleiter, H., Crowe, R. R., Hesselbrock, V., Nurnberger, J. I., . . . Reich, T. (1998). Familial transmission of substance dependence: Alcohol, marijuana, cocaine, and habitual smoking: A report from the Collaborative Study on the Genetics of Alcoholism. *Archives of General Psychiatry, 55*(11), 982–988.

Black, C. (1981). *It will never happen to me*. Denver, CO: M.A.C.

Blum, K., Cull, J. G., Braverman, E. R., & Comings, D. E. (1996). Reward deficiency syndrome. *American Scientist, 84*, 132–145.

Burman, S. (1997). The challenge of sobriety: Natural recovery without treatment and self-help groups. *Journal of Substance Abuse, 9*, 41–61.

Cacciola, J. S., Dugosh, K., Foltz, C., Leahy, P., & Stevens, R. (2005). Treatment outcomes: First time versus treatment-experienced clients. *Journal of Substance Abuse Treatment, 28*(Suppl. 1), S13–S22.

Carr, C. J., Xu, J., Redko, C., Lane, D. T., Rapp, R. C., Goris, J., & Carlson, R. G. (2008). Individual and system influences on waiting time for substance abuse treatment. *Journal of Substance Abuse Treatment, 34*(2), 192–201.

Cunningham, J. A. (1999a). Resolving alcohol-related problems with and without treatment: The effects of different problem criteria. *Journal of Studies on Alcohol, 60*(4), 463–466.

Cunningham, J. A. (1999b). Untreated remissions from drug use: The predominant pathway. *Addictive Behaviors, 24*(2), 267–270.

Daley, D. C., & Marlatt, G. A. (2006). *Overcoming your alcohol or drug problem: Effective recovery strategies. Therapist guide* (2nd ed.). New York, NY: Oxford University Press.

Dawson, D. (1996). Gender differences in the risk of alcohol dependence: United States, 1992. *Addiction, 91*(12), 1831–1842.

Dennis, M. L., & Scott, C. K. (2007). Managing addiction as a chronic condition. *Addiction Science & Clinical Practice, 4*(1), 45–55.

Dennis, M. L., & Scott, C. K. (2003). *Recovery management checkup (RMC) protocol for people with chronic substance use disorders*. Bloomington, IL: Chestnut Health Systems. Retrieved from https://www.ncbi.nlm.nih.gov/pmc/articles/PMC3277866

Dennis, M. L., Scott, C. K., Funk, R., & Foss, M. A. (2005). The duration and correlates of addiction and treatment careers. *Journal of Substance Abuse Treatment, 28* (Suppl. 1), S51–S62.

Eisen, S. A., Lin, N., Lyons, M. J., Scherrer, J. F., Griffith, K., True, W. R., . . . Tsuang, M. T. (1998). Familial influences on gambling behavior: An analysis of 3359 twin pairs. *Addiction, 93*(9), 1375–1384.

Ettner, S. L., Huang, D., Evans, E., Ash, D. R., Handy, M., Jourabchi, M., & Hser, Y. I. (2005). Benefit-cost in the California Treatment Outcome Project: Does substance abuse treatment "pay for itself"? *Health Services Research, 41*(1), 192–213. doi:10.1111/j.1475–6773.2005.00466.x. Retrieved from http://www.blackwell-synergy.com/action/doSearch

Fiore, M. C., Novotny, T. E., Pierce, J. P., Giovino, G. A., Hatziandreu, E. J., Newcomb, P. A., . . . Davis, R. M. (1990). Methods used to quit smoking in the United States. Do cessation programs help? *Journal of the American Medical Association, 263*(20), 2760–2765.

French, M. T., Zavala, S. K., McCollister, K. E., Waldron, H. B., Turner, C. W., & Ozechowski, T. J. (2008). Cost-effectiveness analysis of four interventions for adolescents with a substance use disorder. *Journal of Substance Abuse Treatment, 34*(3), 272–281.

Friedman, A. S., Tomko, I. A., & Utada, A. (1991). Client and family characteristics that predict better family therapy outcome for adolescent drug abusers. *Family Dynamics of Addiction Quarterly, 1*(1), 77–93.

Ghose, T. (2008). Organizational- and individual-level correlates of posttreatment substance use: A multilevel analysis. *Journal of Substance Abuse Treatment, 34*(2), 249–262.

Goodwin, L. R., Jr. (1981). Psychological self-help: A five-step model. *Journal of Humanistic Psychology, 21*(1), 13–27.

Goodwin, L. R., Jr. (2002). *The button therapy book: How to work on your buttons and the button-pushers in your life.* Victoria, BC, Canada: Trafford.

Goodwin, L. R., Jr. (2006). A comprehensive substance abuse counselor education program: From specialty certificate to PhD. *Journal of Teaching in the Addictions, 5*(2), 59–80.

Goodwin, L. R., Jr., & Sias, S. M. (2014). Severe substance use disorder viewed as a chronic condition and disability. *Journal of Rehabilitation, 80*(4), 52–59.

Gossop, M., Stewart, D., & Marsden, J. (2008). Attendance at Narcotics Anonymous and Alcoholics Anonymous meetings, frequency of attendance and substance use outcomes after residential treatment for drug dependence: A 5-year follow-up study. *Addiction, 103*(1), 119–125.

Graves, E., & Goodwin, L. R., Jr. (2008). Pharmacotherapeutic treatment of alcohol dependence: An overview. *Journal of Teaching in the Addictions, 7*(1), 75–95.

Grella, C. E., & Joshi, V. (1999). Gender differences in drug treatment careers among clients in the National Drug Abuse Treatment Outcome Study. *American Journal of Drug and Alcohol Abuse, 25*(3), 385–406.

Hazelden Foundation. (2008). *Results from the fall 2008 national study of public attitudes toward addiction.* Center for Public Advocacy. Retrieved from http://www.hazelden.org

Heyman, G. M. (2013). Quitting drugs: Quantitative and qualitative features. *Annual Review of Clinical Psychology, 9*, 29–59.

Holder, H., Longabaugh, R., Miller, W. R., & Rubonis, A. V. (1991). The cost effectiveness of treatment for alcoholism: A first approximation. *Journal of Studies on Alcohol, 52*(6), 517–540.

Hook, M. K. (2008). Addiction and families. In D. Capuzzi & M. D. Stauffer (Eds.), *Foundations of addictions counseling* (pp. 325–352). Boston, MA: Pearson/Allyn & Bacon.

Hser, Y. I., Anglin, M. D., Grella, C., Longshore, D., & Prendergast, M. L. (1997). Drug treatment careers. A conceptual framework and existing research findings. *Journal of Substance Abuse Treatment, 14*(6), 543–558.

Hser, Y. I., Grella, C., Chou, C. P., & Anglin, M. D. (1998). Relationships between drug treatment careers and outcomes: Findings from the National Drug Abuse Treatment Outcome Study. *Evaluation Review, 22*(4), 496–519.

Humphreys, K., Moos, R. H., & Finney, J. W. (1995). Two pathways out of drinking problems without professional treatment. *Addictive Behaviors, 20*(4), 427–441.

Inaba, D. S., & Cohen, W. E. (2014). *Uppers, downers, all arounders* (8th ed.). Ashland, OR: CNS Publications.

Joanning, H., Quinn, W., Thomas, F., & Mullen, R. (1992). Treating adolescent drug abuse: A comparison of family systems therapy, group therapy, and family drug education. *Journal of Marital and Family Therapy, 18*(4), 345–356.

Kendler, K. S., Aggen, S. H., Tambs, K., & Reichborn-Kjennerud, T. (2006). Illicit psychoactive substance use, abuse and dependence in a population-based sample of Norwegian twins. *Psychological Medicine, 36*(7), 955–962.

Kessler, R. C. (1994). The National Comorbidity Survey of the United States. *International Review of Psychiatry, 6*, 365–376.

Kinney, J. (2003). *Loosening the grip: A handbook of alcohol information* (7th ed.). Boston, MA: McGraw-Hill.

Lawson, A., & Lawson, G. (1983). *Alcoholism and the family: A guide to treatment and prevention.* Austin, TX: PRO-ED.

Leake, G. J., & King, A. S. (1977). Effect of counselor expectations on alcoholic recovery. *Alcohol Health and Research World, 11*(3), 16–22.

Lewis, J. A., Dana, R. Q., & Blevins, G. A. (2015). *Substance abuse counseling* (5th ed.). Stamford, CT: Cengage.

Liddle, H. A., Dakof, G. A., Parker, K., Diamond, G. S., Barrett, K., & Tejeda, M. (2001). Multidimensional family therapy for adolescent drug abuse: Results of a randomized clinical trial. *American Journal of Drug and Alcohol Abuse, 27*(4), 651–688.

Liddle, H. A., & Diamond, G. S. (1991). Adolescent substance abusers in family therapy: The critical initial phase of treatment. *Family Dynamics of Addiction Quarterly, 1*(1), 55–68.

Lynskey, M. T., Agrawal, A., Bucholz, K. K., Nelson, E. C., Madden, P. A., Todorov, A. A., . . . Heath, A. C. (2006). Subtypes of illicit drug users: A latent class analysis of data from an Australian twin sample. *Twin Research and Human Genetics, 9*(4), 523–530.

McCrady, B. S., Horvath, T., & Delaney, S. I. (2003). Self-help groups. In R. H. Hester & W. R. Miller (Eds.), *Handbook of alcoholism treatment approaches: Effective alternatives* (3rd ed., pp. 165–187). Boston, MA: Allyn & Bacon.

Miller, W. R., & Baca, L. M. (1983). Two-year follow-up of bibliotherapy and therapist-directed controlled drinking training for problem drinkers. *Behavior Therapy, 14*, 441–448.

Miller, W. R., Benefield, R. G., & Tonigan, J. S. (1993). Enhancing motivation for change in problem drinking: A controlled comparison of two therapist styles. *Journal of Consulting and Clinical Psychology, 61*(3), 455–461.

Miller, W. R., & Carroll, K. M. (2006). *Rethinking substance abuse: What science shows, and what we should do about it.* New York, NY: Guilford Press.

Miller, W. R., & Rollnick, S. (1991). *Motivational interviewing: Preparing people to change addictive behavior.* New York, NY: Guilford Press.

Miller, W. R., & Rollnick, S. (2002). *Motivational interviewing: Preparing people to change addictive behavior* (2nd ed.). New York, NY: Guilford Press.

Miller, W. R., Wilbourne, P. L., & Hettema, J. E. (2003). What works? A summary of alcohol treatment outcome research. In R. H. Hester & W. R. Miller (Eds.), *Handbook of alcoholism treatment approaches: Effective alternatives* (3rd ed., pp. 13–63). Boston, MA: Allyn & Bacon.

Miller, W. R., Zweben, A., DiClemente, C. C., & Rychtarik, R. G. (1995). *Motivational enhancement therapy manual: A clinical research guide for therapists treating individuals with alcohol abuse and dependence.* Project MATCH Monograph Series (Vol. 2). Rockville, MD: National Institute on Alcohol Abuse and Alcoholism.

Milmoe, S., Rosenthal, R., Blane, H. T., Chafetz, M. E., & Wolf, I. (1967). The doctor's voice: Postdictor of successful referral of alcoholic patients. *Journal of Abnormal Psychology, 72*(1), 78–84.

Moos, R. H., & Moos, B. S. (2005). Sixteen-year changes and stable remission among treated and untreated individuals with alcohol use disorders. *Drug and Alcohol Dependence, 80*(3), 337–347.

National Center on Addiction and Substance Abuse at Columbia University. (2012). *Addiction medicine: Closing the gap between science and practice.* New York, NY: Columbia University Press.

National Institute on Drug Abuse. (1994). *National pregnancy and health survey* [Press release]. Rockville, MD: National Clearinghouse for Alcohol and Drug Information.

National Institute on Drug Abuse. (1999). *Principles of drug addiction treatment: A research based guide.* NIH Publication No. 00–4180. Bethesda, MD: National Institutes of Health.

O'Farrell, T. J., & Fals-Stewart, W. (2003). Alcohol abuse. *Journal of Marital and Family Therapy, 29*(1), 121–146.

O'Farrell, T. J., Murphy, M., Alter, J., & Fals-Stewart, W. (2008). Brief family treatment intervention to promote continuing care among alcohol-dependent patients in inpatient detoxification: A randomized pilot study. *Journal of Substance Abuse Treatment, 34*(3), 363–369.

Office of Applied Studies. (2005). *Treatment episode data set (TEDS): 2002. Discharges from substance abuse treatment services* (DHHS Publication No. SMA 04–3967). Rockville, MD: Substance Abuse and Mental Health Services Administration.

Orleans, C. T., Schoenbach, V. J., Wagner, E. H., Quade, D., Salmon, M. A., Pearson, D. C., . . . Kaplan, B. H. (1991). Self-help quit smoking interventions: Effects of self-help materials, social support instructions, and telephone counseling. *Journal of Consulting and Clinical Psychology, 59*(3), 439–448.

Piercy, F. F., & Frankel, B. R. (1989). The evolution of an integrative family therapy for substance-abusing adolescents: Toward the mutual enhancement of research and practice. *Journal of Family Psychology, 3*(1), 5–25.

Prochaska, J. O., Norcross, J. C., & DiClemente, C. C. (1994). *Changing for good: The revolutionary program that explains the six stages of change and teaches you how to free yourself from bad habits.* New York, NY: William Morrow.

Quinn, W. H., Kuehl, B. P., Thomas, F. N., & Joanning, H. (1988). Families of adolescent drug abusers: Systemic interventions to attain drug-free behavior. *American Journal of Drug and Alcohol Abuse, 14*(1), 65–87.

Robert Wood Johnson Foundation. (2006a, August). *Economic benefits of treating substance abuse outweigh costs.* Research Highlight Number 7. Retrieved from http://www.rwjf.org/en/library/research/2007/05/substance-abuse-treatment-benefits-and-costs.html

Robert Wood Johnson Foundation. (2006b, August). *Treatment of chemical dependency may reduce medical utilization and costs.* Research Highlight Number 6. Retrieved from https://www .drugpolicy.org/docUploads/NewMexicoMedicaidFactSheet.pdf

Robins, L. N., & Regier, D. A. (1991). *Psychiatric disorders in America.* New York, NY: Macmillan.

Roizen, R. (1977). *Barriers to alcoholism treatment.* Berkeley, CA: Alcohol Research Group.

Rowe, C. L., & Liddle, H. A. (2003). Substance abuse. *Journal of Marital and Family Therapy, 29*(1), 97–120.

Satir, V. (1988). *The new peoplemaking.* Palo Alto, CA: Science and Behavior Books.

Schuckit, M. A. (1986). Genetic and clinical implications of alcoholism and affective disorder. *American Journal of Psychiatry, 143*(2), 140–147.

Schuckit, M. A. (2000). Genetics of the risk for alcoholism. *American Journal on Addictions, 9*(2), 103–112.

Scott, C. K., Foss, M. A., & Dennis, M. L. (2005). Pathways in the relapse-treatment-recovery cycle over 3 years. *Journal of Substance Abuse Treatment, 28*(Suppl.), 563–572.

Sias, S. M., & Goodwin, L. R., Jr. (2007). Students' reactions to attending 12-step meetings: Implications for counselor education. *Journal of Addictions and Offender Counseling, 27,* 113–126.

Simpson, D. D., Joe, G. W., & Broome, K. M. (2002). A national 5-year follow-up of treatment outcomes for cocaine dependence. *Archives of General Psychiatry, 59*(6), 538–544.

Sobell, L. C., Ellingstad, T. P., & Sobell, M. B. (2000). Natural recovery from alcohol and drug problems: Methodological review of the research with suggestions for future directions. *Addiction, 95*(5), 749–764.

Stanton, M. D., & Shadish, W. R. (1997). Outcome, attrition, and family-couples treatment for drug abuse: A meta-analysis and review of the controlled, comparative studies. *Psychological Bulletin, 122*(2), 170–191.

Substance Abuse and Mental Health Services Administration. (2013). *Results from the 2012 National Survey on Drug Use and Health: Summary of national findings.* Office of Applied Studies. (NSDUH Series H-46, HHS Publication No. [SMA] 13–4795). Rockville, MD: Author.

Szapocznik, J., Kurtines, W. M., Foote, F., Perez-Vidal, A., & Hervis, O. (1986). Conjoint versus one-person family therapy: Further evidence for the effectiveness of conducting family therapy through one person with drug-abusing adolescents. *Journal of Consulting and Clinical Psychology, 54*(3), 395–397.

Thomas, C. P., Garnick, D. W., Horgan, C. M., Miller, K., Harris, A. H., & Rosen, M. M. (2013). Establishing the feasibility of measuring performance in use of addiction pharmacotherapy. *Journal of Substance Abuse Treatment, 45*(1), 11–18.

Timko, C., Moos, R. H., Finney, J. W., & Lesar, M. D. (2000). Long-term outcomes of alcohol use disorders: Comparing untreated individuals with those in Alcoholics Anonymous and formal treatment. *Journal of Studies on Alcohol, 61*(4), 529–540.

Toneatto, T., Sobell, L. C., Sobell, M. B., & Rubel, E. (1999). Natural recovery from cocaine dependence. *Psychology of Addictive Behaviors, 13,* 259–268.

Vaillant, G. E. (2003). A 60-year follow-up of alcoholic men. *Addiction, 98*(8), 1043–1051.

Valle, S. K. (1981). Interpersonal functioning of alcoholism counselors and treatment outcome. *Journal of Studies on Alcohol, 42*(9), 783–790.

Watson, A. L., & Sher, K. J. (1998). Resolution of alcohol problems without treatment: Methodological issues and future directions of natural recovery research. *Clinical Psychology: Science and Practice, 5,* 1–18.

Wegscheider, S. (1981). *Another chance: Hope and help for the alcoholic family.* Palo Alto, CA: Science and Behavior Books.

White, W. L. (1996). *Pathways from the culture of addiction to the culture of recovery: A travel guide for addiction professionals* (2nd ed.). Center City, MN: Hazelden.

Winters, K. C., Stinchfield, R., Latimer, W. W., & Lee, S. (2007). Long-term outcome of substance-dependent youth following 12-step treatment. *Journal of Substance Abuse Treatments, 33*(1), 61–69.

18

Working With Trauma-Related Mental Health Problems Among Combat Veterans of the Afghanistan and Iraq Conflicts

LINDSEY N. COOPER, RYAN P. HOLLIDAY, NICHOLAS D. HOLDER, JAMYLAH JACKSON, CAROL S. NORTH, AND ALINA M. SURÍS

*T*he conflicts in Iraq and Afghanistan brought large numbers of returning combat veterans home with social, cultural, and psychological issues unique to this cohort. Operation Enduring Freedom (OEF) began in Afghanistan in 2001, Operation Iraqi Freedom (OIF) began in Iraq in 2003, and Operation New Dawn (OND) began in Iraq (a new phase following the end of OIF) in 2010 that officially ended in 2014. OEF/OIF/OND veterans are military personnel enlisted or activated after 2001. Of the more than one million service members deployed to Iraq or Afghanistan, nearly half were deployed more than once. More than 52,000 service members were wounded, with the fatality count approaching 7,000 (U.S. Department of Defense [DoD], 2016). Traumatic combat exposures in Iraq and Afghanistan included mortar, rocket, and artillery fire; small arms fire; multiple high-intensity blasts; roadside bombs; improvised explosive devices (IEDs); rocket propelled grenades; and surprise sniper attacks (Mental Health Advisory Team 5 [MHAT-V], 2008; Seal, Bertenthal, Miner, Sen, & Marmar, 2007; Spelman, Hunt, Seal, & Burgo-Black, 2012). Commonly sustained injuries were blast wounds and soft tissue and orthopedic injuries, including amputations, burns, hearing loss, and traumatic brain injury (TBI) (Grieger et al., 2006).

The OEF/OIF/OND conflicts were the longest sustained U.S. military operations since the Vietnam War and the first extended conflicts to rely on an all-volunteer military (Institute of Medicine [IOM], 2010) at a time when there were fewer active-duty military personnel available than in the previous conflicts. This situation created a different military climate compared with previous sustained military operations, with greater dependence on National Guard and reservists, longer deployment durations, multiple deployments, and shorter intervals between deployments. These more numerous deployments coupled with the shorter intervals between them increased the need for transition and readjustment time for returning soldiers and their families.

Medical advances have increased the survival rates of soldiers with significant injuries. Improvements in body armor and emergency medical care reduced combat fatality-to-injury ratios to their lowest level in history (1:7.2 for OIF, 1:5.0 for OEF, 1:2.6 in

Vietnam, and 1:1.7 in World War II; DoD, 2017; Leland & Oboroceanu, 2010). Therefore, higher proportions of veterans from the OEF/OIF conflicts than ever before returned home with severe combat-related injuries requiring specialized care. Accompanying these physical wounds were the mental wounds of war. Seal et al. (2009) found that 37% of Iraq and Afghanistan veterans accessing Veterans Affairs (VA) health care services received psychiatric diagnoses, with 22% meeting criteria for posttraumatic stress disorder (PTSD) and 17% meeting criteria for depressive disorders; rates were higher among those with repeated deployments.

OEF/OIF military personnel are fundamentally different from those of previous military operations, such as the Gulf War and Vietnam War, in a number of ways. There has been much discussion regarding the uniqueness of the OEF/OIF conflicts in their heavy involvement of National Guard and reservist personnel. Deployed soldiers within today's reservist units are older and more likely to have families than in the Vietnam War era. Reservists and National Guard units also differ in many ways from active-duty military that may affect their psychosocial adjustment. Reservists are less likely to be part of a cohesive unit with the high levels of camaraderie and trust that active component service members who live and train together experience. Reservists generally function as civilians except during monthly weekend trainings and actual deployment. The transition back to civilian life for reservists occurs more abruptly than for active-duty personnel and thus may be more difficult. Family members of reservists are less connected to the military community and do not receive the support of interactions with other families of deployed soldiers in the way that regular military families do.

Women have made up a larger percentage of deployed forces than ever before, comprising 15% of deployed military personnel (DoD, 2014). Between 2002 and 2006, 50% of deployed women using veteran health care had been activated from Reserve or Guard units. Compared with their civilian counterparts, military mothers were three times more likely to be single parents and five times more likely to be married to a military and deployable spouse (Joint Economic Committee U.S. Congress, 2007). National Guard and reservist mothers who were primary caregivers likely found it more difficult to arrange for alternative child care than mothers who were active-duty personnel. Many deployed female soldiers were also mothers of young children and endured long periods of separation from their children and spouses. For deployed women, especially those who were mothers, family disruptions and family-related concerns were superimposed on the other stresses of deployment.

Historically, women have been excluded from direct combat operations. However, legislation passed in January 2013 opened military positions with direct combat roles to women, with full implementation beginning January 1, 2016 (DoD, 2015b). In addition, expansion of support functions (e.g., mechanic, military police, transportation) performed by female military personnel coupled with the nature of the OEF/OIF conflicts (insurgency warfare) increased traumatic exposures among female troops in the war zone (Street, Vogt, & Dutra, 2009). In Iraq, many female soldiers, like their male counterparts, were exposed to surprise ambushes of their convoys, mortar and grenade attacks, gunfire exchange, IEDs, witnessing serious injury or death, and personal threat of serious injury or death (Street et al., 2009). Female soldiers were more likely than male soldiers to experience discrimination and harassment, with half or more acknowledging some form of sexual harassment during each of their years in the military (Lipari, Cook, Rock, & Matos, 2008).

To inform the provision of mental health interventions for OEF/OIF/OND veterans, a thorough understanding of the mental health problems in this population is a necessary first step. This chapter first reviews research on the prevalence and types of mental health problems among OEF/OIF/OND veterans, associated risk factors, and other psychosocial issues. Following this, empirical evidence for treatment in this population is provided. This material provides guidance to clinicians working with mental health and psychosocial problems of veterans of the OEF/OIF/OND conflicts.

PSYCHIATRIC AND READJUSTMENT PROBLEMS OF RETURNING OEF/OIF/OND VETERANS

Mental health problems among OEF/OIF/OND veterans may be divided into PTSD, other psychiatric disorders, and TBI. In addition to all the problems that are known to affect returning military personnel from previous wars, they may also experience a variety of psychosocial issues, many of which may be unique to this special population.

Exposure to Military Trauma

PTSD may develop in relation to a number of different types of trauma such as physical and sexual assault, combat exposure, natural disasters, motor vehicle collisions, and other kinds of accidents. The types of traumatic events most likely to be associated with PTSD represent human acts of intentional physical harm such as combat, assault, and sexual assault (Breslau et al., 1998). Exposure to trauma is difficult to categorize for military combat. The combat theater differs from many other kinds of trauma situations in which the danger is ongoing and recurrent. Some types of threats also vary from one war to another. The types of combat-related traumatic incidents experienced by OEF/OIF/OND veterans have been established through previous research, including a RAND study by Tanelian et al. (2008) building on previous work by Hoge et al. (2004) in OEF/OIF veterans and the earlier work of Castro, Bienvenu, Hufmann, and Adler (2000) with soldiers deployed to Kosovo. The list of traumatic combat incidents can be found in Table 18.1.

Missing from this list of combat experiences, however, is the possibility of prolonged exposure to potential threats that are outside of any of the 15 types of trauma exposures identified in Table 18.1. The types of warfare in the Iraq and Afghanistan conflicts differed from those of earlier conflicts and wars in several ways. There were

TABLE 18.1 TRAUMATIC COMBAT INCIDENTS

Serious injury or death of a friend
Viewing dead or seriously injured noncombatants
Witnessing an accident resulting in serious injury or death
Smelling decomposing bodies
Being physically moved or knocked over by an explosion
Sustaining an injury not requiring hospitalization
Sustaining a blow to the head from any accident or injury
Sustaining an injury requiring hospitalization
Engaging in hand-to-hand combat
Witnessing brutality toward detainees/prisoners
Being responsible for the death of a civilian
Killing enemy combatants
Handling or uncovering human remains
Being attacked or ambushed
Receiving incoming artillery, rocket, or mortar fire

no front lines because it was uncertain when and from where the next attack could come. Thus, the threat was typically constant and ongoing. Especially in Iraq, many of the operations occurred in largely urban areas where civilian crowds made identification of the enemy difficult. Any travel presented ongoing threats of encountering IEDs. Suicide bombers could infiltrate purportedly "safe" zones, creating a sense of prolonged potential for risk even on post in primarily noncombat-related positions. Although this ongoing potential threat was part of the stressful environment of today's combat theater, it does not clearly fulfill the *Diagnostic and Statistical Manual of Mental Disorders*, fifth edition (*DSM-5*) specification of exposure to an immediate physical threat as defined by PTSD criterion A (American Psychiatric Association [APA], 2013). Regardless, this type of stressor has been found to be associated with posttraumatic stress symptoms (Kolkow, Spira, Morse, & Grieger, 2007).

Another established list of traumatic combat incidents (MHAT-IV, 2006) includes 30 different types of OEF/OIF combat experiences. The lack of standardization in the literature regarding what does and does not qualify as combat trauma exposure and the lack of a consistent system of evaluating the severity of combat experiences leaves much to be resolved by clinical judgment. Psychiatric syndromes associated with combat-related stressors that do not meet criterion A cannot, by definition, be determined to represent PTSD or its symptoms, and the possibility that the symptoms may represent another psychiatric disorder should not be overlooked.

Although combat trauma is the type of trauma traditionally identified in association with military experience, OEF/OIF/OND veterans also faced risk of exposure to military sexual trauma (MST), both while deployed and stateside. MST, as defined by the VA, includes both sexual harassment and sexual assault during a military service (Title 38 U.S. Code 1720D). The rates of reported MST have been rising. This is likely because of the rising numbers of women in the military, increased screening, and access to MST services that routinely assess for MST (Kimerling et al., 2010). Barth and colleagues (2016) found that between 2009 and 2011, approximately 41% of women and 4% of men reported experiencing MST. In comparison, national VA statistics between 2002 and 2009 indicated that 22% of female and 1% of male veterans seeking VA health care acknowledged a history of MST (Surís & Smith, 2011). The larger proportion of male service members, however, yields nearly equal numbers of men and women with a history of MST (Surís & Lind, 2008). The DoD has implemented policies attempting to reduce the prevalence of MST, such as the Sexual Assault Prevention and Response (SAPR) policy program in 2006 (DoD, 2015a; Lande, Ghurani, Burton, & Earley, 2016). The current SAPR policy included initiatives for MST prevention, victim assistance, investigation, accountability, and assessment (DoD, 2015a; Lande et al., 2016). The DoD reported a minimal decrease in reported MST incidents from 2014 to 2015 from 6,131 to 6,083 (DoD, 2015a).

Posttraumatic Stress Disorder

PTSD is the psychiatric disorder most likely to arise after OEF/OIF deployments (Seal et al., 2007). According to the *DSM-5* (APA, 2013), the diagnosis of PTSD requires exposure to a traumatic stressor representing a threat to life or limb or sexual violence. The diagnostic criteria allow for four types of qualifying exposures to the traumatic event: direct experience of the event, directly witnessing the event, learning of the experience of a traumatic event by a loved one or a close friend (with the actual or threatened death being either violent or accidental), or experiencing repeated or extreme exposure to aversive details of a traumatic event (not through media, pictures, television, or movies unless work-related). Additionally, trauma-related symptoms that impair functioning or cause clinically significant distress must be present for more than 1 month.

These symptoms must include at least one of five reexperiencing symptoms (Criterion B: intrusive recollections, nightmares, flashbacks, and emotional or physiological distress in response to reminders of trauma), one or both avoidance symptoms (Criterion C: avoidance of or efforts to avoid distressing memories, thoughts, or feelings associated with the trauma or avoidance of or efforts to avoid external reminders—people, places, situations—that arouse memories or feelings associated with the trauma), at least two of seven symptoms signifying negative alterations in cognition or mood associated with the traumatic event (Criterion D: e.g., inability to remember important aspects of the trauma; persistent negative beliefs about oneself, others, or the world; distorted cognitions about the cause of the traumatic event; feelings of guilt; feelings of detachment from others; inability to experience positive emotions; and diminished interest or participation in significant activities), and at least two of six hyperarousal symptoms (Criterion E: sleep disturbance, concentration problems, hypervigilance, exaggerated startle response, jitteriness, irritability).

Recent literature reviews have noted that studies vary widely in their estimates of the prevalence of PTSD among OEF/OIF/OND veterans (Ramchand et al., 2010; Ramchand, Rudavsky, Grant, Tanielian, & Jaycox, 2015), with most studies in these reviews reporting rates between 5% and 30%. For example, Koo, Hebenstreit, Madden, and Maguen (2016) reported that 28% of male OEF/OIF/OND veterans and 23% of female OEF/OIF/OND veterans were diagnosed with PTSD between 2001 and 2013. A meta-analysis by Kok, Herrell, Thomas, and Hoge (2012) reported PTSD prevalence at 13% for OEF/OIF/OND combat units, 6% among deployed OEF/OIF/OND samples, and 3% among nondeployed samples. Variability in the reported prevalence rates may relate in part to substantial methodological variability and limitations in study designs. Major methodological limitations in this research include the use of screening instruments rather than full diagnostic assessments, inconsistent time frames of assessment (e.g., current diagnosis in the last month vs. cumulative prevalence across the entire period since return from war vs. lifetime prevalence), cross-sectional and retrospective designs, and selection bias with underrepresentation of those most severely wounded or removed from duty. The previous prevalence estimates of psychiatric illness in OEF/OIF/OND veterans can be compared with estimates among military veterans of other eras, 2% to 10% for Persian Gulf War veterans (Kang & Bullman, 1996) and 15% for Vietnam era veterans (Schlenger et al., 1992). The lifetime prevalence of PTSD in the general population is 7.5% (Kessler, Sonnega, Bromet, Hughes, & Nelson, 1995). PTSD would be expected to be substantially more prevalent in treatment populations than in the general population (Ramchand et al., 2010, 2015).

Other Psychiatric Disorders

PTSD is not the only clinically important outcome of combat trauma. A review of VA medical records found that PTSD is typically associated with at least one other psychiatric disorder and often several disorders, especially major depressive disorders, substance use disorders, and anxiety disorders (Seal et al., 2009). Medical record reviews also indicated a sixfold increase in psychiatric diagnoses in OEF/OIF veterans between 2002 and 2008 (Cohen et al., 2009; Seal et al., 2007, 2009). It is unclear, however, if this increase in psychiatric diagnoses reflected an actual increase in prevalence or more diligent assessment of psychiatric disorders (Spelman et al., 2012).

A large study of OEF/OIF veterans receiving VA health care identified psychiatric disorders in 37% of the veterans, with more than half (56%) of these cases having at least two disorders. Of those with more than one disorder, 29% had two disorders and 33% had three or more disorders. The most common disorders identified were

PTSD (29%), anxiety disorders (6%), adjustment disorders (6%), depressive disorders (17%), alcohol use disorders (7%), and drug use disorders (3%; Seal et al., 2007, 2009). In a survey of active duty military OEF/OIF/OND service members, Shen, Arkes, and Williams (2012) found that up to 20% of postdeployment veterans met criteria for major depressive disorder. Reviewing VA records of OEF/OIF veterans presenting for treatment, Sayer et al. (2010) found higher rates of diagnosed psychiatric disorders: depressive disorders in 28%, other anxiety disorders in 10%, and substance use disorders in 5%, with an additional 35% screening positive for potential drug or alcohol disorders. Studies using screening instruments have reported higher rates of psychiatric illness compared to studies using full diagnostic assessments. In a study of Iraq War soldiers by Maguen et al. (2010), 32% of veterans screened positive for depression and 25% screened positive for alcohol abuse. The prevalence of psychiatric disorders also varies between branches of the military. In a study examining postdeployment health data for more than 50,000 service members, Mustillo et al. (2015) found the highest risk for and diagnosis rate of PTSD and depression was for active duty Navy personnel and the lowest for Air Force personnel. Alcohol use disorders were least prevalent among the Air Force and highest among Marines (Mustillo et al., 2015). Location of deployment also influenced the likelihood of psychopathology across all branches, with those returning from Afghanistan having higher risks of developing PTSD than service members returning from Iraq.

A direct comparison of PTSD prevalence across eras is problematic because studies did not use the same methodology (i.e., interview vs. symptom checklist). In a representative sample of Vietnam era veterans in the National Vietnam Veterans Readjustment Study (NVVRS), the current prevalence of PTSD was found to be 15% for males and 8% for females (Kulka et al., 1990). Kang, Natelson, Mahan, Lee, and Murphy (2003) used a PTSD symptom checklist to estimate the prevalence of PTSD in a population-based study of Gulf War veterans. They estimated the current prevalence of PTSD in Gulf War veterans to be 2% (Kang et al., 2003). A population-based study of OEF/OIF service members using a symptom checklist reported a current *probable* PTSD prevalence rate of nearly 14% (Schell & Marshall, 2008).

Several studies have focused on alcohol problems. Estimates of alcohol misuse among OEF/OIF/OND service members have ranged from 12% to 40% (Burnett-Zeigler et al., 2011; I. G. Jacobson et al., 2008; Seal et al., 2009). McDevitt-Murphy and colleagues (2010) reported that 26% of veterans screened in VA primary care evidenced hazardous alcohol use. In other studies, one fourth of OEF/OIF veterans seeking treatment at VA primary care and postdeployment clinics screened positive for problem drinking (Jakupcak, Luterek, Hunt, Conybeare, & McFall, 2008; McDevitt-Murphy et al., 2010).

Suicide statistics show an alarming increase in completed suicides in recent years among OEF/OIF/OND–era active-duty service members and veterans. Research has identified several risk factors for suicide among OEF/OIF/OND military personnel and veterans. Indicators of suicide risk include exposure to military combat, significant stressors such as prolonged deployment-related separation from loved ones, relationship problems, PTSD, alcohol and other substance use disorders, TBI, and impulsivity (Kang & Bullman, 2008; Martin, Ghahramanlou-Holloway, Lou, & Tucciarone, 2009; MHAT-V, 2008).

The prevalence of suicidal ideation among OEF/OIF/OND veterans has varied widely, with some studies reporting rates as high as 32% and some as low as 6% (Corson et al., 2013; Lemaire & Graham, 2011). The veterans who reported suicidal ideation also had higher rates of positive PTSD and depression screens and reported more psychosocial problems. The avoidance symptom cluster was specifically associated with suicidal ideation. Both postdeployment social support and a sense of purpose and control were protective. In a sample of OEF/OIF/OND veterans, DeBeer, Kimbrel, Meyer, Gulliver, and Morissette (2014) found that when social support was rated high, PTSD and depression had almost no association with suicidal ideation; however, when social support was rated low, PTSD and depression had a positive relationship with suicidal ideation. In a large study of OEF/OIF/OND veterans registered with the VA, Lemaire and Graham (2011) found that depressive disorders, PTSD, and psychotic disorders were all significantly associated with suicidal ideation. Suicidal ideation was most prevalent among veterans with depressive disorders and second in prevalence among those with PTSD, but the risk was highest among veterans with both of these disorders. There have been conflicting findings regarding suicide risk in OEF/OIF/OND veterans. The Army STARRS study recently found that a current or early deployment was associated with an increased suicide risk (Gilman et al., 2014), but other studies have reported that deployment with or without combat was not associated with suicide (Gilman et al., 2014; LeardMann et al., 2013). These findings underscore the importance of conducting a thorough assessment for other psychiatric disorders, as well as PTSD for veterans exposed to trauma.

Traumatic Brain Injury

TBI is considered a "signature injury" of the Iraq and Afghanistan wars (Defense Health Board Task Force on Mental Health, 2007). *TBI* is defined as traumatically induced structural injury and/or physiological disruption of brain function resulting from an external force, immediately followed by new onset or worsening of at least one of the following clinical signs: any period of loss or a decreased level of consciousness; loss of memory for events immediately before or after the injury (posttraumatic amnesia); alteration in mental state at the time of the injury (e.g., confusion, disorientation, slowed thinking); and neurological deficits (e.g., weakness, loss of balance, change in vision, praxis, paresis/plegia, sensory loss, aphasia) that may or may not be transient (VA/DoD, 2016, p. 6).

TBI commonly involves cognitive difficulties such as problems with attention and concentration, memory, and executive functions. Physical symptoms may include headaches, fatigue, sleep problems, and sensitivity to light and noise. Behavioral and emotional symptoms may include depressed or anxious mood, irritability, impaired impulse control, and aggressive behavior. Mild TBI (mTBI) is also referred to as "a concussion." mTBI symptoms primarily resolve in hours to days, but a small percentage of people report minor transient symptoms persisting beyond 6 months to a year (Bogdanova & Verfaellie, 2012; VA/DoD, 2016).

TBI is a type of major or mild neurocognitive disorder (NCD) in the *DSM-5* (previously termed *postconcussional disorder* in *DSM-IV-TR*; APA, 2000), defined as a syndrome following a head trauma consisting of any rapid movement or displacement of the brain within the skull that causes significant cerebral concussion or injury. To meet diagnostic criteria, the injury must have caused either a loss of consciousness, posttraumatic amnesia, disorientation and confusion, or neurological signs (e.g., positive neuroimaging, new or worsening seizures, changes in visual field, or hemiparesis). Additionally, major or mild NCD following TBI may be accompanied by various other symptoms, including fatigue, disordered sleep, headache, vertigo or dizziness, unprovoked irritability or aggression, anxious/depressed/labile mood, personality change, and apathy/lack of spontaneity beginning after the injury (APA, 2013; Schoenberg & Scott, 2011). These symptoms are often associated with significant impairment in social or occupational functioning (APA, 2013).

TBI has been found to be prevalent among OEF/OIF/OND veterans. The DoD has reported that more than 235,000 OEF/OIF/OND veterans were diagnosed with a TBI between 2000 and 2011 (Centers for Disease Control and Prevention [CDC], 2015; VA/ DoD, 2016). Between 12% and 23% of OEF/OIF/OND veterans are estimated to have sustained a TBI while deployed; however, only 10% to 20% of veterans with a TBI continue to experience post-concussive symptoms after 3 months (O'Neil et al., 2013). Thus, the majority of TBI injuries are classified as mTBI. Many cases of mTBI are comorbid with PTSD and other psychiatric disorders, which may in part reflect difficulties in differentiating it from other disorders or problems. In a literature review by O'Neil et al. (2013), studies reported 50% to 78% of veterans with confirmed mTBI also had psychiatric diagnosis: PTSD in 45%, alcohol use disorder in 28%, and another substance use disorder in 9%. However, the majority of studies reviewed concluded that few, if any, significant mental health outcome differences are evident among veterans with mTBI compared to those without (O'Neil et al., 2013). Additionally, little evidence was found to suggest that cognitive, physical, or psychiatric symptoms were more common in veterans with than without mTBI. A few studies have found cognitive deficits in veterans with mTBI; however, the types of cognitive deficits across studies were inconsistent (O'Neil et al., 2013). A study of OIF soldiers assessed at 3 months postdeployment for mTBI found that loss of consciousness in the incident was associated with a positive screen for PTSD (44%) and major depression (23%; Hoge et al., 2004). In a review of VA records of OEF/OIF veterans presenting for treatment, TBI was diagnosed in 4% of veterans, and 19% were positive for *probable* PTSD or a comorbid drug or alcohol disorder (Sayer et al., 2010).

Risk Factors for Mental Health Problems in OEF/OIF/OND Veterans

Recent research has focused on both pre-trauma and post-trauma risk factors for PTSD. There is considerable evidence that the degree and type of trauma exposure experienced by service members during deployment increase the likelihood of deployment-related mental health problems. The degree of exposure to combat, as represented by the number of firefight exposures, for example, is associated with subsequent development of PTSD (Xue et al., 2015). Severity of both combat exposure and combat injuries has been found to be associated with psychiatric disorders among OEF/OIF veterans (Tanelian et al., 2008). The severity of the soldiers' physical problems was associated with greater likelihood of both PTSD and depression, as combat injuries can reduce veterans' quality of life (MacGregor, Tang, Dougherty, & Galarneau, 2013; Xue et al., 2015).

Discharging a weapon can generate intense memories of the event and increase the likelikhood of PTSD (Xue et al., 2015). A postdeployment study of OIF soldiers found that 40% had to kill during combat. Even after controlling for other types of combat exposure, the experience of having to kill in combat was positively associated with the likelihood of screening positive for PTSD, alcohol abuse, problems with anger and relationships, and impaired psychosocial functioning (Maguen et al., 2010). Multiple deployments also increase the risk for PTSD, presumably through the cumulative effects of exposure to trauma and other deployment stress experienced over a period of time. One study found that 27% of veterans who were deployed three or four times had problems with depression, anxiety, or acute stress, compared with 12% of those deployed only once (MHAT-V, 2008).

Exposure to MST is especially likely to be associated with postdeployment psychiatric problems, and the mental health consequences of MST may combine additively, as well as interactively, with mental health effects of trauma exposures during deployment. Kimerling et al. (2010) found that female veterans exposed to MST were 3.5 times more likely than other female veterans to have a psychiatric disorder. In women, MST has been found to be associated specifically with PTSD, depression, and substance use disorders, as well as with various psychological symptoms (Surís & Lind, 2008) and impaired functioning (Street et al., 2009). Women sexually assaulted during military service may feel trapped in their working environment, as they may be reluctant to report the incident for fear of negative career consequences—especially if the perpetrator is a senior officer (Turchik & Wilson, 2010). Survivors of MST have been betrayed by someone they were supposed to be able to trust, and they may have no choice but to continue to work alongside this person (because military personnel cannot readily transfer their duty station; Street et al., 2009; Surís & Smith, 2011). Survivors are thus placed in a position of having to depend on people they cannot trust, and at the same time, they may also feel distanced from the camaraderie of their fellow soldiers. Military environments create intense camaraderie (e.g., willingness to sacrifice one's life for one's comrades) and trust that are vital for mutual protection and safety of the unit and its members. The sense of betrayal of trust and the alienation from colleagues that accompany MST are thus likely to be even more pronounced than with sexual affronts experienced in civilian environments.

Ethnic group membership, military rank, and branch of military have also been found to be associated with risk of PTSD and other psychiatric disorders among OEF/OIF/OND veterans. Research studies examining age at the time of the traumatic experience have produced varied results, with some showing lower age to be a predictor of mental illness and others finding it unrelated (Kang & Hyams, 2005; Xue et al., 2015). Veteran subgroups with greater risk of psychiatric illness are women, teenagers, ethnic minorities, divorced/separated veterans (Luxton, Skopp, & Maguen, 2010; Tanelian et al., 2008), and enlisted personnel compared with officers. Members of the Army and Marines are up to three times more likely than Navy and Air Force personnel to have PTSD (Kang & Hyams, 2005; Mayo, MacGregor, Dougherty, & Galarneau, 2013; Xue et al., 2015). PTSD has also been found to be more prevalent among reservist personnel than among active-duty soldiers (25% vs. 17%; Milliken, Auchterlonie, & Hoge, 2007).

In 2010, Fontana and Rosenheck reported that newly returning veterans appeared to have a greater burden of PTSD, although with less comorbid substance abuse, than veterans whose deployment ended years ago (Fontana & Rosenheck, 2010). Substance abuse among OEF/OIF/OND veterans is associated with impaired social functioning and other comorbid psychiatric illness.

Veterans entering treatment shortly after service in the war zone have been found to have less psychopathology than veterans entering treatment many years postdeployment (Fontana & Rosenheck, 2008, 2010). They have also been found to have better social functioning, with more education, less unemployment, more intact rather than broken marriages, and fewer legal problems. Based on this research, treatment providers can expect that veterans who seek treatment a long time after return from war may present with more psychopathology and psychosocial problems than those who enter treatment shortly after homecoming.

Psychosocial Problems and Emotional Distress

Although the majority of returning troops do not experience psychiatric illness after homecoming, many experience adjustment problems. The first adjustment for veterans returning home is the loss they may feel on separation from the tight camaraderie of the military unit that some veterans describe as more like family than even their own families (McAndrew et al., 2017). Once home, veterans may experience difficulties reacclimatizing to the rapid transition from a combat zone to civilian life. They may face adjustment issues in relationships disrupted by deployment, problems redefining roles in the home, and other readjustment problems such as negotiating difficult vocational and occupational choices (Gewirtz, Erbes, Polusny, Forgatch, & DeGarmo,

2011; Interian, Kline, Callahan, & Losonczy, 2012; Lester & Flake, 2013; Sayers, 2011). Couples must navigate fluctuations from interdependence to independence and back again, which can create conflicts and role confusion (Sayers, 2011). Marital relationships may become strained as veterans and their partners seek to renegotiate roles and reestablish intimacy, particularly among veterans with PTSD (Erbes, Meis, Polusny, & Compton, 2011; Khaylis, Polusny, Erbes, Gewirtz, & Rath, 2011; Monson, Fredman, & Taft, 2011; Sayer et al., 2011). Spouses of deployed OEF/OIF veterans have been found to have greater prevalence of depression, sleep problems, anxiety disorders, acute stress reactions, and adjustment disorders compared to spouses of nonveterans (Mansfield et al., 2010).

In surveys of returning personnel conducted 1 month postdeployment, approximately 4% of both active duty and reserve service members reported problems with interpersonal conflict; by 6 months, however, 14% of active duty and 21% of reserve service members reported interpersonal conflict (Milliken et al., 2007). These increases in problems over time suggest a process of deterioration in interpersonal relationships during the first several months back home. Immediately after homecoming, many veterans enter a "honeymoon" period, experiencing relief and joy at being rejoined with their families as their predominant feelings, but these positive feelings apparently fade for some veterans as readjustment to civilian life proceeds.

Veterans who are parents may face special challenges. For example, because the veteran's partner has had to assume all parenting functions, the returning veteran may feel left out of parent–child interactions (Gewirtz et al., 2011; Lester & Flake, 2013). On returning, veterans have to adjust to the developmental changes and the new level of maturity their children have achieved during their absence, but some may continue to treat their children as if they were younger. Some returning veterans interact with their children as if they were soldiers, creating distance in the parent–child relationship. Children with a parent returning from deployment may experience problems with regression and acting-out behaviors (Lester et al., 2016; Litz & Orsillo, 2011). The amount of family disruption following a combat-related injury to a family member during an OEF/OIF deployment has been found to be associated with higher levels of distress in children (Cozza et al., 2010). Collectively, these findings point to mental health effects on children associated with parental deployment and family readjustments during departure and on homecoming.

One clinically important area that research appears to address only indirectly is how deployment and readjustment affect the developmental stages of adult life that returning veterans must negotiate. Veterans returning from deployment in their mid to late twenties may find themselves having to choose a new career, as military skills learned and achievements such as rank and leadership may not translate well into civilian jobs. Older veterans leaving military service after many years face a dilemma of whether to retire from work altogether or embark on a new career. Many veterans therefore face stressful mid-life career changes that may necessitate returning to school after a long time away or having to start "at the bottom" in their careers. Injuries or health problems acquired during deployment may force some returning veterans to reconsider their previously chosen career paths. Veterans who opted to join the military in lieu of attending college may be disadvantaged in competition for jobs with civilians who achieved educational degrees and direct experience in their chosen line of work while the veteran was deployed. Repeated deployments are expected to be associated with higher financial and employment stress, especially with the greater composition of older, married soldiers in today's military reserve units.

Among veterans who opt to pursue higher education postdeployment, many report difficulties with their transition from military to college life. These transition difficulties are associated with greater posttraumatic stress symptom severity and less perceived social support (Elliott, Gonzalez, & Larsen, 2011). Many veterans feel uncomfortable seeking support from their academic institutions (Livingston, Havice, Cawthon, & Fleming, 2011), in part because veteran students may feel unwelcome and out of place in their new academic environment (DiRamio, Ackerman, & Mitchell, 2008).

Unemployment is a persisting concern among veteran populations. According to the U.S. Department of Labor (2016), the 2015 unemployment rate for OEF/OIF/OND veterans was 5.8%. These rates exceeded rates for veterans across all eras (4.6%) (U.S. Department of Labor, 2016). One third (33%) of OIF/OEF veterans had at least one service-connected disability (U.S. Department of Labor, 2016) presenting potential barriers to employment. PTSD comorbidity may also contribute to veteran unemployment: Nearly 40% of veterans with PTSD have been found to be rated as more impoverished and to have lower occupational functioning than their civilian counterparts (Elbogen, Johnson, Wagner, Newton, & Beckham, 2012; Murdoch, Hodges, Cowper, & Sayer, 2005). A 2009 report on employment among veterans seeking outpatient PTSD services found that 61% were not working (Desai, Spencer, Gray, & Pilver, 2009). The authors suggested that seeking disability compensation potentially discouraged efforts to achieve stable employment (Drew et al., 2001).

Military deployments may also disrupt social relationships outside of the veteran's family. Returning veterans may find that they are "out of sync" with same-aged peers and friends (Ahern et al., 2015). Their friends may be at different life stages, having moved on with their own careers, family involvements, friendships, and social activities. The veteran may feel disconnected from former friends in the civilian world and may not feel that these friends can understand them. Older veterans who are medically retired from their military careers, or who have enough years of service to retire, may return home to find that they do not have much in common with their civilian peers who continue working for a number of years until their retirements.

Given the many issues surrounding readjustment to civilian life, it is understandable that a substantial proportion of returning veterans may encounter many difficulties in social and interpersonal functioning, productivity, marital and family relationships, occupational and educational endeavors, engaging in community and leisure activities, and anger management after returning from deployment; additionally, stigma toward seeking help and alcohol misuse may further complicate successful adjustment to civilian life (Cornish, Thys, Vogel, & Wade, 2014; Sayer et al., 2010). A review of VA records of OEF/OIF veterans who averaged 42 months past deployment found that 40% acknowledged problems readjusting to civilian life and 25% had difficulties in *all* areas of functioning (Sayer et al., 2010). The most frequently endorsed problem areas were related to interpersonal functioning, such as difficulties confiding personal thoughts and feelings to others and getting along with spouses, children, and friends. The single most frequently reported problem was difficulty controlling anger. Occupational functioning problems, such as difficulties finding or keeping a job and doing what is needed for work or school, were also endorsed. Problems were also reported in functioning at home, such as completing chores; in leisure functioning, such as enjoyment or making good use of free time; and in finding meaning and purpose in life. Increasing use of alcohol and other substances was another problem area identified among veterans after their return from deployment.

Several other studies have found psychosocial functioning problems to be associated with PTSD. Problems readjusting to civilian life endorsed by OEF/OIF/OND veterans were found to be associated with screening positive for *probable* PTSD in a VA medical record study by Sayer et al. (2010, 2011), although many other veterans also reported having such problems. Impairment in psychosocial and occupational functioning and adjustment were found to be associated with PTSD in a study of National Guard and Reserve veterans (Shea, Vujanovic, Mansfield, Sevin, & Liu, 2010). Interpersonal and social problems were specifically associated with avoidance and numbing symptoms, but overall functional impairment and global distress were specifically associated with hyperarousal symptoms. Problems in physical functioning, role functioning, physical pain, and general health were associated with PTSD in a study that reviewed intake data from OEF/OIF veterans seeking health care through a VA postdeployment health clinic (Jakupcak et al., 2008). Disruptions to relationships, especially family relationships, have been found to be more strongly associated with mental health functioning in female than in male veterans (Vogt, Pless, King, & King, 2005).

TREATMENT FOR TRAUMA-RELATED MENTAL HEALTH PROBLEMS OF OEF/OIF/OND VETERANS

Any major review of treatment for trauma-related mental health problems of OEF/OIF/OND veterans must be preceded by an understanding of the substantial barriers to engagement and retention in treatment faced by today's veteran population. Interpersonal and other social problems associated with PTSD may have the unfortunate effect of isolating veterans from social support systems designed to help them (Erbes, Westermeyer, Engdahl, & Johnsen, 2007). Younger cohorts of veterans differ from Vietnam and Persian Gulf era veterans in important ways that may affect their ability to engage and remain in treatment, including gender composition, marital status, legal history, age, and deployment experiences (Fontana & Rosenheck, 2008). For example, many OEF/OIF/OND veterans have young families and are employed. These two factors alone can create scheduling challenges that make it difficult for veterans to repeatedly take time off work or arrange for child care to remain in treatment for long periods of time. In contrast, older veterans may have more job seniority or be retired, and their children may be adults, thus allowing them more scheduling flexibility. It stands to reason that the recent OEF/OIF/OND veteran cohorts may differ from previous cohorts in their treatment needs and responses to approaches geared toward addressing their current issues. A 2008 IOM report on PTSD treatment identified the need for research to determine which kinds of treatment and strategies for delivery are most effective for this particular cohort.

A potential organizational barrier to mental health treatment is a lack of capacity to accommodate veterans' needs for access to care. For example, many veterans may be unable to leave work during hours that treatment is available, and obtaining transportation to an inconveniently located service provider facility may present an insurmountable hardship. VA PTSD clinical teams have historically accommodated Vietnam-era veterans with their more chronic and persistent symptoms than recently returning veterans (Erbes, Curry, & Leskela, 2009), whose treatment needs may be different and whose growing numbers may overwhelm existing service capacities. VA personnel have been added nationally to address the mental health treatment needs of the current OEF/OIF/OND cohorts, but not all facilities received these additional resources.

Stigma has been a longstanding barrier to mental health care for military personnel. Soldiers with mental health problems have been found to be twice as likely as their civilian counterparts to acknowledge concerns related to the stigma surrounding mental illness. In particular, they describe fears of embarrassment, damage to their careers, loss of confidence in them by members of the unit, and being perceived by their peers as weak if their mental illness is discovered; additionally, they have more negative beliefs about treatment (DeViva et al., 2016; MHAT-V, 2008; Milliken et al., 2007; Pietrzak, Johnson, Goldstein, Malley, & Southwick, 2009). Many of their concerns and perceptions may be well founded, as the military has historically maintained a policy of reporting substance abuse and other mental health problems to soldiers' superiors (IOM, 2010). These mandatory reporting rules may discourage personnel who need treatment from seeking and accepting mental health and substance-abuse treatment referrals. Although a desired function of the mandatory mental health/substance abuse reporting requirement is to identify impaired soldiers who could potentially endanger themselves and others, this practice unfortunately acts to reduce the likelihood that those needing treatment receive it. Addressing this issue, the IOM encouraged the DoD to "actively promote an environment to reduce stigma and encourage treatment for mental health and substance use disorders in an effort to improve military readiness and ability to serve" (IOM, 2010, p. 6).

Recently, strategies have been employed to normalize the use of mental health services after combat exposure, including postdeployment evaluations within the military and also at VA facilities upon discharge from the military. Despite these efforts, some veterans deliberately downplay symptoms in efforts to avoid detection of their mental health problems, either as an attempt to achieve more rapid discharge from military service or in hopes that their symptoms abate without professional attention.

Engagement and retention in mental health treatment appear to be especially difficult for current cohorts of returning military veterans. A comparison of treatment adherence among OEF/OIF veterans and Vietnam era veterans found OEF/OIF treatment dropout rates to be more than twice those of Vietnam veterans, and treatment attrition was independent of pretreatment distress levels (Erbes et al., 2009). In a multi era sample of veterans, of those who accepted a referral for specialty mental health care, approximately 25% did not attend the first treatment session; of those who did, 25% did not attend the second session (Lindley, Cacciapaglia, Noronha, Carlson, & Schatzberg, 2010). Studies have estimated the average dropout rate for evidence-based PTSD therapies in veterans at 23% (Steenkamp & Litz, 2013). Evidence regarding the association of treatment adherence with occupational status is mixed (Erbes et al., 2009; Fontana & Rosenheck, 2008). Possible explanations for the especially high treatment attrition rates within OEF/OIF/OND veterans might be heightened sensitivity of this cohort to stigma surrounding mental health problems, or that treatment approaches designed for prior-era veterans may not adequately meet the needs of veterans of the current era wars. Chard, Schumm, Owens, and Cottingham (2010) observed that the chronic PTSD of prior-era veterans does not generally respond as well to treatment as PTSD in newly returning veterans. Fontana and Rosenheck (2008) suggested that premature attrition from treatment may result in worsening symptoms over time, leading to decreased social functioning, particularly occupational functioning. Therefore, receiving effective treatment before the erosion of social support systems and before PTSD becomes persistent is likely to be a particularly important aspect of mental health care for returning veterans.

Overview of Treatment for Trauma-Related Mental Health Problems

Mental health treatment of veterans begins with adequate psychiatric and psychosocial assessment. Accurate diagnosis of psychiatric disorders, such as PTSD, is needed to select the type of treatment most likely to be effective. Just as important, though, is the assessment of psychosocial problems that are likely to occur in association with psychiatric disorders such as PTSD but also commonly occur in the absence of psychiatric illness. Adjustment difficulties, distress, and isolated symptoms can create significant problems for veterans. These issues should not be confused with psychiatric illness and clinicians should avoid pathologizing these kinds of difficulties. At the same time, clinicians should also take care to avoid minimizing the importance of psychosocial problems simply because these problems do not amount to a diagnosable disorder. Although reduction of symptoms is a worthy goal of treatment, restoring psychosocial functioning is also an important consideration. Recognizing and providing assistance with these common problems can make a positive difference in the lives of many veterans.

The mental health assessment of returning OEF/OIF/OND veterans should provide a comprehensive evaluation of psychosocial functioning, including functioning before military service (Litz & Orsillo, 2011). Information should also be obtained regarding the veteran's coping behaviors, trauma history, and specific experiences of deployment that stand out for that veteran. Safety factors such as suicidality and homicidality should be carefully assessed, as well as potential for domestic violence and child abuse. These safety factors and psychosocial functioning should continue to be evaluated along with symptom levels over the course of treatment, as they may change over time.

Treatment should not only be based on the psychiatric diagnosis but should also address specific symptoms. For example, veterans with PTSD who struggle with avoidance behaviors may benefit from therapy that specifically targets avoidance, such as Prolonged Exposure Therapy (PE). Veterans with PTSD who express guilt and self-doubt about a decision they made in combat may benefit more from a therapy that focuses on negative thought patterns, such as Cognitive Processing Therapy (CPT). Veterans with PTSD who are hyperaroused and cannot sleep may benefit from medication that has sedative side effects, and veterans with nightmares may benefit from administration of prazosin. The treatment plan for returning veterans might include two or more therapeutic modalities targeting PTSD and other psychopathology (e.g., individual psychotherapy, group psychotherapy, and medication).

As mental health treatment approaches for OEF/OIF/OND veterans have largely focused on PTSD, this review begins with specific treatments for PTSD and then moves to broader interventions for adjustment problems more generally. The VA and DoD (2010) jointly published a set of Clinical Practice Guidelines outlining the evidence-based treatment approaches for PTSD, recommended as "first-line" treatments. The IOM independently evaluated scientific evidence from 1980 to 2007 for pharmacologic and psychological treatment modalities for PTSD (IOM, 2008). These IOM and VA/DoD treatment reviews and recommendations played a significant role in determining the focus for the review of treatments provided later in this chapter. In general, time-limited therapy approaches may be most desirable for treating returning veterans, given the aforementioned barriers to treatment and relatively high therapy attrition rates in this veteran cohort. Randomized controlled trials (RCTs) are the current standard for determining the effectiveness of a treatment. Although RCTs specifically targeting OEF/OIF/OND veterans' responses to traditional therapy approaches are available, their numbers are still relatively sparse.

Treatments for mTBI in veterans who are still symptomatic are less well established, because the majority fully recover, even without treatment (VA/DoD, 2009). Clinical Practice Guidelines for mTBI noted a lack of evidence establishing direct causality between the brain injury and postconcussive symptoms, and a lack of objective indicators of brain pathology. As postconcussive symptoms do not correlate with objective indicators of brain injury and pathology, the Clinical Practice Guidelines recommend symptomatic treatment for mTBI (VA/DoD, 2009).

Pharmacotherapy

Antidepressants

Selective serotonin reuptake inhibitors (SSRIs), such as paroxetine, sertraline, citalopram, and fluoxetine, are considered a mainstay of treatment for PTSD as first-line pharmacotherapeutic agents (Alexander, 2012; Ipser & Stein, 2012; Ravindran & Stein, 2010; Stein, Ipser, & McAnda, 2009). Although only paroxetine and sertraline are approved by the U.S. Food and Drug Administration (FDA) for the treatment of PTSD, there is extensive evidence from numerous large RCTs of the efficacy of various agents of this class (Alexander, 2012; Ipser & Stein, 2012; Puetz, Youngstedt, & Herring, 2015; Ravindran & Stein, 2010; Stein et al., 2009). Long-term studies have further demonstrated evidence of benefit from SSRIs in maintaining acute-phase gains and preventing relapse (Ravindran & Stein, 2010; Roberts, deRoon-Cassini, & Brasel, 2010). Considerable evidence of efficacy has also accrued for other classes of antidepressants such as serotonin/norepinephrine-specific agents (SNRIs; especially venlafaxine, also mirtazapine), certain tricyclic antidepressants (e.g., amitriptyline, imipramine), monoamine oxidase inhibitors (MAOIs, e.g., phenelzine), and alternative or atypical serotonergic antidepressant agents (e.g., nefazodone; Alexander, 2012; Lee et al., 2016; Puetz et al., 2015; Ravindran & Stein, 2010; Stein et al., 2009).

The strategies and procedures for treating PTSD with antidepressant medications are similar to treatment of major depression with these medications. The effectiveness of these medications is independent of their antidepressant properties. They may also help with the management of common comorbid disorders (depressive disorders and other anxiety disorders such as panic disorder) and troublesome symptoms such as irritability, aggression, and suicidal ideation. The newer SSRIs and SNRIs have fewer adverse effects, favorable safety profiles, and simpler titration schedules compared with tricyclic antidepressants and other older psychotropic agents (Reeves, 2007). An advantage of these newer medications is that nonpsychiatric physicians (such as family practitioners and internists) may be more comfortable prescribing these medications, which may improve patient access to psychotropic treatment of PTSD.

Several reviews of pharmacotherapy for PTSD (Cukor, Spitalnick, Difede, Rizzo, & Rothbaum, 2009; L. W. Davis, English, Ambrose, & Petty, 2001; Puetz et al., 2015; Ravindran & Stein, 2010; Stein, Ipser, & Seedat, 2006) have noted that observed benefit from pharmacotherapy for PTSD in men and in combat veterans is not nearly as robust as that demonstrated in studies of civilian populations and women in particular. Stein and colleagues (2009), lamenting that many patients respond poorly to medication or show only partial reduction in symptoms, emphasized the need for development of better psychotropic agents for treatment of PTSD in the future. In response to incomplete or inadequate response of many patients to pharmacotherapy, augmentation strategies have been devised using agents from various psychoactive medication classes.

Anticonvulsants

Interest in the use of mood stabilizers to augment pharmacotherapy for PTSD arose in conjunction with theories that repeated traumatic experiences may lead to sensitization and kindling of limbic discharges (Reeves, 2007). Anticonvulsants, used in the treatment of seizure disorders in which kindling is implicated, have been demonstrated effective in the treatment of mood disorders as well. Despite a theoretical basis for the use of anticonvulsants in the treatment of PTSD, anticonvulsant medications (as a class) were not found to be efficacious for PTSD in a comprehensive meta-analysis (Lee et al., 2016). This meta-analysis provides strong evidence against the seizure-like kindling theory of PTSD and against the use of anticonvulsants for the treatment of PTSD.

Atypical Antipsychotics

Antipsychotic agents have been widely used as adjunctive medications for PTSD treatment, despite many clinical guidelines recommending against their use in the treatment of PTSD (APA, 2004; International Society for Traumatic Stress Studies, 2005; VA/DoD, 2010). In a comprehensive meta-analysis of PTSD treatments, antipsychotics were found to have a small positive effect as a treatment for PTSD (Lee et al., 2016). However, antipsychotic medications have considerable side effects, including extrapyramidal symptoms (e.g., parkinsonism, tardive dyskinesia), metabolic derangements (e.g., weight gain, dyslipidemia), and cardiovascular (e.g., atrial hypertension, sudden cardiac death) adverse events (De Hert, Detraux, van Winkel, Yu, & Correll, 2012). These potentially serious side effects coupled with the small therapeutic benefits of antipsychotic medication discourage their general use for veterans with PTSD who do not also have psychotic disorders.

Antianxiety Agents

Benzodiazepines have historically been used to treat PTSD for their anti-anxiety and sedative characteristics; however, clinical guidelines recommend against their use (APA, 2004; International Society for Traumatic Stress Studies, 2005; VA/DoD, 2010). Known problems in the use of benzodiazepines include potential for oversedation, cognitive impairment, psychomotor incoordination, respiratory depression, and dangers of overdose (Dell'osso & Lader, 2013). In particular, tolerance and dependence are well-established risks with prolonged use. For patients with substance abuse and certain personality problems, which frequently accompany PTSD, benzodiazepines should be avoided. Dissociative and disinhibitory properties of benzodiazepines may cause problems in management of PTSD. Benzodiazepines may further disinhibit behaviors among patients with impulse control disorders and contribute to dissociative states that may accompany PTSD. In summary, there is little evidence for the efficacy of benzodiazepines for treatment of PTSD, but there is considerable potential for problems emerging from the use of benzodiazepines in PTSD treatment, as well as potential for worsening the PTSD (Ipser & Stein; 2012; Ravindran & Stein, 2010; Reeves, 2007).

Another antianxiety medication that has been unsuccessfully tried for PTSD is buspirone. Although it is a nonaddictive antianxiety medication that is widely used for treatment of anxiety, there is no evidence for its efficacy in treating PTSD (Ravindran & Stein, 2010; Reeves, 2007).

Prazosin for Treatment of Nightmares

Prazosin, an α-1-adrenergic blocker widely used as an antihypertensive agent, has seen increasing application to the treatment of combat-related PTSD in recent years, especially in the targeted management of nightmares and related sleep disturbances. The role of central nervous system adrenergic activity involving norepinephrine metabolism implicated in PTSD provides a theoretical basis for the use of prazosin in the treatment of PTSD. Mounting evidence from case studies, retrospective chart reviews, open-label trials, and RCTs support the use of prazosin as an adjunctive agent targeting specific sleep-related disturbances in OIF/OEF/OND veterans with combat-related PTSD (Cukor et al., 2009; Raskind et al., 2013; Writer, Meyer, & Schillerstrom, 2014).

In summary, although only two medications have been FDA-approved for the treatment of PTSD, there are several medications that can be potentially helpful for PTSD. Recent recommendations have specifically discouraged the use of polypharmacy in treating PTSD (Lee et al., 2016).

"Emerging" Medications for PTSD

Several promising studies have investigated novel treatment approaches for the treatment of PTSD in which medication is paired with fear memory activation to augment memory extinction or interfere with reconsolidation. Medications investigated in this research include d-cycloserine (a partial NMDA receptor glycine agonist), corticosteroids, rapamycin (also known as sirolimus, a protein kinase mTOR [mammalian target of rapamycin] pathway agent), and empathomimetic agents (e.g., 3,4-methylenedioxymethamphetamine [MDMA]), but research with these agents is too preliminary to inform clinical treatment recommendations (Thomas & Stein, 2016). Other novel research agents of potential interest for PTSD are morphine and ketamine (NMDA receptor antagonist), but research on these agents to date is not sufficiently developed to consider these agents as likely treatment candidates (Steckler & Risbrough, 2012).

Psychotherapy

The VA's Office of Mental Health has initiated a national rollout of evidence-based therapies targeting psychiatric and psychosocial problems commonly faced by returning veterans, such as PTSD, major depression, substance abuse, and family problems. The specific therapies being rolled out by the VA, described in detail later, are CPT, cognitive behavioral therapy (CBT), acceptance and commitment therapy (ACT), PE therapy, and integrative behavioral couples therapy (IBCT). Psychotherapies are deemed "evidence-based" only after their efficacy has been supported by RCT equivalent groups and with minimal attrition (Karlin & Cross, 2014; Karlin et al., 2010). These treatments require intensive therapist training and often include post-training consultation to assist with implementation. Many of these therapies have been studied in veteran populations, and recent research has examined their utility with OEF/OIF/OND veterans.

Evidence-based psychotherapies such as CPT and PE have demonsrated evidence of effectiveness but also have well-documented limitations. Dropout rates are high and dropout has been found to be associated with younger age, higher military rank, poor symptom improvement, comorbid substance use, and limited clinician training (Steenkamp, 2016; Szafranski, Gros, Menefee, Norton, & Wanner, 2016; Yehuda & Hogue, 2016). PTSD symptom levels remain high in many veterans, even after completion of an evidence-based therapy (Steenkamp, 2016; Steenkamp, Litz, Hoge, & Marmar, 2015).

CPT for PTSD

CPT (Resick, Monson, & Chard, 2007) is a form of trauma-focused CBT employing both cognitive/behavioral and narrative exposure techniques. Trauma-related beliefs regarding self, others, and the world are addressed with an emphasis on exploring issues of safety, trust, power/control, esteem, and intimacy.

As a manualized treatment, CPT has 12 sessions designed to build on one another, and an additional session is provided for patients with prominent traumatic grief (Galovski, Wachen, Chard, Monson, & Resick, 2015). CPT is offered in individual and group formats, with preliminary evidence that the individual format is more effective than the group format for active duty military personnel (Resick et al., 2016). Therapy begins with psychoeducation focused on common psychological effects of trauma exposure. CPT frames PTSD as a disruption of the normal emotional recovery process following exposure to trauma. It then provides an explanation of the cognitive model and allows patients to practice identifying their own thoughts and resulting feelings related to specific traumatic and nontraumatic events. Throughout the therapy, persistent maladaptive thoughts ("stuck points") are gently challenged using Socratic questioning, and patients are taught cognitive/behavioral techniques to challenge their own negative thoughts. By considering alternate interpretations of events, patients can view their trauma(s) in a more realistic and balanced manner. In a clinical trial comparing treatment outcomes between OEF/OIF/OND veterans receiving CPT or treatment as usual, Alvarez et al. (2011) found CPT to be more effective in reducing posttraumatic stress and depressive symptoms, improving quality of life, improving coping, and reducing distress. In a recent RCT for active duty OEF/OIF/OND military personnel with combat-related PTSD, group CPT outperformed a nontrauma focused group psychotherapy intervention (Resick et al., 2015).

PE Therapy for PTSD

PE therapy has four components. First, therapy begins with psychoeducation providing information about common trauma reactions and normalization of the patient's current avoidant coping strategies. The rationale of treatment and goals of treatment are explained. Second, patients learn breathing retraining to assist with relaxation. The third and fourth components are imaginal exposure (repeated retelling of the traumatic experience story) and in vivo exposure exercises. PE therapy is typically completed in eight to 12 90-minute sessions.

PE is based on emotional processing theory, which posits that PTSD symptoms are a product of cognitive and behavioral avoidance of trauma-related reminders (Rauch & Foa, 2006). During PE, psychotherapists help patients with efforts to interrupt and reverse cognitive and behavioral avoidance through corrective information. PE therapy is thought to decrease distress by allowing patients to approach their fearful memories in the presence of objectively safe reminders of the traumatic experience (Foa, Hembree, & Rothbaum, 2007). Patients learn that the distress related to the memory does not last forever and that they eventually get habituated to it. As anxiety surrounding the memory decreases, patients are able to gain fuller understanding and acceptance of their memories of the traumatic event. Patients also participate in "in vivo" practice sessions with real-life assignments to help them reengage in activities they have been avoiding because they are reminders of the traumatic experience. Through these assignments, patients learn that feared situations such as a crowded shopping mall or watching a military documentary are objectively safe and can be tolerated. Repeated real-life practices in PE therapy result in habituation, with patients becoming less anxious and more actively engaged in their current lives.

To date, no RCTs have been conducted to specifically assess the efficacy of PE in OEF/OIF/OND veterans with PTSD. In a multi-site RCT, PE was significantly more effective than a non-trauma focused comparison condition at reducing PTSD symptom severity for female veterans across multiple service eras (Schnurr et al., 2007). This finding has been replicated by several other studies of veterans from various eras, including OEF/OIF/OND, confirming the effectiveness of PE with veterans (Eftekhari et al., 2013; Goodson, Lefkowitz, Helstrom, & Gawrysiak, 2013).

CBT for Depression

CBT is supported by substantial empirical evidence as a treatment of choice for PTSD and other mental health problems. Through cognitive restructuring techniques, CBT targets unrealistic cognitions that create or contribute to negative emotions that are considered to be central to the psychopathology of depressive disorders. Patients learn to identify and change common patterns of negative thinking known as cognitive distortions. Relationships among thoughts, feelings, and behaviors are explored with an emphasis on using restructured cognitions and behavioral activation to improve mood states (Beck, 2011).

ACT for Depression

ACT is a form of CBT that differs from traditional CBT in that its focus is not on examining or changing one's thoughts, feelings, or memories, but rather on simply recognizing and accepting them. This approach uses mindfulness and acceptance strategies along with commitment toward values-oriented behaviors to promote psychological flexibility and improvements in mood. ACT approaches have been used in the treatment of PTSD, although to date RCTs evaluating its effectiveness for PTSD are not available in the published academic literature. Lang and colleagues (2016) conducted an RCT to determine the efficacy of ACT to treat emotional distress in OEF/OIF/OND veterans by comparing it to Present Centered Therapy. ACT was found to reduce depressive and anxiety symptoms in veterans; however, the effects of ACT did not significantly differ from a present-centered therapy comparison condition.

Seeking Safety

Seeking Safety therapy is designed for simultaneous treatment of posttraumatic stress symptoms and comorbid substance misuse (Najavits, 2002). Seeking Safety is recognized by the International Society for Traumatic Stress Studies as an effective treatment for coexisting PTSD and substance use disorders, and it is widely used across a number of VA settings. This therapy is present-focused rather than trauma-focused. It is manualized for both clinicians and patients. The primary theme throughout the treatment is *safety*: in interpersonal relationships and in management of emotions, thought processes, and behaviors. Seeking Safety incorporates a focus on ideals and values before the development of posttraumatic stress and substance abuse and their related behaviors. Seeking Safety was designed to be adaptable to a number of formats, including group and individual therapy settings. This therapy provides content in case management, as well as cognitive, behavioral, and interpersonal domains. The Seeking Safety materials provide 25 modules, such as safety, recovery cognitions, detaching from emotional pain, and community resources, that can be presented in any order and as needed. Clinician self-care and therapeutic issues are also addressed. Modules have accompanying patient handouts with relevant psychoeducational materials and exercises for developing coping skills and practice assignments to be completed between sessions. The shorter time frame for Seeking Safety may have practical implications for OEF/OIF/OND veterans who have known problems with treatment retention.

Seeking Safety has been applied in a variety of populations, including male and female veterans, homeless individuals, and inmate populations. Outcome studies have demonstrated reduced posttraumatic stress symptoms, stronger problem-solving and coping skills, better social functioning, and an enhanced sense of meaning (see Najavits, 2009, for a review). Seeking Safety has been found effective compared to treatment as usual and wait list control conditions in several RCTs. It has also been found to be associated with decreased drug use, increased treatment attendance, greater client satisfaction, and more active coping (Boden et al., 2012; Lenz, Henesy, & Callender, 2016).

IRT for Nightmares

Imagery rehearsal therapy (IRT) for nightmares is a promising treatment that has been used in varying formats for many years and extensively implemented in VA settings. IRT research has demonstrated treatment-related reductions in trauma-related nightmares and other posttraumatic stress symptoms. van Schagen, Lancee, Spoormaker, and van den Bout (2016) demonstrated in a recent RCT that IRT was effective for a diverse range of psychiatric disorders, including PTSD. A version of the therapy developed by Krakow and Zadra (2010) has been successfully implemented with veterans. This and similar protocols have been found to reduce nightmares and posttraumatic stress symptoms in mixed era veterans (including OEF/OIF/OND veterans), as well as active-duty soldiers (Casement & Swanson, 2012; Forbes et al., 2003; Forbes, Phelps, & McHugh, 2001; Long et al., 2011; Lu, Wagner, Van Male, Whitehead, & Boehnlein, 2009; Moore & Krakow, 2007; Nappi, Drummond, Thorp, & McQuaid, 2010).

Family Therapies

As research has clearly demonstrated that the stressors of deployment and ensuing readjustment issues can negatively affect not only the veteran but also the veteran's family (Pietrzak et al., 2009), the Veterans Health Administration (VHA) Uniform Mental Health Services Handbook (VA, 2008) has established guidelines for mental health care and integration of care across VA programs. This handbook recommends provisions for the family involvement in treatment planning and care when requested by the veteran. Of particular relevance for returning veterans coping with posttraumatic stress or depressive symptoms or with adjustment concerns that also involve the family are two types of therapy: IBCT and a modified version of the Support and Family Education (SAFE) family group.

IBCT was developed by N. S. Jacobson and Christensen (1996) in response to research findings that traditional behavioral therapy for couples suffered from substantial relapse rates, and that efficacy was variable across various populations (N. S. Jacobson & Margolin, 1979). IBCT retains the basic behavioral strategy of traditional behavioral couples therapy such as communication and problem-solving skills training and behavioral exchange interventions, but its primary and initial focus is on emotional acceptance. In this therapy, recurrent problematic interactions within couples are identified and couples are then encouraged to express underlying emotions of hurt and fear along with their anger during these interactions to promote empathy and intimacy. Christensen et al. (2004) and N. S. Jacobson, Christensen, Prince, Cordova, and Eldridge (2000) demonstrated two distinct advantages of IBCT: (a) efficacy with a broader range of couples than served by traditional behavior therapy and (b) indications that the therapeutic benefits may be maintained.

A recent study by Roddy, Nowlan, Doss, and Christensen (2016) reported that the benefits of IBCT have been found to persist for at least 5 years after treatment. Erbes, Polusny, MacDermid, and Compton (2008) developed an adaptation to IBCT that is especially tailored to the needs of returning OEF/OIF veterans and is briefer than standard IBCT, requiring 12 to 14 rather than 24 to 26 sessions. The Erbes et al. (2008) adaptation provides an education component covering deployment-related concerns, PTSD, and various symptoms, incorporating motivational interviewing techniques such as identifying pros and cons of change as needed to enhance motivation to remain in treatment (Miller & Rollnick, 2002). Although this version of IBCT has not yet been empirically tested, Erbes et al. have suggested that reductions in relationship conflict and enhancement of partner empathy and intimacy, combined with education about the effects of PTSD and use of skills training, may decrease the level of distress of both partners and improve relationship functioning after return from deployment. IBCT is also being studied as a web-based intervention for distressed couples as a means of increasing access to treatment (Roddy et al., 2016).

S.A.F.E., developed at the Oklahoma City VA Medical Center (Sherman, 2003), is another form of family therapy designed to help family members cope with the psychological symptoms of the veteran in their family. The focus of the program is broad and addresses several psychiatric disorders, including schizophrenia, depression, and bipolar disorder. The many topics covered in this program require a total of 18 sessions. In response to the influx of OEF/OIF veterans, Bowling, Doerman, and Sherman (2007) adapted and condensed the S.A.F.E. program to address issues specifically relevant to families of returning OEF/OIF veterans such as PTSD and general reintegration problems in a 12-session program with accompanying handouts of resource lists, psychoeducational materials, and exercises involving topics such as parenting, communicating with one's loved one, caring behaviors, and coping with PTSD. The developers of the program suggested holding two group meetings a month, one with veterans attending along with family members and the other for family members only, but facilitators are encouraged to adapt the program as appropriate to their needs. The response of families to this program has been overwhelmingly positive.

Recently, the Reaching Out to Educate and Assist Caring, Healthy Families (REACH) program has been developed and studied in veteran populations. The REACH program is a 9-month psychoeducational multifamily group designed for veterans with PTSD and their family members. Veterans who participated in the REACH program have shown substantial improvement in empowerment, family communication and problem solving, and coping with PTSD symptoms. Family members who participated showed similar improvements in these areas as well (Fischer, Sherman, Han, & Owen, 2013).

Virtual Reality Therapy

Virtual reality therapy (VRE) involves visualization, interaction, and/or manipulation of stimuli through the use of computers. VRE uses technology to provide more consistent and controllable stimuli than what patients' imaginations can produce (Rizzo & Kim, 2005; Rizzo, Schulteis, & Kerns, 2004). VRE uses computer graphics in motion-tracked displays allowing vibrations, sounds, and scent deliveries to enhance the realism of the exposure. This approach has been used with some success to treat PTSD in Vietnam veterans (Rothbaum et al., 2014), Iraq veterans (Rothbaum, Rizzo, & Difede, 2010), and survivors of the 9/11 attacks on New York City's World Trade Center (Difede, Hoffman, & Jaysinghe, 2002). Research has also compared VRE to traditional therapies for PTSD. A recent study found VRE to be effective in reducing posttraumatic stress symptoms; however, PE therapy was found to have greater symptom reduction at 3- and 6-month follow up in active military service members (Reger et al., 2016). VRE was also associated with higher treatment dropout, suggesting that some veterans may have found this therapy too intense to complete (Reger et al., 2016). Limitations of VRE involve associated costs, potential for malfunctioning equipment to disrupt the therapeutic process, and some patients being distracted or overwhelmed by the realism provided by the VRE technology. Additional research is needed comparing VRE to more traditional interventions.

Other Interventions

Brain Stimulation Treatments

Various brain stimulation techniques, including transcranial magnetic stimulation (TMS), deep brain stimulation (DBS), vagal nerve stimulation, and transcranial direct current stimulation (tDCS) have been or are currently being studied as potential treatments for PTSD (Clark et al., 2015; Cleary et al., 2015; Karsen, Watts, & Holtzheimer, 2014; Marin, Camprodon, Dougherty, & Milad, 2014).

TMS uses a pulsed magnetic field to modulate neuronal activity. A coil is placed near the scalp and a variable electric current is pulsed through the coil, creating magnetic waves that penetrate the skull and alter neuronal activity in the targeted area (Clark et al., 2015).

A recent review by Karsen and colleagues (2014) examined eight separate studies of TMS used as the primary treatment for general population members with PTSD. All studies in this review found that TMS reduced PTSD symptoms, and both high and low frequency stimulation were found to be effective. A review and meta-analysis by Berlim and Van Den Eynde (2014) of controlled trials of TMS specifically applied to the dorsolateral prefrontal cortex found similar results, with reductions in posttraumatic stress, general anxiety, and depressive symptoms. A very recent systematic review and meta-analysis by Trevizol et al. (2016) also concluded that active TMS was superior to a control for treatment of PTSD. As the published studies have been limited by small sample sizes, generalizability of results has not been determined, and thus additional research is needed. To date, no published studies have specifically investigated the effectiveness of TMS for veteran PTSD.

Deep brain stimulation has been studied as a potential treatment for several psychiatric disorders. No studies of deep brain stimulation for PTSD have yet been published, although an RCT is currently underway (Koek et al., 2014).

Vagal nerve stimulation is currently being studied in animal models as a possible treatment for PTSD (Marin et al., 2014). Transcranial direct current stimulation has been studied in humans as a treatment for depression, but there are no published studies for PTSD (Marin et al., 2014).

Treating General Postdeployment Adjustment Problems

Although psychosocial and adjustment difficulties on homecoming can be distressing (Shea et al., 2010), these difficulties by themselves do not constitute psychiatric illness and therefore warrant different kinds of interventions. The first step in developing interventions for adjustment problems of returning veterans is a comprehensive assessment of psychosocial functioning that addresses the areas previously identified as well as safety issues, pending legal issues, and all other psychosocial concerns relevant for all service members (Litz & Orsillo, 2011). As veterans recently returning from deployments are especially likely to have protective factors such as intact families, employment and educational aspirations, and fewer legal problems, clinical interventions for returning veterans should be designed to preserve the social assets already present.

An important area to assess is the level of functioning at work or in school. Occupational issues may vary from unemployment and difficulty finding a job, to embarking on a new career after discharge or retirement from the military, to problems of low productivity, anger, and interpersonal difficulties on the job. Veterans making a transition to a different career may benefit from vocational counseling that provides interest inventories and tests of skills and abilities, coaching for interviewing skills, assistance with resume writing, training in a new field, and emotional support and therapy to address potential impediments such as negative self-talk that can undermine confidence. In particular, Individual Placement and Support (IPS) supported employment is an evidence-based vocational rehabilitation model that encourages engagement in competitive employment rather than sheltered jobs (Bond & Drake, 2014). IPS has been shown to enhance psychosocial functioning (i.e., self-esteem and quality of life) as well as increase likelihood of employment (L. W. Davis et al., 2012).

Veterans who anticipate returning to school may benefit from case management assistance to help them identify and apply for educational benefits. Considering that veteran students tend to seek support from their peers (Elliott, Gonzalez, & Larsen, 2011), student veteran groups can potentially increase social support and ease the transition between military and college life (Summerlot, Green, & Parker, 2009). Additionally, veterans may benefit from assistance in developing study skills and support, as well as development of realistic expectations and management of stress associated with returning to school after a long period of time away in a different context.

Assessment of family functioning may also identify problems in veterans after their return from deployment. Couples with relationship problems may benefit from marital therapy. Alternatively, specialized retreats designed for returning veterans and their spouses that are offered by various organizations may allow couples to bypass barriers to formal treatment such as the stigma and inconvenience of multiple sessions (L. W. Davis et al., 2012). Family therapy and parenting classes may also be helpful (Gewirtz, Pinna, Hanson, & Brockberg, 2014; Lester et al., 2012; Murphy & Fairbank, 2013). Specifically tailored programs have been developed to help children adjust to the deployment and return of a military parent. For example, Sesame Workshop (2011) (the nonprofit organization responsible for *Sesame Street*) has developed a collection of videos called the "Talk, Listen, Connect" series to help children learn to cope with the topics of deployment and return of a parent, change in the family, and grief.

The Families Overcoming Under Stress Program (FOCUS) is a therapy program for military families with a deployed parent. The protocol consists of eight sessions with parents, children, and families aimed at developing skills for emotion regulation and recognition, increasing awareness of various perspectives about the deployment, enhancing family coping skills, identifying strengths within the family, collaborative problem solving and goal setting, creating a shared narrative regarding the deployment, and improving access to community resources (Gewirtz et al., 2014; Murphy & Fairbank, 2013). Lester and colleagues (2012) compared outcomes in 331 families that participated in FOCUS and reported significant decreases in anxiety, depression, and overall psychological symptoms after completion of the intervention. Families that completed the program also showed better functioning and their children demonstrated an increased prosocial behavior. An additional follow-up study demonstrated similar success, with boys and younger children having the best outcomes at 1- and 4-month follow ups (Lester et al., 2013). A previous RCT of the FOCUS program conducted with families with parental depression found this intervention to be effective (Bearslee, Wright, Gladstone, & Forbes, 2007). RCTs have not been conducted using FOCUS specifically targeting parental deployment.

Relationships with friends and community involvement should also be assessed. Hypervigilance and anxiety around crowds is a common complaint of returning veterans, and these reactions may lead to withdrawal from activities in the community and isolation from the veteran's natural support systems. Participating in veterans' groups and community projects or volunteer activities of interest to the veteran may help decrease social isolation and provide meaning and a sense of purpose for the veteran. It may help the veteran to learn to make distinctions between "military self" and "home self."

Problems in the area of anger control may have repercussions across all domains of functioning. Assessment of anger-control problems should consider the potential for domestic violence and/or abuse toward children. An option for veterans with anger-control problems is referral to an anger-management group. Anger-management groups for returning veterans should address combat-specific issues, such as helping veterans understand that aggressive expression of anger that may have been adaptive in combat situations is not adaptive in civilian interactions.

Assessment of substance use is essential, given the very high rates of comorbid substance abuse problems in this population. Veterans who have difficulty controlling alcohol intake may feel that alcohol helps them cope with their symptoms and with distress. One focus of treatment for them is the development of healthier alternative coping skills. Referral for formal alcohol treatment may be indicated.

Comprehensive resource and referral lists are valuable for connecting veterans with the myriad of interventions and resources to address the many psychosocial issues they face. Many veterans prefer to seek assistance with their reintegration difficulties through innovative sources such as the Internet (Sayer et al., 2010). Many organizations and agencies have developed websites that include links to resources for OEF/OIF/OND veterans and their families and professionals who treat this population. For example, the National Military Family Association has various camps for children of deployed or injured military parents, as well as support for military spouses. The Defense Centers of Excellence for Psychological Health and Traumatic Brain Injury Project (2011) supported by the National Center for Telehealth and Technology provides a website with information about relevant topics such as families and friendships, anger, stigma, and work adjustment. Self-assessments, informational podcasts and videos, and sections for family members and providers are also available on the website. The National Center for Telehealth and Technology also supports the Military Children Education Coalition (2008), which offers various videos and lesson plans for elementary, middle, and high school level educators to help children cope with parental deployment and subsequent return. A joint project of the Departments of Defense, Labor, and VA created The National Resource Directory (2010), "a website for connecting wounded warriors, Service Members, Veterans, their families with those who support them." The site provides a number of resources at national and local levels that span a broad range of topics, including information on education, training, and employment; housing and homelessness assistance; and support for caregivers. The National Center for PTSD (2016) offers a VA-sponsored website providing information for veterans and families with handouts on subjects related to trauma and PTSD. It also disseminates tools, research data, and other information to support and educate providers who work with veterans.

CONCLUSIONS

This chapter has reviewed the mental health problems of returning veterans of the Iraq and Afghanistan conflicts and mental health treatments and other interventions for them. Returning combat veterans from the Iraq and Afghanistan wars represent a unique cohort of veterans. As their demographic characteristics and mental health issues may differ from previous veteran cohorts, their mental health treatment needs can also be expected to differ. Clinicians working with these veterans should be aware not only of the potential for psychiatric disorders such as PTSD as well as depressive and other comorbidities, including TBI, but also the possibility of postdeployment readjustment problems. Many different modes of mental health treatment and other interventions are available for clinicians to use in efforts to help veterans with these problems. Although research has provided considerable evidence of effectiveness for many treatments, further research into the comparative efficacy of various psychotherapies and psychopharmacologic agents is needed, as well as further development of even more effective and comprehensive treatments.

REFERENCES

Ahern, J., Worthen, M., Masters, J., Lippman, S. A., Ozer, E. J., & Moos, R. (2015). The challenges of Afghanistan and Iraq Veterans' transition from military to civilian life and approaches to reconnection. *PLOS ONE, 10*(7), e0128599.

Alexander, W. (2012). Pharmacotherapy for post-traumatic stress disorder in combat veterans: Focus on antidepressants and atypical antipsychotic agents. *Pharmacy and Therapeutics, 37*(1), 32–38.

Alvarez, J., McLean, C., Harris, A. H., Rosen, C. S., Ruzek, J. I., & Kimerling, R. (2011). The comparative effectiveness of cognitive processing therapy for male veterans treated in a VHA posttraumatic stress disorder residential rehabilitation program. *Journal of Consulting and Clinical Psychology, 79*(5), 590–599.

American Psychiatric Association. (2000). *Diagnostic and statistical manual of mental disorders* (4th ed., text revision). Washington, DC: Author.

American Psychiatric Association. (2004). *Practice guidelines for the treatment of patients with acute stress disorder and posttraumatic stress disorder*. Arlington, VA: American Psychiatric Association.

American Psychiatric Association. (2013). *Diagnostic and statistical manual of mental disorders* (5th ed). Washington, DC: American Psychiatric Press.

Barth, S. K., Kimerling, R. E., Pavao, J., McCutcheon, S. J., Batten, S. V., Dursa, E., . . . Schneiderman, A. I. (2016). Military sexual trauma among recent veterans: Correlates of sexual assault and sexual harassment. *American Journal of Preventive Medicine, 50*(1), 77–86.

Bearslee, W. R., Wright, E. J., Gladstone, T. R., & Forbes, P. (2007). Long-term effects from a randomized trial of two public health preventive interventions for parental depression. *Journal of Family Psychology, 21*(4), 703–713.

Beck, J. S. (2011). *Cognitive behavior therapy: Basics and beyond* (2nd ed.). New York, NY: Guilford Press.

Berlim, M. T., & Van Den Eynde, F. (2014). Repetitive transcranial magnetic stimulation over the dorsolateral prefrontal cortex for treating posttraumatic stress disorder: An exploratory meta-analysis of randomized, double-blind and sham-controlled trials. *Canadian Journal of Psychiatry. Revue canadienne de Psychiatrie, 59*(9), 487–496.

Boden, M. T., Kimerling, R., Jacobs-Lentz, J., Bowman, D., Weaver, C., Carney, D., . . . Trafton, J. A. (2012). Seeking Safety treatment for male veterans with a substance use disorder and post-traumatic stress disorder symptomatology. *Addiction, 107*(3), 578–586.

Bogdanova, Y., & Verfaellie, M. (2012). Cognitive sequelae of blast-induced traumatic brain injury: Recovery and rehabilitation. *Neuropsychology Review, 22*(1), 4–20.

Bond, G. R., & Drake, R. E. (2014). Making the case for IPS supported employment. *Administration and Policy in Mental Health, 41*(1), 69–73.

Bowling, U. B., Doerman, A., & Sherman, M. (2007). *Operation enduring families: Information and support for Iraq and Afghanistan veterans and their families*. Oklahoma City, OK: Oklahoma City VA Medical Center Family Health Program. Retrieved from http://www.ouhsc.edu/oef

Breslau, N., Kessler, R. C., Chilcoat, H. D., Schultz, L. R., Davis, G. C., & Andreski, P. (1998). Trauma and posttraumatic stress disorder in the community: The 1996 Detroit Area Survey of Trauma. *Archives of General Psychiatry, 55*(7), 626–632.

Burnett-Zeigler, I., Ilgen, M., Valenstein, M., Zivin, K., Gorman, L., Blow, A., . . . Chermack, S. (2011). Prevalence and correlates of alcohol misuse among returning Afghanistan and Iraq veterans. *Addictive Behaviors, 36*(8), 801–806.

Casement, M. D., & Swanson, L. M. (2012). A meta-analysis of imagery rehearsal for post-trauma nightmares: Effects on nightmare frequency, sleep quality, and posttraumatic stress. *Clinical Psychology Review, 32*(6), 566–574.

Castro, C. A., Bienvenu, R. V., Hufmann, A. H., & Adler, A. B. (2000). Soldier dimensions and operational readiness in U.S. Army forces deployed to Kosovo. *International Review of the Armed Forces Medical Service, 73*, 191–200.

Centers for Disease Control and Prevention. (2015). *Report to congress on traumatic brain injury in the United States: Epidemiology and rehabilitation*. Atlanta, GA: National Center for Injury Prevention and Control; Division of Unintentional Injury Prevention. Retrieved from http://www.cdc.gov/traumaticbraininjury/pdf/tbi_report_to_congress_epi_and_rehab-a.pdf

Chard, K. M., Schumm, J. A., Owens, G. P., & Cottingham, S. M. (2010). A comparison of OEF and OIF veterans and Vietnam veterans receiving cognitive processing therapy. *Journal of Traumatic Stress, 23*(1), 25–32.

Christensen, A., Atkins, D. C., Berns, S., Wheeler, J., Baucom, D. H., & Simpson, L. E. (2004). Traditional versus integrative behavioral couple therapy for significantly and chronically distressed married couples. *Journal of Consulting and Clinical Psychology, 72*(2), 176–191.

Clark, C., Cole, J., Winter, C., Williams, K., & Grammer, G. (2015). A review of transcranial magnetic stimulation as a treatment for post-traumatic stress disorder. *Current Psychiatry Reports, 17*(10), 83.

Cleary, D. R., Ozpinar, A., Raslan, A. M., & Ko, A. L. (2015). Deep brain stimulation for psychiatric disorders: Where we are now. *Neurosurgical Focus, 38*(6), E2. doi:10.3171/2015.3.FOCUS1546.

Cohen, B. E., Marmar, C., Ren, L., Bertenthal, D., & Seal, K. H. (2009). Association of cardiovascular risk factors with mental health diagnoses in Iraq and Afghanistan war veterans using VA health care. *Journal of the American Medical Association, 302*(5), 489–492.

Cornish, M. A., Thys, A., Vogel, D. L., & Wade, N. G. (2014). Post-deployment difficulties and help seeking barriers among military veterans: Insights and intervention strategies. *Professional Psychology: Research and Practice, 45*(6), 405–409.

Corson, K., Denneson, L. M., Bair, M. J., Helmer, D. A., Goulet, J. L., & Dobscha, S. K. (2013). Prevalence and correlates of suicidal ideation among Operation Enduring Freedom and Operation Iraqi Freedom veterans. *Journal of Affective Disorders, 149*(1–3), 291–298.

Cozza, S. J., Guimond, J. M., McKibben, J. B., Chun, R. S., Arata-Maiers, T. L., Schneider, B., . . . Ursano, R. J. (2010). Combat-injured service members and their families: The relationship of child distress and spouse-perceived family distress and disruption. *Journal of Traumatic Stress, 23*(1), 112–115.

Cukor, J., Spitalnick, J., Difede, J., Rizzo, A., & Rothbaum, B. O. (2009). Emerging treatments for PTSD. *Clinical Psychology Review, 29*(8), 715–726.

Davis, L. L., English, B. A., Ambrose, S. M., & Petty, F. (2001). Pharmacotherapy for post-traumatic stress disorder: A comprehensive review. *Expert Opinion on Pharmacotherapy, 2*(10), 1583–1595.

Davis, L. W., Paul, R., Tarr, D., Eicher, A. C., Allinger, J., & Knock, H. (2012). Operation restoration: Couples reunification retreats for veterans of Operations Enduring and Iraqi Freedom. *Journal of Psychosocial Nursing and Mental Health Services, 50*(11), 20–29.

De Hert, M., Detraux, J., van Winkel, R., Yu, W., & Correll, C. U. (2012). Metabolic and cardiovascular adverse effects associated with antipsychotic drugs. *Nature Reviews. Endocrinology, 8*(2), 114–126.

DeBeer, B. B., Kimbrel, N. A., Meyer, E. C., Gulliver, S. B., & Morissette, S. B. (2014). Combined PTSD and depressive symptoms interact with post-deployment social support to predict suicidal ideation in Operation Enduring Freedom and Operation Iraqi Freedom veterans. *Psychiatry Research, 216*(3), 357–362.

Defense Centers of Excellence for Psychological Health and Traumatic Brain Injury Project. (2011). Retrieved from http://www.afterdeployment.org/web/guest

Defense Health Board Task Force on Mental Health. (2007). *An achievable vision: Report of the Department of Defense Task Force on Mental Health.* Falls Church, VA: Defense Health Board. Retrieved from http://www.ha.osd.mil/dhb/mhtf/MHTF-Report-Final.pdf

Dell'osso, B., & Lader, M. (2013). Do benzodiazepines still deserve a major role in the treatment of psychiatric disorders? A critical reappraisal. *European Psychiatry, 28*(1), 7–20.

Desai, R., Spencer, H., Gray, S., & Pilver, C. (2009). *The long journey home XVIII. Treatment of posttraumatic stress disorder in the Department of Veterans Affairs: Fiscal year 2009 service delivery and performance.* West Haven, CT: Northeast Program Evaluation Center.

DeViva, J. C., Sheerin, C. M., Southwick, S. M., Roy, A. M., Pietrzak, R. H., & Harpaz-Rotem, I. (2016). Correlates of VA mental health treatment utilization among OEF/OIF/OND veterans: Resilience, stigma, social support, personality, and beliefs about treatment. *Psychological Trauma, 8*(3), 310–318.

Difede, J., Hoffman, H., & Jaysinghe, N. (2002). Innovative use of virtual reality technology in the treatment of PTSD in the aftermath of September 11. *Psychiatric Services, 53*(9), 1083–1085.

DiRamio, D., Ackerman, R., & Mitchell, R. L. (2008). From combat to campus: Voices of student-veterans. *NASPA Journal, 45*(1), 73–102.

Drew, D., Drebing, C. E., Van Ormer, A., Losardo, M., Krebs, C., Penk, W., & Rosenheck, R. A. (2001). Effects of disability compensation on participation in and outcomes of vocational rehabilitation. *Psychiatric Services, 52*(11), 1479–1484.

Eftekhari, A., Ruzek, J. I., Crowley, J. J., Rosen, C. S., Greenbaum, M. A., & Karlin, B. E. (2013). Effectiveness of national implementation of prolonged exposure therapy in Veterans Affairs care. *JAMA Psychiatry, 70*(9), 949–955.

Elbogen, E. B., Johnson, S. C., Wagner, H. R., Newton, V. M., & Beckham, J. C. (2012). Financial well-being and postdeployment adjustment among Iraq and Afghanistan war veterans. *Military Medicine, 177*(6), 669–675.

Elliott, M., Gonzalez, C., & Larsen, B. (2011). U.S. military veterans transition to college: Combat, PTSD, and alienation on campus. *Journal of Student Affairs Research and Practice, 48*(3), 279–296.

Erbes, C. R., Curry, K. T., & Leskela, J. (2009). Treatment presentation and adherence of Iraq/Afghanistan era veterans in outpatient care for posttraumatic stress disorder. *Psychiatric Services, 6*, 175–183.

Erbes, C. R., Meis, L. A., Polusny, M. A., & Compton, J. S. (2011). Couple adjustment and posttraumatic stress disorder symptoms in National Guard veterans of the Iraq War. *Journal of Family Psychology, 25*(4), 479–487.

Erbes, C. R., Polusny, M. A., MacDermid, S., & Compton, J. S. (2008). Couple therapy with combat veterans and their partners. *Journal of Clinical Psychology, 64*(8), 972–983.

Erbes, C. R, Westermeyer, J., Engdahl, B., & Johnsen, E. (2007). Post-traumatic stress disorder and service utilization in a sample of service members from Iraq and Afghanistan. *Military Medicine, 172*(4), 359–363.

Fischer, E. P., Sherman, M. D., Han, X., & Owen Jr., R. R. (2013). Outcomes of participation in the REACH multifamily group program for veterans with PTSD and their families. *Professional Psychology: Research and Practice, 44*(3), 127–134.

Foa, E., Hembree, E., & Rothbaum, B. O. (2007). *Prolonged exposure therapy for PTSD*. Oxford, England: Oxford University Press.

Fontana, A., & Rosenheck, R. (2008). Treatment-seeking veterans of Iraq and Afghanistan: Comparison with veterans of previous wars. *Journal of Nervous and Mental Disease, 196*(7), 513–521.

Fontana, A., & Rosenheck, R. (2010). War zone veterans returning to treatment: Effects of social functioning and psychopathology. *Journal of Nervous and Mental Disease, 198*(10), 699–707.

Forbes, D., Phelps, A., & McHugh, T. (2001). Treatment of combat-related nightmares using imagery rehearsal: A pilot study. *Journal of Traumatic Stress, 14*(2), 433–442.

Forbes, D., Phelps, A. J., McHugh, A. F., Debenham, P., Hopwood, M., & Creamer, M. (2003). Imagery rehearsal in the treatment of posttraumatic nightmares in Australian veterans with chronic combat-related PTSD: 12-month follow-up data. *Journal of Traumatic Stress, 16*(5), 509–513.

Galovski, T. E., Wachen, J. S., Chard, K. M., Monson, C. M., & Resick, P. A. (2015). Cognitive processing therapy. In U. Schnyder & M. Cloitre (Eds.), *Evidence-based treatments for trauma-related psychological disorders: A practical guide for clinicians* (pp. 189–204). Cham, Switzerland: Springer.

Gewirtz, A. H., Erbes, C. R., Polusny, M. A., Forgatch, M. S., & Degarmo, D. S. (2011). Helping military families through the deployment process: Strategies to support parenting. *Professional Psychology, Research and Practice, 42*(1), 56–62.

Gewirtz, A. H., Pinna, K. L., Hanson, S. K., & Brockberg, D. (2014). Promoting parenting to support reintegrating military families: after deployment, adaptive parenting tools. *Psychological Services, 11*(1), 31–40.

Gilman, S. E., Bromet, E. J., Cox, K. L., Colpe, L. J., Fullerton, C. S., Gruber, M. J., . . . Kessler, R. C.; Army STARRS Collaborators. (2014). Sociodemographic and career history predictors of suicide mortality in the United States Army 2004-2009. *Psychological Medicine, 44*(12), 2579–2592.

Goodson, J. T., Lefkowitz, C. M., Helstrom, A. W., & Gawrysiak, M. J. (2013). Outcomes of Prolonged Exposure therapy for veterans with posttraumatic stress disorder. *Journal of Traumatic Stress, 26*(4), 419–425.

Grieger, T. A., Cozza, S. J., Ursano, R. J., Hoge, C., Martinez, P. E., Engel, C. C., & Wain, H. J. (2006). Posttraumatic stress disorder and depression in battle-injured soldiers. *American Journal of Psychiatry, 163*(10), 1777–1783; quiz 1860.

Hoge, C. W., Castro, C. A., Messer, S. C., McGurk, D., Cotting, D. I., & Koffman, R. L. (2004). Combat duty in Iraq and Afghanistan, mental health problems, and barriers to care. *New England Journal of Medicine, 351*(1), 13–22.

Institute of Medicine. (2008). *Treatment of posttraumatic stress disorder: An assessment of the evidence.* Washington, DC: National Academies Press.

Institute of Medicine. (2010). *Returning home from Iraq and Afghanistan: Preliminary assessment of readjustment needs of veterans, service members, and their families.* Washington, DC: National Academies Press.

Interian, A., Kline, A., Callahan, L., & Losonczy, M. (2012). Readjustment stressors and early mental health treatment seeking by returning National Guard soldiers with PTSD. *Psychiatric Services, 63*(9), 855–861.

International Society for Traumatic Stress Studies. (2005). *Effective treatments for PTSD* (2nd ed.). Oakbrook Terrace, IL: Guilford Press.

Ipser, J. C., & Stein, D. J. (2012). Evidence-based pharmacotherapy of post-traumatic stress disorder (PTSD). *The International Journal of Neuropsychopharmacology, 15*(6), 825–840.

Jacobson, I. G., Ryan, M. A., Hooper, T. I., Smith, T. C., Amoroso, P. J., Boyko, E. J., . . . Bell, N. S. (2008). Alcohol use and alcohol-related problems before and after military combat deployment. *Journal of the American Medical Association, 300*(6), 663–675.

Jacobson, N. S., & Christensen, A. (1996). *Integrative couple therapy: Promoting acceptance and change.* New York, NY: W. W. Norton.

Jacobson, N. S., Christensen, A., Prince, S. E., Cordova, J., & Eldridge, K. (2000). Integrative behavioral couple therapy: An acceptance-based, promising new treatment for couple discord. *Journal of Consulting and Clinical Psychology, 68*(2), 351–355.

Jacobson, N. S., & Margolin, G. (1979). *Marital therapy: Strategies based on social learning and behavioral exchange principles.* New York, NY: Bruner/Mazell.

Jakupcak, M., Luterek, J., Hunt, S., Conybeare, D., & McFall, M. (2008). Posttraumatic stress and its relationship to physical health functioning in a sample of Iraq and Afghanistan War veterans seeking postdeployment VA health care. *Journal of Nervous and Mental Disease, 196*(5), 425–428.

Joint Economic Committee U.S. Congress. (2007). *Happy Mother's Day? New JEC report reveals military moms face tough challenges to get mental health care, childcare, and family leave.* Washington, DC: Author. Retrieved from https://www.jec.senate.gov/public/index.cfm/democrats/press-releases?ID= EB633779-7E9C-9AF9-72CA-884578253E62

Kang, H. K., & Bullman, T. A. (1996). Mortality among U.S. veterans of the Persian Gulf War. *New England Journal of Medicine, 335*(20), 1498–1504.

Kang, H. K., & Bullman, T. A. (2008). Risk of suicide among US veterans after returning from the Iraq or Afghanistan war zones. *Journal of the American Medical Association, 300*(6), 652–653.

Kang, H. K., & Hyams, K. C. (2005). Mental health care needs among recent war veterans. *New England Journal of Medicine, 352*(13), 1289.

Kang, H. K., Natelson, B. H., Mahan, C. M., Lee, K. Y., & Murphy, F. M. (2003). Post-traumatic stress disorder and chronic fatigue syndrome-like illness among Gulf War veterans: A population-based survey of 30,000 veterans. *American Journal of Epidemiology, 157*(2), 141–148.

Karlin, B. E., & Cross, G. (2014). Enhancing access, fidelity, and outcomes in the national dissemination of evidence-based psychotherapies. *American Psychologist, 69*(7), 709–711.

Karlin, B. E., Ruzek, J. I., Chard, K. M., Eftekhari, A., Monson, C. M., Hembree, E. A., . . . Foa, E. B. (2010). Dissemination of evidence-based psychological treatments for posttraumatic stress disorder in the Veterans Health Administration. *Journal of Traumatic Stress, 23*(6), 663–673.

Karsen, E. F., Watts, B. V., & Holtzheimer, P. E. (2014). Review of the effectiveness of transcranial magnetic stimulation for post-traumatic stress disorder. *Brain Stimulation, 7*(2), 151–157.

Kessler, R. C., Sonnega, A., Bromet, E., Hughes, M., & Nelson, C. B. (1995). Posttraumatic stress disorder in the National Comorbidity Survey. *Archives of General Psychiatry, 52*(12), 1048–1060.

Khaylis, A., Polusny, M. A., Erbes, C. R., Gewirtz, A., & Rath, M. (2011). Posttraumatic stress, family adjustment, and treatment preferences among National Guard soldiers deployed to OEF/OIF. *Military Medicine, 176*(2), 126–131.

Kimerling, R., Street, A. E., Pavao, J., Smith, M. W., Cronkite, R. C., Holmes, T. H., & Frayne, S. M. (2010). Military-related sexual trauma among Veterans Health Administration patients returning from Afghanistan and Iraq. *American Journal of Public Health, 100*(8), 1409–1412.

Koek, R. J., Langevin, J. P., Krahl, S. E., Kosoyan, H. J., Schwartz, H. N., Chen, J. W., . . . Sultzer, D. (2014). Deep brain stimulation of the basolateral amygdala for treatment-refractory combat post-traumatic stress disorder (PTSD): Study protocol for a pilot randomized controlled trial with blinded, staggered onset of stimulation. *Trials, 15*, 356.

Kok, B. C., Herrell, R. K., Thomas, J. L., & Hoge, C. W. (2012). Posttraumatic stress disorder associated with combat service in Iraq or Afghanistan: Reconciling prevalence differences between studies. *Journal of Nervous and Mental Disease, 200*(5), 444–450.

Kolkow, T. T., Spira, J. L., Morse, J. S., & Grieger, T. A. (2007). Post-traumatic stress disorder and depression in health care providers returning from deployment to Iraq and Afghanistan. *Military Medicine, 172*(5), 451–455.

Koo, K. H., Hebenstreit, C. L., Madden, E., & Maguen, S. (2016). PTSD detection and symptom presentation: Racial/ethnic differences by gender among veterans with PTSD returning from Iraq and Afghanistan. *Journal of Affective Disorders, 189*, 10–16.

Krakow, B., & Zadra, A. (2010). Imagery rehearsal therapy: Principles and practice. *Sleep Medicine Clinics, 5*, 289–298.

Kulka, R. A., Schlenger, W. E., Fairbanks, J. A., Hough, R. L., Jordan, B. K., Marmar, C. R., . . . Grady, D. A. (1990). *Trauma and the Vietnam War generation: Report of findings from the National Vietnam Veterans Readjustment Study.* New York, NY: Brunner/Mazel.

Lande, R. G., Ghurani, S., Burton, C. N., & Earley, K. (2016). Evolution of sexual trauma treatment in the military: Experience of a psychiatric partial hospitalization program. In E. C. Ritchie (Ed.), *Intimacy post-injury* (pp. 191–202). New York, NY: Oxford University Press.

Lang, A. J., Schnurr, P. P., Jain, S., He, F., Walser, R. D., Bolton, E., . . . Chard, K. M. (2016). Randomized controlled trial of acceptance and commitment therapy for distress and impairment in OEF/OIF/ OND veterans. *Psychological Trauma: Theory, Research, Practice, Policy.* Advance online publication. http://dx.doi.org/10.1037/tra0000127.

LeardMann, C. A., Powell, T. M., Smith, T. C., Bell, M. R., Smith, B., Boyko, E. J., . . . Hoge, C. W. (2013). Risk factors associated with suicide in current and former US military personnel. *Journal of the American Medical Association, 310*(5), 496–506.

Lee, D. J., Schnitzlein, C. W., Wolf, J. P., Vythilingam, M., Rasmusson, A. M., & Hoge, C. W. (2016). Psychotherapy versus pharmacotherapy for posttraumatic stress disorder: Systemic review and meta-analyses to determine first-line treatments. *Depression and Anxiety, 33*(9), 792–806.

Leland, A., & Oboroceanu, M. J. (2010). *American war and military operations casualties: Lists and statistics.* Washington, DC: Congressional Research Service. Retrieved from http://www.fas.org/sgp/crs/natsec/RL32492.pdf

Lemaire, C. M., & Graham, D. P. (2011). Factors associated with suicidal ideation in OEF/OIF veterans. *Journal of Affective Disorders, 130*(1–2), 231–238.

Lenz, A. S., Henesy, R., & Callender, K. (2016). Effectiveness of seeking safety for co-occurring posttraumatic stress disorder and substance use. *Journal of Counseling & Development, 94*(1), 51–61.

Lester, P., Aralis, H., Sinclair, M., Kiff, C., Lee, K. H., Mustillo, S., & Wadsworth, S. M. (2016). The impact of deployment on parental, family and child adjustment in military families. *Child Psychiatry and Human Development, 47*(6), 938–949.

Lester, P., & Flake, E. (2013). How wartime military service affects children and families. *Future of Children, 23*(2), 121–141.

Lester, P., Saltzman, W. R., Woodward, K., Glover, D., Leskin, G. A., Bursch, B., . . . Beardslee, W. (2012). Evaluation of a family-centered prevention intervention for military children and families facing wartime deployments. *American Journal of Public Health, 102*(Suppl. 1), S48–S54.

Lester, P., Stein, J. A., Saltzman, W., Woodward, K., MacDermid, S. W., Milburn, N., . . . Beardslee, W. (2013). Psychological health of military children: Longitudinal evaluation of a family-centered prevention program to enhance family resilience. *Military Medicine, 178*(8), 838–845.

Lindley, S., Cacciapaglia, H., Noronha, D., Carlson, E., & Schatzberg, A. (2010). Monitoring mental health treatment acceptance and initial treatment adherence in veterans: Veterans of Operations Enduring Freedom and Iraqi Freedom versus other veterans of other eras. *Annals of the New York Academy of Sciences, 1208*, 104–113.

Lipari, R. N., Cook, P. J., Rock, L. M., & Matos, K. (2008). *2006 Gender relations survey of active duty members.* DMDC Report No. 2007–002. Arlington, VA: Department of Defense Manpower Data Center.

Litz, B., & Orsillo, S. M. (2011). The returning veteran of the Iraq War: Background issues and assessment guidelines. In *The Iraq War clinician guide* (2nd ed., pp. 21–32). White River Junction, VT: National Center for PTSD. Retrieved from http://www.ptsd.va.gov/professional/manuals/manual-pdf/iwcg/iraq_clinician_guide_ch_3.pdf

Livingston, W. G., Havice, P. A., Cawthon, T. W., & Fleming, D. S. (2011). Coming home: Student veterans' articulation of college re-enrollment. *Student Affairs Research and Practice, 48*(3), 315–331.

Long, M. E., Hammons, M. E., Davis, J. L., Frueh, B. C., Khan, M. M., Elhai, J. D., & Teng, E. J. (2011). Imagery rescripting and exposure group treatment of posttraumatic nightmares in veterans with PTSD. *Journal of Anxiety Disorders, 25*(4), 531–535.

Lu, M., Wagner, A., Van Male, L., Whitehead, A., & Boehnlein, J. (2009). Imagery rehearsal therapy for posttraumatic nightmares in U.S. veterans. *Journal of Traumatic Stress, 22*(3), 236–239.

Luxton, D. D., Skopp, N. A., & Maguen, S. (2010). Gender differences in depression and PTSD symptoms following combat exposure. *Depression and Anxiety, 27*(11), 1027–1033.

MacGregor, A. J., Tang, J. J., Dougherty, A. L., & Galarneau, M. R. (2013). Deployment-related injury and posttraumatic stress disorder in US military personnel. *Injury, 44*(11), 1458–1464.

Maguen, S., Lucenko, B. A., Reger, M. A., Gahm, G. A., Litz, B. T., Seal, K. H., . . . Marmar, C. R. (2010). The impact of reported direct and indirect killing on mental health symptoms in Iraq War veterans. *Journal of Traumatic Stress, 23*(1), 86–90.

Mansfield, A. J., Kaufman, J. S., Marshall, S. W., Gaynes, B. N., Morrissey, J. P., & Engel, C. C. (2010). Deployment and the use of mental health services among U.S. Army wives. *New England Journal of Medicine, 362*(2), 101–109.

Marin, M. F., Camprodon, J. A., Dougherty, D. D., & Milad, M. R. (2014). Device-based brain stimulation to augment fear extinction: Implications for PTSD treatment and beyond. *Depression and Anxiety, 31*(4), 269–278.

Martin, J., Ghahramanlou-Holloway, M., Lou, K., & Tucciarone, P. (2009). A comparative review of US military and civilian suicide behavior: Implications for OEF/OIF suicide prevention efforts. *Journal of Mental Health Counseling, 31*, 101–118.

Mayo, J. A., MacGregor, A. J., Dougherty, A. L., & Galarneau, M. R. (2013). Role of occupation on new-onset post-traumatic stress disorder and depression among deployed military personnel. *Military Medicine, 178*(9), 945–950.

McAndrew, L. M., Markowitz, S., Lu, S. E., Borders, A., Rothman, D., & Quigley, K. S. (2017). Resilience during war: Better unit cohesion and reductions in avoidant coping are associated with better mental health function after combat deployment. *Psychological Trauma, 9*(1), 52–61.

McDevitt-Murphy, M. E., Williams, J. L., Bracken, K. L., Fields, J. A., Monahan, C. J., & Murphy, J. G. (2010). PTSD symptoms, hazardous drinking, and health functioning among U.S.OEF and OIF veterans presenting to primary care. *Journal of Traumatic Stress, 23*(1), 108–111.

Mental Health Advisory Team IV. (2006). Office of the Surgeon Multi-National Force-Iraq and Office of the Surgeon General United States Army Medical Command. Retrieved from http://armymedicine .mil/Documents/MHAT-IV-Report-17NOV06-Full-Report.pdf

Mental Health Advisory Team V. (2008). Office of the Surgeon Multi-National Force-Iraq and Office of the Command Surgeon and Office of the Surgeon General United States Army Medical Command. Retrieved from http://armymedicine.mil/Documents/Redacted1-MHATV-OIF-4-FEB-2008Report.pdf

Military Child Education Coalition. (2008). Military child facts 2007. Retrieved from www.militarychild.org

Milliken, C. S., Auchterlonie, J. L., & Hoge, C. W. (2007). Longitudinal assessment of mental health problems among active and reserve component soldiers returning from the Iraq War. *Journal of the American Medical Association, 298*(18), 2141–2148.

Miller, W. R., & Rollnick, S. (2002). *Motivational interviewing: Preparing people for change* (2nd ed.). New York, NY: Guilford Press.

Monson, C. M., Fredman, S. J., & Taft, C. T. (2011). Couple and family issues and interventions for veterans of the Iraq and Afghanistan wars. In J. I. Ruzek, P. P. Schnurr, J. J. Vasterling, & M. J. Friedman (Eds.), *Caring for veterans with deployment-related stress disorders* (pp. 151–169). Washington, DC: American Psychological Association.

Moore, B. A., & Krakow, B. (2007). Imagery rehearsal therapy for acute posttraumatic nightmares among combat soldiers in Iraq. *The American Journal of Psychiatry, 164*(4), 683–684.

Murdoch, M., Hodges, J., Cowper, D., & Sayer, N. (2005). Regional variation and other correlates of Department of Veterans Affairs Disability Awards for patients with posttraumatic stress disorder. *Medical Care, 43*(2), 112–121.

Murphy, R. A., & Fairbank, J. A. (2013). Implementation and dissemination of military informed and evidence-based interventions for community dwelling military families. *Clinical Child and Family Psychology Review, 16*(4), 348–364.

Mustillo, S. A., Kysar-Moon, A., Douglas, S. R., Hargraves, R., Wadsworth, S. M., Fraine, M., & Frazer, N. L. (2015). Overview of depression, post-traumatic stress disorder, and alcohol misuse among active duty service members returning from Iraq and Afghanistan, self-report and diagnosis. *Military Medicine, 180*(4), 419–427.

Najavits, L. M. (2002). *Seeking Safety: A treatment manual for PTSD and substance abuse.* New York, NY: Guilford Press.

Najavits, L. M. (2009). Seeking Safety: An implementation guide. In A. Rubin & D. W. Springer (Eds.), *The clinician's guide to evidence-based practice.* Hoboken, NJ: John Wiley.

Nappi, C. M., Drummond, S. P., Thorp, S. R., & McQuaid, J. R. (2010). Effectiveness of imagery rehearsal therapy for the treatment of combat-related nightmares in veterans. *Behavior Therapy, 41*(2), 237–244.

National Center for PTSD. (2016). Washington, DC: United States Department of Veterans Affairs. Retrieved from http://www.ptsd.va.gov

National Resource Directory. (2010). Retrieved from http://www.nationalresourcedirectory.gov

O'Neil, M. E., Carlson, K., Storzbach, D., Brenner, L., Freeman, M., Quiñones, A., . . . Kansagara, D. (2013). *Complications of mild traumatic brain injury in veterans and military personnel: A systematic review.* Washington, DC: Department of Veterans Affairs.

Pietrzak, R. H., Johnson, D. C., Goldstein, M. B., Malley, J. C., & Southwick, S. M. (2009). Perceived stigma and barriers to mental health care utilization among OEF-OIF veterans. *Psychiatric Services, 60*(8), 1118–1122.

Puetz, T. W., Youngstedt, S. D., & Herring, M. P. (2015). Effects of pharmacotherapy on combat-related PTSD, anxiety, and depression: A systematic review and meta-regression analysis. *PLOS ONE, 10*(5), e0126529.

Ramchand, R., Rudavsky, R., Grant, S., Tanielian, T., & Jaycox, L. (2015). Prevalence of, risk factors for, and consequences of posttraumatic stress disorder and other mental health problems in military populations deployed to Iraq and Afghanistan. *Current Psychiatry Reports, 17*(5), 37.

Ramchand, R., Schell, T. L., Karney, B. R., Osilla, K. C., Burns, R. M., & Caldarone, L. B. (2010). Disparate prevalence estimates of PTSD among service members who served in Iraq and Afghanistan: Possible explanations. *Journal of Traumatic Stress, 23*, 59–68.

Raskind, M.A., Peterson, K., Williams, T., Hoff, D. J., Hart, K., Holmes, H., . . . Peskind, E. R. (2013). A trial of prazosin for combat trauma PTSD with nightmares in active-duty soldiers returned from Iraq and Afghanistan. *American Journal of Psychiatry, 170*(9), 1003–1010.

Rauch, S., & Foa, E. (2006). Emotional processing theory (EPT) and exposure therapy for PTSD. *Journal of Contemporary Psychotherapy, 36*, 61–65.

Ravindran, L. N., & Stein, M. B. (2010). The pharmacologic treatment of anxiety disorders: A review of progress. *Journal of Clinical Psychiatry, 71*(7), 839–854.

Reeves, R. R. (2007). Diagnosis and management of posttraumatic stress disorder in returning veterans. *Journal of the American Osteopathic Association, 107*(5), 181–189.

Reger, G. M., Koenen-Woods, P., Zetocha, K., Smolenski, D. J., Holloway, K. M., Rothbaum, B. O., . . . Gahm, G. A. (2016). Randomized controlled trial of prolonged exposure using imaginal exposure vs. virtual reality exposure in active duty soldiers with deployment-related posttraumatic stress disorder (PTSD). *Journal of Consulting and Clinical Psychology, 84*(11), 946–959.

Resick, P. A., Monson, C. M., & Chard, K. M. (2007). *Cognitive processing therapy: Veteran/military version.* Washington, DC: Department of Veterans Affairs.

Resick, P. A., Wachen, J. S., Dondanville, K. A., Pruiksma, K. E., Yarvis, J. S., Peterson, A. L., . . . Young-McCaughan, S. (2016). Effect of group vs. individual cognitive processing therapy in active-duty military seeking treatment for posttraumatic stress disorder: A randomized clinical trial. *JAMA Psychiatry, 74*(1), 28–36.

Resick, P. A., Wachen, J. S., Mintz, J., Young-McCaughan, S., Roache, J. D., Borah, A. M., . . . Peterson, A. L. (2015). A randomized clinical trial of group cognitive processing therapy compared with group present-centered therapy for PTSD among active duty military personnel. *Journal of Consulting and Clinical Psychology, 83*(6), 1058–1068.

Rizzo, A. A., & Kim, G. (2005). A SWOT analysis of the field of virtual rehabilitation and therapy. *Presence: Teleoperators and Virtual Environments, 14*, 1–28.

Rizzo, A. A., Schulteis, M. T., & Kerns, K. (2004). Analysis of assets for virtual reality applications in neuropsychology. *Neuropsycholological Rehabilitation, 14*, 207–239.

Roberts, J. C., deRoon-Cassini, T. A., & Brasel, K. J. (2010). Posttraumatic stress disorder: A primer for trauma surgeons. *Journal of Trauma, 69*(1), 231–237.

Roddy, M. K., Nowlan, K. M., Doss, B. D., & Christensen, A. (2016). Integrative Behavioral Couple therapy: Theoretical background, empirical research, and dissemination. *Family Process, 55*(3), 408–422.

Rothbaum, B. O., Price, M., Jovanovic, T., Norrholm, S. D., Gerardi, M., Dunlop, B., . . . Ressler, K. J. (2014). A randomized, double-blind evaluation of d-cycloserine or alprazolam combined with virtual reality exposure therapy for posttraumatic stress disorder in Iraq and Afghanistan war veterans. *American Journal of Psychiatry, 171*(6), 640–648.

Rothbaum, B. O., Rizzo, A., & Difede, J. (2010). Virtual reality exposure therapy for combat-related posttraumatic stress disorder. *Annals of the New York Academy of Sciences, 1208*, 126–132.

Sayer, N. A., Frazier, P., Orazem, R. J., Murdoch, M., Grazely, A., Carlson, K. F., . . . Noorbalooci, S. (2011). Military to civilian questionnaire: A measure of postdeployment community reintegration difficulty among veterans using Department of Veterans Affairs medical care. *Journal of Traumatic Stress, 24*(6), 660–670.

Sayer, N. A., Noorbaloochi, S., Frazier, P., Carlson, K., Grevely, A., & Murdoch, M. (2010). Reintegration problems and treatment interests among Iraq and Afghanistan combat veterans receiving VA medical care. *Psychiatric Services, 61*, 589–597.

Sayers, S. L. (2011). Family reintegration difficulties and couples therapy for military veterans and their spouses. *Cognitive and Behavioral Practice, 18*(1), 108–119.

Schell, T. L., & Marshall, G. N. (2008). Survey of individuals previously deployed for OEF/OIF. In T. Tanielian & L. H. Jaycox (Eds.), *Invisible wounds of war: Psychological and cognitive injuries, their consequences, and services to assist recovery* (pp. 87–115). Santa Monica, CA: RAND Centre for Military Health Policy Research.

Schlenger, W. E., Kulka, R. A., Fairbank, J. A., Hough, R. L., Jordan, B. K., Marmar, C. R., & Weiss, D. S. (1992). The prevalence of post-traumatic stress disorder in the Vietnam generation: A multimethod, multisource assessment of psychiatric disorder. *Journal of Traumatic Stress, 5*, 333–363.

Schnurr, P. P., Friedman, M. J., Engel, C. C., Foa, E. B., Shea, T., Chow, B. K., . . . Turner, C. (2007). Cognitive behavioral therapy for posttraumatic stress disorder in women: A randomized control trial. *Journal of the American Medical Association, 297*(8), 820–830.

Schoenberg, M. R., & Scott, J. G. (2011). *The little black book of neuropsychology.* New York, NY: Springer Publishing.

Seal, K. H., Bertenthal, D., Miner, C. R., Sen, S., & Marmar, C. (2007). Bringing the war back home: Mental health disorders among 103,788 US veterans returning from Iraq and Afghanistan seen at Department of Veterans Affairs facilities. *Archives of Internal Medicine, 167*, 476–482.

Seal, K. H., Metzler, T. J., Gima, K. S., Bertenthal, D., Maguen, S., & Marmar, C. R. (2009). Trends and risk factors for mental health diagnoses among Iraq and Afghanistan veterans using Department of Veterans Affairs health care, 2002–2008. *American Journal of Public Health, 99*(9), 1651–1658.

Sesame Workshop. (2011). Deployments, homecomings, changes, and grief. Retrieved from http://www.sesameworkshop.org/initiatives/emotion/tlc

Shea, M. T., Vujanovic, A. A., Mansfield, A. K., Sevin, E., & Liu, F. (2010). Posttraumatic stress disorder symptoms and functional impairment among OEF and OIF National Guard and Reserve veterans. *Journal of Traumatic Stress, 23*, 100–107.

Shen, Y. C., Arkes, J., & Williams, T. V. (2012). Effects of Iraq/Afghanistan deployments on major depression and substance use disorder: Analysis of active duty personnel in the US military. *American Journal of Public Health, 102*(S1), S80–S87.

Sherman, M. (2003). Updates and five-year evaluation of the S.A.F.E. program: A family psychoeducational program for serious mental illness. *Community Mental Health Journal, 42*, 213–219.

Spelman, J. F., Hunt, S. C., Seal, K. H., & Burgo-Black, A. L. (2012). Post deployment care for returning combat veterans. *Journal of General Internal Medicine, 27*(9), 1200–1209.

Steckler, T., & Risbrough, V. (2012). Pharmacological treatment of PTSD—Established and new approaches. *Neuropharmacology, 62*(2), 617–627.

Steenkamp, M. M. (2016). True evidence-based care for posttraumatic stress disorder in military personnel and veterans. *JAMA Psychiatry, 73*(5), 431–432.

Steenkamp, M. M., & Litz, B. T. (2013). Psychotherapy for military-related posttraumatic stress disorder: Review of the evidence. *Clinical Psychology Review, 33*(1), 45–53.

Steenkamp, M. M., Litz, B. T., Hoge, C. W., & Marmar, C. R. (2015). Psychotherapy for military-related PTSD: A review of randomized clinical trials. *Journal of the American Medical Association, 314*(5), 489–500.

Stein, D. J., Ipser, J. C., & McAnda, B. A. (2009). Pharmacotherapy for posttraumatic stress disorder: A review of meta analysis and treatment guidelines. *CNS Spectrums, 14*(1), 25–31.

Stein, D. J., Ipser, J. C., & Seedat, S. (2006). Pharmacotherapy for posttraumatic stress disorder (PTSD). *Cochrane Database of Systematic Reviews, 2006*(1), CD002795.

Street, A. E., Vogt, D., & Dutra, L. (2009). A new generation of women veterans: Stressors faced by women deployed to Iraq and Afghanistan. *Clinical Psychology Review, 29*(8), 685–694.

Summerlot, J., Green, S., & Parker, D. (2009). Student veterans organizations. *New Directions for Student Services, 126*, 71–79.

Surís, A., & Lind, L. (2008). Military sexual trauma: A review of prevalence and associated health consequences in veterans. *Trauma, Violence, and Abuse, 9*, 250–269.

Surís, A., & Smith, J. (2011). PTSD related to sexual trauma in the military. In W. Penk & B. Moore (Eds.), *Handbook for the treatment of PTSD in military personnel* (pp. 255–269). New York, NY: Guilford Press.

Szafranski, D. D., Gros, D. F., Menefee, D. S., Norton, P. J., & Wanner, J. L. (2016). Treatment adherence: An examination of why OEF/OIF/OND veterans discontinue inpatient PTSD treatment. *Military Behavioral Health, 4*(1), 25–31.

Tanelian, T., Jaycox, L. H., Schell, T. L., Marshal, G. N., Burnam, M. A., Eibner, C., . . . Vaiana, M. E. (2008). The Invisible Wounds Study Team. *Invisible wounds of war: Summary and recommendations for addressing psychological and cognitive injuries.* Santa Monica, CA: RAND Center for Health Policy Research. Retrieved from http://rand.org/pubs/monographs/2008/RAND_MG720.1.pdf

Thomas, E., & Stein, D. J. (2016). Novel pharmacological treatment strategies for posttraumatic stress disorder. *Expert Review of Clinical Pharmacology, 10*(2), 167–177.

Trevizol, A. P., Barros, M. D., Silva, P. O., Osuch, E., Cordeiro, Q., & Shiozawa, P. (2016). Transcranial magnetic stimulation for posttraumatic stress disorder: An updated systematic review and meta-analysis. *Trends in Psychiatry & Psychotherapy, 38*(1), 50–55.

Tuerk, P. W., Yoder, M., Grubaugh, A., Myrick, H., Hamner, M., & Acierno, R. (2011). Prolonged exposure therapy for combat-related posttraumatic stress disorder: An examination of treatment effectiveness for veterans of the wars in Afghanistan and Iraq. *Journal of Anxiety Disorders, 25*, 397–403.

Turchik, J. A., & Wilson, S. M. (2010). Sexual assault in the U.S. military: A review of the literature and recommendations for the future. *Aggression and Violent Behavior, 15*, 267–277.

U.S. Department of Defense. (2014). *2014 demographics.* Washington, DC: Author. Retrieved from http://download.militaryonesource.mil/12038/MOS/Reports/2014-Demographics-Report.pdf

U.S. Department of Defense. (2015a). *FY15 annual report on sexual assault in the military.* Retrieved from http://www.sapr.mil/public/docs/reports/FY15_Annual/FY15_Annual_Report_on_Sexual_Assault_in_the_Military.pdf

U.S. Department of Defense. (2015b). *Implementation guidance for the full integration of women in the armed forces.* Washington, DC: Author. Retrieved from http://www.defense.gov/Portals/1/Documents/pubs/OSD014303-15.pdf

U.S. Department of Defense. (2016). *U.S. military casualties—OCO casualty summary by casualty type.* Retrieved from https://www.dmdc.osd.mil/dcas/pages/report_sum_reason.xhtml

U.S. Department of Defense. (2017). *DoD casualty reports, 2011.* Retrieved from https://www.defense.gov/casualty.pdf

U.S. Department of Labor. (2016). *Employment situation of veterans—2015.* Retrieved from https://www.bls.gov/news.release/pdf/vet.pdf

U.S. Department of Veterans Affairs. (2008). VA Uniform mental health services in VA medical centers and clinics. In *Veterans health administration handbook 1160.01*. Washington, DC: Author. Retrieved from http://www.va.gov/vhapublications/ViewPublication.asp?pub_ID=1762

U.S. Department of Veterans Affairs and Department of Defense. (2009). *VA/DoD clinical practice guideline for management of concussion/mild traumatic brain injury (mTBI), version 1.0*. Washington, DC: Author. Retrieved from http://www.healthquality.va.gov/mtbi/concussion_mtbi_full_1_0.pdf

U.S. Department of Veterans Affairs and Department of Defense. (2010). *VA/DoD clinical practice guideline. Management of post-traumatic stress*. Washington, DC: Author.

van Schagen, A. M., Lancee, J., Spoormaker, V. I., & van den Bout, J. (2016). Long-term treatment effects of imagery rehearsal therapy for nightmares in a population with diverse psychiatric mental disorders. *International Journal of Dream Research, 9*(1), 67–70.

Vogt, D. S., Pless, A. P., King, L. A., & King, D. W. (2005). Deployment stressors, gender, and mental health outcomes among Gulf War I veterans. *Journal of Traumatic Stress, 18*, 272–284.

Writer, B. W., Meyer, E. G., & Schillerstrom, J. E. (2014). Prazosin for military combat-related PTSD nightmares: A critical review. *Journal of Neuropsychiatry and Clinical Neurosciences, 26*(1), 24–33.

Xue, C., Ge, Y., Tang, B., Liu, Y., Kang, P., Wang, M., & Zhang, L. (2015). A meta-analysis of risk factors for combat-related PTSD among military personnel and veterans. *PLOS ONE, 10*(3), e0120270.

Yehuda, R., & Hoge, C. W. (2016). The meaning of evidence-based treatments for veterans with post-traumatic stress disorder. *JAMA Psychiatry, 73*(5), 433–434. doi:10.1001/jamapsychiatry.2015.2878

19

Users of Assistive Technology: The Human Component*

MARTIN G. BRODWIN, FRANCES W. SIU, AND ELIZABETH CARDOSO

A ssistive technology (AT) has a profound impact on the everyday lives and employ- ment opportunities of individuals with disabilities by providing them with greater independence and enabling them to perform activities not possible in the past. AT is defined in the Technology-Related Assistance of Individuals with Disabilities Act of 1988 (Tech Act; P. L. 100–407) as "any item, piece of equipment, or product system, whether acquired commercially off the shelf, modified, or customized, that is used to increase, maintain, or improve functional capabilities of individuals with disabilities" (Scherer, 2007, p. 185). AT enhances social functioning, recreational activities, and work opportunities, thus decreasing a consumer's functional limitations and help- ing to "level the playing field" between people with disabilities and those without disabilities.

When utilizing AT, a consumer's self-worth, sense of belonging, and the attitudes of others play a dynamic role. Therefore, consumer involvement is imperative to the process. Initially, in the assessment/evaluation phase of rehabilitation, the rehabilitation counselor should help the consumer identify the priorities and motivation for request- ing AT. These should be in the forefront throughout the entire process as they are key to successful implementation and use of AT. By carefully defining achievement goals with the consumer, the counselor will be able to clearly identify what he or she wants to accomplish by using technology. This involves the activities that motivate a consumer to use AT and is crucial to successful adaptation and use.

Self-esteem, self-efficacy, and motivation are described as central elements in increasing a consumer's confidence and belief in self. Good outcomes and efficacy expectations, as well as strong motivation, help lead to successful adaptation to AT. The purpose of this chapter is to present the human component of technology, the rela- tionship between consumers and technological devices/equipment, and the acceptance and use by consumers. Recommendations are offered to assist rehabilitation profes- sionals in helping consumers with accepting, utilizing, and benefiting from technology.

*From "Use of assistive technology: The human component," by M. Brodwin, T. Star, and E. Cardoso, 2003, *Journal of Applied Rehabilitation Counseling, 34*, 23–29. The National Rehabilitation Counseling Association.

TECHNOLOGY ACCEPTANCE AND USE

AT increases functional abilities, independence, and access to mainstream society by individuals with disabilities. Currently, more than 20 million Americans with disabilities are using technology; however, a national survey on AT abandonment found that 29% of devices obtained were discarded later (Riemer-Reiss & Wacker, 2000). These researchers found "those individuals who continued to use their technology had significantly higher mean scores than those who discontinued use of their technology in relation to relative advantage, consumer involvement, and compatibility" (p. 48).

Riemer-Reiss and Wacker (2000) researched technology use and abandonment issues by consumers. Their findings inferred that little documentation existed from the consumer's perspective as to why assistive devices had been abandoned. These authors' goal was to determine factors associated with AT continuance or discontinuance using Rogers's (1995) theory of diffusion, based on a consumer's initial decision to accept a device and later reject it. According to Riemer-Reiss and Wacker (2000), discontinuance happens in two ways: (a) replacement, where one device is discarded for an improved one, and (b) user disenchantment or dissatisfaction. The researchers derived the following as crucial factors for consumers' continued use of AT: advantage, compatibility, trialability, and reinvention.

Carroll and Phillips (1993), in a survey on abandonment of AT by 25 new users, concluded that characteristics of relative advantage (effectiveness, reliability, ease of use, comfort, and enhancement of the user's performance) were significantly related to not abandoning technology. Compatibility, a factor related to use, is the extent to which the device is perceived by consumers to meet their needs. Trialability was defined as the degree to which the consumer could experiment with the AT device or equipment before acquisition. Reinvention occurs when a new model replaces an older one. Riemer-Reiss and Wacker (2000) hypothesized that the relationship between continuance/discontinuance involved a combination of compatibility, advantage, support, trialability, consumer involvement, and changes when making decisions or setting goals. These authors concluded that further research is necessary in the areas of evaluation and whether the provision of technology is meeting the needs and desires of the consumer.

NONUSE OR USE OF AT

The degree to which a device is essential for a consumer's desired function includes his or her particular needs and becomes crucial in determining whether the consumer uses or abandons the product (Scherer, 2002, 2007). To avoid nonuse, rehabilitation counseling professionals need to identify and consider matching technology with aspects of the person's personality and temperament, characteristics of the setting, and the material traits of the assistive device itself.

Optimal Use

Scherer (2007) further described optimal characteristics of the setting in which the AT will be used to include the following: support from others (family, peers, and employer), realistic expectations of family/employer, and an environment that fully supports and rewards use of technology. Positive consumer personality variables involve motivation (how AT will help the consumer accomplish desired tasks), coping skills, capability to use the device, pride in using technology, patience, and self-discipline. Characteristics of the technology that influence consumer use include the following: compatibility with and enhancement of other technologies that the consumer is using, reliability, ease of use, problem-free and timely maintenance, and desirable transportability.

Benefit Expectations

These expectations involve what the consumer wants to accomplish by using AT—the desired tasks that are most important to the consumer. Aspects of technology that will benefit consumers are influenced by the positive and negative attitudes of others. Other areas that may influence continued use are the following: social support, loneliness, isolation, and cultural identity. Research has shown that individuals who do not have social support have an increased chance of discontinuing use of recently acquired technology (Riemer-Reiss & Wacker, 2000; Scherer, 2007). The characteristics related to consumers' acceptance and use include level of technical comfort, cognitive (intellectual) skills, personality traits, adjustment, and outlook, including preexisting temperament and ways of coping. In addition, technological characteristics to consider include design factors, such as weight, ease of setup, and compatibility with other devices, as well as the consumer's level of comfort when using AT (Reed & Saladin, 2008).

THE HUMAN COMPONENT

The National Council on Disability performed a study in 1993 on the impact of ATs on individuals with disabilities and found that (a) approximately 76% of children who received AT were able to stay in a regular classroom and about 45% were able to reduce school-related services; (b) around 62% of working-age persons were able to be less reliant on their family members and 58% were able to cut down on paid assistance; (c) roughly 80% of senior citizens were able to increase their independence and about half were able to avoid institutionalization; (d) nearly 92% of working individuals reported that AT helped them to work efficiently and effectively and 83% indicated that they increased their income; and (e) almost 67% reported that AT had helped them to obtain employment (Stumbo, Martin, & Hedrick, 2009).

AT does not merely increase the functional abilities and independence of the end users; utilization of AT has powerful influences on the attitude, self-worth, self-esteem, and motivation of older individuals and those with disabilities.

Attitudes

Attitudes exhibited by professionals are crucial in establishing trust and confidence in the counselor–consumer relationship. When a consumer forms a relationship with a professional involving how to effectively use AT, the consumer takes the position of initiating a help-seeking role. This role requires developing a level of courage toward, and trust and confidence in, the professional relationship. The rehabilitation counselor needs to maintain a focus on the consumer's best interests and have a positive attitude. Any negative attitudes exhibited by the professional could have adverse consequences for the consumer in his or her achievement of desired outcomes. The goal is to approach providing technology services from the consumer's perspective when defining specific objectives, needs, and desires. According to Scherer (2007), "assistive technologies are used when consumers have goals and see the devices as valuable to goal achievement. When users have significant input into selection of the devices, they become more invested in using them successfully" (p. 131).

Self-Worth

Schaller and DeLaGarza (1999) affirmed that the self-concepts of consumers with disabilities are influenced by the social context in which they interact, validating either positively or negatively self-worth. Supportive relationships for consumers promote a sense of belonging and are necessary for the development of positive self-images and self-acceptance. Positive social support promotes more stability, less emotional stress, and greater psychological well-being by buffering negative life events and easing environmental pressures. Consumers with disabilities usually have knowledge of their needs, but have a difficult time expressing and attaining feelings of belonging. Technology can both heighten feelings of being different (in a negative way) and, at the same time, enhance the ability to interact with others. As noted by Best (2009), children with cerebral palsy who use AT are more capable of interacting with children without disabilities.

Self-Esteem

Behavior and cognition are essential elements that contribute to learning, with an emphasis on learning through observation of others. This is certainly true when consumers are adapting to the use of AT. Self-esteem is highly related to an individual's ability to accomplish tasks and goals. The concepts of self-esteem, self-worth, and self-image are defined as the total dimension of the self, with self-concept relating to a specific area in which individuals evaluate their knowledge, capabilities, and skills (Santrock, 2009).

An ability to cope with a problem rather than avoid it contributes to positive self-evaluative thoughts, which generate self-approval, thus enhancing one's self-esteem. Bandura's (1982) theory of individuals believing that they can master a situation and produce a positive outcome is labeled self-efficacy. It is based on the principle that cognitive events are induced and altered by efforts and persistence demonstrated in a task. Personal experience reinforced by successful performance of a task, including use of AT, enhances an individual's belief that goals attempted can be accomplished (Conyers, Enright, & Strauser, 1998; Cook, Polgar, & Hussey, 2008).

Self-Efficacy Theory

Self-efficacy theory proposes that expectations vary in level of challenge (high or low degree), in strength (ability to persevere), and in flexibility of self-efficacy (whether it will transfer from one area to another). The essential elements previously noted affect the level of self-efficacy and the extent to which an individual is able to cope with obstacles, and it is applicable to the use of technology. In the first element, a consumer feels confident in knowing what to do with AT and how to do it. The second element involves a belief that, if tried out, success will be achieved. A belief that the chosen behavior will have an effect on the outcome (adaptation to technology) is the third element. The final element brings successful reinforcement to the consumer as he or she believes that the device or equipment is of importance. Thus, the enhancement of activities and reduction of functional limitations provide adequate incentives for performing the behavior in the future (Cook et al., 2008; Scherer, 2007).

Efficacy Expectations and Outcome Expectations

Self-efficacy beliefs consist of two components: efficacy expectations and outcome expectations (Conyers et al., 1998). Efficacy expectations concern a person's beliefs about the ability to undertake a given task (in this case, learning to use technology), and range from high to low. Outcome expectations involve whether a person knows what to do in a given situation and believes that the outcomes of effort will be beneficial or not and also have a range of high to low. Both efficacy and outcome expectations need to be relatively high for people to attempt and succeed at using technology. Self-efficacy includes four essential elements that can be related to the use of AT (Bandura, 1982; Mitchell & Brodwin, 1995):

1. In a given situation, an individual knows what to do and how to do it. In the case of AT, the consumer needs the knowledge on how to successfully use the device.
2. The person has the confidence that he or she can succeed in the activity. This relates to a consumer being self-assured that, if given sufficient instruction, he or she can successfully learn to use the device or equipment.
3. The individual believes that what he or she does will have an impact on the end result. This element involves a consumer believing that he or she can learn to use the technology and that this will result in a positive outcome, in that the consumer will be able to accomplish the desired tasks with use of technology.
4. The outcome is of sufficient importance for the person to want what the outcome will provide. The consumer believes that what the device or equipment provides in decreasing functional limitations and enhancing capabilities is what he or she desires.

Consequently, the level of self-efficacy a consumer maintains will determine, in part, whether he or she will accept, try out, and continue to use AT in the future. When the levels of these four components are high, the consumer typically demonstrates goal-oriented, self-assured, and persistent behavior when dealing with the technology. The higher the consumer's self-efficacy, the greater the likelihood of successful adaptation to, and use of, AT (Conyers et al., 1998).

Motivation

The term *motivation* is defined as an inner urge or desire that prompts an individual to perform a behavior; motivation produces a particular action or manifests itself as any influence that promotes positive performance (Scherer, 2007). Self-efficacy provides the foundation for motivation by establishing actions that result in positive, repetitive reinforcement. In the process of delivering technology services to a consumer, motivation may result from any point within the process: the consumer, the activity engaged in, the environment, or the AT system components. As noted by Rubin and Roessler (2008), in dealing with consumers and AT, motivation must always be maintained for there to be a successful end result.

Generally, human behavior may be inspired, intrigued, satisfied, or provide feelings of accomplishment at any point in task engagement that reinforces an intrinsic element expressed as motivation. AT can provide motivation in many ways. Social rewards, such as increased interpersonal interaction, may provide the necessary motivation and desire to use technology. For example, when a student derives pleasure from playing games on a computer, he or she will be more motivated and interested in using the computer for homework. By carefully defining the goals of the potential user, devices can be selected that are meaningful and motivating to the particular consumer.

Achievement Motivation

This kind of motivation is based on the need for achievement and defined by the desire to accomplish some purpose or reach a level of excellence by expending an amount of effort to excel. Achievement-oriented individuals are less likely to have fear of failure; they have stronger hopes for success and are moderate risk takers. To learn to use AT involves taking risks that may result in failure. Factors that influence achievement motivation have been identified as early independence training by parents and interaction within an environment with others engaging in strong social modeling of achievement behavior (Santrock, 2009). One can postulate that consumers with this background will more readily adapt to and persist in using technological devices.

Intrinsic and Extrinsic Motivation

According to Santrock (2009), there are two types of motivation components that have been identified: intrinsic and extrinsic. Intrinsic motivation is defined as confidence in one's ability to be competent and to accomplish something for its own sake. Working hard in school with the goal of a higher paying job is an example of extrinsic motivational behavior. Learning to operate a computer to do better in school or work is another example. Using a computer to interact socially, check email, visit chat rooms, play games, or listen to music is a third example.

Researchers (Rogers, 1995; Santrock, 2009) have identified the role of the environment in promoting high intrinsic motivation. Factors that contribute to motivation are the variety of experiences and the extent to which the family or caregiver encourages competence and curiosity. Extrinsic motivation may include those resulting from social outcomes or successful completion of an activity. Examples of social outcomes involving AT acquisition include conversational discourse, achievement of a goal (moving to a desired location in a power wheelchair), or reinforcement (getting higher grades in school).

BENEFITS AND EXAMPLES OF AT

AT enables consumers with disabilities to reduce and perhaps minimize functional limitations. These devices and equipment may be low-tech (mechanical) or high-tech (electromechanical or computerized) and can compensate for sensory and functional losses. AT provides the means to move (e.g., wheelchairs, scooters, lifts), speak (e.g., augmentative and alternative communication [AAC] devices), read (e.g., Braille input, voice recognition devices), hear (e.g., telecommunication devices for the deaf [TDD], hearing aids), or manage self-care tasks (e.g., remote environmental control systems, prosthetic and orthotic devices). Technology service is "any service that directly assists an individual with a disability in the selection, acquisition, or use of an assistive technology device" (Scherer, 2002, p. 185). Realistically, technology helps equalize the capacities of those individuals with disabilities compared to those without disabilities (Brodwin, 2010).

Technology has many social and recreational applications that enhance the ability of consumers to participate in meaningful activities. For example, a wheelchair with balloon tires allows a consumer to travel on the beach and traverse other rough, outdoor terrain. Greater independence in daily living, including leisure time activities, becomes enhanced with AT. Remote environmental control allows a consumer to do such tasks as turn on lights, a computer, the television, or the radio; answer a telephone; and unlock the front door. Through reasonable accommodations, many consumers are able to remain on their jobs, and others can seek employment if they are not working (de Jonge, Scherer, & Rodger, 2007). A power chair or scooter at work may allow consumer mobility without the use of the excess energy required when walking. An adaptive computer at work may permit a consumer to perform required work functions that were previously time-consuming or not possible. Consumers with expressive communication deficits may be capable of performing work or school functions with increased and enhanced use of computer-based communication (Brodwin, Parker, & DeLaGarza, 2010).

Another form of technology, custom-designed prosthetic and orthotic devices, helps consumers with upper extremity limitations. These devices enhance manual dexterity, bilateral dexterity, and tasks involving eye–hand coordination. Consumers with upper extremity difficulties may be helped by enlarged keyboards, key guards, miniature keyboards, and various specialized user interface switches (optical head pointers, light beams, touch screens) (Rubin & Roessler, 2008). Prosthetic and orthotic devices help consumers with lower extremity limitations perform activities such as standing and walking.

Accommodations for consumers with visual deficits include both optical and nonoptical low-vision devices. Examples of optical devices are magnifiers, specially coated lenses, and telescopes. Nonoptical visual aids include talking clocks, talking calculators, closed-circuit televisions that enlarge print electronically, and personal computers and peripherals with the capability of print magnification, speech output, and optical scanning (Brodwin et al., 2010). In addition, hearing aids, TDD, cochlear implants, electronic ears, amplified telephones, and audio loops are helpful AT devices for consumers who are deaf or hard-of-hearing.

AAC consists of a range of communication tools that allow a person to select symbols, pictures, letters, words, or phrases to generate oral communication. This type of AT is usually employed when working with the population that has autism (especially nonverbal individuals) and with people with speech impediments.

Individuals with learning disabilities often have difficulties with reading, writing, speaking, listening, spelling, reasoning, visual perception, or math. They have trouble taking in information through their senses and processing the information accurately to the brain. Information is scrambled and distorted when communicated to the brain, resulting in confused thinking, disorganization, and avoidance behavior. The person may be able to think logically but not be able to articulate in writing and, consequently, may appear "lazy" or even "stupid." AT along with personal effort can make a difference. For example, listening to the taped version of the book or using screen reading software to read scanned reading materials allows the person to bypass the reading problem. This alternative learning style is favored in the community with learning disabilities since it promotes independence, reduces anxiety, and fosters self-esteem.

RECOMMENDATIONS FOR REHABILITATION COUNSELING PROFESSIONALS

1. Consumer involvement, from initial assessment through selection and adaptation, is essential to the success of AT. A consumer-driven model provides a feeling of ownership and responsibility and is directly related to continued use of AT (Riemer-Reiss & Wacker, 2000).

2. By having the consumer identify priorities and desires he or she wants to accomplish through the use of AT, the rehabilitation counselor learns what is foremost in motivating the consumer to use technology.

3. A careful analysis of costs and benefits of AT from the consumer should be made before selection. The advantage a device provides must outweigh the costs of using it or the device will probably not be used (Riemer-Reiss & Wacker, 2000).

4. Basic, minimal (low-tech) cost solutions should be considered before expensive high-tech ones. Simple devices may be as effective as more complex ones.

5. The devices should be durable, reliable, and effective (Rubin & Roessler, 2008).

6. Provisions need to be in place for technical assistance, repairs, and routine maintenance (Rubin & Roessler, 2008).

7. To ensure increased functioning and independence (the ultimate goals of using technology), the correct match between consumer and the AT must occur. If not, the chances of continued consumer use of the device or equipment will be minimized (Reed & Saladin, 2008).

8. When recommending AT, the consumer should be presented with any possible alternative choices.

9. Each consumer has preferences, perspectives, and expectations. The counselor needs to realize that professionals and consumers see things from very different perspectives (Scherer, 2007).

10. The degree to which a technological device is essential for desired functioning, the more likely it will be used (Carroll & Phillips, 1993).

11. The counselor needs to make sure the consumer really does want the device and that it is not just something someone else really wants him or her to have (Scherer, 2007).

12. The consumer needs the skills to use the device; it should be easy to operate and require little assistance from others for everyday use (Scherer, 2002).

A change in a consumer's needs can result in product discontinuance (Cook, 2002; Scherer, 2007). Therefore, follow-up and periodic reassessment of a consumer's desires and abilities are crucial for continued use of AT devices.

CONCLUSIONS

The goal of AT is to increase functional independence for consumers who have disabilities (Brodwin, 2010; Cook et al., 2008). Therefore, the focus is not on the disability but on the remaining functional (residual) abilities that individuals use to accomplish their chosen objectives and their daily tasks. When technological systems are considered for use, the rehabilitation counselor needs to evaluate the various characteristics of the consumer that will effect successful adaptation. According to Scherer (2007), the single most significant factor associated with technology abandonment is a failure to consider the user's opinions and preferences in device selection—in other words, the device is abandoned because it does not meet the person's needs or expectations. Other reasons that AT may be abandoned include a lack of motivation, insufficient training, ineffective device performance, and accessibility problems (Phillips & Zhao, 1993). There needs to be a close and appropriate fit (match) between the technological device and consumer. Therefore, the need for the counselor to actively listen and engage the consumer in the process is essential to the effectiveness and outcome of AT success. The closer the counselor matches the consumer's various characteristics to the appropriate device, the greater the chance it will continue to be used. In additional, the consumer needs to be knowledgeable and trained in the specific device for it to be used efficiently and effectively.

REFERENCES

Bandura, A. (1982). Self-efficacy mechanism in human agency. *American Psychologist, 37*, 122–147.

Best, S. J. (2009). Cerebral palsy. In M. G. Brodwin, F. W. Siu, J. Howard, & E. R. Brodwin (Eds.), *Medical, psychosocial, and vocational aspects of disability* (3rd ed., pp. 305–318). Athens, GA: Elliott & Fitzpatrick.

Brodwin, M. G. (2010). Assistive technology. In I. B. Weiner & W. E. Craighead (Eds.), *Corsini encyclopedia of psychology* (Vol. 1, 4th ed., pp. 158–160). Hoboken, NJ: John Wiley.

Brodwin, M. G., Parker, R. M., & DeLaGarza, D. (2010). Disability and reasonable accommodation. In E. M. Szymanski & R. M. Parker (Eds.), *Work and disability: Context, issues, and strategies for enhancing employment outcomes for people with disabilities* (3rd ed., pp. 281–323). Austin, TX: PRO-ED.

Brodwin, M. G., Star, T., & Cardoso, E. (2003). Use of assistive technology: The human component. *Journal of Applied Rehabilitation Counseling, 34*, 23–29.

Carroll, M., & Phillips, B. (1993). *Survey on assistive technology abandonment by new users* (Cooperative Agreement No. H133E0016). Washington, DC: National Institute on Disability and Rehabilitation Research.

Conyers, L. M., Enright, M. S., & Strauser, D. R. (1998). Applying self-efficacy theory to counseling college students with disabilities. *Journal of Applied Rehabilitation Counseling, 29*(1), 25–30.

Cook, A. M. (2002). Future directions in assistive technology. In M. J. Scherer (Ed.), *Assistive technology: Matching device and consumer for successful rehabilitation* (pp. 269–280). Washington, DC: American Psychological Association.

Cook, A. M., Polgar, J. M., & Hussey, S. M. (2008). *Cook and Hussey's assistive technologies: Principles and practice* (3rd ed.). St. Louis, MO: Mosby Elsevier.

de Jonge, D., Scherer, M. J., & Rodger, S. (2007). *Assistive technology in the workplace.* St. Louis, MO: Mosby.

Mitchell, L. K., & Brodwin, M. G. (1995). Self-efficacy and rehabilitation counseling. *Directions in Rehabilitation Counseling, 6*, 1–4.

Phillips, B., & Zhao, H. (1993). Predictors of assistive technology abandonment. *Assistive Technology, 5*(1), 36–45.

Reed, B. J., & Saladin, S. P. (2008). Assistive technology. In J. D. Andrew & C. W. Faubion (Eds.), *Rehabilitation services: An introduction for the human services professional* (pp. 188–227). Linn Creek, MO: Aspen Professional Services.

Riemer-Reiss, M. L., & Wacker, R. R. (2000). Factors associated with assistive technology discontinuance among individuals with disabilities. *Journal of Rehabilitation, 66*(3), 44–50.

Rogers, E. M. (1995). *Diffusion of innovations* (4th ed.). New York, NY: Free Press.

Rubin, S. E., & Roessler, R. T. (2008). *Foundations of the vocational rehabilitation process* (6th ed.). Austin, TX: PRO-ED.

Santrock, J. W. (2009). *Life-span development* (12th ed.). New York, NY: McGraw-Hill.

Schaller, J., & DeLaGarza, D. (1999). "It's about relationships": Perspectives of people with cerebral palsy on belonging in their families, schools, and rehabilitation counseling. *Journal of Applied Rehabilitation Counseling, 30*(2), 7–18.

Scherer, M. J. (Ed.). (2002). *Assistive technology: Matching devices and consumers for successful rehabilitation.* Washington, DC: American Psychological Association.

Scherer, M. J. (2007). *Living in the state of stuck: How technology impacts the lives of people with disabilities* (4th ed.). Cambridge, MA: Brookline Books.

Stumbo, N. J., Martin, J. K., & Hedrick, B. N. (2009). Assistive technology: Impact on education, employment, and independence of individuals with physical disabilities. *Journal of Vocational Rehabilitation, 30*(2), 99–110.

20

Religion and Disability: Clinical, Research, and Training Considerations for Rehabilitation Professionals*

BRICK JOHNSTONE, BRET A. GLASS, AND RICHARD E. OLIVER

RELIGION AND HEALTH

Since the dawn of the new millennium, laypersons and health professionals have become increasingly interested in the relationship between health and religion. This was caused in part by the growing religious diversity in the United States (Eck, 2001) and increased attention to different faiths since September 11, 2001. Although the relationship between religion and health has been minimally discussed in the mainstream media in the past, *Newsweek* once published a special issue entitled, "God & Health: Is Religion Good Medicine? Why Science Is Starting to Believe" (Kalb, 2003). In addition, over the past 20 years, television programs with a religious theme have proven to be very popular (e.g., *Touched by an Angel*) and movies with a religious focus have generated much discussion regarding the role of religion in society (e.g., *The Passion of the Christ, Luther*). Traditional beliefs about separation of church and state have even changed over the past two decades, as evidenced by the faith-based health initiatives that were promoted by President Bush in the United States during his term.

Although the impact of religion on health has been infrequently researched in the past, several prominent psychological and rehabilitation journals have published special journal issues/sections on the subject. These include the *American Psychologist* ("Spirituality, Religion, and Health"; Rayburn, 2003), the *Journal of Rehabilitation* ("Spirituality and Disability"; Alston, 2001), and the *Monitor on Psychology* ("Spirituality and Mental Health: In Practice, on Campus and in Research"; American Psychological Association, 2003). Even the *Journal of the American Medical Association* published the proceedings of two conferences that addressed spirituality and health (Koenig, 2002). Furthermore, the National Institutes of Health (NIH) has funded numerous projects investigating the impact of religion on health over the past decade, and private

---

*Brick Johnstone, Bret A. Glass, & Richard E. Oliver (2007). Religion and disability: Clinical, research and training considerations for rehabilitation professionals. *Disability and Rehabilitation, 29*(15), 1153–1163. Reprinted by permission of Taylor & Francis Ltd.

foundations, such as the John Templeton Foundation, are providing significant financial support to research the relationship between religion and health.

This new attention to health care and religion stems from the central role religion plays in the lives of most individuals. For example, Gallup polls from earlier this century indicate that religion is a "very important" part of the lives of 55% of the American public and is "fairly important" to another 29% (The Gallup Poll, 2004). More than 90% of individuals polled in 2003 reported believing in a "God" (FOX News/Opinion Dynamics Poll, 2003) and 66% reported being a member of a church or synagogue (CNN/*USA Today*/Gallup Poll, 2002). In another national survey, McCaffrey, Eisenberg, Legedza, Davis, and Phillips (2004) estimated that one third of adults used prayer for health concerns, and indicated that people who prayed reported high levels of perceived helpfulness. *Newsweek* (2003) further indicated that 84% of Americans think that praying for people who are ill improves their chances of recovery, and 72% state they would welcome the opportunity to discuss their religious beliefs with their physician.

It is clear that laypersons, health professionals, and researchers are interested in addressing the importance of religion in society and in health care. However, if we are to use religion effectively to improve the health of individuals, there is a need to better educate current rehabilitation professionals and students about religion, to critically evaluate the existing literature on disability and religion, and to develop practical suggestions for rehabilitation professionals to appropriately use religion to promote positive health outcomes.

DEFINITIONS OF SPIRITUALITY AND RELIGION

In order to understand the relationships that exist among religion, spirituality, and health, it is first necessary to define *religion* and *spirituality*. These terms can be both complementary and contradictory, but they are often used interchangeably. Spirituality is recognized as an internal experience of personal cultivation motivated by interest in meaning, purpose, and significance, whereas religion is recognized as an external experience of formal expression with associated systems of worship, traditions, practices, doctrines, beliefs, moral codes, and accompanying dogmas that represent specific ideologies shared by a faith-based group (Green, Benshoff, & Harris-Forbes, 2001; McColl et al., 2000; Underwood-Gordon, Peters, Bijur, & Fuhrer, 1997). Regardless of the definitions ascribed to spirituality and religion, it is evident that spirituality is applicable to all persons, whether religious, atheist, agnostic, or uncategorical (Carson, Soeken, Shanty, & Terry, 1990; Forbes, 1994; Goddard, 1995; McFarland & McFarlane, 1997; Treloar, 2000). Although ambiguity exists in the current literature regarding "religion" and "spirituality," it is important for future research in this area to succinctly define and measure these differing constructs.

RELIGION AND HEALTH RESEARCH

As previously indicated, there has been increasing research regarding religion and health over the past decade. Some researchers have focused on the impact of religion on persons with various diseases, including kidney disease (Tix & Fraser, 1998), cancer (Schnoll, Harlow, & Brower, 2000), heart disease (Ai, Dunkle, Peterson, & Bolling, 1998), lung disease (Matthees et al., 2001), HIV/AIDS (Avants, Warburton, & Margolin, 2001), cystic fibrosis (Stern, Canda, & Doershuk, 1992), diabetes (Samuel-Hodge et al., 2000), sickle cell disease (Cooper-Effa, Blount, Kaslow, Rothenberg, & Eckman, 2001), and amyotrophic lateral sclerosis (ALS; Murphy, Albert, Weber, Del Bene, & Rowland, 2000). Other research has focused on the efficacy of specific religious beliefs and practices in promoting health, including traditional Judeo-Christian and Eastern religious practices such as Zen, yoga, and meditation (Seeman, Dubin, & Seeman, 2003).

A review of the literature by Koenig, McCullough, and Larson (2001) identified 724 quantitative studies of religion and health published during the 20th century, and reported that 66% found a statistically significant relationship between religion and better mental health, greater social support, and less substance abuse. Although the existing research suggests that a positive relationship exists between religion and health, some professionals have argued that this research is plagued by methodological problems. For example, it is frequently argued that the positive relationships that are commonly observed between increased religiosity and health are more likely attributable to the lifestyle behaviors of religious individuals rather than religion per se, for example, less alcohol consumption and better dietary habits (King, 1990), increased social support associated with religious congregations (Taylor & Chatters, 1988), and a positive worldview that promotes well-being (McIntosh, 1995).

In order to determine the validity of existing religion and health studies, Powell, Shahabi, and Thoresen (2003) completed a literature review to critically evaluate the most popular hypotheses made regarding the connection between religion/spirituality and physical health (i.e., church attendance decreases mortality, prayer improves recovery, etc.). The authors concluded that there is "persuasive" evidence that church service attendance is associated with declined mortality, that there is "some" evidence that religion and spirituality protect against cardiovascular disease, that being prayed for improves physical recovery from illness, and that religion/spirituality may impede recovery from illness.

RELIGION AND CHRONIC DISABLING CONDITIONS

To date research on religion and health has primarily focused on persons with life-threatening diseases and conditions such as cancer (Schnoll, Harlow, & Brower, 2000), heart disease (Ai, Dunkle, Peterson, & Bolling, 1998), lung disease (Matthees et al., 2001), HIV/AIDS (Avants, Warburton, & Margolin, 2001), kidney disease (Tix & Fraser, 1998), cystic fibrosis (Stern, Canda, & Doershuk, 1992), diabetes (Samuel-Hodge et al., 2000), sickle cell disease (Cooper-Effa, Blount, Kaslow, Rothenberg, & Eckman, 2001), and ALS (Murphy, Albert, Weber, Del Bene, & Rowland, 2000). Persons facing impending death may use religion to help them accept their condition, come to terms with unresolved life issues, and prepare for death.

However, it is arguable that religion may be an equally if not more important coping mechanism for persons with chronic disabilities such as traumatic brain injury (TBI), spinal cord injury (SCI), stroke, arthritis, epilepsy, and so on. These individuals may expect to live for years, even decades, after the onset of their injury or disease and may use religion to help them cope with their disability, give new meaning to their lives based on their newly acquired disabilities, and help them to establish new life goals. For example, a middle-aged man who primarily derives self-esteem from his identification as a masculine, physically fit laborer may need to redefine himself and set new goals if he experiences an SCI. Similarly, a severe TBI may cause a young, intelligent woman studying to be an attorney to develop a new self-concept, as well as to develop new life goals. Religion is likely to be a significant resource for such individuals to help them cope with the significant changes they will experience in their lives. Although many individuals with disabilities turn to religion to help them deal with their situations, to date religion is infrequently discussed in rehabilitation settings and is rarely investigated in rehabilitation research. To better meet the needs of persons with disabilities, this needs to change.

The minimal research that has been conducted on religion and rehabilitation populations to date has generally included only anecdotal case studies (Landsberg, 2003), descriptive information about the religious practices of persons with disabilities (e.g., how many persons with TBI use religion to cope), or correlational analyses (e.g., more spirituality is correlated with better outcomes). For example, in 2001 *The Journal of Rehabilitation* published a special issue on "Spirituality and Disability" (Alston, 2001), although five of the six articles were nonempirical narrative articles, and the only empirical study reported the validation of a measure of spirituality (i.e., the Spiritual Transcendence Scale) based on undergraduate students (and not persons with disabilities). Similarly, Boswell, Knight, Hamer, and McChesney (2001) conducted a qualitative assessment of the spiritual beliefs and practices of six women with physical disabilities and, as expected, reported that spirituality and disability were associated for this small sample. McColl et al. (2000) conducted a similar qualitative evaluation of spiritual issues for 16 persons with either TBI or SCI and developed a matrix of common religious themes reported by this group. McNulty, Livneh, and Wilson (2004) evaluated spiritual well-being in 50 persons with multiple sclerosis and indicated that spirituality is positively correlated with psychosocial adjustment.

Powell, Shahabi, and Thoresen (2003) examined three studies to determine whether depth of religiousness and church/service attendance provided any degree of protection from acquired disability, defined as required institutionalization or required assistance with daily living skills (Colantonio, Kasl, Ostfeld, & Berkman, 1993; Goldman, Korenman, & Weinstein, 1995). The reviewers indicated there was no evidence to suggest that religious/spiritual involvement protects an individual from acquiring a disability. However, Powell, Shahabi, and Thoresen (2003) did find that studies by Haley, Koenig, and Bruchett (2001) and Idler and Kasl (1997) reflected a positive relationship between religious practice and disability, that is, as physical disability became more prevalent, personal religious practices became more frequent. This suggests that those experiencing disabling conditions of increasing severity may have a tendency to engage in religious activities more often.

Unfortunately, there have been few empirical studies with large samples to evaluate the relationship between religion and health outcomes for persons with chronic disabling conditions. The need still exists to determine how individuals with chronic disabilities, compared to life-threatening diseases, use religion to help them cope with and prepare for lifelong handicaps.

RELIGION AS A METHOD TO COPE WITH DISABILITY

In addition to improving the functional abilities of persons with disabilities, one of the primary goals of rehabilitation professionals is to facilitate individuals' adjustment to their disability. There has been considerable research on the different ways in which individuals cope with disabilities, which indicates that persons generally cope with stress by changing the environment, changing themselves, or changing the meaning of the event/issue of relevance. Traditional psychological research on the coping strategies of persons with disabilities has attempted to identify how individuals search for meaning in their disability (Dunn, 1994) and how they integrate their disabilities into their self-concept (Tait & Silver, 1989). Several studies have indicated that many individuals cope by relying on cognitive strategies that promote favorable beliefs about the self in difficult situations (Elliott, Witty, Herrick, & Hoffman, 1991), whereas other studies have shown that people tend to engage in protective and self-enhancing behaviors in order to maintain consistent and positive thoughts of themselves (Synder, 1989). For example, some individuals may cope with disability and promote self-esteem by providing rationalizations for their inability to perform some activity, or they may attempt to direct themselves and others away from problematic situations and toward situations that lead to positive outcomes. In addition, many individuals with disabilities cope by increasing the values they place on personal skills and traits (e.g., intelligence, social skills) and personal relationships they may have previously minimized (Keany & Glueckauf, 1993), while simultaneously decreasing their emphasis on physical attributes or characteristics (Wright, 1983).

In addition to these psychological coping strategies, many individuals with disabilities use spiritual coping strategies to assist them in adjusting to their disabilities. In fact, religious coping has been shown to add unique power to the prediction of positive adjustment for persons with disabilities after controlling for the effects of traditional coping strategies (Pargament, Ensing, et al., 1990; Pargament, Ishler, et al., 1994; Pargament & Park, 1995). Although rehabilitation professionals work with patients with disabilities to promote adjustment to disability, the use of religious coping strategies for persons with disabilities is not even mentioned in rehabilitation psychology training guidelines (Patterson & Hanson, 1995) or in standard rehabilitation medicine and rehabilitation psychology textbooks (Frank & Elliott, 2000; Rosenthal, Griffith, Kreutzer, & Pentland, 1999).

Standard strategies used in rehabilitation to assist individuals in coping with their disabilities include psychological counseling, medications, support groups, and family/peer support. However, many individuals also report relying on religious beliefs, practices, and supportive relationships to help them cope with their disabilities. For example, Cigrang, Hryshko-Mullen, and Peterson (2003) reported that 26% of patients with chronic physical illnesses reported using prayer and religion as a way to cope with their disability. Unfortunately, rehabilitation professionals rarely ask about a person's religion or religious coping strategies, and usually only briefly when taking a patient's history (e.g., asking about their religious affiliation). Some patients may be referred to a hospital chaplain, encouraged to pray, or referred back to their religious networks after discharge. Given the significant number of individuals who report using religion to cope with daily problems, it seems appropriate for rehabilitation professionals to increase their attention to this subject.

Various articles, in fact, propose that rehabilitation professionals and researchers need to consistently consider the religious beliefs and practices of individuals with illness and disability. Specifically, Ray (2004) proposes that religious beliefs should be one of the four components to be considered when evaluating the coping skills of individuals with illnesses or disabilities. The three commonly accepted coping mechanisms used by persons to deal with stressors, which should be uniformly considered by rehabilitation professionals, are (a) knowledge of their condition (i.e., the more one knows about conditions and treatments, the more likely it can be managed), (b) inner resources (e.g., individual beliefs and personality traits, such as optimism vs. pessimism), and (c) social support (i.e., the more the social support, the better the outcome). However, Ray also suggests that spirituality (i.e., individual belief in a higher power) is a fourth, relatively less considered coping mechanism, which is necessary to address when evaluating and treating patients with health disorders.

HOW DOES RELIGION FACILITATE COPING?

For many religious individuals, including laypersons and professionals, the specific manner or mechanism by which religion facilitates adjustment to disability is relatively unimportant. Individuals have their own personal faith and religious practices, and that is all that matters. Conversely, rehabilitation professionals and patients who are not religious may not want to discuss religion because they may not believe that it is a valid method by which to cope with disability, that it is not an appropriate subject to discuss in rehabilitation, or that it is a subject with which they are not comfortable addressing. In fact, some health professionals believe that religion and health care should remain separate, given the personal nature of religion, and that the impact of religion on health cannot be scientifically validated (Lawrence, 2002; Sloan et al., 2000).

From a rehabilitation perspective, the specific mechanisms by which religion facilitates adjustment to disability is of relatively minimal importance, whether it is through divine intervention, the power of repetitive religious practices (e.g., individual or group prayer, chanting, laying on of hands, yoga, anointing ceremonies, sand paintings, etc.), or a placebo effect (which may be the perspective of nonreligious rehabilitation professionals). If religion helps an individual cope with a disability in a positive manner, it should be used accordingly. Regardless of one's personal religious beliefs, it is possible to understand how religion is used to cope with illnesses and disabilities based on two different models of coping: spiritual (faith based) versus psychoneuroimmunological (physiologically based).

Spiritual Model of Religious Coping

For most religious individuals, their faith in a higher power is sufficient for them to deal with their disability. In explaining how spirituality may be used to cope with illness and disability, Koenig (2002) suggests that many persons with illnesses feel helpless and not in control of their condition, but that religion provides them an indirect form of control in that their problem is turned over to a higher power to handle. He also states that prayer can give individuals the belief that they are directly controlling their outcome by praying or meditating about it, and that prayer can improve adjustment to health problems by producing a state of relaxation similar to stress management techniques.

Psychoneuroimmunological Model of Religious Coping

Many rehabilitation professionals may not be comfortable considering the use of religion as a means to cope with disability, and particularly if they are trained in the scientist–practitioner model. As scientists they are trained to consider issues of causality and empirical evidence. However, it is impossible to directly prove the effect of divine intervention or the power of prayer, as these constructs and behaviors are hard to conceptualize, quantify, and measure, although the measurement of spirituality is improving (Hill & Pargament, 2003). For those rehabilitation professionals who may not feel comfortable using religion to assist individuals in coping with their disabilities, it is also possible for them to reframe religious coping in terms of psychoneuroimmunological models.

In general, psychoneuroimmunology is based on the belief that the mind (i.e., thoughts) can directly influence the body and how we adapt to stress. Psychoneuroimmunology can be defined as the study of four bodily systems that interact to promote health and assist the body in handling stress: (a) the mind, (b) endocrine system, (c) central nervous system, and (d) immune system (Ray, 2004). In fact, several studies have shown that the nervous, endocrine, and immune systems all have receptors on critical cells that can receive information from each of the other systems (Dantzer, 2001; Raison & Miller, 2001). Clear relationships between psychological stress and health outcomes have been demonstrated, including studies that have shown that increased stress is associated with respiratory tract infections (Cohen, 1996; Cohen, Tyrrel, & Smith, 1991; Kiecolt-Glaser & Glaser, 1987; Takkouche, Regueira, & Gestal-Otero, 2001) and cancer outcomes (Greer, 1991). Other studies have shown that clear relationships exist between religion and cardiovascular, neuroendocrine, and immunological functions, including traditional Judeo-Christian and Eastern religious practices such as Zen, yoga, and meditation (Seeman, Dubin, & Seeman, 2003). Just as biofeedback, stress management therapies, and mindfulness meditation have been shown to lead to greater control over bodily functions and the ability to cope with stress (Kabat-Zinn et al., 1998; Schmidt, Wijga, Von Zur Mühlen, Brabant, & Wagner, 1997), it is also likely th at other religious beliefs and practices can lead to decreased stress, increased immunological functioning, and better physical and mental health.

Ray (2004) argues that thoughts, feelings, and beliefs can be conceptualized as chemical and electrical activities in our brains, and that these thoughts (i.e., chemical/electrical activities) can change our biology, health, and longevity in some cases. As an example, Ray cited a study (Phillips & King, 1988) that evaluated the death rates of elderly Jewish men the week before and after Passover. Theoretically, the death rates should not differ statistically, although the researchers hypothesized that they might, given that Passover has particular religious significance for elderly Jewish men. In fact, the study indicated that the death rates of elderly Jewish men declined by 24% the week before Passover and increased by 24% the week after. They found no change in the death rates of Jewish women, Jewish children, Black adults, or Asian adults during the same time periods, suggesting that these elderly men were able to delay their deaths due to their will to live. Ray cited a similar study in which the death rates of elderly Chinese women were investigated the week before and after the Chinese Harvest Moon Festival, a holiday that holds special religious significance for elderly Chinese women (Phillips & Smith, 1990). The findings indicated that the death rates of Chinese women aged 75 years and older declined by more than one third the week before the holiday, but rose by 35% the week after the holiday. No differences in death rates were found for younger Chinese women. These studies clearly illustrate that the will to live (i.e., the mind) is very powerful in determining life, death, health, and well-being. Ray concluded that health clinicians and researchers need to promote the investigation of mind–body relationships and develop treatment and research models that incorporate psychological, medical, and religious components.

SPECIFIC RELIGIOUS COPING METHODS

Before religious coping strategies are used with patients, it is necessary to determine their religious affiliation, their beliefs and practices, and the specific manner in which they may use religious coping methods (e.g., prayer, reframing of disability, etc.). Some patients may have little or no desire to use religion to cope with their disability, and not all individuals with disabilities may feel comfortable discussing their religious beliefs with their health care providers. Other patients may have strong religious beliefs and coping strategies that promote adjustment, while some may have religious beliefs and coping strategies that negatively impact their health (e.g., beliefs that their illness/disability is a reflection of God's punishment, Fitchett, Rybarczyk, DeMarco, & Nicholas, 1999). Before encouraging religious coping, rehabilitation professionals need to determine sensitively which people are most appropriate to benefit from religious coping.

Pargament and Brant (1998) have stressed that religion can be an effective or ineffective coping mechanism, depending on the individual and situation. For example, many people draw strength from their religion for coping purposes, while others have negative views of religion or previous negative religious experiences that hinder successful adaptation to disability. Several studies suggest that religious coping may be used most often by females, older individuals, and persons of low income (Neighbors, Jackson, Bowman, & Gurin, 1983), as well as African Americans, persons with less education, widows and widowers, churchgoers, and fundamentalists (Bijur, Wallson, Smith, Lifrak, & Friedman, 1993; Ellison, 1991; Veroff, Douvan, & Kulka, 1981). Other research suggests that religion is most appropriate to use at times of high stress (Maton, 1989). Religious coping can be passive (i.e., a person turns his or her problems over to God) or active (i.e., increase in prayer or religious rituals). For some individuals religious coping can be personal (i.e., direct appeals to God for intervention) or interpersonal (i.e., seeking support from clergy and congregation). In addition, religious coping can be problem focused (i.e., developing specific problem-solving strategies to overcome their illness/disability or adapt to it) or emotion focused (i.e., seeking emotional reassurance from God to gain acceptance of their illness/disability).

Pargament suggests that there are three types of positive religious coping mechanisms to help persons adjust to stress:

(a) **Spiritual religious support.** In this manner of religious coping, individuals generally perceive that they have the support of a higher power (i.e., they trust that God would not let anything bad happen to them) and/or that they will receive guidance from God (i.e., God will show them how to deal with a difficult situation).

(b) **Clergy and congregational support.** Many individuals turn to religious leaders to assist them in coping with difficult situations, including priests, pastors, ministers, rabbis, imams, shamans, and so on, as they are the most appropriate professionals to provide spiritual support. Similarly, many individuals turn to fellow members of their congregations (e.g., temples, dharma centers, mosques, churches), as these people have similar religious beliefs and are the individuals with whom they practice their religion.

(c) **Benevolent religious reframing.** People use this type of cognitive reframing to attribute negative life events to karma or to the will of God (i.e., acceptance that God will work with them in their difficult time for a specific reason), making it easier for them to accept their fate.

Although religion may be used by many individuals to cope with their problems, not all persons are comfortable discussing their religious beliefs with their health professionals. For example, in one poll, 28% of persons stated that religion and medicine should be separate (*Newsweek,* 2003). In fact, not all people use effective religious strategies to cope with adversity. Pargament and Brant (1998) reported several negative religious attitudes and beliefs that can adversely affect the ability of persons to cope with illness and disability, including:

(a) **Discontent with God, a higher power, or their congregation.** Many persons may feel that God has abandoned them in their illness or disability, which may subsequently lead to hopelessness, despair, and resentment. Such hopelessness is associated with poorer health outcomes and is difficult to overcome, even with the help of religious and behavioral health specialists.

(b) **Negative religious reframing.** In contrast to benevolent religious reframing, some individuals may believe that their illness/disability is a reflection of negative karma or of God's punishment. As may be expected, these individuals may have significant difficulties adjusting to their problems, or being motivated to do something about them, believing that God is purposely causing their illness/disability.

In addition to taking into account the attitudes and beliefs that may adversely affect the outcomes of persons with disabilities, it is also necessary for rehabilitation professionals to consider how one can inappropriately promote religion with patients. Specifically, there is the possibility that overly religious professionals may invade the privacy of patients, as religion is a matter of conscience and thus very private for many individuals. Some health professionals may proselytize and attempt to impose their religious beliefs on their patients, thereby coercing patients to engage in religious practices (e.g., praying) that they may not wish to do. Many patients may also feel the need to follow the religious advice of the rehabilitation "expert," given the differences in authority/ power that may be perceived by the patient. Furthermore, some patients from minority religions may feel compelled to discuss religious matters even if they do not want to, perceiving that they may experience religious discrimination if they are not members of the majority religion (Miller & Thoreson, 2003).

PRACTICAL SUGGESTIONS

It is encouraging that religious issues are being more frequently addressed by health care professionals and that there is increased research on the mechanisms by which religious coping strategies can positively influence health outcomes. Unfortunately, to date most religion and health care textbooks and articles provide little if any practical information about how religious coping can be appropriately promoted in rehabilitation. Similarly, most religion and health research has used only correlational analyses to show that increased religion is generally associated with better health outcomes, which is of limited practical value. In order to most effectively use religion in rehabilitation, specific training modules in religion are necessary for health professionals and specific religion-based interventions need to be developed, evaluated, and implemented. Following are several practical suggestions for rehabilitation professionals to (a) utilize religious coping strategies with patients in rehabilitation, (b) educate students regarding basic beliefs and practices of different religions and their relation to health care, (c) develop research programs that systematically investigate the relationship between religion and rehabilitation outcomes, and (d) identify appropriate funding sources for religion and rehabilitation research.

CLINICAL SERVICE ISSUES

Before using religion or spirituality-based coping strategies in rehabilitation, it is important for rehabilitation professionals to be aware of and to monitor their own religious beliefs and potential prejudices, and to understand how these potential prejudices may affect interactions with patients. Rehabilitation professionals also need to become comfortable in addressing religion with their patients and each other, rather than viewing religion as a taboo subject. Although some professionals may feel uncomfortable obtaining information about patients' religious beliefs, it is no different than inquiring about their sexual, psychological, substance use, and legal histories. In fact, it can be argued that religion is such an important part of many individuals' total being that it is inappropriate not to address it, even if briefly. Similarly, rehabilitation professionals will work most effectively with individuals with disabilities when they have an understanding of the individual's worldview, including their religious beliefs and practices. Ignoring these cultural and religious factors can have serious implications regarding the individual's willingness to adhere to or comply with treatment recommendations.

On inpatient rehabilitation units, it may be best to designate one person to initially address the religious beliefs and practices of patients to assure that patients are not inundated with religious inquiries from all rehabilitation professionals. Many disciplines, including psychologists, physicians, rehabilitation therapists, social workers, case managers, or chaplains, could potentially be responsible for addressing these issues, depending on individual practitioners' beliefs and comfort level with religious issues. Chaplains are arguably the most important religious resources in most hospitals, and it may be helpful to have them regularly meet patients who express strong religious beliefs, so that they can address their spiritual needs and serve as the contact person for the patient's religious leaders in their home communities. Similarly, it may be helpful to have hospital chaplains attend rehabilitation team meetings to assist team members in understanding the religious beliefs and practices of patients so that team members can best meet the needs of patients.

It is most appropriate to address religious issues with patients in an initial interview, if the patient is comfortable in doing so. In this situation, it is recommended that the following information be determined:

- Comfort level in discussing religion
- Religious affiliation
- Any specific religious practices/customs that need to be observed (e.g., the need to pray at certain times each day, dietary restrictions, restrictions on physical touching by other genders, etc.)
- Specific religious beliefs regarding their disability (e.g., God's will or punishment), and
- Any religious coping methods they use (e.g., prayer, rituals, benevolent or negative reframing, etc.).

Koenig (2002) provides other suggestions for specific religion-related questions to ask patients, including:

- Do your religious or spiritual beliefs provide comfort and support or do they cause stress?
- How would these beliefs influence your medical decisions if you became really sick?
- Do you have any beliefs that might interfere or conflict with your medical care?
- Are you a member of a religious or spiritual community and is it supportive?
- Do you have any spiritual needs that someone should address?

After gathering this basic information about religion, it may then be determined how rehabilitation professionals can assist their patients in using appropriate religion-based coping strategies, if desired by the patient. Praying with patients may be appropriate based on the comfort levels of both the patient and the provider. Some professionals, particularly psychologists and physicians, are increasingly praying with their patients (Jarvik, 2004; Kersting, 2003). This is an issue which individual providers will need to consider based on their own beliefs. However, the need exists to be sure that there is no coercion, proselytizing, or religious activities based on unrecognized assumptions. Other religious practices important to individuals can also be encouraged, including yoga, reading of religious texts, meditation, laying on of hands, and so on.

Rehabilitation psychologists, counselors, and chaplains should also work together to initiate forgiveness interventions with patients with disabilities when appropriate, and particularly those patients who were injured as the result of the actions of others (e.g., car accidents, violence, etc.). Many religious traditions have explicit ceremonies of forgiveness for oneself and forgiveness of others. When this is the case, the rehabilitation professional should seek the guidance of a religious leader.

When patients are discharged from inpatient rehabilitation units, it may be appropriate to refer them to their existing religious support systems, including their religious organization (i.e., church, synagogue, dharma center, mosque) or religious leaders and congregations. Unfortunately, many health professionals rarely make referrals to clergy

(Koenig, Bearon, Hover, & Travis, 1991). Just as it is common for patients to be referred to their respective community-based resources and social networks (e.g., spouse, parents, friends, coworkers, clubs, support groups, advocacy agencies, etc.), rehabilitation professionals need to increase their interaction with these community-based religious resources. This may include making contact with the religious colleagues of the patient (with their permission) to inform them of the patient's need for spiritual support, both during hospitalization and after discharge.

PROFESSIONAL TRAINING ISSUES

On a professional level, there are an increasing number of health professional training programs (e.g., medical, nursing, psychology, counseling, etc.) that offer courses or training modules on religion, which is particularly important given the increasing religious diversity in America. In fact, *Newsweek* (2003) reported that although only three medical schools offered courses in health and spirituality four decades ago, more than half of the medical schools do so today. Similarly, Cashwell and Young (2004) indicate that psychological counseling programs are offering more classes on spirituality, and that the counseling accrediting body (Council for Accreditation of Counseling and Related Educational Programs, 2001) is giving increased attention to spirituality and religion in training requirements. It is suggested that rehabilitation professional training programs include academic coursework, didactic training, and/or professional supervision in religious issues, including introductory information regarding the most common religions, beliefs, practices, and customs. For example, students should be taught the basic beliefs of Christianity, Judaism, Islam, Buddhism, Hinduism, Native American religions, and so on, and their relevance to health care. It is very important that rehabilitation professionals and students be aware of the different religious customs that should be considered when evaluating and treating individuals in health care settings, including information regarding the appropriateness of physical touching by others, preferences regarding gender-specific services (e.g., expectations for some health services to be provided only by same-gender individuals), dressing and hygiene customs (e.g., requirements to wear certain clothes or headdresses at all times), beliefs regarding death and an afterlife, and so on. Booklets have been written for medical professionals to inform them of specific religious and cultural practices that should be considered when offering health care. For example, Sikhs have specific religious beliefs and customs pertaining to personal hygiene, daily prayers, dietary requirements, reproductive issues, and beliefs about birth and death (Bagnetto, 2004). Many Sikhs wear a steel bracelet (Kara) to signify their unity with God, as well as shorts (Kaccha), which signify sexual morality. Their uncut hair (Kesh) symbolizes spirituality, so health care professionals need to explain carefully why Sikh patients may need to remove their turbans, and allow them to do it themselves. The reference section of this chapter provides a list of relevant readings regarding religion and disability, as does the following website: www.disabilitystudies.com/religion.htm.

RESEARCH ISSUES

Future rehabilitation research will need to determine the efficacy of religious beliefs, behaviors, and coping methods on the physical and mental health of persons with disabilities. In addition, as is the case for all rehabilitation research, the need exists to determine the relationships among these religious variables and community-based outcomes such as the ability to live independently, work, and participate in recreational activities.

Of primary importance, researchers will need to determine the specific religious rituals (e.g., individual prayer, intercessory prayer, ritual participation) and coping mechanisms (e.g., benevolent reframing, prayer, etc.) that are most appropriate to use with different individuals (e.g., persons with strong faiths, persons who become religious after the onset of their disability, atheists or persons with little religious conviction, etc.), different populations (e.g., gender, race, age, etc.), and different disability groups (e.g., physically vs. cognitively impaired, etc.). Although the conceptualization and measurement of religious beliefs and behaviors have been criticized in the past, Hill and Pargament (2003) have reviewed several of the more commonly used and validated religion and spirituality measures that can be used by future religion and health researchers.

Consistent with the recommendations of Ray (2004), rehabilitation professionals are strongly encouraged to investigate mind–body relationships and develop treatment and research models that incorporate psychological, medical, and religious components. Investigation of the relationships that exist among religious beliefs and rituals, religious coping strategies, psychoneuroimmunological functions, and health outcomes will likely produce the most useful information that can be used by rehabilitation professionals in the future. Relatedly, rehabilitation professionals need to collaborate with faith-based organizations to improve the physical and mental health of persons with disabilities, as well as their ability to reintegrate back into their communities. Such collaborations are particularly important given the resources that are available in most community churches (e.g., church vans, counseling services) to assist persons with disabilities with transportation and provision of social support.

Rehabilitation professionals also need to be aware of existing funding sources for such research, as many government agencies and private foundations are increasingly funding religion-based health research. Possible funding sources include the Templeton Foundation (2004), the Department of Health and Human Services Presidential Faith-Based Initiatives (The Center for Faith Based & Community Initiatives, 2006), and NIH (National Institutes of Health, 2006).

ACKNOWLEDGMENT

This chapter was supported with funding from the Center for Religion, the Professions, and the Public at the University of Missouri—Columbia, sponsored by the Pew Charitable Trusts.

REFERENCES

Ai, A. L., Dunkle, R. E., Peterson, C., & Bolling, S. F. (1998). The role of private prayer in psychological recovery among midlife and aged patients following cardiac surgery. *The Gerontologist, 38*(5), 591–601.

Alston, P. (2001). Special issue: Spirituality and disability. *Journal of Rehabilitation, 67*(1), 1–47.

American Psychological Association. (2003). Spirituality and mental health: In practice, on campus and in research. *Monitor on Psychology, 34*, 40–53.

Avants, S. K., Warburton, L. A., & Margolin, A. (2001). Spiritual and religious support in recovery from addiction among HIV-positive injection drug users. *Journal of Psychoactive Drugs, 33*(1), 39–45.

Bagnetto, L. A. (2004). Booklet aids medical professionals in caring for Sikhs. Retrieved from http://www.tandfonline.com/doi/abs/10.1080/09638280600955693?src=recsys&journalCode=idre20

Bijur, P. E., Wallson, K. A., Smith, C. A., Lifrak, S., & Friedman, S. B. (1993). *Gender differences in turning to religion for coping.* Paper presented at the annual meeting of the APA, Toronto, ON, Canada.

Boswell, B. B., Knight, S., Hamer, M., & McChesney, J. (2001). Disability and spirituality: A reciprocal relationship with implications for the rehabilitation process. *Journal of Rehabilitation, 67*, 20–25.

Carson, V., Soeken, K. L., Shanty, J., & Terry, L. (1990). Hope and spiritual well-being: Essentials for living with AIDS. *Perspectives in Psychiatric Care, 26*(2), 28–34.

Cashwell, C. S., & Young, J. S. (2004). Spirituality in counselor training: A content analysis of syllabi from introductory spirituality courses. *Counseling Values, 48*, 96–109.

The Center for Faith Based & Community Initiatives. (2006). DHS Center for Faith Based & Neighborhood Partnerships. Retrieved from http://www.hhs.gov/fbci/

Cigrang, J. A., Hryshko-Mullen, A., & Peterson, A. L. (2003). Spontaneous reports of religious coping by patients with chronic physical illness. *Journal of Clinical Psychology in Medical Settings, 10*, 133–137.

CNN/*USA Today*/Gallup Poll. (2002). Retrieved from http://www.pollingreport.com/religion.htm

Cohen, S. (1996). Psychological stress, immunity, and upper respiratory infections. *Current Directions in Psychological Science, 5*, 86–89.

Cohen, S., Tyrrell, D. A., & Smith, A. P. (1991). Negative life events, perceived stress, negative affect, and susceptibility to the common cold. *Journal of Personality and Social Psychology, 64*(1), 131–140.

Colantonio, A., Kasl, S. V., Ostfeld, A. M., & Berkman, L. F. (1993). Psychosocial predictors of stroke outcomes in an elderly population. *Journal of Gerontology, 48*(5), S261–S268.

Cooper-Effa, M., Blount, W., Kaslow, N., Rothenberg, R., & Eckman, J. (2001). Role of spirituality in patients with sickle cell disease. *Journal of the American Board of Family Practice, 14*(2), 116–122.

Council for Accreditation of Counseling and Related Educational Programs. (2001). *Accreditation procedures manual and application for counseling and related educational programs.* Alexandria, VA: Author.

Dantzer, R. (2001). Can we understand the brain and coping without considering the immune system? In D. M. Broom (Ed.), *Coping with challenge: Welfare in animals including humans* (Vol. 7, pp. 102–110). Berlin, Germany: Dahlem University Press.

Dunn, D. S. (1994). Positive meaning and illusions following disability: Reality negotiation, normative interpretation, and value change. *Journal of Social Behavior and Personality, 9*, 123–138.

Eck, D. L. (2001). *A new religious America: How a "Christian country" has become the world's most religiously diverse nation* (pp. 2–9). San Francisco, CA: HarperSanFrancisco.

Elliott, T. R., Witty, T. E., Herrick, S., & Hoffman, J. T. (1991). Negotiating reality after physical loss: Hope, depression, and disability. *Journal of Personality and Social Psychology, 61*(4), 608–613.

Ellison, C. W. (1991). Spiritual well-being: Conceptualization and measurement. *Journal of Psychology and Theology, 11*, 330–340.

Fitchett, G., Rybarczyk, B. D., DeMarco, G. A., & Nicholas, J. J. (1999). The role of religion in medical rehabilitation outcomes: A longitudinal study. *Rehabilitation Psychology, 44*, 333–353.

Forbes, E. J. (1994). Spirituality, aging, and the community-dwelling caregiver and care recipient. *Geriatric Nursing, 15*(6), 297–302.

FOX News/Opinion Dynamics Poll. (2003). Retrieved from http://www.pollingreport.com/religion.htm

Frank, R. G., & Elliott, T. R. (2000). *Handbook of rehabilitation psychology.* Washington, DC: American Psychological Association.

The Gallup Poll. (2004). Religious tolerance score edged up in 2004. Retrieved from http://www.pollingreport.com/religion.htm

Goddard, N. C. (1995). "Spirituality as integrative energy": A philosophical analysis as requisite precursor to holistic nursing practice. *Journal of Advanced Nursing, 22*(4), 808–815.

Goldman, N., Korenman, S., & Weinstein, R. (1995). Marital status and health among the elderly. *Social Science & Medicine, 40*(12), 1717–1730.

Green, R. L., Benshoff, J. J., & Harris-Forbes, J. A. (2001). Spirituality in rehabilitation counselor education: A pilot survey. *Journal of Rehabilitation Medicine, 67*(3), 55–60.

Greer, S. (1991). Psychological response to cancer and survival. *Psychological Medicine, 21*(1), 43–49.

Haley, K. C., Koenig, H. G., & Bruchett, B. M. (2001). Relationship between private religious activity and physical functioning in older adults. *Journal of Religion and Health, 40*, 305–312.

Hill, P. C., & Pargament, K. I. (2003). Advances in the conceptualization and measurement of religion and spirituality. Implications for physical and mental health research. *American Psychologist, 58*(1), 64–74.

Idler, E. L., & Kasl, S. V. (1997). Religion among disabled and nondisabled persons II: Attendance at religious services as a predictor of the course of disability. *Journals of Gerontology. Series B, Psychological Sciences and Social Sciences, 52*(6), S306–S316.

Jarvik, E. (2004). Prayer doctor–physician believes in tapping spiritual resources. Retrieved from http://deseretnews.com/dn/view/0,1249,575040927,00.html

Kabat-Zinn, J., Wheeler, E., Light, T., Skillings, A., Scharf, M. J., Cropley, T. G., . . . Bernhard, J. D. (1998). Influence of a mindfulness meditation-based stress reduction intervention on rates of skin clearing in patients with moderate to severe psoriasis undergoing phototherapy (UVB) and photochemo-therapy (PUVA). *Psychosomatic Medicine, 60*(5), 625–632.

Kalb, C. (2003, November 10). God & health: Is religion good medicine? Why science is starting to believe. *Newsweek*, pp. 44–56.

Keany, K. C. M.-H., & Glueckauf, R. L. (1993). Disability and value change: An overview and reanalysis of acceptance of loss theory. *Rehabilitation Psychology, 38*, 199–210.

Kersting, K. (2003). Religion and spirituality in the treatment room. *APA Monitor, 34*, 40–42.

Kiecolt-Glaser, J. K., & Glaser, R. (1987). Psychosocial moderators of immune function. *Journal of Behavioral Medicine, 9*, 16–20.

King, D. G. (1990). Religion and health relationships: A review. *Journal of Religion and Health, 29*(2), 101–112.

Koenig, H. G. (2002). An 83-year-old woman with chronic illness and strong religious beliefs. *Journal of the American Medical Association, 288*(4), 487–493.

Koenig, H. G., Bearon, L. B., Hover, M., & Travis, J. L. (1991). Religious perspectives of doctors, nurses, patients, and families. *Journal of Pastoral Care, 45*(3), 254–267.

Koenig, H. G., McCullough, M., & Larson, D. B. (2001). *Handbook of religion and health*. New York, NY: Oxford University Press.

Landsberg, L. F. (2003, fall/winter). The healing power of religious community. *Harvard Divinity Bulletin*, pp. 34–36.

Lawrence, R. J. (2002). The witches' brew of spirituality and medicine. *Annals of Behavioral Medicine, 24*(1), 74–76.

Matthees, B. J., Anantachoti, P., Kreitzer, M. J., Savik, K., Hertz, M. I., & Gross, C. R. (2001). Use of complementary therapies, adherence, and quality of life in lung transplant recipients. *Heart & Lung: The Journal of Critical Care, 30*(4), 258–268.

Maton, K. I. (1989). The stress-buffering role of spiritual support: Cross-sectional and prospective investigations. *Journal for the Scientific Study of Religion, 28*, 310–323.

McCaffrey, A. M., Eisenberg, D. M., Legedza, A. T., Davis, R. B., & Phillips, R. S. (2004). Prayer for health concerns: Results of a national survey on prevalence and patterns of use. *Archives of Internal Medicine, 164*(8), 858–862.

McColl, M. A., Bickenbach, J., Johnston, J., Nishihama, S., Schumaker, M., Smith, K., . . . Yealland, B. (2000). Spiritual issues associated with traumatic-onset disability. *Disability and Rehabilitation, 22*(12), 555–564.

McFarland, G. K., & McFarlane, E. A. (1997). *Nursing diagnosis and intervention: Planning for patient care* (3rd ed.). St. Louis, MO: Mosby.

McIntosh, D. N. (1995). Religion as schema, with implications for the relation between religion and coping. *International Journal for the Psychology of Religion, 5*, 1–16.

McNulty, K., Livneh, H., & Wilson, L. M. (2004). Perceived uncertainty, spiritual well-being, and psychosocial adaptation in individuals with multiple sclerosis. *Rehabilitation Psychology, 49*, 91–99.

Miller, W. R., & Thoresen, C. E. (2003). Spirituality, religion, and health. An emerging research field. *American Psychologist, 58*(1), 24–35.

Murphy, P. L., Albert, S. M., Weber, C. M., Del Bene, M. L., & Rowland, L. P. (2000). Impact of spirituality and religiousness on outcomes in patients with ALS. *Neurology, 55*(10), 1581–1584.

National Institutes of Health. (2006). NIH grants policy statement. Retrieved from http://grants1.nih.gov/grants/ oer.htm

Neighbors, H. W., Jackson, J. S., Bowman, P. J., & Gurin, G. (1983). Stress, coping, and Black mental health: Preliminary findings from a national study. *Prevention in Human Services, 2*(3), 5–29.

Pargament, K. I., & Brant, C. R. (1998). Religion and coping. In *Handbook of religion and mental health* (pp. 111–128). San Diego, CA: Academic Press.

Pargament, K. I., Ensing, D. S., Falgout, K., Olsen, H., Reilly, B., Van Haitsma, K., & Warren, R. (1990). God help me: (I) Religious coping efforts as predictors of the outcomes to significant negative life events. *American Journal of Community Psychology, 18*, 793–823.

Pargament, K. I., Ishler, K., Dubow, E., Stanik, P., Rouiller, R., Crowe, P., . . . Royster, B. J. (1994). Methods of religious coping with the Gulf War: Cross-sectional and longitudinal analyses. *Journal for the Scientific Study of Religion, 33*, 347–361.

Pargament, K. I., & Park, C. L. (1995). Merely a defense? The variety of religious means and ends. *Journal of Social Issues, 51*, 13–32.

Patterson, D. R., & Hanson, S. L. (1995). Joint Division 22 and ACRM guidelines for postdoctoral training in rehabilitation psychology. *Rehabilitation Psychology, 40*, 299–310.

Phillips, D. P., & King, E. W. (1988). Death takes a holiday: Mortality surrounding major social occasions. *Lancet, 2*(8613), 728–732.

Phillips, D. P., & Smith, D. G. (1990). Postponement of death until symbolically meaningful occasions. *Journal of the American Medical Association, 263*(14), 1947–1951.

Powell, L. H., Shahabi, L., & Thoresen, C. E. (2003). Religion and spirituality. Linkages to physical health. *American Psychologist, 58*(1), 36–52.

Raison, C. L., & Miller, A. H. (2001). The neuroimmunology of stress and depression. *Seminars in Clinical Neuropsychiatry, 6*(4), 277–294.

Ray, O. (2004). How the mind hurts and heals the body. *American Psychologist, 59*(1), 29–40.

Rayburn, C. A. (2003). Spirituality, religion, and health. *American Psychologist, 58*, 24–74.

Rosenthal, M., Griffith, E. R., Kreutzer, J. S., & Pentland, B., (Eds.). (1999). *Rehabilitation of the adult and child with traumatic brain injury* (3rd ed.). Philadelphia, PA: F. A. Davis.

Samuel-Hodge, C. D., Headen, S. W., Skelly, A. H., Ingram, A. F., Keyserling, T. C., Jackson, E. J., . . . Elasy, T. A. (2000). Influences on day-to-day self-management of type 2 diabetes among African-American women: Spirituality, the multi-caregiver role, and other social context factors. *Diabetes Care, 23*(7), 928–933.

Schmidt, T., Wijga, A., Von Zur Mühlen, A., Brabant, G., & Wagner, T. O. (1997). Changes in cardiovascular risk factors and hormones during a comprehensive residential three month kriya yoga training and vegetarian nutrition. *Acta Physiologica Scandinavica. Supplementum, 640*, 158–162.

Schnoll, R. A., Harlow, L. L., & Brower, L. (2000). Spirituality, demographic and disease factors, and adjustment to cancer. *Cancer Practice, 8*(6), 298–304.

Seeman, T. E., Dubin, L. F., & Seeman, M. (2003). Religion and spirituality: Linkages to physical health. *American Psychologist, 58*, 36–52.

Sloan, R. P., Bagiella, E., VandeCreek, L., Hover, M., Casalone, C., Jinpu Hirsch, T., . . . Poulos, P. (2000). Should physicians prescribe religious activities? *New England Journal of Medicine, 342*(25), 1913–1916.

Stern, R. C., Canda, E. R., & Doershuk, C. F. (1992). Use of nonmedical treatment by cystic fibrosis patients. *Journal of Adolescent Health, 13*(7), 612–615.

Synder, C. R. (1989). Reality negotiation: From excuses to hope and beyond. *Journal of Social and Clinical Psychology, 8*, 130–157.

Tait, R., & Silver, R. C. (1989). Coming to terms with major negative events. In J. S. Uleman & J. A. Bargh (Eds.), *Unintended thought* (pp. 351–382). New York, NY: Guilford Press.

Takkouche, B., Regueira, C., & Gestal-Otero, J. J. (2001). A cohort study of stress and the common cold. *Epidemiology, 12*(3), 345–349.

Taylor, R. J., & Chatters, L. M. (1988). Church members as a source of informal social support. *Review of Religious Research, 30*, 193–203.

Templeton Foundation. (2004). What are the limits to what we can discover? Retrieved from https://www.templeton.org

Tix, A. P., & Fraser, P. A. (1998). The use of religious coping during stressful life events: Main effects, moderation, and mediation. *Journal of Consulting and Clinical Psychology, 66*(2), 411–422.

Treloar, L. L. (2000). Integration of spirituality into health care practice by nurse practitioners. *Journal of the American Academy of Nurse Practitioners, 12*(7), 280–285.

Underwood-Gordon, L., Peters, D. J., Bijur, P., & Fuhrer, M. (1997). Roles of religiousness and spirituality in medical rehabilitation and the lives of persons with disabilities. A commentary. *American Journal of Physical Medicine & Rehabilitation, 76*(3), 255–257.

Veroff, J., Douvan, E., & Kulka, R. A. (1981). *Mental health in America: Patterns of help seeking from 1957 to 1976.* New York, NY: Basic Books.

Wright, B. A. (1983). *Physical disability: A psychosocial approach* (2nd ed.). New York, NY: Harper & Row.

21

Rehabilitation Professionals and Abuse of Women Consumers

Martin G. Brodwin and Frances W. Siu

*I*n American society, men and women with disabilities have been treated stereotyp- ically with disdain and discrimination. Traditional efforts to promote protection of the "weak and disabled" (a societal stereotype) have inadvertently kept individuals with disabilities from accessing resources and education for protection and advancement (Smart & Smart, 2012; Thiara, Hugue, Bashall, Ellis, & Mullender, 2012). One form of discrimination is manifest through the prevalence of abusive behaviors. Powers and Oschwald (2005) reported that abuse is a serious problem for people who have dis- abilities. Violence is more prevalent among women with disabilities as compared with those without disabilities and with men with disabilities (Nosek, Hughes, Taylor, & Taylor, 2006).

Rehabilitation counselors can begin to assist women with issues of abuse by acknowledging that advocacy and protection from abusive behavior are a priority for many women with disabilities (Chan, 2010). By routinely asking about abuse and addressing issues of safety and control during rehabilitation planning, counselors can provide valuable information, resources, and support that may help prevent abuse from occurring and assist women for whom abuse has occurred (Glover-Graf & Reed, 2006; Powers et al., 2009). Although information pertinent to this area is being disseminated, a network of resources within the community helpful to all parties involved in abuse issues is necessary. Professional referral to psychologists, psychiatric social workers, and vocational training centers can help provide holistic support for consumers. Because of the vulnerability and highly dependent nature of women with disabilities, they rarely complain or voice anger and humiliation. Advocating for these consumers can be a sig- nificant part of rehabilitation counselors' job responsibilities.

ABUSE AND VIOLENCE

Abuse is a serious and underreported problem that is prevalent among women with dis- abilities in the United States. Studies show that the percentage of women with disabili- ties who have been abused is 62% to 67%; these women experience all kinds of abuse for significantly longer periods of time than those without disabilities (Nosek et al.,

2006; Thomas, Joshi, Wittenberg, & McCloskey, 2008). Violence against women cuts across geographic lines and penetrates all socioeconomic levels. Women of all religious, ethnic, economic, and educational backgrounds and of varying ages, physical abilities, and lifestyles are affected by gender-based mistreatment. The phenomenon of violence against women is a complex social, health, criminal justice, and human rights problem occurring throughout the world (Alhabib, Nur, & Jones, 2010).

INTIMATE PARTNER ABUSE

The most common context of violent abuse of women is between intimate partners. This crime is commonly referred to as *domestic violence, intimate partner violence, spousal abuse,* or *wife abuse.* Females constitute the vast majority of victims, whereas males comprise the majority of perpetrators (U.S. Department of Justice, 2015; World Health Organization, 2001). Each year, approximately 5.3 million incidents of intimate partner violence occur in the United States. About 85% of incidents of victimization by intimate partners involved women; about 15% happened to men (U.S. Department of Justice, 2015). Approximately 29.7% of women in America will experience violence in an intimate relationship, and for 24% to 30% of these women, the abuse will be regular and ongoing. The lifetime prevalence of physical violence by an intimate partner is 31.5% for women (National Center for Victims of Crime, 2017). The highest rate of domestic violence occurs among young women between 16 and 24 years of age (National Coalition Against Domestic Violence [NCAD], 2007). As a result, 2 million people are injured and 1,300 killed annually. Intimate partner violence costs this country more than $4 billion in medical expenses and $1.8 billion in loss of productivity; eight million days of paid work is lost, equivalent to the loss of 32,000 full-time jobs each year. An estimated 48% of "victimized" women in the United States do not report their abuse to law enforcement agencies (Centers for Disease Control and Prevention [CDC], 2014).

The genesis of intimate partner violence occurs when a perpetrator exerts power to take control of the victim. As identified by many domestic abuse survivors, a vicious cycle of abuse proceeds in three stages (Hassouneh-Phillips, McNeff, Powers, & Curry, 2005). Stage 1 is the *tension-building* phase, during which the abuser is edgy, moody, unpredictable, easily agitated, and there is an air of heightened anxiety, causing the victim emotional distress; stage 2 is the *explosion* phase, during which the abuser becomes intensely emotional, angry, explosive, violent, and abusive in various ways; and stage 3 is the *honeymoon period,* during which the abuser appears to be regretful, apologizes for abusive actions, and returns to being a loving individual, as if nothing had happened. Over the course of the cycle, the victim experiences many feelings, from anger to love to confusion.

A woman is at increased risk of being stalked and even killed after leaving her abusive relationship, because the victim's choice to leave her abuser is likely to be perceived as a challenge to the perpetrator's ability to maintain power and control (Kopala & Keitel, 2003; Thiara et al., 2012). As a result, considerations of safety should dictate where, when, and how an abused woman decides to leave that relationship. Even if an abused woman eventually leaves her home, the abuse often continues after separation, frequently characterized by different forms of behavior, increased repetitions, and, tragically, increased severity (NCAD, 2003).

Types of Abuse

Domestic violence commonly occurs in the forms of physical, emotional, and sexual abuse, which are often concurrent (CDC, 2014). NCAD (2007) estimated that 1.3 million women are physically assaulted by their intimate partners annually, with more than 80% being stalked by a current or former intimate partner. Nearly 7.8 million women have been sexually assaulted by an intimate partner at some point in their lives; 31% of women who are stalked by a current or former intimate partner are also sexually assaulted by the same person. Approximately one third of women who report abuse to the police are later killed by their spouses or boyfriends (U.S. Department of Justice, 2015). Physical violence and emotional abuse occurring simultaneously is part of a systematic pattern of abusers exercising their need for power and control.

Emotional abuse was characterized as "soul murder" in the Surgeon General's Report on Women's Mental Health (U.S. Department of Health and Human Services [HHS], 2005), which is an apt definition of a crime in which a woman's spirits are significantly diminished. The report addressed serious concerns about the effects of emotional abuse, which negates a woman's existence and is as damaging as physical and sexual abuse. A pattern of emotional abuse is likely to destabilize a woman's perceptions of herself and her reality (Schaller & Fieberg, 1998). For many physically battered women, emotional abuse is an ongoing backdrop against which physical abuse occurs. As a result, a battered woman's symptoms may reflect the stress of dealing with repetitive verbal abuse, threats, and segregation from society (Dutton, Haywood, & El-Bayoumi, 2000).

In recent years, social media has brought attention to bullying as a form of physical and emotional abuse. Olweus (1994) defined *bullying* as unwanted, intentional, aggressive behavior that involves a real or perceived power imbalance that is often repeated over time. A second definition of *bullying* is "any aggressive behavior of a more powerful person or group toward a less powerful person" (Hong, Neely, & Lund, 2015, p. 157). Traditional bullying behaviors range from teasing, name calling, taunting, stealing, and damaging the victim's personal belongings to pushing, shoving, intimidating, threatening with or without a weapon, physical aggression, and shaming the victims to the point where some commit suicide. Cyberbullying is the use of technology to bully others. Technological devices, such as computers and cellphones, and social media like Facebook, YouTube, and Twitter, are used to inflict harm on others (McNamara, 2013).

ABUSERS

Within an abusive relationship, there is a victim and an abuser. The abuser who exerts power to take control of the victim is often referred to as the perpetrator or batterer. These individuals are likely to be men who are known to the victim, including friends, neighbors, husbands, boyfriends, and extended-family members (NCAD, 2007). Bancroft (2002) found the following five principal behaviors to be characteristic of abusers: (a) exerting power to take control; (b) blaming the "victim" for their problems, so as to have someone to take their frustrations out on; (c) enjoying being the center of attention with priority given to their needs; (d) taking complete financial control of the abused woman; and (e) having a history of being abused. Often, abusive individuals project pleasant and charming images, appearing in public to be unusually fun and loving.

Peterman and Dixon (2001) described a batterer as someone who uses all types of abuse and other behaviors to gain control of what he considers "his" woman. Most batterers involved in intimate partner violence do not have criminal records and are rarely violent with anyone except their partners. They frequently have low self-esteem, fear being abandoned by separation and divorce, suspect infidelity or pregnancy, and often choose violence rather than looking for other solutions to perceived problems.

There are three types of batterers: typical batterers, sociopathic batterers, and anti-social batterers.

Typical Batterers

They are the most common type of abuser and are usually not diagnosed to have mental illness or a personality disorder, nor are they violent to people outside the family. Typically, they lack criminal records.

Sociopathic Batterers

These individuals may have been diagnosed with personality disorders, accept violence as a way to deal with problems, are more violent than the typical batterer, and too frequently use weapons to hurt their victims. These individuals are very unlikely to have criminal records, although they may be substance abusers and use power and control both inside and outside the family environment.

Antisocial Batterers

These people constitute a small percentage of the population. They are usually diagnosed with mental illnesses or personality disorders compounded by drug addiction. Their violent acts are far more severe and frequent, with the result that they often have criminal records.

VULNERABILITY TO ABUSE

In addition to experiencing all forms of abuse that happen to women without disabilities, women with disabilities also experience abuse unique to their disabilities and which persists for significantly longer periods, including neglect, coercion, control/restraint, theft of property, arbitrary deprivation of liberty, concealment of medication, restriction of mobility, and the threat of such acts (Nosek et al., 2006). Not only do women with disabilities experience intimate partner abuse, they also may suffer institutional abuse, because they are more likely to be institutionalized and encounter abusive service providers outside their homes.

Nosek, Howland, Rintala, Young, and Chanpong (2001) suggested eight reasons why women with disabilities are more vulnerable to abuse:

- Increased dependence on others for long-term care
- Denial of human rights resulting in perceptions of powerlessness
- Less risk of discovery in the perception of the perpetrator
- Difficulty some survivors have in being believed
- Less education about appropriate and inappropriate sexuality
- Social isolation and increased risk of manipulation
- Physical helplessness and vulnerability in public places
- Attitudes within the field of disabilities valuing mainstreaming and integration, without consideration of each individual's capacity for self-protection

Perpetrators of abuse of women with disabilities include intimate partners, caregivers who are friends, family members, hired personal attendants, and service providers such as health care or independent living personnel in public and private settings (Glover-Graf & Reed, 2006). Moreover, when people with disabilities report abuse, they are often met with skepticism, blunting opportunities to escape further abuse (Powers et al., 2009).

SOCIAL AND PSYCHOLOGICAL ISSUES

Compared with women without disabilities, women with disabilities are more vulnerable and have notably lower self-esteem (Alhabib et al., 2010; Sobsey, 1994). Historically, women with disabilities display defining characteristics. These are (a) having more dependency on others, (b) typically socialized to be passive before other people's wishes and demands, (c) short on self-esteem due to frequent rejections, (d) afraid of being placed in an institutional environment, (e) more accepting of abuse as normal behavior because of the habitual effect, (f) socially isolated, (g) perceived as powerless, (h) less believable by others, (i) naive about sexuality, and (j) directed to mainstream living without resources for self-protection (Glover-Graf & Reed, 2006).

Learned helplessness is a common result of being a victim in an abusive relationship, resulting in beliefs that one cannot leave, fight back, or do anything to control the situation (Deaton & Hetica, 2001). A perception of powerlessness becomes paramount in an individual's thoughts and behavior.

Abuse affects all aspects of a person's life. Many abused individuals' basic survival needs are challenged; a form of abuse peculiar to women with disabilities is deprivation of food, medicine, assistive devices, and mobility (Hassouneh-Phillips & Curry, 2002). The feeling of safety of such women is threatened by the constant fear and hostility they live with daily. As suggested by Maslow's hierarchy theory of needs, it is difficult and often impossible for these individuals to satisfy higher level needs such as love, self-esteem, and self-actualization without first satisfying lower level needs for food, clothing, shelter, and safety. Many abused women acquire multiple disabilities. Approximately 40% have acquired disabilities because of the abuse, and 60% of women seeking help from the Domestic Violence Initiative for Women With Disabilities had disabilities prior to being abused. Others were homicidal or suicidal because of the violence in their lives (Glover-Graf & Reed, 2006).

ABUSE AND EMPLOYMENT

The U.S. Census Bureau (Rubin, Roessler, & Rumrill, Jr., 2016) estimated that 10% of women between ages 16 and 64 have work disabilities. Among these women, only 14% work full time, compared to 52% of women without disabilities and 22% of men with disabilities. Of those between ages 25 and 64 years, 9% have college degrees as compared with 26% of women without disabilities and 13% of men with disabilities. Census research has shown that even when women with disabilities have higher levels of education, they are less likely to be employed.

Because of psychosocial debilitating factors, women with disabilities feel that they must work twice as hard as women without disabilities to gain recognition from their employers. Women with disabilities believe that it is vital to first prove that their disabilities do not hinder their competence and reliability. Only then will they feel that employers appropriately value the work they produce. Several additional factors contribute to employment inequalities for women with disabilities (Doren & Benz, 1998):

- Women are less likely than men to receive occupational or vocational training in secondary school.
- Women with disabilities underuse vocational rehabilitation services in comparison to men with disabilities.
- Because of the ramifications of the earning gap, occupational stereotypes, and gender division in the labor market, women with disabilities are less likely to be employed and more likely to be underemployed.

- Employers may be reluctant to promote an employee with a disability because of the fear that added responsibility or extra workload could worsen the disability. Employers may also believe that women with disabilities are sick and, therefore, fragile.
- Women with disabilities are often literally hidden from sight and kept away from customers because they do not fit the stereotypical female image. In addition, coworkers with preconceived notions about women with disabilities may lack understanding.

Regardless of improvement in employment opportunities for women since the working women's movement in the 1970s, women with disabilities have fewer employment opportunities than women without disabilities and men with disabilities. Women with disabilities are more likely to experience poor post-school employment outcomes, lower earnings, negative employment experiences, and little or no support or accommodation. Doren and Benz (1998) noted that women with disabilities are doubly disadvantaged in the labor market, experiencing dual discrimination because of prejudice toward both gender and disability. Sociologists suggest that minority women with disabilities may experience "triple jeopardy" because they are non-White, "disabled," females. Thus, it stands to reason that abused women with disabilities are very likely to experience "quadruple discrimination."

The economic impact of disability on employment, earnings, and education is more devastating for women than for men (Rubin et al., 2016). Violence in women's lives is yet another significant barrier to employment, which impacts job search and job retention behaviors due to increased mental and physical health hazards (Coulter, 2004). Wettersten et al. (2004) reported that domestic abuse has a profound impact on the prospects of female survivors gaining meaningful employment, possibly as a result of a diminished vocational history and general self-concept that may decrease the ability to work. This group of women have difficulty retaining their jobs and receiving promotions; they often turn to welfare and return to their abusive relationships.

In addition, women may encounter abuse through workplace bullying, a learned behavior of abuse in which the abuser exerts power to take control of the abused individual. Like many other types of abuse, workplace bullying comes in many forms, involves many aspects of life, and impacts the abused individual's loss of productivity in the workplace and unknown psychological distress. Most bullies have an aggressive personality and a strong desire to be in charge; they lack empathy and remorse, and enjoy gossiping and spreading rumors to maliciously exclude their victim(s) from the group. They often intimidate and humiliate their "prey" in person and/or through the use of social media. In general, male bullies are more likely to engage in observable bullying tactics, such as physical aggression, whereas female bullies are more likely to use less observable tactics such as intimidation and encouraging others to stay away from a certain worker (McNamara, 2013).

Abuse is a serious health, economic, and human rights issue associated with numerous social problems (U.S. Department of Justice, 2015). Poor health related to chronic illness and sexually transmitted diseases such as HIV/AIDS are abuse-related health hazards within our society. Although intimate partner abuse involving people with disabilities occurs at all socioeconomic levels, it arises frequently among persons with low incomes (James, Johnson, & Raghavan, 2004). Acts of violence have been found to harm the economy, relating directly to decreased productivity, reduced tax proceeds, and poverty. Other social problems related to domestic abuse include homelessness, substance abuse, criminal activity, child abuse, teen pregnancy, unwanted pregnancy, prostitution, trafficking, and gang activities (NCAD, 2007).

REHABILITATION SERVICES

Because of widespread violence against women with disabilities, it is likely that rehabilitation professionals will serve clients who have experienced abuse or who are in abusive relationships (Brodwin & Siu, 2007; Siu, 2005). Rehabilitation counselors may be the only individuals who are available and trustworthy with whom to discuss these issues. Vocational rehabilitation can provide hope for such women. Rehabilitation services that include job training, vocational programs, and employment opportunities provide battered women with immediate income to support themselves and their children after leaving their abusers. Securing financial resources through employment is a significant motivator to assist abused women in leaving these relationships and becoming independent (Chronister & McWhirter, 2003).

The philosophy of rehabilitation counseling is to use a holistic approach, integrating programs to empower rehabilitation consumers to achieve fulfilling, socially meaningful, and functionally effective interaction within society (Brodwin & Brodwin, 2014; Patterson, Szymanski, & Parker, 2012). Bitter (quoted in Patterson et al., 2012) stated that equality of opportunity affirming the holistic nature and uniqueness of individuals must provide the philosophical foundation for the practice of rehabilitation.

STRATEGIES TO COMBAT VIOLENCE

Cooperative efforts across disciplines, organizations, and individuals are essential to producing positive influences among people dealing with abuse issues in their lives. To reduce violence against people with disabilities in a meaningful way, greater collaboration among professionals is needed for three principal reasons (Sobsey, 1994). First, most abuse-related programs are developed without consideration of addressing limited accessibility and making reasonable accommodation to meet the needs of people with disabilities. Second, most helping professionals deny responsibility for providing special care unique to people with disabilities. Third, multiple-discipline support team members must incorporate a focus on violence and abuse prevention as part of their operations.

The number 1 goal when structuring abuse prevention and intervention teams is to prioritize representation by all relevant disciplines to produce effective interdisciplinary teamwork that inspires reputable working relationships and sensible communication among all team members. Due to the needs of people with disabilities, abuse prevention and intervention team members need to discuss cases with experienced consultants within the social service systems. Psychologists, social workers, counselors, and rehabilitation service providers have the primary responsibility for designing and implementing programs to help survivors of abuse overcome the negative effects of their experiences.

Rehabilitation counselors can assist other team members to work together and promote the recovery of individuals who have been abused (Glover-Graf & Reed, 2006). Rehabilitation professionals, especially rehabilitation counselors, must consider casting themselves as prominent representatives, striving to provide a better quality of life for abused individuals by providing rehabilitation services with sensitivity, caring, and cultural understanding.

Consistent with the objectives of developing rehabilitation plans "with" (not for) consumers with disabilities is the essence of respecting their autonomy. Sobsey (1994) suggested that people with disabilities should be included in meaningful ways in every aspect of violence and abuse prevention. The extent and nature of their involvement should be based on a woman's unique situation. Personnel who care for women must understand that safety is the most essential and valuable need, not only for the women at risk but also for everyone in their families. It is important that direct service providers take an active role in prevention and intervention. The most effective approach is to assemble a violence prevention support team or task force made up of disability specialists, medical experts, and other helping professionals who can share experiences and information, support each other's rights to be free of harassment if there is a report of abuse, and create a formalized violence-related support network (Thomas et al., 2008).

Rehabilitation counselors can begin to assist women with issues of abuse by acknowledging that advocacy and protection from abuse are a priority and necessity for many women with disabilities. By routinely asking about abuse and addressing issues of safety and control during rehabilitation planning, counselors can provide information, resources, and support that may help prevent abuse from occurring and assist women for whom abuse has occurred. Although information pertinent to this area is being disseminated, a network of resources within the community helpful to all parties involved in abusive relationships is needed. Referral to psychologists, social workers, professional counselors, and vocational training centers provides holistic support for consumers. Because of the vulnerability and possible dependent nature of women with disabilities, these persons rarely complain or voice anger and humiliation (Siu, 2005). Advocating for such clients who have abuse issues can be an important part of the rehabilitation counselor's job responsibilities.

The recovery process for abused women with disabilities has two vital goals: (a) establishing safety and (b) restoring control over their lives (Powers et al., 2009). Establishing safety often begins by focusing on control of the body and then moving outward toward control of the environment. Body control focuses on regulating functions consisting of eating, sleeping, and managing symptoms such as anxiety, depression, flashbacks, and states of dissociation. Rehabilitation counselors can assist women in establishing safety and control over their lives through several means. This includes fostering women with disabilities in a self-image as income-generating workers; providing them information about and assisting them in connecting with agencies and resources; supporting them as they establish those connections; empathizing with them about their frustrations, fears, and stresses during the process; and acknowledging their successes, even seemingly minor ones. As a result, efforts to aid recovery from abuse have implications for rehabilitation in the areas of health care, transportation services, attendant care, and vocational/career counseling (Schaller & Fieberg, 1998).

As providers of human services, rehabilitation counselors need to understand that although they are responsible to report suspicion of abuse, they are not responsible for proving its occurrence. Counselors' training should include attention to the principle that when in doubt, contacting domestic violence hotlines for guidance is a viable option.

INCLUSION OF STUDY OF ABUSE IN REHABILITATION EDUCATION CURRICULA

The idea of including the study of abuse in rehabilitation curricula has been echoed in multiple studies (Glover-Graf & Reed, 2006; Hassouneh-Phillips & Curry, 2002; Schaller & Fieberg, 1998). The consistent recommendation has been to include topics addressing abuse in rehabilitation curricula for both preservice and in-service training programs, with the goal of better preparing rehabilitation professionals to deal with consumers' abuse issues that often surface in crisis situations. The sound judgment of rehabilitation professionals could make a difference in the lives and well-being of abused women; discussing issues related to influencing their decision to stay, leave, or return to an abusive relationship is crucial. Such judgment may play a significant role in how post-separation battered women manage their safety while reentering mainstream society. Glover-Graf and Reed (2006) suggested that integrating the content related to the abuse of women with disabilities in rehabilitation counselor training programs is a matter of ethical practice.

Young, Nosek, Walter, and Howland (1998) suggested that to combat violence against women with disabilities, all rehabilitation service providers must (a) take responsibility to be knowledgeable about domestic violence and abuse issues, (b) cultivate a network of resources in the community for helping abuse survivors, and (c) include screening for abuse in routine intake and follow-up procedures. For preservice education, specific content areas on abuse could be added to the curriculum. Additionally, supervised practicum and internship experiences should include opportunities to work with women who have experienced abuse.

Intimate partner violence has a powerful and harmful impact on women with disabilities. Rehabilitation counselors, as primary service providers for people with disabilities, are likely to have opportunities to help these individuals. To better prepare professionals to provide appropriate rehabilitation services with sensitivity rehabilitation, educators must be involved in the design of preservice and in-service training curricula that include issues of domestic violence and disability. Counselors would benefit from additional training to be able to empower domestic violence survivors to take control and improve their quality of life.

RECOMMENDATIONS FOR REHABILITATION PROFESSIONALS

To address abuse issues during rehabilitation, rehabilitation professionals have several responsibilities to (a) learn about violence by using available training related to abuse of people with disabilities; (b) employ universal screening as a routine client-intake procedure; (c) volunteer information, resources, and referrals to clients who are in danger or at risk of an abusive situation; (d) facilitate collaboration with domestic violence shelters to supply personal care services and replace medications and assistive devices left behind in an emergency situation (Hassouneh-Phillips & Curry, 2002); (e) accumulate domestic violence resources to enhance abuse-related services for abuse survivors with disabilities (Hassouneh-Phillips et al., 2005); (f) raise awareness and offer educational activities to reduce the vulnerability of women with disabilities and increase their ability to protect themselves (Nosek, Foley, Hughes, & Howland, 2001); and (g) participate in public awareness campaigns to help inform women about strategies to get help (Juodis, Starzomski, Porter, & Woodworth, 2014).

REFERENCES

Alhabib, S., Nur, U., & Jones, R. (2010). Domestic violence against women: Systematic review of prevalence studies. *Journal of Family Violence, 25,* 369–382.

Bancroft, L. (2002). *Why does he do that? Inside the minds of angry and controlling men.* New York, NY: Berkeley.

Brodwin, M. G., & Brodwin, S. K. (2014). A case study approach, rehabilitation intervention, and the medical specialties. In M. G. Brodwin, F. W. Siu, J. Howard, & E. R. Brodwin (Eds.), *Medical, psychosocial, and vocational aspects of disability* (4th ed., pp. 1–15). Athens, GA: Elliott & Fitzpatrick.

Brodwin, M. G., & Siu, F. W. (2007). Domestic violence against women who have disabilities: What educators need to know. *Education, 127*(4), 548–551.

Centers for Disease Control and Prevention. (2014). *National Center for Injury Prevention and Control: Division of violence prevention: National data on intimate partner violence, sexual violence, and stalking.* Retrieved from https://www.cdc.gov/violenceprevention/pdf/NISVS-Fact-Sheet-2014.pdf

Chan, J. (2010). Combating violence and abuse of people with disabilities: A call to action. *Journal of Intellectual and Developmental Disabilities, 35*(1), 48–49.

Chronister, K. M., & McWhirter, E. H. (2003). Applying social cognitive career theory to the empowerment of battered women. *Journal of Counseling and Development, 81*, 418–425.

Coulter, M. (2004). *The impact of domestic violence on the employment of women on welfare* (Award Number: 1998-WT-VX-0020. Document No.: 205294). Retrieved from https://www.ncjrs.gov/pdffiles1/nij/grants/205294.pdf

Deaton, W. S., & Hetica, M. (2001). *A therapist's guide to growing free—A manual for survivors of domestic violence.* Binghamton, NY: Haworth.

Doren, B., & Benz, M. R. (1998). Employment inequality revisited: Predictors of better employment outcomes for young women with disabilities. *Journal of Special Education, 31*(4), 425–443.

Dutton, M. A., Haywood, Y., & El-Bayoumi, G. (2000). Impact of violence on women's health. In S. J. Gallant, G. P. Keita, & R. Royak-Schalder (Eds.), *Health care for women* (pp. 41–56). Washington, DC: American Psychological Association.

Glover-Graf, N., & Reed, B. J. (2006). Abuse against women with disabilities. *Rehabilitation Education, 20*(1), 43–56.

Hassouneh-Phillips, D., & Curry, M. A. (2002). Abuse of women with disabilities: State of the science. *Rehabilitation Counseling Bulletin, 45*(2), 96–104.

Hassouneh-Phillips, D., McNeff, E., Powers, L., & Curry, M. A. (2005). Invalidation: A central process underlying maltreatment of women with disabilities. *Women & Health, 41*(1), 33–50.

Hong, E. R., Neely, L., & Lund, E. M. (2015). Addressing bullying of students with autism: Suggestions for families and educators. *Interventions in School and Clinics, 50*(3), 157–162.

James, S. E., Johnson, J., & Raghavan, C. (2004). "I couldn't go anywhere"—Contextualizing violence and drug abuse: A social network study. *Violence Against Women, 10*(9), 991–1014.

Juodis, K., Starzomski, A., Porter, S., & Woodworth, M. (2014). What can be done about high-risk perpetrators of domestic violence? *Journal of Family Violence, 29*, 381–390.

Kopala, M., & Keitel, M. A. (Eds.). (2003). *Handbook of counseling women.* Thousand Oaks, CA: Sage.

McNamara, B. E. (2013). *Bullying and students with disabilities: Strategies and techniques to create a safe environment for all.* Thousand Oaks, CA: Sage.

National Center for Victims of Crime. (2017). Crime information and statistics. Retrieved from http://victimsofcrime.org/docs/default-source/ncvrw2015/2015ncvrw_stats_ipv.pdf?sfvrsn=2

National Coalition Against Domestic Violence. (2003). *2003 Domestic violence statistics—Domestic violence facts.* Retrieved from http://www.ncadv.org/files/DV_Facts.pdf

National Coalition Against Domestic Violence. (2007). *2007 Domestic violence statistics—Domestic violence facts.* Retrieved from http://www.ncadv.org/files/domesticviolencefacts.pdf

Nosek, M. A., Foley, C. C., Hughes, R. B., & Howland, C. A. (2001). Vulnerabilities for abuse among women with disabilities. *Sexuality and Disability, 19*(3), 177–189.

Nosek, M. A., Howland, C., Rintala, D. H., Young, M. E., & Chanpong, G. F. (2001). National study of women with physical disabilities: Final report. *Sexuality and Disability, 19*(1), 5–39.

Nosek, M. A., Hughes, R. B., Taylor, H. B., & Taylor, P. (2006). Disability, psychosocial, and demographic characteristics of abused women with physical disabilities. *Violence Against Women, 12*(9), 838–850.

Olweus, D. (1994). Bullying at school: Basic facts and effects of a school based intervention program. *Journal of Child Psychology and Psychiatry, and Allied Disciplines, 35*(7), 1171–1190.

Patterson, J. B., Szymanski, E. M., & Parker, R. M. (2012). Rehabilitation counseling: The profession. In R. M. Parker & J. B. Patterson (Eds.), *Rehabilitation counseling: Basics and beyond* (5th ed., pp. 1–26). Austin, TX: PRO-ED.

Peterman, L. M., & Dixon, C. G. (2001). Assessment and evaluation of men who batter women. *Journal of Rehabilitation, 67*(4), 38–42.

Powers, L. E., & Oschwald, M. (2005). *Violence and abuse against people with disabilities: Experiences, barriers, and prevention strategies.* Retrieved from http://www.disabilities.temple.edu/programs/justice/docs/bibliographyScans/Powers_Oschwald.pdf

Powers, L. E., Renker, P., Robinson-Whelen, S., Oschwald, M., Hughes, R., Swank, P., & Curry, M. A. (2009). Interpersonal violence and women with disabilities: Analysis of safety promoting behaviors. *Violence Against Women, 15*(9), 1040–1069.

Rubin, S. E., Roessler, R. T., & Rumrill, Jr., P. D. (2016). *Foundations of the vocational rehabilitation process* (7th ed.). Austin, TX: PRO-ED.

Schaller, J., & Fieberg, J. L. (1998). Issues of abuse for women with disabilities and implications for rehabilitation counseling. *Journal of Applied Rehabilitation Counseling, 29*(2), 9–17.

Siu, F. W. (2005). Rehabilitation counselors: What we should know about domestic violence. *Rehabilitation Professional, 13*(2), 43–47.

Smart, J. F., & Smart, D. W. (2012). Models of disability: Implications for the counseling profession. In I. Marini & M. A. Stebnicki (Eds.), *The psychological and social impact of illness and disability* (6th ed., pp. 61–78). New York, NY: Springer Publishing.

Sobsey, D. (1994). Abuse, neglect, violence, and disability. In D. Sobsey (Ed.), *Violence and abuse in the lives of people with disabilities: The end of silent acceptance* (pp. 13–50). Baltimore, MD: Brooks.

Thiara, R. K., Hugue, G., Bashall, R., Ellis, B., & Mullender, A. (2012). *Disabled women and domestic violence: Responding to the experiences of survivors*. London, England: Kingsley.

Thomas, K. A., Joshi, M., Wittenberg, E., & McCloskey, L. A. (2008). Intersections of harm and health: A qualitative study of intimate partner violence in women's lives. *Violence Against Women, 14*(11), 1252–1273.

U.S. Department of Health and Human Services. (2005). *Social stress factors and stigma*. In Surgeon General's workshop on women's mental health, November 30–December 1, 2005, Denver, Colorado workshop report. Retrieved from http://www.surgeongeneral.gov/topics/womensmentalhealth/mentalhlth_rpt.pdf

U.S. Department of Justice. (2015). Bureau of Justice Statistics: Criminal victimization. Retrieved from https://www.bjs.gov/content/pub/pdf/cv15.pdf

Wettersten, K. B., Rudolph, S. E., Faul, K., Gallagher, K., Trangsrud, H. B., Adams, K., . . . Terrance, C. (2004). Freedom through self-sufficiency: A qualitative examination of the impact of domestic violence on the working lives of women in shelters. *Journal of Counseling Psychology, 51*(4), 447–462.

World Health Organization. (2001). *WHO fact sheet No 239—Violence against women*. Retrieved from http://www.who.int/mediacentre/factsheets/fs239/en

Young, M. F., Nosek, M. A., Walter, L., & Howland, C. (1998). *A survey of rehabilitation service providers' perceived knowledge and confidence in dealing with abuse of women with disabilities*. Unpublished manuscript.

V

New Directions: Issues and Perspectives

*T*he final section of this text addresses several contemporary issues faced by persons with chronic illness and disabilities (CIDs) that are relevant to counselors and practice. In addition to psychosocial adjustment, multiple other variables affect adaptation and overall well-being of persons with CID. The authors in Part V discuss newer challenges that these individuals face, including obesity, poor nutrition, poverty, suicide, threat of terrorism, and depression, all of which are on the rise in the United States. They also discuss implications of the natural aging process for persons with disabilities. It is essential to understand how such variables impact the physical and mental health of individuals seeking employment, continuing education, careers, and a wellness-oriented lifestyle. At one end of the spectrum are individuals who thrive and are resilent in life, sometimes against tremendous odds, whereas at the other end are individuals who are hindered by mental and physical health problems, struggle through school, or experience chronic unemployment difficulties. No single factor accounts for such mental and physical health disparities. Rather, they are the result of complex variables that include, but are not limited to, personality characteristics and traits, cognitive functioning, social and emotional intelligence, resiliency and coping skills, internal locus of control, and critical aspects related to 'socioeconomic and cultural status. Overall, Part V provides the justification for the seventh edition of this text, expanding on current areas of interest in the fields of rehabilitation, counseling, and psychology.

MAJOR HIGHLIGHTS IN PART V

- The authors of Chapter 22 explore common conditions affecting those with CID, and discuss the growth of positive psychology and its application to this population. They ask the question, "What does it mean to live a good life?"—and even provide an answer that focuses on essential concepts of self-acceptance, purpose in life, personal growth, mastery over one's environment, and autonomy.
- The *International Classification of Functioning, Disability and Health* (ICF; WHO, 2001) encapsulates contemporary thinking on disability. In attempting to move away from the narrow pathological classifications of mental and physical disabilities found in the *Diagnostic and Statistical Manual of Mental Disorders (DSM-5*; American Psychiatric Association, 2013) and the *International Classification of Diseases and Related Health Problems (ICD-10*; World Health Organization, 2016)

the *ICF* takes a more holistic approach in considering not only the diagnosed disability but also the psychological, social, and environmental factors that may exacerbate a condition. The authors of Chapter 23 explore the *ICF* classifications, including various models of disability, future research directions, and implications. All educators and counselors should become familiar with and begin using this authoritative text, which provides a holistic approach to working with the psychosocial needs of clients with CIDs.

- Empathy fatigue is a natural artifact of serving others at the most intensive levels of counseling. A state of psychological, emotional, mental, physical, spiritual, and occupational exhaustion, it occurs as counselors' own wounds are continually revisited by their clients' life stories of chronic illness, disability, trauma, grief, and loss. Empathy fatigue is both similar to and different from other professional fatigue syndromes such as compasson fatigue and burnout. The authors of Chapter 24 provide guidelines for assessing and recognizing the associated symptoms of empathy fatigue that can decrease a counselor's ability to remain empathetic to client needs. Guidelines for self-care are offered that draw on the principles of resiliency, positive coping, and the field of positive psychology.

- Chapter 25 addresses the epidemiological significance of obesity in the United States, and various medical and physical conditions that predispose individuals to CIDs. The authors discuss the incidence of obesity and obesity-related complications such as type 2 diabetes, heart disease, and musculoskeletal problems, and explore the psychosocial and vocational implications of these conditions. They note that obesity will cost the U.S. health care system over $3 trillion by 2050 if a radical change in people's lives is not made. As individuals who are overweight and obese are often subjected to ridicule and discrimination in both their personal and professional lives, the authors explore societal attitudes and employment discrimination toward this population.

- Increasing numbers of immigrants, refugees, internally displaced persons, and asylum seekers from war-torn countries are seeking safe haven in the United States and other nations that value human life and civil liberties. This emerging population has multiple needs beyond food, shelter, and clothing. The medical and mental health challenges facing countries involved in resettlement are vast. Chapter 26 explores both problems and solutions, and offers guidelines for the counselors working with such groups. Although the research in this area is quite new, it builds on the foundation and perspectives of multicultural counseling.

- Individuals who are aging successfully with a disability comprise an emerging population and a new direction for resources and services. Many of these individuals are members of the "baby boomer" generation. These older Amercians have unique needs that extend beyond medical/physical care and financial support. Historically, older individuals have been marginalized and stigmatized by society. Thus, authors in Chapter 27 explore how to live well into one's older years despite diminished mental and physical abilities. This includes planning for retirement jobs and continuing educational opportunities. Personal assistance needs and accommodation to maintain independent living are also discussed. Chapter 27 comes full circle from the earlier chapters of this book in noting, once again, that societal and environmental barriers can sometimes be more disabling than the disability itself.

- The authors of Chapter 28 discuss the stress of military deployment and return for veterans and their families. Within a family systems framework, the authors explore family dysfunction and family coping strategies for dealing with successful reintegration of a deployed family member. The nuances of receiving notification and deployment, the attachment model, resiliency, children's reactions, family adaptation while a loved one is deployed, and reunion and reintegration are all discussed in relation to the psychological and social implications for the veteran and his or her family. Strategies for counselors in working with this population are provided.

- Chapter 29 presents the most recent research related to social justice counseling. It explores variables such as oppression, poverty, and disability, bringing to light and into focus future directions in this core area of psychosocial counseling. The author contends that promoting a just society challenges the injustice done to racial, ethnic, and other cultural minorities. Indeed, people with disabilities are among the most disenfranchised groups internationally. Thus, supporting human and civil rights is a natural part of the social justice counseling approach. Many times clients who have been consistently denied equal opportunities and who experience discrimination in employment, education, housing, and recreational and social activities, as well as other life areas, are at risk for mental and chronic medical/physical health conditions. Guidelines for increasing their awareness, knowledge, and skills offer social justice counselors increased opportunities for building optimal therapeutic relationships.

- Finally, in Chapter 30, the book's editors, Marini and Stebnicki, write a compelling and provocative reflection on the counseling profession. They summarize salient aspects of dealing with culture and disability that reflect how services are provided in an evidence-based practice environment. Each editor offers opinions and considerations for counseling professionals in the 21st century. Together, they hypothesize an inconvenient and potentially frightening future for Americans, particularly those of lower socioeconomic status, many of whom are minorities with disabilities. The ramifications of social class and classism are explored, whereby social injustice perpetuates and exacerbates classism. In particular, Marini and Stebnicki call on counselors and related helping professionals to take a more active role in advocating beyond their traditional narrowly focused job duties of working almost exclusively with the client to adapt and survive in an able-bodied world.

REFERENCES

American Psychiatric Association. (2013). *Diagnostic and statistical manual of mental disorders* (5th ed.). Arlington, VA: American Psychiatric Press.

World Health Organization. (2001). *International classification of functioning, disability, and health: ICF.* Geneva, Switzerland: Author.

World Health Organization. (2016). *International statistical classification of diseases and related health problems.* Geneva, Switzerland: Author.

22

Application of Well-Being Therapy to People With Disability and Chronic Illness*

BARRY NIERENBERG, GILLIAN MAYERSOHN, SOPHIA SERPA, ALEXIA HOLOVATYK, EVAN SMITH, AND SARAH Cooper

> *It is not external events themselves that cause us distress, but the way in which we think about them, our interpretation of their significance. It is our attitudes and reactions that give us trouble. We cannot choose our external circumstances, but we can always choose how we respond to them.*
>
> —Epictetus (CE 55–135)

*I*t is nearly 70 years since the publication of Meyerson's (1948) groundbreaking article, "Physical Disability as a Social and Psychological Problem"; the field of rehabilitation psychology can rightfully look back on a full and rich history since then. Part of this history includes some work that has not only endured but is now considered to be foundational to the field. From the start, a pattern that has characterized the field's growth is its ability to use data from current research findings to improve interventions. Over time, however, these foundational principles have slowly moved to the background of our work and are now, in some circles, ignored (Weiten, Dunn, & Hammer, 2011). A fresh examination of where we came from could, and should, be informing new approaches and new understandings of people living with chronic illness and disability (Dunn, 2014). In this chapter, we look back at the historic foundational principles of RP and show the links to current research on the psychology of well-being and explore implications for providing meaningful interventions that could improve the lives of persons with disability and chronic illness.

One place to start is Wright's classic 1983 work elucidating the 20 value-laden beliefs that continue to guide our field (Dunn, 2014). One important principle among those is the charge to constantly review and update these beliefs. It is instructive to

---

briefly examine Wright's original writing and reflect on where it can extend the effectiveness of our current work. As has been written elsewhere, the influence of Kurt Lewin's work on the 20 value-laden beliefs is evident (Dunn, 2014; Trieschmann, 1988). Let us take, for example, the second principle on the list ("The severity of a handicap can be increased or diminished by environmental conditions"; Wright, 1983, p. xi). This represents an obvious use of Lewin's (1943) construct of behavior being best understood as a product of the person–environment interaction. This principle has led to a recent reconceptualization of disability not as a characteristic of the person, but as an outcome of each person's interaction with the immediate environment (National Institute on Disability and Rehabilitation Research, 2013). To make this clear to people currently living without a disability, loss of electricity caused by extreme weather may provide a useful analogy. People living an extended period under these conditions have learned how disabling life can be without modern conveniences that are dependent on electricity (e.g., climate control, refrigeration, lights). They are effectively disabled by environmental conditions.

Wright's (1983) Principle 3 states: "Issues of coping and adjusting to a disability cannot be validly considered without examining reality problems in the social and physical environment" (p. xvii) and Principle 5 states: "The significance of a disability is affected by the person's feelings about the self and his or her situation" (p. xvii). Together, these two principles imply it is not only what happens to the individual that is important but also how the individual understands it that moderates the behaviors and feelings that arise from it. This is captured by Lewin's (1943) famous formula, $B = f(P, E)$, demonstrating the interrelationships between persons (P) and their environments (E). This formula represents the interaction that effectively determines individuals' ability to manage situations associated with their disability.

Wright's (1983) Principles 1 and 7 lead directly to *person-first thinking*, where the person is seen first and not the particular disability. Specifically, they state "1. Every individual needs respect and encouragement; the presence of a disability, no matter how severe does not alter these fundamental rights" (p. xvii) and "7. The client is seen not as an isolated individual but as a part of a larger group that includes other people, often the family" (p. xvii). When we place individuals first in our understanding, and our exploration of their living with a disability second, they take the foreground and the disability is then put in its place as being but one factor in their lives impacting their lifespace (Lewin, 1943), that is, their idiosyncratic person–environment fit. In other words, no amount of disability erases a person's assets.

Another concept expanded on in Wright's (1983) book is the concept of coping versus succumbing (p. 195). Here she highlights the significant differences between (a) the instances in which individuals demonstrate active coping by focusing on remaining strengths and viewing problems as surmountable and (b) times these same people passively succumb by focusing on losses and things they cannot change. The importance of coping and focusing on remaining strengths following an acquired disability goes back to at least Trieschmann's (1978) article articulating the role for psychologists in a spinal cord injury (SCI) unit. Here Trieschmann argued, "The clinical psychologist can play a significant role in the treatment of spinal injury as a behavioral consultant to the rehabilitation team, as a researcher into the rehabilitation process, *as an evaluator of the psychological strengths and assets of the person with spinal injury,* and as a therapist and counselor" (original boldface replaced with italics; Trieschmann, 1978, p. 217). As others have pointed out (Dunn, 2014; Dunn & Dougherty, 2005; Dunn, Uswatte, & Elliott, 2009), this focus on one's remaining personal assets lends itself to an exploration of what it takes to "live the good life with disability."

The relatively new field of positive psychology (PP) came into being as an attempt to address exactly this ancient philosophical question: "What does it mean to live the good life?" This question takes on added dimensions when we examine the implications of living with a disability and could be understood as a direct extension of RP's original principles. Recent findings from PP give us a framework to understand the various answers for those living with a disabling condition (Dunn, 2014). How do we begin to enumerate our "assets" as a person with or without a disability?

Before we go further, it is important to address a common misconception of PP. It is a misreading of this relatively new field to view PP simply as an iteration of "looking on the sunny side of the street" and "don't worry, be happy." Instead, the data from this approach suggest new perspectives can become available once we take *a more-balanced look* at current person–environment interactions. Within the PP framework, constructs, such as optimism, hope, well-being, grit, and happiness, are explored using a variety of therapeutic techniques (e.g., mindfulness, acceptance, and commitment therapy). This approach argues that a more balanced and comprehensive evaluation can lead to an increased appreciation for both the strengths remaining in each person's "new normal" circumstances and the challenges and problems that were never asked for that remain frustratingly present. In this manner, rehabilitation professionals can have a more realistic, balanced picture of the people they serve. In addition, people living with chronic illness and disability can have a more realistic picture of their present. In fact, there may be some basis for considering changing "coping versus succumbing" to "coping *and* succumbing." People both cope and succumb throughout the course of a lifetime, and the word *versus* connotes "bad adjustment" and failure to cope. Taking this more-balanced approach leads one to see that succumbing is in reality neither "bad" nor a failure.

In the body of this chapter, we review how PP approaches have been used for people with disabilities (PWD), present an overview of the development and structure of well-being therapy (WBT), including a literature review, and then demonstrate how it could be applied to people with SCI. The chapter concludes with a discussion of the broader implications for utilizing these approaches more widely in RP as well as a cautionary note.

PP APPROACHES TO PWD

A review of the existing literature on PP approaches to PWD is somewhat hampered by fragmentation due to a lack of a universally accepted definition of which interventions are considered to be included in this category. An exhaustive review of the field is beyond the scope of this chapter; however, some reports in the literature nonetheless bear consideration to examine the data supporting this approach.

One of the arguments for a PP approach to rehabilitation stated, "Positive psychology of rehabilitation should do more than just focus on treatment issues or adaptation to disability—it must capitalize on people's psychosocial strengths to maintain or enhance psychological and physical well-being and to prevent pathology" (Dunn & Dougherty, 2005, p. 307). This clearly is resonant with the fourth value-laden principle: "The assets of the person must receive considerable attention in the rehabilitation effort." One of the earliest explorations of PP in rehabilitation looked at psychological well-being (PWB) following amputation (Dunn, 1996) wherein researchers examined the beneficial effects of finding positive meaning in persons secondary to limb loss. Dunn (1996) hypothesized that finding meaning and being an optimist would be significantly predictive of lower levels of depressive symptoms and higher levels of self-esteem. Results of the study showed 77% of participants indicated something positive happened as a result of their amputation. The report concluded that given that dispositional optimism was a particularly strong predictor of both measures of PWB, rehabilitation professionals should consider helping patients to foster this sense of optimism during the rehabilitation phase. Additionally, heightened perceptions of control served to enhance individuals' beliefs in personal autonomy and mastery over their physical condition and influence their activities during rehabilitation and beyond. The article concluded that rehabilitation professionals should find ways to promote a primary sense of perceived control by pointing out aspects of individuals' behavior or environment that can be altered. One can view this study's hypothesis and results as firmly rooted in Principle 5: "The significance of a disability is affected by the person's feelings about the self and his or her situation" (Wright, 1983, p. xvii).

Optimism has been linked to improved physical functioning and fewer physical symptoms in a study of rheumatoid arthritis patients (Fournier, de Ridder, & Bensing, 2002). Additionally, optimism has been linked to better psychosocial adjustment (Brenner, Melamed, & Panush, 1994) and higher levels of PWB in a longitudinal study of rheumatoid arthritis patients (Treharne, Lyons, Booth, & Kitas, 2007). There is also evidence in the literature that PWB plays a buffering role in coping with stress and has a favorable impact on disease course: A study by Mangelli, Gribbin, Büchi, Allard, and Sensky (2002) examined pain, disease activity, disability, depression, and anxiety in outpatients at a rheumatology clinic. They found lower levels of PWB in the clinical sample compared to an able-bodied community sample, and each of the well-being scales showed significant correlations, in the predicted direction, with both depression and anxiety. They argued that well-being levels should be able to help identify individuals who are more vulnerable to depression and that these individuals should then be targeted to receive some intervention.

For people living with traumatic brain injury (TBI), a number of researchers have attempted to use PP constructs that are tied to foundational principles. A recent overview of PP approaches in brain injury (Evans, 2011, p. 118) argued one of the more significant impacts of brain injury on the individual is the decreased ability to experience the "engaged life" (Evans, 2011). Under some conditions, cognitive and/or physical impairments can reduce one's personal autonomy, relationship satisfaction, ability to work or enjoy leisure activities, and cause an overall disruption in one's sense of self and identity, thus impairing an individual's sense of well-being. Evans (2011) further pointed out that PP potentially offers a framework for conceptualizing changes in mental health (positive and negative) following brain injury. However, he stressed the fact that, to date, little research has been done in this area.

In the first recorded trial of PP interventions for individuals with acquired brain injury, researchers used two types of PP interventions: (a) a gratitude journal and (b) a "signature strengths" intervention (Andrewes, Walker, & O'Neill, 2014). For the latter, individuals identified their key strengths via Peterson and Seligman's (2004) Value in Action Inventory of Strengths and were encouraged to find a new way to use these every day for a week. Andrewes et al.'s (2014) stated goal here was for individuals to be more easily guided toward a more realistic, positive sense of identity. The authors reported that individuals who received the PP intervention scored higher on a happiness index following the intervention and at the end of the 12-week program when compared to baseline and control group scores. However, no differences were found between groups on a self-concept score. It should be noted here the authors did not link their work to the foundational principles, thereby missing an opportunity to give their study more grounding in accepted RP theory.

Another group looking at people with acquired brain injury—Bertisch, Rath, Long, Ashman, and Rashid (2014)—represents one of the first explorations of the relationships between PP constructs (character strengths, resilience, and positive mood) and rehabilitation-related variables (perceptions of functional ability postinjury and beliefs about treatment) at several time points (baseline, 6 months follow-up, and longitudinally). They found that measures of character strengths and resilience were associated with rehabilitation-related variables within the baseline set and the follow-up set as well as longitudinally. They concluded that their "preliminary findings support relationships between character strengths, resilience, and positive mood states with perceptions of functional ability and expectations of treatment, respectively, which are primary factors in treatment success and quality of life outcomes in rehabilitation medicine settings" (Bertisch et al., 2014, p. 585).

DEVELOPMENT AND STRUCTURE OF WBT

As indicated earlier, an exhaustive review of the field is beyond the scope of this chapter. However, one way to begin exploring an integration of some PP approaches is to look at well-articulated factors that have been proven to be an integral part of "living the good life." A number of researchers in this area have argued that in the English language, the word *happiness* is used correctly in numerous nonrelated situations and is too ambiguous and vague a concept to be effectively utilized, so they have argued it should be replaced by the term *well-being* (Ryff, 1989; Seligman, 2011). With more than 25 years of data behind the study of well-being, an examination of the ideas of Carol Ryff is warranted. In Ryff's (1989) article exploring the theoretical aspects of well-being, she outlined six key dimensions of well-being. These are enumerated in Table 22.1.

Along with her colleagues, Ryff developed a structured, self-report instrument to measure these dimensions, and subsequent factor analysis supported this dimensional structure (Ryff, 1989). The original instrument was initially completed by 321 men and women. The test–retest reliability coefficients for the 20-item scale over a 6-week period on a subsample of respondents ($n = 117$) were all between 0.81 and 0.85. Ryff's Psychological Well-Being Scale additionally showed good validity on the basis of analyses of overlap with other instruments and the distinctness of factors (Ryff, 1989). One of the more intriguing findings was an almost perfect inverse relationship between positive and negative affective states (Fava, Rafanelli, Cazzaro, Conti, & Grandi, 1998).

Fava and colleagues (1998) explored the relatively high depression relapse rates that are repeatedly documented in the literature (Hooley & Teasdale, 1989; Teasdale et al., 2000). Given the finding of a strong inverse relationship between positive and negative affective states, he hypothesized that the relapse rate may be a function of a

TABLE 22.1 RYFF'S WELL-BEING FACTORS

Factor	Definition
Self-Acceptance	The capacity to see and accept one's strengths and weaknesses
Purpose in Life	Having goals and objectives that give life meaning and direction
Personal Growth	Feeling that personal talents and potential are being realized over time
Positive Relations With Others	Having close, valued connections with significant others
Environmental Mastery	Being able to manage the demands of everyday life
Autonomy	Having the strength to follow personal convictions, even if they go against conventional wisdom

Source: Adapted from Ryff (1989).

deficit in well-being rather than the presence of depressive states. Using Ryff's (1989) instrument, he compared the well-being of individuals who had been treated success-fully for their depression with psychopharmacological agents and therapy to a group of individuals who did not meet criteria for pathology as defined by the *Diagnostic and Statistical Manual of Mental Disorders* (4th ed., text rev.; *DSM-IV-TR*; American Psychiatric Association, 2000). Both groups ostensibly did not qualify for a *DSM-IV-TR* diagnosis; however, he found that the group of previously depressed individuals had 40% less well-being than did their "normal" counterparts.

This led to the question of whether previously depressed individuals could improve their well-being and the extent to which this would affect their relapse rates. Utilizing cognitive behavioral techniques, researchers taught them to increase these fac-tors over eight sessions, each 30 to 50 minutes long, occurring every other week. Fava, Ruini, Rafanelli, et al. (2004) found that participants' well-being increased and depres-sion significantly decreased in the pre- and posttest design. Concerning relapse rates, he retested the original group 6 years later, hypothesizing the therapeutic effects of the intervention would persist over time (Fava, Ruini, Rafanelli, et al., 2004). His group persisted on elevated levels of well-being, even after a lengthy time, with only a 40% depression relapse rate. A similar intervention for anxiety yielded equally strong results.

In considering the application of this concept to PWD, we could use SCI as an exam-ple. We know from the literature that individuals who experience an SCI are at a greater risk of developing psychological disorders. Migliorini, Tonge, and Taleporos (2008) found that individuals with an SCI have higher prevalence rates of depression (37%), anxiety (30%), and posttraumatic stress disorder (PTSD; 8.4%) when compared to a control group. Furthermore, additional studies have found that the prevalence of depression within this population ranges between 10% and 60% (Bombardier, Richards, Krause, Tulsky, & Tate, 2004; Elliott & Frank, 1996; Kalpakjian & Albright, 2006). Pollard and Kennedy (2007) showed that these symptoms of depression appear to remain stable over an extended period of time. Importantly, the researchers found that coping strategies 12 weeks postinjury pre-dicted approximately one third of the variance in depression at year 10. Before exploring the possible application of WBT to people with SCI, an examination of WBT is in order.

WBT is a structured, directive, and problem-oriented model based on an educa-tional model. Self-observation is emphasized through the use of a structured diary and patient–therapist interactions (Emmelkamp, 1974; Fava, Ruini, Rafanelli, et al., 2004). WBT, as conceptualized by Fava, Ruini, Rafanelli, et al. (2004), is a short-term psycho-therapeutic strategy that extends over 8 to 12 sessions, each 30 to 50 minutes long, which may occur either weekly or biweekly. Although the standard format of WBT is outlined as eight sessions, the number of sessions may vary according to the patient's needs and collaboration with other therapies. For example, if the patient has already undergone a course of traditional, symptom-oriented cognitive behavioral therapy (CBT) and, therefore, is familiar with the concepts of the homework and the diary, the number of sessions needed may be decreased.

Fava and colleagues' (1998) model of WBT is based on Carol Ryff's conceptualiza-tion of PWB (Ryff, 1989). This model was selected on the basis of its easy applicability to clinical populations (i.e., residual phase of affective disorders, recurrent depression, generalized anxiety disorder) as well as its 25-year history of good reliability and valid-ity (Fava, Mangelli, & Ruini, 2001; Fava & Tomba, 2009; Rafanelli et al., 2002). Within Ryff's (1989) model of PWB, the therapist's goal is to assist the patient in moving from an impaired to an optimal level within Ryff's six dimensions of PWB. Rather than obtaining the highest possible levels in all dimensions, patients are encouraged to obtain balanced functioning (Table 22.2). Optimal-balanced well-being varies from patient to patient, according to factors such as personality traits, social rules, and cultural and social contexts (Ryff & Singer, 2008).

WBT Session Development

Initial Sessions

The beginning sessions of WBT focus on identifying episodes of well-being and putting them into a situational context, no matter how short the episodes were. Patients report episodes of well-being on a scale of 0 to 100 (with 0 being absence and 100 being the most intense well-being) in a structured diary. The initial phase usually extends over a couple of sessions; yet, its duration is dependent on factors that impact any of the homework assignments, including issues of resistance and noncompliance.

Intermediate Sessions

After patients properly recognize instances of well-being, they transition to the next phase of treatment, which involves the identification of thoughts and beliefs that lead to the premature interruption of their well-being. This phase is crucial because it allows the therapist to determine which areas of well-being are not impacted by irrational or automatic thoughts in addition to those that are saturated with them. The focus of this phase is on self-monitoring for moments and feelings of well-being. Notably, the therapist refrains from suggesting any technical or conceptual alternatives, unless patients have achieved a satisfactory degree of self-observation. This phase may extend over two or three sessions depending on the patients' motivation and ability.

Final Sessions

Monitoring the course of episodes of well-being permits the therapist to identify specific impairments across the well-being dimensions as described in Ryff's (1989) conceptual framework. At times, an additional source of information may be provided via the administration of Ryff's (1989) Psychological Well-Being Scale self-rating inventory. The six dimensions of PWB are introduced to the patients progressively, as long as the material in the patient's diary lends itself to it. For example, if a patient discloses struggles with independence, the therapist could explain that autonomy consists of having an internal locus of control, independence, and self-determination or that personal growth consists of being open to new experiences and considering the self as expanding over time. The therapist then engages in cognitive therapy techniques by discussing cognitive distortions and introducing alternative interpretations to the patient's thinking errors.

The factor that differentiates WBT from other standard cognitive therapies is that the primary focus of WBT is on instances of emotional well-being rather than psychological distress. In addition, the goal in WBT is the promotion of PWB as defined by Ryff (1989), as opposed to the goal of standard cognitive therapy, which is on the reduction of psychological distress through one's ability to control and/or contrast automatic thoughts. WBT is conceptualized as a specific strategy within the broad continuum of self-therapies because it shares similar techniques to other cognitive modalities (Fava, 2000). Finally, WBT "refrains from explaining from the onset to the patient its rationale and strategies, but relies on his/her progressive appraisals of positive self" (Fava & Ruini, 2003, p. 54). For example, it may help the individual who struggles with anxiety to view anxiety as an unavoidable element of everyday life, which can be "counteracted by a progressive increase in environmental mastery and self-acceptance" (Fava & Ruini, 2003, p. 54).

The current iteration of WBT is firmly rooted in a CBT approach (Fava, Ruini, & Rafanelli, 2004). Other foundations could logically be applied if assumptions inherent in utilizing this cognitive focus are not met. For example, in the case of people with

TABLE 22.2 MODIFICATIONS OF PSYCHOLOGICAL WELL-BEING FOLLOWING WELL-BEING THERAPY OR OTHER POSITIVE INTERVENTIONS

Ryff Psychological Well-Being Factors	Low Level	Balanced-Functional Level	Excess Level
Environmental Mastery	Has difficulties managing everyday affairs. Feels unable to change or improve surrounding context. Is unaware of surrounding opportunities. Lacks sense of control over external world.	Has a sense of mastery and competence in managing the environment. Controls complex array of external activities. Makes effective use of surrounding opportunities. Is able to create or choose contexts suitable to personal needs and values.	Is unable to savor positive emotions and hedonic pleasure. Is unable to relax.
Autonomy	Is concerned about the expectations and evaluations of others. Relies on judgments of others to make important decisions. Conforms to social pressures to think and act in certain ways.	Is self-determining and independent. Is able to resist social pressures to think and act in certain ways. Regulates behavior from within. Evaluates self by personal standards.	Is unable to get along with other people, to work in a team, and to learn from others. Spends time and energy fighting for opinions and rights. Relies only on self to solve problems. Is unable to ask for advice or help.
Self-Acceptance	Feels dissatisfied with self. Is disappointed with what has occurred in past life. Is troubled about certain personal qualities. Wishes to be different from what he or she is.	Possesses a positive attitude toward the self. Acknowledges and accepts multiple aspects of self, including good and bad qualities. Feels positive about past life.	Has narcissistic and egocentric traits. Has difficulty admitting own mistakes and rigidity.
Purpose in Life	Lacks a sense of meaning in life. Has few goals or aims. Lacks sense of direction. Does not see purpose in past life. Has no outlooks or beliefs that give life meaning.	Has goals in life and a sense of directedness. Feels there is a meaning to the present and past life. Holds beliefs that give life purpose. Has aims and objectives for living.	Has obsessional passions. Is unable to admit failures. Manifests persistence and rigidity. Is unable to change perspective and goals. Finds excessive hope paralyzing and hampers facing negativity and failures.

(*continued*)

TABLE 22.2 MODIFICATIONS OF PSYCHOLOGICAL WELL-BEING FOLLOWING WELL-BEING THERAPY OR OTHER POSITIVE INTERVENTIONS   (*continued*)

Ryff Psychological Well-Being Factors	Low Level	Balanced-Functional Level	Excess Level
Positive Relations With Others	Has few close, trusting relationships with others.	Has warm, satisfying, and trusting relationships with others.	Feels pain and distress of others due to exaggerated empathy.
	Finds it difficult to be warm, open, and concerned about others.	Is concerned about the welfare of others.	Sacrifices own needs and well-being for others due to exaggerated altruism.
	Is isolated and frustrated in interpersonal relationships.	Is capable of strong empathy, affection, and intimacy.	May mask low self-esteem and sense of worth through extreme forgiveness and gratefulness.
	Is not willing to make compromises to sustain important ties with others.	Understands give and take of human relationships.	
Personal Growth	Has a sense of personal stagnation.	Has a feeling of continued development.	Is unable to process negativity.
	Lacks a sense of improvement or expansion over time.	Sees self as growing and expanding.	Forgets or does not give enough emphasis to past negative experiences.
	Feels bored and uninterested with life.	Is open to new experiences.	Cultivates benign illusions that do not fit with reality.
	Feels unable to develop new attitudes or behaviors.	Has a sense of realizing his or her potential.	Sets unrealistic standards for overcoming adversities.
		Sees improvement in self and behavior over time.	
		Is changing in ways that reflect more self-knowledge and effectiveness.	

Adapted from Ruini and Fava (2012) and Ryff (1989).

SCI, the nature of their difficulties may not lie in "dysfunctional core beliefs," but may alternatively lie in assumptions inherent in their perception of living with their "new normal" postinjury status. Here it would be possible to use an acceptance and commitment therapy (ACT) approach connecting Ryff's (1989) factors to related values that each person's behaviors are supporting or blocking.

Hayes (2004) defines *ACT* as

A functional contextual therapy approach based on Relational Frame Theory which views human psychological problems dominantly as problems of psychological inflexibility fostered by cognitive fusion and experiential avoidance. In the context of a therapeutic relationship, ACT brings direct contingencies and indirect verbal processes to bear on the experiential establishment of greater psychological flexibility primarily through acceptance, defusion, establishment of a transcendent sense of self, contact with the present moment, values, and building larger and larger patterns of committed action linked to those values. (as cited in Bach & Moran, 2008, p. 6)

Developed by Hayes, Levin, Plumb-Vilardaga, Villatte, and Pistorello (2013), ACT is built on empirically based principles utilizing mindfulness and behaviorally based principles to undermine unhelpful language processes and increase psychological flexibility. Within the framework of ACT, the following assumptions are made: (a) Pain in life is inevitable and (b) feelings of joy and sadness are two sides of the same coin (Hayes et al., 2013). In keeping with the examination of what it means to live the good life, Russ Harris stated, "The aim of ACT is to create a rich, full, meaningful life while accepting the pain that inevitably goes with it" (Harris, 2009, p. 2). Although ACT is similar to CBT because it also developed from behaviorism (Hayes et al., 2013), it posits that neither the thought nor the emotional responses can be either controlled or made to go away and, therefore, places emphasis on the person's attempts to control the emotional consequences of the thought rather than attempts to control the thought itself, as in CBT. Ultimately, ACT seeks to generate psychological flexibility via behavioral activation on the basis of an individual's values.

LITERATURE REVIEW OF WELL-BEING THERAPY

Although gradually increasing, the body of empirical literature examining the use of WBT for all populations is limited. Likewise, the literature related to the efficacy of WBT for rehabilitation populations, such as SCI, is even scarcer. However, given that the literature has demonstrated WBT is associated with positive effects for depression, affective disorders, anxiety, and psychosomatic medicine, a review of the existing literature on efficacy is warranted. Studies utilizing WBT were identified through four major database searches: PubMed, PsycINFO, ERIC, and Social Science Citation Index, as well as Google Scholar (http://scholar.google.com). Keywords included throughout the search were as follows: *WBT, PWB, Ryff's PWB,* and *WBT.* Compiled manuscripts were reviewed to determine whether they used Ryff's definition of PWB and/or explicitly used Ryff's Psychological Well-Being Scale as an outcome measure. Because there are several definitions of well-being within the field of PP, we chose the aforementioned criteria in order to maintain consistency across the studies reviewed. PWB as defined by Carol Ryff was chosen due to the comprehensive nature of the foundations that formed the basis of her established and well-validated measure. For the purposes of this review, any study, including dissertations, for which the full text was available was included. A total of 11 met the criteria for inclusion.

Fava and colleagues (2005) used WBT to increase the length of remission in individuals with generalized anxiety disorder. Participants received either eight sessions of standard CBT or the sequential administration of four sessions of CBT followed by four sessions of WBT (CBT–WBT). The two groups were compared posttreatment, and results revealed a significant advantage for the CBT–WBT intervention. Additionally, a significantly higher degree of improvement across all of the PWB scales was evidenced among the CBT–WBT participants. Fava et al. (2005) hypothesized that changes in well-being may impact the balance of positive and negative affect that characterizes anxiety disorders, thus leading to an increased level of well-being. The data from this study are in "keeping with the complexity of the balance of positive and negative effects in health and disease, the emerging models of positive mental health, and the clinical needs of sustained recovery in patients with mood and anxiety disorders" (Fava et al., 2005, p. 30).

Moeenizadeh and Salagame (2010) randomly assigned patients diagnosed with depression to either CBT or WBT in an effort to evaluate treatment efficacy related to improvement in well-being and reduction of depressive symptoms among these patients. Although pre- and posttreatment comparisons demonstrated that both patients treated with CBT and those treated with WBT endorsed significant symptom reduction, results indicated those in the WBT condition experienced greater relief of depressive symptomatology. The authors concluded WBT effectively decreased the cognitive–affective and somatic–vegetative factors. Furthermore, those who completed the WBT intervention demonstrated a significant increase in PWB compared to the CBT group, and this improvement in PWB was inversely related to the experience of depressive symptomatology. The authors suggested that treating depressive symptoms of well-being with WBT could be more effective than CBT, because all patients who took part in eight sessions of WBT group improved their close relationships, optimism, happiness, innocence, success, and socialization with others when compared to the CBT group.

A substantial body of evidence has indicated the influences of well-being on vulnerability to disease (Mangelli et al., 2002; Ryff & Singer, 1998) and quality of life (Fava & Sonino, 2000; Ryff & Singer, 2000). Increased well-being may buffer or prevent possible feelings of demoralization and loss that can be present in individuals with chronic diseases. As a result, increased well-being may improve individual coping abilities and offer more balance to times of succumbing.

WBT may yield clinical benefits/improvements in quality of life, coping style, and social support for individuals with chronic and life-threatening illnesses (Emmelkamp & van Oppen, 1993). In addition, there is evidence that well-being can act as a mitigating factor in coping with stress and has a positive impact on disease course (Fava, 1992, 1996; Ryff & Singer, 1998); it also has some positive effects on the immunological and endocrine systems (Fava & Sonino, 2000). Further clinical examples in the literature include anxiety and hope in the course of medical disorders (Heszen-Niejodek, Gottschalk, & Januszek, 1999), the relationship between life satisfaction and cardiac variables (Majani et al., 1999), and the role of optimism and coping style in transplantation outcomes (Stilley, Miller, Manzetti, Marino, & Keenan, 1999).

Mangelli and colleagues (2002) further investigated the findings mentioned in the studies previously, along with the evidence that cognitive therapy for individuals with rheumatoid arthritis led to positive changes (Sharpe et al., 2001). They studied pain, disease activity, disability, depression, and anxiety among outpatients at a rheumatology clinic. Results indicated lower levels of well-being within the participants compared to those individuals in the community sample from the study performed by Ryff, Lee, Essex, and Schmutte in 1994. This discrepancy appeared across all of the six dimensions; however, it was most prominent within the domains of personal growth and purpose in life. Also, there were significant inverse bivariate correlations between depression or anxiety and each of the PWB subscale scores. Notably, these correlations were stronger for depression than anxiety. Environmental mastery and self-acceptance evidenced the strongest negative correlations with depression. Reduced level of autonomy was associated with anxiety, whereas low levels of positive relations with others was associated with depression (Mangelli et al., 2002). Findings from this study (Mangelli et al., 2002) need to be replicated because they have valuable implications for treatment of not only rheumatoid arthritis but also other chronic illnesses.

Another study examining well-being in individuals with a chronic medical condition was conducted by Cosci, Pennato, Bernini, and Berrocal (2011). The authors investigated whether well-being predicted negative affect in patients with fibromyalgia. Participants included 48 females with fibromyalgia and 48 matched-age controls. Results indicated the participants living with fibromyalgia had significantly higher scores on depression, functional impairment, and pain than did controls. Purpose in life and positive relationships were found to be significant predictors of functional impairment among fibromyalgia patients. The authors concluded from their data that having higher levels of purpose in life and positive relationships prevent diminished daily functioning, which in turn prevents depression. Moreover, having an optimal level of self-acceptance prevents anxiety, thereby protecting the individual from depression.

The biopsychosocial model of fibromyalgia suggests stress has a possible etiology in the disorder and that stress-related factors, such as anxiety, can perpetuate symptoms and disability (Van Houdenhove & Egle, 2004). The results of this study suggested that certain dimensions of well-being might protect individuals living with fibromyalgia from the effects of the adversity on ill-being. Cosci et al. (2011) suggested that WBT might be useful for individuals with fibromyalgia, given that the intervention works on strengthening the dimensions of well-being. The aforementioned could diminish anxiety levels, enhance daily functioning, and, ultimately, prevent depression.

We argue that given these reports, the use of WBT within populations of individuals living with chronic illnesses and/or disability should be effective and could lead to positive treatment outcomes.

THE CASE FOR CLINICAL APPLICATION OF WBT: PEOPLE WITH SCI

Individuals with a SCI who experience depression are likely to experience longer hospitalizations, increased pain, decreased functional improvement, higher rates of pressure ulcers, and higher financial expenditures, as well as decreased self-efficacy and diminished quality of life (Elliott & Frank, 1996; Fann et al., 2011; Middleton et al., 2007). Depression among this population can be considered a comorbid complication as opposed to an adaptive process in adjustment (Elliott & Kennedy, 2004). Living with depression can severely impact a person's quality of life, mobility, and family functioning (Elliott & Frank, 1996). Active self-care can significantly reduce the occurrence of pressure ulcers, skin injuries, and urinary tract infections; however, sustaining a self-care regimen if one is suffering from depression is more difficult.

Applying WBT to this population can lead to an alternative way of understanding why some individuals mainly succumb to their acquired disabilities, whereas others are more able to balance this by also coping effectively at times. Ryff and Singer (1996) suggested that under some circumstances, it is actually *the absence of well-being* that leads to individuals' being vulnerable to potential future hardships. If true, they argued, then the route to more positive and enduring adaptation lies not entirely on eliminating the negative but instead on building the positive. From another standpoint, this can be understood as a logical extension of the foundational RP principles of (a) no amount of physical disability erases a person's assets and (b) individuals able to cope tend to balance a focus on their old and newly found strengths, whereas those who mostly succumb tend to mainly be aware of their losses (Trieschmann, 1988).

Just such an approach focused on understanding positive coping is demonstrated by the work of Hammell (2004), who examined quality of life among people with SCI and enumerated factors that significantly contribute to quality of life. Emergent themes found within Hammell's interviews were as follows: autonomy, meaningful use of time, "doing and being" (p. 610), relationships, belonging, support and reciprocity, refocusing values, the need to have something to wake up for, ability to explore new opportunities, and the need to envision future time engaged in meaningful activities. It is interesting that without referencing Ryff's work, on examination, one can see Hammell's themes are quite similar to and significantly reflect Ryff's six factors (Table 22.3).

The RP literature reveals added support for applying Ryff's PWB formulation to SCI. As can be seen in Table 22.3, each of her factors has been found to apply to persons with

TABLE 22.3 RYFF'S SUBJECTIVE WELL-BEING FACTORS AND CORRESPONDING SUPPORT IN SPINAL CORD INJURY (SCI) LITERATURE

Ryff's Well-Being Factors	Related Factors in Persons With SCI
Environmental Mastery	*Physical environment*: Challenges with physical access, urban infrastructure, and the availability and accessibility of transportation. *Economic environment:* Cost of health care for individuals with SCI. *Political/legal environment:* Difficulties surrounding accessibility to resources such as medical assistance, transportation, and insurance. *Social environment:* Negative impact on those with SCI and the associated stigma, fewer social connections (Hammell, 2007).
Autonomy	Autonomy has been linked to the opportunity to live in the community, to direct one's own personal care, to make decisions, and to act on choices. Factors that can influence one's autonomy are the ability to have a job or continue engaging in daily functions such as driving and also the level and type of injury. This research suggests that autonomy is linked with a higher quality of life and is a key factor of assessment and goal of treatment for individuals with SCI. Similar to self-efficacy. Scivoletto, Petrelli, Di Lucente, and Castellano (1997) examined factors linked with anxiety and depression in individuals with SCI and found that rates were significantly associated with a lack of autonomy. Hammell (2004) identified autonomy as being essential for attaining quality in living.
Self-Acceptance	Problems associated with the self and the perception of a "disabled" body can have a significant impact on the lives of many people with SCI (Hammell, 2007). Redefining disability and changing their own subjective experience of disability has led participants to a gradual rediscovery of self and provided them with an avenue by which a personal interpretation of disability could be made, not in terms of inadequacy or limitations but in terms of personal potential and self-confidence (Carpenter, 1994). Emotional adjustment, particularly self-perception and self-acceptance, is considered one of the more crucial indicators of achievement of rehabilitation goals (Ben-Sira, 1981; Cohen & Lazarus, 1983; Oliver, Zarb, Silver, & Salisbury, 1988; Trieschmann, 1988; Zola, 1982).
Purpose in Life	Research findings indicate that purpose in life is a powerful predictor of adjustment after SCI, mediating the effects of personality variables and locus of control (Dunn, 1994; Thompson, Coker, Krause, & Henry, 2003). To demonstrate the link between purpose in life and psychological well-being, Crewe (1997) examined narratives of people's lives with long-term SCI and found that individuals who identified a purpose in life and found meaning from their injury adapted well compared to those who did not report a purpose in life.
Positive Relations With Others	Previous research has found that traumatic spinal cord injury can lead to disrupted social relationships (Kleiber, Brock, Lee, Dattilo, & Caldwell, 1995). The research supports the significance of the need for warm, trusting, understanding social relationships that correlate with overall psychological well-being. Factors and priorities differ from those of the general population (i.e., accomplishments such as achieving sitting balance and wheelchair-to-toilet transfers) and contribute to a sense of separation from the "real world," which alienates them from their personal life and social context (Cogswell, 1983).
Personal Growth	Hammell (2007), who examined factors of quality of life and adjustment to SCI, found that those who adjusted well to SCI perceived their growth process as a continuity of their personal life biography, focusing on capability and competence rather than inadequacy and limitation. These individuals viewed themselves as able, not disabled, acknowledging that they are the same person preinjury but just have more challenges, such as difficulty getting around and different body functioning. Leisure activities such as good acts (e.g., volunteering) or good habits (e.g., regular exercise) can contribute to posttraumatic growth by providing opportunities to discover unique abilities and hidden potential, build companionship and meaningful relationships, make sense of traumatic experience and finding meaning in everyday life, and generate positive emotions. This is also consistent with Crewe's (1997) findings.

Source: Ryff (1989).

SCI well-being, lending further credence to utilizing this construct. By assessing each individual according to Ryff's Psychological Well-Being Scale, greater clarity could be gained regarding in which domain individuals may benefit from an increase in well-being.

It is an empirical question whether achieving an optimal level of well-being as defined by Ryff will help individuals with SCI live a purposeful, engaged, independent, and meaningful life. However, using a well-being framework is consistent with previous research findings on positive adaptation following SCI. By assessing an individual on Ryff's six factors, one could identify areas in need of improvement. Then it would be possible to intervene in each of these identified areas by using Fava's CBT approach to increasing well-being, moving individuals toward a more-balanced, functional level. This would effectively replace traditional clinical psychology's psychopathology paradigm focusing solely on alleviating negative affective states.

> Less attention has been devoted to the understanding of individuals who adapt successfully to SCI and the factors that facilitate successful adaptation. . . . It is important to understand how individuals successfully adapt as it could provide the basis for developing interventions for bolstering or establishing skills, attitudes, or beliefs that facilitate positive outcomes after the onset of disability. (Kortte, Gilbert, Gorman, & Wegener, 2010, p. 40)

Contemporary approaches within the field of RP are refocusing on the foundational principles that recognize that no amount of physical disability erases one's assets as a person and that disability is a product of the person–environment interactions. This is diametrically opposed to viewing the patient as "victims of cruel fate, objects of prejudice or pity, or simply health-preoccupied, passive recipients of medical care" (Dunn et al., 2009, p. 652). Rather than concentrating on the loss a person has experienced, the trend is to sharpen the focus on the positive aspects of a person's life. Similarly, well-being places attention on the positive aspects of the self and, therefore, gives people with SCI autonomy and power over their recovery process.

One of the many goals of a rehabilitation psychologist is to help individuals with a disability attain the highest possible level of well-being. By utilizing PP interventions such as a model of WBT, it may be possible to effectively increase well-being and decrease instances of depression and other psychological disorders such as anxiety or PTSD among individuals with a chronic illness or disability. Finally, it is expected that individuals who are able to achieve optimal well-being across the six dimensions identified by Ryff (1989) may expend more effort in the rehabilitation process, which could in turn decrease future hospitalizations, decrease instances of depression and other psychological disorders, and improve coping and adjustment to the disability. Individuals with increased well-being may make more functional improvements after rehabilitation, have decreased hospitalizations, and have decreased secondary complications. This, of course, is an empirical question that begs to be answered with data, given the current search for ways to prevent disease and increase health.

The overarching goal of using WBT is not only to lower instances of psychopathology in people with chronic illness or disability but also to improve their quality of life, increase well-being, and decrease future rehospitalizations. As mentioned previously, adjusting to living with a disability can be challenging. As Trieschmann (1988) stated in discussing the personal dimension of living with an SCI, "people with SCI are a fairly heterogeneous group but they have one thing in common: the disability penalizes them and reduces their freedoms" (pp. 4–5). It seems possible that by engendering the positive aspects of one's life and focusing on the different areas of well-being, we could assist PWD to increase their well-being and possibly prevent the development or relapse of a psychological condition such as depression, PTSD, or anxiety. The use of this intervention could, and we argue should, be expanded to other rehabilitation diagnoses such as limb loss, orthopedic conditions, mild brain injuries, and chronic illnesses.

The efficacy of this approach in other diagnoses needs further study; however, data in our current literature do suggest that WBT could lead to a significant improvement in quality of life and well-being in a rehabilitation population.

Utilizing PP approaches such as WBT may prove to be an effective intervention to help improve quality of life and increase well-being, coping, and adjustment to disability. There are unanswered questions that need to be addressed such as optimal timing for implementation of an intervention to be maximally effective. Should WBT be used as a sequential treatment to evidence-based interventions to address psychopathology such as CBT, as a stand-alone treatment, or in combination with other psychotherapeutic approaches? Additionally, it is essential to identify during which phase of recovery and adjustment this intervention would be most appropriate: inpatient acute, postacute, or postdischarge? More specifically, the question remains as to whether these interventions should be used as a prevention method, as an intervention in the active phase of psychological disorders, or as a relapse-prevention treatment.

For example, do groups receiving WBT shortly after injury experience lesser rates of depression than do those who do not? One can infer from the current literature that individually, for example, people living with SCI tend to do well. However, as a cohort, this population psychologically fares worse than do their counterparts living without an SCI. If this group does prove to benefit significantly with WBT, this intervention could be implemented as part of routine care for acute patients with SCI to circumvent a host of negative consequences associated with depression. In speaking with board members of an SCI support group in Miami, Florida, all of whom are living with SCI, they agreed this form of prophylactic intervention may be most useful in the immediate outpatient phase of treatment, when patients must return home to deal with the hassles of everyday life without the support of their inpatient care team. This transition phase, from full-time support from a medical care team to caring for oneself at home, can be lonely and emotionally traumatic for patients with a new SCI. In sum, this vulnerable period wherein patients have time to process their experience without the social support network that is built into an inpatient setting may be the most optimal time to implement a well-being intervention. Again, research must be done to corroborate this hypothesis. It remains an empirical question as to the optimal timing for WBT. Is there a critical time period for WBT effectiveness? Can it be useful for people years after their injury? Does it serve a protective function in individuals not experiencing a deficit in their well-being levels?

In addition, data are necessary to address the issue of potential efficacy (or lack thereof) for individuals not showing an impairment in their well-being levels. Further studies could help clarify the optimal period to implement this type of intervention. Moreover, further studies are required to assess the efficacy of these approaches in combination with an antidepressant or anxiolytic medication.

PP is not a one-size-fits-all solution for increasing well-being and quality of life, and therefore, the use of customized treatment is encouraged (e.g., taking into account the areas of well-being that are below optimal level to the specific individual). This leads to another empirical question, namely: Are differing variants of WBT necessary for different conditions? In what ways, if any, should WBT for people with amputations differ from WBT for individuals living with TBI? Examining the six dimensions as described by Ryff's model of PWB within people with chronic conditions could lead to a more individualized treatment and, potentially, to a more efficacious treatment.

To use one example, the financial costs associated with living with SCI are high. Without taking into account the wage loss, fringe benefits, and productivity after having an SCI, the annual estimated costs are $730,000 for individuals with paraplegia who were 25 years old at the age of injury and are as high as $2.185 million for individuals with tetraplegia who were 25 years old at the age of injury (National Spinal Cord Injury Statistical Center [NSCISC], 2013). In addition, individuals with an SCI have decreased employment rates. One year postinjury, only 12% of people with SCI are employed, and 20 years postinjury only approximately 33% of individuals are employed (NSCISC, 2013). All of these factors can significantly contribute to decreased well-being and higher incidents of psychopathology such as depression and anxiety. It is an empirical question as to what degree, if any, these adverse outcomes could be affected by a WBT intervention. Research data investigating psychological contributions to preventing or mitigating both financial and emotional costs associated with preventable complications would be both timely and welcome additions to current health care debates. If the data warrant inclusion, PP interventions, such as WBT, could become a standard aspect of medical care instead of an elective add-on.

Ryff and Singer (1996) posited that the treatment of psychopathology that focuses exclusively on the alleviation of negative symptoms leaves people vulnerable to future relapses. However, focusing on bolstering one's positive attributes may serve to create a buffer against future adversities. In a preventative model, building a "wall" of positive psychological defenses has the potential to prepare individuals to weather the emotional pitfalls of coping with the substantial life change that accompanies a physical disability or chronic illness. Reconnecting people with the values and goals that are most dear to them (regardless of physical disability), giving people the means to shore up their cognitive skill set to achieve those goals, teaching self-compassion, and creating a feeling of connectedness with others are a few examples of the building blocks that PP uses to build positive psychological defenses.

One should not assume that the alleviation of negative symptoms in itself will result in an increase in well-being. In fact, facilitating the growth of positive factors may work through an entirely separate mechanism (Ryff & Singer, 2006). In the same vein, it should not be assumed that the bolstering of positive affect will remove negative affect throughout the active phase of an illness. At present, there is no evidence to suggest that interventions such as WBT can effectively be used independently from standard treatments such as CBT or pharmacotherapy; therefore, more research must be conducted before WBT is used independently or even in conjunction with standard care during the active phase of an illness.

A CAVEAT

Dunn an colleagues (2009) issued the following caveat, however: "Resiliency and growth should be encouraged, not required" (p. 658). A PP approach, they argued, must not be forced on people living with chronic illness or disability, because there is no correct way to respond. The authors pointed out that among some well-intentioned researchers and therapists, there still exists a sizable cohort who believe people with acquired physical disabilities need to "properly mourn their loss of function" and that any failure to properly grieve for loss of a premorbid self is seen as psychological denial or another defensive reaction. However, as Trieschmann (1988, p. 69) pointed out, this "requirement of mourning" is rooted in the assumption that a display of depression is necessary for "healthy adjustment," and it endures despite data showing quite the opposite. It is important to keep in mind that individuals cope in their own way, which is generally syntonic with how they have dealt with adversity previously, on the basis of their individual differences.

CONCLUSIONS

There is power in revisiting the underlying foundational principles of our past and looking at how they can inform our present and future functioning. Clearly, the basic ideas put forth by Lewin, Meyerson, Wright, and Treischmann that underlie our field lead logically to the examination of some approaches within the realm of PP and especially the data-based approaches of researchers such as Carole Ryff and Giovanni Fava. Once examined, ideas like WBT come to the foreground, and data need to be collected on whether this logical extension of some of our foundational principles can be effective in assisting those people living with chronic illness and disability.

REFERENCES

American Psychiatric Association. (2000). *Diagnostic and statistical manual of mental disorders* (4th ed., text rev.). Washington, DC: Author.

Andrewes, H. E., Walker, V., & O'Neill, B. (2014). Exploring the use of positive psychology interventions in brain injury survivors with challenging behaviour. *Brain Injury, 28*, 965–971. doi: 10.3109/02699052.2014.888764

Bach, P. A., & Moran, D. J. (2008). *ACT in practice: Case conceptualization in acceptance and commitment therapy.* Oakland, CA: New Harbinger.

Ben-Sira, Z. (1981). The structure of readjustment of the disabled: An additional perspective on rehabilitation. *Social Science & Medicine. Part A, Medical Sociology, 15*(5), 565–580.

Bertisch, H., Rath, J., Long, C., Ashman, T., & Rashid, T. (2014). Positive psychology in rehabilitation medicine: A brief report. *NeuroRehabilitation, 34*(3), 573–585.

Bombardier, C. H., Richards, J. S., Krause, J. S., Tulsky, D., & Tate, D. G. (2004). Symptoms of major depression in people with spinal cord injury: Implications for screening. *Archives of Physical Medicine and Rehabilitation, 85*, 1749–1756. doi:10.1016/j.apmr.2004.07.348

Brenner, G. F., Melamed, B. G., & Panush, R. S. (1994). Optimism and coping as determinants of psychosocial adjustment to rheumatoid arthritis. *Journal of Clinical Psychology in Medical Settings, 1*, 115–134. doi:10.1007/BF01999741

Carpenter, C. (1994). The experience of spinal cord injury: The individual's perspective–implications for rehabilitation practice. *Physical Therapy, 74*(7), 614–628; discussion 628.

Cogswell, B. (1983). Readjustment of paraplegics in the community. In L. W. Mechanic (Ed.), *Handbook of health care and the health professions* (pp. 156–163). New York, NY: Free Press.

Cohen, F., & Lazarus, R. (1983). Coping and adaptation in health and illness. In L. W. Mechanic (Ed.), *Handbook of health care and the health professions* (pp. 608–635). New York, NY: Free Press.

Cosci, F., Pennato, T., Bernini, O., & Berrocal, C. (2011). Psychological well-being, negative affectivity, and functional impairment in fibromyalgia. *Psychotherapy and Psychosomatics, 80*, 256–258. doi:10.1159/000322031

Crewe, N. (1997). Life stories of people with long-term spinal cord injury. *Rehabilitation Counseling Bulletin, 41*, 26–42.

Dunn, D. S. (1994). Positive meaning and illusions following disability: Reality negotiation, normative interpretation, and value change. *Journal of Social Behavior and Personality, 9*, 123–138.

Dunn, D. S. (1996). Well-being following amputation: Salutary effects of positive meaning, optimism and control. *Rehabilitation Psychology, 41*, 285–302. doi:10.1037/0090-5550.41.4.285

Dunn, D. S. (2014). *The social psychology of disability.* New York, NY: Oxford University Press.

Dunn, D. S., & Dougherty, S. B. (2005). Prospects for a positive psychology of rehabilitation. *Rehabilitation Psychology, 50*, 305–311.

Dunn, D. S., Uswatte, G., & Elliott, T. R. (2009). Happiness, resilience, and positive growth following physical disability: Issues for understanding, research, and therapeutic intervention. In S. J. Lopez & C. R. Snyder (Eds.), *Oxford handbook of positive psychology* (2nd ed., pp. 651–664). New York, NY: Oxford University Press.

Elliott, T. R., & Frank, R. G. (1996). Depression following spinal cord injury. *Archives of Physical Medicine and Rehabilitation, 77*, 816–823. doi:10.1016/S0003-9993(96)90263-4

Elliott, T. R., & Kennedy, P. (2004). Treatment of depression following spinal cord injury: An evidence-based review. *Rehabilitation Psychology, 49,* 134–139.

Emmelkamp, P. M. G. (1974). Self-observation versus flooding in the treatment of agoraphobia. *Behaviour Research and Therapy, 12,* 229–237. doi:10.1016/0005-7967(74)90119-3

Emmelkamp, P. M. G., & van Oppen, P. (1993). Cognitive interventions in behavioral medicine. *Psychotherapy and Psychosomatics, 59*(3–4), 116–130.

Evans, J. J. (2011). Positive psychology and brain injury rehabilitation. *Brain Impairment, 12,* 117–127. doi:10.1375/brim.12.2.117

Fann, J. R., Bombardier, C. H., Richards, J. S., Tate, D. G., Wilson, C. S., & Temkin, N.; PRISMS Investigators. (2011). Depression after spinal cord injury: Comorbidities, mental health service use, and adequacy of treatment. *Archives of Physical Medicine and Rehabilitation, 92*(3), 352–360.

Fava, G. A. (1992). The concept of psychosomatic disorder. *Psychotherapy and Psychosomatics, 58,* 1–12. doi:10.1159/000288605

Fava, G. A. (1996). The concept of recovery in affective disorders. *Psychotherapy and Psychosomatics, 65,* 2–13. doi:10.1159/000289025

Fava, G. A. (2000). Cognitive behavioral therapy. In M. Fink (Ed.), *Encyclopedia of stress* (pp. 484–497). San Diego, CA: Academic Press.

Fava, G. A., Mangelli, L., & Ruini, C. (2001). Assessment of psychological distress in the setting of medical disease. *Psychotherapy and Psychosomatics, 70,* 171–175. doi:10.1159/000056249

Fava, G. A., Rafanelli, C., Cazzaro, M., Conti, S., & Grandi, S. (1998). Well-being therapy: A novel psychotherapeutic approach for residual symptoms of affective disorders. *Psychological Medicine, 28,* 475–480. doi:10.1017/S0033291797006363

Fava, G. A., & Ruini, C. (2003). Development and characteristics of a well-being enhancing psychotherapeutic strategy: Well-being therapy. *Journal of Behavior Therapy and Experimental Psychiatry, 34,* 45–63. doi:10.1016/S0005-7916(03)00019-3

Fava, G. A., Ruini, C., & Rafanelli, C. (2004). Psychometric theory is an obstacle to the progress of clinical research. *Psychotherapy and Psychosomatics, 73,* 145–148. doi:10.1159/000076451

Fava, G. A., Ruini, C., Rafanelli, C., Finos, L., Conti, S., & Grandi, S. (2004). Six-year outcome of cognitive behavior therapy for prevention of recurrent depression. *American Journal of Psychiatry, 161,* 1872–1876. doi:10.1176/appi.ajp.161.10.1872

Fava, G. A., Ruini, C., Rafanelli, C., Finos, L., Salmaso, L., Mangelli, L., & Sirigatti, S. (2005). Well-being therapy of generalized anxiety disorder. *Psychotherapy and Psychosomatics, 74,* 26–30. doi: 10.1159/000082023

Fava, G. A., & Sonino, N. (2000). Psychosomatic medicine: Emerging trends and perspectives. *Psychotherapy and Psychosomatics, 69,* 184–197. doi:10.1159/000012393

Fava, G. A., & Tomba, E. (2009). Increasing psychological well-being and resilience by psychotherapeutic methods. *Journal of Personality, 77,* 1903–1934. doi:10.1111/j.1467-6494.2009.00604.x

Fournier, M., de Ridder, D., & Bensing, J. (2002). Optimism and adaptation to chronic disease: The role of optimism in relation to self-care options of type 1 diabetes mellitus, rheumatoid arthritis and multiple sclerosis. *British Journal of Health Psychology, 7,* 409–432. doi:10.1348/135910702320645390

Hammell, K. W. (2004). Quality of life among people with high spinal cord injury living in the community. *Spinal Cord, 42,* 607–620. doi:10.1038/sj.sc.3101662

Hammell, K. W. (2007). Quality of life after spinal cord injury: A meta-synthesis of qualitative findings. *Spinal Cord, 45,* 124–139. doi:10.1038/sj.sc.3101992

Harris, R. (2009). *ACT made simple: An easy-to-read primer on acceptance and commitment therapy.* Oakland, CA: New Harbinger.

Hayes, S. C. (2004). Acceptance and commitment therapy, relational frame theory, and the third wave of behavioral and cognitive therapies. *Behavior Therapy, 35,* 639–665.

Hayes, S. C., Levin, M. E., Plumb-Vilardaga, J., Villatte, J. L., & Pistorello, J. (2013). Acceptance and commitment therapy and contextual behavioral science: Examining the progress of a distinctive model of behavioral and cognitive therapy. *Behavior Therapy, 44,* 180–198. doi:10.1016/j.beth.2009.08.002

Heszen-Niejodek, I., Gottschalk, L. A., & Januszek, M. (1999). Anxiety and hope during the course of three different medical illnesses: A longitudinal study. *Psychotherapy and Psychosomatics, 68,* 304–312. doi:10.1159/000012348

Hooley, J. M., & Teasdale, J. D. (1989). Predictors of relapse in unipolar depressives: Expressed emotion, marital distress, and perceived criticism. *Journal of Abnormal Psychology, 98,* 229–235. doi:10.1037/0021-843X.98.3.229

Kalpakjian, C. Z., & Albright, K. J. (2006). An examination of depression through the lens of spinal cord injury: Comparative prevalence rates and severity in women and men. *Women's Health Issues, 16,* 380–388. doi:10.1016/j.whi.2006.08.005

Kleiber, D. A., Brock, S. C., Lee, Y., Dattilo, J., & Caldwell, L. (1995). The relevance of leisure in an illness experience: Realities of spinal cord injury. *Journal of Leisure Research, 27*, 283–299.

Kortte, K. B., Gilbert, M., Gorman, P., & Wegener, S. T. (2010). Positive psychological variables in the prediction of life satisfaction after spinal cord injury. *Rehabilitation Psychology, 55*, 40–47. doi: 10.1037/a0018624

Lewin, K. (1943). Defining the "field at a given time." *Psychological Review, 50*, 292–310. doi:10.1037/h0062738

Majani, G., Pierobon, A., Giardini, A., Callegari, S., Opasich, C., Cobelli, F., & Tavazzi, L. (1999). Relationship between psychological profile and cardiological variables in chronic heart failure: The role of patient subjectivity. *European Heart Journal, 20*, 1579–1586. doi:10.1053/euhj.1999.1712

Mangelli, L., Gribbin, N., Büchi, S., Allard, S., & Sensky, T. (2002). Psychological well-being in rheumatoid arthritis: Relationship to "disease" variables and affective disturbance. *Psychotherapy and Psychosomatics, 71*, 112–116. doi:10.1159/000049354

Meyerson, L. (1948). Physical disability as a social psychological problem. *Journal of Social Issues, 4*, 2–10. doi:10.1111/j.1540-4560.1948.tb01513.x

Middleton, J., Tran, Y., & Craig, A. (2007). Relationship between quality of life and self-efficacy in persons with spinal cord injuries. *Archives of Physical Medicine and Rehabilitation, 88*(12), 1643–1648.

Migliorini, C., Tonge, B., & Taleporos, G. (2008). Spinal cord injury and mental health. *Australian and New Zealand Journal of Psychiatry, 42*(4), 309–314.

Moeenizadeh, M., & Salagame, K. K. (2010). The impact of well-being therapy on symptoms of depression. *International Journal of Psychological Studies, 2*, 223–230. doi:10.5539/ijps.v2n2p223

National Institute on Disability and Rehabilitation Research. (2013). National Institute on Disability and Rehabilitation Research: Long-range plan for fiscal years 2013–2017. Retrieved from https://www.federalregister.gov/articles/2013/04/04/2013–07879/national-institute-on-disability-and-rehabilitation-research-long-range-plan-for-fiscal-years

National Spinal Cord Injury Statistical Center. (2013). Spinal cord injury model systems: 2013 annual report: Complete public version. Retrieved from https://www.nscisc.uab.edu/PublicDocuments/reports/pdf/2013%20NSCISC%20Annual%20Statistical%20Report%20Complete%20Public%20Version.pdf

Oliver, M., Zarb, G., Silver, J., & Salisbury, V. (1988). *Walking into darkness: The experience of spinal cord injury.* London, England: Macmillan Press.

Peterson, C., & Seligman, M. E. (2004). *Character strengths and virtues: A handbook and classification.* New York, NY: Oxford University Press.

Pollard, C., & Kennedy, P. (2007). A longitudinal analysis of emotional impact, coping strategies and post-traumatic psychological growth following spinal cord injury: A 10-year review. *British Journal of Health Psychology, 12*, 347–362. doi:10.1348/135910707X197046

Rafanelli, C., Conti, S., Mangelli, L., Ruini, C., Ottolini, F., Fabbri, S., . . . Fava, G. A. (2002). Benessere psicologico e sintomi residui nei pazienti con disturbi affettivi: II. Confronto tra well-being therapy e terapia cognitivo-comportamentale [Psychological well-being and residual symptoms in patients with affective disorders: II. Comparison of well-being therapy and cognitive behavioral therapy]. *Rivista di Psichiatria, 37*, 179–183.

Ruini, C., & Fava, G. A. (2012). Role of well-being therapy in achieving a balanced and individualized path to optimal functioning. *Clinical Psychology & Psychotherapy, 19*(4), 291–304.

Ryff, C. D. (1989). Happiness is everything, or is it? Explorations on the meaning of psychological well-being. *Journal of Personality and Social Psychology, 57*, 1069–1081. doi:10.1037/0022-3514.57.6.1069

Ryff, C. D., Lee, Y. H., Essex, M. J., & Schmutte, P. S. (1994). My children and me: Midlife evaluations of grown children and of self. *Psychology and Aging, 9*, 195–205. doi:10.1037/0882-7974.9.2.195

Ryff, C. D., & Singer, B. (1996). Psychological well-being: Meaning, measurement, and implications for psychotherapy research. *Psychotherapy and Psychosomatics, 65*, 14–23. doi:10.1159/000289026

Ryff, C. D., & Singer, B. (1998). The contours of positive human health. *Psychological Inquiry, 9*, 1–28. doi:10.1207/s15327965pli0901_1

Ryff, C. D., & Singer, B. H. (2000). Biopsychosocial challenges of the new millennium. *Psychotherapy and Psychosomatics, 69*, 170–177. doi:10.1159/000012390

Ryff, C. D., & Singer, B. H. (2006). Best news yet on the six-factor model of well-being. *Social Science Research, 35*, 1103–1119. doi:10.1016/j.ssresearch.2006.01.002

Ryff, C. D., & Singer, B. H. (2008). Know thyself and become what you are: A eudaimonic approach to psychological well-being. *Journal of Happiness Studies, 9*, 13–39.

Scivoletto, G., Petrelli, A., Di Lucente, L., & Castellano, V. (1997). Psychological investigation of spinal cord injury patients. *Spinal Cord, 35*, 516–520. doi:10.1038/sj.sc.3100437

Seligman, M. (2011). *Flourish: A new understanding of happiness, well-being-and how to achieve them.* London, England: Nicholas Brealey Publishing.

Sharpe, L., Sensky, T., Timberlake, N., Ryan, B., Brewin, C. R., & Allard, S. (2001). A blind, randomized, controlled trial of cognitive-behavioural intervention for patients with recent onset rheumatoid arthritis: Preventing psychological and physical morbidity. *Pain, 89*(2–3), 275–283.

Stilley, C. S., Miller, D. J., Manzetti, J. D., Marino, I. R., & Keenan, R. J. (1999). Optimism and coping styles: A comparison of candidates for liver transplantation with candidates for lung transplantation. *Psychotherapy and Psychosomatics, 68*, 299–303. doi:10.1159/000012347

Teasdale, J. D., Segal, Z. V., Williams, J. M., Ridgeway, V. A., Soulsby, J. M., & Lau, M. A. (2000). Prevention of relapse/recurrence in major depression by mindfulness-based cognitive therapy. *Journal of Consulting and Clinical Psychology, 68*, 615–623. doi:10.1037/0022-006X.68.4.615

Thompson, N. J., Coker, J., Krause, J. S., & Henry, E. (2003). Purpose in life as a mediator of adjustment after spinal cord injury. *Rehabilitation Psychology, 48*, 100–108. doi:10.1037/0090-5550.48.2.100

Treharne, G. J., Lyons, A. C., Booth, D. A., & Kitas, G. D. (2007). Psychological well-being across 1 year with rheumatoid arthritis: Coping resources as buffers of perceived stress. *British Journal of Health Psychology, 12*, 323–345. doi:10.1348/135910706X109288

Trieschmann, R. B. (1978). The role of the psychologist in the treatment of spinal cord injury. *Paraplegia, 16*, 212–219. doi:10.1038/sc.1978.37

Trieschmann, R. B. (1988). *Spinal cord injuries: The psychological, social, and vocational rehabilitation* (2nd ed.). New York, NY: Demos Medical Publishing.

Van Houdenhove, B., & Egle, U. T. (2004). Fibromyalgia: A stress disorder? Piecing the biopsychosocial puzzle together. *Psychotherapy and Psychosomatics, 73*, 267–275. doi:10.1159/000078843

Weiten, W., Dunn, D., & Hammer, E. (2011). *Psychology applied to modern life: Adjustment in the 21st century.* Belmont, CA: Cengage.

Wright, B. A. (1983). *Physical disability—A psychosocial approach* (2nd ed.). New York, NY: Harper & Row.

Zola, I. K. (1982). Denial of emotional needs to people with handicaps. *Archives of Physical Medicine and Rehabilitation, 63*(2), 63–67.

23

Classifying Functioning, Disability, and Health: The ICF

DAVID B. PETERSON

*T*he *International Classification of Functioning, Disability and Health* (*ICF*; World Health Organization [WHO], 2001), and its predecessors—the *International Classification of Impairments, Disabilities and Handicaps* (*ICIDH* and *ICIDH-2*; WHO, 1980, 1999)—have been influential in the conceptualization of the construct of disability in the United States and internationally for more than three decades. Any discussion of the psychological and social impact of illness and disability would be incomplete without considering the *ICF*'s influences on this social discourse.

We begin with a brief overview of the history of classification of health and illness, and the role that different conceptualizations of disability have played along the way. We then review the development of the *ICF* within the context of these conceptualizations and introduce its key concepts, conceptual framework, and a brief orientation to its use. We conclude with consideration of the current and future impact of the *ICF* on conceptualizing psychological and social aspects of illness and disability.

In a chapter that reviews the *ICF*, it is difficult to avoid being redundant with other similar publications. A variety of reviews have discussed and critiqued the *ICF* (see Bruyère, & Peterson, 2005b; Peterson & Kosciulek, 2005). Several book chapters have been written for seminal handbooks in the counseling and psychology professions (Peterson, 2009, 2015a, 2015b, 2017; Peterson & Elliott, 2008; Peterson, Mpofu, & Oakland, 2010; Peterson & Threats, 2016), and a text focusing on the psychological aspects of functioning, disability, and health (Peterson, 2011). These publications notwithstanding, any explanation of the *ICF* can and should be referenced back to the *ICF* itself (WHO, 2001).

CONCEPTUALIZATIONS OF DISABILITY: *ICD, ICIDH,* AND *ICF*

The concept of disability has manifested itself in various ways across stakeholders in our health care system. An awareness of the prevailing perspectives on disability can inform intervention targeting and the evaluation of health care intervention outcomes, and is therefore very informative in conceptualizing clinical work with people with disabilities. At the same time, a concise review of the medical, social, and biopsychosocial models of disability illustrates the development of the *ICF* and its predecessors.

Several texts have compared and contrasted various models of disability, including a chapter in the present volume. Previous iterations of this text (Dell Orto & Power, 2007; Marini & Stebnicki, 2012) provided detailed reviews of how disability has been defined and conceptualized in the literature. *The Handbook of Counseling Psychology* (S. D. Brown & Lent, 2008) includes a chapter discussing advancements in conceptualizing disability (Peterson & Elliott, 2008). More recently, the text *Psychological Aspects of Functioning, Disability and Health* (Peterson, 2011) provides a review of models of disability as they relate to the *ICF*. We begin with a concise review of the medical, social, and biopsychosocial models of disability, highlighting perspectives held by various stakeholders in the health care system, which may inform our collaboration with multiple disciplines in today's health care environment.

Origins of Classifications of Health

The international classification of population health began with a focus on the prevalence of medical diagnoses and causes of death with the *International Statistical Classification of Diseases and Related Health Problems* (*ICD*, now in its 10th revision, WHO, 2016). A brief review of the *ICD* is important to understanding the conceptual development of the construct of disability, as well as knowing that the *ICD* serves as the sister classification for the *ICF*; more on that in a moment. The *ICD* provides an etiological classification of health conditions (e.g., diseases, disorders, injuries) related to mortality (death) and morbidity (illness). The *ICD* was first formalized in 1893 as the Bertillon Classification or the International List of Causes of Death; the *ICD* acronym persists to date.

The United States recently adopted the *ICD-10*. Initially approved by the World Health Assembly in 1992, it is scheduled to be updated to the *ICD-11* within the next few years. The *ICD-11* promises to be a global, multilingual, multidisciplinary system of classification, and its development transparent and free from commercial input. The system's context will allow for interactive information sharing using modern technology and integrated into health informatics systems worldwide. The new system will be intended for daily clinical use with simpler diagnostic criteria (Martin, 2009).

Although various stakeholders in the health care system hold varying and opposing views on how to conceptualize disability, making consensus difficult to achieve, it is important to define disability so that those who are disadvantaged by their experience of disability can be identified, their life experiences compared with those who are not disabled, and disparities in life experiences can be noted so that inequalities can be observed, measured, and ultimately remedied (Leonardi, Bickenbach, Ustun, Kostanjsek, & Chatterji, 2006).

Medical Model

The medical model has been the dominant force in health care service provision, focusing on the diagnosis of a disease, disorder, or injury (G. N. Wright, 1980). The medical model can be described as a treatment process that first identifies a pathogen or cause of injury or other disease processes (often classified by the *ICD*), and then selects an appropriate treatment protocol for the condition identified (Reed et al., 2008). Within the United States, a classification of procedures associated with treatment of illness or injury employed in this treatment process is the Current Procedural Terminology or CPT codes (American Medical Association [AMA], 2017).

The medical model has focused neither on contextual factors (e.g., social and environmental factors) nor on the subjective experiences of individuals with disabilities. Disability within this context tends to be conceptualized as a personal problem that requires treatment by a medical professional (WHO, 2001). More contemporary perspectives on disability have posited that behavioral and social factors affect the course of chronic disease and disability over the life span, moving the focus from the individual to one's context.

The medical model and related diagnostic information have limited utility for assessment and treatment due to the lack of focus on important contextual factors in health and functioning. Historical evidence suggests that diagnostic information alone, without functional data, may not adequately reflect an individual's health condition (see Peterson, 2005; Reed et al., 2005). Disease or impairment may manifest differently across individuals; similar functioning does not imply similar health conditions. Diagnoses alone have not sufficiently predicted length (McCrone & Phelan, 1994) or outcome of hospitalization (Rabinowitz, Modai, & Inbar-Saban, 1994), level of necessary care (Burns, 1991), service needs (National Advisory Mental Health Council, 1993), work performance (Gatchel, Polatin, Mayer, & Garcy, 1994), receipt of disability benefits (Bassett, Chase, Folstein, & Regier, 1998; Massel et al., 1990; Segal & Choi, 1991), or social integration (Ormel, Oldehinkel, Brilman, & vanden Brink, 1993).

For instance, someone with the diagnosis of major depressive disorder, according to the *Diagnostic and Statistical Manual of Mental Disorders* (5th ed.; *DSM-5;* American Psychiatric Association [APA], 2013), must experience at least five of the nine possible characteristic symptoms in order to qualify for the diagnosis. These symptoms can range from a diminished ability to concentrate to significant weight gain or loss. The functional implications of any of the nine symptoms may be quite disparate, and the possible combinations of the five symptoms required for the diagnosis will have varying clinical presentations. When one considers the possible combinations of presentations, it becomes clear that diagnostic information alone is limited without clear descriptions of function that inform the diagnosis.

Notwithstanding the limitations of the medical model, it is very important to note that it has not been without utility. The medical model contributed to advances in science that helped researchers to better describe disease processes and related etiology, and so allowed more rapid and effective response to the acute needs of persons with physical disabilities and other chronic health conditions. The medical model also informed early initiatives to address issues of improved care, survival, and quality of life. Medical definitions of disability provide the cornerstone for determining disability for legal and occupational purposes, and for determining eligibility for financial assistance (Peterson & Elliott, 2008). Although it continues to be influential, limitations of the medical model and the focus on the civil rights-related and disability activism helped to develop the opposing *social model* of disability.

Social Model

The medical model was challenged by the civil rights era and related disability advocacy efforts, encouraging a movement away from the medical model of disability and functioning toward a social model that considered the role of environmental barriers in health and functioning (Peterson & Elliott, 2008; Rusk, 1977; Smart, 2005; G. N. Wright, 1980; B. A. Wright, 1983). As just reviewed, diagnostic information alone, without functional data, may not adequately reflect an individual's health condition (see Peterson, 2005, 2011; Reed et al., 2005). Disease or impairment may manifest differently across individuals; similar functioning does not imply similar health conditions.

Beyond the variety of presentations of diagnoses and potential functional limitations that may or may not present in an individual, Leonardi et al. (2006) wrote that the quality of life experience of a person dealing with health issues is an important focus of clinical attention. It was their position that it is important to distinguish between objective descriptions of the "disability experience" and an individual's satisfaction with that experience: "data about quality of life, well-being, and personal satisfaction with life are useful for health and policy planning; but these data are not necessarily predicted by the presence or extent of disability" (p. 1220).

In contrast to the medical model, the social model of disability highlights the importance of a person's subjective experience as it relates to facilitators and barriers that the environment may present, their impact on health and functioning, and ultimately an individual's quality of life (Elliott, Kurylo, & Rivera, 2002; Hurst, 2003; Smart, 2005; Ueda & Okawa, 2003). In the social model of disability, disability is no longer a simple personal attribute, but a complex social construct reflecting the interaction between the individual and his or her environment (WHO, 2001, p. 20).

The social paradigm focuses on the barriers and facilitators to functioning, such as daily activities, life skills, social relations, life satisfaction, and participation in society. This model suggests that any problem related to disability is influenced by, if not due in large part to, societal attitudes and barriers in the environment. Within the social model paradigm, the individual is seen as the organizing core, but impairments are defined by the environment (Olkin, 1999; Olkin & Pledger, 2003). The environment is typically construed as the "major determinant of individual functioning" (Pledger, 2003, p. 281). The social model highlights the need for increased access and opportunities for people with disabilities, and it has historically been favored by advocates for the civil rights of persons with disabilities, who historically have disapproved of the medical model in general.

Limitations associated with the social model of disability include that it has neither clearly distinguished who qualifies as a person with a disability nor how disability is measured or determined. Further, researchers in this area have not established a distinct body of scholarship that systematically posits empirically testable and potentially falsifiable hypotheses (Peterson & Elliott, 2008). Perhaps this is due to the fact that some supporters of the social model of disability regard psychological theory and scholarship as part and parcel of the medical model where disability is equated with person-based pathology, largely independent of environmental and social factors (see Olkin & Pledger, 2003).

Biopsychosocial Model

The origins of the biopsychosocial framework can be traced back to an article from the 1970s arguing for a new medical model for biomedicine (see Engel, 1977). The biopsychosocial model of disability integrates useful aspects of both the medical and social models of disability, addressing biological, individual, and societal perspectives on health. Planning treatments and documenting outcomes of interventions from the body, individual, and societal perspectives can improve the quality of health care service provision and consequently the quality of life of people with disabilities, as well as increase the participation of individuals with disabilities in society (Peterson & Threats, 2005). The biopsychosocial perspective defines health care in the broadest sense by using a universal, culturally sensitive, integrative, and interactive model of health and disability that is sensitive to social and environmental aspects of functioning (Peterson, 2005, 2011).

The *ICF* integrates the medical and social models of disability, addressing biological, individual, and societal perspectives on health in a biopsychosocial approach (Peterson, 2005; WHO, 2001). Ultimately, the biopsychosocial model integrates all that is useful in both the medical and social models of disability. Next, we turn to a discussion about the evolution of the *ICF* and its influence on the international discourse on functioning, disability, and health.

ICD, ICIDH to the ICF

The development of the *ICF* began in 1974, when two separate classifications were developed, the first addressing impairments related to changes in health and the second handicaps that considered the role of the environment in disability and functioning. Discussions generated from work since 1972 were formally submitted for consideration at the October 1975 International Conference for the Ninth Revision of the *International Classification of Diseases*. In May 1976, the 29th World Health Assembly adopted a resolution that approved the trial publication of the supplementary classification of impairments and handicaps as a complement to the *ICD*. The first edition of the *ICIDH*, the *ICF*'s predecessor, was published in 1980 for trial purposes. This trial edition of the *ICIDH* presented the origins of a more holistic model of disability, stressing the role of environmental determinants in the performance of day-to-day activities and fulfillment of social roles by persons with disabilities (Brandsma, Lakerveld-Heyl, Van Ravensberg, & Heerkens, 1995; De Kleijn-De Vrankrijker, 2003).

The *ICIDH* was instrumental in defining key concepts within the Americans with Disabilities Act (ADA). Two critical terms, *impairments* and *disability*, were defined parallel to those employed in the *ICIDH*. S. C. Brown (1993) argued for advantages of linking the *ICIDH* with the ADA such as the creation of a uniform framework for discussion and a standardized measurement tool for data collection. For a succinct overview of contributions of the *ICIDH* in the development of the ADA definitions and implementation, see Nieuwenhuijsen (1995).

The revision of the *ICIDH* began with its reprinting in 1993, which ultimately led to the provisionally titled *ICIDH-2*. It was referred to and incorporated in the Standard Rules on the Equalization of Opportunities for Persons with Disabilities (United Nations Department of Public Information [UNDPI], 1993), which was adopted by the United Nations General Assembly at its 48th session in December 1993. The *ICIDH-2* was accepted as one of the United Nations' social classifications, subsequently affecting international human rights mandates as well as national legislation.

At a 1996 meeting in Geneva, work from various collaborating centers was collated and an alpha draft was produced, which was pilot tested from May 1996 through February 1997. Comments and suggestions were compiled at the WHO headquarters, and primary issues were identified and circulated to contribute to the ongoing revision process. The primary principle held that the classification should contain a culturally meaningful order of categories relying on consensus from potential stakeholders, including professionals in health care service provision, insurance, Social Security, and other entitlement programs; labor; education; economics; social policy development; and allied corporate entities. Another guiding principle for the *ICIDH-2* revisions was respect for the different languages represented in the international community. They maintained that the *ICF* should be attractive to its users and should appeal to managers and policy makers who would support its use and that it needed to have continuity with previous classification systems in order to complement systems already in place (WHO, 2001).

Feedback obtained during testing of the alpha draft of the *ICIDH-2* was used to develop a beta-1 draft that was tested from June 1997 through December 1998. These results were used to inform development of a beta-2 draft, which underwent testing from July 1999 through September 2000, which is when the writer became involved with the *ICIDH-2* development efforts.

Feasibility and reliability studies of case evaluations were conducted during the beta-2 field trials that involved 24 countries, 1,884 case evaluations, and 3,216 evaluations of case summaries. Focus groups and various other studies contributed to the beta-1 and 2 revision processes. The revisions formulated for the beta-2 draft of the *ICIDH-2* signified the shift from a focus on impairment and disorder to a focus on health. These revisions were designed to reflect changes in disability policy development and reforms of health care systems internationally and also mirror the medical, social, and biopsychosocial perspectives on disability just reviewed, as well as their development over time.

International field testing occurred in over 50 countries (WHO, 2001) at various centers and nongovernmental and intergovernmental organizations affiliated with the United Nations through the efforts of more than 1,800 scientists, clinicians, persons with disabilities, and other experts. Results of the studies led to several conclusions including that the *ICIDH-2* was a useful and meaningful public health tool. It was agreed that training was needed in the implementation of the system, particularly in the application of its conceptual framework.

After preliminary review of the systematic beta-2 field trial data, the prefinal draft was completed in October 2000 and presented at a revision meeting the following month. Suggestions from the meeting were incorporated into the version submitted to the WHO Executive Board in January 2001. The final draft was presented at the 54th World Health Assembly in May 2001. The Assembly voted for the adoption of the *ICIDH-2* and elected to rename the system from the second edition of the *ICIDH (ICIDH-2)* to the *International Classification of Functioning, Disability and Health*, or the *ICF*. A summary of the *ICIDH/ICF* revision process can be found in the seventh annex of the *ICF* (WHO, 2001).

Prior to its most current form as the *ICF* in 2001, Hurst (2003) challenged the *ICIDH* development efforts by saying that it perpetuated the medical model, countered the social model of disability, and presented barriers to the understanding of issues related to social justice and disability among health care providers. In response to this criticism, the WHO made a concerted effort to involve people with disabilities and disability rights advocates in the *ICIDH* revision process that produced the *ICF*. Such criticism had great influence on the evolution of the *ICF* and its increased focus on contextual factors, and ongoing participation of international stakeholders will continue to shape the *ICF* in its future iterations.

From a disability rights activist perspective, the interactive model informing the *ICF*'s conceptual framework is complementary to the social model of disability (disability being an interaction among impairment, functioning, and environment). The social model of disability is very helpful in describing how environmental factors are key to understanding disability and how advocacy occurs through social change (Hurst, 2003). The name was changed from the *ICIDH* to the *ICF* to reflect the paradigm shift away from a focus on consequences of disease as found in the 1980 version toward a focus on the components of health found in the current version (WHO, 2001). Rather than an emphasis on "impairment, disability, and handicap" exclusively, the revised classification incorporated the terms *activity* and *participation* to denote positive experiences related to function and health. In the current version of the classification, the term *impairment* is defined as a problem with a body function or structure and the term *handicap* has been replaced with the term *participation restriction*, meaning a problem an individual may experience in life situations.

The evolution of the *ICIDH* to the current iteration of the *ICF* reflects the international zeitgeist to embrace a biopsychosocial model of disability rather than a medical or social model exclusively. We now have at our disposal an etiologically neutral framework and classification that was created through global consensus building to identify all aspects of a person's health experience at the individual and contextual levels (Stucki, Ustün, & Melvin, 2005).

INTERNATIONAL CLASSIFICATION OF FUNCTIONING, DISABILITY, AND HEALTH

The *ICF* (WHO, 2001) was published in 2001 as the latest addition to the WHO family of classifications, as a new taxonomy of health and functioning that promotes the use of universal classifications of function that are complementary to the use of diagnostic information in health care service provision. A sister classification to the *ICD* defined earlier, the two systems are used together to classify a holistic conceptualization of health and functioning.

The *ICF* embraces a biopsychosocial approach for conceptualizing and classifying mental and physical health functioning (body functions and structures), disability (activity limitations and participation restrictions), environmental barriers, and facilitators; collaborating with the person being assessed in determining these factors (personal factors); targeting interventions; and evaluating treatment efficacy. These terms are further defined in the next section.

The *ICF* is a significant development in health care, as it can be used as a standard for defining concepts, building constructs, hypothesizing relationships, and proposing new theories that will further research and practice in counseling (Bruyère & Peterson, 2005a; Bruyère, Van Looy, & Peterson, 2005). Detailed classification of functioning requires reading the *ICF* and receiving training in its use, so an overview of its details is outside the scope of this chapter. However, the reader is referred to various published references to become familiar with the full classification system and oriented to its use (Peterson, 2005, 2011; Peterson & Paul, 2009; WHO, 2001).

ICF Conceptual Framework

For our purposes, the *ICF* conceptual framework is reviewed here as a potential template to inform health care professionals working with people with disabilities. The *ICF* is based on a universal, culturally sensitive, integrative, and interactive model of health and functioning that provides sensitivity to psychosocial and environmental aspects of health and disability (Simeonsson et al., 2003; Ustün et al., 2003). The *ICF* conceptual framework portrays health as a dynamic interaction between a person's functioning and disability within a given context (Figure 23.1).

The conceptual framework of the *ICF* consists of two parts: *Functioning and Disability* and *Contextual Factors*. Each part contains two components; within the first part, the *Body* component consists of two parallel classifications, *Body Functions* and *Body Structures*. The second component, *Activities and Participation*, covers domains of functioning from an individual and a societal perspective. Health care professionals conceptualizing a case can use this framework to first explore biological bases of behavior (body functions and body structures). Once the physical and mental health and functioning of an individual are clarified at the individual level, then how that person functions in his or her environment can be explored with respect to potential (activity) versus actual ability to participate within a social context (participation). The discrepancy between identified potential (activity) and actual participation can serve as the focus of clinical attention for intervention targeting.

The second part of the *ICF* classification addresses *Contextual Factors* through two components; the first is *Environmental Factors*, or factors in the physical, social, or attitudinal world ranging from the immediate to more general environment. The biopsychosocial model has supported the utility of considering facilitators and barriers present

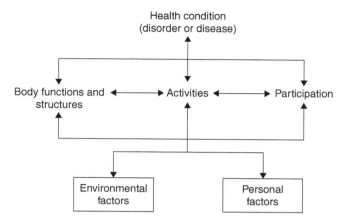

FIGURE 23.1 Interactions among the components of *ICF*.

ICF, International Classification of Functioning, Disability and Health.

in the environment when planning treatment interventions for people with disabilities. The second component is *Personal Factors*, calling attention to the need to consider unique factors such as gender, race, age, fitness, religion, lifestyle, habits, upbringing, coping styles, social background, education, profession, past and current experience, overall behavior pattern and character, individual psychological assets, and other health conditions (WHO, 2001).

Key Concepts

Within the *ICF*, the term *health* refers to components of health that are a focus of health care professionals (e.g., hearing, learning, remembering, seeing, speaking, walking) as well as health-related components of well-being that are not typically a focus of health care systems (e.g., education, labor, social interactions, transportation). As reviewed earlier, the literature suggests that attending to contextual factors that are not typically a focus of health care systems can lead to improved treatment outcomes. The *ICF* conceptual framework can help clinicians account for various contextual factors that may be influencing someone's health and functioning as impacted by *disorder* or *disease*, including factors that may escape the focus of many health care providers.

Functioning within the *ICF* conceptual framework is defined as all body functions, activities, and participation in society. *Disability* refers to any impairments, activity limitations, or participation restrictions, or "the outcome or result of a complex relationship between an individual's health condition and personal factors, and of the external factors that represent the circumstances in which the individual lives" (WHO, 2001, p. 17). Note that the terms used in the *ICF* are capitalized to distinguish them from their lay uses (Threats & Worrall, 2004).

APPLYING THE ICF CONCEPTUAL FRAMEWORK

The following scenario will help illustrate the utility of the biopsychosocial framework and the *ICF* for case conceptualization. Consider a 22-year-old man who due to a head trauma has a neurocognitive disorder, as well as a co-occurring diagnosis of major depressive disorder, single episode, severe, without psychotic features. We will use this scenario to illustrate several points.

A clinician may encounter a variety of perspectives across and within health care agencies. Understanding these perspectives can help to identify allies and inform strategies to address barriers in the system. For instance, if a clinician is encountering a health care entity focused on the medical model of service provision, the clinician's advocacy efforts can focus on social and contextual factors to encourage a holistic program of health care.

In our example, the treating hospital may be focused on medical presentations of impairment related to his head trauma and the degree of depressive symptomology and related risks. The *ICF*'s conceptual framework addresses these foci through body functions and body structures (which do include the brain). In addition, the biopsychosocial approach embraced within the *ICF*'s conceptual framework will take into careful account contextual issues such as the client's family system, social circles, and greater community. Further, through a consideration of activities and participation, the client's potential based on his functioning and impairments can be compared with how his current context facilitates or hinders his functioning.

Clinicians may find that some health care systems are more open to the biopsychosocial approach than others. It is important to capitalize upon the strengths inherent in a given system and to carefully suggest ideas that may enhance treatment based on a framework like that proposed within the *ICF*. They can in turn use the *ICF* conceptual framework to highlight the role of contextual factors in facilitating or hindering healthy functioning.

CLASSIFYING WITH THE *ICF*

The size and scope of the *ICF*, with just under 1,500 categories of classification, may make it appear difficult to use at first. It is important to review the *ICF* in its entirety and participate in available training opportunities in order to become proficient with the *ICF*. For the purpose of introduction, a general overview of using the *ICF* is available in a journal article by Peterson (2005), and specific application to working with psychological impairments is available in a text by Peterson (2011).

To provide some encouragement and perspective on the *ICF*, one could compare its use with that of any comprehensive reference; it is not necessary or practical to read most reference material from cover to cover in a brief time period; rather, one searches for specific information according to a specific need. Once familiar with the basic structure of the *ICF*, the user can search purposefully for information related to health and functioning with some facility.

There are two versions of the *ICF*: the full version that provides all four levels of classification detail and the short version that provides two levels of classification. In either case, units of classification are qualified with numeric codes that specify the magnitude or extent of disability or function in a given category as well as the extent to which an environmental factor is a facilitator or a barrier. To allow quick and easy classification, the WHO has created an electronic version of the *ICF* that is searchable through the *ICF* Browser or CD-ROM (WHO, 2001). An alphabetical index is also available in the hardcopy version of the *ICF*.

One-Level Classification

The categories of function for a given domain begin at a general level of detail and expand to levels of greater detail. The one-level classification of the *ICF* expands on the core structure as follows: (a) The body functions component contains eight chapters that address "physiological functions of body systems (including psychological functions)" (WHO, 2001, p. 12); (b) the body structures component contains eight chapters that parallel the body functions component and deal with "anatomical parts of the body such as organs, limbs, and their components" (p. 12); (c) the activities and participation component contains nine chapters, with activities addressing "the execution of a task or action by an individual" and participation addressing "involvement in a life situation" (p. 14); and (d) the environmental factors component contains five chapters focusing on "the physical, social, and attitudinal environment in which people live and conduct their lives" (p. 171), organized from the immediate to more general environment. The maximum number of codes available at the one-digit level of classification is 34.

Two-Level Classification

The two-level classification is the first branching level of the *ICF*, comprising specific chapter headings. Alphanumeric codes begin with a letter (b for body functions, s for body structures, d for activities and participation, and e for environmental factors) and a three-digit numeric classification indicating the chapter and specific categories within each chapter. For example, the classification associated with the psychological function of emotion is found in the first chapter of body functions (its code begins with "b") under the specific mental function section, called emotional functions, or alphanumeric code b152. The two-level items total 362 distinct, three-digit codes.

Detailed Classification

The detailed classification with definitions lists all categories within the *ICF* along with their definitions, inclusions, and exclusions, providing greater levels of detail using four- and five-digit numeric codes. The level of classification used depends on the clinical context. Examining emotional functions, examples of level of detail include appropriateness of emotion (b1520), regulation of emotion (b1521), and range of emotion (b1522). Code groups also offer other specified (e.g., b1528) and unspecified (e.g., b1529) codes for functions not detailed in the current classification.

Codes at the detailed level of classification number up to 1,424 items. However, the *ICF* suggests that typical use of the system in a health or health-related setting for surveys and clinical outcome evaluation will generate a set of 3 to 18 codes to describe a case with two-level (three-digit) precision. The more precise four-level codes would be used for more specialized services (rehabilitation outcomes, geriatrics, and mental health) and research.

Hierarchical, Mutually Exclusive Code Example

Within components, as units of classification become more detailed, there is the assumption that more detailed units share the attributes of the broader units in the hierarchy order in which they fall. For example, range of emotion b1522 shares the attributes of the higher level of classification of emotional function b152. It is worth mentioning again that categories within the same level are designed to be mutually exclusive. More than one category may be used to accurately classify specific functioning as warranted.

Let us consider an example within the *ICF* from the mental functions chapter, page 49, the orientation functions (b114) section of global mental functions (b110–139), which are second-level codes. Orientation functions can be classified more precisely to address orientation to person (b1142, a third-level code) and even more precisely as orientation to others (b11421), a five-digit code. This represents the pathway from a two-level code in mental functions to a more detailed classification.

Qualifiers

Qualifiers provide inherent meaning to the *ICF* codes, reflect the magnitude of the issue classified, and appear as one, two, or three digits after the decimal point that follows the *ICF* code. Students of the *ICF* will benefit from a review of the second annex of the *ICF* (pp. 219–233) that provides coding guidelines, including an overview of the *ICF* organization and structure and general and specific coding rules. Annex Four of the *ICF* (pp. 238–241) provides specific case examples for applying the *ICF*. However, there is work to be done with respect to the consistent clinical implementation of the *ICF*.

CLINICAL IMPLEMENTATION OF THE *ICF*

Manual

Although the *ICF* was adopted as the complement to the *ICD-10*, the 191 member states that are encouraged by the WHO to use it must generate their own resources to guide its clinical implementation. These efforts have not been consistent or well coordinated across the member states. In order to facilitate implementation of the *ICF* in clinical settings in the United States, the APA and WHO formed a series of interdisciplinary teams of experts to develop *The Procedural Manual and Guide for the Standardized Application of the ICF: A Manual for Health Professionals* (Reed et al., 2005, 2008). Meanwhile, the WHO turned its attention to a more concise guide for the use of the *ICF*, *A Practical Manual for Using the International Classification of Functioning, Disability and Health (ICF)*, which was posted on the WHO's website as an exposure draft for comment in October 2013. Training needs to be developed to promote consistent coding of guidelines from the WHO and its collaborating centers (Reed et al., 2008). Clinical judgment, assessment biases, and interactional dynamics between rater and participants are further areas of complexity to address in standard use of the *ICF*, so much work lies ahead.

Ethical Use of the *ICF*

The *ICF* incorporates a set of ethical provisions that, when applied responsibly and used with consumer participation in a collaborative and informational process, assures ethical use of the *ICF*. The *ICF* is not something that is done to someone; rather, it is *done with* or in collaboration with a person (Peterson & Threats, 2005; Threats & Worrall, 2004). The 11 ethical provisions are actually a part of the *ICF*'s classification system. In order to maintain the spirit of its intended use, it is important for *ICF* users to be informed by the ethical provisions when applying the *ICF* to practice.

The 11 ethical provisions were established in the sixth annex of the *ICF* to reduce the risk of disrespectful or harmful use of the classification system. The provisions address three general areas: (a) respect and confidentiality, (b) clinical use of the *ICF*, and (c) social use of *ICF* information (WHO, 2001, pp. 244–245). The sixth annex of the *ICF* prefaces the ethical guidelines for the use of *ICF* as follows:

> Every scientific tool can be misused and abused. It would be naïve to believe that a classification system such as *ICF* will never be used in ways that are harmful to people. As explained in Appendix 5, the process of the revision of *ICIDH* has included persons with disabilities and their advocacy organizations from the beginning. Their input has led to substantive changes in the terminology, content and structure of *ICF*. This annex sets out some basic guidelines for the ethical use of *ICF*. It is obvious that no set of guidelines can anticipate all forms of misuse of a classification or other scientific tool, or for that matter, that guidelines alone can prevent misuse. This document is no exception. It is hoped that attention to the provisions that follow will reduce the risk that *ICF* will

be used in ways that are disrespectful and harmful to people with disabilities. (WHO, 2001, p. 244)

The 11 provisions are listed here according to three broad themes.

Respect and Confidentiality

1. *ICF* should always be used so as to respect the inherent value and autonomy of individual persons.
2. *ICF* should never be used to label people or otherwise identify them solely in terms of one or more disability categories.
3. In clinical settings, *ICF* should always be used with the full knowledge, cooperation, and consent of the persons whose levels of functioning are being classified. If limitations of an individual's cognitive capacity preclude this involvement, the individual's advocate should be an active participant.
4. The information coded using *ICF* should be viewed as personal information and subject to recognized rules of confidentiality appropriate for the manner in which the data will be used.

Clinical Use of ICF

5. Wherever possible, the clinician should explain to the individual or the individual's advocate the purpose of the use of *ICF* and invite questions about the appropriateness of using it to classify the person's levels of functioning.
6. Wherever possible, the person whose level of functioning is being classified (or the person's advocate) should have the opportunity to participate and in particular to challenge or affirm the appropriateness of the category being used and the assessment assigned.
7. Because the deficit being classified is a result of both a person's health condition and the physical and social context in which the person lives, *ICF* should be used holistically.

Social Use of ICF Information

8. *ICF* information should be used, to the greatest extent feasible, with the collaboration of individuals to enhance their choices and their control over their lives.
9. *ICF* information should be used toward the development of social policy and political change that seeks to enhance and support the participation of individuals.
10. *ICF*, and all information derived from its use, should not be employed to deny established rights or otherwise restrict legitimate entitlements to benefits for individuals or groups.
11. Individuals classed together under the *ICF* may still differ in many ways. Laws and regulations that refer to *ICF* classifications should not assume more homogeneity than intended and should ensure that those whose levels of functioning are being classified are considered as individuals (WHO, 2001, pp. 244–245).

FUTURE DIRECTIONS FOR THE *ICF*

The WHO wrote in the eighth annex of the *ICF* that the *ICF* is owned by all its users. There is much left to be done by the international community owners of this important but developing system. WHO suggested the following foci for future work with the *ICF*:

1. Promote the use of the *ICF* at the country level for development of national databases.
2. Establish an international dataset and the framework to permit international comparisons.

3. Identify algorithms for eligibility for social benefits and pensions.

4. Study disability and functioning of family members (e.g., a study of third-party disability due to the health condition of significant others).

5. Develop the personal factors component.

6. Develop precise operational definitions of categories for research purposes.

7. Develop assessment instruments for identification and measurement.

8. Provide practical applications by means of computerization and case recording forms.

9. Establish links with quality-of-life concepts and the measurement of subjective well-being.

10. Research into treatment or intervention matching.

11. Promote use in scientific studies for comparison between different health conditions.

12. Develop training materials on the use of *ICF*.

13. Create *ICF* training and reference centers worldwide.

14. Research environmental factors to provide the necessary detail for use in describing the standardized and current environment (WHO, 2001, pp. 251–252).

The literature reviewed in this chapter suggests that considerable progress has been made in meeting the goals suggested by the WHO. It is an exciting time to be involved with the development of the *ICF* as its owners take responsibility for making the system the best it can be for society. We conclude this chapter with a review of important future developments for the *ICF*.

Mental Health Parity

The *ICF* was designed to be etiologically neutral, addressing health and function regardless of diagnosis. Consequently, the *ICF* promotes parity between physical and mental health care service provision. For example, difficulties in attention are classified the same regardless of whether they are caused by problems with physical pain, the effects of medication, or depression. When functioning becomes the focus of describing health, the differences between physical and mental impairments are not a focus of attention, supporting aspirations for mental health parity (Peterson & Threats, 2005).

Unfortunately, mental health-related services are often relegated to mental health carve outs that are not as well resourced as services for physical medicine. Although mental health care parity legislation was passed in the United States, it has yet to effectively challenge the lack of parity with respect to third-party resources provided for the treatment of physical versus mental disabilities. The *ICF* has brought international attention to this dilemma through the associated Mental Health Task Force (see Kennedy, 2003).

If health care classification becomes more etiologically neutral and focuses on functioning (what a person does, what he or she can do given the opportunity), the rationale for mental health parity becomes more salient. It is to be hoped that, the *ICF* will continue to play an important role in achieving mental health parity and in treating people with mental disorders comparably to people dealing with physical disorders. For a thorough review of the important work of the Mental Health Task Force described in our historical development discussion of the *ICF*, see the study by Kennedy (2003).

Social Justice and Disability Advocacy

Although the original *ICIDH* (WHO, 1980) was developed in close circles of rehabilitation professionals who did not systematically consult with people with disabilities, efforts began in 1993 to revise the classification system with input sought from the disability community, including individuals with disabilities and related organizations. Disabled Peoples' International contributed its time and energies to the revision process, and the *ICF* reflects their important input (Duggan, Albright, & LeQuerica, 2008; Hurst, 2003; WHO, 2001, p.

242). Subsequently, the United Nations recognized the *ICIDH*'s value and endorsed its use "as a basis for human rights advocacy around the world" (Üstün et al., 2003, p. 569). Future efforts to revise the *ICF* will present an international opportunity for those interested in social justice to meaningfully contribute to the *ICF*'s ongoing development.

Advocacy is an ethical responsibility of all health care professionals. The ethical provisions of the *ICF* encourage health care professionals to use the *ICF* to facilitate the empowerment and inclusion of persons with disabilities in society. One way to advocate social justice for those who may be marginalized by society is to include them in the development of practical solutions, as was done in the development of the *ICF* (Peterson & Threats, 2005). The *ICF* greatly benefited from significant input from all of its stakeholders, an example of social justice in action.

The disability community was also involved in and had an important impact on the identification of key constructs within the classification during latter phases of the development of the *ICF* (see Hurst, 2003; Üstün et al., 2003). For example, the term *handicap* was eliminated from the classification because of its pejorative connotations in English. Disability was purposefully avoided as a name of any component of the *ICF* and is used as an umbrella term that is operationalized as activity limitations or participation restrictions (see definitions described previously).

Another important outcome of the disability community's involvement was the establishment of the Environmental Task Force (ETF), one of the three task forces created for the recent revision process. ETF was funded by the Centers for Disease Control and chaired by Rachel Hurst, a disability rights activist (Hurst, 2003). People with disabilities were the majority of the members of the ETF, representing WHO-based geographic regions and expertise in environmental factors and disability. The work of the ETF resulted in the development of the environmental factors component of the *ICF*, which encouraged consideration of the influence of interactions between an individual and his or her environment rather than focusing on the person's impairment exclusively (Schneidert, Hurst, Miller, & Üstün, 2003).

The contextual factors (environmental and personal factors) developed in collaboration with the disability community provided a more holistic picture of health and functioning. Classifying health and functioning in light of contextual factors facilitates more effective health care service provision for people with disabilities and greater social justice. Social policy developers can consider contextual factors and related databases when establishing legislation, services, and interventions for people with disabilities (Hurst, 2003; Schneidert et al., 2003).

Future Research

Literature generated by *ICF* stakeholders suggest a number of areas of ongoing research on the *ICF* (Peterson, 2005; Peterson & Rosenthal, 2005; Peterson et al., 2010). Validity studies are necessary to provide evidence to support the model of disability and functioning proposed by the WHO. Further operationalization and quantification of *ICF* codes and qualifiers are necessary. Researchers must collect data on the various constructs presented, explore associations, and hypothesize and confirm causal links. *ICF* core sets have been and continue to be developed in order to assemble useful collections of disability-specific code sets. As research progresses on more specific applications of the *ICF*, evidence for the validity of specific applications will become apparent (Peterson & Paul, 2009).

Chute (2005) proposed that the evolving knowledge base of medical information has outgrown our ability to consume it effectively. Systems like the *ICF* and its sister classification, the *ICD*, in electronic and searchable formats, can help construct shared semantics, vocabularies, and terminologies that are accessible and clinically useful in a way that helps us to use medical knowledge effectively for treating people in health care settings. Medical informatics is a very complex area of research. Aspects of health and functioning are important metrics of well-being and so are important to include in this evolving research area (Chute, 2005).

The *ICF* contributes to an increasingly unified global discourse about the health and well-being of groups including people with disabilities. Researchers involved in clinical practice and in using the *ICF* need to continue developing international and interdisciplinary collaborations to facilitate this discourse (Martin, 2009). Ongoing clinical implementation efforts will help us understand the *ICF*'s utility in conceptualizing functioning, disability, and health within this international and multidisciplinary paradigm.

Some believe that the *ICF* is still missing important aspects of life and living currently summarized under the personal component of contextual factors. Ueda and Okawa (2003) suggest that the entire "subjective dimension" or "experience" is missing from the *ICF* entirely. They define the "subjective experience of disability" as

> A set of cognitive, emotional and motivational states of mind of any person, but particularly of a person with health condition and/or disability. ... It is a unique combination of, on one hand, a disability experience, i.e. a reflection (influence) of existing health conditions, impairments, activity limitations, participation restrictions and negative environmental factors (obstacles) into the person's mind (negative subjective experience), and on the other hand an experience of a positive nature, which includes, among other things, the psychological coping skills developed, often unconsciously, in order to overcome these negative influences (positive subjective experience). (p. 599)

It is reasonable to propose that there may be considerable overlap between subjective experience and personal factors, which are currently undefined within the contextual part of the *ICF*. To the *ICF*'s credit, developing this component is prioritized as important future work for the *ICF* (WHO, 2001, p. 251).

CONCLUSIONS

The *ICF* promises to inform our international health efforts by providing a unified language of health and functioning that will facilitate the exchange of information worldwide. Future assessment, treatment, and research efforts using the *ICF* can revolutionize the way we think about physical and psychological functioning, disability, and health; improve the quality of care for individuals internationally; generate and disseminate universal research data on disability and functioning; and ultimately influence culturally sensitive global health policy.

Those who want to learn more about the *ICF* should consult the *ICF* itself for more precise coding guidelines, paying close attention to annexes at the end of the document, specifically, Annexes 2, 3, and 4; seek training from WHO affiliates knowledgeable in the *ICF*; and read more of the seminal references noted in this chapter.

REFERENCES

American Medical Association. (2017). *Current procedural terminology*. Washington, DC: Author.

American Psychiatric Association. (2013). *Diagnostic and statistical manual of mental disorders* (5th ed.). Arlington, VA: American Psychiatric Publishing.

Bassett, S. S., Chase, G. A., Folstein, M. F., & Regier, D. A. (1998). Disability and psychiatric disorders in an urban community: Measurement, prevalence and outcomes. *Psychological Medicine, 28*(3), 509–517.

Brandsma, J. W., Lakerveld-Heyl, K., Van Ravensberg, C. D., & Heerkens, Y. F. (1995). Reflection on the definition of impairment and disability as defined by the World Health Organization. *Disability and Rehabilitation, 17*(3–4), 119–127.

Brown, S. C. (1993). Revitalizing "handicap" disability research. *Journal of Disability Policy Studies, 4*, 55–73.

Brown, S. D., & Lent, R. (Eds.). (2008). *Handbook of counseling psychology* (4th ed.). Hoboken, NJ: John Wiley.

Bruyère, S. M., & Peterson, D. B. (2005a). Introduction to the special section on the *International Classification of Functioning, Disability and Health (ICF)*: Implications for rehabilitation psychology. *Rehabilitation Psychology, 50*, 103–104.

Bruyère, S. M., & Peterson, D. B. (Eds.). (2005b). Special section on the *International Classification of Functioning, Disability and Health (ICF)*: Implications for rehabilitation psychology. *Rehabilitation Psychology, 50*.

Bruyère, S. M., Van Looy, S. A., & Peterson, D. B. (2005). *The International Classification of Functioning, Disability and Health (ICF)*: Contemporary literature review. *Rehabilitation Psychology, 50*, 113–121.

Burns, C. (1991). Parallels between research and diagnosis: The reliability and validity issues of clinical practice. *Nurse Practitioner, 16*(10), 42–45, 49–50.

Chute, C. G. (2005, June). *The spectrum of clinical data representation: A context for functional status.* Symposium conducted at the meeting of the World Health Organization's North American Collaborating Center, Mayo Clinic, Rochester, MN.

De Kleijn-De Vrankrijker, M. W. (2003). The long way from the *International Classification of Impairments, Disabilities and Handicaps (ICIDH)* to the *International Classification of Functioning, Disability and Health (ICF)*. *Disability and Rehabilitation, 25*, 561–564.

Dell Orto, A. E., & Power, P. W. (Eds.). (2007). *The psychological and social impact of illness and disability*. New York, NY: Springer Publishing.

Duggan, C. H., Albright, K. J., & LeQuerica, A. (2008). Using the ICF to code and analyse women's disability narratives. *Disability and Rehabilitation, 30*(12–13), 978–990.

Elliott, T., Kurylo, M., & Rivera, P. (2002). Positive growth following an acquired physical disability. In C. R. Snyder & S. Lopez (Eds.), *Handbook of positive psychology* (pp. 687–699). New York, NY: Oxford University Press.

Engel, G. L. (1977). The need for a new medical model: A challenge for biomedicine. *Science, 196*(4286), 129–136.

Gatchel, R. J., Polatin, P. B., Mayer, T. G., & Garcy, P. D. (1994). Psychopathology and the rehabilitation of patients with chronic low back pain disability. *Archives of Physical Medicine and Rehabilitation, 75*(6), 666–670.

Hurst, R. (2003). The International Disability Rights Movement and the *ICF*. *Disability and Rehabilitation, 25*(11–12), 572–576.

Kennedy, C. (2003). Functioning and disability associated with mental disorders: The evolution since ICIDH. *Disability and Rehabilitation, 25*(11–12), 611–619.

Leonardi, M., Bickenbach, J., Ustun, T. B., Kostanjsek, N., & Chatterji, S.; MHADIE Consortium. (2006). The definition of disability: What is in a name? *Lancet, 368*(9543), 1219–1221.

Marini, I., & Stebnicki, M. (Eds.). (2012). *The psychological and social impact of illness and disability* (6th ed.). New York, NY: Springer Publishing.

Martin, S. (2009). Improving diagnosis worldwide. *Monitor on Psychology, 40*(9), 62–65.

Massel, H. K., Liberman, R. P., Mintz, J., Jacobs, H. E., Rush, T. V., Giannini, C. A., & Zarate, R. (1990). Evaluating the capacity to work of the mentally ill. *Psychiatry, 53*(1), 31–43.

McCrone, P., & Phelan, M. (1994). Diagnosis and length of psychiatric in-patient stay. *Psychological Medicine, 24*(4), 1025–1030.

National Advisory Mental Health Council. (1993). Health care reform for Americans with severe mental illness: Report of the National Advisory Mental Health Council. *American Journal of Psychiatry, 150*, 1447–1465.

Nieuwenhuijsen, E. R. (1995). The ICIDH in the USA: Applications and relevance to ADA goals. *Disability and Rehabilitation, 17*(3–4), 154–158.

Olkin, R. (1999). *What psychotherapists should know about disability*. New York, NY: Guilford Press.

Olkin, R., & Pledger, C. (2003). Can disability studies and psychology join hands? *The American Psychologist, 58*(4), 296–304.

Ormel, J., Oldehinkel, T., Brilman, E., & vanden Brink, W. (1993). Outcome of depression and anxiety in primary care. A three-wave 3 ½-year study of psychopathology and disability. *Archives of General Psychiatry, 50*(10), 759–766.

Peterson, D. B. (2005). *International Classification of Functioning, Disability and Health (ICF)*: An introduction for rehabilitation psychologists. *Rehabilitation Psychology, 50*, 105–112.

Peterson, D. B. (2009). *The International Classification of Functioning, Disability & Health*: Application to professional counseling. In M. A. Stebnicki & I. Marini (Eds.), *The professional counselor's desk reference* (pp. 529–542). New York, NY: Springer Publishing.

Peterson, D. B. (2011). *Psychological aspects of functioning, disability and health*. New York, NY: Springer Publishing.

Peterson, D. B. (2015a). Mental health management in vocational rehabilitation and disability evaluation: Applying the *International Classification of Functioning, Disability and Health (ICF)* conceptual framework. In R. Escorpizo, S. Brage, D. Homa, & G. Stucki (Eds.), *Handbook of vocational rehabilitation and disability evaluation: Application and implementation of the ICF* (pp. 295–316). Switzerland: Springer.

Peterson, D. B. (2015b). The *International Classification of Functioning, Disability & Health*: Applications for professional counseling. In I. Marini & M. Stebnicki (Eds.). *The professional counselor's desk reference* (2nd ed. pp. 329–336). New York, NY: Springer Publishing.

Peterson, D. B. (2017). Conceptualizing functioning, disability and health (Revision). In D. R. Falvo & B. Holland, *Medical and psychosocial aspects of chronic illness and disability* (6th ed. pp. 1–9). Burlington, MA: Jones & Bartlett.

Peterson, D. B., & Elliott, T. R. (2008). Advances in conceptualizing and studying disability. In S. Brown & R. W. Lent (Eds.), *Handbook of counseling psychology* (4th ed., pp. 212–230). Hoboken, NJ: Wiley.

Peterson, D. B., & Kosciulek, J. F. (Eds.). (2005). Special issue on the *International Classification of Functioning, Disability & Health (ICF). Rehabilitation Education, 19*.

Peterson, D. B., Mpofu, E., & Oakland, T. D. (2010). Concepts and models in disability, functioning, and health. In E. Mpofu & T. Oakland (Eds.), *Rehabilitation and health assessment: Applying ICF guidelines* (pp. 3–26). New York, NY: Springer Publishing.

Peterson, D. B., & Paul, H. (2009). Using the *International Classification of Functioning, Disability and Health* (ICF) to conceptualize disability functioning in psychological injury and law. *Psychological Injury and Law, 2*(3–4), 205–214.

Peterson, D. B., & Rosenthal, D. (2005). The *International Classification of Functioning, Disability and Health*: A primer for rehabilitation educators. *Rehabilitation Education, 19*, 81–94.

Peterson, D. B., & Threats, T. T. (2005). Ethical and clinical implications of the *International Classification of Functioning, Disability and Health (ICF)* in rehabilitation education. *Rehabilitation Education, 19*, 129–138.

Peterson, D. B. & Threats, T. T. (2016). The World Health Organization Model of Health: What evidence is needed? In K. Olson, R. A. Young, & I. Z. Schultz (Eds.), *Handbook of qualitative health research for evidence-based practice* (pp. 61–76). New York, NY: Springer.

Pledger, C. (2003). Discourse on disability and rehabilitation issues. Opportunities for psychology. *The American Psychologist, 58*(4), 279–284.

Rabinowitz, J., Modai, I., & Inbar-Saban, N. (1994). Understanding who improves after psychiatric hospitalization. *Acta Psychiatrica Scandinavica, 89*(3), 152–158.

Reed, G. M., Dilfer, K., Bufka, L. F., Scherer, M. J., Kotzé, P., Tshivhase, M., . . . Stark, S. L. (2008). Three model curricula for teaching clinicians to use the ICF. *Disability and Rehabilitation, 30*(12–13), 927–941.

Reed, G. M., Lux, J. B., Jacobson, J. W., Stark, S., Threats, T. T., Peterson, D. B., et al. (2005). Operationalizing the *International Classification of Functioning, Disability and Health* (ICF) in clinical settings. *Rehabilitation Psychology, 50*, 122–131.

Rock, M. (2005, June). *Welcome WHO/ICF NACC to Mayo clinic*. Symposium conducted at the meeting of the World Health Organization's North American Collaborating Center, Mayo Clinic, Rochester, MN.

Rusk, H. A. (1977). *Rehabilitation medicine* (4th ed.). St. Louis, MO: Mosby.

Schneidert, M., Hurst, R., Miller, J., & Ustün, B. (2003). The role of environment in the *International Classification of Functioning, Disability and Health (ICF). Disability and Rehabilitation, 25*(11–12), 588–595.

Segal, S. P., & Choi, N. G. (1991). Factors affecting SSI support for sheltered care residents with serious mental illness. *Hospital & Community Psychiatry, 42*(11), 1132–1137.

Simeonsson, R. J., Leonardi, M., Lollar, D., Bjorck-Akesson, E., Hollenweger, J., & Martinuzzi, A. (2003). Applying the *International Classification of Functioning, Disability and Health* (ICF) to measure childhood disability. *Disability and Rehabilitation, 25*(11–12), 602–610.

Smart, J. (2005). The promise of the *International Classification of Functioning, Disability & Health* (ICF). *Rehabilitation Education, 19*, 191–199.

Stucki, G., Ustün, T. B., & Melvin, J. (2005). Applying the ICF for the acute hospital and early post-acute rehabilitation facilities. *Disability and Rehabilitation, 27*(7–8), 349–352.

Threats, T. T., & Worrall, L. (2004). Classifying communication disability using the ICF. *Advances in Speech-Language Pathology, 6*, 53–62.

Ueda, S., & Okawa, Y. (2003). The subjective dimension of functioning and disability: What is it and what is it for? *Disability and Rehabilitation, 25*(11–12), 596–601.

Ustün, T. B., Chatterji, S., Bickenbach, J., Kostanjsek, N., & Schneider, M. (2003). The *International Classification of Functioning, Disability and Health*: A new tool for understanding disability and health. *Disability and Rehabilitation, 25*(11–12), 565–571.

United Nations Department of Public Information. (1993). *The standard rules on the equalization of opportunities for persons with disabilities.* Adopted by the United Nations General Assembly, 48th session, resolution 48/96, annex, of 20 December, 1993.

World Health Organization. (1980). *International classification of impairments, disabilities, and handicaps (ICIDH).* Geneva, Switzerland: Author.

World Health Organization. (2016). *International statistical classification of diseases and related health problems, tenth revision (ICD-10).* Geneva, Switzerland: Author.

World Health Organization. (1999). *ICIDH-2: International classification system of functioning and disability: Beta-2 draft, short version.* Geneva, Switzerland: Author.

World Health Organization. (2001). *International classification of functioning, disability and health: ICF.* Geneva, Switzerland: Author.

Wright, B. A. (1983). *Physical disability: A psychosocial approach* (2nd ed.). New York, NY: Harper & Row.

Wright, G. N. (1980). *Total rehabilitation.* Boston, MA: Little, Brown.

24

From Empathy Fatigue to Empathy Resiliency

Mark A. Stebnicki

*I*n traditional Native American philosophy, it is said that each time you heal some-one you give away a piece of yourself. The journey to become a medicine man or woman requires an understanding that the healer at some point in time will become wounded and require healing (Tafoya & Kouris, 2003). Nouwen (1972) refers to this experience as *the wounded healer*, whereby the helper may detach or withdraw into himself or herself, creating a space for no one else to enter. In Native American culture as well as others that discuss professional fatigue syndromes, many counseling profes-sionals in the West also encounter a wounded healer type of experience. I refer to this phenomenon as *empathy fatigue*. It results from a state of psychological, emotional, mental, physical, spiritual, and occupational exhaustion that occurs as the counselors' own wounds are continually revisited by his or her clients' life stories of chronic illness, disability, trauma, grief, and loss (Stebnicki, 1999, 2000, 2001, 2007, 2008, 2012). It is of paramount importance that professional counselors, counselor educators, clinical supervisors, and concerned others recognize this negative shift within the professional counselor's mind, body, and spirit that may signal an empathy fatigue experience. This chapter offers (a) a description of the empathy fatigue construct as it relates to other professional fatigue syndromes, (b) a recently developed tool (Global Assessment of Empathy Fatigue [GAEF]) that may be useful for screening and identifying professionals who may be experiencing empathy fatigue, and (c) resources for self-care of empathy fatigue and building resiliency.

Many counselors spend a tremendous amount of time and energy acting in com-passionate and empathic ways searching for the meaning of their clients' mind, body, and spirit that has been lost to trauma, incest, addictions, and other stressors that prompt questions concerning the meaning of their lives. As a consequence, profes-sional counselors become affected by the same persistent or transient physical, emo-tional, and psychological symptoms as their clients. Thus, empathy fatigue is a type of counselor impairment that affects the whole self: mind, body, and spirit. Identifying counselor impairment or fatigue syndromes requires the use of self-care practices to maintain competent and ethical practice in the counseling profession (Herlihy & Corey, 2015). As Schneider Corey and Corey (2016) suggest, helpers feel a great pressure being intimately connected with the welfare of their clients. This type of professional work-related stress has a psychological, physical, and behavioral cost that may result in the symptoms of depression, anxiety, and emotional exhaustion. From the empathy fatigue perspective, there is a cost to one's mind, body, and spiritual growth.

COMPARING EMPATHY FATIGUE WITH COUNSELOR IMPAIRMENTS

Similar observations and measurements of counselor impairment and fatigue syndromes have been noted in the nursing, psychology, counseling, and mental health literature. Compassion fatigue was first introduced in the nursing literature by Joinson (1992) and then expanded by Figley (1995, 2002), Pearlman and Saakvitne (1995), and Stamm (1995), as well as others later on in the psychology literature. Early in its development, compassion fatigue hypothesized that therapists who deal with survivors of extraordinarily stressful and traumatic events are more prone to compassion fatigue or a secondary traumatic stress (STS) type of reaction as a result of feeling compassion and empathy toward others' pain and suffering. McCann and Pearlman (1989) refer to this experience as "vicarious traumatization," in which the therapist becomes deeply emotionally affected by the client's traumatic stories. Consequently, the professional counselor experiences a special type of burnout (Maslach, 1982, 2003), where there is an organizational–environmental impact on the person who feels emotionally and physically exhausted, depleted, and has reached the point of depersonalization with his or her professional colleagues.

More recent, Stamm (2010) has noted that more than 500 papers, books, articles, and 130 dissertations have been written on or related to compassion fatigue. Stamm has developed the Professional Quality of Life Scale (ProQOL), which is based on the foundations of the compassion fatigue construct. It is beyond the scope of this chapter to describe the ProQOL; therefore, readers should consult the Resources list for a comprehensive discussion given the breadth of this work by Stamm.

Empathy Fatigue as the Wounded Spirit

Clearly, the search for personal meaning in one's chronic illness, disability, or traumatic experience is an existential and spiritual pursuit (Stebnicki, 2006). Multiple client stories of extraordinarily stressful and traumatic events, as well as exposure to clients with chronic illness and life-threatening disabilities, many times place the professional helper at risk of feeling helpless and hopeless. Many professional helpers search for spiritual and existential meaning within the context of their clients' pain and suffering. Such questions as *How could life and death, joy and suffering, love, self-acceptance, and healing exist all within the same day in the lives of my clients?* can be quite overwhelming and disorienting. So the question becomes: Who pays attention to, and takes care of, the wounded healer? Nouwen (1972) speaks about this type of counselor fatigue experience from his concept of the wounded healer. He suggests that, paradoxically, we withdraw into ourselves, thus creating a sacred space for no other person to enter. Miller (2003) suggests that from the wounded healer concept, as the counselor brings a compassionate spirit to the counseling relationship, the client's expectation of the counselor is that he or she does not have any psychological, emotional, or spiritual vulnerabilities. Thus, the counselor is seen as a role model for emotional and spiritual wellness by the client who feels wounded.

Spirituality is a natural part of being human (Assagioli, 1965; Jung, 1973; Worthington, 1988). In many cultures, one of the most significant and meaningful questions relates to where we came from before birth and where we will transcend at the time of our death (Pedersen, 2000), a deep spiritual and existential question. Accordingly, professional counselors have an ethical obligation to explore the spiritual identity of their clients' lives (Association of Spiritual, Ethical, and Religious Values in Counseling [ASERVIC], 2014; Pargament & Zinnbauer, 2000; Shafranske & Malony, 1996). Indeed, spirituality plays a prominent role in the lives of individuals from many different cultural and ethnic backgrounds. Spiritual connectedness is a cultural attribute and can be a form of social support that empowers individuals with chronic illnesses and disabilities to cope with their environment (Harley, Stebnicki, & Rollins, 2000). Thus, to work effectively with the client's spiritual identity and worldview, it has been suggested throughout the literature that counselor educators and supervisors need to intentionally prompt their supervisee to inquire about the client's spiritual health (Bishop, Avila-Juarbe, & Thumme, 2003; Cashwell & Young, 2004; Polanski, 2003; Stebnicki, 2006).

Overall, a major departure from the construct of empathy fatigue with other fatigue syndromes is the spiritual aspect. Facilitating empathic approaches in the counseling relationship requires that we help our clients unfold the layers of their stress, grief, loss, or traumatic experiences by searching through their emotional scrapbooks. The search for personal meaning and purpose of our client's pain and suffering may contribute to our own spiritual fatigue experience. If counselors are mindful of this experience, and view this as an opportunity for nurturing personal growth and development, then they may create opportunities for resiliency so that they can replenish their wounded spirits.

A NEW LOOK AT COUNSELOR IMPAIRMENT AND FATIGUE SYNDROMES

One of the most troubling aspects of counselor impairment and fatigue syndromes is that counselor educators, supervisors, and professional counseling associations have been slow to prepare counselor supervisees for cultivating self-care approaches. We do a good job of preparing competent and ethical practitioners for diagnosing and treating a variety of mental health conditions and addressing other counseling-related issues. However, the role and function of professional counselors have expanded significantly in the past 10 years. Today, many counselors provide mental health and disaster relief services to those involved in a multitude of extraordinarily stressful and traumatic events (e.g., hurricanes, fires, floods, school shootings, workplace violence, exposure to combat). Consequently, providing the mental health rescue to those at the epicenter of critical incidents profoundly affects the mind, body, and spirit of professional counselors.

Maintaining personal and professional wellness in one's career goes beyond acquiring continuing educational credits at conferences and workshops. Rather, some counselors will require a transformative personal experience to continue in their chosen profession. There appears to be some promise for addressing issues in counselor impairment and fatigue syndromes that have drawn the interest of some state and national professional counseling associations. For example, the American Counseling Association (ACA) Taskforce on Counselor Wellness and Impairment was formed in 2003 to recognize the importance of self-care approaches to increase counselor wellness (ACA, 2014). The ACA website (www .counseling.org) provides a variety of stress and compassion fatigue self-reporting instruments for the identification and prevention of counselor impairment and fatigue syndromes. It also offers resources for building capacity for occupational and career wellness.

EMPATHY: A NATURAL WAY OF BEING FOR PROFESSIONAL COUNSELORS

Throughout the history of the helping professions, the most fundamental approach to helping others has been rooted in compassion and empathy. In fact, empathy has a rich history of being at the core of most humanistic theoretical orientations within counselor education and training programs. Accordingly, possessing the skills of empathy is a prerequisite for becoming a competent helper and is a person-centered approach that practitioners can facilitate to increase interpersonal effectiveness and enhance client outcomes (Corey & Corey, in press; Egan, 1998; Ivey & Ivey, 1999; Truax & Carkhuff, 1967). The richness of using the skills of basic- and advanced-level empathy can build a strong client–counselor relationship. If facilitated competently by the therapist, empathy can (a) help increase client self-awareness; (b) be a motivation for personal growth and change; and (c) cultivate new ways of thinking, feeling, and acting to achieve optimal levels of mind, body, and spiritual wellness.

Rogers (1980) talked passionately about empathy and empathic listening as a "way of being" with a client. However, there is an emotional and physical cost to entering the private perceptual world of the client because the counselor may be a "sponge" for his or her client's emotional and physical pain. The conscious and unconscious absorption of the client's emotional, physical, spiritual, and existential issues is a natural artifact of helping others at intense levels of service. This is because many counselors are in "high-touch" professions and are at the epicenter of their client's life stories. Many client stories contain themes of extraordinarily stressful and traumatic events, pain and suffering, and result in client transference and negative countertransference of toxic energy during the session. Accordingly, there is a shadow side to facilitating empathic approaches with clients during counseling interactions. If the experience of empathy fatigue is not recognized by self and others, then it can potentially lead to a deterioration of the counselor's resiliency or coping abilities.

Rogers (1980) appeared to have an understanding of counselor fatigue syndromes. He observed a significant need for therapists to rebalance their minds, bodies, and spirits after spending countless hours in psychotherapy sessions. As I have observed, counselors who work in a variety of professional practices experience professional fatigue. This includes professionals who work with clients who have experienced loss of a loved one (i.e., grief, divorce, extramarital affairs); trauma (combat, intimate-partner sexual abuse, and violence); substance abuse (i.e., family, legal, career issues); career development issues (i.e., company downsizing, work-related job stress, career transitions); chronic health conditions (i.e., cancer, HIV/AIDS); and generalized anxiety and depression, as well as other general stress conditions.

This chapter's author hypothesizes that empathy fatigue may be different from other types of counselor impairment and fatigue syndromes. This is primarily because empathy fatigue (a) is viewed as a counselor impairment that can occur early on in one's career due to an interaction of variables that include, but are not limited to, personality traits, general coping resources, age and developmental-related factors, opportunities to build resiliency, organizational and other environmental supports, and the interrelationship among the person's mind, body, and spiritual development; (b) many times goes unrecognized by the individual and the professional counseling setting or environment because of its subtle characteristics; (c) may be experienced as both an acute and cumulative type of emotional, physical, and spiritual stressor that does not follow a predictable linear path to total burnout or fatigue; (d) is a highly individualized experience for most individuals, because the counselor's perception toward the client's story and life events differs depending on the issues presented during the session; and (e) is a dynamic construct where the search for personal meaning in one's chronic illness, disability, traumatic experience, pain, and suffering is an existential and spiritual pursuit (Stebnicki, 2006).

In view of this hypothesis, professional counselors who experience empathy fatigue appear to have a diminished capacity to listen and respond empathically to their client's stories that contain various themes of acute and cumulative psychosocial stress, not necessarily stories of acute and posttraumatic stress. Client stories that have themes such as addictions, physical or sexual abuse, and psychological trauma can adversely affect the mind, body, and spirit of the counselor. Remembering emotions related to such painful or traumatic events and recreating an internal "emotional scrapbook" can be extremely painful and difficult for clients as well as counselors. This is especially relevant for new professional counselors who have not had the opportunity to cultivate self-care strategies for professional wellness.

Carl Jung appeared to have an understanding of counselor fatigue syndromes as he observed the need for therapists to rebalance their mind, body, and spirit after spending countless hours in psychotherapy sessions with their clients. Jung was inspired by the belief that humans are spiritual beings, not just biological, instinctual, or behavioral organisms. He explored manifestations of the soul and the process of transforming the mind, body, and spirit into a greater awareness of the self to increase one's purpose in life. In Jung's view, regaining psychic equilibrium, soul searching, and self-discovery appear to be paramount in maintaining one's therapeutic practice.

New studies on the mind–body connection report that the shared emotions and physiological arousal experienced between client and therapist can contribute to our knowledge of how empathic connections are developed during counseling sessions. For example, Marci, Ham, Moran, and Orr (2007) looked at 20 client–therapist pairs, with the client being treated for mood and anxiety disorders. The researchers specifically focused on the therapeutic relationships that were formed during psychotherapy sessions. They then took measures of the physiological reactions of both client and therapist and the client's perceived level of empathy as expressed by the therapist. They found that when high positive emotions and empathy were experienced by the client and therapist, then similar physiological responses were experienced as measured by electrical skin conductance recordings, heart rate, voice dynamics, and body movement.

It appears that a much stronger working alliance or social–emotional attachment is formed in therapy than once perceived. Because an empathetic connection forms between client and therapist, there appears to be a potential for some degree of emotional and physical exhaustion experienced by intense, cumulative, and regular therapeutic interactions.

Emotions and the Brain: The Neuroscience of Empathy Fatigue

In the study of emotions and the brain, it is hypothesized that there are discrete, basic, and universal emotions that persons react to on a mind, body, and spiritual dimension (Bar-On & Parker, 2000; Barone et al., 2005; Mayne & Bonanno, 2001). Advances in neuroimaging have provided scientific tools to measure the emotional and physiological experiences of empathic therapeutic interactions, showing a significant positive correlation between developing strong empathic ties and interactions and enhanced client and patient outcomes (Riess, 2010). Despite the fact that many individuals express universal emotions (e.g., anger, love, happiness, sadness) with varying levels of experience and intensity, Mayne and Ramsey (2001) indicate that this only constitutes a measure of personal experience and a self-report of emotional expression. From a purely dynamic physiological state, emotions involve different body systems and are measured much differently by neuroscientists than experimental psychologists. This is important to understand because our individual perception of critical events will determine how our parasympathetic and sympathetic nervous systems are activated during times of an actual or anticipated stressful event. After prolonged periods of physiological stress, such as those seen by professionals who work with the traumatized, it is evident that chronic activation of the stress response has both a physiological and emotional cost. As a consequence, professionals who work at such intense levels of service may experience anxiety and depressive disorders and may account for some aspects of the emotional and physical fatigue experienced by those who report counselor fatigue syndromes such as empathy fatigue.

Kabat-Zinn (1990; see Berger, 2006) indicates that empathy fatigue can be scientifically measured in the brain because there are specific neurological pathways to empathetic responses. The complexities of studying how emotions affect our mind, body, and spirit require studying such problems from a multidisciplinary perspective that includes the fields of psychology, neurology, immunology, and biology. The discipline of psychoneuroimmunology (PNI) has provided a model by which researchers can study emotions and the brain. The task of PNI researchers is a difficult one because as Sapolsky (1998) suggests, our emotions, particularly the stress response, have their own unique physiological arousal patterns of magnitude, frequency, and intensity. This is so, in part, because people differ in how they turn on their stress mechanism and other emotional responses in the brain. As Sapolsky (1998) notes, if we are constantly trying to mobilize energy, we never have the opportunity to store it; therefore, we can use this source of energy for calm and relaxed states of consciousness. Accordingly, there is a physical and emotional cost to persistent sympathetic arousal because of the heavy secretion of glucocorticoids released in the body that are markers for depression and anxiety disorders.

Brothers (1989) points to the brain's amygdala–cortical pathway as part of the key neural circuitry that underlies the emotions associated with the empathy response. The amygdala appears to be the specific structure of the brain that orchestrates the most intense electrical activation when reading, interpreting, or trying to understand the emotions of others. Over time, the counselor's inability to express a healthy and facilitative emotional response (such as empathy) based on the client's expression of feelings such as stress, grief, or trauma appears to have a biopsychosocial–spiritual cost to the counselor. In other words, the chronic and cumulative activation of the emotional brain and habitual repression of emotions can compromise our immune system, which increases our resistance to infections, chronic illness, and diseases (Pert, Dreher, & Ruff, 2005; Sapolsky, 1998; Weil, 1995).

Although we have no control over our autonomic nervous system, we do have some degree of control over our voluntary nervous system, such as that observed during a biofeedback session. Thus, becoming attuned to things we do have control over in life is central to the care we can provide for ourselves and our clients.

RISK FACTORS IN EMPATHY FATIGUE

Stebnicki (2000) offers a functional risk-factor assessment for empathy fatigue that may assist professional counselors, counselor educators, and supervisors to identify and recognize risk factors. The items in this particular functional assessment were developed from a meta-analysis of similar counselor impairments and fatigue conditions as noted in the literature (e.g., burnout, compassion fatigue, STS, depression, substance abuse, other mental health conditions). In the current development of an empathy fatigue measure, consideration will be given to content items that address the spiritual dimension. There is a constellation of areas to consider within the experience of empathy fatigue that includes, but is not limited to, the professional's:

1. **Current and preexisting personality traits and states:** type A personality traits, unrealistic or high expectations by the person, need for recognition, and pattern of cynicism

2. **History of emotional or psychiatric problems:** underlying mental health issues or behaviors that may interfere with the counselor's competency, direct or indirect exposure to critical incidents, lethality issues, or harm to self and others
3. **Maladaptive coping behaviors:** patterns of alcohol or substance abuse, increased use of tobacco, caffeine, and food
4. **Age- and experience-related factors:** younger professionals new to counseling versus older professionals' coping abilities, experience in working with different types of clients/consumers, and experience in crisis response
5. **Organizational and system dynamics at the counselor's place of work:** an organization or system is insensitive to or unappreciative of the emotional needs of the counselor, organization, or system's openness to trying new approaches
6. **Specific job duties of counselor in which the counselor is employed:** direct service versus supervisory, caseload size, work overly demanding and time-consuming
7. **Unique sociocultural attributes:** values, beliefs, and cultural identities that may be different from that of the organization/employer
8. **Response to handling past critical and other stressful life events:** level of exposure to trauma or STS and counselor's ability to cope and identification of any counselor isolation, detachment, or dissociative issues
9. **Level of support and resources:** individual, group, or family support, ability to seek out assistance
10. **Spirituality:** counselor questioning the meaning and purpose of life, occupation, spiritual, and/or religious beliefs; anger toward god or religious affiliation; any spiritual emergencies

Generally, there are multiple risk factors in empathy fatigue that complicate one's competence and ethics, impair one's personal and professional relationships, and hinder one's capacity for personal coping and resiliency. Thus, consideration must be given to assessing empathy fatigue from a holistic perspective. Developing domains before scale items is essential in the scale development process. Other analysis and statistical procedures will also assist the researcher in the design process. The following domains are suggested to measure the construct of empathy fatigue.

- **Individual traits:** current and preexisting personality traits, any history of emotional or psychiatric problems, maladaptive coping behaviors
- **Family:** level of support and resources, family history of poor coping abilities, lack of clear expectations and rules for occupation or career
- **Sociocultural:** worldview, personal cultural identity, choice of occupation, family and extended family members, coping resources, age, gender, race, ethnicity, disability
- **Developmental level:** experience level of counselor: practicum, internship, postgraduate, or expert
- **Occupational setting:** organizational and system dynamics, setting where professional is employed, specific job duties, responsibilities, and position within the organization
- **Physical attributes:** medical–physical status, chronic illness, disability, health status, nutritional intakes, and lifestyle factors related to health
- **Cognitive behavioral:** dysfunctional thought patterns, ability to motivate oneself, flexibility in problem-solving tasks
- **Religious–spiritual:** connection to higher power, God, spirit helpers, and patterns of religious practices in terms of rituals and ceremonies

GLOBAL ASSESSMENT OF FUNCTIONING IN THE THEORETICAL MEASUREMENT OF EMPATHY FATIGUE

The GAEF rating scale is a theoretical measure of the holistic experience of empathy fatigue (Table 24.1). The GAEF is categorized according to five different levels of functioning. Level V indicates the highest level and level I the lowest level of the hypothetical construct of empathy fatigue. It is hypothesized that professional helpers may experience and project this felt sense of empathy fatigue in seven distinct content areas that are contained within each of the five levels: (a) cognitively, (b) behaviorally, (c) spiritually, (d) in process/counseling skills, (e) emotionally, (f) physically, and (g) occupationally. Table 24.1 delineates each of these areas that may be observed by self and others in the professional helper's environment. The theoretical constructs involved in measuring this type of counselor impairment are currently being researched. As the GAEF is in its theoretical stage of development, the construct of empathy fatigue is differentiated theoretically from other counselor impairment and fatigue syndromes. There is no empirical evidence as yet to report, however.

The intent and purpose of the GAEF in its early stage of development are to provide a means of viewing the overall level of functioning as the professional helper experiences empathy fatigue. The content contained within each of the five levels of functioning is based on a comprehensive review of the counselor impairment and fatigue literature in counseling, psychology, and mental health, as well as biopsychosocial research in the fields of nursing and medicine (see Stebnicki, 2008). The GAEF rating scale was also guided by the present author's clinical experiences.

Counselor impairments appear to involve a constellation of states, traits, behaviors, and other factors that encompass the person's experience of working with clients who have a diversity of issues ranging from daily hassles and life adjustment issues to extraordinarily stressful and traumatic events. It is difficult to determine universal traits or states of counselor impairment because each professional experiences and perceives his or her clients' general levels of stress differently. It is much like the difficulties in studying stressful life events. Overall, it is hypothesized that there are both conscious and unconscious factors that relate to the professional counselor's experience of stress and fatigue. Furthermore, the frequency, intensity, level of intrusion, and avoidance of critical issues are considered to be both acute and cumulative in nature. Thus, some counselors may perceive more relevance of certain characteristics within each of the content areas in the GAEF than other areas. The theoretical continuum ranging from level V (most impaired) to level I (least impaired), it is hoped, can provide an anchor or benchmark for the optimal level of functioning for professional helpers within each of the content domains.

Use of Different Raters

The GAEF should be used to rate the professional helper's current level of functioning. Because individual behaviors, states, and traits are often dependent on the environment in which they are observed, observations should be documented based on multiple raters as listed subsequently. A time sampling method should be used because the individual may differ in his or her experience of empathy fatigue with regard to events that take place at different times throughout the day (e.g., mornings, afternoons, evenings, weekends, before client sessions, after client sessions, and every other day). Persons considering rating themselves and/or others using the GAEF should be open to, and understand, the limitations and bias that are found in other subjective ratings of experiences such as mood, affect, personality, stress, attitude, motivation, level of satisfaction, and job burnout, as well as measures of spiritual well-being.

TABLE 24.1 GLOBAL ASSESSMENT OF EMPATHY FATIGUE RATING SCALE (GAEF)

Content Area	Level V	Level IV	Level III	Level II	Level I
Cognitive	• Diminished concentration • Preoccupied • Disorganized thoughts • Detachment from client	• Diminished concentration • Preoccupied • Slightly disorganized thoughts • Detachment • Possible irrational thinking	• Exhibits some diminished concentration • Somewhat preoccupied • Thought organization is loose • Fair focus on the therapeutic process • Quiet attending of counselor to internal thoughts and feelings • Having an "off day"	• Slight problems in concentration • Occasionally preoccupied • Need to continually refocus • Good focus on therapeutic process • Some response to internal thoughts and feelings • Thoughts of hopefulness • Physical signs of being restless or impatient, but controls behavior • Eye contact good • Occasionally strained vocal quality and pace of speech	• Slight problems in concentration and thought organization • More preoccupied than usual • Responding to internal thoughts and feelings more than usual, but therapeutic process good
Behavioral	• Impatience • Irritability • Aggression • Cynical with client • Hypervigilance • Poor eye contact • Strained, erratic, or slow- or fast-paced speech	• Impatient • Irritable • Competitive • Very cautious • Eye contact fair • Somewhat strained, erratic, or slow- or fast-paced speech • Somewhat cynical with clients	• Exhibits signs of restlessness or impatience • Slightly inattentive eye contact • Slightly strained vocal tone and pace of speech	• Exhibits physical signs of restlessness or impatience, but controls behavior • Eye contact good • Vocal quality and pace of speech good, but sometimes strained	

(continued)

TABLE 24.1 GLOBAL ASSESSMENT OF EMPATHY FATIGUE RATING SCALE (GAEF) (continued)

Content Area	Level V	Level IV	Level III	Level II	Level I
	• Detached from spiritual support • Lack meaning and purpose in faith or spiritual beliefs • Communication of these deficits	• Lacks some meaning and purpose with regard to faith or spiritual beliefs • Some detachment of spiritual support • Communication of lack of meaning and purpose spiritually	• Confusion regarding meaning and purpose with regard to faith or spiritual beliefs • Separation from spiritual support	• Sense of awareness of refocusing on meaning and purpose with regard to faith or spiritual beliefs • Attempts to remain connected spiritually • Makes attempts to become reconnected to spiritual support	• Sense of connectedness to faith restored after self-reassurance • Attempts to become reconnected to spiritual support
Process skills	• Lack of rapport with client • Strained working alliance • Nonexistent attending and listening • No genuine empathetic responses • Resistant • Apprehensive • Hypersensitive • High degree of countertransference • Lack of open-ended questioning • Lack of solution-focused probes • Diminished use of brainstorming techniques	• Rapport difficult to establish • No working alliance • Poor attending and listening • Gather information in session vs. processing client story • Superficial empathic responses • Some degree of countertransference • Little use of open-ended questioning • Little use of solution-focused probes • Little use of brainstorming techniques with clients	• Longer time to establish rapport • Working alliance achieved more slowly • Listening and attending to clients fair to good • Empathetic responses more genuine • Session involves gathering basic information • Some missed opportunities in therapeutic interactions • Responses have only basic empathy • Somewhat resistant or apprehensive • Little nonverbal interest during the session • Some degree of countertransference	• Working alliance takes longer to achieve but remains stable • Empathic response more genuine, deeper, and more frequent • Session goes beyond data gathering • Nonverbal incongruences in session • Avoids dealing with countertransference • Uses some open-ended questioning, solution-focused probes, or brainstorming techniques • Rapport takes longer to establish, but eventually is good • Working alliance takes longer to achieve	• Rapport takes slightly longer to establish • Working alliance takes somewhat longer to achieve, but work with client remains intact and stable • Attending and listening are appropriate • Integration of client content, experience, and affect better • Few missed therapeutic opportunities • Empathic responses somewhat deeper • Somewhat hesitant to explore new areas of client support and resources • Some nonverbal incongruences

TABLE 24.1 GLOBAL ASSESSMENT OF EMPATHY FATIGUE RATING SCALE (GAEF) *(continued)*

Content Area	Level V	Level IV	Level III	Level II	Level I
	• Basic information gathering sessions vs. processing client story • Misses opportunities to integrate client content, experience, and affect	• Somewhat resistant or apprehensive during session • Shows little nonverbal interest during testing	• Little use of open-ended questioning • Little use of solution-focused probes • Little use of brainstorming techniques	• Ongoing therapeutic work with client remains intact and stable • Attending and listening are good	• Increased interest in understanding • Open-ended questioning, solution-focused probes, and brainstorming techniques used
Emotional	• Diminished affective state • Moodiness • Sadness • Tearfulness • Negative • Pessimistic • Clear high and low emotions • Depleted • Exhausted	• Somewhat diminished affective state • Moodiness • Slight mood swings • Moderate level of sadness • Emotionally fatigued • Exhausted • Negative • Pessimistic	• Affective state fair • Slight moodiness • Dysthymic • Appears emotionally tired • Negative • Pessimistic	• Affective state good • Sense of dysthymic mood • Slightly emotionally tired • Feeling negative or pessimistic	• Affective state could be better • Sense of a slightly "down" mood • Somewhat emotionally tired • Slightly negative • Pessimistic, but initiates self-correction
Physical	• Shallow breathing • Sweating • Fatigue • Discomfort while sitting	• Shallow breathing • Slight sweating • Fatigue • Facial grimacing	• Exhibits tiredness • Sighs of frustration with breath • Facial grimacing • Lack of appetite	• Exhibits slight tiredness but takes steps to avoid fatigue • Occasional signs of frustration • Uses internal dialogue to relax • Some discomfort while sitting	• Slight tiredness • Takes steps to avoid fatigue • Occasional signs of frustration • Uses internal dialogue to relax

(continued)

TABLE 24.1 GLOBAL ASSESSMENT OF EMPATHY FATIGUE RATING SCALE (GAEF) *(continued)*

Content Area	Level V	Level IV	Level III	Level II	Level I
	• Dizziness • Nausea • Disturbance in visual acuity • Facial grimace of pain • Muscle tremors or twitches • Severe headache	• Feelings of wooziness • Lack of appetite due to upset stomach • Occasional muscle tremors or twitches • Moderate degree of headache • Disturbance in visual acuity	• Occasional muscle twitches • Slight sense of headache • Dry eyes	• Appetite and eating habits somewhat irregular • Muscles slightly tense • Needs constant reminder to rebalance physical wellness	• Appetite and eating habits somewhat irregular • Muscles feel slightly tense • Constant reminder to rebalance wellness
Occupational	• Missing at least 1 day of work per week • Canceling sessions • Not showing up for sessions • Avoids meetings • Avoids colleagues at work • Leaves work early every day • Sick or cynical sense of humor • Poor coping skills • Shows little resiliency • Difficulty separating professional and personal life	• Missing 2–3 days of work per month • Rescheduling client appointments • Avoids meetings • Avoids colleagues at work • Leaves work early on average • Consistently cuts sessions short • Exhibits cynical sense of humor • Difficulties separating professional and personal life • Struggling • Exhibiting decreased coping abilities and resiliency	• Missing 1–2 days of work per month • Some avoidance of starting session on time • Hope for client "no shows" • Cuts session shorter than usual • Makes excuses to try and leave meetings and work early • Superficial contact with colleagues at work • Exhibits inappropriate sense of humor • Some difficulties separating professional and personal life • Some difficulties with coping abilities and resiliency	• May feel the need to take off 2 days of work per month • Has thoughts of client "no shows" • Occasionally makes excuses for leaving meetings early • Minimal contact with colleagues at work • Has difficulties transitioning to social self • Some difficulties separating professional and personal life • Better coping abilities and resiliencies	• May feel the need to take off 2 days of work per month • Thoughts of client "no shows" • Conducts sessions on time and for usual duration • Will make excuses for leaving meetings early • Contact with colleagues less than usual • Exhibits usual sense of humor • Difficulties transitioning to social self • Some difficulties separating • Better coping skills and resiliency

- **Self-ratings by the professional:** The individual himself or herself may use the GAEF as a self-report measure.
- **Ratings by the professional's colleagues:** The professional may request the involvement of his or her clinical supervisor, peer mentor, or another professional to rate his or her observations independently on the GAEF measure.
- **Ratings by clients/consumers:** Ratings may be carried out according to a well-designed scheme within the work environment that uses interrater agreement by the therapist's client/consumer and/or a triad of raters (i.e., client, therapist, and independent observer).
- **Ratings by independent observers outside the work environment:** The therapist may request ratings by close professional colleagues.
- **Ratings by another objective individual:** The professional may request ratings by others (i.e., personal therapists) who are closely committed to the professional's personal goals of self-care and personal growth.

As the rater(s) view the GAEF rating scale shown in Table 24.1, they should rate the level of empathy fatigue experienced primarily within the past 2 weeks. Although the professional helper may not relate with all characteristics within each level, the therapist should choose the attributes that he or she identifies with more so than not. Furthermore, the rater(s) may consider using the GAEF levels (V, IV, III, II, and I) for each of the seven content areas and derive a rating (i.e., level V in Cognitive Behavioral; level III in Spiritual, Physical).

CULTIVATING COUNSELOR RESILIENCY

A consistent finding in resiliency psychology research suggests that persons' attitudes and beliefs play a key role in the degree of resiliency that is exhibited or expressed. Resilient professionals almost always appear to possess a higher degree of internal locus of control, and are inwardly directed, self-motivated, and thrive despite adverse conditions. Professional helpers who have bounced back from adversity in their lives, such as substance addiction, divorce, loss of a loved one, career transition, or traumatic stress, have chosen to live in an optimal state of mental and physical well-being. They have incorporated the following principles, some of which are universal, in cultivating a resilient mind, body, and spirit.

Making a Choice

Professional helpers make a thinking, feeling, and behavioral choice on a daily basis when they must deal with client adversity. At the end of the day, counselors can choose to vent with their colleagues (and be a good listener for others) and not take home all their clients' stories of adversity. If they take on this stress (consciously or unconsciously), it may be added to their own already wounded soul. Thus, the alternative would be to choose more healthy thoughts and emotions. The act of choosing a healthier outlook basically is a choice to take responsibility for one's own thoughts and emotions. There will always be a professional responsibility of helping another person in a compassionate and empathic way. However, resilient professionals know how to manage client adversity throughout their work, home, social, and interpersonal lives. Thus, not moving forward into one's own program of personal wellness would be self-defeating. The alternative would inevitably be bleak by constantly ruminating over the client's adversity at the end of the day. Thus, making a choice to change one's stream of thoughts and emotions about a client's adversity can be very empowering for some therapists. Negative and destructive thought patterns must be replaced with a plan of personal self-care and wellness. This must be reinforced and supported by colleagues and others in the counselor's environment to be successful. Accordingly, professional counselors need to create opportunities to help cultivate personal wellness and self-care approaches.

Positive Thinking

The power of positive thinking is about believing in yourself, having faith in your abilities, and having a high level of confidence that you can effect a positive outcome with your clients. As counselors struggle with their own as well as their clients' issues, it is easier for therapists to see the barriers and obstacles to living from a positive frame of reference. The counselor may have many negative recurring thoughts about the client's life in general. However, this can turn into a self-fulfilling prophecy. Professional counselors need to practice positive redirection in their thinking so that it can become a routine and intentional way of living.

Taking Self-Responsibility

Shifting blame to others does not provide an opportunity for the therapist to develop resiliency behaviors (e.g., "My clients drive me crazy sometimes by really pushing my buttons; if they think that they have problems, they should have seen the client from my previous session"). Metaphorically, "when you point a finger at someone else, there are four fingers pointing back at you." Taking responsibility is a challenge for many counselors, even though we advocate the same with our clients. Many professionals were never taught how to do this. For example, some clients may be in denial of their son's or daughter's substance abuse behaviors and may enable the adolescent. The consequences of the adolescent's bad choices may be hindered by the therapist who has taken on all the emotional responsibility, or perhaps by identifying with the adolescent's parent. Taking self-responsibility is learned behavior that can generalize to other areas of the therapist's life. We all need to learn how to model self-responsibility and give up some control to the client. Allowing our clients to take safe risks and fail can be very therapeutic at times. It can build resiliency and promote healthy choices. Meanwhile, we may learn how our clients can live without our assistance. Overall, we should be internally responsible for our own thoughts, emotions, and actions and learn how to build resiliency traits.

Self-Motivation

Resilient individuals find their own unique style of internal motivation from school, work, and home, socially, emotionally, and in other ways. Persons who have bounced back and pulled through adverse critical incidents demonstrate to others that they know how to achieve optimal and realistic control in their lives. These types of professional helpers tend to have an increased level of emotional, physical, and spiritual well-being. They are persistent with the tasks they take on and have an innate sense for knowing how to achieve their life goals. Many professionals have had the opportunity to observe healthy role models in their environment. They were fortunate to have a colleague, clinical supervisor, life coach, teacher, religious or spiritual leader, or others who have cared about them to help them overcome the more difficult challenges in their lives.

CONCLUSIONS

The experience of empathy fatigue is both similar and different from other types of counselor impairment or professional fatigue syndromes. Thus, it is hypothesized that the cumulative effects of multiple client sessions throughout the week may lead to a deterioration of the counselor's resiliency or coping abilities. Professional counselors who interact with clients who experience daily hassles and stressful life events may be at the same risk level as those professionals who assist those who are traumatized.

As the professional counselor engages in therapeutic interactions, this may predispose the counselor to experience an empathy fatigue reaction that ranges on a continuum of low, moderate, and high. However, there are multiple risk factors that should be considered as identified in the GAEF. Consequently, the cumulative effects of multiple client stories can result in the depletion of the professional counselor's empathic energies, resulting in empathy fatigue. Developing a clearer understanding of the risk factors associated with empathy fatigue is pivotal in developing self-care strategies for the professional counselor.

RESOURCES

Al Siebert Resiliency Center: resiliencycenter.com. Dr. Siebert (1934–2009) has been a resiliency researcher, trainer, and practitioner for well over 35 years. The resiliency center has, over the years, developed a culture of resiliency, as opposed to "managing ones' stress," which is counter to the resiliency philosophy. The center has a plethora of resources and research articles on resiliency.

American Counseling Association's Taskforce on Counselor Wellness and Impairment: www.counseling.org/wellness_taskforce/tf_resources.htm. The ACA is the largest professional counseling association in North America. This is a very comprehensive source for counselor self-care. There are multiple assessment and screening tools for professional counselors that include wellness, professional quality of life, traumatic stress, and a variety of other assessments.

Gift From Within: www.giftfromwithin.org. Gift is an international not-for-profit organization for survivors of traumatic stress. This particular organization is dedicated to PTSD survivors and advocates multiple supports from family, friends, and peers. Educational materials, list of retreats, workshops, and online support are offered.

Green Cross Foundation and Green Cross Academy of Traumatology: www.greencross.org. Green Cross is a professional organization of traumatologists founded by Dr. Charles Figley and colleagues, who have developed the foundational research and educational materials related to compassion fatigue.

Mark Lerner Associates, Inc.: www.marklernerassociates.com. Dr. Lerner is a clinical psychologist and traumatic stress consultant with an international reputation in organizations and individuals who have experienced extraordinarily stressful and traumatic events in their lives. Dr. Lerner offers consultations, workshops, and educational and training materials for individuals and organizations to thrive and survive after traumatic events.

RECOMMENDED READING

Brennan, B. A. (1987). *Hands of light: A guide to healing through the human energy field*. New York, NY: Bantam Books.

Davis, M., Robbins Eshelman, E., & McKay, M. (1995). *The relaxation and stress reduction workbook* (4th ed.). Oakland, CA: New Harbinger.

Fanning, P. (1994). *Taking control of your life*. Oakland, CA: New Harbinger.

Figley, C. R. (2002). *Treating compassion fatigue*. New York, NY: Brunner-Routledge.

Fox, M., & Sheldrake, R. (1996). *The physics of angels: Exploring the realm where science and spirit meets*. San Francisco, CA: Harper San Francisco.

Goodwin, L. R. (2002). *The button therapy book: A practical psychological self-help book and holistic cognitive counseling manual for mental health professionals*. Victoria, Canada: Trafford.

Hauck, R. (1994). *Angels: The mysterious messengers*. New York, NY: Ballantine.

Ingerman, S. (1991). *Soul retrieval: Mending the fragmented self.* San Francisco, CA: Harper San Francisco.

Kabat-Zinn, J. (1990). *Full catastrophe living: Using the wisdom of your body and mind to face stress, pain, and illness.* New York, NY: Dell.

Kabat-Zinn, J. (1994). *Wherever you go there you are: Mindfulness meditation in everyday life.* New York, NY: Hyperion.

LeShun, L. (1974). *A self-discovery guide of how to meditate.* Boston, MA: Bantam.

Maslach, C. (2003). *Burnout: The cost of caring.* Cambridge, MA: Malor Books.

McKay, M., Davis, M., & Fanning, P. (1997). *Thoughts and feelings: Taking control of your moods and your life.* Oakland, CA: New Harbinger.

Mehl-Madrona, L. (1997). *Coyote medicine: Lessons from Native American healing.* New York, NY: Fireside/ Simon & Schuster.

Merton, T. (1961). *New seeds of contemplation.* New York, NY: New Directions.

Mitchell, K. K. (1994). *Reiki: A torch in daylight.* St. Charles, IL: Mind Rivers.

Monaghan, P., & Diereck, E. G. (1999). *Meditation: The complete guide.* Navato, CA: New World Library.

Moodly, R., & West, W. (2005). *Integrating traditional healing practices into counseling and psycho-therapy.* Thousand Oaks, CA: Sage.

Myers, J. E., & Sweeney, T. J. (2005). *Counseling for wellness: Theory, research, and practice.* Alexandria, VA: American Counseling Association.

Schaper, D., & Camp, C. A. (2004). *Labyrinths from the outside in: Walking to spiritual insight—A beginner's guide.* Woodstock, VT: Skylight Paths.

Seaward, B. L. (1997). *Stand like mountain flow like water.* Deerfield Beach, FL: Health Communications.

Seaward, B. L. (2006). *Essentials of managing stress.* Sudbury, MA: Jones & Bartlett.

Siebert, A. (2005). *The resiliency advantage: Master change, thrive under pressure, bounce back from setbacks.* San Francisco, CA: Berrett-Koehler.

Weiss, L. (2004). *Therapist's guide to self-care.* New York, NY: Brunner-Routledge.

REFERENCES

American Counseling Association. (2014). *ACA taskforce on counselor wellness and impairment.* Retrieved from http://www.creating-joy.com/taskforce/tf_wellness_strategies.htm

Assagioli, R. (1965). *Psychosynthesis.* New York, NY: Viking Press.

Association of Spiritual, Ethical, and Religious Values in Counseling. (2014). Competencies in addressing spiritual and religious issues in counseling. Retrieved from http://www.aservic.org/resources/spiritual-competencies

Bar-On, R., & Parker, J. D. (2000). *The handbook of emotional intelligence: Theory, development, assessment, and application at home, school, and in the workplace.* San Francisco, CA: Jossey-Bass.

Barone, D. F., Hutchings, P. S., Kimmel, H. J., Traub, H. L., Cooper, J. T., & Marshal, C. M. (2005). Increasing empathetic accuracy through practice and feedback in a clinical interviewing course. *Journal of Social and Clinical Psychology, 24*(2), 156–171.

Berger, R. M. (2006). Prayer: It does a body good. *Sojourners Magazine, 35*(2), 17.

Bishop, D. R., Avila-Juarbe, E., & Thumme, B. (2003). Recognizing spirituality as an important factor in counselor supervision. *Counseling and Values, 48*(1), 34–46.

Brothers, L. (1989). A biological perspective on empathy. *American Journal of Psychiatry, 146*(1), 10–19.

Cashwell, C. S., & Young, J. S. (2004). Spirituality in counselor training: A content analysis of syllabi from introductory spirituality courses. *Counseling and Values, 48*(2), 96–109.

Egan, G. (1998). *The skilled helper: A problem-management approach to helping* (6th ed.). Pacific Grove, CA: Brooks/Cole.

Figley, C. R. (1995). *Compassion fatigue: Coping with secondary traumatic stress disorder in those who treat the traumatized.* Bristol, PA: Brunner/Mazel.

Figley, C. R. (2002). Compassion fatigue: Psychotherapists' chronic lack of self care. *Journal of Clinical Psychology, 58*(11), 1433–1441.

Harley, D. A., Stebnicki, M. A., & Rollins, C. W. (2000). Applying empowerment evaluation as a tool for self-improvement and community development with culturally diverse populations. *Journal of Community Development Society, 31*(2), 348–364.

Herlihy, B., & Corey, G. (2015). *Boundary issues in counseling: Multiple roles and responsibilities.* Alexandria, VA: American Counseling Association.

Ivey, A. E., & Ivey, M. B. (1999). *Intentional intervention and counseling: Facilitating client development in a multicultural society.* Pacific Grove, CA: Brooks/Cole.

Joinson, C. (1992). Coping with compassion fatigue. *Nursing, 22*(4), 116, 118–119, 120.

Jung, C. G. (1973). Psychology and religion: East and west. In W. McGuire & R. F. C. Hull (Eds. and Trans.), *The collected works of C. G. Jung* (Vol. 11, pp. 5–105). Princeton, NJ: Princeton University Press. (Original work published 1937)

Kabat-Zinn, J. (1990). *Full catastrophe living: Using the wisdom of your body and mind to face stress, pain, and illness.* New York, NY: Dell.

Marci, C. D., Ham, J., Moran, E., & Orr, S. P. (2007). Physiologic correlates of perceived therapist empathy and social-emotional process during psychotherapy. *Journal of Nervous and Mental Disease, 195*(2), 103–111.

Maslach, C. (1982). *The burnout: The cost of caring.* Englewood Cliffs, NJ: Prentice Hall.

Maslach, C. (2003). *Burnout: The cost of caring.* Cambridge, MA: Malor Books.

Mayne, T. J., & Bonanno, G. A. (2001). *Emotions: Current issues and future directions.* New York, NY: Guilford Press.

Mayne, T. J., & Ramsey, J. (2001). The structure of emotion: A nonlinear dynamic systems approach. In T. J. Mayne & G. A. Bonanno (Eds.), *Emotions: Current issues and future directions* (pp. 1–37). New York, NY: Guilford Press.

McCann, L., & Pearlman, L. A. (1989). Vicarious traumatization: A framework for understanding the psychological effects of working with victims. *Journal of Traumatic Stress, 3*(1), 131–149.

Miller, G. (2003). *Incorporating spirituality in counseling and psychotherapy: Theory and technique.* Hoboken, NJ: John Wiley.

Nouwen, H. J. M. (1972). *The wounded healer.* New York, NY: An Image Book/Doubleday.

Pargament, K. L., & Zinnbauer, B. J. (2000). Working with the sacred: Four approaches to religious and spiritual issues in counseling. *Journal of Counseling and Development, 78*, 162–171.

Pearlman, L. A., & Saakvitne, K. W. (1995). *Trauma and the therapist: Self-care issues for clinicians, researchers, and educators.* Lutherville, MD: Sidran Press.

Pedersen, P. (2000). *A handbook for developing multicultural awareness* (3rd ed.). Alexandria, VA: American Counseling Association.

Pert, C. B., Dreher, H. E., & Ruff, M. R. (2005). The psychosomatic network: Foundations of mind-body medicine. In M. Schlitz, T. Amorok, & M. Micozzi (Eds.), *Consciousness and healing: Integral approaches to mind-body medicine* (pp. 61–78). St. Louis, MO: Elsevier, Churchill, & Livingstone.

Polanski, P. J. (2003). Spirituality and supervision. *Counseling and Values, 47*(2), 131–141.

Riess, H. (2010). Empathy in medicine—A neurobiological perspective. *Journal of the American Medical Association, 304*(14), 1604–1605.

Rogers, C. R. (1980). *A way of being.* Boston, MA: Houghton Mifflin.

Sapolsky, R. M. (1998). *Why zebras don't get ulcers: An updated guide to stress, stress-related diseases, and coping.* New York, NY: W. H. Freeman.

Schneider Corey, M., & Corey, G. (2016). *Becoming a helper* (7th ed). Boston, MA: Cengage.

Shafranske, E. P., & Malony, H. N. (1996). Religion and the clinical practice of psychology: The case for inclusion. In E. P. Shafranske (Ed.), *Religion and the clinical practice of psychology* (pp. 561–586). Washington, DC: American Psychological Association.

Stamm, B. H. (1995). *Compassion fatigue: Coping with secondary traumatic stress disorder in those who treat the traumatized.* New York, NY: Brunner-Routledge.

Stamm, B. H. (2010). The concise ProQOL manual. Retrieved from https://nbpsa.org/images/PRP/ProQOL_Concise_2ndEd_12-2010.pdf

Stebnicki, M. A. (1999, April). *Grief reactions among rehabilitation professionals: Dealing effectively with empathy fatigue.* Presentation made at the NRCA/ARCA Alliance Annual Training Conference, Dallas, TX.

Stebnicki, M. A. (2000). Stress and grief reactions among rehabilitation professionals: Dealing effectively with empathy fatigue. *Journal of Rehabilitation, 6*(1), 23–29.

Stebnicki, M. A. (2001). Psychosocial response to extraordinary stressful and traumatic life events: Principles and practices for rehabilitation counselors. *New Directions in Rehabilitation, 12*(6), 57–71.

Stebnicki, M. A. (2006). Integrating spirituality in rehabilitation counselor supervision. *Rehabilitation Education, 20*(2), 137–159.

Stebnicki, M. A. (2007). Empathy fatigue: Healing the mind, body, and spirit of professional counselors. *Journal of Psychiatric Rehabilitation, 10*(4), 317–338.

Stebnicki, M. A. (2008). *Empathy fatigue: Healing the mind, body, and spirit of professional counselors.* New York, NY: Springer Publishing.

Stebnicki, M. A. (2012). Psychosocial impact of empathy fatigue on professional helpers. In I. Marini & M. A. Stebnicki (Eds.), *The professional counselor's desk reference* (pp. 423–432). New York, NY: Springer Publishing.

Tafoya, T., & Kouris, N. (2003). Dancing the circle: Native American concepts of healing. In S. G. Mijares (Ed.), *Modern psychology and ancient wisdom: Psychological healing practices from the world's religious traditions* (pp. 125–146). New York, NY: Haworth Integrative Healing Press.

Truax, C. B., & Carkhuff, R. R. (1967). *Towards effective counseling and psychotherapy.* Chicago, IL: Aldine.

Weil, A. (1995). *Spontaneous healing.* New York, NY: Ballantine.

Worthington, E. L. (1988). Understanding the values of religious clients: A model and its application to counseling. *Journal of Counseling Psychology, 35*(2), 166–174.

25

Obesity as a Disability: Medical, Psychosocial, and Vocational Implications*

MARIA G. ROMERO AND IRMO MARINI

*U*ntil recently, the American social condition of being overweight or obese had not received much attention from researchers or the media. The medical, psychosocial, and vocational implications of obesity have quickly moved to the forefront of study for researchers, counselors, and the medical community. Obesity is now considered the second leading cause of preventable death after cigarette smoking, and it is estimated that more than 300,000 people die each year in the United States from obesity-related complications (Fontaine & Bartlett, 1998; Puhl & Brownell, 2001). In much greater numbers, however, are the rapidly growing secondary disabilities associated with obesity, which have direct, indirect, and personal costs to the individual and the community (Seidell, 1999). In the United States, where more than $33 billion is spent by consumers each year on weight loss/management remedies and where less than 5% of the population is able to keep the weight off, it seems apparent this epidemic requires a greater understanding and better treatment alternatives (Seidell, 1999; Seligman, 1994).

In this chapter, a range of topics related to obesity, including its prevalence, medical aspects, and associated complications, are explored. Other relevant areas include the psychosocial factors pertaining to societal attitudes and individual mental health issues, vocational implications concerning work/wage discrimination, Social Security regulations, and Americans with Disabilities Act (ADA) protections. The implications for rehabilitation counselors regarding vocational and mental health counseling are also discussed.

DEFINING OVERWEIGHT AND OBESITY

Before any issues related to being overweight or obese are discussed, it is important to understand the medical definitions of each. Obesity is determined by using the body mass index (BMI) in which a person's weight in kilograms is divided by the person's height in meters squared. BMI is a measurement tool used to determine a

*From *Journal of Applied Rehabilitation Counseling*, 2006, *37*(1), 21–29. Reprinted with permission from the National Rehabilitation Counseling Association.

person's excess body weight using the following categories: overweight is a BMI of 25 kg/m² or more, obesity is a BMI of 30 kg/m² or greater, and severe obesity is BMI of 40 kg/m² or more. Consequently, a BMI under 18.5 kg/m² is defined as underweight, and a BMI between 18.5 and 24.9 is considered normal weight (Visscher & Seidell, 2001). BMI identifies persons considered to be at increased risk of weight-related disorders and premature death (Hunter, Reid, & Noble, 1998). Cross-sectional studies have also shown that a large waist circumference, considered to be in excess of 102 cm in men and 88 cm in women, is also associated with increased morbidity (Molarius & Seidell, 1998). The Metropolitan Life Insurance (MLI) Company tables have established mortality rates based on height-and-weight ratios. The MLI tables list mild obesity as being 20% to 40% over ideal weight, moderate obesity as 41% to 99% over ideal weight, and morbid obesity at 100% or more over ideal weight (MLI, 1996). The MLI tables and BMI calculations can be found at www.halls.md/body-mass-index.

Aside from this mathematical definition, *obesity* is also defined as an excessively high amount of body fat or adipose tissue in relation to lean body mass (Centers for Disease Control and Prevention [CDC], 2004). The amount of body fat (or adiposity) includes the distribution of fat throughout the body and the size of the adipose tissue deposits (CDC, 2004).

Changes in Prevalence Rates and the Current State of Overweight and Obesity

Currently, 69.2% of Americans are either overweight or obese, according to the CDC (2004). This continues to be seen as one of the biggest threats to the health of adults and children living in the United States and globally. Recent data from the Behavioral Risk Factor Surveillance System indicated that no U.S. state met the goal set forth by the *Healthy People 2010* initiative, pushing for a reduction of the proportion of obesity among adults to 15% (Obesity Society, 2014). Thirty states were within 10 percentage points above the goal. More recently, The State of Obesity (2016) report has further added that Louisiana is now the state with the highest obesity rate (36%), along with other southern states such as Alabama and Mississippi. Colorado was reported to be the state with the lowest (20%) obesity rates. Furthermore, four states (Minnesota, Montana, New York, and Ohio) have seen obesity rates decrease, which marks the first time any type of decrease for obesity rates has been seen since Washington, DC, reported a decrease in 2010 (The State of Obesity, 2016). The *Healthy People 2020* target is to reduce obesity by 13% or reduce the proportion of adults who are obese to 31% (Office of Disease Prevention and Health Promotion [ODPHP], 2016).

PREVALENCE

The sudden rise in numbers of children and adults who are obese has led researchers and global health organizations, such as the World Health Organization (WHO), to identify obesity, especially among children, as one of the most critical "health challenges" of the 21st century (WHO, 2016, para. 1). Half a billion people worldwide are considered obese, a health problem affecting industrialized and developing countries alike. In the United States, adults reportedly gain about 1 to 2 pounds per year, which translates to about 40 to 80 pounds of weight gain over the course of adulthood (Berger, 2014). Presently, this puts the health of children and adults at risk and raises the total cost of preventable health conditions up to a possible $210 billion (The State of Obesity, 2016), when in 2008, estimates of the annual medical burden of obesity and overweight were about $147 billion (Kirby, Liang, Chen, & Wang, 2012). Annually, medical costs for people with obesity are about $1,400 more than a normal weight adult (CDC, 2016). In light of these numbers, some recent reports have indicated that rates of obesity may be slowing down, or even reaching a plateau in the United States (Berger, 2014; The State of Obesity, 2016), findings that may be attributable to the push of programs designed to increase and promote health awareness and an interest in healthier eating habits.

Recent estimates by the CDC (2016c) indicate that 79% of adults older than 20 years are overweight, including 36.5% of individuals with obesity. Youth with obesity are reported to be at 17% where the largest increases were among adolescents (12–19 years) rather than younger children (Carroll, Navaneelan, Bryan, & Ogden, 2015).

Gender

Several characteristics, such as gender, race, ethnicity, and socioeconomic factors, seem to play a part in the variability and the prevalence of obesity (De Silver, 2013). For example, recent data by the CDC (2016c) and the Pew Research Center (De Silver, 2013) suggest that culture and gender may be playing a larger role in the numbers of Americans who are overweight or obese, such that this tends to be less prevalent among women with higher income and a college education. Researchers have yet to find a significant relationship between obesity and men with higher income or education (De Silver, 2013). The CDC (2016c) indicated that obesity is higher among non-Hispanic Black and Mexican American men with higher incomes compared to low-income men. Women, aged 20 through 59 years, with obesity outnumber men (Ogden, Carroll, Fryar, & Flegal, 2015). More than one third of women (38%; aged 25–65 years) are obese (BMI greater than 30), and 20% of these are morbidly obese (BMI greater than 40) compared to 12% of men (Berger, 2014).

Ethnicity

Since the publication of this chapter in 2012, the prevalence of obesity continues to affect certain racial/ethnic groups disproportionately (CDC, 2016c; Kirby et al., 2012), especially among women (Wang & Beydoun, 2007). Several studies (Kirby et al., 2012; Wang & Beydoun, 2007) indicate that about half of African American women are obese compared to one third of White women and 37% of Black men. As for men, it was previously mentioned that obesity is higher among non-Hispanic Black and Mexican American men when income increased (CDC, 2016c). Asian Americans experience less obesity than any other group (10%), compared with 32% for Whites, 43% for Hispanics, and 47% for Blacks (De Silver, 2013).

Among youth, Hispanic and African American female youth face substantially higher rates of overweight and obesity than their same-aged White peers (Fradkin et al., 2015; The State of Obesity, 2016; Wang & Beydoun, 2007). The National Health and Nutrition Examination Survey (NHANES) data from 2011 to 2014 reported that 15% of White youth are obese, compared to 22% of Hispanic youth and 20% of African American youth, and only 8% of Asian American youth (The State of Obesity, 2016). Other studies have examined the role of income on obesity in youth, such that children coming from higher socioeconomic status (SES) have lower rates of obesity, but the same cannot be said for Hispanic and African American youth (Fradkin et al., 2015; Ogden, Lamb, Carroll, & Flegal, 2010).

MEDICAL IMPLICATIONS

The medical community has been reluctant to educate or dictate to patients the impact obesity has on the body (Cleator et al., 2002). In one study, nearly 50% of obese patients indicated that their physician had not recommended any treatment for weight loss and

75% reported that they had little or any faith in their physician to assist them with weight loss (Wadden et al., 2000; Wee, McCarthy, Davis, & Phillips, 1999). Relatedly, physicians have generally reported a negative bias toward overweight patients (Ajzen & Fishbein, 1977; Eagly & Chaiken, 1993; Teachman & Brownell, 2001). Indeed, physicians may not only perceive overweight and obese patients differently, but some have also been found to spend less time with heavier patients (approximately 9 minutes) and have less of a desire to help them (Hebl & Xu, 2001). Hebl, Xu, and Mason (2003) found that although male overweight patients did not perceive their quality of care to be lower than that of nonoverweight patients, female overweight patients did perceive poorer quality care from their physicians.

Secondary Complications of Obesity

As noted earlier, the health effects of obesity make it the second leading cause of preventable death (Puhl & Brownell, 2001). Independent of this, however, are the tens of millions of persons at risk of developing more serious chronically disabling conditions. The Obesity Society (2014) reports that obesity is associated with more than 30 medical conditions with very strong evidence linked with at least 15 secondary conditions. The highest prevalence ratio is linked with high blood pressure—essentially the heavier one is, the greater the likelihood of having this condition. The Obesity Society reports that more than 75% of hypertension cases can be directly attributed to obesity, and the risk of developing hypertension is 5 to 6 times greater than that in nonobese individuals between 20 and 45 years of age (Obesity Society, 2014; Diamanti-Kandarakis & Bergiele, 2001). Hypertension related to obesity has been found across all age and ethnic groups, gender, and SES. Hypertension is further related to cardiovascular disease as a result of high blood lipid levels (triglycerides or bad cholesterol—low-density lipoproteins) and eventually coronary heart disease across all groups.

The incidence of coronary heart disease follows the same prevalence trajectory as hypertension in that the higher an individual's BMI, the higher the percentage of reported coronary heart disease. For example, the prevalence of coronary heart disease among women with a BMI of 18.5 to 24.9 is 6.87%, whereas the prevalence among women with a BMI of greater than 40 is 19.22% (NHANES III, 1988–1994). Other circulatory-related disorders associated with obesity include chronic venous insufficiency, deep vein thrombosis, and stroke.

A third strong risk factor with high prevalence rates related to obesity is type 2 diabetes (NHANES III, 1988–1994). The Obesity Society (2014) projects that as many as 90% of persons with type 2 diabetes are overweight or obese, and this is especially true for certain minority groups such as Hispanics and American Indians. As the BMI rises, there is a proportionate increase in the percentage of persons with diabetes. Obesity has been found to be the strongest environmental influence for type 2 diabetes onset (Obesity Society, 2014). The medical ramifications of obesity with diabetes are that obesity increases insulin resistance, thereby making drug treatment less effective.

A fourth major complication of obesity is the effect of excessive weight on the body's musculoskeletal system, leading to a higher prevalence of osteoarthritis (NHANES III, 1988–1994). Prevalence percentages for persons with a BMI greater than 40 are 17% for women and 10% for men. Obesity has been correlated with the development of osteoarthritis in the back, knees, hips, and hands. It has also been associated with rheumatoid arthritis, carpal tunnel syndrome, low back pain, joint pain, and heel spurs (Obesity Society, 2014; Onyike, Crum, Lee, Lyketsos, & Eaton, 2003; Visscher & Seidell, 2001).

Finally, there are a host of other complications that have been associated with obesity, including mental health issues (primarily depression and anxiety), pancreatitis, sleep apnea, urinary stress incontinence, chronic odor, liver disease, impaired immune response, impaired respiratory function, gallbladder disease, and a variety of cancers, including breast cancer, esophageal and gastric cancer, colorectal cancer, endometrial cancer, and renal cell cancer (Obesity Society 2014; Mustillo et al., 2003; Onyike et al., 2003; Palinkas, Wingard & Barrett-Connor, 1996; Ross, 1994; Visscher & Seidell, 2001).

PSYCHOSOCIAL IMPLICATIONS OF OBESITY

Societal Attitudes

Negative societal attitudes toward persons who are obese generally begin at a young age. Early research indicated that children as young as 6 years describe obese children as lazy, dirty, stupid, ugly, and cheaters (Staffieri, 1967). Current research on obesity indicates that there remains a "widespread, culturally acceptable stereotype and negative attitude of obese people" (Cossrow, Jeffery, & McGuire, 2001, p. 208) and that culture determines what is attractive. Other research findings have shown that being obese is associated with negative attitudes such as being aesthetically unpleasant to look at (Wooley & Wooley, 1979), morally and emotionally impaired (Keys, 1955), and alienated from one's sexuality (Millman, 1980). The implications of such attitudes can lead to prejudice and discrimination, in part due to a largely held belief that obesity is something that is controllable and that persons who are overweight are lazy and weak willed (Myers & Rosen, 1999; Wadden & Stunkard, 1985). This perception elicits the concept of attribution of blame on the individual and/or the family for not being strong enough to control the problem (Gordon-Larsen, 2001; Neumark-Sztainer, 1999; Puhl & Brownell, 2001). Although there is evidence that obesity is part genetically and part environmentally caused, most laypersons continue to believe obesity to be largely environmentally based (Neumark-Sztainer, 1999). Puhl and Brownell (2003) note how attributional explanations of weight stigma are related to the Protestant work ethic and "just-world bias" (p. 216) in blaming the individual. This attitude tends to be more prevalent in cultures that promote individualism and thinness.

Employer Attitudes

Although the implications of employer discrimination toward persons who are obese are discussed later, suffice it to note that employer discrimination against overweight or obese persons is found at virtually all stages of employment, including hiring (Klesges et al., 1990), placement (Bellizzi, Klassen, & Belonax, 1989), compensation (Register & Williams, 1990), promotion (Bordieri, Drehemer, & Taylor, 1997), discipline (Bellizzi & Norvell, 1991), and discharge (Kennedy & Homant, 1984). Klesges et al.'s (1990) laboratory study found that even though qualified overweight candidates were mostly preferred over unqualified normal-weight candidates, overweight candidates were most often assessed with qualities such as lacking self-control and discipline, being depressed, and having an offensive appearance. Other studies have suggested that employers perceive that obese job applicants lack self-discipline, have low supervisory potential, are less ambitious, and lack poor personal hygiene and appearance (Larkin & Pines, 1979; Rothblum, Miller, & Garbutt, 1988).

Mental Health

Although obesity has been associated with physical and chronic medical conditions fairly consistently, the effect that obesity has on severe psychiatric disorders is more contradictory (Onyike et al., 2003; Wadden & Stunkard, 1985). It has not been shown that overweight persons have any more serious psychological disturbance than the general population (Wadden & Stunkard, 1985). Conversely, Fontaine and Bartlett (1998) indicate that it is well known that obesity has a negative impact on health and has an effect on other important aspects of life. Obesity has been closely associated with depression, eating disorders in children and adults, and behavior problems among children such as oppositional defiant disorder (Burrows & Cooper, 2002; Li et al., 2004; Onyike et al., 2003). Studies have shown both positive and negative correlations between depression and obesity (Crisp, Queenan, Sittampaln, & Harris, 1980; Palinkas et al., 1996; Paykel, 1977). Palinkas and colleagues (1996), however, discuss the concept of "jolly fat," which proposes that obese people are jolly and not depressed. This hypothesis stems from the theory that the dietary habits of obese persons may protect them against depression, anxiety, and dysphoria.

Because an individual's perception about himself or herself is to a degree influenced by the attitudes of others, overweight individuals "may suffer low self-esteem, have negative self-images, think others dislike them, and thus have high levels of depression" (Ross, 1994, p. 64). Wadden and Stunkard (1985) indicate that although it is believed that being overweight and obese are closely linked to emotional disturbance, recent research has suggested that disturbances among individuals may in some cases be the consequence of obesity and the social prejudice and discrimination that are demonstrated against them (Puhl & Brownell, 2003). Li and colleagues (2004) indicate, however, that societal attitudes toward obesity and its impact on individuals are culture specific.

Self-Esteem

In Western societies where billions of dollars in advertising are spent annually on the rewards of being thin, the stigmatization of being obese can impact an individual's self-esteem and radically change his or her behavior in a quest for the glorified, yet often unrealistic, perfect body (Carlisle-Duncan & Robinson, 2004; Seligman, 1994). Self-esteem is regarded as a socially derived state, such as when a person who is obese does not measure up to society's view of thinness, which can cost him or her potential employment and marital opportunities (Klesges et al., 1990; Pingitore, Dugoni, Tindale, & Spring, 1994; Sobal, 1984). Although some studies show being obese does not affect one's level of self-esteem (Grilo, Wilfley, Brownell, & Rodin, 1994), other studies suggest that self-esteem is indeed impacted (Burrows & Cooper, 2002; Goodman & Whitaker, 2002; Gordon-Larsen, 2001; Lumeng, Gannon, Cabral, Frank, & Zuckerman, 2003; C. T. Miller, Rothblum, Brand, & Felicio, 1995; Mustillo et al., 2003).

C. T. Miller and Downey (1999) suggest that gender is the factor that determines how weight affects self-esteem. In the United States, the standards of thinness are more extreme for women than they are for men, and self-esteem may be more of an important aspect for women than for men (Grilo et al., 1994). Women are more dissatisfied with their bodies than are men and are more likely to work hard toward achieving the thin ideal (Jambekar, Quinn, & Crocker, 2001). They are also more likely to diet, suffer from eating disorders (C. T. Miller & Downey, 1999), and feel poorly about themselves when they cannot achieve the thin ideal (Jambekar et al., 2001).

Socioeconomic Status

There is some evidence to suggest that obesity may be more prevalent among those of lower SES and with lower levels of education, factors that tend to be interrelated (Averett

& Korenman, 2001; Gordon-Larsen, 2001; Gortmaker, Walker, Weitzman, & Sobol, 1990; Rosmond & Björntorp, 1999). There also appears to be a stronger relationship of obesity among women in comparison to men in relation to SES from traditionally being paid less in the workforce. Researchers hypothesize a cycle of low education associated with lower paying jobs, and lower income is further associated with poorer food and nutritional consumption behavior, including the inexpensiveness of the more fatty foods (Averett & Korenman, 2001; Rosmond & Björntorp, 1999). This cycle is further influenced by employer discrimination toward persons who are overweight or obese in that if they are not skilled or educated, women more so than men, they are hired in lower paying jobs if they are hired at all (MacDonald, 1999; Pagan & Davila, 1997; Roehling, 1999). When ethnicity is considered, there are numerous studies indicating a high prevalence of obesity among middle-aged Hispanic and African American women of low SES (Winkleby, Gardner, & Taylor, 1996).

Fat Pride

In 1969, the National Association to Advance Fat Acceptance (NAAFA) was established with the overall objective of improving the quality of life for fat people. Its mission is to eliminate discrimination based on body size, self-empower overweight persons, educate its members on nutritional information, and provide support for improving self-image and being comfortable with one's body size (NAAFA, 1994). NAAFA believes its mission is similar to that of the civil rights movement and other related movements, and although changing attitudes has been slow, business marketing trends are catering more to oversized persons as evident in their magazines and commercials.

VOCATIONAL IMPLICATIONS

The issue of weight discrimination in employment has received greater interest over the past several years due to the growing increase in the incidences of obesity, the greater number of lawsuits based on weight discrimination, and employer concerns about health care-related costs (Johnson & Wilson, 1995; Lipman, 1998; Taussig, 1994; Zablocki, 1998). This section explores existing legislative protections concerning employment discrimination of persons who are obese and existing evidence toward prevalence of employment discrimination.

Legislative Protections

Two relevant areas fall within this purview: protections set forth from the Rehabilitation Act of 1973 (RHA) and protections from Title I of the ADA of 1990. The Social Security Administration follows the Clinical Guidelines in the classification of obesity using the BMI described earlier.

Before October 1999, obesity was considered an impairment in which applicants for benefits could be awarded solely for being obese (*Federal Register*, 2002). Subsequent to the October 1999 ruling deleting obesity as a primary disabling condition, the administration added paragraphs to the prefaces of musculoskeletal, respiratory, and cardiovascular body system listings, reminding adjudicators that the effects of obesity secondary to other impairments can have a greater impact on functioning than by considering each impairment separately. Despite the ruling, however, obesity can still "equal" (classify as disabled) a listing by itself if it is classified as "severe" in addition to considering an individual's age, education, and past work history (*Federal Register*, 2002). Unfortunately, as shown by its definition, there is no specific BMI level that differentiates between "severe" and "nonsevere" obesity. As such, Administrative Law Judges have much discretion in deciding what is severe. Generally, there will have to be some other disabling condition such as a musculoskeletal, respiratory, or heart condition that significantly limits the individual completing activities of daily living (Roehling, 1999).

Regarding other federal protection under ADA or RHA, both have parallel definitions of disability and neither law specifically mentions obesity as a disability. Instead, both laws define an individual with a disability as someone with a mental or physical impairment that substantially limits one or more major life activities. Legally, the courts have consistently ruled using the Equal Employment Opportunity Commission regulations that coverage of obesity as a disability will be considered a rare occurrence. To establish obesity as a disability, two factors must be met: Obesity was caused by a physiological condition and the employee must be morbidly obese or 100% over his ideal body weight (*Cook v. Rhode Island*, 1993). This requirement is, of course, extremely difficult to prove, and statistically less than 1% of Americans are considered morbidly obese (Rodin, 1993). Even when plaintiffs can show a physiological cause for morbid obesity, the Supreme Court has ruled that ADA definitions of disability do not cover conditions that are medically correctable as obesity arguably can be (*Albertson's Inc. v. Kirkingburg*, 1999; *Murphy v. United Parcel Service*, 1999).

Although there appears to be scant protection for obesity discrimination in employment, there are two additional laws that can be more favorable for those filing employment discrimination lawsuits. The first is "perceived disability," which stems from the ADA and RHA definitions considering an employee who is "regarded as" disabled. In the 1993 *Cook v. Rhode Island* decision, the plaintiff did not have to prove he had a disability, but rather that the employer perceived he had one (i.e., regarded as) and was suffering from a weight condition and assumed he could not perform the functions of the job.

Other protections fall under Title VII of the 1964 Civil Rights Act addressing "disparate treatment and disparate impact" categories of discrimination (*Gerdom v. Continental Airlines, Inc.*, 1983). The first refers to cases where an employer treats some employees differently, as apparent in the Continental Airlines case where the court determined that the airline's hire/fire policies treated employees differently based on gender due to differences in male versus female flight attendant weight restriction policies. This disparate treatment category also takes into consideration whether the established job requiring characteristic (slender female flight attendants) is a bona fide occupational qualification. If an employer can prove that having heavier female flight attendants will somehow hurt their business, then they are not obligated to hire the individual. The disparate impact discrimination category refers to whether an employer's hiring policies have a disparate impact on a designated group of people based on gender, age, or race. If, for example, an employer wanted to hire males exclusively, and had no bona fide occupational qualification as to how the business might be negatively impacted by hiring women, the employer would be liable under the disparate impact category of discrimination (Roehling, 1999).

Prevalence of Employment Discrimination

Discrimination against overweight employees occurs in the employment arena as well involving hiring, promotion, termination, and insurance coverage (Bordieri et al., 1997; Klesges et al., 1990; Register & Williams, 1990). Despite the fact that over 99% of persons who are overweight or obese are not protected or recognized under existing disability legislation, research in this area continues to show a link between employment discrimination and obesity irrespective of court rulings (Roehling, 1999).

It has been reported that Caucasian women who weighed an average of 65 pounds more earned approximately 7% less than their slimmer coworkers; however, no significant differences existed among minority women. Gortmaker et al. (1990) found that obese women earned approximately $6,700 less than slender women. Haskins and Ransford (1999) studied the relationship between weight and career payoffs among 306 women and found that weight had no effect on income when education, length of service, and age were controlled. It did, however, have an effect on level of career access, with 65% of the thinner women holding professional and managerial positions compared with only 39% of the overweight women. For blue-collar workers, a reverse trend was observed. There are also reported cases where overweight employees must pay higher health care premiums (Paul & Townsend, 1995), are denied benefits altogether due to their weight, or are terminated because of their weight (Rothblum, Brand, Miller, & Oetjen, 1990).

Evidence also suggests that persons who are overweight or obese are disadvantaged in not only being hired but also the type of position they may be hired for (Puhl & Brownell, 2001). Several studies note that when business students or managers are asked to rate identical candidates' résumés, overweight persons are often not selected for the job, or they are hired in less desirable positions (Decker, 1987; Klassen, Jasper, & Harris, 1993; Larkin & Pines, 1979; Rothblum et al., 1988).

COUNSELING IMPLICATIONS

The implications of working with persons who are obese or overweight may be broken down into mental health counseling and/or vocational counseling. Although each of these is discussed separately, it is important to note that clients may come in for assistance with overlapping concerns.

Mental Health Counseling

Although a relationship between obesity and psychiatric disorders, such as depression, is not well established, there are several studies that indicate depression to be most consistently correlated with severe obesity in women (Carpenter, Hasin, Allison, & Faith, 2000; Noppa & Hällström, 1981; Roberts, Kaplan, Shema, & Strawbridge, 2000). Because, however, other chronic medical conditions related to obesity, such as diabetes, arthritis, or musculoskeletal pain, often coexist with obesity, it is difficult to distinguish what role obesity itself has in depression (Katon & Ciechanowski, 2002; Katon & Sullivan, 1990). Other possible coexisting contributors that can impact an individual's mental health previously discussed include unemployment or underemployment in lower paying jobs (Bordieri et al., 1997; Pagan & Davila, 1997), lower SES (Sobal & Stunkard, 1989), and being discriminated against in employment, by family members, and treating medical professionals (Adams, Hicken, & Salehi, 1988; Crandall, 1995; Price, Desmond, Krol, Snyder, & O'Connell, 1987; Teachman & Brownell, 2001).

In working with the mental health needs of persons who are obese, Olkin (1999) has advocated for disability-affirmative therapy, whereby counselors must explore their own biases and beliefs about obesity, recognize and acknowledge the inequity and discrimination directed at those who are obese, and view the counseling process from a social construct approach that does not attribute blame to the individual, but rather stems from negative societal attitudes. It is also important that counselors do not make a client's size the salient issue in counseling. Automatically assuming a client's size is the cause of his or her problems cannot only derail establishing rapport, but also offend the client (Rush, 1998). Olkin (1999) recommends directly asking clients whether they perceive their medical condition as having an impact as to their seeking counseling. In situations in which this is the case, cognitive reframing can be an excellent strategy in changing a client's perspective in placing a lesser value on his/her physique and instead focusing on other positive interpersonal attributes (Leahy, 2001; Wright, 1983).

Additional strategies counselors can use when clients' weight is a precipitating factor in their mental health could include behavior modification, rational emotive therapy, reality therapy, support groups, and bibliotherapy. Behavior modification strategies could focus around establishing a baseline for eating behavior, times of day, diary recording of what one's affect is like before/after eating (i.e., anxious, stressed, sad), and subsequently replacing eating behaviors for healthier behaviors (Spiegeler & Guevremont, 1998). Rational emotive therapy could be effective in changing clients' perceptions toward building self-esteem; however, they should recognize that many of their beliefs about being discriminated against are likely true and must be validated by the counselor (Ellis & Maclaren, 1998; Wessler & Wessler, 1988). Reality therapy again must be used with caution in that it assumes individual responsibility for one's situation (Glasser, 2000). Support groups or group counseling can be effective in helping clients to validate each others' perceptions regarding discrimination, motivating each other to overcome their difficulties, and providing friendship in situations outside of the group (Jacobs, Masson, & Harvill, 2002). Finally, bibliotherapy can be effective in educating clients across a gambit of areas, including weight control, exercise, and eating behaviors.

Vocational Counseling

When obesity is a factor in vocational counseling, counselors again must first acknowledge the fact that employer discrimination does exist and empower clients if relevant with information about legislation involving disparate treatment and disparate impact. As with counseling other persons with disabilities, clients who are obese should be encouraged to focus on what their qualifications are to perform jobs. Counselors and clients must also work together in dispelling myths and misconceptions about overweight employees.

In assessing clients with obesity for vocational opportunities, it is important to know whether there are other secondary disabilities such as respiratory, musculoskeletal, diabetes, or heart disease problems. This would typically be detailed in client medical records and should be verified as to severity with the client regarding functional limitations. With this in mind, counselors have a better understanding of clients' physical capabilities in performing work and in conducting a transferable skills analysis. Client education, past work experience, occupational interests, and age play a significant role in successfully placing clients. Typically, higher level of education generally corresponds with work that is less physically demanding. For those clients with lower levels of education (i.e., less than grade 12), counselors should explore the unskilled, sedentary, and light levels of work that are generally less strenuous. Such positions may include video surveillance monitor, parking lot attendant, ticket taker, garment sorter, clothing or other production inspectors, machine operators, assembly workers, and file clerks. Those clients with higher levels of education are generally easier to place in less physically demanding jobs and have been shown in the literature to be less discriminated against by employers when they are qualified (Klesges et al., 1990).

Vocational counseling should also encompass any perceived anxiety clients who are obese may have regarding employment. Although ability to perform the job would generally not be a concern for qualified clients, dealing with negative or stereotypical attitudes of employers and coworkers may carry some trepidation. Clients can be empowered through role-playing mock job interviews by teaching clients to focus on strengths/assets to perform the job, to know their rights, and to convey these in a nonthreatening manner to employers. Being prepared to respond appropriately to possible coworker degradation comments would be beneficial to practice as well. Similarly, clients' self-esteem may be enhanced by refocusing cognitions of self-worth away from physique/physical appearance, and direct cognitions more toward one's abilities to perform the work.

Finally, counselors may benefit from being familiar with the stages of change theory. Some clients may not perceive having a problem and therefore obesity may be viewed as an addictive behavior. R. W. Miller and Rollnick (2004) describe the stages from precontemplation (not acknowledging a problem), contemplation (suspecting a problem; however, being unsure as to wanting to change), determination (making a cognitive decision to change), action (engaging in change behaviors), maintenance/exit, or in some cases relapse. Understanding motivational interviewing can assist counselors in helping clients to move toward recognizing and developing a more healthy lifestyle.

SUMMARY

Obesity and related medical complications have soared to the forefront of medical conditions that lead to premature death, discrimination in employment, compromised quality of life, and negative psychosocial implications. Its prevalence is statistically found across all groups and ages, particularly so among persons of minority groups and low SES. The impact of being obese affects individuals in a number of nonmedical ways as well: being the subject of negative societal attitudes and affecting one's self-esteem, the type of job one obtains, and potentially one's mental health. Counselors who are aware of the medical, psychosocial, and vocational implications of obesity can assist clients in a variety of ways, keeping Olkin's (1999) recommendations in mind regarding disability-affirmative therapy. Although legislatively obesity is not recognized for over 99% of its arguable population, research has shown this stigmatized group is nevertheless discriminated against as any other minority group might be. As such, it would benefit rehabilitation counselors to be well prepared to work with this ever-increasing population.

REFERENCES

Adams, G. R., Hicken, M., & Salehi, M. (1988). Socialization of the physical attractiveness stereotype: Parental expectations and verbal behaviors. *International Journal of Psychology, 23*, 137–149.

Ajzen, I., & Fishbein, M. (1977). Attitude-behavior relations: A theoretical analysis and review of empirical research. *Psychological Bulletin, 84*, 888–918.

Albertson's Inc. v. Kirkingburg, 199 S. Ct. 2162 (1999).

Averett, S., & Korenman, S. (2001). The economic reality of the beauty myth. *Journal of Human Resources, 31*, 304–330.

Bellizzi, J. A., Klassen, M. L., & Belonax, J. J. (1989). Stereotypical beliefs about overweight and smoking and decision-making in assignments to sales territories. *Perceptual and Motor Skills, 69*(2), 419–429.

Bellizzi, J. A., & Norvell, D. W. (1991). Personal characteristics and salesperson's justifications as moderators of supervisory discipline in cases involving unethical sales force behavior. *Journal of the Academy of Marketing Science, 19*, 11–16.

Berger, K. S. (2014). *The developing person through the life span* (9th ed.). New York, NY: Worth.

Bordieri, J. E., Drehemer, D. E., & Taylor, D. W. (1997). Work life for employees with disabilities: Recommendations for promotion. *Rehabilitation Counseling Bulletin, 40*, 181–191.

Burrows, A., & Cooper, M. (2002). Possible risk factors in the development of eating disorders in overweight pre-adolescent girls. *International Journal of Obesity and Related Metabolic Disorders, 26*(9), 1268–1273.

Carlisle-Duncan, M., & Robinson, T. T. (2004). Obesity and body ideals in the media: Health and fitness practices of young African-American women. *Quest, 56*, 77–104.

Carpenter, K. M., Hasin, D. S., Allison, D. B., & Faith, M. S. (2000). Relationships between obesity and *DSM-IV* major depressive disorder, suicide ideation, and suicide attempts: Results from a general population study. *American Journal of Public Health, 90*(2), 251–257.

Carroll, M. D., Navaneelan, T., Bryan, S., & Ogden, C. L. (2015). *Prevalence of obesity among children and adolescents in the United States and Canada (NCHS Data Brief, No. 211).* Hyattsville, MD: National Center for Health Statistics.

Centers for Disease Control and Prevention. (2004, June 24). Overweight and obesity: Nutrition and physical activity. Retrieved from http://www.cdc.gov/nccdphp/dnpa/obesity/index.htm

Centers for Disease Control and Prevention. (2016a, June 13). Obesity and overweight. Retrieved from http://www.cdc.gov/nchs/fastats/obesity-overweight.htm

Centers for Disease Control and Prevention. (2016b, June 16). Defining overweight and obesity. Retrieved from https://www.cdc.gov/obesity/adult/defining.html

Centers for Disease Control and Prevention. (2016c, September 1). Adult obesity facts. Retrieved from https://www.cdc.gov/obesity/data/adult.html

Cleator, J., Richman, E., Leong, K. S., Mawdsley, L., White, S., & Wilding, J. (2002). Obesity: Under-diagnosed and under-treated in hospital outpatient departments. *International Journal of Obesity and Related Metabolic Disorders, 26*(4), 581–584.

Cook v. Rhode Island Department of Mental Health, 10F.2d 17, 2AD 1476(1ˢᵗ Cir. 1993).

Cossrow, N. H., Jeffery, R. W., & McGuire, M. T. (2001). Understanding weight stigmatization: A focus group study. *Journal of Nutrition Education, 33*(4), 208–214.

Crandall, C. S. (1995). Do parents discriminate against their heavy-weight daughters? *Personality and Social Psychology Bulletin, 21*, 724–735.

Crisp, A. H., Queenan, M., Sittampaln, Y., & Harris, G. (1980). "Jolly fat" revisited. *Journal of Psychosomatic Research, 24*(5), 233–241.

Decker, W. H. (1987). Attributions based on managers' self-presentation, sex, and weight. *Psychological Reports, 61*, 175–181.

De Silver, D. (2013, November 13). Obesity and poverty don't always go together. Pew Research Center. Retrieved from http://www.pewresearch.org/fact-tank/2013/11/13/obesity-and-poverty-dont-always-go-together

Diamanti-Kandarakis, E., & Bergiele, A. (2001). The influence of obesity on hyperandrogenism and infertility in the female. *Obesity Reviews, 2*(4), 231–238.

Eagly, A., & Chaiken, S. (1993). *The impact of attitudes on behaviors. The psychology of attitudes.* London, England: Harcourt Brace.

Ellis, A., & Maclaren, C. (1998). *Rational emotive behavior therapy: A therapist guide.* San Luis Obispo, CA: Impact.

Federal Register. (2002, September 12). SSR 02–01 p: Policy ruling Titles II and XVI.

Fontaine, K. R., & Bartlett, S. J. (1998). Estimating health-related quality of life in obese individuals. *Disease Management & Health Outcomes, 3*(2), 61–70.

Fradkin, C., Wallander, J. L., Elliot, M. N., Tortolero, S., Cuccaro, P., & Shuster, M. A. (2015). Associations between socioeconomic status and obesity in diverse young adolescents: Variation across race/ethnicity and gender. *Health Psychology, 54*, 1–9. doi:10.1037/hea0000099

Gerdom v. Continental Airlines, Inc., 692, 30 FEP 235 (9th Cir. 1982; en banc), cert denied, 460 U.S. 1074 (1983).

Glasser, W. (2000). *Reality therapy in action.* New York, NY: HarperCollins.

Goodman, E., & Whitaker, R. C. (2002). A prospective study of the role of depression in the development and persistence of adolescent obesity. *Pediatrics, 110*(3), 497–504.

Gordon-Larsen, P. (2001). Obesity-related knowledge, attitudes, and behaviors in obese and non-obese urban Philadelphia female adolescents. *Obesity Research, 9*(2), 112–118.

Gortmaker, S. L., Walker, D. K., Weitzman, M., & Sobol, A. M. (1990). Chronic conditions, socioeconomic risks, and behavioral problems in children and adolescents. *Pediatrics, 85*(3), 267–276.

Grilo, C. M., Wilfley, D. E., Brownell, K. D., & Rodin, J. (1994). Teasing, body image, and self-esteem in a clinical sample of obese women. *Addictive Behaviors, 19*(4), 443–450.

Haskins, K. M., & Ransford, H. E. (1999). The relationship between weight and career payoffs among women. *Sociological Forum, 14*(2), 295–318.

Hebl, M. R., & Xu, J. (2001). Weighing the care: Physicians' reactions to the size of a patient. *International Journal of Obesity and Related Metabolic Disorders, 25*(8), 1246–1252.

Hebl, M. R., Xu, J., & Mason, M. F. (2003). Weighing the care: Patients' perceptions of physician care as a function of gender and weight. *International Journal of Obesity and Related Metabolic Disorders, 27*(2), 269–275.

Hunter, J. D., Reid, C., & Noble, D. (1998). Anaesthetic management of the morbidly obese patient. *Hospital Medicine, 59*(6), 481–483.

Jacobs, E. E., Masson, R. L., & Harvill, R. L. (2002). *Group counseling: Strategies and skills* (4th ed.). Pacific Grove, CA: Brooks/Cole.

Jambekar, S., Quinn, D. M., & Crocker, J. (2001). The effects of weight and achievement messages on the self-esteem of women. *Psychology of Women Quarterly, 25*, 48–56.

Johnson, T., & Wilson, M. C. (1995). An analysis of weight-based discrimination: Obesity as a disability. *Labor Law Journal, 46*(4), 238–244.

Katon, W., & Ciechanowski, P. (2002). Impact of major depression on chronic medical illness. *Journal of Psychosomatic Research, 53*(4), 859–863.

Katon, W., & Sullivan, M. D. (1990). Depression and chronic medical illness. *Journal of Clinical Psychiatry, 51* (Suppl.), 3–11; discussion 12.

Kennedy, D. B., & Homant, R. J. (1984). Personnel managers and the stigmatized employee. *Journal of Employment Counseling, 21*, 89–94.

Keys, A. (1955). Obesity and heart disease. *Journal of Chronic Diseases, 1*(4), 458–461.

Kirby, J. B., Liang, L., Chen, H. J., & Wang, Y. (2012). Race, place, and obesity: The complex relationships among community racial/ethnic composition, individual race/ethnicity, and obesity in the United States. *American Journal of Public Health, 102*(8), 1572–1578.

Klassen, M. L., Jasper, C. R., & Harris, R. J. (1993). The role of physical appearance in managerial decisions. *Journal of Business and Psychology, 8*, 181–198.

Klesges, R. C., Klem, M. L., Hanson, C. L., Eck, L. H., Ernst, J., O'Laughlin, D., . . . Rife, R. (1990). The effects of applicant's health status and qualifications on simulated hiring decisions. *International Journal of Obesity, 14*(6), 527–535.

Larkin, J. C., & Pines, H. A. (1979). No fat persons need apply: Experimental studies of the overweight stereotype and hiring preference. *Sociology of Work Occupations, 6*, 312–327.

Leahy, R. L. (2001). *Overcoming resistance in cognitive therapy.* New York, NY: Guilford Press.

Li, Z. B., Ho, S. Y., Chan, W. M., Ho, K. S., Li, M. P., Leung, G. M., & Lam, T. H. (2004). Obesity and depressive symptoms in Chinese elderly. *International Journal of Geriatric Psychiatry, 19*(1), 68–74.

Lipman, H. (1998). Courts weigh in on obesity. *Business and Health, 63*, 53–54.

Lumeng, J. C., Gannon, K., Cabral, H. J., Frank, D. A., & Zuckerman, B. (2003). Association between clinically meaningful behavior problems and overweight in children. *Pediatrics, 112*(5), 1138–1145.

MacDonald, S. M. (1999). Obesity: Worldwide prevalence and trend. *Healthy Weight Journal, 13*(6), 84–92.

Metropolitan Life Insurance Company. (1996). *Weigh in!* New York, NY: Author.

Miller, C. T., & Downey, K. T. (1999). A meta-analysis of heavy-weight and self-esteem. *Personality and Social Psychology Review, 3*(1), 68–84.

Miller, C. T., Rothblum, E. D., Brand, P. A., & Felicio, D. M. (1995). Do obese women have poorer social relationships than nonobese women? Reports by self, friends, and coworkers. *Journal of Personality, 63*(1), 65–85.

Miller, R. W., & Rollnick, S. (2004). *Motivational interviewing: Preparing people for change.* New York, NY: Guilford Press.

Millman, M. (1980). *Such a pretty face: Being fat in America.* New York, NY: W. W. Norton.

Molarius, A., & Seidell, J. C. (1998). Selection of anthropometric indicators for classification of abdominal fatness—A critical review. *International Journal of Obesity, 22*, 719–727.

Murphy v. United Parcel Service, 119 S. Ct. 2133 (1999).

Mustillo, S., Worthman, C., Erkanli, A., Keeler, G., Angold, A., & Costello, E. J. (2003). Obesity and psychiatric disorder: Developmental trajectories. *Pediatrics, 111*(4 Pt 1), 851–859.

Myers, A., & Rosen, J. C. (1999). Obesity stigmatization and coping: Relation to mental health symptoms, body image, and self-esteem. *International Journal of Obesity and Related Metabolic Disorders, 23*(3), 221–230.

National Association to Advance Fat Acceptance. (1994). *Fighting size discrimination and prejudice.* Sacramento, CA: Author.

National Health and Nutrition Examination Survey. (1988–1994). National Center for Health Statistics. Plan and operation of the Third National Health and Nutrition Examination Survey, 1988–1994. Series III: Programs and collection procedures. *Vital Health Stat, 1*, 1–407.

Neumark-Sztainer, D. (1999). The weight dilemma: A range of philosophical perspectives. *International Journal of Obesity and Related Metabolic Disorders, 23 Suppl 2*, S31–S37.

Noppa, H., & Hällström, T. (1981). Weight gain in adulthood in relation to socioeconomic factors, mental illness and personality traits: A prospective study of middle-aged women. *Journal of Psychosomatic Research, 25*(2), 83–89.

Obesity Society. (2014). Obesity statistics. Retrieved from http://www.obesity.org/resources/facts-about-obesity/what-is-obesity

Office of Disease Prevention and Health Promotion. (2016). Physical activity, nutrition, and obesity. In *Healthy People 2020*. Washington, DC: U.S. Department of Health and Human Services. Retrieved from https://www.healthypeople.gov/2020/leading-health-indicators/infographic/nutrition-physical-activity-and-obesity

Ogden, C. L., Carroll, M. D., Fryar, C. D., & Flegal, K. M. (2015). *Prevalence of obesity among adults and youth: United States, 2011-2014* (NCHS Data Brief No. 219). Hyattsville, MD: National Center for Health Statistics.

Ogden, C. L., Lamb, M. M., Carroll, M. D., & Flegal, K. M. (2010). *Obesity and socioeconomic status in children and adolescents: United States, 2005–2008* (NCHS Data Brief No. 51). Hyattsville, MD: National Center for Health Statistics.

Olkin, R. (1999). *What psychotherapists should know about disability*. New York, NY: Guilford Press.

Onyike, C. U., Crum, R. M., Lee, H. B., Lyketsos, C. G., & Eaton, W. W. (2003). Is obesity associated with major depression? Results from the Third National Health and Nutrition Examination Survey. *American Journal of Epidemiology, 158*(12), 1139–1147.

Pagan, J. A., & Davila, A. (1997). Obesity, occupational attainment, and earnings. *Social Science Quarterly, 78*, 756–770.

Palinkas, L. A., Wingard, D. L., & Barrett-Connor, E. (1996). Depressive symptoms in overweight and obese older adults: A test of the "jolly fat" hypothesis. *Journal of Psychosomatic Research, 40*(1), 59–66.

Paul, R. J., & Townsend, J. B. (1995). Shape up or ship out? Employment discrimination against the overweight. *Employee Responsibilities Rights Journal, 8*, 133–145.

Paykel, E. S. (1977). Depression and appetite. *Journal of Psychosomatic Research, 21*(5), 401–407.

Pingitore, R., Dugoni, B. L., Tindale, R. S., & Spring, B. (1994). Bias against overweight job applicants in a simulated employment interview. *Journal of Applied Psychology, 79*(6), 909–917.

Price, J. H., Desmond, S. M., Krol, R. A., Snyder, F. F., & O'Connell, J. K. (1987). Family practice physicians' beliefs, attitudes, and practices regarding obesity. *American Journal of Preventive Medicine, 3*(6), 339–345.

Puhl, R. M., & Brownell, K. D. (2001). Bias, discrimination, and obesity. *Obesity Research, 9*(12), 788–805.

Puhl, R. M., & Brownell, K. D. (2003). Psychosocial origins of obesity stigma: Toward changing a powerful and pervasive bias. *Obesity Reviews, 4*(4), 213–227.

Register, C. A., & Williams, D. R. (1990). Wage effects of obesity among young workers. *Social Science Quarterly, 71*, 130–141.

Roberts, R. E., Kaplan, G. A., Shema, S. J., & Strawbridge, W. J. (2000). Are the obese at greater risk for depression? *American Journal of Epidemiology, 152*(2), 163–170.

Rodin, J. (1993). Cultural and psychosocial determinants of weight concerns. *Annals of Internal Medicine, 119*(7 Pt 2), 643–645.

Roehling, M. V. (1999). Weight-based discrimination in employment: Psychological and legal aspects. *Personnel Psychology, 52*(4), 696–1016.

Romero, M. G., & Marini, I. (2006). Obesity as a disability, Medical, psychosocial, and vocational implications. *Journal of Applied Rehabilitation Counseling, 37*(1), 21–29. Retrieved from http://nrca-net.org/jarc_indices.html

Rosmond, R., & Björntorp, P. (1999). Psychosocial and socio-economic factors in women and their relationship to obesity and regional body fat distribution. *International Journal of Obesity and Related Metabolic Disorders, 23*(2), 138–145.

Ross, C. E. (1994). Overweight and depression. *Journal of Health and Social Behavior, 35*(1), 63–79.

Rothblum, E. D., Brand, P. A., Miller, C. T., & Oetjen, H. A. (1990). The relationship between obesity, employment discrimination, and employment-related victimization. *Journal of Vocational Behavior, 37*, 251–266.

Rothblum, E. D., Miller, C. T., & Garbutt, B. (1988). Stereotypes of obese female job applicants. *International Journal of Eating Disorders, 6*, 277–283.

Rush, L. L. (1998). Affective reactions to multiple social stigmas. *Journal of Social Psychology, 138*, 421–430.

Seidell, J. C. (1999). The burden of obesity and its sequelae. *Disease Management & Health Outcomes, 5*(1), 13–21.

Seligman, M. E. P. (1994). *What you can change & what you can't*. New York, NY: Knopf.

Sobal, J. (1984). Marriage, obesity, and dieting. *Marriage and Family Review, 7*, 115–139.

Sobal, J., & Stunkard, A. J. (1989). Socioeconomic status and obesity: A review of the literature. *Psychological Bulletin, 105*(2), 260–275.

Spiegeler, M. D., & Guevremont, D. C. (1998). *Contemporary behavior therapy* (3rd ed.). Pacific Grove, CA: Brooks/Cole.

Staffieri, J. R. (1967). A study of social stereotype of body image in children. *Journal of Personality and Social Psychology, 7*(1), 101–104.

Taussig, W. C. (1994). Weighing in against discrimination: Cook v. Rhode Island, Department of Mental Health, Retardation, and Hospitals and the recognition of obesity as a disability under the Rehabilitation Act and the Americans with Disabilities Act. *Boston College Law Review, 35*, 927–963.

Teachman, B. A., & Brownell, K. D. (2001). Implicit anti-fat bias among health professionals: Is anyone immune? *International Journal of Obesity and Related Metabolic Disorders, 25*(10), 1525–1531.

The State of Obesity. (2016). Adult obesity rates down in four states. Retrieved from http://stateofobesity.org/adult-obesity

Visscher, T. L., & Seidell, J. C. (2001). The public health impact of obesity. *Annual Review of Public Health, 22*, 355–375.

Wadden, T. A., Anderson, D. A., Foster, G. D., Bennett, A., Steinberg, C., & Sarwer, D. B. (2000). Obese women's perceptions of their physicians' weight management attitudes and practices. *Archives of Family Medicine, 9*(9), 854–860.

Wadden, T. A., & Stunkard, A. J. (1985). Social and psychological consequences of obesity. *Annals of Internal Medicine, 103*(6 (Pt 2)), 1062–1067.

Wang, Y., & Beydoun, M. A. (2007). The obesity epidemic in the United States–gender, age, socioeconomic, racial/ethnic, and geographic characteristics: A systematic review and meta-regression analysis. *Epidemiologic Reviews, 29*, 6–28.

Wee, C. C., McCarthy, E. P., Davis, R. B., & Phillips, R. S. (1999). Physician counseling about exercise. *Journal of the American Medical Association, 282*(16), 1583–1588.

Wessler, R. A., & Wessler, R. L. (1988). *The principles and practice of rational-emotive therapy* (5th ed.). San Francisco, CA: Jossey-Bass.

Winkleby, M. A., Gardner, C. D., & Taylor, C. B. (1996). The influence of gender and socioeconomic factors on Hispanic/White differences in body mass index. *Preventive Medicine, 25*(2), 203–211.

Wooley, S. C., & Wooley, O. W. (1979). Obesity and women: I. A closer look at the facts. *Women's Studies International Quarterly, 2*, 69–79.

World Health Organization. (2016, June). Obesity and overweight fact sheet. Retrieved from http://www.who.int/mediacentre/factsheets/fs311/en

Wright, B. A. (1983). *Physical disability: A psychosocial approach* (2nd ed.). New York, NY: Harper & Row.

Zablocki, E. (1998). Weight and work. *Business and Health, 16*(8 Suppl. A), 20–24.

26

Immigrants, Refugees, and Asylum Seekers: The Psychosocial Cost of War on Civilians

MARK A. STEBNICKI

*T*he world has been at war since the beginning of time. The majority of deaths that occur during times of war do not involve military personnel. Rather, 90% are composed of civilian casualties (Wiist et al., 2014). Since World War II, there have been 127 different wars fought globally with more than 40 million civilian deaths (Hanson & Vogel, 2012). World War II alone was responsible for more than 27.3 million civilian casualties (War Chronicle, 2016). Other examples since the mid-20th century include over 5.4 million civilian deaths in the Democratic Republic of Congo; two million civilian deaths related to the Khmer Rouge killing fields; 2 million civilian deaths in Rwanda; and 200,000 civilian deaths from the Bosnian civil war in the Balkins (Genocide Intervention Network, 2016). Our most recent conflicts, Operation Iraqi Freedom, Operation Enduring Freedom, and Operation New Dawn, have resulted in more than 210,000 civilian casualties. Civilian causalities (direct and indirect) owing to enemy combatants are difficult to obtain because there are no standardized reporting procedures for these (Physicians for Social Responsibility [PSR], 2016). PSR suggests that the U.S. military and the Department of Defense do not do an accurate accounting of civilian causalities during war time.

Global security is reportedly in one of its most capricious states in modern times. Some would say that we are in the midst of World War III as a result of the Islamic State of Iraq, al Qaeda, the Taliban, Russia, China, and other hostile insurgencies where civilians are at the epicenter of armed conflict and the quest for power and control of land and resources. Geographic relocation to the United States and other countries is no longer just for immigrant job seekers or a quest to improve one's quality of life. Rather, the journey is long, perilous, and primarily for the purpose of basic survival, just to be able to breathe, and have basic food, shelter, and clothing.

What is at stake is the safety and security of U.S. citizens and other global civilian populations' mental and physical well-being. We are confronted by simultaneous technological, person-made, and biological threats perpetrated by antigovernment groups, terrorist networks, such as the Islamic State in Iraq and Syria (ISIS), and other dark entities that have flown under the radar for decades (Joint Chiefs of Staff, Unified Combatant Commands, & Office of the Secretary of Defense, 2016).

The United States has been blessed with a democracy that respects and upholds civil liberties for the most part. It has a strong humanitarian base of nonprofit organizations and faith-based groups to help those in need of food, clean water, shelter, clothing, and mental and physical health care. However, the same opportunities are not afforded to civilians in war-torn countries where torture, rape, imprisonment, and execution are daily threats to minority and disempowered indigenous groups. As a consequence, millions of immigrants, refugees, internally displaced persons, and asylum seekers from war-torn countries seek to find safe havens in the United States and other nations that value human life and civil liberties.

DEFINITIONS

The U.S. Citizenship and Immigration Services (USCIS; 2016c) under the U.S. Department of Homeland Security delineates the complex law and path to citizenship as it relates to immigrants, refugees, and asylum seekers. The USCIS (2016a) makes decisions based on policies and laws that were first introduced in the Immigration and Nationality Act (INA). The INA was shaped by the McCarren–Walter bill in 1952, which created Public Law 82–414. An extensive policy manual exists (USCIS, 2016b), which provides full disclosure of all policies related to rights, responsibilities, and processes of naturalization, continuous residence, individuals and groups under temporary protected status (TPS), and overall policies related to immigration. The intent of the chapter is to provide transparency to all public, private, and governmental entities. The law itself is quite complex and is beyond the scope of this chapter to be discussed comprehensively. However, definitions are described in the following sections so as to clarify the individuals who comprise the populations and cultures we refer to as immigrants, refugees, and asylum seekers.

Immigrant

The term *immigrant* is defined as a person who is a migrant from another country, either lawfully or unlawfully, with the intent to take up permanent residence (Homeland Security, 2016). If granted legal residency, he or she is provided the status of a *permanent resident alien*. Those who migrate from another country unlawfully are also referred to as *immigrants,* but not in legal status and not as a *permanent resident alien.* The uninformed and culturally insensitive often use the term *illegal aliens* for immigrants who have entered the United States unlawfully. There is a certain degree of stigma and stereotype associated with the term *alien* because of its dehumanizing aspects. Thus, it becomes more humanistic and culturally appropriate to use the terms *permanent resident* and *U.S. citizen* when referring to those who immigrated lawfully to the United States and have been granted residency or citizenship status. The term *unauthorized immigrant* likewise reflects a greater degree of humanism as opposed to *alien.*

The Secretary of Homeland Security has the power to designate individuals and groups from foreign countries under the TPS, which grants foreign nationals temporary residence in the United States. This would typically be done in cases in which returning to his or her country of origin would likely result in imprisonment and/or harm would come to him or her; in many circumstances the individual's return would result in death. At the time of this writing, foreign nationals from the following countries have been granted TPS by the U.S. government: El Salvador, Guinea, Haiti, Honduras, Liberia, Nepal, Nicaragua, Sierra Leone, Somalia, South Sudan, Sudan, Syria, and Yemen.

Refugee

The USCIS (2016c) defines a *refugee* as someone who (a) is located outside the United States and is in need of humanitarian assistance; (b) demonstrates he or she has been persecuted owing to race, religion, nationality, political opinion, or membership within a particular social group, and is not firmly resettled in another country; and (c) meets all the requirements for admission contingent on background screenings (i.e., mental, physical, criminal).

Asylum Seeker

Each year people come to the United States seeking asylum because of threats to their safety and fear of persecution. The USCIS defines an *asylum seeker* as a person who, because of race, religion, nationality, membership in a particular social group, or political opinion, has been threatened with violence, persecution, and fear that he or she will suffer persecution. Asylum seekers are a new phenomenon to the United States and European nations for the 21st century because of the immense volume of populations seeking safety and security from war-torn countries. This sociopolitical phenomenon requires governments to seriously consider the human, moral, and ethical issues related to accepting and not accepting, screening, and adjudicating such populations of individuals. Issues related to terrorism, criminality, pandemic viruses, and other consequences are quite challenging for the mental and physical health and welfare of the civilized world today.

PREVALENCE, INCIDENCE, AND ETIOLOGY

Worldwide there are more than 51 million refugees, asylum seekers, and internally displaced persons from war-torn countries forced to flee their homelands (United Nations High Commissioner for Refugees [UNHCR], 2016). The UNHCR's global trend report compiled by governments and nongovernmental-partnering organizations shows an enormous increase in these indigenous populations because of war and threats of safety and security. At the time of this writing, the largest number of refugees have come from Afghanistan (2.5 million), Syria (2.4 million), Somalia (more than 1.1 million), Sudan (650,000), Democratic Republic of the Congo (500,000), Myanmar (480,000), Iraq (402,000), Columbia (307,000), and Vietnam (314,000). In January 2016, there were 51,000 Afghan, Syrian, and Iraqi refugees who traveled through the harsh winter conditions over the Mediterranean Sea (Mercy Corps, 2016) to seek asylum in various other countries. All were forced out of their homelands and spread geographically across bordering countries because of war. Presently, over 1.1 million people worldwide have submitted applications for asylum with an additional 25,300 asylum seekers who are children separated from or unaccompanied by their parents. The parents of these children were likely seriously injured or killed as casualties of war.

Despite some of the hysteria among American citizens, the majority of applications for asylum are being handled by Germany and other European nations, not the United States. However, since 1975, the U.S. State Department has welcomed over three million refugees from all over the world (U.S. State Department, 2016). There are multiple governmental and nongovernmental organizations in all 50 states that have provided basic needs for these indigenous groups. Since 2000, the State Department has handled more than 600,000 applications from immigrants, refugees, and asylum seekers. As a result of the war in Syria, more than 11,000 Syrians have applied for U.S. refugee status since 2006. The status of these applications varies from month to month and statistics do not accurately depict who remains in the United States and who does not.

The etiology of this worldwide epidemic is clear. It is war that is at the foundation of all human suffering as millions are forced to relocate geographically. This person-made disaster points to the overall lack of respect and empathy for human life perpetrated by brutal governments, religious zealots, and other indigenous tribal warring groups. The known causes are also exemplified by civil and religious armed conflicts; continuous bombing of villages and towns; violence perpetrated by drug warlords; forced sexual prostitution and slavery; human trafficking; imprisonment by the government for possessing the "wrong" sociopolitical or religious beliefs; racism; discrimination; forced isolation/internal displacement; detention camps; deprived access to adequate mental and physical health care; and withholding of basic food, water, shelter, and clothing for warmth. Overall, it is an incomprehensible task for any one government, organization, or agency to provide assistance for all those in critical need.

SOCIOCULTURAL FAMILIAL IMPACT OF WAR

Acts of genocide, ethnic cleansing, political persecution, and other atrocities have wounded the soul of indigenous populations. The mental health field is only beginning to understand the impact that war has on cultures and civilian families. Children are especially vulnerable and profoundly affected by war because of long-term exposure to political and cultural violence. In the United States, it is estimated that approximately 43% of all refugees are children (American Psychological Association, 2010). Many families are often forcibly separated or relocated, creating a family crisis accompanied by the loss of family rituals and identity. There is the significant loss of parents, family, friends, homes, schools, and other familiar daily routines. Since the 1990s, there have been well over two million children who have been killed, 6 million disabled, and 20 million left homeless as the result of war (Stichick & Bruderlein, 2001). The United Nations (2016) reports that between January 2011 and June 2015, about 1,400 boys and girls have been abducted in Iraq by al Qaeda and ISIS. In addition, more than 3,000 children have died as the result of improvised explosive device (IED) explosions.

There are severe mental, physical, social, emotional, psychological, and spiritual consequences to these cultures, which has created a historical trauma that is passed down to many future generations. This humanitarian crisis requires a long-term plan to bridge the gap between Western mental health treatment strategies and adapting culturally relevant approaches for indigenous groups exposed to war (Hanson & Vogel, 2012; Miller & Rasmussen, 2010). The complex trauma acquired by armed conflict, poverty, malnutrition, and displacement into overcrowded and impoverished refugee camps has created mental and physical trauma resulting in permanent disabilities. The destruction of social networks and those who are survivors of forced child military service, sexual assault, and the loss of social and material support, as well as widows and orphans, has created a complex trauma that cannot be addressed purely from Western models of mental health treatment. Rather, exposure to war on civilians requires integrative culturally sensitive approaches to heal the symptoms of posttraumatic stress and the daily stressors of survival on war-affected indigenous populations.

A humanitarian crisis of epic proportions exists on a global basis for immigrants, refugees, internally displaced persons, and asylum seekers from war-torn countries. The complex global security both at home and abroad has far-reaching implications for the sociocultural and psychosocial health, safety, and welfare of all the planet's populations. The complex trauma experienced by immigrants, refugees, and asylum seekers appears to be a silent epidemic for most Americans. The critical challenges for these indigenous/ethnic groups rarely come into the consciousness of "things to worry about" for most Americans, unless of course one or more of these groups live in your community. It certainly becomes an issue for Americans who identify or belong to the ethnic heritage of these groups. The reality is that there is no amount of money or donations that can heal the suffering of foreign nationals, which can be viewed on the nightly news and other 24-hour electronic media news outlets.

Fear and ignorance are easily spread by some U.S. politicians who misuse language (i.e., illegal aliens, Muslim terrorists), which ultimately stigmatizes ethnic minority groups. Truly, language has the potential to harm or heal. Stigmatizing language communicated about different minority groups has the potential to perpetrate overt acts of prejudice, discrimination, and intentional/unintentional racism. Misuse of language by well-intentioned U.S. lawmakers who have created legal terms, such as *Hispanic*, also has the potential to stigmatize minorities because it does not consider cultural identity (i.e., Latina[o], Columbian, Mexican American) and within-group differences. The various terms we use to describe other cultures tend to seep into the unconsciousness of many Americans. Consequently, we normalize the stigmatizing language used to describe different minorities and can easily become intolerant of others, which hinders our ability for compassion and empathy.

As mental health professionals, we must deflect the negative attitudes and overt prejudices that are sustained in the larger society. The groups most affected have sustained enough harsh treatment for one lifetime. Thus, we have an ethical obligation to build cultural awareness, knowledge, and skills to work with others who are culturally different. Unfortunately, the majority of practitioners do not have training to work with the complex trauma experienced by immigrants from war-torn countries (Stebnicki, 2015). Despite training in multicultural counseling, most practitioners do not have the language skills and cultural knowledge to work with these indigenous populations. This should not prevent mental health professionals from responding to the humanitarian need in an empathic way of being. Accordingly, special training is required to work competently and ethically with immigrants from places in the far reaches of the globe, which is discussed later in this chapter.

GOVERNMENT-DRIVEN DISASTER RESPONSE AND STRATEGIC INITIATIVES

There is a human cost to living in an unpredictable world that has experienced person-made disasters perpetrated on defenseless and disempowered civilians who are exposed to war. There are no peaceful political resolutions in many scenarios. As a consequence, there are always civilian casualties as a result of war. Historically, there has always been a humanitarian response in times of large-scale disasters. Therefore, having some faith there will always be humanitarian efforts, as well as compassion for others, requires a determined, hopeful, positive, and optimistic view of the world.

Humanitarian efforts are seen in many corners of the Earth where agencies and organizations have mobilized to cobble together basic services for food, clean water, shelter, clothing, and medical health care. It may be the nature of humans that every non-profit agency, faith-based organization, or government entity has its own conceptual idea of assisting with food, clean water, shelter, clothing, health care, and financial support. However, it is critical that some organizations can take charge of planning, coordinating, organizing, and leading a unified coalition of care providers and volunteers to be effective in large-scale disaster response, such as the masses of immigrants, refugees, and asylum seekers fleeing their homelands and geographically relocating all over the world.

The Strategic Foresight Initiative (SFI) action plan developed by the Federal Emergency Management Agency (FEMA, 2012) is one example of an agency that has stepped up to the challenge of addressing the needs of immigrants, refugees, and asylum seekers in the United States and has projected and anticipated potential crisis outcomes up to the year 2030. Although FEMA's mission is not humanitarian in nature, the SFI action plan provides a comprehensive crisis response plan for handling the influx of indigenous/ethnic populations. This transformative crisis response and disaster plan is intended to advance strategic planning at the local, county, state, and federal government levels to be prepared for potential associated risks of epidemics, pandemic health, illness and disease concerns, biological risks, and other crises that might erupt as a result of populations from war-torn countries arriving to the United States.

The guideposts presented in FEMA's SFI report explore and highlight other critical areas of epidemic concerns such as the (a) increasing complexity and decreasing predictability of living in a secure homeland environment; (b) evolving mental, medical, and physical health care needs of all Americans and at-risk populations; and (c) future resource constraints of fiscal, technological, and highly trained personnel to work at the epicenter of disaster. An abbreviated list of SFI scenarios includes understanding the preparation, prevention, protection, and disaster response in dealing with the health care of older aging adult populations, persons with chronic illnesses and disabilities, technology, terrorism in the homeland, pandemics, drought, and multiple other critical incidents that deal with the strain of economic resources, the deteriorating infrastructure, and other major threats that are person-made and biological in nature.

The United States is the world's strongest nation enjoying the advantages of civil rights for all cultural minority groups (e.g., persons of racial/ethnic diversity; persons with disabilities; persons that identify as lesbian, gay, bisexual, and transgender [LGBT]), state–federal programs for disability benefits (e.g., workers compensation, supplemental security income [SSI], Social Security disability insurance [SSDI]), technology, energy, and alliances and partnerships with other countries to decrease security threats on multiple levels. Despite these strengths, there are countries, governments, and other dark entities that would like to undo the benefits and progress afforded to Americans.

For example, the 2015 report of the military's contribution to national security (Joint Chiefs of Staff, Unified Combatant Commands, & Office of the Secretary of Defense, 2016) identifies threats to our national security. These include, but are not limited to (a) Russia—which has repeatedly demonstrated a lack of respect for the sovereignty of its neighboring countries and other actions that violate multiple human rights agreements; (b) Iran—which also has interest in pursuing nuclear and missile delivery technologies and state-sponsored terrorism, and has undermined stability in Middle Eastern countries such as Israel, Lebanon, Iraq, Syria, and Yemen; (c) North Korea—which is also very active in the pursuit of nuclear weapons, ballistic missile testing, and cyber-attacks, and has repeatedly and contentiously confronted and bullied Korea and Japan with harm; and (d) China—which has added much anxiety and tension to the Asia-Pacific region not only militarily, but by claiming its territories that include nearly the entire South China Sea.

The key point is that the government and antigovernment groups that make up these suppressive cultures have unpredictable behaviors that threaten the health, safety, and welfare of Americans and all other reasonable countries' indigenous populations around the world. Regardless of your political, moral, and philosophical beliefs regarding the engagement in war, the presence and actions of the U.S. military, its allies, and its partners are critical to deter aggression and defeat extremist groups in key global hot spots.

History has shown that the real victims of war are defenseless and disempowered civilians. As a result of enduring national interests, national security, and a plethora of international critical incidents and issues, one gets the impression that the United States has multiple and complex concerns that are a potential threat to the health, security, and overall well-being of the homeland.

Presently, we have incurred multiple limitations that exceed our resources in respond to complex multiple critical events occurring simultaneously (e.g., terrorism, conflict/war, cyber security, natural disasters, and biological threats). From some socio-political perspectives, issues related to immigrants, refugees, and asylum seekers have become low priority for government agencies and present a challenge of epic proportions. Thus, it is critical that we set an example of service and respond to the humanitarian needs of others, creating opportunities for healing the mind, body, and spirit of critical populations.

GUIDELINES FOR MENTAL HEALTH SCREENINGS FOR NEWLY ARRIVED REFUGEES AND ASYLUM SEEKERS

The Centers for Disease Control and Prevention (CDC; 2016) and the Division of Global Migration and Quarantine published guidelines in June 2015 for evaluating the mental and physical health needs of newly arrived refugees and asylum seekers. The long journey of refugees and asylum seekers is a testament to their psychological, emotional, and physical resiliency. However, many die along this perilous journey. Exposure to profound stressors and traumatic events predisposes refugees and asylum seekers to a life of chronic and persistent mental and physical health conditions, causing permanent disability. More specific, the chronic and persistent risk factors that predispose refugees and asylum seekers to a lifetime of disabilities include depression, posttraumatic stress symptoms, anxiety and panic attacks, substance use disorders, somatization, and traumatic brain injuries.

The etiology and underlying cause of refugees' and asylum seekers' mental and physical conditions are well documented in the literature (CDC, 2016; Craig, MacJajua, & Warfa, 2009; Fazel, Wheeler, & Danesh, 2005; Hanson & Vogel, 2012; Higson-Smith, 2013; Miller & Rasmussen, 2010; Pells & Treisman, 2012). It is unimaginable for most Americans to understand the horrific life that some have endured. This includes, but is not limited to, exposure to war and combat at an early age, state-sponsored violence and oppression, torture, internment camps, human trafficking, displacement from one's home and country, loss of family members and prolonged separation, the stress of adapting to a new culture, and living in poverty and unemployment. Indeed, the process of resettlement and psychosocial adjustment to living in a new country does in fact require medical and mental health interventions.

Triage of Refugees and Asylum Seekers

Under the authority of the INA and the Public Health Service Act, the Secretary of Health and Human Services and the CDC's Division of Global Migration and Quarantine outline regulations for medical and mental health screenings of refugees seeking admission to the United States. Other government agencies involved in the medical and mental health screenings are the Department of State (DOS) and the USCIS. The process and regulations are quite complex. Thus, the reader should consult the References section for a more comprehensive review.

One of the first steps in this process is developing health clinics in the homeland and overseas for the purpose of triaging refugees and asylum seekers. Clinicians perform a variety of medical and mental health evaluations using medically trained American-born interpreters and bicultural interpreters. Based on the severity of symptoms presented by the refugee patient and his or her ability to function in daily life, the medical evaluations are triaged into three separate groups. Group I includes those refugees with chronic, serious, and acute health conditions that require immediate follow-up. Group II includes refugees with less acute mental health or psychiatric symptoms that only require routine follow-up care. Group III involves refugees without any identified mental or physical symptoms that require routine or immediate care.

Refugees' Mental and Physical Assessment

Guidelines and procedures for the mental and physical assessment are comprehensive and mandatory for all refugees and asylum seekers coming to the United States. The goal is to prevent, detect, and intervene in mental or physical health conditions that require urgent or immediate attention and to generally assess those refugees that require referral and follow-up care with other providers. The following are mandatory evaluations completed by medical and mental health professionals:

- Review of any available premigration medical and mental health records from the refugees' country of origin
- Current medical history, physical exam, use of prescription medications, allergies, and particularly screening for such neurological conditions as traumatic brain injury
- Exposure to any occupational hazards as many indigenous minority groups have worked in agriculture, mining, and factory occupations that have a high-risk exposure to toxins
- The level of exposure to combat and other traumatic events, particularly screening for symptoms of posttraumatic stress
- Screening for other mental health conditions such as depression, anxiety, and substance use disorders; screenings for drug and alcohol use also include any use of traditional herbal indigenous substances such as khat
- Specialized child screenings that include childhood immunizations, vaccinations, allergies, any malnutrition, maltreatment, scars, physical deformities, the child's patterns of normal development, level of education, and any somatic complaints
- Social–familial–cultural history, as well as educational, occupational, or literacy levels

If significant positive findings emerge from any of these assessments, it is quite typical that follow-up clinical observations and assessments are warranted. All critical information is provided to resettlement agencies so that individual needs can be met. It is particularly important that on initial assessment vulnerable populations are identified because of some unique needs requiring follow-up care. Some vulnerable populations include the following individuals: (a) pregnant women and infants; (b) severely disabled individuals and those who have chronic illnesses; (c) those who exhibit chronic and persistent psychiatric symptoms; (d) those who are developmentally disabled and those who possess other neurocognitive conditions; and (e) those who are aged, elderly, or frail.

CULTIVATING A WORKING ALLIANCE WITH REFUGEES: CONSIDERATIONS FOR MENTAL HEALTH PROFESSIONALS

It is of paramount importance that mental health professionals use culturally sensitive approaches when interacting with refugees, many of whom are significantly culturally different from the professional's background. Rapport building is at the foundation of cultivating a strong working alliance. The use of culturally appropriate empathy and other therapeutic techniques is discussed in more detail in other chapters of the book. However, mental health professionals should anticipate some level of difficulty during rapport building, which is a natural artifact of working with immigrants, refugees, and asylum seekers. Some examples of these difficulties exist because:

- Many cultural groups distrust Americans because they were taught to fear them by their country of origin.
- The U.S. military may have invaded their country, which destabilized their government and destroyed their homeland.
- Americans are many times viewed as violent people as portrayed in movies and other electronic media.
- Some indigenous groups may view mental health professionals as an extension of their previous punitive government.
- Some indigenous groups may not understand the American lifestyle behaviors as portrayed in the electronic and social media.
- Most indigenous groups do not have a mental health provider system such as the United States, and many do not endorse mental health counseling because they were taught not to disclose personal problems and issues to strangers.

Facilitating culturally sensitive approaches with refugees and asylum seekers also requires some knowledge, awareness, and skills in the following areas:

- Knowledge of the geographic location and salient aspects of the refugee's culture (i.e., religious and spiritual beliefs, occupations, daily lifestyle habits, form of government, system of health care and education)
- Competencies in the use of cultural empathy (i.e., use of eye contact, nonverbal language, spatial distance, time orientation)
- Administration and use of all assessments (standardized and nonstandardized) and an understanding that most assessments were not culturally normed on the population being served
- The mental health professional's overreliance on Western mental health counseling theories and techniques
- The mental health counselor's overuse of diagnosing and treating mental health disorders as they relate to *Diagnostic and Statistical Manual of Mental Disorders* (5th ed.; *DSM-5*; American Psychiatric Association, 2013) criteria

First Steps in Cultivating a Working Alliance

Many refugees and asylum seekers want to escape their countries of origin because of mental and physical torture, mass violence and genocide, witnessing the killings of family members and friends, sexual abuse, kidnapping of children and women to be used in forced sexual prostitution, looting of personal possessions by the government/military, starvation, and deprivation of food, shelter, and clothing. The acts of brutality perpetrated on these indigenous groups have created distrust among almost everyone except the friends and family whom they journeyed with to find safe haven. Accordingly, mental health professionals can cultivate a working alliance possessing awareness, knowledge, and skills in the following areas:

- Use language interpreters when necessary for communicating and always attend to the person you are speaking to, not the interpreter. It is preferable to use an interpreter from the indigenous group you are serving.
- Find a tribal leader, elder, or some other member of the refugee group who has knowledge of the specific culture and the needs of his or her own people.

- Collaborate, support, and coordinate services, working through one or two persons who are indigenous to the culture, which can help build trust among others in the group.
- Understand that "silence" does not imply resistance. Rather, many refugees have a natural reluctance toward Americans or engage in Western models of therapeutic services from someone outside their culture.
- Understand how to interpret the emotions and cognitions of refugees, which is critical to engaging in therapeutic alliances. For instance, many refugees may exhibit feelings of rage and anger. This should not be anthologized. Rather, anger and rage are many times experienced as inconceivable betrayal by the government they once trusted. There are many other emotions that require other interpretations.
- Use natural spaces or the natural environment to build a rapport and working alliance with someone. An office space or building can potentially intimidate many indigenous populations and may retraumatize these individuals as a representation of the brutal government from which they fled.

Second Steps in Cultivating a Working Alliance

There are no words to describe the horrific trauma that many refugees have experienced. A seasoned humanitarian mental health professional understands the refugee's risk factors and long-term mental health problems, and knows how to reduce further traumatic exposure by creating a *circle of trust*. This trust can potentially be developed by the strategies offered in the section "First Steps in Cultivating a Working Alliance" and can be strengthened by the following therapeutic culturally endorsed interventions:

- Mental health professionals should view refugees as "survivors" rather than "victims." There are extraordinary stories of survival that can help build resiliency among others in the refugee groups. Shared storytelling among group members that are matched appropriately (men to men; women to women) is critical. Individual therapeutic interaction for many indigenous groups is not a natural way of healing. Thus, the group is only as strong and resilient as those that comprise the group. Refugee groups can draw to one another because they have earned the circle of trust.
- The numbness and shock of being a survivor of the horrific extraordinary stressful and traumatic events experienced by the refugee may linger much longer than anticipated. Everyone heals at his or her own rate and pace; however, the level of intensity and posttraumatic stress symptoms may endure for months after an arrival to a safe haven country.

CONCLUSIONS

The etiology of the worldwide epidemic of immigrants, refugees, and asylum seekers is clear. It is war that is at the foundation of all human suffering as millions are forced to relocate geographically. This epidemic of person-made disaster points to the overall lack of respect and empathy for human life perpetrated by brutal governments, religious zealots, and other indigenous tribal warring groups. The known causes are also exemplified by civil and religious armed conflicts, continuous bombing of villages and towns, violence perpetrated by drug warlords, forced sexual prostitution and slavery, imprisonment by the government for possessing the "wrong" sociopolitical or religious beliefs, racism, discrimination, forced isolation/internal displacement and detention camps, deprived access to adequate mental and physical health care, and the withholding of basic food, water, shelter, and clothing for warmth. Overall, disaster mental health responders who commit to work with specific indigenous populations of global cultures require a much different approach to provide culturally sensitive interventions and strategies. This chapter offers some guidelines to mental health professionals to begin working globally with the new culture of immigrants, refugees, and asylum seekers.

REFERENCES

American Psychiatric Association. (2013). *Diagnostic and statistical manual of mental disorders* (5th ed.). Arlington, VA: American Psychiatric Publishing.

American Psychological Association. (2010). Resiliency and recovery after war: Refugee children and families in the United States. Retrieved from http://www.apa.org/pubs/info/reports/refugees-full -report.pdf

Centers for Disease Control and Prevention. (2016). Guidelines for mental health screening during the domestic medical examination for newly arrived refugees. Retrieved from http://www.cdc.gov/ immigrantrefugeehealth/pdf/mental-health-screening-guidelines.pdf

Craig, T., MacJajua, P., & Warfa, N. (2009). Mental health care needs of refugees. *Psychiatry, 8*(9), 351–354.

Fazel, M., Wheeler, J., & Danesh, J. (2005). Prevalence of serious mental disorder in 7000 refugees resettled in western countries: A systematic review. *Lancet, 365*(9467), 1309–1314.

Federal Emergency Management Agency. (2012). Crisis response and disaster resilience 2030: Forging strategic action in an age of uncertainty. Progress report highlighting the 2010 to 2011 insights of the Strategic Foresight Initiative. Retrieved from https://www.fema.gov/media-library -data/20130726-1816-25045-5167/sfi_report_13.jan.2012_final.docx.pdf

Genocide Intervention Network. (2016). Annual report 2008. Retrieved from http://www.footprint network.org/content/images/uploads/Global_Footprint_Network_2008_Annual_Report.pdf

Hanson, E., & Vogel, G. (2012). The impact of war on civilians. In L. L. Levers (Ed.), *Trauma counseling: Theories and interventions* (pp. 412–433). New York, NY: Springer Publishing.

Higson-Smith, C. (2013). Counseling torture survivors in contexts of ongoing threat: Narratives from sub-Saharan Africa. *Journal of Peace Psychology, 19*(2), 164–179.

Homeland Security. (2016). Definition of terms. Retrieved from http://www.dhs.gov/definition-terms# permanent_resident_alien

Joint Chiefs of Staff, Unified Combatant Commands, & Office of the Secretary of Defense. (2016). *The national military strategy of the United States of America 2015: The United States military's contribution to national security.* Retrieved from http://www.jcs.mil/Portals/36/Documents/ Publications/2015_National_Military_Strategy.pdf

Mercy Corps. (2016). Top stories. Retrieved from https://www.mercycorps.org

Miller, K. E., & Rasmussen, A. (2010). War exposure, daily stressors, and mental health in conflict and post-conflict settings: Bridging the divide between trauma-focused and psychosocial frameworks. *Social Science & Medicine, 70*(1), 7–16.

Pells, K., & Treisman, K. (2012). Genocide, ethnic conflict, and political violence. In L. L. Levers (Ed.), *Trauma counseling: Theories and interventions* (pp. 389–411). New York, NY: Springer Publishing.

Physicians for Social Responsibility. (2016). Body count: March 2015 report. Retrieved from http://www .ippnw.de/commonFiles/pdfs/Frieden/Body_Count_first_international_edition_2015_final.pdf

Stebnicki, M. A. (2015, October). *The psychosocial cost of war on non-military civilian populations: A global perspective.* Presentation made at the Annual Conference of the Licensed Professional Counseling Association of North Carolina, Raleigh, NC.

Stichick, T., & Bruderlein, C. (2001). Children facing insecurity: New strategies for survival in the global era. Harvard Program on Humanitarian Policy and Conflict Research. Retrieved from http:// reliefweb.int/sites/reliefweb.int/files/resources/F067BD96BAD2F990C12571D900437781-Harvard -May2001.pdf

United Nations. (2016). New UN report warns of "abhorrent violations" against children in war-torn Iraq. Retrieved from https://childrenandarmedconflict.un.org/new-un-report-warns-of-abhorrent -violations-against-children-in-war-torn-iraq

United Nations High Commissioner for Refugees. (2016). World refugee day: Global forced displacement tops 50 million for the first time in post-WWII era. Retrieved from http://www.unhcr.org/ 53a155bc6.html

U.S. Citizenship and Immigration Services. (2016a). Immigration and Nationality Act. Retrieved from https://www.uscis.gov/laws/immigration-and-nationality-act

U.S. Citizenship and Immigration Services. (2016b). Policy manual. Retrieved from https://www.uscis .gov/policymanual/HTML/PolicyManual.html#introduction

U.S. Citizenship and Immigration Services. (2016c). Refugees and the refugee process. Retrieved from https://www.uscis.gov/humanitarian/refugees-asylum/refugees

U.S. State Department. (2016). Diplomacy in action. Retrieved from http://www.state.gov

War Chronicle. (2016). Estimated war dead World War II. Retrieved from http://warchronicle.com/ numbers/WWII/deaths.htm

Wiist, W. H., Barker, K., Arya, N., Rhode, J., Donohoe, M., White, S., . . . Hagopain, A. (2014). The role of public health in the prevention of war: Rationale and competencies. *American Journal of Public Health, 106*(4), 34–37. doi:10.2105/AJPH.2013.301778

27

Key Concepts and Techniques
for an Aging Workforce*

Susanne M. Bruyère, Debra A. Harley, Charlene M. Kampfe, Sara VanLooy, and John S. Wadsworth

Older workers are one of the fastest growing subsets of the American workforce. According to the U.S. Bureau of Labor Statistics (2012), one in five American workers is older than 65 years, and it is predicted that between 2014 and 2024, the number of workers 55 years and older will grow by 19.8%, with much of that growth made up of people older than 65 (Toosi, 2015; U.S. Bureau of Labor Statistics, 2015). As the baby boom generation continues to age, the number of 65- to 74-year-olds in the labor force is projected to increase more than workers in other age groups, and workers aged 75 years and older are expected to have the fastest growth of all (U.S. Bureau of Labor Statistics, 2015). The Social Security Administration (SSA) projects that by 2080, 23% of the total population will be aged 65 or older, while the general working age population will shrink to 54%. Consequently, the Social Security system is experiencing a declining worker-to-beneficiary ratio, which will fall from 3.3 to 2.1 in 2040 (Reznik, Shoffner, & Weaver, 2005). As employers draw human capital from the general population, and as the population ages, so does the workforce. The aging population is likely to result in an increasing number of people with disabilities in the workforce who may have difficulty with work performance and staying employed (McDonald & Harder, 2004).

Effective counseling practices must increasingly include attention to preparing both individuals and their workplaces for the impact of the aging process. Proactive education on ways to maximize the productivity of an aging workforce, effective case management, and workplace accommodations can significantly contribute to maximizing aging-worker retention. Increasingly cited as a workplace accommodation among older workers is the desire for flexible work arrangements (e.g., alternative schedules, reduced working hours, nonmonetary benefits; Tishman, VanLooy, & Bruyère, 2012).

*Susanne Bruyère's efforts on this chapter were supported in part by a grant from the National Institute on Disability, Independent Living, and Rehabilitation Research (NIDILRR grant number 90RT5010-01-00). NIDILRR is a center within the Administration for Community Living (ACL), Department of Health and Human Services (HHS). The contents of this chapter do not necessarily represent the policy of NIDILRR, ACL, HHS, and you should not assume endorsement by the federal government.

Older persons frequently experience dehumanizing situations or attitudes. They are often devalued by society, discriminated against with regard to employment, discouraged from making their own decisions about a variety of aspects of their lives, and forced to make residential relocations into institutions that may not encourage or allow independence of thought or action (Kampfe, 2015). The professional counselor's philosophy is antithetical to these practices.

Employment is a key aspect of the current social effort to promote financial independence, emotional health, and physical wellness among the growing population of older individuals (Gonzales, Matz-Costa, & Morrow-Howell, 2015). Both the need for economic support and the personal and social benefits of work may be important for persons of all ages. While the "baby boom" generation is moving into an age group with a much lower workforce participation rate (Toosi, 2015), many older workers will need to work longer for the income it brings to ensure adequate postretirement incomes to address increased life spans, and for life satisfaction associated with productivity (Institute on Rehabilitation Issues, 2009; Kampfe, 2015; U.S. Department of Labor, 2010).

THEORETICAL AND CLINICAL CONSIDERATIONS

The aging process is unique to every individual. Professional counselors have many opportunities to provide interventions that improve the quality of life for older persons (Hershenson, 2015). However, theoretical and philosophical models used in counseling older individuals are overwhelmingly grounded in the medical model, which emphasizes the identification and treatment of pathological physical changes that are associated with growing older (Bowling & Dieppe, 2005). The medical model identifies a diagnosis, prescribes a protocol for intervention, and offers a prognosis. As a dominant paradigm, this model asserts that the body is a physical mechanism that can be studied quantitatively through measurement of physiological function (e.g., lab work, CT scan, EKG) and can be treated as well at a strictly physical level (e.g., medications, physical therapy, surgery). In many ways, the medical model disregards psychological concepts, emotional reactions, and subjective data. In addition, the medical model looks within the individual for a diagnosis of the problem, placing the physician above the person, and ignores the person's physical and social environment (Kampfe, 2015). This emphasis may lead counselors to anchor assessment results on biases against older adults. Ultimately, the medical model is rigid, restrictive, and disempowering because it adheres to the notion that aging itself is a type of impairment that with appropriate treatment can be either ameliorated or cured.

Developmental Models of Aging

A number of important theories and approaches (e.g., psychosocial theory, activity theory, continuity theory, disengagement theory) germane to counseling, public health, and social work are salient for a better understanding of aging. One approach is more closely aligned with the developmental model (Erikson, 1959). Erikson described human life in terms of stages—sequential developmental occurrences in which individuals experience developmental crises (e.g., change in employment status, loss, and grief). He pointed out that old age is a time when people struggle to find meaning in the life they have lived, a sense of ego, integrity, and satisfaction with a life well spent. The stage of life designated as *old age* involves numerous transitions (e.g., retirement, loss of autonomy, and impaired health). The advantage of applying the developmental model to older people is its focus on wellness, planning for successful adaptations, and empowerment to realize the developmental goal and reach their full potential.

Developmental frameworks for counseling intervention have been reported to be successful in addressing a wide variety of concerns that impact older persons. Sexuality for older persons may be addressed through holistic and developmental frameworks that stress the potential for lifelong capacity to enjoy intimacy and sensual enjoyment. Career development may be presented as a lifelong, dynamic process that requires individuals to engage throughout their lifetime in the ongoing assessment, analysis, and synthesis of information about the world of work and self.

Socioecological Models of Aging

Another approach is the socioecological model, which is most closely associated with Bronfenbrenner (1986). Applied to older adults, the model places the elder at the center of four nested systems consistent with an elder-centered approach to prevention and intervention (Quandt, McDonald, Bell, & Arcury, 1999). The socioecological model considers the influence and interaction of the individual at four levels: (a) microsystem (biological and personal factors that converge to influence how individuals behave as well as risk factors for adverse outcomes), (b) mesosystem (focuses on close relationships to explore how such relationships promote well-being and quality of life), (c) exosystem (identifies community contexts in which social relationships occur), and (d) macrosystem (includes broad ideological values, norms, and institutional patterns that may foster a climate in which older adults are either encouraged or prohibited; Harley & Teaster, 2016).

Integration of Life Experiences

An individual who is aging successfully has a more integrative experience that includes acceptance of the past, resolution of conflicts, and reconciliation of reality with the ideal self than a person who utilizes escape and obsessive reminiscence of the past. Life reviews may allow clients to integrate life experiences and create new meaning to promote the resolution of conflicts and reconciliation with others in preparation for life transitions and the termination of life. Life planning may assist older persons in clarifying transferable vocational or leisure skills, planning for age-related change, and setting goals.

Personal control is vital in maintaining mental health and life satisfaction (Kampfe, 2015). The ability to make decisions, self-regulate behavior, and control the environment is positively associated with psychological well-being. Paid work is recognized as an important source of well-being for older men and women because work provides a sense of independence and competence outside of immediate family networks. Counseling interventions that encourage personal control rather than focus on diagnosis and pathology may be more effective in promoting the well-being of older persons.

Counseling and Case Management

The aging population requires multiple services from various professionals (e.g., counselors, health care providers, and employment human resource departments). To better facilitate positive outcomes for aging populations, interagency collaboration offers an opportunity for enhanced employment outcomes. Casework is the common denominator, which cuts across various service professionals and is relevant to deconstructing disincentives for either maintaining or returning to work. (See Harley, Donnell, & Rainey, 2003, for strategies and implications for functional integration collaboration for crossing professional borders.)

Counseling can assist older adults in coping and meeting their needs in changing situations. However, fewer older adults than younger ones use mental health services and other related counseling services. Older individuals may associate counseling treatment with institutionalization or believe it is reserved for extremely disturbed individuals. They may also attribute emotional difficulties to the normal process of growing older, and they may believe that the inability to cope with difficulties is a sign of failure to age successfully.

Assessment of Older Adults

Assessment should involve special considerations for older consumers because age-related limitations are often misinterpreted. It is important to recognize that physical and mental disabilities can manifest themselves differently in older adults. For example, mobility limitations can influence older adults' mental functioning, which in turn impact their concentration and responsiveness. Appropriate assessment leads to subsequent planning and service delivery. Older adults may not have recent experiences in standardized testing and may find some assessments threatening. Thus, older adults may require additional explanation to clarify what the test measures, its relevance to the questions at hand, and the benefits of the actual results (Kampfe, 2015). To ensure optimal performance, older adults should be prepared in advance for testing and given prior notice to bring all assistive devices (American Psychological Association [APA], n.d.).

Testing instruments must be chosen to be appropriate (Kampfe, 2015; Kampfe, Wadsworth, Mamboleo, & Schonbrun, 2008). Norms are not available on some instruments for age cohorts beyond 60 or 65 (e.g., Holland's *Self-Directed Search*; Holland, 1994). Even instruments that include older persons in the norm groups often only go to age 89 or 90 years and thus would not necessarily be applicable to 100-year-olds (e.g., Wechsler Adult Intelligence Scales–Revised III [WAIS III]; Wechsler, 1997). Furthermore, the age range for older persons (e.g., 65–105 years) is wide; there are very different functional levels, needs, and appropriate assessments within the age groups of 65 to 105 (Kampfe, 2015). Test administrators need to assume responsibility for recognizing deficiencies of the instruments and selecting other appropriate instruments, if available.

In addition to vocational and intelligence assessment, consideration should be given to making a comprehensive geriatric assessment a part of the overall assessment process (i.e., medical status, functional capabilities, psychosocial status). When the test administrator has knowledge of the older adult's medical problems, prescribed and over-the-counter medications, and use of alcohol or any other drug, this information should be weighed in the interpretation of test results. Information from a comprehensive assessment can assist the test administrator in a more accurate interpretation of test results.

Endurance must be a consideration in scheduling tests. People with sensory impairments, reduced energy levels, or disabling physical or mental conditions may exhibit fatigue and can benefit from accommodations during testing. Many older adults commonly report restrictions in their ability to carry out meaningful activities of daily living, as well as require assistance from other people (U.S. Department of Health and Human Services, 2013). Reflex speed typically decreases and sensory loss increases with age, so power or practical tests may be more meaningful than speed tests (Kampfe, 2015). Abbreviated screening instruments may also be useful—shortened instruments to assess depression have been found to be as effective as longer ones, and a four-test short form of the WAIS III has been found as effective as the full form in determining intellectual functioning in persons more than age 65. Situational assessments (also known as ecological evaluations) or job trials may be more relevant to older persons than paper-and-pencil testing. Behavioral assessment is an important adjunct.

In the assessment of older adults, because of the physical, cognitive, and sensory changes that often accompany aging, the APA (n.d.) emphasizes that (a) the testing environment should be modified to ensure optimal performance; (b) the test administrator must be flexible in the testing process and interpretation of results; and (c) qualitative indices are, at times, of more importance than quantitative indicies. Often, the social aspects of older adults' lives (e.g., adverse living conditions, financial stressors, personal support system, family or interpersonal difficulties) produce effects that can alter test results. In addition, both quantitative and qualitative data should be examined in the context of the older adult's beliefs, education, ethnicity, culture, and stage-of-life issues.

Functional Assessment of Older Adults

Tests of functional level can be an important source of information in vocational assessments and can further assist in career planning with older adults who wish to return to work. However, the use of functional assessments to evaluate change in older adults is complicated by a lack of consensus as to which assessment is most suitable (Wales, Clemson, Lannin, & Cameron, 2016). Specific instruments have been developed to determine functional status of older persons. For example, the Instrumental Activities of Daily Living Scale (Nourhashémi et al., 2001) has been effectively used with women aged 75 years and older to assess independent living functioning and to predict successfully risk factors of frailty in older women who, at the time of the assessment, were healthy and living at home. Other functional assessment instruments that appear to be promising for use with older adults include the Functioning Autonomy Measurement System (SMAF) and the Assessment of Motor and Process Skills (AMPS). Both are responsive to change when applied to older adults (Wales et al., 2016). Although Universal Design for Learning (UDL) provides a means for designing assessments that are fair, equitable, and supportive of variation in learner ability and offers benefits in career assessment and vocational evaluation practices (Smith, Leconte, & Vitelli, 2012), it has yet to be used with older adults to assess how they learn, work, behave, and interact with information and their environment.

Assessment of decision-making capacity in older adults is becoming increasingly important in evaluating workplace performance. Although mental capacity is not a predictor of job performance in older adults, it is relevant in measuring decision making and scope to perform specific tasks related to cognitive and procedural skills (e.g., independent living, giving consent).

CONSIDERATIONS FOR OLDER WORKERS

The aging population is at a state of development that is not as focused on employment, and thus has difficulty finding its place in a society that defines people by their careers. However, greater life expectancy, the need for income in later life, and changes in the structure of retirement programs have caused increasing numbers of older people to remain in the workforce, where they are presented with numerous barriers (Sass, 2016; Turner, 2008).

People who are older are more likely than younger people to be adapting to the effects of sensory loss; to see themselves as being closer to death; to have a loss of role models for social demands they encounter; to experience significant loss of cohort groups, long-term friendships, and family members; to experience role changes, role reversals, and alterations in role expectations; to perceive changes in social support; and to experience changes in perception of time. Counselors can assist with adjustment to these critical life events.

As people age, chronic physical and mental health conditions are more prevalent (Kampfe, 2015). These conditions often do not decrease people's ability to work, live independently, and conduct activities of daily living. Variables such as lifestyle, coping abilities, activity accommodations, medical care, external supports, physical and social environments, therapeutic regimens, and rehabilitation may mediate the severity of functional limitations and subsequent development of disabilities (Ng & Law, 2014).

Premorbid personality is an important component in adaptation to disability. Both negative and positive traits may be associated with adjustment to disability or illness (Frank, 2011). Although some individuals manage to adapt to the implications and limitations of their disability, others fail to accept this situation, manifesting depressive symptoms, expressions of anger, or persistent denial (Psarra & Kleftaras, 2013). On the one hand, for example, some research indicates that after the onset of disability, people initially experience sharp drops in life satisfaction, and the ability to regain lost life satisfaction is at best partial (Infurna & Wiest, 2016). On the other hand, other studies have suggested that the impact on life satisfaction is significantly moderated by predisability personality (Boyce & Wood, 2011). Infurna and Wiest (2016) found that people who acquired a disability in young adulthood and old age reported stronger declines in life satisfaction and were less likely to adapt in the years thereafter. Factors associated with maintaining life satisfaction were less severe disability and higher levels of social participation. Conversely, Boerner (2004) found a critical role of accommodative coping for adaptation, with beneficial effects on mental health more pronounced in the case of high disability for younger participants, suggesting that dealing with disability may pose more of a mental health risk in middle than in late adulthood. Apparently, old age may be a time with significant challenges, especially for those with disabilities and chronic illness, but it is not a time when quality of life and adjustment are inevitably poor (Akman, 2004). The effects of endurance, resilience, energy level, and stress are important in rehabilitation planning for persons of all ages and even more important when chronic, multiple, and severe conditions are combined with effects of aging.

A particular concern of older workers is their risk of disability-related changes in sensory acuity. Approximately 9.4% of all individuals aged 65 to 74 years in the general population experience a hearing impairment. Visual impairments are also common, affecting approximately 4.4% of people in that age category (Erickson, Lee, & von Schrader, 2016). Sensory impairments are a particularly significant source of functional limitation, regardless of chronological age, and these conditions often lead to a diminished ability to participate in everyday life (Kampfe, 2015). Employers are less familiar with accommodations for these types of impairments than for other disabilities, make them less frequently than they do other accommodations, and find them more difficult to make than other accommodations (Bruyère, Erickson, & VanLooy, 2006). This lack of experience lessens the likelihood that employers are prepared to deal with these disabilities. This barrier to continued productivity may affect older workers disproportionately.

People who are older experience the full range of disability, including mental illness and substance abuse. Among adults aged 65 to 74 years, the prevalence of mood disorder is 5.7%, anxiety is 9.5%, and the prevalence of any personality disorder is 13.2% (Reynolds, Pietrzak, El-Gabalawy, Mackenzie, & Sareen, 2015). These may be long-existing conditions, or may result from more recent situations (such as severe depression related to medications), or may result from a combination of these. Although older people are less likely to receive a diagnosis of major depression, they report higher rates of depressive symptoms on checklists, suggesting that the diagnostic criteria may underestimate the prevalence of depression among older people (Fiske, Wetherell, & Gatz, 2009).

Substance abuse in older individuals can be a continuation of a past addiction; a new coping strategy; an abuse of prescription medication; or a condition associated with anxiety, depression, or cognitive disorders. It may resemble conditions that are associated with aging such as chronic pain, fatigue, or depression, or be exacerbated by medication interactions. Once identified, however, those who have this disorder may benefit from treatment (Blow & Barry, 2012).

Information regarding various social norms imposed on older individuals within different cultures, including marginalized ethnic and racial groups (e.g., roles, status, and issues of respect), is needed. For example, older people from ethnic and racial minorities or Appalachian populations may rely heavily on informal networks and indigenous influence for intervention.

Although it is true that as workers age, they experience some decline in cognitive and physical functioning, there is little evidence of a link between aging and work performance. Baltes and Baltes (1990) proposed a model of aging that suggests that older workers adapt to the loss of personal resources by making adjustments, referred to as *selection, optimization, and compensation*, or SOC. This framework describes how the process of aging causes people to select and refine their goals in life and work, to optimize how they allocate their personal resources to achieve those goals, and to choose compensatory strategies to ensure they reach those goals and maintain the functioning needed to do so. In the process, older workers can leverage the resources they have gained from a lifetime of work, find new purposes and possibilities, and enhance their own well-being and their work productivity (Ng & Law, 2014). A complex set of issues exist around the intersection of aging, disability, and employment (i.e., onset of disability, severity of disability, type of disability). Several significant challenges affect older workers' ability to work: (a) their health; (b) more likely to work in physically demanding jobs rather than those that are technology based; and (c) not considering themselves as having a disability, but simply seeing themselves as aging. As a result, many older workers do not seek accommodations from their employers or seek services from the public workforce and vocational rehabilitation systems that might help them stay on the job or return to work (Heidkamp, Mabe, & DeGraaf, 2012). For older workers, employment considerations should be examined within the context of physical and psychological complications of job stress and appropriate interventions to minimize those risk factors (Merz, Bricout, & Kock, 2001).

PROACTIVE EMPLOYER RESPONSE

A major issue for aging workers and their employers is the work environment, and whether it might be unfriendly and perhaps even discriminatory toward older workers. A significant factor influencing the decision to retain or eject older workers is no doubt the culture of the workplace itself. Another factor is the misperception that older workers are more costly in terms of health insurance, low productivity, and missed days of work.

Research suggests that employers discriminate against older workers in the job application process (American Association of Retired Persons, 2014; Bendick, Brown, & Wall, 1999; Bendick, Jackson, & Horacio, 1997; Johnson & Neumark, 1996; Lahey, 2008; Perry et al., 2017; von Schrader & Nazarov, 2016). In addition, the stereotypes that younger workers have of their older peers can greatly influence workplace dynamics. Traditional stereotypes of older workers (e.g., being inflexible, sick, and unwilling to learn new technology) continue to persist at many levels (Ng & Feldman, 2012;

Posthuma & Campion, 2009). Such stereotypes clearly have had an influence on older workers' labor force participation in the past. Workers who experience age discrimination are more likely to leave their current employment setting and less likely to remain employed. Age-based stereotyping perpetuates discriminatory practices and discourages elderly workers from remaining in or returning to the workplace (Kampfe et al., 2007).

Around 30,000 charges are filed annually in the United States under the Age Discrimination in Employment Act of 1967 (ADEA), a law that protects workers 40 and over from discrimination in employment on the basis of age. Although the majority of ADEA charges cite termination-related issues (63%), a growing number over the last 20 years cite issues of employment relations (including harassment and discipline). The age group with the highest charge rate (number of charges per 10,000 in the labor force) is those approaching full retirement age (62- to 64-year-olds), indicating that these workers are perhaps feeling pushed out of the workforce prematurely (von Schrader & Nazarov, 2016). Age discrimination in the workplace is often difficult to detect, and can be hidden within management practices that target older workers, such as incentivized layoffs, restriction of training to new hires, and internal ranking systems (Woolever, 2013). Age discrimination may also manifest as disability discrimination: nearly 60% of disability discrimination claims filed under the Americans with Disabilities Act (ADA) come from people more than age 40 (Bjelland et al., 2010), and 16% are filed by people older than 55 years (Bruyère, von Schrader, Coduti, & Bjelland, 2010).

Keeping the senior worker not only preserves valuable institutional knowledge and memory but also creates beneficial diversity in the workplace. Incentives and workplace supports will be needed to encourage employers to retain older workers and to encourage older workers to remain in the workforce. Employers must create workplace policies and practices and effective intergenerational inclusion initiatives that support worker retention. This process may include adopting new management styles and work setting protocols that focus on an age-diverse workforce. Human resource policies and practices should reflect alternatives that will respond to the older workers' desire for flexible working hours, part-time positions, and the ability to choose what part of the day they work. Flexible workplace, telecommuting options, and flex-time agreements can help fill this need (Kampfe, 2015; von Schrader, Bruyère, Malzer, & Erickson, 2013).

Benefit plans may also create disincentives for retaining older workers. Many plans can send mixed messages to older workers; some create incentives to retire while others encourage continued labor force activity. Some employers are creating health care and retirement policies that offer incentives to older workers to stay engaged in the workforce, such as phased retirement, "in demand" workforce for specialized consulting, senior staff mentors for new workers, casual/part-time workers' programs, discounts on pharmaceuticals, specialized health screenings, long-term care insurance, preretirement planning, and prorated benefits for employees on flexible work schedules (Tishman et al., 2012; von Schrader et al., 2013).

Managers play an important role in retaining older workers. Managers may perpetuate stigma about aging or disability and fail to recognize workplace issues as they arise—or they avoid performance discussions and encourage the use of disability leave rather than addressing issues in the work environment (Coduti, Tugman, Bruyère, & Malzer, 2015). Managers also have a strong impact on the workplace culture, and employees who report to managers who are aware of their organization's policies about disability and diversity are less likely to experience bias or discriminiation (Nishii & Bruyère, 2014). The second most common basis for disability discrimination charges is "retaliation," which includes harassment and discipline issues. These are areas in workplace culture where supervisory influence can make a great deal of difference (Bruyère et al., 2010). When managers, and the organization, foster a culture of flexibility and accommodation, all employees see requests for accommodations as less unusual, and are more likely to accept accommodations as supports that improve productivity (Nishii & Bruyère, 2016).

Employers may find that some HR practices considered "universal" are in practice less fit for the needs of older workers, and may wish to examine their current HR management in terms of sets of practices centered around development of existing skills, maintaining current levels of functioning, utilization of existing resources, and accommodation of new issues (Kooij, Jansen, Dikkers, & de Lange, 2014). These categories of practice parallel and support the SOC framework of aging.

Finally, it is important to address intergenerational conflict and concerns. Positive exposures to team members of different ages through selective work group composition or focused interventions may support a positive organizational climate for aging (Truxillo, Cadiz, & Hammer, 2015).

COUNSELOR PRACTICE, TRAINING, AND RESEARCH IMPLICATIONS

Employers and their aging employees will need further information to support an expanding older cohort in the workforce, who very much want to continue working and yet may incur disabilities. Counselors can provide individual supports to older clients who are experiencing disabilities that may impact work performance, and they can also offer consultation to employers about the accommodation process. To be able to confront myths and stereotypes, counselors will need to have knowledge of the intellectual, social, and emotional well-being of older adults, as well as accommodations that can mitigate the limitations that may naturally occur in the aging process. Counselor educators can prepare counselors-in-training for this task by including aging issues in the counselor education curriculum.

Personal experiences with various groups of people and social learning experiences shape one's viewpoint toward a group. Counselors-in-training may have had prior exposure to negative stereotypes about persons with disabilities, have been repeatedly exposed to negative stereotypes about aging (ageism), have a prejudice against older persons (gerontophobia), have a fear of aging or of associating with older persons, or have other attitudinal barriers or misconceptions (Kampfe, 2015). Both personal and societal attitudes toward the aging process and older populations are appropriate to explore in specific courses such as psychosocial, cultural diversity, counseling theories, career development, and human growth and development coursework. The ultimate goal is for issues on aging to be infused throughout the curriculum. Inclusion of material on multicultural aspects of human relationships is intended to increase trainees' multicultural awareness, knowledge, and skills through developing an understanding of one's personal values, attitudes, motivations, and behaviors.

Retraining, adaptive devices, physical therapy, and occupational therapies can assist workers injured on the job, regardless of their ages. However, counselors should be aware that age-related changes in stamina and healing may require that older employees who do receive on-the-job injuries may need to be afforded additional time and extended therapy to fully restore optimal functioning.

Infusion of information regarding this population into existing counselor accreditation–approved curricula is vital if the counseling profession is to become a resource for the development of strategies to maintain the economic independence of older citizens. Such courses can also expose counselors-in-training to the issues and attitudes that impact the employment of older workers, particularly those with disabilities (Kampfe, Harley, Wadsworth, & Smith, 2007; Kampfe, Wadsworth, Smith, & Harley, 2005).

Research is needed on the issues of aging workers, such as training needs, career transition issues, and retirement planning. Research is also needed on which accommodations, workplace modifications, and changes to policies and practices positively impact the retention and continued productivity of an aging workforce. Counselor practitioners are in a unique position to contribute to needed research design conceptualization, metrics, and analyses to test the multiplicity of interventions we will be exploring in the coming years to keep our aging workforce healthy and intellectually engaged in the employment environment. Counselors are experientially qualified to provide the needed services to keep this population productive and more fully engaged in their communities and continuing employment.

RESOURCES

National Organizations/Associations

Administration of Aging: https://www.acl.gov/about-acl/administration-aging
Adult Development and Aging, Division 20 of the American Psychological Association: www.apa.org/about/division/div20.html
American Association of Geriatric Psychiatry: www.aagponline.org/
American Association of Retired Persons (AARP): www.aarp.org
The American Geriatrics Society: www.americangeriatrics.org
Association for Adult Development and Aging, A Division of the American Counseling Association: www.aadaweb.org
Council for Accreditation of Counseling Related Educational Programs (CACREP) Gerontological Counseling Standards: www.cacrep.org. (See yearly counseling standards under "Programs.")
Johnson, R. W., & Neumark, D. (1996). *Age discrimination, job separations, and employment status of older workers: Evidence from self-reports* (NBER Working Paper Series No. 5619). Cambridge, MA: National Bureau of Economic Research.
National Council on Aging: www.ncoa.org

REFERENCES

Age Discrimination in Employment Act of 1967, Pub L. No. 90–202, 29 USC 621.
Akman, J. S. (2004). The developmental psychology of aged persons. In S. Carta (Ed.), *Encyclopedia of life support systems, Vol. 2—Psychology*. Paris, France: UNESCO-EOLSS. Retrieved from http://www.eolss.net/index.aspx
American Association of Retired Persons. (2014). *Staying ahead of the curve 2013 : The AARP work and career study*. Washington, DC: Author. Retrieved from http://www.aarp.org/content/dam/aarp/research/surveys_statistics/general/2014/Staying-Ahead-of-the-Curve-2013-The-Work-and-Career-Study-AARP-res-gen.pdf
American Psychological Association. (n.d.). *What practitioners should know about working with older adults*. Washington, DC: Author. Retrieved from http://www.nova.edu/gec/forms/practitioners_older_adults.pdf
Baltes, P., & Baltes, M. (1990). Psychological perspectives on successful aging: The model of selective optimization with compensation. In P. Baltes & M. Baltes (Eds.), *Successful aging: Perspectives from the behavioral sciences* (pp. 1–34). New York, NY: Cambridge University Press.
Bendick, M. J., Brown, L. E., & Wall, K. (1999). No foot in the door: An experimental study of employment discrimination against older workers. *Journal of Aging & Social Policy, 10*(4), 37–41. doi:10.1300/J031v10n04

Bendick, M. J., Jackson, C. W., & Horacio, J. (1997). Employment discrimination against older workers. *Journal of Aging & Social Policy, 8*(November), 37–41. doi:10.1300/J031v08n04

Bjelland, M. J., Bruyère, S. M., von Schrader, S., Houtenville, A. J., Ruiz-Quintanilla, A., & Webber, D. A. (2010). Age and disability employment discrimination: Occupational rehabilitation implications. *Journal of Occupational Rehabilitation, 20*(4), 456–471.

Blow, F. C., & Barry, K. L. (2012). Alcohol and substance misuse in older adults. *Current Psychiatry Reports, 14*(4), 310–319. doi:10.1007/s11920-012-0292-9

Boerner, K. (2004). Adaptation to disability among middle-aged and older adults: The role of assimilative and accommodative coping. *Journals of Gerontology, 59*(1), P35–P42.

Bowling, A., & Dieppe, P. (2005). What is successful ageing and who should define it? *BMJ, 331*(7531), 1548–1551.

Boyce, C. J., & Wood, A. M. (2011). Personality prior to disability determines adaptation: Agreeable individuals recover lost life satisfaction faster and more completely. *Psychological Science, 22*(11), 1397–1402.

Bronfenbrenner, U. (1986). The ecology of the family as a context for human development: Research perspectives. *Developmental Psychology, 22*, 723–742.

Bruyère, S. M., Erickson, W. A., & VanLooy, S. A. (2006). The impact of business size on employer ADA response. *Rehabilitation Counseling Bulletin, 49*(4), 194–206.

Bruyère, S. M., von Schrader, S., Coduti, W., & Bjelland, M. (2010). United States employment disability discrimination charges: Implications for disability management practice. *International Journal of Disability Management, 5*(2), 48–58. doi:10.1375/jdmr.5.2.48

Coduti, W. A., Tugman, K., Bruyère, S. M., & Malzer, V. (2015). Aging workers: Work environment as a factor in employee mental health. *International Journal of Disability Management, 10*(4), 935–963. Retrieved from https://doi.org/10.1017/idm.2015.4

Erickson, W., Lee, C., & von Schrader, S. (2016). 2014 Disability status report. Retrieved from http://www.disabilitystatistics.org/StatusReports/2014-PDF/2014-StatusReport_US.pdf

Erikson, E. H. (1959). *Identity and the life cycle: Psychological issues.* New York, NY: International Universities Press.

Fiske, A., Wetherell, J., & Gatz, M. (2009). Depression in older adults. *Annual Review of Clinical Psychology, 5*, 363–389. doi:10.1146/annurev.clinpsy.032408.153621

Frank, R. (2011). Premorbid personality. In J. S. Kreutzer, J. Deluca, & B. Caplan (Eds.), *Encyclopedia of clinical neuropsychology* (p. 2010). New York, NY: Springer Publishing.

Gonzales, E., Matz-Costa, C., & Morrow-Howell, N. (2015). Increasing opportunities for the productive engagement of older adults: A response to population aging. *The Gerontologist, 55*(2), 252–261. doi:10.1093/geront/gnu176

Harley, D. A., Donnell, C., & Rainey, J. (2003). Interagency collaboration: Reinforcing professional bridges to serve aging populations with multiple service needs. *Journal of Rehabilitation, 69*, 32–37.

Harley, D. A., & Teaster, P. (2016). Theories, constructs, and applications in working with LGBT elders in human services. In D. A. Harley & P. B. Teaster (Eds.), *Handbook of LGBT elders: An interdisciplinary approach to principles, practices, and policies* (pp. 3–26). Cham, Switzerland: Springer International.

Heidkamp, M., Mabe, W., & DeGraaf, B. (2012 May). The public workforce system: Serving older job seekers and the disability implications of an aging workforce. Retrieved from https://www.dol.gov/odep/pdf/ntar_public_workforce_system_report_final.pdf

Hershenson, D. B. (2015). The individual plan for retirement: A missing part of plan development with older consumers. *Rehabilitation Counseling Bulletin, 59*(1), 9–17.

Holland, J. L. (1994). *Self-directed search.* Odessa, FL: Psychological Assessment Resources.

Hoyer, W. J., & Roodin, P. A. (2003). *Adult development and aging* (5th ed.). Boston, MA: McGraw-Hill.

Infurna, F. J., & Wiest, M. (2016). The effect of disability onset across the adult life span. *Journal of Gerontology: Psychological Sciences.* Advance online publication. doi:10.1093/geronb/gbw055

Institute on Rehabilitation Issues. (2009). *The aging workforce.* Hot Springs: University of Arkansas.

Johnson, R. W., & Neumark, D. (1996). *Age discrimination, job separations, and employment status of older workers: Evidence from self-reports* (NBER Working Paper Series No. 5619). Cambridge, MA: National Bureau of Economic Research.

Kampfe, C. M. (2015). *Counseling older people: Opportunities and challenges.* Alexandria, VA: American Counseling Association.

Kampfe, C. M., Harley, D. B., Wadsworth, J. S., & Smith, S. M. (2007). Methods and materials for infusing aging issues into the rehabilitation curriculum. *Rehabilitation Education, 21*, 107–116.

Kampfe, C. M., Wadsworth, J. S., Mamboleo, G. I., & Schonbrun, S. L. (2008). Aging, disability, and employment. *Work, 31*(3), 337–344.

Kampfe, C. M., Wadsworth, J. S., Smith, S. M., & Harley, D. A. (2005). The infusion of aging issues in the rehabilitation curriculum: A review of the literature. *Rehabilitation Education, 19*, 225–233.

Kooij, D. T. a. M., Jansen, P. G. W., Dikkers, J. S. E., & deLange, A. H. (2014). Managing aging workers: A mixed methods study on bundles of HR practices for aging workers. *International Journal of Human Resource Management, 25*(15), 2192–2212. doi:10.1080/09585192.2013.872169

Lahey, J. N. (2008). Age, women, and hiring: An experimental study. *Journal of Human Resources, 43*(1), 30–56. doi:10.1353/jhr.2008.0026

McDonald, T., & Harder, H. G. (2004). Older workers and disability management. *International Journal of Disability, Community & Rehabilitation, 3*(3). Retrieved from http://www.ijdcr.ca/VOL03_03_CAN/articles/harder3.shtml

Merz, M. A., Bricout, J. C., & Koch, L. C. (2001). Disability and job stress: Implications for vocational rehabilitation planning. *Work, 17*(2), 85–95.

Ng, E. S. W., & Law, A. (2014). Keeping up! Older workers' adaptation in the workplace after age 55. *Canadian Journal on Aging, 33*(1), 1–14. doi:10.1017/S0714980813000639

Ng, T. W. H., & Feldman, D. C. (2012). Evaluating six common stereotypes about older workers with meta-analytical data. *Personnel Psychology, 65*(4), 821–858. doi:10.1111/peps.12003

Nishii, L. H., & Bruyère, S. M. (2014). *The workplace and people with disabilities: Past, present, and future* (Webcast Archive). Ithaca, NY: Cornell ILR School. Retrieved from http://www.cornell.edu/video/workplace-people-with-disabilities-past-present-future

Nishii, L. H., & Bruyère, S. M. (2016). Conducting case studies. In S. M. Bruyère (Ed.), *Disability and employer practices: Research across the disciplines* (pp. 125–148). Ithaca, NY: Cornell University Press.

Nourhashémi, F., Andrieu, S., Gillette-Guyonnet, S., Vellas, B., Albarède, J. L., & Grandjean, H. (2001). Instrumental activities of daily living as a potential marker of frailty: A study of 7364 community-dwelling elderly women (the EPIDOS study). *Journals of Gerontology. Series A, Biological Sciences and Medical Sciences, 56*(7), M448–M453.

Perry, E. L., Golom, F. D., Catenacci, L., Ingraham, M. E., Covais, E. M., & Molina, J. J. (2016). Talkin' 'bout your generation: The impact of applicant age and generation on hiring-related perceptions and outcomes. *Work, Aging and Retirement, 3*(2), 186–199. doi:10.1093/workar/waw029

Posthuma, R. A., & Campion, M. A. (2009). Age stereotypes in the workplace: Common stereotypes, moderators, and future research directions. *Journal of Management, 35*(1), 158–188. doi:10.1177/0149206308318617

Psarra, E., & Kleftaras, G. (2013). Adaptation to physical disabilities: The role of meaning in life and depression. *European Journal of Counselling Psychology, 2*(1), 79–99 doi:10.5964/ejcop.v2i1.7

Quandt, S. A., McDonald, J., Bell, R. A., & Arcury, T. A. (1999). Aging research in multi-ethnic rural communities: Gaining entrée through community involvement. *Journal of Cross-Cultural Gerontology, 14*(2), 113–130.

Reynolds, K., Pietrzak, R. H., El-Gabalawy, R., Mackenzie, C. S., & Sareen, J. (2015). Prevalence of psychiatric disorders in U.S. older adults: Findings from a nationally representative survey. *World Psychiatry, 14*(1), 74–81. doi:10.1002/wps.20193

Reznik, G. L., Shoffner, D., & Weaver, D. A. (2005). Coping with the demographic challenge: Fewer children and living longer. *Social Security Bulletin, 66*(4), 37–45.

Sass, S. A. (2016). *How do non-financial factors affect retirement decisions?* Report No. 16–3. Boston, MA: Center for Retirement Research at Boston College.

Smith, F. G., Leconte, P., & Vitelli, E. (2012). The VECAP position paper on universal design for learning for career assessment and vocational evaluation. *Vocational Evaluation and Career Assessment Journal, 8*(1), 13–26.

Tishman, F. M., VanLooy, S. A., & Bruyère, S. M. (2012). *Employer strategies for responding to an aging workforce*. New Brunswick, NJ: NTAR National Leadership Center. Retrieved from http://www.dol.gov/odep/pdf/NTAR_Employer_Strategies_Report.pdf

Toosi, M. (2015, December). Labor force projections to 2024: The labor force is growing, but slowly. *Monthly Labor Review*. Retrieved from http://www.bls.gov/opub/mlr/2015/article/pdf/labor-force-projections-to-2024.pdf

Truxillo, D. M., Cadiz, D. M., & Hammer, L. B. (2015). Supporting the aging workforce: A review and recommendations for workplace intervention research. *Annual Review of Organizational Psychology and Organizational Behavior, 2*, 351–381. doi:10.1146/annurev-orgpsych-032414-111435

Turner, J. A. (2008). Era of living longer. *Benefits Quarterly, 24*(3), 20–25.

U.S. Bureau of Labor Statistics. (2012, January). Labor force projections to 2020: A more slowly growing workforce. *Monthly Labor Review*, p. 50.

U.S. Bureau of Labor Statistics. (2015). Career outlook: Projections of the Labor Force, 2014–2024. Retrieved from http://www.bls.gov/careeroutlook/2015/article/projections-laborforce.htm

U.S. Department of Health and Human Services. (2013). *A profile of older Americans: 2013*. Retrieved from https://www.acl.gov/sites/default/files/Aging%20and%20Disability%20in%20America/2013_Profile.pdf

U.S. Department of Labor. (2010, March). *Record unemployment among older workers does not keep them out of the job market. Issues in Labor Statistics*. Washington, DC: Author. Retrieved from http://www.bls.gov/opub/ils/pdf/opbils81.pdf

von Schrader, S., Bruyère, S. M., Malzer, V., & Erickson, W. A. (2013). *Absence and disability management practices for an aging workforce*. Ithaca, NY: Cornell University Press. Retrieved from http://digitalcommons.ilr.cornell.edu/edicollect/1320/

von Schrader, S., & Nazarov, Z. E. (2016). Trends and patterns in Age Discrimination in Employment Act (ADEA) charges. *Research on Aging, 38*(5), 580–601. doi:10.1177/0164027515593989

Wales, K., Clemson, L., Lannin, N., & Cameron, I. (2016). Functional assessments used by occupational therapists with older adults at risk of activity and participation limitations: A systematic review. *PLOS ONE, 11*(2), e0147980.

Wechsler, D. (1997). *WAIS-III administration and scoring manual*. San Antonio, TX: Psychological Corporation.

Woolever, J. (2013). Human resource departments and older adults in the workplace. In P. Brownell & J. J. Kelly (Eds.), *Ageism and mistreatment of older workers: Current reality, future solutions* (pp. 111–134). Dordrecht, Germany: Springer Science and Business Media. doi:10.1007/978-94-007-5521-5

28

Risk and Resilience in Military Families Experiencing Deployment: The Role of the Family Attachment Network*

SHELLEY A. RIGGS AND DAVID S. Riggs

*M*ilitary deployment is a significant risk condition entailing an increased probability of maladjustment in a number of critical life domains. Service members returning from deployment often experience depression, anxiety, substance abuse, suicidal ideation, interpersonal conflict, and aggressiveness (Hoge, Auchterlonie, & Milliken, 2006; Hoge et al., 2002). Three out of every five service members deployed around the world in support of Operation Enduring Freedom (OEF) and Operation Iraqi Freedom (OIF) also leave families at home (Johnson et al., 2007). These families face unique stressors through the course of military service and deployments, including frequent relocations and reconfigurations of the family system, ambiguous loss and fear for a loved one's safety, and high levels of stress and/or dysfunction among family members (Flake, Davis, Johnson, & Middleton, 2009; Huebner, Mancini, Wilcox, Grass, & Grass, 2007). In spite of the apparent increase in marital and family difficulties during the last decade, the majority of veterans and their families demonstrate positive adaptation during and after deployment (Peterson, Park, & Castro, 2011). So what distinguishes resilient military families from those who develop psychological and/or relational problems?

Unfortunately, the theoretical and empirical literature examining military families is scarce, so our understanding of this distinction is limited. According to Walsh (2003), resilience involves "the interplay of multiple risk and protective processes over time, including individual, family, and larger sociocultural influences" (p. 400). Recent reviews suggest that the most robust protective factors for resilient adaptation to various adversities are sensitive and responsive parenting among children, and supportive family or other social networks among adults (Charuvastra & Cloitre, 2008). Based on these findings, we conceptualize individual resilience within the relational context of family bonds. At the level of individual development, attachment relationships contribute to intra- and interpersonal processes underlying risk and resilience throughout the life span. At a broader level, family systems theory conceives of individuals and

---

relationships as developing within the larger attachment network of the family. From a systemic perspective, stressful experiences affect the whole family and the impact on all members and relationships is mediated by key family processes (Walsh, 2006).

Although attachment and family system theories overlap in many complementary ways, Kozlowska and Hanney (2002) argued that conceptual confusion has resulted when the dyadic constructs from attachment theory have been applied to family processes and patterns. In particular, despite the resemblance of three major family patterns (adaptive, disengaged, enmeshed) to the three primary attachment categories (secure, avoidant/dismissing, anxious–ambivalent/preoccupied), these patterns do not always map onto each other on a one-to-one basis (Vetere & Dallos, 2008). In spite of these difficulties, promising efforts to present a family-wide perspective on attachment processes have appeared in the literature, positing constructs such as the secure family base (Byng-Hall, 1995) and the emotional security hypothesis (Davies, Cummings, & Winter, 2004). In this chapter, we present a family attachment network model to describe the adaptation of military families during the stress of deployment and their adjustment during the reintegration process. The family attachment network consists of multiple relationships existing at multiple system levels (e.g., individual, dyadic, subsystem, and system-wide interaction patterns), each of which has rules and attributes that are distinct and do not exist at other levels, yet are inextricably intertwined with other levels and the larger system (Kozlowska & Hanney, 2002). Similarly, within the family system, each attachment relationship is unique, such that a child's attachment behaviors toward different caregivers can vary, siblings can demonstrate different attachment strategies with the same caregiver, and parent–child attachment relationships often diverge from spousal attachment patterns (Berlin & Cassidy, 1999).

NOTIFICATION AND DEPLOYMENT

Military deployments constitute a series of events and stressors that begin at the point when service members are notified that they will be deployed, encompass the time that they are deployed, and continue through their return home and their reintegration back into their family and community. The demands of the U.S. military's involvement in Iraq and Afghanistan have required troops to be deployed multiple times for extended periods ranging from 3 to 24 months (Jumper et al., 2005),[*] resulting in what has been termed the "cycle of deployment." This section describes expected family processes during the predeployment and deployment phases when military members are first notified and sent overseas. The proposed network model assumes that attachment and family processes function and interact simultaneously at the individual, dyadic, and family levels (Kobak, Cassidy, Lyons-Ruth, & Ziv, 2006). However, given the difficulty of focusing on the unique properties of all system levels at the same time (Kozlowska & Hanney, 2002), separate graphic representations are presented. First, a diathesis–stress diagram depicts the role of the attachment system in the psychological functioning of nondeploying parents and children during the deployment phase (Figure 28.1). In addition, a set of four diagrams illustrates optimal pre-/postdeployment family functioning and potential structural adaptations to deployment of the larger family system (Figures 28.2–28.5). Conceptually, the developmental trajectories of individual family members and attachment dyads depicted in Figure 28.1 are embedded within the family system

---

[*]Total length of time families reported service members deployed or mobilized between January 2003 and September 2005: 24% reported 6 months or less, 66% reported 7 to 18 months, and 9% reported 19 months.

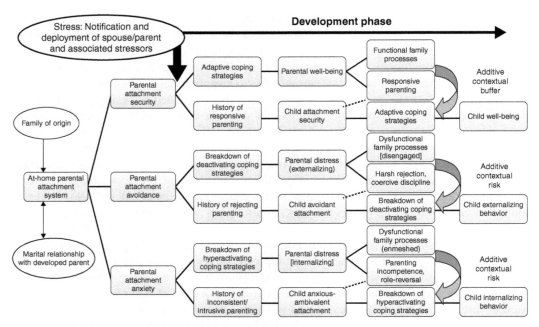

FIGURE 28.1 Family attachment network model depicting diathesis–stress response to deployment.

circles presented in Figures 28.2 to 28.5. Furthermore, the model recognizes that the family system is situated in and affected more broadly by the military unit and wider sociocultural context.

The Attachment System

Attachment and Coping

The attachment system can be understood as a biologically evolved strategy to manage stress (Kobak et al., 2006). Deployment constitutes a threat to all family members' sense of safety because the secure base of an attachment figure becomes unavailable (Vormbrock, 1993). The mechanism underlying the attachment-related risk or resilience is the "internal working model" (IWM), which is a dynamic mental representation of self and other formed in early attachment relationships and carried forward to provide an internal template used to cope with stress, regulate emotions, and interact in close relationships (Bowlby, 1980). Secure individuals have positive IWMs of both self and other that are associated with adaptive coping, high self-efficacy, and psychological well-being (Mikulincer & Florian, 1998). Secure adults are more likely to have secure relationships with their spouses (Mikulincer & Shaver, 2007) and generally provide sensitive and responsive parenting, which contributes to secure attachment in their children (De Wolff & van Ijzendoorn, 1997).

In contrast, people with insecure attachment systems have negative IWMs of self and/ or others that translate into high levels of attachment anxiety and/or attachment avoidance. Individuals with a history of rejection by attachment figures develop negative models of others characterized by attachment avoidance, which is associated with distrust and a deactivating coping strategy involving the minimization of emotions and attachments, denial, and avoidance of intimacy (Mikulincer & Shaver, 2007). On the other hand, when early caregiving is inconsistent or intrusive, individuals develop negative models of self, characterized by attachment anxiety, which is associated with fears of abandonment and a hyperactivating coping strategy involving exaggerated emotional reactions, overdependency,

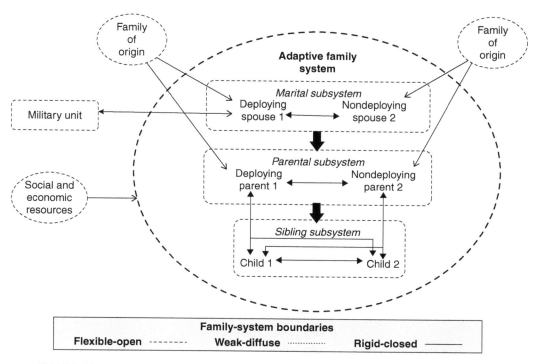

FIGURE 28.2 Pre- and postdeployment normal operations: Adaptive family system.

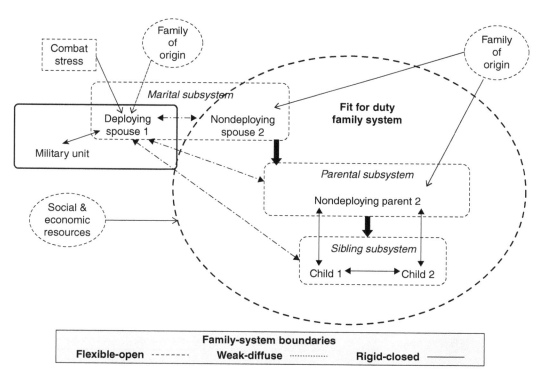

FIGURE 28.3 Deployment adaptation: The fit-for-duty family system adapts well to deployment separation from military spouse/parent.

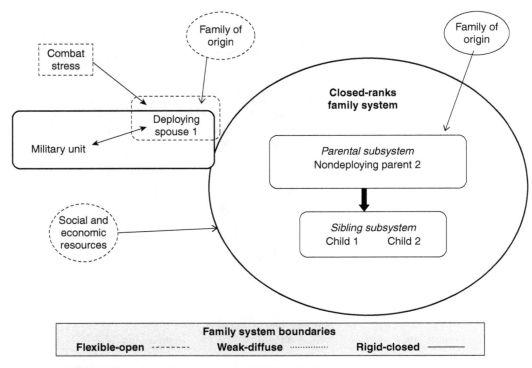

FIGURE 28.4 Deployment maladjustment: The closed-ranks family is characterized by disengagement and rigid boundaries, closed communication, lack of support, and permanent redistribution of deploying member's roles.

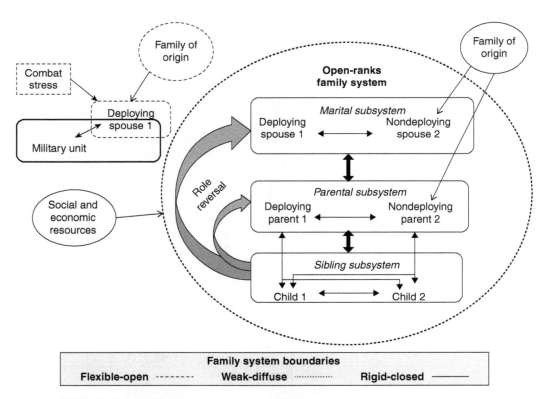

FIGURE 28.5 Deployment maladjustment: The open-ranks family is characterized by diffuse boundaries, inappropriate communication, role reversals, and failure to redistribute deploying member's roles.

and ambivalence toward attachment figures (Mikulincer & Shaver, 2007). When attachment figures are abusive or neglecting, the attachment system develops along an atypical, disorganized trajectory associated with increased risk for poor outcomes in multiple domains (Cassidy & Mohr, 2001; S. A. Riggs, 2010). Negative IWMs of self and others manifest in high levels of both attachment anxiety and attachment avoidance (also known as "fearful attachment"), which place individuals doubly at risk because they are unable to determine the viability of any coping strategy and consequently demonstrate an ineffective and confusing mixture of both hyperactivating and deactivating coping behaviors (e.g., approach/avoidance conflict) or become completely paralyzed (Simpson & Rholes, 2002).

Attachment as Diathesis

Despite some excitement regarding the opportunity to use their military training in defense of their country, notification of deployment orders is likely to be perceived as an immediate threat to security, thereby activating the attachment systems of service members and their families. The degree of threat is heightened when the military parent is sent to a combat zone, where physical safety is endangered. As the anticipated separation approaches, all family members, regardless of attachment status, are likely to experience increased anxiety and tension (Pincus, House, Christensen, & Adler, 2001). Based on Bowlby's (1980) delineation of grief/separation responses, normal and expected behavior during this period includes vacillations among angry protest, denial, and sadness in anticipation of loss. As suggested by the literature (e.g., Davies, Sturge-Apple, & Cummings, 2004), individual distress may contribute to marital and family conflict, which can interfere with parenting and family routines, negatively affecting children, who may respond with fear, regression, and acting-out behaviors (Pincus, House, Christensen, & Adler, 2001).

   When the military spouse or parent departs, even in the context of a secure attachment network, family members initially may experience numbness or disorientation, a sense of abandonment, and mood and sleep problems, followed by a period of emotional and behavioral disorganization, anger, and resentment (Pincus et al., 2001). The diathesis–stress model in Figure 28.1 posits those individual differences in the attachment system of nondeploying home during deployment. To reduce complexity, only the three primary attachment dimensions (secure, avoidant, anxious) are included, but it is assumed that the combination of the two insecure dimensions entails even greater risk for dysfunction manifested in an unpredictable, bewildering mixture of anxious and avoidant behaviors and outcomes (S. A. Riggs et al., 2007; Simpson & Rholes, 2002). For each dimension, one row shows the nondeploying parent's hypothesized trajectory and a second row shows the hypothesized trajectory of that parent's child(ren).

Nondeployed Spouse/Parent's Reactions

In response to deployment separation, the positive mind-set of secure individuals functions as a buffer against maladaptive reactions and stimulates the active mobilization of internal resources and social support (Mikulincer & Shaver, 2007). Adaptive coping contributes to the secure parent's ability to maintain psychological well-being, continue providing responsive parenting, and establish new functional family processes in the absence of the military parent. Separately, attachment anxiety and attachment avoidance are considered "good enough" strategies for adequate functioning under normal circumstances (Collins & Feeney, 2004). However, insecure attachment creates a vulnerability for dysfunction that is most likely to emerge under conditions of high stress (Kobak et al., 2006). Deployment of a spouse not only takes away a primary attachment figure, but also entails a loss of emotional support, loneliness, financial strain, role shifts or conflicts, and the role overload of single parenthood (Flake et al., 2009; Vormbrock,

1993; Warner, Appenzeller, Warner, & Grieger, 2009). So when their typical coping strategies break down under the additive contextual stress associated with deployment, insecure parents are likely to become distressed.

Emotional detachment and withdrawal may be observed in some spouses (Pincus et al., 2001), who are likely to endorse attachment avoidance. Theoretically, other attachment-related responses include anxious–ambivalent behaviors, such as clinginess and anger at the deploying spouse or parent, or disorganized behaviors characterized by simultaneous approach or avoidance. Continuing anger, depression, and psychological dysfunction among at-home parents in the deployment phase have been reported (Bey & Lange, 1974; Jensen, Martin, & Watanabe, 1996; Kelley, 1994; Medway, Davis, Cafferty, Chappell, & O'Hearn, 1995; Zeff, Lewis & Hirsch, 1997). Research supports the diathesis–stress model's assumption that individual differences in the attachment organization will affect the psychological functioning of nondeploying parents, which in turn affects family processes. In several studies, the level of emotional distress during deployment reported by at-home wives of National Guard members was correlated with insecure attachment and the degree of family disruption during separation (Cafferty, Davis, Medway, O'Hearn, & Chappell, 1994; Medway et al., 1995).

Children's Reactions

Research suggests that many children exhibit remarkable resilience throughout the deployment cycle (Lester et al., 2010; Zeff et al., 1997). At the same time, other findings indicate that some children of deployed parents demonstrate more anxiety, withdrawal, anger, noncompliance, or other emotional or behavior problems than children whose parents are not deployed (Flake et al., 2009; Kelley et al., 2001). Individual differences in children's responses to deployment separation will be related to developmental level, their attachment bonds with the deploying and nondeploying parents, and the overall psychological and behavioral functioning of the at-home parent. If deploying parents, whether mothers or fathers, have acted as key attachment figures for their children, their departure represents a significant loss that will lead to grief responses. Younger children tend to exhibit fear and regressive behaviors (e.g., clinginess, crying, wetting the bed; Pincus et al., 2001), whereas older school-age and adolescent children often experience emotional dysregulation, anger, aggression, sense of abandonment, withdrawal, or academic difficulties (Huebner et al., 2007; Lincoln, Swift, & Shorteno-Fraser, 2008).

The impact of the deploying parent's departure will be mitigated if children feel securely bonded to a nondeploying parent who copes effectively and maintains relatively stable parenting practices. As shown in Figure 28.1, secure parenting practices and adaptive family processes contribute to the resilience of secure children, who continue to cope adaptively in order to maintain their psychological well-being. In addition, the dashed line reflects reciprocal influences in the parent–child relationship, such that child attachment security assists the nondeploying parent to preserve responsive parenting practices. On the other hand, an insecure attachment system in the nondeploying parent increases risk for children. Most important, insecure adult attachment is associated with nonoptimal parenting practices that lead to the insecure attachment in the offspring (De Wolff & van Ijzendoorn, 1997). In addition, insecure adults are more likely to experience psychological distress (Kobak et al., 2006), which interferes with their ability to provide adequate parenting and appropriately modify family routines and structure to reassure and comfort children. Evidence indicates that the at-home parent's functional or emotional impairment can interfere with basic family routines (Kelley, 1994) and is the best predictor of child outcomes related to military deployment (Flake et al., 2009; Lester et al., 2010; Medway et al., 1995).

Consistent with the previous research (Chandra et al., 2010; Flake et al., 2009; Jensen, Martin, & Watanabe, 1996; Luthar, 2006), the proposed network model predicts that the relationship between parental deployment and the emotional well-being of children at all developmental levels is at least partially mediated by the nondeploying parent's psychological adjustment, parenting practices and stress, and the degree of family disruption. Specifically, Figure 28.1 illustrates the hypothesis that high attachment avoidance and the breakdown of deactivating coping strategies in the nondeploying parent will foster psychological distress, coercive parenting, harsh discipline, and disengaged family processes. These factors create additional risk for the breakdown of avoidantly attached children's coping strategies and the development of externalizing problems. The model also posits that high attachment anxiety and the breakdown of hyperactivating coping strategies in the nondeploying parent will foster psychological distress, incompetent and role-reversing parenting practices, and enmeshed family processes. These factors create additional risk for the breakdown of anxiously attached children's coping strategies and the development of internalizing problems. Finally, the dashed lines represent reciprocal family influences suggesting that children who are insecurely attached may behave in ways that contribute to parenting difficulties. Based on the existing literature (S. A. Riggs et al., 2007; Simpson & Rholes, 2002), the risk for poor outcomes is substantially increased if the nondeploying parent has high levels of both attachment anxiety and avoidance. In extreme cases, child neglect or abuse can occur among overwhelmed parents (Gibbs, Martin, Kupper, & Johnson, 2007), particularly when high attachment avoidance and anxiety are both present.

The Family System

Resilient Family Processes

The entries and exits of a deploying spouse or parent disrupt the family, creating stress and disorganization in the family system, subsystems (e.g., marital, parent–child, sibling), and individual members. Walsh (2006) suggested that key processes for family resilience in the face of this kind of stress include family belief systems, communication processes, and organizational patterns. The importance of family belief systems is supported by research showing that spouses adapted well to deployment when they were able to "make meaning" of the situation (Hammer, Cullen, Marchand, & Dezsofi, 2006). Beliefs that potentially contribute to better functioning in military families include optimism for the future, a sense of mastery, spiritual philosophies, and a positive outlook on military life and its purpose, including patriotism and a sense of pride in the contribution of the deploying spouse or parent. Military families at home will also benefit from increasing the quality and quantity of family communication (Figley, 1993), especially when characterized by clarity and honesty, open emotional expression (e.g., mutual empathy, tolerance, humor), and collaborative problem solving (Walsh, 2006). Unfortunately, research indicates that many adolescents perceive heightened negative family emotion and conflict during deployment, and believe they need to keep their own emotions or thoughts to themselves to protect other family members (Huebner et al., 2007).

Walsh (2006) referred to structural or organizational patterns as the family's "crisis shock absorbers" (p. 84). High-functioning families demonstrate flexibility in adapting to new challenges and connectedness (i.e., cohesion) in the provision of mutual support and respect (Walsh, 2006). A central organizational concept that links the multiple levels of the family network is the "secure family base," defined as a reliable network of attachment relationships that share responsibility for ensuring that every family member will be cared for and feel secure enough to explore and develop freely (Byng-Hall,

1995). Research with adolescents suggests that the perception of a secure family base contributes to better mental health (Woodhouse, Dykas, & Cassidy, 2009). Each time a service member deploys, family flexibility is tested, as the system structure and organization necessarily shift, and family roles and power dynamics are renegotiated. In the midst of major change, reestablishing the secure family base and maintaining simple routines, such as family dinners or bedtime rituals, can enhance the family's adjustment (Luthar, 2006; Walsh, 2006).

Adequate functioning and authoritative leadership by the nondeploying parent is critical in the adaptation of families during deployment. Major family theorists (e.g., Minuchin, 1974; Walsh, 2006) highlight the vital function of parents in creating and maintaining a strong hierarchical organization with clear structural boundaries inside the family, as well as between the family and the outside world. The external boundary should allow cohesion within its borders, and should be permeable enough to allow families to benefit from social and economic resources (Walsh, 2006). For military families, helpful external resources might involve the mobilization of extended kin and friends, and community or military support organizations, as well as financial and job security (Figley, 1993).

Family Adaptation During Deployment

A central feature of the proposed network model is the essential interconnection of multiple levels in the family system, which include individual members, the marital subsystem, the parental subsystem, the sibling subsystem, and the complete nuclear family system. In Figures 28.2 to 28.5, the large circle in each diagram marks the external boundary separating the outside world from the family system, within which are several rectangles representing various subsystems that encompass the individual and dyadic processes depicted in Figure 28.1. The white space between external and subsystem boundaries comprises the family processes described earlier that can facilitate or impair adjustment to the experience of a deployment. Other important contextual layers are intergenerational processes, the military unit, and the family's social and economic resources.

Figure 28.2 represents the "normal ops" of a well-functioning military family before and after deployment. Both internal and external boundaries are flexible and open, dyadic attachments are strong and form a secure family base (solid bidirectional arrows), and the appropriate hierarchical power structure (unidirectional arrows among subsystems) is present. Figures 28.3 to 28.5 depict various ways the multilevel family system might adapt to deployment. Hill (1949) conceptualized positive coping to military-induced separation in terms of flexibility in expressing emotion and effective redistribution of the absent spouse's family roles. We have labeled these well-functioning families "fit-for-duty" (see Figure 28.3) and adopted Hill's labels to refer to two types of poor family adjustment: "close-dranks" (see Figure 28.4) and "open-ranks" (see Figure 28.5).

In Figure 28.3, fit-for-duty families demonstrate effective coping by maintaining strong leadership in the nondeploying spouse, temporarily redistributing the absent member's roles and responsibilities, communicating openly, and retaining comforting family routines, or creating new rituals to replace lost ones. By preserving open internal and external boundaries, the family is able to provide support to one another and effectively use supportive resources outside of the family. It is important to note that although the deploying spouse or parent now exists primarily as part of his or her military unit, and outside of the functional family system, the secure internal working models of each family member sustain strong dyadic attachments over time and distance and are reinforced with frequent contact. Consequently, fit-for-duty families remain able to perform their primary tasks in supporting ongoing individual and family functioning in a secure, productive, and effective manner throughout the deployment.

According to Hill (1949), closed-ranks families disengaged and blamed the separation on the absent spouse or parent, devalued the deploying member's role, and redistributed his responsibilities permanently. Theoretical extension of these findings suggests that these families are headed by a nondeploying parent who has high levels of attachment avoidance. As shown in Figure 28.4, rigid internal and external boundaries prevent open communication and limit family members' ability to support each other or obtain assistance from outside sources. The nondeploying parent will maintain strict discipline, shut down emotional expression, and communicate a "get on with it" attitude with no patience for weakness. In contrast to practical limitations soldiers often place on family communication, due to regulations or the need to control distractions (Durham, 2010), an avoidant at-home spouse may initiate an emotional cutoff that entails severe restrictions on contact between family members and the deploying spouse or parent. Closed-ranks families reorganized family roles and established a fairly efficient system during the deployment, but experienced greater difficulties during reintegration (Hill, 1949).

Figure 28.5 depicts the weak external and internal boundaries of an open-ranks family, which is likely headed by a nondeploying parent with high attachment anxiety. Especially useful in the conceptualization of weak boundaries in military families is Boss's (1999) construct of "ambiguous loss," which refers to (a) the psychological presence of a family member despite his or her physical absence, or (b) the psychological absence of a family member despite his or her physical presence. As described by Hill (1949), open-ranks families keep a strong bond with the absent parent, but unlike the fit-for-duty families who also maintain close connections, these families appear overly dependent on the absent spouse or parent and do not reassign his or her responsibilities or decision-making powers. The gray letters and lines in Figure 28.5 represent the psychological presence and unfilled roles of the deployed spouse or parent despite his or her physical absence. Ambiguous loss of a spouse or parent contributes to blurred boundaries regarding who belongs in the family, which creates role confusion, interferes with task accomplishment, blocks decision making, and prevents the adaptive reorganization of the family system (Boss, 1999). Consistent with this assumption, Hill's open-ranks families experienced extensive disruption during deployment. However, research with families of service members missing in action (MIAs) suggests that some dimensions of psychological presence (e.g., maintaining MIA's image and role in the family) appear to be functional for children and family processes, but not for spouses (Boss, 1980). The MIA status of the military parent may explain these differences, but further investigation is needed to determine why, how, and for whom maintaining psychological presence is useful.

In addition to ambiguous external boundaries in open-ranks families, the combination of the prolonged absence of a military spouse and an at-home parent with high attachment anxiety creates an environment ripe for internal parent–child boundary violations involving enmeshment and role reversals, such as spousification (i.e., parent turns to child for companionship and intimacy) or parentification (e.g., excessive caregiving responsibility for siblings or a dysfunctional parent; Jacobvitz, Riggs, & Johnson, 1999). Consistent with this hypothesis, findings indicate that military adolescents express frequent concerns regarding the at-home parents' psychological state and complain of significant changes in family roles and responsibilities, wherein they were expected to take on more chores and care for younger siblings (Huebner et al., 2007). Although some degree of assistance from older children contributes to positive family adaptation and functioning (Minuchin, 1974), research suggests that extensive parent–child boundary violations can have a negative impact on children's psychological well-being (Jacobvitz, Hazen, Curran, & Hitchens, 2004).

POSTDEPLOYMENT FAMILY NETWORK

Family Reunion and Reintegration

After the military spouse or parent returns home, individual family members' attachment relationships and the functioning of the family system and subsystems generally do not return to the exact state that existed before the deployment. The extent to which service members, spouses, and children have been changed by the experience of deployment will increase the complexity of the reintegration process. Although family members typically are excited about their reunion and are eager to welcome home their returning spouse or parent, a number of factors can make the experience frustrating and unsettling (Figley, 1993; Hill, 1949; Vormbrock, 1993). In addition to joy and anxious contact seeking, the attachment literature suggests that normative responses among both secure and insecure groups may include some degree of ambivalence, anger, and emotional disengagement for a period of time after reunion (Vormbrock, 1993). Wives of Vietnam veterans retrospectively reported resentment, emotional distance, and lower marital intimacy on reunion, despite a desire for renewed connection (Bey & Lange, 1974). Returning soldiers also longed for closeness despite feeling unneeded and jealous of their wives' attention to the children (Hunter, 1984). Evidence suggests that a secure attachment style may promote positive adjustment during reintegration, including higher positive affect, greater marital satisfaction, and less conflict 4 months after reunion (Cafferty, et al, 1994).

Reunions with children can also be challenging. The U.S. military's current practice of deploying service members for multiple tours with relatively little time at home in between means that some military parents are absent for a large portion of their child's life, often during key developmental periods (Lester et al., 2010). At this time, very little is known about the impact of single or multiple deployment separations on children and the developmental or contextual factors that may contribute to their risk or resilience. However, Chandra et al. (2010) reported that the duration of deployment is related to children's difficulties during and after a parent's absence. Theoretically, the same factors that are influential during the deployment separation will be important for children during reintegration: age, previous attachment to the returned parent, and current relationship with the nondeploying parent. Drawing on the extensive attachment literature with nonmilitary children, very young children with no memory of the deployed parent initially will display normal fear responses to a stranger. However, older children who were bonded to the military parent and grieved the loss of their attachment figure can remain detached and ignore the returned parent for a period of time. Longer separations will be associated with greater detachment and longer periods of readjustment after reunion. In the transition period from detachment to reattachment, contradictory emotions and behaviors shifting from anger and bitterness to fretfulness and excessive clinginess may be observed.

In all likelihood, most children with secure attachment bonds before deployment will ultimately adapt and settle into a positive relationship with a returned parent who demonstrates healthy adjustment. On the other hand, children who had an insecure attachment to the military parent before deployment are at an increased risk for further problems, such as intense separation anxiety, depression, anger, or oppositional behavior. For both the returned military spouse or parent and children, a secure attachment bond with the at-home spouse or parent will facilitate adjustment, and insecurity in this relationship will complicate the reintegration process.

As the family begins to reorganize to accommodate the return of the military member, stress and conflict can arise regarding major decisions, confusion in altered roles or routines, independence and control, criticism or disagreements about child rearing, and family shifts in social support (Drummet et al., 2003; Figley, 1993; Hunter, 1984). Bowling and Sherman (2008) suggested that the major tasks of reintegration are redefining family roles, managing strong emotions and replacing emotional con-striction with relational intimacy, and creating shared meaning. Earlier research indi-cates that families who maintained the service member's psychological presence in the family during deployment separation (fit-for-duty and open-ranks) exhibit more flexibility and adaptability when difficulties occur (McCubbin, Dahl, Lester, & Ross, 1975). However, in open-ranks families, enmeshed relationships or role reversals between the at-home parent and children may create jealousy on the part of both the returning parent and the involved children. In closed-ranks families who func-tionally replaced and/or emotionally cut off the deployed spouse or parent from the family system, a power struggle may ensue between the returning military spouse, who begins to reassert previous family roles, and the at-home spouse who resents giving up hard-earned independence and decision-making authority (Drummet et al., 2003; Pincus et al., 2001). Children in both these types of families may also fight the returned parent's efforts to resume a family role taken on by the children during the parent's absence. Qualitative findings suggest that adolescents, who matured and assumed substantial household responsibilities during the deployment, resent being treated like a younger child by the returned parent, who expects everything to be the same (Huebner et al., 2007). As a result, they may rebel and resist the returned parent's discipline.

Veteran's Psychological State and Postdeployment Family Functioning

Resilience among military personnel is more often the rule than the exception, with many service members demonstrating constructive transformations. A secure attach-ment system will contribute to positive adaptations, which might include active coping efforts, religious commitment, or an in-depth reevaluation of the self and the impor-tance of significant others (Mikulincer & Shaver, 2007). These reactions may stimulate aspirations for betterment in the form of educational pursuits, occupational achieve-ment, or a rededication to family life that may be viewed as psychological, spiritual, or social growth.

However, the physical and emotional challenges encountered by service mem-bers during deployments may lead to significant difficulties with their reintegration into the family and community. Although deployed, military personnel may develop or strengthen their ability to suppress fears and emotions, and develop an inability to relax a vigilant stance of suspicion and secrecy (Basham, 2008). Whereas these abilities are unquestionably adaptive to a combat environment, they create numer-ous problems in the family home. Research has consistently shown that returning veterans face increased difficulties in intimate relationships, particularly when the veteran suffers psychological problems. Veterans' depressive and trauma symptoms are related to marital difficulties (e.g., poor communication, intimacy problems, rela-tionship dissatisfaction, domestic violence, divorce), parenting problems (e.g., paren-tal dissatisfaction, coparenting disagreement), and maladaptive family functioning (e.g., high conflict, low cohesion and flexibility; Cook, Riggs, Thompson, Coyne, & Sheikh, 2004; Hendrix, Erdmann, & Briggs, 1998; Kessler, 2000; Sayers, Farrow, Ross, & Oslin, 2009).

A number of factors contribute to these relationship difficulties. First, insecure attachment is a risk factor for poor psychological and relational outcomes. Relative to veterans without posttraumatic stress disorder (PTSD), those with PTSD are more likely to endorse insecure attachment, especially dismissing or fearful styles that are characterized by high-attachment avoidance (Ghafoori, Hierholzer, Howsepian, & Boardman, 2008; Renaud, 2008). Insecure attachment is also associated with romantic relationship dysfunction (Mikulincer & Shaver, 2007). Veterans with PTSD often exhibit behaviors associated with insecure attachment, such as difficulties with the following: communication, emotional expressiveness, trust, self-disclosure, self-absorption, isolation, sociability, anger control, hostility, and physical aggression (Carroll, Rueger, Foy, & Donahoe, 1985; Rosenheck & Thomson, 1986). These problems and avoidant defenses, such as denial and emotional numbing, affect the capacity for intimacy with romantic partners, and can interfere with the ability to bond and remain attached to children (Scaturo & Hayman, 1992). For example, a maladaptive pursuer–distancer marital pattern may develop when an avoidantly attached service member's lack of emotion and distancing strategies trigger a secure or anxiously attached spouse's fears of abandonment and subsequent pursuit of connection, which in turn actually intensifies the avoidant partner's distancing reaction.

In addition, sleep disturbance and self-medicating substance abuse can disrupt family routines and contribute to marital strain. Military personnel who experience these and other psychological problems after deployment may be physically present in the family system, but absent from the family both emotionally and functionally. In addition to causing service members difficulty in their roles as spouse and parent (Rosenheck & Thomson, 1986), this situation represents an ambiguous loss for families and affects their reorganization because the lack of clarity regarding family roles leads to uncertain boundaries and can immobilize other family members (Dekel, Goldblatt, Keidar, Solomon, & Polliack, 2005). Without adequate organization, chaotic home environments and greater tension in the family may trigger or aggravate the veteran's posttraumatic symptoms (Tarrier, Sommerfield, & Pilgrim, 1999), which can then exacerbate problematic family interactions. If the negative cycle continues, a prevailing sense of insecurity in the family attachment network develops, even among families that were secure before deployment. As a result, families of veterans with PTSD may be characterized by rigidity, high levels of scapegoating and conflict, but low levels of independence, cohesion, expressiveness, and openness (Hendrix et al., 1998; D. S. Riggs, Byrne, Weathers, & Litz, 1998; Rosenheck & Thomson, 1986; Solomon, Waysman, & Mikulincer, 1990).

Trauma symptoms, such as intense hostility and reexperiencing episodes, can be frightening and contribute to psychological distress in spouses and emotional or behavioral disturbance in children (Figley, 1993). Cross-cultural evidence of the emotional toll of living with a veteran has emerged in research examining spouses of veterans with PTSD in the United States, Israel, and the Netherlands (Alessi, White Ray, Ray, & Stewart, 2001; Dirkzwager, Bramsen, Adèr, & van der Ploeg, 2005; Solomon et al., 1992). Symptom profiles of spouses included lower subjective well-being, neurotic concerns, somatic complaints, poor social relations and support, sleeping problems, and posttraumatic intrusion, avoidance, and hyperarousal symptoms. Dekel (2007) reported that among wives of Israeli former prisoners of war, husbands' PTSD symptoms and attachment style explained over half the variance in overall symptom level of wives, with husbands' attachment style being the strongest contributor to the wives' psychological health and posttraumatic growth.

Some researchers have suggested that military personnel with PTSD are unable to provide a secure environment that promotes the healthy development of their children (Caselli & Motta, 1995). Parental deployment alone has been linked to children's later emotional problems (Jensen et al., 1996), but the addition of parental PTSD symptoms can further disrupt the parent–child relationship (Haley, 1984) and increase the risk of children developing internalizing and externalizing problems (Caselli & Motta, 1995). Veterans with PTSD report that their children act afraid or not warm toward them (Sayers et al., 2009), suggesting that posttraumatic symptoms frighten children and might engender disorganization in the parent–child attachment relationship. Children's development of symptoms will be related to how much PTSD affects the veteran's and spouse's parenting skills, attachment with their children, and level of hostility and violence in the home.

CONCLUSIONS

A central assumption of the proposed model is that attachment relationships and family systems are fundamental contexts for risk and resilience between military members and their families during the deployment cycle. Given the incomplete literature regarding military families, the family attachment network model presents theory-based hypotheses for future researchers to test. Undoubtedly there are other viable explanatory approaches and it is our hope that investigators will improve on the current model's limitations. In particular, because each level of the multilevel family system is interconnected in multiple ways, it was not possible to represent all potential network connections in this chapter. Also, the model applies only to two-parent families; clearly single parents who are deployed face additional stressors not considered in the model. Furthermore, the model does not account for the predeployment presence of family maltreatment or domestic violence, which is associated with disorganization in the attachment system (Cassidy & Mohr, 2001) and chaos in the family system (Alexander, 1992). Although high rates of maltreatment and violence in military families (Rentz et al., 2006) indicate that a thorough consideration of these destructive processes in relation to the deployment cycle is warranted, the attachment and systemic interactions in these maltreating families are too complex and unpredictable to address within the scope of this chapter. In addition, intergenerational trauma is a worthy consideration, particularly given strong evidence that childhood trauma is a reliable predictor of PTSD in adulthood (Luthar, 2006).

It remains to future researchers to test the assumptions of the network model. Researchers should consider potential moderators, such as sex of parent or child, various deployment characteristics (e.g., frequency, duration, location, extent of family contact, etc.), and external resources (e.g., social/kin support, financial stability, military services to families, etc.). Another question is the extent to which postdeployment family functioning is related to preexisting individual and family factors, the unique contribution of deployment experiences, and/or the interaction between the two variables. The cross-fertilization of attachment and family systems theories can offer valuable insights to inform research questions and design. In particular, given the relevance of the attachment system to separation experiences, surprisingly little research has examined adult attachment strategies in military populations, and none has investigated parent–child attachment relationships in military families. Increased federal funding for these and other family-based research is clearly warranted and could provide data to assist in developing programs and treatment approaches for military members and their families.

Until that time, health providers may find it useful to consider attachment and family processes in their work with military personnel, spouses, and children. Some scholars have recommended that military families separated by deployment strive to maintain adequate contact and stretch system boundaries to preserve the psychological presence of the deployed service member, while redistributing his or her practical roles and responsibilities (Drummet et al., 2003; Vormbrock, 1993). Following extended deployments, it may be particularly important to address the need to reestablish potentially healing attachments between service members and their spouses and children. In addition, counselors should focus on helping the family develop or strengthen family resilience processes that facilitate reintegration, such as active coping strategies, improving the quality and quantity of family communication, increasing flexibility regarding roles and responsibilities, and decreasing isolation through the use of community and social support (Figley, 1993; Hammer et al., 2006).

REFERENCES

Alessi, M. W., White Ray, J., Ray, G. E., & Stewart, S. J. (2001). Personality and psychopathology profiles of veterans' wives: Measuring distress using the MMPI-2. *Journal of Clinical Psychology, 57*(12), 1535–1542. doi:10.1002/jclp.1115

Alexander, P. C. (1992). Application of attachment theory to the study of sexual abuse. *Journal of Consulting and Clinical Psychology, 60*(2), 185–195. doi:10.1037/0022-006X.60.2.185

Basham, K. (2008). Homecoming as safe haven or the new front: Attachment and detachment in military couples. *Clinical Social Work Journal, 36*, 83–96. doi:10.1007/s10615-007-0138-9

Berlin, L., & Cassidy, J. (1999). Relations among relationships: Contributions from attachment theory and research. In J. Cassidy & P. R. Shaver (Eds.), *Handbook of attachment: Theory, research, and clinical applications* (pp. 688–712). New York, NY: Guilford Press.

Bey, D. R., & Lange, J. (1974). Waiting wives: Women under stress. *American Journal of Psychiatry, 131*(3), 283–286.

Boss, P. (1999). *Ambiguous loss: Learning to live with unresolved grief.* Cambridge, MA: Harvard University Press.

Boss, P. G. (1980). The relationship of psychological father presence, wife's personal qualities and wife/family dysfunction in families of missing fathers. *Journal of Marriage & the Family, 42*, 541–549. doi:10.2307/351898

Bowlby, J. (1980). *Attachment and loss: Vol. 3. Loss, sadness and depression.* New York, NY: Basic Books.

Bowling, U. B., & Sherman, M. D. (2008). Welcoming them home: Supporting service members and their families in navigating the tasks of reintegration. *Professional Psychology: Research and Practice, 39*, 451–458. doi:10.1037/0735-7028.39.4.451

Byng-Hall, J. (1995). Creating a secure family base: Some implications of attachment theory for family therapy. *Family Process, 34*(1), 45–58. doi:10.1111/j.1545-5300.1995.00045.x

Cafferty, T. P., Davis, K. E., Medway, F. J., O'Hearn, R. E., & Chappell, K. D. (1994). Reunion dynamics among couples separated during Operation Desert Storm: An attachment theory analysis. In D. Perlman (Ed.), *Attachment processes in adulthood.* (pp. 309–330). London, England: Jessica Kingsley.

Carroll, E. M., Rueger, D. B., Foy, D. W., & Donahoe, C. P. (1985). Vietnam combat veterans with posttraumatic stress disorder: Analysis of marital and cohabitating adjustment. *Journal of Abnormal Psychology, 94*(3), 329–337. doi:10.1037/0021-843X.94.3.329

Caselli, L. T., & Motta, R. W. (1995). The effect of PTSD and combat level on Vietnam veterans' perceptions of child behavior and marital adjustment. *Journal of Clinical Psychology, 51*(1), 4–12. doi:10.1002/1097-4679(199501)51:1<4::AID-JCLP2270510102>3.0.CO;2-E

Cassidy, J., & Mohr, J. J. (2001). Unsolvable fear, trauma, and psychopathology: Theory, research, and clinical considerations relate to disorganized attachment across the life span. *Clinical Psychology: Science and Practice, 8*, 275–298. doi:10.1093/clipsy.8.3.275

Chandra, A., Lara-Cinisomo, S., Jaycox, L. H., Tanielian, T., Burns, R. M., Ruder, T., & Han, B. (2010). Children on the homefront: The experience of children from military families. *Pediatrics, 125*(1), 16–25. doi:10.1542/peds.2009-1180

Charuvastra, A., & Cloitre, M. (2008). Social bonds and posttraumatic stress disorder. *Annual Review of Psychology, 59*, 301–328. doi:10.1146/annurev.psych.58.110405.085650

Collins, N., & Feeney, B. (2004). An attachment theory perspective on closeness and intimacy. In D. Mashek & A. Aron (Eds.), *Handbook of closeness and intimacy* (pp. 163–187). Hillsdale, NJ: Erlbaum.

Cook, J. M., Riggs, D. S., Thompson, R., Coyne, J. C., & Sheikh, J. I. (2004). Posttraumatic stress disorder and current relationship functioning among World War II ex-prisoners of war. *Journal of Family Psychology: Journal of the Division of Family Psychology of the American Psychological Association (Division 43), 18*(1), 36–45. doi:10.1037/0893-3200.18.1.36

Davies, P. T., Cummings, E. M., & Winter, M. A. (2004). Pathways between profiles of family functioning, child security in the interparental subsystem, and child psychological problems. *Development and Psychopathology, 16,* 525–550. doi:10.1017/S0954579404004651

Davies, P. T., Sturge-Apple, M. L., & Cummings, E. M. (2004). Interdependencies among interparental discord and parenting practices: The role of adult vulnerability and relationship perturbations. *Development and Psychopathology, 16*(3), 773–797. doi: 10.1017/S0954579404004778

De Wolff, M. S., & van Ijzendoorn, M. H. (1997). Sensitivity and attachment: A meta-analysis on parental antecedents of infant attachment. *Child Development, 68*(4), 571–591.

Dekel, R. (2007). Posttraumatic distress and growth among wives of prisoners of war: The contribution of husbands' posttraumatic stress disorder and wives' own attachments. *American Journal of Orthopsychiatry, 77*(3), 419–426. doi:10.1037/0002-9432.77.3.419

Dekel, R., Goldblatt, H., Keidar, M., Solomon, Z., & Polliack, M. (2005). Being a wife of a veteran with posttraumatic stress disorder. *Family Relations: An Interdisciplinary Journal of Applied Family Studies, 54,* 24–36. doi:10.1111/j.0197-6664.2005.00003.x

Dirkzwager, A. J., Bramsen, I., Adèr, H., & van der Ploeg, H. M. (2005). Secondary traumatization in partners and parents of Dutch peacekeeping soldiers. *Journal of Family Psychology, 19*(2), 217–226. doi:10.1037/0893-3200.19.2.217

Drummet, A. R., Coleman, M., & Cable, S. (2003). Military families under stress: Implications for family life education. *Family Relations, 52,* 279. doi:10.1111/j.1741-3729.2003.00279.x

Durham, S. W. (2010). In their own words: Staying connected in a combat environment. *Military Medicine, 175*(8), 554–559.

Figley, C. R. (1993). Coping with stressors on the home front. *Journal of Social Issues, 49,* 51–71.

Flake, E. M., Davis, B. E., Johnson, P. L., & Middleton, L. S. (2009). The psychosocial effects of deployment on military children. *Journal of Developmental and Behavioral Pediatrics, 30*(4), 271–278. doi:10.1097/DBP.0b013e3181aac6e4

Ghafoori, B., Hierholzer, R., Howsepian, B., & Boardman, A. (2008). The role of adult attachment, parental bonding, and spiritual love in the adjustment to military trauma. *Journal of Trauma & Dissociation, 9*(1), 85–106. doi:10.1080/15299730802073726

Gibbs, D. A., Martin, S. L., Kupper, L. L., & Johnson, R. E. (2007). Child maltreatment in enlisted soldiers' families during combat-related deployments. *Journal of the American Medical Association, 298*(5), 528–535. doi:10.1001/jama.298.5.528

Haley, S. A. (1984). The Vietnam veteran and his preschool child: Child rearing as delayed stress in combat veterans. *Journal of Contemporary Psychotherapy, 14,* 114–121. doi: 10.1007/BF00956740

Hammer, L. B., Cullen, J. C., Marchand, G. C., & Dezsofi, J. A. (2006). Reducing the negative impact of work-family conflict on military personnel: Individual coping strategies and multilevel interventions. In T. W. Britt (Ed.), *Military life: The psychology of serving in peace and combat (Vol. 3): The military family.* (pp. 220–242). Westport, CT: Praeger.

Hendrix, C. C., Erdmann, M. A., & Briggs, K. (1998). Impact of Vietnam veterans' arousal and avoidance on spouses' perceptions of family life. *American Journal of Family Therapy, 26,* 115– 128.

Hill, R. (1949). *Families under stress: Adjustment to the crises of war separation and return.* Oxford, England: Harper.

Hoge, C. W., Auchterlonie, J. L., & Milliken, C. S. (2006). Mental health problems, use of mental health services, and attrition from military service after returning from deployment to Iraq or Afghanistan. *Journal of the American Medical Association, 295*(9), 1023–1032. doi:10.1001/jama.295.9.1023

Hoge, C. W., Lesikar, S. E., Guevara, R., Lange, J., Brundage, J. F., Engel, C. C., …Orman, D. T. (2002). Mental disorders among U.S. military personnel in the 1990s: Association with high levels of health care utilization and early military attrition. *American Journal of Psychiatry, 159*(9), 1576–1583. doi:10.1176/appi.ajp.159.9.1576

Huebner, A. J., Mancini, J. A., Wilcox, R. M., Grass, S. R., & Grass, G. A. (2007). Parental deployment and youth in military families: Exploring uncertainty and ambiguous loss. *Family Relations, 56,* 112–122.

Hunter, E. (1984). Treating the military captive's family. In F. Kaslow & R. Ridenour (Eds.), *The military family: Dynamics and treatment* (pp. 167–196). New York, NY: Guilford Press.

Jacobvitz, D., Hazen, N., Curran, M., & Hitchens, K. (2004). Observations of early triadic family interactions: Boundary disturbances in the family predict symptoms of depression, anxiety, and attention-deficit/hyperactivity disorder in middle childhood. *Development and Psychopathology, 16*(3), 577–592. doi:10.1017/S0954579404004675

Jacobvitz, D., Riggs, S., & Johnson, E. (1999). Cross-sex and same-sex family alliances: Immediate and long-term effects on sons and daughters. In N. D. Chase (Ed.), *Burdened children: Theory, research, and treatment of parentification.* (pp. 34–55). Thousand Oaks, CA: Sage.

Jensen, P. S., Martin, D., & Watanabe, H. (1996). Children's response to parental separation during Operation Desert Storm. *Journal of the American Academy of Child and Adolescent Psychiatry, 35*(4), 433–441. doi:10.1097/00004583-199604000-00009

Johnson, S. J., Sherman, M. D., Hoffman, J. S., James, L. C., Johnson, P. L., Lochman, J. E., . . . Stepney, B. (2007). *The psychological needs of US military service members and their families: A preliminary report.* Retrieved from https://www.apa.org/pubs/info/reports/military-deployment-summary.pdf.

Jumper, C., Evers, S., Cole, D., Raezer, J. W., Edger, I., Johner, M., & Pike, H. (2005). National Military Family Association report on the cycles of deployment. Retrieved on from https://www.purdue.edu/hhs/extension/docs/HowToHelp_FamilyFriendNeighbor-print-INDIANA.pdf.

Kelley, M. L. (1994). Military-induced separation in relation to maternal adjustment and children's behaviors. *Military Psychology, 6,* 163–176.

Kelley, M. L., Hock, E., Smith, K. M., Jarvis, M. S., Bonney, J. F., & Gaffney, M. A. (2001). Internalizing and externalizing behavior of children with enlisted Navy mothers experiencing military-induced separation. *Journal of the American Academy of Child and Adolescent Psychiatry, 40*(4), 464–471. doi:10.1097/00004583-200104000-00016

Kessler, R. C. (2000). Posttraumatic stress disorder: The burden to the individual and to society. *Journal of Clinical Psychiatry, 61*(Suppl. 5), 4–12; discussion 13.

Kobak, R., Cassidy, J., Lyons-Ruth, K., & Ziv, Y. (2006). Attachment, stress, and psychopathology: A developmental pathways model. In D. Cicchetti & D. J. Cohen (Eds.), *Developmental psychopathology, (2nd ed., Vol 1): Theory and method* (pp. 333–369). Hoboken, NJ: John Wiley.

Kozlowska, K., & Hanney, L. (2002). The network perspective: An integration of attachment and family systems theories. *Family Process, 41*(3), 285–312.

Lester, P., Peterson, K., Reeves, J., Knauss, L., Glover, D., Mogil, C., ...Beardslee, W. (2010). The long war and parental combat deployment: Effects on military children and at-home spouses. *Journal of the American Academy of Child and Adolescent Psychiatry, 49*(4), 310–320. doi:10.1097/00004583-201004000-00006

Lincoln, A., Swift, E., & Shorteno-Fraser, M. (2008). Psychological adjustment and treatment of children and families with parents deployed in military combat. *Journal of Clinical Psychology, 64*(8), 984–992. doi:10.1002/jclp.20520

Luthar, S. S. (2006). Resilience in development: A synthesis of research across five decades. In D. Cicchetti & D. J. Cohen (Eds.), *Developmental psychopathology, Vol. 3: Risk, disorder and adaptation* (pp. 739–795). Hoboken, NJ: John Wiley.

McCubbin, H. I., Dahl, B. B., Lester, G. R., & Ross, B. A. (1975). The returned prisoner of war: Factors in family reintegration. *Journal of Marriage & the Family, 37,* 471–478. doi:10.2307/350511

Medway, F. J., Davis, K. E., Cafferty, T. P., Chappell, K. D., & O'Hearn, R. E. (1995). Family disruption and adult attachment correlates of spouse and child reactions to separation and reunion due to Operation Desert Storm. *Journal of Social and Clinical Psychology, 14,* 97–118.

Mikulincer, M., & Florian, V. (1998). The relationship between adult attachment styles and emotional and cognitive reactions to stressful events. In J. Simpson & W. S. Rholes (Eds.), *Attachment theory and close relationships* (pp. 143–165). New York, NY: Guilford Press.

Mikulincer, M., & Shaver, P. R. (2007). *Attachment in adulthood: Structure, dynamics, and change.* New York, NY: Guilford Press.

Minuchin, S. (1974). *Families and family therapy.* Cambridge, MA: Harvard University Press.

Peterson, C., Park, N., & Castro, C. A. (2011). Assessment for the U.S. Army Comprehensive Soldier Fitness program: The Global Assessment Tool. *American Psychologist, 66*(1), 10–18. doi:10 .1037/a0021658

Pincus, S. H., House, R., Christensen, J., & Adler, L. E. (2001). *The emotional cycle of deployment: A military family perspective.* Retrieved from https://msrc.fsu.edu/system/files/The%20Emotional%20Cycle%20of%20Deployment%20-%20A%20Military%20Family%20Perspective.pdf

Renaud, E. F. (2008). The attachment characteristics of combat veterans with PTSD. *Traumatology, 14,* 1–12. doi:10.1177/1534765608319085

Rentz, E. D., Martin, S. L., Gibbs, D. A., Clinton-Sherrod, M., Hardison, J., & Marshall, S. W. (2006). Family violence in the military: A review of the literature. *Trauma, Violence & Abuse, 7*(2), 93–108. doi:10.1177/1524838005285916

Riggs, D. S., Byrne, C. A., Weathers, F. W., & Litz, B. T. (1998). The quality of the intimate relationships of male Vietnam veterans: Problems associated with posttraumatic stress disorder. *Journal of Traumatic Stress, 11*(1), 87–101.

Riggs, S. A. (2010). Childhood emotional abuse and the attachment system across the life cycle: What theory and research tell us. *Journal of Aggression, Maltreatment & Trauma, 19,* 5–51. doi:10.1080/10926770903475968

Riggs, S. A., Paulson, A., Tunnell, E., Sahl, G., Atkison, H., & Ross, C. A. (2007). Attachment, personality, and psychopathology among adult inpatients: Self-reported romantic attachment style versus Adult Attachment Interview states of mind. *Development and Psychopathology, 19*(1), 263–291. doi:10.1017/S0954579407070149

Rosenheck, R., & Thomson, J. (1986). "Detoxification" of Vietnam War trauma: A combined family-individual approach. *Family Process, 25*(4), 559–570. doi:10.1111/j.1545-5300.1986.00559.x

Sayers, S. L., Farrow, V. A., Ross, J., & Oslin, D. W. (2009). Family problems among recently returned military veterans referred for a mental health evaluation. *Journal of Clinical Psychiatry, 70*(2), 163–170. doi:10.4088/JCP.07m03863

Scaturo, D., & Hayman, P. (1992). The impact of combat trauma across the family life cycle: Clinical considerations. *Journal of Traumatic Stress, 5,* 273–288. doi:10.1002/jts.2490050212

Simpson, J. A., & Rholes, W. S. (2002). Fearful-avoidance, disorganization, and multiple working models: Some directions for future theory and research. *Attachment & Human Development, 4*(2), 223–229. doi:10.1080/14616730210154207

Solomon, Z., Waysman, M., Belkin, R., Levy, G., Mikulincer, M., & Enoch, D. (1992). Marital relations and combat stress reaction: The wives' perspective. *Journal of Marriage & Family, 54,* 316–326. doi:10.2307/353063

Solomon, Z., Waysman, M., & Mikulincer, M. (1990). Family functioning, perceived societal support, and combat-related psychopathology: The moderating role of loneliness. *Journal of Social and Clinical Psychology, 9,* 456–472.

Tarrier, N., Sommerfield, C., & Pilgrim, H. (1999). Relatives' expressed emotion (EE) and PTSD treatment outcome. *Psychological Medicine, 29*(4), 801–811. doi:10.1017/S0033291799008569

Vetere, A., & Dallos, R. (2008). Systemic therapy and attachment narratives. *Journal of Family Therapy, 30,* 374–385. doi:10 .1111/j.1467-6427.2008.00449.x

Vormbrock, J. K. (1993). Attachment theory as applied to wartime and job-related marital separation. *Psychological Bulletin, 114,* 122–144. doi:10.1037/0033-2909.114.1.122

Walsh, F. (2003). Family resilience: Strengths forged through adversity. In F. Walsh (Ed.), *Normal family processes: Growing diversity and complexity.* (pp. 399–423). New York, NY: Guilford Press.

Walsh, F. (2006). *Strengthening family resilience* (2nd ed.). New York, NY: Guilford Press.

Warner, C. H., Appenzeller, G. N., Warner, C. M., & Grieger, T. (2009). Psychological effects of deployments on military families. *Psychiatric Annals, 39,* 56–63. doi:10.3928/0048571320090201-11

Woodhouse, S. S., Dykas, M. J., & Cassidy, J. (2009). Perceptions of secure base provision within the family. *Attachment & Human Development, 11*(1), 47–67. doi:10.1080/14616730802500792

Zeff, K. N., Lewis, S. J., & Hirsch, K. A. (1997). Military family adaptation to United Nations Operations in Somalia. *Military Medicine, 162*(6), 384–387.

29

Social Justice, Oppression, and Disability: Counseling Those Most in Need

Irmo Marini

*I*nequality is perhaps America's most egregious, embarrassing, and least desirable trait as an industrialized nation. Although some would argue the United States ideally upholds egalitarian values and traditions, its history chronicles a plethora of contradictions dating back to the country's formation (David, 2014; Fox & Marini, 2012; Hughes & Avoke, 2010; Liu, 2011; Ramsey & Marini, 2016; Smiley & West, 2012; Stiglitz, 2013). If Gandhi, Churchill, Hubert Humphrey, Pope John Paul II, Dostoyevsky, and others' observations that a society is judged by how it treats its most vulnerable members (paraphrased) is accurate, then the United States has surely failed. Indeed, with the greed and corruption of corporate America embedded and arguably controlling the political system with financial contributions supporting their causes, there is no voice to advocate for its poor and most in need citizens (Huffington, 2003, 2010; Marini & Stebnicki, 2012; Ramsey & Marini, 2016; Smiley & West, 2012; Stiglitz, 2013; Warren, 2014).

The root causes of social injustice are in part centralized around wealth inequities, politicians, and legislation favoring the wealthy, discrimination, and a Darwinian mentality (Greenwald, 2011; Marini, 2012b; Warren, 2014). Whereas Darwin and his followers in the late 19th century espoused natural selection in that the strong will survive and the weak shall perish regarding eugenics, Marini (2012b) states the 21st-century mantra has morphed into a more surreptitious "survival of the financially fittest" social psyche (p. 490). The eugenics movement in its extreme during Hitler's Nazi regime murdered an estimated 300,000 German citizens with disability deemed "undesirables" and "useless eaters." Survival of the financially fittest in today's era, however, is much less conspicuous in the overall harm it afflicts on its most vulnerable citizens. When the life expectancy for Americans living in one ZIP code differs by 20+ years compared to those living several miles away in another code due partially to wealth disparities, it behooves us as a society to solve such social and moral problems (Bloch, 2013).

In this chapter, we explore the ramifications of social injustice in America focusing on those with disabilities. The ripple effect of poverty, oppression, and disability, and its subsequent deleterious impact for equitable treatment and opportunity, is discussed. Beginning with prevalence statistics regarding poverty in general and disability specifically, the chapter segues into an exploration of the domino and vicious cycle effect of inequitable education, employment, health care, and health. The resulting psychosocial impact on minorities and those with disabilities is a reciprocal occurrence between these populations interfacing with an arguably apathetic societal and political populace. Finally, a dialogue regarding the social justice counselor and strategies for counseling and advocating for this most ignored and disenfranchised population in America is discussed.

POVERTY AND DISABILITY IN AMERICA

Poverty in America has remained relatively unchanged during the past 5 years. In the Current Population Survey (2015), the U.S. Census Bureau indicates that more than 46 million, or 14.8%, of Americans continue to live in poverty. It is interesting to note that poverty rates did edge up between 2013 and 2014 for individuals with disabilities, those with bachelor's degrees or higher, and married couples, indicating even those with a postsecondary education or perhaps two incomes were at risk. As with previous years, approximately one in five children lived in poverty according to federal guidelines. The 2014 U.S. federal poverty rate for single, younger persons under 65 was $11,670. For single parents, the rate was $15,730 with one child; comprised of 30.6% for a female single parent and 15.7% for a single male parent. For two-parent households with two children, the poverty rate was $23,850 per year. As in previous years, minorities had significantly higher poverty rates. African Americans led the way at 27.4%, Hispanic/Latinos at 26.6%, Asian Americans at 12.1%, and Caucasians at 9.9% (U.S. Department of Health and Human Services, 2014).

For persons with disabilities in 2014, the poverty rate differed depending on one's age. For children younger than 5 years, 34% of their primary caregivers surveyed lived in poverty (Annual Disability Statistics Compendium, 2014). This rate dropped to 32.6% between ages 5 and 17 years, and lowered further to 28.2% for those between 18 and 64 years of age. For the same adult age group of persons without disabilities, the comparative rate was only 13%; therefore, the rate for those with disabilities living in poverty was more than double that for those without disabilities with the same demographics. A similar near doubling trend was also observed between those with and without disabilities at the other age groups as well. The prevalence with which persons with disabilities require some type of assistance gradually increases with age; roughly less than 10% at age less than 15 years and more than 50% at age 80 years or older (Brault, 2012).

When combining disability and minority status, persons with disabilities who are a minority are by far the largest population living in poverty, and especially so for disabled female minority parents (Brault, 2012; Hughes & Avoke, 2010). Greater than one in four children with disabilities live below the poverty level, with the greatest prevalence being single female minority families (Parish, Rose, & Andrews, 2010). Smiley and West (2012) cite the vicious cycle of poverty begetting poverty, and the difficulty that impoverished individuals have climbing out of the cycle of poverty. Fremstad (2009) argues that although the poverty and disability literature overlap significantly, they are rarely jointly discussed or connected. He cites that not only are persons of minority with disabilities more likely to be unemployed or surviving off government benefits, but they are also more likely to incur medical costs not otherwise covered by Medicare or Medicaid. The connection among disability, minority status, poverty, and oppression is further detailed subsequently.

THE SOCIAL AND ECONOMIC COST OF OPPRESSION
AND DISENFRANCHISEMENT

The cost of inequitable treatment of persons with disabilities and/or minorities is delete-rious not only to these populations, but society as well both socially and economically. During any election cycle, Medicare, Medicaid, and Social Security are always topics of discussion, generally with politicians acknowledging the increased costs, but few will-ing to take any steps to actively address solutions. Brault (2012) noted approximately 59% of working age adults with severe disabilities receive some form of public assis-tance in terms of Social Security, subsidized housing, food stamps, and cash assistance. Approximately 20% receive Supplemental Security Income (SSI), which is the Social Security Administration's income assistance for persons with disabilities who qualify as being poor. Ouellette, Burstein, Long, and Beecroft (2004) further note that simply cit-ing poverty rates does not fully capture the material hardship that individuals endure. The nuances of living in poverty include housing instability, food insufficiency, living in unsafe neighborhoods, the ongoing stress of potential utility and telephone disconnec-tion, and inadequate or no health care.

Nam, Huang, Heflin, and Sherraden (2012) note the racial and ethnic disparities in America regarding food insufficiency. They and others cite that approximately 17.2 million families in the United States suffer long-term effects of not having enough food and the uncertainty of being able to feed one's family on a daily basis. This, in turn, has a negative effect on children's physical and cognitive development and ability to fight chronic diseases, impairs academic achievement, contributes to higher dropout rates, and hurts one's potential for competitive employment in adulthood (Jyoti, Frongillo, & Jones, 2005; Whitaker, Phillips, & Orzol, 2006). The overrepresentation of minorities with disabilities generationally living in a cycle of continued poverty is alarmingly high and contributes to the large life expectancy discrepancy noted earlier between the haves and have-nots in America (Stiglitz, 2013).

The social cost to persons and/or minorities with disabilities is that they become "stuck" in a continuing ill-conceived poverty cycle, which does not allow SSI recipients to be competitively employed and keep their medical coverage (Marini & Reid, 2001; Marini & Stebnicki, 1999). In addition, the social cost to one's self-concept and self-esteem is diminished by not being a contributing member to society (Marini, 2012a). The American work ethic has long since been idealized as a primary pathway from rags to riches, and simplistically thought by many to be easily determined by one's drive, perseverance, and motivation to succeed. Although there are social programs that facilitate these efforts (Ticket to Work), there are also government policies (Medicare work restrictions) that fiscally inhibit efforts of those with disabilities from entering the workforce (Marini & Reid, 2001; Marini & Stebnicki, 1999).

In addition to the self-esteem costs to unemployed individuals who otherwise would like to work is the ever-continuing shaming and negative societal attitudes toward those who are perceived as living off the system (Rose & Baumgartner, 2013). Rose and Baumgartner (2013) studied what we today term *public shaming* regarding media cov-erage of almost 50 years regarding poverty in the United States. Specifically, the authors cite numerous media outlets (newspapers, magazines, books, etc.) as well as politicians who frame topics that sway public opinion. They note that framing of the poor in the 1960s was projected as the poor being victims of living in an unfair economic system with poor health options, attending underfunded dysfunctional schools, and subject to racial discrimination. The result of such attitudes and media framing culminated in the

War on Poverty, and the government response to eradicate poverty was immediate and effective, reducing the poverty level from 22% to 12% within 15 years as social program assistance increased from 3% to 8%.

In the early 1970s, however, the discourse on poverty began to change, largely when Ronald Reagan was campaigning for president. Politicians and the media began framing persons living in poverty as lazy, cheaters, and welfare queens having children who were also living off the system (Hancock, 2004; Rose & Baumgartner, 2013). Much like disability, concepts related to the poor are socially constructed and subsequently can shape public policy. Hancock (2004) believed this new discourse largely impacted President Clinton's 1990s Welfare Reform, which saw funding cuts and 5-year maximums for persons on welfare. This sentiment continues to exist today, especially among so many in the Republican Party, as Mitt Romney demonstrated in a 2012 Florida speech to wealthy donors, citing about 47% of Americans who live off the system. During the same 2012 campaign, House Speaker Newt Gingrich's famous sound bite that President Obama would be "the best food stamp President in American history" also demonstrated the disdain toward the poor and those in government who are perceived as enablers of free taxpayer giveaways to the poor. Although many see the issue of poverty as a rather simplistic dichotomous personal choice of being lazy or alternatively motivated to work, we next turn to how this topic is much more complex when considering the impact of social injustice and oppression in America.

Education

Researchers of social economics who focus on the economic complexities of social policies and their impact begin to unravel the stark differences between the haves and have-nots, and the impact of oppression and inequalities, from an early age (Hughes & Avoke, 2010; Liu, 2011; Stiglitz, 2013). These and other authors argue there is a ripple effect for families living in poverty. Poor families typically live in low-income neighborhoods with low property tax revenues to adequately finance local public schools. Hughes and Avoke (2010) note that poorly funded schools may be dilapidated, have poor heating, are underfunded and understaffed, have lower teacher expectations, and statistically experience higher dropout rates. These schools are predominantly in low-income minority neighborhoods, and Balfanz and Legters (2004) cite a 50% dropout rate among African American students and a 40% dropout rate among Hispanics from such neighborhoods.

For students with disabilities, the statistics are equally grim. A U.S. Department of Education (2009) report found that minority students with severe disabilities were more likely to be placed in special education and segregated from the general education population. The curriculum in special education ideally is supposed to focus on developing self-determination and essential job skills needed for employment; however, the special education curriculum often falls far short of curricular expectations (Wehman & Kregel, 1997). Without the opportunity for a quality education or to learn entry-level job skills for the competitive labor market, students with disabilities from underfunded low-income neighborhoods essentially have no skills to become employed. Newman, Wagner, Cameto, and Knokey (2009) found that post-high school, youth diagnosed with a developmental disability had only a 31% mostly part-time employment rate, 14% lived independently or semi-independently, 26% had a checking account, and 7% attended some postsecondary education. Newman et al. concluded that disability and poverty combine for poorer educational opportunities, lower graduation rates, higher dropout rates exceeding 50%, and ultimately poor employment options and rates among youth with disabilities, particularly those of minority status.

Overall, there are statistically poorer economic and employment outcomes for children with disabilities living in low-income neighborhoods who attend underfunded schools when compared to nondisabled children in better funded schools. The dropout, graduation, and ultimately employment rates are drastically different for low-income children with disabilities, and their opportunity to climb out of poverty is marginal at best. Attempting to learn while one is hungry or cold due to insufficient school heating becomes difficult, as is the ability to concentrate on one's studies when living in low-income, unsafe neighborhoods.

Employment

The ripple effect of a poor or inadequate education for the variety of reasons noted previously ultimately impacts one's ability for competitive employment. Braddock and Parish (2001) cite an 80% unemployment rate among adults with disabilities raised in poverty conditions in the United States. Being a minority female with a disability ranks highest among those most unemployed. Brault (2012) indicates that employment opportunities for persons with disabilities who have not been afforded a quality education and an opportunity to obtain a postsecondary education are relegated to largely entry-level minimum wage occupations performing primarily physical labor. This is not the case for those with mobility impairments, but rather those with cognitive or developmental disabilities if they are capable of performing competitive employment. For those with mobility but no cognitive impairments, there continues to be an approximate 70% unemployment rate overall for this group as well.

One of the major disincentives Marini and Reid (2001) have previously argued, however, is that in the majority of states where the minimum wage remains $7.25 per hour or just more than $15,000 per year (without deducting income tax), combined with the likelihood of losing one's medical benefits, it is simply not worth the risk for those collecting disability benefits for a minimum wage job. For those single individuals collecting SSI benefits, their maximum earnings are $733 per month. As such, for most individuals collecting SSI amounting to $8,800 per year with medical benefits and given the choice to earn a few thousand dollars more working 40 hours per week with minimal if any medical benefits, it is simply not worth taking the risk. Of all beneficiaries historically on the Social Security roles, less than 1% ever leave to return to the workforce (Marini, 2012a). This same Catch-22 exists for persons with physical impairments who require home care assistance to complete activities of daily living (ADL). All states have maximum daily limits regarding the number of hours per week of home care assistance; however, one must be homebound and services are not provided for those who want/can work and/or drive. Although the archaic Medicare homebound rules allow for an individual to attend adult day care, they are not allowed to work to qualify for activities of daily living (ADL) home care services. The incentive should be to support employment efforts by providing such assistance rather than penalizing those with disabilities who want to work but need home care assistance to do so.

Health Care and Health Costs

Individuals without health insurance decreased from 2013 to 2014 largely due to the Affordable Care Act and the mandate for insurance companies to provide coverage for those with preexisting conditions. There was an approximate 23% decrease of uninsured Americans from 41.8 million people in 2013 down to 33 million in 2014 (Current Population Survey, 2015). In her book, *Money Driven Medicine*, Mahar (2006) cites health care practices and costs that demonstrate approximately seven of 10 personal bankruptcies filed by Americans are due to extraordinary medical bills that most hospitals are elusive at attempting to explain. Several days of hospitalization for relatively minor surgery can easily exceed more than $100,000, and for the majority of Americans poor or otherwise without adequate insurance, these costs can never be paid. An estimated 15% of private hospitals have also been known to practice "patient dumping" whereby high-cost patients who have been stabilized but do not have insurance are literally dumped off at the door of another hospital or elsewhere (Rice & Jones, 1991). The authors note that the uninsured are made up largely of minorities who generally do not seek medical services until it is an emergency.

As noted earlier, the overall significance of social injustice toward poor minorities with disabilities can result in more than a 20-year difference in life expectancy between this population and those with greater wealth. Although living a long and healthy life is partially an individual's responsibility, statistics cannot ignore the higher mortality rates among poor minorities who have a disability living in lower income housing, obtaining poorer health care, having an insufficient income to eat healthy, and living in unsafe or hazardous environments and neighborhoods. A two-tier system of inequitable treatment in health care, housing, employment, and education between the haves and have-nots ultimately ends with higher and younger mortality rates for the have-nots (Brault, 2012; Liu, 2011; Mahar, 2006; Smiley & West, 2012; Stiglitz, 2013).

Environmental Inequities

Persons with disabilities and other minorities have been subtly subjected to social injustices via environmental and social barriers as well. Again, these inequities are related to low socioeconomic status where statistically a majority of minorities and those with disabilities reside. These populations are more likely to live in unsafe neighborhoods without a nearby grocery store or park for recreation and exercise (Liu, 2011). The stark diversity in urban planning between wealthy and poor neighborhoods creates an unhealthy environment for those living in poverty. Individuals living in low-income neighborhoods without a vehicle must travel many miles to a local grocery store, and have difficulty purchasing healthy foods. As such, these neighborhoods typically have convenience stores stocked with high calorie, high sugar, inexpensive foods that are more affordable and available. Obesity and the multitude of secondary health-related complications (e.g., diabetes, hypertension, cardiovascular disease) from being obese are much more prevalent among those living in poverty and in impoverished neighborhoods (Ramsey & Marini, 2016; Romero & Marini, 2012).

Those living in low-income housing also face other environmental hazards. Johnston, Werder, and Sebastian (2016) cite the decades-old common practice of environmental injustice, whereby environmentally hazardous industries take up residence in low-income, mostly minority areas. The authors cite a disproportionately higher number of waste disposal facilities across the country, including oil and gas wastewater disposal wells. The recent publicity of contaminated water wells and the deleterious health impact on the cognitive and physical development of children and adults is appalling. Similarly, although the poisonous health impact (e.g., seizures, mental retardation, nervous system abnormalities) of lead paint have been known for more than 75 years, corporate lead paint proponents successfully lobbied to keep using it, particularly in low-income housing developments, up until the late 1970s (Ludden, 2016).

Lynch and Stretesky (2012) also discuss the environmental injustices imposed on Native Americans and the environmental hazards to which they have been exposed. The authors describe the poverty and income disparities between Native Americans living on the reserve in comparison to non-Native Americans. They cite poverty rates of 37% on nongaming reservations and 27% on gaming reservations. Educational achievement is also much lower with only 11% holding college degrees on nongaming reserves and 16% on gaming reserves. Housing conditions for many American Indians on non-gaming reserves are also dismal, with a reported 24% of houses lacking indoor plumbing and 26% lacking a complete kitchen. There is no adequate health care coverage on the reserves, leaving families often having to travel great distances to a public hospital. Native Americans have a much higher than average risk for advanced cancer, cardiovascular disease, substance abuse, and suicide. Like other minorities, they too have been exposed to hazardous waste sites from commercial and military toxic waste facilities being built around the communities where they reside.

For persons with disabilities, environmental barriers continue despite the now 27-year-old Americans with Disabilities Act (ADA) of 1990. Recent studies of Americans with disabilities continue to express their daily frustrations with pockets of noncompliance across the country in the areas of transportation, public accommodations, employment protections, and health care access (Graf, Marini, & Blankenship, 2009; Marini, Bhakta, & Graf, 2009). From medical facilities having inaccessible exam tables for wheelchair users, to hospitals and/or medical clinics not offering translators for persons who are deaf, these entities continue to be in violation of the law. ADA filings under the Equal Employment Opportunity Commission (just Title I) since 1997 to 2015 have ranged and gradually climbed from approximately 15,000 to almost 27,000 complaints annually regarding alleged employment discrimination alone (U.S. Equal Employment Opportunity Commission, n.d.). Public accommodations complaints have exceeded these numbers. For most entities that have not made the appropriate ADA changes by now, many of them have taken an apathetic "so sue me" type attitude.

THE PSYCHOSOCIAL COST OF OPPRESSION

David (2014) in his edited book *Internalized Oppression: The Psychology of Marginalized Groups* notes the impact of oppression on persons of minority status and those with disabilities. David and associates note how after years of discrimination and microaggressions, many marginalized individuals succumb to feeling, and ultimately believe, they are devalued or second class citizens. Wright (1988) similarly addressed this concept of succumbing. Ramsey and Marini (2016) also address the psychosocial impact of being devalued and dehumanized by negative societal attitudes. Dohrenwend (2000) found a correlation between perceived discrimination and higher levels of depression and anxiety among minority groups. David (2014) similarly found that individuals who internalized oppression also experienced stress, depression, and anxiety.

Aside from feelings of low self-worth, persons with disabilities who perceive they are discriminated against also report to be less likely to socialize with friends and family, less likely to go to the movies or a restaurant, and more likely to perceive their lives will become worse rather than better (National Organization on Disability, 2004, 2010). Many persons with disabilities living under the poverty level worry about their health and well-being, finances, limited community support, and unsafe or unhealthy living conditions (Cooper, Korman, O'Hara, & Zovistoski, 2009). Besides such daily worries for those minorities with few resources, persons with disabilities continue to experience daily hassles and frustrations dealing with inaccessible businesses, fragmented medical services, and the perceived negative attitudes of others (Graf et al., 2009; Li & Moore, 1998; Marini et al., 2009).

In further exploring the mental and physical health implications for individuals who are, or perceive to be, oppressed and/or discriminated against, a number of interesting studies show the significance of the person–environment interaction and its implications. Aguinaldo (2008), for example, studied the concept of gay oppression as a determinant of gay men's health, citing the premise, "homophobia is killing us." In his literature review, Aguinaldo notes the mental and physical health problems of gay men living in a society that oppresses, discriminates, and is blatantly prejudiced toward them. The resulting fear, physical and verbal abuse, felt hatred, and anger gay males often endure by others carries a heavy psychological toll, sometimes resulting in depression, anxiety, lacking self-worth, shame, self-destructive behaviors such as suicide, inferiority, and self-defeating behaviors (Dempsey, 1994).

Generalized stress and stress-related illnesses have also been linked to others who are oppressed and feel discriminated against (Turner & Avison, 2003). Turner and Avison found that African Americans reported higher occurrences of discriminatory experiences including violence, death, and daily discrimination resulting in chronic stressors when compared with White study participants. Perlow, Danoff-Burg, Swenson, and Pulgiano (2004) noted how discrimination negatively impacts one's sense of control, and feelings of hopelessness can ultimately lead to a variety of mental health disorders.

If societal discrimination and oppression simply stopped there, the negative physical and mental health impact of oppressed individuals would be alarming in and of itself. Unfortunately, the peripheral implication of perceived prejudice toward an individual or group has further negative ramifications that can exacerbate health problems (Kessler et al., 2003; Krieger, 1999). Numerous studies show the resulting ripple effect of discrimination, including unemployment or underemployment, lower socio-economic status, poorer health care, lower educational attainment, and poverty (Eaton & Muntaner, 1999; Kessler et al., 2003; Krieger, 1999; Ramsey & Marini, 2016; Williams, Yan, Yu, Jackson, & Anderson, 1997).

Hughes and Avoke (2010) describe the elephant in the room in relation to poverty, disability, and unemployment or underemployment of persons with disabilities. They note that individuals who live under these circumstances are chronically exposed to inadequate housing opportunities, educational opportunities, transportation, poor finances, and concerns about their health or well-being. Current public policies have failed to remedy many of these ongoing problems despite decades-old fair housing legislation, the Individuals with Disabilities Education Act, and the ADA. Much like the 1964 Civil Rights Act has taken decades to gradually remedy the impact of oppression and discrimination, the full equal rights of minorities and those with disabilities have yet to be reconciled and continue to be violated to this day. Marini (2012b) poses the question as to whether the glass is half-full or half-empty concerning the human rights of persons with disabilities.

In measuring the pulse of American politics regarding disability equal rights, the ADA in all probability will remain in effect for the foreseeable future to be the last major effort to better the lives of persons with disabilities. In the 2016 presidential race, for example, neither party campaigned on any further improvements to or strengthening of the civil rights of persons with disabilities. Even with such promises, the gaps in the law and the lack of legal oversight to enforce the law leave much of it relatively ignored across parts of the country, and left up to individual citizens with disabilities to police their own law and file suits.

SOCIAL JUSTICE

The American Counseling Association (ACA) has led the way only recently in considering social justice to be a valid counseling specialization. Specifically, in its 2014 revised code of ethics, ACA cites "when appropriate, counselors advocate at the individual, group, institutional, and societal levels to examine potential barriers and obstacles that inhibit access and/or growth and development of clients" (ACA, 2014, p. 5). The ACA has also approved the new Division for Counselors for Social Justice within the ACA. On its 2010 homepage defining what social justice counseling entails, the Division for Counselors for Social Justice cites:

> Social justice counseling represents a multifaceted approach to counseling in which practitioners strive to simultaneously promote human development and the common good through addressing challenges related to both individual and distributive justice. Social justice counseling includes empowerment of the individual as well as active confrontation of injustice and inequality in society as they impact clientele as well as those in their systemic contexts. In doing so, social justice counselors direct attention to the promotion of four critical principles that guide their work; equity, access, participation, and harmony. This work is done with a focus on the cultural, contextual, and individual needs of those served. (Counselors for Social Justice, American Counseling Association, n.d., para. 5)

Greenleaf and Williams (2009) discuss the view that the counseling profession has been largely driven or entrenched by the medical model paradigm, one that focuses exclusively on the individual and treating his or her impairments. This represents a pathological orientation to diagnosis and treatment described earlier, and is perhaps no better evident than our reliance on the *Diagnostic and Statistical Manual of Mental Disorders* (5th ed., *DSM-5*, American Psychiatric Association, 2013). However, to truly consider a holistic approach toward working with people with disabilities, we must consider the 81-year-old writings of Lewin (1936) concerning the person–environment interaction discussed in Chapter 5. Specifically, our behavior is a function of our individual traits and characteristics in response to our interactions with our environment ($B = f[P \times E]$). Numerous empirical studies have shown that regardless of how strong a character someone has, with a perceived discriminatory social environment, the individual's physical and mental health may be negatively affected (Dohrenwend, 2000; Gee, 2002; Li & Moore, 1998; Ramsey & Marini, 2016; Rumbaut, 1994; Williams & Williams-Morris, 2000).

The Social Justice Counselor

The paradigm shift in how we work with clients must extend beyond simply working with them and their families, to ultimately exploring what, if any, societal and environmental barriers may likely block their goals (Neville & Mobley, 2001). It has been suggested that social advocacy is the "fifth force" within the counseling profession, essentially an extension and complement to the multicultural movement (Ratts, D'Andrea, & Arredondo, 2004, p. 28). The ecological approach to counseling acknowledges the impact that an unfriendly environment can have on the well-being of clients (Wilson, 2003). Ivey and Ivey (1998) describe the Developmental Counseling and Therapy model, noting how external stressors can impact intrapsychic changes in clients. The authors cite the progression and reciprocal effect of these interactions, including (a) environmental or biological insult, which may lead to; (b) stress and physical/emotional pain, which may lead to; (c) sadness/depression, which may lead to; (d) defense against the pain, possibly mental disorders.

In providing a holistic approach to helping clients with disabilities, counselors must be willing to not only acknowledge social injustice exists but also willing to go the extra mile to do something about it. As the Division for Counselors of Social Justice web page indicates, "Social justice counseling includes empowerment of the individual as well as active confrontation of injustice and inequality in society as they impact clientele as well as those in their systemic contexts." In defining exactly what "active confrontation of injustice and a quality in society" means, counselors must be aware of what their job's contractual limitations are, if any, regarding Congressional letter writing, advocacy, peaceful protests, and other legal remedies to confront injustice and inequality. The ACA has been quite effective over the years in rallying its 43,000 plus constituents by providing them with legislative alerts, synopsis of relevant legislative bills being introduced for passage, who their congressional leaders are, and sample letters for counselors to use as a template. The ACA Advocacy Competencies (Lewis, Arnold, House, & Toporek, 2003) concerning social justice advocacy in counseling recognizes the ecological model; oppression and discrimination are socially constructed and have a damaging physical and mental health impact on individuals who are functioning within a toxic reciprocal person–environment atmosphere (Bronfenbrenner, 1977; Wilson, 2003).

Several recent school counselor education publications have addressed active steps in preparing counselors for social justice (Bemak & Chung, 2008; Steele, 2008). Bemak and Chung (2008), for example, describe ACA advocacy competencies in relation to promoting systems advocacy, student empowerment, identifying specific advocacy strategies to communicate to colleagues, and stressing the need to further disseminate information to other constituents. These competencies emphasize strength in numbers and group action in promoting equality in educational funding, adequate resources, and a safe learning environment. To passively sit back and counsel students in a dysfunctional or antiquated learning environment is inadequate. The authors cite potential counselor concerns as to why they may not want to become involved in remedying social injustice problems. Some obstacles include general apathy, being labeled as a troublemaker, fear of retribution, a sense of powerlessness, and anxiety that can lead to guilt for not advocating. Bemak and Chung offer recommendations to assist counselors; for example, aligning social justice advocacy with organizational mission and goals, using data-driven strategies, having the courage to speak out, taking calculated risks, recruiting colleagues and others in the cause, developing political partners, becoming politically knowledgeable, and keeping faith (Bemak & Chung, 2008, pp. 379–380).

In considering social justice regarding persons with disabilities, counselors and case managers can influence a number of possible inequities in health care, education, housing, and employment. Persons with disabilities and especially those of minority status are statistically the most disenfranchised population in the United States (National Organization on Disability, 2004). Counselors have to acknowledge environmental inequities as well as the implications that oppression and discrimination can have on clients who can succumb to and give up trying (Dempsey, 1994; Dohrenwend, 2000; Gee, 2002). Thesen (2005) discusses how he and other physicians often knowingly or unknowingly treat patients in a dehumanizing and oppressive manner. He indicates that this type of behavior is counterproductive to patient health and can leave them feeling powerless and without any control. Thesen calls for medical professionals to instead empower their patients by including them in the decision-making process, educating them, and acknowledging their concerns. Bham and Forchuk (2008) illustrated empirically Thesen's (2005) premise in their interview of 336 current and former psychiatric and/or physically disabled clients. Specifically, the authors found that patients with comorbid conditions of a psychiatric and physical disability perceived themselves to be more discriminated against and oppressed by health care professionals. This, in turn, positively correlated with psychiatric problem severity, self-rated general health, and poorer life satisfaction and well-being. Counselors should be prepared to step in and advocate for clients when they witness the negative attitudes of health care professionals.

In other life domains concerning clients with disabilities, counselors and case managers should be prepared to tackle social injustice issues that impede client progress in the social and vocational realm. Despite the 20-year-old ADA, environmental barriers still exist that have been shown to result in some persons with disabilities feeling frustrated, angry, socially anxious, and depressed at times (Charmaz, 1995; Di Tomasso & Spinner, 1997; Graf et al., 2009; Hopps, Pepin, Arseneau, Frechette, & Begin, 2001; Li & Moore, 1998; Marini et al., 2009). Counselors can assist clients in constructing letters to business owners demanding removal of access barriers, filing complaints with the Office of Civil Rights, referring clients to Client Assistance Programs (CAPs), and finding an ADA lawyer if necessary (Blackwell, Marini, & Chacon, 2001; Blankenship, 2005; Marini et al., 2009). There appears to be little doubt from numerous empirical studies showing negative or perceived hostile environmental conditions can, and do, have a negative impact on client well-being. For counselors to concern themselves just with assisting clients to deal with living in an able-bodied world, it is a job that is left unfinished or incomplete.

ADVOCACY

Social justice and advocacy are sometimes used interchangeably and are often considered synonymous concepts. The primary difference, however, is that social justice is a broader concept recognizing unequal power, unearned privilege, and oppression (Alston et al., 2006). Advocacy is more behavioral and action oriented, and is an activity that often involves actions to correct some social injustice. As such, several authors discuss social justice advocacy in relation to some perceived social inequity. O'Day and Goldstein (2005) interviewed 16 disability advocacy and research leaders regarding the top contemporary advocacy issues concerning persons with disabilities. Disability advocacy organizations, such as the Consortium of Citizens with Disabilities (CCD), Not Dead Yet (NDY), Americans with Disabilities for Attendant Programs Today (ADAPT), American Association of People with Disabilities (AAPD), and others, are involved with grassroots advocacy, ongoing events, rallies, and information dissemination regarding important legislative issues toward enhancing full inclusion of persons with disabilities. O'Day and Goldstein found the top 5 contemporary issues were affordable and accessible health care, employment, access to assistive technology, long-term care, and civil rights enforcement concerning Titles II and III (public services and public accommodations) of the ADA. Similar concerns have been reported elsewhere (Graf et al., 2009; Marini et al., 2009).

Advocacy can take several forms in terms of action. The simplest form of advocacy involves letter writing to local and state constituents in attempts to bring attention to some social inequity, such as accessible housing. Arguably, more extreme forms can involve peaceful protests, such as occupying lawmakers' offices and sometimes subsequent citations for trespassing. The group ADAPT has been relentless and fairly successful over the past several decades in promoting disability rights, with its successful start in the early 1980s fighting for public accessible transportation in major cities, including city buses, subways, and Greyhound bus lines. The group would organize; primarily the wheelchair users would block buses, chain themselves, and otherwise occupy legislators' offices to be heard. In time, the majority of their efforts were successful in bringing major change across America, where persons with physical disabilities were unable to use public transportation. During the past decade or so, ADAPT has focused its fight on community-based care, whereby persons who require assistance with activities of daily living do not have to live in a nursing home. Their motto is "free our people," arguing that more than two thirds of federal and state monies are successfully lobbied into nursing homes instead of the money following the person who chooses to live at home. For counselors and case managers who work for the state or federal government, the central question becomes whether this type of advocacy to support such causes has any job repercussions. If conducted on our own time, there generally is no adverse impact; however, counselors are encouraged to be familiar with their agency's workplace policies. Too often when we advocate, we do so for our own interests and to protect our jobs or territory and disguise it as client beneficence.

Ericksen (1997) indicates that advocacy is conceptually a cross between public policy, public relations, and conflict resolution. Lee (1998) defines advocacy as becoming the voice of the clients and taking action to make environmental changes that may impede barriers to a client's career, academic, personal, or social goals. Semivan and White (2006) noted that the skills needed for effective advocacy include passion, fact-finding, knowledge, data-based research, and goal-oriented concrete objectives. They must also know the limits of their professional roles and be able to separate highly charged emotions from their actions. Stewart, Gibson-Semivan, and Schwartz (2009) cited practical advocacy strategies to include (a) identifying the target population and the nature/facts of the injustice; (b) developing a rationale as to how advocacy will affect the advocate and target population chosen; (c) developing clearly and concisely how advocating will fit the therapist's role, and fits within the scope of practice or ethics for the counselor; (d) conducting research on the background and nature of the social injustice thoroughly, including speaking to individuals who have been affected by it; (e) developing a list of references and resources for dissemination; (f) outlining the broader and then individual measurable goals of the advocacy project and reviewing them regularly for refining if necessary; and (g) after selecting goals, determining what the first steps are and whose responsibility it is to carry out each activity (Stewart et al., 2009).

So how can rehabilitation educators, researchers, and counselors either directly or indirectly become better advocates for persons with disabilities? For educators, teaching students about relevant advocacy community services, such as CAPs, legal aid, guardianship, and services provided by Centers for Independent Living (CILs), becomes important in knowing about nonmedical services that can help in social injustice situations (Blankenship, 2005; Marini et al., 2009). In addition, educators can teach students about legislation pertaining to persons with disabilities, provide legislative alerts, and show students how to write to legislators on behalf of persons with disabilities. Two organizations that are extremely effective in providing information and education on these topics are the National Rehabilitation Association and the ACA. Educators can also have letter-writing campaigns for important legislation as part of a class grade, and/or attend or develop local information sessions about impending legislation. Overall, teaching students how to advocate effectively can then be passed on to teaching clients with disabilities once students graduate.

For rehabilitation education researchers, studying the impact of teaching and empowering persons with disabilities about how to advocate for themselves can minimize years of dependency on others who have traditionally made decisions for them (Brinckerhoff, 1994). Brinckerhoff noted how teaching adolescents affected by learning disability self-advocacy skills regarding effectively managing their college experience can be self-empowering and enhance self-esteem (Van Reusen & Bos, 1990). Research topics could include a control and experimental group design, provide the experimental group with tangible training skills to become more proficient at some self-advocacy task, and then measure the psychosocial impact of empower-ment, locus of control, and self-efficacy. Anecdotally, it would seem self-evident that individuals who are taught skills to become more proficient in mastering or control-ling parts of their environment would enhance client self-esteem and self-confidence.

Counselors working directly with persons with disabilities in a variety of settings and in a variety of ways can work with clients directly regarding advocacy and self-empowerment issues. Although many counselors have been empowering clients for years regarding job clubs, job search strategies, interview skills training, and so on, oth-ers may tend to "do for" rather than "do with" clients, which can be counterproductive. Brodwin, Star, and Cardoso (2007), for example, discuss the importance of including clients in selecting assistive technology or adaptive equipment, because without client input, many clients will not use or will discard the device. As noted with educators, counselors can refer clients to appropriate advocacy agencies, assist in writing letters of complaint or letters to congressional leaders, and teach assertiveness and advocacy skills in presenting their case.

CONCLUSIONS

In many ways, rehabilitation and other counselors have become somewhat desensitized to the unchanging 70% plus unemployment and underemployment rate among persons with disabilities (Houtenville, 2000, National Organization on Disability [NOD], 2004), alarmingly high dropout rates for students (NOD, 2004), higher poverty rates (Hughes & Avoke, 2010; McNeil, 2001), poorer and inadequate health care (Berk, Schur, & Cantor, 1995), social oppression and discrimination (Ratts et al., 2004), and ongoing physical access barriers for persons with disabilities (Graf et al., 2009; Marini et al., 2009). The Social Justice Counselor is a relatively new breed of counselor who actively advocates for change in the community and among policy makers when part of the client's issues has an environmental basis. Counselors in training should not only learn about how to assist clients with disabilities with coping skills to live in an able-bodied world but also empower and actively assist clients to combat social injustice and oppression in their lives.

REFERENCES

Aguinaldo, J. P. (2008). The social construction of gay oppression as a determinant of gay men's health: "Homophobia is killing us." *Critical Public Health, 18*(1), 87–96.

Alston, R. J., Harley, D. A., & Middleton, R. (2006). The role of rehabilitation in achieving social justice for minorities with disabilities. *Journal of Vocational Rehabilitation, 24,* 129–136.

American Counseling Association. (2014). Code of ethics. Retrieved from http://www.counseling.org/docs/default-source/ethics/2014-aca-code-of-ethics.pdf?sfvrsn=fde89426_5

American Psychiatric Association. (2013). *Diagnostic and statistical manual of mental disorders* (5th ed.). Arlington, VA: American Psychiatric Publishing.

Annual Disability Statistics Compendium. (2014). Poverty in the US. Retrieved from https://disability compendium.org/sites/default/files/user-uploads/Archives/PreviousDisabilityCompendium Releases/2014%20Compendium%20Release.pdf

Balfanz, R., & Legters, N. E. (2004). Locating the dropout crisis: Which high schools produce the nation's dropouts? In G. Orfield (Ed.), *Dropouts in America: Confronting the graduation crisis* (pp. 57–84). Cambridge, MA: Harvard Education Press.

Bemak, F., & Chung, R. C. (2008). New professional roles and advocacy strategies for school coun-selors: A multicultural/social justice perspective to move beyond the nice counselor syndrome. *Journal of Counseling & Development, 86,* 372–382.

Berk, M. L., Schur, C. L., & Cantor, J. C. (1995). Ability to obtain health care: Recent estimates from the Robert Wood Johnson Foundation National Access to Care Survey. *Health Affairs, 14*(3), 139–146.

Bham, A., & Forchuk, C. (2008). Interlocking oppressions: The effect of a comorbid physical disability on perceived stigma and discrimination among mental health consumers in Canada. *Health & Social Care in the Community, 17*(1), 63–70.

Blackwell, T. M., Marini, I., & Chacon, M. (2001). The impact of the Americans with Disabilities Act on independent living. *Rehabilitation Education, 15*(4), 395–408.

Blankenship, C. J. (2005). Client assistance programs and protection and advocacy services. In W. Crimando & T. F. Riggar (Eds.), *Community resources: A guide for human service workers* (pp. 218–224). Long Grove, IL: Waveland Press.

Bloch, J. (2013). Hopkins conference tackles link between wealth and health. *BaltimoreBrew.* Retrieved from https://www.baltimorebrew.com/2013/04/24/hopkins-conference-tackles-link-between-wealth-and-health

Braddock, D., & Parish, S. (2001). An institutional history of disability. In G. Albrecht, K. Seelman, & M. Bury (Eds.), *Handbook of disability studies* (pp. 11–68). Thousand Oaks, CA: Sage.

Brault, M. W. (2012). *Americans with disabilities: 2010. Current Population Reports*, P70-131. Washington, DC: U.S. Census Bureau.

Brinckerhoff, L. C. (1994). Developing effective self-advocacy skills in college-bound students with learning disabilities. *Intervention in School & Clinic, 29*(4), 229.

Brodwin, M. G., Star, T., & Cardoso, E. (2007). Users of assistive technology. In A. E. Dell Orto & P. W. Power (Eds.), *The psychological and social impact of illness and disability* (pp. 505–519). New York, NY: Springer Publishing.

Bronfenbrenner, U. (1977). Toward an experimental ecology of human development. *American Psychologist, 32,* 513–531.

Charmaz, N. (1995). The body, identity, and self: Adapting to impairment. *Sociological Quarterly, 36,* 657–680.

Cooper, E., Korman, H., O'Hara, A., & Zovistoski, A. (2009). *Priced out in 2008: The housing crisis for people with disabilities.* Boston, MA: Technical Assistance Collaborative. Retrieved from http://www.tacinc.org

Counselors for Social Justice, American Counseling Association. (n.d.). What is social justice in counseling. Retrieved from https://counseling-csj.org

Current Population Survey. (2015). Income, poverty and health insurance coverage in the United States. Retrieved from https://www.census.gov/newsroom/press-releases/2015/cb15-157.html

David, E. J. R. (2014). *Internalized oppression: The psychology of marginalized groups.* New York, NY: Springer Publishing.

Dempsey, C. L. (1994). Health and social issues of gay, lesbian, and bisexual adolescents. *Families in Society: The Journal of Contemporary Human Services, 75*(3), 160–167.

Di Tomasso, E., & Spinner, B. (1997). Social and emotional loneliness: A re-examination of Weiss' typology of loneliness. *Personality and Individual Differences, 22,* 417–427.

Dohrenwend, B. P. (2000). The role of adversity and stress in psychopathology: Some evidence and its implications for theory and research. *Journal of Health and Social Behavior, 41*(1), 1–19.

Eaton, W. W., & Muntaner, C. (1999). Socioeconomic stratification and mental disorder. In A. V. Horwitz & T. L. Scheid (Eds.), *A handbook for the study of mental health: Social contexts, theories, and systems* (pp. 259–283). New York, NY: Cambridge University Press.

Ericksen, K. (1997). *Making an impact: A handbook on counselor advocacy.* Washington, DC: Taylor & Francis/Accelerated Development.

Fox, D. D., & Marini, I. (2012). History of treatment toward persons with disabilities in America. In I. Marini & M. Stebnicki (Eds.), *The psychological and social impact of illness and disability* (pp. 3–12). New York, NY: Springer Publishing.

Fremstad, S. (2009). *Half in ten: Why taking disability into account is essential to reducing poverty and expanding economic unclusion.* Washington, DC: Center for Economic and Policy Research. Retrieved from http://www.cepr.net/documents/publiclications/poverty-disability-2009-09.pdf

Gee, G. C. (2002). A multilevel analysis of the relationship between institutional racial discrimination and health status. *American Journal of Public Health, 5,* 109–117.

Graf, N. M., Marini, I., & Blankenship, C. (2009). 100 words about disability. *Journal of Rehabilitation, 75*(2), 25–34.

Greenleaf, A. T., & Williams, J. M. (2009). Supporting social justice advocacy: A paradigm shift towards an ecological perspective. *Journal for Social Action in Counseling and Psychology, 2*(1), 1–12.

Greenwald, G. (2011). *With liberty and justice for some: How the law is used to destroy equality and protect the powerful.* New York, NY: Metropolitan Books.

Hancock, A. M. (2004). *The politics of disgust: The public identity of the welfare queen*. New York: New York University Press.

Hopps, S., Pepin, M., Arseneau, I., Frechette, M., & Begin, G. (2001). Disability related variables associated with loneliness among people with disabilities. *Journal of Rehabilitation, 67*(3), 42–48.

Houtenville, A. (2000). *Economics of disability research report #2: Estimates of employment rates for persons with disabilities in the United States by state, 1980 through 1998*. Ithaca, NY: Cornell University, Research and Rehabilitation Training Center for Economic Research on Employment Policy for Persons with Disabilities.

Huffington, A. (2003). *Pigs at the trough: How corporate greed and political corruption are undermining America*. New York, NY; Crown Publishers.

Huffington, A. (2010). *Third world America: How our politicians are abandoning the middle class and betraying the American dream*. New York, NY: Crown.

Hughes, C., & Avoke, S. (2010). The elephant in the room: Poverty, disability, and employment. *Research & Practice for Persons With Severe Disabilities, 35*(1–2), 5–14.

Ivey, A. E., & Ivey, M. B. (1998). Reframing *DSM-IV*: Positive strategies from developmental counseling and therapy. *Journal of Counseling and Development, 76*, 334–350.

Johnston, J. E., Werder, E., & Sebastian, D. (2016). Wastewater disposal wells, fracking, and environmental injustice in Southern Texas. *American Journal of Public Health, 106*(3), 550–556.

Jyoti, D. F., Frongillo, E. A., & Jones, S. J. (2005). Food insecurity affects school children's academic performance, weight gain, and social skills. *Journal of Nutrition, 135*(12), 2831–2839.

Kessler, R. C., Berglund, P., Demler, O., Jin, R., Koretz, D., Merikangas, K. R., . . . Wang, P. S.; National Comorbidity Survey Replication. (2003). The epidemiology of major depressive disorder: Results from the National Comorbidity Survey Replication (NCS-R). *Journal of the American Medical Association, 289*(23), 3095–3105.

Krieger, N. (1999). A review of concepts, measures, and methods for studying health consequences of discrimination. *Journal of Health Services, 29*, 295–352.

Lee, C. C. (1998). Counselors as agents for social change. In C. C. Lee & G. R. Walz (Eds.), *Social action: A mandate for counselors* (pp. 3–16). Alexandria, VA: American Counseling Association.

Lewin, K. (1936). *Principles of topological psychology*. New York, NY: McGraw-Hill.

Lewis, J., Arnold, M. S., House, R., & Toporek, R. (2003). *ACA advocacy competencies*. Retrieved from http://www.counseling.org/Publications

Li, L., & Moore, D. (1998). Acceptance of disability and its correlates. *Journal of Social Psychology, 138*(1), 13–25.

Liu, W. M. (2011). *Social class and classism in the helping professions: Research, theory, and practice*. Thousand Oaks, CA: Sage.

Ludden, J. (2016). Baltimore struggles to protect children from lead paint. *National Public Radio* aired on March 21, 2016. Retrieved from http://www.npr.org/2016/03/21/471267759/baltimore-struggles-to-protect-children-from-lead-paint

Lynch, M. G., & Stretesky, P. B. (2012). Native Americans in social and environmental justice: Implications for criminology. *Social Justice, 38*(3), 104–124.

Mahar, M. (2006). *Money-driven medicine: The real reason health care costs so much*. New York, NY: Collins.

Marini, I. (2012a). The psychosocial world of the injured worker. In I. Marini, N. Graf, & M. Millington (Eds.), *Psychosocial aspects of disability: Insider perspectives and counseling strategies* (pp. 235–256). New York, NY: Springer Publishing.

Marini, I. (2012b). What we counsel, teach, and research regarding the needs of persons with disabilities: What have we been missing. In I. Marini, N. Graf, & M. Millington (Eds.), *Psychosocial aspects of disability: Insider perspectives and counseling strategies* (pp. 481–498). New York, NY: Springer Publishing.

Marini, I., Bhakta, M. V., & Graf, N. (2009). A content analysis of common concerns of persons with physical disabilities. *Journal of Applied Rehabilitation Counseling, 40*(1), 44–49.

Marini, I., & Reid, C. R. (2001). A survey of rehabilitation professionals as alternative provider contractors with Social Security: Problems and solutions. *Journal of Rehabilitation, 67*(2), 36–41.

Marini, I., & Stebnicki, M. (1999). Social Security's alternative provider program: What can rehabilitation administrators expect. *Journal of Rehabilitation Administration, 23*(1), 31–41.

Marini, I., & Stebnicki, M. A. (2012). *The psychological and social impact of illness and physical disability* (6th ed.). New York, NY: Springer Publishing.

McNeil, J. (2001). *Americans with disabilities 1997. Current population reports* (pp. 70–73). Washington, DC: U.S. Census Bureau.

Nam, Y., Huang, J., Heflin C., & Sherraden, M. (2012). *Racial and ethnic disparities in food insufficiency: Evidence from a statewide probability sample of White, African American, American Indian, and Hispanic infants.* St. Louis, MO: Center for Social Development, Washington University.

National Organization on Disability. (2004, June 24). *Landmark survey finds pervasive disadvantages* [press release]. Washington, DC: Author.

National Organization on Disability. (2010). *Kessler Foundation/NOD2010 Survey of Americans with Disabilities.* Washington, DC: Author. Retrieved from http://www.2010disablitysurveys.org/pdfs/surveyresults.pdf

Neville, H. A., & Mobley, M. (2001). Social identities in contexts: An ecological model of multicultural counseling psychology processes. *Counseling Psychologist, 29,* 471–486.

Newman, L., Wagner, M., Cameto, R., & Knokey, A. M. (2009). *The post-high school outcomes of youth with disabilities up to 4 years after high school. A report of findings from the National Longitudinal Transition Study-2 (NLTS2).* Menlo Park, CA: SRI International. Retrieved from https://www.nlts2-org/reports/2009_04/nlts2_report_2009_04_complete.pdf

O'Day, B., & Goldstein, M. (2005). Advocacy issues and strategies for the 21st century. *Journal of Disability Policy Studies, 15*(4), 240–250.

Ouellette, T., Burstein, N., Long, D., & Beecroft, E. (2004). *Measures of material hardship.* Final Report. Washington, DC: U.S. Department of Health and Human Services.

Parish, S. L., Rose, R. A., & Andrews, M. E. (2010). Income poverty and material hardship among U.S. women with disabilities. *Social Service Review, 83,* 33–52.

Perlow, H. M., Danoff-Burg, S., Swenson, R. R., & Pulgiano, D. (2004). The impact of ecological risk and perceived discrimination on the psychological adjustment of African American and European youth. *Journal of Community Psychology, 32,* 375–389.

Ramsey, W., & Marini, I. (2016). Social justice and counseling the oppressed. In I. Marini & M. Stebnicki (Eds.), *The psychological and social impact of illness and disability* (pp. 585–591). New York, NY: Springer Publishing.

Ratts, M., D'Andrea, M., & Arredondo, P. (2004). *Social justice counseling: "Fifth force" in field.* Retrieved from http://www.counseling.org/content/NavigationMenu/Publications/Counselingtodayonline/July2004/SocialJusticeCounsel.htm

Rice, M. F., & Jones, W. (1991). The uninsured and patient dumping: Recent policy responses in indigent care. *Journal of the National Medical Association, 83*(10), 874–880.

Romero, M. G., & Marini, I. (2012). Obesity as a disability: Medical, psychosocial, and vocational implications. In I. Marini & M. Stebnicki (Eds.), *The psychological and social impact of illness and disability* (pp. 435–447). New York, NY: Springer Publishing.

Rose, M., & Baumgartner, F. R. (2013). Framing the poor: Media coverage and U.S. poverty policy, 1960–2008. *Policy Studies Journal, 41*(1), 22–48.

Rumbaut, R. (1994). The crucible within: Ethnic identity, self-esteem, and segmented assimilation among children of immigrants. *International Migration Review, 28,* 748–794.

Semivan, S. G., & White, M. A. (2006). *Advocacy: The key to a counselor's success.* Poster session presented at annual American Counseling Association Conference, Montreal, QB, Canada.

Smiley, T., & West, C, (2012). *The rich and the rest of us: A poverty manifesto.* New York, NY: Smileybooks.

Steele, J. M. (2008). Counselor preparation: Preparing counselors to advocate for social justice: A liberation model. *Counselor Education & Supervision, 48,* 74–85.

Stewart, T. A., Gibson-Semivan, S., & Schwartz, R. C. (2009). The art of advocacy: Strategies for psychotherapists. *Annuals of the American Psychotherapy Association, 12*(2), 54–59.

Stiglitz, J. E. (2013). *The price of any quality: How today's divided society endangers our future.* New York, NY: W. W. Norton.

Thesen, J. (2005). From oppression towards empowerment in clinical practice–offering doctors a model for reflection1. *Scandinavian Journal of Public Health, 66,* 47–52.

Turner, R. J., & Avison, W. R. (2003). Status variations in stress exposure: Implications for the interpretation of research on race, socioeconomic status, and gender. *Journal of Health and Social Behavior, 44*(4), 488–505.

U.S. Department of Education. (2009). *28th Annual report to Congress on the implementation of the Individuals with Disabilities Education Act, 2006.* Washington, DC: Author.

U.S. Department of Health and Human Services. (2014). 2014 Poverty guidelines. Retrieved from http://aspe.hhs.gov/poverty/14poverty.cfm

U.S. Equal Employment Opportunity Commission. (n.d.). Disability discrimination. Retrieved from https://www.eeoc.gov/laws/types/disability.cfm

Van Reusen, A., & Bos, C. (1990). I plan: Helping students communicate in-planning conferences. *Teaching Exceptional Children, 22*(4), 30–32.

Warren, E. (2014). *A fighting chance.* New York, NY: Metropolitan Books.

Wehman, P., & Kregel, J. (1997). *Functional curriculum for elementary, middle, and secondary age students with special needs.* Austin, TX: PRO-ED.

Whitaker, R. C., Phillips, S. M., & Orzol, S. M. (2006). Food insecurity and the risks of depression and anxiety in mothers and behavior problems in their preschool-aged children. *Pediatrics, 118*(3), e859–e868.

Williams, D. R., & Williams-Morris, R. (2000). Racism and mental health: The African American experience. *Ethnicity & Health, 5*(3–4), 243–268.

Williams, D. R., Yan Yu, Jackson, J. S., & Anderson, N. B. (1997). Racial differences in physical and mental health: Socio-economic status, stress and discrimination. *Journal of Health Psychology, 2*(3), 335–351.

Wilson, F. R. (2003). *What is ecological psychotherapy?* [Electronic Version], pp. 1–3. Retrieved from http:// ecologicalcounseling.org/wilsonart2,html

Wright, B. A. (1988). Attitudes and the fundamental negative bias: Conditions and corrections. In H. E. Yuker (Ed.), *Attitudes towards persons with disabilities* (pp. 3–21). New York, NY: Springer Publishing.

30

Reflections and Considerations

Part A: Reflections on the View From Here

Irmo Marini

*J*ust over 30 years ago in the Northern Ontario city of Thunder Bay, I was in the middle of a game as a Lakehead University varsity hockey player. During the last minute of the second period, I was tripped and collided headfirst into the end boards, fracturing my neck at the C5 to C6 vertebral level. In the blink of an eye, I went from an all-around athlete, 13-year bodybuilder, to an almost totally dependent wheelchair user. The almost 11 months of hospitalization and rehabilitation began a long journey back mentally, physically, and philosophically. I emerged back into a world that I was now viewing differently from a seated position and realized some people were viewing me differently, too, with pity, curiosity, and sympathy. I needed to somehow make them see me as I was before—strong, independent, witty, disciplined, and emotionally stable. After all, I was still the same guy. For me, being paralyzed from the chest down now meant I had to reinvent myself from athlete to intellectual using my brain instead of my brawn.

Many of the chapters in this book are a reflection of not only some of my personal experiences but also the common lived experiences of others with various disabilities. Throughout this text, we have explored a variety of psychosocial issues related to chronic illness and disability. However, if this was all the book was about, it would be fairly straightforward and discipline-specific for rehabilitation counseling and related professionals. But unlike most of the social sciences, the complexities of human behavior, as we have discussed, are often reciprocally interdependent on societal attitudes, environmental access or barriers, and social justice.

In Chapter 1, Fox and Marini discussed the legal and blatant discrimination and exclusion of Americans with disabilities concerning the 1924 Immigration Act, involuntary sterilization, and forbidding some with disabilities to legally marry. The ramifications of social Darwinism regarding natural selection and the 20th-century mantra "survival of the fittest" have morphed into something else in 21st-century America. It has become increasingly apparent that we are in an era of "survival of the financially fittest." The social injustice inflicted on people with disabilities, especially minorities with disabilities who are uneducated and poor, is subconsciously and undeniably ingrained in American social behavior. Although America strives for an egalitarian society ideal,

Liu (2011) cites a plethora of literature painting a very different picture on the negative impact of social classism.

In Liu's book titled *Social Class and Classism in the Helping Professions*, he cites numerous studies exploring the discriminatory and deleterious impact of classism and oppression. Although rags-to-riches stories are often inspiring, the statistical reality of such instances is rare. For most people growing up in poverty, an often perpetuated and generational lineage occurs for numerous complex reasons, both individual and socio-structural. In other words, as we discussed in Chapter 7 and the concept of somatopsy-chology, the interrelationship between individual factors (e.g., intelligence, motivation, and resilience) and an individual's environment (e.g., societal attitudes, availability of health care, physical access, and family support and income) dictate potential success-ful adaptation or conversely succumb to one's circumstances. Liu argues that the fallout from classism and oppression stacks the deck against individuals and their children from ever climbing the social status ladder.

People with disabilities who are female and part of a minority represent the most disenfranchised population in America, but millions of other disabled and/or minorities face a number of sociostructural barriers that can overwhelm even the most resilient of individuals. The cascading cycle of poverty, poor education, poor health care, and poor living conditions exacerbates social injustice and "haves versus have nots." This vicious cycle of low income can be traced to the need to purchase less expensive, often more fat-laden food, which can lead to obesity, subsequent poor health, and disability (e.g., type 2 diabetes), as well as sporadic employment. This stressful toll negatively impacts mental health and is often correlated with depression and anxiety (Garland et al., 2005; Marini, 2011; Minkler, Fuller-Thomson, & Guralnik, 2006; Schaefer-McDaniel, 2009). The less control individuals feel they have over their circumstances, the greater the feelings of hopelessness, learned helplessness, and psychological distress (Evans, 2004, 2006).

The growing economic and class disparity in America is unquestionably reaching a tipping point as it did during the Great Depression (Huffington, 2010; Reich, 2010). Where will this leave people with disabilities and their families who are already living statistically at the lower end of the spectrum? Will the United States ever adopt universal health care as so many countries already have, or will corporatism, capitalism, and the "I am not my brother's keeper" mentality continue to force everyone to go down with the ship? Survival of the financially fittest will become meaningless if citizens revolt against the system as they have in other countries where all civility comes to a halt. With a Trump presidency and the Republicans in power, there have been daily demonstra-tions across the country in some parts of the world against his initial exclusive policies. So how do rehabilitation counselors, educators, and related helping professionals even begin to address these seemingly insurmountable and arguably uncontrollable events? Are any of us even motivated to try?

SMALL STEPS AND THE POWER OF ALTRUISM

There needs to be a quantum shift in how we perceive the scope of our jobs, our ethical and moral responsibilities to our clients and ourselves, and the motivation to want to get out from behind our desks and do more. To pretend to ignore or simply remain igno-rant of the changing realities conveys a laissez-faire attitude and/or violates the ethical principle of beneficence if we know we can do more for our clients but choose not to. As I point out in Chapter 29 on social justice, depression, and disability, we simply need to do more for those most in need.

Short of giving one's time to counsel individuals following such traumatic events, counselors and related professionals can also volunteer their time at the local level, assisting those in need by collecting for food banks, educational tutoring, clothing drives, Habitat for Humanity, and so on. Offering free counseling services, which are generally offered at many nondenominational churches, is another excellent way of helping others during troubled times. Various fund-raising activities by the local Masons, Centers for Independent Living, Easter Seals, March of Dimes, and other organizations are also frequently occurring.

At a more professional level, counselors can assist clients with disabilities by writing letters of complaint to businesses that are still not physically accessible to all. Teaching clients how to advocate for themselves and the fact that they have the power to implement change can be very empowering (Graf, Marini, & Blankenship, 2009; Marini, Bhakta, & Graf, 2009). Clients can also be referred to Client Assistance Programs, which have the legal expertise in filing formal complaints with the Office of Civil Rights and filing lawsuits when needed. It is unfortunate that 27 years after the passage of the Americans with Disabilities Act, such lawsuits must still be pursued as observed by the thousands of ongoing new suits filed each year (Blackwell, Marini, & Chacon, 2001).

I do not believe we can any longer afford to ignore the plight of those in need, not only because of the embarrassment it conveys about us as a society but also because of the social and economic ramifications of a morally and financially bankrupt society. Americans have been known to rise with great resilience and compassion at critical junctures of their history. As rehabilitation professionals, we must do our part to see the larger picture, to know the global and cultural issues, and to be more than just what our job description reads. Our piece of the puzzle is to assist people with disabilities, empower them, and educate society and advocate for social justice. Seligman (2002) in his book *Authentic Happiness* indicates that we can only be truly happy by giving and caring for others. The power of altruism is a reciprocal reward both to ourselves and to the recipients. Ultimately, when we are helping others, we are helping ourselves.

REFERENCES

Blackwell, T. M., Marini, I., & Chacon, M. (2001). The impact of the Americans with Disabilities Act on independent living. *Rehabilitation Education, 15*(4), 395–408.

Evans, G. W. (2004). The environment of childhood poverty. *American Psychologist, 59*(2), 77–92.

Evans, G. W. (2006). Child development and the physical environment. *Annual Review of Psychology, 57*, 423–451.

Garland, A. F., Lau, A. S., Yeh, M., McCabe, K. M., Hough, R. L., & Landsverk, J. A. (2005). Racial and ethnic differences in utilization of mental health services among high-risk youths. *American Journal of Psychiatry, 162*(7), 1336–1343.

Graf, N. M., Marini, I., & Blankenship, C. (2009). 100 words about disability. *Journal of Rehabilitation, 75*(2), 25–34.

Huffington, A. (2010). *Third world America: How our politicians are abandoning the middle class and betraying the American dream*. New York, NY: Crown.

Liu, W. M. (2011). *Social class and classism in the helping professions: Research, theory, and practice*. Thousand Oaks, CA: Sage.

Marini, I. (2011). The history of treatment toward persons with disabilities. In I. Marini, N. M. Graf, & M. J. Millington (Eds.), *Psychosocial aspects of disability: Insider perspectives and counseling strategies* (pp. 1–46). New York, NY: Springer Publishing.

Marini, I., Bhakta, M. V., & Graf, N. (2009). A content analysis of common concerns of persons with physical disabilities. *Journal of Applied Rehabilitation Counseling, 40*(1), 44–49.

Minkler, M., Fuller-Thomson, E., & Guralnik, J. M. (2006). Gradient of disability across the socioeconomic spectrum in the United States. *New England Journal of Medicine, 355*(7), 695–703.

Reich, R. B. (2010). *After shock: The next economy and America's future.* New York, NY: Alfred A. Knopf.

Schaefer-McDaniel, N. (2009). Neighborhood stressors, perceived neighborhood quality, and child mental health in New York City. *Health & Place, 15*(1), 148–155.

Seligman, M. E. (2002). *Authentic happiness: Using the new positive psychology to realize your potential for lasting fulfillment.* New York, NY: Free Press.

Part B: Reflections

MARK A. STEBNICKI

MY PERSONAL JOURNEY INTO THE HELPING PROFESSION

I started my career at a community rehabilitation center (sheltered workshop) around 1979 in Murphysboro, Illinois, a small rural town in southern Illinois close to the border of Kentucky and Missouri. Besides doing work adjustment training, job placement activities, and job coaching with these clients, I also drove the bus to pick them up for work in the morning and dropped them off at the end of the day. I really got to know their family members and the psychosocial challenges of individuals with mental and physical disabilities living in rural America. This was my introduction to working with people who had a variety of medical, physical, developmental, neurocognitive, psychiatric, and chronic health conditions that were disabling. I remembered this as a very rewarding opportunity that helped launch my career, which has spanned more than 30 years. Metaphorically, driving the "short bus" placed me in the position of leadership, guiding people to find their way through work, education, and career opportunities, and then independent or supported living arrangements. In my consciousness, I never really left this small rural community because it reflected who I was and how it taught me some important life lessons from "salt-of-the-earth" people with humble beginnings. I could relate with this group of individuals.

Since then, my professional journey took me to live in four different states and work in a variety of settings with a diverse range of individuals. I have worked in vocational rehabilitation; mental health and substance abuse treatment settings in state, county-operated, and private practices; client advocacy and case-management; neuro-rehabilitation and traumatic brain injury (TBI) units; and residential psychiatric, substance abuse, and rehabilitation facilities; as well as engaging in teaching, research, and service activities at two different universities. The chapters presented in this text indeed are an accurate depiction of researchers and practitioners who have worked their careers in attempts to improve the quality of lives for persons with chronic illnesses and disabilities. I am proud to be part of such a project where so many authors have provided qualitative and quantitative depictions of working in one-on-one relationships with the psychological, social, emotional, spiritual, vocational, independent living, and disability rights aspects that challenge people with disabilities on a day-to-day basis.

HISTORICAL SIGNIFICANCE

Historically, the care, treatment, and attitudes toward people with physical and psychiatric disabilities in America have not been healthy or empowering. In fact, since the 1960s, circumstances within this unique cultural group have stayed somewhat the same despite attempts in trying to achieve optimal levels of independent living, accessible transportation, accessibility in public places, jobs and career opportunities, and overall integration into American society. For many Americans, the attitudes and perceptions toward persons with disabilities have not changed, especially when you have leaders in high government positions that mock and portray people with disabilities as a "drain on society." As the text points out, there are many factors that are transparent examples of how many agencies, organizations, and government policies hinder opportunities for persons with disabilities. They are intentionally perpetrated by a range of sociopolitical resistance, social and civil justice challenges, and multiple other factors that hinder the ability to achieve a "level-playing-field" to compete for jobs, educational opportunities, health care, and overall integration and participation in life.

Historically, there are within-group differences in how this culture of "people with disabilities" wants to be viewed. From a multicultural perspective, the person himself or herself chooses a cultural identity because of his or her own unique cultural experiences, characteristics, attributes, needs, and motivations. Indeed, living with a disability requires ongoing support and resources to achieve optimum levels of psychosocial adjustment and adaptation. In reality, one cannot "get closure" with a life-altering event that affects one's medical, physical, cognitive, mental, emotional, psychological, social, spiritual, career/vocational, environmental health, and independent living needs.

A PIVOTAL SHIFT IN THE HELPING PROFESSION

Over the last 20 years or so, there is evidence of a pivotal shift among the helping professions. The two counselor accreditation bodies in the United States, the Congress of Racial Equality (CORE) and Council for Accreditation of Counseling and Related Educational Programs (CACREP), have merged into one counseling organization (CACREP) with one set of accreditation standards. This shift is perhaps motivated by individuals, groups, professional associations, and accrediting bodies that call for restrictions in the eligibility, licensure, ability to collect third-party payment, and other practice restrictions on professional counselors such as licensed professional counselors (LPCs). The same restrictions do not apply for clinical social workers and psychologists in settings such as the Veterans Administration (VA), the Tricare military health insurance program, and Medicare provider status. Consequently, the counseling profession itself, particularly rehabilitation counselors, do not have a level playing field by which to serve persons with disabilities. The political rhetoric and campaign of disinformation becomes translated into a common core language of "who is a qualified provider" to treat persons with mental and physical disabilities. Although on the surface these well-lobbied disciplines appear to have the client's best interests in mind, in actuality it has always been a turf war of who gets a larger piece of the counseling pie dollars.

One example of this pivotal shift that has isolated a segment of the counseling profession is the RAND Corporation's study (RAND Corporation, 2014) of community-based providers' cultural competence for providing mental health services to military populations. The RAND Corporation indicated that only 24% of therapists participating in the Tricare military-based health insurance program meet the criteria for cultural competence in providing military mental health services. Additionally, this study notes that LPCs, many from a rehabilitation counseling background, have the highest quality of services and training in evidence-based practices to serve the mental health needs of military populations. Yet, the VA and many military bases hire clinical social workers or psychologists as the primary preferred provider. Many LPCs are not accepted on the Tricare insurance panel and are unable to work on military installations or for the VA system without being a clinical social worker or psychologist. More recent, LPCs must be graduates of CACREP-accredited programs and pass the Certified Clinical Mental

Health Counselor (CCMHC) exam to provide services. The CCMHC credential alone does not prepare LPCs to work with military cultures. Rather, its original intention was to diagnose and treat mental health disorders in the general community-based nonmilitary mental health sector. Thus, it is anticipated that there will be fewer service providers to take care of the mental health needs of active duty personnel, veterans, veterans with disabilities, and family members because of this exclusionary policy. This is just one of many examples of the changing professional environment and political landscape that intentionally isolates professional helpers from important services that can be offered, particularly to service personnel and veterans with disabilities. The harmful effects of limiting eligibility are that service personnel and veterans have limited choices to deal with a complexity of medical/physical and co-occurring mental health conditions.

The list of challenges grows every year. Extraordinary times require extraordinary efforts. It requires our full attention to advocate best practices and the most qualified providers to serve persons with disabilities. The federal/state programs and policy development of health care related to serving people with disabilities rarely seeks input from individuals receiving such services. In addition, the policy makers, boards, and other organizations seldom have persons with a disability represented as decision makers. As many have found in their careers, if you do not have a seat at the table of the core decision makers, then the voices are not heard. Perhaps it is time to look back into the history of our respected leaders, organizers, and advocates that helped form the counseling profession and turn our attention to the people we serve and what is in *their best interest.*

THE FUTURE OF PSYCHOSOCIAL REHABILITATION

The future of the counseling profession requires individuals, groups, organizations, associations, and public and private sector health care entities to listen to the people they serve with an empathic heart. As this text documents, many individuals who have struggled with and transcended issues of addiction, chronic illness, life-threatening disease, disability, and other extraordinary stressful and traumatic events have cultivated a personal wisdom so they could achieve optimal wellness and balance. We need to be mindful of how these challenges were transcended and be intentional in our efforts to serve individuals based on their own cultural belief system about healing (Stebnicki, 2016). Despite our professional training and background in providing evidence-based practices in a formal treatment setting, our client's cultural wisdom can tell us many things about healing the mind, body, and spirit. There is evidence that many persons with disabilities have healed with minimal assistance from a professional counselor. Some have followed Dr. Andrew Weil's advice in his book *Spontaneous Healing* (Weil, 1995) as they have taken control of their own illness and disease and empowered themselves with wisdom of the mind, body, and spirit. This text is replete with discussions and personal testimonials of persons with disabilities. Competent and ethical professionals know how to attune themselves to the person's culture and collective wisdom they seek for healing the mind, body, and spirit, especially in times of extraordinary stressful or traumatic life-altering events (Stebnicki, 2017). Thus, the future of the counseling profession must be grounded in the roots of compassion, empathy, and listening with our heart-chakra to the persons we serve.

REFERENCES

RAND Corporation. (2014). Community-based mental health providers need more preparation to better care for veterans. Retrieved from http://www.rand.org/news/press/2014/11/12/index1.html

Stebnicki, M. A. (2016). Integrative approaches in counseling and psychotherapy: Foundations of the mind, body, and spirit. In I. Marini & M. A. Stebnicki (Eds.), *The professional counselor's desk reference* (2nd ed., pp. 593–604). New York, NY: Springer Publishing.

Stebnicki, M. A. (2017). *Disaster mental health counseling: Responding to trauma in a multicultural context*. New York, NY: Springer Publishing.

Weil, A. (1995). *Spontaneous healing*. New York, NY: Ballantine.

DISCUSSION QUESTIONS

1. In your own life, what are the characteristics that may contribute to the perception of your own wellness?
2. Considering positive psychology, how might your self-esteem or sense of self-worth be affected if you were frequently surrounded by people without disabilities who ignored, devalued, and treated you like a child?
3. Can there be an objective standard for "successful aging," or is such a concept strictly a subjective belief, different for all of us?
4. What factor does Stebnicki discuss regarding empathy fatigue that all counselors should be aware of and self-monitor against, and what are some strategies to reduce it from occurring?
5. What are the economic, psychosocial, and medical implications as to why obesity is on the rise in the United States?
6. In what ways (cognitive, behavioral, and emotional) can counselors assist obese clients if requested to do so?
7. Why do you think rehabilitation professionals have been absent from the debate on euthanasia and physician-assisted suicide? Is it now possible to enter this conflictual discussion? Why?
8. How might you counsel persons nearing retirement with or without a disability? Specifically, what are the unique considerations for aging and/or retiring persons?
9. What are the unique concerns for, and how would you best counsel, persons with or without disabilities who are anxious and stressed about the continual threat of terrorist attacks?
10. In the final chapter, what are the current concerns Marini and Stebnicki have for the United States, and what specific strategies can you do or become involved in to reduce these potentially impending economic, psychosocial, and societal problems?

Appendix A: Perspective Exercises

We have selected six perspective exercises to prompt the reader to explore further the meaning of disability in one's life. These exercises enlarge the opportunity to personalize many of the disability-related issues explained in the text. Each one of the exercises challenges us to confront our personal beliefs when these beliefs are impacted by the disability experience.

PERSPECTIVE EXERCISE 1

Common Pain, Mutual Support

Perspective

A harsh reality of illness and disability is that individuals within a family are often abandoned, isolated, and left on their own. Group counseling and peer support can provide a helpful alternative for those challenged by a variety of illnesses, losses, and changes by providing structure, role models, perspective, support, and resources at a time of ongoing crisis. When thinking about group counseling and self-help alternatives, it is important to recognize that many individuals are not accustomed to sharing feelings with strangers and may resist the group counseling experience.

Exploration

1. List five ways group counseling or peer support could help a person with a disability adjust to living with the effects of the disability or other major life events.
2. If you had a disability, would you voluntarily enter a group? Why or why not?
3. What would be the most difficult aspect of group counseling for you as a group member?
4. Are there certain people with illnesses or disabilities you would not want to associate with?
5. List the characteristics of group members that make you uncomfortable.
6. If you could choose a group leader to lead a group of persons and families experiencing major life changes, what would be the characteristics you would like this person to have?
7. What are the characteristics of a group leader or peer leader that would put you off?
8. Identify the most upsetting situation that could occur for you as a group member.
9. Should people with a disability and people without a disability be in the same group? Why or why not?
10. Should persons with a brain injury be in a group with individuals who are living with AIDS, spinal cord injury, or mental retardation?

PERSPECTIVE EXERCISE 2

Who Needs This Kind of Help?

Perspective

When families are in a state of crisis, they need to be listened to, responded to, and treated with sensitivity, care, and respect. Often, the stress of health care and rehabilitation environments creates a situation in which professional and nonprofessional staff do not provide help but rather create pain by insensitive and nonhelpful remarks.

Exploration

1. List examples of how health care and human service professionals could be helpful in dealing with the impact of a disability.

Helpful responses:

(Example: It is not easy but we will be there to help.)

a.
b.

Not helpful responses:

(Example: After all, your daughter was an alcoholic who should not have been driving.)

a.
b.

PERSPECTIVE EXERCISE 3

Is the Person With a Disability More Important Than the Family?

Perspective

The occurrence of a severe disability often focuses all of the family's emotional resources on the person who has sustained the injury. Often this focusing is essential to contain the fallout from the injury and to stabilize the total family system. However, in order for families to realign their goals and to establish a different balance in their lives, they must make a transition. This transition should consider the individual needs of family members; the total needs of the family; and the emerging, changing needs of the family and family members living with the opportunities, and problems, associated with an illness or disability.

Exploration

1. In coping with the demands of a disability in a family, how should the emotional resources be allocated? The financial resources?
2. Is it ever possible to regain balance in the family following an illness or disability? If so, how?
3. How long is a long time?
4. Consider a severely disabled child with a grandparent with Alzheimer's disease and the other grandparent with a preexisting psychiatric disorder. How should the emotional resources of a sibling be allocated?

PERSPECTIVE EXERCISE 4

Enough Is Enough

Perspective

An often overlooked factor in addressing the needs of a person with a disability and his or her family is the impact of additional illnesses on the patient, other family members, and/or primary caregivers. This can be a major issue because the resources of the support system can be greatly stressed. An example of this would be the following case overview.

June

June was a 54-year-old wife and mother of four children when she had a stroke. She had lived a very active, vigorous life and was the central figure in her family system. Caring for and managing were facilitated by the commitment of her husband, John, who felt it was a privilege to care for his wife and best friend. Although their children were living in the same town, they were able to maintain their separate lives due to the commitment and investment of their father. A major crisis occurred when their father suffered a severe heart attack and was in need of complete care himself. A temporary plan was to have an unmarried daughter move home to stabilize the situation. This worked for 3 weeks, until the daughter suffered a severe back injury while trying to lift her mother off the floor.

Faced with a decision to either place the mother in a nursing home or have her move in with one of the children, the family was forced to realize that they had to become involved at a higher level of commitment and personal sacrifice. This decision never had to be made because both the mother and father died within 1 month. This case overview illustrates several points: (a) viable caregiving arrangements can suddenly change and (b) multiple illnesses can have a synergistic effect, overwhelming the resources of both caregiver and family.

Exploration

1. Having read the aforementioned case synopsis, list other additional factors that could have further complicated this case.
2. Consider a specific family challenged by a stroke that had to deal with the impact of multiple illnesses. What was the outcome? Were there any intergenerational issues? What would have been helpful?
3. What are some areas of competence that are important for the family's caregiving for a family member who has a stroke?
4. What are the assets and limitations of being involved with a self-help group?
5. Do you think that families can ever be normal again after a stroke?
6. Identify those extended family members who would not be helpful to you or your immediate family. State why.

PERSPECTIVE EXERCISE 5

Fragile: Handle With Care

Perspective

When families are forced by reality to address the complexity and permanence of a disability, there is an urgent need for them to be listened to, appreciated, valued, and understood.

By listening, caring, and responding, the family is validated and given the opportunity to establish a communication process that is based on real issues, mutual respect, and hope, based on reality and not on desperation.

Exploration

1. Develop a list of what is needed to maintain a sense of well-being and a positive family life.

    a.

    b.

    c.

    d.

    e.

2. Develop a list of what is needed or would be needed to help negotiate the stress of a disability experience within the family.

    a.

    b.

    c.

    d.

    e.

PERSPECTIVE EXERCISE 6

I Am in Love With a Stranger

Perspective

Most relationships are based on common goals, mutual respect, interpersonal concerns, and emotional security. For these and a variety of other reasons, people choose to be with each other and enter a long-term relationship. Unfortunately, illness in general and disability in particular can introduce elements into a relationship that are stressful, challenging, and sometimes overwhelming. Some relationships can negotiate these challenges, whereas others struggle and the relationship erodes away.

Exploration

1. Think of a couple you believe has an ideal relationship. How would this change if one of them acquired a disability? Who could cope the best as a caregiver? As a patient?

2. If you know a couple who has successfully experienced a major trauma, discuss what enabled them to survive.

3. If they did not do as well as they could have, what would they have needed?

Appendix B: Personal Perspectives

*A*vailable to the authors are the many dynamic stories of those who use different coping strategies to live and to grow despite a serious disability or illness. These personal perspectives are living illustrations of how to be productive while experiencing significant life challenges. We wish to include some personal perspectives here that can broaden the reader's understanding of living with and beyond an illness or disability and also show that different perspectives of coping and living only enrich an understanding of the dimensions of the total human experience. These personal perspectives enlarge on Irving Kenneth Zola's conviction, clearly stated in the foreword of the third edition of *The Psychological and Social Impact of Disability* (Marinelli & Dell Orto, 1991): "Disability was not merely a personal problem to be solved by individual effort . . . as much a social problem created and reinforced by social attitudes and prejudices whose solution would require governmental resources, protections, and interventions" (p. xv).

These personal statements also further emphasize and extend the implications of the disability-related issues identified in Parts I to V of this book. The personal journeys of Robert Neumann and Tosca Appel that you will read illustrate both the material discussed in Part II by Livneh and Antonak on psychological adaptation to chronic illness and disability and the chapters in Part III on Family Issues in Illness and Disability. These family issues are further highlighted by the narrative experiences of Judy Teplow, Karen's mother, and both Chris and his mother. Paul Egan's poignant account brings to life many of the concepts identified in the chapters in Part II. With the description of David's experience, all of these personal statements provide the reader with an opportunity to understand the varied models of disability, discussed clearly in the chapter by Smart and Smart in Part I.

CHRIS AND HIS MOTHER: HOPE AND HOME

CHRIS MOY

The following personal perspective presents the often irrational life experience that can test and strengthen the human mind, body, and spirit. A son and his mother share their journey, as well as the hopes and dreams that had to be let go as well as aspired to.

Reprinted from Power and Dell Orto (2004).

Chris's Perspective

Before my injury in July 1991, my family had endured its share of trials and tribulations. I guess you could say we were a typical middle-class family. At least we considered ourselves middle class. Actually, we were on the low-income end of middle class, but we were happy. We never felt deprived of anything; even though we didn't have a lot of money for clothes or extras, we never went without. My two older brothers and I shared many wonderful times with our parents. Everyone was always very close: church every Sunday, dinners together, and always discussions on how things were going. My parents, to my knowledge, never missed a sporting event or school function. Everyone was treated fairly, given the same opportunities, and encouraged to grow and learn by experiencing new things. We were always given the freedom to choose our activities, but we were expected not to quit halfway through. If we started something, we were always expected to give it a fair chance before deciding not to continue with it. I guess that's where I developed much of my determination.

My father and mother shared the responsibilities of keeping the household going. When my father lost his job, he took over all the household chores and my mother continued to work full time. Dad was always the athletic type, and he instilled in us the belief that hard work, determination, and self-confidence would not only help us athletically, but later in our lives as we began to go out into the world. Our friends were always welcome in our house. I'll never forget how my Dad would fix lunch every day for me and my best friend during our senior year. There aren't too many guys who would want to go home every day for lunch, but I always felt very comfortable with it.

Mom has always been the matriarch of the family. Being an optimist, she was able to see the good in everything. Although she's a petite woman, she had a quiet, gentle strength about her. I never tried to "pull one over on her," as she always had a way of finding things out. When one of us boys would do something we shouldn't have, mom always found out. This still amazes me.

My oldest brother was always quiet and kind of shy. Acting as a role model for me and my other brother, he worked hard in school and pursued extracurricular activities. At the time of my injury, he was out of school and living on his own. As the middle child, my other brother was more aggressive and outgoing. Striving for independence, he couldn't wait to be out on his own. As the youngest of the three boys, I was always on the go. I was very popular in school and gifted athletically. I had just graduated from high school and had secured a baseball scholarship at a nearby university. It had always been my dream to play professional ball. It seemed I had been preparing my whole life to play in the "big show." Little did I know that I was really preparing for the challenge of my life.

After graduating from high school, I was carefree and looked forward to a great future. I was planning on attending Walsh University, where I had been awarded the baseball scholarship, where I would major in business. I could not wait to start college, become independent, and meet new people. New challenges and new opportunities occupied my thoughts.

The summer after my graduation was a time I remember vividly. Playing 80-odd games in 6 weeks and enjoying my new freedom with friends, I thought I had it all. I figured as long as I had baseball, friends, and family, I had everything I would ever need. What I did not figure on was losing baseball, being separated from friends, and becoming almost completely dependent on my family.

On July 29, 1991, a friend and I went to the mall to do some school shopping. Afterward we decided to hang out at the local strip and see what was going on. We ran into two of our friends, Valerie and Bobby Joe. The four of us talked and cruised around enjoying the cool summer night. Around 10:30 p.m., we decided to stop off at Taco Bell to go to the restroom and get some drinks. When we entered the Taco Bell, I noticed nothing unusual so we proceeded to order. It was supposed to be a fun night out on the town, and it probably would have ended that way had the conclusion of the night not found me lying in a coma, fighting for my life.

As we were leaving the restaurant, I still hadn't noticed anything unusual. As I proceeded out the door a couple of steps behind my friends, I was struck in the face by a fist. Swinging around to see who had struck me, I was disoriented. As soon as I swung around, I felt a glass bottle shatter over my right temporal lobe. I immediately fell to the ground where I was kicked and beaten for what felt like an eternity, but was actually only a few minutes. Afterward, I slowly tried to regain consciousness. I was rushed to the hospital where I fell into a coma for a month.

Emerging from my coma was the greatest challenge of my life, a challenge I will never forget. It called for every resource I had if I were to breathe and walk again. It was like I was alone in a dense, thick fog groping for a familiar hand, yet unable to find anything concrete and strangely aware of a vast emptiness and solitude. This is a faint reflection of my coma. As I lay there, I experienced repeated flashes of light . . . my brain inevitably reacted. I wondered where the light came from! Had I really seen it or was it only a figment of my imagination? I convinced myself that the flash of light was real and thus my only hope of finding my way back home. From a great distance, I heard the distinct voices of my mother, father, and brothers, and Amy, the girl next door. Each time I heard their encouragement, I drew one step closer to the light. Although I felt like falling into despair, a word of love from God, my family, and my friends urged me forward. Without such love I would not have advanced even one step. Along with these words of love, I also heard the muffed voices of doctors and the high-pitched whispers of nurses as they wondered what they could do to help me. Eventually, they concluded that I would not make it. I was determined to prove them wrong.

Every day, I fought the coma with all of my might. Every day, I drew a little closer to the light. Finally, the day came when I opened my eyes and saw the heartbroken tears of the people I loved and longed to be with. Meanwhile, I could not move a single muscle in my body. I could not even talk. However, this did not bring my spirits down; somewhere deep within I knew that I had just answered the greatest challenge of all, the challenge of coming back from virtual death.

After awakening from my coma, I slowly began to realize what had happened. I went from a fully functional young adult to practically a vegetable in a blink of an eye. I was left totally immobile, not able to talk, and my world had seemed to crumble to dust. My family and friends were there to support me; if not for them, I think I would have died.

During the ensuing weeks, the doctors and nurses gave me little hope for recovery, but through persistent pleading, my mother convinced the doctors to give me time before decisions were made to institutionalize me. My family and I vowed to meet this brain injury head on and give it our best. I slowly regained mobility and could see gradual improvements. The doctors also saw my progress and decided to send me to a rehabilitation hospital to continue therapy.

It was at the rehabilitation hospital that my attitude and commitment to recovery preceded all other thoughts. My family, friends, therapist, nurses, and doctors were my team, and they were counting on me to bring them to victory. You see, it was the ninth inning, the game was tied, the bases were loaded, and I was at the plate facing a full count. It was the kind of situation I thrived on. It was do-or-die time. I could dig in, face the challenge, and try, or I could drop my bat, strike out, and die.

The choice was mine. What did I do? Well, I stepped up to the box, dug my feet in, and my mind focused on the pitcher, or in this case, the injury. I saw the ball coming; it was like a balloon. I stepped toward the ball, made a smooth swing, and then I heard a crack. The ball ricocheted off my bat like a bullet from a gun. I just stood there and watched it soar high and long; I knew in an instant it was gone. As I touched each base, a part of my recovery passed, and before I knew it, I was home, starting school, and enjoying life again.

Although my recovery is not yet complete, I play a game every day in my head, and with every hit, catch, and stolen base, a part of my recovery passes. My next home run could be the one that brings me full circle. The pursuit of this dream is encompassed by the determination and hope that one day I will make it back to my ball field. All I can do is try and pray that everything will turn out right, and if it does not, I will still go on because I know I gave it my best.

The road to recovery has been long and wearisome, but I have already put many miles behind me and I know I will emerge completely triumphant. This experience has taught me many valuable lessons. Above all, it has convinced me that the human will can overcome obstacles that many consider insurmountable. I have walked through the valley of the shadow of death and have come out, not unscathed but undaunted. I am among the few people who can say that they have experienced near-death and were able to live and talk about it. I consider myself lucky and remain grateful to all who have helped me recover from this disaster. My experience has indisputably helped make me the person I am today.

Although many things helped my family overcome this catastrophe, the most helpful was first and foremost our faith in God and belief that He would make everything all right. Second, it was the overwhelming support we received from family and friends. How could we not make it with such kindness and compassion? The third thing was becoming knowledgeable about brain injury. This seemed to make us feel more in control of the situation, instead of relying on doctors and nurses for details of what was happening. Throughout the injury, we kept a positive outlook on life, knowing that we would pull through. The family, as a whole, had a kind of inner strength, which told each member that things would work out in the end. Finally, we came to accept the situation and the consequences it has brought. The past cannot be changed, but the present and future can.

Intervention was never offered to my family. I often wonder why, but I guess no one ever thought to ask what the family needed. Interventions that would have been helpful to my family include

- A team of doctors who would offer in-depth knowledge on the subject of head injury, or offer literature or reading material in a layperson's terms
- Counseling for the family because just being able to talk to someone about what was happening would have helped; information on support groups and meeting other families who have experienced such trauma would have been extremely soothing
- Someone offering assistance with a list of attorneys, if needed, or other medical facilities better equipped and able to help a patient progress
- Someone who would have been able to structure a program that would have fit my family's needs, for example, phone numbers of groups or organizations that offer help, and, if out of town, assistance with lodging, meals, churches, and so forth

After reading and realizing the lack of professional help my family had, I have to wonder what really helped us get through this experience. It seemed that everything that was needed by the family, the family provided. I thank God for giving us the strength, courage, and wisdom to endure each day and for watching over us as we struggle through my head injury.

His Mother's Perspective

I remember lying in bed the night we got the phone call. I was wondering why Chris was late. It was 10:30 p.m. He had gone school shopping at the mall with a friend. It wasn't like him not to call if he was going to stop somewhere else.

Just the weekend before, he had finished up a grueling summer baseball schedule, playing 80-odd games in 6 weeks. He had worked so hard on getting a scholarship, and we were very proud of him. I remember his last tournament game. When they lost, he quickly tossed his uniform, like only a ballplayer could, to get ready for the drive to Walsh University where he would be attending in the fall. It was orientation weekend, but he had come back to play his final game. His dad had said, "Well, Chris, that was your last game." A strange feeling passed through me, and I quickly added, "Until you get to college." As we later drove to the hospital that night, that conversation kept floating through my thoughts.

We really didn't know how bad things were until we arrived at the hospital. When they told us he was having seizures and would need immediate brain surgery, we were devastated. Some friends of ours had gone through a similar experience just the year before, so were all too aware of the seriousness of the situation. As friends and family gathered at the hospital to keep a constant vigil, the pain and devastation set in. So many questions kept going through our minds. Would he live? If he did, how would he be? Why was this happening to us? The nurses were very helpful and brought much-needed comfort during the long weeks while he was in a coma. My husband and I could not bear to leave the hospital. The doctors did not seem to be educated enough to deal with the situation, so we finally had to make the agonizing decision to have him moved. All along we prayed to God to give us the strength, courage, and wisdom to make the right decisions.

My husband was offered a job, and the decision was made for him to go to work as I stayed with Chris. My husband quickly took over all the responsibilities of working and running the household, plus handling all the stacks of paperwork. I, on the other hand, was learning, right along with Chris, about therapy. Together we struggled to help him get better. For him, it was a matter of working relentlessly to make his body do what he wanted it to do. For me, it was the anguish of watching and being there for my child, but not really being able to make it all better. It was a feeling of helplessness. I was determined to learn everything I could about head injury. Somehow being more knowledgeable on the subject made me feel more in control. I always tried to keep a cheerful, encouraging face on for Chris even though my heart was breaking. My other two sons were great. The middle son remained at home with his father and did everything he could to help out. My oldest son visited Chris daily and opened his bachelor apartment, which he was sharing with two other guys, to me.

Although the outlook was bleak, we never gave up hope that Chris would return to normal. But as we've learned, nothing is ever normal. Our lives are constantly changing. As Chris begins to have more and more control over his body, he seems more content. When Chris started school again after his injury, I never imagined he would do this well or go this far. Having him transferred so far from home has been hard on the whole family, but he seems so happy that it's hard not to be happy for him. From the beginning, he was always accepted for who he was, not for what his body had trapped him into. The son we had was taken from us, but the son we were given back is even better in so many ways. Chris is a constant inspiration to all who come in contact with him. There is not a doubt in my mind that he will succeed in life.

As I reflect back, the pain and hurt will never go away, but I developed a tolerance for it. Life for all of us in this world is a challenge. You draw strength to meet those challenges through those around you. Things are so unpredictable, but would we really want to know how things will turn out? All we can hope for is to be surrounded by love and the courage to face what life has to offer. A Garth Brooks song better explains this point: "Yes my life is better left to chance. I could have missed the pain, but I'd had to miss the dance" (Arata, 1990).

DISCUSSION QUESTIONS

1. If you were engaged and your fiancé/fiancée had a traumatic brain injury, what would you do? What would your family suggest?

2. How would you respond if you or a family member were brain injured as a result of violence?

3. Discuss the athletic frame of reference that Chris had and how it was an asset in his treatment, recovery, and rehabilitation.

4. Why was Chris's family able to rally in a time of crisis?

5. If your loved one were not expected to survive, what would you do if faced with the decision concerning the use of life supports?

6. After reading this personal perspective, would you consider rehabilitation at any cost?

7. What did Chris mean when he stated, "I know I gave it my best."

8. How can people learn to adapt to change as Chris and his family did?

KAREN—MY DAUGHTER FOREVER

LINDA STACEY

Medical History: Karen

I am the mother of Karen. Although it is she who must bear the trauma, the pain, and the limitations, it is I who suffer with her and sometimes, truthfully, because of her.

After writing Karen's brief medical history (see table), I thought I would try to compute the hours spent in and traveling to and from hospitals. I found it impossible—the hours are uncountable. Worse, I think, is the life-or-death surgery with comparatively little follow-up or routine orthopedic surgery, which requires trips to Boston (20 miles one way), three times a week for physical therapy. It has been almost a year since

Age	Medical Problem
4 weeks (4½ pounds)	Open-heart surgery
10½ months	Cerebral palsy diagnosed
2½ years	Brace on leg to allow for walking
6 years	Heel cord surgery
7 years	Open-heart surgery
10 years	Muscle transplant—arm

Reprinted from Power and Dell Orto (1980).

the last surgery, and we are still making the trip twice a month. The exercises are never ending, the casts must be continually replaced, and trying to motivate acceptance of these responsibilities by Karen was, until recently, next to impossible.

She is mine forever, I sometimes think. I will never forget the doctor's response when I asked when all this would stop. His answer was to the point: "When her husband takes over." To him, she is not a person but an arm or a leg, depending on where the problems lay at the time.

I think back to her day of birth—thrilled with another girl. Karen was preemie weight but full term. Because she nursed well, she was allowed to come home with me. Symptoms began to appear within a few weeks, but nothing that seemed too unusual. A doctor who cared enough saw her once or twice a week to check and called me often when I didn't call him. Because he cared enough to keep a close watch, he was able to diagnose a congenital heart defect before it was too late—he saved her life. I had never dreamed of a problem of such magnitude.

The diagnosis was a septal defect in the heart. In other words, a hole in the heart that allowed oxygenated blood to mix with deoxygenated blood. Emergency surgery was needed to repair the defect. The doctors would not give us any odds on Karen's survival of the surgery, but she had no chance at all if surgery was not performed. Karen was, at the time, one of the smallest (although not the youngest) infants to survive this surgery. We thought our problems were over until we discovered (when she was 10½ months old) that Karen had cerebral palsy. It was years before I could say those last two words: cerebral palsy. I always said that she had damage to the motor area of the brain. Somehow that didn't seem so bad.

The cause will always remain unknown. It could be congenital, it could be due to a lack of oxygen before the corrective heart surgery, or it could have happened during the surgery at a time when techniques were not perfected for working on such a small child (she was hooked up to an adult-sized heart–lung machine, for example). The cause is unimportant. It is the effects that we must deal with.

At first, the attention a family gets in these circumstances is unbelievable. You're special, everyone wants to help, and there is a certain amount of glory or martyrdom involved. "How do you manage?" they ask. They could never do it. Well, the answer to that is, you do it because you have to. There is no one else to do it for you. You only wonder how you managed after the latest crisis has passed. Then it's on to the next crisis—always another one to look forward to. It's almost as if this child will be mine forever—in the sense that I will always be responsible for her. Although this may sound selfish, I can't imagine any parents wanting to keep their children with them for the rest of their lives. Cop out? Maybe it is, but I can't help it.

How do we feel about Karen? It was a long time before I could say that sometimes I hate her for all the problems she presents. A parent cannot easily voice this emotion regarding a child, especially a handicapped child—it's almost inhuman. Karen's sisters could say "hate" much easier—children's feelings are much closer to the surface than those of adults.

On the other hand, these same sisters who sometimes hate her will rise to her defense when they see that she is treated badly. She is not, however, an easy child to get along with. Although Karen functions well in school with a great deal of supportive help (resource room, counseling, etc.), she is socially immature and has no real friendships to rely on. It is we at home who care for her who must bear the brunt of her frustrations—acting out and generally behaving abominably.

Of course, we love Karen, but it is often difficult to show openly. A child of Karen's temperament can drain your emotions. The more affection and attention you give, the more she wants. I often feel as though I am bled dry. She is all-consuming.

Sometimes, I feel pity. What will she be able to do? Because she appears almost normal, people expect normalcy from her. For that matter, so do we, for I am always afraid of selling her short. We demand that she perform tasks that are within her capabilities—even more. If I tie her shoes for her now, who will do it when I'm not here? She needs to know how to tie shoes with one hand. She must learn in spite of herself.

Often I feel compassion. How do you console a child who has no "real" friends? What playmates she does have are not above tormenting her in insidious ways. What do you say when she tells you that the kids at school call her "mental"? How does it feel knowing that if someone comes to call for you, it is only because no one else can come out to play? Telling her not to pay attention is almost ludicrous. These things hurt us both, but it is very difficult to build self-image in a child who is "different" and intelligent enough to know it.

I always feel guilty—not because I've somehow done this to her, but because she is so much better off than other victims of cerebral palsy. Cerebral palsy can be devastating to the point of total immobility and retardation. Karen is neither. Why then should I complain? I guess I can only say that this is our problem, and it is we who must deal with it.

At night, I cry when I see her sleeping. She sleeps relaxed, the spasticity is gone, and the cerebral palsy seems to have disappeared for 12 hours or so. But in the morning, Karen still limps, her hand is still misshapen, and she still has trouble with school work and social adjustment. I cry now.

What will Karen be when she grows up? My head knows that there's a place for her somewhere—my heart wonders if she'll find it.

Update: 30 years later, Karen is married and is working.

DISCUSSION QUESTIONS

1. What role do siblings play in the developmental process of a sibling who is disabled?
2. What role does birth order play in the area of sibling rivalry for an adolescent with a disability?
3. How can the family be a liability in the school-to-work transition for an adolescent with a disability?
4. How has the AIDS issue created additional concerns for families of adolescents with special needs?
5. How would you and your family feel if you had a child like Linda's child, and who was making great strides in managing the particular disability, but then was diagnosed with another debilitating disease?
6. What advice, help, or insight would you give a family member who may not stop focusing on what he or she has lost because of the caring demands associated with the severe disability of a child?

LIVING IN SPITE OF MULTIPLE SCLEROSIS

Tosca Appel

Multiple sclerosis (MS) was something I knew nothing about or even considered being part of my life. Even if I did, it was more an illness for those who were young adults.

Reprinted from Power, Dell Orto, and Blechar-Gibbons (1988).

However, I was one of those rare cases of MS that occur before the age of 20 years—I was 11 years, 9 months old when my first symptom occurred.

My first attack of MS took the form of a lack of motor coordination of my right hand. I was unable to hold utensils, and my hand was turned inward. My parents, in their concern, rushed me to the emergency room of the hospital. The intern who saw me at the emergency room told my parents without any exam that I had a brain tumor. Needless to say, this shocked my parents because, other than this attack, limited to my right hand, I was otherwise normal and healthy. I was admitted to the hospital, where I stayed for 12 days. Ten days after the initial attack, the symptoms abated. Two days later, I was discharged from the hospital and was totally back to normal. The doctors had put the blame of the attack on a bad case of nerves. Before the attack, I was enrolled in Grove Lenton School of Boston. This was a very high-pressured school. From my A average in grammar school, my grades had dropped to roughly a B average. I was worried, and I spent many sleepless nights crying myself back to sleep. I could not handle the pressure of going to a private school. Consequently, I transferred to a public junior high school. Without the pressure, my grades went up to an A average. I was happier and everything was fine.

My second attack occurred when I was 16 years old and in the 11th grade. My mother and I were planning my Sweet-16 birthday party. My mother rented a room in a nightclub. I was all excited, planning who I was going to invite, what it was going to be, and what the room was going to be like. One day before the party, my history teacher asked me a question. I stood up to answer, and my speech came out all garbled. I was unable to string the words into a sentence. I was even unable to utter words. All that came out were sounds. I clutched my throat to help the words come out easier. At times they did, but at times it came out a garbled mess. I remembered the teacher's look. He looked at me in utter surprise and a little bit helplessly. In total utter shock, my attempts at speech sounded so ludicrous to me—so totally as if it did not belong to my head, and so totally foreign that I started laughing hysterically. I couldn't be serious about the sounds I was making. Again, my parents rushed me to the hospital where again another intern did his initial workup on me. However, the sounds that came out of me were so funny that I again started laughing almost hysterically, because I was well aware of what I wanted to say and I was also well aware that it was not coming out of my mouth right. The intern, in his wisdom, thought that this behavior was an attention-getter. He thought I was faking the whole thing.

After the first attack, my mother had decided that this time she would not let me be admitted to the hospital. I was then not admitted, but I was instead seen on an out-patient basis. The inability to speak lasted roughly 2 weeks. I had the party and had a good time. But pictures were taken during this time, and I hated them. Why? My smile came out cockeyed. I smiled with the left half of my mouth, without moving the right side. To me it was quite ugly. After my speech returned, the doctors said that the right side of my mouth and tongue were numb and paralyzed, thus making it very hard for me to talk. Overall, I do not remember the attack. Two weeks after this attack, I again went into complete remission.

In 1967, at the age of 19 years, I applied to and was accepted at Northeastern University. However, during the fall term, I started having trouble seeing. My father drove me to the train station so that I would be able to take the trolley to school. But after I got on the trolley, I took it beyond my stop, and went to the Massachusetts Eye and Ear Infirmary to have my eyes checked out. I did not tell my family about my concerns because I did not want to worry anybody. A doctor put me through a whole eye workup, and he said that he could not promise how much sight I would get back in my eye but that he would do all he could. Considering that I was an English major and I loved to read, this freaked me out. I asked him if glasses would help, and he said no, that he might be able to get all my sight back or none of it, but that he could not promise me anything. I had to call my mother after I left him. I first went into the restroom and cried. I controlled myself long enough to call my mother. I got off the phone with my mother as quickly as possible and left for school on the train.

During the ride, I was attempting to figure out if it would have been better to have been born blind and never have seen anything than to lose sight after having it and know what you are missing. As a result of this thinking process, I came to the conclusion that it would have been better for me to have been born blind, because I now knew the beauties of a sunset, of reading, of a flower, of all the things that people who have sight take totally for granted. I do not know how I would rationalize it now.

When I got to school I went into the cafeteria, sat with my friends, and began crying. Once I stopped crying, I got it all out of my system and my friends and I decided that crying would not solve anything, and the best thing I could do was to go home, take some medication, and see if my sight returned. When I returned home, I did not initially tell my parents of what the doctor had said about the possibility that my sight might not return. I decided that my parents always got very nervous when something happened to me and that there was no need to worry them about me.

So, I did not say anything until my mother mentioned that she had spoken to my neurologist. At this time, unbeknownst to me, I was diagnosed as having MS. My neurologist had told my mother of the diagnosis and told her to tell me. My mother had refused. The doctor then told her that I would never forgive her if she did not tell me. She said that was something that she would have to deal with and did not want to tell me. Consequently, following my mother's wishes, the doctor naturally did not tell me.

The loss of sight in my left eye lasted 3 weeks, and then I went back to college and continued the daily routine of living. Still my mother had not told me about the MS. She bore it alone and did not tell anyone for 6 months after she knew. The only person she spoke to about my MS was my older sister, who is 6 years older than I am. When my mother would become depressed, she would call my sister and cry about the injustice of this happening to me rather than to herself.

My mother's rationale for not telling me was basically twofold. First, she felt that she should not burden me with the knowledge of my chronic degenerative disease because the knowledge of MS could deter me from doing what I wished to do. Second, when my mother saw me running out of the house to go on a date or to a party, she would get scared and sad, thinking about the day that I would not be able to go out and enjoy myself. My mother felt that the knowledge would hang like a cloud over my head, so she made it her responsibility that I was not to know.

However, this conspiracy of silence put my doctors in a difficult position when I went to see them. I would beg the doctor to tell me what was wrong, but he could not because of a promise made to my mother. Because I remembered when a doctor had told me I might have had a brain tumor, which was incorrect, I asked my neurologist if I was going to die of a brain tumor—to which he said, "You can only die of a brain tumor if you have a brain." This may have been a joke to him; it was not for me! The worry about the brain tumor was a preoccupation of mine. My fingers would tingle, or I would feel something go wrong with my balance, and I would be worried that it might be caused by a brain tumor. I was really worried about dying. I found no comfort in the silly remark that I would need a brain to have a brain tumor. At the time,

I told the doctor that I was not kidding and that I was very worried. To that, he replied that they did not know what was wrong with me, but when they discovered a pill for it they would rush it to me. I left his office feeling very depressed, very alone, and not understood.

Finally, when my mother told me I had MS, I was sad and confused, but also very much relieved. Now there was a basis for my physical concerns. Because I had long periods of remission over the next 10 years, there were the low points of exacerbation but the long periods of life, living, and the pursuit of happiness. It was great to be a young adult who was living life and running ahead of the long-reaching shadow of MS.

At age 28 years, I reached a major crisis point in my life. I was faced with the reality of ongoing deterioration. My sight reached the point where I was not able to read the newspaper. In addition, I lost what functional use I had in my left hand. Although these losses may not seem to be catastrophic issues to the nondisabled, they were catastrophic to me. The reason was that they reaffirmed the reality that I had little control of my body and of what was happening to it.

The feeling intensified when I had to resign myself to the fact that I needed to use a wheelchair. To me, this was an admission of defeat and that my disease was getting the best of me. Although I made the cognitive decision to continue to struggle, it was very difficult when the little physical control I had was slowly eroding away. As a result, I made the choice to live, rather than to deteriorate or die. Although this is easy to verbalize, it is often not easy to implement. I can choose to actualize myself, but I am limited by physical and emotional resources to follow through completely in that process.

My unique situation is that I was dependent on my family, with whom I lived. I was also dependent on my mother to provide me with the assistance I needed, such as cooking and partial dressing. Even though I wanted to live independently, I had to accept that I had a wonderful home life, caring parents, and a loyal brother.

The next major transition occurred when my father and mother died, both within the same year. While initially having to deal with the impact of the loss of people I care about, I also had to face the question of what would happen to me. Fortunately, when my parents became ill, I made the choice to get an apartment and to develop the independent-living support systems I would need. Another possibility for me was to extend the relationship with my boyfriend, to whom I was once engaged and whom I had been dating for 15 years. However, this possibility is questionable, for there were reasons we did not get married and they are still real concerns.

This is my response to the disease that has plagued me for 24 years and has altered the course of my life. I will not let it beat me. What motivates me is the memory of my parents and the knowledge of my heritage. My mother and father spent years in a concentration camp, and many of my other family members perished there. I feel the obligation to make the best of my situation and draw on the strength of those persons who suffered far more than I am suffering. As I see it, the key to my ability to survive is the memory, support, and encouragement of others. They have made the difference, accepting me as I am and helping me to resolve my feelings about not being what I was or could have been.

DISCUSSION QUESTIONS

1. What is your reaction to how Tosca was told about her MS?
2. What are the family issues with Tosca that helping professionals should be aware of?

3. After reading her personal perspective, if you were in Tosca's situation, would you consider marriage or having a child?

4. How do societal roles and expectations for women create stress for women with disabilities?

5. Do you think that the mental health needs of women with disabilities are different from those of men with disabilities? If so, please explain in what way(s)?

6. How would you feel if your parents decided, when you were 17 and had a crippling disability, to place you in another caring environment so that better care could be given to your sibling who also had a devastating illness?

SURVIVING AMYOTROPHIC LATERAL SCLEROSIS: A DAUGHTER'S PERSPECTIVE

JUDY TEPLOW

Betty Miller: Beloved Wife, Mother, and Grandmother, September 4, 1986, Age 70 Years

In the early spring, when the ground is soft, I will lay a marker on my mother's grave, a permanent marker to commemorate the life of a very special lady. The inscription will be short, impersonal, and incomplete—and somehow not befitting a woman who courageously struggled against a devastatingly cruel terminal illness.

I cannot inscribe her story in stone, but I can set it on paper as a lasting tribute. I hope it will be a comfort to those who are afflicted with a serious or terminal illness, and a help to the families and health professionals who are involved in their care and treatment.

It was going to be an unbearable, oppressive day, but my mother had no intention of sitting in her small, air-conditioned apartment. She set out early with her walking buddies on their 5-mile jaunt and, as usual, took the lead. She was amused that her companions, who towered over her 5-foot frame, could not keep up with her brisk pace.

Everything seemed to be going well for her and my dad. Retirement for them was not sedentary life, but rather one that was full and gratifying. In a few weeks, they would return to their apartment in Boston for 5 months of relief from Florida's intolerable heat.

But for now, Betty was enjoying her walk and thinking about how rich her life was. As she turned the bend, her thoughts were cut off abruptly by a stiffening in her left leg—perhaps a cramp—but she did not have the pain associated with a cramp. Her gait slowed down considerably, and in a minute she found herself lying on her side. She was stunned by this unexpected interruption. She did not stumble over a rock or a crack in the roadside. What should she attribute this weakness to?

It took 5 months for the doctors to make an accurate diagnosis. An electromyogram was performed at the Brigham and Women's Hospital, and it was this test that ultimately determined that my mother had amyotrophic lateral sclerosis (ALS), Lou Gehrig's disease, a progressive, degenerative disease that is terminal. It is probably the most dreaded neurological disease and is one with no known cause or cure.

Within 1 year of the first visible symptom, Betty would be a virtual paraplegic, confined to a wheelchair, unable to talk or to feed herself. Breathing and swallowing would become progressively more difficult. At no time would the disease affect her mental faculties, and she would always be aware of the creeping paralysis.

Reprinted from Power and Dell Orto (2004).

My initial reaction to the diagnosis was one of disbelief, devastation, and helplessness. How could such an active and health-conscious person be stricken with such a catastrophic illness? I felt a sadness for my parents, and I had real concerns about my dad's health also. It was conceivable to me that this tragedy could destroy him as well, and I prepared myself for the worst.

The family and doctors were in total agreement as to how much to tell my mother. She had always been petrified of doctors and hospitals and was by nature very nervous and anxious. We knew that she could not cope with such outrageous news.

She was told that she had a chronic neuromuscular disease and that she would need intensive therapy. We did not offer her hope of a cure, nor did we inform her that she was terminally ill. She asked very few questions, wanted to know as little as possible about her disease, and became adept at tuning out whatever she was not ready to hear.

Like my mother, my aunt, my father, and my brother went to great lengths to avoid the truth. Denial became a protective measure they were to use effectively throughout the course of the illness. As much as I tried to beat through this barrier, I was met with resistance. It was this resistance that was to become a great source of frustration and anger for me. My aunt held out the longest, talking about the research, cures, and the possibility of people living several years. My brother, who never coped with adversity too well, did not become an integral part of the team, and his visits to the nursing home were often sporadic and brief.

I had to know all the medical aspects of the disease, so I asked a lot of questions and read many books on ALS, and on death and dying. Someone had to take charge, to plan, and to carry the family through this crisis.

From the Brigham and Women's Hospital, my mother was transferred to the Braintree Rehabilitation Hospital. It was there that she was put on a daily regimen of physical, speech, and occupational therapies. She was extremely tense and frightened, but the staff was very professional and experienced and knew how to respond to her emotional and physical needs. This was really not a time for rehabilitation as much as a time for enormous adjustment. It also allowed the family to make plans for home health care. I wished that my mother could stay at Braintree indefinitely, for I feared that the support systems at home would not be adequate.

My fears were well founded. She was not home 2 months when all systems began to breakdown. My mother required constant attention, and the Visiting Nurse's Association and private-home health professionals were not able to keep up with her demands. Oftentimes, my father was left without help, and he had to assume the role as a primary caregiver. Tensions mounted and tempers began to flare, and what was once a very happy marriage now appeared to be very strained. My dad's health was deteriorating as well as my mother's, and they looked to me for a quick solution.

I knew that my mother required round-the-clock care in a skilled nursing facility, but I did not want to be responsible for initiating the search. I could not find it in my heart to do this to her, especially when she threatened to commit suicide before she would enter a nursing home. My grandmother had taken her own life because she could not cope with a painful illness, so I was worried about my mother's intentions. I began to get pressure from her sister, also, in defiance of any plan to move my mom from her home. We were in a crisis, and we needed help quickly.

I was fortunate to find a psychologist who would help me accept and confront problems that were difficult and painful. He helped me see issues more clearly when everything seemed overwhelming and confusing. It was through him that I began to understand the complexities surrounding chronic and terminal illnesses. His continued support and genuine concern were to sustain me through some very difficult times, the first of which was my mother's move to a nursing home.

The transition from the apartment to the nursing home was traumatic for the family. Ostensibly, the home was attractive and meticulous, with spacious rooms and beautiful furnishings. In sharp contrast to this orderliness was a picture of deterioration—of very old people in their 80s and 90s ravaged by debilitating diseases, marked with permanent deformities, hooked up to life-supporting machines, impaired by mental illness—an aura of sadness and loneliness, and a sense that many of these people were deserted by their families.

I wished that I could put blinders on my mother's eyes—to shut out a world that was so unreal, but yet only too real and disheartening. My mother was only 69 years old and looked 10 years younger. How could we do this to her! I knew that there was no alternative, but I was stricken with guilt, a guilt that was to stay with me for a long time. It took a good 3 months before I could walk into the nursing home without feeling sick—without feeling very, very shaken.

I don't think my mother ever adjusted to nursing-home life. I think she resigned herself to her fate. I know she often felt very sad, lonely, and misunderstood, but I do not think she felt abandoned. She knew that the family was there for her, and it was this prevailing sense of security that kept her from slipping into a deep depression.

A schedule was worked out, wherein one or two family members would visit daily. This was arranged, mostly out of love, partly out of guilt, and out of an acute awareness that strangers would not minister to her needs the way family would. We also knew that if we were going to survive this ordeal, we would have to share the responsibilities, for each of us had a history of medical problems. Often, the burden of responsibility rested on my shoulders, and at times I felt overwhelmed. But I also felt that if my mother could cope with the effects of a very disabling disease, I could deal with any problems that arose.

I do not know how she endured all the suffering, and I do not understand what held her together. She certainly did not triumph over her disease—she did not write a book, or paint by mouth, or engage in anything that was extraordinary. She just tried to get through the day. There were many tears and many moments of anguish, but even in her despair, she insisted on getting up, getting dressed, and—above all—having her hair done weekly. Thank God there was a hairdresser on the premises, and thank God she still cared about her appearance. Throughout her illness, she never lost her sense of humor or her ability to smile and laugh. But the laughing was done for the staff, and most of the crying was done with the family.

We tried to maintain a sense of equilibrium, but it was difficult to keep control when all systems were failing. The disease was progressing at an alarming rate, and we knew she would need the strong support of the family and the specialized services of many health care professionals. Some services were effective, but most fell short. Many professionals were not familiar with or could not cope with the demands of ALS. They were uneasy in treating a terminally ill patient, or clearly had an attitude problem toward the sick and the elderly. I must acknowledge, though, that most people did try to help, and I cannot fault them for their human limitations in dealing with a very difficult case.

I also believe that my mother's inability to speak had a lot to do with the quality of care she received. This was a great source of frustration for her and for the health professionals who worked with her. The family members were the only ones who had the patience to make use of the communication boards. We acted as liaison between my mother and the staff, so our involvement in her care was crucial.

We also acted as her advocates and protectors. There were aspects of nursing-home care that were unsettling, but because we had a very good working relation with the staff, most of our grievances were worked out. I can only think of one incident that was offensive and repulsive, and it was due to a personality conflict between my mother and an aide. An aide had lost control and, out of anger and impatience, threw a sheet over my mother's head. This was a gross violation of my mother's right to be treated as a living human being until the day she died.

The only other situation that disturbed me occurred outside the home. A week before my mother died, her doctor was called to check on her deteriorating condition. To our dismay, we learned that the doctor was on vacation and had left instructions for the covering physician. Her doctor had promised to leave explicit directions regarding heroic measures. This was not an insignificant oversight. I had chosen this doctor because he had been highly recommended by another physician and was on staff at a hospital directly opposite the nursing home. Because of his close proximity, I thought that he would be accessible to my mother and the family, but unfortunately we found him to be very impersonal and distant.

Without the encouragement and concern of a handful of people, the experience would have been unbearable. There were three exceptionally caring people who made a great impact on my mother.

Janet, a nurse's aide, became my mother's guardian angel, and she was to watch over her and attend to all her needs while she was in the nursing home. There was such a strong attachment between them that on the day my mom died Janet was unable to work.

Margaret, the assistant director of nursing at the nursing home, had lost her mother to ALS, and she was familiar with the disease and its effects on the family. She was always available to us, and it was not unusual for her to interrupt a busy schedule to explain what comfort measures should be used. She was also instrumental in educating the staff about the nature of the disease. She was my inspiration and a great source of strength.

Bobby was a close friend of the family. He had experienced the loss of a loved one, so he was no stranger to personal tragedy. He attended many workshops with Elizabeth Kübler-Ross and was involved in hospice, and he knew how to relate to the terminally ill. Bobby showered my mother with gifts and flowers and made her feel very special. He was the only one who could talk to her about death and life after death and ultimately helped her accept her mortality. He was a good friend to me, also, and I was able to talk with him about my greatest fear—the use of life-support systems.

The issue of support systems was always a source of great pain and anguish for me. My anxiety was heightened by my mother's refusal to discuss these matters and the inability of family members to agree on a specific course of action. I personally believed that the use of heroic measures, in my mother's case, would be cruel and inhumane—a prolongation of inexorable suffering pain—and an interference with the natural order of things.

But I had to know where my mother stood on these issues for, ultimately, it was her life and her decision. Three months before her death, she began to make her wishes known. She slowly spelled out the word die every day. She made it quite clear to me that she could no longer tolerate living. She finally came to terms with her death, knew it was imminent, and had an urgency to express her grief and fears about dying. Once she accepted her death, she became more tranquil.

I did not want my mother to die in the arms of strangers, nor did I want her to experience death alone. I was fortunate to be with her at the final moment of death. My aunt and I sat by her side and held her hands, and except for a brief interruption by staff, this was a family affair. We exchanged a few words of support and comfort, but we were mostly caught up in remembering and recollecting. I wondered if my mother saw her life flashing before her, and if she were passing through the dark tunnel toward Omega, but I could not be sure.

DISCUSSION QUESTIONS

1. What aspects of Judy's mother's transition from the apartment to the nursing home were most traumatic for the family?
2. How does the slow deterioration of an elderly parent emotionally affect the immediate members of his or her family?
3. What is the meaning of the statement: "My mother's inability to speak had a lot to do with the quality of care she received"? What is the relationship between those two factors?
4. Are there additional roles, other than advocate and protector, that an adult child of a chronically ill parent must play during the illness?
5. Of the three "exceptionally caring people who made a great impact on my mother," who would you choose if you could only select one to care for your own mother who may be chronically ill and needs caregiving efforts?
6. If you were in a similar situation with an elderly, chronically ill parent, what would be your reaction to the statement, "She made it quite clear to me that she could no longer tolerate living"?

MY LIFE WITH A DISABILITY: CONTINUED OPPORTUNITIES

Paul Egan

For me life began very comfortably more than 57 years ago, in a then affluent suburb of Greater Boston. I was the third son of a prominent up-and-coming general contractor. I also had an older sister. A month before I was born, tragedy befell the family when the firstborn son, then aged 6 years, died of diphtheria. So, when I arrived healthy and sound, I was a most welcome addition to a grieving mother and father. Just before I turned 2, another brother was born.

In September 1944, I entered the U.S. Navy and, after completing boot camp, I was initially assigned to motor-torpedo boats in the Philippines. I was then assigned to a yard minesweeper with a team of 22 officers and men. Our assignment consisted of sweeping (dragging) the shipping channels and ports of the Philippine Islands. During this time, my job performance was classified as outstanding, and I received many promotions. However, my life suddenly came apart. While I was moving a keg of concentrated ammonia across the deck, it blew up in my face. The ammonia burned my eyes, the linings of my nose and throat, and also the skin around my facial area. I was rendered unconscious, and on regaining consciousness 3 days later, the doctor told me that my eyes were badly burned and that I would have to be patient and pray for a miracle to take place.

One year, seven hospitals, and several operations later, vision returned to my right eye to the degree of 20/70 with corneal scarring. Other complications emerged as my head and my right hand had a constant tremor. This ailment was incorrectly diagnosed

From Power, Dell Orto, and Blechar-Gibbons (1988). Reprinted with permission.

as a nervous anxiety reaction. So I became a psychiatric bouncing ball. In May of 1947, I was discharged with a 70% Veterans Affairs (VA) compensation.

I immediately went to work for a friend, pumping gas in a gas station. But I had greater ambitions, and I enrolled at Boston Business Institute in a business administration curriculum for 2 years. Shortly after returning to school, my mother developed cancer and passed away on December 15, 1947. This was a profound loss to all of us, as my mother was always on hand with her guidance and sense of fortitude. She was always there to listen, to encourage me to make the most of myself and to go back to school. In fact, in the initial stages of my readjustment to civilian life and to my own disability, it was mom's positive attitude, including her expectations for me, that inspired me to move forward. Her philosophy of making one's residual assets work for the fulfillment of goals is one that I have adopted in my own life.

In June 1948, I married Marietta, a girl I had known before I entered the service. Around this time, my father went on a trip to Newfoundland, his place of birth, and came back a few months later, married. He had married his brother's housekeeper, a plain-appearing woman who was 25 years younger than he was. They immediately isolated themselves from all family and friends for years to come.

In June 1949, I graduated from business school and started experimenting with the real world. Although I was very fortunate in not being unemployed for more than a month during the next 24 years, my choice of expanding my horizons was limited greatly by an uninformed business environment. Time after time when applying for positions for which I was qualified, ignorance, fear, stigmatization, and prejudice were barriers I found most difficult to overcome.

During the next 20 years, my wife gave birth to five daughters, we moved to a larger house, and I was employed in various jobs. Shortly after the birth of our first daughter, I began a series of operations on my left eye. These operations climaxed with an unsuccessful corneal transplant, which resulted in the surgical removal of my left eyeball. Soon after the birth of our second daughter, I had a laminotomy. I understood this operation as involving the transaction of the thin layers of connective tissues around the optic nerve. The pain and suffering endured were the most excruciating of my life. But I was able to get through all of this because of the support of my wife. We didn't think about the past or about my other disabilities. We focused on the present, and together we often discussed our mutual concerns. This was a tremendous help to get through my own sufferings. But in 1968, my tremors got worse, and I went into a VA hospital for a brain operation. After doing an encephalogram, the doctor thought that the risks were too high. Instead of the operation, a new experimental drug was tried, but that increased the body involvement and was quickly discontinued.

Moreover, a trauma occurred in our family, on a night in January 1970 when the temperature was 25 degrees below zero, our oil-burning furnace exploded, destroying our home and all of our possessions. All of our neighbors came to our support, and they held a fund-raising party for us that resulted in not only a substantial amount of money but also in donations of services in our efforts to rebuild. Another factor in our rebuilding effort was that after an absence of more than 20 years, my father reappeared and lent us the remaining necessary funds to rebuild. After we had made a few repayments he said, "You've shown good faith," tore up the note, and then chose to go back into hibernation with his wife. I tried on numerous occasions to visit with him on his 90-acre farm, but he was always "out" or had to go some place in a hurry.

After getting settled into our new home in June 1970, our life returned to a semblance of normalcy until late in 1973 when I lost my job. My employment was not the only loss, however, for I also lost my sense of dignity and self-respect, and I drifted aimlessly in a sea of self-pity and depression for nearly 4 years. Though my family was very supportive of me during this time, I knew this was my own struggle and they themselves had to survive. My daughters were married, had their own families, but seemed to be there when I needed someone to share my feelings.

In June 1977, I was classified as blind. That November I entered the VA Blind Rehabilitation Center at West Haven, Connecticut, and from that time on life took on a new perspective. After 14 weeks of intensive training and guidance, I was again doing things for and by myself. The educational-testing evaluations done at the center indicated a potential for higher education. So in September 1978, I returned to school with the goal of becoming a social worker. In May 1982, I received my BS from Suffolk University, and then in 1984, I earned an MS from Boston University. In April of that year, I began a new career as a field representative and outreach-employment specialist with the Blind Veteran's Association. Yet as I look back now on all of these years of family life, of living with my disabilities, and then finally becoming blind, I often think of my own family, with their patience and understanding. They made the difference so often during my many rehabilitation efforts. Even when I became depressed, they urged me to continue, for somehow they appreciated what I could still do. Probably I would never have gone back to school without their encouragement. Even my father, who died in 1978 and who really never got over the shock of seeing his first financial empire disintegrate, was there one time when we really needed some assistance. To all of my family, I say thank you.

DISCUSSION QUESTIONS

1. After reading the personal perspective by Paul Egan, at what time during the progressive deterioration of his eyesight do you think that family intervention would have been most effective?

2. After reading the chapters in Part IV related to intervention approaches and resources, what do you consider the role of spirituality and could it be applicable to Paul Egan's family?

3. If disability or a severe illness occurred in your own family, and considering Brodwin, Siu, and Cardoso's chapter "Users of Assistive Technology: The Human Component," how would you access the resources that could provide assistive technology?

4. Discuss the issues related to the following statement: "I really can't have any effective contact with a family that is living with a disability situation unless I have a degree in family counseling or family therapy."

EXPERIENCING SEXUALITY AS AN ADOLESCENT WITH RHEUMATOID ARTHRITIS

ROBERT J. NEUMANN

It was a walk I'd taken many times before, down to the train station of our town in suburban Chicago to watch the sleek yellow Milwaukee Road streamliners pass through. Usually it was nothing for the healthy 12-year-old kid that I was. Just seven or eight

From Power, Dell Orto, and Blechar-Gibbons (1988). Reprinted with permission.

shady, tree-lined blocks—but today it felt like miles. With every step, my right knee was aching more, feeling more stiff.

My friend Terry was walking along with me. I gritted my teeth against the rising pain and struggled to maintain a steady gait. I didn't want Terry to know. I sensed that this was no ordinary ache, and I feared he would not understand. I was right on both counts.

Finally, I could stand it no longer. "You know, Terry, my right knee's feeling awfully stiff and sore," I said.

Without missing a beat, my horror-film-aficionado friend shot back, "Must be rigor mortis!"

Happily, rigor mortis it wasn't, just rheumatoid arthritis. Yet it would be 5 painful months before I and my family had even the small comfort of that diagnosis. But, in a way, Terry was right: It was the demise of the lifestyle I had known for my entire previous 12 years.

By my 12th birthday, I was just beginning to feel that things were going really well. I enjoyed getting out of the house by taking long rides on my bicycle; the guys were actually beginning to seek me out to play baseball with them; I was positively ecstatic when my parents allowed me to take my first long-distance train trip all alone to visit an aunt in Pittsburgh.

The arthritis changed all that. Literally within days my right knee became so stiff, swollen, and sore that it was all I could do to hobble from bedroom to bathroom to kitchen. I began seeing a bewildering succession of doctors who could not even arrive at a diagnosis, much less an effective treatment. They hypothesized tuberculosis or cancer of the bone. Their treatments were progressively more drastic aspiration of the knee, a leg brace, exploratory surgery. None accomplished much more than aggravating the condition physically and sending me emotionally even deeper into fear and depression. This was the late 1950s, and apparently in those days even the medical profession was less aware that rheumatoid arthritis can and does affect people of all ages, young and old.

Early in 1960, I went to the Mayo Clinic, where my arthritis was diagnosed at last and where more appropriate treatment was prescribed. Nonetheless, even this was not able to halt the progression of the disease to my other joints. First, it was my other knee, then my ankles, then my fingers, then my elbows, then my neck, then my hips, then. . . . With a sort of gallows humor, I'd say I had joined the Joint-of-the-Month Club. But behind this facade, I was terrified at how my body was progressively deteriorating before my eyes. Actually, I would avoid seeing it—or letting others see me—as much as possible. I would refuse all invitations to go to the beach or park for fear I would have to wear shorts that would expose my spindly, scarred legs. I would wear hot, long-sleeved shirts on even the most blistering summer days to avoid anyone's seeing my puny arms.

One day, almost by chance, I could avoid it no longer. I caught a good look at myself in a full-length mirror and was appalled at what I saw. I had remembered myself as having an able body. The person I saw looking back at me had a face swollen from high doses of cortisone, hands with unnaturally bent fingers, and legs that could barely support his weight.

I felt devastated. But as I look back on it now, I believe that experience of seeing myself as I really was, was the first step in becoming comfortable with the person I am. Of course, what I did not realize then was that I was a victim, not just of a disease, but of that even more insidious social phenomenon that Beatrice Wright (1983) has identified as the idolization of the normal physique. As a society, we celebrate the body beautiful, the body whole. As Dion, Berscheid, and Walster's (1972) research has demonstrated, we believe that what is beautiful in conventional terms is good, and we equate physical attractiveness with greater intelligence, financial success, and romantic opportunities. Media images of all types reinforce the notion that being young, active, and attractive is the ticket to the good life. Lose that attractiveness, lose that physical perfection, the images imply, and gone as well are the chances for success in love and life. This is definitely not the type of foundation on which an adolescent's fragile self-concept is likely to develop a solid, confident base.

But, painful as it was, looking at myself in the mirror and seeing myself as I really was, was the prerequisite for self-acceptance. It was acknowledging the physical facts, if not liking them. It was not until years later when I was in graduate school that I attended a seminar given by a marvelous person named Jesse Potter, and came to understand that our culture's body-beautiful emphasis is only one way—one narrow, constricting way—of viewing reality. She helped me redefine my experience and understand that a person's attractiveness, a person's value, depends on who one is, not on how one appears. Simple as it sounds, for me that was a revelation and a liberation to realize that in the words of the Velveteen Rabbit (Williams, 1975), "once you are real, you can't be ugly—except to those who don't understand."

If my rheumatoid arthritis was a trauma for me, its effects also extended to stress other members of the family. My mother was a quiet source of support and preferred to keep her feelings about the disease to herself. Often she would cry alone in her room; she told me this only years later. But nowhere were the effects of the disease more evident than on my father. A traveling salesman with stubborn ways and volatile temperament, my father would frequently return from business trips edgy, angry, and generally out of sorts. This in turn caused me to dread these homecomings because as an adolescent I had no way of predicting what mood he might be in or what might set him off. It was only after I had moved from home and was employed as a hospital-based psychologist that he felt free enough to tell me how he could do nothing but think of me at home while he was spending those long hours driving the expressways and lonely country roads, worried by how sick I was and frustrated by his own powerlessness to do anything about it—if only he had been able to express those feelings openly and directly 20 years earlier.

One subject my father was able to express himself directly on was the topic of education and my future. He put it in his customary unvarnished manner: "Bob, you don't have much of a body. But you got a good mind. If you're going to succeed, you've got to use it." And, as I was growing up, there never was any question I would succeed. It was simply assumed I would do well in school, go on to college, and get well-paid employment. Clearly, I internalized these expectations for academic success even more than my father intended. But there is no doubt his high expectations functioned as a self-fulfilling prophecy. In large measure, I owe the PhD after my name, the jobs I have had, and many of the wonderful people I have met to my father's simple belief that I could and would. And today, when I work with clients, it is a particular frustration to see how many parents needlessly limit their disabled children's life possibilities through well-intentioned but misguided protectionism or realism that lowers expectations for success by focusing on all the problems rather than on the potentials.

During my high school days, my social life was virtually nonexistent. Because I received physical therapy at home in the afternoon and because my stamina was poor in any event, I only attended school until about 1 p.m. This eliminated any possibility of interacting with peers in extracurricular activities. To complicate the situation further, because my life revolved around classes and studying, I routinely received unusually good grades and routinely broke the class curve, much to the animosity of those peers I did interact with. But perhaps most significant, the school I attended was a Catholic, all-boys high school. This removed me from any contact whatsoever with the female part of the population at a time when my interest was anything but dormant. I literally had only one date, with the daughter of family friends, during my entire 4 years of high school. This situation bothered me enough that I eventually discussed it with my biology teacher. A layman, he suggested that things would be better when I got to college, a response that was only partially more reassuring and accurate than that of the priests who counseled cold showers when issues like these arose.

These less-than-satisfying experiences have led me to be a strong advocate of mainstreaming. From one perspective, I was fortunate to have experienced a limited form of mainstreaming in an era before the advent of Public Law 94–142. At least the interactions I had with male peers gave me a basic idea of how able-bodied adolescent males view the world. Unfortunately, neither the school authorities nor my parents understood how important it was to ensure that deficits in social skills would not develop through lack of informal, out-of-classroom socialization with male peers and the total lack of contact with any female ones. Meanwhile, I unsuspectingly continued to study and dream of the day I would start college and the active love life I had fantasized about for so long.

Finally, the big day arrived. Armed with a body of knowledge about women derived solely from TV, James Bond movies, and the *Playboy* magazines my younger brother smuggled in, I arrived at a small Midwestern college never dreaming I was, in reality, as green as the lovely pines that graced the campus.

It took only a short while before I noticed that my actual accomplishments with women were falling far short, not only of my expectations, but also of the experiences of my friends and acquaintances. Within a few months, most of the people I knew, both men and women, had developed ongoing intimate relationships. Everywhere the couples were obvious: sitting together in classes, dining together in the cafeteria, partying together at dances, studying together, walking together, and sleeping together. I, on the other hand, became frustratingly adept at performing all these activities alone.

Actually, I was quite good at developing nonsexual friendships with women, especially those who had other boyfriends. I could relate well to them because there was no need for me to do the mating dance, no need for me to call on sociosexual skills I had never learned. These friendships were a mixed blessing. They provided emotional support and the beginning of much-needed learning about the opposite sex. But inevitably there were many poignant moments when my friend would go off to her lover, and I would go off alone. As unpracticed as I was in picking up social cues, I continually confused friendship and romantic messages when meeting apparently available new women. A poem I wrote at that time unintentionally reflected the confusion:

> LOST
> I like you
> when we joked and laughed 'bout people that we knew. I wanted
> you
> when you softly said
> that you must have love too. I love you
> then you took his hand, and oh, I knew, I knew.

It was a depressing pattern. A woman would express an incipient interest; I would misread the cues and respond inappropriately, then feel crushed when the relationship died. Rejection and depression became themes that were only too familiar. I became convinced I was unlovable.

Finally, my roommate Michael decided to do something about the situation. A self-styled ladies' man with the body and bravado of a Greek god, Michael, appointed himself my teacher. My first assignment was to read a book he provided me with called *Scoremanship* (Gray, 1969). Once I had finished the book, Michael proclaimed me ready for field experience. It was late on Friday afternoon, and Michael and I were having an early supper in the cafeteria.

"Bob," he nudged me. "Isn't that that Jane over there you've been wanting to go out with?"

"Yeah," I responded dubiously, looking at a woman several tables from us. "Well, remember the book. Just go up and ask her to go to a movie tonight." "Tonight?" I nearly choked. "But it's too late. She's probably got ten dozen things to do."

"Self-defeating talk is unknown to the Scoreman," Michael smiled serenely. "Just go and do it!"

Michael would not let me back out, so I figured I had no alternative but to go forward and experience my next rejection. Slowly I walked over to her table. "Oh, hi, Jane!" I said, as if I'd just noticed her. "You know, uh, seeing you here reminds me. I was thinking of going to a movie tonight. Would you like to come?" Listening to myself, I was sure she'd never buy this one. "Why I'd love to!" she enthused. "Pick me up at my dorm in a half hour!"

I could hardly believe it. I rushed back to our table. "My God! She actually said yes. She actually said yes! What do I do now?"

Michael gazed at me with a smile of patient superiority. "You take her to the movie. Then you bring her back to our room. I'll fix everything up. Don't you worry about a thing."

The date itself was fine. The movie was enjoyable, and the conversation relaxed and friendly. She even agreed to come back to the room for a drink.

I put the key in the door. As I opened it, I discovered just how much fixing Michael had done. Out billowed clouds of incense. Inside the room, candles everywhere cast their flickering light on *Playboy* magazines that had been artfully strewn about and opened to the most suggestive pages. Clothes and books were piled high on all the furniture except my bed. (So she would have to sit right beside me, Michael later explained.) But the crowning touch came when I noticed that on the night table beside my bed, Michael had arranged a little altar, complete with candles, a small *Playboy* calendar, and an opened package of condoms. I could have died.

Needless to say, seeing all this, Jane instantly developed a headache that required her immediate return to her dorm. After she had set out for her dorm, and though Michael had been trying to be a friend, I was embarrassed and set out to find him and relate my feelings.

Obviously, my role models were not always the most appropriate. And being the only disabled person on that small campus meant I did not have the benefit of interacting with and learning from other disabled peers. Nonetheless, I was learning, observing which things I did worked and which did not. Over time, even I could see that I was gradually improving my relationships.

My senior year eventually arrived, and I celebrated my 21st birthday—still without ever having experienced a physical relationship. Chronologically, I had come of age, but emotionally I still felt insecure, lacking the physical experience that symbolized manhood. I assumed my disability was largely to blame, since by then I knew I could develop nonsexual friendships with ease. Increasingly I came to view my virginity as a barrier in need of being surmounted. But this was not just a matter of desire, a stirring of hormones. To me it was also a matter of self-worth and self-esteem. For as long as I was valued by others only for my companionship and intelligence, I still was not being related to as a whole person, a person with sexual dimensions and emotional, intellectual, and spiritual ones—and I feared for whether I ever would be a whole person.

As it happened, that doubt was soon to be laid to rest in a manner I could never have foreseen. It was a Saturday night, and my friend Justin and I had just finished viewing an on-campus theatrical production by the Garrick Players when we encountered Sarah in the foyer. Justin had been friends with her for some time, but I knew her only peripherally from having shared a class or two and an occasional meal in the cafeteria. Generally, Sarah traveled in a different circle from mine. But tonight she was alone, so after some discussion we three agreed it would be fun to drive to town to get a drink.

We stopped at the Nite-N-Gale, a popular campus hangout, and had a couple of glasses of wine. But mostly we just talked. The conversation was good: comfortable and convivial, a pleasant mix of the light-hearted and the more serious. After a while, we headed back to Sarah's room on campus and continued in the same vein. Midnight arrived, and Justin declared himself tired and left for his room, leaving Sarah and me alone.

The conversation turned more serious. She asked me what it was like to live with arthritis. I told her about the Joint-of-the-Month Club and looking in the mirror. She in turn shared some of the hurts she felt in growing up in poverty with parents in ill health. Finally, I noticed it was approaching 2 a.m. "Well, I guess it's time to go," I said.

"You don't sound too wild about it, Bob."

I was surprised she had picked up on a reluctance I thought I was not showing. "Yeah, you're right," I sighed. "It's just that when I get back to the room I'll find Michael there with his girlfriend. It's damn depressing. Hell, I met her before he did! I liked her too!"

For a long second, Sarah just stared at me. Then a smile, warm and tender like I had never before seen, began to cross her face. "Bob, you know you don't have to," she said.

I will never forget Sarah, perhaps more than most people will never forget their first. What we shared was physical, but also far more. With her, I did not have to worry about how to handle the issue of my disability because to my astonishment, she did not view my disability as an issue: The mere fact that our relationship was physical confirmed as nothing else could that this, too, was possible. The effect on my self-esteem was tremendous. As a disabled colleague once remarked, "When most of your problems have been on a physical level, it's on the physical level that you're most strongly reassured." That statement has always stayed with me, even though I would amend the thought somewhat. Self-esteem is most enhanced when one's positive expectations converge with the reality of one's experience. Lack one or the other, and the individual suffers. At any rate, I still recall how brilliantly the sun was shining the next day as Sarah and I walked across the campus.

DISCUSSION QUESTIONS

1. What was your reaction to the statement by Neumann: "Self-esteem is most enhanced when one's positive expectations converge with the reality of one's experiences"?
2. Who should be responsible for sex education programs for adolescents coping with disabilities?
3. What role has society played in the formulation of attitudes toward the sexuality of persons with disabilities?

4. Would there be a significant difference in the critical issues with a young woman who has had an experience similar to that of Neumann as related in his personal perspective?

5. How is an adolescent's search for self-identity complicated by a serious, chronic disability?

6. What is the role of the health professional in working with parents concerned about the sexuality of their children?

MY LIFE WITH MUSCULAR DYSTROPHY: LESSONS AND OPPORTUNITIES

Robert P. Winske

I am 41 and the middle son of three boys born with a rare form of muscular dystrophy known as *nemaline rod myopathy*. To date, there is still little information known about the disease, as was the case at the time when we were born in the early to mid-1960s, though it is clear that it is a progressive condition and is passed from mother to son. At the time of each of our births, what made the case more baffling to the doctors was how this occurred. As I stated, muscular dystrophy is a congenital impairment that is passed through the X-chromosomes of the mother. To my mother's knowledge, however, she herself didn't have the disability.

When my older brother was born, the doctors requested that my parents check the family tree and see whether there was anyone on either side of the family who may have had muscular dystrophy. However, as requested, my parents, with the assistance of their parents, did check each side and their efforts proved unsuccessful. To their knowledge, no one on either side of the family had ever been diagnosed and treated for any form of the impairment. Though my mother did have a physical disability, to her knowledge it was polio not muscular dystrophy. She became sick as a young child in the late 1940s, which was at the height of the polio epidemic that extended into the early fifties. Growing up, my mother always talked about getting sick when she was a young girl when her muscles got weak, especially in her lower extremities, and was told by her parents that it was polio. She had no reason to doubt this information because her mother was a registered nurse. She was also treated in hospital wards where several children her age were being treated for the same condition and some were worse than she was. My mother was still able to walk, which was not so for most of the children.

As there were no signs of the disease found on either side of the family, the doctors believed that the occurrence of muscular dystrophy was a fluke. There was no reason why it occurred, and they informed my parents that to their understanding, the odds to their having another child with the birth defect were unlikely. This led them to decide to have another child. Like my brother, I also was born with the same form of muscular dystrophy. This really perplexed the doctors not only because my parents had another baby with the disease but also because I wasn't as severely impacted by its limitations.

However, following the birth of a second child with the neuromuscular condition, the doctors again insisted that someone on one side of the family had to have had the condition. They even wondered whether a family member had a baby with the same or similar condition, but never took the baby home. This was common at that time as children with birth defects were generally institutionalized because it was an

Reprinted from Power and Dell Orto (2004).

embarrassment to families to have children with impairments. It was also believed that parents couldn't provide the needed, specialized care. If this were the case, the doctors believed that whoever in the family may have had a child with muscular dystrophy wouldn't want to admit to it, being ashamed or embarrassed, because of the belief that everyone wants the perfect baby.

Following the doctor's recommendation, my parents again went back to their parents to examine both sides of the family. It was emphasized that it was important to know whether there was any family history of muscular dystrophy so the doctors could more efficiently treat me and my brother. Again, as with the previous search, the second attempt to identify anyone in the family who may have had the same or similar condition also proved unsuccessful. No one in the family reported having any family members with any physical disabilities. Because of the absence of any disclosure, it was suggested that my parents not have any more children because it couldn't be guaranteed that they wouldn't have another child with the physical impairments. With each of our births, it was also recommended that they not bring us home, as the doctors attempted to tell my parents that we would never grow up to be anything, to have independent lives, and would demand a lot of care. Such communication was especially true after I was born. The doctors tried to explain that my parents already had their hands full with taking care of a child with a severe physical impairment. Trying to take care of two would be too much and too overwhelming. In both cases, my parents opted not to listen to the doctors, so they took me home with them; about 2 years later, they had their third child. Again, a boy was born with the same physical impairments, but with less impairment than I had.

Following the birth of my parents' third child, the physicians were perplexed as to how parents who had no history of muscular dystrophy on either side of the family could have three children with the condition. The only thing they were left to believe was that my mother as a child had been misdiagnosed as having polio. They believed that it could have been an easy mistake because at the time many children were getting sick with polio, and the symptoms my mother recalled experiencing as a child were similar to the impairments experienced with polio. This perception existed for several years until my younger brother was 15 years old. Around that time, my mother and he had, concurrently, a muscle biopsy, a process in which they had a small piece of muscle removed from their thigh to be analyzed. This analysis revealed that each had the same condition, and then these results were compared to the biopsy results my older brother and I had as young children. Thus, as had long been expected, my mother did in fact have muscular dystrophy.

But our lives continued, and my parents successfully raised three children with muscular dystrophy. Each of us completed high school and went on to college. My older brother obtained a job as an advocate for individuals with various impairments after leaving Boston University; I was a senior at Northeastern University, and my younger brother entered the first year at the University of Massachusetts at Amherst after earning an AA degree from Newbury Junior College. However, after my brothers and I had begun to move forward with our lives, my mom found that her mother started to have slight problems with memory, which in the early days was minimal but then slowly progressed. This would eventually lead her to bring her mother to be seen by a doctor because she was concerned that there may be something more serious than normal aging. She was told that her mother did in fact have major health problems and that she was in the early stages of Alzheimer's.

As the disease would progress, my mom would be faced with one of the most difficult decisions that no child ever looks forward to making regarding one's parent. She would realize that despite existing support systems, her mother was no longer safe living on her own, and my mom would have to make the decision that she was unable to care for her mother's needs and would have to put her in a nursing home. She knew that her mother wouldn't want that as she'd always made it clear that she wanted to remain and die in her own home with her dignity. However, my mom knew that a nursing home was the only real option available, fearing that not acting so would result in her mother doing something that would result in serious injury or worse yet, put a neighbor at risk in the elderly housing complex where she was living.

During this process of placing her mother in a nursing home, my mother needed to obtain a variety of information about her mother for the nursing home, which included a determination of eligibility for Medicaid, which is the insurance company that covers the nursing home expenses. One item needed was my grandmother's birth certificate, leading my mother to call the city hall in the town of Kennebunkport, Maine. That is the town where my grandmother had always reported being born and raised. However, this was unsuccessful because when speaking with the town's city hall administrator, my mother was told that there was no record of anyone with the name my mother had provided. A bit confused, my mother followed the recommendation of the city hall employee, which was to check neighboring towns in the event my grandmother had been mistaken. Though my mother found it difficult to believe that her mother wouldn't know the town where she'd been born, she wondered whether she had been born in a different city and just raised in Kennebunkport. My mother spent days calling numerous city halls in those cities and towns surrounding Kennebunk port. All of these calls were unsuccessful, as none of the cities or towns had any record of anyone being born there with her mother's name.

After days of numerous phone calls, feeling frustrated, my mother contacted her mother's sister to ask for assistance and inquired where her mother was born. To my mother's shock, she found out that her mother was adopted as a child. This frustrated my mother. She could only think of why her mother never mentioned this, especially, during the early years in which she and my father were checking both of their family's backgrounds to see whether there was any history of muscular dystrophy on either side of the family. In further conversation with her aunt, my mother indeed discovered that her mother was aware that she did in fact have muscular dystrophy. But for reasons my own mother will never understand, her mother was apparently embarrassed by this diagnosis, and her mother told the doctors treating my mother as a child to tell her it was polio, not muscular dystrophy.

After this revelation, my mother was extremely confused, understandably frustrated, and angry that her mother kept this information from her. Her mother was a registered nurse and should have known that muscular dystrophy is a genetic disorder and not the result of something she or my mother had done wrong that resulted in this impairment. Even more aggravating for my mother was how her mother could remain silent about this information when she, my father, and the doctors were working with both sides of the family to explore whether there was any history of the impairment. My mother found herself not knowing how she should feel or how to approach this topic with her mother. Her mother probably wouldn't have a clear understanding of her reasoning behind the decision or understand the frustration my mother was dealing with. Alzheimer's had robbed her mother of an ability to comprehend anything beyond simple child-like questions and reasoning. She had to figure out herself how to deal with the anger and frustration she had toward her mother, which she knew would be difficult. My mom was unable to resolve questions regarding her mother's decision making, as well as how to set aside these feelings. She knew she had to do this, because she could see her mother quickly withering away day by day as the Alzheimer's progressed, and knew that things were only going to get worse. Therefore, for her mother to be properly cared for at that time and in the later years of her life, and knowing the effects Alzheimer's would continue to have, she had to put these feelings aside if she were to make sure that her mother's needs were met.

Though my mother didn't—and probably never would—totally understand or forgive her mother for what she did at that time, my mother was able to put these feelings aside and put her mother into a nursing home where she was properly cared for during the final few years of her life. I don't know how my mother was able to do this as I knew how she felt, though I do know it took a great deal of strength. She would have drawn on the same strength and courage it took to raise three children with physical impairments during a time when most parents would have had their children placed in an institution, which was recommended when my brother and I were born.

During my lifetime, I've gone through numerous changes due to the progression of my impairment. I started as an individual who was able to walk, then to one who walked and used a manual wheelchair when having to go for any distances or when my legs were sore and weak due to fatigue, and then to one who used a manual chair at all times because I was no longer able to walk, though I was able to perform all activities of daily living. Currently, I require the use of an electric wheelchair for mobility and rely on a personal care attendant to assist me with all activities of daily living.

Though I have dealt with and will continue to deal with rough times that are associated with a progressive form of a physical impairment, I truly can't complain about my life. I have completed both bachelor's and master's degrees from two major universities in Boston and have always had a great job. In most instances, such accomplishments are not true for individuals with major impairments. When people first meet me, whether they are personal care attendants, colleagues, students, or clients, they tend to be surprised at my positive outlook on life. I think they believe they probably would be angry if they were in my situation. But, perhaps, they would not be angry, since I believe that most people with various limitations learn to make the most out of life. Of course, there will always be some people who will never be able to accept their life, choosing instead to be bitter and angry about their situation and wishing they were dead. Some of these people will indeed die, whether through willing themselves to die or from self-induced or assisted suicide.

Concerning my positive outlook on life, I attribute most of this attitude to my parents. They wouldn't allow me or my two brothers to sit back and feel sorry for ourselves, or use our disability as an excuse for not doing something. My mother particularly served as a personal inspiration for us. Though she also has muscular dystrophy, she taught us through example how to live and make the most out of life. She believes that having a disability doesn't entitle one to look for pity from others, or to feel sorry for oneself.

My mother even advocated early in my life, fighting with the local school board, that my brothers and I be integrated and mainstreamed into regular classes with our nondisabled peers, years before the Massachusetts public law, Chapter 766, was enacted guaranteeing equal public education for children with disabilities.

Feeling sorry for ourselves was not an option. While in high school, it was instilled in us that we were expected to go to college, and to get ahead in life and to get a good job. Continued education was a necessity. Though I received Social Security benefits as an individual with a disability, my parents made it clear it was only while in school that I would collect benefits and would not do so for life. Having a job was an important value for my parents, and they insisted that my brothers and I were to have jobs every summer, with a majority of the money to be set aside to pay for college. This value is one that stuck with me. Since earning a bachelor's degree, I've always had a job, even when, because of a dramatic change in my impairment, I had to take time off from work. Each time I knew I would return to work. Not working was never an option in my mind though the doctors would have preferred that I only collect disability benefits. I believe that having a job is important because it allows people to understand that individuals with disabilities are capable of working and can be productive members of society who shouldn't feel sorry for themselves because of their limitations.

Another belief I value that allows me to have a positive outlook on life is that there is always someone worse off than myself. When I was 11 years old and had recently undergone surgery for scoliosis, I was sent to a residential school for children with disabilities for 4 years. This school was wired via television cameras to the classrooms, which allowed me to participate in the school curriculum while recuperating from the surgery. Because the local junior high school where I was born and raised was inaccessible to individuals with physical impairments, I attended this "hospital school." While attending the school, I went home on weekends and holidays. I realized that half of the students lived there like myself because their family wanted nothing to do with them, choosing to make them wards of the state and to be forgotten about. But as a young boy I hated to be away from my family, and during this time I gained an appreciation of how fortunate I was. I realized that my parents cared for and loved me and only sent me to this "hospital school" because it was the only viable option for my junior high education.

Many at this school had no one and would be there until they were 21. Then they would leave the school and at that time not know what would happen to them. I also feel fortunate because I was born with my disability and it's the only life I've known. Compared to those who acquire an impairment due to a traumatic event or an illness, I've always said that if I had to have a disability, I'm glad I was born with it. Yes, there have been changes in my condition resulting in a loss of independence. But I grew up knowing that I was going to experience exacerbations with this neuromuscular impairment. The only thing I had to live with was not knowing when the condition would get worse, and to what extent the change would be. If an individual acquires his or her impairment later in life, with one's life turned upside down with no warning that the life he or she was used to is suddenly taken away, for that person the adjustment is extremely difficult if he or she does make any adjustment at all.

In addition, I've always been thankful that my impairment affects my body and not my mind. I do not consider myself better than someone else with a different condition. But I'd rather have it the way that I am even though I depend a great deal on assistance from others. Importantly, despite my physical limitations, I'm able to understand my needs and direct others on how to assist me with my needs, and with my intact cognitive functions I have earned two college degrees and maintain a great job. These are just my personal beliefs, and I do not ever intend to insult those who have severe, cognitive impairments, such as traumatic brain injuries or Alzheimer's disease.

My final belief that has allowed me to maintain a positive attitude is the conviction that God doesn't put more on one's plate than one is able to manage. Though I am not a very religious individual, I do not want to convey the impression that I've never been angry about my situation or bitter, and depressed wishing that I was dead. There have been numerous times when I wonder why I don't understand what it's all about, and why it happened to me; I can't wait to ask God what it was all about. However, in time I always come around to the beliefs that have allowed me to adjust and make the most out of my life and realize how lucky I am.

I have always been asked, "If there was a cure for muscular dystrophy would I take it?" People are usually amazed when I state that I would decline. Why I decline a hypothetical cure is because this is the only life I know and I feel, because of the reasons discussed, that I am truly blessed for my life. I believe that having this impairment allows me, despite my limitations, to serve as an example that one is still able to have a happy and productive life.

LIFE LESSONS TAUGHT TO ME BY MY DISABILITY

Alfred H. DeGraff

At the age of 18 years, I dove off a pier on Martha's Vineyard and experienced a cervical spinal cord injury. I became, and remain, a quadriplegic dependent on motorized wheelchair mobility, daily physical help from personal assistants (PAs), and enough prescription medications to make several pharmaceutical companies financially dependent on me.

That was almost 40 years ago. I'm convinced from experience that my severe physical disability becomes more valuable to me and to society with each passing year. Although it initially takes a burst of courage and coping skills to acknowledge and "accept" a fresh disability in its infancy, the real test of skills is one's adequacy to support and maintain his or her disability lifestyle over the long haul, decade after decade. Does the person have the staying power to survive daily health crises, hundreds of whining and immature PAs, and, for many, a chronic depression that makes addictions and suicide seem so attractive?

For some people, I'm convinced that the disability lifestyle is no longer viewed as a meaningless tragedy, but instead as a meaningful gift teaching life lessons. People with disabilities encounter an endless stream of opportunities for unique experiences, learning, and growth.

My disability has gifted me with wisdom about humanity that I wouldn't have been able to realize, or realize in such detail and depth, had I been able bodied. This wisdom has given the disability a sense of worth. What follows is my "top ten" list of life lessons—my personal statement of what my disability has meant to me by way of personal experiences, learning, and growth. To many of my able-bodied peers without insightful experiences, these are nice clichés—the text of refrigerator magnets. Instead, for many of us with disabilities, these are lessons acquired from repeated experiences or crises. While coping with an active crisis, these lessons reveal themselves in response to our often-desperate plea to make sense of the situation, "Please show me what I'm to learn from this experience."

I have learned that I have the choice of living this disability lifetime as a victor or a victim. Although I attempt to live optimistically as a victor, I have found that no matter how deeply I might occasionally slip into the victim role, a return route is always made available to me.

Living with a lifelong disability isn't easy. I have found that much of my success or failure has been dependent on how I view life. There is a big difference between whether I choose to be a victim or a victor. And I truly do always have a choice.

As a victim at various times, I have chosen to go through life in a semi-hopeless frame of mind. "Why me? I'll never get ahead, because I'm stuck in this wheelchair." Those who take up full-time residence as a victim erroneously believe they find comfort in wallowing in the anger, grief, sorrow, depression, and despair.

As a victor, I'm presented with the same rough times as the victim; however, I work hard at staying in control of my disability and the quality of my life. As a victim, the nucleus of my daily life is my disability, and my lifestyle becomes a consequence of what my disability permits. As a victor, my soul or spirit is my nucleus, and the disability, like other personal characteristics, is one of many electrons orbiting around my soul or spirit.

I have learned the importance of taking the time to formally grieve a loss, instead of unemotionally trivializing or dismissing it with denial.

Life with a disability is one with many losses. We have lots of opportunities and need to practice grieving. We repeatedly have the choice of grieving now, or grieving later—of paying now, or paying later. There are many factors, outside the scope of this essay, that give us no choice but to grieve later or grieve over a long duration in bite-size pieces.

When we delay, we are sometimes sentenced to carry the weight of the loss's baggage. Grief baggage can manifest itself in many forms, including sorrow, frustration, anger, and depression.

When possible, I try to grieve my losses soon, to defuse grieving of its depressing power, and to move on. The relative absence of unaddressed grief is one of the elements that can reward us with that desirable state we call inner peace.

I have learned that life does not randomly expose me to coincidences, accidents, or seemingly meaningless tragedies. Instead, I am routinely meant to encounter learning and growth opportunities that are sent to me in a variety of disguises.

The Rolling Stones have sung, "You can't always get what you want, but if you try sometimes you get what you need." The Dalai Lama was articulate in countering with, "Remember that not getting what you want is sometimes a wonderful stroke of luck." More recent, there has been yet another outlook that states, "Be careful of what you ask for, you might receive it."

My personal experience has shown me that if I am open to recognizing and learning from life's lessons, and flowing with life's rhythms instead of fighting or fleeing from them, then a whole world of benefits can open up to me.

I have learned that if I were given the opportunity either to shed my disability and return to the experiences, knowledge, and values that I had at the time of my disabling injury, or to keep my current disability with the wisdom it has taught me, I would usually choose to retain my disability.

What about those unique experiences—some joyful and some painful—that I would not have encountered without my paralysis? I usually take full advantage of them. Regardless of whether they were good or bad memories, I have usually succeeded in learning and growing because of them.

I have had firsthand experience in needing, receiving, and then returning human compassion. My disability has also given me first-person insights into prejudice, bigotry, discrimination, injustice, poverty, caring, love, support, integrity, and many other human qualities and inequalities.

I'm not saying I enjoy having my disability; however, it has enabled me to learn much more about humanity and life than I could have learned in an able-bodied lifetime. It's now been almost 40 years of these specialized experiences, learning, and growth. Were I actually presented with the chance of walking away from my wheelchair—but also the need to leave behind the insights I've acquired—I really doubt I'd accept walking back to the starting line of wisdom.

I have learned that it is never appropriate for me to try to shift my responsibilities, which are rightfully mine and for which I am capable of managing, to others, and then to blame them when my needs aren't accommodated.

I have learned that I should never blame any provider for not doing what I should be doing for myself. In addition, I am always ultimately responsible for an aide failing to do a task, or doing it incompletely. Most of the assistance an aide gives me is the face-to-face kind. I am right there, and have a continual responsibility to do QC, or quality control. If an aide has helped me get dressed, and I arrive at my downtown office to find that I am wearing shoes but no socks, is my morning aide to blame? I don't think so.

Sure, I am annoyed that the aide totally spaced out on where my socks were this morning, after remembering them for the previous 7 months. However, I have decided that my responsibility to watch my help providers is more realistic than to attempt to hold anyone responsible for performing my help routine flawlessly with no mistakes. Indeed, I never hold a PA responsible for memorizing every detail of my routine. In the books I've written about PA management, I refer to working with an aide as analogous to dancing. I expect each PA in each work shift to occasionally forget a detail—a dance step. As the PA and I dance through the routine's tasks, and I sense he or she has forgotten the next "step," it's my responsibility to subtly remind the PA of the next step so we can keep on dancing.

I have learned that I am the only valid source for my own joy, sorrow, and inner peace. My own inner peace most often occurs when my actions are in harmony and authentic with my perception of spiritual intentions.

Not only am I solely responsible for my own happiness, for answers to my own life questions, and for coordinating the help required to maintain my health, but no one else will care as much as I if I fail to reach my goals or permit my health to decline.

A rock star who became addicted to drugs and then went through recovery acknowledges that others can't be held responsible for his happiness or the consequences of not achieving happiness. This rock star believed that "we are who we choose to be" . . . "you've got to save yourself . . ." and "nobody knows what you want . . . and nobody will be as sorry if you don't get it."

I have learned that there is a difference between physical pain and emotional suffering. Physical pain is objective and physiological; emotional suffering is subjective and psychological. While I sometimes cannot control the physical pain, I usually do have the choice and ability to control the much more powerful suffering that is created in my mind.

There are psychological ways of alleviating many kinds of emotional suffering. What the mind has the power to create, it also has the power to take away. From many personal experiences, I have learned the difference between the different feelings of physical pain and emotional suffering. I can assure myself of my ability to control suffering, and this has saved my life several times.

I have learned about the powerful advantages and life-sustaining utility there are in making maximum use of mental discipline. I've participated in many workshops and seminars that taught me skills of self-hypnosis, healing mental imagery, and progressive relaxation. I had been routinely using these skills to consciously lower stress and relax, mindfully reduce constrictive asthma, and even attempt to imagine genital orgasms that I could no longer feel. My increasing skills at mind control had resulted in perhaps a 90% success rate for these varied objectives, while enabling me to occasionally reduce my need for prescription medications.

I have learned to live for today—in the present—because yesterday is gone and tomorrow might never happen. Today's events will never happen again, nor should they. Perhaps the predominant, daily challenge I have in living with my disability is in creating and maintaining a set of activities and goals that make life sufficiently interesting and important to merit my getting out of bed each morning.

When I first acquired my disability, I spent a lot of time living in the past. I would look at what I could no longer physically do and think back to the good old days when I was able-bodied and could do those things. This is, of course, a setup for depression—concentrating and aspiring to do what we cannot. If someone with diabetes lies in bed all day and thinks about hot fudge sundaes, he will get depressed. Crosby, Stills, and Nash, in the song "Judy Blue Eyes," sing, "Don't let the past remind us of what we are not now."

People with disabilities should be cautious about reminiscing constantly about missing their able-bodied past or fantasizing about the shape of the future after their ship comes in (example, after they win the lottery) and how much better than their current lifestyle the future will be. Sometimes, when I repeatedly procrastinate about becoming involved in interesting events, I think of Stephen Levine. In his book *A Year to Live,* he cites one quite effective way to identify one's current life purpose: vividly imagine that you are going to die exactly 1 year from today. Ask yourself what priorities you consequently have during this final year of your life!

I have learned the difference between accepting my own disability and society accepting it. For my own acceptance, I should formally acknowledge it, accept my limitations, and then concentrate instead on living within my abilities. If I concentrate on limitations and loss, I will become depressed. For the social acceptance of my disability, I should mostly ignore it. If I speak mostly about my disability instead of my true personal self and interests, it is unfortunately my disability that people will most remember.

During my undergraduate years, I lived purposely in a campus residence hall to facilitate my socialization. Disability-related discussions would crop up occasionally, but for a tiny minority of time. I didn't deny I had a disability, or forbid my dorm mates "to talk about it"; instead, we had more important and interesting topics. One evening, a couple of friends popped into my room and asked if I wanted to join them in casing out a new bar within walking distance from our living area. Out of curiosity, I asked whether the entrance or interior had unavoidable steps. In response, they looked at each other and became very apologetic, "Oh, Al, we're so sorry, we forgot that was a concern." I grinned ear to ear and assured them they weren't guilty of anything. Indeed, they primarily invited me and my personal interests, and not the wheelchair. I felt quite honored that those were my friends' priorities!

So in conclusion to this essay, while I stay in continual communication with the physical and psychological aspects of my disability, it is essential that I concurrently transcend—rise above—this disability and its limitations. It is important that I be able to look beyond the limitations of the disability in order to see the benefits that it offers.

As my abilities decrease with progressing years and disability, it has become increasingly important for me to use my daily time, energy, and stamina as efficiently as possible. My daily aerobic workouts, my requirement for "smart food" quality nutrition, and other health measures are more important to me than to my able-bodied peers.

It has been said that freedom in life is not necessarily doing what one wishes, whenever one wishes to do so. Instead, true freedom is the ability to face, cope with, and successfully get through each of life's unpredictable crises. I believe that my disability and limitations have ironically taught me many lessons about freedom—wisdom that I would not have realized as an able-bodied person.

REFERENCES

Arata, T. (1990). The dance [Recorded by G. Brooks]. On *If tomorrow never comes* [CD]. Nashville, TN: Capitol Nashville.

Dion, K., Berscheid, E., & Walster, E. (1972). What is beautiful is good. *Journal of Personality and Social Psychology, 24,* 285–290.

Gray, F. (1969). *Scoremanship: The sensational new approach to success with women.* New York, NY: Bantam.

Levine, S. (1997). *A year to live: How to live this year as If it were your last.* New York, NY: Bell Tower.

Marinelli, R. P., & Dell Orto, A. E. (1991). *The psychological and social impact of disability* (3rd ed.). New York, NY: Springer Publishing.

Power, P. W., & Dell Orto, A. E. (1980). *Role of the family in the rehabilitation of the physically disabled.* Baltimore, MD: University Park Press.

Power, P. W., & Dell Orto, A. E. (2004). *Families living with chronic illness and disability* (pp. 271–277). New York, NY: Springer Publishing.

Power, P. W., Dell Orto, A. E., & Blechar-Gibbons, M. (1988). *Family interventions throughout chronic illness and disability.* New York, NY: Springer Publishing.

Williams, M. (1975). *The velveteen rabbit.* New York, NY: Avon.

Wright, B. (1983). *Physical disability: A psychosocial approach* (2nd ed.). New York, NY: Harper & Row.

Index

abuse, 371–372
    employment and, 375–376
        economic impact of disability, 375–376
        psychosocial debilitating factors, 375
        women with disabilities, 375–376
    inclusion of study, in rehabilitation
        education curricula, 378–379
    intimate partner, 372
    recommendations, for rehabilitation
        professionals, 379
    rehabilitation services, 376
    social and psychological issues, 375
    types of, 372–373
    vulnerability to, 374
abusers, 373–374
academic disciplines, 61
acceptance and commitment therapy (ACT)
        approach, 327, 395–396
    definition, 395
    for depression, 329
acceptance of disability (AD), 83
ACT. *See* acceptance and commitment
        therapy
adjustment theories, 95. *See also* chaos and
        complexity theory (CCT)
    chronic sorrow, 112
    coping versus succumbing framework, 95
    good-fortune comparison, 110
    history of, 95
    impact of environmental barriers, 96
    negative societal attitudes, 96
    psychosocial adjustment, 110
    reevaluation changes, 95
    somatopsychology, 100–101
    stage models of, 96
        assumptions, 96
        defense mobilization, 97–98
        final adjustment/reintegration, 100
        initial impact, 96
        initial realization, 98–99
        retaliation, 99

value change system, 110
    containment of disability effects, 110
    enlargement of scope of values, 110
    subordination of physique, 110
    transformation, comparative to asset
        values, 110
adolescents with disabilities, 94
aesthetic–sexual aversion, 19
African American culture, and disability, 154
    cultural perspectives of, 154–155
    family perspectives, 155
    religion, impact of, 155–156
    socioeconomic status effects, 155
aging workforce, 471–480
    assessment of older adults, 474–475
    considerations, for older workers, 475–477
        physical and mental health conditions, 476
        premorbid personality, 476
        prevalence of disorders, 476
        risk of disability-related changes, 476
    counseling and case management, 473–474
    counselor practice, 479–480
    developmental models of, 472–473
    functional assessment, 475
    integration of life experiences, 473
    proactive employer response, 477–479
        age discrimination, 478
        beneficial diversity in workplace, 478
        culture of workplace, 477
        role, of managers, 478
    socioecological models, 473
    theoretical and clinical considerations, 472
    training and research implications, 479–480
alcohol use disorders
    treatment approaches for, 299
American colonies, and mental illness, 31
American Organization of Asylum Physicians, 31
American Psychological Association (APA),
        130–131
American Society of Addiction Medicine
        (ASAM), 295

567